ISAAC ASIMOV

Asimov's Guide to Shakespeare

VOLUME ONE
The Greek, Roman, and Italian Plays

VOLUME TWO
The English Plays

ILLUSTRATIONS BY RAFAEL PALACIOS

AVENEL BOOKS
New York

This book was originally published in two volumes as
*Asimov's Guide to Shakespeare, Volume One: The Greek, Roman,
and Italian Plays* and *Asimov's Guide to Shakespeare,
Volume Two: The English Plays.*

Copyright © MCMLXX by Isaac Asimov
All rights reserved.
This edition is published by Avenel Books,
distributed by Crown Publishers, Inc.
by arrangement with Doubleday & Company, Inc.,
e f g h
AVENEL 1978 PRINTING
Manufactured in the United States of America

Library of Congress Cataloging in Publication Data

Asimov, Isaac, 1920-
  Asimov's guide to Shakespeare.

  Originally published in 2 v. by Doubleday, New York.
  Includes index.

  CONTENTS: v. 1. The Greek, Roman, and Italian
plays.—v. 2. The English plays.

  1. Shakespeare, William, 1564-1616—Criticism and
interpretation. I. Title. II. Title: Guide to
Shakespeare.
[PR2976.A73 1978]   822.3'3   78-11321
ISBN 0-517-26825-6

To the memory of my father,
JUDAH ASIMOV (1896–1969)

Introduction

THOSE of us who speak English as our native tongue can count a number of blessings. It is a widespread language that is understood by more people in more parts of the world than any other* and it is therefore the language that is most nearly an open door to all peoples.

Its enormous vocabulary and its relatively simple grammar give it unequaled richness and flexibility and more than make up for its backward spelling. Its hospitality to idiomatic phrases and to foreign words gives it a colorful and dramatic quality that is without peer.

But most of all, we who speak English can read, in the original, the writings of William Shakespeare, a man who is certainly the supreme writer through all the history of English literature and who, in the opinion of many, is the greatest writer who ever lived—in *any* language.

Indeed, so important are Shakespeare's works that only the Bible can compare with them in their influence upon our language and thought. Shakespeare has said so many things so supremely well that we are forever finding ourselves thinking in his terms. (There is the story of the woman who read *Hamlet* for the first time and said, "I don't see why people admire that play so. It is nothing but a bunch of quotations strung together.")

I have a feeling that Shakespeare has even acted as a brake on the development of English. Before his time, English was developing so rapidly that the works of Geoffrey Chaucer, written shortly before 1400, had become unreadably archaic, two centuries later, to the Englishmen of Shakespeare's time. Yet now, after three and a half centuries, Shakespeare's plays can be read quite easily and with only an occasional archaic word or phrase requiring translation. It is almost as though the English language dare not change so much as to render Shakespeare incomprehensible. That would be an unacceptable price to pay for change.

In this respect, Shakespeare is even more important than the Bible. The King James version of the Bible is, of course, only a translation, although a supremely great one. If it becomes archaic there is nothing to prevent newer translations into more modern English. Indeed, such newer translations exist.

* Chinese has more speakers than English, but it is understood on a large scale only in eastern and southeastern Asia.

How, though, can anyone ever dream of "translating" Shakespeare into "modern English"? That would do, perhaps, if one were merely interested in the contents of Shakespeare. (It is, by analogy, in the contents of the Bible that we are interested, not in its exact syllables.)

But who can bear to have nothing more than the contents of Shakespeare's plays? What translation, even merely from one form of English into another form, could possibly reproduce the exact music and thunder of Shakespeare's syllables, and without that—

Yet in one respect Shakespeare recedes from us no matter how faithfully we follow the very syllables he uses. He wrote for all time, yes (whether he knew it or not), but he also wrote for a specific audience, that of Elizabethan Englishmen and -women. He gave its less educated individuals the horseplay and slapstick they enjoyed, and he gave its more educated individuals a wealth of allusion.

He assumed the educated portion of the audience were thoroughly grounded in Greek and Roman mythology and history, since that was part (and, indeed, almost the whole) of the classical education of the upper classes of the time. He assumed, also, that they were well acquainted with England's own history and with the geography of sixteenth-century Europe.

Modern Americans, however, are for the most part only vaguely aware of Greek mythology or Roman history. If anything, they are even less aware of those parts of English history with which Shakespeare deals.

This is not to say that one cannot enjoy Shakespeare without knowing the historical, legendary, or mythological background to the events in his plays. There is still the great poetry and the deathless swing of his writing. —And yet, if we *did* know a little more of what that writing was *about,* would not the plays take on new dimensions and lend us still greater enjoyment?

This is what it is in my mind to do in this book.

It is not my intention to discuss the literary values of the plays, or to analyze them from a theatrical, philosophical, or psychological point of view. Others have done this far beyond any poor capacity I might have in that direction.

What I can do, however, is to go over each of the thirty-eight plays and two narrative poems written by Shakespeare in his quarter century of literary life, and explain, as I go along, the historical, legendary, and mythological background.

In the process, I will, in some places, spend many pages on a single short speech which requires a great deal of background knowledge for its proper *total* appreciation. I may, in other places, skip quickly through whole acts which require nothing more than an understanding of a few archaic words to be crystal clear. (On the whole, I shall make no attempt to translate simple archaisms. This is done, quite adequately, in any briefly annotated edition of Shakespeare.)

In dealing with the plays, I will quote whatever passage inspires an explanation, but I will quote very little else. If the reader is reasonably familiar with a particular play, he will be able to read through the chapter devoted to it without needing to refer to the play itself. If he is *not* familiar with a particular play, it would probably help to keep it at hand for possible reference.

One matter over which I hesitated for a considerable length of time was the question of the order of presentation of the plays. The traditional order, as found in most editions of Shakespeare's collected works, groups the comedies first, then the histories, then the tragedies. This traditional order is very far removed from the order in which the plays were written. Thus, *The Tempest,* which is the first play in the ordinary editions, is the last play that Shakespeare wrote without collaboration. *The Two Gentlemen of Verona,* which is next, is one of the earliest.

It is possible to prepare an edition in which the plays are presented roughly in the order of their writing, something of value to those who study Shakespeare's developing techniques and ideas. This order can only be rough because it is not always certain in exactly which year a particular play was written. Worse yet, placing the plays in the chronological order of writing disrupts the histories and places them out of order as far as the historical events they deal with are concerned.

Since I am chiefly interested in this book in the historical, legendary, and mythological background of the events described in the various plays, I have decided to place the plays in the chronological order of those historical events as far as possible.

To begin with, I divide the plays into four broad groups: Greek, Roman, Italian, and English.

The Greek plays will include those that have their basis in Greek legend, as for instance, *Troilus and Cressida;* or in Greek history (however faintly), as *Timon of Athens.* It will also, however, include pure romances, with no claim whatever to any historical value, except that the background is arbitrarily set in a time we recognize as Greek—as *The Winter's Tale.*

The Roman plays include those that are based on actual history, as *Julius Caesar,* or on utterly non-historical, but Rome-based, inventiveness, as *Titus Andronicus.* (As it happens, even historical fiction such as *The Winter's Tale* and *Titus Andronicus* can be faintly related to actual historical events. No fiction writer is an island and no matter how he tries to draw on his imagination alone, the real world *will* intrude.)

The Italian plays are those set in a Renaissance Italian setting (or in nearby places such as France, Austria, or Illyria) which cannot be pinned down to any specific period of time. I will present the plays in this section in the order in which Shakespeare (as best we can tell) wrote them.

The English plays include not only the sober historical plays such as *Richard II* or *Henry V,* but also those which deal with the legendary period of English history before the Norman conquest or even, in the case of *King Lear* and *Cymbeline,* before the Roman conquest.

There is some overlapping. The Greek plays set latest in time are later than the earliest Roman plays; and the latest Roman plays are later than the earliest English plays. The radical difference in scene, however, makes it convenient to ignore this slight chronological inconsistency. With that out of the way, the order of plays and narrative poems in this volume will carry us through some twenty-eight centuries of history, from the time of legendary Greece before the Trojan War, to Shakespeare's own time.

To make a reasonably even division of the book into two volumes, the Greek, Roman, and Italian plays—in that order—will be grouped into Volume One. This will leave the English plays, to which I have devoted a little more than half the book, to form Volume Two.

In preparing this book, I have made as much use as I could of all sorts of general reference books: encyclopedias, atlases, mythologies, biographical dictionaries, histories—whatever came to hand.

To one set of books, however, I owe an especial debt. These are the many volumes of "The Signet Classic Shakespeare" (General Editor, Sylvan Barnet, published by New American Library, New York). It was, as a matter of fact, while reading my pleasurable way through these volumes that the notion of *Asimov's Guide to Shakespeare* occurred to me.

Volume One

THE GREEK, ROMAN, AND ITALIAN PLAYS

Contents

CONTENTS

III. Italian

PART I

Greek

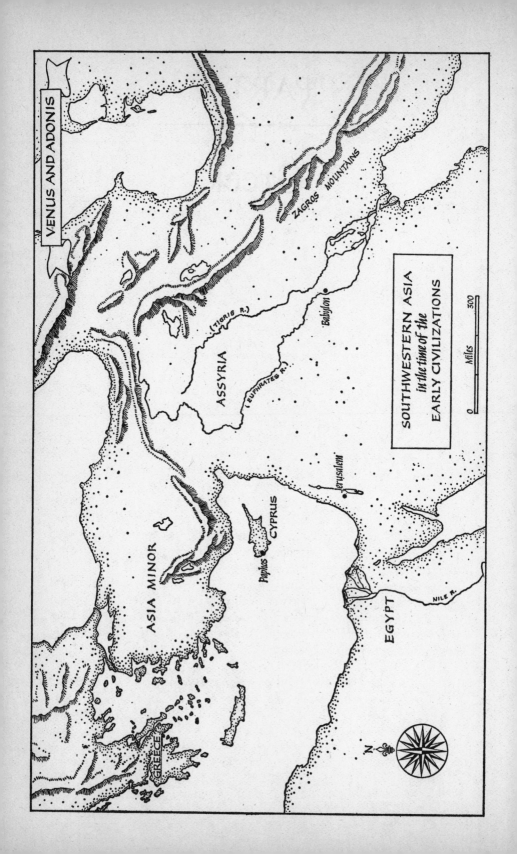

VENUS AND ADONIS

SOUTHWESTERN ASIA
In the time of the
EARLY CIVILIZATIONS

Miles

0   300

ZAGROS MOUNTAINS

Babylon

(TIGRIS R.)

ASSYRIA

(EUPHRATES R.)

Jerusalem

ASIA MINOR

CYPRUS

Paphos

EGYPT

NILE R.

GREECE

N

VENUS AND ADONIS

OF ALL Shakespeare's writings, *Venus and Adonis* is the most straightforwardly mythological and traces farthest backward (if only dimly so) in history. For that reason, I will begin with it.

. . . Earl of Southampton . . .

"Venus and Adonis" bears a dedication:

> *To the Right Honourable Henry Wriothesley, Earl of South-ampton, and Baron of Tichfield.*
>
> —Dedication

Southampton was a well-educated youth of considerable wealth, who was presented at the court of Queen Elizabeth I in 1590, while he was still a boy in his teens. He quickly became a generous patron of poets, Shakespeare among them.

It is suggested that one of Shakespeare's early plays, *Love's Labor's Lost* (see page I–421) was written for a premiere performance at Southampton's house before an assemblage of his friends and guests. If so, the play must have pleased Southampton tremendously; his patronage to Shakespeare extended (so at least one report goes) to the gift of a thousand pounds—an enormous sum in those days—for the completion of some purchase. Perhaps it is no wonder, then, that Shakespeare made his dedication to *Venus and Adonis* florid, indeed.

Nevertheless, considering that we know Shakespeare as a transcendent genius, and that Southampton was merely a rich young man who was no more than twenty years old when *Venus and Adonis* was published, there is something unpleasantly sycophantic about the dedication. Shakespeare pretends to worry, for instance—

> *—how the world will censure me for choosing so strong a prop to support so weak a burthen;*
>
> —Dedication

Can he really doubt his own power so, or overestimate the young man so egregiously? Surely not. Can he be indulging in sarcasm? That would be foolishly risky and nothing in Shakespeare's career would lead us to suppose him a devil-may-care. He was rather the reverse.

Well then, is he merely buttering up a patron with a fat money belt? Perhaps so. It is easy to believe that this is the ordinary language of poets to patrons but it would still hurt us to suppose that Shakespeare would conform to so degrading a custom.

But, to be complete, it is also possible that there was a homosexual attachment and Shakespeare was writing out of love. This is possible. Some think most of Shakespeare's 154 sonnets were written in this period of his life; most of them seem addressed to a young man, possibly (but not certainly) to Southampton.* The twentieth sonnet seems to have the frankest homosexual content. It begins:

> *A woman's face, with Nature's own hand painted,*
> *Hast thou, the master mistress of my passion;*
>
> —lines 1–2

But it denies overt homosexuality, ending:

> *And for a woman wert thou first created,*
> *Till Nature as she wrought thee fell a-doting*
> *And by addition me of thee defeated*
> *By adding one thing to my purpose nothing.*
> *But since she prick'd thee out for women's pleasure,*
> *Mine be thy love, and thy love's use their treasure.*
>
> —lines 9–14

In addition, there are a number of events in Shakespeare's plays that can be interpreted from a homosexual point of view, yet which Shakespeare presents most sympathetically. There are the close male friendships, even to threatened death, as is Antonio's for Bassanio in *The Merchant of Venice* (see page I-501). There is Lucius' passion for Fidele in *Cymbeline* (see page II-72) and the scene in which Orlando woos Ganymede in *As You Like It* (see page I-571).

But too little is known of Shakespeare's life to go any further than this. Any speculations as to his homosexual urges and to the extent to which he gave in to them, if they existed, can never be anything more than speculations.

---

* Shakespeare's sonnets, and a handful of other short poems attributed to him, are not taken up in this book. They are primarily emotional and personal, with little or none of the type of background I am dealing with here.

. . . the first heir of my invention . . .

Shakespeare goes on to say, in his dedication,

> *. . . if the first heir of my invention prove deformed, I shall be sorry it had so noble a godfather . . .*
>
> —Dedication

Venus and Adonis was published about April 1593, at which time Shakespeare was just twenty-nine. He had already established himself as a competent actor and had probably done considerable patching of old plays; notably *Henry VI, Part One* (see page II–640). *Henry VI, Part Two* and *Henry VI, Part Three* were mostly or entirely his and it is possible he had already written two comedies: *The Comedy of Errors* and *Love's Labor's Lost.* It is even possible that two more plays, *Titus Andronicus* and *Richard III* were in the process of production.

These works, however, were meant to be played, not read, and it was to be years before they were actually published. *Venus and Adonis* was the first piece of Shakespeare's writings that actually appeared in print, and it was in that sense only "the first heir of my invention."

Shakespeare seems, by the way, to have turned to narrative poetry only because of a siege of enforced idleness. The London theaters were closed between mid-1592 and mid-1594 as a result of a heightened incidence of plagues, and Shakespeare used the additional time on his hands to write *Venus and Adonis* and *The Rape of Lucrece.*

Rose-cheek'd Adonis . . .

The poem begins early in the day, with Adonis making ready to hunt:

> *Even as the sun with purple-colour'd face*
> *Had ta'en his last leave of the weeping morn,*
> *Rose-cheek'd Adonis hied him to the chase.*
> *Hunting he lov'd, but love he laugh'd to scorn.*
>
> —lines 1–4

Adonis is the Greek version of a Semitic vegetation god. From the beginnings of agriculture, there must have been a kind of relief each year among the farmers that, after the death of vegetation in the fall, there was a rebirth in the spring. Rituals personifying this death-and-rebirth were invented and they must have been looked upon as a kind of flattering homage to Nature (or even as a hint to a possibly forgetful Nature), inducing her to continue. The feeling would surely arise at last that only a thoroughgoing carrying through of the ritual each year would bring about a fertile growing season and a good harvest, and upon that, life through the barren winter would depend.

In that sense, the type of myth of which the tale of Venus and Adonis is representative (though prettied-up from its straightforward origins by the sophisticated imaginations of the later classical poets), reflects the historic birth of agriculture. It can be tied to the great event, some seven thousand years before the Trojan War, that saw the first deliberate cultivation and harvest of wild grain in the foothills of the Zagros Mountains in what is now western Iran.

The Sumerians, about 2000 B.C., represented the agricultural cycle with a god, Dumu-zi, who died and was resurrected; a death-and-resurrection which was celebrated each year by the people of the land. The myth and the ritual were adopted by the later Babylonians and Assyrians—the Semitic peoples who succeeded the Sumerians in the land of the Tigris and Euphrates. In the Semitic language of Babylonia, the name of the vegetation god became Tammuz.

In the Tammuz myth, the god descends into the underworld after his death and all vegetation dies with him. A wailing goddess (variously described as his sister, mother, or wife) manages to rescue him. In the most familiar form of the myth, the rescuer is Ishtar, his wife or love.

The passionate rites for Tammuz were exceedingly attractive to women in particular. They found emotional relief in the wailing and utter grief that symbolized Tammuz' death and in the almost orgiastic joy that came when the priests raised the cry that he was reborn.

The stern prophets of Israel had a hard job keeping the Israelite women from joining in this pagan rite. The tale of Jephthah's daughter was possibly an attempt to solve the problem by converting the rite into a patriotic commemoration. The Israelite general Jephthah had beaten the enemy, after making a rash vow to sacrifice the first living thing that came to greet him on his return. It turned out to be his daughter, whom he sacrificed. The Bible goes on to explain: "And it was a custom in Israel, That the daughters of Israel went yearly to lament the daughter of Jephthah the Gileadite four days in a year" (Judges 11:39–40).

If so, this pious wile did not work. Ezekiel, at the time of the Judean exile in Babylon, enumerated the sins of the Jews of the time and said that in the very Temple in Jerusalem "there sat women weeping for Tammuz" (Ezekiel 8:14).

And in one way, Tammuz has remained in Jewish consciousness ever since. The Babylonians named a month in honor of the god and the exiled Jews, in adopting the Babylonian calendar, adopted the month too. Even today, one of the months of the Jewish calendar (falling in the latter half of June and the earlier half of July) is called Tammuz.

The rites of a dead-and-resurrected God occur in the Greek myths too.

There is the case of Demeter (the grain goddess), whose daughter, Persephone, is abducted by Hades, the god of the underworld. While Persephone is gone, all grain withers, but finally Demeter manages to rescue her daughter under conditions that allow herself and Hades to share her, each for part of the year. The Eleusinian Mysteries, secret religious rites among the Greeks, seem to have involved the celebration of this death-and-resurrection, expanding it to include the resurrection of the human soul after the death of the human body.

As the Greeks and the Semites of the East gained more and more in the way of cultural interchange, the Tammuz version entered Greek mythology directly. Tammuz became Adonis.

The name shift is no mystery. Names of gods are always a little difficult to handle in any culture that considers the name of an object to be almost the equivalent of the object itself. To touch the name with one's own tongue and breath is a form of blasphemy and so circumlocutions are used. Instead of saying Tammuz, one says Lord (just as, in the Bible, Lord is used in place of Yahveh).

The Semitic term for "Lord" is "Adonai" and it was "Adonai," rather than "Tammuz," that was adopted by the Greeks. They added the final s, which is an almost invariable ending on Greek proper names, making it "Adonis."

Since Ishtar was the lover of Tammuz in the Babylonian myth, the equivalent of Ishtar would have to be the lover of Adonis in the Greek myth. The Greek equivalent of Ishtar was Aphrodite, the goddess of love and beauty.

The Greek myth had Adonis born the son of King Theias of Assyria. No such king existed in actual history, to be sure, but this is a hint of the Babylonian origin of the myth. We might suppose, therefore, that the scene of the poem is Babylonia, though Shakespeare never indicates any particular place—and perhaps gave the matter no thought at all.

Adonis' mother was Myrrha, who was herself the daughter of Theias. Myrrha had conceived an incestuous passion for her father and managed to sneak into his bed, with the result that she became pregnant by him. When the shocked father discovered the truth, he would have killed her, but the pitying gods changed her into the myrrh tree.

The myrrh tree yields a bitter resinous sap (myrrh), which oozes out when the bark is split. (The word "myrrh" is from an Arabic word meaning "bitter.") The sap is valued for its uses as incense and in cosmetics and embalming. (It was one of the three gifts brought to the infant Jesus by the wise men—"they presented unto him gifts; gold, and frankincense, and myrrh," Matthew 2:11.)

The sap on being exposed to air hardens into resinous drops called "tears," and these are supposed to represent the tears of Myrrha over the terrible thing she had done. (Working backward, we can suppose that this

part of the myth arose over the attempt to explain why a tree should seem
to weep.)

In the Greek myth, the myrrh tree into which Myrrha had been changed
split after nine months, and the infant Adonis emerged. Aphrodite (who
had inspired Myrrha's fatal love in the first place) felt remorse at the event
and rescued Adonis. She placed him in a box and gave him to Persephone,
goddess of the underworld, for temporary safekeeping. Persephone, noting
the beauty of the child, refused to give him back and there was a quarrel
that ended with each having him part of the time.

Here again is the tale of winter (Adonis with Persephone) and summer
(Adonis with Aphrodite), enlivened, in the Greek way, by a story of forbidden love.

This, at least, is the myth as told by Apollodorus, an Athenian poet who
lived in the second century B.C. Shakespeare does not follow this. He begins with Adonis as a grown man, says nothing of his origins, and concerns
himself only with the final stage of the myth, following a version given by
Ovid.

Ovid, who seems to have been Shakespeare's favorite classical author,
is the Roman poet whose name in full was Publius Ovidius Naso. About
A.D. 1 he was writing his most famous work—a version, in Latin verse, of
those Greek myths that involved the transformation ("metamorphosis")
of one living thing into another.

Ovid's book is therefore called *Metamorphoses,* and the myth of Adonis
is included, since his mother had been turned into a myrrh tree.

Sick-thoughted Venus . . .

In the final couplet of the first stanza, Shakespeare introduces the other
member of the mythical duo:

> *Sick-thoughted Venus makes amain unto him*
> *And like a bold-fac'd suitor gins to woo him.*

—lines 5–6

This is not Aphrodite, notice, as it would be if Shakespeare were following the work of the Greek poet Apollodorus. Shakespeare is using the name
of a Roman goddess instead, the name used by Ovid.

The Romans in the early centuries of their history had a primitive religion, with numerous gods and goddesses of a rather arid nature who were
not to be compared with the sophisticated deities of the much more cultivated Greeks. From the third century B.C. onward, the Romans fell more
and more under the spell of Greek culture and were impelled to adopt the
beautiful and intricate Greek mythology. They could not very well drop

their own deities; instead they compromised by identifying their own gods with the roughly corresponding gods of the Greeks and retold the Greek myths using the Roman names.

Here is a list of the chief gods and goddesses in their Roman and Greek versions:

Roman	Greek	
Jupiter	Zeus	chief of the gods
Juno	Hera	his wife
Minerva	Athena	goddess of wisdom and practical arts
Diana	Artemis	goddess of the moon and the hunt
Mercury	Hermes	messenger of the gods
Mars	Ares	god of war
Vulcan	Hephaestus	god of fire and the forge
Venus	Aphrodite	goddess of love and beauty
Neptune	Poseidon	god of the sea
Vesta	Hestia	goddess of the hearth and home
Dis	Hades	god of the underworld
Ceres	Demeter	goddess of grain and agriculture
Proserpina	Persephone	goddess of the underworld

One major god had, apparently, no Roman equivalent at all, which is not strange, for he was the most Greek of all the Greek gods. He was Apollo, the god of youth and the fine arts (and in later poetry, of the sun as well). The Romans used the Greek name, therefore. They also used Hades or, its equivalent, Pluto, in preference to their own Dis, since Dis (a fearsome underground deity) was not popular with them and they avoided naming him.

Two of the mortal heroes that people the Greek legends, and who play a prominent part in Shakespearean allusions, have altered names given them by the Romans. Thus, the greatest and strongest of all the Greek heroes was Heracles, but the Romans called him Hercules. Again, the wiliest of the Greeks at the siege of Troy was Odysseus, whom the Romans called Ulysses.

In medieval Europe the Greek myths reached the west only through such Roman filters as Ovid and therefore the names used were all Roman. Shakespeare uses the Roman names of the gods invariably.

I will conform to Shakespearean usage, though it goes against the grain to do so, since it is far more appropriate to use the Greek names in dealing with Greek myths. I will ease my conscience, therefore, by occasionally placing the Greek name in parentheses, just to remind the reader of its existence.

Shakespeare departs from his source material in one important way. He makes Adonis reluctant to respond to Venus. "Hunting he loved, but love he laughed to scorn" and Venus, out of sheer necessity, must reverse the role of the sexes and "like a bold-fac'd suitor" be the aggressor.

There is precedent for this in Greek mythology. There was, for instance, Hermaphroditus, the son of Hermes and Aphrodite. He was beloved by a fountain nymph, Salmacis, but he repulsed her coldly. Once, however, when he was bathing in her spring, she was able to unite with him in love, and fearing that she might never be able to repeat the act, prayed the gods that she might remain united with him physically forever.

Her prayer was granted and thereafter Hermaphroditus had the genital equipment of both sexes. The word "hermaphrodite" has, in consequence, entered the English language to represent that pathological bisexual condition.

A much better known example is mentioned by Venus herself in this poem. She complains of Adonis' coldness and accuses him of loving only himself. She warns him he runs risks in consequence, saying:

> *Narcissus so himself himself forsook,*
> *And died to kiss his shadow in the brook.*
>
> —lines 161–62

The tale of Narcissus begins with a nymph, Echo, who had, at Jupiter's orders, kept Juno busy with prolonged and idle gossip while Jupiter busied himself with various nymphs. When Juno found out, she punished Echo by depriving her of her voice—except that she was permitted to repeat the last words of anything said to her.

Unhappy Echo fell in love, thereafter, with Narcissus, a handsome youth who would love no one. She tried to woo him, but could only repeat his last words, and he fled from her impatiently, so that Echo pined away until only her voice was left.

And then one day Narcissus came across a clear spring in which he saw his own face. He had never seen his face before and, staring at it now, fell in love with it. He attempted to woo it, but the shadow could not respond and, in effect, rejected him, so that "himself himself forsook." Attempting, finally, to kiss his shadow, Narcissus drowned, and he too added a word to our language—"narcissism," the morbid love of one's self.

This trick of having Adonis cold to Venus gives Shakespeare a chance to turn his poetic powers to a less hackneyed motif than that of a man's praise of womanly beauty. He can turn to the harder and less familiar task of a woman's praise of manly beauty.

Then too, if we go along with the homosexual component of Shakespeare, it may be significant that a poem dedicated to young Southampton features the prolonged praise of manly beauty and a prolonged pleading for a love that is not, and cannot, be given.

. . . god of war

Venus points out that she is rarely refused when she asks for love:

> *"I have been wooed, as I entreat thee now,*
> *Even by the stern and direful god of war,*
>
> —lines 97–98

One of the most famous tales of Venus/Aphrodite is her love affair with Mars/Ares. The tale is told in the *Odyssey* (Homer's epic poem concerning the voyages of Odysseus), in which Venus is pictured as married to Vulcan/Hephaestus, the ugly and lame smith god. Venus is, under these conditions, quite ready to respond to the wooing of Mars.

Vulcan, suspecting that Venus is being unfaithful, rigged up a device whereby an unbreakable net could fall upon the bed and catch Venus and Mars in the position of love. This was done; Mars and Venus were helplessly bound together while the angry Vulcan called in the other gods to witness his wife's criminal behavior. Unfortunately for himself, the reaction of the gods was not one of sympathy for Vulcan, but rather of envy for Mars.

And Titan . . .

By now, the sun was high in the sky:

> *And Titan, tired in the midday heat,*
> *With burning eye did hotly overlook them,*
> *Wishing Adonis had his team to guide,*
> *So he were like him, and by Venus' side.*
>
> —lines 177–80

In the Greek myths, Jupiter/Zeus and his fellow deities had not always ruled the universe. Before them had been a race of older gods whom they supplanted. (Perhaps this is a reflection in myth of the supercession of the pre-Greeks of the Balkan peninsula by the invading Greek tribes.)

These older gods were called Titans, and their chief was Cronus, whom the Romans called Saturn.

The Titan who served as the god of the sun was Hyperion. One way of saying this, mythologically, was to make him the father of Helios (the Greek word for "sun"). Both "Hyperion" and "Helios" are thus used in classic-minded literature to represent the sun. Since both are considered Titans, the sun can be called, as here, "Titan."

The sun was always pictured as a blazing, golden chariot, driven by a team of wild, fiery horses. It is with this in mind that Shakespeare pictures the "Titan" as wishing Adonis held the reins and he himself were lying by Venus.

In later Greek poetry, Apollo was made the god of the sun, and Shakespeare, in the course of his writing, uses "Apollo" to symbolize the sun too. The Titaness Phoebe, a sister of Hyperion, was the goddess of the moon, and the myths make Apollo a grandson (on his mother's side) of Phoebe. He inherits the ancient name in its masculine form, then, and is called Phoebus or Phoebus Apollo, "Phoebus" too is used by Shakespeare to represent the sun.

Thy mermaid's voice . . .

Adonis is only irritated by Venus' pleadings. While she keeps him back from the hunt with her attempted love-making, his stallion spies a mare and breaks loose. Adonis fails to recapture him and petulantly scolds Venus, blaming her for the loss.

Venus laments that she suffers twice, first because he will not speak to her, and second because when at last he does, it is to scold her. She says:

> *Thy mermaid's voice hath done me double wrong;*
>
> —line 429

The Greeks had, in their myths, tales of beautiful young women, called sirens, who rested on the rocks of a seashore and sang in heavenly voices. Sailors passing by would be attracted by them and, steering their boats nearer, would meet death upon the rocks.

Originally sirens may have been wind spirits carrying off the souls of the dead, and were sometimes pictured with birds' bodies. However, the wind was more deadly on sea than on land, and the sirens became more and more closely associated with the sea until they were pictured as creatures who were women down to the waist and fish below that.

These are the "mermaids" ("sea-maids"), who bewitch sailors to their doom on the rocks, as they sit combing their long hair and singing. The famous German poem "Die Lorelei" is of such a creature.

So when Venus speaks of Adonis' "mermaid voice" she means a beautiful voice that is luring her to doom.

. . . worse than Tantalus' . . .

The day is drawing to a close and Adonis finally manages to get Venus to promise to leave him alone if he kisses her. He proceeds to do so but she returns the embrace in such full measure that he has all he can do to disengage himself. He then reveals that the next day he intends to hunt boar.

At this Venus is sent into a paroxysm of fear, lest he be killed in so dangerous a pursuit. She seizes him and they fall to the ground in the very position of love. Yet even so, to Venus' frustration, he will do nothing.

> *That worse than Tantalus' is her annoy*
> *To clip Elysium and to lack her joy.*
>
> —lines 599–600

Tantalus was a Peloponnesian king who was an intimate friend of Jupiter and the other gods. He was admitted to their feasts and in return he invited them to his house. For some reason, perhaps to test their divine knowledge, he served them the flesh of his own son when they were feasting at his house. The gods were horrified. They restored the son to life, and, for his detestable crime, Tantalus was killed by Jupiter's lightning bolt. What's more, Tantalus was sent to Tartarus, the region beneath Hades where particularly wicked people were specially punished.

Tantalus' punishment was to stand in water up to his neck in eternal frustration. He was consumed by thirst, but every time he stooped to drink, the water swirled downward. Fruit-laden branches hovered temptingly near and he was famished, but every time he reached to snatch a fruit, it whisked away. It is from this that the word "tantalize" is derived.

For Venus, to have Adonis exactly where he ought to be and yet have him make no use of the fact seems a frustration worse than that of Tantalus. She was in Tartarus, even though she was "clipping" (holding) Elysium, which was the Greek version of Paradise.

In the Homeric writings, Elysium or "the Elysian plain" existed in the far west, the dimly explored (and therefore wonder-filled) western regions of the Mediterranean Sea, where heroes were taken after death to live in eternal bliss. By later writers this had to be transported beyond the ocean rim, for explorers reached the westernmost point of the Mediterranean shores without finding Elysium. The Greek poet Hesiod, writing a century after Homer, speaks of "the Islands of the Blest" lying out in the Atlantic.

As geographic knowledge continued to broaden, the Roman poet Vergil, writing six centuries after Hesiod, was forced to move Elysium underground, making it a portion of Hades devoted to delight. It was suffused with an eternal spring. Its flowers, groves, and fountains were lit by soft sunshine during the day and by the familiar constellations at night. There the righteous, resting on banks of resilient and perfumed flowers, lived in never-ending felicity.

. . . modest Dian . . .

Venus urges Adonis to hunt foxes or hares, anything that is not dangerous, rather than boars. Adonis, having paid his kiss, finds that he still cannot disengage himself from her wild grasp. It is night already and he is annoyed at this, for it will be hard to find his way. Venus turns this too into praise of Adonis' beauty.

> *So do thy lips*
> *Make modest Dian cloudy and forlorn,*
> *Lest she should steal a kiss and die forsworn.*
>
> *Now of this dark night I perceive the reason:*
> *Cynthia for shame obscures her silver shine,*
>
> —lines 724–28

The Titaness who served as goddess of the moon was Phoebe. However, Hyperion, the Titan god of the sun, had not only Helios as a son but Selene as a daughter. "Selene" is the Greek word for "moon" and that name was the most common mythological representation of the moon.

The later poets, however, transferred the duty of serving as goddess of the moon to Diana/Artemis, the sister of Apollo. She is also called Cynthia because she was supposed to have been born on a mountain called Cynthus on a small island in the Aegean Sea. Apollo is therefore, but much less frequently, called Cynthius.

Diana is, of all the Greek goddesses, the most insistently virgin. Venus therefore says that Adonis may lose his way or trip because the night is dark; and the night is dark because the moon hides herself, lest while shining on Adonis' beautiful face she be unable to resist kissing him, thus ruining her rigid chastity.

A purple flower . . .

Venus' urgings are all in vain. The next day he hunts the boar and is slain. The horrified Venus finds him:

> *And in his blood, that on the ground lay spill'd*
> *A purple flower sprung up, check'red with white,*
> *Resembling well his pale cheeks and the blood*
> *Which in round drops upon their whiteness stood.*
>
> —lines 1167–70

The flower that arose out of the blood, according to the myth, was the anemone, and its appearance makes a second reason why the tale qualifies for inclusion in Ovid's *Metamorphoses*.

This is not the only flower that was supposed to have originated out of the blood of a mortal loved by a god.

There was the case, for instance, of a beautiful Spartan prince, Hyacinthus, with whom Apollo fell in love. (The Greeks had a tolerant and even approving attitude toward male homosexuality, and the Greek gods indulged in it too.) The West Wind was also in love with Hyacinthus and when Apollo and Hyacinthus were exercising by throwing the discus, the West Wind, out of jealousy, blew the discus against the boy's head, killing him. From the blood of Hyacinthus sprang the hyacinth, which carries on its petals markings that look like the first two letters of the name of Hyacinthus (in Greek), two letters which, coincidentally, mean "woe."

. . . to Paphos . . .

Shakespeare's version of the story ends there, with the disastrous climax of Adonis' death. The last, and 199th, stanza, reads:

> *Thus weary of the world, away she hies*
> *And yokes her silver doves, by whose swift aid*
> *Their mistress, mounted, through the empty skies*
> *In her light chariot quickly is convey'd,*
> > *Holding their course to Paphos, where their queen*
> > *Means to immure herself and not be seen.*
> > —lines 1189–94

The doves, for their amorous dispositions, their whiteness and gentleness, are fitting representations of romantic love and are therefore associated with Venus. Shakespeare makes a number of allusions to her doves in the course of his writings.

Paphos is a town on the western shore of the island of Cyprus, a town particularly dedicated to the worship of Venus. She is sometimes called the "Paphian goddess" as a result and sometimes "Cypris."

In the Greek myth, however, the tale of Adonis does not end with his death and Venus' mourning. In the proper fashion of death-and-resurrection, Venus goes to Jupiter and persuades him to make an arrangement whereby Proserpina, queen of the underworld, can have Adonis for half the year and she for the other half. And thus, Adonis, like the vegetation god he is, dies and is resurrected each year.

A MIDSUMMER NIGHT'S DREAM

THESSALY

Aegean
Sea

Thebes
Athens
Corinth
Argos
Sparta

NAXOS

N

Knossos

CRETE

GREECE *in the time of* THESEUS

0   Miles   100

2

A MIDSUMMER

NIGHT'S DREAM

THE TITLE of this play sets its tone. "Midsummer" refers to the summer solstice, when the noonday sun reaches the most elevated point in the heavens. By our present calendar, this is June 21. (To be sure this is only the beginning of summer by modern convention and by temperature considerations.)

The actual calendar day of the solstice has varied at different times because calendars themselves have. The Midsummer Day in English tradition is June 24, which is celebrated as the birthday of John the Baptist and which therefore has a Christian distinction as well as an earlier pagan one. The preceding night would be "Midsummer Night."

There is a folk belief that extreme heat is a cause of madness (hence the phrase "midsummer madness") and this is not entirely a fable. The higher the sun and the longer it beats down, the more likely one is to get sunstroke, and mild attacks of sunstroke could be conducive to all sorts of hallucinatory experiences. Midsummer, then, is the time when people are most apt to imagine fantastic experiences.

In calling the play *A Midsummer Night's Dream,* then, Shakespeare is deliberately describing it as a piece of utter fantasy. It does *not* imply, however, that the play actually takes place on Midsummer Night. Only one reference in the play seems to set a time and that makes it seem considerably earlier; see page I-45.

. . . fair Hippolyta . . .

The play opens in a spirit of high festivity. A marriage is about to take place. The scene is set in the palace of Theseus, Duke of Athens, and it is he who speaks:

> Now, fair Hippolyta, our nuptial hour
> Draws on apace. Four happy days bring in
> Another moon;

—Act I, scene i, lines 1–3

Theseus was the great hero of Athens, who (according to Greek legend) was the first to unify the peninsula of Attica under the rule of the city of Athens. He was supposed to have lived in the generation before the Trojan War and we may therefore put the time of the play as about 1230 B.C. (which makes this play the earliest from the standpoint of background chronology, so that I place it immediately after *Venus and Adonis*.)

As the centuries wore on, the imaginative Athenians invented more and more hero tales with which to adorn the life of their founder until, finally, he was second only to Hercules in the number of adventures he was given.

One tale involving Theseus concerns his expedition to a land of warrior women. The women, the legend tells us, cauterized the left breast in infancy so that it never developed and left that side free for the maneuvering of a shield. They were called "Amazons," from a Greek word meaning "breastless."

Theseus defeated the Amazons and captured their queen, Antiope, keeping her as his love. He married her and by her had a son, Hippolytus. The name of Hippolytus was famous in Greek legend because he was the center of a very famous tale involving the hopeless love for him of his stepmother, Phaedra.

A feminine version of Hippolytus' name, Hippolyta, worked its way backward therefore and was given to his mother in place of the older name, Antiope. This was all the easier to do because in the tale of another expedition against the Amazons, that of Hercules, Hippolyta was indeed given as the name of their queen. Shakespeare makes use of Hippolyta as the name of Theseus' Amazon queen, not only here, but also in *The Two Noble Kinsmen* (see page I-56).

Theseus is listed in the cast of characters as "Duke of Athens." This is an anachronism, for Athens was not a duchy or anything analogous to it in Theseus' time. It was what we would today call a kingdom and Theseus was its king.

The title "Duke of Athens" did not, however, come out of nowhere. In 1204 a party of Crusaders from the West overthrew the Byzantine Empire, which then ruled Greece, took and sacked its capital, Constantinople, and divided up what they could of the Empire among themselves, fashioning new states, Western style. One of these fragments was the "Duchy of Athens," which included the regions about Athens and Thebes.

The Duchy of Athens continued in existence for two and a half centuries. Finally, in 1456, it was absorbed into the empire of the Ottoman Turks. Shakespeare's play, probably written about 1595, was only a century and a half removed from this Duchy of Athens, and the title of "Duke" would seem a natural one to the Elizabethan audience.

Since *A Midsummer Night's Dream* centers about a wedding, since it is gay and frothy and all about love and lovers, it seems natural to suppose that it was written for, and originally produced as, part of the entertainment at a wedding feast. Scholars have tried to guess which wedding it might have been and six different ones have been suggested, but none is very likely. The marriages of the two men most likely to have the use of Shakespeare's services in this way, the Earl of Southampton (see page I-3), and the Earl of Essex (Elizabeth's favorite and a great friend of Southampton), both took place in 1598, which is too late for the play.

. . . Cupid's strongest bow

The marriage festivities of Theseus and Hippolyta serve as the background plot, or the "frame," of the play. In the foreground are three other sets of events, involving totally disparate groups of characters whom Shakespeare cleverly weaves together.

The first of these subplots is introduced at once, as a set of well-born Athenians break in upon Theseus. At their head is Egeus, who is vexed and annoyed because his daughter, Hermia, will not agree to marry a young man named Demetrius. Hermia insists stubbornly that she is in love with Lysander, of whom her father does not approve.

Lysander himself points out that Demetrius had previously been in love with Helena, a friend of Hermia's, and that Helena still returned that love.

All will not do. Despite Hermia's emotion and Lysander's reason, Egeus insists on having his way, as is his legal right. Theseus decides that by his own wedding day Hermia must have agreed to obey her father. The alternatives are death or lifelong celibacy. All then leave the stage, but Lysander and Hermia.

No recourse but flight seems left them. Lysander suggests that Hermia meet him in the wood outside Athens and that they flee to a rich aunt of his who lives outside Athenian territory. There they can marry.

Hermia agrees to meet him that very night, swearing to do so in a lyrical outburst of romantic vows:

> I swear to thee, by Cupid's strongest bow,
> By his best arrow with the golden head,
> By the simplicity of Venus' doves,
> By that which knitteth souls and prospers loves,
> And by that fire which burned the Carthage queen,
> When the false Troyan under sail was seen,
> —Act I, scene i, lines 169–74

Cupid is the Latin version of the Greek Eros, both of whom were personifications of sexual passion. Cupid (Eros) is earliest mentioned in the works of the Greek poet Hesiod, who wrote in the eighth century B.C. There he represented the impersonal force of attraction that created all things. In later centuries Cupid was personified as a young man, then as a boy, and finally as an infant rather like the cherubs in our own art.

In the Greek myths he was given various sets of parents; Venus and Mars (see page I–11) in the best-known version. He was considered to be mischievous, of course, as anyone could see who witnesses the ridiculous events brought about by love. He was sometimes depicted as blind, since love seemed to afflict the most mismatched couples (mismatched by all standards except those clearly visible to the lovers themselves).

He was supposed to possess a bow and arrows, for the onset of love (which is sometimes sudden, or seems sudden in later reminiscence) resembles a quick arrow in the heart. In later tales, Cupid was given two types of arrows, one with a golden tip to produce love, and another with a leaden tip to produce hate. Sometimes the hate arrows were made the property of a companion deity, Anteros ("opposed to Eros").

Doves were birds sacred to Venus (see page I–15) and they too served as appropriate vehicles for lovers' oaths.

The "Carthage queen" is a reference to one of Shakespeare's favorite personages in classical legend and one to which he often refers. She is Dido, who in 814 B.C. (according to legend), founded the North African city of Carthage, which in later centuries dominated the western Mediterranean and rivaled Rome itself.

The best-known story in connection with Dido involves the Trojan hero Aeneas. Aeneas is one of the fighters on the Trojan side who survived the destruction of Troy. Indeed, at one point in the *Iliad,* Aeneas is on the point of being destroyed by the invincible Achilles, and is saved by the intervention of the gods. The excuse is that Jupiter (Zeus) "intends that Aeneas shall rule the surviving Trojan stock, and his children's children after him."

Naturally, numerous tales were later invented that gave Aeneas adventures after the fall of Troy. Of these, the one that is best known today was not told by a Greek at all but by a Roman poet, Publius Vergilius Maro (best known among English-speaking people as Vergil). In the reign of Augustus, first of the Roman emperors, in the last decades of the first century B.C., Vergil wrote a tale, in imitation of Homer, regarding the escape of Aeneas from burning Troy and his wanderings over the Mediterranean Sea. The epic poem he wrote was named *Aeneid* for its hero.

Eventually, Aeneas lands in Carthage and meets Queen Dido. (To be sure, the Trojan War was in 1200 B.C. and Queen Dido lived in 800 B.C., making four centuries between them, but Vergil didn't care about that and neither—if the truth be known—do we, in reading the *Aeneid.*)

Dido falls desperately in love with the handsome Trojan stranger; their love is consummated and for a moment it seems that all will be happy. But Aeneas is a "false Troyan" who betrays the Queen. The gods warn him that his divinely appointed task is to go to Italy, there to found a line which was eventually to give rise to Rome. Quietly, he sneaks away.

Dido, in despair, builds a funeral pyre on the shore, sets it on fire, and throws herself on the flames, dying with her eyes fixed on the disappearing ship. Few readers can feel any sympathy for Vergil's rather pallid hero. Despite Vergil's own attempt to make it all seem very pious of Aeneas to follow the divine dictates, our hearts are all with the injured Carthaginian and not with the scuttling Trojan. Dido has remained ever since an epitome of the betrayed woman.

Of course, it is anachronistic of Hermia to speak of Dido and Aeneas, since that took place after the Trojan War and Theseus lived before—but, again, that is a matter of little moment.

. . . when Phoebe doth behold

Helena now enters. She is a bosom friend of Hermia's and the friendship has remained unbroken, apparently, even though Demetrius, whom Helena desperately loves, is as desperately wooing Hermia.

The two lovers softheartedly decide to tell Helena of their own plan of flight, in order to reassure her that the obstacle to her love of Demetrius will be removed. Lysander says their flight will take place:

> Tomorrow night, when Phoebe doth behold
> Her silver visage in the wat'ry glass
> —Act I, scene i, lines 209–10

Phoebe is a way of referring to the moon, making use of the oldest moon goddess in classical myth and harking back to the Titaness (see page I-12).

It is odd, though, that Lysander should refer to the moon as lighting up the night, for at the very beginning of the play, Theseus has specifically stated that it is only four nights to the next new moon. This means that the old moon is now a crescent which appears only in the hours immediately preceding the dawn.

Yet it is to be understood that the entire magic night that is soon to follow is moonlit. In a way, it is essential. The soft moonlight will be just enough to make things seem not quite what they are. Who would argue with it? Let there be a full moon throughout the night even if astronomy says it is impossible.

Of course, the kindly motive that led Hermia and Lysander to tell Helena their plans makes trouble at once. Helena, virtually mad with love, promptly tells Demetrius of the plan, hoping thereby to gain his gratitude (and failing).

. . . all our company . . .

The second scene of the play introduces a third strand of plot, one that does not involve aristocrats, but laboring men. Indeed, the second scene is laid in the house of one of them, a carpenter.

These laborers have none of the aura of Athenian aristocrat about them; indeed, they are in every respect, even down to their names, comic Englishmen. This sort of thing is true in all of Shakespeare's plays. Of whatever nationality and historical period the main characters are represented as being, the lower classes are always portrayed as Englishmen of Shakespeare's own time.

The leader of the group, the one in whose house they are meeting, looks about and asks, portentously,

> *Is all our company here?*
>
> —Act I, scene ii, line 1*

This leader is Peter Quince, the carpenter, and it is possible in his case and in all the others to see a connection between the name and the occupation. According to a footnote in the Signet Classic Shakespeare edition, "quines" are blocks of wood used for building and therefore characteristic of carpenters.

The other men of the company are:

Nick Bottom the weaver; one of the numerous meanings of "bottom" is a "skein of thread."

Francis Flute, the bellows-mender, which is apt since the sides of a bellows are fluted.

Tom Snout, the tinker, who deals largely with the repair of kettles, which are characterized by a snout (or spout).

Snug the joiner, an occupation which joins pieces of wood, it is to be hoped snugly.

Finally, there is Starveling the tailor, a name which is evidence that there has long been a tradition that tailors are weak, cowardly, effeminate creatures, perhaps because they work so much on women's clothes and because it is so easy to assume that a manly man would not be interested in such an occupation.

---

* In numbering the lines for reference there would be no problem if nothing but verse were involved, as in *Venus and Adonis* and in the first scene of *A Midsummer Night's Dream*. Then the identity and numbering of the lines are fixed. Where we encounter prose, as we do now for the first time, the lines depend on the design of type and the width of the columns. The numbering then varies from edition to edition and can alter the number in passages of verse too, if they follow passages of prose in the same scene. In this book, I am using the numbering system given in "The Signet Classic Shakespeare." If the reader is referring to some other edition, he will often have to look a little to either side of the line number, so to speak, but he will not be far off and his search will not be difficult.

". . . Pyramus and Thisby"

The six laborers have met in order to arrange the production of a play intended to celebrate the marriage of Theseus and Hippolyta. Quince announces the name of the play:

> *. . . our play is, "The most lamentable comedy, and most cruel death of Pyramus and Thisby."*
> —Act I, scene ii, lines 11–13

The tale of Pyramus and Thisbe is found in Ovid's *Metamorphoses* (see page I–8) and has no known source beyond that.

Pyramus and Thisbe were a youth and maiden of Babylon who lived in adjoining houses and who loved each other but were kept separate by the enmity of their parents. They talked through a chink in the wall that separated the estates and arranged to meet outside the city one night.

Thisbe got there first, but was frightened by a lion and fled, leaving her veil behind. The lion, who had just killed an ox, snapped at the veil, leaving it bloody. Pyramus arrived, found the lion's footprints and the bloody veil. Coming to a natural conclusion, he killed himself. When Thisbe returned, she found Pyramus' dead body and killed herself as well.

There is a strange similarity between this tale and that of *Romeo and Juliet,* a play that was written at just about the time *A Midsummer Night's Dream* was being written. Did Shakespeare's satirical treatment of the Pyramus-Thisbe story get him interested in doing a serious treatment of it? Was the serious treatment already written and was he now poking a little good-natured fun at it? We can never tell.

. . . play Ercles rarely . . .

The workmen are among Shakespeare's most delightful creations: naïve and yet well-meaning. And of them all, the most naïve and the best-meaning is Bottom. Bottom no sooner hears the name of the play but he says, pompously:

> *A very good piece of work, I assure you, and a merry.*
> —Act I, scene ii, lines 14–15

Since the tale of Pyramus and Thisbe was well known to any Elizabethan with the slightest education, and known to be an utterly tragic one designed for reducing softhearted maidens to floods of tears, Bottom's own characterization of it reveals him at once. He is illuminated as the cocksure know-it-all who knows nothing; the fool who thinks himself wise, and yet who, through the very enormity of his folly, makes himself lovable.

The workmen are each assigned a role in the play and Bottom is given the part of Pyramus the hero. Despite Bottom's pretense of knowledge concerning the play, it promptly turns out that he doesn't know what kind of part Pyramus is. He is told that Pyramus is a lover and he is wistful over the possibility of other roles, saying:

> . . . *my chief humor is for a tyrant. I could play Ercles rarely, or a part to tear a cat in, to make all split.*
>
> —Act I, scene ii, lines 29–31

"Ercles" is Bottom's mispronunciation of Hercules (and much of the humor in Shakespeare's plays rests with the mangling of the English language by the uneducated—something sure to raise patronizing chuckles from the better classes in the audience).

Hercules (Heracles) was the greatest of the legendary heroes of the Greeks. He was a child of Jupiter (Zeus) by an illicit amour with a mortal woman. He thus incurred the vengeful enmity of Juno (Hera). As a result of a crime committed during one of his periodic fits of madness, he was condemned to perform twelve labors for an unworthy relative, Eurystheus, King of Argos.

The tale of his labors (which may originally have been inspired by the progress of the sun through the twelve constellations of the zodiac) were elaborated and interlarded before, between, and afterward by so many additions illustrative of his superhuman strength that Hercules became the most storied individual in Greek legend. He remained popular through all succeeding ages.

Since Hercules' forte was sheer brute strength, mingled with madness, he had to be played broadly with a rolling, bass voice, with rage and threats and much flexing of muscles.

The poorer plays of Elizabethan times were notorious for overacting, something beloved of the lower classes. Certainly Hercules could scarcely be portrayed satisfactorily without overacting, and it was just the sort of role a lovable dimwit like Bottom would yearn for and want to portray.

The "part to tear a cat in, to make all split" is probably a reference to Samson, the Israelite analogue of Hercules. At one time, the young Samson encountered a lion. "And the Spirit of the Lord came mightily upon him, and he rent him as he would have rent a kid, and he had nothing in his hand" (Judges 14:6). Samson would clearly have suited Bottom every bit as much as Hercules would have.

The remaining parts are then given out, with the proceedings interrupted at every point by Bottom's yearnings to play each part as it is described, offering to do it in any way that might be desired. It is only when he is told how unimaginably handsome Pyramus is that Bottom recognizes that only he can play the young man and reconciles himself to the task.

They then all agree to rehearse the play secretly in the wood outside Athens so that no outsiders learn their plans and steal their thunder (the same wood in which Lysander and Hermia have been scheming to meet).

. . . the moon's sphere

The second act opens in this very wood, but with neither the well-born lovers nor the low-born actors in view. The wood is already occupied and we are now introduced to still another strand of plot, one that involves sheer fantasy, for it concerns fairies (drawn from Celtic legend rather than Greek mythology, but that doesn't bother anybody).

Two spirits meet to open the act. The more grotesque spirit asks the more graceful one (named simply "Fairy") where it is going. The answer is, in part:

> *I do wander everywhere,*
> *Swifter than the moon's sphere;*
>
> —Act II, scene i, lines 6–7

Here we have a little Greek astronomy. The Greeks believed that the sun, the moon, and the various planets were each set in a transparent sphere. The various spheres were nested one beyond the other, all centered on the earth, which was the very core and midpoint of the universe.

The spheres moved in various complicated fashions and the end result was to cause the heavenly object attached to it to move against the background of the stars in the fashion observed by human astronomers. The smaller, inner spheres turned more rapidly than the larger, outer ones. The moon was attached to the innermost, smallest sphere and therefore, since that sphere turned most rapidly, it moved against the stars most rapidly. —The Fairy boasts it can move even swifter than the swiftest heavenly body, the moon and its sphere.

The notion that all the spheres turned about the earth as a center was seriously challenged by the Polish astronomer Nicholas Copernicus in 1543. The issue was strongly disputed and was not finally settled in favor of Copernicus till after Shakespeare's death. Indeed, Copernicus' theory was not inconsistent with spheres (centered about the sun, rather than the earth) and it was not till Kepler showed that the planets moved in elliptical orbits (in 1609) that the notion of the celestial spheres began to die.

Shakespeare does *not*, be it noted, take the advanced position of agreeing with Copernicus. In science he is a thoroughgoing conservative who clings tightly to Greek teachings, and the notion of the spheres is a favorite of his. He refers to them in a number of places.

. . . *the Fairy Queen*

The Fairy continues to describe her duties:

> *And I serve the Fairy Queen*
> *To dew her orbs upon the green.*
>
> —Act II, scene i, lines 8–9

Nowadays we think of fairies (when we think of them at all) as tiny little creatures with butterfly wings, suitable characters for children's tales. Tinkerbell, the fairy in *Peter Pan,* is a prize example.

This is strictly a modern, watered-down version, however; a notion to which, actually, the fairies of this very play, *A Midsummer Night's Dream* have greatly contributed.

In earlier centuries fairies were taken much more seriously, and well they might be, for they originated in part out of a dim memory of the pagan sprites of the woodlands: the fauns, satyrs, and nymphs of the Greco-Roman mythology, together with the gnomes, elves, and kobolds of the Teutonic imaginings and the sorcerers and "little folk" of Celtic tales. They were the mysterious forces of nature, usually capricious, often malevolent.

The vague old beliefs clung among the country folk and became old wives' tales, while the Church, recognizing their pagan origins, strove against them.

Naturally the fairies would have a king and queen, though their names and powers vary from region to region. (For a mythology to become standard, a sophisticated literature is required, and this could scarcely be found in the case of a set of beliefs driven by the Church into refuge among the rude and unlettered.)

To us, the most familiar name of the Fairy Queen is "Titania," which is the name Shakespeare uses. But it is familiar to us *only* because Shakespeare uses it in this play. As far as we know, he was the first ever to use that name for the Fairy Queen.

We can only speculate what inspired Shakespeare to use it. The most likely guess points to Ovid's *Metamorphoses,* which Shakespeare used so often. At one point Ovid uses the name "Titania" for the moon, referring to Phoebe (see page I–12) by the same line of reasoning that causes one to use "Titan" to refer to the sun (see page I–11).

This, after all, is a moon-drenched play, a tale of fantastic doings in the dim-lit night. It may have pleased Shakespeare to have the Fairy Queen a version of the moon goddess.

The "orbs upon the green" are circles of darker grass that can be found here and there on lawns. These are the result of a mushroom's activities: a mushroom which sends out threads in all directions and fruits now and then in gradually wider circles, or parts of circles. Those with sufficient imagination see in these circles the existence of tiny ballrooms for fairies (here viewed as miniature creatures). They are called "fairy rings."

. . . Oberon is passing fell . . .

The grotesque spirit, on hearing that the other is part of the train of the Fairy Queen, says:

> *The King doth keep his revels here tonight.*
> *Take heed the Queen come not within his sight,*
> *For Oberon is passing fell and wrath,*
> —Act II, scene i, lines 18–20

The name "Oberon" is not a creation of Shakespeare's. Indeed, it dates back to ancient Teutonic times. The old Germanic legends told of a variety of earth spirits. The dwarfs (undersized, deformed creatures, usually malevolent) had, as their chief occupation, mining. (This is still so, even in Disney's *Snow White and the Seven Dwarfs*.) We can only wonder whether the legend arose in part out of the first sight by Germanic hunters of miners, caked with soil—with most of them children or undersized adults, since a small body was at a premium for writhing through the underground passages.

In any case, the king of the dwarfs in the Teutonic tales was Alberich, who is best known to us today for the part he plays in the Nibelung tale as told in Richard Wagner's four operas that begin with the Rhinemaidens and end with the Twilight of the Gods. Alberich is the fiendish dwarf who steals the gold from the Rhinemaidens. When the gold is taken from him in turn, he lays a curse upon all future holders of the gold and it is the working out of this curse that finally ends the universe.

"Alberich" is softened into "Oberon" in the French. As king of the fairies, rather than of the dwarfs, he plays a part in a popular medieval romance called *Huon of Bordeaux*. Huon kills the son of Charlemagne in this tale and is sent off on a dangerous quest in punishment. He meets Oberon, who is described as the son of a most curious pair of parents: Julius Caesar of Roman history and Morgan le Fay of Celtic legend. (Yet is that so curious? Medieval French culture represented a mingling of the Celtic peoples of ancient Gaul with the Roman conquerors—together with the later Germanic conquerors, represented by Charlemagne. Huon and Oberon may represent the meeting of Frank with Gallo-Roman.—But never mind, it's Shakespeare I'm talking about in this book.)

Huon of Bordeaux was translated into English about 1540 by an English statesman and author, John Boucheir, 2d Baron Berners. Shakespeare must surely have been aware of it, and he borrowed "Oberon" from it.

Oberon and Titania are both in the heavens now. The German-English astronomer William Herschel, who had discovered the planet Uranus in 1781, detected its two outermost satellites (it has five altogether, as far as we know today) in 1787. Departing from the then universal habit of naming bodies of the solar system after Greco-Roman gods and goddesses, he resorted to Shakespeare and named them Titania and Oberon. Oberon is the outermost.

. . . *so sweet a changeling*

The reason for the quarrel between Titania and Oberon is explained to the audience at once, for the ungainly spirit says that Oberon is angry with Titania:

> *Because that she as her attendant hath*
> *A lovely boy, stolen from an Indian king;*
> *She never had so sweet a changeling.*
> *And jealous Oberon would have the child*
> —Act II, scene i, lines 21–24

It was one of the more fear-provoking legends concerning fairies that it was their habit to steal healthy infants from their cradles, substituting sickly or deformed ones. The substituted infants found by the mothers were "changelings." The true horror of this legend lay not so much in the needless fear it provoked among parents but in the fact that when a deformed, retarded, or sickly child was indeed born, that poor infant was sometimes mistreated in order that the fairies might be induced to take it away again.

In this case, Shakespeare mistakenly refers to the stolen normal child as the changeling.

This speech, by the way, contains one of the numerous indications in the play that the fairies are very small in size, for the spirit says that whenever Oberon and Titania meet, they quarrel vehemently so that:

> *—all their elves for fear*
> *Creep into acorn cups and hide them there.*
> —Act II, scene i, lines 30–31

The best that can be done on the stage, of course, is to have the fairies played by children, and that is really quite small enough, for in *The Merry Wives of Windsor* children pretend to be fairies (see page I-446) and succeed in fooling one of the characters, who is not portrayed as wondering that fairies are so large. Shakespeare may deliberately have reduced the fairies in this play to minuscule size to add to the fantasy.

Oberon and Titania, at least, give the appearance of being full-sized humans, if we consider what Shakespeare says of them.

. . . Robin Goodfellow

By this time the Fairy has recognized the spirit to whom it has been speaking. It says:

> *Either I mistake your shape and making quite,*
> *Or else you are that shrewd and knavish sprite*
> *Called Robin Goodfellow.*
>
> —Act II, scene i, lines 32–34

The Fairy recites the mischievous deeds of Robin Goodfellow, but adds:

> *Those that Hobgoblin call you, and sweet Puck,*
> *You do their work, and they shall have good luck.*
>
> —Act II, scene i, lines 40–41

Puck, a king of the elves in Scottish mythology, was pictured as an evil demon, to begin with. His role diminished with time to that of a mere mischief-maker and it is this role Shakespeare gives him.

To avert the mischief, it was necessary to flatter him, to call him "sweet Puck" or use the euphemism "Goodfellow," with the friendly given name of "Robin" (of which "Hob" is the diminutive).

The Germans had a kind of earthy, mischievous creature in their legends, who behaved much like Shakespeare's Puck, and who were called "kobolds." "Goblin" may be a form of that word, so that "hobgoblin" means "Robin the Kobold." (People were sufficiently fearful of Puck's knavishness to make "hobgoblin" become synonymous with a besetting fear.)

Puck proudly admits his identity and describes himself as Oberon's jester, making the rather dour Fairy King laugh at the practical jokes the tricksy sprite plays on people.

. . . the shape of Corin . . .

Puck is scarcely finished when Oberon enters from one side and Titania from the other, each with their attendant elves. Both are angry at once and in no time at all are shrewishly raking up past infidelities. Titania says:

> *. . . I know*
> *When thou hast stolen away from fairy land*
> *And in the shape of Corin sat all day,*
> *Playing on pipes of corn, and versing love*
> *To amorous Phyllida.*
>
> —Act II, scene i, lines 64–68

It is not moderns only who long for a simpler past and who imagine a world of country joy and pastoral pleasures. The city folk of Shakespeare's time, and for that matter, those of ancient times, likewise turned away from what they conceived to be the corrupting influence of city life and longed for a magical land of shepherds and milkmaids ("Arcadia") that never really existed.

Pastoral plays and poetry were a fad in Shakespeare's time and one conventional name for the shepherd-hero was Corin. Indeed, Shakespeare makes use of that name for a shepherd in his own pastoral play *As You Like It* (see page I–568). As for Phyllida, that is a version of "Phyllis," a traditional name for a pastoral heroine, and a good one too, since it means "leafy" in Greek.

Titania accuses Oberon, further, of having arrived in Athens from India only to be at Theseus' wedding because he himself has been a past lover of Hippolyta.

Accusations like these make us think of Oberon and Titania as full-sized. To be sure, they can take any shape they wish (Oberon made love to Phyllida "in the shape of Corin") but it is difficult to think of them being lovingly interested in coarse humans if they themselves are dainty enough to fit in an acorn cup.

. . . Ariadne and Antiopa

Oberon, furious at Titania's scandalous allegations, accuses her in turn of being in love with Theseus and having caused him to betray earlier loves of whom she had been jealous. Oberon says:

> *Didst not thou lead him through the glimmering night*
> *From Perigenia, whom he ravishèd?*
> *And make him with fair Aegles break his faith,*
> *With Ariadne and Antiopa?*
>
> —Act II, scene i, lines 77–80

These were women whom Theseus met in the course of his adventures. Thus, Perigenia was the daughter of Sinis, a wicked bandit who lived at the Corinthian Isthmus. Sinis would bend the tops of pine trees to the ground and tie some luckless traveler's right foot to one pine tree, and left foot to the other. He would then release the trees, which would spring upright, tearing the traveler in two.

Theseus wrestled with him and killed him, then discovered the bandit's daughter hiding in terror. She fell in love with him at once. Theseus had a child by her, but then gave her to one of his companions.

Aegles and Antiopa are two other loves of Theseus. In fact, Antiopa (Antiope) is the name of the Amazonian Queen, for which Shakespeare substituted the name "Hippolyta."

By all odds, the most famous of the forsaken maidens is Ariadne. She was the daughter of King Minos of Crete, who, when Theseus was a youth, held Athens under tribute, demanding seven youths and seven maidens each year. These were sacrificed to the Minotaur, a bull-headed monster. (This is a legendary memory of the time, prior to 1400 B.C., when Crete was the greatest naval power in the Mediterranean, and when bull worship was an important factor in its religion.)

Theseus had himself selected as one of the seven youths and sailed to Crete to place an end to the tribute once and for all.

The Minotaur was hidden in the center of a labyrinth so intricate that no one entering could expect to find his way out even if he were so fortunate as to kill the monster. (This may well have been a Grecian memory of the great palace at Knossos, the Cretan capital, which had so many rooms that the unsophisticated Greeks of the day must have wondered how anyone could find his way around within it.)

Minos' daughter, Ariadne, having fallen in love with Theseus, gave him a magic ball of twine which would unwind before him, leading him to the Minotaur, and which he could then trace back for the return. Theseus followed the twine, killed the Minotaur, and returned.

The Athenian had promised to make Ariadne his wife in return and when he left Crete, he took her with him. They landed on the Aegean island of Naxos and while she slept, Theseus and his party stole away and made for Athens without her. Why he deserted her the myths don't say, though Mary Renault has a fascinating conjecture concerning it in her novel *The King Must Die*.

. . . angry winter . . .

Titania, womanlike, dismisses the charges scornfully as fantasies born of jealousy. She speaks bitterly of their quarreling as having caused the very seasons to have grown confused (a clear reflection of the role of the fairies as nature spirits):

> *The spring, the summer,*
> *The childing autumn, angry winter, change*
> *Their wonted liveries; and the mazèd world,*
> *By their increase, now knows not which is which.*
>
> —Act II, scene i, lines 111–14

The interest here lies in that some critics see this to be a contemporary reference. The years 1594–96 were horrible, from the standpoint of weather, in England, and if the play had been written in 1595, Shakespeare might have been referring to the weather at this time.

Oberon points out that to end the quarreling, all that need be done is for Titania to give up the Indian changeling, but this Titania flatly refuses to do, and they part.

. . . certain stars shot madly . . .

The chafed Oberon decides to teach Titania a lesson. He calls Puck to him and reminds him of a time they listened to a mermaid (see page 1–12) sing. Oberon says:

> *. . . the rude sea grew civil at her song,*
> *And certain stars shot madly from their spheres,*
> *To hear the sea maid's music.*
>
> —Act II, scene i, lines 152–54

This represents the romantic belief that even inanimate nature responds to beautiful music. This is most commonly aired in connection with Orpheus, the musician of Greek legend, and a beautiful song on that subject is to be found in *Henry VIII*.

The Greeks supposed that the stars possessed a sphere of their own. The stars do not move relative to each other (they are "fixed stars" as opposed to the planets) and all were affixed to a single sphere, therefore. Shakespeare, however, mistakenly supposes each star to have its individual sphere and therefore says the stars shot madly from their "spheres."

The thought that a star could leave its sphere arises from the sight of "shooting stars," which are not stars at all, of course, but fragments of matter, often no larger than a pinhead, which in their travels about the sun collide with the earth and are heated to white brilliance by friction with the air.

. . . a fair vestal . . .

Oberon goes on:

> *That very time I saw, but thou couldst not,*
> *Flying between the cold moon and the earth,*
> *Cupid all armed. A certain aim he took*
> *At a fair vestal thronèd by the west,*
> —Act II, scene i, lines 155–58

But Cupid's arrow, for a wonder, missed:

> *And the imperial vot'ress passèd on,*
> *In maiden meditation, fancy-free.*
> —Act II, scene i, lines 163–64

Vesta was the Roman goddess of the hearth; that is, of the household fire. The six priestesses in her service had, as their chief duty, the guarding of a sacred flame which must never be allowed to go out. This is perhaps a memory of a time when the art of lighting a fire at will was new and difficult, and when the loss of a household fire meant an uncomfortable period of cold and uncooked food. (It would be something like a breakdown in electric service these days.)

The priestesses were required to be virgins and to maintain an absolute chastity on pain of torture and death, and it is recorded that in eleven hundred years only twenty cases of violation of that rule were recorded.

The Vestal Virgins were venerated and had many privileges, taking precedence even over the Emperor on certain ceremonial occasions. The term "vestal" has come to be synonymous with "virgin" in the English language because of them.

Shakespeare's reference to the "fair vestal thronèd by the west" can be to none other than to Elizabeth I who, at the time the play was written had been reigning thirty-seven years, was sixty-two years old, and had never married. Non-marriage need not necessarily be equated with virginity, of course, and Elizabeth had had several favorites (including the Earl of Essex at the time the play was written) but her subjects accepted her virginity as fact.

In the early years of her reign, her failure to marry was of great concern to her advisers, for children were required if the succession was to be made sure. As the years passed and she grew too old to have children anyway, the best had to be made of it, and Elizabeth's reputed virginity became a source of pride. She became known as the "Virgin Queen," and when in the 1580s the first English settlers attempted to found colonies on what is now the east-central shore of the United States, they named the region "Virginia" in her honor.

Shakespeare's delicate picture of Elizabeth as a "fair vestal" whom not even "Cupid all armed" could defeat and who remained "in maiden meditation, fancy-free" must surely have pleased the aged Queen, who had always been terribly vain of her good looks, and who insisted on being treated as a beauty even after she had long ceased to be one. The terrible anachronism of placing her in the reign of Theseus would bother no one.

. . . a girdle round about the earth

Cupid's arrow, which misses the fair vestal, hits a flower which Oberon describes as:

> Before milk-white, now purple with love's wound,
> And maidens call it love-in-idleness.
>
> —Act II, scene i, lines 167–68

The flower referred to is more commonly spoken of nowadays as the pansy. Oberon orders Puck to:

> Fetch me this herb, and be thou here again
> Ere the leviathan can swim a league.
>
> —Act II, scene i, lines 173–74

It is foolish, of course, to try to attach literal meaning to what is obviously poetic hyperbole, but—just for fun—"leviathan" is the whale, which can swim as speedily as twenty miles an hour. To swim a league (three miles) would require nine minutes.

Puck answers:

> I'll put a girdle round about the earth
> In forty minutes.
>
> —Act II, scene i, lines 175–76

It is interesting to note that Puck outdoes even the modern astronaut, who requires ninety minutes to go around the earth. To circumnavigate the planet in forty minutes means moving at the rate of 37,500 miles an hour or a little over 10 miles a second. Puck would be hard put to manage to stay close to the earth's surface at this speed, for he would well exceed the escape velocity.

However, Shakespeare was writing a century before Newton had worked out the law of gravity, and, in any case, we can assume that such mundane universal laws of the universe would not apply to Puck.

In the nine minutes allowed him by Oberon, by the way, Puck could, at this speed, flash to a point twenty-seven hundred miles away and back again. In short, he could fly from Athens to England and back with several minutes to spare, and it must have been in England that Oberon saw Cupid aiming at the fair vestal. —So through all the fantasy, Shakespeare manages (without meaning it, I'm sure) to allow Puck enough time.

Oberon plans to use the juice of the plant he has sent Puck for as a love philter. It will serve to make Titania fall in love with something abhorrent, and thus Oberon will have his revenge.

. . . you hardhearted adamant

At this point, Demetrius (warned by Helena of the lovers' flight) comes upon the scene in search of Lysander and Hermia, intent on killing the former and dragging the latter back to Athens. Helena tags after him, although Demetrius, utterly ungrateful for her help, does his best to drive her away. But poor Helena cries out:

> You draw me, you hardhearted adamant;
> But yet you draw not iron, for my heart
> Is true as steel.
> —Act II, scene i, lines 195–97

The word "adamant" is from a Greek expression meaning "not tamed." It was applied to a mythical substance that was so hard it could not be cut or broken and in that sense could not be tamed. The word has been applied to the hardest naturally occurring substance; that is, to diamond, and, as a matter of fact, "diamond" is a corruption of "adamant."

In the Middle Ages "adamant" was falsely related to the Latin expression "adamare," meaning "to attract," so that it came to be applied to the magnet. Helena cleverly uses the word in both senses at once, for Demetrius attracts her as though he were a magnet and his cruel heart is diamond-hard.

Apollo flies . . .

Demetrius desperately tries to escape her importunities, and Helena, still pursuing him, says sadly:

Apollo flies, and Daphne holds the chase;

—Act II, scene i, line 231

Daphne was a nymph, daughter of the Peneus River (which cuts across Thessaly in northern Greece). Apollo fell in love with her and when she refused him, he tried to rape her. She fled and Apollo ran after. Even as his hands were clutching at her shoulder, she prayed to the earth goddess, who changed her into a laurel tree.

To Helena, it seems that the old myth reverses itself in her case. Oberon, overhearing, pities her. He decides to use the love juice for Demetrius as well as for Titania. In this way do the fairy plot and the lovers plot intertwine.

Oberon does not count, however, on a second pair of Athenians creeping through the fairy-haunted wood. Lysander and Hermia, coming on stage, are overcome by weariness and lie down to sleep. Puck, returning with the love juice, is told by Oberon to anoint the eyes of an Athenian youth in the woods. Puck finds Lysander and Hermia sleeping, assumes Lysander is the youth meant by Oberon, and places the juice on his eyes.

Next comes Demetrius running through, outdistancing the panting Helena. Helena, who can run no more, finds Hermia and Lysander sleeping, wonders if they are dead, and wakes Lysander. He sees Helena through his juice-moistened eyes and falls madly in love with her immediately.

Helena assumes she is being mocked and runs away. Lysander pursues her and Hermia wakes to find herself alone.

. . . a bush of thorns . . .

Meanwhile, in that spot of the woods where Titania lies sleeping (having earlier been lulled to sleep by a fairy-sung lullaby), the Athenian laborers come blundering in to work out the production problems of *Pyramus and Thisbe.*

Those problems are many and difficult to their unsophisticated minds. Bottom points out, for instance, that when Pyramus draws a sword to kill himself, he will frighten the ladies in the audience. What's more, introducing a lion will frighten them even more. It will be necessary, Bottom explains, to have a prologue written that will explain that no harm is intended, that the lion is not a real one, and so on.

There is next the question of moonlight. Will there be a moon that night? Quince checks the almanac and says:

Yes, it doth shine that night.

—Act III, scene i, line 55

This is odd, since the play is to be given at Theseus' wedding and Theseus himself has said it will take place on the night of the new moon, which means there will be *no* moon in the sky.

But it really doesn't matter. Even if there is no moon to shine naturally upon the stage, Quince has an alternative.

> . . . *one must come in with a bush of thorns and a lantern, and say he comes to disfigure, or to present, the person of Moonshine.*
> —Act III, scene i, lines 59–61

A man holding a lantern on high is an obvious representation of the moon. But why a bush of thorns?

The vague shadows on the moon's face, visible to the naked eye, are the marks of the "seas," relatively flat circular areas surrounded by the lighter cratered and mountainous areas. In the days before telescopes, the nature of the markings could not be known and an imaginative peasantry concerted the shadows into figures; most commonly the figure of a man. This was the "man in the moon."

Somehow the feeling arose that the man in the moon had been hurled there as a punishment and the particular crime was thought to have been described in the Bible. The crime took place when the Israelites were wandering in the wilderness on their way to the Promised Land. "And while the children of Israel were in the wilderness, they found a man that gathered sticks upon the sabbath day. And they that found him gathering sticks brought him unto Moses and Aaron" (Numbers 15:32–33).

It is clearly stated that this sabbath breaker was stoned to death. Nevertheless, an alternate non-biblical version of his punishment arose and grew popular. This was that for breaking the sabbath he was exiled to the moon with the sticks he had gathered. The sticks gradually elaborated into a thornbush and a dog was often added too (either as a merciful gesture of company for the man or as an unmerciful representation of the devil, who forever torments him). When in the final act of *A Midsummer Night's Dream* the little play is actually put on at Theseus' wedding, the dog appears with Starveling the Tailor, who plays Moonshine.

. . . *at Ninny's tomb*

Puck enters, having taken care (as he supposes) of Demetrius, and now all ready to place the love juice on Titania's eyes. He finds, to his amazement, the rehearsal in progress. Bottom (as Pyramus) delivers his lines and exits, while Flute (as Thisbe) calls after him:

I'll meet thee, Pyramus, at Ninny's tomb.

—Act III, scene i, line 98

"Ninny's tomb" is Flute's mangling of "Ninus' tomb." Ninus, according to Greek legend, was the founder of the Assyrian Empire and the builder of Nineveh, its capital, which, as was thought, was named after him. Since the tale of Pyramus and Thisbe takes place in Babylon, which was an important part of the Assyrian Empire, a mention of Ninus' tomb is useful local color.

The Greek versions of Assyrian history are, of course, completely distorted. There was no historical character such as Ninus. There was, however, an early Assyrian conqueror, Tukulti-Ninurta I, who reigned about the time of the Trojan War. His fame may have dimly reached across Asia Minor, and his long name could have been shortened to the first half of the second part, with a final *s* (which ended almost all Greek names) added.

. . . make an ass of me . . .

The mischievous Puck sees his chance to improve on the instructions given him by Oberon. He follows Pyramus offstage and works a charm that places an ass's head on his shoulders. When Bottom returns, unaware of the change, he finds that his frightened companions take one look at him and flee. Their cries to the effect that he is monstrously changed leave him puzzled. Finally, he says:

> *I see their knavery. This is to make an ass of me; to fright me, if they could.*

—Act III, scene i, lines 121–22

Bottom, who, figuratively speaking, has proved himself all through the play to have an ass's head, now owns one literally; and he is as unaware of his literal ass's head now as he had been of his figurative one earlier.

But he remains lovable in his folly even now. Titania, who has had the juice placed on her eyes, wakes at this moment and at once falls in love with Bottom in his grotesque disguise. She places her retinue of tiny fairies at his disposal, and Bottom, taking it all as his due, allows himself, most complacently, to be worshiped and adored.

. . . the gun's report

Delighted, Puck races to report the event to Oberon. He describes the scene when Bottom returns with his ass's head and the other workmen scatter and fly:

> *As wild geese that the creeping fowler eye,*
> *Or russet-pated choughs, many in sort,*
> *Rising and cawing at the gun's report,*
>
> —Act III, scene ii, lines 20–22

Either Puck can foresee the future with remarkable clarity or this is a particularly amusing anachronism—guns in the time of Theseus.

. . . th' Antipodes

Oberon is pleased, but asks about the Athenian lovers, and Puck says he has taken care of that too.

But in comes Demetrius. He has found Hermia, who is berating him bitterly for having killed Lysander. Only Lysander's death could explain his having left her while asleep. She would not for one moment accept the possibility that he had crept away from her willingly:

> *I'll believe as soon*
> *This whole earth may be bored, and that the moon*
> *May through the center creep, and so displease*
> *Her brother's noontide with th' Antipodes.*
>
> —Act III, scene ii, lines 52–55

The ancient Greeks were the first to realize that the earth was spherical in shape. (To be sure, they were not the Greeks of Theseus' time. The first who thought so lived seven and a half centuries after Theseus.) They realized that people who lived on the other side of the globe from themselves would have their feet pointing upward, so to speak, in the direction opposite from that in which their own feet pointed.

The people on the other side of the globe would therefore be "antipodes" ("opposite-feet"). The name was applied to the other side of the globe itself as a result.

. . . the Tartar's bow

Demetrius desperately denies having killed Lysander, but Hermia scolds him fiercely and leaves. Demetrius, wearied, lies down to sleep. Oberon, seeing Puck's mistake, sends him angrily after Helena so that the mistake can be corrected. Puck, eager to calm his angry king, says:

I go, I go; look how I go,
Swifter than arrow from the Tartar's bow.

—Act III, scene ii, lines 100–1

Europe, through its ancient and medieval history, has been periodically plagued by nomadic horsemen thundering west from the steppes of central Asia. The Cimmerians, Scythians, Sarmatians, Huns, Avars, and Magyars each in turn terrorized European territories. The nomads won their victories through superior mobility; through the dash of their swift and hardy horses, from whose backs the riders shot arrows that galled their slower-moving European adversaries.

The last and most terrible of the nomadic invaders were the Tatars or Mongols, who in the first half of the thirteenth century conquered both China and Russia. In 1240 the speeding Mongol horsemen darted into central Europe, smashing every clumsy army of armored knights that was raised to stop them, and spreading ruin and desolation almost to the Adriatic.

Far back in central Asia their ruler died and all the Mongol armies (undefeated) swept back to take part in the decision as to the succession. In 1241, therefore, the Mongols left and, as it happened, never returned.

The Europeans, however, were long to remember the dreadful period of 1240–41. They called the horsemen Tartars, rather than Tatars, thinking of them not as men but as demons from Tartarus (see page I–13). The Tartars' arrows remained in mind and Shakespeare could use them as a metaphor for speed (even though they had entered European consciousness twenty-five centuries after the time of Theseus).

. . . high Taurus' snow

Oberon places the juice on Demetrius' eyes and Puck brings back Helena as ordered. With Helena, however, is Lysander, still under the influence of the juice and still pleading love. Helena persists in thinking Lysander is making cruel fun of her. The noise they make wakes Demetrius, who is now also in love with Helena.

Demetrius addresses her in the most elaborate lover's fashion, saying:

That pure congealèd white, high Taurus' snow,
Fanned with the eastern wind, turns to a crow
When thou hold'st up thy hand: O, let me kiss
This princess of pure white . . .

—Act III, scene ii, lines 141–44

Helena is obviously a fair-skinned blonde, which in medieval times represented an ideal of beauty. Her skin is whiter than the snows of the Taurus Mountains, a range in southeastern Asia Minor.

When the German tribes tore the western provinces of the Roman Empire apart, they established themselves as an aristocracy over a Celto-Roman peasantry. The Germans were taller than the Celto-Romans on the average, and fairer. Over the centuries, therefore, fair skin, blond hair, blue eyes, and tall stature came to be associated with aristocracy and beauty; the reverse with peasanthood and ugliness.

Helena, completely confused, decides that both men have combined for some insane reason to make fun of her. Then, when Hermia enters and acts astonished, Helena maintains that her old girlfriend has also joined in the joke.

. . . you Ethiope

Poor Hermia can make nothing of what is going on. All she knows is that she has found Lysander again, but that Lysander is acting most peculiarly. She approaches Lysander timidly to find out what it is all about, but the erstwhile tender lover turns on the poor girl savagely and says:

> Away, you Ethiope!
>
> —Act III, scene ii, line 257

The expression "Ethiopian" is from Greek words meaning "burnt faces"—faces that have been darkened by exposure to the sun. It was applied to the races living south of Egypt and was eventually used for African blacks generally.

Here, then, the same principle that brings about praise for Helena's fair beauty brings contempt for poor Hermia's darker complexion.

Hermia has trouble understanding this, but when she does she leaps at once to the conclusion that Helena has stolen her love. She cries out furiously about Helena:

> Now I perceive that she hath made compare
> Between our statures; she hath urged her height,
> And with her personage, her tall personage,
> Her height, forsooth, she hath prevailed with him.
>
> —Act III, scene ii, lines 290–93

She advances upon Helena, nails unsheathed, and Helena fearfully shrinks away as both men vie in protecting her.

The exasperated Hermia accepts every remark as a reference to her plebeian shortness and Lysander, sensing her sensitivity, throws the fact of it in her face, saying:

Get you gone, you dwarf;
You minimus, of hind'ring knotgrass made;
You bead, you acorn!

—Act III, scene ii, lines 328–30

Knotgrass, a common weed, was supposed to stunt growth if eaten.

Lysander and Demetrius, angered with each other over their common love for Helena, as earlier they had been over their common love for Hermia, stride offstage to fight. At this, Helena, left alone with Hermia, flees, and Hermia follows.

. . . as black as Acheron

Oberon is terribly irritated and virtually accuses Puck of having done all this deliberately. Puck denies having done it on purpose, though he admits the results have turned out fun.

Oberon orders him to begin mending matters:

. . . Robin, overcast the night.
The starry welkin cover thou anon
With drooping fog, as black as Acheron;
And lead these testy rivals so astray,
As one comes not within another's way.

—Act III, scene ii, lines 355–59

Acheron is the name of one of the five rivers which the classical writers described as encircling the underworld. For some reason, the name of this particular river came to be applied to the underworld generally, so that "Acheron" came to be a synonym for "Hades."

Once the night is made dark, Puck is to mislead Lysander and Demetrius, weary them to sleep once more, rearrange their affections, entice them into considering it all a dream, and send all four safely back to Athens.

. . . Aurora's harbinger

Puck agrees, but urges haste:

For night's swift dragons cut the clouds full fast,
And yonder shines Aurora's harbinger;

—Act III, scene ii, lines 379–80

Aurora (known to the Greeks as Eos) is the goddess of the dawn. She is the third child of the Titan Hyperion (see page I–11), a sister of Helios, god of the sun, and Selene, goddess of the moon.

Her harbinger is the planet Venus, shining as the morning star and rising only an hour or two before the sun and therefore not long before the dawn.

Oberon agrees and Puck accomplishes the task, sending all four Athenians into a scrambling confusion that wearies them to sleep once more. He then anoints Lysander's eyes in such a way that when all four awake, all shall be straightened out. Or, as Puck says:

> Jack shall have Jill;
> Nought shall go ill;
> The man shall have his mare again, and all shall be well.
> —Act III, scene ii, lines 461–63

"Jack and Jill" is a stock phrase for a man and his sweetheart or wife. Jack is clearly a generic name for a man generally, since it is so common (a diminutive of Jacob, which in one form or another—James in England, Hamish in Scotland, Jacques in France, Iago or Diego in Spain and Portugal, and Giacopo in Italy—was an extremely popular name all over western Europe).

Jill is far less common and is usually considered a short version of Juliana. It was used, probably, because a one-syllabled girl's name starting with the J sound was needed, though it seems to me that Joan would have been more fitting. In any case, we ourselves know Jack and Jill primarily from the nursery rhyme that sends them to the top of a hill to fetch a pail of water.

Nor is this the only complication unraveled. Oberon meets Titania, who, in her entranced adoration of the ass-headed Bottom, freely gives up her Indian boy. She then has Bottom sleep with his long-eared head in her lap, and Oberon finally takes pity on her. He releases her from her spell and orders Puck to remove the ass's head from Bottom and send him back to Athens too.

And so at last are Oberon and Titania reconciled.

. . . with Hercules and Cadmus . . .

Now that the complications of the subplots are solved, Theseus and Hippolyta come on the scene again. They are following the hunt and Hippolyta says, in reminiscence:

> I was with Hercules and Cadmus once,
> When in a wood of Crete they bayed the bear
> With hounds of Sparta.
> —Act IV, scene i, lines 115–17

The world of orthodox Greek myth comes swimming back. Hercules was indeed a contemporary of Theseus and the two are made companions in several myths.

Cadmus, in the legends, was a Phoenician prince. He had come to Greece in search of Europa, his sister. She had been kidnapped by Zeus in the shape of a bull and brought to Crete, where Minos was to reign and the Minotaur was to be found. As a matter of fact, Minos was the son of Europa.

Cadmus never found Europa (so that it isn't quite right to place him in Crete). Wandering in Greece itself, he founded the city of Thebes. The Greek legend has it that it was Cadmus who taught the letters of the alphabet to the Greeks. This is interesting since the alphabet did, in actual fact, originate with the Phoenicians and it is entirely appropriate that the Greeks be taught it by Cadmus, a Phoenician prince.

Sparta is mentioned in this passage too. In Theseus' time it was a city in southern Greece that was not particularly remarkable, though it was soon to become the home of Helen, whose beauty sparked the Trojan War. In later centuries Sparta was to become the most militarized and, for a time, the most militarily successful of the Greek cities.

. . . Thessalian bulls

Theseus says that his own hounds are of the same breed as the "hounds of Sparta" Hippolyta has mentioned:

> . . . their heads are hung
> With ears that sweep away the morning dew;
> Crook-kneed, and dew-lapped like Thessalian bulls;
>
> —Act IV, scene i, lines 123–25

Thessaly is a fertile plain region in northeastern Greece, much different from the rocky, mountainous area to the south where Greece's most famous cities, including Athens, Sparta, Thebes, and Corinth, were located. It would be naturally a place where horses would be useful and where cattle would be profitably bred. A Thessalian bull would be larger and better than a bull bred elsewhere in Greece.

The rite of May

In the wood, the hunting party, which includes Egeus, the father of Hermia, comes upon the four young people, still sleeping where Puck had left them.

Egeus frowns and begins to ponder on the meaning, but Theseus, depicted throughout the play as courtly and kind, quickly places a harmless interpretation on the matter. He says:

> No doubt they rose up early to observe
> The rite of May;
>
> —Act IV, scene i, lines 135–36

May Day, the first of May, was a day of nature celebration in ancient times. Spring was definitely established by then; the greenery was growing; it was warm enough to spend the evening outdoors. It was a time for revelry and youth, and no doubt a time when the fertility of nature might best be imitated by the celebrants.

The Maypole about which the young people danced may well be what was left of a phallic symbol. Indeed, earlier in the play, Hermia had made use of just such an implication, perhaps. When she was terribly irritated at being scorned for her shortness, she turned on Helena and said,

> How low am I, thou painted maypole? Speak!
>
> —Act III, scene ii, line 296

Not only does Hermia in this way refer disparagingly to Helena as tall and skinny (and perhaps with as little figure as a maypole), but she also implies that the men, Lysander and Demetrius, are dancing about her with immoral intent.

Theseus' reference places the play well before Midsummer Day, by the way.

. . . Saint Valentine . . .

Perhaps Theseus is not unaware of the coarser ways of celebrating May Day, for as the hunting horns sound and the Athenian lovers rouse themselves, Theseus says, with light mockery:

> Good morrow, friends. Saint Valentine is past:
> Begin these wood birds but to couple now?
>
> —Act IV, scene i, lines 142–43

St. Valentine's Day is certainly past, for, as we all know, it falls on February 14. Valentine's Day commemorates the martyred death of St. Valentine on February 14, 270 (which makes it a terribly anachronistic comment in the mouth of Theseus).

The romantic symbolism of the day antedated the good saint. There is a folk belief that the birds began to mate on this day (which is what Theseus is referring to) and this may have initiated fertility rites in pagan days. The Church would attempt to transfer the rites to a Christian commemoration and soften them too, and the story arose that St. Valentine made anonymous gifts of money to help poor girls to a dowry that would find them husbands. Thus, he became the patron saint of romantic love.

The ferocious Egeus, hearing Lysander confess he had intended to elope with Hermia, calls for his death and the marriage of Hermia to Demetrius. Demetrius, however, confesses that he now loves Helena. Theseus, listening politely, decides that each loving pair is now to be married, Lysander to Hermia, and Demetrius to Helena.

Meanwhile Bottom also rouses himself, finds his natural head restored, dismisses his vague memories as a dream, and returns to Athens and to his mourning comrades. They are delighted to meet him and continue to prepare their play.

"The battle with the Centaurs . . ."

The time of the wedding of Theseus and Hippolyta is now at hand. Theseus has heard of the events of the magic night in the woods and dismisses them as fantasy. He turns to the list of entertainments proposed for the wedding feast and reads off the first item:

> "The battle with the Centaurs, to be sung
> By an Athenian eunuch to the harp."
> We'll none of that. That have I told my love,
> In glory of my kinsman Hercules.

> —Act V, scene i, lines 44–47

Centaurs were common monsters of Greek myths, composite creatures with the head and torso of men affixed to the body of a horse. They were supposed to have been natives of Thessaly. Perhaps the notion originated with the first sight of men riding horses. The southern Greeks, in their narrow valleys, having been unused to horses for generations, would find men on horseback in the plains of Thessaly when they marched northward in battle and tales of centaurs would drift back to stay-at-homes.

The centaurs were considered to be barbaric creatures of the senses, given to gross eating, to drunkenness and lechery. The chief tale in which centaurs are prominent involves the marriage of Pirithous, a friend of Theseus (he does not appear in this play but he has a minor role in *The Two Noble Kinsmen*, see page I-56).

Pirithous, who was of the Thessalian tribe of the Lapiths, invited his kinsmen and friends to the wedding, Theseus among them. He also invited a party of centaurs. The centaurs, however, drank too much and, in a drunken fury, created a disturbance and tried to carry off the bride. At once a fight broke out and the Lapiths, with Theseus' stanch help, drove off the centaurs, killing many.

It could not be this tale that was to be sung by the eunuch, for Hercules is not involved and Theseus refers to a battle with centaurs that redounded to Hercules' honor. But then, Hercules had several encounters with centaurs and won every battle.

Theseus here and in *The Two Noble Kinsmen* (see page I–58) refers to "my kinsman Hercules." They were both great-grandchildren, through their mothers, of Tantalus (see page I–13).

. . . the tipsy Bacchanals

A second item on the list is:

> *"The riot of the tipsy Bacchanals,*
> *Tearing the Thracian singer in their rage."*
>
> —Act V, scene i, lines 48–49

The Thracian singer was Orpheus, who played the lyre and sang so beautifully that wild beasts were calmed and the very trees and rocks left their place to follow him. He married Eurydice, whom he deeply loved, and when she was bitten by a snake and died, he descended into the underworld to reclaim her. So beautiful was his music that he even touched the cold heart of Hades, who agreed to let him take Eurydice back, provided he didn't turn to look at her till he was out of the underworld.

They were almost out, the light of day was ahead, when Orpheus, suddenly fearful that he was being tricked by a counterfeit, turned to look— and Eurydice slipped forever away from him.

He emerged to wander about inconsolably. He met a group of bacchanals, women engaged in the wild and drunken rites that celebrated Bacchus, god of the vine. When Orpheus seemed oblivious to them, they interpreted his sad silence as scorn. They tore him apart and threw his head into the river. It floated down to the sea, still singing as it went.

. . . I from Thebes . . .

Theseus gives his opinion of the Orpheus item curtly:

> *That is an old device; and it was played*
> *When I from Thebes came last a conqueror.*
>
> —Act V, scene i, lines 50–51

The myths do contain accounts of a victorious war fought against Thebes by Theseus. As a matter of fact, that war plays an important part in *The Two Noble Kinsmen* (see page I–59) where it is fought immediately before the wedding.

"The thrice three Muses . . ."

A third item is:

> *"The thrice three Muses mourning for the death*
> *Of Learning, late deceased in beggary."*
> —Act V, scene i, lines 52–53

Theseus dismisses that as a satire too sharp to fit a wedding ceremony.

The nine Muses ("thrice three") were daughters of Jupiter (Zeus) who were the goddesses of the various branches of learning.

Some critics have tried to pick out some particular person meant by "Learning" in this passage. It is suggested, for instance, that the reference is to the death of the Italian poet Torquato Tasso, who died in 1595.

However, it seems most likely that Shakespeare is merely poking fun at the chronic complaints in his time (and in ours, for that matter) that everything is going to the devil, that the great feats of the past will never be equaled, and that the public taste is degenerating. To show that this was felt even in Theseus' time would be amusing.

But then Theseus' eye catches the notice of the play about Pyramus and Thisbe, and though the master of the revels snobbishly dismisses it as the pathetic attempt of ignorant workers and Hippolyta expresses her nervousness over their possible failure, Theseus nobly indicates he will hear it and that nothing can be a failure if it is presented with honest good will and out of a sense of duty.

. . . like Limander . . .

Now Bottom and company present their play, which, in the actual practice, turns out to be lamer and more ridiculous than even the rehearsals had prepared us for. They mangle classical references, as when Bottom (Pyramus) says:

And, like Limander, am I trusty still.
> —Act V, scene i, line 197

Flute (Thisbe) replies to this:

And I like Helen, till the Fates me kill.
—Act V, scene i, line 198

There is no "Limander" anywhere in the corpus of Greek legends. If Flute really means "Helen," that must be the famous Helen of Troy, that paragon of beauty who was the cause of the Trojan War (see page I–76). In that case, Limander must mean Alexander, which is one of the alternate names for Paris, who eloped with her.

On the other hand, it is more likely that by Limander, Bottom meant Leander, the well-known hero of the romantic tale of a lover who nightly swam the Hellespont to be with his love and who, one stormy night, drowned in the attempt. In that case the girl would be Hero, not Helen.

. . . Shafalus to Procrus . . .

Bottom (Pyramus) also protests:

Not Shafalus to Procrus was so true.
—Act V, scene i, line 199

This is a mangling of Cephalus and Procris, a rather affecting myth about a loving husband and wife. Cephalus, an ardent hunter, had a spear that never missed. He went out hunting early every morning and finally Procris decided to follow him to see if he might not be meeting another woman. Cephalus, heated with hunting, rested and called on the breeze to cool him. Procris, imagining he was calling a woman, sprang from her hiding place and Cephalus, in reflex action, threw his never-missing spear and killed her.

O Sisters Three

The Play of Pyramus and Thisbe ends with a pair of the most terrific death scenes ever seen as first Pyramus and then Thisbe commit elaborate suicide. Thisbe cries out in her turn:

O Sisters Three,
Come, come to me,
With hands as pale as milk;

> *Lay them in gore,*
> *Since you have shore*
> *With shears his thread of silk.*

> —Act V, scene i, lines 338–43

The "Sisters Three" are the Fates, who govern all events and whose edicts neither gods nor men can defy. There are three of them by the natural division of time into past, present, and future.

Clotho represents the past and she spins the thread of life, causing life to originate and an individual to be born. Lachesis guides the thread, representing the present and its events. Dreadful Atropos is the future, for she carries the shears with which she snips the thread and brings death.

The three Fates play a much more serious part in *Macbeth* (see page I-160).

. . . the triple Hecate's team

The play within a play ends with a dance and with its audience amused and ready for bed.

Nothing remains but the final bit of entertainment, supplied by the fairy band. Puck comes on the stage alone to say that with the coming of night once more the fairies are back:

> *. . . we fairies, that do run*
> *By the triple Hecate's team,*
> *From the presence of the sun,*
> *Following darkness like a dream,*
> *Now are frolic.*

> —Act V, scene i, lines 385–89

Hecate was supposed to be one of the Titanesses in Greek mythology, but in the struggle that resulted in their supplanting by Jupiter (Zeus) and the other later gods, Hecate sided with Jupiter and remained in power. She was probably another personification of the moon.

There were three common goddesses of the moon in the later myths: Phoebe, Diana (Artemis), and Hecate. All three might be combined as the "triple Hecate" and Hecate was therefore frequently portrayed with three faces and six arms.

Later mythologists also tried to rationalize the difference in names by saying that Phoebe was the moon goddess in the heavens, Diana on earth, and Hecate in the underworld.

This connection with the underworld tended to debase her and make her a goddess of enchantments and magic spells, so that the fairies in following "triple Hecate's team" were following not only the pale team of horses that guided the moon's chariot (hence were active at night rather than by day) but also shared her power of enchantment and magic.

Her enchantments and magic made her sink further in Christian times until Hecate finally became a kind of queen of witches, and she appears in this guise in *Macbeth* (see page II–185).

Now in come Oberon and Titania with the rest of their fairies. They make their concluding pretty speeches, placing a good luck charm on all the couples being married in the play (and perhaps on the couple being married in the audience, if *A Midsummer Night's Dream* was performed to celebrate a marriage). Puck then delivers the epilogue and the play is over.

Nothing in the play indicates a tragic end to the love tale of Theseus and Hippolyta, and though it seems a shame to mention it after such a happy time, I will.

The Amazons, offended at Theseus' kidnapping of their queen, mounted an attack against him. They were defeated, but Hippolyta, fighting Amazonlike at the side of her husband, and against her own subjects of the past, was killed.

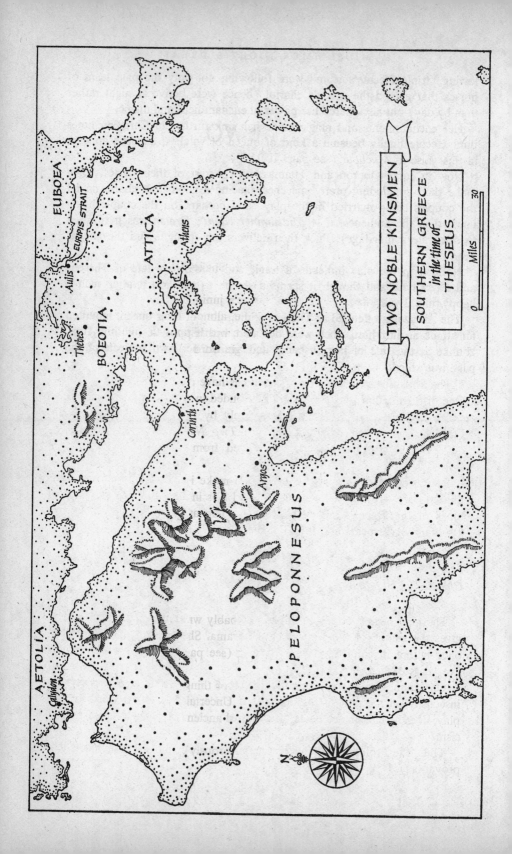

TWO NOBLE KINSMEN

SOUTHERN GREECE
in the time of
THESEUS

Miles
0   30

EUBOEA

EURIPIS STRAIT

Aulis

AETOLIA

Calydon

BOEOTIA

Thebes

ATTICA

Athens

Corinth

Argos

PELOPONNESUS

N

3

THE TWO

NOBLE KINSMEN

I N 1613, at the very end of his career, Shakespeare collaborated with John Fletcher in writing two plays.

Fletcher was fifteen years Shakespeare's junior and between 1606 and 1625 (he died in the latter year) he wrote, alone or in collaboration, some fifty plays. The most notable of these were with Francis Beaumont, so that "Beaumont and Fletcher" is almost a single word in the history of English literature.

The Shakespeare-Fletcher collaborations have all but vanished, as such. One of them, *Henry VIII* is generally included in editions of Shakespeare's collected works and is presented as solely by him, with no mention of Fletcher. The other collaboration, *The Two Noble Kinsmen,* is treated quite the reverse. It is generally omitted from Shakespeare's collected works.

Recent scholarship, however, seems to make it reasonably certain that Shakespeare wrote a major part of it, and it is included as one of the volumes of the Signet Classic Shakespeare. The authorship is given as by "William Shakespeare and John Fletcher."

Chaucer, of all admired . . .

The play begins with a Prologue (probably written by Fletcher) which gives the source of the content of the drama. Shakespeare had done this once before in connection with *Pericles* (see page I–181), written some five years earlier.

One cannot help wondering if this sort of thing isn't a sign of a certain insecurity on the part of the playwright. Uncertain as to the worth of the play, does he call on the name of a revered ancient as a shield against criticism?

Thus, the Prologue, hoping (rather timorously) that the play meets approval, says:

It has a noble breeder, and a pure,
A learned, and a poet never went
More famous yet 'twixt Po and silver Trent.
Chaucer, of all admired, the story gives:

—Prolog, lines 10–13

Geoffrey Chaucer was born about 1340 and died in 1400. He was at the peak of his fame during the reign of Richard II (see *Richard II*). His wife was a lady in waiting to the second wife of John of Gaunt, an uncle of Richard II and an important character in the play of that name. What's more, she was sister to John of Gaunt's third wife.

Chaucer is widely considered the first great writer in English (as opposed to the older Anglo-Saxon or Norman-French languages) and as the father of English literature. Placing him among the most prominent poets of western Europe (between the Po River in northern Italy and the Trent River in central England) is not an undue exaggeration.

Chaucer's masterpiece is the *Canterbury Tales,* published in the last decade of his life. This pictured a group of twenty-nine varied individuals, united in the accident that all were on a pilgrimage to Canterbury. They planned to amuse themselves on the way by each telling (according to the original plan) two stories, making fifty-eight in all. Only twenty-three stories actually appear, so that less than half the original plan was carried through, but what exists is still splendid because of the wide variety in content and style and because of the interesting characterization of each pilgrim, both in description and in the story he or she chooses to tell.

One of the pilgrims was a knight, and his tale was the first to be told. This "Knight's Tale," which serves as the source of *The Two Noble Kinsmen* is itself taken from the poem *La Teseida* of Giovanni Boccaccio.

It is a tale of courtly love, treating with seriousness that artificial game of man and woman popularized by the troubadours of southern France in the time of the Crusades. By the conventions of courtly love, a woman was treated in a semifeudal, semireligious manner, with the lover serving her as both a vassal and a worshiper. The lover had to fulfill every whim of his mistress and suffer the extremes of emotion in a manner that had little if any relation to real life, but has affected storybook romance down to our own day. Such love could not exist in marriage but, according to convention, had to face insuperable barriers, such as the marriage of the mistress to someone else. Courtly love was mock passion, mock heroics, mock poetry, with nothing real but the noise it made.

Near the beginning of his career as a playwright, Shakespeare satirized courtly love rather amusingly in his *Love's Labor's Lost* (see page I–437). (It was far more effectively blasted in the great Spanish novel *Don Quixote de la Mancha* by Miguel de Cervantes, the first part of which appeared in 1605. The love of Don Quixote for Dulcinea del Toboso reduced the conventions of courtly love to ridicule once and for all.)

In *The Two Noble Kinsmen* Shakespeare and Fletcher treat courtly love seriously, but so lost are its conventions to us of the twentieth century that we cannot—even when Shakespeare asks us to. And at that, perhaps Shakespeare didn't try very hard to win us over. Those portions of the play which he wrote seem to have been pageantlike in nature. Shakespeare was writing "spectacle."

Than Robin Hood

The pageantry and spectacle of the play may even have been forced upon it by the pressure of having to live up to its Chaucerian source (like a modern trying to make a musical out of a Shakespearean play). At least, Fletcher, in the Prologue, begs the audience not to hiss lest Chaucer turn in his grave and say:

> "*O fan*
> *From me the witless chaff of such a writer*
> *That blasts my bays and my famed works makes lighter*
> *Than Robin Hood!*"
>
> —Prolog, lines 18–21

That great folk hero, Robin Hood, was known to the English public through a series of popular ballads which first appear (as far as modern knowledge is concerned) in Chaucer's lifetime. These ballads were enormously popular but as serious poetry were quite insignificant. They were analogous, in a way, to our own enormously popular but literarily insignificant TV westerns.

. . . child of Ver

The play opens with a scene which is thought to be Shakespearean.

Hymen enters. He is the Greek god of marriage, and is a mere personification concerning whom there are no well-known myths. Following Hymen are a variety of nymphs and then a wedding party—a groom, a bride, the groom's friend, the bride's sister. Everything is joyous and springlike and the first words of the play are a song about early flowers:

> *Primrose, first-born child of Ver,*
> *Merry spring-time's harbinger,*
>
> —Act I, scene i, lines 7–8

"Ver" is an obsolete term for spring, from the French *vert* (meaning "green"—from which such words as "verdure" and "verdant" are also derived).

The marriage that is being so celebrated is between none other than Theseus and Hippolyta, the same couple who were being married at the start of *A Midsummer Night's Dream* (see page I–18). In fact, some critics suggest that Shakespeare used Chaucer's "Knight's Tale" as the original inspiration of *A Midsummer Night's Dream,* borrowing the marriage as the frame and then filling it with his own subplots. Here in *The Two Noble Kinsmen* he follows Chaucer in the subplot as well.

In *The Two Noble Kinsmen,* Theseus is supplied with a friend, Pirithous, who was lacking in *A Midsummer Night's Dream.* Pirithous is an authentic mythological character. It was at his marriage that a famous battle with centaurs took place (see page I–46).

The best-known myth concerning Theseus and Pirithous deals with an occasion when the latter decided to gain for himself the hand of none other than Proserpina, queen of the underworld (see page I–15). Theseus loyally offered to help and the two invaded Hades. There both were magically imprisoned in chairs from which they could not rise, and it seemed, in punishment for their presumption, that this situation would last eternally. Hercules, however, eventually rescued them. According to some versions, he rescued only Theseus and left Pirithous forever imprisoned in Hades.

Hippolyta in this play is given a sister whom she did not have in *A Midsummer Night's Dream.* This is Emilia, a character who does not belong to classical myth at all, but to medieval fiction. She is to be the heroine of this play, the puppet about whom will circle the mummery of courtly love.

. . . cruel Creon . . .

Before the marriage can take place, however, three queens enter. Each kneels, pleading, before a separate member of the wedding party, and a stately back-and-forth begins. The First Queen (given no other name in the play) falls at the feet of Theseus, and says:

> *We are three queens, whose sovereigns fell before*
> *The wrath of cruel Creon; who endured*
> *The beaks of ravens, talons of the kites,*
> *And pecks of crows, in the foul fields of Thebes.*
> *He will not suffer us to burn their bones,*
> *To urn their ashes . . .*

> —Act I, scene i, lines 39–44

It was in Thebes that the famous legend of Oedipus was set. Oedipus, who had been cast away as an infant and had been brought up far away from Thebes, did not know he was the son of the Theban King and Queen. Visiting Thebes, he unknowingly killed the King and married the Queen—killing his father and marrying his mother, whence we get the expression "Oedipus complex." By his own mother Oedipus had two sons, Eteocles and Polyneices, and two daughters, Ismene and Antigone.

After the truth of the matter came out, Oedipus blinded himself and went into voluntary exile, while his mother-wife, Jocasta, committed suicide.

Jocasta's younger brother, Creon, became effective ruler of Thebes. Creon supported Eteocles, Oedipus' elder son, for the succession. Polyneices, the younger son, went into exile and talked certain leaders of the city of Argos, sixty miles southwest of Thebes, into leading an army against his city.

Five Argive leaders took up the struggle. With them was not only Polyneices, but also Tydeus, who was a refugee in Argos because he had fled his home town after accidentally killing his brother. Tydeus was the father of Diomedes, who was to be an important Greek warrior at the siege of Troy and an important character in Shakespeare's *Troilus and Cressida* (see page I-79).

The tale of the expedition of these leaders against Thebes is usually called "The Seven Against Thebes," though in *The Two Noble Kinsmen* the number is reduced to three.

The seven were defeated, and Creon remained master of the field. As a punishment for the aggressors (and particularly for Polyneices, who had warred against his own city—an act of treason for which no personal wrongs were deemed sufficient excuse), Creon ordered the fallen warriors on the Argive side to remain in the field unburied, a prey to carrion birds and beasts.

This was a terrible fate for Greeks, who felt that until a dead body had been burned with appropriate rites, its shade must wander restlessly about the border of Hades. In fact, it was held impious of Creon to dictate such a fate, since it was wrong to inflict it even on hated enemies.

The Greek playwright Sophocles wrote one of the greatest of the surviving Greek dramas on this subject. Entitled *Antigone,* it dealt with Oedipus' younger daughter, who felt that the religious obligation to bury her fallen brother, Polyneices, transcended all other considerations. She accomplishes the deed even though it means her own death.

The three queens apparently have attempted to do Antigone's deed but have failed, and now they have come to ask Theseus to invade Thebes, punish Creon, and see to it that the fallen warriors are duly burned.

King Capaneus . . .

Theseus is sympathetic to the appeal, for he has met the First Queen before. He says:

> *King Capaneus was your lord. The day*
> *That he should marry you, at such a season*
> *As now it is with me, I met your groom.*
>
> —Act I, scene i, lines 59–61

Capaneus was one of the seven against Thebes and his death was dramatic. He had placed a ladder against Thebes's wall and, climbing it, boasted that not even Jupiter (Zeus) could keep him out of the city now. Promptly, he was struck by a lightning bolt and killed. He had a son, named Sthenelus, who was to be at the siege of Troy as companion and friend of Diomedes. Sthenelus appears in the *Iliad* but not in Shakespeare's *Troilus and Cressida*.

Capaneus' wife was named Evadne, and presumably it is she who is the First Queen.

. . . his Nemean hide

On the occasion of the marriage of Capaneus and Evadne, Theseus met the bride as well and found her beautiful. Nor was he the only one. Theseus says:

> *Hercules our kinsman,*
> *Then weaker than your eyes, laid by his club:*
> *He tumbled down upon his Nemean hide*
> *And swore his sinews thawed.*
>
> —Act I, scene i, lines 66–69

The reference is to the first labor (see page I-24) of Hercules. That was to kill a lion that infested the valley of Nemea, ten miles southwest of Corinth. This Nemean lion was no normal beast, but an enormous monster whose hide was impenetrable to any weapon.

Hercules tried arrows, sword, and club, but nothing would make an impression. He therefore seized the beast's throat and throttled it to death. He then flayed the creature with the only thing that could cut through its hide, its own razor-sharp claws. Forever after, he wore the lion's hide as a protective shield.

. . . the helmeted Bellona . . .

Theseus orders the Queen to stand, and accepts the task, saying:

> *O no knees, none, widow,*
> *Unto the helmeted Bellona use them,*
> *And pray for me your soldier.*
>
> —Act I, scene i, lines 74–76

Bellona is not a member of the Greek mythological group. She is a Roman war goddess (the Latin word for war is *bellum*) and was considered either the wife or sister of Mars. There was a temple to Bellona outside the city of Rome, and the Senate met there when negotiating with foreign ambassadors, or when greeting the return of victorious generals.

. . . the banks of Aulis . . .

The Second Queen pleads with Hippolyta, the Third with Emilia. Both are sympathetic but Theseus naturally wishes to continue with the wedding before taking care of Creon. The queens (and even Hippolyta and her sister) plead with Theseus to reverse matters and make war with Creon first.

Theseus agrees at last and says to an officer:

> *Hence you,*
> *And at the banks of Aulis meet us with*
> *The forces you can raise . . .*
>
> —Act I, scene i, lines 210–12

Aulis was famous as the place where the ships of the Greek host gathered (in the generation after Theseus) to sail to Troy. Shakespeare could not resist, therefore, having Theseus gather *his* army there.

Aulis is on the seacoast of Greece, just where the large island of Euboea comes nearest the mainland, leaving a strait, the Euripus, not more than a mile wide. In these constricted waters a fleet can gather in safety. From Aulis there is a sea voyage of 170 miles northeast, as the crow flies, to reach Troy.

Of what use, however, to assemble at a seaport in order to send an army from Athens to Thebes, since the two cities are separated by land? Thebes is thirty-five miles northwest of Athens, and to travel to Aulis improves the situation very little. Besides, Aulis is in Theban-dominated territory and an Athenian army would very likely have to fight a battle as soon as it gets to Aulis.

Dear Palamon . . .

The scene now shifts to Thebes, and, specifically, to two young Theban soldiers. One of them begins:

> *Dear Palamon, dearer in love than blood*
> *And our prime cousin . . .*
>
>   —Act I, scene ii, lines 1–2

The speaker is Arcite. Needless to say, nowhere in the Greek body of myth are Palamon and Arcite to be found. They are creations strictly of the medieval romancers. They are ideal medieval knights, brave, noble, chivalrous beyond all qualification, and devoted one to the other.

They are apparently of the family of Oedipus, for as they bemoan the corruption and decadence of Thebes, Palamon begins to lay the worst of the blame on an individual that Arcite guesses at once, saying:

> *Our uncle Creon.*
>
>   —Act I, scene ii, line 62

However, the news of Theseus' invasion comes and the two young soldiers, who had been planning to leave Thebes, realize that whatever their disenchantment with the city, they must fight for it against foreign invaders.

. . . great Apollo's mercy . . .

The battle is won by Theseus and the bodies of the dead warriors are rescued. They will be given all the proper funeral rites by the queens.

Theseus' victory over Thebes is mentioned, in passing, in *A Midsummer Night's Dream* (see page I-47). An affecting tale concerning Evadne, the First Queen, is not mentioned in *The Two Noble Kinsmen*. When her dead husband, Capaneus, was being burned, Evadne found she could not bear to part with him. She threw herself, living, on the fire, and burned to death.

The battle had had another result as well. It brought Palamon and Arcite into Athenian hands as prisoners. The Theban youths fought marvelously, but were overwhelmed and are wounded and near death. Theseus has, however, been impressed by their fighting and orders that physicians attempt to save their lives. He says:

For our love
And great Apollo's mercy, all our best
Their best skill tender.

—Act I, scene iv, lines 45–47

Apollo is the god of the fine arts, and apparently medicine was considered one of them. (He was also the god of disease, for it was his arrows which were pictured as striking down the population of a city struck by the plague.) Asclepius, who is described in the myths as a specific god of medicine, is a son of Apollo.

. . . *a Parthian quiver* . . .

Whereas the entire first act is considered Shakespeare's, most of the second, third, and fourth acts are considered Fletcher's.

Palamon and Arcite are recovered from their wounds, but they are in an Athenian prison now. They are guarded by a jailer who has a pretty daughter. Neither is given a name, but are called merely "Jailer" and "Daughter" in the stage directions. There is also a young man who is in love with the daughter, and he is called only "Wooer."

The two Thebans expect to remain in prison for life and together they mourn the joys they shall never taste again, such as hunting:

No more now must we halloo, no more shake
Our pointed javelins, whilst the angry swine
Flies like a Parthian quiver from our rages,
Struck with our well-steeled darts.

—Act II, scene i, lines 107–10

The Parthians were an ancient people who ruled over what is now Iraq and Iran and who were noted for their ability as horse archers. The Romans fought them for centuries and were occasionally defeated by them. A boar struck by many darts would be as full of arrows as a Parthian quiver.

The remark is anachronistic, of course, if we consider the time to be really that of Theseus. Parthia did not develop as a nation until about 250 B.C., a full thousand years after the time of Theseus. On the other hand, if we allow our mind to wander forward to medieval times in the Palamon and Arcite scenes, the reference to Parthia ceases to be an anachronism.

. . . a noble kinsman

Still, the two young men have each other and it occurs to them that while they are together, they have an important part of life. Each hymns the other's friendship, until it seems that their enforced company brings them to the height of bliss and that such friendship as theirs could not possibly be severed.

At that moment, though, Emilia and a maid come into the garden adjoining the prison. They gather flowers and Emilia comments on the myth of Narcissus (see page I-10).

Even while Palamon and Arcite are swearing total friendship, first Palamon, then Arcite, sees Emilia from a window and instantly (such is the convention of courtly love) falls entirely in love with her to the point where there is no room for any other emotion.

The two friends are suddenly competitors and Palamon claims sole right to the love since he saw Emilia first and called Arcite's attention to her. Arcite, however, points out that he too is subject to passions and says:

> *Why then would you deal so cunningly,*
> *So strangely, so unlike a noble kinsman,*
> *To love alone?*
>
> —Act II, scene i, lines 250–52

Here is the reference from which the title of the play is taken. Palamon and Arcite are "the two noble kinsmen."

. . . against the Maying

The quarrel between them is suspended when Arcite is called away. The news is quickly brought back to Palamon that Arcite, on Pirithous' request, has been released from prison, but banished forever from Athens.

Palamon fears that Arcite, free, may yet lead an army back to Athens to try to win Emilia. Arcite, on the other hand, as he takes the road back to Thebes, fears that Palamon, in Athens, though imprisoned, may have an opportunity to woo and win Emilia.

At this point, Arcite comes upon a group of country people intent on a holiday. One of them says, in fact:

> *Do we all hold, against the Maying?*
>
> —Act II, scene ii, line 36

Here, as in *A Midsummer Night's Dream,* that other play set against the

Theseus-Hippolyta marriage, we have a group of members of the lower classes arranging a rustic performance. It is a May Day celebration, and *A Midsummer Night's Dream* seems to have taken place at May Day too (see page I-45).

Arcite decides to violate the exile order, join the countrymen, and in rustic guise participate in the athletic contests that accompany the May Day celebration.

As we might expect, he wins at wrestling before the eyes of Theseus and the court (who fail to recognize him—all disguises are effective in Shakespearean plays). Arcite even has the happiness of talking to Emilia and being accepted as her servant.

. . . the King of Pigmies

Arcite does not, however, have it all his own way. The Jailer's Daughter has fallen in love with Palamon and has let him out of his jail cell, though unable, at the moment, to arrange his liberation from the chains upon him.

Palamon finds Arcite and challenges him to a duel, but their old friendship is not entirely gone. Arcite helps him hide, then gets him food and wine, together with files with which to remove the shackles. They even try to reminisce fondly about earlier loves that did not come between them, but then Emilia's name comes up and they are ready for slaughter again.

Meanwhile, however, the poor Daughter, in a series of short scenes by herself, makes a gradual descent from love for Palamon, to a passionate search for him so that she might file off the shackles, to heartbreak at being unable to find him and fearing him dead, and, at last, to madness. She begins to talk nonsense built about her desire to know of the lost and absent Palamon:

> *Would I could find a fine frog; he would tell me*
> *News from all parts o'th'world; then would I make*
> *A carack of a cockleshell, and sail*
> *By east and north-east to the King of Pigmies,*
> *For he tells fortunes rarely.*
>
> —Act III, scene iv, lines 12–16

The Pygmies are first mentioned in Homer's *Iliad,* as a dwarfish people who perpetually war against cranes (and who, one would suppose, are therefore small enough to be eaten by cranes). The very word "pygmy" comes from a Greek word meaning the length of the arm from elbow to knuckles, which would imply that the little creatures were about a foot high. They were supposed to live somewhere in Ethiopia, the Greek name for the mysterious regions south of Egypt.

By modern times the Pygmies were dismissed as but another figment of the fertile Greek imagination, but then, oddly enough, a race of short human beings (not one foot high, to be sure, but averaging some four feet high) were discovered in central Africa in the nineteenth century.

It seems fairly reasonable to suppose that some of them were encountered by Egyptian armies adventuring southward, for, in the time of their stronger dynasties, the Egyptians controlled regions far into what is now the Sudan. Individual pygmies were very likely brought back as prisoners and rumors of such human beings, with the shortness exaggerated, would then serve as the basis for the Greek legend.

The Daughter also sings a sad song which deals with a maiden who searches for her love, and then, worn out and weary, she adds:

> O for a prick now like a nightingale,
> To put my breast against! I shall sleep like a top else.
> —Act III, scene iv, lines 25–26

The nightingale's song can be heard all night long and it was a common folk belief that it had to lean against a thorn so that the pain would keep it awake and singing.

. . . Meleager and the boar

The countrymen have now worked out a dance with which to amuse and please Theseus and Hippolyta, who are out hunting. (This is reminiscent of the play *Pyramus and Thisbe* which entertained the same couple in *A Midsummer Night's Dream*.)

The countrymen are under the direction of a pedantic schoolmaster who interlards his speech with unnecessarily learned allusions. Thus, he tells them all to hide in the thicket and come out on signal to surprise Theseus:

> I fling my cap up—mark there—then do you,
> As once did Meleager and the boar,
> Break comely out before him . . .
> —Act III, scene v, lines 17–19

Meleager, in the Greek myths, was a king of Calydon in Aetolia. He is best known in connection with a monstrous boar who had been sent by Diana (Artemis) to ravage the Calydonian countryside. A huge expedition was organized to track down and kill the "Calydonian boar," and, as a matter of fact, Theseus and Pirithous were among the heroes present on the occasion.

At one point in the hunt, the boar came dashing out of the thicket at Theseus, whose hastily thrown javelin went wide. He might have been killed but for the fact that Meleager, who was on the spot, threw more accurately, diverted the beast, then killed him.

Under the circumstances, the schoolmaster's allusion is most inappropriate.

. . . dance a morris

As the countrymen take their places, it turns out that one girl is missing. For a moment, it looks as though all is ruined, but the Jailer's Daughter, quite mad, wanders onto the scene and she is at once pressed into service.

Theseus and his party are now coming. The countrymen hide and the schoolmaster confronts Theseus, saying:

> We are a merry rout, or else a rabble
> Or company, or by a figure Chorus,
> That 'fore thy dignity will dance a morris.
>
> —Act III, scene v, lines 105–7

The "morris dance" was part of the May Day celebration. In its origins it was probably some kind of magical rite, involving men in the guise of animals, who are shot at. This may have been a way of ensuring successful hunting, and there may also have been included some general fertility rituals, involving a King and Queen of the May.

Indeed, the schoolmaster mentions them when he enumerates the company. He himself appears first, he says, and then:

> The next the Lord of May, and Lady bright,
>
> —Act III, scene v, line 124

There were other characters as well, including one at least who made the fertility nature of the celebration unmistakable. He was a farcical fool called the "Bavian" who was equipped with a tail which perhaps showed his descent from the tailed satyrlike fertility spirits of the wildwood. The schoolmaster, in preparing his muster earlier, was concerned lest the fool go too far, for he said:

> Where's the Bavian?
> My friend, carry your tail without offense
> Or scandal to the ladies;
>
> —Act III, scene v, lines 33–35

But it is clear that the tail is not the only appendage the Bavian has. He has a phallus too, and a prominent one, which can scarcely avoid giving offense if the ladies are in the least delicate. Nevertheless, the schoolmaster in introducing the company before Theseus and his party officiously points out what needs no pointing out:

> . . . and next the Fool,
> The Bavian with long tail, and eke long tool,
> > —Act III, scene v, lines 130–31

Perhaps to lessen the pagan character of the May Day celebration and reduce churchly opposition, new and popular characters were introduced in the form of Robin Hood and Maid Marian (as the King and Queen of the May) together with other members of his band. After all, Robin hunted deer and so completely lived in the forest as to be considered almost a spirit of the wildwood. He would fit the celebration, and his popularity would help make the morris dance respectable.

Why morris dance, by the way? One theory is that the dance was brought in from Spain in the time of King Edward III (when his son, the Black Prince, campaigned for a time in that land; see page II–260). It was, according to that view, a Moorish military dance, and from Moorish dance to morris dance is but a step. Another theory is that the dancers blacked themselves as part of their disguise and were Moorish in that sense.

The dance, when given, adds another bit of pageantry to the play.

By Castor . . .

Arcite and Palamon are now ready for their duel. They help each other into armor with every sign of affection and with mutual praise, but they fight in earnest, for the requirements of courtly love are that a knight must sacrifice all else.

Theseus and his company, still hunting, come upon the duelers. Theseus is furious, for dueling is against the law. He says, angrily, even before he knows the identity of the fighters:

> By Castor, both shall die.
> > —Act III, scene vi, line 137

It is unusual to swear by Castor alone, for he is one of an inseparable pair, Castor and Polydeuces (or Pollux). They were twin brothers who were the model of fraternal affection. They were born of Leda and were brothers of Helen, whose beauty later caused the Trojan War.

To swear by Castor is inappropriate for another reason, for Castor and his twin brother were contemporaries of Theseus and were still alive. They had not yet attained the status of gods.

In any case, Theseus' vow does not stand. Everyone, Pirithous, Hippolyta, and Emilia, pleads with him to let the warriors fight it out. Since Emilia refuses to choose between them but offers to accept the winner—quite in line with the conventions of courtly love—Theseus gives them a month's grace and then each, accompanied by three friends apiece, can join battle formally for the hand of the lady.

. . . as Iris

The Jailer's mad Daughter is back at home now and her faithful Wooer comes anxiously to learn of her. He had seen her roaming the countryside in her madness and had found her as beautiful

> . . . as Iris
> Newly dropped down from heaven.
> —Act IV, scene i, lines 87–88

The name "Iris" means "rainbow" and she was the representation of that phenomenon. Since the rainbow seems like a delicate bridge in the sky, it was easy to imagine that it served as a route between heaven and earth. From the route itself, the name was applied to a messenger who plied that route, and Iris was therefore a messenger, carrying divine orders to mortals and serving Juno (Hera) in particular.

. . . wanton Ganymede

Emilia has her problems. She is distressed that either Palamon or Arcite should die for her. She could prevent it if only she could choose between them, but she can't. She has a picture of each, and each she in turns admires. Of Arcite, she says:

> Just such another wanton Ganymede
> Set Jove a-fire with and enforced the god
> Snatch up the goodly boy . . .
> —Act IV, scene ii, lines 15–17

Ganymede, in the Greek myths, was a beautiful Trojan prince, with whom Jupiter (Zeus) fell in love. Jupiter took on the guise of an eagle and carried Ganymede off, taking him to heaven where he became the wine pourer of the gods. This is another case of homosexuality attributed to the gods, as in the case of Apollo and Hyacinthus (see page I–15)—this time of Jupiter himself.

The use of Jove for Jupiter, as in this passage, is common. Jove is from a Latin word that means simply "god."

. . . Pelops' shoulder

Of Arcite's brow, Emilia goes on to say that it is

> *Arched like the great-eyed Juno's, but far sweeter,*
> *Smoother than Pelops' shoulder!*
> > —Act IV, scene ii, lines 20–21

Pelops was the son whom Tantalus killed and served as food for the gods (see page I–13). The gods recognized what was being served them and, with one exception, did not eat of the food. The exception was Demeter, who, sorrowing over Proserpina (see page I–7), had absent-mindedly eaten some of the shoulder. The gods, in bringing Pelops back to life, replaced the missing part with ivory so that Pelops' shoulder served, in literature, as a standard for smoothness.

—But then Emilia looks at Palamon's picture and thinks he is equally wonderful. She cannot choose.

. . . a piece of silver . . .

While this is going on, the Jailer has brought a doctor to treat his mad daughter. All she can do is talk of Palamon, nothing but Palamon. She thinks Palamon is dead and that in the next world Dido will abandon Aeneas (see page I–20) for Palamon's sake. The reference to Dido is as anachronistic here as it was in *A Midsummer Night's Dream*.

She seems to be thinking of death herself, to join Palamon in the afterworld. This requires certain rites, of course:

> *. . . you must bring a piece of silver on the tip of your tongue,*
> *or no ferry.*
> > —Act IV, scene iii, lines 19–21

The Greeks felt that Charon, the ferrier of the underworld, would not take a shade over the Styx River into Hades unless he were paid, and for the purpose a small coin was usually placed in the corpse's mouth.

. . . pick flowers with Proserpine . . .

The Daughter imagines that once in the Elysian Fields (see page I-13), all would be well:

> *we shall come there, and do nothing all day long but pick flowers with Proserpine. Then will I make Palamon a nosegay . . .*
>
> —Act IV, scene iii, lines 24–26

Proserpina was picking flowers when she was carried off by Hades (see page I-7) and that action is therefore associated with her.

The doctor, listening to all this, decides that the only way the Daughter can possibly be cajoled out of her madness is to let her think she has Palamon. He therefore urges the Wooer to play the part of Palamon in all possible ways. The Wooer agrees and the Daughter accepts him in this role. Mad or not, the play ends happily for these two.

. . . methought Alcides . . .

The tournament between the knights led by Arcite and by Palamon is ready to begin, and in the fifth act Shakespeare's pen takes over for heavy pageantry. Both warriors must offer prayer to the gods. Arcite chooses to pray to Mars (Ares), the god of war, and receives the approval of his request for victory in the form of a short burst of thunder.

Palamon chooses to pray not to Mars but to Venus, the goddess of love (a wiser choice by the rules of courtly love), and he receives a positive sign too, in the form of music and doves.

Emilia prays also, to the virginal Diana (Artemis), asking that the one who best loves her should win her. She receives an answer as the sole rose falls from a rosebush.

The tournament is nip and tuck, but it is fought offstage. At first the cries seem to make Palamon the winner, but in the end it is Arcite by a narrow margin and Mars's omen is fulfilled.

Theseus greatly admires both. Palamon, the loser, is highly praised:

> *. . . methought Alcides was*
> To him a sow of lead.
>
> —Act V, scene iii, lines 119–20

Greeks generally had a single name. There was considerable chance of duplication, therefore, and it was necessary to identify people by their native cities or by their father's name. One might say "Diomedes, son of Tydeus" (see page I–57), or simply "son of Tydeus," as another way of referring to Diomedes. In Greek fashion, "son of Tydeus" would be "Tydides."

It was difficult to call Hercules by the name of his father, since he was the son of Jupiter, who had come to his mother Alcmene in the guise of her husband Amphitryon. With Amphitryon notoriously cuckolded, the mythmakers could scarcely call him "Amphitryonides." They evaded the issue by naming him for his grandfather, Alcaeus, Amphitryon's father. He is therefore called Alcides.

And yet though Arcite has won the battle by Mars's grace, Palamon wins the lady by Venus' grace. Arcite, in triumph, mounts a horse who, through accident, throws him and falls upon him. Arcite is brought onstage, dying, and gives his right to Emilia to Palamon. This is justified by Theseus' statement that Arcite had admitted, after all, that Palamon had seen the lady first.

With that, all the rules of courtly love are satisfied and the play can come to an end.

4

The History of

TROILUS AND CRESSIDA

THE MOST famous event in the early history of Greece was the Trojan War, fought a generation after the time of Theseus—or shortly before 1200 B.C. Concerning that war, we have only the legendary tale told by Homer, a Greek poet who supposedly lived in the ninth century B.C.

Whether Homer actually lived, or whether the poems ascribed to him were written by one man or many, has exercised the ingenuity of literary critics for over two thousand years, but that is not the sort of problem that concerns us here.

What does concern us is that the Homeric poems have (along with the Bible and Shakespeare's plays) been the most notable and influential works of literature ever produced in the Western world, and that in 1601 Shakespeare wrote his own version of the Homeric tale.

Shakespeare was by no means the first, nor was he the last, to do a version of Homer.

Homer's poem may have first been put together about 850 B.C. and have been sung or recited by bard after bard, the tale being carried on from generation to generation through oral tradition. About 500 B.C. it was carefully edited by Athenian scholars and placed into the form we now have.

Homer tells the tale of but a single episode in the long Trojan War, which, according to legend, lasted ten years. The episode takes place in the tenth and last year and deals with a quarrel between two of the Greek leaders, with the near disaster that befalls the Greek cause as a result, and with the dramatic reconciliation that follows after all the participants have suffered tragic losses.

In the course of the epic, hints are given as to events that took place before the incident of the quarrel and of events that were to take place after the reconciliation. The popularity of Homer's tale led later Greek poets and dramatists to try their hand at telling other portions of the tale, based on Homer's references and on other legends then extant but not surviving today.

Other ancient writers even tried retelling the tale of the quarrel itself in their own way, and the habit of doing so continued through the Middle Ages and into modern times. In 1925, for instance, the American writer

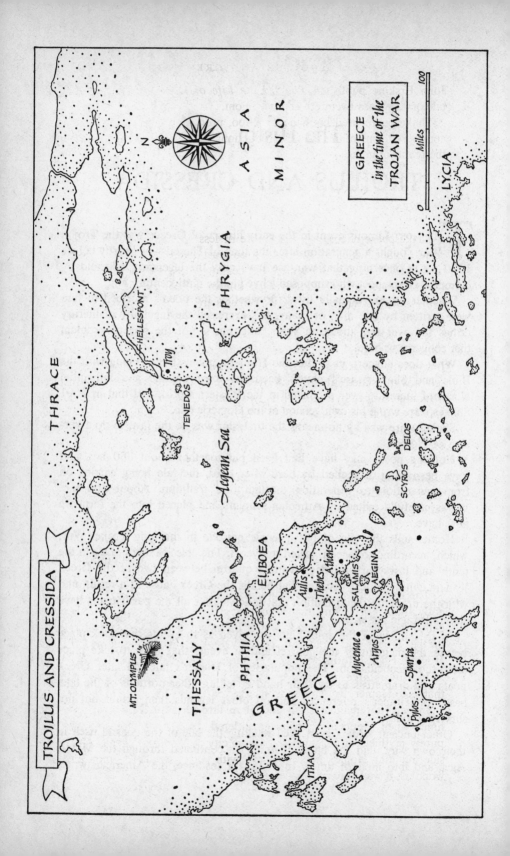

TROILUS AND CRESSIDA

GREECE
in the time of the
TROJAN WAR

Miles
0   100

THRACE

HELLESPONT

Troy

TENEDOS

ASIA

MINOR

PHRYGIA

Aegean Sea

SCYROS

DELOS

LYCIA

MT. OLYMPUS

THESSALY

EUBOEA

PHTHIA

Aulis

Thebes

Athens

SALAMIS

AEGINA

GREECE

Mycenae

Argos

Sparta

Pylos

ITHACA

John Erskine published *The Private Life of Helen of Troy,* putting the tale of Troy into twentieth-century idiom.

Shakespeare tried his hand at it too, producing, alas, a play that is not considered one of his better productions and is by no means worthy of the grand original.

In Troy . . .

Shakespeare chooses to tell (more or less) the same incident that concerns Homer, which means that he too must concentrate on the final stages of a long siege. Where Homer was dealing with incidents in a war which (in his time) must have been well known to all Greeks, with its heroes' names being household words, Shakespeare was not quite in the same position.

Educated Englishmen in Shakespeare's time knew of the Trojan War, but chiefly through writings on the subject in Roman and medieval times. It was only toward the end of the sixteenth century that Homer's poem itself was translated into English by George Chapman (whose work inspired a famous sonnet by John Keats two centuries later). At the time *Troilus and Cressida* was being written, only a third of that translation had yet appeared, so it is doubtful how much firsthand knowledge of Homer's actual tale Shakespeare himself had and how much he had to depend on later (and distorted) versions of the Troy tale.

Shakespeare did not apparently feel safe in starting, as Homer did, toward the end of the war, and inserts a somewhat apologetic Prologue to set the stage. The Prologue begins directly:

> *In Troy there lies the scene.*
>
> —Prologue, line 1

The name of the walled city which endured the long siege was, apparently, Ilion (or Ilium, in the Latin spelling). Homer's poem is therefore called the *Iliad.* The region in which Ilium was located was known as Troas or the Troad, and from this, the city took the alternate name of Troia. It is the English form of this latter name, Troy, that is most familiar to us.

It is over three thousand years now since Troy was destroyed and yet, thanks to Homer, its name remains forever fresh to us.

Indeed, it remained fresh and alive through a period in early modern times when skeptical scholars considered the Trojan War to have been purely mythical and were sure that no city of Troy had ever existed. Considering that Homer filled his tale with gods, goddesses, monsters, and wonders, it was easy to feel skepticism.

However, after all the overlay of the marvelous has been scraped away, a core remains and, as it turns out, that core has value.

A German businessman, Heinrich Schliemann, who implicitly believed the essential truth of the *Iliad* (minus its gods), amassed wealth and in the late nineteenth century used it to go to Greece and Turkey, where he hoped to dig up the ruins of Troy and some of the great Greek cities of the time. From the 1860s to his death in 1890, he achieved phenomenal success, locating the site of Troy and other places mentioned in the *Iliad*.

Historians now know quite a bit about the early phase of Greek history, which they call the Mycenaean Age. From what they have learned, we find that Homer's tale is a surprisingly faithful rendering (though with a few anachronisms) of Mycenaean society. Historians are now just as certain that there *was* a siege of Troy, as a century ago they were certain there was not.

. . . isles of Greece

The Prologue goes on to describe those who were attacking Troy:

> *From isles of Greece*
> *The princes orgulous, their high blood chafed,*
> *Have to the port of Athens sent their ships,*
>
> —Prologue, lines 1–3

According to the legend, it was a combined expedition of Greek forces drawn from all the petty kingdoms that were then to be found in Greece. In theory, all acknowledged an overlord who ruled in the southern portion of the peninsula and it was this overlord who acted as commander in chief of the expedition.

The overlordship was not tight, however, and the leaders of the various contingents were very aware of their own rights and privileges. There was a strong resemblance between the situation in Mycenaean Greece and that in medieval Europe, where a king was titular overlord but could only with the greatest difficulty induce his various dukes and counts to obey him. Shakespeare was not so far removed from this stage of history to fail to understand it, hence his reference to the princes "orgulous"; that is, "haughty."

The Greek forces, coming from various regions, had to meet at some gathering place to form a unified fleet. According to legend, that meeting place was at Aulis, a harbor in Boeotia, protected by the long island of Euboea (see page I–59).

Shakespeare here makes the gathering place Athens, which is incorrect.

. . . toward Phrygia

Having gathered, the united fleet now moves on across the Aegean Sea toward Troy. The total number of ships is given:

> *. . . Sixty and nine, that wore*
> *Their crownets regal, from th'Athenian bay*
> *Put forth toward Phrygia;*
>
> —Prologue, lines 5–7

In Mycenaean times, a people we now call the Phrygians were in control of western Asia Minor. They still dominated the area in the supposed time in which Homer lived, three and a half centuries after the Trojan War, so he could speak of them familiarly. Their power was not destroyed till about 700 B.C. when the nomadic Cimmerians from the regions north of the Black Sea invaded Asia Minor and wreaked widespread destruction. The name "Phrygia" was still applied to a region of west central Asia Minor throughout ancient times, however.

The chances are that the Trojans (although pictured in the *Iliad* as being in no way different from the Greeks in language, customs, or religion) were Phrygians.

Shakespeare's mention of 69 ships is an extremely modest underestimate of the legendary number. The *Iliad* lists the numbers of ships brought by each Greek contingent in Book Two and the total comes to 1186. Christopher Marlowe in his play *Dr. Faustus* is closer to Homer, by far, when he has Faustus cry out at seeing the shade of the beautiful woman who, according to legend, brought on the war, "Was this the face that launched a thousand ships—"

The ravished Helen . . .

The basic cause of the expedition was undoubtedly most unromantic. Troy controlled the narrow waters between the Aegean Sea and the Black Sea and was, therefore, master of an important trade route. By charging tolls for passage, they grew rich, and this made the city a valuable prize for any freebooting expedition.

Not only did Troy's wealth form a tempting target, but the Mycenaeans were being prodded from behind. New tribes of Greeks from the north, relatively uncivilized ones called Dorians, were making their pressure felt. Conditions at home were less settled than they had been and the urge to take part in piratical expeditions overseas increased.

Indeed, the time of the Trojan War was one of great turmoil throughout the civilized world and it was not only Troy that was suffering harm from sea raiders. Other raiders ravaged the coast of Egypt and Canaan, for instance. Certain contingents of these raiders settled down on the Canaanite coast and became the Philistines, who strongly influenced Israelite history.

By Homer's time a much more trivial, but much more romantic, cause had been given for the expedition. Shakespeare gives it briefly here. The Greeks, he says, have sworn

> *To ransack Troy, within whose strong immures*
> *The ravished Helen, Menelaus' queen,*
> *With wanton Paris sleeps—and that's the quarrel.*
> —Prologue, lines 8–10

In ancient times piratical raids were common. Ships would come ashore and armed men would suddenly snatch up cattle and people, then sail away again. If the people captured (and intended for the slave-market) included any of prominent family, reprisal raids might be carried through. The immediate cause of the Trojan War could well have been such a raid, of which the Trojans may have been guilty or which it suited the Greeks to say that the Trojans were guilty.

With time, the details of the abduction were adorned and elaborated with complicated myth, and this particular one has become world-famous. I'll give it briefly.

At a certain wedding (involving a bride and groom who will appear later in this chapter) all the gods and goddesses had been invited—with one exception. Eris, the Goddess of Discord, had been overlooked. She appeared unbidden and in anger tossed a golden apple (the "Apple of Discord") among the guests. It bore the label "To the Fairest."

At once three goddesses claimed it: Juno (Hera), the wife of Jupiter (Zeus); Minerva (Athena), the Goddess of Wisdom; and Venus (Aphrodite), the Goddess of Beauty.

The goddesses agreed to accept the decision of Paris, a Trojan prince, and each goddess tried her best to bribe him. Juno offered him power, Minerva offered him wisdom, and Venus offered him the fairest woman in the world for his bride. He chose Venus, which was probably the honest choice in any case.

There was a complication, though. The fairest woman in the world was Helen, who was already married to Menelaus, King of Sparta.

Guided by Venus, Paris arrived as a guest in Sparta, was royally treated by Menelaus, and then, when Menelaus was off on state affairs, Paris seized the opportunity to abduct the willing Helen (Paris was very handsome) and carry her off to Troy.

Menelaus was rightly angry over this and the result was the Greek expedition against Troy.

To Tenedos . . .

The journey of the Greek fleet is followed:

> *To Tenedos they come,*
> *And the deep-drawing barks do there disgorge*
> *Their warlike fraughtage. Now on Dardan plains*
> *The fresh and yet unbruisèd Greeks do pitch*
> *Their brave pavilions.*
>
> —Prologue, lines 11–15

Tenedos is a small island about four miles off the shore of Asia Minor near Troy.

Troy itself is several miles inland and the plain between itself and the sea is the "Dardan plain." Dardania is a name for a section of the Trojan coast. The name is derived, according to the myth, from Dardanus, a son of Jupiter. A grandson of Dardanus was Tros, from whose name Troy was derived.

Having brought the Greeks to Troy, the Prologue now warns the audience that the play will not start at the beginning:

> *. . . our play*
> *Leaps o'er the vaunt and firstlings of those broils,*
> *Beginning in the middle,*
>
> —Prologue, lines 26–28

. . . Troilus, alas . . .

Yet though the play begins in the middle of a war, it does not begin with martial scenes or even with martial speeches. It begins with a rather sickly speech of love.

The fault lies not in Homer but in medieval distortions of the tale. In Shakespeare's time the most popular version of the tale of Troy was a twelfth-century French romance, written by Benoît de Sainte-Maure, called *Roman de Troie*. Even that wasn't based on Homer directly, but on works written in late Roman times which were themselves altered versions of the original account.

The *Roman de Troie* was written when the devices of courtly love (see page I-54) were taking France by storm, so that Homer's vigorously masculine tale became prettified with the addition of an artificial love story. It was the love story, rather than the Homeric background, that interested later writers such as Boccaccio in Italy and Chaucer in England, and through them, Shakespeare.

The first scene of *Troilus and Cressida* is in Troy. A young Trojan warrior comes on the scene, sulky and petulant because he is being frustrated in love. He is taking off his armor and won't fight, saying:

> *Each Troyan that is master of his heart,*
> *Let him to field; Troilus, alas, hath none.*
>
> —Act I, scene i, lines 4–5

As the name of the play tells us, the action is to revolve to a large extent about Troilus, but who is he?

In Homer's *Iliad* he is dead before the action starts, and he receives exactly one mention. Toward the very end of the book, when the aged King of Troy is making ready to go to the Greek camp to try to ransom the dead body of his most heroic son, he berates his remaining sons, saying,* "Your dead brothers were the best soldiers in my dominions. Mestor, Troilus the Chariot-Fighter, and Hector, a very god among men—yes, his aspect was rather divine than human—fallen and gone, and mere dregs left me."

That is all; nothing more.

The later poets and commentators filled in the gap, though, and invented various tales concerning Troilus that agreed in only one respect: he was eventually killed by Achilles, the greatest of the Greek warriors.

Since Troilus is heroic and since his tale is not told (and therefore fixed) by Homer, there is room left for addition in medieval fashion, when the medieval writers took their turn. It was Troilus to whom the tale of courtly love was affixed.

I'll not meddle . . .

With Troilus is an older man, Pandarus, who listens impatiently to the young hero's sighs. Apparently he has been doing his best to bring the love affair to a happy conclusion. Now he pretends to lose patience, saying:

> *Well, I have told you enough of this. For my part,*
> *I'll not meddle nor make no farther.*
>
> —Act I, scene i, lines 13–14

Who is Pandarus? In the *Iliad* there is indeed a character by this name. He is pictured as an expert archer and appears in Homer's tale on two separate occasions.

His first appearance is in Book Four of the *Iliad*. A truce has been de-

---

* In my quotations from the *Iliad,* I am making use of the recent translation by Robert Graves, *The Anger of Achilles* (Doubleday, 1959).

clared between the armies and for a moment it seems as though the war may end in a compromise with Helen returned and Troy left standing. Pandarus, however, treacherously shoots an arrow at Menelaus and wounds him. The war goes on.

Pandarus makes a second appearance in Book Five. He shoots an arrow at Diomedes, one of the major Greek heroes, and wounds him slightly. A little later, he encounters the enraged Greek at close range and is himself killed. Exit Pandarus.

Shakespeare's Pandarus has no more in common with this other one than the name. In *Troilus and Cressida* Pandarus is a genial old man, very interested in sex—a kind of voyeur, in fact—and so unashamed in his vicarious delight over the whole matter that he has given the word "pander" to the English language.

To be sure, it is not Shakespeare who is entirely responsible for this change. Pandarus appears as Pandaro in a short poem ("Filostrato") about this love affair published by the Italian writer Giovanni Boccaccio in 1338. In "Filostrato" Pandaro is the cousin of the girl whom Troilus loves.

The English poet Chaucer (see page I–54) published in 1385 *Troilus and Criseyde,* a much longer work, based on "Filostrato." In it Pandaro, the girl's cousin, became Pandare, the girl's uncle.

It was Shakespeare next who, using Chaucer's poem as a main source, wrote *Troilus and Cressida* and changed Pandare to Pandarus.

. . . fair Cressid . . .

Bumblingly, Pandarus urges patience on Troilus, and Troilus retorts that he is already superhumanly patient. He says:

> *At Priam's royal table do I sit,*
> *And when fair Cressid comes into my thoughts—*
> —Act I, scene i, lines 31–32

Priam is King of Troy, the figure of a royal patriarch. He has, all told, fifty sons and twelve daughters by various wives, and Troilus is one of the sons. When the Greek expedition arrived before the walls of Troy, Priam was too old to fight, but he was still in full authority as king.

As for "fair Cressid," who is she? She is Pandarus' niece in the play and it is she with whom Troilus is in love, but where does she come from? She is not mentioned, not once, in the *Iliad.*

Yet, even so, we can trace her origin from the very first book of the *Iliad.* In that first book, Homer relates the cause of a quarrel between Agamemnon, the commander in chief of the Greek forces, and the greatest warrior in those forces, Achilles.

The army, it seems, has conducted a raid, carried off captives, and divided the loot. Agamemnon's share included a girl named Chryseis, while Achilles' share included another girl named Briseis. (The similarity in names is unfortunate and is a sure source of confusion.)

It turns out that Chryseis is the daughter of Chryses, a priest of Apollo. The priest comes to the camp to retrieve his daughter but when he is brusquely turned away by Agamemnon, Apollo (answering his priest's prayer) sends plague into the Greek camp. As a result, Achilles urges Agamemnon to return Chryseis and Agamemnon pettishly insists that, in that case, he will appropriate Briseis in return.

The quarrel flares and Achilles, in a rage, declares he will retire to his tent. He and his warriors will fight no more on behalf of this miserable leader. (And surely, our sympathies are all with the wronged Achilles at the start.)

The argument rests entirely on a matter of prestige. Agamemnon's view is that his prerogative as commander in chief is unassailable. Achilles insists that the commander in chief cannot hide behind his office while committing an injustice. The matter of the girls is a trifling symbol of the clash between central authority and individual rights. Homer does not introduce the thought that Agamemnon might be in love with Chryseis or Achilles with Briseis; certainly not in the medieval sense.

Later writers, however, more romantic than Homer and far less able, cannot resist stressing the love story, and make Achilles in love with Briseis.

In Benoît's medieval *Roman de Troie,* another factor is brought in to further complicate the matter and make the love tale even more interesting. The Trojan prince Troilus is also in love with Briseis, so that now there is a triangle of men, Agamemnon, Achilles, and Troilus, all competing for her.

Benoît distorts the name, and "Briseis" becomes "Briseide." Since it is almost impossible to avoid confusing "Briseis" with "Chryseis," "Briseide" easily becomes "Criseide." Hence Chaucer wrote of Troilus and Criseyde; and by a further small change Shakespeare wrote of Troilus and Cressida.

. . . Hector or my father . . .

Poor Troilus also complains that he must hide his aching heart and conceal the fact that he is hopelessly in love:

> *Lest Hector or my father should perceive me*
> —Act I, scene i, line 38

Hector was Priam's oldest son, his father's surrogate in the field, the commander in chief of the Trojan armies. He is the best and greatest warrior on the Trojan side, second only to Achilles as a fighter. He is one of the most attractive personalities in the *Iliad* and is the picture of patriotism.

The bias in his favor is far more pronounced in medieval versions of the tale, since the Trojans were supposed to be the ancestors of the Romans, and Rome always had a "good press" in the Middle Ages. Such a bias may also be expected in Shakespeare's play and it is there. Shakespeare consistently pictures Hector as braver and better than Achilles, for instance.

Why Troilus should be so reluctant to let Priam or Hector know of his love is not made clear in the play. One might argue that it was a time to fight and not to love and that father and older brother would object to having young Troilus moon away his time when the city was in such peril. More likely, however, courtly love is, by convention, supposed to be barred by tremendous hurdles; barriers of law or caste, parental disapproval, royal disfavor, and so on. Troilus must not be allowed to have it too easy, therefore.

. . . somewhat darker than Helen's

As for Pandarus, it is his task at the moment to keep Troilus' love in flame by a skillful praising of Cressida, saying:

> *An her hair were not somewhat darker than Helen's*
> —Act I, scene i, lines 43–44

He does not go on and really, the implication that Cressida might almost be compared with Helen can only be considered humorous.

Ever since the tale of the Trojan War has been extant, Helen has been considered beauty incarnate and beyond comparison. Notice, though, the implication that darker hair is, in itself, a blot on beauty (see page I–436).

. . . Cassandra's wit . . .

Pandarus continues to praise Cressida. Having compared her physical attributes with Helen's, in bumbling style, he searches for a way of praising her mind. He says:

> *. . . I would somebody had heard her talk yesterday, as I did.*
> *I will not dispraise your sister Cassandra's wit, but—*
> —Act I, scene i, lines 47–49

Cassandra was one of Priam's daughters and the most tragic of them. She was beloved by Apollo and had promised to yield to him if he would give her the gift of prophecy. When he had granted her that favor she nevertheless remained obdurate. The divine gift could not be withdrawn, but in revenge Apollo decreed that no one would ever believe her true prophecies. In other words, people believed her mad.

The comparison, then, with Cassandra in matter of wit is but another bumble, calculated, perhaps, to draw a laugh from the more knowing in the audience.

. . . behind her father . . .

Troilus continues to bemoan his fate, oblivious to Pandarus' wheedling. The go-between therefore tries the other extreme. Violently, he disowns the whole business and washes his hands of it. He will do nothing further for Troilus and says:

> *She's a fool to stay behind her father. Let her to the Greeks, and so I'll tell her the next time I see her.*
> —Act I, scene i, lines 83–85

Cressida's father is Calchas, a priest of Apollo. If Cressida's name is derived from the *Iliad's* Chryseis, her father's name must be derived from the name of Chryseis' father, Chryses. He too was a priest of Apollo.

Why "Calchas" from "Chryses"? Because there is also a Calchas in the *Iliad*. He is a skilled prophet or soothsayer on the Greek side, and can interpret the omens. It is he, for instance, who explained that the plague striking at the Greeks was the result of Agamemnon's refusal to surrender Chryseis to her father. Both Chryses and Calchas are thus involved in the demand that Agamemnon surrender Chryseis.

There is no hint in the *Iliad* that Calchas is anything but a Greek and certainly there is no confusion between him and Chryses. In later stories, however, the confusion arises. Chryses the Trojan priest of Apollo and Calchas the Greek soothsayer are combined and the story arises that Calchas, a Trojan priest of Apollo, knowing through his prophetic arts that Troy must fall, deserts to the Greeks.

The story of the lost daughter is retained, though. Since Calchas/Chryses has now turned voluntarily to the Greeks to remain with them permanently, he can't be trying to retrieve a daughter from the Greeks. After all, *he's* there. He must, therefore, be trying to retrieve a daughter from the Trojan camp, a daughter he left behind in deserting to the Greeks. And it is this Trojan daughter, Cressida/Chryseis, whom Troilus loves.

. . . thy Daphne's love

Troilus is at once anxious to placate Pandarus, who, after all, remains the only bridge by which he can reach Cressida. Pandarus, however, pushing his advantage, rushes off, leaving Troilus behind to sing Cressida's praises, calling on Apollo (the god of poetry) to help him:

> *Tell me, Apollo, for thy Daphne's love,*
> *What Cressid is . . .*
>
> —Act I, scene i, 102–3

It is interesting that Apollo, the personification of male beauty, is so often tragically unsuccessful in his loves. Cassandra refused him, for instance, and Daphne (see page I-36) is an even more famous love.

What news, Aeneas . . .

Troilus' soliloquy ends when another Trojan warrior enters. He is in full armor, on his way to the battle, and is rather puzzled that Troilus is lingering in Troy. Troilus asks:

> *What news, Aeneas, from the field today?*
>
> —Act I, scene i, line 112

Aeneas, in the legends, is a son of none other than Venus, though his father, Anchises, was a mortal man. Aeneas was not a Trojan exactly, but a Dardanian; that is, the inhabitant of a district neighboring Troy proper. He attempted to maintain neutrality in the war at first but the attacks of Achilles forced him to join forces with Priam and his sons.

None of this is in the *Iliad*. In the *Iliad* he is an ardent Trojan fighter, second only to Hector. He is a darling of the gods and is saved by Venus and Apollo when about to be killed by Diomedes, and on another occasion by Neptune, when it is Achilles who is about to kill him.

Homer makes it quite plain that Aeneas is not fated to die in the general sack that destroys Troy (see page I-209). This was the basis of Vergil's plot in the *Aeneid*, which deals with the wanderings of Aeneas after the destruction of Troy.

Because Aeneas was viewed as the ancestor of the Romans, he had to be treated with particular care by Western poets. The English had to be even more careful, for they aped the Romans in their search for a glorious beginning.

Several medieval chroniclers in England composed versions of a legendary past that traced the early Britons back to Troy. It seems, according to them, that Aeneas had had a great-grandson, Brute, who, having inadvertently killed his father, fled Italy and finally landed in the northern island, which got its name of "Britain" from him.

There is absolutely nothing to it, of course, other than the accidental similarity between the common Roman name Brute or Brutus and the name of Britain. Nevertheless it gave the English a profound interest in the tale of Troy and a strong pro-Trojan sympathy. In particular, Aeneas must be, and is, idealized. In *Troilus and Cressida* he is gay, debonair, and the perfect medieval knight.

. . . Menelaus' horn

Aeneas tells Troilus that Paris has been wounded in a duel with Menelaus. (Such a duel is described in Book Three of the *Iliad* and it is after that duel, which Menelaus wins, that a truce is negotiated, a truce which is broken by Pandarus' arrow—see page I–79).

Troilus shrugs it off:

> *Let Paris bleed; 'tis but a scar to scorn:*
> *Paris is gored with Menelaus' horn.*
>
> —Act I, scene i, lines 115–16

There was an accepted convention in Shakespearean England that a betrayed husband had horns; invisible ones, of course. This may be from a consideration of the sexual life of the polygamous stags, who fight each other for the possession of a harem of does. The deceived husband is, perhaps, likened to a defeated stag; hence his horns.

The husband whose wife had fooled him was universally viewed with amused contempt in Shakespeare's time. This attitude arose, perhaps, from the conventions of courtly love, (see page I–54) where the knight was, ideally, supposed to love the wife of another. In all such tales, the husband was the villain (witness the well-known romance of Tristan and Iseult) and the audience cheered when the horns were, so to speak, placed on his forehead.

The betrayed husband was therefore an inexhaustible theme for comedy and any mention of horns or horned animals, even any reference to foreheads, was the signal for laughter—and Shakespeare made the most of that.

Thus it is that Troilus scorns poor wronged Menelaus. To modern ears, which do not find adultery either as serious or as comic as the Elizabethans did, such jests fall flat.

Queen Hecuba . . .

The scene shifts to Cressida now. She enters with her servant, Alexander, looking after two women who have hastened by. She inquires who those were who passed and Alexander answers:

> *Queen Hecuba and Helen.*
>
> —Act I, scene ii, line 1b

Queen Hecuba (or Hecabe, in the Greek form) was the second wife of Priam. She bore him nineteen of his sixty-two children, including Hector, Paris, Troilus, and Cassandra of those mentioned so far. Because of her sufferings, she was a favorite character in tragic dramas devoted to the Trojan War and, indeed, in *Hamlet* Shakespeare makes use of this fact indirectly (see page II–115). Here, in *Troilus and Cressida,* however, she never appears onstage.

He chid Andromache . . .

Apparently the two women are hastening to the walls to see the battle, for they fear it may be going poorly. After all, even Hector is perturbed, or as the servant says:

> *Hector, whose patience*
> *Is as a virtue fixed, today was moved.*
> *He chid Andromache, and struck his armorer,*
>
> —Act I, scene ii, lines 4–6

Andromache is Hector's wife. The last part of Book Six of the *Iliad* is devoted to a scene in which she hurries with her infant son, Scamandrius, to meet Hector before he leaves the city on his way to the battle. It is the most touching scene of married love in Homer. Andromache pleads with Hector to stay in the city, for all her own relatives are dead. "So, dear Hector," she says, "you are now not merely my husband—you are father, mother, and brother, too!"

But Hector must go and he reaches out his arms to give his son a farewell and to pray over him, hoping that someday the child's feats will be such that all will agree that "His father was the lesser man!" Alas, it was not to be, for Hector's son was killed when Troy was destroyed.

A lord of Troyan blood . . .

To make Hector scold Andromache, something most unusual must have
happened. Cressida asks what that might be and is told:

> *. . . there is among the Greeks*
> *A lord of Troyan blood, nephew to Hector;*
> *They call him Ajax.*
> —Act I, scene ii, lines 12–14

Ajax plays a great role in the *Iliad.* He is one of two men in the epic
that bears the name. Since the one here referred to is particularly large,
he is called "Ajax the Greater." Of the two, only "the Greater" appears
in *Troilus and Cressida,* so it suffices to call him Ajax.

In the *Iliad* Ajax is the strongest of the Greeks, save only for Achilles,
but is considerably more renowned for his strength than for his subtlety.
He is never wounded in the *Iliad,* and he is the only important hero who
never at any time personally receives the help of a god or a goddess. He
is the epitome of success through hard work, without inspiration.

He is not, in the *Iliad,* of Trojan blood; nor is he a nephew to Hector.
The attribution of Trojan blood to Ajax is probably the result of confusion with Ajax's half brother (see page I–103).

. . . a gouty Briareus . . .

Alexander goes on to describe Ajax and makes him out to be a parody
of the picture presented in Homer; as nothing more than a stolid, dim-
witted man-mountain. He says of Ajax:

> *. . . he is a gouty Briareus, many hands and no use, or*
> *purblind Argus, all eyes and no sight.*
> —Act I, scene ii, lines 29–30

Briareus was an earthborn monster with fifty heads and a hundred
arms. The most important myth in which he figured was one in which the
tale of a revolt against Jupiter is central. The other gods, led by Neptune
and Apollo, succeed in binding Jupiter, and he might have been overthrown, but for the action of a sea nymph, who hastily brought Briareus
to the rescue. The monster untied Jupiter and by his presence cowed the
other gods.

As for Argus, he was a monster with a hundred eyes who was sent by
Juno (Hera) in order that he might watch the nymph Io. Io had been one
of Jupiter's many loves, and that god had turned her into a heifer to hide

her from Juno, but unsuccessfully. Argus' vigilance (his eyes never closed in unison; fifty at least were always open and alert) would prevent Jupiter from ever turning Io back into human form.

Jupiter sent Mercury (Hermes) to the rescue. Mercury lulled Argus to a simultaneous hundred-eyed sleep with a soothing lullaby and then cut off his head. Juno placed Argus' many eyes in the tail of her favorite bird, the peacock.

Alexander's description of Ajax, in other words, is that of a man who has all the physical attributes required for a warrior but who lacks the intelligence to make those attributes work for him.

And, apparently, what bothers Hector is that this mule of a man has struck him down. Hector cannot help but feel the shame of it.

That's Antenor . . .

Pandarus arrives on the scene and at once begins busily to praise Troilus, hoping to arouse Cressida's ardor. Cressida, who knows exactly what he is doing, teases him unmercifully by never allowing his praises to stand but turning everything on its head.

Soon the men are returning from the field at the close of the day, and Pandarus decides to let Troilus' own appearance do the talking. He leads Cressida to a place where she can see them, continuing to promise her Troilus, but naming the others as they pass.

Aeneas passes first and is praised, of course. (Aeneas is always praised—he must be.) Then comes another, and Pandarus says:

> That's Antenor. He has a shrewd wit, I can tell you; and he's man good enough—he's one o' the soundest judgments in Troy whosoever . . .
>
> —Act I, scene ii, lines 197–99

In the *Iliad* Antenor was one of the elders of Troy. He was a councilor of Priam and a man of good judgment, as Shakespeare says, but far too old to fight. There is undoubtedly confusion here with Agenor, his son, who in the *Iliad* plays an important role as a Trojan warrior.

That's Helenus . . .

Pandarus' fussing becomes funnier and funnier. Hector and Paris pass and he praises them with forced enthusiasm, but keeps watching for Troilus and growing constantly more upset because Troilus doesn't appear.

When Cressida asks the name of one of the passing warriors, Pandarus answers absently:

> *That's Helenus. I marvel where Troilus is. That's Helenus.*
> *I think he went not forth today. That's Helenus.*
>
> —Act I, scene ii, lines 227–29

Helenus was another son of Priam and Hecuba, and, according to some accounts, a twin brother of Cassandra. He was likewise blessed with the powers of a soothsayer and was a priest. He was the only one of Priam's sons to survive the fall of Troy (perhaps because of his priestly character) and in the end, according to some of the later tales, married Andromache, Hector's widow. Together they ended their lives ruling over Epirus, a district in northwestern Greece.

. . . That's Deiphobus

But Cressida is still teasing Pandarus unmercifully. She clearly knows all the men whom Pandarus is identifying. In fact, she sees Troilus before Pandarus does and asks in mock disdain:

> *What sneaking fellow comes yonder?*
>
> —Act I, scene ii, line 234

And, at the crisis, Pandarus fails to recognize him after all, saying:

> *Where? Yonder? That's Deiphobus.*
>
> —Act I, scene ii, line 235

Only belatedly does he realize it is Troilus.

Deiphobus is still another son of Priam and Hecuba. After Paris dies in battle, it is he who next marries Helen. As a result, when Troy is taken, he is killed by Menelaus and his corpse is hideously mangled.

Pandarus makes up for his tardiness in recognizing Troilus by setting up such a caterwauling after him that Cressida is embarrassed; not so embarrassed, however, that she fails to continue her teasing.

It is only after Pandarus leaves that she reveals in a soliloquy that she is actually in love with Troilus, but holds off because she thinks women are valued only as long as they are not attained.

. . . after seven years' siege . . .

With the third scene we find ourselves in the Greek camp for the first time.

There is a general air of depression over the camp and Agamemnon, the commander in chief, is trying to instill heart in the warriors. Their troubles are, after all, long-standing ones, so why be disheartened now?

> *. . . is it matter new to us*
> *That we come short of our suppose so far*
> *That after seven years' siege yet Troy walls stand;*
> —Act I, scene iii, lines 10–12

If this is the last year of the war, as it must be, then Troy's walls have been standing nine years, not seven—but that is a small error that makes no difference.

Agamemnon goes on to point out that the difficulty of the task but tests their mettle and tries their worth.

Agamemnon is in a difficult position, for as commander in chief of the Greek army, the chief odium will fall upon him if the expedition fails. He is commander in chief because he is the king of Mycenae, which at the time of the Trojan War was the chief city of Greece and gave its name to the Mycenaean Age. It declined soon after the Trojan War thanks to the devastation that accompanied the Dorian conquest of much of Greece. It was but a disregarded village in the days of Greece's greatest period, centuries later.

Mycenae, located in the northeastern Peloponnesus, six miles north of Argos, has been excavated in the last century, and ample evidence has been discovered of past greatness.

Agamemnon was the grandson of Pelops (see page I–68) and, in theory, he ruled over all of Greece, though in actual fact the princes of northern Greece (Achilles among them) were restive in the face of the claims of leadership on the part of the southern city, Mycenae.

He was married to Clytemnestra, the daughter of Tyndareus, King of Sparta, a city located some fifty-five miles south of Mycenae.

The younger sister of Clytemnestra was none other than Helen, over whom the Greeks and Trojans were fighting. Helen's beauty was such that her life, from beginning to end, was one of fatal attraction to men. While she was still a young girl of twelve, she was kidnapped, according to the legends, by the Athenian hero Theseus. She was rescued by her brothers, Castor and Polydeuces, and after she was restored, her father, Tyndareus, decided to marry her off and let her husband have the responsibility of holding her.

That was easier said than done, for when the word went out that Helen's hand was to be given in marriage, all the heroes of Greece came to Sparta to compete for her. It seemed impossible to choose one without making enemies of all the others.

It was Ulysses who had the solution. He had no real hope of gaining Helen for himself. He suggested to Tyndareus, therefore, that the competing heroes all be required to take an oath to agree to whatever decision was made as to Helen's husband and to promise to support that husband against anyone who might attempt to take Helen away from him. This was done and Ulysses was rewarded with the hand of Penelope, Helen's cousin.

It was Menelaus who was chosen as Helen's husband. For one thing, he was wealthy; for another, he was the younger brother of the King of Mycenae, Agamemnon.

Agamemnon himself could not compete for Helen because he was already married, but he pressed hard on behalf of his younger brother, and it was very likely because of the prestige and pressure of the "Great King" that Menelaus was accepted.

This was a good stroke of policy on Agamemnon's part. Menelaus succeeded to the throne of Sparta, as Helen's husband. Since Menelaus was a rather passive character, dominated by his more forceful brother, Agamemnon found himself greatly strengthened by his indirect control of the important city of Sparta.

By the same token, Paris' abduction of Helen was a serious blow to Agamemnon, for it weakened Menelaus' claim on the Spartan throne (which was Helen's rather than his own). Agamemnon had to push hard for a punitive expedition on Troy, and it may have been, again, the influence of the Great King, rather than any vow, which gathered the feudal lords of Greece into the expedition.

In the *Iliad* Agamemnon does not shine. His quarrel with Achilles, in which the Great King is entirely in the wrong, nearly wrecks the Greek cause, and on more than one occasion Homer (who is always respectful to him) shows him being deservedly corrected by others.

. . . Nestor shall apply

When Agamemnon is done, the oldest of the Greek leaders stands up to second his words:

> *With due observance of thy godlike seat,*
> *Great Agamemnon, Nestor shall apply*
> *Thy latest words.*

—Act I, scene iii, lines 31–33

In the *Iliad* Nestor is active among the Greeks despite the fact that he is described as ruling over the third generation of subjects. Although he is so old, he survives to see Troy sacked. Then, ten years after the fall of that city, when the last of the Greek warriors returns home, Nestor is still alive and still ruling in his city of Pylos on the southwestern shore of Greece. Pylos, like Mycenae, was an important center in the time of the Trojan War, but faded away in later times. It left not even a village behind.

The frequent reference to Nestor's age made some of the Roman writers grant him two hundred years, but that is not really necessary. In the Mycenaean Age it is quite likely that the life expectancy would be no more than twenty-five to thirty years, and that few men would reach forty before violence or disease laid them low. If Nestor was seventy years old at the time of the play he would be ruling over the third generation of men, and even ten years after the fall of Troy, he would be only eighty.

An occasional person could reach such an age, even in the short-lived times of the ancients, but certainly he would represent a marvel.

In the *Iliad* Nestor is shown in the field, driving his chariot. He does not actually engage in combat, but he is always there overseeing his forces. What's more, he is constantly giving advice in long-winded speeches, and although no one in the *Iliad* ever indicates that he is bored by Nestor, it seems clear that Nestor is a bore just the same. He is forever recalling the feats of his youth and one gets the idea that the same feats must surely have been recalled over and over again. The old man seems more obviously a bore in Shakespeare's version.

The gentle Thetis . . .

Nestor seconds Agamemnon's views. The old man points out that anyone can succeed when the task is easy, but that great enterprises call out the best in man. On calm seas, any ship can sail, but on stormy seas, it is the strong vessel that makes its mark. Nestor says:

> But let the ruffian Boreas once enrage
> The gentle Thetis, and anon behold
> The strong-ribbed bark through liquid mountains cut,
> Bounding between the two moist elements
> Like Perseus' horse,
>
> —Act I, scene iii, lines 38–42

Boreas is the personification of the north wind and Thetis is used here as the personification of the ocean, but that is wrong. There is common confusion between Thetis and Tethys. The latter was a Titaness and the wife of Oceanus (who is clearly the god of the ocean), so that Tethys can serve as a feminine version of the personification.

Thetis, in her own right, plays an important role in the Greek myths and in the *Iliad* particularly. She is a sea nymph (all the easier to confuse her with Tethys) and it was she who brought Briareus to the rescue of Jupiter (see page I-86).

Thetis' beauty was such that both Jupiter and Neptune tried to win her, until they found out she was fated to have a son stronger than his father. It was unsafe for either god, or any god, to marry her in that case, and she was forced to marry a mortal. The mortal chosen was a Thessalian prince named Peleus, and at the marriage (pushed through much against the will of Thetis) all the gods and goddesses assembled.

It was at this wedding that Eris appeared with her Apple of Discord. What's more, born of this marriage was Achilles, who was, indeed, far stronger than his father Peleus.

In the *Iliad* Thetis makes several appearances in her role as Achilles' mother, bewailing the fact that her son was fated to endless glory but short life.

The reference to Perseus' horse is to the famous winged stallion Pegasus. Perseus was a Greek hero in the generations before the Trojan War, whose great feat was the destruction of Medusa, one of the three Gorgons, whose appearance was so fearful that they turned to stone anyone who looked at them. With divine help, Perseus was able to cut off the head of Medusa. The blood that dripped from it, on striking the ground, gave rise to Pegasus, who leaped up at once and winged his way into the sky. In that sense, he was Perseus' horse, though there was no further connection between the two.

. . . hear Ulysses speak

When Nestor is finished, the shrewdest of the Greeks arises, and addressing the two preceding speakers says:

> *. . . let it please both*
> *Thou great, and wise, to hear Ulysses speak.*
> —Act I, scene iii, lines 68-69

As Nestor is the very personification of the rather tedious wisdom of age, so Ulysses (Odysseus) is the very personification of shrewdness and clever, but not always ethical, strategy. This comes out even better in Homer's companion poem, the *Odyssey*, which deals with Ulysses' return home after the fall of Troy, and of the ten years of adventures he survives through cleverness and endurance.

The later tales of the Troy cycle attributed to Ulysses all the clever stratagems devised by the Greeks, notably that of the wooden horse itself, with which the fall of Troy was finally encompassed. Since cleverness easily degenerates into slyness and rascality, some of the later myths picture Ulysses as a deceitful coward. None of that, however, appears anywhere in Homer, where Ulysses is depicted as uniformly admirable. Nor does it appear in Shakespeare's play.

. . . Prince of Ithaca

Agamemnon says at once:

> *Speak, Prince of Ithaca;*
>
> —Act I, scene iii, line 70

Ithaca is the home island of Ulysses; its exact location is not certain. Indeed, it has been an interesting game among classical scholars to try to determine which Greek island it might be from the descriptions given in the *Odyssey*.

The general feeling is that it is one of the Ionian Islands off the west coast of Greece. The particular island (called "Ithake" on modern maps) is small, only thirty-six square miles in area, and some twenty miles from the mainland. It is surrounded by larger islands, which presumably also represented part of Ulysses' domain.

. . . rank Thersites . . .

Agamemnon states that there is as much chance that Ulysses will utter folly as that:

> *When rank Thersites opes his mastic jaws,*
> *We shall hear music, wit, and oracle.*
>
> —Act I, scene iii, lines 73–74

Thersites plays one small part in the *Iliad*. He is the only common man, the only non-aristocrat, mentioned by name, and Homer has a field day at his expense, describing him as: "—a certain Thersites, who had no control over his tongue, and poured out an endless stream of abuse against his superiors, saying whatever came into his head that might raise a laugh. Thersites was by far the ugliest man in the Greek army: bandy-legged, lame, hump-backed, crook-necked and bald."

His appearance is in Book Two, where as a result of a miscalculation by Agamemnon, the Greek army is about to break up and make for home. Ulysses is desperately trying to stop them when Thersites breaks into invective against Agamemnon and keeps it up until he is stopped by a blow from Ulysses and some stern words.

That is all! It must be remembered that the *Iliad* was written about aristocrats and for an aristocratic audience, and, moreover, that it was aristocratic patronage that kept bards in comfort. Homer and those like him could scarcely afford to portray a common man successfully running down warriors and noblemen.

And yet, if one reads Thersites' speech in the one scene given him, it makes good sense. He scolds Agamemnon for hogging the best of the loot and for offending Achilles, on whom the Greek victory most depends. It was all true enough, and the blow he received did not alter that fact. Homer may have been having his moment of grim fun with the aristocrats.

Shakespeare, who was likewise patronized by aristocrats and who likewise rarely showed the common people in a good light, adopted Thersites as part of the comic relief in the play, though it is black comedy indeed. Thersites' mastic (that is, abusive) jaws never open without spewing out untold bitterness, and we are prepared for that in this comment of Agamemnon's.

. . . the glorious planet Sol

Ulysses points out that the trouble with the Greek force rests in its divisions, the existence within it of factions that neutralize its efforts. This lack of central authority, he maintains, is against nature itself, for inanimate nature shows the beneficial effects of order even in the heavens, where the planets move through the sky in strict accordance with certain rules:

> And therefore is the glorious planet Sol
> In noble eminence enthroned and sphered
> Amidst the other; whose med'cinable eye
> Corrects the influence of evil planets,
>
>   —Act I, scene iii, lines 89–92

"Sol" is the Latin word for "sun" and is the personification of the sun in the Roman myths.

This passage sounds as though Shakespeare, through Ulysses' mouth, is proclaiming the sun to be the ruler of the planets, for he is "in noble eminence enthroned" and he governs and controls the others.

If so, this is a startlingly modern view, not only for Ulysses, but even for Shakespeare, for it seems to refer to the heliocentric theory of the solar system, which places the sun at the center and makes the planets (including the earth itself) revolve about it. The mere fact that the sun is at the center would make it appear to rule the planetary system (so that it is a *solar* system), and Isaac Newton eventually showed, some sixty-seven years after Shakespeare's death, that the sun's overwhelming gravitational force did, indeed, keep the planets in their place.

It is surprising that Shakespeare should seem to be giving this impression, for all through his plays he shows himself a complete conservative as far as science is concerned and accepts only the Greek view of the universe. To be sure, some Greeks, notably Aristarchus of Samos, about 250 B.C., claimed the sun was the center of the planetary system, but few listened to them, and the Greek majority view continued to place the earth at the center. This latter doctrine was made final by the grand synthesis of the astronomer Ptolemy, about A.D. 150. (The earth-at-center theory is therefore called the "Ptolemaic system" in consequence.)

In 1543 Copernicus advanced the same notion that Aristarchus once had, but with much more detailed reasoning. His view was not accepted by most scholars for a long time, and in Shakespeare's lifetime the Copernican view was still widely considered rather far out and blasphemous.

Can Shakespeare, then, be taking the progressive Copernican view against the conservative Ptolemaic attitude?

No! That he remains conservative is clear at several points. He refers, for instance, to the "planet Sol." The Greeks observed that several heavenly bodies shifted position constantly against the background of nonshifting of "fixed" stars. These bodies they called "planets," meaning, in English, "wanderers." The known planets included the sun, the moon, Mercury, Venus, Mars, Jupiter, and Saturn, seven bodies in all.

Once the Copernican view of the planetary system was established, it seemed unreasonable to call the sun a planet, since it didn't wander among the stars, really, but was thought to be the motionless center of the planetary system.

It fell out of fashion to call the sun a planet, therefore. The name "planet" was then applied only to those bodies which revolved about the sun. This meant that the earth itself would have to be viewed as a planet. The moon revolves about the earth, the only body to retain its Ptolemaic position, and it is not, strictly speaking, viewed as a planet any longer. It is a satellite. Of the Greek planets, therefore, only Mercury, Venus, Mars, Jupiter, and Saturn retain the name and to these are added the earth and the planetary bodies since discovered: Uranus, Neptune, Pluto, and a host of tiny bodies called planetoids or asteroids.

Shakespeare refers to Sol as a planet, however, thus insisting that the sun moves and is not the center of the planetary system. He has the sun not merely enthroned but also "sphered." That is, it is embedded in a sphere that encircles the earth (see page I–25), whereas if it were the center of the planetary system, it could not be part of a sphere.

Finally, in speaking of the necessity of order in the heavens, Shakespeare has Ulysses say, a bit earlier in the speech:

> The heavens themselves, the planets, and this center
> Observe degree, priority, and place.
>
> —Act I, scene iii, lines 85–86

That makes a clear distinction between the planets and "this center," that is, earth.

If the sun is "in noble eminence enthroned," then, it is only because, in Shakespeare's view, it is the brightest and most magnificent of the planets and not because it has a central position.

In evil mixture . . .

Ulysses goes on to point out the harmful effects of disorder in the heavens:

> But when the planets
> In evil mixture to disorder wander,
> What plagues, and what portents, what mutiny,
>
> —Act I, scene iii, lines 94–96

This seems to reflect the universal belief in astrology in Greek times, in Shakespeare's times, and, for that matter, in our own times. The planets were supposed to influence matters on earth by their ever changing positions against the stars and relative to each other. Certain positions foreboded evil and therefore represented "the planets in evil mixture."

And yet the motions of the planets followed a fixed pattern that could be worked out, and was worked out, by Greek astronomers (a thousand years after the Trojan War, to be sure) so that such "evil mixture" could not really represent disorder. They followed inevitably from planetary motion.

There were, however, some heavenly phenomena which were very spectacular and which took place only rarely; notably eclipses of the sun and of the moon. These therefore were particularly baleful and frightening, and remained signs of apparent disorder in the heavens even after they had been explained astronomically and had been proven to be predictable.

Still more frightening and disorderly were the occasional appearances of comets, whose comings and goings seemed utterly erratic and were shown to be governed by the sun's gravitational field only two centuries *after* Shakespeare's death.

The great Achilles . . .

Having established (most eloquently) the general principle that only in centralized authority accepted by all, only in an established hierarchy of mastery, is order and efficiency to be found, Ulysses descends to specifics. Agamemnon should be the autocratic head of the enterprise against Troy, but his subordinates flout him and, in particular:

> *The great Achilles, whom opinion crowns*
> *The sinew and the forehand of our host,*
> *Having his ear full of his airy fame,*
> *Grows dainty of his worth, and in his tent*
> *Lies mocking our designs.*
>
> —Act I, scene iii, lines 142–46

Achilles was certainly the foremost hero on the Greek side and in the *Iliad* he is by no means treated as a conceited fop. Before the poem opens, he has been the mainstay of the army; his expeditions have subdued the Trojan dominions in Asia Minor; he has fought harder than anyone.

It is only when Agamemnon tries to take away his lawful prize, the girl Briseis, and scorns him before the gathered army, that Achilles loses his temper and withdraws from the fight. He proves himself to be vengeful and cruel thereafter, but at least he has a reasonable cause for his anger.

In Roman and medieval times, however, the legend of the Roman descent from Aeneas swung popular opinion heavily in favor of the Trojans. Achilles was therefore downgraded and there seemed nothing wrong in having him sulk in his tent out of vainglorious conceit, rather than in righteous wrath. Furthermore, the proponents of courtly love did not fail to make use of later myths concerning Achilles' love for a Trojan princess. That will appear later in the play as a cause for his malingering.

. . . With him Patroclus

Nor is Achilles alone. He has a friend:

> *With him Patroclus*
> *Upon a lazy bed the livelong day*
> *Breaks scurril jests,*
>
> —Act I, scene iii, lines 146–48

Patroclus is one of the important characters in the *Iliad* and is pictured there as the bosom friend of Achilles. Homer makes nothing of the relationship beyond that of loving friendship, but the later Greeks casually assumed more. They saw nothing wrong in homosexuality and even felt it to be a superior form of love. Consequently they had no hesitation in seeing Achilles and Patroclus as lovers in the literal sense of the word. This did not prevent Patroclus from being portrayed as a noble character (indeed, the gentlest of the Greeks) and a brave warrior.

In Christian Europe, however, homosexuality was an abomination and the Greek outlook could not be retained on its own terms. Shakespeare is forced to present Patroclus as effeminate, though he does not deprive him of all our sympathy either.

. . . roaring Typhon . . .

Ulysses is offended at the fact that Patroclus mimics the Greek leaders for Achilles' amusement. Vehemently, Ulysses insists that the imitations are poor ones, though he does not hesitate to describe them with a realism that must surely be sufficient to embarrass the ones being imitated.

He describes Patroclus pretending to be Agamemnon, for instance, with an affectation of great self-importance and melodramatic language (undoubtedly not too much an exaggeration of the way Agamemnon should be played). The language Patroclus uses, says Ulysses indignantly, is so ridiculously exaggerated that:

> . . . *from the tongue of roaring Typhon dropped,*
> *Would seem hyperboles.*
> —Act I, scene iii, lines 160–61

Typhon, in the Greek myths, was the largest monster ever born. His arms were a hundred miles long, his legs were serpents, his eyes flashed fire, and his mouth spewed forth flaming rocks. He may have been a personification of a volcano or, possibly, of a hurricane.

The gods themselves fled in terror before him and he was even able to capture Jupiter and for a while incapacitate him. Typhon was, however, eventually defeated and buried under Mount Etna, the largest and most fearsome volcano known to the ancient world.

Whether volcano or hurricane, it is clear that Typhon had a roaring voice, and that is the point of the metaphor.

. . . Vulcan and his wife

Ulysses next describes Patroclus imitating Nestor getting ready to speak, or to answer a night alarm, meticulously demonstrating how he acts the old, old man (again presumably very much the way Nestor is really acted). And Ulysses says indignantly:

> *That's done, as near as the extremest ends*
> *Of parallels, as like as Vulcan and his wife,*
> —Act I, scene iii, lines 167–68

Since parallels never meet, they can be extended infinitely in either direction. The imitation is as far from reality, Ulysses' words are saying, as is an infinite distance in one direction from an infinite distance in the other.

The other comparison of opposites is Vulcan (Hephaestus) and his wife, Venus (see page I–11).

He hath a lady . . .

Ulysses does not go on to say that Patroclus imitates Ulysses as well, but one can easily imagine he does and that that is what really annoys the Ithacan.

But further discussion is interrupted by a messenger who arrives from Troy. It is Aeneas, debonair and gay, bringing a challenge from Hector, offering single combat with any Greek. As a cause for combat, he sends a message which Aeneas delivers as:

> *He hath a lady wiser, fairer, truer,*
> *Than ever Greek did compass in his arms;*
> —Act I, scene iii, lines 275–76

This is straight out of the medieval tales, when knights were supposed to fight in the names of their ladies in accord with the rules of courtly love (see page I–54). Agamemnon rises to the occasion, following the silly conventions on his own account, saying:

> *This shall be told our lovers, Lord Aeneas;*
> *If none of them have soul in such a kind,*
> *We left them all at home. But we are soldiers;*
> *And may that soldier a mere recreant prove,*
> *That means not, hath not, or is not in love!*
> —Act I, scene iii, lines 284–88

It is hard to believe that such lines can be read seriously in surroundings that even hint at the grandeur with which Homer surrounded the Trojan War.

. . . the great Myrmidon

Agamemnon leads Aeneas off to carry the challenge to the various tents, but it is clear that it is meant for Achilles.

When he is gone, Ulysses huddles with Nestor. Ulysses has an idea— Why send Achilles against Hector? Suppose by some accident Achilles is wounded. With Achilles known to be their best man, that would be disastrous.

If, on the other hand, someone other than Achilles is sent, and loses, it will still be taken for granted that Achilles would have won if he had fought. On the other hand, if the lesser man should win, not only would that be a terrific gain for the Greeks, but Achilles himself, suddenly finding himself in second place behind a new champion, would leave off his posturing and laziness and would buckle down to the serious business of fighting. Ulysses' advice is that they:

> . . . make a lott'ry;
> And by device let blockish Ajax draw
> The sort to fight with Hector; among ourselves
> Give him allowance for the better man,
> For that will physic the great Myrmidon
> Who broils in loud applause, and make him fall
> His crest that prouder than blue Iris bends.
>
> —Act I, scene iii, lines 373–79

At the start of Book Seven of the *Iliad,* Hector *does* challenge the Greek champions, though not with a silly make-believe excuse involving courtly love. Several Greek champions did accept the challenge, lots were drawn, and the choice *did* fall on Ajax, though Homer makes no mention of any device to do so.

As for the Myrmidons, they were a tribe in Phthia in southern Thessaly over whom Achilles ruled, hence the reference to him as "the great Myrmidon." The word seems to contain the Greek *myrmex,* meaning "ant," and the ancient mythmakers invented an explanation for this.

Aeacus, the grandfather of Achilles, ruled the small island of Aegina near Athens. Either it was not populated to begin with or its population was destroyed by a plague. In either case, Aeacus prayed to Zeus that he be given men to rule and in response the god converted the ants on the island into men. These Myrmidons followed Aeacus' son, Peleus, to Thessaly and from there a contingent went with Peleus' son, Achilles, to the Trojan War.

Iris is usually the personification of the rainbow (see page I–67), but here she is used to represent the sky generally.

. . . as Cerberus

Now we are ready to have our first glimpse of Ajax and Thersites. A proclamation has been posted concerning Hector's challenge and Ajax wants to know what it says. Since Ajax is illiterate, he must ask Thersites to read it for him and Thersites is not in an obliging mood. (He never is.)

Thersites scolds Ajax most viciously and eloquently and Ajax, who can speak only with his fists, uses those as arguments. Thersites strikes back (with words) where he knows it will hurt most, saying:

> Thou grumblest and railest every hour on Achilles, and thou art as full of envy at his greatness as Cerberus is at Proserpina's beauty . . .
> —Act II, scene i, lines 33–35

Cerberus is the ugly, slavering, three-headed dog that guards the gateway to the underground abode of the dead, serving to prevent any living from invading those regions and any of the dead from escaping. Proserpina, on the other hand, is the beautiful queen of the underworld, the daughter of Ceres, whom Hades had carried off (see page I–7).

. . . Achilles' brach . . .

Achilles and Patroclus come on the scene and prevent Ajax from striking Thersites further. Achilles is clearly amused at Thersites and encourages him to continue his scurrilous comments concerning Ajax, to the latter's huge annoyance. Nor does Thersites spare Achilles himself, and when the gentle Patroclus tries to quiet the lowborn railer, Thersites says, sarcastically:

> I will hold my peace when Achilles' brach bids me, shall I?
> —Act II, scene i, lines 119–20

"Brach" is an archaic word for a bitch and Patroclus is thus compared with a female animal. This is one of the few explicit and contemptuous references to homosexuality to be found in Shakespeare.

Thersites then departs, leaving Achilles to read the news of Hector's challenge to Ajax (pretending to care little about the matter for himself).

. . . Let Helen go

In the *Iliad*, the duel between Ajax and Hector takes up a good portion of Book Seven. It ends with both champions alive but with Hector having had clearly the worst of it. (This is reflected in the earlier statement in *Troilus and Cressida* that Ajax had beaten Hector down on one occasion, see page I-87.)

At the end of the duel, therefore, it is reasonable that the disheartened Trojans hold a conference and consider whether or not to offer to give up Helen, pay an indemnity, and buy off the Greeks. Antenor counsels this line of action, but Paris insists he will not give up Helen, and when the offer of an indemnity without Helen is made, the Greeks (heartened by Ajax's showing) refuse, so the war goes on.

Shakespeare changes this. Hector's challenge has been issued and it has not yet been taken up, yet the Trojans are now seen in council trying to reach an important decision. Nestor, on behalf of the Greeks, has offered to end the war if the Trojans surrender Helen and pay an indemnity. It seems unreasonable to suppose that the Greeks would make such an offer or the Trojans consider one while the issue of the duel remained in doubt.

Yet the council proceedings are presented. In Shakespeare, it is Hector who makes the plea for a peace even at the price of a virtual surrender, saying in part:

> . . . *modest doubt is called*
> *The beacon of the wise, the tent that searches*
> *To the bottom of the worst. Let Helen go.*
> —Act II, scene ii, lines 15–17

This is in character for Shakespeare's Hector and for Homer's Hector too. In the *Iliad* Hector is never pictured as a fire-eater for the sake of battle. He is pictured as knowing well that Troy is in the wrong and that Paris' abduction is indefensible, but he fights because Troy is his city. He is a fighter in a poor cause, but his own character enforces respect nevertheless.

. . . for an old aunt . . .

Paris argues the hawkish view in the *Iliad*, but it is Troilus who speaks first here. He points out that it was the Trojans who first suffered loss at the hands of the Greeks and that the abduction of Helen was but a retaliation that all the Trojans favored at the time it was carried through. He goes on to describe Paris' retaliation:

> *And for an old aunt whom the Greeks held captive*
> *He brought a Grecian queen, whose youth and freshness*
> *Wrinkles Apollo's and makes pale the morning.*
> —Act II, scene ii, lines 77–79

The "old aunt" is Hesione, a sister of King Priam. When Hercules captured and sacked Troy, he carried off Hesione into captivity. She was never returned despite Trojan demands.

The capture of Hesione plays no part in the Homeric tale, and the abduction of Helen could, in any case, never be viewed as a fair return for an earlier outrage. Hesione was captured as a war prisoner, and however deplorable we consider such things now, this was considered legitimate in ancient times. Paris, on the other hand, had taken Helen not as the spoils of war, but by treachery and at the cost of violating what was due his host, Menelaus, who was entertaining him with all hospitality. The two actions simply weren't comparable.

The tale of Hesione has another point of impingement on the tale of Troy. She was awarded to Telamon, the brother of Peleus. By her, Telamon had a son named Teucer, who is therefore first cousin to Achilles. Teucer does not appear in *Troilus and Cressida* but he does appear in the *Iliad* as a skilled archer.

Telamon, by a previous wife (an Athenian woman), had another son, who was none other than Ajax. Ajax is therefore first cousin to Achilles and half brother to Teucer. In the *Iliad* Teucer is always fighting at the side of Ajax and the two half brothers are devoted to each other.

Teucer, notice, is half Trojan through his mother and is actually a nephew of Priam and a first cousin to Hector, Troilus, Paris, and the rest, as well as to Achilles. At the beginning of the play, when Ajax is first mentioned to Cressida, he is described as "a lord of Troyan blood, nephew to Hector," which he isn't. The confusion is with Teucer, who is a lord of Trojan blood, cousin to Hector.

Our firebrand brother . . .

The council is interrupted by Cassandra, Priam's mad daughter, whose prophecies are always true, but never believed. She wails:

> *Cry, Troyans, cry! Practice your eyes with tears!*
> *Troy must not be, nor goodly Ilion stand;*
> *Our firebrand brother, Paris, burns us all.*
>
> —Act II, scene ii, lines 108–10

Just before Paris was born (according to legends that play no part in the *Iliad*) Hecuba dreamed she was delivered of a burning firebrand. A soothsayer, when consulted, said that this meant that Troy would be burned and destroyed because of the child about to be born. He urged that the child be killed as soon as born.

Priam, unable to bring himself to do the job or witness its being done, had a herdsman take the child, instructing him to kill it. The herdsman could not do it either, but exposed the child in an uninhabited place. There it was found by a she-bear, which suckled it.

The herdsman, finding the child alive when he returned after some days, decided to bring it up as his own son, and it was while the young man was engaged in herding that the three goddesses Juno, Minerva, and Venus came down to have him decide which was the most beautiful.

After this, Paris, still in his role as herdsman, entered certain games being held in Troy, did marvelously well, even against Hector, and was recognized by Cassandra as the long-lost Paris. There was no thought of killing him; he was restored to his royal position and, eventually, proved his title to the firebrand dream by sailing to Sparta and abducting Helen.

. . . whom Aristotle . . .

Hector refers to Cassandra's cries as proof that Helen ought to be returned and the war ended, but Cassandra is simply dismissed as mad by Troilus. Paris rises and places himself on Troilus' side.

Hector is not convinced. He says his two younger brothers argue:

> *. . . but superficially: not much*
> *Unlike young men, whom Aristotle thought*
> *Unfit to hear moral philosophy.*
>
> —Act II, scene ii, lines 165–67

This is, actually, one of the most amusing anachronisms in Shakespeare. The dramatist forgets, for the moment, that he is discussing a war that took place in 1200 B.C., and has Hector refer to a philosopher who died in 322 B.C.—nine centuries later.

And yet, although Hector denigrates the arguments of Troilus and Paris, he cannot manage to stand against the kind of arguments that refer to such abstractions as honor, glory, and patriotism. It is decided (as in the *Iliad*) to keep Helen and let the war go on.

. . . *thy caduceus* . . .

The scene shifts back to the Greek camp, where Thersites, standing outside Achilles' tent, is brooding over his recent beating by Ajax. He inveighs against the stupidity of both heroes, Achilles as well as Ajax, and invokes the vengeance of the gods upon them, saying:

> *O thou great thunder-darter of Olympus, forget that thou art Jove, the king of gods; and, Mercury, lose all the serpentine craft of thy caduceus, if ye take not that little, little, less than little wit from them that they have;*
>
> —Act II, scene iii, lines 10–14

Jupiter (Zeus) was, in all likelihood, a storm god originally. His home would naturally be on a mountaintop where the clouds gather. Olympus was the one chosen by the Greeks, and it was a logical choice, for it is the highest mountain in Greece—although not so terribly high at that, only 1.8 miles. It is located in northern Thessaly, about 170 miles northwest of Athens.

As a storm god, Jupiter would naturally be in charge of the lightning. He would therefore be a thunder-darter, or, more correctly, a thunderbolt-darter.

Mercury (Hermes) was, in many myths, the messenger of the gods, a kind of male version of Iris (see page I-67). It is because of Mercury's swiftness in fulfilling his errands that he is usually pictured with small wings on his sandals and hat.

In carrying the messages of Jupiter, he was acting as Jupiter's herald or substitute and therefore carried with him the aura of Jupiter's majesty. In token of that he carried a staff, as earthly heralds did. In earliest times, the staff may have had flexible twigs at the end which would be wound back over the body of the staff.

In later times, these twigs, shown in representations of Mercury and misunderstood, became serpents. It is this serpent-bound staff, called the caduceus, which became a characteristic mark of Mercury. The caduceus was further confused in still later times with a magical wand, the agent by which Mercury, at the behest of Jupiter, brought about supernatural effects. Thersites therefore speaks of the "craft of thy caduceus."

. . . the Neapolitan bone-ache . . .

Having wished evil on Ajax and Achilles specifically, Thersites goes on to curse the Greeks generally:

> *After this, the vengeance on the whole camp! Or, rather, the Neapolitan bone-ache, for that, methinks, is the curse depending on those that war for a placket.*
>
> —Act II, scene iii, lines 18–21

The "Neapolitan bone-ache" is syphilis. This was not recognized as a serious, contagious disease until the early sixteenth century. Indeed, the story arose that it first appeared in Italy during battles at which some of Columbus' sailors were present. It therefore seemed that those sailors had picked up syphilis in the New World from the Indians and brought it back to Europe. (Europe sent the Indians smallpox in return.)

This may not be so and the disease may have occurred in Europe earlier, and been considered one of the forms of leprosy, perhaps; but if so, syphilis occurred less frequently then and less virulently. If the sixteenth century did not find it a new disease, it found it at least a more serious version of an old one, and it still required a new name.

This was difficult to find, for it was early recognized that contagion most easily resulted through sexual intercourse, so that it became shameful to admit the disease or even discuss it. It was natural for any group to consider it characteristic of a neighboring group. The French, for instance, would call it the "Neapolitan bone-ache," while the Italians would call it the "French disease."

In 1530 an Italian physician, Girolamo Fracastoro, wrote a Latin epic poem which was a mock myth about a shepherd who offended Apollo and who fell victim to what Fracastoro called the "French disease." The shepherd's name was the Greek-sounding one (but not real Greek) of Syphilis, and it is this which gave the present name to the disease.

In Shakespeare's time the disease was still less than a century old in European consciousness. It had the doubtful virtue of novelty and of being associated with sex. Any reference to it, then, was good for a laugh, especially if it was arranged to have the laugh at the expense of foreigners. Thersites not only affixes it to the Neapolitans (making the reference doubly anachronistic, since Naples was not to be founded till some five centuries after the Trojan War) but makes use of the sexual angle as well by insisting it is to be what is expected for any army that wars for a placket (a petticoat, and therefore a coarse term for a woman).

References to syphilis abound in Shakespeare, usually at the expense of the French, but since moderns don't find the subject as humorous as the Elizabethans did, I shall pick up such references as infrequently as I can.

. . . a privileged man . . .

Thersites assumes, in this scene, a totally un-Homeric role. He is a jester; a man of quick wit (or perhaps slightly addled brains) whose remarks and responses are a source of amusement. He had apparently fulfilled that function for Ajax but Ajax had beaten him and he was now seeking employment with Achilles instead.

In return for amusing his master (in days when amusement was not yet electronified and easy to come by at the flick of a dial) a jester was allowed extraordinary leeway in his mockery and much more freedom of speech than anyone else might have. Naturally, this worked best when the jester's patron was powerful and could suppress the hurt feelings of underlings who might otherwise break the jester's neck.

Thus, when Thersites begins to perform for Achilles, Patroclus reacts with the beginnings of violence to one of Thersites' scurrilous remarks and Achilles restrains him by saying:

> *He is a privileged man. Proceed, Thersites.*
> —Act II, scene iii, line 59

Such a jester was often called a "fool" and many a Shakespearean play has someone listed as "Fool" in the cast of characters. This was not necessarily because they were foolish, but because very often they hid their sharp satire behind oblique comments in such a way that the points were not immediately apparent and therefore seemed foolish to the dull-witted. It also helped keep the jester from broken bones if he played the fool so that those he mocked might not be certain whether his remarks were deliberately hurtful or whether they were perhaps just the aimless maunderings of a lackwit.

Thersites is given this name a little later in the scene when Ajax is inveighing against Achilles and Nestor is surprised at the spleen of those remarks. Ulysses explains:

> *Achilles hath inveigled his fool from him.*
> —Act II, scene iii, line 93

. . . and a cuckold . . .

Thersites' bitter jesting for the benefit of Achilles, and largely at the expense of Patroclus, is interrupted by the arrival of a deputation from the Greeks. Achilles promptly retires into the tent, unwilling to talk to them, and before leaving himself, Thersites expresses his opinion of both sides of this inter-Greek friction:

Here is such patchery, such juggling, and such knavery.
All the argument is a whore and a cuckold . . .

—Act II, scene iii, lines 73–75

The whore is Helen, of course, and the cuckold (that is, the deceived husband) is Menelaus.

Why cuckold? The word is a form of "cuckoo." The common European species of cuckoo lays its egg in the nest of another and smaller bird, leaving to the foster parents the task of rearing the cuckoo fledgling. The male adulterer also lays his egg in the nest of another, to use the ribald analogy that must have occurred as long ago as Roman times, for the Romans called an adulterer a "cuckoo." The word shifted to "cuckold" and the name passed from the adulterer to the adulterer's victim. The name, or any guarded reference to it, was as sure-fire a source of laughter in Elizabethan times as any remark concerning horns (see page I–84).

. . . rely on none

The deputation of Greeks who have arrived at Achilles' tent intend to urge him to fight more vigorously.

This parallels, in a way, Book Nine of the *Iliad,* where the Greeks, having had some trouble in an immediately preceding battle, gloomily anticipate more and decide to try to win over Achilles once again.

A deputation of three, Ajax, Ulysses and Phoenix (the last an old tutor of Achilles), are sent. They offer to return the girl Agamemnon took from Achilles, together with additional rich gifts as compensation for Achilles' humiliation. By now, however, Achilles has so consumed himself with anger that he prefers his grievance to all else and he absolutely refuses.

In the *Iliad* Achilles puts himself in the wrong at this point, so that in the end he will have to suffer too, as well as Agamemnon and his Greek army. But if Achilles puts himself in the wrong, he does it at least in a grand fashion.

In *Troilus and Cressida* Achilles can offer nothing but petulance. Ulysses enters the tent and emerges to say that Achilles will not fight. When Agamemnon asks the reason, Ulysses replies:

He doth rely on none,

—Act II, scene iii, line 165

This is mere sulkiness, or, as it turns out later, lovesickness and treason, which is even worse. Shakespeare thus continues his Trojan-biased downgrading of the Homeric picture of the great Greek hero.

. . . more coals to Cancer . . .

It is time for the Greeks to make do without Achilles as best they can, obviously, and they begin to flatter Ajax into accepting the duel with Hector.

Thus, when Agamemnon suggests that Ajax be sent into the tent to plead with Achilles, Ulysses demurs grandiloquently and says that Achilles is not worth so great an honor as having a man like Ajax demur to him:

> *That were to enlard his fat-already pride,*
> *And add more coals to Cancer when he burns*
> *With entertaining great Hyperion.*
> —Act II, scene iii, lines 197–99

Hyperion (the sun, see page I-11) makes a complete round of the sky against the background of the stars in the course of one year. The stars in its path are divided into twelve constellations, which, all together, make up the Zodiac. (This is from a Greek phrase meaning "circle of animals" because so many of the constellations are visualized as animals.)

On June 21 the sun enters the sign of Cancer (the Crab) and summer starts on that day. Ulysses refers to summer heat in the notion of Cancer burning because of the entry of great Hyperion. Ajax kowtowing to Achilles would but make summer heat hotter; that is, it would make proud Achilles prouder.

Bull-bearing Milo . . .

The flattery grows grosser and grosser and Ajax, delighted, accepts it all. Ulysses says, in praise of Ajax:

> *. . . for thy vigor,*
> *Bull-bearing Milo his addition yield*
> *To sinewy Ajax.*
> —Act II, scene iii, lines 247–49

Milo was an athlete of Croton, a city on the coast of the Italian toe, whose feats of strength had grown legendary. The most famous tale was that he lifted a particular calf onto his shoulders every day. It grew heavier with age, of course, and finally Milo was lifting a full-grown bull. This was the reason for his addition (that is, title) of "Bull-bearing," a title which, Ulysses was saying, he would now have to yield to Ajax.

This is another anachronism, of course, almost as bad as the one about Aristotle. Milo was not a myth but an actual historical figure (though the stories about him might be exaggerated, to be sure). He died about 500 B.C., seven centuries after the Trojan War.

Fresh kings . . .

Ajax is now thoroughly softened up and has played the scene as an utter puppet in the hands of Ulysses. This is completely unclassical, for Ajax is a truly heroic figure in the *Iliad* and was viewed as a sympathetic and tragic figure in later tales. Partly this was because he was considered an Athenian, for he was from the small island of Salamis, which, in the century when the *Iliad* was edited into its final form, had just been annexed by Athens.

Yet there is an echo of the classic too. After Achilles' death there was a competition for his armor, which narrowed down to Ulysses and Ajax. Ulysses won out and Ajax, in grief and shame, went mad. Ajax, it would seem, in one way or another, is always at the mercy of Ulysses.

This part of the task done, Ulysses now suggests that Agamemnon call a council of war, at which the arrangement to put up Ajax against Hector be completed. He says:

> *Please it our great general*
> *To call together all his state of war;*
> *Fresh kings are come to Troy.*
>
> —Act II, scene iii, lines 260–62

It would not have been reasonable to suppose that the city of Troy, all by itself, could have withstood a huge expeditionary force of a united Greece. Rather, it stood at the head of a large combination of forces itself. The tribes of Asia Minor stood with it and one of the most prominent Trojan heroes in the *Iliad* was Sarpedon, a prince of Lycia in southwestern Asia Minor, some three hundred miles south of Troy. He does not appear in *Troilus and Cressida,* but Pandarus, who does, is also a Lycian—at least in the *Iliad.*

In Book Ten of the *Iliad,* immediately after the unsuccessful deputation to Achilles, there is, indeed, the tale of a new reinforcement of the Trojans. This is Rhesus, a Thracian king who has led both men and horses to the aid of the Trojans. Thrace is in Europe, to be sure, but it lies to the northeast of Greece and was inhabited by non-Greeks. (Nor did it ever become Greek in the future. It is the region that makes up the modern kingdom of Bulgaria.)

In the *Iliad* Ulysses and Diomedes sneak into the Trojan camp under the cover of night and assassinate Rhesus, nullifying the effect of his reinforcement, but nothing of the sort takes place in *Troilus and Cressida.* The reference to fresh kings coming to Troy is all that is left.

O Cupid, Cupid, Cupid

As Act Three opens, Pandarus has finally made arrangements to bring Troilus and Cressida together for a night and has come to Priam's palace to persuade Paris to cover for Troilus, so that no one may suspect where the young prince is.

This gives Shakespeare a chance to place Helen herself on stage—in one scene only.

In the *Iliad* Helen's beauty is made overwhelming. All are victims of it and all are affected by it. Homer places her praise, with exceeding effectiveness, in the mouths of the old men of Troy, showing that even impotent age feels the influence. He says:

"At Helen's approach, these grey-beards muttered earnestly among themselves. 'How entrancing she is! Like an immortal goddess! Yes, marvellously like one! I cannot blame the Trojans and Greeks for battling over her so bitterly!' "

And Helen is her own victim too. She is conscious of herself as the cause of immense misery; she is contrite and ashamed, and, in the same scene referred to above, she says to Priam:

" 'I ought to have died before eloping with Prince Paris—imagine, leaving my home, my family, my unmarried daughter, and so many women friends of my own age! But leave them I did, and now I weep for remorse. . . . Oh, I am a shameless bitch, if ever there was one.' "

Furthermore, Helen is intelligent and in the *Odyssey,* when, ten years after the fall of Troy, she is once again the wife of Menelaus and the two are entertaining the son of Ulysses in their home, Helen is clearly more quick-witted than her husband.

But how does Shakespeare present Helen in the one scene in which she appears? She appears as a vain, silly woman, with an empty head, unaware of (or uncaring about) what she has caused, and incapable, apparently, of making an intelligent remark.

Helen scarcely allows Pandarus the chance to make his arrangements with Paris and insists he sing for her, saying:

> *Let thy song be love. This love will undo us all.*
> *O Cupid, Cupid, Cupid!*
>
> —Act III, scene i, lines 111–12

Cupid (Eros) is the god of love (see page I-19).

This is Helen as viewed through the eyes of courtly love. By the convention of the troubadours, a woman need not deserve love, she need merely be a woman.

. . . be thou my Charon

The arrangements with Paris are made and Pandarus hurries back to bring Troilus and Cressida together. Troilus is waiting for him in a fever of impatience, and says:

> *I stalk about her door*
> *Like a strange soul upon the Stygian banks*
> *Staying for waftage. O, be thou my Charon,*
> *And give me swift transportance to those fields*
> *Where I may wallow in the lily beds*
> *Proposed for the deserver.*

> —Act III, scene ii, lines 7–12

The Stygian banks are those that border the river Styx, which, according to the Greek myths, flows about Hades, separating it from the abode of mortal men. The spirits of dead men must wait upon those banks until a ferry, under the guidance of an underworld deity called Charon (see page I–68) ferried him across.

It is not to Hades itself that Troilus demands passage, of course, but to the Elysian Fields (see page I–13) where he can "wallow in the lily beds."

"As false as Cressid"

The lovers meet, with Pandarus licking his chops lecherously and doing everything but forcing them into embrace. The two young people make eloquent speeches to each other, protesting their love. Troilus swears his constancy, adding a new simile to the common comparisons for truth:

> *"As true as Troilus" shall crown up the verse*
> *And sanctify the numbers.*

> —Act III, scene ii, lines 183–84

Cressida, similarly, makes up a series of similes for falseness, adding a new and climactic one, in case she should ever be unfaithful:

> *Yea, let them say, to stick the heart of falsehood,*
> *"As false as Cressid."*

> —Act III, scene ii, lines 196–97

Pandarus too chimes in:

> *I have taken such pains to bring you together, let all pitiful*

goers-between be called to the world's end after my name;
call them all Pandars.

—Act III, scene ii, lines 201-3

All these wishes came true, as Shakespeare knew they would, for they were already current in his time, thanks to Chaucer's earlier tale. And, indeed, goers-between are still called Pandars (panders) to this day.

Let Diomedes . . .

But the young lovers have no sooner met and consummated their passion than the clouds begin to gather. In the Greek camp, remember, is Calchas, the renegade Trojan (the analogue of Chryses in the *Iliad*).

His services have been such that Agamemnon has always been willing to ask the Trojans to surrender Cressida in return for some Trojan who might be prisoner of the Greeks. They have always refused. But now the Greeks have captured Antenor and he is so important to the Trojans, says Calchas, that they will surely give up Cressida to have him back.

It is curious how this reverses the situation in the *Iliad*. In the *Iliad* Chryses the priest asks Agamemnon to return his daughter, Chryseis, who is held in the Greek camp. In *Troilus and Cressida* Calchas the priest asks Agamemnon to obtain his daughter, Cressida, who is held in the Trojan camp. In the *Iliad* Agamemnon refuses the request; in *Troilus and Cressida* he agrees.

Agamemnon says:

> *Let Diomedes bear him,*
> *And bring us Cressid hither; Calchas shall have*
> *What he requests of us.*

—Act III, scene iii, lines 30-32

Diomedes is the son of Tydeus, who was one of the seven against Thebes (see page I-57). Diomedes and the sons of the other fallen leaders swore to avenge that defeat. They were called the Epigoni ("after-born") and succeeded where their fathers had failed—taking and sacking Thebes.

Not long after that, Diomedes and his friend Sthenelus, the son of Capaneus (see page I-58), joined the expedition to Troy, leading the men of Argos.

In the *Iliad*, Diomedes is one of the most effective of the Greek warriors, third only to Achilles and Ajax. Indeed, in Book Five Diomedes wreaks havoc among the Trojans and not even Hector can stand against him. It is only in post-Homeric times that his role in the Troilus-Cressida story was invented.

. . . great Mars to faction

Diomedes is also taking the message to Hector that the Trojan's challenge has been accepted and that Ajax will fight with him.

With that done, Ulysses now tightens his net about Achilles. He suggests that the Greek princes pass the great hero by with slight regard, while he follows behind to explain to the startled Achilles that what is past is easily forgotten and that man's reputation depends on what he is doing, not on what he has done. It is Ajax who is now the darling of the army because he is going to fight Hector, and Achilles, who is doing nothing, is disregarded. Yet Achilles, he admits, is one

> *Whose glorious deeds, but in these fields of late,*
> *Made emulous missions 'mongst the gods themselves*
> *And drave great Mars to faction.*
>
> —Act III, scene iii, lines 187–89

In the *Iliad* the gods themselves take sides in the fighting. Most active on the Greek side are Juno and Minerva (who lost out in the contest before Paris) and Neptune (who had once built walls for Troy and then been defrauded of his pay). Most active on the Trojan side are Venus (who won the contest before Paris), her loving Mars, and Apollo (who had also been defrauded in the matter of the walls, but apparently didn't care).

At one point Mars actually joined in the spearing and killing as though he were human, until Diomedes, guided by Minerva, wounded him and drove him from the field.

The gods do not appear in *Troilus and Cressida,* and their fighting leaves behind but this one reference by Ulysses.

. . . one of Priam's daughters

Achilles says brusquely that he has his reasons for remaining out of the fight, whereupon Ulysses explains, dryly, that the reasons are not private:

> *'Tis known, Achilles, that you are in love*
> *With one of Priam's daughters.*
>
> —Act III, scene iii, lines 192–93

The daughter in question is Polyxena. She does not appear in the *Iliad,* but later poets, anxious to add love and romance to Homer's austere tale, supplied her. Achilles was supposed to have fallen in love with her and to have been ready to betray the Greeks for her sake. Others write, variously, that she was indeed married to him eventually and that it was at the marriage rites that Achilles was slain by Paris (with Polyxena's treacherous help, according to some). Other versions are that she killed herself after he died, or was sacrificed at his burial rites.

. . . Pluto's gold

Achilles writhes in embarrassment, but Ulysses says calmly that it is not at all surprising that his secret is known:

> The providence that's in a watchful state
> Knows almost every grain of Pluto's gold
> —Act III, scene iii, lines 196–97

Pluto, as the god of the underworld, was naturally related to gold and to other forms of mineral wealth found in the ground. It was an easy transition to imagine Pluto to be the god of wealth. Actually, the personification of wealth was given the name "Plutus," a close variant of "Pluto."

In later myths Plutus was imagined to be the son of Ceres (Demeter). She is the harvest goddess and the reference to wealth in the grounds can refer to the richly growing grain as well as to the minerals. But then, Pluto (Hades) was the son-in-law of the same goddess, since it was he who carried off Proserpina, Ceres' daughter.

To be pedantically correct, one should speak only of Plutus in connection with wealth, but the mistake is a small one.

. . . young Pyrrhus . . .

Ulysses further turns the knife in the wound:

> But it must grieve young Pyrrhus now at home,
> When fame shall in our islands sound her trump,
> And all the Greekish girls shall tripping sing,
> "Great Hector's sister did Achilles win,
> But our great Ajax bravely beat down him."
> —Act III, scene iii, lines 209–13

Pyrrhus (also known as Neoptolemus) is Achilles' son, and his birth came about as follows.

Before the expedition to Troy began, Thetis had hidden her young son Achilles on the island of Scyrus, for she knew that if he went to Troy he would win deathless fame but die young. She preferred to have him live a quiet but long life. She had him disguised as a maiden at the court of the Scyran ruler.

The Greeks came searching for him in response to Calchas' warning that they could not take Troy without Achilles. Ulysses cleverly discovered which maiden was Achilles by presenting a display of jewels and finery, among which a sword was hidden. Where the real girls snatched at the jewels, Achilles seized the sword.

Apparently, Achilles also revealed himself to the other maidens in such a fashion as to father a son on one of them. That son, Pyrrhus, remained in Scyrus while Achilles was at Troy.

The accretion of myths and elaborate tales about the central pillar of Homer's story has made hash of the chronology of the affair.

For instance, it is at the wedding of Peleus and Thetis that the Apple of Discord is flung among the guests, and it is immediately afterward that Paris, still a herdsman, must choose among the goddesses. Paris must be a teen-ager at the time and Achilles is not yet born, so Paris must be at least fifteen years older than Achilles.

Eventually, Paris abducts Helen and the Trojan War starts. Now Achilles is old enough to go to war. Let us say he is fifteen at the start of the war and has already left a girl with child. By the time of the last year of the war, in which both the *Iliad* and *Troilus and Cressida* are set, Achilles is twenty-four and Paris is thirty-nine. Since Hector is the oldest son of Priam, he must be in his late forties at least.

This is bearable, perhaps, but now consider that Pyrrhus, at Achilles' death in the last year of the war, can scarcely be much more than ten years old. Yet according to the later legends, he is brought to Troy and fights with surpassing bravery in the final battles, to say nothing of being one of the cruelest of the sackers at the end (see page I–209).

Such things did not bother those who listened to the tales, of course, and they don't really bother us, either, since the value of those tales does not depend on such mundane matters as precise chronology. However, it is a curiosity and so I mention it.

A valiant Greek . . .

Achilles is left shaken after Ulysses departs and Patroclus urges his great friend to return to the wars. (This Patroclus also does in the *Iliad*.) But Achilles cannot yet bring himself to do this. He suggests only that Ajax, after the combat, invite Hector and the other Trojan leaders to visit him under a flag of truce.

Meanwhile, Diomedes has brought Antenor to Troy. He is greeted by Paris and Aeneas and Paris says:

A valiant Greek, Aeneas; take his hand.
Witness the process of your speech, wherein
You told how Diomed, a whole week by days,
Did haunt you in the field.

—Act IV, scene i, lines 7–10

This reflects a passage in the *Iliad*, but one that is considerably softened in Aeneas' favor. In Book Five of the *Iliad*, the one dominated by the feats of Diomedes, Aeneas and Diomedes meet in the field and the latter has much the better of it. With a great boulder, Diomedes strikes down Aeneas and would surely have killed him except that first Venus and then Apollo swooped down to save him.

. . . Anchises' life

Aeneas is all chivalrous graciousness, in the best tradition of medieval gallantry, and says:

Now, by Anchises' life,
Welcome indeed!

—Act IV, scene i, lines 21–22

Anchises is Aeneas' father. Venus fell in love with the handsome young Anchises and had Aeneas by him. She made Anchises promise, however, that he would never reveal the fact that he was the goddess' lover. Incautiously, Anchises let out the secret and was in consequence paralyzed, blinded, or killed (depending on which version of the story you read).

Anchises was far better known to Shakespeare's audience than one might expect from the Greek myths alone. He is the subject of a dramatic story in Vergil's *Aeneid*. The aged Anchises cannot walk (this fits in with the suggestion that he was paralyzed because of his indiscretion concerning Venus) and was therefore helpless at the time of the sack and destruction of Troy. Aeneas, therefore, bore him out of the burning city on his back, thus setting a greatly admired example of filial love, a love that is reflected backward by having Aeneas swear by his father's life.

By Venus' hand . . .

Aeneas goes on to combine hospitality and martial threat in courtly manner:

> *By Venus' hand I swear,*
> *No man alive can love in such a sort*
> *The thing he means to kill more excellently.*
>
> —Act IV, scene i, lines 22–24

The mention of Venus' hand makes sense in light of the events in Book Five of the *Iliad*. When Aeneas lies felled by Diomedes' boulder, sure to be killed if the gods did not intervene, Venus (Aeneas' mother) flew down from Olympus to save him. The furious Diomedes cast his spear even at the goddess and wounded her in the hand. She fled, screaming, and it was only when the much more powerful Apollo took her place that Diomedes was forced to retire. Thus, Aeneas was swearing by that part of his mother which had been hurt on his behalf.

. . . *Some say the Genius*

On the very morning after their night together, the news comes to Troilus that he must give up Cressida and send her to the Greek camp.

Brokenhearted, Troilus and Cressida vow eternal fidelity. Troilus gives Cressida a sleeve (an arm cover which in medieval times was a separate article of clothing, not sewn to shirt or robe) and Cressida returns a glove.

The deputation waits outside for Cressida to be turned over to them, and when Aeneas calls out impatiently, Troilus says:

> *Hark! You are called. Some say the Genius*
> *Cries so to him that instantly must die.*
>
> —Act IV, scene iv, lines 50–51

To the Romans, every man had a personal spirit (the equivalent of what we would call a guardian angel) which they called a "Genius." Every woman, similarly, had her "Juno," and Genius may be a masculine form of Juno. To this day, we speak of a man who is supremely gifted as a "genius," though we forget that by this we mean that the divine spirit is speaking through him with particular effectiveness.

Hosts of superstitions naturally arose concerning these Geniuses. It would warn the person it guarded of imminent death, for instance, as Troilus says here.

Fie, fie upon her

Cressida is brought to the Greek camp, where she is suddenly a different person. She has been flirtatious and a little hypocritical with Troilus, teasing and a little ribald with Pandarus, but nothing so bad. In the Greek camp, however, she is suddenly a gay wanton, joking with the Greek leaders and eager to kiss them all—even Nestor.

Only the clear-eyed Ulysses refuses, insulting her openly, and saying to Nestor after she leaves:

> *Fie, fie upon her!*
> *There's language in her eye, her cheek, her lip;*
> *Nay, her foot speaks. Her wanton spirits look out*
> *At every joint and motive of her body.*
> —Act IV, scene v, lines 54–57

Without warning, Cressida is pictured as an utterly worthless woman.

Why so sudden a change? Surely there must have been room to express Cressida's side of the matter in at least one speech. She is torn away from home, and from love at the very moment of that love's height, with only her father at her side, frightened, uncertain, weak. Chaucer, in his version, presents Cressida's dilemma far more sympathetically and lets us pity her in her fall. Shakespeare only lets us despise her.

Might we speculate that Shakespeare is being savage to Cressida and showing her in the worst possible fashion because he wishes to make a point outside the play?

The play seems to have been performed first in 1602, and Shakespeare may have been writing it in 1600–1. Is there a possibility, then, that Shakespeare was influenced by a dramatic event that took place in the time when he was writing the play?

Shakespeare's patron, Henry Wriothesley, Earl of Southampton (see page I–3), with whom Shakespeare may have been on the closest possible terms, was himself a member of the faction of Robert Devereux, 2nd Earl of Essex.

About the time that Shakespeare was beginning his career as a dramatist, Essex had become the favorite and lover of Queen Elizabeth I (who was thirty-three years older than he was).

Essex longed for a successful military career, though the sensible Queen saw that although he might be suitable for a lover, he was not suitable for a general. In 1596, however, he finally persuaded her to allow him to lead an expedition to Spain (with which England was still carrying on a desultory war, a war of which the defeat of the Armada in 1588 had been the high point). Southampton accompanied him on this expedition.

The expedition had a certain success, for the city of Cádiz was seized and sacked. Elizabeth I did not consider the results of the expedition to have been worth its expense, however—she was always a most careful lady with a shilling—and Essex did not receive the credit that he (and his faction, including Southampton and, presumably, Shakespeare) felt he deserved.

Essex, however, became more of a war hawk than ever, having tasted the delights of victory. In 1599 he talked the reluctant Elizabeth (who by now was beginning to feel he was becoming entirely too ambitious to be a safe subject) into letting him lead an expedition into Ireland to put down a rebellion there. Again Southampton left with him, but this time Elizabeth called him back, to his deep discomfiture.

The Essex faction had high hopes for the Irish adventure, and Shakespeare, writing *Henry V* while Essex was in Ireland, refers to the expedition most flatteringly in the chorus that precedes Act V of that play (see page II–508).

The expedition, however, proved a complete fiasco and Essex returned to England in absolute fury at what he, and his faction, believed to be the machinations of the anti-Essex group at the English court. It seemed to them that they had deliberately intrigued against Essex to prevent him from achieving military renown.

In desperation, Essex began to plot rebellion. Southampton arranged to have Shakespeare's play *Richard II* revived. It dealt with the deposition of an English monarch (see page II–304) and Elizabeth did not miss the point. Both Southampton and Essex were arrested, tried for treason, and convicted in February 1601. Essex was, indeed, executed on February 25, but Southampton's sentence was commuted to life imprisonment and, after Elizabeth's death in 1603, he was released.

It is tempting to think that Shakespeare wrote *Troilus and Cressida* under the deep shadow of the misfortunes of Essex and Southampton.

To him, the expedition against Troy may have seemed very much like Essex's expeditions against Cádiz and, later, against Ireland. These expeditions were fought for what seemed to Shakespeare, perhaps, to be a most ungrateful and worthless woman who was oblivious to the sufferings of her faithful servants and whom he may have envisioned as amusing herself with Essex's rival, Sir Walter Raleigh, while the faithful Essex was suffering in the field. Could this be why Shakespeare draws Helen as so contemptible (see page I–111)?

The factions that disrupted the Greek effort on the fields of Troy were magnified by Shakespeare, perhaps as a bitter satire on the factions at the English court that had, in the view of the Essex faction, stabbed Essex in the back.

And Cressida, of course, would then be another aspect of Elizabeth—that false woman who had betrayed her lover and sent him to the gallows. Could Shakespeare have been working on the fourth act just when the execution of Essex came to pass (with Southampton still in prison)? Could he have turned to his pen for revenge on Cressida, making no effort whatever to explain her or excuse her? Did he want her defection to be as bare and as disgraceful as possible so that Ulysses' "Fie, fie upon her!" might reflect as strongly as possible upon the Queen?

The youngest son . . .

At last we are ready for the duel between Hector and Ajax. Since Ajax is a relative of Hector's (here again is the confusion between Ajax and Teucer) it is agreed that the fight is not to be to the death.

While they prepare, Agamemnon asks the name of a sad Trojan on the other side. Ulysses answers:

> *The youngest son of Priam, a true knight,*
> *Not yet mature, yet matchless . . .*
>
> —Act IV, scene v, lines 96–97

It is Troilus being described here, in the very highest terms. The praise has nothing directly to do with the play, and one cannot help but wonder if Shakespeare intends it to refer to the betrayed and executed Essex; if it is his epitaph for that rash person.

This is an example, by the way, of the curious way in which in *Troilus and Cressida* the combatants on either side don't seem to know each other until they are introduced, although they have presumably been fighting each other for years.

This is true in the *Iliad* as well. In Book Three of that poem, when Paris and Menelaus are getting ready for their duel, Priam and his councilors sit on the wall and view the Greek army. Helen is there too, and Priam has her identify several of the Greek champions: Agamemnon, Ulysses, Ajax. Surely after nine years of war Priam ought to know these people. Perhaps the war was much shorter in the earliest legends (and, for all we know, in truth) but grew longer to accommodate the numerous tales added to the primitive story by later poets—and perhaps Homer's tale was tailored to correspond, unavoidably leaving inconsistencies as a result.

Not Neoptolemus . . .

The duel between Ajax and Hector is fought and ends in a draw and in a graceful speech by the chivalrous Hector, as does the similar duel in Book Seven of the *Iliad* (where, however, Hector clearly gets the worse of the exchanges).

Ajax, who is not very good at speaking, manages to express his disappointment at not having beaten Hector definitely.

To which Hector, rather vaingloriously, replies:

Not Neoptolemus so mirable,
On whose bright crest Fame with her loud'st "Oyes"
Cries, "This is he!" could promise to himself
A thought of added honor torn from Hector.

—Act IV, scene v, lines 141–44

The only Neoptolemus in the Greek myths was the son of Achilles (see page I–116), who was also known as Pyrrhus, meaning "ruddy," the latter possibly being a nickname. This is possibly an anachronism on Shakespeare's part, for Hector could scarcely be speaking of a boy who had not yet appeared in the war—or else it is Achilles who is being referred to rather than his son.

I knew thy grandsire . . .

The Trojan leaders are then invited to the Greek camp under conditions of truce (as Achilles had asked, see page I–116). There they greet each other with careful courtesy, and old Nestor says to Hector:

I knew thy grandsire,
And once fought with him.

—Act IV, scene v, lines 195–96

Hector's grandfather was Laomedon, who built the walls of Troy. According to legend, he built them with the aid of Poseidon and Apollo, who were condemned to earthly labor by Zeus for their rebellion against him (which Thetis and Briareus thwarted, see page I–86). When the walls were complete, Laomedon refused the gods their pay and in revenge they sent a sea monster to ravage the Trojan coast.

The Trojans had to sacrifice maidens periodically to the monster, and eventually Laomedon's own daughter, Hesione, was exposed to him. She was rescued by Hercules. It was when Laomedon broke his word again and refused certain horses which he had promised in return for the rescue, that Hercules sacked the city and took Hesione captive. He also killed Laomedon and all but one of his sons. The sole surviving son was Priam.

Nestor is not recorded as having fought with Laomedon (either for him or against him, in either meaning of the phrase). There is, however, an odd coincidence here. Hercules is also recorded as having made war against Neleus, Nestor's father, to have slain Neleus and all but one of his sons and to have placed the one survivor, Nestor, on the throne of Pylos. In this respect, Priam and Nestor had a good deal in common.

. . . your Greekish embassy

Hector also greets Ulysses (who has cleverly cut off what promises to be a flood of Nestorian reminiscence) and says:

> *Ah, sir, there's many a Greek and Troyan dead,*
> *Since first I saw yourself and Diomed*
> *In Ilion, on your Greekish embassy.*
> > —Act IV, scene v, lines 213–15

This represents a point of difference from the *Iliad*. Before the fighting began, the Greeks had sent Ulysses and Menelaus (not Diomedes) to Troy, under a flag of truce, to demand the return of Helen. This is referred to in Book Three of the *Iliad*.

It is, however, very easy to associate Diomedes with Ulysses, for they often acted in concert in the legends about Troy. In the *Iliad* it is Ulysses and Diomedes who act in concert in Book Ten to kill Rhesus the Thracian.

In later myths they are also joined. Thus, the two together sneak into Troy itself in order to steal the Palladium, an image of Minerva (Athena), who bore the alternate name of Pallas, after which the object, holy to her, was named. This was supposed to guard the city and it was not until it was stolen that the city became vulnerable.

Tomorrow do I meet thee . . .

As the fourth act ends, it would seem that a well-rounded climax is clearly being prepared. Troilus approaches Ulysses to ask where Calchas' tent might be located. Ulysses has shown that he admires Troilus and despises Cressida, and it is no great feat to guess that he will be the instrument whereby Troilus will learn of Cressida's infidelity.

As for Achilles, Ulysses' plan has worked wonderfully. He is a new man and when Hector twits him for not fighting, he says:

> *Dost thou entreat me, Hector?*
> *Tomorrow do I meet thee, fell as death;*
> > —Act IV, scene v, lines 267–68

What, then, ought we to expect in the fifth act? Troilus will learn of Cressida's faithlessness, we can be sure, and will go raving out on the field to avenge himself on the Greeks. Perhaps he is to be killed by Diomedes, perhaps by Achilles—but he must die. Troilus dies, in the Greek legends that deal with him, before Achilles' spear, and of what dramatic value is it to survive under the conditions of the tragedy as outlined in this play?

Achilles must also kill Hector, since that is an absolute necessity; all versions of the Troy legend agree there. In the *Iliad* Achilles returns to the fight only after Hector has killed Patroclus, but perhaps Shakespeare might not have needed that part of Homer's plot. After all, Shakespeare's presentation of Patroclus scarcely fits the notion of that effeminate as a doughty warrior. (Homer's presentation of Patroclus was quite different.) Shakespeare might well have felt it would be more satisfactory to have Ulysses' plan stand as the spring that set Achilles to fighting again.

Then, Cressida must die too. Perhaps by her own hand out of contrition or perhaps, in shame, after being cast off by a disgusted, or sated, or callous Diomedes.

Indeed, a century before *Troilus and Cressida* was written, a Scottish poet named Robert Henryson had written a continuation of Chaucer's tale and called it *Testament of Cresseid*. It was so close an imitation of Chaucer that for a while it was considered authentically Chaucerian and in 1532 was actually included in an edition of Chaucer's works.

In the *Testament* Diomedes grows tired of Cressida and casts her off. Cressida rails against Venus and Cupid and is stricken by them with leprosy in punishment. Her face and body utterly altered by this loathsome disease, she begs by the roadside, and Troilus, magnificent on his horse, passes her and tosses her a coin, without recognizing her.

It is a crude denouement, and a savage one, and we could hope that the gentle Shakespeare might never have felt tempted to adopt it, but it was popular and shows what an audience would like in the way of dramatic retribution.

What does Shakespeare really do, then?

Very little, really. The fifth act falls apart and *Troilus and Cressida,* which is tight enough and sensible enough through the first four acts, becomes a rather unsatisfactory play as a result of the fifth act. While it is not my intention in this book to make literary judgments, it appears that the fifth act is so poor that some critics have suggested that Shakespeare did not write it.

We can imagine such a possibility. Suppose that Essex's execution had taken place while Shakespeare was writing *Troilus and Cressida*. He might have written the fourth act savagely, putting Cressida in her place, and then have found the whole thing too unpleasant to continue. If he abandoned the play, some other member of the actors' company of which Shakespeare was a member may have worked up an ending for the play; one that could not match what had gone before, naturally.

Or perhaps we don't have to go that far. It is not absolutely essential to absolve Shakespeare of every inferior passage in his plays. He may have been the greatest writer who ever lived but he was still a man and not a god. He could still write hurriedly; he could still write halfheartedly. And with Essex's execution burning him, he may have botched the last act himself.

. . . a letter from Queen Hecuba

Just as the fifth act begins there is a sudden retreat from the situation as it had been developed at the end of the fourth act. Suddenly Thersites delivers a letter to Achilles, who reads it and says:

> My sweet Patroclus, I am thwarted quite
> From my great purpose in tomorrow's battle.
> Here is a letter from Queen Hecuba,
> A token from her daughter, my fair love,
> Both taxing me and gaging me to keep
> An oath that I have sworn. I will not break it.
>
> —Act V, scene i, lines 38–43

So all of Ulysses' careful planning, all his wisdom and slyness, go suddenly for nothing, and when Achilles is brought to battle it will be in Homer's fashion. In that case, why should Shakespeare have introduced Ulysses' plot at all? It is almost as though another hand, taking up the fifth act, having no idea as to what Shakespeare intended, fell back on Homer in default of anything else.

. . . Ariachne's broken woof . . .

Meanwhile Ulysses has guided Troilus to Calchas' tent, where the young man quickly sees that Cressida is false. The conversation is one long, shallow flirtation of Cressida with Diomedes. She even gives him as a token the very sleeve that Troilus had given her.

The brokenhearted Troilus tries to chop logic and convince himself that he does not really see his Cressida; that there are two Cressidas. One is Diomedes' Cressida, a faithless, worthless woman; and the other, secure in his own mind, is his ideal Cressida, faithful and true. Yet he must admit that this separation is not real, that somehow the two are one:

> And yet the spacious breadth of this division
> Admits no orifex for a point as subtle
> As Ariachne's broken woof to enter.
>
> —Act V, scene ii, lines 147–49

Arachne (not "Ariachne," a change Shakespeare makes to save the meter, apparently) was a Lydian woman so proud of her skill as a weaver that she challenged Minerva (Athena) herself to compete with her. In the competition, Arachne produced a tapestry into which those myths that were uncomplimentary to the gods were woven. When she was done, Minerva could find no fault with it and petulantly tore it to shreds. Arachne tried to hang herself, but Minerva, somewhat remorsefully, saved her life, changed the girl into a spider and the rope into a strand of spider web.

Troilus is saying that not even the finest strand of a spider's web can really be fit between the two Cressidas he is trying to conjure up. He realizes that there is only one Cressida and that he has been betrayed.

. . . The fierce Polydamas

And now suddenly the play explodes into a battle scene, something which the *Iliad* is fiercely crammed with. It begins with Hector arming himself for the fray despite the pleas of his wife Andromache, his sister Cassandra, and his father Priam. Troilus, on the other hand, urges him into the battle with savage forcefulness, for he longs for revenge on Diomedes.

The tide of battle goes against the Greeks to begin with and Agamemnon comes on stage to rally his men:

> *Renew, renew! The fierce Polydamas*
> *Hath beat down Menon;*
>
> —Act V, scene v, lines 6–7

Polydamas appears briefly in the *Iliad* as a friend of Hector's, one who counsels moderation. In Book Twelve, when the Trojan fortunes are beginning to ride high, Polydamas cautions against cocksureness and predicts the end may be disaster. Trojans are winning victories because Achilles is not fighting, but what if he rejoins the battle?

It is to him that Hector makes a famous rejoinder. In quite an un-Homeric mood, he derides all the omens, all the worries about whether birds are flying on the right or on the left, and says: "A divine message? The best divine message is: 'Defend your country!'."

. . . Palamedes

Menon, whom Polydamas has "beat down," does not appear in the *Iliad,* nor do most of the other names that Agamemnon calls out, recounting the tale of defeats in sonorous syllables.

One name, however, perhaps by accident, is memorable, though he does not appear in the *Iliad*. Agamemnon speaks of:

> *. . . Palamedes*
> *Sore hurt and bruised.*
>
> —Act V, scene v, lines 13–14

Palamedes appears in the later myths as a man almost as shrewd as Ulysses himself. When the heroes were gathering to go to Troy, Menelaus and Palamedes traveled to Ithaca to urge Ulysses to come. Ulysses had learned from an oracle that if he went he would not return for twenty years and then penniless and alone, so he pretended to be mad. He guided a plow along the seashore, sowing salt instead of seed. Palamedes watched the display cynically, and suddenly placed Ulysses' one-year-old son, Telemachus, in the path of the plow. Ulysses turned it aside and his pretense of madness was broken.

Ulysses never forgave Palamedes and eventually engineered his death by having him framed for treason. This happened before the *Iliad* opens and there is no hint concerning it in Homer's tale.

This speech of Agamemnon's reflects the situation in Book Fifteen of the *Iliad*. Achilles obdurately refuses to fight; a number of the Greek chieftains, including Agamemnon, Diomedes, and Ulysses, have been wounded, and the Trojan fortunes are at their peak. The Greeks have fallen back to their very ships and the Trojans, with Hector leading them on, are bringing the torches with which to set those ships on fire.

Patroclus ta'en . . .

But in the course of Agamemnon's cry, however, one significant phrase creeps in:

> *Patroclus ta'en or slain.*
>
> —Act V, scene v, line 13

Thus, in four words, is masked the most dramatic portion of the *Iliad*. Achilles, having brutally rejected Agamemnon's offer of amends in Book Nine, forfeits the side of right and must, in his turn, begin to pay.

That payment comes in Book Sixteen, when Patroclus, horror-stricken at the Greek defeat and at the imminent burning of their ships, begs Achilles to let him enter the fight. Achilles agrees. He allows Patroclus to wear Achilles' own armor, but warns him merely to drive the Trojans from the ships and not to attempt to assault the city.

Patroclus does well. The Trojans are driven back, but the excitement of battle causes him to forget Achilles' advice. He pursues the fleeing Trojans, is stopped by Hector, and killed.

. . . bear Patroclus' body . . .

Agamemnon's remark that Patroclus is either taken or slain is soon settled in favor of the latter alternative. Nestor enters, saying:

> *Go, bear Patroclus' body to Achilles,*
>
> —Act V, scene v, line 17

Again, in a few words, many dramatic deeds in the *Iliad* are slurred over. In Book Seventeen there is a gigantic struggle over Patroclus' body. Hector manages to strip the dead man of the armor of Achilles, but the Greeks save the body itself in a fight in which Menelaus and Ajax do particularly well. In the *Iliad* it is Menelaus who sends the message to Achilles, not Nestor, but then it is Nestor's son, Antilochus (who does not appear in *Troilus and Cressida*), who actually carries the message.

. . . Great Achilles

Events follow quickly. Ulysses comes onstage, crying:

> *O courage, courage, princes! Great Achilles*
> *Is arming, weeping, cursing, vowing vengeance!*
> *Patroclus' wounds have roused his drowsy blood,*
>
> —Act V, scene v, lines 30–32

So it happens in the *Iliad.* Achilles, paid back for his intransigence, realizes too late that he has sulked in his tent too long. In the *Iliad,* however, he doesn't arm so quickly. He has no armor, for he had given it to Patroclus, who had lost it to Hector.

A new set of armor must be forged for Achilles by Vulcan himself, something to which Book Eighteen of the *Iliad* is devoted. In Book Nineteen there is the formal reconciliation of Agamemnon and Achilles, and only then, in Book Twenty, does Achilles join the battle.

. . . I'll hunt thee for thy hide

In Books Twenty, Twenty-one, and Twenty-two, Achilles is at war, and none can stand before him. Indeed, in those three books, no Greek warrior but Achilles is mentioned. It is as though he, a single man, fights alone against the Trojans (with occasional help from one god or another) and defeats them.

In Book Twenty-two, when the Trojan army has fled within the walls of Troy in fear of the raging Achilles, Hector at last comes out alone to meet him in the climactic battle of the *Iliad*. But the issue is never in doubt.

The onrush of Achilles daunts even Hector, and at the last moment he turns to flee, trying to find his way safe through one of the city gates. Achilles heads him off and three times they run completely round the city (which can only be village-size by modern standards).

Only then does Hector turn, perforce, to face Achilles, and is killed!

None of this can appear in *Troilus and Cressida*. The medieval poets, with their pro-Trojan/Roman prejudice, had to treat Hector much more gently, and Shakespeare inherits that attitude from them.

He has the two champions fight indeed, but it is Achilles who has to fall back, weakening. Hector says, gallantly,

> *Pause, if thou wilt.*
>
> —Act V, scene vi, line 14

And Achilles goes off, muttering that he is out of practice.

Yet something must be done to account for the fact that Hector does indeed die at the hands of Achilles, so Shakespeare makes the former do a most un-Hectorish thing. Hector meets an unnamed Greek in rich armor and decides he wants it. When the Greek tries to run, Hector calls out:

> *Wilt thou not, beast, abide?*
> *Why then, fly on, I'll hunt thee for thy hide.*
>
> —Act V, scene vi, lines 30–31

Nowhere in Homer, nor anywhere else in this play, does Hector give anyone reason to think he would ever call a foeman "beast" or take the attitude that war is a hunt, with other men playing the role of animals, and it is partly because of this that some critics doubt that Shakespeare wrote the last act. And yet it is necessary for Hector to do something of this sort, in order that he might earn the retribution that now falls upon him.

. . . Troy, sink down

Hector catches his prey and kills him. It is late in the day and Hector decides the day's fight is over. Perhaps he is helped to that decision by his eagerness to try on the new armor he has won. At any rate, he takes off his own armor, stands unprotected—and at that moment, Achilles and a contingent of his Myrmidons appear on the scene.

Hector cries out that he is unarmed, but Achilles orders his men to kill, and then says, in grim satisfaction:

> So, Ilion, fall thou next! Come, Troy, sink down!
> Here lies thy heart, thy sinews, and thy bone.
> —Act V, scene viii, lines 11–12

For Achilles to kill Hector in this way is unthinkable in a Homeric context and must strike any lover of the *Iliad* as simple sacrilege. But there it is—the medieval pro-Trojan, pro-Hector view.

. . . wells and Niobes . . .

Troilus bears the news of Hector's death to the Trojan army:

> Go in to Troy, and say there Hector's dead.
> There is a word will Priam turn to stone,
> Make wells and Niobes of the maids and wives,
> —Act V, scene x, lines 17–19

Niobe was a Theban queen, a daughter of Tantalus (see page I–13), whose pride in her six sons and six daughters led her to boast herself the superior of the goddess Latona (Leto), who had only one of each. Latona's children, however, happened to be Apollo and Diana.

To avenge the taunt, Apollo and Diana shot down all twelve children, the twelfth in Niobe's arms. She wept continuously after that, day after day, until the gods, in pity, turned her to stone, with a spring of tears still bubbling out and trickling down.

. . . no more to say

This essentially ends the play. As Troilus says:

> Hector is dead; there is no more to say.
> —Act V, scene x, line 22

To be sure, Troilus promises revenge on the Greeks and on Achilles particularly, but that is just talk. There can be no revenge. Troy must fall.

Nor has Troilus revenge on Diomedes or Cressida. Diomedes still lives and still has Cressida.

The fifth act is an ending of sorts, but it is not the ending toward which the first four acts were heading.

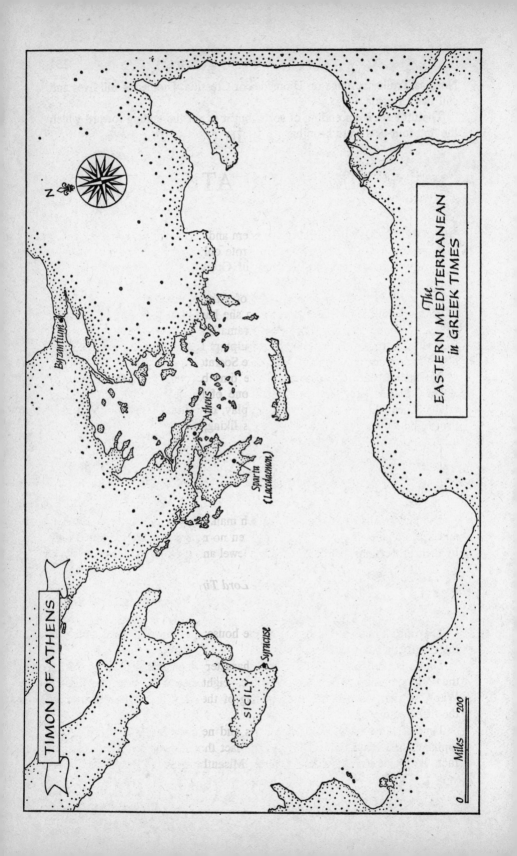

TIMON OF ATHENS

The
EASTERN MEDITERRANEAN
in GREEK TIMES

Byzantium

Athens

Sparta
(Lacedaemon)

SICILY

Syracuse

0   200
Miles

5

The Life of

TIMON OF ATHENS

SHAKESPEARE wrote a narrative poem and three plays set in the legendary days of Greek history. He wrote only one play that was based—in a very tenuous way—in the days of Greece's greatest glory, the fifth century B.C.

This century was the Golden Age of Athens, when she beat off giant Persia and built a naval empire, when she had great leaders like Themistocles, Aristides, and Pericles; great dramatists like Aeschylus, Sophocles, Euripides, and Aristophanes; great sculptors like Phidias; great scientists like Anaxagoras; great philosophers like Socrates and Plato.

But Shakespeare chose to mark the time by writing a play, *Timon of Athens,* that is generally considered one of his least satisfactory. Many critics consider it to be an unfinished play, one that Shakespeare returned to on and off, never patching it to his liking, and eventually abandoning it.

. . . the Lord Timon . . .

The play opens in the house of a rich man. A Poet, a Painter, a Jeweler, and a Merchant all enter. They are given no names but are identified only by their professions. The Jeweler has a jewel and the Merchant says:

> *O pray let's see't. For the Lord Timon, sir?*
> —Act I, scene i, line 13

The Lord Timon is the owner of the house; the center toward which all these and others are tending.

Timon is, apparently, a historical character who lived in Athens during the Peloponnesian War (431–404 B.C.—eight centuries after the Trojan War), so that we may set the opening of the play in the last quarter of the fifth century B.C.

Timon's fame to his contemporaries and near successors, such as Aristophanes and Plato, lay entirely in the fact that he was a misanthrope. In fact, he was referred to as "Timon Misanthropos" ("Timon the Man-

Hater"). He lived by himself, professed to hate mankind and to detest human society. To the sociable Greeks, to whom conversation and social intercourse were the breath of life, there was something monstrous in this.

Plutarch, in his "Life of Mark Antony," describes how, at a low point in his career, Antony decided for a while to imitate Timon and withdraw from human society. Shakespeare may have come across this while working on his play *Antony and Cleopatra* (see page I–370) and conceived the idea of writing a play centered on the condition of misanthropy. And, indeed, *Timon of Athens* seems to have been written immediately after *Antony and Cleopatra,* in 1606 or 1607.

The senators of Athens . . .

Additional men enter and the Poet identifies them, saying:

> *The senators of Athens, happy men!*
>
> —Act I, scene i, line 40

Throughout the play Shakespeare treats Athens, with whose social and political life he is unacquainted, as though it were Rome, a city with which he was much more at home. Athens had no senators or anything quite equivalent to the well-known legislators of Rome. Yet Shakespeare, throughout the play, has the rulers of Athens act like the stern, irascible, grasping Roman aristocrats, rather than like the gay, impulsive, weather-cock democrats they really were.

Indeed, so anxious does Shakespeare appear to be to deal with Rome rather than with Athens, that almost every character in the play has a Roman name. This is quite out of the question in reality, of course. No Roman name was ever heard of in Athens of Timon's time. Rome itself had never been heard of. If Rome had forced itself on the attention of any Athenian of the time, it would have seemed only a barbarian Italian village of utterly no account.

Feigned Fortune . . .

But Timon is not yet Misanthropos. He is, at the beginning of the play, an extremely wealthy man of almost unbelievable benevolence. He seeks for excuses to give money away and every man there is trying to get his share.

Yet the Poet, at least, is not entirely fooled by the superficial appearance of wealth and happiness that surrounds Timon. He speaks of his poetry to the Painter, and describes its content by saying:

Sir, I have upon a high and pleasant hill
Feigned Fortune to be throned.

—Act I, scene i, lines 63–64

The goddess of fortune (Fortuna to the Romans and Tyche to the Greeks) became popular in the period that followed Greece's Golden Age. Alexander the Great had come and gone like lightning across the skies, bringing Greece vast conquests and vast derangements. The individual Greek cities came to be helpless in the grip of generals and armies; culture decayed as materialism grew and the rich grew richer while the poor grew poorer.

Fortune was a deity of chance and was just right for the age following Alexander the Great; an age which saw the passing of youth and confidence, and in which good and evil seemed to be handed out at random and without any consideration of desert.

The Poet explains that Fortune beckons benignly and Timon mounts the hill, carrying with him all those he befriends. But Fortune is fickle and Timon may be kicked down the hill by her. In that case, none of the friends he took up the hill with him will follow him down.

Shakespeare is, in this way, preparing the audience for the consideration of what it was that made Timon a misanthrope.

Plutarch says only that ". . . for the unthankfulness of those he had done good unto and whom he took to be his friends, he was angry with all men and would trust no man."

Another similar treatment of Timon at much greater length was by a Greek writer, Lucian, born in Syria about A.D. 120. He had written twenty-six *Dialogues of the Gods,* in which he poked satirical fun at conventional religion, but so pleasantly that even the pious must have found it difficult to take offense.

His best essay is considered to be "Timon," in which he uses the theme of a man who has become misanthropic through the ingratitude of others to poke fun at Jupiter and at Wealth. He expands on the hint in Plutarch and makes Timon out to have been, originally, a fantastically generous man who beggared himself for his friends and then found none who would help him.

Shakespeare adopted this notion, but removed all the fun and humor in Lucian's dialogue and replaced it with savagery.

. . . a dog

Timon himself now enters, and moves among all those present with affability and generosity, giving to all who ask, denying no one. He accepts their rather sickening sycophancy with good humor, but accepts it.

There is only one sour note and that is when the philosopher Apemantus enters. He is churlish and his every speech is a curt insult.

The Painter strikes back with:

> *Y'are a dog.*
>
> —Act I, scene i, line 202

This is not a mere insult, but, in a way, a statement of fact, if a slightly anachronistic one.

About 400 B.C. a philosopher named Antisthenes taught that virtue was more important than riches or comfort and that, indeed, poverty was welcome, for wealth and luxury were corrupting. One of his pupils was Diogenes, who lived near Corinth about 350 B.C. and who carried Antisthenes' teachings to an extreme.

Diogenes lived in the greatest possible destitution to show that people needed no belongings to be virtuous. He loudly derided all the polite social customs of the day, denouncing them as hypocrisy.

Diogenes and those who followed him made ordinary men uncomfortable. These grating philosophers seemed to bark and snarl at all that made life pleasant. They were called *kynikos* ("doglike") because of their snarling, and this became "cynic" in English.

Diogenes accepted the name and became "Diogenes the Cynic." Apemantus is pictured in this play as a Cynic a century before the term became fashionable, and when the Painter calls him a dog, he is really dismissing him as a Cynic.

Apemantus' insults extend even to Timon. When the Poet tries to defend Timon, Apemantus considers it mere flattery and says, crushingly:

> *He that loves to be flattered is worthy o' th' flatterer.*
>
> —Act I, scene i, lines 229–30

This is the first clear statement that Timon, despite appearances, is not entirely to be admired. He is extremely generous, but is it in order to do good, or in order to be flattered and fawned upon? There is something so public, ostentatious, and indiscriminate in his benevolences that they grow suspect.

'Tis Alcibiades . . .

A messenger comes in with the announcement of new visitors;

> *'Tis Alcibiades and some twenty horse,*
>
> —Act I, scene i, line 246

Alcibiades is the only character in the play who has an important role in Athenian history. He was an Athenian general of noble birth, handsome and brilliant, who in the end turned traitor and did Athens infinite harm.

He is brought into the play because Plutarch uses him as an occasion for an example of Timon's misanthropy. The one man Timon made much of was Alcibiades, and when asked why that was, Timon answered, harshly, "I do it because I know that one day he shall do great mischief unto the Athenians."

This is rather better and more specific insight than individuals are likely to have, and in all probability the story is apocryphal and was invented long after Alcibiades had demonstrated the harm he did Athens.

. . . Plutus, the god of gold

Timon is giving a feast that night as he is wont to do. In fact, one Lord who means to partake of it says of him:

> He pours it out. Plutus, the god of gold,
> Is but his steward . . .
> —Act I, scene i, lines 283–84

Plutus is related, by name and origin, to Pluto, the king of the underworld, and represents the wealth of the soil, both mineral and vegetable (see page I–115).

The later Greeks considered Plutus to be a son of Fortune, who had been blinded by Jupiter so that he gives his gifts indiscriminately. In Lucian's dialogue, Wealth is also pictured as blind and as giving his gifts to anyone he happens to bump into. Thus, once again, Timon's wealth is associated with chance and its slippery nature made plain.

What's more, Timon will give, but won't receive. He says as much to Ventidius, one of his guests at the feast. Ventidius tries to thank him for favors received, but Timon says:

> You mistake my love;
> I gave it freely ever, and there's none
> Can truly say he gives, if he receives.
> —Act I, scene ii, lines 9–11

In this respect, though, Timon seems to aspire to be a god, since surely only a god can always give, never receive. Furthermore, Timon would deprive others of the act of giving, which he apparently considers the supreme pleasure. Would he reserve the supreme pleasure exclusively for himself?

It is almost as though Timon were divorcing himself from mankind through the unique act of giving without receiving. He will not condescend to be human and in that respect he (so to speak) hates mankind. Perhaps Shakespeare meant to show (if he could have polished the play into final form) that a man does not become a misanthrope unless he has been one all along. Perhaps he meant to show that Timon did not pass from benevolence to misanthropy but merely changed from one form of misanthropy to another.

A thousand talents . . .

The banquet ends in a general donation to everyone by Timon, so that cynical Apemantus guesses that Timon will be going bankrupt soon. The guess is correct and even conservative, for though Timon doesn't know it (scorning, like a god, to inquire into the status of his wealth) he is already deep in debt.

His creditors (whom his steward has long been holding off) will be restrained no longer, and not long after the banquet Timon is told the situation. All astonished, he finds out that all his land is sold, all his cash is spent, all his assets gone. Yet he will not accept the reproaches of his steward but is cheerfully confident he can borrow from his many adoring friends.

He sends his servants to various people who are in debt to him for past favors and tells them to ask, casually, for large sums. The steward, Flavius, he sends to the senators so that the city treasury may reward him for money he had in the past given it. He tells Flavius:

> Bid 'em send o'th'instant
> A thousand talents to me.
>
> —Act II, scene ii, lines 208–9

A talent was a huge sum of money. It is equal to nearly sixty pounds of silver, and by modern standards it is equivalent to about two thousand dollars. What Timon was so cavalierly asking for "o'th'instant" was two million dollars. The city of Athens could not possibly have made available that sum of money to a private person "o'th'instant."

The ridiculous size of the sum requested is sometimes taken as an indication that Shakespeare did not know how much a talent was worth, and either hadn't done the necessary research by the time he abandoned the play, or, if he had, never got around to changing the figures throughout.

What is even more likely to be a mistake appears a little later, as scene after scene passes in which Timon's servants vainly try to borrow money from those whom earlier the once rich man had so loaded with benefits. Thus, Lucius, one of those so benefited, says, incredulously, to one of the pleading servants:

> *I know his lordship is but merry with me.*
> *He cannot want fifty five hundred talents.*
>
> —Act III, scene ii, lines 40–41

He cannot indeed. That would be some 160 *tons* of silver. A private person of Timon's time simply could not have had so much wealth to hand out on the moment. Perhaps Shakespeare was dithering between fifty talents and five hundred talents, wondering if the latter was too great, and, having written in both, never got around to erasing one or the other by the time he had abandoned the play.

It is tempting to despise those whom Timon had so benefited and who were now so lost to gratitude. But let us be reasonable. Timon had *forced* the benefits on his friends, eager to demonstrate godlike generosity. Should those friends now deliver their money to someone who had displayed such abysmal lack of understanding of personal finance? Whatever they gave him would surely be lost forever and at once.

Naturally, Timon did not look at it that way at all. His pretensions to superhuman wealth and benevolence had been punctured and he found himself in a towering rage of frustration and humiliation as a result.

At Lacedaemon . . .

Meanwhile, Alcibiades is having an argument of his own with the Athenian Senate. Some soldier is under sentence of death for murder and Alcibiades is pleading for a reversal of the sentence on the grounds that death came as a result of an honorable duel fought in anger that had come about because the man under sentence had been bitterly offended.

Who the soldier is, what the occasion, why the Senate is so harsh or Alcibiades so insistent are not explained. Shakespeare had inserted the scene, perhaps the best in the play, but had never gotten around to supplying the mortar that would connect it properly to what had gone before. It seems clear, though, that Shakespeare is setting up a subplot to show another facet of the "ingratitude" theme. Alcibiades says of the soldier:

> *His service done*
> *At Lacedaemon and Byzantium*
> *Were a sufficient briber for his life.*
>
> —Act III, scene v, lines 60–62

This vaguely suits the Peloponnesian War, which was going on in the lifetime of Timon and Alcibiades. Athens was fighting a coalition led by the city of Sparta, of which an alternate (and, in some respects, more nearly official) name was Lacedaemon.

However, the speech makes it sound as though there was fighting at Lacedaemon, and that wasn't so. The city of Sparta, protected by its unparalleled army, was unapproachable throughout the sixth and fifth centuries B.C. It was not until Sparta suffered a shattering defeat at the hands of Thebes, thirty years after the Peloponnesian War, that the city became vulnerable.

Nor were there important battles at Byzantium (the later Constantinople and the still later Istanbul), though it occupied a strategic position at the straits between the Aegean Sea and the Black Sea, not very far from where Troy had once been situated.

We banish thee . . .

When Alcibiades continues to plead the soldier's cause, the First Senator, austere and obdurate in Roman rather than Athenian manner, finally says:

> *Do you dare our anger?*
> *'Tis in few words, but spacious in effect:*
> *We banish thee for ever.*
>
> —Act III, scene v, lines 95–97

In actual history, Alcibiades was indeed banished from Athens, but not for so personal and trivial a cause. In 415 B.C. he had urged that Athens end the long war with Sparta by a very daring move, nothing less than an invasion of Sicily and the capture of its chief city, Syracuse, which had been supporting the Spartan cause financially.

A victory in Sicily would have transferred Syracuse's navy and wealth to the Athenian side, given Athens a secure base in the west, and broken the morale of the Spartan coalition. It was a desperate gamble, but under Alcibiades it might just possibly have succeeded.

The Athenians, however, voted another general, Nicias, as cocommander, and this was a terrible mistake. Nicias was an "appeaser," anxious to make a deal with Sparta, and couldn't possibly be expected to supply vigorous leadership—especially since he was a most incompetent general in any case.

To make matters worse, just before the expedition was to set sail, certain religious statues in the city were blasphemously mutilated, and suspicion fell upon Alcibiades, who was a known agnostic.

To be sure, Alcibiades would scarcely have been so insane as to have chosen this time to play the scoffer in so ostentatious a manner. Although the mystery of who mutilated the statues has never been solved, most historians feel it must have been Alcibiades' enemies who did it, and that Alcibiades was framed.

At first, proceedings against Alcibiades were ordered suspended till the Sicilian expedition was over, but then after the fleet got under way, the Athenians changed their mind and recalled Alcibiades. Alcibiades was certain that he couldn't possibly escape conviction and so he went voluntarily into exile.

The Sicilian expedition, be it noted, came to utter grief without him. A huge Athenian force, both men and ships, was utterly destroyed and Athens never truly recovered. She was never again, after the Sicilian expedition, what she had been before it. Because it was Alcibiades who had urged it on, he had brought great harm to Athens (as Timon, according to Plutarch, had foreseen) and was yet to do more.

. . . hated be of Timon . . .

Back we go to Timon's house, where Timon has called back his friends for another banquet. All the men who had just refused to lend Timon money are now back at their old places. They don't know how Timon has managed to recover, but if he is conducting feasts, they intend to be at the trough.

They are as servile as ever and Timon appears as affable as ever, but when it is time to eat of the covered dishes, Timon reveals them to be full of water and nothing more. Timon throws the water in their faces, curses them, and drives them away, crying out:

> Burn house, sink Athens, henceforth hated be
> Of Timon man and all humanity.
>
> —Act III, scene vi, lines 105–6

There is the transition. Timon goes from universal benevolence to universal malevolence. In both roles, he has held himself far removed from ordinary mankind, but in the latter he at least requires no wealth.

Timon leaves his home and the city. He finds himself a cave outside Athens and spends his time in cursing. He digs and finds gold (a device borrowed from Lucian's dialogue), but that does not soften his hardened heart or soothe his poisoned soul.

This fell whore . . .

Now a parade of people comes seeking Timon in the cave. (After all, he is rich again.) The first, by accident rather than by design, for Timon's wealth is not yet known, is Alcibiades, who is marching against Athens at the head of a rebel army and who at first fails to recognize Timon.

Alcibiades is accompanied by two prostitutes whom Timon does not fail to condemn. He says to Alcibiades concerning one of them:

> *This fell whore of thine*
> *Hath in her more destruction than thy sword,*
> *For all her cherubin look.*
>
> —Act IV, scene iii, lines 62–64

The "fell whore" in question is Phrynia, whose name is inspired by a famous Athenian courtesan named Phryne who flourished in the time of Alexander the Great, a century after Alcibiades. She grew immensely rich from her earnings, for she had as her customers the most distinguished men of the time and she charged healthy fees. The most famous story told of her is that once when she was brought before a court, accused of profaning certain religious rites, she exposed her breasts to the judges and was acquitted on the spot.

. . . proud Athens on a heap

Alcibiades expresses sympathy for Timon, offers him money, and begins:

> *When I have laid proud Athens on a heap—*
>
> —Act IV, scene iii, line 102

The historical Alcibiades, when he fled Athens, went to Sparta, his city's bitter enemy, and there advised that enemy how best to conduct its war. For a period of time he virtually directed Sparta's armies, much more intelligently and effectively than Spartan generals had been able to do. In that sense, Alcibiades was marching against Athens.

But when, in the play, Alcibiades talks of destroying Athens, Timon interrupts to wish him all success in that task, together with the destruction of himself afterward. And before they go, he heaps bitter speeches on the courtesans as he gives them quantities of his own gold.

The middle of humanity . . .

Apemantus now comes in. The old and practiced Cynic can now bandy insults with the new-made Misanthropos. Shakespeare bases this on a tale of Plutarch's, intending to show how Timon, in his universal hatred, outdid the Cynics. He tells how Apemantus once, when dining with Timon, they two being all the company, commented on how pleasant it was to feast alone without hated mankind present, and Timon answered morosely, "It would be, if you were not present."

Thus, when in the play Apemantus offers to give Timon food, and mend his diet, Timon says:

> *First mend my company, take away thyself.*
> —Act IV, scene iii, line 284

But Apemantus is not fooled. He was not impressed by Timon playing god, and he is not impressed by Timon playing dog. (It is odd that in English, god and dog are the same letters in mirror image.) Apemantus says, cynically:

> *Art thou proud yet?*
> —Act IV, scene iii, line 278

He says even more sharply:

> *The middle of humanity thou never knewest, but the extremity of both ends.*
> —Act IV, scene iii, lines 301–2

The rumor of Timon's gold spreads. Thieves come to relieve him of it, but he gives it to them with such malevolent glee at the harm it will do them that they leave most uneasily.

His old steward, Flavius, arrives weeping, and asks only to continue to serve Timon. Even Timon's withered heart is touched and he is forced to retreat one inch from his universal hatred. He says:

> *I do proclaim*
> *One honest man. Mistake me not, but one.*
> —Act IV, scene iii, lines 505–6

Here Timon seems to have faced mankind and found himself momentarily to be neither god nor dog, but "the middle of humanity." Had he found himself permanently back to that middle, the play might have been more satisfactory, but Shakespeare blunders onward through the thicket of unrelieved misanthropy.

. . . hang himself

The Poet and the Painter arrive to get their share of the gold by pretending selfless love of Timon, but Timon overhears their plotting and drives them away.

Then come Athenian Senators, pleading with Timon to take over the leadership of the city's forces in order to turn back Alcibiades, who is battering at the city's walls, but Timon states bitterly that he doesn't care what Alcibiades does to Athens. Shakespeare now makes use of still another anecdote in Plutarch.

He announces one favor he will do Athens. He has a tree that he is about to chop down, but he urges the Senators to announce to all Athenians who wish to take advantage of the offer to:

> Come hither ere my tree hath felt the ax,
> And hang himself.
>
> —Act V, scene i, lines 212–13

Those enemies of Timon's . . .

Timon dies, unreconciled to the end, and Athens must surrender to Alcibiades.

This did not happen quite so in history.

Rather, Alcibiades finally fell out with the Spartans (the story is that he was a little too familiar with one of the Spartan queens and the Spartan King resented it) and returned to Athenian allegiance. They welcomed him back because the war was going more and more badly and they needed him. In 407 B.C. he made a triumphant return to Athens and in that sense, Athens might be viewed as having surrendered to him.

The Athenians, however, could never bring themselves to trust him, and the next year he was exiled again, this time permanently.

The play does not go that far. It ends with the reconciliation, as Alcibiades says:

> Those enemies of Timon's and mine own
> Whom you yourselves shall set out for reproof,
> Fall, and no more.
>
> —Act V, scene iv, lines 56–58

Alcibiades lets himself be placated and reconciled, where Timon did not, and it is plain that the former is displayed as the preferable course.

Timon is dead by then, but the epitaph he wrote for himself is brought in and Alcibiades reads it—Timon's final word (taken from Plutarch).

> *Here lie I, Timon, who alive all living men did hate.*
> *Pass by and curse thy fill, but pass, and stay not here thy*
> *gait.*

—Act V, scene iv, lines 72–73

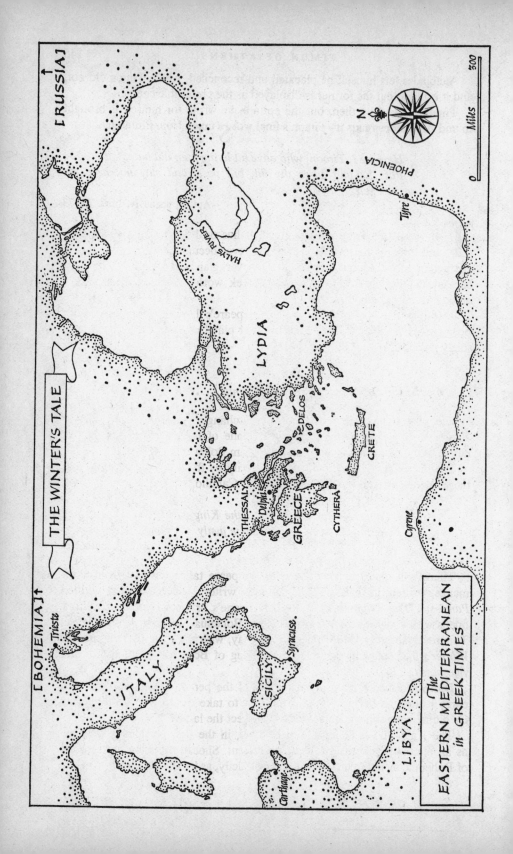

[RUSSIA]

[BOHEMIA]

THE WINTER'S TALE

Trieste

ITALY

SICILY

Syracuse.

Carthage

LIBYA

GREECE

THESSALY

Delphi

CYTHERA

CRETE

DELOS

LYDIA

Cyrene

HALYS RIVER

PHOENICIA

Tyre

N

The
EASTERN MEDITERRANEAN
in GREEK TIMES

0   Miles   300

6

THE WINTER'S TALE

THE WINTER'S TALE is a romance. It has no historical basis whatever and none of the events it describes ever occurred; nor are any of its characters to be found in history, however glancingly. Nevertheless, its background lies in the pre-Christian Greek world. I therefore include it among the Greek plays.

It seems to have been one of Shakespeare's latest plays, too, having been written as late as 1611. The only later play for which Shakespeare was solely responsible was *The Tempest*.

. . . the King of Sicilia means to pay Bohemia . . .

The play opens with two courtiers exchanging graceful compliments. The scene is set in Sicilia (Sicily) and one of the courtiers, Camillo, is native to the place. The other is a vistor from Bohemia.

The occasion is a state visit paid to Sicily by the King of Bohemia, and there may be a return visit in consequence. Camillo says:

> *I think this coming summer the King of Sicilia means to pay Bohemia the visitation which he justly owes him.*
>
> —Act I, scene i, lines 5–7

There is a queer reversal here. Shakespeare takes the plot from a romance written in 1588 by the English writer Robert Greene, entitled *Pandosto. The Triumph of Time*. In Greene's original romance the story opens with a visit of the King of Sicily to Bohemia, rather than the reverse. This reversal is carried all through the play, with the King of Sicily in *The Winter's Tale* playing the role of the King of Bohemia in *Pandosto*, and vice versa.

Did Shakespeare make a casual slip of the pen to begin with and then carry it through because he was too lazy to take the trouble to correct it? Or did he have some good reason?—I suspect the latter.

The King who is being visited behaves, in the first portion of the play, as an almost psychotically suspicious tyrant. Should this king be the King of Bohemia, as in Greene, or the King of Sicily, as in Shakespeare?

Suppose we look back into history. In 405 B.C., just ten years after the ill-fated Sicilian expedition of Athens (see page I–140), a general, Dionysius, seized control over Syracuse, the largest and strongest city of Sicily. By 383 B.C. he had united almost the entire island under his rule.

Dionysius is best known for the manner in which he kept himself in power for thirty-eight years in an era when rulers were regularly over-thrown by palace coups or popular unrest. He did so by unending suspicion and eternal vigilance. For instance, there is a story that he had a bell-shaped chamber opening into the state prison, with the narrow end con-necting to his room. In this way, he could secretly listen to conversations in the prison and learn if any conspiracies were brewing. This has been called the "ear of Dionysius."

He arrested people on mere suspicion and his suspicion was most easily aroused. Naturally, he left the memory of himself behind in most unsavory fashion and though he died in peace, he is remembered as a cruel and sus-picious tyrant.

If Shakespeare had to choose between Bohemia and Sicily as a place to be ruled by a tyrant, was it not sensible to choose Sicily?

Of course, King Leontes of Sicily, the character in the play, is not to be equated with Dionysius. The Sicilian tyrant of old may simply have made Sicily seem the more appropriate scene for tyranny, but there all resem-blance ends and nothing in the play has any relationship to the life of Dionysius.

Nevertheless, because of this tenuous connection between Leontes and Dionysius, and the fact that Dionysius lived a generation after Timon, I am placing this play immediately after *Timon of Athens*.

As for Bohemia . . . Later in the play there will be scenes of idyllic pas-toral happiness in the kingdom of the visiting monarch. Shall that other kingdom then be Sicily, as in Greene, or Bohemia, as in Shakespeare?

To be sure, in ancient times Sicily was an agricultural province that served as the granary of early Rome. It might therefore be viewed as an idyllic place in contrast to citified and vice-ridden Rome itself. However, Sicily was also noted for its brutal wars between the Greeks and Carthage and, later, the Romans and Carthage. Still later, it was the scene of horrible slave rebellions.

What of Bohemia by contrast? The Bohemia we know is the western-most part of modern Czechoslovakia and is no more a pastoral idyll than anywhere else. This Bohemia is inhabited by a Slavic people, in Shake-speare's time as well as in our own, and its origin, as a Slavic nation, dates back to perhaps the eighth century, something like a thousand years after the time of Dionysius.

This discrepancy in time did not bother Greene, or Shakespeare either, and would not bother us in reading the play. However, is it necessarily our present real-life Bohemia that Shakespeare was thinking of? Was there another?

Shortly after 1400, bands of strange people reached central Europe. They were swarthy-skinned nomads, who spoke a language that was not like any in Europe. Some Europeans thought they came from Egypt and they were called "gypsies" in consequence. (They still are called that in the United States, but their real origin may have been India.)

When the gypsies reached Paris in 1427, the French knew only that they had come from central Europe. There were reports that they had come from Bohemia, and so the French called them Bohemians (and still do).

The gypsy life seemed gay and vagabondish and must have been attractive to those bound to heavy labor or dull routine. The term "Bohemian" therefore came to be applied to artists, writers, show people, and others living an unconventional and apparently vagabondish life. Bohemia came to be an imaginary story land of romance.

Well then, if Shakespeare wanted a land of pastoral innocence and delights, should he pick Sicily or Bohemia? —Bohemia, by all means.

. . . tremor cordis . . .

The courtiers let the audience know that Leontes of Sicily and Polixenes of Bohemia were childhood friends and have close ties of affection. In the next scene, when the two kings come on stage themselves, this is made perfectly clear.

Polixenes has been away from home for nine months and pressing affairs must take him away. Leontes urges him strenuously to remain, and when Polixenes is adamant, the Sicilian host asks his Queen, Hermione, to join her pleas with his. She does, and after joyful badinage, Polixenes gives in.

Then, quite suddenly, without warning at all, a shadow falls over Leontes. He watches his gay Queen and the friend she is cajoling (at Leontes' own request) and he says in an aside:

> *Too hot, too hot!*
> *To mingle friendship far is mingling bloods.*
> *I have tremor cordis on me . . .*
> —Act I, scene ii, lines 108–10

An unnatural physical effect, a palpitation of the heart ("tremor cordis") has come over him. A sickness, an abnormality, makes of the genial host, without real cause, a jealous tyrant.

The sickness grows on itself. He wonders if he has been cuckolded (see page I–108) and is at once convinced he is. He seeks supporting opinion and consults his courtier, Camillo, who listens in horror and recognizes the situation as a mental illness:

> Good my lord, be cured
> Of this diseased opinion, and betimes,
> For 'tis most dangerous.
>
> —Act I, scene ii, lines 296–98

. . . sighted like the basilisk

Camillo's clear wisdom is greeted by Leontes with a howl of rage. The King makes it clear that if Camillo were a loyal subject he would poison Polixenes. Reluctantly, Camillo agrees to accept the direct order, provided the King will then offer no disgrace to his Queen.

By now, however, Polixenes notes that the warm friendship that had surrounded him but a short time ago has vanished and he is aware of an intensifying frigidity. He meets Camillo and questions him but Camillo can only speak evasively, and still in the metaphor of sickness:

> I cannot name the disease; and it is caught
> Of you, that yet are well.
>
> —Act I, scene ii, lines 387–88

He is referring, of course, to the insane jealousy of which Polixenes is the unwitting and undeserved cause. Polixenes cannot understand and says:

> How caught of me?
> Make me not sighted like the basilisk.
> I have looked on thousands, who have sped the better
> By my regard, but killed none so.
>
> —Act I, scene ii, lines 388–91

Another name for the basilisk is the cockatrice, a word that may have originated as a distortion of crocodile. The medieval European had little contact with crocodiles, though he had heard of them in connection with the distant Nile.

The crocodile, like the serpent, is a deadly reptile. It might almost be viewed as a gigantic, thick snake, with stubby legs. To Europeans, unfamiliar with the crocodile except by distant report, the snaky aspects of the creature could easily become dominant.

Once "cockatrice" is formed from "crocodile," the first syllable becomes suggestive, and the fevered imagination develops the thought that the monster originates in a cock's egg and is a creature with a snake's body and a cock's head.

The cockatrice is pictured as the ultimate snake. It kills not by a bite but merely by a look. Not merely its venom, but its very breath is fatal. Because the cockatrice is the most deadly snake and therefore the king of snakes, or because the cockscomb may be pictured as a crown, the cockatrice came to be called "basilisk" (from Greek words meaning "little king").

Camillo cannot resist Polixenes' pleadings for enlightenment. He advises the Bohemian King to flee at once. Since Camillo is now a traitor, saving the man he was ordered to kill, he must fly also. Together, they leave Sicily.

A sad tale's best . . .

Meanwhile, at the court, Mamilius, Leontes' little son, is having a pleasant time with the ladies in waiting. His mother, Hermione, it now turns out, is rather late in pregnancy. (Polixenes, remember, had been at the Sicilian court for nine months.)

The Queen asks her son for a story, and Mamilius says:

> *A sad tale's best for winter; I have one*
> *Of sprites and goblins.*
> —Act II, scene i, lines 25–26

There's the reference that gives the play its title. The play is a sad tale of death—but also of rebirth. For winter does not remain winter always, but is followed by the spring.

. . . sacred Delphos . . .

The childish tale is interrupted by the arrival of the King and his courtiers. Leontes has learned of Polixenes' flight with Camillo and that is the last straw. He accuses Hermione of adultery and orders her to prison.

Neither her indignant and reasonable claims to innocence nor the shocked testimony of faith in her on the part of his own courtiers will turn Leontes in the slightest. His tyranny is in full course now.

But he will go this far—he will rely on divine assurance. He says:

> *I have dispatched in post*
> *To sacred Delphos, to Apollo's temple,*
> *Cleomenes and Dion . . .*
> —Act II, scene i, lines 182–84

This more than anything else proves the play to be placed in ancient Greek times, when the oracle at Delphi (*not* Delphos) was in greatest repute.

The oracle, a very ancient one, was located on the Greek mainland about six miles north of the center of the Gulf of Corinth and seventy miles northwest of Athens. Its location was originally called Pytho and it contained a shrine to the earth goddess that was served by a priestess known as the Pythia. This priestess could serve as the medium through which the wishes and wisdom of the gods could be made known.

The oracle, along with the rest of Greece, was inundated by the Dorian invasion that followed after the Trojan War. When Greece began to climb out of the darkness in the eighth century B.C., Pytho had a new name, Delphi, and the nature of the shrine had changed. It served Apollo rather than the earth goddess.

Greek myths were devised to explain the change.

Those myths told that when the Titaness Latona (Leto) was about to give birth to children by Jupiter, the jealous Juno made her life miserable in a variety of ways. She sent a dragon or giant snake, named Python, to pursue her, for instance. Eventually Latona bore twin children, Apollo and Diana. Apollo made his way back to Pytho, where the Python made its home, and killed it. Apollo then took over the shrine itself and gave it its new name (though the priestess remained the Pythia).

For centuries Delphi remained the most important and sacred of all the Greek oracles. It was beautified by gifts made to it by all the Greek cities and many foreign rulers. It served as a treasury in which people and cities kept their money for safekeeping, since no one would dare pollute the sacred shrine by theft.

On the other hand, there is also a place called Delos, a tiny island no larger than Manhattan's Central Park, located in the Aegean Sea about a hundred miles southeast of Athens.

It too is involved with the tale of Latona and her unborn children. Juno, who was persecuting Latona in every way possible, had forbidden any port of the earth on which the sun shone to receive her. Tiny Delos, however, was a floating island which Jupiter covered with waves so that the sun did not shine on it. There Apollo and Diana were born. Thereafter, Delos was fixed to the sea floor and never moved again.

As a result, Delos was as sacred to Apollo as Delphi was, and it was easy to confuse the two. Thus, one could imagine the oracle at Delphi to be located on the island of Delos, and speak of the combination as the "island of Delphos." Greene does this in *Pandosto* and Shakespeare carelessly follows him.

. . . Dame Partlet . . .

In prison, Hermione is delivered of her child and it turns out to be a beautiful little girl. Paulina, the wife of the courtier Antigonus, is a bold woman with a sharp tongue. Passionately loyal to Hermione and uncaring for the consequences, she offers to take the child to Leontes in the hope that the sight of the babyish innocence might soften him.

With the child, Paulina forces her way into Leontes' presence. He won't look at the child and cries out impatiently to Antigonus:

> *Give her the bastard,*
> *Thou dotard, thou art woman-tired, unroosted*
> *By thy Dame Partlet here.*
> —Act II, scene iii, lines 72–74

This refers to an extremely popular medieval cycle of animal stories, in which human failings are placed in animal guise, a device that dates back to Aesop in the Western tradition. The cycle is known as a whole as "Reynard the Fox," for the fox is the rascal hero (much like Br'er Rabbit in the Uncle Remus stories).

The tales reached their final form about 1100 and grew so popular that some of the names of the animals entered the common language. Even more familiar than "Reynard" for fox is "Bruin" for bear, for instance.

"Dame Partlet" is the hen and Leontes is saying in angry, insulting tones that Paulina is an old biddy who has henpecked her foolish husband into giving up the roost; that is, the dominating position in the house.

Antigonus can scarcely deny it at that. When Leontes tells him he should be hanged for not quieting his wife, Antigonus says, resignedly:

> *Hang all the husbands*
> *That cannot do that feat, you'll leave yourself*
> *Hardly one subject.*
> —Act II, scene iii, lines 108–10

". . . of high treason . . ."

Leontes' madness continues in full course. He orders Antigonus to carry off the baby girl to some desert spot and leave it there to die.

The King then gets news that Cleomenes and Dion, the ambassadors to the Delphos, are returning, and he hastens to prepare a formal trial for the Queen. She is brought out of prison to face her indictment. The officer of the court reads it out:

> *"Hermione, Queen to the worthy Leontes, King of Sicilia,*
> *thou art here accused and arraigned of high treason, in com-*
> *mitting adultery with Polixenes, King of Bohemia, and con-*
> *spiring with Camillo to take away the life of our sovereign*
> *lord the King, thy royal husband . . .*
>
> —Act III, scene ii, lines 12–17

There must have seemed a strange familiarity in this scene to Englishmen, for scarcely three quarters of a century before, not one but two English queens had stood accused of a very similar charge. These were two of the six wives of Henry VIII (who had died in 1547, seventeen years before Shakespeare's birth). One was Anne Boleyn, Henry's second wife, tried for adultery in 1536, and the other was Catherine Howard, his fifth wife, tried for adultery in 1542. Both were convicted and beheaded, the former at the age of twenty-nine and the latter at the age of about twenty-two.

The Emperor of Russia . . .

Again Hermione defends herself with dignity and sincerity, carrying conviction to all but the insane Leontes. While she waits for the word of the oracle, she says:

> *The Emperor of Russia was my father.*
> *Oh that he were alive, and here beholding*
> *His daughter's trial!*
>
> —Act III, scene ii, lines 117–19

Russia was not, of course, in existence in the time when Sicily was under Greek domination. The Russian people first swam into the light of history in the ninth century when Viking adventurers from Sweden took over the rule of the land and established a loose congeries of principalities under the vague overlordship of Kiev. This "Kievan Russia" was destroyed in 1240 by the Mongol invasion.

A century before Shakespeare's birth, however, Russia was beginning to emerge from the Mongol night. In 1462 Ivan III ("the Great") became Grand Prince of Muscovy. He managed to annex the lands of Novgorod, a northern city, which controlled the sparsely settled lands up to the Arctic Ocean. This first gave Muscovy a broad realm, larger in terms of area than that of any other nation in Europe. With that, Muscovy became Russia.

In 1472 Ivan married the heir to the recently defunct Byzantine Empire and laid claim to the title of Emperor.

His successors, Basil III and Ivan IV ("the Terrible"), continued the policy of expansion. Ivan IV, who reigned from 1533 to 1584 (through Shakespeare's youth, in other words), defeated the remnant of the Mongols and extended the Russian realm to the Caspian Sea.

Not only did Ivan the Terrible's victories put Russia "on the map," but during his reign England gained personal knowledge of the land. In 1553 an English trade mission under Richard Chancellor reached Ivan's court, so that Shakespeare's reference to "The Emperor of Russia" was rather topical.

"Hermione is chaste . . ."

Cleomenes and Dion now bring in the sealed message from Delphos. It is opened and read. It states:

> *"Hermione is chaste, Polixenes blameless, Camillo a true subject, Leontes a jealous tyrant, his innocent babe truly begotten, and the King shall live without an heir, if that which is lost be not found."*
>
> —Act III, scene ii, lines 130–33

This is clear, straightforward, and dramatic—and lacks all resemblance to the kind of oracles actually handed out by the real Delphi. In fiction, oracles may interpret present and foretell future with faultless vision; in actual fact, they can do nothing of the sort.

The real oracle at Delphi was extremely practiced at giving out ambiguous statements that could be interpreted as correct no matter what the eventuality. The most famous example of this (though by no means the only one) took place in 546 B.C. when Croesus of Lydia, in western Asia Minor, was considering a preventive attack on the growing Persian kingdom to the east of the Halys River, Lydia's boundary.

Croesus consulted the oracle at Delphi, of which he was one of the most munificent patrons. He was told: "When Croesus passes over the river Halys, he will overthrow the strength of an empire."

Croesus attacked at once, and realized too late that the oracle was carefully phrased so as to remain true whether he won or lost. He lost and it was his own realm that was overthrown. It is for reasons such as this that "Delphic" and "oracular" have come to mean "evasive," "ambiguous," "double-meaning."

Apollo, pardon

And still Leontes does not give in. Like Pharaoh in the Bible, his heart hardens with each new thrust and he dismisses the statement of the oracle as falsehood.

But at this very moment a servant rushes in to say that Leontes' young son, Mamilius, ill since his mother was arrested, has died. At the news, Hermione faints and Paulina declares she is dying.

The King is stricken. The death of his son at the instant of his blasphemy against Apollo punishes that blasphemy and demonstrates the truth of the oracle ("the King shall live without an heir") simultaneously.

As suddenly as the disease of jealousy had seized upon him, it leaves him. In one moment, he is sane again, and cries out in heartbreak:

> *Apollo, pardon*
> *My great profaneness 'gainst thine oracle.*
>
> —Act III, scene ii, lines 150–51

He is anxious now to undo all he has done, but he cannot bring Mamilius back to life, he cannot unkill the Queen, he cannot find the child he has ordered exposed. He is doomed to live in endless remorse until "that which is lost" be found.

He can only bow his racked body before the harsh and indignant vituperation of Paulina.

. . . The deserts of Bohemia

But what of Antigonus and the little baby girl he had been ordered to expose?

In *Pandosto* the child is given to sailors by the Bohemian King. These take her to the sea and expose her in a boat during a storm. The boat, carrying the child, is carried to the seacoast of Sicily.

But Shakespeare has reversed the kingdoms. It is the Sicilian King, Leontes, who hands out the girl to be exposed. If the reversal is to continue, the ship must land on the seacoast of Bohemia, rather than that of Sicily, and so it does. Act III, scene iii has its scene set on "Bohemia, the seacoast."

The trouble with this is that while Sicily has a seacoast on every side, Bohemia—the real Bohemia—both in our day and in Shakespeare's is an inland realm and has no seacoast. It is, in fact, two hundred miles from the closest seacoast, at Trieste (nowadays part of Italy).

Shakespeare must have known this, of course, but what difference does it make, when Bohemia is not a real land at all, but is the Bohemia of idyll, and may have a seacoast just as well as it may have anything else?

Of course, if we want to be literal, there was a time when the real Bohemia had a seacoast. It was at the height of its power under the reign of Ottokar II ("the Great"), who ruled from 1253 to 1278. In 1269, at a time when the Holy Roman Empire was going through a period of weakness, Ottokar conquered what is now Austria and ruled over an enlarged Bohemia that stretched over much of central Europe, right down to the head of the Adriatic Sea. For four years, then (before the Holy Roman Empire regained these lost lands), and four years *only,* from 1269 to 1273, Bohemia had a seacoast in the neighborhood of modern Trieste.

The ship carrying Antigonus and the baby reaches land and Antigonus says to the sailors:

> *Thou art perfect then our ship hath touched upon*
> *The deserts of Bohemia?*
>
> —Act III, scene iii, lines 1–2

By "deserts" Antigonus merely means an unoccupied region. If we are not contented with Bohemia as an imaginary kingdom but insist on the real one, we can pretend that Bohemia has its mid-thirteenth-century boundaries and that the ship has landed near Trieste. This is not bad. It would mean that Antigonus traveled from Sicily, through the length of the Adriatic Sea, a distance of some seven hundred miles.

Antigonus has seen Hermione in a dream and she has bidden him name the little girl Perdita ("the lost one"). He puts the baby down together with identifying materials, in case she should happen to be found and brought up. But even as he makes his way back to the ship, he encounters a bear and there follows the most unusual direction in Shakespeare's plays, for it reads "Exit, pursued by a bear."

. . . things new born

As Antigonus leaves, an old Shepherd and then his son come on the scene. The son is referred to in the cast of characters as "Clown," but in its original meaning of "country bumpkin."

The Clown has seen the ship destroyed by a storm and Antigonus eaten by the bear, but the Shepherd has found Perdita and says to his son:

> *Now bless thyself; thou met'st with things dying, I with things*
> *new born.*
>
> —Act III, scene iii, lines 112–13

It is the turning point of the play. Until now, the theme of the play has been a kind of dying, as Leontes went insane and drove person after person into flight, exile, or death. But the winter's tale is over and the spring begins, for Perdita the pretty child will not die. She has been found by the Bohemian shepherds and she will live.

. . . slide o'er sixteen years . . .

There comes a huge lapse of time between Act III and Act IV. The lapse is necessary and also occurs in *Pandosto,* which has as its secondary title *The Triumph of Time.*

This is a particularly radical violation of the "unities." There were three of these, according to the prescription in Aristotle's *Poetics.* There was the unity of time, since the entire action of a play should take no more than twenty-four hours; of place, since the entire action should be in one place; and action, since every incident in the play should contribute to the plot and there should be no irrelevancies.

These classical unities were taken up by the French dramatists of the seventeenth century, when France was the cultural leader of Europe.

Shakespeare could adhere to the unities if he chose (he did so, almost entirely, in *The Comedy of Errors*) but he felt no compulsion about it. His plays veered widely from place to place and covered events that took up the course of years. His plays had plots and subplots and occasional total irrelevancies. For this, he was sneered at by the classicists, who considered his plays to be crude, formless, and barbaric, though not without a kind of primitive vigor.

We don't think so at all nowadays. The observance of the unities can go along with great power in the hand of a genius. (No one can fault Sophocles' *Oedipus Rex,* which observes them rigorously.) On the other hand, in the hand of anyone less than a genius, the unities almost force tedium on a play, as they make it necessary to report action at an earlier time and a different place entirely through reports, so that all the play consists of one character explaining to another (for the benefit of the audience) what has happened or what is happening.

Shakespeare let time and place flash across the stage and by piling scene upon scene with spatial and temporal jumps lent his plays such a whirlwind speed that an audience could not help but be enraptured with action that never stopped and never allowed them to catch their breath.

Yet even Shakespeare must have felt that at this point in *The Winter's Tale* he might be going a little too far. (He had done much the same in *Pericles,* see page I–195, which he had written a year or two earlier.) He brings in Time as a kind of chorus, opening the Fourth Act, explaining the lapse of time and apologizing for it too:

> *Impute it not a crime*
> *To me, or my swift passage, that I slide*
> *O'er sixteen years* . . .
> —Act IV, scene i, lines 4–6

. . . Florizel I now name to you . . .

Time mentions one specific involved in the passing of years—the existence of a son of Polixenes. He had been casually mentioned early in the play, but he is now named for the first time. Time says:

> *I mentioned a son o'th'King's, which Florizel*
> *I now name to you* . . .
> —Act IV, scene i, lines 22–23

We can suspect, if we have the slightest experience with romances, that Florizel will fall in love with the grown-up Perdita, so that a king's son will woo a girl who is (to all appearances) a shepherd's daughter.

This happens, of course, and "Florizel" became the epitome of the "Prince Charming," the handsome man who comes to sweep the poverty-stricken young girl out of her cottage and into the palace. Heaven only knows how many marriages have been ruined because real life could not fulfill the dreams of romance-fed girls.

To at least one actual woman there was a kind of literal fulfillment. In the early 1780s an actress named Mary Robinson was wooed by a rather dissipated young man, who called her Perdita and himself Florizel in the letters he sent her. He happened to be the Prince of Wales, the eldest son of King George III of England. He later became Prince Regent during his father's madness and King George IV in 1820 upon his father's death.

He never married Miss Robinson, of course, and he was a poor excuse for a Florizel anyway, except for his rank, as he became fatter, grosser, and more dissipated with each successive year. He was a most unlovable man and very unpopular with his subjects.

. . . named me Autolycus . . .

But we are in mythical Bohemia now, where Polixenes, grown older, is as virtuous as he ever was and still cherishes the good Camillo. Camillo longs to see Sicily again, for the repentant Leontes calls for him. Polixenes will not release him, however, and suggests instead that they find out why Prince Florizel haunts a certain shepherd's cottage.

But Bohemia contains more than virtue. Striding onstage is a peddler, singing happily. He makes his living by being a petty thief and confidence man. He says:

> *My father named me Autolycus, who being, as I am, littered under Mercury, was likewise a snapper-up of unconsidered trifles.*
>
> —Act IV, scene iii, lines 24–26

Mercury (Hermes) was the god of thieves. It was appropriate, therefore, that there be myths involving a description of the clever thefts carried through by the god.

Thus, almost immediately after he was born, Mercury killed a tortoise, made the first lyre out of it, and used that to sing a lullaby that put his mother, the nymph Maia, to sleep. Freed of her supervision he went out into the world, found a herd of fifty cattle belonging to Apollo, and stole them, placing improvised shoes on their feet to confuse the tracks and forcing them to walk backward to make them seem to have gone in the opposite direction.

The furious Apollo found them at last and saw through Mercury's defense of being an innocent babe. Mercury could only placate him by giving Apollo the lyre.

Mercury, incidentally, was the patron god not only of thieves but of merchants as well, which indicates the rather mixed opinion that the ancients had of merchants—possibly with some justice.

A son of Mercury was Autolycus, who, like his father, was a master thief. He could steal cattle undetectably and helped himself to the herds of Sisyphus. As Sisyphus watched his herds melt away, he found himself suspecting Autolycus without being able to obtain proof. He therefore made markings on the soles of his cattle's hoofs and eventually found Autolycus in possession of cattle on whose hoofs were marked "Stolen from Sisyphus."

Autolycus' daughter married Laertes of Ithaca and their son was none other than Ulysses (see page I–92), who was the epitome of all that was shrewd and clever.

The peddler Autolycus in the play glories in his name and what that signifies and has a chance to demonstrate it at once. The Clown comes along, on his way to buy things for the great sheepshearing festival that is about to take place. Autolycus promptly pretends to have been robbed and beaten by a rogue, and the kindly Clown, helping him, has his pocket picked as a reward.

. . . but Flora

Back at the shepherd's cottage, Perdita, now a beautiful girl of sixteen, is the mistress of the feast and is dressed accordingly. Prince Florizel, overcome by her beauty, says to her:

> *These your unusual weeds to each part of you*
> *Do give a life; no shepherdess, but Flora,*
> *Peering in April's front.*
>
> —Act IV, scene iv, lines 1–3

Flora was the Roman goddess of flowers and the spring. Her festival was celebrated at the end of April and the beginning of May.

. . . the green Neptune

But Perdita is very nervous. Florizel stumbled upon her father's house when pursuing an escaped falcon and has fallen in love with her. Now he is attending the feast dressed as a shepherd and calling himself Doricles. Perdita fears his father the King will find him out and be furious. But Florizel says that even the gods stooped to low appearances for love:

> *Jupiter*
> *Became a bull, and bellowed; the green Neptune*
> *A ram, and bleated; and the fire-robed god,*
> *Golden Apollo, a poor humble swain,*
> *As I seem now.*
>
> —Act IV, scene iv, lines 27–31

Jupiter (Zeus) fell in love with Europa, a princess of Phoenicia. To win her, he turned himself into a snow-white bull and joined the Tyrian herd. Europa saw the new bull and was fascinated by it. It proved so gentle, she climbed on its shoulders at last, whereupon it ambled to the sea, plunged in, and swam westward. It arrived at Crete (a tidy swim of 550 miles) and there he eventually had three sons by her.

As for Neptune (Poseidon), called "green" because he was god of the sea, he loved Theophane. To steal her away from her other suitors, he turned her into a ewe and himself into a ram. Their offspring was a golden ram which, after death, yielded the famous Golden Fleece for which Jason adventured.

Apollo (called "fire-robed" and "golden" because he was god of the sun) had once offended Jupiter by killing the Cyclops, who forged the lightning which served as Jupiter's spears. Apollo was condemned to serve a Thessalian king, Admetus, as shepherd for punishment. Admetus treated the temporarily demoted god with every consideration, and in return, Apollo, still in shepherd's disguise, helped Admetus accomplish certain difficult tasks required for the winning of the beautiful Alcestis.

. . . Dis's wagon

Perdita's fears are well based, for Polixenes and Camillo do indeed come to the sheepshearing festival to spy on Florizel/Doricles' doings. They are greeted warmly by the unsuspecting Perdita in her role as hostess, and appropriate flowers are handed out. Perdita bemoans the lack of spring flowers that she might give the young ladies and says:

> O Proserpina,
> For the flow'rs now, that, frighted, thou let'st fall
> From Dis's wagon.
> —Act IV, scene iv, lines 116–18

Dis (Hades) had abducted Proserpina while she was picking flowers in the fields of central Sicily (see page I–7). She dropped those flowers as she was carried, shrieking, into the underworld.

. . . Cytherea's breath

Perdita describes some of these flowers, saying, for instance:

> . . . violets, dim,
> But sweeter than the lids of Juno's eyes,
> Or Cytherea's breath;
> —Act IV, scene iv, lines 120–22

Cytherea is an alternate name for Venus (Aphrodite). It comes from the island of Cythera off the southeast tip of the Greek mainland. On that island, as in Paphos (see page I–15), Venus had a well-known temple. Some versions of Venus' birth state that she rose from the sea, and, of course, some place the point of the rising near Paphos and some near Cythera.

. . . a tawdry-lace . . .

The disguised Polixenes and Camillo can't help but be taken by the pretty and sweet Perdita. The shepherds and shepherdesses dance; gaiety expands; and suddenly Autolycus appears at the door as a singing peddler and ballad seller.

The Clown, who is in love with Mopsa, a shepherdess, wants to buy her something, but he has reneged on previous promises and Mopsa says to him impatiently:

> *Come, you promised me a tawdry-lace, and a pair of sweet gloves.*
>
> —Act IV, scene iv, lines 250–51

The expression "tawdry-lace" has a rather complicated background. It dates back to Anglo-Saxon England, much of which in the seventh century was still pagan. Egfrith, King of Northumbria, had a wife named Etheldreda, who listened with interest to Christian missionaries. She became a nun and established a religious community on land in her father's kingdom of East Anglia, becoming its first abbess in 673.

Etheldreda was eventually sainted and her name day, October 17, was celebrated at the site of the convent with a large fair, which drew crowds of the peasantry. With time, the Anglo-Saxon name of the saint was shortened to Audrey, so that it was the Fair of Saint Audrey that was celebrated.

At these fairs there was a brisk sale of souvenirs (as in modern fairs), and, in particular, cheap jewelry and showy lace could be bought—nothing really valuable, but strong on garish colors and elaborate frills. By further slurring the name of Saint Audrey, one came to speak of "tawdry lace," for instance, in connection with a cheap and showy specimen of that material. As a consequence, "tawdry" has now come to refer to anything of low quality that is cheap and tasteless.

. . . than Deucalion . . .

Ballads are talked of and a dance of satyrs is presented. It is all pastorally delightful, but Polixenes and Camillo, still in disguise, grow less and less happy. They encourage the disguised Florizel (who does not recognize them) to tell his love. He does so, in complete abandon, and is willing to pledge betrothal to Perdita on the spot, and before witnesses, a deed that is equivalent to marriage.

Polixenes asks Florizel if he has a father who might attend the wedding. Florizel admits he has but says flatly that his father must remain ignorant of this. At that, Polixenes, in a passion, strips off his disguise. He threatens the Shepherd with death, and Perdita with mutilation to mar her beauty. He says further that if his son ever as much as thinks of Perdita again—

> *. . . we'll bar thee from succession;*
> *Not hold thee of our blood, no not our kin,*
> *Farre* [farther] *than Deucalion off.*
>
> —Act IV, scene iv, lines 433–35

Deucalion was a legendary ruler of southern Thessaly, and might be termed the Greek Noah. Zeus had sent a great flood over the earth to wipe out the human race, but Deucalion (warned by his father, the Titan Prometheus) built an ark in which he and his wife, Pyrrha, rode out the flood, coming to rest on Mount Parnassus after it was over.

They then prayed that mankind might be renewed and were told by a divine voice to turn their heads away and throw the bones of their mother behind them. The two reasoned that Mother Earth was meant. Turning their heads away they threw stones over their shoulder. The stones Deucalion threw became men and those Pyrrha threw women.

In this way the race of men and women could trace their descent to Deucalion and Pyrrha, and all men were related to at least the extent of being common descendants of Deucalion—except that Polixenes was going to deny Florizel even that much if he disobeyed.

. . . make for Sicilia

Polixenes leaves, but Florizel is not disturbed. He intends to marry Perdita even if it means losing his kingdom. Camillo, much impressed by Perdita and longing to see his own country, now plans to do for Florizel what sixteen years before he had done for Florizel's father—help him escape and go with him. Florizel has prepared a ship for the escape and Camillo says, earnestly:

> *. . . make for Sicilia,*
> *And there present yourself and your fair princess*
> *(For so I see she must be) 'fore Leontes.*
>
> —Act IV, scene iv, lines 547–49

To get Florizel as far as the ship, Camillo disguises him in different fashion by making him change clothes with Autolycus, who now comes on the scene glorying in the success of his ballad selling and pocket picking.

The Shepherd and his son, the Clown, having been threatened with death by the King, are meanwhile in a state of abject terror. The Clown urges his father to reveal the fact that Perdita is not really a relative by showing the relics that had been found with her. In this way, the Shepherd and the Clown, proving not to be related to the real criminal in this matter of the enchantment of the prince, might escape punishment.

Autolycus overhears this and (in Florizel's clothes) pretends he is a courtier and easily cons the poor bumpkins into coming with him. He decides to bring them to Florizel on a gamble that this may bring him advancement.

Great Alexander . . .

For the last act the scene shifts back to Sicily, where Leontes' life is one long, wretched repentance. His courtiers are urging him to marry again, for the land is without an heir and the perils of civil war loom.

Paulina, however, the wife of old Antigonus, who had been eaten by a bear, is against it. The oracle from "Delphos" had predicted that the King would remain without an heir till "that which is lost" be found. Paulina considers this to mean the long-ago-exposed girl. She says to Leontes:

> Care not for issue,
> The crown will find an heir. Great Alexander
> Left his to th'worthiest: so his successor
> Was like to be the best.
>
> —Act V, scene i, lines 46–49

Actually, this was a poor analogy. When Alexander the Great died suddenly in 323 B.C. (about two generations *after* the time of Dionysius of Syracuse, at which time I have arbitrarily placed the action of this play) at the age of thirty-three, he left behind a termagant mother, a foreign wife, a mentally retarded half brother, a half sister, and an unborn child. Not one could serve as a successor and the natural choice would therefore have rested among the very capable generals who had been trained by Alexander and his father, Philip.

Alexander might have chosen any one of the generals and his dying vote might have fixed that general in the throne and brought about the consolidation of the new and gigantic Macedonian Empire, changing the history of the world. Unfortunately, Alexander (for whatever reason) is supposed to have said, with his last breath, "To the strongest" when asked to whom he left his Empire.

If there had been a strongest, that would have been well, but there wasn't. No one general was strong enough to defeat and dominate all the rest. The result was that for thirty years a civil war raged among the generals. At the end, Alexander's Empire was worn out and fragmented. The fragments continued to war against each other with the result that within three centuries of Alexander's death, the eastern half of his Empire was retaken by native tribes and the western half was taken by Rome.

Surely this is not the fate for Sicily that Paulina was urging on Leontes.

In fact, she has other plans. She urges Leontes to vow never to marry
anyone not chosen by herself. Leontes, who can never punish himself
sufficiently, agrees.

. . . from Libya

Florizel is now introduced, arriving in Sicily with Perdita. Leontes greets
the young man tearfully and inquires, with wonder, of the beautiful Perdita. Florizel, attempting to mask the truth as deeply as possible, says:

> *Good my lord,*
> *She came from Libya.*
>
> —Act V, scene i, lines 156–57

Libya was the name given by the ancient Greeks to the entire north
African coast west of Egypt. The two chief cities of Libya in the time of
Dionysius of Syracuse were Cyrene, a Greek city five hundred miles to the
southeast of Sicily, and Carthage, a non-Greek city, a hundred miles to the
southwest.

. . . Julio Romano . . .

Events hasten now. Even while Florizel is embroidering his lie by mak-
ing Perdita the daughter of a Libyan king, news arrives that Polixenes and
Camillo are in Sicily. Polixenes sends a message demanding the arrest of
Florizel.

However, the audience need not be alarmed. It is at once revealed
that the Shepherd and the Clown are also in Sicily and they can reveal the
truth of Perdita's identity.

What happens next is offstage. We would think that there should be a
grand reconciliation scene as Perdita is shown to be Leontes' daughter,
and there is, but not onstage. We learn of it only through a discussion
among three Gentlemen.

This is odd and we might speculate that in the original form of the play
the recognition and restoration of Perdita was the climax. Perhaps this ending turned out to be weak—after all, a very similar climax had been used
only a year or two before by Shakespeare in *Pericles* (see page I-199).
Pressure might have been applied to Shakespeare to make some alteration
in that ending.

As a result, Shakespeare thrust Perdita's recognition offstage and prepared an even more dramatic scene involving Queen Hermione.

Paulina had reported her dead in Act III, and there has been no hint since that the report was wrong. Indeed, at the end of Act III, when Antigonus is taking the little baby girl off to exposure, he dreams that Hermione's ghost appears to him, and this would make it seem that Shakespeare really did consider her dead.

Shakespeare, in his revision (assuming there was one), did not trouble to go back and put in some indication of Hermione's remaining alive, nor does he expunge the reference to the ghost, which is useful in explaining the name "Perdita."

Instead, he begins at this late date in the fifth act to start preparing the audience. The Third Gentleman mentions, for the first time, a statue:

> . . . the Princess, hearing of her mother's statue, which is in the keeping of Paulina—a piece many years in doing and now newly performed by that rare Italian master, Julio Romano . . .
>
> —Act V, scene ii, lines 101–5

Julio Romano was a real Italian artist, known for his painting rather than for his sculpture, who had died in 1546, a little over half a century before *The Winter's Tale* was written. This is a startling anachronism, of course.

The Second Gentleman adds another vital item in the new build-up. Concerning Paulina, he says:

> she hath privately, twice or thrice a day, ever since the death of Hermione, visited that removed house.
>
> —Act V, scene ii, lines 113–15

Of course, the statue turns out to be the living Hermione after all. Why she has been kept from the so repentant King for sixteen years and been condemned to a life of solitary imprisonment; why Paulina has undertaken the backbreaking task of feeding and caring for her and keeping the secret; why the King has not had curiosity to see the progress of the statue during all the "many years" in which it was being made—these points are not explained. All this lack of explanation lends substance to the theory that the last half of the fifth act is a new ending, patched on imperfectly.

There is the final reconciliation scene and all ends in happiness. Paulina (who has now learned of her husband's death) marries Camillo, and even the Shepherd and the Clown now find themselves enriched, so that Autolycus, swearing to reform, is taken under their protection.

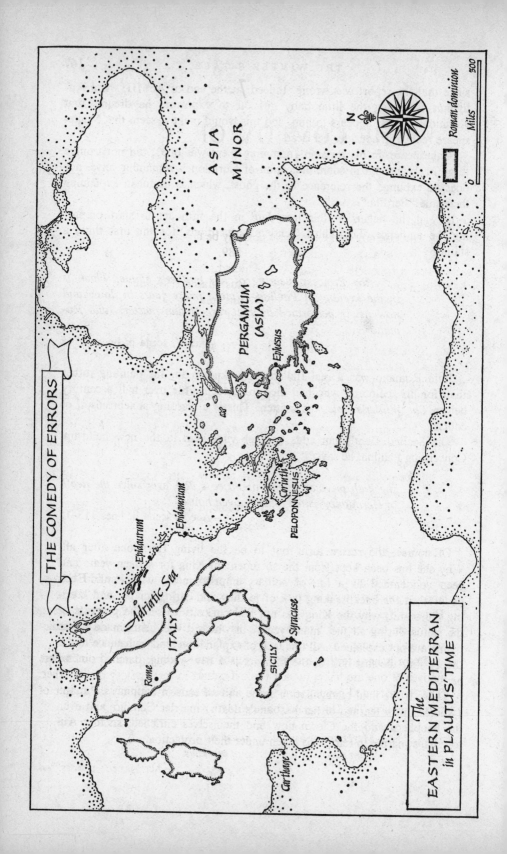

THE COMEDY OF ERRORS

The
EASTERN MEDITERRAN
in PLAUTUS' TIME

ASIA MINOR

PERGAMUM (ASIA)

Ephesus

Epidaurum

Epidamnum

Adriatic Sea

ITALY

Rome

SICILY

Syracuse

Carthage

Corinth

PELOPONNESUS

N

Roman dominion

0   300
        Miles

7

THE COMEDY OF ERRORS

THE COMEDY OF ERRORS may possibly be the very first play Shakespeare wrote, perhaps even as early as 1589.

It is a complete farce, and it is adapted from a play named *Menaechmi*, written by the Roman playwright Titus Maccius Plautus about 220 B.C. If we assume that the events in Plautus' play reflect the time in which it was written (although Plautus borrowed the plot from a still earlier Greek play) we can place the time a century and a half after that of Dionysius of Syracuse. It is for that reason I place this play immediately after *The Winter's Tale*.

Plautus' play *Menaechmi* tells of the comic misadventures of twin brothers separated at birth. One searches for the other and when he reaches the town in which the second dwells, finds himself greeted by strangers who seem to know him. There are constant mistakes and cross-purposes, to the confusion of everyone on the stage and to the delight of everyone in the audience.

Shakespeare makes the confusion all the more intense by giving the twin brothers each a servant, with the servants twins as well. The developments are all accident, all implausible, and—if well done—all funny.

Merchant of Syracusa . . .

The play begins seriously enough in Ephesus. Solinus, Duke of Ephesus, appears onstage, with Egeon, a merchant of Syracuse. The title "Duke of Ephesus" is as anachronistic as "Duke of Athens" (see page I-18) and with even less excuse, since there never was a Duchy of Ephesus in medieval times as there was, at least, a Duchy of Athens.

There is hard feeling between Ephesus and Syracuse, to the point where natives of one are liable to execution if caught in the territory of the other. The Syracusan, Egeon, caught in Ephesian territory, stands in danger of this cruel law. The Duke says, obdurately:

> Merchant of Syracusa, plead no more;
> I am not partial to infringe our laws.
>
> —Act I, scene i, lines 3–4

In the time of Plautus, the Greek city-states were as logically the scene of romantic comedy as were the Italian city-states in Shakespeare's own time. In both cases, the city-states were in decline but lingered in a golden afterglow.

Syracuse was no longer as great as it had been under Dionysius. It lived rather in the shadow of the growing Roman power, with which it had allied itself in 270 B.C.

In the course of the Second Punic War, fought in Plautus' middle age, Rome looked, for a while, as though it were going to lose, when the Carthaginian general Hannibal inflicted three spectacular defeats upon it between 218 and 216 B.C. Syracuse hastily switched to the Carthaginian side in order to be with the winner, but this proved to be a poor move.

Rome retained sufficient strength to lay siege to Syracuse and, after more than two years of warfare, took and sacked it in 212 B.C. Syracuse lost its independence forever. Plautus may have written *Menaechmi* in the last decade of Syracusan independence, but even if he wrote after its fall, it is not hard to imagine him as seeing it still as the important city-state it had been for the past five centuries.

For the other city, Plautus did not use Ephesus (as Shakespeare does) but he could have. Ephesus is a city on the Aegean coast of Asia Minor. Asia Minor fell under the control of various Macedonian generals after the death of Alexander the Great in 323 B.C., but individual cities flourished and retained considerable powers of local self-government. Indeed, Ephesus, in Plautus' lifetime, was geographically part of the kingdom of Pergamum, which made up the western third of the peninsula of Asia Minor. The city was at the very peak of its wealth and its commercial prosperity.

Of course, neither was in a position to carry on petty feuds with each other, and there is no historical basis for the opening situation in the play—but that is just to get the story moving.

To Epidamnum . . .

Duke Solinus points out that the penalty for being caught in Ephesian territory is a thousand marks. In default of payment of the fine, Egeon must be executed.

Egeon seems to think death will be a relief and the curious Duke asks why. Egeon sighs and begins his tale. In Syracuse, he had married a woman he loved:

> *With her I lived in joy, our wealth increased*
> *By prosperous voyages I often made*
> *To Epidamnum . . .*
>
> —Act I, scene i, lines 38–41

Epidamnum (or Epidamnus) was a Greek city-state on what is now the coast of Albania; on the site, indeed, of Durrës, Albania's chief port.

Epidamnum is, actually, the other city used by Plautus, in place of Shakespeare's Ephesus, and in a way it is more suitable. Epidamnum is three hundred miles northeast of Syracuse; Ephesus twice as far; and one might suppose that the nearer neighbors two cities are, the more likely they are to quarrel.

Epidamnum became Roman in 229 B.C., so that Plautus was writing the play not long after the end of the city's independence.

Why did Shakespeare switch from Epidamnum to Ephesus? Perhaps because Ephesus was far more familiar to Christians. Two centuries after Plautus' death it became one of the centers of the very early Christian church. One of the letters in the New Testament attributed to St. Paul is the Epistle to the Ephesians.

Of Corinth . . .

At one point, though, Egeon had had to make a long stay at Epidamnum, and after six months his wife followed him there, although she was nearly at the point of giving birth. In Epidamnum she was delivered of twin sons in an inn where a lowborn woman was also being delivered of twin sons. Egeon bought the lowborn twins as slaves for his own sons.

They then made ready to return home, but were caught in a bad storm not far off Epidamnum. When the ship was deserted by its crew, Egeon's wife tied one child and one servant child to a small mast and Egeon tied the other child and the other servant child to another mast. For security, they tied themselves to masts as well and waited for the ship to be driven to land.

What's more, rescue seemed close:

> The seas waxed calm, and we discoverèd
> Two ships from far, making amain to us;
> Of Corinth that, of Epidaurus this.
>
> —Act I, scene i, lines 91–93

Corinth was located on the narrow isthmus that connected the Peloponnesus to the rest of Greece. This favored position gave it a footing that placed it on the sea, looking east toward Asia Minor and also looking west toward Italy. Throughout Greece's history it remained one of its most important cities and one of its most prosperous parts. In Plautus' lifetime it was the wealthiest city in Greece. That prosperity was destroyed for a century when Roman forces, for inadequate reasons, sacked it in 146 B.C., a generation after Plautus' death.

Epidaurus was a Greek city-state on the eastern shores of the Peloponnesus, only twenty-five miles from Corinth. It would spoil the effect of the story to have two ships come from such closely spaced cities.

Fortunately, there is another Epidaurus (or, in this case, Epidaurum), which is located on the eastern shore of the Adriatic Sea, some 130 miles up the coast from Epidamnum. That gives us our picture. The wrecked ship, not far from Epidamnum, is being approached by a ship from Epidaurus, sailing from the north, and by another ship from Corinth, sailing from the south.

Before the rescuers can reach the ship on which Egeon and his family are adrift, that ship hits a rock and is split in two. Egeon, with one son and servant child, is picked up by the ship from Epidaurus; his wife, with the other son and servant child, is picked up by the ship from Corinth. The two ships separate and the family is permanently split in two.

. . . farthest Greece

Egeon and his half of the family return to Syracuse, but the other half of the family has proceeded to some destination unknown to him and he never hears of them again.

Egeon's son and his servant, once grown, want to try to find their twins. They leave on the search, and after they are gone for a period of time, Egeon sets out in his turn to find them:

> *Five summers have I spent in farthest Greece,*
> *Roaming clean through the bounds of Asia,*
> *And coasting homeward, came to Ephesus,*
> —Act I, scene i, lines 132–34

"Greece" had a broader meaning in ancient times than it has today, and "Asia" a narrower one. Greece (or "Hellas" as the Greeks, or Hellenes, themselves called it) was the collection of the thousand cities of Greek-speaking people, whether those cities were located on the Greek peninsula proper or elsewhere. From Massilia (the modern Marseilles) on the west, to Seleucia on the Tigris River on the east, all is "Greece." Egeon had thus been searching not just Greece proper but wherever the Greek tongue was spoken.

As for Asia, this term was applied in Roman times (and in the New Testament, for instance) not to the entire Asian continent in the modern sense, but to the western half of Asia Minor only, the territory of the kingdom of Pergamum actually. Egeon, scouring Asia Minor, would naturally return to Syracuse by way of Ephesus, the largest city of the region.

The Duke is affected by the sad story, but insists that it is either a thousand marks or death.

. . . stay there, Dromio . . .

Egeon and his listeners get off the stage and now the coincidences begin, for his son and servant, the very ones for whom he is searching, have just landed in Ephesus; while his wife and other son and servant, for whom the first son and servant are searching, have been in Ephesus all the time. The entire family is in the same city and no one guesses it till the very end of the play, although that is the obvious and only way of explaining the extraordinary things that are to happen.

Indeed, everyone is extraordinarily obtuse, for the merchant who has brought the Syracusan son to Ephesus warns him:

> *Therefore, give out you are of Epidamnum,*
> *Lest that your goods too soon be confiscate.*
> *This very day a Syracusian merchant*
> *Is apprehended for arrival here,*
>
> —Act I, scene ii, lines 1–4

Does the son ask who this Syracusian (a countryman, after all) might be? No, for if he does, the plot is ruined. The events can only follow if no character in the play ever sees the plainest point, and the audience must co-operate and accept the obtuseness for the sake of its own pleasure.

The son has a supply of money with him which he orders his servant to deposit for safekeeping at the inn where they are to stay:

> *Go bear it to the Centaur, where we host,*
> *And stay there, Dromio, till I come to thee;*
>
> —Act I, scene ii, lines 9–10

It is stated by Egeon, but not explained, that both servants bore the same name. This is necessary since even if the twins' faces were alike, the confusion could only be complete if their names were alike too. This identity in names passes the bounds of the credible, yet it must be accepted or else all must be given up.

The servants are both named Dromio, which comes from a Greek word meaning "racecourse." It is appropriate, for all through the play each servant is sent racing, now on this errand, now on that, usually coming to grief, for they are forever meeting not their master but their master's twin, without realizing it.

As for the masters, they are both named Antipholus, from Greek words meaning "opposed in balance." They are so alike, in other words, that if each were placed on the opposite end of a balance, the balance would remain unmoved.

In order to identify them in the play, the masters have to be called "Antipholus of Syracuse" and "Antipholus of Ephesus." The servants are "Dromio of Syracuse" and "Dromio of Ephesus."

It is Antipholus of Syracuse who sends Dromio of Syracuse to the Centaur.

. . . as I am a Christian . . .

Dromio of Syracuse runs off and Antipholus of Syracuse explains to the merchant that he is in search of his mother and twin brother. Suddenly Dromio of Ephesus races on the scene. His master, Antipholus of Ephesus, is a married man and dinner at home is waiting for him. Dromio of Ephesus sees Antipholus of Syracuse and begs him to come home.

Antipholus of Syracuse naturally wants to know what home and what dinner Dromio is talking about and why he hasn't stayed at the Centaur and what happened to the money. Just as naturally, Dromio of Ephesus wants to know what money.

Now here is Antipholus of Syracuse madly searching for a twin brother with a twin-brother servant, and here comes what seems to be his servant who obviously is talking about an utterly inappropriate set of events. Ought not Antipholus of Syracuse instantly suspect it as his servant's twin brother mistaking him for his own twin brother?

Not at all. The thought never occurs to Antipholus of Syracuse (or to Dromio of Syracuse) for an instant, even though these cross-purposes multiply. (Antipholus of Ephesus and Dromio of Ephesus are more to be excused. They are not consciously looking for their twins and so they are mentally unprepared to consider the twins' existence as explanation for the errors.)

As the cross-purposes continue (and they require each set of twins to wear identical costumes, if any further multiplication of implausibility is required), Antipholus of Syracuse cries out:

> Now, as I am a Christian, answer me,
> In what safe place you have bestowed my money;
> Or I shall break that merry sconce of yours
> > —Act I, scene ii, lines 77–79

Here, certainly, we depart from Plautus, in whose lifetime Christianity had not yet arisen. —And since Dromio of Ephesus can give no satisfaction, he is beaten.

. . . war against her heir

The cross-purposes continue and grow worse. Antipholus of Syracuse hastens to the Centaur, finds his money safe there, and calculates it was impossible to have seen Dromio when he had seen him. (Does he suspect? Not on your life!)

In comes Dromio of Syracuse and Antipholus of Syracuse asks him if he has recovered his senses. Dromio of Syracuse naturally doesn't know what he is talking about and denies that he ever denied he had the gold. So he is beaten too. (The Dromios are constantly being beaten for no fault of their own.)

In comes Adriana, the wife of Antipholus of Ephesus, and the wife's sister, Luciana. They accost Antipholus of Syracuse and demand he come home to dinner with them. Antipholus of Syracuse is flabbergasted and suspects witchcraft (he suspects anything and everything but the obvious fact that his twin brother is involved), yet eventually accompanies the two women.

Now, at last, Antipholus of Ephesus appears on the scene, ordering a necklace from a Merchant for his wife. He is further complaining that Dromio of Ephesus (who is with him) is telling some ridiculous story about himself denying that he is married.

Antipholus of Ephesus invites the Merchant home for dinner and when they reach his house they find the doors barred. Voices within insist that Antipholus of Ephesus is an imposter, for the master of the house is within and at dinner. Dromio of Ephesus and Dromio of Syracuse even engage in conversation (with a closed door between) and suspect nothing.

Antipholus of Ephesus, in high rage, thinking his wife is entertaining some lover, decides to take the necklace and give it to a courtesan rather than to his wife.

Indoors, meanwhile, Antipholus of Syracuse is attracted to Luciana, the wife's sister, and she, embarrassed, urges him to be sweet and kind to his wife instead. When she leaves, Dromio of Syracuse enters and tells his master that a fat cook claims him as her husband.

The two of them, Antipholus of Syracuse and Dromio of Syracuse, begin a satirical (and to our modern ears, cruel) catalogue of the charms of the lady.

Dromio of Syracuse says she is as spherical as a globe and that countries could be located on her. Antipholus of Syracuse begins to test this, in Shakespeare-contemporary manner, all thought of the supposedly Greek background forgotten. Thus he inquires about Ireland and America, though neither was known in Plautus' time.

The answer to one of the questions offers a possible way of dating the play. Antipholus of Syracuse asks about the location of France on the cook's body and Dromio replies:

> *In her forehead, armed and reverted, making war against her*
> *heir.*
>
> —Act III, scene ii, lines 126–27

The reference must be to Henry IV, who in 1589 had become King of France on the death of his second cousin, Henry III. However, Henry IV was a Protestant and Catholic France (in particular, Catholic Paris) would not accept him. For several years France made "war against her heir."

Henry IV won an important victory at Ivry in 1590 and then in 1593 abjured Protestantism and accepted Catholicism. Between his victory and his repentance, enough of the Catholic opposition was won over to end the war. Since Dromio of Syracuse makes it sound as though the revolt is continuing, one can suppose that *The Comedy of Errors* was written no later than 1593 and no earlier than 1589.

. . . the mermaid's song

Antipholus of Syracuse continues to suppose that witchcraft is at work and decides to get out of Ephesus on the first ship. He sends Dromio of Syracuse to locate such a ship.

Antipholus dislikes the woman who claims to be his wife and feels a strong attraction to her sister, which, he suspects, is a specific result of enchantment. He feels he must not give in to all this:

> *But, lest myself be guilty to self-wrong,*
> *I'll stop mine ears against the mermaid's song.*
>
> —Act III, scene ii, lines 168–69

Here is another example of a reference to the dangerous singing of the mermaids or sirens (see page I–12).

. . . in Tartar limbo . . .

The cross-purposes continue. The Merchant from whom Antipholus of Ephesus has ordered a chain meets Antipholus of Syracuse and forces it on him, refusing to take money at the moment, saying he will take it at suppertime. Antipholus of Syracuse plans to be gone from the city by suppertime but the Merchant will not listen.

However, the Merchant unexpectedly encounters a creditor of his own and decides to get the money sooner. This time it is Antipholus of Ephesus he meets, coming from the courtesan's place with Dromio of Ephesus.

This Antipholus sends his servant to buy a rope, with which he intends to chastise his wife and servants for locking him out of the house.

The Merchant asks for his money and Antipholus of Ephesus denies receiving the chain. The Merchant is so enraged at this denial that he calls in the police and demands that Antipholus of Ephesus be arrested.

It is at this point that Dromio of Syracuse arrives with the news that he has located a ship leaving Ephesus. Antipholus of Ephesus knows nothing about a ship and Dromio of Syracuse knows nothing about a rope. Antipholus of Ephesus has no time, however, to worry about this particular cross-purpose. He needs bail and he sends Dromio of Syracuse to his wife's place to get the money.

In delivering the message, Dromio of Syracuse explains to Adriana that his master is in trouble:

> . . . he's in Tartar limbo, worse than hell:
> —Act IV, scene ii, line 32

The Greek notion of the afterlife in Hades was a rather gray one. It was a place of shadows where the shades of men and women remained in weakness and forgetfulness; where they suffered no torture but experienced no joy.

Beneath this colorless Hades was Tartarus (see page I-13), which helped inspire later Christian theologians with their notion of hell. In place of the mild Hades itself, Christians imagined a region called limbo at the border of hell. This receives its name from the Latin word for "border" and, like Hades, is a gray place of no punishment and no hope.

We might say, then, that in the Christian sense, hell is worse than limbo, while in the Greek sense, Tartarus is worse than Hades. To say, as Dromio does, that "Tartar limbo" is "worse than hell" is a queer mixture of terms that probably tickled an audience more aware of these theological and classical distinctions than moderns are.

. . . Lapland sorcerers . . .

Antipholus of Syracuse, still waiting for news of a ship, still impatient to be gone, marvels at how everyone seems to know him and think highly of him.

> Sure, these are but imaginary wiles,
> And Lapland sorcerers inhabit here.
> —Act IV, scene iii, lines 10–11

Lapland is an ill-defined area making up the Arctic regions of Scan-

dinavia and northwestern Russia, inhabited by Lapps, who are the Old
World equivalent of the New World Eskimos. They might easily be con-
fused, in Shakespeare's time, with the Finns of Finland, for Lapps and
Finns are similar in race and language.

The comment of Antipholus of Syracuse would seem to refer to Finland
rather than Lapland, for Finnish mythology is unusual in the emphasis it
places on song and magic. Their heroes are magicians rather than strong
men, Merlin rather than Hercules. The most famous Finnish literary
work is their national epic, the *Kalevala,* which is pre-Christian in inspiration and the hero of which is the singing magician Wainamoinen.

Satan, avoid . . .

The apparent enchantments continue. Dromio of Syracuse comes panting in with the money given him by Adriana to bail Antipholus of Ephesus.
Dromio of Syracuse hands it to Antipholus of Syracuse, who naturally
doesn't know what it is. He asks about the ship instead and Dromio of
Syracuse insists he has already given him that news.

In comes the courtesan to whom Antipholus of Ephesus has promised
the chain. She sees it around the neck of Antipholus of Syracuse and asks
for it. Antipholus answers violently:

> *Satan, avoid! I charge thee, tempt me not!*
> —Act IV, scene iii, line 49

The harassed Antipholus of Syracuse, already convinced he is the victim
of witchcraft, is sure that the light wench is the devil himself come to tempt
him to sin. The exclamation is a form of Jesus' reproof to Satan on the occasion of the temptation in the wilderness. Jesus is then quoted as saying
"Get thee hence, Satan" (Matthew 4:10).

(When Shakespeare quotes the Bible, he cannot very well quote the
exact wording of the King James version with which we ourselves are so
familiar. That version was not published till 1611, some twenty years
after *The Comedy of Errors* was written and nearly at the close of Shakespeare's writing career.)

The courtesan naturally decides he is mad and goes off to warn his
wife.

. . . the kitchen vestal . . .

Meanwhile, Antipholus of Ephesus is still waiting for the bail which
Dromio of Syracuse delivered to Antipholus of Syracuse. In comes Dromio

of Ephesus with the rope that *he* had been sent for just before Antipholus of Ephesus had been arrested. Naturally he gets beaten.

Adriana and Luciana arrive now with the courtesan. With them they bring a schoolmaster, Mr. Pinch, whom they hope is wise enough to cure Antipholus of Ephesus of his madness. Antipholus of Ephesus, to whom it seems the rest of the world is mad, is driven to distraction by this.

He insists that, despite his wife's protestations, he had been barred from his own house at dinner. He calls on Dromio of Ephesus to confirm this and for once master and man are on the same side. When Antipholus of Ephesus points out that the very kitchenmaid railed at him, Dromio of Ephesus says:

> *Certes, she did; the kitchen vestal scorned you.*
> —Act IV, scene iv, line 76

The vestals were the Vestal Virgins (see page I–33) but this can scarcely be taken to mean that the kitchenmaid was a virgin. In Shakespeare's time, this was scarcely likely if she was over twelve. Apparently it is only a comically high-flown way of saying that she was in charge of the fire, as the vestals were in charge of the sacred fire.

. . . Circe's cup

But there is further trouble. Antipholus of Ephesus still wants to know where the bail money is and Luciana says she sent it. Dromio of Ephesus denies that he received it or that he was even sent for it, and Antipholus of Ephesus, in his rage, begins to act mad indeed. He and Dromio of Ephesus are seized and dragged away.

In come Antipholus of Syracuse and Dromio of Syracuse on their way to the waterfront. The Merchant, who has just had Antipholus of Ephesus arrested, sees him apparently at liberty, with the chain for which he was arrested openly around his neck. There is a fight and Antipholus of Syracuse and Dromio of Syracuse escape into a nearby abbey. The Abbess emerges and refuses to let anyone else enter.

But the day is coming to a close. (This play and *The Tempest* are the only two plays in which Shakespeare kept the action within the bounds of a single day in accordance with the Greek "unities"—see page I–158.) Egeon is being led to his death, since he has not been able to raise the thousand marks he has been fined. Adriana seizes the opportunity to accost the Duke of Ephesus and beg him to persuade the Abbess to release her poor, mad husband.

But Antipholus of Ephesus and Dromio of Ephesus have escaped from their own jailers and have come furiously on the scene. Antipholus of

Ephesus demands justice against his wife, who, he claims, is conspiring to imprison him after having barred him from his own house.

The Duke, listening to the babble of confusing testimony from all sides, says:

> *Why, what an intricate impeach is this!*
> *I think you all have drunk of Circe's cup.*
>
> —Act V, scene i, lines 270–71

Circe is the name of a sorceress who appears in the *Odyssey*. She lived on a Mediterranean island and had visitors drink wine from her cup. The drink would turn them into animals, who were then enslaved by her.

Ulysses' men, in the course of their return from fallen Troy, come to Circe's island, drink from her cup, and are changed into swine. Ulysses himself, with the help of an antidote supplied him by Mercury, overcomes her.

The Duke, by this reference to Circe's cup, implies that all about him have lost their ability to reason but are as confused as senseless beasts.

Egeon interrupts to say the man seeking redress is his son Antipholus. But it is Antipholus of Ephesus he indicates and that Antipholus at once denies any knowledge of Egeon. The Duke backs him up, saying he has known Antipholus of Ephesus all his life and that Antipholus has never been in Syracuse. (The Duke is as dull as the rest; he doesn't catch on either.)

It is only when the Abbess emerges with Antipholus of Syracuse and Dromio of Syracuse, and the two Antipholuses and Dromios face each other, that all is clear at last. The Abbess turns out, of course, to be Egeon's wife.

All the conflicting events of the day are sorted out; Egeon is liberated; and the play ends in utter happiness. It is even clear that Antipholus of Syracuse will marry Luciana so that the two brothers will also be brothers-in-law.

8

PERICLES,

Prince of Tyre

T HE DATE of this play is usually given as 1608, and the last three acts are characteristically late Shakespearean in style. The first two acts are, however, considered much inferior, and many critics feel that, except for a touch here and there, they were not written by Shakespeare.

Whether that is so or not, the play, as it stands, is included in the collections of Shakespeare's plays and, for better or worse, will forever bear his name.

. . . ancient Gower . . .

The play begins with an introduction. An old man comes on stage and says:

> *To sing a song that old was sung,*
> *From ashes ancient Gower is come,*
>
> —Act I, Introduction, lines 1–2

John Gower was a fourteenth-century English poet (c. 1330–1408) and a friend and contemporary of Chaucer's (see page I-54). Gower was considered by his contemporaries, though not by moderns, to have been almost Chaucer's equal, and though it might be thought they would have borne each other the ill will of competitors, they did not. They dedicated books to each other.

One of Gower's principal works is *Confessio Amantis* (*Confession of a Lover*), first published in 1383. In this work, a number of romances are told in English couplets. The tales are by no means original with Gower. What he does is retell stories from ancient and medieval sources, choosing the most popular ones.

In the eighth book of *Confessio Amantis* Gower tells a tale, taken from a Greek source, of which a version is presented in this play. A prose version of the same story, "The Pattern of Painful Adventures," was published in 1576 by Laurence Twine. Some scenes in *Pericles* are drawn from Twine, but Gower is the major influence.

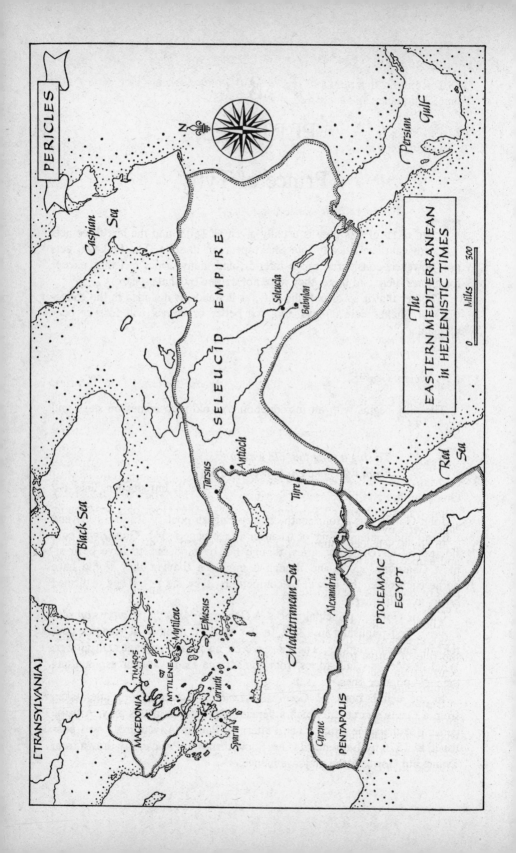

It is only in this play and in *The Two Noble Kinsmen* (see page I-54) that Shakespeare so openly announces his source.

. . . Antiochus the great

Gower lays the scene of the play:

> *This Antioch, then; Antiochus the great*
> *Built up this city for his chiefest seat,*
> *The fairest in all Syria—*
>
> —Act I, Introduction, lines 17–19

This alone tells us that the time in which the tale is supposed to take place is in the Hellenistic period; that is, in the couple of centuries that followed the death of Alexander the Great. In this period, Greek-language monarchies were established in Egypt and western Asia.

The largest of these was established south and east of Asia Minor in 321 B.C. by Seleucus I, who had been one of Alexander's generals. The realm is, in his honor, usually called the Seleucid Empire in the histories.

Seleucus had made his first capital in ancient Babylon, but quickly abandoned it as too alien and un-Greek. In its place, he constructed Seleucia on the Tigris, about twenty miles north of Babylon. It became a thoroughly Greek city.

Although the Empire covered vast tracts of what are now the nations of Iraq, Iran, and Afghanistan, the portion most under the influence of Greek culture and therefore most valued by the Greek-speaking and Greek-cultured descendants of Seleucus was the westernmost part, commonly called Syria by the Greeks.

In Syria Seleucus founded a city which served as his western capital and named it Antiocheia, after his father, Antiochus. In English, we know it as Antioch. It was located fifteen miles from the sea, near the northeastern corner of the Mediterranean, and is now located in southwestern Turkey.

About a century and three quarters after the founding of the Seleucid Empire, almost all the eastern provinces had fallen away and come under the rule of native princes. What was left of the Greek kingdom was concentrated in the westernmost provinces and what had been the Seleucid Empire came more and more to be called simply Syria.

Despite the vicissitudes of the Empire, however, Antioch continued to grow and became a great metropolis. In the days of the Roman Empire, when Rome had finally absorbed the last remnant of the Seleucid realm, Antioch was the third largest city of the Empire. Only Rome itself and Alexandria in Egypt were larger.

The question is, now, which monarch is referred to by Gower as "Antiochus the great"? It is no use to try to decide by the actual events of the play, since these are all fictitious.

There were thirteen monarchs of the Seleucid kingdom named Antiochus, but one of them, the third of the name, did call himself Antiochus the Great. This Antiochus III ruled from 223 to 187 B.C. In the first part of his reign, he brought back into the Seleucid fold (very temporarily) some of the large eastern provinces that were breaking away, marching through the east almost like another Alexander in doing so. It was this which gave him the idea of calling himself "the Great."

Once that was accomplished, he attempted to annex Egypt, which was governed by a boy king at the time, and also Asia Minor. Had he succeeded, he would have united almost all of Alexander's Empire under his rule.

Unfortunately for himself, Antiochus III fell afoul of the rising power of Rome. Challenging that Western nation, he invaded Greece, but was defeated there in 191 B.C. The Romans followed him into Asia Minor and defeated him again in 190 B.C. Antiochus ended his reign in defeat and failure.

Considering that in *Pericles* Antiochus the Great is pictured as ruling in magnificence and glory (at least at the beginning), we might arbitrarily place the fictitious events of this play about 200 B.C. This is twenty years after the suggested time of *A Comedy of Errors* and so *Pericles* becomes the eighth and last of Shakespeare's Greek plays.

. . . her to incest . . .

Gower goes on to explain that "Antiochus the great" was left a widower with a beautiful daughter:

> *With whom the father liking took,*
> *And her to incest did provoke.*
>
> —Act I, Introduction, lines 25–26

Incest is treated here as a horrible and unspeakable crime, and so it is considered in most societies; though, it must be admitted, not in all. The Egyptian Pharaohs routinely married their sisters, feeling perhaps that only their sisters had blood aristocratic enough to make a marriage suitable. (Or perhaps it was a relic of matrilineal descent; of the times when the nature of fatherhood was not understood and when property could only be inherited through the mother. By marrying his sister, the Pharaoh could make sure that the sister's son, who later was to inherit the throne, would also be his own.)

After the death of Alexander the Great, one of his generals, Ptolemy, seized Egypt and established the "Ptolemaic kingdom." For nearly three centuries Egypt was ruled by his descendants, all of whom were named Ptolemy. The Ptolemies carefully adhered to Egyptian customs in order to remain popular with their subjects. Ptolemy II took for his second wife, for instance, his full sister, Arsinoe. As a result, first she, and then he, received the surname Philadelphus ("sibling lover"). He did not have children by her. Cleopatra, the last of the Ptolemaic rulers of Egypt (see page I–318), was married in turn to two of her brothers, though each marriage was purely formal, for both were children at the time of the marriage.

Furthermore, in the Persian dominions in the days before Alexander's conquest, incest was not abhorred and father-daughter unions were allowed. Antiochus the Great ruled over most of the core of the old Persian Empire. It is not on record that he followed Persian custom in this respect, but that old custom may have been in the mind of the anonymous Greek writer who first invented the tale which worked its way down the centuries and came to rest in Shakespeare's *Pericles*.

. . . Prince of Tyre . . .

To keep his luscious daughter from the princely suitors that sought her hand, Antiochus forced all to attempt to solve a riddle. Failure to solve the riddle was punished with death and numerous suitors had already suffered that penalty.

The play itself begins before the palace at Antioch, where a young suitor has come to present himself for the hand of the princess. Antiochus says:

> *Young Prince of Tyre, you have at large received*
> *The danger of the task you undertake.*
>
> —Act I, scene i, lines 1–2

Tyre is a city on the Mediterranean coast, about 220 miles south of Antioch. It is much the more ancient of the two cities, for it was a flourishing town in the thirteenth century B.C. when the ancient Egyptian Empire was at its height.

Tyre was an important port of the Canaanites, who were called Phoenicians by the Greeks. Its ships ventured far through the Mediterranean, founding what eventually became the still greater city of Carthage on the north African shore. Tyrian ships even ventured outside the Mediterranean, reaching Britain on the north and, as one tale has it, circumnavigating the African continent to the south.

Tyre's stronghold was on a rocky island off the shore and this, combined with her navy, kept her secure against the land-based empires of Asia. She maintained her independence not only against David's Israelite Empire but against the much more dangerous Assyrian and Chaldean empires. Nebuchadrezzar subjected it to a thirteen-year siege from 587 to 574 B.C. and managed only a partial victory.

The real end of Tyre's independence came in 332 B.C., when one much greater than Nebuchadrezzar banged against its gates. This was Alexander the Great himself. He had been sweeping through Asia Minor with scarcely any resistance and was now heading toward Egypt, when Tyre unexpectedly refused to yield. Even Alexander required seven full months to take Tyre, and when he completed the job, he was vengeful enough to have ten thousand of its citizens executed and another thirty thousand sold into slavery.

Although Tyre recovered to some extent, it remained only a shadow of its former self, first under the Ptolemies of Egypt, then under the Seleucid Empire, and finally under the Roman Empire.

It was in 198 B.C., just about the suggested time of the events of this play, that Antiochus the Great wrested the southern part of Syria from Egypt.

Tyre vanished from the view of western Europe after the breakup of the Roman Empire, but reappeared in the time of the Crusades. The Crusaders captured it in 1124 and for over a century it remained one of the chief cities of the Christian "Kingdom of Jerusalem." When the Crusaders were finally driven out of the East, Tyre was destroyed. A small village, still bearing the old name, exists on its site now, in southern Lebanon.

The original Greek version of the story of *Pericles* is lost, but a Latin prose romance based on that Greek version exists. It begins with the incest and riddle of Antiochus, and the young man who comes to win the princess is "Apollonius of Tyre." The "of Tyre" merely means he was born there, or lives there. To make him *Prince* of Tyre is an anachronism, for Tyre did not have independent rulers in Hellenistic times.

Shakespeare did not use the name Apollonius. He was influenced, apparently, by a character in *Arcadia,* a romance written in 1580 by Sir Philip Sidney, which had as one of its heroes a character named Pyrocles. Pyrocles' nobility was something like that which Shakespeare had in mind for his own hero, and, perhaps for that reason, he used the name, converting it to the more common Greek form of Pericles.

The only important historical Pericles was the leader of democratic Athens from 460 to 429 B.C. Under him, Athens was at the height of its power and culture and his rule may be taken as coinciding with the Golden Age of Greece. It must be emphasized, though, that the Pericles of Shakespeare's play has nothing whatever to do with Pericles of Golden Age Athens.

. . . this fair Hesperides

Pericles declares himself aware of the danger of wooing Antiochus' daughter, and she is brought out before him—a vision of loveliness. Antiochus says:

> Before thee stands this fair Hesperides,
> With golden fruit, but dangerous to be touched;
> For deathlike dragons here affright thee hard.
> —Act I, scene i, lines 28–30

This is a reference to the eleventh of the twelve labors which Hercules was supposed to undergo in the Greek myths. The Hesperides are so named from a Greek word meaning "west." They were the three daughters of Hesperus, the Evening Star (which always appears in the west after sunset), according to one version of the myth. Another version has them the daughters of the Titan Atlas, who gave his name to the Atlantic Ocean and who was associated with what was, to the Greeks, the Far West.

On the far western section of the north African coast there was supposed to be a garden containing a tree bearing golden apples (oranges, I wonder?), which was guarded by an ever watchful dragon. Hercules achieved this task, as he did all others, but Antiochus seems to doubt that Pericles can do the equivalent.

. . . to Tharsus

Antiochus presents the riddle Pericles must solve. It is a silly riddle and quite transparent. Pericles sees the answer at once and is horrified. He carefully hints at the truth and Antiochus is, in his turn, horrified.

Pericles sees that to have solved the riddle is as dangerous as to have missed it and leaves hurriedly for Tyre. Antiochus sends a servant after the young prince to poison him.

Even at Tyre, Pericles is uneasy. He is not far enough from Antioch and he feels that Antiochus will come against him with an army and bring misery on the whole city. (And well he might, for in actual history, Tyre became part of Antiochus' dominions in 198 B.C.)

Pericles tells his loyal lord, Helicanus, the story and says he intends to go into exile:

> Tyre, I now look from thee then, and to Tharsus
> Intend my travel . . .
> —Act I, scene ii, lines 115–16

No city named Tharsus is to be found in the gazetteers.

The name is very similar to Tarsus, an important city on the southern coast of Asia Minor, best known to us as the place where Antony and Cleopatra first met (see page I–343) a century and a half after the time of Pericles, and where St. Paul was born a few decades later still.

Tarsus, however, is only about 170 miles west of Antioch and was as firmly in the Seleucid grip as was Tyre itself. It is interesting to wonder if perhaps Tharsus is a distortion of Thasos, a small island in the northern Aegean Sea. There are places in the play where Thasos would fit well.— However, it is most likely that Tharsus is a completely fictitious place, no more to be located on the map than the Bohemia of *The Winter's Tale* (see page I–156).

. . . the Trojan horse . . .

Pericles leaves Tyre just in time to escape Antiochus' poisoning emissary, but he finds matters in Tharsus not well. Its governor, Cleon, and his wife, Dionyza, bewail the fact that the prosperous city has been reduced by a two-year famine to a point of near cannibalism. Even as they are wailing, a fleet of ships appears on the horizon. At first they suspect it is an enemy come to take advantage of their weakness, but it is the noble Pericles. He enters with his attendants and says:

> . . . *these our ships you happily* [i.e., perhaps] *may think*
> *Are like the Trojan horse* [which] *was stuffed within*
> *With bloody veins expecting overthrow,*
> *Are stored with corn to make your needy bread,*
> —Act I, scene iv, lines 91–94

The Trojan horse was the final stratagem of the Greeks, who after ten years' siege of Troy (see page I–89) had abandoned hope of conquest by direct attack. The climactic scene of the war is not described in Homer's *Iliad* or in Shakespeare's *Troilus and Cressida*. It is, however, described in Vergil's *Aeneid*.

The Greeks built a giant hollow horse, filled it with their best warriors, then pretended to abandon the siege and sail away. The Trojans were easily convinced that the horse was an offering to Minerva (Athena) and that it was a good luck token which, if accepted, would forever protect the city against conquest. It was accordingly taken into the city and that night the Greek warriors emerged and opened the gates to the remainder of the army (which had secretly returned). Then began the bloody task of sacking the city.

Pericles' ships, however, were not filled with warriors, but with food.

. . . our country of Greece . . .

Gower emerges at the beginning of the Second Act to explain that Pericles is treated with great honor at Tharsus but that word comes to him from Tyre that Antiochus is indeed anxious to have him killed and that even Tharsus will not be safe.

Pericles therefore takes to the sea again and this time is wrecked. He is washed on shore all alone, all his companions and goods gone.

The Second Act opens, then, on the shore of the Pentapolis, which apparently is where Pericles has been washed up. He approaches some fishermen, asking their help for pity, pointing out that he has never had to beg before. The First Fisherman replies sardonically:

> *No, friend, cannot you beg? Here's them in our country of*
> *Greece gets more with begging than we can do with working.*
> —Act II, scene i, lines 67–69

The Pentapolis ("five cities") is a district on the north African shore about 550 miles west of Alexandria and 950 miles southwest of Antioch. The chief of the five cities was Cyrene, and the region is still called Cyrenaica today. It is the northeasternmost section of the modern nation of Libya and was much in the news in 1941 and 1942, when the British and Germans were fighting back and forth across it in the Desert War.

Obviously, the Pentapolis is not in Greece in the modern sense, where that is specifically the land occupying the southernmost portion of the Balkan peninsula. Yet Shakespeare, or whoever wrote this scene, was (perhaps unknowingly) not really incorrect in the wider sense of Greece as including any area where Greek language and culture was dominant (see page I-172).

A knight of Sparta . . .

The ruler of Pentapolis is Simonides, and his daughter, Thaisa, is having a birthday the next day. Various knights are to fight at a tournament in her honor (a queer intermingling of medieval custom with the ancient background).

Pericles no sooner hears this than fishermen come in dragging a suit of armor which has entangled their nets in the sea. It is Pericles' own armor, lost in the shipwreck. Now he too can join the tournament and engage in a second type of contest for the beautiful daughter of a king.

Simonides and Thaisa appear in the next scene, seated in a pavilion in the fashion of medieval sponsors of a tournament. The competing knights pass by, presenting their shields with the identifying device on each.

Thaisa describes the first for her father:

A knight of Sparta, my renownèd father;
And the device he bears upon his shield
Is a black Ethiop reaching at the sun.
The word, Lux tua vita mihi.

—Act II, scene ii, lines 18–21

Sparta was at one time the leading military city of Greece, but in 371 B.C., nearly two centuries before the apparent time of the play, it had been catastrophically defeated by Thebes at the Battle of Leuctra. From that time on, Sparta sat paralyzed, refusing to change with the times, and never admitted it was no longer the leader of Greece. In 200 B.C. it was in its last stages of independence and still produced good fighters.

There is nothing impossible, then, in the appearance of a Spartan in the competition, although he could scarcely be a "knight" in the medieval sense. Nor is it at all likely that he would have a Latin motto ("Thy light is life to me") on his shield, since in the time of Antiochus the Great, Latin was, to the cultivated Greeks, a barbarous and uncouth native Italian dialect, nothing more.

A prince of Macedon . . .

The second knight is described by Thaisa as:

A prince of Macedon, my royal father;
And the device he bears upon his shield
Is an armed knight that's conquered by a lady;
The motto thus, in Spanish, Piu per dolcessa che per forza.

—Act II, scene ii, lines 24–27

Macedon was a kingdom on the northwest shore of the Aegean Sea, Greek in language and culture, but backward in the time of Athens' Golden Age, and playing little part in Greek history at the time.

It rose to prominence in 359 B.C. when a remarkable man, Philip II, began his period of rule over it. Under his guidance, it came to dominate Greece, and under his son, Alexander the Great, it conquered the Persian Empire.

Macedon was greatly weakened by the conquest, in point of fact, as most of its soldiers and best citizens departed forever to rule over distant areas in Asia and Africa. It suffered also from barbarian invasions in the third century B.C. Nevertheless, Macedon managed to maintain control over the entire Balkan peninsula, including Greece proper. In 200 B.C., however, it stood at the brink of downfall, for war with Rome was beginning and this war Macedon was eventually to lose utterly.

It is not inappropriate that a Macedonian should be represented here, but what is he doing with a motto "in Spanish," a language which did not yet exist and would not for nearly a thousand years? (The Signet Shakespeare gives the motto in Italian, anyway, another language which did not yet exist. It means "More by gentleness than by force.")

. . . a fire from heaven . . .

The third knight is from Antioch, the fourth and fifth are not identified geographically, and the sixth knight, in rusty, shabby armor, is Pericles. It is Pericles, of course, who wins the tournament, and Thaisa is much taken with his handsome appearance. There is a gala celebration and it looks as though Pericles' luck has turned.

As for Antiochus, his luck has taken a final downturn. At Tyre, Helicanus, who rules in Pericles' absence, tells what has happened. Apparently the gods are annoyed at Antiochus' incest and, as Helicanus says:

> *Even in the height and pride of all his glory,*
> *When he was seated in a chariot*
> *Of an inestimable value, and*
> *His daughter with him, a fire from heaven came,*
> *And shriveled up their bodies, even to loathing.*
> —Act II, scene iv, lines 6–13

In actual history, Antiochus the Great did not die such a death. His defeat by Rome placed a heavy burden on him in the way of tribute. He tried to raise the money by forcing the priesthood to disgorge the treasures hoarded in their temples. He was supervising the stripping of such a temple when the populace, aroused by the priests, mobbed and killed him in 187 B.C.

A younger son of Antiochus III, Antiochus IV, ruled from 175 to 163 B.C., and he may well have contributed to the picture Shakespeare draws of "Antiochus the great." It was Antiochus IV who particularly beautified Antioch as the eastern provinces fell farther and farther away. It was Antiochus IV who made a name for himself in history as a king of intolerable wickedness, which also fits the picture in *Pericles*.

Antiochus IV, like his father, was browbeaten by Rome (not even daring to meet them in battle) and, partly out of chagrin at that, turned against those Jews of his kingdom who would not accept Greek culture. The Jews rose in bloody revolt and the tale of that revolt is told in the Books of Maccabees, which form part of the Apocrypha but are accepted in the Catholic version of the Bible.

Antiochus IV died of tuberculosis during a campaign in the eastern provinces. In the First Book of Maccabees (a sober historical account) his death is recounted undramatically, except that he is reported to have, in rather unlikely fashion, died regretting his actions against the Jews and recognizing that he was being punished for what he had done.

In the Second Book of Maccabees (a more emotional account, and filled with tales of martyrdom and miracles) Antiochus is supposed to have died in agony, swarming with worms and rotting away while still alive: "and the filthiness of his smell was noisome to all his army. And the man, that thought a little afore he could reach to the stars of heaven, no man could endure to carry for his intolerable stink" (2 Maccabees 9:9–10).

The death of Antiochus IV as reported in 2 Maccabees undoubtedly contributed to the death of Antiochus in *Pericles,* for Helicanus says that after Antiochus and his daughter had shriveled under the fire from heaven:

> . . . *they so stunk*
> *That all those eyes adored them ere their fall*
> *Scorn now their hand should give them burial.*
>
> —Act II, scene iv, lines 11–13

. . . *make for Tharsus*

Pericles' fortune continues to climb, for he marries Thaisa and then hears from Tyre that Antiochus is dead and that the Tyrians long for Pericles' return.

He and his now pregnant wife, Thaisa, go on board ship to return to Tyre. Once again a storm strikes and at its height Thaisa goes into labor and is delivered of a baby girl. She apparently dies in the process and the superstitious sailors will not have a corpse on board. They place her in a coffin and shove it overboard.

The battered ship is near Tharsus and Pericles feels they cannot make Tyre. He cries out:

> O make for Tharsus!
> There will I visit Cleon, for the babe
> Cannot hold out to Tyrus. There I'll leave it
> At careful nursing.
>
> —Act III, scene i, lines 77–80

To go from the Pentapolis to Tyre and be driven by the storm toward Tharsus is within belief if it is really Tarsus that the name implies; but it is much less credible if Tharsus is Thasos.

. . . through Ephesus . . .

The scene now shifts to Ephesus and the home of Cerimon, a skillful doctor. A follower says to him:

> *Your honor has through Ephesus poured forth*
> *Your charity, and hundreds call themselves*
> *Your creatures, who by you have been restored;*
> —Act III, scene ii, lines 43–45

Ephesus, the great and prosperous city of the time of *The Comedy of Errors,* is still great and prosperous in the time of *Pericles.*

This queen will live . . .

At this moment, servants enter with a chest that has been cast up from the sea. It is the casket containing Thaisa, along with a note from Pericles asking that if the dead body be found, it be piously buried.

But Cerimon is a skillful physician indeed. He says:

> *This queen will live: nature awakes; a warmth*
> *Breathes out of her. She hath not been entranced*
> *Above five hours.*
> —Act III, scene ii, lines 94–96

If Tharsus were really Tarsus, this would be impossible. The Queen's body was consigned to the sea at a time when the ship was near Tharsus and to reach Ephesus would require it to drift westward the length of Asia Minor and then northward, half the length of the Aegean coast of that peninsula—an about six-hundred-mile journey. To drift at 120 miles an hour is quite a picture.

On the other hand, suppose the storm had driven the ship to Thasos. From there to Ephesus would be only 250 miles, which would require a drift of 50 miles an hour.

But at Tharsus, Pericles asks when Tyre can be reached and a sailor says:

> *By break of day, if the wind cease.*
> —Act III, scene i, line 76

From Thasos to Tyre is more than a night's journey.

So it's best to ignore geography. Tharsus cannot be placed anywhere on the map in such a way as to have a plausible relationship to Ephesus,

Tyre, and Pentapolis, all three of which have positions that are known and fixed.

And Aesculapius . . .

To restore Thaisa to life is, of course, an arduous task even for Cerimon, who ends by saying:

> *And Aesculapius guide us!*
>
> —Act III, scene ii, line 112

Aesculapius (the Latin version of the Greek Asclepius) was, in Greek myth, a son of Apollo who was supremely skilled as a physician. So skillful was he that he could restore life to the dead. This enraged Hades, who apparently felt himself to be endangered by technological unemployment. He complained to Jupiter (Zeus), who solved matters by killing Aesculapius with a thunderbolt. After death, Aesculapius was raised to divine rank and became the god of medicine.

It is in his divine role that Cerimon appeals to him on this occasion.

Marina . . .

At Tharsus Pericles is greeted warmly as the savior of the time of the famine, but he cannot linger. He must go to Tyre, leaving behind:

> *My gentle babe,*
> *Marina, who, for she was born at sea,*
> *I have named so . . .*
>
> —Act III, scene iii, lines 12–16

"Marina" is the feminine form of the Latin word meaning "of the sea." The baby is left in the care of Cleon and his wife Dionyza.

Diana's temple . . .

In Ephesus Thaisa is now fully recovered and, thinking that Pericles died in the shipwreck, says she will live in religious retreat. Cerimon, the doctor, says:

> *Madam, if this you purpose as ye speak,*
> *Diana's temple is not distant far,*
> *Where you may abide . . .*
>
> —Act III, scene iv, lines 11–13

Ephesus in ancient times was known for its temple to Diana (Artemis). An early version of this temple was completed about 420 B.C. and was impressive enough to be considered one of the Seven Wonders of the World.

In October 356 B.C. the temple was destroyed by fire and it proved to be a case of deliberate arson. When the culprit was captured, he was asked why he had done this deed. He replied that he did it in order that his name might live forever in history. He was executed and to defeat his desire it was ordered that his name be erased from all records and never be spoken. (However, the man had his wish after all, for a name purporting to be his survives somehow. It is Herostratus.)

This was a century and a half before the time of *Pericles,* but the temple was rebuilt, of course. Indeed, it is most famous to moderns because it plays a distant role in the New Testament, some two centuries after the time of *Pericles* and four centuries after Herostratus' crime.

St. Paul, in Ephesus on a missionary voyage, denounced idolatry and roused the hostility of the silversmiths of the city, who did a roaring business in the manufacture of little religious objects for tourists who came to visit the temple of Diana. Not foreseeing the time when their successors would do equally well, if not better, with small crucifixes and statues of the Virgin Mary, the silversmiths were horrified at St. Paul's denunciation of idolatry. There were riots in the city and the crowd was "full of wrath and cried out, saying, Great is Diana of the Ephesians" (Acts of the Apostles 19:28).

To be sure, Shakespeare knew Diana as the virgin goddess of the moon and the hunt (see page I–14), as she was in classical Greek mythology. The Diana of the Ephesians was another goddess altogether, a representation of fecundity, a fertility goddess with her chest covered by breasts, representing, perhaps, the nourishing earth. Diana's temple in Ephesus was surely not an appropriate life for a quiet existence, free from the sexual lusts of the world, but in the play it is taken as such.

. . . *dove of Paphos* . . .

The fourth act once again opens with Gower, who covers this time a passage of fourteen years, during which Marina grows to young womanhood in Tharsus. (The actual length of the time is specified later, when Pericles refers to her as fourteen years old.)

This is very similar to *The Winter's Tale,* where another baby girl, Perdita, separated from her parents, also grows to young womanhood (see page I–158). In both cases the father of the young girl is a ruler and the mother is thought to be dead but isn't really.

One difference in the two plays is that Perdita grows up in *The Winter's*

Tale to know only love and admiration, while Marina in *Pericles* is not so lucky.

Cleon and Dionyza have a daughter of their own named Philoten, who is completely overshadowed by Marina. Gower describes the hopelessness of Philoten's case:

> . . . *so*
> *With dove of Paphos might the crow*
> *Vie feathers white.*
>
> —Act IV, Introduction, lines 31–33

The dove of Paphos (see page I–15) is one of those doves that draw Venus' chariot.

. . . rob Tellus . . .

Dionyza plots, out of jealousy, to have Marina murdered despite the great debt owed Pericles by Tharsus. Her vile plan is made the easier since Marina's nurse, who has been with her since her birth, has just died and Marina has lost a natural guardian. Indeed, Marina makes her first appearance in the play mourning her nurse's death. She is carrying a basket of flowers and speaks sadly at the grave of the dead woman:

> *No, I will rob Tellus of her weed*
> *To strew thy green with flowers . . .*
>
> —Act IV, scene i, lines 13–14

Tellus is one of the names of the Roman goddess of the earth, Terra being the other, and more familiar, one.

. . . Mytilene is full . . .

Dionyza urges Marina to take a walk on the seashore with a man who has been ordered to murder her. Providentially, a band of pirates come ashore and seize Marina before she can be killed.

Marina's situation has not improved by much, however, for the scene shifts to a brothel in Mytilene where the pander in charge is having problems. He says to his men:

> *Search the market narrowly! Mytilene is full of gallants.*
> *We lost too much money this mart by being too wenchless.*
>
> —Act IV, scene ii, lines 3–5

Mytilene is the chief city on the island of Lesbos in the eastern Aegean. It is one of the larger Aegean islands and of the other places mentioned in the play it is nearest to Ephesus. It is only about a hundred miles northwest of Ephesus in a direct line, though the sea voyage would require working round a promontory of land and would be longer.

It is, on the other hand, 150 miles southeast of Thasos and, if that island were "Tharsus," it would be easy to imagine the pirates making for Mytilene, which, as a sailors' haven, is apparently a good market for prostitution.

The poor Transylvanian . . .

In rather revolting terms, the pander and a bawd continue to talk about the shortage of girls. The pander says:

> *The poor Transylvanian is dead that lay with the little*
> *baggage.*
> —Act IV, scene ii, lines 22–23

This is an indication that the few girls they have are riddled with disease. Of course, the use of the term "Transylvanian" is an anachronism. Transylvania is a region which now makes up the central portion of modern Romania, or, as it was known to the Romans, Dacia. The term "Transylvania" did not come into use until the twelfth century. It means "beyond the forests" and was first used by the Hungarians, from whose standpoint Transylvania was indeed a land beyond the forests.

It is to Mytilene that the pirates have brought Marina, and they sell her, still untouched (virgins bring high prices) to the brothel.

The petty wrens of Tharsus . . .

At Tharsus Cleon is horrified at what Dionyza has done. She faces it out, however, and maintains that Pericles need never know. She wants to know if Cleon is:

> *. . . one of those that thinks*
> *The petty wrens of Tharsus will fly hence*
> *And open this to Pericles.*
> —Act IV, scene iii, lines 21–23

This is in line with the old superstition that birds will tell of crimes, from which comes our own phrase "a little bird told me."

One possible source of the idea rests in a popular Greek tale concerning a poet, Ibycus, en route to Corinth, who was set upon by thieves and killed. As he was dying, he cried out to cranes passing overhead, urging them to tell the world of the crime.

The Corinthian populace was stunned and horrified at the death of the popular poet and the thieves were uneasy at the stir they had created. During the course of a play which they were watching along with the rest of the Corinthians, the Furies (spirits who avenge crimes) were presented in such horrid fashion that the thieves were terrified. And when, just at this moment, cranes happened to fly overhead, the distraught thieves cried, "The cranes of Ibycus! The cranes of Ibycus!" and gave themselves away.

Another possible source for the superstition rests in a verse in the Bible which says: "Curse not the king, no not in thy thought; and curse not the rich in thy bedchamber: for a bird of the air shall carry the voice, and that which hath wings shall tell the matter" (Ecclesiastes 10:20). This can be interpreted as a warning that kings and powerful men have spies and sycophants in plenty who are always ready to earn gratitude by accusing others of treasons. However, there is a temptation to take anything in the Bible literally and the notion of telltale birds entered the language.

Thetis, being proud . . .

It seems that Pericles' miseries are never done. Gower emerges yet again in the next scene to describe how Pericles comes to Tharsus to get his daughter (why the long delay?) and finds her dead, with a monument built to her in the market place; on which is an inscription that reads in part:

> . . . *at her birth*
> *Thetis, being proud, swallowed some part o'th'earth*
> —Act IV, scene iv, lines 38–39

Thetis was a sea nymph whom Shakespeare here, as elsewhere (see page I-91), confuses with Tethys, a goddess of the sea.

. . . the god Priapus . . .

Meanwhile, the brothel at Mytilene is the scene of a new kind of trouble. Marina has been installed as one of the prostitutes, but she remains untouched. Those who approach her are quickly converted to virtue and leave with the determination to patronize brothels no more. The bawd is horrified, saying:

> *Fie, fie upon her! She's able to freeze the god Priapus . . .*
> —Act IV, scene vi, lines 3–4

Priapus is a god of fertility, pictured as a dwarfish, ugly creature with a gigantic penis in a perpetual state of erection (whence our own medical term "priapism").

When Lysimachus, the governor of Mytilene, comes to the house, Marina quickly converts him too and sends him away virtuous. In despair, the pander and bawd hand Marina over to a servant to be deflowered, thinking that then she might become more amenable to their purposes. Marina, however, persuades him to make an effort to hire her out as a governess instead, capable of teaching many maidenly accomplishments.

The music of the spheres . . .

Pericles' ship, returning from Tharsus to Tyre, passes by Mytilene. (If Tharsus is Tarsus, this is impossible. If Tharsus is Thasos, it is quite possible.)

The governor of Mytilene, Lysimachus, boards the ship and finds Pericles sitting there, speechless with grief. He is saddened by the sight and says that there is a girl in Mytilene who can console him. Marina is brought on board and, before long, it turns out that the two are father and daughter.

At the discovery, Pericles hears music the others cannot. He says:

> *The music of the spheres! List, my Marina.*
> —Act V, scene i, line 232

This is a reference to a mystical Greek notion. The philosopher Pythagoras of Samos discovered that twanging cords with lengths related to each other by small whole numbers emitted harmonious notes. It set him to thinking of the importance of numbers in the universe and he and his disciples evolved many odd beliefs based on numbers.

The Pythagoreans later developed the notion of the individual planets being set in spheres (see page I–25) at distances relative to each other such that they could emit harmonious notes. Perhaps at first this "music of the spheres" was considered metaphorically only, but eventually it was taken literally and came to mean a celestial sound that was far more beautiful than could be imagined on earth.

Pericles was finally being rewarded for having endured so much misfortune so patiently.

. . . goddess argentine

At the sound of the music, Pericles falls asleep and in his sleep the goddess Diana appears to him. Pericles is ordered to go to the Ephesian temple, there to make known his story to the people. He wakes and says:

> *Celestial Dian, goddess argentine,*
> *I will obey thee . . .*
>
> —Act V, scene i, lines 252–53

Diana (Artemis) is goddess of the moon, which is silver, rather than the sun's bright gold. The Latin word for silver is *argentum,* so that Diana as the silver goddess of the moon is the "goddess argentine."

The nation of Argentina was so named because the earliest explorers found the natives wearing silver ornaments. The river which they were exploring became the Río de la Plata (Spanish for "Silver River"). The nation that grew up about that river as a nucleus became the Latinized version of the same idea, Argentina.

As a result, the term "goddess argentine" would nowadays be rather ambiguous.

In Ephesus Pericles discovers his wife Thaisa and so, after fourteen years, the family is reunited. It is left to Gower to explain that Marina will be married to Lysimachus and that Pericles visited vengeance on Cleon and Dionyza by returning to Tharsus and burning them in their palace.

PART II

—◆—

Roman

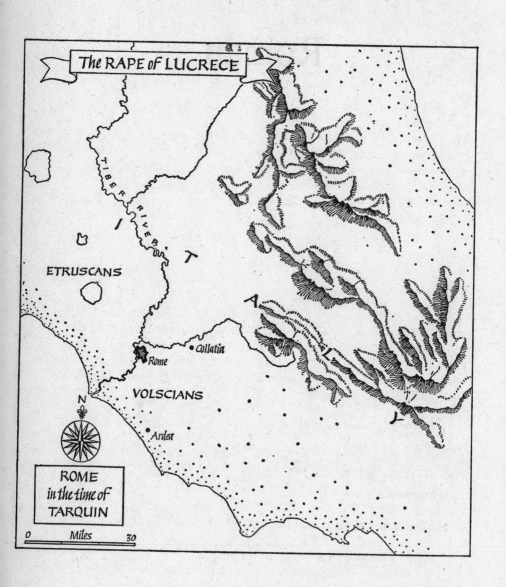

The RAPE of LUCRECE

ETRUSCANS

TIBER RIVER

I T A L Y

• Collatia
Rome

VOLSCIANS

• Ardea

N

ROME
in the time of
TARQUIN

0   Miles   30

9

THE RAPE OF LUCRECE

SHAKESPEARE wrote four plays and one narrative poem dealing with Roman history, real, legendary, or fictional. Of these, it is the poem, *The Rape of Lucrece,* that deals with the earliest event, the legendary fall of the Roman monarchy in 509 B.C.

If I were treating all Shakespeare's works in a single chronological grouping, *The Rape of Lucrece* would be placed between *Troilus and Cressida* and *Timon of Athens.* However, since I am segregating the Greek and Roman works, *The Rape of Lucrece* appears as the first of the Roman group.

The love . . .

The Rape of Lucrece was published about May 1594, a year after *Venus and Adonis.* This later poem is both longer and more serious than the earlier, and makes for harder reading too. Like the earlier poem, it is dedicated to Southampton (see page I–3), and the additional year seems to have increased the intimacy between Shakespeare and his young patron. At least the dedication begins:

> *The love I dedicate to your Lordship is without end;*
> —Dedication

Lust-breathed Tarquin . . .

The first stanza of the poem plunges the story into action at once:

> *From the besieged Ardea all in post,*
> *Borne by the trustless wings of false desire,*
> *Lust-breathed Tarquin leaves the Roman host*
>
> —lines 1–3

The year, according to legend, is 509 B.C., and Rome is still no more than a city-state. It had been founded about two and a half centuries before (753 B.C. is the traditional date) and has been governed by a line of kings. Ruling in the city now is the seventh king to sit on the Roman throne. His name is Lucius Tarquinius (better known in English as Tarquin) and he has been given the surname Superbus, meaning "proud," because of his arrogant tyranny.

Tarquin forced the senatorial aristocracy into submission by executing some on trumped-up charges and by refusing to replace those who died a natural death.

He kept himself in power by gathering an armed guard about himself, and ruled as a military despot. Nevertheless, he maintained a kind of popularity with the common people by a program of public works and by an aggressive foreign policy that brought in loot from surrounding tribes.

The aristocracy could only wait and hope that some particular event would take place to alienate the populace generally from the despotic monarch.

It is not, however, King Tarquin who is referred to in the third line of the poem, but his son, Tarquinius Sextus, the heir to the throne.

The Roman army is engaged in a war against the Volscians, a tribe who occupied territory just south of Rome. The Romans were at this time laying siege to Ardea, one of the Volscian cities, just twenty miles south of Rome, and it is from this siege that Tarquin Sextus is hurrying.

. . . Lucrece the chaste

The incident Shakespeare is about to relate is to be found in the first book of the *History of Rome* by Titus Livius (better known as Livy to English-speaking people), and also in the *Fasti* (*Annals*), written by Shakespeare's favorite ancient writer, Ovid.

Despite the fact that the incident is taken from ancient writers, it is not at all likely that it is historically accurate. In 390 B.C., a little over a century after the time of Tarquin, Rome was taken and sacked by the barbarian Gauls and the historical records were destroyed. All of Roman history prior to 390 B.C. is a mass of legends based on uncertain kernels of fact.

The legends narrated by Livy and others were, however, accepted as sober fact right down to modern times, and certainly Shakespeare accepted this tale as such. He goes on for the remainder of the first verse to tell the reason for the prince's haste:

> *And to Collatium bears the lightless fire*
> *Which, in pale embers hid, lurks to aspire*
> *And girdle with embracing flames the waist*
> *Of Collatine's fair love, Lucrece the chaste.*

—lines 4–6

Prince Tarquin has a cousin, also named Tarquin, whose estates are near Collatia (which Shakespeare calls "Collatium"), a small town ten miles east of Rome. He was therefore Tarquin of Collatia, or in Latin: Tarquinius Collatinus. In order to distinguish him from Tarquinius Superbus, the King, and from Tarquinius Sextus, the prince, he may be called simply Collatinus, or, in English, Collatine.

At the siege of Ardea (and a siege is usually a boring occupation) the Roman aristocrats, it seems, fell to discussing their wives, each boasting of the virtue and chastity of his own. This is the sort of thing one would scarcely think men would seriously do, yet it is common in romances. Shakespeare uses such a discussion as the mainspring of part of the action in *Cymbeline* (see page II–58), for instance.

In fact, the unreal romanticism of this discussion is part of what causes historians to suspect the account of the Rape of Lucrece to be a fable. It is very likely a tale made up long after Tarquin's reign to account for the establishment of the Republic; a historical romance, to begin with, later taken as sober history.

But, history or fiction, this is the tale. Of the Roman aristocrats, Collatine was most emphatic in maintaining the chastity and sobriety of his wife, Lucretia, a name of which Lucrece is a shortened version.

It came down to a wager eventually, and the Romans decided to leave the siege temporarily so that they might dash home to Rome to check on their wives' activities. Doing so, they found that all the wives but Lucrece were having a good time; dancing, laughing, gossiping, feasting. Lucrece, however, was at home, alone except for her maids, and was gravely engaged in the housewifely task of spinning.

Collatine had won his wager, but in a deeper sense, he had lost, for Prince Tarquin, having seen Lucrece's beauty and chastity, conceived a powerful desire to make love to her. Once all the aristocrats were back at the siege, he left again, this time alone, in order to gratify that desire.

. . . had Narcissus seen her . . .

Tarquin is not at ease. He is not an utterly abandoned villain and he feels the guilt and disgrace of the reprehensible thing he is doing—yet he cannot help himself. After having arrived, he is treated as a welcome guest and Lucrece asks for news of her husband. Tarquin muses on her beauty and says to himself that, on hearing her husband was well

> . . . *she smiled with so sweet a cheer*
> *That, had Narcissus seen her as she stood,*
> *Self-love had never drown'd him in the flood.*
> —lines 264–66

Narcissus is the young man in Greek myths who loved only himself, and drowned trying to kiss his reflection in water (see page I–10).

. . . a cockatrice' dead-killing eye

When night comes, Prince Tarquin invades Lucrece's bedroom and tells her that if she will not yield, he will take her anyway and kill a slave, whom he will accuse as her lover. The situation paralyzes Lucrece with horror, which the poem indicates by stating:

> Here with a cockatrice' dead-killing eye
> He rouseth up himself and makes a pause;

—lines 540–41

Tarquin's words have the effect on her that a cockatrice's eye would have. The legendary cockatrice, the infinitely poisonous snake, kills with a mere glance (see page I–150).

A similar metaphor from the other direction is then used:

> So his unhallowed haste her words delays,
> And moody Pluto winks while Orpheus plays.

—lines 552–53

The reference is to Orpheus' descent into the underworld to win back his wife Eurydice (see page I–47). His music charmed even Pluto, and as the harsh king of the underworld was made captive by beauty, so chaste Lucrece was paralyzed by evil.

. . . still-pining Tantalus . . .

Tarquin rapes Lucrece, then hastens away, miserable and guilty, leaving her behind, miserable and innocent.

To Lucrece, all the world is now fit only for cursing. There is no comfort anywhere or in anything. What good is wealth, for instance? The aged miser, having accumulated his hoard, finds his health gone, and cannot buy youth back with his gold:

> But like still-pining Tantalus he sits
> And useless barns the harvest of his wits,

—lines 858–59

Tantalus is always the very personification of punishment through frustration (see page I–13).

. . . Fortune's wheel

Nor does time heal matters in her now utterly pessimistic view. It but makes matters worse; merely serving to

> *. . . turn the giddy round of Fortune's wheel.*
>
> —line 952

Fortune (Tyche), an important goddess to the later Greeks (see page I-135), was often pictured with a turning wheel. That represented the manner in which men's fortunes rose and fell in indifferent alternation.

. . . lamenting Philomele . . .

One thing she determines. She will tell her husband the truth, so that he might not imagine his desecrated wife to be whole, and so that Tarquin might not be able to smile secretly at Collatine's ignorance. This conclusion brings her solace and she ends her wailing for a while:

> *By this, lamenting Philomele had ended*
> *This well-tun'd warble of her nightly sorrow,*
>
> —lines 1079–80

Philomela was a young woman in the Greek myths who (in Ovid's version of the tale) had undergone an even crueler rape than that of Lucrece, and who was eventually turned into a nightingale which nightly sang the sad song of her misery. Philomela is therefore a poetic synonym for "nightingale" and is frequently used in this way by Shakespeare.

Indeed, Shakespeare used this particular myth in detail in *Titus Andronicus* (see page I-405), which was written shortly before *The Rape of Lucrece*.

The rapist in Philomela's case was a Thracian king named Tereus, and Lucrece sees the comparison, for she says to the nightingale she imagines before her:

> *For burthen-wise I'll hum on Tarquin still,*
> *While thou on Tereus descants better skill;*
>
> —lines 1133–34

She then makes use of the legend of the nightingale leaning against a thorn to keep awake all night (see page I-64) to hint at suicide:

> *. . . wretched I*
> *To imitate thee well, against my heart*
> *Will fix a sharp knife . . .*

> —lines 1136–38

. . . Pyrrhus' proud foot . . .

She will not kill herself, however, until Collatine finds out the truth, and she writes a letter, begging him to hasten home. While she waits she has a chance to study and comment on an elaborate painting of the Greek siege of Troy, which had taken place seven centuries before her time.

(Actually in 509 B.C. Rome was completely under Etruscan cultural influence and was far removed from the world of Greek art and literature. It is extremely unlikely that the real Lucrece would be so knowledgeable of Greek mythology or have an opportunity to study paintings of the Trojan War. However, Shakespeare's high-flown style in this poem made such abundant classical allusion necessary.)

The painting is described. It is

> *. . . made for Priam's Troy*
> *Before the which is drawn the power of Greece,*
> *For Helen's rape the city to destroy,*

> —lines 1367–69

The Trojan War had had its cause, according to legend, in the rape (i.e., abduction) of Helen by Paris (see page I–76), and there is, therefore, an analogy to Lucrece's situation.

The individual Greek heroes are mentioned:

> *In Ajax' eyes blunt rage and rigour roll'd;*
> *But the mild glance that sly Ulysses lent*
> *Show'd deep regard and smiling government.*

> *There pleading might you see grave Nestor stand,*
> *As 'twere encouraging the Greeks to fight,*

> —lines 1398–1402

Ajax was, next to Achilles, the strongest of the Greeks; Ulysses (Odysseus) the craftiest; Nestor the wisest. All play important parts in *Troilus and Cressida* (see pages I–86, I–91, and I–92) and their listing here symbolizes Troy being assailed by strength, cunning, and wisdom.

Beyond that, Troy is confronted also by irresistible fate, as epitomized by the transcendent hero Achilles:

. . . for Achilles' image stood his spear,
Grip'd in an armed hand; himself behind
Was left unseen . . .

—lines 1424–26

The spear was symbol enough; the obscured hero was more an impersonal and relentless force than a man. He too plays his part, in an all-too-human fashion, in *Troilus and Cressida* (see page I–114).

What's more, the picture shows the Trojan War in its various stages. At another place, Lucrece sees Troy fallen and finds in it a face with sorrows to match her own:

. . . she despairing Hecuba beheld,
Staring on Priam's wounds with her old eyes,
Which bleeding under Pyrrhus' proud foot lies.

—lines 1447–49

This incident is past the ending of Homer's *Iliad* and of Shakespeare's *Troilus and Cressida*. It represents the tendencies of the later mythmakers to pile horror on horror and to multiply the tragedy of Troy's final destruction.

The Trojan King, Priam (see page I–79), had witnessed his city besieged for ten years and, one by one, nearly every one of his fifty sons killed. Now at last the Greeks were gone, but they had left behind a large wooden horse (see page I–188). Priam and the Trojans are persuaded to drag the horse into the city and the Greek warriors hidden within emerge at night, open the gates for the remainder of the army, and begin their slaughter.

Priam and his aged wife, Hecuba (see page I–85), flee to an altar of Zeus where they might be safe. Polites, one of Priam's very few surviving sons, comes running madly toward the altar too. Behind him is Pyrrhus (or Neoptolemus) (see page I–115), the son of Achilles.

Pyrrhus has been brought to the field of Troy after his father has been killed by an arrow in the heel from the bow of Paris. He quickly proves himself as brave and as cruel as his father.

Now it is his cruelty that is predominant. He kills Polites even at the altar and in the presence of his parents. Priam, driven mad at the sight, feebly casts a spear at Pyrrhus, who promptly kills him as well.

. . . perjur'd Sinon . . .

Lucrece sadly views the depicted miseries of falling Troy:

Lo, here weeps Hecuba, here Priam dies,
Here manly Hector faints, here Troilus sounds [swoons]
                              —lines 1485–86

Hector was the greatest of the Trojan warriors (see page I-188), but in the medieval versions of the story of Troy, it is his younger brother, Troilus, who rises to prominence, and it is Troilus who is the titular hero of *Troilus and Cressida.*

Lucrece finally concentrates, however, on a Greek captive, taken by the Trojans after the Greeks had built their wooden horse. This captive, Sinon, who pretended to be a refugee from the Greeks, told a false story that the wooden horse was an offering to Athena and would forever protect Troy from conquest if brought within the city. He is therefore described as:

> *. . . perjur'd Sinon, whose enchanting story*
> *The credulous old Priam after slew;*
>   —lines 1521–22

The story which Priam believed brought about the death of the old king. It is to Sinon, the very symbol of treachery in aftertime, that Lucrece compares Tarquin.

. . . Brutus drew

Finally Collatine arrives home from the siege, anxious to know what emergency had caused his wife to write. With him are other men of senatorial rank. To them all, Lucrece tells the story, and while they stand there horrified, she draws her knife and kills herself.

For a moment, all stand transfixed. Lucretius, her father, throws himself in sorrow on her body:

> *And from the purple fountain Brutus drew*
> *The murd'rous knife . . .*
>   —lines 1734–35

This is the first mention of Lucius Junius Brutus, an aristocrat who had escaped the deadly attentions of King Tarquin by pretending to be a moron and therefore harmless. ("Brutus" means "stupid," and this name was, supposedly, given to him because of his successful play acting. However, the truth may be the reverse. It may have been known that one of the destroyers of the Tarquinian kingdom was named Brutus and for lack of other hard details after the Gallic sack in 390 B.C., the meaning of the name was allowed to inspire the tale of his pretending to be a moron.)

Brutus had good reason to play it safe in any way he could, for according to the legend, his father and older brother had been among those executed by Tarquin—something which did not cause him to love the king either.

Now, seeing the shock, horror, and hatred sweeping the spectators, Brutus feels that he will be able to head a popular movement against the kingdom. He no longer needs his pretense of stupidity:

> Brutus, who pluck'd the knife from Lucrece' side,
> Seeing such emulation in their woe,
> Began to clothe his wit in state and pride,
> Burying in Lucrece' wound his folly's show.
>
> —lines 1807–10

Brutus rouses the crowd and the poem ends with a final (and 265th) verse:

> They did conclude to bear dead Lucrece thence,
> To show her bleeding body thorough Rome,
> And so to publish Tarquin's foul offence;
> Which being done with speedy diligence,
>   The Romans plausibly [with applause] did give consent
>   To Tarquin's everlasting banishment.
>
> —lines 1850–55

Thus did the Roman kingdom come to an end. In its place was established the Roman Republic, which five centuries later was to rule all the Mediterranean world.

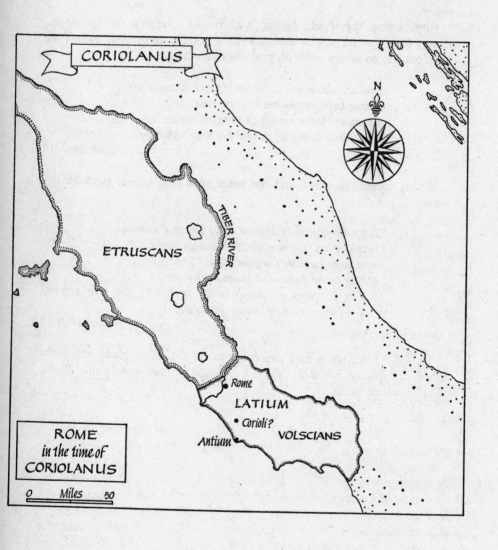

ROME
in the time of
CORIOLANUS

0   Miles   50

10

The Tragedy of

CORIOLANUS

O NE OF the most popular of the ancient historians was Plutarch, a
Greek who was born in Chaeronea, a town about sixty miles northwest of Athens, in A.D. 46. In his time, Greece had long passed the days of
its military splendor and was utterly dominated by Rome, then at the very
height of its empire.

Anxious to remind the Romans (and Greeks too) of what the Greeks
had once been, Plutarch wrote a series of short biographies about A.D. 100
in which he dealt with men in pairs, one Greek and one Roman, the two
being compared and contrasted. Thus, Theseus (see page I–18), the legendary unifier of the Attic peninsula under Athens, was paired with Romulus, the legendary founder of Rome. For this reason, the book is commonly
called *The Parallel Lives*. Plutarch's style is so pleasing that his book,
with its gossipy stories about great historical figures, has remained popular
ever since.

It was put into English in 1579 (from a French version) by Sir Thomas
North, who did it so well that his book turned out to be one of the prose
masterpieces of the Elizabethan Age. Shakespeare read it and used it as the
basis for three of his plays. He paid the translation the ultimate compliment
of scarcely changing its words in some cases. They made almost perfect
blank verse as they stood.

Shakespeare wrote *Coriolanus* about 1608 and it was the last of his
three Plutarchian plays. Its subject matter was, however, the earliest in
time, so I am placing it first.

The action opens in 494 B.C. (according to legend), only fifteen years
after the rape of Lucrece, the expulsion of the Tarquins, and the establishment of the Republic by Brutus (see page I–211). The events described in
the play are therefore of extremely dubious value historically, for they take
place a century before the destruction of the Roman annals by the Gallic
invaders (see page I–204).

Nevertheless, with Plutarch's guidance, Shakespeare can draw upon a
complete and interesting story, though perhaps one that is too romantic to
sound completely true.

. . . to die than to famish

Coriolanus opens in the streets of Rome, with citizens hurrying onstage in a fever of agitation, carrying weapons. Some crisis is taking place and the men are desperate. Their leader is called "First Citizen" in the play and he calls out to them:

> *You are all resolved rather to die than to famish?*
> —Act I, scene i, lines 4–5

Only fifteen years before, King Tarquin had been driven out of Rome and the institution of the monarchy had been destroyed. The Roman Republic was set up and was to last for five centuries. Control was placed in the hands of the aristocracy (the "patricians"), with numerous checks and balances, to make sure that no one of the aristocrats could gain so much power as to make himself a king and start the round of tyranny and revolt over again.

That did not mean, however, that Rome had become a little corner of heaven. The patricians, now that they had power in their hands, intended to keep it there. They reserved to themselves virtually all the rights, both political and economic, and yielded very little to the common people ("plebeians").

The plebeians in those days were small farmers who were expected to leave their farms and fight the city's battles whenever duty called. In the years after the first founding of the Republic, duty called frequently, for the exiled king tried to regain his position and made use of neighboring tribes as allies. Rome had to fight for its life.

As a result of those wars, though, the plebeian soldier might return from battle to find his farm neglected, or even ravaged, and would be in need of capital to begin again. The city did not consider itself economically responsible for its farmers and the loans a plebeian could get from the patricians were on harsh terms; and if they were not repaid, he and his family could be sold into slavery.

Furthermore, when food was scarce there was nothing to prevent the patricians (who had the capital for it) from buying up the supplies and then reselling it to the plebeians at a profit, thus capitalizing on the general misfortune.

It would be utterly inhuman to expect that the plebeians would sit still for all this. Undoubtedly, their lot had worsened under the Republic and they found it intolerable that they were expected to give their lives for the patricians while getting nothing in return.

. . . Caius Marcius . . .

The riotous citizens onstage are rebelling plebeians, then, and the First Citizen reminds them whom they are chiefly to blame for their misfortunes. He cries out:

> *First you know, Caius Marcius is chief enemy to the people.*
> —Act I, scene i, lines 7–8

Caius Marcius is the proper name of the hero of the play. He is to gain the surname of Coriolanus under circumstances to be described later.

Caius Marcius came from an old patrician family. According to Plutarch (in a passage Shakespeare quotes later in the play) he was a descendant of Ancus Marcius, the fourth king of Rome. This did not mean that Caius Marcius, as the descendant of a king, was necessarily a royalist.

Rome's seven kings could be divided into two groups, in fact, with Ancus Marcius belonging to the older. When he became king, he established an advisory body consisting of a hundred of the older representatives of the various clans that made up the city's people. This group of older men was the "Senate," so called from the Latin word for "old men." These senators were called "patricians" from the Latin word for "father," because they were, in theory, the fathers of the people. The word was then extended to all the old families from whom senators might be drawn.

According to tradition, Ancus Marcius brought in new colonists from among conquered tribes outside Rome, since the growing city could use the extra hands. These, however, were not granted the political powers of the old Romans. It was their descendants who became plebeians.

Ancus Marcius was not succeeded by his sons, but by a king called Tarquinius Priscus ("Tarquin the Elder"), who was an Etruscan from the north. (The Etruscans to the north of Rome were at that time the dominant people in Italy, and the succession of Tarquinius Priscus may be actually a sign of Etruscan overlordship of Rome—a situation softened in the Roman legends out of Roman pride.)

Under Tarquinius Priscus, Rome prospered materially, but the power of the king increased at the expense of the patricians. He was finally assassinated by those on the side of the old kings, but eventually the son of Tarquinius Priscus gained the throne. This was the Tarquinius Superbus who was expelled from Rome after the events outlined in *The Rape of Lucrece* (see page I–211).

Caius Marcius, by family tradition, then, would be against the Tarquinian notion of monarchy. And he would be strongly pro-patrician and anti-plebeian.

. . . dog to the commonalty

When the Second Citizen, a less extreme leader of the plebeian mob, expresses reservations against aiming at Marcius particularly, the First Citizen replies firmly:

> *Against him first: he's a very dog to the commonalty.*
>
> —Act I, scene i, lines 28–29

This is the key to Marcius' character. He is a "dog" to his enemies. He snarls and bites. Plutarch says of him: "he was so choleric and impatient, that he would yield to no living creature, which made him churlish, uncivil, and altogether unfit for any man's conversation."

That is his tragedy: the tragedy of his personality. What he might have gained, and ought to have gained for the better qualities within himself, he threw away by his perpetual anger and willfulness.

It may have been just this which was the challenge that interested Shakespeare and made him decide to write the play. In *Antony and Cleopatra* (see page I–317), which he had written a year or so earlier, Shakespeare shows us a flawed hero, Mark Antony, who sacrificed honor and worldly ambition to love and to sexual passion. In *Coriolanus* he shows us the reverse, a hero who served only military honor and who allowed nothing to stand in his way (with one exception).

Yet although Antony is loaded to the breaking point with weaknesses, while Marcius is stuffed to the bursting point with virtues, we end by loving Antony and feeling a cold dislike for Coriolanus. Surely Shakespeare is far too good a playwright to have done this by accident. Might not *Coriolanus* be viewed as a frigid satire of the military virtues; as an example of Shakespeare's distaste for war, a distaste that shows through even the official idolatry of the English hero-king in *Henry V* (see page II–481)?

. . . to please his mother . . .

When the Second Citizen urges in Marcius' defense that he has served his country well, the First Citizen admits that much but insists it was not done for Rome. He says:

> *. . . though soft-conscienced men can be content to say it was for his country, he did it to please his mother . . .*
>
> —Act I, scene i, lines 37–39

There is Marcius' one weakness. He loves his mother. And even that weakness is, looked at superficially, another piece of nobility. Why should not a man love his mother? Certainly the United States of today, with its Mother's Day and its semiofficial matriolatry, is no society in which to argue that to love one's mother is wrong, or even a weakness.

Yet it is made plain as the play progresses that the love-of-mother in Coriolanus' case is extreme. It is the clearest case of an Oedipal fixation in Shakespeare, far clearer than in the dubious case of Hamlet.

According to the legend, Marcius' father died while he was very young and the boy was then brought up by his mother. The rearing was successful in establishing a close relationship between them. Here are Plutarch's words: ". . . touching Marcius, the only thing that made him to love honor was the joy he saw his mother did take of him. For he thought nothing made him so happy and honorable, as that his mother might hear everybody praise and commend him, that she might always see him return with a crown upon his head, and that she might still embrace him with tears running down her cheeks for joy."

This sort of thing, we can see, is not calculated to endear him to Rome generally. Those plebeians who got only the rough side of Marcius' tongue and the harsh side of his advice on policy might not feel any necessity to be grateful for something he did only to please his mother. Let his mother reward him, not the people, and this is what the First Citizen seems to be implying.

Furthermore, Marcius' attitude as described by Plutarch and as adopted by Shakespeare is that of a boy, not a man. Marcius is a boy who never grew up, except physically. Emotionally he remains a boy, not only with respect to his mother but with respect to everything else. If we are to understand the play, this point must not be forgotten.

. . . To th'Capitol

While the citizens talk, there are shouts from offstage which seem to signify the revolt is spreading. The First Citizen cries out impatiently:

Why stay we prating here? To th'Capitol!
—Act I, scene i, lines 48–49

The city of Rome eventually spread out over seven hills. One of the earliest to be occupied was the Capitoline Hill. This had steep sides in some directions, which made it suitable for defense. A large temple to Jupiter was built upon it which could also serve as a last-ditch fortress.

The name of the hill is from a Latin word meaning "head," and the legend arose that a head or skull was uncovered when the foundations of the temple were being dug. The Senate met in the Capitol fortress and so it was the center of the city's politics; in that sense the hill was the head (or most important part) of the city, and perhaps that is how the name really arose.

Naturally, the plebeians would want to storm the Capitol and seize control of it.

Worthy Menenius Agrippa . . .

But now a patrician steps on the scene who is not assaulted. He is a very unusual patrician; one who can speak to the people bluffly and pleasantly and make himself liked by them—the antithesis of Marcius. The newcomer is Menenius Agrippa, and the Second Citizen identifies him at once as:

> Worthy Menenius Agrippa, one that hath always loved the people.
>
> —Act I, scene i, lines 52–53

Even the extremist First Citizen says, rather churlishly:

> He's one honest enough; would all the rest were so!
>
> —Act I, scene i, lines 54–55

Menenius Agrippa's role in history (even the legendary history of the times before 390 B.C., as purveyed by Livy and Plutarch) is confined to the one incident that is about to be related. Nothing else is known of him either before or after. Everything else about him in this play is Shakespeare's own invention.

In the actual tale told by Livy and Plutarch, the occasion is not a brawl in the street but, in a way, something more serious. The plebeians have decided to secede altogether. If Rome takes all and gives nothing, she is not a true mother and the plebeians will make one for themselves. They withdraw to a neighboring hill and prepare to found a city of their own.

This is a deadly danger for the patricians, for they need plebeian hands on the farms and in the army. What's more, Rome cannot endure the founding of a neighboring city that is bound to become and remain a deadly enemy. The plebeians must be brought back and, for a wonder, the Senate tried persuasion and gentleness. They sent Menenius Agrippa, a patrician with a reputation for good humor and with no record of animosity toward the plebeians.

A pretty tale . . .

Menenius urges the citizens to desist, saying the shortage of food is the fault of the gods, not of the patricians. The First Citizen answers bitterly that the patricians have cornered the food market and now grind the faces of the poor for their own profit. We are strongly tempted to believe the First Citizen, for all he speaks in prose where Menenius orates in gentle pentameters, especially since Menenius drops the subject and decides to be more indirect. He says:

> *I shall tell you*
> *A pretty tale; it may be you have heard it;*
> —Act I, scene i, lines 90–91

The tale he tells is the fable of the organs of the body rebelling against the belly. The organs complain that they do all the work while the belly gets all the food. The belly answers that it is his function to digest the food and send it out to all the body. Without the belly, all the rest of the organs would weaken and die. The Senate and the patricians are then compared to the belly by Menenius. Through their careful management of the commonwealth, the patricians distribute benefits to all.

The fable may sound well, but surely to the plebeians of the time it must have been unconvincing, since it was precisely their complaint that the patricians were *not* distributing benefits to all the commonwealth but were reserving them for themselves.

Plutarch says of the tale, "These persuasions pacified the people conditionally." Note the word "conditionally." Words alone were not enough. The people demanded a reform of the government and got it.

. . . let me use my sword . . .

Before Shakespeare gets to these reforms, however, he wants to bring on Marcius and display him as he is. Marcius comes whirling in, acknowledges Menenius' greetings in the briefest possible way, and grates out harshly to the citizens:

> *What's the matter, you dissentious rogues*
> *That, rubbing the poor itch of your opinion,*
> *Make yourself scabs?*
> —Act I, scene i, lines 165–67

Menenius is attended because he speaks gently. Does Marcius think he can get anywhere by scolding? It doesn't matter whether he does or not, for there is no other way he can act, and the First Citizen indicates that by his dryly ironic rejoinder:

> *We have ever your good word.*
>
> —Act I, scene i, line 167b

Marcius continues to rail, denouncing them as utterly untrustworthy. He says:

> *Trust ye?*
> *With every minute you do change a mind,*
> *And call him noble that was now your hate,*
> *Him vile that was your garland.*
>
> —Act I, scene i, lines 182–85

This is, of course, a standard complaint against the common people; that they are fickle and unreasoning. This dates back to the Greek historians, who showed that the Athenian democracy was subject to radical changes in its policies and that Athenian politicians suffered drastic changes in fortune at the hand of the fickle public—in contrast to the steady policies of Sparta, which was certainly no democracy. (And yet who would prefer the death-in-life of Sparta to the brilliance of Athens?)

Roman writers referred to the *mobile vulgus* ("fickle multitude") and about half a century after Shakespeare's death this was abbreviated to "mob," a word now used for any dangerous and disorderly crowd of people. Had Shakespeare had the use of the word it would undoubtedly have appeared somewhere in this speech.

In Elizabethan England, with its strong oligarchy, the view of the public by "gentlemen" was very much like the view of the Roman patricians. Shakespeare himself was born of a prosperous middle-class family and certainly held himself superior to those he considered plebeian. Furthermore, he was patronized by the aristocracy and liked to identify himself with them.

When, therefore, he had occasion to speak of the common people, he was rarely kind or sympathetic. He makes much of their dirtiness, greasiness, and bad breath. And he is never quite as unkind to them as in this play. This is one reason why *Coriolanus* is not one of Shakespeare's more popular plays in modern times. His social views embarrass mid-twentieth-century America.

It may be that Shakespeare is antiplebeian in this play partly because of the conditions in England at the time the play was written. The unpopular Scottish king, James VI, was on the English throne now as James I and there was a rising clamor against him. Voices from below were beginning to be heard against James's theory of absolute monarchy and against his contention that decisions in religion were entirely in the hand of the King. Those voices were to grow louder until (a generation after Shakespeare's death) they led England into revolution and James's son to the headsman's ax.

If Shakespeare was writing with at least part of his attention fixed on securing the approval of the aristocratic portion of his audience, on whose approval so much depended from an economic standpoint, this was the time for harsh words against the commons. The application would be seen.

The amazing thing, though, is that with all the animus against the commons which Shakespeare possesses, for both personal and economic reasons, he does not therefore make Marcius sympathetic. His integrity as a writer and his hatred of war forces Shakespeare to display Marcius' reaction to the commons as an overreaction, and the patrician champion loses us at the very start.

His response to the cry of the people for food, to their protest that they are starving, is:

> *Would the nobility lay aside their ruth,*
> *And let me use my sword, I'd make a quarry*
> *With thousands of these quartered slaves, as high*
> *As I could pick my lance.*
>
> —Act I, scene i, lines 198–201

We are acquainted, of course, with people who think the proper answer to the protesting poor is the policeman's club, the cattle prod, and the gun. Such people are difficult to like, and Marcius is one of them.

Five tribunes . . .

But then Marcius must grumble forth the news that the patricians have not done as he would have liked them to do. They have compromised instead and granted the plebeians a new kind of officer. Marcius describes them as:

> *Five tribunes to defend their vulgar wisdoms,*
> *Of their own choice. One's Junius Brutus—*
> *Sicinius Velutus, and—I know not. 'Sdeath!*
> *The rabble should have first unroofed the city,*
> *Ere so prevailed with me . . .*
>
> —Act I, scene i, lines 216–20

It was the grant of the tribunes, rather than Menenius' fable, that brought the plebeians back to Rome. The tribunes were officials drawn from the plebeian ranks and elected by the plebeians only. Their purpose was to safeguard the interests of the plebeians and to keep the patricians from passing laws they felt would be unfair to the common people. Eventually, indeed, the tribunes gained the power of stopping laws they disapproved of by merely crying out "Veto!" ("I forbid!"). Not all the power of the government could pass a law against a tribune's veto.

Actually, the institutions of the Republic developed only gradually and received their familiar form only by 367 B.C. However, later Roman historians tended to push back several of the features into the undocumented period before 390 B.C. to give them the added sanctity of extra ancientness. The history of the tribunate during the fifth century B.C. is quite obscure and the supposed first tribunes listed by Plutarch (he names only two out of the five and Shakespeare follows him in this) make no mark in actual history.

Is Junius Brutus a descendant or relative of the Lucius Junius Brutus who helped found the Republic (see page I-210)? From the name one would suppose so, yet if he were, he would be a patrician and it is of the essence that the tribunes are plebeians. Or was there some dim feeling on the part of the legendmakers that since a Junius Brutus was one of the first two consuls of the Republic, a Junius Brutus ought also to be one of the first two tribunes?

From the standpoint of the play, of course, it doesn't matter.

. . . the Volsces . . .

In any case, civil broils must now be buried in the face of a foreign menace. A messenger hurries on the scene asking for Marcius. He says:

> *The news is, sir, the Volsces are in arms.*
> —Act I, scene i, line 225

At this early stage in their history, the Romans were still fighting for the control of Latium, that section of west-central Italy that occupies a hundred miles of the coast southeast of Rome. It is the home of the Latin language.

The Volscians were the tribes occupying the southeastern half of Latium. Under the last kings of Rome, they along with the other Latin tribes had been part of a loose confederacy headed by Rome, and it may be that all were more or less under Etruscan control. With the expulsion of the Roman kings and the weakening of the Etruscan hold, the Latin tribes squabbled among themselves. The Volscians fought with the Romans throughout the fifth century B.C. and were in the end defeated. In Marcius' time, however, the long duel was only beginning.

Attend upon Cominius . . .

A deputation of senators comes to see Marcius now. He is their best warrior and they need his help. Marcius has no illusions that the fight will be an easy one, for the Volscians have a gallant leader, Tullus Aufidius. A senator says:

> Then, worthy Marcius,
> *Attend upon Cominius to these wars.*
> —Act I, scene i, lines 238–39

Cominius is one of the two consuls of Rome at this time. They were the chief executives of the city, having replaced the office of the ousted king. The consuls were elected for a one-year term, since the Romans felt that one year was insufficient for any consul to build up a large enough personal following to serve in making himself a king.

Two consuls were chosen, rather than one, since the rule was that no action could be taken without agreement between them. It seemed reasonable to suppose that neither consul could take any real steps toward tyranny without the other jealously stepping in to stop him.

The chief duties of the consuls were to be in charge of the armed forces of Rome and to lead the Roman armies in warfare. Cominius, as consul, was to be the army leader, and Marcius, who was not a consul, would have to be a subordinate officer.

The senators are clearly not at all certain that Marcius will agree to this; a commentary on his sullen spirit of self-absorption. Cominius says hastily:

> *It is your former promise.*
> —Act I, scene i, line 239

This time, at least, Marcius gives in at once and all sweep off the stage, leaving behind only the two newly appointed tribunes, Sicinius and Brutus. They had come in with the senators but had remained silent. Left alone, they make it clear that they resent Marcius' pride and his harsh taunts.

Sicinius wonders that Marcius can bear to serve as an underling with Cominius commanding, and Brutus suggests a cynical interpretation, saying that Marcius shrewdly schemes to avoid responsibility in case of disaster:

> *For what miscarries*
> *Shall be the general's fault, though he perform*
> *To th'utmost of a man; and giddy censure*
> *Will then cry out of Marcius "O, if he*
> *Had borne the business!"*
>
> —Act I, scene i, lines 267–71

Nowhere in the play, however, is Marcius given credit for so devious a nature. Brutus is simply putting his own style of shrewdness into Marcius' mind. What is much more likely is that Marcius doesn't care who commands and who does not, whom Rome praises and whom she does not. All he wants is a chance to fight so that, in any office, he can win his mother's praise.

. . . to guard Corioles

The fast Roman response to the Volscian threat forces the Volscians to hasten their own plans. Tullus Aufidius is consulting with the Volscian council and one of the Volscian senators says:

> *Noble Aufidius,*
> *Take your commission; hie you to your bands:*
> *Let us alone to guard Corioles.*
>
> —Act I, scene ii, lines 25–27

This council of war is taking place in Corioli (or Corioles), a town whose location is now uncertain, and this, in itself, is one of the signs that the story of Coriolanus is legendary. At the time of the traditional date of this war, 493 B.C. (a year after the plebeian uprising, although Shakespeare, in the interest of speeding the action, makes it take place immediately afterward), what records we have indicate that Corioli was not a Volscian city but was in alliance with that portion of Latium which was under Roman leadership.

It is very likely that the tales of Coriolanus that were dimly remembered had to be adjusted to account for the name. Why should Marcius be remembered as Coriolanus unless he had played a key role in the conquest of that city? So the conquest was assumed.

And why was Marcius eventually given the name of Coriolanus if it was *not* because of the conquest of the city? No one will ever know. For that matter, can we be certain that such a man as Coriolanus ever existed at all?

. . . Hector's forehead . . .

Now, at last, Marcius' mother, Volumnia, is introduced. So is his wife, Virgilia. Virgilia is, however, a shrinking girl, much dominated by her mother-in-law, who is pictured as the ideal Roman matron. She is a most formidable creature and we cannot help but wonder if Marcius' little-boy love for her is not intermingled with more than some little-boy fear.

Shakespeare makes it plain that Marcius has become something that is his mother's deliberate creation. Even when he was young, she tells her daughter-in-law proudly, all she could think of was how honor (that is, military glory) would become him. She says:

> To a cruel war I sent him, from whence he returned, his
> brows bound with oak.
> > —Act I, scene iii, lines 14–16

(An oak wreath was the reward granted a soldier who had saved the life of a fellow soldier.)

Virgilia timidly points out that Marcius might have been killed, but Volumnia says, grimly:

> I had rather had eleven die nobly for their country than
> one voluptuously surfeit out of action.
> > —Act I, scene iii, lines 25–27

And when Virgilia gets a little queasy over Volumnia's later reference to possible blood on Marcius' brow, Volumnia then says, in scorn at the other's weakness:

> Away, you fool! It [blood] more becomes a man
> Than gilt his trophy. The breasts of Hecuba,
> When she did suckle Hector, looked not lovelier
> Than Hector's forehead when it spit forth blood
> > —Act I, scene iii, lines 42–46

In later centuries the Romans invented a legend to the effect that they were descended from the Trojan hero Aeneas (see page I-20), and it is natural to read this back into early Roman history and to imagine that the early Romans identified strongly with the Trojans. Hector (page I-81) was Troy's greatest fighter.

. . . a gilded butterfly . . .

Volumnia's bloodthirsty and single-minded approach to the notion of military honor makes it plain why Marcius, trained by her, is what he is. But can it be that Shakespeare approves of this sort of mother and finds the product of her training to be admirable? Let's see what follows immediately!

Valeria, a friend of the family, comes to visit, and describes something she has observed that involves Marcius' young son. She says:

> *I saw him run after a gilded butterfly; and when he caught it, he let it go again; and after it again; and over and over he comes, and up again; catched it again; or whether his fall enraged him, or how 'twas, he did so set his teeth, and tear it.*
> —Act I, scene iii, lines 63–68

The promising child, in other words, plays cat-and-mouse with a butterfly and ends by killing it in a rage. But why a butterfly? Surely nothing can be as pretty, harmless, and helpless as a butterfly. It isn't possible that we can feel sympathetic for a child that would deliberately and sadistically kill one. And this is clearly the product of Volumnia's bringing up.

But can we really apply the unreasoning action of a young child to the behavior of the adult Marcius? Surely we can, for Shakespeare makes certain that we do. What does he have Volumnia say to Valeria's tale? She says, calmly:

> *One on's father's moods.*
> —Act I, scene iii, line 70

It seems reasonable to suppose that Shakespeare admires neither Volumnia's philosophy nor the individuals it produces.

. . . another Penelope . . .

Valeria wants Virgilia to come out on the town with her but Virgilia will not. Like a loyal wife, she will stay at home till her husband is back from the wars. Valeria says, cynically:

> *You would be another Penelope; yet, they say, all the yarn she spun in Ulysses' absence did but fill Ithaca full of moths.*
> —Act I, scene iii, lines 86–88

Penelope is the very byword of the faithful wife. Married to Ulysses

(see page I–90) but a couple of years when he went forth to Troy, she remained faithful for twenty years in his home island of Ithaca, till he returned. In the last several years, he was rumored dead and many suitors
clamored for her hand. She put them off with one ruse or another, the most
famous being that she wanted first to finish a shroud she was weaving for
Ulysses' aged father, Laertes. Every day she wove and every night she
ripped out what she had woven, keeping it up a long time before she was
caught. The story of Penelope and the suitors makes up a major portion
of Homer's *Odyssey*.

. . . to Cato's wish . . .

The Roman forces under Marcius and Titus Lartius (another valiant
Roman) are meanwhile laying siege to Corioli. They are met with Volscian
resolution and are beaten back at the first assault. Marcius, yelling curses
at his soldiers in his usual manner, rushes forward and manages to get
inside the city gates, which close behind him. He is alone in an enemy city.

Titus Lartius, coming up now, hears the news, and speaks of him as
already dead. He says, apostrophizing the as-good-as-dead Marcius:

> *Thou wast a soldier*
> *Even to Cato's wish, not fierce and terrible*
> *Only in strokes; but with thy grim looks and*
> *The thunder-like percussion of thy sounds*
> *Thou mad'st thine enemies shake . . .*
>
> —Act I, scene iv, lines 57–61

This is taken almost verbatim from Plutarch, where that biographer
describes Marcius as a soldier after Cato's heart. The Cato referred to is
Marcus Porcius Cato, often called Cato the Censor (an office which he held
with vigor), for he was a model of old-fashioned Roman virtue. He was
completely honest and completely bound to duty, but he was cold, cruel,
sour, miserly, and narrow-minded. He was heartless to his slaves and
lacked any tender feelings for his wife and children. As censor, he was
perfectly capable of fining a Roman patrician for kissing his own wife in
the presence of their children.

It was perfectly proper for Plutarch to quote Cato in this connection,
for he lived over three centuries after Cato. Shakespeare, however, is guilty
of negligence in placing the remark in Lartius' mouth without making the
necessary modification, for it now becomes an amusing anachronism. The
siege of Corioli took place, according to legend, in 493 B.C., and Cato
wasn't born till 243 B.C., two and a half centuries later (and didn't become
censor till 184 B.C.).

Caius Marcius Coriolanus

But Marcius is not dead. If the tale were not a legend, magnified in the telling, even if we allow a kernel of truth, he would undoubtedly be dead. Perhaps this part of the tale of Marcius was inspired by a similar incident in the life of Alexander the Great.

In 326 B.C. Alexander was conducting his last major campaign in what was then called India, but in a region which is now part of Pakistan. They laid siege to a town called Multan, which is located about 175 miles southwest of Lahore, on one of the chief tributaries of the Indus. In a fever of excitement, Alexander pressed forward to the walls and managed to climb them and leap into the city without looking to see whether the army was following or not.

For a while, he was alone in the midst of enemies. One or two men managed to join him and when Alexander was struck down and seriously wounded they protected him until the army made its way into the city. Alexander survived, but it was a very near thing.

Marcius does better than that, however. No one joins him and he appears on the battlements, bleeding, but not seriously wounded. Only now does the rest of the army, in a fever of enthusiasm, storm the city and take it.

Marcius then leads part of the army to join Cominius and together they defeat the Volscians under Tullus Aufidius.

Now the army rings with praises for Marcius, but when Titus Lartius tries to put those praises into words, Marcius says, gruffly:

> *Pray now, no more. My mother,*
> *Who has a charter to extol her blood,*
> *When she does praise me grieves me.*
> —Act I, scene ix, lines 13–15

This sounds like modesty, like superhuman modesty, but is it? Marcius is a loner. His universe consists of himself alone, plus his mother. He is willing to enter Corioli alone, to fight alone against an army; the soldiers under his command are but a source of annoyance to him.

Why, then, should he want their praise? Who are they to praise him? Far from this being a true mark of modesty, it might rather be interpreted as the sign of a most confounded arrogance. Only his mother has a right to praise him and even that is not entirely acceptable to him. In the remark, further, he naïvely reveals the fact that he places his mother (as far as the right of praise is concerned) above Rome.

Nevertheless, he is not to get away without some mark of favor. Cominius, the consul, gives him an added name, saying:

> . . . from this time,
> For what he did before Corioles, call him,
> With all th'applause and clamor of the host,
> Caius Marcius Coriolanus.
>
> —Act I, scene ix, lines 62–65

It was a Roman custom, when one of their generals won a signal victory over some particular foreign enemy, to give him an additional name taken from the conquered place or people. Sometimes the individual was thereafter known by his new title almost exclusively.

The most renowned case of this in Roman history is that of Publius Cornelius Scipio. Scipio was the final conqueror of Hannibal, the Carthaginian general, the greatest and most feared enemy Rome ever had in the days of its greatness, and certainly one of the most remarkable captains in the lamentable history of warfare. The battle in which Scipio finally overcame Hannibal was fought at Zama in 202 B.C., a city in northern Africa. As a consequence, the title "Africanus" was added to Scipio's name.

"Coriolanus" is formed in the same fashion. From this point on in the play, his speeches are marked "Coriolanus" rather than "Marcius" and it is the former name that is given to the tragedy itself.

. . . Lycurguses . . .

Back at Rome, the citizens are still waiting for news from the army. The two tribunes, Brutus and Sicinius, cannot help but hope for a little bad news, since that would weaken the position of Marcius (they don't yet know his new title).

Menenius, the friend of Marcius and one who, because of his age, considers himself practically a foster father of the younger man, is also on-stage and rails wittily at the uncomfortable tribunes, who lack the verbal agility to stand up to him. Menenius is particularly annoyed because the tribunes call Marcius proud, and at one point he says to them:

> Meeting such wealsmen as you are—I cannot call you
> Lycurguses . . .
>
> —Act II, scene i, lines 54–56

"Wealsmen" are statesmen, a term Menenius uses ironically, since he considers them anything but that. And lest their denseness allow them to mistake his remark for a compliment, he specifically denies that they can be compared to Lycurgus.

Lycurgus, according to tradition, was a Spartan leader of the ninth century B.C. who devised the social, economic, and political system under which the Spartans lived in ancient times. The Spartan aristocracy devoted themselves to a military regime that made even the Roman system look pallid. (Actually it was developed in the seventh century B.C. and may have been attributed to the legendary Lycurgus to give it greater authority.)

It was a narrow, constricted, miserable way of life that won the Spartans many victories and therefore gained them much praise by those who valued victories for themselves and who did not have to live in Sparta at the time. It cost Sparta everything else but military victory, and in the end the narrow and inflexible outlook it gave them cost them victory as well.

Nevertheless, Lycurgus remained as the byword for the statesman and lawgiver.

Menenius grows wordier and more articulate with each speech as the tribunes become more and more beaten down. Finally, he makes the direct comparison:

> Yet you must be saying Marcius is proud; who, in a cheap
> estimation, is worth all your predecessors since Deucalion.
> —Act II, scene i, lines 92–94

Deucalion was the sole male survivor of a great flood in the Greek legends (see page I–164) and from him all later men were considered to be descended.

. . . in Galen . . .

But now the three women enter—Volumnia, Virgilia, and Valeria—with news that Marcius is returning in victory. They have letters and there is one for Menenius.

The voluble old man is so elated at the news, and especially at the grand tale that there is a letter for him, that he throws his cap in the air and declares it is the best medicine he could have. He says:

> The most sovereign prescription in Galen is but empiricutic
> [quackish], and, to this preservative, of no betier report than
> a horse-drench.
> —Act II, scene i, lines 119–21

This is an even more amusing anachronism than the reference to Cato. Galen was a Greek physician who practiced in Rome and whose books, throughout the Middle Ages and into early modern times, were considered the last word in medical theory and practice. The only trouble is that he was at the height of his career about A.D. 180, nearly seven centuries *after* the time of Menenius.

. . . the repulse of Tarquin . . .

Menenius and Volumnia now engage in a grisly counting of wounds and scars on Marcius' body. Volumnia says:

> He received in the repulse of Tarquin seven hurts i'th'body.
> —Act II, scene i, lines 154–55

After the eviction of Tarquin (see page I–211), the ex-King made several attempts to regain power, first with the aid of the Etruscans and then with the aid of other Latin cities. He was defeated at each attempt, the final battle coming at Lake Regillus in 496 B.C., only two years before the date of the opening scene of *Coriolanus*.

I warrant him consul

Coriolanus himself comes now, and his new title is announced to the entire city. He kneels first of all to his mother, and only after her reminder does he address his wife. The city is wild over him and it is clear he can receive whatever honor or office it can bestow on him. Volumnia states, with satisfaction, what is in many minds:

> Only
> There's one thing wanting, which I doubt not but
> Our Rome will cast upon thee.
> —Act II, scene i, lines 206–8

It is the consulship itself obviously, and Volumnia, as usual, continues to guide her son toward the heights.

The two tribunes are also aware of the waiting consulship, and they are worried. Sicinius says:

> On the sudden,
> I warrant him consul.
> —Act II, scene i, lines 227–28

From their standpoint, nothing could be worse. Coriolanus' reactionary beliefs are well known. He would have killed the plebeians rather than compromise with them in the matter of tribunes. As a willful and determined consul, he might cancel that compromise. As Brutus says:

> Then our office may,
> During his power, go sleep.

—Act II, scene i, lines 228–29

Their only hope is that Coriolanus, through his own pride, will ruin his own chances.

At sixteen years

We move swiftly to the Capitol, the seat of the government, where the people are gathered to elect the new consuls, of whom Coriolanus is odds-on favorite to be one.

However, to achieve the goal, Coriolanus must get the vote of the people, and the way in which this was done was to flatter and cajole them, very much as in our own time. In early Roman times, it was customary for a candidate for the consulate to dress humbly, speak softly, and show the scars won in battle. He did so in an unadorned white toga (hence our word "candidate," from the Latin word for "dressed in white").

The routine begins with the equivalent of a nominating speech from Cominius, the then-consul, and it sounds very much (allowing for changes in times and manners) like a nominating speech one might make today. Cominius begins:

> At sixteen years,
> When Tarquin made a head for Rome, he fought
> Beyond the mark of others.

—Act II, scene ii, lines 88–90

If we allow Tarquin's earliest battle to regain Rome to have been in 509 B.C. and if Coriolanus was sixteen then, we can say he was born in 525 B.C. and was thirty-two years old at the taking of Corioli. If the reference is to one of Tarquin's later attempts, then Coriolanus was younger than thirty-two.

Be taken from the people

The eloquent summary by Cominius of a career of heroic battling wins over the patricians and Menenius says it remains only to speak to the people. Coriolanus demurs rather churlishly, and the tribunes, seeing their chance, at once demand that the candidate live up to the letter of the custom.

Coriolanus has this to say of the custom:

> *It is a part*
> *That I shall blush in acting, and might well*
> *Be taken from the people.*
>
> —Act II, scene ii, lines 145–47

The tribunes could ask no better attitude than that. To say baldly that he wishes to take privileges from the people is absolutely no way to get their vote, and the tribunes rush away to see to it that the plebeians are made aware of Coriolanus' attitude.

. . . ask it kindly

Coriolanus does put on the uniform of humility, grumbling fiercely at every stage of the game and keeping poor Menenius in a sweat, for the old man is working overtime to keep him quiet and respectful just long enough.

Coriolanus cannot be so. Try as he might, he ends by being contemptuous as the voting citizens approach. He asks one of them:

> *Well then, I pray, your price o'th'consulship?*
>
> —Act II, scene iii, lines 77–78

To which the citizen makes a most reasonable reply, giving the price of anything requested, however deserving it may be:

> *The price is, to ask it kindly.*
>
> —Act II, scene iii, line 79

And that is precisely what Coriolanus, thanks to his mother's teachings, cannot do.

. . . in free contempt

Almost creaking in the attempt, Coriolanus manages to bend an absolute minimum so that he might make it seem, to inquiring citizens, that he does indeed "ask it kindly." That, combined with his great reputation of the moment, lures the people into promising to vote for him.

It is only afterward, by comparing notes, that they realize his bending was more seeming than actual and that he did not, for instance, actually show his scars to anyone. (This too sounds like modesty, but it can be interpreted as the result of arrogance. He will not stoop to win the approval of anyone. He wants it as his right and without question.)

The tribunes are disgusted that the plebeians have been so easily fooled, and Brutus demands impatiently:

> Did you perceive
> He did solicit you in free contempt
> When he did need your loves; and do you think
> That his contempt shall not be bruising to you
> When he hath power to crush?
>
> —Act II, scene iii, lines 205–9

The plebeians, seeing the good sense in this, veer about and decide to withdraw their approval while there is still time and the official vote has not yet been taken.

(Plutarch says that Coriolanus actually showed his scars and won their favor more fairly. It was only when, on the actual voting day, he showed up with an escort of patricians, in all his pomp and pride, that the plebeians turned from him. Shakespeare's modification fits better the personality the dramatist has decided to portray.)

. . . Numa's daughter's son

The plebeians are rather embarrassed at having to reverse their votes and the tribunes offer to take the blame. They say the plebeians might claim to have been against Coriolanus all along but that the tribunes had talked them into favoring him. Now, in turning against him, they had merely shaken off the tribunes' propaganda.

This seems awfully poor. The tribunes were the very spearhead of the antipatrician and, in particular, anti-Coriolanus, movement. Could the patricians for a moment believe that they had spoken in favor of Coriolanus? Or was Shakespeare merely seizing the opportunity to insert a passage from Plutarch that would lend another bit of historical authenticity to the play?

He has Brutus tell them all the wonderful things the tribunes would have said about Coriolanus in persuading the plebeians to vote for him:

> The noble house o'th'Marcians, from whence came
> That Ancus Marcius, Numa's daughter's son,
> Who after great Hostilius here was king;
> Of the same house Publius and Quintus were
> That our best water brought by conduits hither;
>
> —Act II, scene iii, lines 244–48

This is straight out of North's translation of Plutarch, almost word for word.

The Numa referred to is Numa Pompilius, who reigned as second king of Rome, coming to the throne, according to legend, in 716 B.C., after the death of Romulus, Rome's founder. He was a mild and exemplary king, upon whom Roman legend fixed the founding of Roman religion. There was peace in his reign and he was always looked back to as an ideal ruler.

He reigned till 673 B.C. and was followed by Tullus Hostilius, who ruled till 641 B.C. and who is also mentioned in this passage.

Following Hostilius, the throne was voted to Ancus Marcius, who, as the passage states, was a grandson of Numa on his mother's side. Thus, Coriolanus was descended from two of Rome's seven kings.

So much is legendary. The next is probably anachronistic. The city of Rome, in its great days, had its water supplied through aqueducts. No other city of ancient or medieval times had such an elaborate water system. In fact, Rome had a better water system than Shakespeare's London did. Naturally, writers of both ancient and later times tended to be awed by Rome's aqueducts and, if anything, to overemphasize them.

The Rome of Coriolanus' day was still a small town, quite rude and uncivilized. It certainly had no elaborate aqueducts, but relied on wells and on the Tiber River. The first important aqueducts to be built were constructed in 312 B.C., nearly two centuries after Coriolanus' time.

And Censorinus . . .

Brutus continues listing Coriolanus' ancestors:

> *And Censorinus that was so surnamed*
> *And nobly named so, twice being censor,*
> *Was his great ancestor.*
> —Act II, scene iii, lines 244–51

It is very unlikely that Censorinus could have existed. He too must be an anachronism born of the deliberate putting back of Roman customs into the legendary days before the Gallic sack. In Coriolanus' time, there had scarcely been time for one man to serve as censor twice, especially since the office was not founded till 443 B.C., half a century after the events in this play.

. . . to Antium

While waiting for the vote, Coriolanus discusses foreign affairs with the other soldiers, Cominius and Titus Lartius. The Volscians, while defeated, have not been crushed, and Tullus Aufidius, their great champion, still lives. Titus Lartius had seen him under a safe-conduct and says:

> On safeguard he came to me; and did curse
> Against the Volsces, for they had so vilely
> Yielded the town. He is retired to Antium.
>
> —Act III, scene i, lines 9–11

Antium is a coastal Latin town, thirty-three miles south of Rome. (That is the measure of Rome's as yet infant state, that its chief enemies, even after a retreat, were yet little more than thirty miles away.)

Antium's original fame was as a Volscian stronghold, as it is in this play, and it was not made fully subject to Rome till 341 B.C., a century and a half after Coriolanus' time. In the days of Rome's greatness, it was a favorite seaside resort of wealthy Romans. The Emperor Nero was born there and built a magnificent villa there.

The modern Italian version of its name is Anzio and under that name it gained a grisly, if fleeting, notoriety during World War II. An Allied amphibious force landed there on January 22, 1944, forming the Anzio bridgehead. It was hoped that this would link up quickly with other forces advancing up the Italian peninsula, but strong German resistance kept the bridgehead bloodily in being for four months, the linkage with the main Allied forces not taking place till May 25.

. . . this Triton . . .

As Coriolanus and his friends move on to the Senate, they are stopped by the tribunes and get the astonishing news that Coriolanus, who thought he had clinched the vote, is in disfavor with the plebeians after all and is to be denied the consulship. The tribunes make no effort to soften the blow and present the matter arrogantly in the hope that Coriolanus will burst into a rage and harm his own cause further.

He does. Rather than attempt to placate the tribunes, he plainly states his extreme rightist position concerning the plebeians.

Then, when the tribune Sicinius orders the raging Coriolanus to remain where he is and peremptorily forbids him to advance toward the Capitol, Coriolanus repeats Sicinius' words with the utter scorn of the born patrician for someone he views as a lowborn rascal. He says:

> Shall remain!
> Hear you this Triton of the minnows? Mark you
> His absolute "shall"?
>
> —Act III, scene i, lines 88–90

Triton was a son of Neptune (Poseidon) in the Greek myths and was pictured as a merman—fish from the waist down. He was usually depicted as blowing a blast on a large sea shell, a blast that might either rouse the winds or calm the sea. In either case, he controlled the waves. Thus, the tribune was being mocked as one who controlled a herd of insignificant rabble and thought he was powerful in consequence. He was a Triton, but of nothing but minnows.

. . . Hydra here . . .

Coriolanus turns on the patricians as well, for he maintains that they have given rise to this trouble by foolishly appeasing the plebeians and granting them rights instead of beating them down by force. He says:

> *You grave but reckless senators, have you thus*
> *Given Hydra here to choose an officer,*
> —Act III, scene i, lines 92–93

The Hydra was a monster that was killed by Hercules as his second labor (see page I–24). It was pictured as a huge sea creature with a dog-like body and eight or nine heads, one of which was immortal. (The picture may have arisen as an improvement on the eight-tentacled octopus.)

Later mythmakers improved matters by giving the Hydra fifty heads, or one hundred, or even ten thousand. Furthermore, as each head was cut off, two new ones grew into place instantly. Again, the creature was pictured as so poisonous its very odor could kill, and so on.

Hercules managed anyway. Each time he cut off a head, he had an assistant sear the stump with fire to prevent new growths. The immortal head he buried under a huge rock and thus, finally, the monster was killed.

But this made the Hydra a byword for anything with many heads, or anything which reappeared when dispatched. An intricate social difficulty, which bobs up again after each effort made to cure matters, is "Hydra-headed," and in our own times it would seem that all social problems are of this nature.

Again, the word may well be applied to a mob and it is this metaphor that is being used by Coriolanus. The decision as to the choice of consul has been handed over to the many-headed multitude.

The aediles . . .

Coriolanus continues in this way, in overwhelming rage, despite all attempts by Menenius and other patricians with common sense to stop him.

Finally, he threatens to take away the plebeians' political gains by force.

Now the tribunes have all they want. Not only has Coriolanus lost any possible chance of gaining the plebeian vote; he has committed actual treason by advocating unconstitutional methods of procedure. Brutus cries out:

> *The aediles, ho! Let him be apprehended.*
>
> —Act III, scene i, lines 171–72

The aediles were plebeian officials who had come into existence at the same time the tribunes had. They had a number of responsibilities in their time. They were in charge of the streets, of the distribution of grain, of the public celebrations. Here they appear in their role as protectors of the tribunes; officers empowered to arrest those who threatened the tribunal safety.

. . . to th'rock Tarpeian . . .

Naturally, Coriolanus is not going to submit tamely to arrest; nor, for that matter, are the patricians ready to see him arrested. The aediles can do nothing by themselves, but in a moment the stage swarms with plebeians coming to the aid of their tribunes. A full-fledged riot is in progress, despite everything Menenius can do to try to calm matters.

The tribune Sicinius manages to seize the floor and denounces Coriolanus, demanding not only his arrest, but his instant conviction of treason and his execution.

> *Therefore lay hold of him;*
> *Bear him to th'rock Tarpeian, and from thence*
> *Into destruction cast him.*
>
> —Act III, scene i, lines 211–13

The Tarpeian Rock is a cliff that formed part of the Capitoline Hill (see page I–217). To explain its name a legend arose in later times that went as follows:

In the first decades of Rome's existence, when it was under its founder and first king, Romulus, there was war with the Sabines, a tribe of the vicinity. The Sabines laid siege to the Capitoline Hill and their chance at victory came through Tarpeia, the daughter of the Roman commander who held sway over the defending forces.

The Sabines managed to persuade Tarpeia to open the gates for them in return for what they wore on their left arms. (Tarpeia set that condition with reference to the gold bracelets they wore there.) That night she secretly opened the gates, and the first few Sabines, as they entered, threw their shields at her, for they wore their shields on their left arms too. The Sabines, who (like most people) were willing to make use of traitors, but didn't like them, in this way kept their bargain.

The first criminal to be executed on the Capitoline Hill gave her name, therefore, to the later place of execution. (The story was undoubtedly made up to account for the name and is very unlikely to have even the slightest foundation in historical fact.)

. . . his trident

Coriolanus draws his sword. He is certainly not going to be led tamely to execution, and the riot sharpens. When the plebeians are temporarily driven off, Menenius and the other patricians manage, just barely, to persuade Coriolanus to leave. He is forced away for his own safety and because there can be no peacemaking as long as he is there to fire up popular resentment with his own strident tongue.

Menenius says of him when he is gone:

> *His nature is too noble for the world:*
> *He would not flatter Neptune for his trident,*
> *Or Jove for's power to thunder. His heart's his mouth:*
> —Act III, scene i, lines 254–56

Jupiter (Jove) has the lightning bolt as his chief weapon. Neptune's trident ("three teeth") is the three-pointed spear with which he (like Triton and his shell) calmed the waves or drove them to fury. Both lightning bolt and trident were unique attributes, and if Coriolanus would not stoop to beg for them, how much less would he stoop for a mere consulship.

And yet does Menenius really believe that this is a sign of nobility—or of stupidity? In his very next speech, he bursts out:

> *What the vengeance!*
> *Could he not speak 'em fair?*
> —Act III, scene i, lines 261–62

When the plebeians return, Menenius just barely manages to talk them out of their determination for instant execution and gains Coriolanus the chance of a trial.

I muse my mother

Coriolanus is at home, utterly unrepentant. He feels he has done completely right and would do it again at whatever risk. Only one thing bothers him. His mother, somehow, is not happy. Coriolanus says:

> *I muse my mother*
> *Does not approve me further, who was wont*
> *To call them* [the plebeians] *woolen vassals . . .*
>
> —Act III, scene ii, lines 7–9

And when his mother comes in, he says to her in a child's aggrieved tone:

> *I talk of you:*
> *Why did you wish me milder? Would you have me*
> *False to my nature? Rather say I play*
> *The man I am.*
>
> —Act III, scene ii, lines 13–16

But she *does* wish him milder. It is not because she (or Menenius for that matter) are more liberal than Coriolanus or less likely to use harsh measures. It is a matter of being more politic. First get the consulship, by any means, and then, with power, crush the plebeians. She says:

> *I have a heart as little apt as yours,*
> *But yet a brain that leads my use of anger*
> *To better vantage.*
>
> —Act III, scene ii, lines 29–31

Menenius and the rest are urging him now to stand trial voluntarily, to repent his words and, in effect, crawl a little. Coriolanus is horrified at the very thought, but his mother adds her pleas, saying in one phrase exactly what is wrong with him:

> *You are too absolute;*
>
> —Act III, scene ii, line 39

But that, of course, is her own fault, since she taught him to treat the world as though it consisted of nothing but gilded butterflies which he might tear apart at a mindless whim.

She tells him now flatly that he must treat this as a stratagem of war. He would play a part to deceive an enemy in arms and cajole a town to surrender. Let him now play a part to deceive the plebeians. (There is no thought in the mind of Volumnia or the other patricians—or probably in those of Shakespeare's audience—that such a course of action is dishonorable.)

To force Coriolanus to do this, Volumnia does not scruple to pull hard at the Oedipal ties that bind him to her:

> *I prithee now, sweet son, as thou hast said*
> *My praises made thee first a soldier, so,*
> *To have my praise for this, perform a part*
> *Thou hast not done before.*
>
> —Act III, scene ii, lines 107–10a

That is it. Coriolanus would not be swayed by thoughts of his own safety, by the city's danger, by his friend's reasoning, but once his mother has pled, he says:

> *Well, I must do't.*
>
> —Act III, scene ii, line 110b

For a moment, though, his resolution wavers even now. He can't go through with it. Thereupon Volumnia throws up her hands and tells him angrily to do as he pleases. At that, Coriolanus promptly gives in, out of the absolute terror of being in the position of disobeying his mother's wishes. He says, in little-boy terms:

> *Pray, be content:*
> *Mother, I am going to the marketplace;*
> *Chide me no more.*
>
> —Act III, scene ii, lines 130–32

And yet, after all that, when he comes to trial, he can no more hold his tongue than he can jump to the moon. It is an easy task for the tribunes to irritate him into madness again. He is convicted of treason and condemned, not to death at the Tarpeian Rock, but to lifelong exile. (This is actually supposed to have taken place in 491 B.C.)

It is a politic commutation of sentence, for the tribunes could now say that Coriolanus had deserved death, but that they had shown mercy out of consideration for his services in war.

. . . to pluck from them their tribunes . . .

Coriolanus leaves the city, after showing himself surprisingly cheerful, firm, resolute, and in good heart, cheering up his mother and his friends. (Plutarch describes the leave-taking similarly.)

Shakespeare has him make a significant comment, however. Coriolanus says:

> *I shall be loved when I am lacked.*
>
> —Act IV, scene i, line 15

This is a strange optimism on his part. He does not show elsewhere in this play any such general confidence in his fellowmen. It almost sounds as though he has something specific in mind; that he has firm information that his friends intend to take action to bring him back; even unconstitutional action.

That this may be so is strengthened by an odd scene that follows hard thereafter and which seems somewhat irrelevant to the action. A Roman named Nicanor and a Volscian named Adrian meet somewhere between Rome and Antium. Their speeches are ascribed merely to "Roman" and "Volsce." They appear nowhere else in the play and the only purpose of the scene is to highlight gathering treason in Rome on the part of the patricians.

The Roman says:

> . . . *the nobles receive so to heart the banishment of that worthy Coriolanus, that they are in a ripe aptness to take all power from the people and to pluck from them their tribunes forever.*
>
> —Act IV, scene iii, lines 21–25

To attain this end, it may be that the patricians are even considering allying themselves with the common enemy. The Volscian had said of his own people:

> . . . *they are in a most warlike preparation, and hope to come upon them* [the Romans] *in the heat of their division.*
>
> —Act IV, scene iii, lines 17–19

The Roman's response to this news of the Volscian activity is:

> *I am joyful to hear of their readiness . . .*
>
> —Act IV, scene iii, lines 48–50

My birthplace hate I . . .

Yet the next scene does not follow this up. There is a sudden break. Coriolanus has made his way to Antium. It is his intention to seek out Tullus Aufidius himself and throw himself upon his mercy. He says:

> *My birthplace hate I, and my love's upon*
> *This enemy town. I'll enter. If he slay me,*
> *He does fair justice; if he give me way,*
> *I'll do his country service.*
>
> —Act IV, scene iv, lines 23–26

What happened? According to the previous scene, it looked as though there were a conspiracy to bring Coriolanus back, even with Volscian help. Nothing further of that is mentioned in the play. Plutarch, to be sure, says that the nobles turned against Coriolanus, but only after the exiled man had joined the Volscians. As for his motive in joining the enemy, Plutarch cites merely rage and desire for revenge.

Yet it almost seems as though Shakespeare had something better in mind . . .

It often happened in the history of the Greek cities that there were internal disturbances between the social classes and that the leaders of one side or the other would be exiled. In such cases, it was common for the exiles to join a foreign enemy and fight their own city with the aid of their sympathizers within, as was the case of Alcibiades, for instance (see page I–142), some eighty years after the time of Coriolanus. (Indeed, Plutarch gives his biographies of Coriolanus and Alcibiades as a pair, showing himself aware of the similarities in their histories.)

It was this constant civil war and almost constant treason that helped bring down the Greeks and place them at last at the mercy of first the Macedonians and then the Romans.

It never happened in Rome. There were internecine struggles within the city in plenty throughout the history of the Republic, but *never* in the face of an outside enemy. When the foreign armies invaded, all Romans locked arms and this was never so remarkable or admirable as when Hannibal nearly ruined the realm two and a half centuries after the time of Coriolanus. It was this which saved Rome and brought her to world empire at last.

It would almost seem, then, as though there were a missing scene here. Perhaps there should be a scene in Rome after the meeting of the Roman and Volsce, one in which the patricians are meditating treason. The news of the Volscian invasion comes, and after some soul searching, Cominius might rise and insist that the city must come before class and that even Coriolanus must be sacrificed in the greater need of the defense of Rome. And with that the conspiracy would collapse.

. . . our dastard nobles . . .

Coriolanus, hearing of this, is more than disappointed. It is the last straw. *Everyone* has deserted him. Surely it must be this which makes him turn to the Volscians. Plutarch doesn't have it this way, but Plutarch is only repeating a legend and in my opinion he could have worked it out better at this point. Shakespeare seems to have started in this direction and then never wrote or dropped out the crucial scene.

It is only that missing scene that can explain what happens next. Coriolanus makes his way, in disguise, to the house of Tullus Aufidius, who is there presiding over a feast to the Volscian nobles, and reveals himself as a suppliant. He tells Aufidius he has nothing left but his name:

> *The cruelty and envy of the people,*
> *Permitted by our dastard nobles, who*
> *Have all forsook me, hath devoured the rest.*
>   —Act IV, scene v, lines 78–80

Why "dastard nobles?" How have they "forsook" him? Only that missing scene would make this plain and account for the colossal bitterness of Coriolanus during the remainder of the play, against not only the plebeians, but the entire city.

The Coriolanus legend up to this point, by the way, bears a suspicious resemblance to the tale of Themistocles, a famous Athenian who was actually a contemporary of Coriolanus (except that Themistocles is a historical character and Coriolanus is not).

Themistocles was the moving spirit behind the Athenian-led Greek victory over the Persians in 480 B.C. (thirteen years after the supposed capture of Corioli). After the defeat, however, when Athens was secure, Themistocles' growing pride offended the Athenians. About 472 B.C. he was exiled from the city. In exile, evidence of treason was found against him and he had to make his way to Persia itself as the only place he could be safe.

On his way there he passed through the city of a man who was his personal enemy—Admetus, King of the Molossians. (Molossia was later known as Epirus and is, in modern times, called Albania.)

Themistocles came to Admetus in disguise and appealed to him as a fugitive, just as Coriolanus appealed to Aufidius.

Here the stories part company, however. Themistocles was accepted by Admetus and finally made his way to Persia, where he lived out the remainder of his life. He never took any actual action against Athens.

Coriolanus did not wish escape. He wished revenge.

Joined with Aufidius . . .

Aufidius accepts Coriolanus' help joyfully. In fact, he offers him generalship over half the army, for what may seem to us perfectly valid reasons. It may seem odd to take the chance of turning over half his forces to someone who until recently had been the chief enemy of the Volscians, but by now Aufidius must know Coriolanus' character well. He must know that Coriolanus has in his mind room for nothing but rage. If the rage is now turned against Rome, the breach between man and city will be made permanent. Coriolanus will have to continue aiding the Volscians, placing his fighting ability and his inside knowledge of Rome at Volscian disposal. And then, when Rome is utterly defeated and wiped out, Coriolanus can be taken care of.

Rome, meanwhile, is in a temporary state of utter peace and the tribunes congratulate themselves at having brought things to such a happy conclusion. The bad news comes soon enough, however. A messenger dashes in saying:

> *It is spoke freely out of many mouths,*
> *How probable I do not know, that Marcius,*
> *Joined with Aufidius, leads a power 'gainst Rome,*
> > —Act IV, scene vi, lines 65–67

Perhaps this is why the missing scene is missing (either taken out or never written). For the missing scene to have worked, there would have had to be news of a Volscian advance, followed by a patrician refusal to abandon the city, so that Coriolanus would have had to join the enemy in a rage. But then he would merely be joining a marching army as a hanger-on.

This way, the Volscians don't move until Coriolanus joins them, and the news arrives that not only is the enemy approaching but the exiled Coriolanus is at their head. So, for the sake of this added drama, the missing scene is removed. It means that the meeting between the Roman and the Volsce is made irrelevant and Coriolanus' desertion to the Volscians and his anger against the "dastard nobles" left inadequately motivated. In this case, apparently, Shakespeare had his choice of two lines of development and did not manage to make a clear decision.

. . . cowardly nobles . . .

The failure to make a clear decision between the two courses of development haunts this sixth scene of the fourth act. At first the patricians seem rather exultant about Coriolanus' assault. Cominius says of the Volscians:

> *they follow him*
> *Against us brats with no less confidence*
> *Than boys pursuing summer butterflies,*
> —Act IV, scene vi, lines 93–95

Cominius is actually proud of Coriolanus' ascendancy over the Volscians, but note the picture of butterfly killing again. It is as though Shakespeare were reminding us that a child who is brought up as a butterfly killer may end as a city destroyer.

In the absence of the missing scene, it is perhaps here that the patricians ought to overcome their sympathy and admiration for Coriolanus and decide that patriotism takes priority. The necessary speech does not occur (perhaps because it was originally in the lost scene and was not shifted when the scene was lost). That it may have at one time been present might be indicated by a bitter remark of Menenius to the tribunes:

> *We loved him, but, like beasts*
> *And cowardly nobles, gave way unto your clusters.*
> —Act IV, scene vi, lines 122–23

Of course, it might refer to the patricians acceding to the sentence of exile.

. . . more proudlier

Yet all is not well with Coriolanus, either. He is still Coriolanus and can no more bend to the Volscians, now that he is leading them, than he could ever bend to the Romans. The Volscian officers are uneasy and even Tullus Aufidius is unhappy, saying:

> *He bears himself more proudlier,*
> *Even to my person, than I thought he would*
> *When first I did embrace him; yet his nature*
> *In that's no changeling . . .*
> —Act IV, scene vii, lines 8–11

And yet he must be used, for he is conquering Rome without even having to fight. Aufidius says:

All places yield to him ere he sits down,
And the nobility of Rome are his;
The senators and patricians love him too.
—Act IV, scene vii, lines 28–30

Apparently, even though the patricians of Rome have agreed to resist, there remain some who cling more tightly to party than to country. And even those who are intending to resist can do so with only half a heart.

And yet can the patricians honestly think that the Volscians are willing to serve as nothing more than a bunch of errand boys for them, to help them back to power out of love and kindness? The outside power, brought in to help in an internal fight, stays (all history shows) to help itself at the expense of all. And Aufidius says, at the end of the scene, apostrophizing the absent Coriolanus (to whom he refers by the familiar first name as though the man is someone he can now consider a tool or servant):

When, Caius, Rome is thine,
Thou art poor'st of all; then shortly art thou mine
—Act IV, scene vii, lines 56–57

The patricians who decide to resist Coriolanus may be moved by abstract love of country, but they may also be moved by a realization of the danger of accepting foreign help under any circumstances. This is something the Greeks never learned (and few nations since).

. . . one poor grain or two . . .

Soon Rome knows the worst. It is Coriolanus' vengeful desire to burn it to the ground. Surrender will not satisfy him; only destruction will. (This is purely psychotic unless the patricians had specifically deserted Coriolanus in the scene I postulate to be missing.)

Cominius, the ex-consul, and Coriolanus' old general, had gone to plead and had been met coldly. Cominius had reminded Coriolanus of his friends in the city and reports that:

His answer to me was,
He could not stay to pick them in a pile
Of noisome musty chaff. He said 'twas folly,
For one poor grain or two, to leave unburnt
And still to nose th'offense.
—Act V, scene i, lines 24–28

Even at best, with all possible motive, Coriolanus seems to have skirted the edge of madness here, for as Menenius points out:

> *For one poor grain or two!*
> *I am one of those; his mother, wife, his child,*
> —Act V, scene i, lines 28–29

There seems little hope for penetrating the red veil of madness that has closed over Coriolanus' vengeful mind. Cominius says:

> *. . . all hope is vain*
> *Unless his noble mother and his wife,*
> *Who (as I hear) mean to solicit him*
> *For mercy to his country.*
> —Act V, scene i, lines 70–74

Wife, mother, child . . .

Even this faint possibility seems to wither. Menenius is urged to try his luck with Coriolanus, but he is thrust scornfully away and Coriolanus denies that anyone, even his dearest, can sway him. He says to Menenius:

> *Wife, mother, child, I know not. My affairs*
> *Are servanted to others.*
> —Act V, scene ii, lines 83–84

Has Coriolanus the strength to turn against his own mother? Perhaps, but only because he has a substitute. He remains the little boy who must have parental approval. Having brutally turned away Menenius, he turns to Aufidius and seeks approval with what might almost be a simper:

> *This man, Aufidius,*
> *Was my beloved in Rome; yet thou behold'st.*
> —Act V, scene ii, lines 93–94

Aufidius knows his man. Gravely, he gives him what he wants and tells him he is a good boy:

> *You keep a constant temper.*
> —Act V, scene ii, line 95

. . . I'll speak a little

But now the women come: his wife, his mother, the fair Valeria. His young son is also there.

Coriolanus kneels to his mother, but holds firm, saying:

> *Do not bid me*
> *Dismiss my soldiers, or capitulate*
> *Again with Rome's mechanics. Tell me not*
> *Wherein I seem unnatural. Desire not*
> *T'allay my rages and revenges with*
> *Your colder reasons.*
>
> —Act V, scene iii, lines 81–86

He is determined to place his own grievances above Rome and wishes to cancel his mother's arguments even before she makes them.

But now Volumnia, in a speech of noble eloquence, shows that she places Rome before him and herself. Too late she tries to teach him that life is not a matter of blows and rages alone; that there are softer and nobler virtues:

> *Think'st thou it honorable for a noble man*
> *Still* [always] *to remember wrongs?*
>
> —Act V, scene iii, lines 154–55

And when Coriolanus remains obdurate, she rises to return to Rome to die and then uses the one remaining weapon at her disposal, and the most terrible of all:

> *Come, let us go.*
> *This fellow had a Volscian to his mother;*
> *His wife is in Corioles, and his child*
> *Like him by chance. Yet give us our dispatch.*
> *I am hushed until our city be a-fire,*
> *And then I'll speak a little.*
>
> —Act V, scene iii, lines 177–82

With a terrible understatement, she makes it clear that when the city is burning, she will call down a dying mother's curse upon her son.

O my mother, mother . . .

And before this Coriolanus cannot stand. He collapses utterly and cries out:

> *O my mother, mother! O!*
> *You have won a happy victory to Rome;*
> *But, for your son—believe it, O, believe it!—*
> *Most dangerously you have with him prevailed,*
> *If not most mortal to him.*
>
> —Act V, scene iii, lines 185–89

He turns away; he will not fight further against Rome; and he asks Aufidius to make peace. Aufidius is willing to do so. With Coriolanus not in the fight, Rome will be difficult to take. It would be better to make the peace, use the results against Coriolanus, and perhaps fight Rome another time when Coriolanus is not present either to help or to hinder. So much we can assume. Aufidius actually says, in an aside, that he is glad at this development since it will help him ruin Coriolanus.

. . . made for Alexander

In Rome Menenius is gloomy. He tells an anxious Sicinius that he doesn't think Volumnia will prevail; after all, he himself did not. He describes Coriolanus in the most forbidding terms as nothing but a war machine:

> *He sits in his state as a thing made for Alexander.*
>
> —Act V, scene iv, lines 22–23

He is, in other words, as immobile, as aloof, as untouched by humanity as a statue of Alexander the Great. This is an anachronism, for Alexander lived nearly a century and a half after Coriolanus and died in 323 B.C.

But almost at that moment comes the news that Coriolanus has given in and that the army is gone. Rome goes mad with joy and flocks to the gates to greet Volumnia.

. . . thou boy of tears

The Volscian army is back in Corioles now and Aufidius is ready to strike and rid himself of the incubus he had earlier accepted; an incubus that would have been worth its cost if it had brought them the destruction of Rome. But it had not, for, as Aufidius says bitterly:

> *. . . at his nurse's tears*
> *He whined and roared away your victory;*
>
> —Act V, scene vi, lines 97–98

Coriolanus, stupefied, calls on Mars, the god of war, and Aufidius says, with contempt:

> *Name not the god, thou boy of tears!*
> —Act V, scene vi, line 101

For the first time, Coriolanus has been openly called what he is. He is a boy; a tearful, butterfly-killing mamma's boy who never grew up except in muscles; who did all his warlike deeds so that his mother might clap her hands over him; and who broke up at last when his mother said "Bad boy!"

Coriolanus cannot accept Aufidius' sneer because in his heart he knows it is true, and he dare not let himself know it consciously. He keeps repeating that word, shouting:

> *"Boy!" False hound!*
> *If you have writ your annals true, 'tis there,*
> *That, like an eagle in a dovecote, I*
> *Fluttered your Volscians in Corioles.*
> *Alone I did it. "Boy"?*
> —Act V, scene vi, lines 113–17

His last boast is of his feat at Corioli in entering the city and fighting *alone*. At the end as at the beginning he is alone in the universe, he with his mother. Is that being a boy, he asks? Of course it is. A foolish act of boyish braggadocio is no less foolish because it succeeds.

And once again, Coriolanus' rage and tactlessness draws down anger upon himself. He is killed by numerous swords that have been prepared for the purpose by Aufidius himself.

The Volscian nobles are taken aback. They regret the sudden killing without trial, but one says of Coriolanus:

> *His own impatience*
> *Takes from Aufidius a great part of blame.*
> *Let's make the best of it.*
> —Act V, scene vi, lines 145–47

It is at this point of the climax of self-ruin that Shakespeare ends the tale.

Plutarch tells a little more. Coriolanus is honorably buried and the city of Rome pays homage to the mother, if not the son, by allowing her to mourn for him the full period of ten months that was then customary.

And at some time, in a future battle, Tullus Aufidius died in arms against Rome. Roman power grew steadily and Volscian power declined, and in the end it was Rome, Rome, Rome, over all Latium, all Italy, all the Mediterranean world.

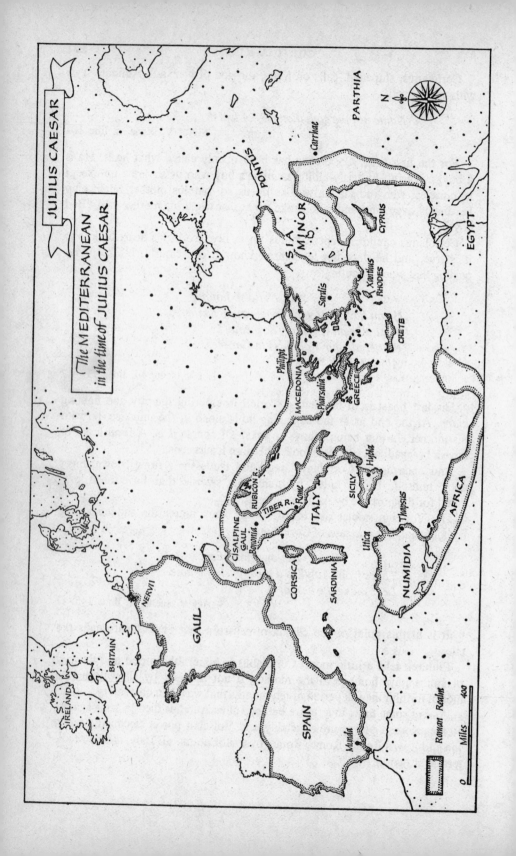

JULIUS CAESAR

The MEDITERRANEAN
in the time of JULIUS CAESAR

N

PARTHIA

Carrhae

PONTUS

ASIA
MINOR

CYPRUS

EGYPT

Sardis

Xanthus
RHODES

CRETE

Philippi

MACEDONIA

Pharsalia

GREECE

RUBICON R.

CISALPINE
GAUL

Bononia

TIBER R.

Rome

ITALY

SICILY

Hippo

NERVII

GAUL

CORSICA

SARDINIA

Utica

Thapsus

NUMIDIA

AFRICA

IRELAND

BRITAIN

SPAIN

Munda

Roman Realm

Miles

0   400

11

The Tragedy of

JULIUS CAESAR

THE FIRST Plutarchian play (see page I–213) written by Shakespeare (probably in 1599) concerned the time four and a half centuries after Coriolanus. Rome had survived the Gallic sack and the onslaught of Hannibal of Carthage. It had spread itself west and east over the shores of the Mediterranean Sea and now all those shores were either Roman territory or under the control of some Roman puppet king.

But Rome's troubles were coming from within. There was no longer any serious question of conquest from without. That was impossible and would remain impossible for several centuries. Now, however, there had come an inner struggle. For half a century there had been a sputtering string of conflicts, between generals, for control, and the play opens when the conflict seems to have been decided.

The victor is the greatest Roman of them all—Julius Caesar.

. . . get you home

The events of the first scene, in the streets of the city of Rome, are those of October 45 B.C. Caesar has just returned from Spain, where he defeated the last armies of those adversaries that had stood out against him.

He was now undisputed master of all the Roman realm, from end to end of the Mediterranean Sea. It seemed Rome was ready now to experience a rich and prosperous period of peace under the great Julius.

Not all of Rome is delighted by this turn of events, however. Those who had opposed Caesar and his policies might have been beaten into silence, but not into approval—and not even always into silence.

Caesar stood for an utter and thoroughgoing reform of the political system of the Roman Republic, which in the last century had fallen into decay and corruption. In this, he was supported chiefly by the commons and opposed chiefly by the senators and the aristocratic families.

In the first scene, though, Shakespeare pictures not the aristocratic opposition, but that of a pair of tribunes, Flavius and Marullus. This is odd, for the office of tribune was originally established to protect the commons against the aristocrats (an event which is at the core of the events in *Coriolanus,* see page I–222). One would have thought they would be more likely to support Caesar than oppose him.

Actually, however, the matter of the tribunes is borrowed by Shakespeare from Plutarch, but is moved earlier in time. If the incident had been left in its Plutarchian place, it would have seemed more apt.

At any rate, in Shakespeare's version the populace is swarming out to greet the homecoming Caesar, when they are met by the tribunes. One of them, Flavius, cries out:

> *Hence! Home, you idle creatures, get you home!*
>
> —Act I, scene i, line 1

. . . rejoice in his triumph

One of the populace, a cobbler, explains the activity:

> . . . *indeed, sir, we make holiday to see Caesar and to rejoice in his triumph.*
>
> —Act I, scene i, lines 33–34

The "triumph" was an old Roman custom borrowed from the ancient Etruscans centuries before Caesar's time. A victorious general entered the city in state, preceded by government officials and followed by his army and captured prisoners. The procession moved along decorated streets and between lines of cheering spectators to the Capitol, where religious services were held. (It was rather analogous to the modern ticker tape procession down Fifth Avenue.)

The day was a high festival, with plenty of food and drink for all at government expense, so that the populace was delighted partly with the aura of victory and partly with the fun. For the general himself, it represented the highest possible honor.

In July 46 B.C., more than a year before the play opens, Caesar had returned to Rome after nine years of conquest in Gaul and three years of civil war in Greece, Egypt, Asia Minor, and Africa. He had then broken all public records for magnificence by holding four triumphs, one after another, over each of four sets of foreign enemies he had conquered. These were the Gauls, the Egyptians, the Pontines of Asia Minor, and the Numidians of Africa.

After that, he went to Spain for one last victorious battle and now he was returning for one last triumph.

What tributaries . . .

The cobbler's reply but further irritates the tribune Marullus, who cries out in anguish:

> *Wherefore rejoice? What conquest brings he home?*
> *What tributaries follow him to Rome,*
> *To grace in captive bonds his chariot wheels?*
>   —Act I, scene i, lines 35–37

Marullus has a point here. The whole purpose of a triumph was to demonstrate the victories of Romans over their non-Roman enemies—over foreigners. Civil wars in themselves could bring no true conquests; Roman fought Roman so that a Roman victory necessarily implied a Roman defeat as well and a triumph was impossible.

Caesar, in the course of the civil war, had beaten armies under Roman generals, but he had been careful not to celebrate such victories in specific triumphs. He had brought as prisoners only foreigners who had fought against him, even when these (the Numidians, for instance) had been fighting as allies of Roman factions and even though the Roman soldiers who opposed him bore the brunt of the defeat.

In his last battle in Spain, however, there were no foreign enemies. He had fought only Romans and if he had a triumph it could be only over Romans. He did not bring home a true "conquest," no true "tributaries," and why, therefore, a triumph?

Knew you not Pompey . . .

The tribunes can be even more specific. Marullus says:

> *Knew you not Pompey? Many a time and oft*
> *Have you climbed up to walls and battlements,*
> *To tow'rs and windows, yea, to chimney tops,*
> *Your infants in your arms, and there have sat*
> *The livelong day, with patient expectation,*
> *To see great Pompey pass the streets of Rome.*
>   —Act I, scene i, lines 40–45

Gnaeus Pompeius (usually known as Pompey to English-speaking people) was born in 106 B.C. and made a great name for himself as a general at quite an early age, largely because of his talent for being on the right side in the right place at the right time. He won important victories in Spain, for instance, in 77 B.C. against a rebellious Roman general, largely because that general happened to be assassinated at the crucial moment.

He was given the right to append "Magnus" ("the Great") to his name as a result of early victories, which accounts for the tribune's reference to "great Pompey."

In 67 B.C. he accomplished something really surprising. Pirates had been infesting the Mediterranean Sea for a long time. They had evaded all Roman force and had all but made trade impossible, when Pompey was called to the task of suppressing them. He was put in charge of the entire Mediterranean coast to a distance of fifty miles inland for three years and was told to use that time for destroying the pirates. He managed to clear them all out in three months!

He was then put in charge of the Roman armies in Asia Minor. Again, this was a tremendous piece of luck for him. An earlier Roman general, competent but unpopular, had almost completed the job when his troops rebelled. Pompey took over, cleared up the last remaining forces of the enemy, and got all the credit.

In 61 B.C. he returned to Rome and at the age of forty-five received the most magnificent triumph Rome had seen up to that time. It is presumably partly with reference to this triumph that the tribunes spoke of the people waiting to see the great Pompey.

Pompey was not of a great aristocratic family himself and would have been proud to be accepted by the senators as one of their own. The senators, however, had learned from experience that successful generals of the non-aristocratic classes could be dangerous, and they watched Pompey carefully.

Yet Pompey had done his best to earn senatorial approval. On returning to Italy in 61 B.C. after his victories, he had disbanded his army and had taken his place in Rome as a private citizen. This had merely gained him a total loss of influence. He could not even persuade the Senate to approve the award of bonuses to his faithful soldiers.

Pompey was forced to turn elsewhere. He formed an alliance with Marcus Licinius Crassus, the richest man in Rome, and with a skillful and charming orator and politician, Julius Caesar. Caesar was then an impoverished aristocrat (who nevertheless opposed the Senators) in the employ of Crassus.

The three together, in 60 B.C., formed the First Triumvirate (*triumvir* means "three men") and ruled Rome.

The three took advantage of their power to parcel out provinces for themselves. Caesar, born in 100 B.C., and by far the most capable of the three, obtained for himself the governorship of that portion of Gaul ruled by Rome (a portion that included what is now northern Italy and southern France). He used that as a base from which to conquer the rest of Gaul. Fighting his first battles at the age of forty-four, he surprised everyone by showing himself to be a military genius of the first rank.

Pompey, who was assigned the governorship of Spain, but who let deputies run it while he himself remained in Rome, was not entirely pleased by Caesar's sudden development of a military reputation. As for Crassus, he was jealous enough to take an army to the east to fight the Parthians, who ruled over what had once been the eastern part of the Persian Empire. In 53 B.C. he lost a catastrophic battle to them at Carrhae, and lost his life as well.

Pompey and Caesar now shared the power, with no third party to serve as intermediary.

By now the senatorial conservatives, frightened by Caesar's success and recognizing Pompey as far the less dangerous of the two, had lined up solidly behind the latter.

Pompey, flattered by aristocratic attentions, let himself be wooed into open opposition to his erstwhile ally. When Caesar's term as governor of Gaul came to an end, the Senate, buoyed up by Pompey's support, arrogantly ordered Caesar to return to Rome at once without his army. This was technically in order since it was treason for any Roman general to bring a provincial army into Italy.

Caesar, however, knew that if he arrived in Rome without his army, he would be arrested at once on some charge or other, and might well be executed.

So after hesitating at the Rubicon River (the little Italian creek which was the boundary of Italy proper, in the Roman view) he made his decision. On January 10, 49 B.C., he crossed the Rubicon with a legion of troops and a civil war began.

Pompey found, much to his own surprise, that Caesar was far more popular than he, and that soldiers flocked to Caesar and not to himself. He was forced to flee to Greece and the senatorial party fled with him. Caesar followed and at a battle in Pharsalia, Greece, on June 29, 48 B.C., Caesar's army smashed that of Pompey.

Pompey had to flee again, almost alone, to Egypt, which was then still independent of Rome. The Egyptian government, however, was afraid to do anything that might displease Caesar, who was clearly the coming man. They therefore assassinated Pompey the instant he landed on Egyptian soil.

Caesar followed, and remained in Egypt for a while. There he met Cleopatra, its fascinating young queen.

Caesar next traveled to Asia Minor, and then to Africa, to defeat diehard armies allied to those who shared the views of the dead Pompey and the senatorial party. Only then did he return to Rome for his quadruple triumph.

. . . Pompey's blood

In no part of that quadruple triumph did Caesar commemorate his victory over Pompey himself. In fact, as a deliberate stroke of policy, Caesar forgave such of the Pompeian partisans as he could and did his best to erase hard feelings. His mission, as far as possible, was to unite Rome and put an end to the civil broils through conciliation.

And yet the Roman tribunes in their harangue to the populace bring up Pompey, reproachfully, in connection with this last triumph of Caesar, and Marullus says to the gathered people:

> *And do you now put on your best attire?*
> *And do you now cull out a holiday?*
> *And do you now strew flowers in his way*
> *That comes in triumph over Pompey's blood?*
>
>   —Act I, scene i, lines 51–54

By "Pompey's blood" is not meant Pompey's death in defeat, as might seem, but Pompey's kinsmen.

Pompey had two sons, the elder of whom shared his father's name and was Gnaeus Pompeius Magnus also. We can call him Gnaeus Pompeius to differentiate him from his father, whom we can still call simply Pompey.

Gnaeus Pompeius remained with the senatorial party after his father's death. He had a fleet in his charge and he brought it to Africa (where the modern nation of Tunis exists), putting it at the service of the largest remaining senatorial army. When Caesar defeated it in April 47 B.C., Gnaeus Pompeius escaped to Spain.

After the quadruple triumph, only Spain was left in opposition. Caesar took his legions there and in March 45 B.C. a battle took place at Munda in southern Spain.

The senatorial army fought remarkably well and Caesar's forces were driven back. For a time, indeed, Caesar must have thought that years of invariable victory were going to be brought to ruin in one last battle (as had been the case of Hannibal of Carthage a century and a half earlier). So desperate was he that he seized a shield and sword himself, rushed into battle (he was fifty-five years old then), and shouted to his retreating men, "Are you going to let your general be delivered up to the enemy?"

Stung into action, the retiring legions lunged forward once more and carried the day. The last senatorial army was wiped out. Gnaeus Pompeius escaped from the field of battle, but was pursued, caught, and killed. (Pompey's younger son escaped and lived to play a part in the events that took place some six years later, and in another of Shakespeare's plays, *Antony and Cleopatra*.)

Now, returning from Spain, Caesar was celebrating his victory over Gnaeus Pompeius and it was in this sense that he came in "triumph over Pompey's blood."

. . . the feast of Lupercal

The populace disbands and leaves the stage, presumably returning to their houses in guilt. The tribune, Flavius, then suggests that they tear down the decorations intended for the triumph. Marullus hesitates, for it may be sacrilege. He says:

> May we do so?
> You know it is the feast of Lupercal.
> —Act I, scene i, lines 69–70

The Lupercalian festival was an ancient fertility rite whose origins are lost in antiquity and probably predate civilization. It involved the ritual sacrifice of goats, which were noted for being ruttish animals.

Strips of the skin of the sacrificed goats were cut off by the priests in charge. They then ran about the Palatine Hill, striking out with those thongs. Anyone struck would be rendered fertile, supposedly, and sterile women therefore so placed themselves at the rites as to make sure they would be struck.

The "feast of Lupercal" was held each year on February 15 and this was not the day of Caesar's last triumph at all (as would appear from the play), but four months later. Shakespeare, however, commonly compresses time in his historical plays (a compression that is a dramatic necessity, and even a dramatic virtue), and here he lets the four months pass between the driving off of the populace and the next speech of the tribunes. There is no further talk of the triumph.

One would suppose from this first scene that the triumph was somehow aborted and never took place. It *did* take place, of course. The chief point of the scene is to show that there is opposition to Caesar.

. . . in servile fearfulness

Flavius shrugs off the possibility of sacrilege. It is more important to resist Caesar's pretensions. He says:

> These growing feathers plucked from Caesar's wing
> Will make him fly an ordinary pitch,
> Who else would soar above the view of men
> And keep us all in servile fearfulness.
> —Act I, scene i, lines 75–78

The battle in Caesar's time did not really involve liberty in our modern sense. On the one hand was a time-honored but distorted and corrupt senatorial government, inefficient and dying. On the other was the one-man dictatorship of Julius Caesar, intent on fundamental reform and a centralized government.

There would have been no freedom for the common people anywhere, even in Rome, under either form of government. Under Caesar, however, the government would certainly have been more efficient and the realm more prosperous. That this is so is demonstrated by the fact that when Caesar's heir and successor founded a Caesar-type government (the Roman Empire), it led to two centuries of unbroken peace and prosperity.

During that peaceful time, however, literary men had leisure to look back on the decades before the establishment of the Empire and to regret the hurly-burly of politics and the active drama of contending personalities. It seemed to them that they and their senatorial patrons lived in a gilded prison (and indeed the senators sometimes suffered, when suspicious emperors suspected treason among them). It became fashionable to look back with nostalgic sadness to the days of the Roman Republic.

The senatorial party of Caesar's time then came to be called "Republicans" and to be viewed as exponents of "liberty." They were entirely idealized and in this fashion were passed on to Shakespeare and to us. We need not be deluded, however. The senatorial notion of "liberty" was the liberty of a small group of venal aristocrats to plunder the state unchecked.

Calphurnia

The scene shifts now to another part of Rome, where Caesar and many with him are on their way to attend the Lupercalian rites. Caesar's first word in the play is to call his wife:

> *Calphurnia!*

—Act I, scene ii, line 1

Caesar had three wives altogether. He married his first wife in 83 B.C. when he was not yet seventeen. She was the daughter of a radical antisenatorial politician, and it was from this connection, probably, that Caesar began to get his own antisenatorial philosophy. When Caesar's father-in-law was killed and the conservatives gained control and initiated a bloodbath (the radicals had had their turn previously), Caesar was ordered to divorce his wife. He refused! It might have then gone hard with him as a result, but the young man's aristocratic connections saved his life.

Caesar's first wife died in 67 B.C. and he made a politically convenient second marriage, taking as wife Pompeia, the daughter of Pompey, who was then at the height of his career.

In 62 B.C. a certain young scapegrace named Publius Clodius (called "Pulcher" or "good-looking") played a rather foolish practical joke. He dressed himself in women's clothing and got himself into Caesar's house at a time when a religious festival was in process which only women could attend.

He was caught and it was a great scandal. Many whispered that it could not have been done without the co-operation of Pompeia and even wondered if Clodius might not be Pompeia's lover. Pompeia was almost certainly innocent, but Caesar divorced her at once with the famous remark that "Caesar's wife must be above suspicion." Actually, he was probably tired of her and was glad of a face-saving excuse for the divorce.

After Caesar had formed the triumvirate with Pompey and Crassus, he married again, for the third and last time, to Calpurnia (or Calphurnia, as Shakespeare calls her). She was a daughter of one of Pompey's friends, and it was therefore, in a sense, another political marriage.

. . . in Antonius' way

Caesar has a simple direction for Calphurnia:

> *Stand you directly in Antonius' way*
> *When he doth run his course.*
> —Act I, scene ii, lines 3–4

Antonius, it seems, will be one of those who will race along wielding the goat-hide thongs at the Lupercalian festival. Since Calphurnia has had no children, and Caesar would like a direct heir, it will be useful for her to be struck.

The Antonius referred to is Marcus Antonius, far better known, in English, as Mark Antony. He was born in 83 B.C. and was thirty-eight years old at the time of this Lupercalian festival. He was related to Julius Caesar on his mother's side and had joined the general while he was in Gaul. He had remained loyally pro-Caesar ever since.

Mark Antony had been tribune in 49 B.C. when Pompey and the Senate were trying to force Julius Caesar to come to Italy without his army. Mark Antony and his fellow tribune did what they could to block senatorial action, then fled to Caesar's army, claiming they were in danger of their lives. Since tribunes were inviolate and might not be harmed, Caesar had the excuse he needed to cross the Rubicon with his army.

While Caesar was in Greece and Egypt fighting the civil war, Mark Antony held the fort in Rome itself and didn't do a very good job of it.

Caesar continued to value him for his absolute loyalty, however, and they remained together to the end.

. . . the ides of March

And then a voice calls Caesar's name. It is a soothsayer, a man who foresees the future. This time his message is a simple one:

> Beware the ides of March.
> —Act I, scene ii, line 18

To understand the matter of "the ides" we must consider the Roman calendar, which must set some sort of record for inconvenience.

Each of the Roman months has three key dates and the other days are defined as "so many days before the such-and-such key date." Nor are the key dates regularly spaced or quite the same from month to month.

The first day of each month is the "calends" of that month.

Not long after the calends come the "nones." The nones fall on the fifth day of January, February, April, June, August, September, November, and December, and on the seventh day of March, May, July, and October.

The word "nones" means "nine" because it falls nine days before the third key date, the "ides," where the nine days count the day of the ides itself. The ides, therefore, fall on the fifteenth day of March, May, July, and October, and on the thirteenth day of the other months.

From all this we gather that the "ides of March" is what we could call March 15 today. The Lupercalian festival, which falls on February 15, is not, however, on the "ides of February," for that date would be what we now call February 13.

I am not gamesome . . .

Calmly, Caesar ignores the mystic warning and passes on to the festival. The incident of the soothsayer is not a Shakespearean invention, but is referred to in Plutarch.

That, of course, does not necessarily make it authentic. The event of the ides of March was so dramatic and so clearly a turning point of history that numerous fables arose afterward of all sorts of supernatural omens and forebodings preceding it. The incident of the soothsayer is only the most restrained and dramatically satisfying one of them.

After Caesar and his party pass on, two men remain behind: Brutus and Cassius. Cassius asks if Brutus intends to watch the festival and Brutus says he won't, for:

I am not gamesome: I do lack some part
Of that quick spirit that is in Antony.
                                        —Act I, scene ii, lines 28–29

No, he is not gamesome (that is, "merry" or "gay"). The Romans, somehow, usually aren't in literature. They are generally presented as grave, portentous, dignified men, given to declamations in high-sounding phrases, and that is exactly how Brutus is presented.

He is Marcus Junius Brutus, born in 85 B.C., and therefore just past forty at this time.

Brutus was the "Republican" most idealized by later historians, but he was by no means an admirable character in real life.

To begin with, he was a nephew of Cato, one of Caesar's most obdurate and steadfast enemies. It is not surprising, then, that Brutus was also an enemy of Caesar's to begin with. Indeed, he fought on Pompey's side in Greece and was taken prisoner when Pompey was defeated.

Caesar, however, followed a consistent policy of leniency toward his enemies, feeling, perhaps, that in this way he converted them to friends and healed the wounds inflicted by civil war. So Brutus was pardoned and set free.

The policy seemed to have worked in Brutus' case, for he behaved as though he were converted from a Pompeian into a sincere Caesarian. When Caesar went to Africa to take care of the senatorial armies there, those had, as one of their most important leaders, Cato, who was Brutus' uncle. And yet Brutus remained one of Caesar's lieutenants and served him loyally in the province of Cisalpine Gaul (in what is now northern Italy).

Later on, crucially and fatally, he abandoned Caesar once again. The later idealization of Brutus has him acting out of conviction and principle, but a glance at his career before the opening scenes of *Julius Caesar* would make it seem that he was, rather, a self-serving turncoat.

. . . *Cassius* . . .

Brutus is unwilling that his lack of gamesomeness should interfere with Cassius' pleasures. He says:

>   *Let me not hinder, Cassius, your desires;*
>   *I'll leave you.*
>   —Act I, scene ii, lines 30–31

Cassius' full name is Gaius (or Caius) Cassius Longinus, and he is a capable soldier. He went with Crassus to the East as second-in-command. After the disastrous defeat which almost destroyed the Roman army, thanks in good part to Crassus' incapacity, Cassius took over and brought what was left of the army safely back to Roman territory.

He was also with Pompey at first, but after Pompey's defeat he reassessed the situation. He had not been captured, but it seemed to him that Caesar was sure to win, and Cassius intended to be on the winning side. He followed Caesar into Asia Minor and threw himself on the conqueror's mercy. Caesar pardoned him and let him serve under him.

Cassius married Junia, the sister of Brutus, and was, therefore, Brutus' brother-in-law.

Your hidden worthiness . . .

But now that Brutus makes ready to leave Cassius, Cassius gently restrains him. He has a use for Brutus and to serve that use he begins, carefully, to seduce him with praise. He tells Brutus that he is too modest and does not sufficiently value himself, saying:

> . . . it is very much lamented, Brutus,
> That you have no such mirrors as will turn
> Your hidden worthiness into your eye,
> That you might see your shadow.
>
> —Act I, scene ii, lines 35–38

Somehow the general idealization of Brutus is such that most of those who read or see this play imagine that Brutus is presented in heroic colors; and, indeed, the play is often produced with Brutus as the hero. Yet a close reading seems to show that Shakespeare is utterly out of sympathy with Brutus and makes him rather a despicable character.

Cassius bemoans Brutus' modesty, but there is no modesty in Brutus as portrayed by Shakespeare. Brutus always listens complacently to those who praise him, and praises himself often enough. Nor does Cassius for a moment really believe that Brutus is modest, for in the rest of the scene his attempt to win over Brutus to a desired line of action is pitched entirely to Brutus' overweening vanity.

. . . Caesar for their king

Cassius' smoothly scheming flattery is interrupted by the sound of shouting in the distance, and Brutus cries out:

> What means this shouting? I do fear the people
> Choose Caesar for their king.
>
> —Act I, scene ii, lines 79–80

The word "king" had a dread sound to Romans throughout their great days, a dread that dated back to the hated Tarquin (see page I-211). The tale of Tarquin was a heritage of every Roman schoolboy, as the tale of George III is of every American schoolboy, and a stanch republicanism was inculcated in the former case as it is in the latter.

Then too, in the two centuries preceding Julius Caesar's period of power, Rome had been more or less continuously at war with the various Hellenistic nations of the eastern Mediterranean, all of which were ruled by kings. Kings were the enemy and were therefore hated; and the kings were always defeated by the Roman republicans, so that the institution of monarchy had the aura of defeat about it.

Consequently, Caesar was in a dilemma when he took power over Rome. He simply had to reform the government, which had come to be utterly stagnant and unworkable, but he could not do so by ordinary legal means. That would require working through the Senate, and the Senate was hostile and obstructionist. Hence, he had to rule dictatorially, by decree.

The Roman system of government allowed for rule by decree under certain conditions. A special official could be elected for six months who would have the power to rule by decree. He was a "dictator" (from a Latin word meaning "to say," because what he said became law without further ado). A famous early (and legendary) dictator was Cincinnatus, who in 458 B.C. held the dictatorship for only a few days to meet an emergency.

In later times the device was broadened. In 81 B.C. the Roman general Lucius Cornelius Sulla made himself dictator and held the post for two years. This was with the connivance of the Senate, whose cause Sulla favored.

Caesar took advantage of the broadening and turned it against the Senate. He had taken the power of a dictator during the civil war and at the time of the quadruple triumph had had himself declared dictator for a term of ten years. After the Spanish triumph, which opens this play, he was made dictator for life.

He used the dictatorship to bring about his program of reform. He tried to reform the Senate by wrenching it out of the hands of the few oligarchs who monopolized it and allowing the entry of important families from the provinces. He broadened the base of citizenship, revised the taxation procedure, reconstructed cities, improved trade, passed laws designed to strengthen the moral structure of society, and reformed the calendar so that it was almost the one we use today. He even established the first public library.

Yet although he was dictator for life, Caesar felt it was not enough. As merely dictator, his death would be the sign for a new struggle for power, and all his reforms would be undone. That placed a premium on his death and made his opponents eager for an assassination. If he were king, however, his power would merely descend to his nearest heir upon his death, and there would be far less point to killing him.

It was this desire of Caesar to make himself king—a desire imputed to him by the senatorial conservatives, and probably justly so—that was the chief weapon against him. The conservatives, who hated him and his reforms, emphasized his ambition for the kingship, hoping that the hated word would turn the populace against Caesar.

On the other hand, the conservatives also feared that the popularity of his reforms might more than make up for the fearsomeness of the word, and that the infatuated populace, caught up on the occasion of some holiday such as the present Lupercalian festival, would be stampeded into declaring him king and that the Senate would then be forced, much against its will, to go along. Once that was done, it would be too late to expect to turn back the tide of reform.

It was exactly this that Brutus feared when he heard the shouting.

. . . the waves of Tiber

Brutus' outspoken fear of Caesar as king heartens Cassius. He plays on that fear by describing the indignity of having to bow down to one who after all is but a man and perhaps not even as good a man as oneself. To make his point, he tells a tale of a contest between himself and Caesar.

One cold day Caesar challenged Cassius to swim across the river. Caesar wearied first and cried out for help. Cassius says:

> I, as Aeneas, our great ancestor,
> Did from the flames of Troy upon his shoulder
> The old Anchises bear, so from the waves of Tiber
> Did I the tired Caesar.
> —Act I, scene ii, lines 112–15

The Tiber River is 252 miles long and is the second longest river in Italy. It would bear little distinction as a river were it not that, like some other short rivers, such as the Thames, the Seine, and the Spree, a great capital was located on its banks. The city of Rome was founded twenty miles upstream from its mouth.

Here again there is a reference to Aeneas as the ancestor of the Romans (see page I-20).

Like a Colossus . . .

In all Cassius' clever speaking, he doesn't once accuse Caesar of tyrannical behavior or of cruelty; he doesn't say his reforms are wicked or evil.

He concentrates entirely on Caesar's physical weakness and poor health, for he is endeavoring to show Brutus that Caesar is inferior, hoping that Brutus' inordinate vanity would then rebel at bowing down to such a ruler.

He labors to find a way to describe the greatness of Caesar and the comparative littleness of Brutus in such a way as to force Brutus to rebel. Cassius says:

> Why, man, he doth bestride the narrow world
> Like a Colossus, and we petty men
> Walk under his huge legs and peep about
> To find ourselves dishonorable graves.
> —Act I, scene ii, lines 135–38

The Colossus is a statue of the sun god built in the island of Rhodes in 280 B.C. to commemorate the successful defense against a siege by a Macedonian general, Demetrius. Why the name "colossus" was applied to a huge statue is unknown, but this Rhodian statue, the largest in the Greco-Roman world, 105 feet tall, was *the* Colossus of Rhodes. It was considered one of the Seven Wonders of the ancient world.

It did not, however, remain long to gladden the eyes of those who value size in art. In 224 B.C., little more than half a century after it had been built, it was toppled by an earthquake.

Once it was gone, the description of what it had looked like while it was standing gradually grew more grandiose, until finally the tale arose that it had straddled Rhodes' harbor and that ships had sailed between its legs in and out of that harbor. This is, of course, quite impossible, for the ancient Greeks had lacked the materials and technique to build a statue so large in a position that would place so much strain on the legs.

The picture is nevertheless a dramatic one, and Cassius, by whose time the statue had been out of existence for nearly two centuries, uses it to fire up Brutus' vanity and envy.

. . . a Brutus once . . .

Cassius plays on Brutus' pride of ancestry too, saying:

> There was a Brutus once that would have brooked
> Th'eternal devil to keep his state in Rome
> As easily as a king.
> —Act I, scene ii, lines 159–61

Brutus considers himself to be descended from Lucius Junius Brutus, who, according to legend, helped overthrow King Tarquin and set up the Roman Republic (see page I–211).

. . . and Cicero

Brutus' vanity is not proof against Cassius' skillful seduction, and he admits that he resents Rome's present situation.

Before matters can go further, though, Caesar comes back onstage, returning from the festival with others crowding around him.

Caesar is clearly angry and those about him look perturbed. Brutus, surprised at this, says to Cassius:

> *Calphurnia's cheek is pale, and Cicero*
> *Looks with such ferret and such fiery eyes*
> *As we have seen him in the Capitol,*
> *Being crossed in conference by some senators.*
>
> —Act I, scene ii, lines 185–88

Marcus Tullius Cicero, though he plays only a small part in this play, was actually the most important man in Rome in Caesar's time, next to Caesar himself.

He was born in 106 B.C. of middle-class family and received an excellent education in Greece. He returned to Rome in 77 B.C. and quickly became Rome's outstanding lawyer and orator (the two went together). He made himself famous by prosecuting one of the particularly crooked Roman provincial governors of the time, Gaius Verres, in 74 B.C.

In 63 B.C. he reached the pinnacle of his career when, as consul, he scotched a dangerous conspiracy against the Roman government by a debt-ridden nobleman, Lucius Sergius Catilina (known in English as Catiline), and had its leaders executed.

He never reached such heights again. He was not brave enough or skillful enough to be an effective opponent of Caesar. In fact, Caesar had his lackey, Publius Clodius (the same who invaded the women's religious festival and made it possible for Caesar to divorce his second wife), to so vilify and harass Cicero as to drive the latter out of Italy altogether in 59 B.C.

Mark Antony had an undying hatred for Cicero, since Antony's foster father had been an associate of Catiline and had been among those executed at the instigation of Cicero. Cicero returned the hatred.

Cicero was a friend of Pompey, who, he thought, would be able to dominate Rome and defeat Caesar. When Pompey found he could not retain Italy and fled to Greece, Cicero, greatly disconcerted, left Italy with him. Cicero grew more and more disturbed at developments among the Pompeian forces and after the Battle of Pharsalia returned to Italy, determined to take a chance on Caesar's mercy rather than fight on with the remnants of a doomed cause. Caesar did not disappoint him; he pardoned Cicero and treated him kindly. Thereafter, Cicero displayed a wary neutrality, neither opposing Caesar's reforms openly nor supporting them, either.

Cicero was a debater rather than a warrior, and he was at home in the battle of words in the Senate rather than in the battle of swords on the field. Hence his angry red eyes (a ferret's eyes are red) reminded Brutus of his appearance when he was opposed in senatorial debate.

. . . always I am Caesar

But even while Brutus and Cassius observe Caesar and his company in astonishment, Caesar is observing them as well. He remarks upon Cassius, particularly, to Antony, in a famous and much quoted passage:

> Yond Cassius has a lean and hungry look;
> He thinks too much: such men are dangerous.
> > —Act I, scene ii, lines 194–95

But after elaborating on Cassius' gravity and on his inability to have fun and thus allow his possible feelings of envy to evaporate in pleasure, Caesar adds hastily:

> I rather tell thee what is to be feared
> Than what I fear; for always I am Caesar.
> > —Act I, scene ii, lines 211–12

Caesar, as portrayed by Shakespeare, strikes wooden poses constantly. He is like a speaking statue, rather than a human being.

This is not and cannot be historical. All our sources seem to unite in assuring us that Caesar had infinite charm and could win over almost anyone, given half a chance. He was second only to Cicero as an orator and his surviving Commentaries, in which he describes his wars in Gaul and the civil war, are ample evidence of his ability as a writer.

He was a remarkably witty and intelligent man; a most human man. He was miles removed from the cardboard strutter in Shakespeare and was in real life much more like George Bernard Shaw's portrayal of him in Caesar and Cleopatra.

Why does Shakespeare portray him so woodenly then? Unfortunately, it was the fashion to describe ancient Romans like that. This fashion stems from the plays of the Roman philosopher Lucius Annaeus Seneca, who wrote about a century after Caesar's death. His are among the most fustian plays ever written, full of emotional sound and fury, blood and horror, and empty, high-sounding speeches.

The general public loved them so that they survived to be copied, alas, by playwrights in early modern times. Shakespeare himself wrote tragedies after the style of Seneca, notably *Titus Andronicus* (see page I-391).

A French poet, Marc Antoine Muret, wrote a tragedy entitled *Julius Caesar* in Latin in 1553. He followed the style of Seneca and made Caesar into a wooden poseur. This was popular too, and one theory is that when Shakespeare wrote his tragedy, he had to keep Caesar in this form because the audience expected it and would not accept any other version.

We might imagine that Shakespeare did so against his will, for he follows Caesar's pompous claim to fearlessness with an immediate confession of weakness on the part of the great man. Caesar goes on to say to Mark Antony:

> Come on my right hand, for this ear is deaf,
> And tell me truly what thou think'st of him.
>
> —Act I, scene ii, lines 213–14

. . . *a crown offered him* . . .

Caesar and his followers leave again, but one remains behind, held back by Brutus. The man stopped is Casca, who is pictured by Shakespeare as a rough, coarse individual, the kind who has no "book learning" and is proud of it. He is Publius Servilius Casca in full, and his only mark in history is his participation in the conspiracy which Cassius is now working up.

Casca is asked as to the events at the festival that caused Caesar to look so put out. Casca says:

> Why, there was a crown offered him; and being offered him,
> he put it by with the back of his hand, thus; and then the
> people fell a-shouting.
>
> —Act I, scene ii, lines 220–22

Apparently Mark Antony took the occasion of the festival, when public spirits were high, and enthusiasm for Dictator Julius was loud, to offer him a linen headband wreathed in laurel. The laurel wreath was well within the Roman tradition. It was a symbol of victory, borrowed from the Greek custom of crowning the victors of the Olympian games in laurel wreaths.

The linen headband was, however, a "diadem," the symbol of monarchy among the kings of the East. For Caesar to put on this particular laurel wreath was tantamount to claiming the position of king. (In later times, gold replaced linen and it was a gold circlet, or crown, that became the symbol of royalty. Shakespeare transmutes the diadem into a crown so that the audience might understand.)

Caesar's stratagem seems obvious. The diadem is made to look as harmless and as Roman as possible by means of the laurel decoration. Ostentatiously, he refuses it, hoping that the crowd, in its enthusiasm, will demand that he accept it. Caesar would then graciously accede to their clamor and become king by the will of the people.

Unfortunately, the crowd did not react this way. Instead of demanding he accept the diadem, they cheered him for refusing it. Twice more Mark Antony tried, and twice more the crowd cheered the refusal. No wonder Caesar had looked angry. His stratagem had failed and he had come close to making a fool of himself.

To Cassius and others of his mind, the intention behind the stratagem is obvious. Caesar wanted to be king and if the trick today had failed, another tomorrow might not—and this must be stopped at all costs.

. . . foamed at mouth . . .

Caesar's anger and disappointment are described most graphically by Casca. He relates that after the third refusal, Caesar:

> . . . fell down in the market place, and foamed at mouth, and
> was speechless.
> —Act I, scene ii, lines 252–53

In short, he had had an epileptic fit. The tale that Caesar was an epileptic may not be a reliable one, however. The Roman historian Gaius Suetonius Tranquillus wrote a scandal-filled set of biographies of the early Roman emperors a century and a half after Caesar's time, and he said that Caesar had twice had "the falling sickness" in the time of battle. It is always doubtful how far one can believe Suetonius, however.

Shakespeare has Casca make another notable comment, meant literally, which has become a very byword in the language. Asked if Cicero said anything, he answered that Cicero had spoken in Greek:

> . . . those that understood him smiled at one another and
> shook their heads; but for mine own part, it was Greek to me.
> —Act I, scene ii, lines 282–84

. . . put to silence

Casca then says:

> *I could tell you more news too: Marullus and Flavius, for*
> *pulling scarfs off Caesar's images, are put to silence.*
> —Act I, scene ii, lines 284–86

Marullus and Flavius are the tribunes of the first scene and this seems to hark back to their activities at the Spanish triumph months before. Actually, their activities then are purely Shakespearean and have no source in history.

Plutarch associates them, rather, with the incident at the Lupercalian festival. After the refusal of the diadem, someone apparently placed it on the head of a statue of Caesar, as though he were still trying to fire the Roman populace with enthusiasm for Caesar as king. One of the tribunes plucked it off and the people cheered him, and that is the germ for Shakespeare's first scene.

Shakespeare says the tribunes were "put to silence," which sounds almost as though they were executed. Plutarch, however, merely says they were turned out of their office.

. . . he loves Brutus

Casca leaves, and then Brutus. Cassius is left alone to smile grimly and remark in soliloquy at how easy Brutus is to handle:

> *Well, Brutus, thou art noble; yet I see*
> *Thy honorable mettle may be wrought*
> *From that it is disposed . . .*
> —Act I, scene ii, lines 308–10

Brutus is constantly being called honorable and noble throughout the play, yet he never seems so in action. Not only is he vain and envious, but he is rather stupid too. Cassius plans to throw letters into Brutus' window, disguised in various hands, all praising him and calling him to save the state. He is certain that Brutus' colossal vanity and less than colossal intelligence will make this rather childish stratagem a success.

Why should Cassius want such a vain fool as Brutus on his side? Can Brutus be trusted not to ruin any conspiracy of which he forms a part? (Actually, no, for his vain folly ruins this one, as Shakespeare makes amply clear.) Cassius gives the answer in his soliloquy:

Caesar doth bear me hard, but he loves Brutus.
—Act I, scene ii, line 313

Later historians emphasized Caesar's partiality toward Brutus since it made succeeding events all the more dramatic. On the other hand, there is one instance which seems to show Caesar's feeling in terms of hard action.

When Caesar first returned in triumph to Rome, Cassius and Brutus both asked for the post of praetor of the city (an office rather like the modern mayor). Caesar granted the post to Brutus, though he is supposed to have admitted that Cassius was the more fit for it.

Caesar's surprising partiality for Brutus and the fact that he was supposed to have once been friendly with Brutus' mother gave rise to the scandalous tale that Brutus was an illegitimate son of Caesar's. However, scandalmongers, then as now, prefer a dramatic guess to a sober fact, and we need not take this very seriously.

However, one can see that Cassius values Brutus partly because through Brutus conspirators may probe Caesar's inner defenses more easily.

. . . to the Capitol tomorrow

Between the second and third scenes another month passes, unmarked by the onrushing action of the play. Casca meets with Cicero in the third scene. Casca looks wild and, on Cicero's question, Casca tells of numerous supernatural events he has just witnessed. Cicero seems unmoved. He dismisses the tale and asks, practically:

Comes Caesar to the Capitol tomorrow?
—Act I, scene iii, line 36

It is, in other words, the night before the ides of March. It is March 14 and Caesar has called the Senate into session for the next day for some matter of great moment.

Caesar was planning to head eastward with an army to make war on the Parthians, who had destroyed Crassus and most of his army nine years before—a Roman defeat that had as yet gone unavenged. Before Caesar could leave, certain matters had to be cleared up.

One possibility is that Caesar did not want to leave Rome without settling the question of kingship, and that he was calling the Senate into session in order to force them to offer him the crown.

Was this so? Would he really accept a grudged title, then depart from Rome for perhaps an extended period, leaving the city to almost certain war? Might it not be that he was merely calling the Senate into session for a formal declaration of war against the Parthians and for the establishment of a kind of "regency" to govern Rome while he was gone? Who can tell now.

The conspirators, however, thought they knew what Caesar planned. They were sure that Caesar was going to make the irrevocable grab for the crown and that there was only one last chance to stop him—before the Senate actually had a chance to meet.

Because they thought so, the next day, March 15, 44 B.C., was to be a key date in world history, and later legend got busy to fill the night before with supernatural portents. It is those legends which Shakespeare incorporates into his play.

Our own materialist age has no difficulty whatever in rejecting out of hand any tales of supernatural occurrences on the night of March 14–15. We can dismiss them even in terms of the Romans themselves. If the eve of the ides had really been so riddled with horror, the conspirators would probably have been cowed from their project by superstition.

. . . save here in Italy

Cicero leaves and Cassius enters. He too is full of the prodigies of the night and he begins to sound out Casca's feelings with regard to Caesar. Casca passes on one rumor as to Caesar's plans for the next day:

> Indeed, they say the senators tomorrow
> Mean to establish Caesar as a king;
> And he shall wear his crown by sea and land,
> In every place save here in Italy.
>
> —Act I, scene iii, lines 85–88

Was this Caesar's intention? It seems, on the surface, a reasonable compromise. Italy at that time still ruled the Roman realm, and it was the Italians alone who were Roman citizens, and it was Roman citizens alone who had the traditional objection to monarchy. The provinces outside Italy lacked the Roman tradition and many of them were, in fact, accustomed to kings. They would accept a King Julius without objection and Italy would continue under Dictator Julius.

It would, however, be a useless compromise as it stood. The permanence of monarchy would exist only in the provinces, which were without military power, while in Italy itself, where lay the control of the armies, Caesar's death would still be the signal for civil war.

What is more likely, if such a compromise were pushed through, is that it would be intended to be temporary. How long after Caesar became king elsewhere would it be before he were king in Italy as well? The

Roman populace, accustomed to hearing of Caesar as king, would come to accept him as such.

Unquestionably, those who opposed Caesar and his reforms would realize this, so that any offer to renounce kingship for Italy only would be completely unsatisfactory. The mere thought of it drives Casca to agree to join the conspiracy Cassius is forming.

'Tis Cinna . . .

Another enters. Casca is at once cautious (he is dealing in a dangerous plot which, if it fails, means death). Cassius reassures him:

> 'Tis Cinna; I do know him by his gait;
> He is a friend.
>
> —Act I, scene iii, lines 132–33

It is Lucius Cornelius Cinna. His father, with the same name, had also been the father of Caesar's first wife. The elder Cinna had been one of Rome's most radical politicians, and had striven against the senatorial government even to the point of leading a revolution. His troops mutinied against him, however, and killed him in 84 B.C. The younger Cinna, however, had now joined the conspiracy against Caesar and in behalf of the senatorial party.

It is amazing how many of the conspirators were in one way or another beholden to Caesar—Brutus most of all. That is probably one reason why the conspiracy succeeded; Caesar considered them all friends.

. . . Decius Brutus and Trebonius . . .

Other conspirators are mentioned. Cinna doesn't recognize Casca at first. He says:

> . . . Who's that? Metellus Cimber?
>
> —Act I, scene iii, line 134

Then, a little later, when Cassius prepares to have the entire group meet at a particular site, he asks:

> Is Decius Brutus and Trebonius there?
>
> —Act I, scene iii, line 148

Gaius Trebonius was of the aristocracy, like Caesar, but, again like

Caesar, he took an active part in the reform movement and worked hard in the Senate on behalf of measures favored by Caesar. He served as a general under Caesar in the wars in Gaul and in 45 B.C. (just the year before) Trebonius served as consul, the chief magistrate of Rome, thanks to Caesar's influence. To be sure, the consul had little real power while Caesar was dictator, but it was a most honorable position.

As for "Decius Brutus," the name is an error that Shakespeare made in following North's translation of Plutarch, where the same error is to be found. The correct name is Decimus Junius Brutus. He belonged to the same family as did Marcus Junius Brutus, who is *the* Brutus of this play. This second Brutus is referred to as "Decius" throughout the play and I will do so too, since that will conveniently prevent confusion between the two Brutuses.

Decius was another one of Caesar's generals during the Gallic conquest. In fact, he commanded the fleet at one point, and after Caesar's victory he served as governor of Gaul for a couple of years. His relationship to Caesar was so close that the Dictator even named Decius as one of his heirs, in case no member of his own family survived him.

. . . the noble Brutus . . .

Yet despite the importance of the individuals in the conspiracy, the need is felt for something more. Cinna says:

> *O Cassius, if you could*
> *But win the noble Brutus to our party—*
> —Act I, scene iii, lines 140–41

Casca explains a little later:

> *O, he sits high in all the people's hearts;*
> *And that which would appear offense in us,*
> *His countenance, like richest alchemy,*
> *Will change to virtue and to worthiness.*
> —Act I, scene iii, lines 157–60

There is another reason why Brutus is desired: to cast a respectable cloak over what otherwise might seem a heinous deed.

But Cassius explains his scheme of deluding "noble" Brutus with fake messages and even has them help in distributing them.

. . . no personal cause . . .

The scene now shifts to Brutus' house. Brutus has been unable to sleep. He wishes to join the conspiracy, but what he needs is some high-sounding noble reason to do so. He can't admit to the world, or even to himself, that he is being driven to it by Cassius' skillful appeal to his own vanity. He says:

> *I know no personal cause to spurn at him,*
> *But for the general. He would be crowned.*
> *How that might change his nature, there's the question.*
>
> —Act II, scene i, lines 11–13

That seems to be the key to the noble cause he seeks—how power might change Caesar. He decides he will

> *. . . think him as a serpent's egg*
> *Which hatched, would as his kind grow mischievous,*
> *And kill him in the shell.*
>
> —Act II, scene i, lines 32–34

What Brutus is now thinking of is a kind of preventive assassination. Caesar must be killed not because he is tyrannical but because he may grow tyrannical.

There is appeal in this argument. Power does tend to corrupt, as history has amply proven, and it is tempting to reason that a tyrant is best removed before he has a chance to show that corruption. What if Adolf Hitler had been assassinated in 1932?

And yet, it is a dangerous view. Once we accept the fact that assassination is justified to prevent tyranny rather than to punish it, who would be safe? What ruler could be sure of not being regarded by someone somewhere as being on the high road to tyranny, which he would reach someday?

. . . Erebus itself . . .

Brutus has been receiving the faked letters Cassius has prepared for him and he has managed to talk himself into believing in the nobility of the enterprise. It is clear he intends to join the conspiracy and yet he is still uneasy about it.

When the conspirators arrive at his house, cloaked in masks and darkness, he is aware of the intrinsic shame of conspiracy. He apostrophizes personified conspiracy and says it must assume a false front, for

> . . . *thy native semblance on,*
> *Not Erebus itself were dim enough*
> *To hide thee from prevention.*
> —Act II, scene i, lines 83–85

In some of the more poetic tellings of the Greek myths, Erebus is pictured as the son of Chaos, the brother of Night, and the father of the Fates. There are no tales told of him, however, and in poetry he is merely, as here, used as the personification of darkness. (The word is also used, sometimes, to describe an underground region en route to Hades.)

. . . what of Cicero . . .

The conspirators are now all together and Brutus is formally accepted among their ranks. Should still others be recruited? Cassius asks:

> *But what of Cicero? Shall we sound him?*
> *I think he will stand very strong with us.*
> —Act II, scene i, lines 141–42

Cicero had a very high reputation in Rome in some ways. In an age of general corruption, Cicero was widely recognized as an honest man of high ideals. He was a true republican and favored republican institutions backed by an honest and upright Senate. He would certainly be opposed to Caesar as king. All agree at once, therefore, that Cicero would be an excellent addition.

All but Brutus, that is, for he says:

> *O name him not! Let us not break with* [confide in] *him;*
> —Act II, scene i, line 150

According to Plutarch's tale, Cicero was not approached because it was felt he lacked the necessary resolution and might, in a pinch, betray the conspiracy.

And, indeed, although he was personally upright, he was indeed a physical coward and could not, through most of his life, face actual danger without quailing.

When that aristocratic hoodlum Clodius (see page I–261) set about harassing Cicero and attacking his retinue with his gang of toughs, Cicero was not the man to face him out. Cicero fled the country and satisfied himself with writing rather whining letters of complaint. When Clodius was finally killed by a rival gang leader, Milo, in 52 B.C., Cicero undertook to defend Milo but was scared into voicelessness by hostile crowds.

Again, in the civil war between Pompey and Caesar, Cicero made a rather miserable spectacle of himself as he tried to keep from being ground to death between the two, and feared to commit himself too far and too dangerously in either direction.

With this background, the conspirators would be justified in not wishing to risk their mutual safety to Cicero's courage.

This, however, is not the view Shakespeare presents Brutus as holding. He has Brutus give as his reason:

> *For he* [Cicero] *will never follow anything*
> *That other men begin.*
> —Act II, scene i, lines 151–52

Brutus objects to Cicero's vanity and to his penchant for insisting on leading an operation or refusing to join. It is indeed true that Cicero was terribly vain, but not more so than Brutus is portrayed to be in this play.

Indeed, one can easily suspect that Brutus does not want Cicero because he does not want a rival; that it is Brutus himself whose vanity will never allow him to "follow anything that other men begin."

He has just joined the conspiracy which other men have begun, to be sure, but he is already calmly taking over the decision-making power and dictating the direction of the conspiracy. Cassius proposes Cicero and Brutus vetoes it. This, in fact, continues throughout the play. Cassius is constantly making solid, practical suggestions, which Brutus as constantly vetoes.

. . . *sacrificers, but not butchers* . . .

Almost at once Brutus forces a wrong decision on the conspirators, one that makes ruin inevitable.

Cassius suggests that Mark Antony be killed along with Caesar. This is a sensible view if we accept the notion of the assassination in the first place. In planning any attack, it is only practical to take into account the inevitable counterattack and take measures to blunt it. Even if Caesar is killed, Mark Antony, an experienced general who is popular with his troops, would have the ability and the will to strike back, if he is allowed to live. Why not kill him then to begin with?

But Brutus says:

> *Our course will seem too bloody, Caius Cassius,*
> *To cut the head off and then hack the limbs,*
> *Like wrath in death and envy afterwards;*
> *For Antony is but a limb of Caesar.*
> *Let's be sacrificers, but not butchers, Caius.*
> —Act II, scene i, lines 162–66

Is this Brutus' nobility? If so, Shakespeare takes considerable pains to neutralize it in the assassination scene an act later, where the conspirators do act like butchers and Brutus urges them to it.

Is it Brutus' obtuse stupidity? Perhaps, but even more so it is an example of how he, not Cicero, "will never follow anything that other men begin."

Perhaps Brutus might himself have suggested taking care of Mark Antony along with Caesar, if only Cassius hadn't mentioned it first. Now, however, that Brutus is in the conspiracy he will lead it, and the one way to do that is to contradict any initiative on the part of the others.

Cassius, uneasily appalled by Brutus' blindness, tries to argue against it. Cassius says of Mark Antony:

> *Yet I fear him;*
> *For in the ingrafted love he bears to Caesar . . .*
> —Act II, scene i, lines 183–84

But Brutus won't even let him finish. Brutus has spoken, and that's that.

. . . Count the clock

At this point there is the sound of a clock striking, and Brutus says:

> *Peace! Count the clock.*
> —Act II, scene i, line 192

This is one of the more amusing anachronisms in Shakespeare, for there were no mechanical clocks in the modern sense in Caesar's time. The best that could be done was a water clock and they were not common, and did not strike. Striking clocks, run by falling weights, were inventions of medieval times.

Indeed, the very same scene, at the beginning, shows Brutus speaking of time telling in a way far more appropriate to his period. He says then, peevishly, as he sleeplessly paces his bedroom:

> *I cannot, by the progress of the stars,*
> *Give guess how near to day.*
> —Act II, scene i, lines 2–3

. . . Cato's daughter

Some last arrangements are made. Decius volunteers to make certain that Caesar doesn't change his mind and that he does come to the Capitol.

There is talk of adding new conspirators and of the exact time of meeting. The conspirators then leave and Brutus is left alone.

But not for long. His wife enters, and demands to know what is going on. Who are these men who came? Why is Brutus acting so strangely? She feels she has a right to know, for

> *I grant I am a woman; but withal*
> *A woman that Lord Brutus took to wife.*
> *I grant I am a woman; but withal*
> *A woman well reputed, Cato's daughter.*
> —Act II, scene i, lines 292–95

Cato was the Pompeian leader referred to earlier, who led the anti-Caesar forces in Africa. His full name was Marcus Porcius Cato, and he is usually called "Cato the Younger," because his great-grandfather, another Marcus Porcius Cato (see page I–227), was also important in Roman history. Cato the Younger was a model of rigid virtue. He deliberately conducted his life along the lines of the stories that were told of the ancient Romans.

Since he was always very ostentatious about his virtue, he annoyed other people; since he never made allowances for the human weaknesses of others, he angered them; and since he never compromised, he always went down to defeat in the end.

Later generations, however, who didn't have to deal with him themselves, have greatly admired his stiff honesty and his unbending devotion to his principles.

Cato, after the defeat of the anti-Caesarian forces in Africa at the Battle of Thapsus in 46 B.C., was penned up with the remnants of the army in the city of Utica (near modern Tunis). Rather than surrender, he killed himself, so that he is sometimes known to later historians as "Cato of Utica." (Meanwhile the "noble" Brutus, far from emulating his uncle's steadfastness, had switched to Caesar's side and was serving under him.)

Cato had a daughter, Porcia, or "Portia" as the name appears in this play, who was thus Brutus' first cousin. The two had married in 46 B.C. and were thus married about two years at the time of the conspiracy. It was the second marriage for each.

. . . a voluntary wound

Portia is an example of the idealized view of the Roman matron—almost repulsive in their high-minded patriotism, as in the case of Volumnia (see page I–225). Thus, Shakespeare follows an unpleasant story told by Plutarch and has Portia say:

I have made strong proof of my constancy,
Giving myself a voluntary wound
Here in the thigh; can I bear that with patience,
And not my husband's secrets?

—Act II, scene i, lines 299–302

According to Plutarch, she slashed her thigh with a razor, and then suffered a fever, presumably because the wound grew infected. She recovered and, showing Brutus the scar, said this indicated how well she could endure pain and ensured that even torture would wring no secrets out of her.

Roman legend spoke frequently of the manner in which Romans could endure pain in a patriotic cause. There is the tale, for instance, of Gaius Mucius, who in the very early days of the Roman Republic was captured by the general of the army laying siege to Rome. Mucius had invaded the general's tent with the intention of assassinating him and now the general demanded, under threat of torture, information on Rome's internal condition.

Mucius then deliberately placed his right hand in a nearby lamp flame and held it there till it was consumed, to indicate how little effect torture would have on him. Perhaps Portia's self-inflicted wound was inspired by the Mucius legend. And perhaps the tale concerning Portia is no more true than that concerning Mucius.

If the matter of Portia's wound were true, then the fact that Brutus was unaware of a bad wound in his wife's thigh until she showed it to him gives us a surprising view of the nature of their marriage.

Caius Ligarius . . .

Before Brutus can explain the situation to Portia, however, a new conspirator enters and she must leave. Brutus greets him:

Caius Ligarius, that Metellus spake of.

—Act II, scene i, line 311

Plutarch calls him Caius Ligarius, but he is named Quintus Ligarius in other places. In either case, he is a senator who supported Pompey and held out for him with Cato the Younger. He was taken prisoner after the Battle of Thapsus, but was pardoned by Caesar after he had been brought to trial, with Cicero as his defender.

Ligarius would have joined the conspiracy sooner but he is sick. As soon as he hears of the details, however, he says:

> *By all the gods that Romans bow before,*
> *I here discard my sickness!*
> > —Act II, scene i, lines 320–21

This story too is from Plutarch, and it is another example of the kind of heroism Romans loved to find in their historical accounts.

The heavens themselves . . .

That same night on which Casca has seen supernatural prodigies and Brutus has joined the conspiracy, Caesar himself has had a restless sleep. His wife, Calphurnia, has had nightmares. What's more, she has heard of the sights men have seen and she doesn't want Caesar to leave the house the next day, fearing that all these omens foretell evil to him.

Caesar refuses to believe it, maintaining the omens are to the world generally and not to himself in particular. To which Calphurnia replies:

> *When beggars die, there are no comets seen;*
> *The heavens themselves blaze forth the death of princes.*
> > —Act II, scene ii, lines 30–31

The comets, appearing in the skies at irregular intervals, and, with their tails, taking on a most unusual shape, were wildly held to presage unusual disasters. For anything else, their appearance is too infrequent. Similarly, the unusual portents of the night must apply to some unusual person.

This makes sense provided astrology in general does.

Caesar does not go so far as to scorn astrology, but he does scorn fear in a pair of famous lines:

> *Cowards die many times before their deaths;*
> *The valiant never taste of death but once.*
> > —Act II, scene ii, lines 32–33

Their minds may change

Nevertheless, Calphurnia continues to beg and eventually Caesar is sufficiently swayed to grant her her wish and to agree to send Mark Antony in his place.

It is morning by now, however, and Decius comes to escort Caesar to the Capitol. The news that Caesar has changed his mind and will not come staggers him. Quickly, he reinterprets all the omens and hints the senators will laugh. Not only does he make use of the threat of ridicule, but he also says:

> . . . *the Senate have concluded*
> *To give this day a crown to mighty Caesar.*
> *If you shall send them word you will not come,*
> *Their minds may change.*

—Act II, scene ii, lines 93–96

This seems true enough. Caesar is trying to pull off a coup that runs counter to the deepest Roman prejudices and it was bound to be a near thing. He had failed, at the Lupercalian festival, to gain a crown by popular acclamation. If he now missed a chance to force the Senate to give him one, he would be giving his opponents a chance to mobilize their forces and the whole project might be ruined. The historic Caesar won many successes by striking when the iron was hot and it isn't likely that he would let such a crucial moment pass.

Caesar changes his mind once again and makes the fateful decision to go.

. . . Read it, great Caesar

Caesar's progress toward the Capitol is attended by further warnings, according to Plutarch's story, which Shakespeare follows. The soothsayer is there and Caesar tells him ironically that the ides of March are come (presumably implying that all is well). To which the soothsayer answers, portentously:

> *Ay, Caesar, but not gone.*

—Act III, scene i, line 2

Another man, Artemidorus, attempts to give Caesar a warning. According to Plutarch, he was a Greek professor of rhetoric from whom a number of the conspirators had been taking lessons. (In those days, rhetoric, the art of oratory, was indispensable to a public career.) He had picked up knowledge of their plans, presumably because they spoke carelessly before him, and he was anxious to reveal those plans to Caesar (perhaps out of pro-Caesarian conviction or perhaps out of the hope of profiting by Caesar's gratitude).

In any case, he passes a note of warning to Caesar, telling him of the plot. According to Plutarch, Caesar tried several times to read the note but was prevented from doing so by the press of people about him. Shakespeare makes it more dramatic, showing Caesar, by his arrogance, bringing his fate upon himself.

Artemidorus, in an agony of impatience, cries out, as other petitions are handed Caesar:

> *O Caesar, read mine first; for mine's a suit*
> *That touches Caesar nearer. Read it, great Caesar.*
> —Act III, scene i, lines 6–7

But Caesar answers grandly:

> *What touches us ourself should be last served.* *Climax?*
> —Act III, scene i, line 8

And thus he condemns himself.

Et tu, Brute . . .

In what follows, Shakespeare follows Plutarch very closely. The conspirators crowd around Caesar on the pretext that they are petitioning for the recall of the banished Publius Cimber, the brother of Metellus Cimber. Caesar refuses, in a fine oratorical display of unyieldingness, saying:

> *. . . I am constant as the Northern Star*
> *Of whose true-fixed and resting quality*
> *There is no fellow in the firmament.*
> —Act III, scene i, lines 60–62

The Northern Star (Polaris) does not itself move. Rather, all the other stars circle about it as a hub (in reflection, actually, of the earth's rotation about its axis, the northern end of which points nearly at Polaris). Caesar's picture of himself as the unchanging Northern Star about which all other men revolve is an example of what the Greeks called *hubris* ("overweening arrogance") and it is followed quickly by what the Greeks called *ate* ("retribution"). It is the biblical "Pride goeth before . . . a fall."

The conspirators have now surrounded him so that the onlookers cannot see what is happening, as each approaches on pretense of adding his own pleas to the petition. When Brutus makes his plea, Caesar is embarrassed. The Dictator has repulsed Metellus Cimber haughtily but he cannot use similar language to the beloved Brutus. All he can say is an uneasy:

> *What, Brutus?*
> —Act III, scene i, line 54

Then, later, when Decius begins his plea, Caesar points out that he cannot do it even for Brutus, saying:

> *Doth not Brutus bootless kneel?*
>
> —Act III, scene i, line 75

At which point Casca strikes with his dagger, crying:

> *Speak hands for me!*
>
> —Act III, scene i, line 76

According to Plutarch, they each proceed to strike at Caesar, having made an agreement among themselves that each conspirator must be equally involved in the assassination. No one of them must be able to try to escape at the expense of the others by pleading he did not actually stab Caesar.

Caesar tried vainly to avoid the blows until it was Brutus' turn. Brutus, according to Plutarch, struck him "in the privities." That was the last straw for Caesar. When Brutus lifted his weapon to strike, Caesar cried out, "Thou also, Brutus!" and attempted no further to avoid the strokes. His outcry, in Latin, was so famous that Shakespeare made no attempt to translate it, but kept it as it was, a small patch of Latin in the midst of the play:

> *Et tu, Brute? Then fall Caesar.*
>
> —Act III, scene i, line 77

. . . in Caesar's blood

So died Julius Caesar, on March 15, 44 B.C., hacked to death by twenty-three stabs. Brutus had earlier made an apparently noble speech to the effect that they not "hack the limbs" and that they "be sacrificers, but not butchers" (see page I–279). He had meant it figuratively with reference to the possible death of Mark Antony, but now that speech takes on a grislier aspect, when it turns out that Caesar has, deliberately, been hacked and butchered to death.

Was Shakespeare sardonically contrasting Brutus' brutal acts with his "noble" words? What should we think? Perhaps Brutus merely went along with the general feeling of the conspirators that the assassination be carried out by universal hacking. This seems doubtful since in every other case in the play he insists on having his own way even though the consensus is against him. Then too, Shakespeare has Brutus go on to say:

Stoop, Romans, stoop,
And let us bathe our hands in Caesar's blood
Up to the elbows, and besmear our swords.
Then walk we forth, even to the market place,
And waving our red weapons o'er our heads,
Let's all cry "Peace, freedom, and liberty!"
                                —Act III, scene i, lines 105–10

Plutarch merely says the swords were bloodied, but Shakespeare has Brutus suggest that they deliberately bloody their arms. Does this not give them all the precise appearance of butchers? Does this not deliberately belie Brutus' plea to "be sacrificers, but not butchers"?

It is precisely as butchers that Brutus would have them all go out to the market place; that is, the forum. The Latin word *forum* means "market place." It was located in the valley between the Capitoline and Palatine hills, the first two hills to be occupied by the city. The market place is a natural site for people to gather, trade news, and discuss business, so that the word "forum" has now come to mean any public place for the discussion of ideas.

. . . on Pompey's basis . . .

When Cassius foretells grimly that this scene will be re-enacted in tragedies through future centuries, the "noble" Brutus evinces no sorrow. Rather, he lends himself to this lugubrious fantasy and says:

How many times shall Caesar bleed in sport,
That now on Pompey's basis lies along
No worthier than the dust!
                                —Act III, scene i, lines 114–16

The reference to "Pompey's basis" is to the pedestal of the statue of Pompey that stood at the Capitol. The statues and trophies of Pompey which had come to grace the Capitol in the time of Pompey's greatness had been taken away in the aftermath of Caesar's victory at Pharsalia by those in Rome who thought to ingratiate themselves with the victor in this way. Caesar, on his return, ordered them replaced, forgiving the memory of Pompey even as he had forgiven so many of Pompey's followers.

And yet not only was he assassinated by those he had forgiven, but in death he was dragged by them (probably deliberately) to the base of Pompey's statue in order that he might lie there a symbolic victim at the feet of the man he had defeated.

. . . no harm intended . . .

At the realization that Caesar was dead, the Capitol emptied itself of the panicked spectators. Who knew, after all, how broad and general the plot was and how many were marked for death?

It was necessary, therefore, for the conspirators to calm the city at once lest a panicked populace, once it regained its breath, break out in uncontrollable rioting of which no one could foresee the end. One senator, Publius, too old and infirm to fly with the rest, remains on the scene terrified. He is accosted gently and sent with a message. Brutus says:

> Publius, good cheer;
> There is no harm intended to your person,
> Nor to Roman else. So tell them, Publius.
>
> —Act III, scene i, lines 89–91

. . . to lie in death

Mark Antony is a special case. He knew that if the plot extended to even one person beyond Caesar himself, he would be the one. So far he had been spared; he had even been taken aside at the time of the assassination. It was necessary now for him to play for time and gain, temporarily, the friendship of the conspirators, or at least allay their suspicions.

In Shakespeare's version, Mark Antony sends a messenger to Brutus with a most humble message:

> If Brutus will vouchsafe that Antony
> May safely come to him and be resolved
> How Caesar hath deserved to lie in death,
> Mark Antony shall not love Caesar dead
> So well as Brutus living; but will follow
> The fortunes and affairs of noble Brutus
> Through the hazards of this untrod state
> With all true faith.
>
> —Act III, scene i, lines 130–37

It is a careful speech, appealing to Brutus' vanity and giving him the necessary adjective "noble." Mark Antony tempts Brutus with the picture of himself taking the place of Caesar, while Mark Antony continues as loyal assistant. It would seem that Antony judges Brutus to be not so much interested in stopping Caesar as in replacing him, and perhaps he is right.

Nor is Mark Antony a complete hypocrite. The message does not promise unqualified submission to Brutus. It sets a condition. Brutus must arrange to have Mark Antony "be resolved" as to the justice of the assassination; that is, to have it explained to his satisfaction.

Of course, Mark Antony has no intention of allowing the assassination to be explained to his satisfaction, but Brutus cannot see that. The unimaginably vain Brutus feels the assassination to be necessary; how then can anyone else doubt that necessity once Brutus explains it?

Your voice shall be as strong . . .

Brutus is won over at once, as he always is by praise, but Cassius is not. He says:

> *But yet have I a mind*
> *That fears him much . . .*
>> —Act III, scene i, lines 144–45

Brutus, with his usual misjudgment, brushes that aside and welcomes Mark Antony, who now comes onstage with a most magnificent piece of bluffing. He speaks in love and praise of Caesar, and grandly suggests that if they mean to kill him, now is the time to do it, in the same spot and with the same weapons that killed Caesar. Yet he is careful to join the offer with flattery:

> *No place will please me so, no mean of death,*
> *As here by Caesar, and by you cut off,*
> *The choice and master spirits of this age.*
>> —Act III, scene i, lines 161–63

The flattery further melts the susceptible Brutus, of course, and he offers conciliatory words to Mark Antony. The practical Cassius realizes that Brutus is all wrong and feels the best move now is to inveigle Mark Antony into sharing the guilt by offering to cut him in on the loot. He says:

> *Your voice shall be as strong as any man's*
> *In the disposing of new dignities.*
>> —Act III, scene i, lines 177–78

. . . what compact . . .

Mark Antony makes no direct reply to the offer of loot, but proceeds to strike those attitudes of nobility he knows will impress Brutus. He ostentatiously shakes the bloody hands of the conspirators yet speaks eloquently

of his love for Caesar, once Brutus professes that he himself had loved
Caesar.

Cassius, rather desperately, breaks into the flow of rhetoric with a practical question to Mark Antony:

> *But what compact mean you to have with us?*
> *Will you be pricked in number of our friends,*
> *Or shall we on, and not depend on you?*
>
> —Act III, scene i, lines 215–17

Where we write names with chalk on slate, or with pen and pencil on
paper, the Romans were apt to scratch them in the wax coated on a wooden
tablet. Where we check off names with a $\checkmark$, they would prick a little hole
next to the name. Hence the question "Will you be pricked in number of
our friends . . ."

. . . do not consent . . .

Again, Mark Antony evades a direct commitment. He still wants an
explanation of Caesar's crimes, which Brutus is still confident he can give.
What's more, Antony adds a casual request:

> *. . . that I may*
> *Produce his* [Caesar's] *body to the market place,*
> *And in the pulpit, as becomes a friend,*
> *Speak in the order of his funeral.*
>
> —Act III, scene i, lines 227–30

It seems a moderate request. After all, Caesar, though assassinated,
deserves an honorable funeral and a eulogy by a good friend; especially
a friend who seems to have joined the conspiracy. Brutus agrees at once.

The clear-seeing Cassius is horrified. He pulls Brutus aside and whispers
urgently:

> *You know not what you do; do not consent*
> *That Antony speak in his funeral.*
>
> —Act III, scene i, lines 232–33

Cassius knows, after all, that Mark Antony is a skillful orator and that
if he catches the attention of the populace he can become dangerous.

Nothing, however, can win out over Brutus' vanity. It is the mainspring
of all the action. Brutus points out that he will speak first and explain the
assassination (he is always sure that he has but to explain the deed and

everyone will understand and be satisfied) and that Mark Antony can, after that, do nothing. To make doubly sure, Brutus sets conditions, saying to Antony:

> *You shall not in your funeral speech blame us,*
> *But speak all good you can devise of Caesar*
> *And say you do't by our permission;*
> > —Act III, scene i, lines 245–48

Brutus was worse than vain; he was a fool to think that such conditions could for one moment stop an accomplished orator and force him to make the conspirators seem noble and magnanimous. Later on, when Mark Antony does speak, he keeps to those conditions rigorously, and it does the conspirators no good at all.

. . . Caesar's spirit . . .

Mark Antony is left alone with Caesar's body and, in an emotional soliloquy, apologizes to the corpse for his show of affection with the conspirators. He predicts the coming of civil war and says:

> *And Caesar's spirit, ranging for revenge,*
> *With Ate by his side come hot from hell,*
> *Shall in these confines with a monarch's voice*
> *Cry "Havoc," and let slip the dogs of war,*
> > —Act III, scene i, lines 270–73

Ate is visualized here as the personified goddess of retribution, and "Havoc" is the fearful cry that sounds out at the final fall of a besieged city. It is the signal for unrestrained killing and looting when all real fighting is done. (The word "hawk" is from the same root and one can see in the swoop of the hawk the symbol of the surge of a conquering army on its helpless victims.)

The reference to "Caesar's spirit" may be taken literally in any society that believes in ghosts, and these include both Mark Antony's and Shakespeare's. Indeed, Caesar's spirit makes an actual appearance in Plutarch's tale and therefore in this play as well.

. . . Octavius Caesar . . .

It is but a small leap, however, to interpret "Caesar's spirit" in another way too. His spirit may be the spirit of his reforms and his attempt to reorganize the Roman government under a strong and centralized rule. This could live on and come "ranging for revenge." And that spirit might well be embodied in another man.

As though to indicate this, Antony's soliloquy is followed by the immediate entrance of a "Servant"; a messenger coming to announce his master is on his way. It follows only six lines after the reference to "Caesar's spirit" and Mark Antony recognizes the newcomer, saying:

> *You serve Octavius Caesar, do you not?*
>
> —Act III, scene i, line 276

Octavius Caesar, whose proper name is Gaius Octavius, is the only living close relative of Julius Caesar. He is the grandson of Caesar's sister, Julia, and is therefore the grandnephew of Julius. He was born in 63 B.C. and was nineteen years old at the time of the assassination.

Octavius was a sickly youth. He had joined Caesar in Spain (just before the opening of the play) but he was obviously unsuited for war. Nor was his greatuncle anxious to push him into warfare. In default of living children of his own, the Dictator needed Octavius as an heir. Therefore, when Caesar was making ready to move east against Parthia, he ordered the boy to remain in Greece at his studies.

Octavius was still in Greece when news of the assassination reached him, and at once he decided to make for Rome, there to demand what he could of his greatuncle's inheritance.

Antony does not welcome the news of the coming of Octavius. He may have loved Julius Caesar, but that does not require him to love Caesar's grandnephew. After all, Antony could reasonably argue that he, as Caesar's loyal lieutenant and a mature man of war, is more realistically Caesar's heir than some sickly child who happens to be related to Caesar by accident of birth. The presence of the boy would merely produce complications and Antony does his best to keep him away. He sends back a message:

> *Here is a mourning Rome, a dangerous Rome,*
> *No Rome of safety for Octavius yet.*
>
> —Act III, scene i, lines 288–89

. . . I loved Rome more

The next scene moves directly to Caesar's funeral. Actually, it took place on March 20 and the five days between assassination and funeral were busy ones. The conspirators had hurriedly taken hold of the spoils. Many of them have had provinces assigned to them: Brutus will govern

Macedonia; Cassius will take over Syria; Decius will have Cisalpine Gaul; Trebonius, part of Asia Minor; Metellus Cimber, another part of Asia Minor; and so on.

For men supposedly actuated only by a noble concern for the commonwealth, they were extraordinarily quick to place themselves in positions of power. Nor was Brutus behindhand in taking his share.

But Shakespeare ignores this and proceeds directly to the funeral.

Brutus begins by addressing a hostile crowd in the forum, offering to explain the circumstances of the assassination. He does so in prose; stilted prose, at that, with laboriously balanced sentences. He insists he loved Caesar and killed him only for the greater good of Rome:

> Not that I loved Caesar less, but that I loved Rome more.
> —Act III, scene ii, lines 21–22

The essence of his defense is that Caesar had grown too ambitious for Rome's safety; that is, Caesar was ambitious to be king. Brutus says (and here he is almost convincing):

> As Caesar loved me, I weep for him; as he was fortunate, I rejoice at it; as he was valiant, I honor him; but as he was ambitious, I slew him.
> —Act III, scene ii, lines 24–27

Brutus then prepares to keep his promise of letting Mark Antony speak on behalf of Caesar. With fatuous vanity, he urges the crowd to listen to Antony and himself hurries away as though he is convinced that he has so turned the crowd against Caesar and toward himself that nothing Mark Antony can say will undo matters.

. . . Brutus is an honorable man

Now Mark Antony is there with Caesar's corpse. Quietly, he begins one of the most famous passages Shakespeare has ever written. (Whatever Antony said in reality—and it must have been effective, for he gained Rome thereby—it is hard to believe that he could possibly have scaled the heights Shakespeare wrote for him.) He begins:

> Friends, Romans, countrymen, lend me your ears;
> I come to bury Caesar, not to praise him.
> —Act III, scene ii, lines 75–76

He admits that if (*if*) Caesar were ambitious, that was a bad fault and he has certainly been punished for it. As he promised Brutus, he explains that he speaks by permission of the conspirators and he does nothing but praise them:

> *Here, under leave of Brutus and the rest*
> *(For Brutus is an honorable man,*
> *So are they all, all honorable men),*
> *Come I to speak in Caesar's funeral.*
>
> —Act III, scene ii, lines 83–86

The phrase "Brutus is an honorable man" is to be repeated and repeated by Mark Antony. He gives the praise to Brutus in precisely the fashion Brutus most enjoys, crying out how honorable and noble he is. Yet the skillful repetition, in rising tones of irony, builds the anger of the crowd to the point where the very epithet "honorable" becomes an insult.

Speaking in short and moving phrases, as though he were choked with emotion, Mark Antony disposes of the charge of ambition:

> *He was my friend, faithful and just to me;*
> *But Brutus says he was ambitious.*
> *And Brutus is an honorable man.*
> *He hath brought many captives home to Rome,*
> *Whose ransoms did the general coffers fill;*
> *Did this in Caesar seem ambitious?*
> *When that the poor have cried, Caesar hath wept;*
> *Ambition should be made of sterner stuff.*
> *Yet Brutus says he was ambitious;*
> *And Brutus is an honorable man.*
> *You all did see that on the Lupercal*
> *I thrice presented him a kingly crown,*
> *Which he did thrice refuse. Was this ambition?*
> *Yet Brutus says he was ambitious;*
> *And sure he is an honorable man.*
>
> —Act III, scene ii, lines 87–101

Antony's arguments are, of course, irrelevant. By "ambition," Brutus meant Caesar's desire to be king, and nothing Antony says disproves that desire. Caesar might be a good personal friend, yet plan to be a king. He might donate ransom money to the public treasury and express pity for the poor, but intend these acts only to build up the good will with which to buy the crown. If he did refuse the crown, it was only to force the mob to insist he take it, and he regretted the failure of the scheme.

But all that, of course, doesn't matter. Antony's speech is almost hypnotic in its force, and, properly presented, it can win over a modern audience which had earlier been prepared to sympathize with Brutus.

. . . *'tis his will*

The crowd is indeed moved and Mark Antony senses that without difficulty. It is time for the next step, to appeal directly and forcefully to the powerful emotion of greed. He says:

> But here's a parchment with the seal of Caesar;
> I found it in his closet; 'tis his will.
> Let but the commons hear this testament,
> Which, pardon me, I do not mean to read,
> And they would go and kiss dead Caesar's wounds,
> > —Act III, scene ii, lines 130–34

Yes indeed, Antony has not been idle in the interval between assassination and funeral either. The very night following the assassination, having made a temporary peace with the conspirators, he took a crucial action. He seized the funds which Caesar had gathered for his projected Parthian campaign and persuaded Calphurnia to let him have access to all of Caesar's papers, among which he found the will.

The funds would be important when it came to bribing senators and hiring soldiers. The will—well, that would be used now.

Naturally, once Antony mentions the will and declines to read it, the crowd howls for it to be read. Antony hangs back and the more he does so, the more violently insistent the crowd becomes. Choosing his moment with artistic care, Antony advances his reason for hesitating:

> I fear I wrong the honorable men
> Whose daggers have stabbed Caesar; I do fear it.
> > —Act III, scene ii, lines 153–54

And one man in the crowd calls out with passion:

> They were traitors. Honorable men!
> > —Act III, scene ii, line 155

There is hatred in the repetition of that phrase so often applied to Brutus, and which Brutus so loves. Another man in the crowd cries out.

> They were villains, murderers! The will! Read the will!
> > —Act III, scene ii, lines 157–58

. . . the Nervii

Mark Antony has them now, but it is still not enough. He intends to make them virtually insane with rage. He descends from the rostrum and has them gather round Caesar's corpse. Antony holds up the cloak Caesar was wearing when he was killed:

> *You all do know this mantle; I remember*
> *The first time ever Caesar put it on:*
> *'Twas on a summer's evening, in his tent,*
> *That day he overcame the Nervii.*
>
> —Act III, scene ii, lines 172–75

The Nervii were a fierce Gallic tribe living in what is now Belgium, and Caesar had beaten them in 57 B.C. This was a skillful allusion, too, for it reminded the crowd of Caesar's conquests, not over Romans, but over barbarian Gauls (whom Romans particularly hated because of the memory of the ancient Gallic sack of Rome in 390 B.C.).

To be sure, this passage doesn't square with actual history. Mark Antony couldn't possibly remember the evening of the day on which Caesar overcame the Nervii, since he didn't join Caesar in Gaul till three years later. Moreover, is it likely that Caesar on the supreme day on which he expects to be crowned king will put on a thirteen-year-old cloak? All our information concerning him agrees that he was a dandy, and meticulous with his grooming.

However, it is an effective passage and the real Mark Antony would have used it, regardless of accuracy, if he had thought of it.

. . . the most unkindest cut of all

Now Mark Antony begins to point to the bloodied rents in the mantle where swords had sliced through (and this he actually did, according to Plutarch). What's more, he has progressed to the point where he can begin to stab the conspirators with pointed words.

> *Look, in this place ran Cassius' dagger through;*
> *See what a rent the envious Casca made;*
> *Through this the well-beloved Brutus stabbed,*
>
> —Act III, scene ii, lines 176–78

Antony lingers on Brutus' stroke, for it was this man who had instructed him to praise the conspirators, and it is Brutus therefore whom he chiefly wants to destroy with praise. He says:

> *. . . Brutus, as you know, was Caesar's angel.*
> *Judge, O you gods, how dearly Caesar loved him!*
> *This was the most unkindest cut of all;*
>> —Act III, scene ii, lines 183–85

Now he whips away the cloak to reveal Caesar's own gashed body, and that is the equivalent of crying "Havoc," for the maddened crowd breaks out with:

> *Revenge! About! Seek! Burn! Fire! Kill! Slay! Let not a traitor live!*
>> —Act III, scene ii, lines 206–7

. . . When comes such another

But still Mark Antony is not through. He calms them yet again, still keeping to his promise to praise Brutus, by saying:

> *I am no orator, as Brutus is;*
> *But (as you know me all) a plain blunt man*
>> —Act III, scene ii, lines 219–20

It is a piece of praise that openly laughs at Brutus, and there is still, after all, the will to read. Antony begins the reading and says:

> *To every Roman citizen he gives,*
> *To every several man, seventy-five drachmas.*
>> —Act III, scene ii, lines 243–44

There is more:

> *Moreover, he hath left you all his walks,*
> *His private arbors, and new-planted orchards,*
> *On this side Tiber; he hath left them you,*
> *And to your heirs forever; common pleasures,*
> *To walk abroad and recreate yourselves.*
>> —Act III, scene ii, lines 249–53

That brings Antony to his climax. He has wrought on the crowd with pity, with greed, and with gratitude, and they are in the highest state combustible. He gives them one last shout:

> *Here was a Caesar! When comes such another?*
>> —Act III, scene ii, line 254

With that, the crowd explodes. They are utterly mad and ready to destroy the conspirators and Rome with them if necessary. Mark Antony watches them rush off, raving, and says grimly:

> *Now let it work; Mischief, thou art afoot,*
> *Take though what course thou wilt.*
>
> —Act III, scene. ii, lines 263–64

. . . his name's Cinna

Shakespeare shows the mob at its frightening work in one incident taken from Plutarch, which involves a minor poet named Helvius Cinna. He was a friend of Caesar's and no relative of Lucius Cornelius Cinna, the conspirator.

Cinna the poet is stopped by elements of the mob who demand he identify himself. He says:

> *Truly, my name is Cinna.*
>
> —Act III, scene iii, line 27

The crowd at once sets up its howl and though the poor fellow shrieks that he is not Cinna the conspirator but merely Cinna the poet, they will not listen, crying:

> *It is no matter, his name's Cinna;*
>
> —Act III, scene iii, line 33

. . . rid like madmen . . .

Soon enough, the conspirators realize the two deadly mistakes Brutus has made for them; letting Antony live, and letting him speak. The mere name of "conspirator" is now enough to kill.

The servant who had appeared in the earlier scene to talk of Octavius appears soon after the conclusion of Antony's great speech to announce:

> *. . . Brutus and Cassius*
> *Are rid like madmen through the gates of Rome.*
>
> —Act III, scene ii, lines 271–72

They hoped at first merely to retire to some nearby town till Rome had cooled down, and then to return. This was not to happen, however. Rome did not cool down; Mark Antony remained in control. The conspirators scattered, some to the respective provinces they had been assigned, some elsewhere. Brutus and Cassius are the only conspirators with whom the play concerns itself in the last two acts. They retire to the eastern provinces.

. . . Octavius is already come . . .

But Mark Antony was not to have it all his own way. He had no way of knowing it, but the day of his funeral speech was the climax of his life, the apex of his power. He had ended it with the rhetorical cry: "Here was a Caesar! When comes such another?" and eleven lines later that question is answered.

The servant who brings the news of the flight of Brutus and Cassius also announces news concerning his master:

> *Sir, Octavius is already come to Rome.*
> —Act III, scene ii, line 265

Here was another Caesar. He was that literally, for he adopted the name; and he was that figuratively too, for he was even more capable than Julius, winning that for which the older man had died without getting.

There was no way of telling this when Octavius first came; young, sickly, and seeming to be of little account in comparison to the great, magnetic charisma that now clung to Mark Antony. Antony underestimated him (everyone did) and could not tell that, as he himself had been Brutus' nemesis, so Octavius was fated to be his—something that will be made clear enough in Shakespeare's *Antony and Cleopatra*.

But even without foreseeing the future, Antony can see that Octavius' coming is a serious embarrassment. Caesar's will, which Antony had read with such consummate skill at the funeral, contained clauses he tried to suppress. Caesar, in his will, had named Octavius as his heir and, what's more, had adopted him as his son. This meant that Octavius owned all of Caesar's funds (which Mark Antony had appropriated) and would have become the next king if Caesar had lived long enough to gain the monarchy.

Mark Antony wanted the will ratified and had persuaded the Senate to do so by agreeing to allow them also to declare an amnesty for the conspirators. However, Antony fought against the ratification by the Senate of that part of the will that dealt with Octavius. Just the same, Gaius Octavius changed his name to Gaius Julius Caesar Octavianus, to indicate his new status as Caesar's adopted son, and is thereafter known to English-speaking historians as Octavian. In this play, however, he remains "Octavius" throughout and I will call him so.

The change in name was a shrewd move. It enabled him to call himself "Caesar" and capitalize on the magic of that name. What's more, Cicero rallied to him, out of hatred for Mark Antony, and Cicero's oratory was a tower of strength.

He and Lepidus . . .

There was also the question of the army. In the play, when Mark Antony hears Octavius is in Rome, he asks his whereabouts and is told:

> *He and Lepidus are at Caesar's house.*
>
> —Act III, scene ii, line 267

The reference is to a Roman general, Marcus Aemilius Lepidus. On the day of the assassination, he just happened to have a legion of troops on the outskirts of the city. He was preparing to move with them to his province in southern Gaul, but when the news of the assassination came, he occupied Rome instead. If he had been a strong character, this accident of being on the scene at the crucial moment might have made him master of the Roman realm.

Lepidus was, however, a weakling. He lacked Octavius' name, Antony's reputation, and the resolution of both. In later years he remained a pawn.

. . . to Octavius

Antony, hearing that Octavius is in Rome and with Lepidus, doesn't hesitate. He says to the Servant:

> *Bring me to Octavius.*
>
> —Act III, scene ii, line 274

The short mob scene involving Cinna the poet intervenes and the fourth act then opens with Antony, Octavius, and Lepidus in triple conference. As far as the play is concerned, little time has elapsed.

In actual history, however, more than a year and a half of intensive political and military jockeying has intervened between the funeral of Caesar and the three-way meeting of Antony, Octavius, and Lepidus.

After the funeral, Antony found himself in annoying difficulties. He was not the politician Caesar had been and he found Octavius a curiously capable enemy for the sickly youngster he seemed to be. What's more, Cicero now rose to new prominence and his oratory flamed to new heights. Cicero's hatred for Mark Antony showed itself in a succession of unbelievably vituperative speeches that wrecked Antony's popularity almost as much as Antony's funeral speech had wrecked Brutus'.

Antony felt he could best regain lost ground by military victory. Decius (Decimus Brutus) was in control of Cisalpine Gaul and he was the closest of the conspirators. Antony turned against him, despite the senatorial amnesty of the conspirators, and thus began a new civil war.

As soon as Antony had marched out of Rome at the head of his troops, however, Octavius persuaded the Senate to declare him a public enemy. With senatorial backing gone, Mark Antony could not make head against Decius, but was forced, in April 43 B.C. (a full year after the assassination), to march his army into Gaul. He had failed militarily as well as politically.

Octavius, master of Rome, now forced the Senate to recognize him at last as heir to Caesar. In September 43 B.C. he himself led an army against Decius. Octavius was no fighter, but the name of Caesar succeeded where Antony had failed. Decius' soldiers deserted in droves, and Decius himself had to flee. He was captured and executed and Octavius' reputation skyrocketed.

By that time, though, Brutus and Cassius had consolidated their power over the eastern half of the Roman realm. It was clear that if Antony and Octavius continued to maneuver against each other, they would both lose and the conspirators would yet emerge in control.

Lepidus therefore labored to bring Antony and Octavius together in a compromise settlement, and succeeded. All three met in Bononia (the modern Bologna) on November 27, 43 B.C., twenty months after the assassination.

The three agreed to combine in a three-man government, an agreement resembling the one that had been made by Caesar, Pompey, and Crassus seventeen years before. In fact, the new agreement is called the Second Triumvirate. The fourth act opens after the Second Triumvirate has been formed.

. . . with a spot . . .

Shakespeare presents the Triumvirate at the moment they make a grisly bargain to seal their compact.

What they chiefly need, after all, is money. One way of obtaining it is to declare certain well-to-do individuals guilty of treason, execute them, and confiscate their estates. This also gives each triumvir a chance to get rid of personal enemies as well. The enemy of one, however, might be the friend or relative of another member of the Triumvirate; and if one of them sacrifices a friend or relative he would naturally expect the other two to make a similar sacrifice.

The proscriptions (that is, arbitrary condemnations) include, for instance, Lepidus' brother. As quid pro quo, Antony must allow his nephew to be marked with a prick in the wax (see page I–290), indicating he is listed for execution. Antony says, with a kind of gruesome magnanimity:

> He shall not live; look, with a spot I damn him.
> —Act IV, scene i, line 6

What Mark Antony demands (something that does not appear in the play at this point) and Octavius is forced to concede, is Cicero's life. Cicero had labored for Octavius and had made all the difference when the young man had first come to Rome as an almost ignored young man, and now Octavius, grown to power, delivers the great orator to his enemy. However much we might excuse it as practical politics, however much we might argue that Octavius had no choice, it remains the blackest single act of Octavius' long and illustrious career.

Are levying powers . . .

With the immediate financial problem ironed out by means of the proscriptions, the Triumvirate can turn to military matters. Antony says:

> And now, Octavius,
> Listen great things. Brutus and Cassius
> Are levying powers; we must straight make head.
> —Act IV, scene i, lines 40–42

The united Caesarians must face the united conspirators. Brutus had been in Macedonia for a year now and Cassius in Syria. In the face of the gathering of their enemies, they were getting armies ready for battle and planning to unite their forces.

. . . this night in Sardis . . .

At once the action moves to the conspirators, who are meeting each other in Asia Minor, and for the first time the setting of the play is outside the city of Rome.

The scene is laid in the camp of Brutus' army outside Sardis, and one of Brutus' aides, Lucilius, tells him with reference to Cassius' approaching army:

> They mean this night in Sardis to be quartered;
> —Act IV, scene ii, line 28

Sardis is a city in western Asia Minor, forty-five miles east of the Aegean Sea. In ancient times it was the capital of the Lydian monarchy, which reached its height under Croesus, who reigned there from 560 to 546 B.C. The wealth of Sardis and the kingdom of Lydia at that time was such that the Greeks used to say "as rich as Croesus," a phrase that is still used today.

It was captured by the Persians in 546 B.C. Then when Alexander the Great destroyed the Persian Empire two centuries later, Sardis fell under the rule of Macedonian generals and monarchs.

In 133 B.C. it became Roman and continued to remain a great city for over a thousand years more. It was finally destroyed in 1402 by the hosts of Tamerlane, the Mongol conqueror, and has lain in ruins ever since.

. . . *an itching palm*

Once Brutus and Cassius meet in the former's tent, they have at each other, for both have accumulated grievances. Brutus scorns Cassius for his avarice:

> *Let me tell you, Cassius, you yourself*
> *Are much condemned to have an itching palm,*
> *To sell and mart your offices for gold*
> *To undeservers.*
>
> —Act IV, scene iii, lines 9–12

The difficulty with the conspirators, as much as with the Triumvirate, is money. Soldiers must be paid or they will desert, and the money must be obtained. Cassius therefore sold appointments to high positions for ready cash, and it is this Brutus scorns.

Another source of money was from the surrounding population. The helpless civilians had no way of resisting the armies, and during the early part of 42 B.C., for instance, Cassius stripped the island of Rhodes of all its precious metals. Asia Minor felt the squeeze too. Wherever Cassius' army passed, the natives were stripped bare and, in some cases, killed when they had given the last drachma. Brutus scorns this too, for he says:

> . . . *I can raise no money by vile means.*
> *By heaven, I had rather coin my heart*
> *And drop my blood for drachmas than to wring*
> *From the hard hands of peasants their vile trash*
> *By any indirection.*
>
> —Act IV, scene iii, lines 71–75

This sounds good, but in the course of the Pompeian war, Brutus, as an actual historical character, had spent some time on the island of Cyprus. There he had oppressed the provincials heartlessly, squeezing money out of them without pity, and writing complaining letters that he was prevented from squeezing still more out of them by other officials.

Then too, while Cassius was draining Rhodes, Brutus demanded money of the city of Xanthus in Asia Minor, and when the city would not (or could not) pay, he destroyed it. He is supposed to have felt remorse after the destruction of Xanthus and to have ceased trying to collect money in this fashion.

And yet he lists one of his grievances against Cassius as:

> *I did send to you*
> *For certain sums of gold, which you denied me;*
>
> —Act IV, scene iii, lines 69–70

It is immediately after that that he says unctuously that he "can raise no money by vile means." In other words, he cannot steal but he is willing to have Cassius steal, share in the proceeds, and then scorn Cassius as a robber. Neither Brutus' intelligence nor his honesty ever seem to survive the words Shakespeare carefully put into his mouth.

. . . swallowed fire

In the quarrel, it is Cassius who backs away, and the scene ends in a reconciliation. Characteristically, Brutus praises himself unstintingly as one who is slow to anger and quick to forgive. He says:

> *O Cassius, you are yokèd with a lamb*
> *That carries anger as the flint bears fire,*
> *Who, much enforcèd, shows a hasty spark,*
> *And straight is cold again.*
>
> —Act IV, scene iii, lines 109–12

Brutus further explains his momentary anger by telling Cassius that his wife, Portia, is dead:

> *Impatient of my absence,*
> *And grief that young Octavius with Mark Antony*
> *Have made themselves so strong—for with her death*
> *That tidings came—with this she fell distract*
> *And (her attendants absent) swallowed fire.*
>
> —Act IV, scene iii, lines 151–55

According to Plutarch, she choked herself by putting hot embers into her mouth. This seems so strange a way of committing suicide as to be almost unbelievable. Is it possible that this is a distortion of a much more likely death—that she allowed a charcoal fire to burn in a poorly ventilated room and died of carbon monoxide poisoning?

. . . farewell, Portia . . .

And now an odd thing happens. An officer, Marcus Valerius Messala, comes in with news from Rome. Brutus maneuvers him (with considerable effort) into revealing the fact that Portia is dead. Without saying he already knows the fact, Brutus says calmly:

> *Why, farewell, Portia. We must die, Messala.*
> *With meditating that she must die once,*
> *I have the patience to endure it now.*
> —Act IV, scene iii, lines 189–91

Brutus adhered to that school of philosophy called Stoicism. It had been founded, some three centuries earlier, by a Greek philosopher, Zeno of Citium (who possibly had Phoenician ancestry as well). He lectured at a *Stoa Poikile* (a "painted porch"; that is, a corridor lined with frescoes) in Athens. From this porch the philosophy took its name.

Stoicism saw the necessity of avoiding pain, but did not feel that choosing pleasure was the best way to do so. The only safe way of living the good life, Stoics felt, was to put oneself beyond both pleasure and pain: to train oneself not to be the slave of either passion or fear, to treat both happiness and woe with indifference. If you desire nothing, you need fear the loss of nothing.

Brutus, with his "Why, farewell, Portia," was greeting the death of a loved one with the proper Stoic response.

But why didn't he tell Messala that he already knew of the death in detail and had just been discussing it with Cassius? One theory is that, having written the proper Stoic scene with its "farewell, Portia," Shakespeare felt it presented Brutus in an unsympathetic light. He felt, perhaps, that an English audience could scarcely feel the proper sympathy for so extreme a Roman attitude; they would feel it repellently heartless. He therefore wrote the earlier scene in which Brutus is still Stoical but shows enough feeling to grow angry with Cassius. Then, the theory goes on, both versions appeared, through carelessness, in the final printed copy of the play.

Yet it seems to me that this cannot be so. Shortly after Messala enters, Cassius, still brooding over the news, says to himself:

Portia, art thou gone?

—Act IV, scene iii, line 165a

To this Brutus makes a hasty response:

No more, I pray you.

—Act IV, scene iii, line 165b

It is as though he does more than merely neglect to tell Messala of his knowledge. He takes special pains to keep Cassius from telling him.

Why? Perhaps precisely so he can strike the proper Stoic note. Since he already knows and the shock is over, he can greet the news with marvelous calm, and strike a noble pose.

We might find an excuse for him and say that he was seizing the opportunity to be ostentatiously strong and Stoical in order to hearten his officers and his army with a good example. On the other hand, he might have done it out of a vain desire for praise. After all, as soon as Brutus makes his Stoic response, Messala says, worshipingly:

Even so great men great losses should endure.

—Act IV, scene iii, line 192

If this is so, and certainly it is a reasonable supposition, what a monster of vanity Shakespeare makes out Brutus to be.

Cicero is dead

Before Messala has the news of Portia's death forced out of him, he delivers the news of the proscriptions of the Second Triumvirate. Dozens of men of senatorial rank have been executed. What's more, says Messala:

Cicero is dead,
And by that order of proscription.

—Act IV, scene iii, lines 178–79

As soon as the Second Triumvirate was formed, Cicero, knowing that any accommodation between Octavius and Antony would have to be at his own expense, tried to escape from Italy. Contrary winds drove his ship back to shore, however, and before he could try again, the soldiers sent to kill him had arrived.

Those with him, his servants and retainers, made as though to resist, but Cicero, sixty-three years old and tired of the wild vicissitudes of public life, found at the end the physical courage he had so conspicuously lacked throughout his life. Forbidding resistance, he waited calmly for the soldiers and was cut down on December 7, 43 B.C., twenty-one months after Julius Caesar's assassination.

. . . toward Philippi

Brutus, meanwhile, has told of the news he himself has received; news to the effect that the triumvirs are on the move eastward, taking the offensive. He says:

> Messala, I have here received letters
> That young Octavius and Mark Antony
> Come down upon us with a mighty power,
> Bending their expedition toward Philippi.
> —Act IV, scene iii, lines 166–69

Philippi was an important city in the province of Macedonia, and was located about ten miles north of the Aegean Sea. It had been built up on the site of an earlier village in 356 B.C. by Philip II, King of Macedon and father of Alexander the Great. The city was named for Philip.

. . . taken at the flood . . .

The question now is how best to react to the Triumvirate offensive. Cassius takes the cautious view. He suggests their forces remain on the defensive.

> 'Tis better that the enemy seek us;
> So shall he waste his means, weary his soldiers,
> Doing himself offense, whilst we, lying still,
> Are full of rest, defense, and nimbleness.
> —Act IV, scene iii, lines 198–201

Brutus, however, disagrees. He points out that the provinces between the enemy army and themselves are angered by the looting they have undergone and would join Antony and Octavius. Their own army, on the other hand, is as large as it is ever likely to be, and if they wait it will start declining. He says, sententiously, in a famous passage:

> *There is a tide in the affairs of men*
> *Which, taken at the flood, leads on to fortune;*
> *Omitted, all the voyage of their life*
> *Is bound in shallows and in miseries.*
>
> —Act IV, scene iii, lines 217–20

Once again, Brutus contradicts Cassius and has his way and the result proves his judgment to be wrong. Throughout the play, Brutus consistently misjudges the moment when the tide is at the flood, and to place this passage in his mouth seems to intend irony.

. . . this monstrous apparition

Brutus makes ready for sleep, in an almost family atmosphere of concern for his servants (and he is portrayed most nearly noble, in good truth, here). He settles down to read a book when suddenly he cries out:

> *Ha! Who comes here?*
> *I think it is the weakness of mine eyes*
> *That shapes this monstrous apparition.*
>
> —Act IV, scene iii, lines 274–76

It is the ghost of Caesar, which Brutus boldly accosts. It tells him only that they will meet again at Philippi.

One might suppose that this was a Shakespearean invention, introduced for dramatic effect, for the chance of turning lights low, producing shadows, and chilling the audience, but, in actual fact, Shakespeare does not have to invent it. The report that Caesar's ghost appeared to Brutus is to be found in Plutarch.

It is with a forward look to this scene, perhaps, that Shakespeare had had Mark Antony speak earlier of "Caesar's spirit."

It proves not so . . .

The fifth act opens in the plains near Philippi, with the opposing armies facing each other and waiting for battle. Octavius, looking at the scene with grim satisfaction, says:

> *Now, Antony, our hopes are answered;*
> *You said the enemy would not come down,*
> *But keep the hills and upper regions.*
> *It proves not so . . .*
>
> —Act V, scene i, lines 1–4

What had happened between the acts was this. Brutus and Cassius, crossing the straits into Macedonia from Asia Minor, encountered a portion of the triumvir army near Philippi. If the conspirators had attacked at once, they ought to have won, but before they could do so, the rest of the triumvir army arrived and it was a standoff.

The triumvir army now outnumbered the conspirators but was weaker in cavalry. What is more, it was Brutus and Cassius who had the strong position in the hills, while Antony and Octavius occupied a marshy and malarial plain.

Brutus and Cassius had only to stay where they were. It would have been suicidal for Antony and Octavius to try to charge into the hills. Yet to stay on the plains would expose them to hunger and disease.

Indeed, Octavius was already sick, although this doesn't appear in the play. Octavius seemed always to be sick before a battle. In this case, he fell sick at Dyrrhachium (on the coast of what is now Albania) and had to be carried by litter the 250 miles to Philippi.

Cassius opposed battle, maintaining that by waiting it out, the enemy would sooner or later have to retreat and that the effect would be one of victory for the conspirators. He was manifestly correct in this and Antony, putting himself grimly in the conspirators' place, was sure that was exactly what they would do.

Antony still did not count on the egregious stupidity of Brutus. Brutus again opposed Cassius and favored immediate battle. Once again Brutus insisted on having his way. Once again Cassius gave in.

. . . the Hybla bees

A parley between the opposing commanders was arranged before the battle. Perhaps an accommodation could be arranged. That could not be, however, for the conversation quickly degenerated into recriminations. At one point, Cassius refers bitterly to Antony's oratory (thinking perhaps of the funeral speech) and says:

> But for your words, they rob the Hybla bees,
> And leave them honeyless.
>
> —Act V, scene i, lines 34–35

Hybla was a town in Sicily, on the southern slopes of Mount Etna, and some forty miles northwest of Syracuse. It was famous, almost proverbial, for its honey.

. . . Brutus, thank yourself

In the wordy quarrel, Antony does have the best of it and Cassius finally is forced to become aware of Brutus' misjudgments. He says to Brutus angrily:

> *. . . Now, Brutus, thank yourself;*
> *This [Antony's] tongue had not offended so today,*
> *If Cassius might have ruled.*

> —Act V, scene i, lines 45–47

Surely he must have thought how, in all likelihood, the conspirators would have been long in control of Rome if only Antony had been killed along with Caesar, as he had advised.

Was Cassius born

There is nothing, then, but to make ready for the actual battle. Cassius is seriously depressed, perhaps because it has been borne in upon him, forcefully, how wrong Brutus has been all through, and because he bitterly regrets all the times he gave in wrongly.

It is now October 42 B.C., more than two and a half years since the assassination of Caesar, and Cassius says to his aide:

> *Messala,*
> *This is my birthday; as this very day*
> *Was Cassius born.*

> —Act V, scene i, lines 70–72

Since we don't know in what year Cassius was born, we can't say how old he was on the day of the Battle of Philippi. However, Plutarch refers to him as older than Brutus (a view Shakespeare adopts) and Brutus may have been born in 85 B.C. It would seem then that Cassius must be in his mid-forties at least and possibly pushing fifty.

Cassius does not find the fact that the battle will be fought on his birthday to be a good omen. He does not want to fight it. He says to Messala:

> *Be thou my witness that against my will*
> *(As Pompey was) am I compelled to set*
> *Upon one battle all our liberties.*

> —Act V, scene i, lines 73–75

This is a reference to the fact that it is Brutus, not Cassius, who is pushing for battle. Cassius, who let himself be overruled, reminds himself, sadly, that Pompey was similarly forced into battle at Pharsalia, six years before, by the hotheads among his councilors, when cautious delay might have served his cause better.

. . . I held Epicurus strong

To unavailing regret that he had allowed himself to be swayed by Brutus, Cassius finds trouble in supernatural omens. He says:

> *You know that I held Epicurus strong,*
> *And his opinion; now I change my mind,*
> *And partly credit things that do presage.*
>
> —Act V, scene i, lines 76–78

Epicurus of Samos was a Greek philosopher who was a contemporary of the Zeno who had founded Stoicism. Epicurus' philosophy (Epicureanism) adopted the beliefs of certain earlier Greek philosophers who viewed the universe as made up of tiny particles called atoms. All change consisted of the random breakup and rearrangement of groups of these atoms and there was little room in the Epicurean thought for any purposeful direction of man and the universe by gods. Omens and divine portents were considered empty superstition.

Now, however, Cassius begins to waver. It seems two eagles, having accompanied the army from Sardis to Philippi, have now flown away, as though good luck were departing. On the other hand, all sorts of carrion birds are now gathering, as though bad luck were arriving.

. . . the rule of that philosophy . . .

Cassius' pessimism forces him to question Brutus as to his intentions in case the battle is lost. Brutus answers in high Stoic fashion. His actions will follow:

> *Even by the rule of that philosophy* [Stoicism]
> *By which I did blame Cato for the death*
> *Which he did give himself . . .*
>
> —Act V, scene i, lines 100–2

Stoicism held it wrong to seek refuge in suicide. The good man must meet his fate, whatever it is, unmoved.

Cassius asks, sardonically, if Brutus is ready, then, in case of defeat, to be led in triumph behind the conqueror's chariot through the Roman streets (and, undoubtedly, with the jeers of the Roman populace ringing in his ears).

At once, Brutus' Stoicism fails him. As long as his Stoic demeanor brings him praise, it is well. If it is going to bring him disgrace he abandons it. But he does so with characteristic self-praise:

> No, Cassius, no; think not, thou noble Roman
> That ever Brutus will go bound to Rome;
> He bears too great a mind.
>
> —Act V, scene i, lines 110–12

Since both plan to die in case of defeat, they may never meet again. Brutus says:

> Forever, and forever, farewell, Cassius!
>
> —Act V, scene i, line 116

Cassius answers in kind and both are now ready for the battle, which takes up the rest of the play.

. . . the word too early

On both sides there was double command. Cassius on the seaward side opposed Antony; Brutus on the inland side opposed Octavius. The fortunes differed on the two flanks. Brutus had the advantage over Octavius and advanced vigorously. He sends messages of victory to the other flank by Messala, saying:

> . . . I perceive
> But cold demeanour in Octavius' wing,
> And sudden push gives them the overthrow.
> Ride, ride, Messala!
>
> —Act V, scene ii, lines 3–6

But even now, in the midst of victory, Brutus judges wrongly. Brutus should, at all cost, have kept his part of the army from advancing in such a way that they could not support the other part in case of need. Instead, his men are overvictorious and fall to looting, when they ought to have wheeled down upon Antony's men.

Antony's army manages instead to drive hard against Cassius' wing. That wing breaks and flies and can receive no help. Titinius, Cassius' aide, says bitterly:

> *O Cassius, Brutus gave the word too early,*
> *Who, having some advantage on Octavius,*
> *Took it too eagerly; his soldiers fell to spoil,*
> *Whilst we by Antony are all enclosed.*
>
> —Act V, scene iii, lines 5–8

In Parthia . . .

Cassius' depression now costs him the final price. He does not realize the exact magnitude of Brutus' victory and therefore does not understand that even allowing for his own defeat, the battle is no worse than drawn.

A band of Brutus' horsemen making their way toward him is mistaken by him for the enemy. When his aide, Titinius, reconnoitering, embraces them gladly, the nearsighted Cassius thinks he is taken prisoner and that his own capture is imminent.

Cassius therefore calls his servant, Pindarus, saying:

> *In Parthia did I take thee prisoner;*
> *And then I swore thee, saving of thy life,*
> *That whatsoever I did bid thee do,*
> *Thou shouldst attempt it.*
>
> —Act V, scene ii, lines 37–40

In Parthia, at the Battle of Carrhae, eleven years before, Cassius had carried through the greatest military achievement of his life. He had carefully husbanded the downhearted remnants of a defeated army and had safely brought them back to Syria.

He had not despaired then, but he did now. He orders his slave to kill him with the same sword that had once pierced Caesar. It is done and Cassius dies.

The last of all Romans . . .

When the news of Cassius' death is brought to Brutus, he comes to view the body and says:

> *O Julius Caesar, thou art mighty yet!*
> *Thy spirit walks abroad, and turns our swords*
> *In our own proper entrails.*
>
> —Act V, scene iii, lines 94–96

His eulogy over Cassius is:

> *The last of all Romans, fare thee well!*
> *It is impossible that ever Rome*
> *Should breed thy fellow . . .*
>
> —Act V, scene iii, lines 99–101

The statement is a gross exaggeration. Except for his conduct at the Battle of Carrhae, Cassius had shown little real ability. Even in organizing the successful conspiracy that killed Caesar, his weakness in allowing the stupid Brutus to guide affairs ruined all.

Caesar, now be still

Shakespeare has the battle continuing as though it were all one piece. That is not so in actual history.

After the drawn battle in which Cassius killed himself unnecessarily and Brutus was victorious on his wing, the two armies withdrew to lick their wounds.

Brutus' army still held the stronger position and, what's more, Brutus controlled the sea approaches so that supplies were denied Antony and Octavius. He had but to stay where he was and he would still win.

But he could not. The habit of wrong judgments could not be broken and this time there wasn't even Cassius present to argue vainly with him. After twenty days he marched to the attack again in a straightforward head-to-head battle.

He lost again, brought the remnants back to a strong position once again, and might have sold his last bit dear, but that his soldiers refused to fight any more.

There was nothing left to do but find somebody to kill him. This service was performed for him by his servant, Strato, who held the sword while Brutus ran upon it, saying:

> *Caesar, now be still:*
> *I killed not thee with half so good a will.*
>
> —Act V, scene v, lines 50–51

To the end the talk is of Caesar.

. . . the noblest Roman of them all

There remains only the eulogy to be delivered over Brutus. Antony, surveying the dead body, says:

> *This was the noblest Roman of them all.*
> *All the conspirators save only he*
> *Did that they did in envy of great Caesar;*
> *He, only in a general honest thought*
> *And common good to all, made one of them.*
> —Act V, scene v, lines 68–72

Plutarch reports that "it was said" that Antony had, on a number of occasions, said something like this. Was it to win over those who had been on Brutus' side for the war that was to follow between himself and Octavius? Was it out of gratitude, since Brutus had refused to allow Antony to be killed on the ides of March? Did Antony really believe what he said?

In terms of Shakespeare's play, this final eulogy is so devastatingly wrong, it can be accepted only as irony. How can we possibly follow Antony in saying that Brutus was the only one who didn't act out of envy, when Shakespeare shows us that he was the only one who *surely* acted out of envy.

In the great seduction scene in Act I, scene ii, Cassius turns all his arguments against Brutus' weak point, his monstrous vanity. He paints a world in which Caesar is all and Brutus nothing, knowing that Brutus cannot bear such a thought. Finally, he makes the comparison a brutally direct one:

> *Brutus and Caesar: what should be in that "Caesar"?*
> *Why should that name be sounded more than yours?*
> *Write them together, yours is as fair a name;*
> *Sound them, it doth become the mouth as well;*
> *Weigh them, it is as heavy; conjure with 'em,*
> *"Brutus" will start a spirit as soon as "Caesar."*
> —Act I, scene ii, lines 142–47

It might be argued that Cassius was speaking generally, comparing Caesar to any other Roman citizen, but the fact is that he made the comparison to *Brutus* specifically, and Brutus listened. Take this together with Brutus' character as painstakingly revealed in every other facet of the play and we can be certain that he was *not* the only conspirator not driven by envy. On the contrary, he was the one conspirator who was driven *only* by envy.

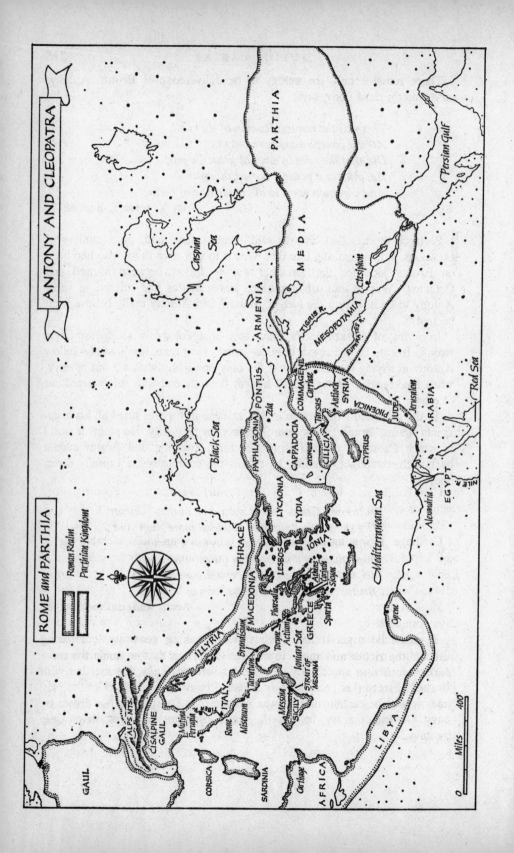

12

The Tragedy of

ANTONY AND CLEOPATRA

I N 1607 Shakespeare returned to North's edition of Plutarch, from which eight years before he had taken material for *Julius Caesar*. Using Plutarch's biography of Mark Antony, Shakespeare wrote what was virtually a continuation of the earlier play, and made it the most Plutarchian of the three plays he derived from that source.

Antony and Cleopatra begins almost at the point where *Julius Caesar* had left off.

Brutus and Cassius have been defeated at the double battle at Philippi in 42 B.C. by the troops under Mark Antony and Octavius Caesar. These two, together with Lepidus, the third member of the Triumvirate (see page I–301), are now in a position to divide the Roman realm among themselves.

Octavius Caesar took western Europe for his third, with the capital at Rome itself. It was what he could best use, for it left him with the Senate and the political power-center of the realm. Octavius was a politician and the battles he could best fight (and win) were battles of words with the minds of men at stake.

Lepidus was awarded the province of Africa, centering about the city of Carthage. It was an inconsiderable portion for an inconsiderable man, and Lepidus was and remained a mere appendage of Octavius Caesar. Lepidus grew important only when someone was required to act as go-between where the two major partners were concerned.

Mark Antony had the East and this suited him very well. Except for the days immediately following Julius Caesar's assassination, Antony had never gotten along well in Rome. He preferred the Eastern provinces, which were far the richer and more sophisticated portion of the Roman realm. Mark Antony was a hedonist; he knew how to appreciate pleasure, and in the great cities of the East he knew he would find it.

He was also a soldier who welcomed war, and in the East he knew he would find that too. The Parthians were to be found there. Eleven years before they had destroyed a Roman army (see page I–257) and for that they had never been punished. Antony hoped to deliver that punishment.

. . . this dotage of our general's . . .

All Antony's plans went awry, however, when in 41 B.C. he encountered
Cleopatra, the fascinating Queen of Egypt. He fell sufficiently in love with
her to forget the necessity of beating the Parthians and to neglect the threat
of the slow, crafty advance of Octavius Caesar in Rome.

The love story of Antony and Cleopatra has captured the imagination of
the world, and has left generations sighing. (And never has it been as ap-
pealingly and as majestically described as in this play.) In its own time,
however, the affair must have been viewed with impatience by those soldiers who were bound to Antony and who found themselves neglected,
their chance for loot and glory vanishing.

The play opens in Cleopatra's palace in Alexandria, the capital of Egypt.
Two soldiers, Demetrius and Philo, come onstage. Philo, who knows the
situation, expresses his soldierly displeasure to Demetrius, who apparently is a newcomer fresh from Rome. Philo says:

> *Nay, but this dotage of our general's*
> *O'erflows the measure. Those his goodly eyes*
> *That o'er the files and musters of the war*
> *Have glowed like plated Mars, now bend, now turn*
> *The office and devotion of their view*
> *Upon a tawny front.*

> —Act I, scene i, lines 1–6

The expression "tawny front" means "dark face" and this represents
a misconception concerning Cleopatra that has been common in later times
and that can never be corrected, in all likelihood. Because she was the
ruler of an African land and because she was an "Egyptian," she has been
presumed to be dark, dusky, swarthy, even perhaps part Negress. She may
have been dark, to be sure, but she was no darker, necessarily, than any
other Greek, for she was *not* of Egyptian descent.

Egypt had become the kingdom of Cleopatra's forebears back in 323
B.C. when Alexander the Great had died. Alexander had conquered the
entire Persian Empire, of which Egypt was part, and after his death one
of his generals, Ptolemaios (or Ptolemy, as he is known in English), seized
Egypt. In 305 B.C. Ptolemy adopted the title of king and from then on, for
two and a half centuries, his descendants, each named Ptolemy, ruled
Egypt.

Ptolemy I, the first of the kings of Ptolemaic Egypt, was a Macedonian,
a native of the Greek-speaking kingdom of Macedon, lying just north of
Greece proper. All the Ptolemies married Greeks and all the rulers of
Ptolemaic Egypt, down to and including Cleopatra, were completely Greek.
Cleopatra's father had been Ptolemy XI, the great-great-great-great-great-

great-grandson of Ptolemy I. There had been a number of Ptolemaic queens, by the way, who bore the name of Cleopatra (a perfectly good Greek name meaning "glory of her father," and not Egyptian at all). The one in Shakespeare's play is actually Cleopatra VII, but she is the only one remembered today and the name without the numeral is enough. There is no danger of confusion with any of the first six.

The notion of Cleopatra as a dark African is carried on further as the speech continues, with Philo saying of Antony:

> *His captain's heart,*
> *Which in the scuffles of great fights hath burst*
> *The buckles on his breast, reneges all temper*
> *And is become the bellows and the fan*
> *To cool a gypsy's lust.*
> —Act I, scene i, lines 6–10

The word "gypsy" means simply "Egyptian" here, but although Cleopatra was an Egyptian by nationality, she was not one by descent. Indeed, the true Egyptians were a "lower class" to the ruling Greeks, as the natives of India once were to the ruling British. Cleopatra would undoubtedly have been terribly offended to have been considered an "Egyptian."

Furthermore, the word "gypsy" by Shakespeare's time had come to be applied to a wandering group of men and women of unknown origin. Popular rumor had them coming from Egypt, hence "gypsy," but it is much more likely they came from India (see page I–149). To call Cleopatra a "gypsy," then, is to call up visions of swarthy women in markedly non-Western costume, both to Shakespeare's audience and our own.

The triple pillar of the world . . .

Antony, Cleopatra, and their train of maids and eunuchs are entering now, and Philo says of Mark Antony, more bitterly still:

> *Take but good note, and you shall see in him*
> *The triple pillar of the world transformed*
> *Into a strumpet's fool.*
> —Act I, scene i, lines 11–13

Antony is one of the three members of the Second Triumvirate. All three together support and rule the Roman realm, hence "triple pillar."

Rome is referred to here as "the world." In a way, it was to the ancients, for it included the entire Mediterranean basin and virtually all the lands that the Greeks and Romans considered "civilized."

Thus, in the Bible, the Gospel of St. Luke speaks of a decree by Caesar Augustus (the very same Octavius Caesar of this play—but a generation later) to the effect that the Roman realm be taxed. The biblical verse phrases it this way: "And it came to pass in those days, that there went out a decree from Caesar Augustus, that all the world should be taxed" (Luke 2:1).

Of course, such phraseology is exaggerated. The Romans (and Shakespeare too) knew that the Roman government didn't rule over all the earth. There were barbarian tribes north of the northern limits of Rome, tribes who would make their presence felt all too painfully in a couple of centuries. And even if the view is confined to civilized areas, the Romans (and Shakespeare too) knew that the Roman government didn't rule over all the civilized earth. To the east of the eastern limits of Rome was the Parthian Empire, a civilized region that had already beaten Rome once and continued to remain a deadly danger to it. (There were also civilizations in China and India, but these lay beyond the Roman horizon.)

In this particular play, however, the transmutation of Rome into the world is dramatically advantageous. Antony is playing for the rule of the whole realm, and loses it, partly through his own miscalculations, and partly through his love affair with Cleopatra. It becomes intensely dramatic, then, to be able to say, he "lost the world." It becomes even more dramatic to say he lost it for love.

In fact, the English poet John Dryden in 1678 wrote his version of the tale of Antony and Cleopatra (far inferior to Shakespeare's), which he called, in the most romantic possible vein, *All for Love; or the World Well Lost.*

. . . tell me how much

Antony and Cleopatra speak now and they are engaged in the foolish love talk of young lovers. Cleopatra is pouting:

> *If it be love indeed, tell me how much.*
> —Act I, scene i, line 14

Yet Cleopatra is not a schoolgirl. She is an experienced woman who has lived and loved fully. She was born in 69 B.C., so she was twenty-eight years old when she met Antony.

Cleopatra's father, Ptolemy XI, died in 51 B.C. and her younger brother, the thirteen-year-old Ptolemy XII, succeeded to the throne. Cleopatra, then nearly eighteen, ruled jointly with him. She got tangled up in palace politics, however, and fled to Syria to raise an army with which to seize undisputed control of the country.

It was at this time, 48 B.C., that Pompey appeared in Egypt, fleeing from the defeat inflicted on him at Pharsalia by Julius Caesar (see page I–257). Pompey was killed by the Egyptians and Julius Caesar landed in Alexandria soon after.

Cleopatra realized that the real power in the Mediterranean basin rested with Rome. Egypt was the only remaining independent power of any consequence along all the Mediterranean shore, and even she could not do a thing without Roman permission. She couldn't even play her game of internal politics if Rome seriously objected. Cleopatra also realized that Julius Caesar was now the most powerful Roman. If she could gain him to her side, then, he would certainly place her on the throne.

She had herself smuggled in to Julius Caesar (so the story goes) wrapped in a carpet. The later storytellers insist that when the carpet was unwrapped, she stepped out nude.

Julius Caesar did see the merits of her case (however persuaded) and spent a year in Alexandria, needlessly interfering in Egyptian politics and running considerable danger himself. During this interval, Cleopatra is supposed to have been his mistress. (He was fifty-two years old at the time, she twenty-one.) At least she bore a son which, she insisted, was his, and called him Ptolemy Caesar. The son was known, popularly, as Caesarion.

In 47 B.C. Caesar left Alexandria, went to Asia Minor to fight a brief battle, then turned westward to win victories in Africa and Spain, and finally came back to Rome as Dictator. He was assassinated just as he was about to make himself king.

There is a story that he brought Cleopatra to Rome and that she managed to get away and return to Egypt after the assassination. This, however, is based on an ambiguous line in one of Cicero's letters, and is very probably not so. Caesar was far too clever a politician to complicate his plans by bringing a "foreign queen" to Rome and setting her up as his mistress. What's more, Cleopatra was far too clever a queen to want to leave her turbulent country for others to control and loot just so she could be a hated mistress to an aging Roman politician.

She very likely stayed in Alexandria between 47 B.C., when Caesar left, and 41 B.C., when she met Mark Antony.

Fulvia perchance is angry . . .

The love murmurings of Antony and Cleopatra are interrupted, however, by messengers from Rome. Antony is annoyed at having his mood punctured and wants the messengers to be brief and leave. Cleopatra, however, is always petulant at any mention of Rome, any hint of the great affairs that might take Antony away from her as once they had taken Julius Caesar. She grows peevishly sarcastic:

Nay, hear them, Antony.
Fulvia perchance is angry . . .

—Act I, scene i, lines 19–20

Fulvia is Mark Antony's third wife; a fierce and ambitious woman, not inferior to Cleopatra in fire, but, presumably, lacking Cleopatra's sexual fascination. At least she didn't fascinate Antony.

Antony was her third husband. Her first husband had been that Publius Clodius who had been the occasion for Julius Caesar's divorce from his second wife (see page I–261) and who had turned into a gang leader who made Cicero his particular prey.

When Cicero was killed as a result of the proscriptions that followed the establishment of the Second Triumvirate (see page I–306), Fulvia had his head brought to her as proof of his death. When it was in her hands, she drove her hairpin through the dead tongue of the great orator with savage glee, as vengeance against the eloquence that had so lacerated two of her husbands, Clodius and Antony.

· Antony had headed east, after his division of the world with Octavius Caesar and Lepidus, without bothering to take the formidable Fulvia with him. (No doubt that was not an oversight, either.) Any mention of his fierce wife undoubtedly embarrassed Mark Antony, and Cleopatra knew it.

. . . the scarce-bearded Caesar . . .

Cleopatra went further than that. The news might not be merely from Fulvia; it might be from Octavius Caesar. She says:

. . . or who knows
If the scarce-bearded Caesar have not sent
His pow'rful mandate to you.

—Act I, scene i, lines 20–22

This must sting. Antony is forty-one years old when the play opens; a grizzled warrior more than a score of years in the field. Octavius Caesar is nineteen years his junior, only twenty-two years old now. Antony had to resent the fact that so young a man should be able to hold himself on an equal plane with the mature warrior.

(Incidentally, in this play Octavius Caesar is always referred to as "Caesar," where he was always referred to as "Octavius" in *Julius Caesar*. I shall call him "Octavius Caesar" in order to avoid confusing him with Julius Caesar.)

Cleopatra gets what she wants. The baited Antony cries out:

Let Rome in Tiber melt, and the wide arch
Of the ranged empire fall! Here is my space,
—Act I, scene i, lines 33–34

He refuses to hear the messengers and leaves.

. . . prized so slight

The soldiers, Philo and Demetrius, who have watched these proceedings
with surprise and disapproval, cannot believe that Antony can be so careless of his own interests. Demetrius says:

Is Caesar with Antonius prized so slight?
—Act I, scene i, line 56

Demetrius, fresh from Rome, knows what Octavius Caesar is doing, if
Antony does not.

Octavius Caesar, young though he was, was one of the master politicians of history. He lost no time in frivolity of any kind. He was a cold,
shrewd man, who never made a serious mistake, and whose destiny it was
to carry through to a conclusion the plans of his great-uncle, Julius Caesar.
He was not, perhaps, as brilliant as the great Julius in war or literature, but
he was even wiser in politics, for he carried through the necessary governmental reforms without ever making use of the hated word "king," but
making himself in the end far greater than a king.

Nor did Octavius Caesar have the romantic appeal of Antony, or Antony's ability to orate, or his talent for putting on a kind of bluff, hail-
fellow-well-met exterior that made him tremendously popular with the
soldiers. Octavius could never be loved till age, and the realization at last
of his greatness, had made him a father figure to the people.

Antony always underrated him and did not realize that the young man
was building a network of alliances with politicians and generals, binding
them to himself by self-interest rather than love, and weaving a net that
would end by making him all-powerful.

Shakespeare too underprizes him, but this is necessary for the sake of
the drama. The audience sympathy must be with the lovable profligate and
not with the cool politician.

Nevertheless, though all audiences must "root" for Antony (for Shakespeare wills it so, and wins me over too), truth compels one to say that
Octavius Caesar was by far the greater man of the two and that it would
have been a world tragedy if circumstance had allowed Mark Antony to
beat him.

. . . the common liar . . .

Demetrius goes on to say:

> *I am full sorry*
> *That he approves the common liar, who*
> *Thus speaks of him at Rome;*
> —Act I, scene i, lines 59–61

Octavius Caesar, in his ceaseless war against Antony, made skillful use of propaganda. When the two triumvirs were at peace, Octavius carefully sapped the other's strength in the West by spreading tales of his profligacy.

Cicero's fiery and vituperative speeches in the last year of his life had covered Antony with slime. And though Cicero's invective was remorselessly exaggerated, much of it stuck. Antony, who did carouse and who loved luxury, gave all too much ground for believing much worse about him than was true.

Octavius Caesar made use of Cicero's speeches and also made use of the new matter that Antony offered. Antony was with this "foreign queen." Rome had fought many wars with Eastern monarchs and it was easy to escalate this affair with Cleopatra into threatened treason.

In contrast, Octavius Caesar never stopped playing the part of the true Roman, industrious, grave, honorable, and devoted to public affairs.

He himself was in love with no exotic temptress. He had been married twice to fine Roman girls. He had had no sons, though. His first wife was childless and his second had one daughter. He was soon to marry a third and last time, however, to the best one yet, a girl named Livia.

Livia was not yet twenty, but she was already married, had a fine young son, and was pregnant with (as it turned out) a second son. She divorced her husband to marry Octavius Caesar, but there was no stigma attached to divorce in those days. She became a model Roman matron, who remained Octavius' wife for the rest of his long life; they remained married for fifty-two years, a phenomenal length of time for a marriage in those days. Livia then lived on as his revered widow for fifteen more years. What's more, although she had no children by Octavius Caesar, her own children by her earlier marriage proved capable warriors and one of them succeeded his stepfather to the rule of all Rome.

The city of Rome was filled, then, with talk of how wicked Mark Antony was and how noble and good Octavius Caesar was, and this played an important part in Octavius' schemes. It was part of Antony's folly that he continually gave men cause to look upon these exaggerated rumors as true (as Demetrius points out) and that he never made an effort to set up effective counterpropaganda of his own. He was entirely too trusting in his own reputation and capacity as a warrior. —As though that were every-thing.

. . . Herod of Jewry . . .

The scene shifts to Cleopatra's palace, where we find the Queen's ladies in waiting having fun at the expense of a soothsayer, who nevertheless makes some statements which turn out to have dramatic irony. He pre-dicts, for instance, that Cleopatra's lady in waiting Charmian will outlive her mistress, and so she does in the end—by about a minute.

At one point, though, Charmian asks him to predict some ridiculous fortunes, including:

> . . . let me have a child at fifty, to whom Herod of Jewry
> may do homage . . .
>
> —Act I, scene ii, lines 27–28

This serves to set the time of the play in a way peculiarly useful to Shake-speare's audience. It is the time in which Herod "the Great" is on the throne of Judea.

Judea had lost its independence in 63 B.C. (twenty-two years before the time this play opens), when Pompey (see page I–255) had absorbed it into the Roman realm. It had been given some internal freedom, however, and Pompey made the capable Antipater its king. Antipater was from Idumaea (the biblical Edom) and was not a Jew by birth, though he had become one by conversion. He was assassinated in 43 B.C., just a year after Julius Caesar had been.

His eldest surviving son, Herod, also a converted Jew, and now thirty years old, was the natural successor, but the Eastern provinces were in a ferment. Brutus and Cassius were trying to strengthen themselves for the fight against Mark Antony and Octavius, and the Parthians were doing their best to take advantage of the disorder in Rome. In fact, after the Battle of Philippi, the Parthians swarmed all over Syria and Judea, and Herod was forced to flee.

He came to Antony for support, and this Antony gave him and con-tinued to give him even though Cleopatra bitterly opposed Herod. Herod became King of Judea, then, at just about the time that Charmian refers to him so jestingly. Still, things didn't settle sufficiently for Herod actually to enter Jerusalem and take the throne till 37 B.C.

The reference to the child to whom Herod might do homage is clear enough too. Whenever the political fortunes of the Jews declined, their hopes for an ideal king or "anointed one" rose. (The Hebrew word for "anointed one" is "Messiah.")

Now that the briefly independent Jewish kingdom under the Maccabees had fallen and the Romans were in control, Messianic hopes rose. All Judea seemed to wait for some child to be born who would be the ideal king and under whom the world system would finally break apart, with Jerusalem becoming the capital of the world and all the nations confessing the one true God.

Undoubtedly, non-Jews heard of these longings and were amused. Charmian suggests, then, that perhaps when she is fifty she may give birth to this Messiah, this true King of the Jews, to whom Herod, a mere earthly king, will have to do homage. And, indeed, Jesus was born before the end of Herod's reign at a time when Charmian, had she lived, would have been not much more than fifty.

Good Isis . . .

The mischievous Charmian also asks the soothsayer to prophesy for the courtier Alexas, who had brought the soothsayer to court for Cleopatra's amusement. She asks that a series of unsatisfactory wives be foretold for him. She says, laughingly:

> Good Isis, hear me this prayer, though thou deny me a matter
> of more weight: good Isis, I beseech thee!
>
> —Act I, scene ii, lines 68–70

Isis was the chief goddess of the Egyptian pantheon. For the most part, the Egyptian deities made little impact on the culturally snobbish Greeks and, therefore, on the Western world, which draws most of its culture from Greek sources.

Isis was the chief exception. For one thing, she was an extraordinarily attractive goddess; a thoroughly human female amid an array of animal-headed deities. She plays a sympathetic role in the Egyptian version of the vegetation-cycle myth (see page I-5). Her brother-husband, Osiris, was killed through treachery by Set, the god of darkness. Osiris' body was cut to pieces and scattered throughout Egypt. The lovely and sorrowing Isis painstakingly searched the land, collected the pieces, put them together, and brought Osiris back to life.

Isis' influence was felt outside the borders of Egypt. As the beautiful "Queen of Heaven" her worship penetrated Rome itself in the dark days of Hannibal's onslaught, when the Romans felt the shortcomings of their own gods and snatched at others. In the days of the Roman Empire (in the centuries following the time of Antony and Cleopatra) temples to Isis were built and her rites celebrated, even in the far-off island of Britain, two thousand miles from the Nile.

After Christianity was established, the spell of Isis still continued to make itself felt. As the goddess of birth and motherhood, she was frequently portrayed with her child, Horus, on her lap. The popular concept of mother and child was transferred to Christianity in the form of the Virgin and the infant Jesus, so that the aura of Isis lingers over the world even now.

A Roman thought . . .

In comes Cleopatra in dark humor, for she can't find Antony. She says:

> He was disposed to mirth; but on the sudden
> A Roman thought hath struck him.
>
> —Act I, scene ii, lines 83–84

The thought of the messengers and what the news might be had apparently gnawed at Antony. Part of him is Roman still, and he left to find them.

. . . my brother Lucius

The news is disturbing indeed, for it deals with war, and a particularly embarrassing one too, for it is Antony's wife, of all people, who is conducting it. The Messenger says:

> Fulvia thy wife first came into the field.
>
> —Act I, scene ii, line 89

Fulvia, her eyesight sharpened, perhaps, by the anger and humiliation she felt at her husband's preoccupation with the Egyptian enchantress, saw what Mark Antony did not—that Octavius Caesar would win it all if he were not stopped.

She therefore did her best to instigate war against Octavius, raising an army and putting it in the field. It probably did not escape her calculation that if she caused enough mischief, her husband's hand would be forced and he would have to come back to Italy to fight—and rejoin her.

Mark Antony is stupefied. He asks:

> Against my brother Lucius?
>
> —Act I, scene ii, line 90

Lucius was Mark Antony's younger brother, and had held a variety of important political posts. In 41 B.C., after the Battle of Philippi and the following division of Rome among the triumvirs, Lucius Antony was made consul.

Actually, the consulate had become an unimportant office by now, for Octavius Caesar was the only real power in Rome, but it still had its prestige. It was a bow to Mark Antony's importance that his brother should be consul. Furthermore, it gave Mark Antony a foothold, so to speak, in the capital, though unfortunately for Antony, not a very competent one.

It was Lucius Antony's duty as consul to oppose the rebellious Fulvia, so that at the very first they seemed to be at war with each other. This was what occasioned Antony's surprise, that his wife should begin a war that would have to be against his brother.

Apparently, that war did not last long. Fulvia talked Lucius into joining her. The Messenger explains:

> . . . soon that war had end, and the time's state
> Made friends of them, pointing their force 'gainst Caesar,
> Whose better issue in the war, from Italy
> Upon the first encounter drave them.
> —Act I, scene ii, lines 92–95

It wasn't quite that quick a victory for Octavius Caesar, but it was quick enough. Octavius' armies drove the forces of Fulvia and Lucius northward and penned them up in the city of Perusia (the modern Perugia, a hundred miles north of Rome). There the forces lay under siege for some months before the city was taken. This short conflict is called the Perusine War.

The war was a disaster for Mark Antony, because he knew everyone would believe that he was behind it (though he was not) and it would give Octavius Caesar all the excuse he needed to picture himself as the innocent victim of wanton aggression.

If Fulvia had to fight, she might at least not have been so quickly defeated, so that Antony might have had something to offset the propaganda victory that had been handed Octavius Caesar. Worse still was the manner of the defeat. The food supply in the city was small and it was reserved for the soldiers of Fulvia and Lucius, who let the civil population starve. Moreover, the final surrender was made on condition that the army's leaders be spared. So they were, but the city itself was sacked in 40 B.C.

This callousness on the part of Fulvia and Lucius Antony, who saved their skins at the expense of thousands of common people, was not lost on the Roman populace. They were execrated and some of the execrations were bound to fall on Mark Antony, whose reputation in Italy took another serious drop.

. . . with his Parthian force

But there is worse news still. It is not only inside the Roman realm that army fights army. The external enemy is tearing at the Eastern provinces and has reached a peak of power. The Messenger says:

> *Labienus—*
> *This is stiff news—hath with his Parthian force*
> *Extended Asia; from Euphrates*
> *His conquering banner shook, from Syria*
> *To Lydia and to Ionia,*
>
> *—Act I, scene ii, lines 100–4*

Quintus Labienus had fought on the side of Brutus and Cassius and had refused to abandon the cause even after the Battle of Philippi and the death of the two conspirators. Instead, he fled to the Parthians, whose armies hovered along the course of the Euphrates River, east of Asia Minor and Syria.

Parthia was originally the name of an eastern province of the Persian Empire. It was conquered by Alexander the Great and, after Alexander's death in 323 B.C., it was incorporated in the Seleucid Empire (see page I–183). The Seleucid grip remained rather loose.

In 171 B.C., while Antiochus IV was the Seleucid king (see page I–183), Mithradates I became ruler of Parthia. He made his land fully independent, and under the weak successors of Antiochus IV, the Parthians drove westward. In 147 B.C. they took over control of the Tigris-Euphrates valley, the home of the ancient civilizations of Sumeria and Babylonia, and in 129 B.C. they founded their own capital of Ctesiphon on the Tigris River.

The last Seleucid kings were penned into the constricted area of Syria itself, with Antioch as their capital, and in 64 B.C. that was made into a Roman province by Pompey.

Across the Euphrates, Rome and Parthia now faced each other. Under Orodes II, Parthia defeated Crassus in 53 B.C.; he was still king when the Battle of Philippi was fought in 42 B.C. He remained eager to do Rome all the harm he could and when Labienus, a trained Roman soldier, defected to him, he was delighted and promptly placed a Parthian army at his disposal.

In 40 B.C. the Parthians under Labienus moved westward, and in short order almost all of Syria and Asia Minor was occupied, with various Roman garrisons joining the renegade general. Lydia was an ancient kingdom in western Asia Minor (and still served as the name of a region of the peninsula when it was under Roman domination), while Ionia was the territory along the western seacoast of Asia Minor. The mention of the two districts by the Messenger shows that all of the peninsula was now under Parthian control. (It was from this Parthian advance that Herod fled, and in 40 B.C. the Parthians, for the only time in their history, marched into Jerusalem.)

All this is bitter for Mark Antony, for it took place in his half of the realm. He, the great soldier, has done nothing to prevent it, and he himself realizes that to Rome it will now look as though he lounged languidly with Cleopatra even while foreign armies were tearing Rome apart.

Mark Antony must realize that while he can get away with mere profligacy as long as he can win battles, the loss of his military reputation as well will cause him to lose everything. He mutters:

> *These strong Egyptian fetters I must break*
> *Or lose myself in dotage.*
> —Act I, scene ii, lines 117–18

From Sicyon . . .

But another Messenger waits and Antony calls for him:

> *From Sicyon, ho, the news!*
> —Act I, scene ii, line 114

Sicyon is a Greek city in the northwest Peloponnesus, fifty miles west of Athens. It was at the peak of its power about 600 B.C. when it was the rule of three generations of benevolent "tyrants," a one-man rule that lasted longer without interruption than in any other case in Greek history. After the fall of the tyranny in 565 B.C., Sicyon was usually dominated by the larger and more powerful cities of Sparta or Corinth. Only after Corinth was destroyed by the Romans in 146 B.C. did Sicyon experience another period of prominence. When Corinth was rebuilt, however, Sicyon began its final decline and the event that the Messenger is about to tell is very nearly the last of importance in its history.

The news is brief, for the Messenger says:

> *Fulvia thy wife is dead.*
> —Act I, scene ii, line 119

Fulvia reached Sicyon in her flight from Italy and then died there in 40 B.C. Antony is stricken. Now that she is gone, he recognizes in her that energy and drive which has recently been missing in himself and says:

> *I must from this enchanting queen break off:*
> *Ten thousand harms, more than the ills I know,*
> *My idleness doth hatch.*
> —Act I, scene ii, lines 129–31a

. . . Enobarbus

Antony is doing his best to make up his mind to leave Cleopatra, and he calls his most reliable aide:

> Ho now, Enobarbus!
>
> —Act I, scene ii, line 131b

Enobarbus is a shortened form of Ahenobarbus, and the person being called is, in full, Gnaeus Domitius Ahenobarbus. His father had fought with Pompey against Caesar and had died at the Battle of Pharsalus.

Enobarbus himself had fought with Brutus and Cassius against Mark Antony and Octavius Caesar and had commanded the fleet, in fact. Even after the Battle of Philippi, Enobarbus had held out as a pirate until he was won over by Mark Antony in 40 B.C., just before this play opens. He then became one of the most ardent of Antony's adherents.

. . . Sextus Pompeius

It is not surprising that Antony must leave for Rome. He must take care of the Parthian menace and he cannot do it if he leaves an angry Octavius Caesar in his rear. He must mend fences there, explain away the actions of his wife and brother, and patch up an understanding. Then, and only then, can he turn on the Parthians. In addition, there is trouble in the West, for that matter. Antony says to Enobarbus:

> . . . the letters too
> Of many our contriving friends in Rome
> Petition us at home. Sextus Pompeius
> Hath given the dare to Caesar and commands
> The empire of the sea.
>
> —Act I, scene ii, lines 183–87

Sextus Pompeius (also called Pompey the Younger) was the younger son of Pompey the Great. He had been in Greece with his father when the Battle of Pharsalus had been lost and he was in the ship with his father when Pompey fled to Egypt. He remained in the ship as his father was rowed to the Egyptian shore and witnessed his father being stabbed and killed when he reached that shore. He was about twenty-seven years old then.

Some years later Sextus was in Spain when his older brother, Gnaeus Pompeius, held out against Julius Caesar. He was at the Battle of Munda, in which Gnaeus was defeated and slain in 45 B.C. (see page I–258). Sex-

tus escaped and during the confusion that followed the assassination of
Julius Caesar, quietly built up his strength at sea.

By 40 B.C. he was in control of the Mediterranean. He had seized Sicily
soon after the assassination and was still holding it. This cut off Rome's
grain supply, part of which came from Sicily itself, with the rest coming
from Africa and Egypt in ships that Sextus could easily intercept. What it
amounted to was that this younger son of Pompey had his hand at the
throat of Rome, and Octavius Caesar, who lacked a navy, could do nothing
about it.

Naturally, since nothing succeeds like success, there was the danger
that Sextus' increasing power would breed still further access of power. As
Antony says:

> Our slippery people,
> Whose love is never linked to the deserver
> Till his deserts are past, begin to throw
> Pompey the Great and all his dignities
> Upon his son;

—Act I, scene ii, lines 187–91

(In this play Sextus' lines are identified as those of "Pompey," but I
shall call him Sextus or Sextus Pompeius in order not to confuse him with
his father, Pompey the Great.)

. . . Nilus' slime . . .

Enobarbus tells Cleopatra of the forthcoming separation (Antony has
been with her a year), and she goes seeking Antony himself to confirm the
news.

Poor Antony is in a dilemma. He is no match for Cleopatra and can
only fluster and fume. He tries to be consoling and reassuring, but she
will have none of it. He even tries to explain to her that her greatest fear
(that he will return to his wife, Fulvia) is gone, since Fulvia is dead. She
turns even that against him, saying:

> O most false love!
> Where be the sacred vials thou shouldst fill
> With sorrowful water? Now I see, I see,
> In Fulvia's death, how mine received shall be.

—Act I, scene iii, lines 62–65

In view of what is to happen in Act IV, this is dramatic irony, for Antony
will react quite differently to the report of Cleopatra's death.

In frustration, Antony protests that he is faithful to her even though he must leave. He says:

> *By the fire*
> *That quickens Nilus' slime, I go from hence*
> *Thy soldier-servant . . .*
>
> —Act I, scene iii, lines 68–70

Egypt is a desert land where it never rains. What makes life possible there is the presence of the Nile River. (The name is of unknown origin. The Egyptians called it simply "The River"; but the Greeks named it "Neilos," which is "Nilus" in Latin spelling and "Nile" to us.)

The Nile is an unfailing source of water for drinking and irrigation. Once a year, moreover, its level rises as the snow on the distant Abyssinian and Kenyan mountains melt. The river waters flood the banks and deposit silt brought down from east-central Africa. The water-soaked fresh soil is outstandingly fertile and in the hot African sun ("the fire that quickens Nilus' slime") generous harvests grow.

. . . *this Herculean Roman* . . .

When Cleopatra's perversity finally moves Antony to rage, she still fleers at him, accusing him of merely pretending anger. She says:

> *Look, prithee, Charmian,*
> *How this Herculean Roman does become*
> *The carriage of his chafe.*
>
> —Act I, scene iii, lines 82–84

The sneer refers to one of Antony's more ridiculous pretensions (though it was taken seriously in his time). Roman noblemen liked to pretend they were descended from the gods and from mythical heroes. The Julian family, of which Julius Caesar was a member, was supposed to have descended from Venus. In similar fashion, the Antonian family, of which Mark Antony was a member, claimed to be descended from Anton, a mythical son of Hercules. Mark Antony himself did everything he could to model himself on the strong man of legend.

In the end, then, Mark Antony is forced to leave angrily, defeated in the battle of words with Cleopatra.

. . . *the queen of Ptolemy*

The scene now shifts to Octavius Caesar's house in Rome. Octavius

Caesar is not much better off in Rome than Mark Antony is in Alexandria. He too is beset with problems, and he is annoyed that Mark Antony's inaction makes it necessary for himself to be all the more industrious.

He is saying bitterly to Lepidus (the third member of the Triumvirate) as he reads a letter:

> *From Alexandria*
> *This is the news: he fishes, drinks, and wastes*
> *The lamps of night in revel; is not more manlike*
> *Than Cleopatra, nor the queen of Ptolemy*
> *More womanly than he;*

—Act I, scene iv, lines 3–7

The phrase "the queen of Ptolemy" brings up an additional point that made Cleopatra unpopular with the Romans. In ancient Egypt it had long been the custom of the Pharaohs to marry their sisters. Since the Pharaonic blood was considered divine, it would not do to have one marry a mortal. Only a woman of the same line was a fit consort. At least, that was the rationalization.

When the Ptolemies ruled Egypt, they made it a point to adopt as many Egyptian customs as possible, in order to keep the populace quiet. This included brother-sister marriages, and Cleopatra was born of a family that had many times been involved in incest (see page I–185), something that was as repulsive to the Romans as it would be to us.

In fact, when Cleopatra's father died, Cleopatra and her brother, Ptolemy XII, were made joint rulers and were, in fact, married. It was expected that eventually they might have offspring who would succeed to the throne. Ptolemy XII, however, died in the course of Julius Caesar's small war in Alexandria in 48 B.C., and Cleopatra's rule was joined with a still younger brother, Ptolemy XIII.

Ptolemy XIII was only ten years old at the time, and in 44 B.C., when the news of Julius Caesar's assassination reached her, Cleopatra had the boy killed and then ruled jointly with her son, Caesarion, only three years old at the time. The new king was Ptolemy XIV.

Octavius Caesar's reference to her as "queen of Ptolemy" stressed the fact that she had been married to her brothers, and we can be sure that this was included in the whispering campaign that was conducted against Mark Antony.

. . . beaten from Modena . . .

Messages of disaster greet Octavius Caesar as they had greeted Antony. Octavius learns that Sextus Pompeius grows stronger along the coast and that pirates control the sea where Sextus himself does not. Daily Octavius Caesar's control over Rome grows shakier as its food supply dwindles.

Octavius Caesar broods resentfully over the fact that he isn't being helped by Antony. Unaware that Antony is on his way westward, Octavius Caesar cries out:

> *Antony*
> *Leave thy lascivious wassails. When thou once*
> *Was beaten from Modena, where thou slew'st*
> *Hirtius and Pansa, consuls, at thy heel*
> *Did famine follow, whom thou fought'st against*
> *(Though daintily brought up) with patience more*
> *Than savages could suffer.*
> —Act I, scene iv, lines 55–61

The reference is to the period following the assassination of Julius Caesar and deals with events not mentioned in Shakespeare's *Julius Caesar*. The events fall in the interval between Acts III and IV of that play (see page I–301).

Decimus Brutus (called "Decius" by Shakespeare) was in control of Cisalpine Gaul in northern Italy, and Mark Antony led an army northward to attack him. Decius fortified himself in Mutina, the modern Modena, 220 miles north of Rome. While Mark Antony fought there, Octavius Caesar, back in Rome, persuaded the Senate to declare war against Antony and to send an army against him led by the consul Hirtius; then another, led by the other consul, Pansa.

Mark Antony left his brother, Lucius, to conduct the siege of Mutina with part of the army, and then led the remainder against the consuls. Antony was badly defeated, but both Roman consuls were killed. (This was a stroke of luck for Octavius, for with both consuls dead, he was in full control of a victorious army.)

Antony had to retreat over the Alps into Gaul, and that retreat was attended by extraordinary suffering and hardship. Antony, in one of his better times, shared that suffering with his men and did so with such stoic patience that he endeared himself to the army. The tale of his nobility in this respect was undoubtedly told and retold with exaggeration, as we can see from the repulsive details Shakespeare has Octavius list:

> *Thou didst drink*
> *The stale [urine] of horses and the gilded [scum-covered]*
> *puddle*
> *Which beasts would cough at.*
> —Act I, scene iv, lines 61–63

The demi-Atlas . . .

Back in Alexandria, Cleopatra already misses Antony and is in a state of delicious self-pity. She says:

> *Give me to drink mandragora.*
>
> —Act I, scene v, line 4

Mandragora is an older form of "mandrake," a plant of the potato family which is native to the Mediterranean region. It has its uses as a cathartic, emetic, and narcotic. Which effect predominates depends on the dose, but Cleopatra thinks of the narcotic aspect, for when asked why she wants it, she says:

> *That I might sleep out this great gap of time*
> *My Antony is away.*
>
> —Act I, scene v, lines 5–6

She thinks longingly of Antony, saying:

> *O, Charmian,*
> *Where think'st thou he is now? Stands he, or sits he?*
> *Or does he walk? Or is he on his horse?*
> *O happy horse, to bear the weight of Antony!*
> *Do bravely, horse, for wot'st thou whom thou mov'st?*
> *The demi-Atlas of this earth . . .*
>
> —Act I, scene v, lines 18–23

Atlas was one of the Titans who warred against Jupiter (see page I–11). In fact, he may have been their general, for he was punished worse than the others. He was condemned to support the heavens on his shoulders.

As time went on, it became difficult to picture Atlas as holding up the sky. The Greeks learned more about astronomy and knew that there was no solid sky to support. The notion arose, then, of Atlas supporting the earth rather than the sky.

Cleopatra pictures Antony here as supporting the weight of the problems of the Roman world. He shared this weight with Octavius Caesar, of course, so he himself was but a demi-Atlas; that is, half an Atlas.

. . . Phoebus' amorous pinches . . .

In contrast, the self-pitying Cleopatra seems to herself to be ugly and old. She says:

> *Think on me,*
> *That am with Phoebus' amorous pinches black*
> *And wrinkled deep in time. Broad-fronted Caesar,*
> *When thou wast here above the ground, I was*
> *A morsel for a monarch; and great Pompey*
> *Would stand and make his eyes grow in my brow;*
> —Act I, scene v, lines 27–32

Phoebus is, of course, the sun, and to be black with the sun's pinches would be to be sun-tanned. A queen like Cleopatra, however, would certainly not allow herself to grow sun-tanned. That was for peasant girls.

What is meant is that she is dark by nature because she dwelt in a tropic land. It is part of the Egyptian-Negress notion of Cleopatra, the usual false picture.

Nor is she honestly "wrinkled deep in time." At this point in the story, she is twenty-nine years old; past her first youth, perhaps, but by no means old and wrinkled.

Still it is human for her to think of herself as she was nine years before, only twenty-one, when Julius Caesar knew her; and even earlier when she met not Pompey himself, but his older son, who bore the same name.

Her opulent throne . . .

But now comes a messenger to Cleopatra from Antony, with the gift of a pearl and with a pretty speech. He says:

> *"Say the firm Roman to great Egypt sends*
> *This treasure of an oyster; at whose foot,*
> *To mend the petty present, I will piece*
> *Her opulent throne with kingdoms. All the East*
> *(Say thou) shall call her mistress."*
> —Act I, scene v, lines 43–46

The story was indeed spread in Rome that Antony was planning to hand over Roman provinces to Cleopatra; even to make her Queen of Rome (with himself as king, of course); that a foreign ruler would thus raise an exotic throne upon the Capitol. In the end, this, more than anything else, was to embitter Rome against Antony.

Shakespeare gets a little ahead of history here. The threat of turning the East over to Cleopatra comes later.

At the moment, Mark Antony and Octavius Caesar, each waist-deep in trouble, were going to have to be friends whether they liked it or not, for only by working together could they survive.

But Cleopatra is not concerned with practical politics now. She is delighted with Mark Antony's remembrance and is ashamed of herself for so much as remembering Julius Caesar and Gnaeus Pompeius. When Charmian teases her with her onetime love of Julius Caesar, she dismisses it with a much quoted line, saying:

> My salad days,
> When I was green in judgment, cold in blood,
>> —Act I, scene v, lines 73–74

And indeed, one of the most interesting aspects of this play is that it is a paean to the ecstasies of mature love, rather than of the teen-age passions so often celebrated.

. . . every hour in Rome

The second act opens in Messina, Sicily, at the camp of Sextus Pompeius, who is in conversation with his captains, Menecrates and Menas. Sextus is rather euphoric, confident that his hold on Rome's food supply gives him the trump card and that Octavius Caesar and Lepidus can do nothing without Antony's military ability. As for Mark Antony, Sextus has full confidence in Cleopatra's charms. He says:

> Mark Antony
> In Egypt sits at dinner, and will make
> No wars without doors.
>> —Act II, scene i, lines 11–13

He is, however, overconfident. Another one of his captains, Varrius, comes with unwelcome news:

> This is most certain, that I shall deliver:
> Mark Antony is every hour in Rome
> Expected.
>> —Act II, scene i, lines 28–30

There is hope, of course, that upon arrival, Mark Antony will fall to quarreling with Octavius. This is tentatively advanced as a possibility by Menas, but Sextus shakes his head. They may have cause enough to quarrel, but as long as the danger from the sea exists, they will have to make friends. At the end of the short scene, things look as bad for Sextus as, at the start, they had looked good.

Hark, Ventidius

In Rome, in Lepidus' house, it is now late in 40 B.C. The confrontation between Octavius Caesar and Mark Antony is about to take place and poor Lepidus is in a sweat lest the two collide destructively. He has undoubtedly done his best to influence Octavius Caesar to be accommodating, and he pleads with Enobarbus to do the same with respect to Mark Antony.

From opposite sides approach the two triumvirs, each with friends, and each pretending to be deep in private discussion so that, for effect, he can seem to be ignoring the other.

Antony speaks first to the general at his side—his thoughts, to all appearances, on military matters in the East:

> *If we compose well here, to Parthia.*
> *Hark, Ventidius.*
>
> —Act II, scene ii, lines 15–16a

Here he goes off, apparently, into military talk unheard by the audience and undoubtedly meant to impress Octavius.

Ventidius is Publius Ventidius Bassus, who in early life had been a poor man who made a living renting mules and carriages. He rose to become a general serving under Julius Caesar in Gaul and remained loyal to Julius Caesar during the war with Pompey. After the assassination of the great Julius, Ventidius served Mark Antony and has remained loyal to him since.

Maecenas; ask Agrippa

As for Octavius Caesar, he is speaking with two men. Of what we can't say, but it is probably politics. Octavius affects carelessness. All we hear him say is:

> *I do not know,*
> *Maecenas; ask Agrippa.*
>
> —Act II, scene ii, lines 16b–17

Maecenas and Agrippa are Octavius Caesar's closest associates, then and afterward. Gaius Cilnius Maecenas was a man of peace. He was several years older than Octavius Caesar and had been a friend of his since the latter was a schoolboy. In later years Maecenas was always left at home to take care of Rome when Octavius Caesar was forced to be away on war or diplomacy. In his eventual retirement, Maecenas used the wealth he had gathered to support and patronize writers and artists. So earnestly did he do this and so great were those he helped that forever after a patron of the arts has been called "a Maecenas."

Marcus Vipsanius Agrippa, on the other hand, was the man of war, the good right arm of Octavius Caesar, the general who fought all his master's battles, and who made it possible for Octavius to win military victories. (Why didn't Agrippa win them for himself? Because he was intelligent enough to know that he needed Octavius' brain to direct his arm. In the same way, Mark Antony needed Julius Caesar's brain to direct his arm, but he never really understood that.)

Agrippa was the same age as Octavius Caesar, was with him at school when the news of the assassination of Julius Caesar had arrived, and went with him to Italy. He did not play much of a part in the war against the conspirators, for he was still young. After the Battle of Philippi, however, Agrippa began to shine. It was he, for instance, who led the armies that penned up Fulvia and Lucius Antonius in Perusia and then defeated them.

. . . time to wrangle . . .

Softly and eagerly, Lepidus draws the two men together. Stiffly, they sit and confront each other. Each raises the matter of his grievances. Octavius Caesar has the better of this, for he can bring up the war fought against him by Fulvia and Lucius, claiming Antony set them on. Antony objects that the war was against his own policy, and ungallantly places full blame upon his dead wife, saying, in terms that must have raised a wry smile from many a husband in the audience:

> As for my wife,
> I would you had her spirit in such another.
> The third o' the world is yours, which with a snaffle
> You may pace easy, but not such a wife.
>
> —Act II, scene ii, lines 65–68

Nevertheless, argumentation continues till Enobarbus roughly points out the necessity of a compromise, however insincere:

> . . . if you borrow one another's love for the instant, you may, when you hear no more words of Pompey, return it again: you shall have time to wrangle in when you have nothing else to do.
>
> —Act II, scene ii, lines 107–10

It doesn't make pleasant listening, but it is a fair appraisal of the situation. A practical means of accommodation must be sought.

Admired Octavia . . .

Agrippa comes up with a suggestion at once. He says to Octavius Caesar:

> *Thou hast a sister by the mother's side,*
> *Admired Octavia: great Mark Antony*
> *Is now a widower.*
>
> —Act II, scene ii, lines 123–25

This sounds as though Agrippa is referring to a half sister, but he isn't. Octavia is a daughter of the same mother as Octavius Caesar as well as of the same father.

Octavius Caesar had two sisters, both older than he. The older one, Octavia Major, was a half sister, by his father's first wife. The second, Octavia Minor, was a full sister and the one to whom Agrippa refers.

She was by no means a young virgin, but was in her mid-twenties by this time (not much younger than Cleopatra) and had been married since her early teens, bearing two daughters and a son. Her husband, Gaius Marcellus, had died the year before, so what was being proposed was the marriage of a widow and a widower.

Mark Antony agrees to the marriage and thus is produced what is hoped will be a permanent bond between the two triumvirs, someone who will be a common love and who will labor to smooth over all irritations. There is a precedent for this, in connection with the First Triumvirate, when Pompey and Julius Caesar were much in the position that Mark Antony and Octavius Caesar are now.

In 58 B.C., when Julius Caesar was leaving for Gaul, he arranged to have Pompey marry Julia, his daughter, who was in her mid-twenties at the time. It turned out to be a love match. Pompey doted on her and while the marriage lasted, peace was maintained between the two men. In 54 B.C., however, Julia died at the age of only thirty. The strongest link between the two men snapped. The civil war that followed might have been prevented had Julia lived.

It was this precedent which was now being followed. If only Mark Antony could love Octavia as Pompey had loved Julia, all might be well (and better, too, for Octavia was destined to live for thirty years more and was not to die young as Julia had done).

. . . my sword 'gainst Pompey

The agreement among the triumvirs was aimed particularly against Sextus Pompeius, and this was rather embarrassing to Mark Antony, who says:

I did not think to draw my sword 'gainst Pompey,
For he hath laid strange courtesies and great
Of late upon me.

—Act II, scene ii, lines 159–61

It was more than that, in fact. The two were making definite overtures toward an alliance. When Antony's mother fled Italy after the Perusine War, Sextus was ostentatiously kind to her. In fact, in a later scene, Sextus reminds Antony of this, saying:

When Caesar and your brother were at blows,
Your mother came to Sicily and did find
Her welcome friendly.

—Act II, scene vi, lines 44–46

Sextus was not doing this, of course, out of sheer goodness of heart. He expected the Perusine War would lead to a greater civil war and he was prepared to choose sides for his own greater benefit. Since Octavius Caesar was closer to himself and the more immediate enemy, he was ready to ally himself with Antony, and this kindness to Antony's mother was a move in that direction.

Indeed, Antony would have welcomed such an alliance, and in 41 B.C. the first steps toward such an understanding had been taken. Undoubtedly, if it had not been for the terrible Parthian menace, the Sextus-Antony combination would have become reality. As it was, though, Antony had to have peace with Octavius Caesar, and to get that the alliance with Sextus had to be abandoned and even war on Sextus had to be considered.

. . . Mount Mesena

If the triumvirs were now to turn against Sextus Pompeius, it was none too soon. Sextus had even established strong bases on the shores of Italy itself. Antony asks where he is, and Octavius Caesar answers:

About the Mount Mesena.

—Act II, scene ii, line 166

Mount Mesena is a promontory that encloses a harbor about which the ancient town of Misenum was located. That town, now long gone, was fifteen miles west of Naples. In later years, Agrippa was to construct a strong naval base there, but now it belonged to Sextus.

. . . the river of Cydnus

The triumvirs leave, so that Mark Antony might meet Octavia and perform whatever perfunctory rites of courtship might seem advisable. Maecenas and Agrippa remain behind with Enobarbus for a little light conversation.

Naturally, this means there is a chance for a little leering in connection with Cleopatra. Maecenas and Agrippa want all the inside information from Enobarbus. Enobarbus is only too glad to comply:

> *When she first met Mark Antony, she pursed up his heart,*
> *upon the river of Cydnus.*
> —Act II, scene ii, lines 192–93

That takes us back to the previous year, 41 B.C., when Antony, in the aftermath of Philippi, had taken over the East and was traveling through Asia Minor, gouging money out of the miserable population for the war against Parthia he was planning. Unfortunately for him, there wasn't much money to be had, squeeze he ever so tightly. Brutus and Cassius had been there the year before (see page I-303) and they had scoured the land clean.

Antony made his headquarters in Tarsus, a city on the southeastern coast of Asia Minor, at the mouth of the Cydnus River. (In Tarsus, a generation later, St. Paul was to be born.) It seemed to Antony that the logical solution to his dilemma was to squeeze Egypt. That land, nominally independent, but actually a Roman puppet, had the greatest concentration of wealth in the Mediterranean world—wealth wrung out of an endlessly fertile river valley and an endlessly patient and hard-working peasant population.

There had been reports that Egypt had helped Brutus and Cassius, and this was very likely, for Egypt was in no position to refuse help to any Roman general who was in her vicinity with an army. Mark Antony understood that well, but what interested him was that this help could be used as an excuse to demand money. He planned to demand a great deal, and for that reason he summoned the Queen of Egypt to come to him in Tarsus and explain her actions. He had briefly seen the Queen in Alexandria in the days when Julius Caesar was there, seven years before, but not since.

Cleopatra, perfectly aware of what Mark Antony intended, and also perfectly aware of his reputation as a woman chaser and of herself as a supreme quarry, decided to come to him in conditions of the greatest possible luxury, with herself beautified to the extreme of art. Plutarch describes the scene well, but Shakespeare improves on it and places it, for greater effect, in the mouth of Enobarbus, the rough soldier, to show that even the least poetic man had to be affected by Cleopatra's unparalleled stage setting of herself.

Enobarbus, in an unbelievable outburst of sheer lyricism, says:

> The barge she sat in, like a burnished throne,
> Burned on the water: the poop was beaten gold;
> Purple the sails, and so perfumèd that
> The winds were lovesick with them; the oars were silver,
> Which to the tune of flutes kept stroke and made
> The water which they beat to follow faster,
> As amorous of their strokes. For her own person,
> It beggared all description: she did lie
> In her pavilion, cloth-of-gold of tissue,
> O'erpicturing that Venus where we see
> The fancy outwork nature: on each side her
> Stood pretty dimpled boys, like smiling Cupids,
> With divers-colored fans, whose wind did seem
> To glow the delicate cheeks which they did cool,
> And what they undid did.
>
> —Act II, scene ii, lines 197–211a

Agrippa, listening, can only mutter in envy:

> O, rare for Antony.
>
> —Act II, scene ii, line 211b

Cleopatra's strategy worked to perfection. Antony found himself sitting at the pier on a throne in Roman state—but utterly alone. He was completely upstaged as everyone crowded to watch the approaching barge. He himself was overcome. When Cleopatra invited him on board the barge, he went in what was almost a hypnotic trance, and was her slave from that moment. The Parthians were forgotten until they charged into the Eastern provinces and forced themselves upon Antony's unwilling notice.

Age cannot wither . . .

Agrippa and Maecenas grow uneasy at the description. The entire accommodation of the triumvirs rests upon the stability of the marriage of Antony and Octavia. Maecenas points out that now Antony must leave her, but Enobarbus answers in an immediate and positive negative; composing in the process the most effective description of complete feminine charm

the world of literature has to offer. He says of the possibility of Antony's
leaving Cleopatra:

> *Never; he will not;*
> *Age cannot wither her, nor custom stale*
> *Her infinite variety: other women cloy*
> *The appetites they feed, but she makes hungry*
> *Where most she satisfies; for vilest things*
> *Become themselves in her, that the holy priests*
> *Bless her when she is riggish.*
>
> —Act II, scene ii, lines 240–46

And what can the others offer in place of this? Maecenas can only say,
rather lamely:

> *If beauty, wisdom, modesty, can settle*
> *The heart of Antony, Octavia is*
> *A blessed lottery to him.*
>
> —Act II, scene ii, lines 247–49

Thy daemon . . .

Antony pledges himself to Octavia, but on leaving her and Octavius
Caesar, he encounters the soothsayer, who has apparently accompanied
his train to Italy. Antony asks whose fortune will rise higher, his own or
Octavius Caesar's. The soothsayer answers:

> *Caesar's.*
> *Therefore, O Antony, stay not by his side.*
> *Thy daemon, that thy spirit which keeps thee, is*
> *Noble, courageous, high, unmatchable,*
> *Where Caesar's is not. But near him thy angel*
> *Becomes afeared, as being o'erpow'red: therefore*
> *Make space enough between you.*
>
> —Act II, scene iii, lines 18–24

The Greeks came to believe that with each individual was associated a
divine spirit through which the influence of the gods could make itself
felt. It was when this influence was most strongly felt that a man could attain heights otherwise impossible to him. Where a particular spirit was
most continually effective, the man himself would be of unusual power and
ability. In some cases, this belief was elaborated to the point where each

individual was thought to have two such spirits, one for good and one for evil, the two continually fighting for mastery.

To the Greeks, such a spirit was a "daimon" (meaning "divinity") and in the Latin spelling this became "daemon." To the later Christians these daemons, being of pagan origin, could only be evil, and therefore we get our present "demon," meaning an evil spirit. However, the Greek notion lives on with but a change of name, and we still speak of guardian angels and we sometimes even envisage an individual as being influenced by his better or worse nature.

The soothsayer is saying that though Octavius Caesar's daemon is inferior to Antony's it can nevertheless win over the latter. In present parlance, we might say that Octavius Caesar plays in luck whenever he encounters Mark Antony. And yet this is hard to accept. It wasn't luck that kept Octavius Caesar on top through all a long life, but ability.

The Latin equivalent, by the way, of the Greek daimon was "genius" (see page I–118).

I'th'East . . .

The soothsayer, in warning Antony to stay far away from Octavius Caesar, is but telling Antony what he wants to hear. (This is the supreme art of the soothsayer in all ages and places.) Antony therefore says, after the soothsayer leaves:

> I will to Egypt:
> And though I make this marriage for my peace,
> I'th'East my pleasure lies.
>
> —Act II, scene iii, lines 39–41a

Eventually, yes, but right now he can't. There are problems he must attend to and until those are resolved, he must remain married to Octavia and must stay out of Egypt.

And some of the problems are in the East and won't wait for his personal presence. His general, Ventidius, comes on scene, and Antony says:

> O, come, Ventidius,
> You must to Parthia. Your commission's ready:
> Follow me, and receive't.
>
> —Act II, scene iii, lines 41b–43

. . . be at Mount

If the Parthians must be dealt with, so must Sextus Pompeius. He was the nearer and the more immediate menace.

The new agreement between the triumvirs and, in particular, Antony's betrayal of his earlier moves toward an alliance had embittered Sextus, and he now escalated his own offensive. In the winter of 40–39 B.C. Sextus' hand about Rome's throat tightened. Virtually no food entered the capital city and famine threatened. When the triumvirs tried to calm the populace, they were stoned.

They had no choice but to try to come to an agreement with Sextus and to allow him to enter the combine. This would make four men (a quadrumvirate) in place of three. To discuss this, the triumvirs agreed to come to Misenum, Sextus' stronghold, to confer with him.

Shakespeare skips over the hard winter, passing directly from Antony's marriage to Octavia to the moment when the triumvirs are leaving for Misenum. Lepidus, Maecenas, and Agrippa come on scene in a whirlwind of activity, and Maecenas says:

> *We shall*
> *As I conceive the journey, be at Mount*
> *Before you, Lepidus.*
>
> —Act II, scene iv, lines 5–7

The "Mount" is the Misenum promontory where the meeting with Sextus will take place.

. . . his sword Phillipan

Back in Alexandria during that same winter, Cleopatra spends a moody, restless time. She longs for the period of happiness she had experienced with Antony and says, in reminiscence, to Charmian:

> *I laughed him out of patience; and that night*
> *I laughed him into patience; and next morn,*
> *Ere the ninth hour, I drunk him to his bed;*
> *Then put my tires and mantles on him, whilst*
> *I wore his sword Philippan.*
>
> —Act II, scene v, lines 19–23

Cleopatra may laugh with delight as she remembers, but the picture of Antony drunk by midafternoon (the ninth hour of a twelve-hour day would be about 3 P.M.) and snoring red-faced while wearing women's clothes was undoubtedly the sort of thing Octavian propaganda was scattering all over Rome to the scandal of all good citizens.

It was the fashion of warriors in medieval legend to give names to their swords. The best-known example is that of King Arthur's Excalibur. Mark Antony's sword, Philippan, is named for the Battle of Philippi—Antony's greatest victory.

. . . a Fury crowned with snakes

Clearly, Cleopatra has not heard the news about Octavia and a frightened Messenger comes in to deliver it.

The Messenger begins by assuring Cleopatra that Antony is well, but he hesitates and the Queen senses that something is wrong. Yet he does not seem sufficiently distraught to be bringing news of death at that. She says to him, concerning his news:

> If not well,
> Thou shouldst come like a Fury crowned with snakes,
> —Act II, scene v, lines 39–40

The Greeks included in their myths three terrible goddesses, the Erinyes ("angry ones"), whose task it was to pursue and madden those who were guilty of particularly terrible crimes, such as the slaying of close kinsmen. They were depicted and described as so ferocious in appearance that the mere sight was maddening. They carried snakes in their hands, or else their hair was made up of living, writhing snakes. (Perhaps they symbolized the raging of conscience.)

To avoid offending them, the Greeks sometimes spoke of them by the euphemistic term "Eumenides" ("the kindly ones"). Aeschylus wrote a powerful play by that name, dealing with part of the Agamemnon myth. Agamemnon (see page I-89) is killed by his wife Clytemnestra on his return from Troy. To avenge his father, Agamemnon's son, Orestes, kills his mother and is pursued by the Erinyes in consequence.

The Romans called these fell goddesses "Furiae," from their word for raging madness, and the word is "Furies" in English.

. . . the feature of Octavia . . .

The Messenger finally blurts out the news of Antony's marriage to Octavia. Cleopatra falls into a towering rage and beats the Messenger, shouting horrible imprecations upon him:

Hence,
Horrible villain! Or I'll spurn thine eyes
Like balls before me: I'll unhair thy head,
Thou shalt be whipped with wire and stewed in brine,
Smarting in ling'ring pickle.

—Act II, scene v, lines 62–66

The whole scene, properly done, shows Cleopatra in a spitting, fantastic fury, and one can only feel that such rage would make Cleopatra the more attractive to Antony ("vilest things become themselves in her"). Compared with that, the gentle and modest Octavia must have seemed utterly pallid and insipid to Antony, in bed as well as out.

(I cannot resist repeating the story of the two respectable English matrons who were viewing a showing of *Antony and Cleopatra* a century ago, in the reign of Queen Victoria. When this scene passed its shattering course upon the stage, one of the matrons turned to the other and whispered in a most shocked manner: "How different from the home life of our own dear Queen!")

But Cleopatra's rage does not entirely wipe out her shrewdness. She questions the trembling Messenger yet again to make sure there is no possibility of mistake and says to him bitterly when the news is confirmed again and yet again:

Hadst thou Narcissus in thy face, to me
Thou wouldst appear most ugly.

—Act II, scene v, lines 96–97

Narcissus is, of course, the lovely youth, irresistible to women, who fell in love with his own reflection (see page I–10).

With that settled, and the Messenger retiring, Cleopatra ponders her next step. She orders a courtier to go after the Messenger and question him further:

Go to the fellow, good Alexas; bid him
Report the feature of Octavia; her years,
Her inclination, let him not leave out
The color of her hair.

—Act II, scene v, lines 111–14

Thou dost o'ercount me . . .

The scene shifts to Misenum, where the triumvirs meet with Sextus. There is an exchange of hostages, threats, harsh language from either side.

Mark Antony tells Sextus that on land the triumvirs "o'ercount" (out-number) him. Sextus responds sardonically:

> At land indeed
> Thou dost o'ercount me of my father's house:
> —Act II, scene vi, lines 26–27

Here the word "o'ercount" is used in an alternate sense, meaning "cheat." The reference is to a house Antony had bought of Pompey the Great once and had then never paid for, since the civil war between Pompey and Julius Caesar intervened. Civil wars always end in enrichment for the victors at the expense of the losers.

. . . wheat to Rome

Octavius Caesar, however, coldly keeps his temper, and his steady urging of the real point causes Sextus Pompeius to bring up a suggested compromise. Sextus says:

> You have made me offer
> Of Sicily, Sardinia; and I must
> Rid all the sea of pirates; then, to send
> Measures of wheat to Rome;
> —Act II, scene vi, lines 34–37

In actual fact, the offer was rather more generous than that. Sextus Pompeius already had Sicily, but to it was added not only Sardinia, but Corsica also, and these three large islands half encircle Italy. In addition, since all these were taken from Octavius Caesar's share of the realm, Sextus was to have Greece as well, so that Antony had to pocket a share of the loss.

In return for becoming the fourth man of the group, Sextus would have to take his hand from Rome's throat.

. . . Apollodorus carried

Sextus Pompeius accepts the compromise and all the parties fall to shaking hands and expressing affection, though Antony, as always, finds he must be the target of a continual lewd curiosity on the part of the others concerning Cleopatra.

Sextus brings up the famous story of how Cleopatra first met Julius Caesar. He says:

And I have heard Apollodorus carried—
—Act II, scene vi, line 68

It had been Apollodorus, a Sicilian Greek, who had delivered the rolled-up carpet containing Cleopatra (possibly nude) to Julius Caesar. Clearly, to bring up tales of Cleopatra's earlier amours could scarcely be calculated to please Antony, and Enobarbus manages to quiet Sextus and head him off.

Thy father, Pompey . . .

Not everyone is satisfied. When the chief characters leave, Menas, one of Sextus' captains, remains behind with Enobarbus. Menas mutters to himself:

Thy father, Pompey, would ne'er have made this treaty.
—Act II, scene vi, lines 82–83

The implication is that Sextus' father, Pompey the Great, would have had too much military and political sense to give up the trump card (starving Rome) for so little, but would have driven a much harder bargain. In this respect, Menas was being more sentimental than accurate, for Pompey the Great had been a poor politician and would undoubtedly have agreed to such a treaty or a worse one.

Later, Menas is frank enough to put the matter even more strongly to Enobarbus:

For my part, I am sorry it is turned to a drinking.
Pompey doth this day laugh away his fortune.
—Act II, scene vi, lines 104–5

The accuracy of Menas' judgment would make itself evident soon enough.

. . . holy, cold and still . . .

But then Menas too starts probing for information about Cleopatra and is thunderstruck when Enobarbus tells him Antony is married to Octavia. Surely, this can only be a marriage of convenience.

Enobarbus agrees:

I think so, too. But you shall find the band that seems to tie

their friendship together will be the very strangler of their
amity: Octavia is of a holy, cold and still conversation.

—Act II, scene vi, lines 120–23

Clearly, Enobarbus doesn't think this is the sort of thing that will hold a man like Antony. He says, confidently:

He will to his Egyptian dish again.

—Act II, scene vi, line 126

. . . the flow o'th'Nile

The quadrumvirs are on Sextus' galley off Misenum, having a grand time, and are hilarious over their wine. Antony is in his element; he can carry his liquor better than any of them and, as an expert on Egypt, a strange and exotic land, he can regale the others with wonders. He says:

Thus do they, sir: they take the flow o'th'Nile
By certain scales i'th'pyramid. They know
By th'height, the lowness, or the mean, if dearth
Or foison [plenty] follow. The higher Nilus swells,
The more it promises . . .

—Act II, scene vii, lines 17–21

Antony is correct here. The Egyptian priesthood kept a careful watch on the changes in the level of the Nile and through long records had learned to forecast from early variations what the final flood level would be and from that what the likelihood of a particularly poor harvest might be. Such studies had also made the Egyptians aware of the 365-day cycle of the seasons very early in their history and had given them an accurate solar calendar, while other civilizations of the time had struggled with the much more complicated lunar calendars.

The pyramids were not, however, used as scales for the level of the Nile. Throughout history, people have wondered at the uses of the pyramids and have been reluctant to accept the fact that those monstrous piles were merely elaborate tombs. They have been accused of every other purpose but that, and some moderns have considered them the repository of the wisdom of the ages, a means of forecasting the future, and an early method of launching spaceships. But they are tombs, just the same, and nothing more.

Your serpent of Egypt . . .

Lepidus is gloriously drunk; drunk enough to wish to shine as an Egyptian authority himself. He says with enormous gravity:

> *Your serpent of Egypt is bred now of your mud by the operation of your sun; so is your crocodile.*
>
> —Act II, scene vii, lines 26–28

This represents the ancient belief in "spontaneous generation," the thought that unwanted or noxious species of plants or animals arise of themselves from dead or decaying matter. (How else explain the prevalence of these species despite human efforts to wipe them out.)

Antony humors the drunken Lepidus by agreeing with him, but it is quite certain that the Egyptians knew that serpents and crocodiles developed from eggs laid by the adult female. The eggs were quite large enough to see.

The situation was less certain with creatures that laid eggs small enough to overlook. It was not until half a century after Shakespeare's death that it was shown that maggots did not arise from dead meat, but from tiny eggs laid on that dead meat by flies. And it wasn't till the mid-nineteenth century that it was shown that microscopic creatures did not arise from dead matter but only from other living microscopic creatures.

Lepidus goes on to deliver a piece of egregious patronization. He says:

> *. . . I have heard the Ptolemies' pyramises are very goodly things; without contradiction I have heard that.*
>
> —Act II, scene vii, lines 35–37

Of course, they were not the Ptolemies' pyramises (or pyramids, as we would say) except in the sense that they were to be found in the land ruled by them. They were built by native Egyptian Pharaohs who ruled more than two thousand years before the first Ptolemy mounted the Egyptian throne. They were as ancient to the Ptolemies as the Ptolemies are to us.

And "goodly things"? Yes indeed. Considering the technology of the time, the pyramids are the most colossal labors of man the planet has seen, with the possible exception of the Great Wall of China. They impress us now even in their ruins as mere piles of huge granite blocks. When they were new, they had white limestone facings that gleamed smoothly and brightly in the sun and were surrounded by enormous temple complexes.

The Greeks, who notoriously admired no culture but their own, humbly included these non-Greek structures among their Seven Wonders of the World; and of all the Seven Wonders only the pyramids still remain.

Antony cannot resist poking fun at the besotted Lepidus, describing the crocodile in grave but non-informative phrases, ending in the portentous:

> . . . *and the tears of it are wet.*
>
> —Act II, scene vii, line 51

Any mention of crocodiles would irresistibly bring tears to mind, for the most famous (but thoroughly untrue) legend concerning the crocodile is that it sheds tears over its prey while swallowing it. Hence the expression "crocodile tears" for hypocritical sorrow.

. . . *lord of all the world*

Menas, meanwhile, has been whispering to Sextus Pompeius and pulling at his sleeve. Sextus, who is enjoying the nonsense at the table, is unwilling to leave and follows Menas only with reluctance.

Once to one side, Menas whispers:

> *Wilt thou be lord of all the world?*
>
> —Act II, scene vii, line 63

The half-drunken Sextus stares in surprise and Menas is forced to explain:

> *These three world-sharers, these competitors,*
> *Are in thy vessel. Let me cut the cable;*
> *And when we are put off, fall to their throats.*
> *All there is thine.*
>
> —Act II, scene vii, lines 72–75

Sextus, sobered by the suggestion, is tempted, but then says, sorrowfully:

> *Ah, this thou shouldst have done,*
> *And not have spoke on't. In me 'tis villainy,*
> *In thee 't had been good service.*
>
> —Act II, scene vii, lines 75–77

This story is told by Plutarch and yet I wonder if it can be true. It is conceivable that the thought would have occurred to Menas and that

Sextus might have shrunk from the perfidiousness of the deed. But is it conceivable that the triumvirs would have placed themselves in Sextus' grasp without taking precautions against just such an act? If Lepidus were too stupid to foresee the possibility and Antony too careless, I would not believe it of Octavius. He would not step into the lion's jaw without some sort of rod so placed as to hold that jaw firmly open.

However, the story is a good one, true or false, and I would hate to lose it, particularly since it displays so neatly the exact moment when Sextus Pompeius reached and passed the peak of his power.

. . . my brave emperor

Octavius Caesar is the only one who is reluctant to drink. He cannot carry his liquor well and he does not enjoy losing his iron control of himself. The rough Enobarbus says to him with some irony:

> *Ha, my brave emperor!*
> *Shall we dance now the Egyptian bacchanals*
> *And celebrate our drink?*
> —Act II, scene vii, lines 105–7

The word "emperor" is from the Latin *imperator,* meaning "commander." It was a title given a successful general by his troops. It was one of the titles granted Julius Caesar by the Senate. He was not merely one of many imperators; he was *the* imperator of the Roman armies as a whole— the generalissimo.

Octavius Caesar eventually received the title too, and since control of the army was, at bottom, the secret of the control of the Roman state, his position as "Roman Imperator" was crucial. Through distortion we know the title as "Roman Emperor," and the state became the "Roman Empire."

Enobarbus uses the term "emperor" in its less exalted but more accurate aspect as "commander." Both Octavius Caesar and Mark Antony are referred to now and then throughout the play as "emperor."

. . . darting Parthia . . .

While Sextus Pompeius is being alcoholically neutralized in the West, Parthia is being defeated outright in the East. Leaving Antony in Italy, Ventidius sailed to Asia Minor, where in 39 B.C. he drove the Roman renegade Labienus into the eastern mountains and there defeated and killed him.

The Parthian army, under Pacorus, the son of King Orodes, still occupied Syria and Judea, however. In 38 B.C. Ventidius took his army to Syria and defeated the Parthians in three separate battles (and it was only after this was done that Herod could take his throne in Jerusalem).

In the last of the three victories over Parthia, Pacorus himself was slain. That last battle was fought (according to the story) on the fifteenth anniversary of the fateful day on which Crassus had lost his army at the Battle of Carrhae.

The third act opens, then, a year after the gay celebration at Misenum, with Ventidius returning in triumph from these wars. The dead body of the Parthian prince is being carried along with the army and Ventidius says:

> *Now, darting Parthia, art thou struck; and now*
> *Pleased fortune does of Marcus Crassus' death*
> *Make me revenger. Bear the King's son's body*
> *Before our army. Thy Pacorus, Orodes,*
> *Pays this for Marcus Crassus.*

> —Act III, scene i, lines 1–5

Parthia is called "darting" because of its reliance on archers in its battles. The Parthian arrows were their most effective weapon.

. . . *Media, Mesopotamia* . . .

Ventidius' aide, Silius, eagerly urges the general to pursue the enemy, to follow up the victory crushingly, and put an end to the Parthian menace forever. He says:

> *Spur through Media,*
> *Mesopotamia, and the shelters whither*
> *The routed fly.*

> —Act III, scene i, lines 7–9

Mesopotamia ("between the rivers") is the name given by the Greeks to the upper portion of the Tigris-Euphrates valley. It was the area within which Crassus had fought and died. The Romans struggled to grasp and hold it for centuries after Crassus' time, and from time to time succeeded. Nearly seven centuries went by before the region passed definitively out of their hands.

Media lay immediately to the east of Mesopotamia. It had been controlled by the Persians, conquered by Alexander the Great, and ruled by the early Seleucids, but at no time, then or later, could Roman force extend itself so far.

I have done enough . . .

Ventidius resists the temptation to continue the war. He might argue that a limited victory is safest. History is full of generals who could have gained greatly through initial victories and then went on to grasp for too much and to lose all. Adolf Hitler of Germany is only the latest example of this.

There have been exceptions, of course; Alexander the Great being the most notorious. It is hard to say how many generals have been lured to destruction by the specter of Alexander and by the fact that they themselves were not the military genius he was.

Ventidius does not advance such reasonable military grounds. He prefers instead to answer with the wisdom of the practical politician.

> *O Silius, Silius*
> *I have done enough: a lower place, note well,*
> *May make too great an act. For learn this, Silius,*
> *Better to leave undone, than by our deed*
> *Acquire too high a fame when him we serve's away.*
> —Act III, scene i, lines 11–15

Perhaps this is true in Antony's case, and if so it is another weakness of his. Since military valor was Antony's great recommendation, he could not endure having his subordinates display too much of it, lest people decide they can do without Antony.

Octavius Caesar had no difficulty of this sort. He was no military man, but he was a political genius. His generals could cover themselves with glory in his name for all he, or anyone, would care—as long as they followed his orders and left the political machinations to him.

. . . to Athens . . .

As the Parthian menace is ended, at least temporarily, in victory, so the difficulties with Sextus Pompeius are ended, at least temporarily, in compromise. The quadrumvirs are separating and Mark Antony must go east again to look after his affairs. But still not to Alexandria. He must yet maintain peace with Octavius Caesar and that means maintaining the marriage with Octavia.

In Syria the victorious Ventidius has heard of Antony's move. He says to Silius:

> *He* [Antony] *purposeth to Athens . . .*
> —Act III, scene i, line 35

Athens was no longer the great warlike power it had been in the time of Alcibiades and Timon (see page I–140) four centuries before. While its fleet had been in being, it was a city to be reckoned with, but its last fleet had been destroyed at the Battle of Amorgos (an island in the Aegean Sea) in 322 B.C.

After that, it was at the mercy of the Macedonians and could at best only wriggle a bit when Macedon was in trouble. In 146 B.C. all of Greece, including Athens, came under direct Roman control as the province of Achaea, and the last vestige of Athenian independence was gone.

Yet Athens could, and did, make one last gamble. In 88 B.C. the kingdom of Pontus in the northeastern stretches of Asia Minor under its able king, Mithradates VI, attacked Rome. Rome was having internal troubles and was caught flat-footed. The Pontine blitz captured all of Asia Minor. For a wild moment, Greece thought that the Greek-speaking Pontines would lead the way to Greek freedom once more. Athens declared for Pontus and moved into opposition against Rome.

Rome, however, sent its able and ruthless general, Sulla, eastward. He laid siege to Athens, quite without regard to its past glories, and Mithradates of Pontus was utterly unable to send help. In 86 B.C. Athens was taken and sacked and that was the final end. Never again, throughout ancient times, was Athens ever to take any independent political or military action. It settled down to the utter quiet of a university town and for two and a half centuries it was to know complete peace at the price of complete stagnation.

It is to somnolent Athens that Antony now comes and it is there he will stay, with Octavia, for over two years.

This is too long a time for the purposes of the play, of course, since Shakespeare is anxious to show the love affair between Antony and Cleopatra to follow an absolutely irresistible course. He must therefore give the impression that Antony's connection with Octavia is fleeting.

To do this, there is a scene, following that which involves Ventidius, which shows Antony leaving with Octavia for Athens, and then, immediately afterward, one which shows Cleopatra still questioning the Messenger who brought her news of the marriage.

While tremendous events are transpiring in the outside world—a year of campaigning in Parthia and Syria, a year of negotiation in Italy—it is yet the same day in Cleopatra's palace. She is still planning to win Antony back from Octavia, and the Messenger, well knowing what is expected of him, gladly describes Octavia as short, round-faced, with a low forehead and a shambling walk.

New wars 'gainst Pompey . . .

Antony's establishment of his capital in Athens is, in itself, an invitation to more trouble. It was part of the compromise agreement with Sextus that the latter be given Greece as one of his provinces. Antony never lived up to that part of the bargain and may have deliberately come to Athens to make sure that Greece remained his.

Once Sextus realized that Antony was not going to keep his part of the treaty, he was naturally infuriated, and once again began his offensive against Rome's food supply. The pact of Misenum was in ruins before it really got a chance to work.

Shakespeare mentions none of this. When he turns to Antony's house in Athens, he pictures Antony as infuriated at events in Italy and placing all the blame for the renewed trouble on Octavius Caesar. Antony is saying angrily to Octavia, concerning her brother:

> . . . *he hath waged*
> *New wars 'gainst Pompey; made his will, and read it*
> *To public ear;*
> *Spoke scantly of me . . .*
> —Act III, scene iv, lines 3–6

Naturally, Octavius must fight Sextus again; when Sextus begins to stop the grain shipments, Octavius has no choice but to regard it as an invitation to war.

Since Sextus' pretext is the withholding of Greece, which is Antony's act, Octavius Caesar can scarcely keep from suspecting that Antony is behind Sextus; that the two have an understanding. He therefore renews the propaganda offensive against Antony ("spoke scantly of me").

Furthermore, Octavius Caesar shored up his own popularity with the Romans by preparing a will donating money and property to the people in case of his death. He carefully let that will be made public. (Mark Antony once read Julius Caesar's will to the public, see page I–295, and he knows well how powerful a weapon a proper will can be.)

Antony might not have been so angry if Octavius Caesar's struggle with Sextus Pompeius had gone badly for the former. The situation had changed from what it was before, however. When Sextus closed off Rome's life line he found out why Menas had been opposed to the compromise agreement at Misenum. Octavius had used the respite to stock Rome and to fill its storehouses. It would take a long time before it could be choked once more and meanwhile Octavius could strike back. Sextus found that while Antony and Octavius could easily undo their part of the agreement, he could not undo his; he could not withdraw the food he had allowed into Rome.

It was still necessary to fight Sextus, however, even if Rome was not starving. Octavius Caesar twice sent out ships to fight Sextus, and twice Sextus' hardened sea fighters won.

Octavius Caesar therefore set to work in earnest. He placed Agrippa in charge and ordered him to build a fleet. Through the whole of 38 and 37 B.C., Agrippa was hard at work on this project, and Antony did not like it. The last thing he wanted was an Octavian victory at sea, for that would mean that Octavius Caesar would be free to turn to the East and would have a fleet to do it with.

Antony's impulse, then, is to engage in open hostilities, now, while Sextus can still be his ally and while Octavius is still without real power at sea. (Antony himself can always have the Egyptian fleet at his disposal, in addition to his own ships.)

Yourself shall go between's . . .

Now comes time for the purpose of the marriage of Octavia to show itself. Octavia pleads for peace between husband and brother and urges Antony to let her serve as peacemaker. Antony agrees, saying:

> . . . as you requested,
> Yourself shall go between's: the meantime, lady,
> I'll raise the preparation of a war
> Shall stain your brother.
>
> —Act III, scene iv, lines 24–27

Octavia may try to make the peace, then, but if she fails, Antony will make war. Actually, she succeeded. She met her brother and managed to arrange another meeting between Antony and Octavius Caesar at Tarentum in southern Italy in 37 B.C. Peace between them continued.

So much the worse for Antony, however, and the marriage with Octavia proved a disaster for him. The peace she arranged was one in which Antony agreed to, and did, suspend his preparations for war; and in which Octavius Caesar agreed to, but did not, suspend his own preparations for sea mastery. In the interval of peace between the triumvirs, Octavius Caesar continued to build his fleet.

. . . wars upon Pompey

Shakespeare skips this second reconciliation altogether. Immediately after the scene with Octavia in which she is sent off as mediator, Enobarbus and another of Antony's captains, Eros, rush in to discuss military matters. Eros has news, and says:

Caesar and Lepidus have made wars upon Pompey.
—Act III, scene v, lines 4–5

This sounds like the same wars that Antony has been complaining about in the previous scene, especially since Enobarbus responds by saying:

This is old.
—Act III, scene v, line 6

Actually, it is a new war, begun *after* Octavia has brought about the meeting at Tarentum and the reconciliation.

On July 1, 36 B.C., Agrippa's new fleet set out in three squadrons, Agrippa at the head of one, Octavius of a second, and Lepidus of a third. For two months these ships and those of Sextus met, with victory usually resting with Sextus. At one point, Octavius' squadron was nearly wiped out.

Finally, on September 3, 36 B.C., Sextus was forced to accept battle with Agrippa near the Strait of Messina, which separates Sicily and Italy. This time Sextus was defeated by sea and land, and his power was utterly destroyed. He managed to get away himself and fled eastward, hoping to find safety with Antony.

. . . denied him rivality . . .

Antony could now see into what catastrophe Octavia's mediation had led him. Octavius Caesar had beaten Sextus and Antony had lost his chance to make vigorous war against Octavius in combination with Sextus. Making that same war without Sextus and with Octavius equipped now with a victorious navy was another, and worse, matter altogether.

Nor was this the full extent to which matters had turned against Antony. Eros has more news, about Lepidus:

Caesar, having made use of him [Lepidus] *in the wars 'gainst Pompey, presently denied him rivality, would not let him partake in the glory of the action; and not resting here, accuses him of letters he had formerly wrote to Pompey; upon his own appeal, seizes him; so the poor third is up, till death enlarge his confine.*
—Act III, scene v, lines 7–13

What happened was that after Sextus Pompeius was defeated, Octavius Caesar added all the conquered areas (Sicily, Sardinia, Corsica, and so on) to the provinces controlled by himself. Lepidus, who controlled only Africa, felt that since he had shared in the fighting, he ought to get some of the loot. This Octavius Caesar refused ("would not let him partake in the glory of the action").

Lepidus attempted to use force but this Octavius Caesar scotched at once. He entered Lepidus' camp with a small body of troops, sure that Lepidus' portion of the army would not support their general (probably he had made arrangements with Lepidus' troops in advance). He was right. Lepidus' men deserted him.

Lepidus was therefore demoted from his triumviral status and Africa was taken from him. He was not imprisoned, however, for he was not that dangerous. He was sent back to Rome and was allowed to keep the purely honorary title of Pontifex Maximus ("high priest"), in which role he had many harmless duties to perform. He kept the job for the remaining quarter century of his life and never bothered anyone again.

And threats the throat . . .

Octavius Caesar is now without a rival in the West. He rules all the provinces and is stronger than ever before. Antony, who had lost his chance for effective military action, can now only rage. Eros describes his actions:

> He's walking in the garden—thus, and spurns
> The rush that lies before him; cries "Fool Lepidus!"
> And threats the throat of that his officer
> That murd'red Pompey.

—Act III, scene v, lines 17–20

Sextus Pompeius, fleeing from the lost battle near Sicily, had gone first to the Aegean island of Lesbos, and then to Asia Minor. There he had been taken by a contingent of Antony's troops, and the officer in charge, assuming him to be an enemy, killed him. That was the end of Sextus Pompeius, just three years after he might have been the lord of all the world by merely cutting a hawser first and then three throats.

The officer who killed Sextus had acted hastily, however. He still had his name and he might have been a most useful pawn to Antony against Octavius. Now he was gone and Antony could only curse the excess zeal of his own loyal officer.

The situation in 36 B.C., then, was this. From a quadrumvirate there had come a diumvirate—two men, Octavius Caesar and Mark Antony.

The disappearance of the other two, Lepidus and Sextus, had resulted in their strength being added entirely to that of Octavius.

In Alexandria . . .

Between the scene just described and the next, there is a historical lapse of two years, which Shakespeare passes over in silence, though they are eventful.

For one thing, Antony, thoroughly disillusioned with the political effect of the marriage with Octavia, left her. The marriage had served Octavius Caesar's purpose only.

In 36 B.C., therefore, he left Athens and returned to Alexandria. He abandoned Octavia and returned to Cleopatra, whom he had not seen in three years. He was forty-seven years old now, and she was thirty-three, and from this point on to the end of their lives, nothing came between them.

Of course, there were still world affairs to deal with. Antony could expect no further agreements with Octavius Caesar. There was going to be war as soon as one or the other felt strong enough to push it.

Antony wanted the strength and to get it he turned and pushed against the Parthians. In a way, this was wasteful, for Antony was turning away from the main enemy (at the moment) and expending energy on a lesser foe. Perhaps we can see his reasoning, though . . .

Octavius Caesar had won considerable military prestige through his victory over Sextus (even though the credit belonged to Agrippa), and since military prestige was Antony's chief stock in trade he had to balance that gain somehow. The Parthians were still reeling from Ventidius' strokes and might be an easy prey. Then too, once they were beaten, Antony could face westward without having to worry about his rear.

Without provocation, then, Antony opened a campaign against the Parthians and proceeded to do what Ventidius had refused to do. He pursued the Parthians deep into their own fastnesses.

For his pains, he was trapped in the mountains and was able to escape only with the loss of more than half his army. It was almost as bad a defeat as Crassus had suffered and only the fact that he himself did not die as Crassus had done obscured the fact.

The next year, 35 B.C., he tried to retrieve matters by attacking Armenia, a much weaker adversary than Parthia. Here he won, capturing the King and bringing him back to Alexandria, where he celebrated a mock triumph. (A real triumph would have had to take place in Rome.)

Antony had returned to Alexandria with his military reputation much tarnished as a result of his Eastern adventure, rather than made glistening as he had hoped. Had he come back an easy and glorious victor over Parthia he might well have turned against Octavius at once. As it was, he seems to have decided in favor of settling for half.

He would build an Eastern empire about Egypt as a base and with Alexandria as its capital. He would assume a defensive stance and await events. In doing so, however, he could not help assuming the posture of an Egyptian king.

After all, life with Cleopatra had become a settled thing. She had had twin children—a boy and a girl—soon after he had left her, back in 40 B.C. Now he recognized them as his. They were named Alexander Helios ("the sun") and Cleopatra Selene ("the moon"). He even married Cleopatra with all solemnity, and the marriage was recognized as valid in the provinces controlled by him, even though he was still married to Octavia. (He didn't formally divorce Octavia till 32 B.C.)

It was at this point, too, that he began to hand over Roman territory to Cleopatra, as he had earlier promised.

Octavius, who had been continuing to build his strength in the West and had been preparing public opinion for an offensive against the East, found all this a godsend.

It is here that Shakespeare takes up the story. Immediately after the scene in which the fate of Lepidus and Sextus is described, the scene shifts to Rome, where Octavius Caesar is describing Antony's activity to Maecenas:

> Contemning Rome, he has done all this and more
> In Alexandria. Here's the manner of't:
> I'th'marketplace on a tribunal silvered,
> Cleopatra and himself in chairs of gold
> Were publicly enthroned; at the feet sat
> Caesarion, whom they call my father's son,
> And all the unlawful issue that their lust
> Since then hath made between them. Unto her
> He gave the stablishment of Egypt; made her
> Of lower Syria, Cyprus, Lydia,
> Absolute queen.
>
> —Act III, scene vi, lines 1–11

Caesarion is, of course, the reputed son of Julius Caesar. Julius Caesar was the great-uncle of Octavius Caesar, actually, but in his will Julius had adopted Octavius as his son, and Octavius therefore always refers to Julius as his father. (A good propaganda point, of course.)

In a way, Antony was restoring to Cleopatra territory that had belonged to the Ptolemies at the peak of their power two centuries before. He also restored Cyrene (which Shakespeare does not mention), which Rome had annexed in 96 B.C.

What's more, their children are also endowed. Octavius Caesar goes on to say:

> *His sons he there proclaimed the kings of kings:*
> *Great Media, Parthia, and Armenia*
> *He gave to Alexander; to Ptolemy he assigned*
> *Syria, Cilicia, and Phoenicia.*
>
> —Act III, scene vi, lines 12–16

This is not as bad as it sounds. Alexander is Alexander Helios, who at this time (34 B.C.) was six years old. The kingdoms he was given were not really Roman, so that they represented a phantom rule. Ptolemy (that is, Caesarion, who is called Ptolemy XIV) received lands that had once been Ptolemaic.

However, we can be sure that Octavius Caesar made the most of Antony's rash family-centered actions. He made it seem to the Roman populace that Antony was giving away Roman provinces to a powerful foreign queen. What's more, he had made himself king (hated word) and loved Alexandria more than Rome. He held triumphs there and Octavius Caesar found a will which he said was Antony's and which directed that Antony be buried in Alexandria rather than in Rome.

It was easy to make it appear that Antony planned to conquer the West and then not only set himself up as king in Rome but make Cleopatra queen. Accusations such as these, skillfully spread, and made plausible by Antony's own actions, utterly destroyed any credit Antony might have in the West.

My lord, Mark Antony

And in upon Octavius Caesar, at this moment, comes Octavia, apparently on her errand of mediation. She says:

> *My lord, Mark Antony,*
> *Hearing that you prepared for war, acquainted*
> *My grieved ear withal; whereon I begged*
> *His pardon for return.*
>
> —Act III, scene vi, lines 57–60

It would appear that Octavia, who left Mark Antony two scenes before, now arrives in Rome. All the events that took place over three years—the defeat and death of Sextus Pompeius, the demotion of Lepidus, the campaigns of Mark Antony in Parthia and Armenia (to which Octavius makes reference in passing)—are all hastened over in the one intervening scene.

This serves a purpose. In many places in the play, Mark Antony is whitewashed to make him a more sympathetic hero. Here he is made to seem worse than he is so that the love story with Cleopatra can be made more dramatic.

In actual fact, he returned to Cleopatra only after three years, when his marriage to Octavia proved to be politically worthless—or worse. Here in the play, it appears that even while Octavia is on her way to intercede for Antony with her brother, the faithless Antony deserts her.

Octavius asks her where Antony is and when she innocently says that he is in Athens, her brother says:

> No, my most wronged sister, Cleopatra
> Hath nodded him to her.
>
> —Act III, scene vi, lines 65–66

Cleopatra's power over Antony thus seems enormous. The truth of Antony's return would have considerably diminished the glamour of the love affair.

The kings o'th'earth . . .

Indeed, Octavius goes on to say, Antony is preparing for war:

> He hath given his empire
> Up to a whore, who now are levying
> The kings o'th'earth for war. He hath assembled
> Bocchus, the King of Libya; Archelaus,
> Of Cappadocia; Philadelphos, King
> Of Paphlagonia; the Thracian king, Adallas;
> King Mauchas of Arabia; King of Pont;
> Herod of Jewry; Mithridates, King
> Of Comagene; Polemon and Amyntas,
> The kings of Mede and Lycaonia;
> With a more larger list of scepters
>
> —Act III, scene vi, lines 66–76

This list of kings sounds impressive; the sonorous syllables roll off the tongue. They are at best, however, a set of puppet kinglets, with very little power except for what prestige their names can lend Antony. Cappadocia, Paphlagonia, Pont (Pontus), Comagene, and Lycaonia are all regions in Asia Minor. Herod and Mauchas represent small kingdoms in southern Syria, and so on. Indeed, one of the kings listed, Bocchus of Libya, actually fought on Octavius Caesar's side.

Nevertheless, this sort of thing was undoubtedly used by Octavius to rouse the Roman populace with the fear that Antony was turning the whole mysterious East loose upon them.

. . . denounced against us . . .

Between this scene and the next, further crucial events take place.

Toward the end of 32 B.C. Octavius finally had the situation exactly where he wanted it. The Senate and the people had grown so exasperated that the former declared war against Cleopatra and the latter supported it avidly.

This was utterly clever. The war was not against Mark Antony, who could be pictured as a Roman general deceived and besotted by a wicked foreign queen; it was against the wicked foreign queen herself. It was not a civil war; it was a patriotic war against the dangerous kingdom of Egypt. (The fact that Egypt was helpless and harmless and that Cleopatra, minus Mark Antony, had no military power at all, could be ignored. The public knew nothing of that.)

Naturally, Mark Antony had to fight. But he had to fight now against Rome and on the side of the foreigner. Desperately he shifted his armies to Greece and prepared to invade Italy.

Cleopatra, in a decision as foolish as that of Octavius Caesar had been wise, decided to accompany Antony, and together they are now at Actium, a promontory in northwestern Greece.

The next scene, then, opens in Actium, where Cleopatra is raging against Enobarbus, who objects to her presence there. She points out that the war, after all, was declared against her:

> Is't not denounced against us? Why should not we
> Be there in person?
> —Act III, scene vii, lines 5–6

But Cleopatra was unintentionally fighting on Octavius Caesar's side in this respect. As a foreign queen, she was no more popular with Antony's soldiers than with the enemy.

And take in Toryne

Indeed, it is the spirit of Antony's forces that is their weakest point, and Octavius Caesar knows it. Anti-Cleopatra propaganda reaches them and the desertions are numerous. The men won't fight for an Egyptian against Rome. Antony's movements are slowed and made uncertain by the increasingly doubtful loyalty of his men.

Octavius Caesar's general, Agrippa, moves quickly, however. Where it had been Antony's hope to invade Italy, it was Agrippa instead who swept across from that peninsula and landed in Greece. Antony comes in with his general, Canidius, brooding about it:

> *Is it not strange, Canidius,*
> *That from Tarentum and Brundusium*
> *He could so quickly cut the Ionian sea*
> *And take in Toryne?*
> —Act III, scene vii, lines 20–23

Tarentum and Brundusium are ports in the "heel" of Italy. The Ionian Sea is the stretch of water between southern Italy and western Greece. Toryne is a small harbor in northwestern Greece, thirty-five miles up the coast from Actium.

. . . not well manned

Octavius Caesar's rapid movement (or, rather, Agrippa's, in his name) has cut Antony's line of communication and put him in the peril of running short of supplies. It is to Antony's interest to force a land battle; he has eighty thousand troops to Octavius Caesar's seventy thousand and it is Antony who is the better tactician on land.

On the other hand, it is to Octavius Caesar's best interests to fight a sea battle. He has only four hundred ships to Antony's five hundred, but he still would have the advantage there. Enobarbus points this out to Antony, saying:

> *Your ships are not well manned;*
> *Your mariners are muleters, reapers, people*
> *Ingrossed by swift impress. In Caesar's fleet*
> *Are those that often have 'gainst Pompey fought;*
> *Their ships are yare, yours, heavy . . .*
> —Act III, scene vii, lines 34–38

The growing desertions from Antony's standards have left his ships shorthanded, and their crews have had to be fleshed out by the drafting of non-sailors from the surrounding population. And, of course, though you can force a man onto a ship, you cannot force him to be a sailor.

The logical course of action would have been to retreat inland and force

Octavius to follow and then fight a land battle. Even an ordinary soldier begs him to take that strategy, saying:

> *O noble Emperor, do not fight by sea,*
> *Trust not to rotten planks.*
>
> —Act III, scene vii, lines 61–62

It is Cleopatra, though, who holds out strongly for a sea engagement. We can speculate why. The hardships of an army march might have excluded her and sent her back to Alexandria. A sea victory, on the other hand, would include the Egyptian fleet and entitle her to a share in the glory and the profits. She points out:

> *I have sixty sails, Caesar none better.*
>
> —Act III, scene vii, line 49

And Antony rejects the advice of his seasoned warriors, decides on the sea battle Cleopatra wants, and loses his last chance.

With all their sixty . . .

There follows the sea battle, the Battle of Actium, on September 2, 31 B.C. It is one of the crucial clashes of history.

The battle is, of course, not shown onstage, but Enobarbus supplies the vision of its crucial moment. In agony, he turns away from the sight:

> *Naught, naught, all naught! I can behold no longer.*
> *Th'Antoniad, the Egyptian admiral,*
> *With all their sixty, fly . . .*
>
> —Act III, scene x, lines 1–3

When the battle began, Octavius' ships could at first make little impression on Antony's large vessels, and the battle seemed to be a useless one between maneuverability and power. Finally, though, Agrippa's superior seamanship maneuvered Antony's fleet into stretching its line, and Agrippa's ships began to dart through the openings that resulted, making straight for Cleopatra's fleet of sixty that lay in reserve.

At this point, Cleopatra ordered her flagship, the *Antoniad* (named in honor of Antony, of course), to turn and carry her to safety. The remainder of her fleet went with her.

The easy interpretation is that it was simply cowardice. Or perhaps the cowardice wasn't that simple; she felt the battle was lost and that retreat was necessary. She had to preserve herself from capture (with reason—

for with her a captive the war would be lost), and also the treasure chest, which was aboard the ship.

The noble ruin of her magic . . .

Scarus, another officer, enters in wild passion, for even worse has developed. He tells Enobarbus that, once Cleopatra sailed away:

> The noble ruin of her magic, Antony,
> Claps on his sea wing, and (like a doting mallard)
> Leaving the fight in height, flies after her.
> —Act III, scene x, lines 18–20

This is the point at which the world is lost and Antony is forever disgraced. There might be reasons for Cleopatra running away; the only reason for Antony is an impulse of love. This impulse might be understandable, even admirable, to romantics, and surely there is nothing so worth a sigh as to witness some great game tossed away for love.

Yet we must admit that however admirable it may be to ruin oneself for love, however noble to go down to personal death for love, it is not noble to cast away the lives and fortunes of thousands of others for love.

Antony abandoned a fleet that was fighting bravely on his behalf, and in the confusion and disheartenment that followed his flight, many men died who might have lived had he remained. What's more, he abandoned thousands of officers and men on the nearby mainland, who had been prepared to die for him, leaving them only the alternative of useless resistance or ignoble surrender.

We may understand Antony, but we cannot excuse him.

He at Philippi . . .

Antony well understood his own disgrace. After Actium, he played awhile with the idea (according to Plutarch) of retiring from the world in an agony of misanthropy and self-pity—like Timon of Athens. (It may have been the reading of this passage, indeed, that inspired Shakespeare to try his hand, rather unsuccessfully, at Timon of Athens immediately after he had finished Antony and Cleopatra.)

Antony cannot bring himself to be a Timon, however, and he must crawl back to the only place that will now receive him—Alexandria. Only Egypt is now his who once ruled half the world, and it will remain his only until Octavius Caesar comes to get him.

Antony broods madly on this same Octavius:

> *He at Philippi kept*
> *His sword e'en like a dancer, while I struck*
> *The lean and wrinkled Cassius; and 'twas I*
> *That the mad Brutus ended . . .*
>
> —Act III, scene xi, lines 35–38

It is true. The Battle of Philippi was all Antony and Octavius' portion of the army was defeated. For that matter, Octavius' portion of the fleet was defeated by Sextus, and Octavius was sick during the Battle of Actium, so that the last two victories were all Agrippa.

Yet Octavius, always beaten, was somehow the winner because what he had he kept and what he lost one way he won another. He could use other men well and he had brains and a cool judgment, and that stands head and shoulders over mere "style."

Fall not a tear . . .

There is no more room for glory in Antony. Shakespeare, for what is left of the play, intends only to recoup for Antony all the sympathy he has lost by his folly in another way; he will win it all back and more by showing Antony the lover.

With all he has lost, Antony can only reproach Cleopatra sorrowfully. When she says that she did not realize he would follow her, he replies:

> *Egypt, thou knew'st too well*
> *My heart was to thy rudder tied by th'strings,*
> *And thou shouldst tow me after.*
>
> —Act III, scene xi, lines 56–58

And when she weeps and begs for pardon he says:

> *Fall not a tear, I say; one of them rates*
> *All that is won and lost. Give me a kiss;*
> *Even this repays me.*
>
> —Act III, scene xi, lines 69–71

What an incredible fool! What an exasperating idiot! But then why do the tears come? And they will continue. Those who can sit through the rest of the play dry-eyed are either seeing an incredibly poor performance or are afflicted with an incredibly impoverished heart.

. . . her all-disgracèd friend

Antony has no choice now but to sue for peace and get what terms he can. He has no kings to send now; they have all deserted him in the aftermath of Actium. He sends his children's tutor to approach Octavius Caesar.

For Cleopatra, he asks that she remain Queen of Egypt only, giving up all the additions Antony has given her. For himself he asks that he remain in Egypt with her or, still less, that he be allowed to remain in Athens as a private citizen. Octavius replies to the Ambassador:

> *For Antony*
> *I have no ears to his request. The Queen*
> *Of audience nor desire shall fail, so she*
> *From Egypt drive her all-disgracèd friend*
> *Or take his life there.*
>
> —Act III, scene xii, lines 19–23

Octavius knows his own military deficiencies as well as Antony does. He knows that all his victories are the work of his allies and subordinates and that he himself has contributed nothing in the field. What he desires more than anything else, then, is a glorious triumph in Rome, such as his famous great-uncle had received. It is very likely that for himself he required no such trumperies, but he must surely have realized that his hold on the Roman people would not be complete without some public celebration of victories associated (however unfairly) with his name.

For the purpose of a triumph, Antony is useless. He is a Roman and could not be dragged at the chariot wheels, and even if he were, that would arouse dangerous sympathies. Nor could he be left alive, even as a private citizen in Athens. How long would he remain a private citizen? How soon would he begin to intrigue to regain what he had lost? For Antony, it had to be death.

Cleopatra, however, must live. She was a foreigner. She was feared to an unimaginable (and undeserved) extent. Her reputation as a charmer and as an insidious schemer against Rome was so impossibly high that the sight of her in chains walking behind Octavius Caesar's triumphant chariot would drive Rome wild with exultation and turn Octavius, truly, into another Julius. Octavius Caesar might have a triumph without Cleopatra; but without her it would be a poor thing and leave his life in that one respect forever incomplete.

Octavius was therefore ready to offer Cleopatra anything, make her any promise, in order to keep her alive.

. . . the boy Caesar . . .

The news of Octavius Caesar's terms is brought to Antony and he says to Cleopatra bitterly:

> *To the boy Caesar send this grizzled head,*
> *And he will fill thy wishes to the brim*
>> —Act III, scene xiii, lines 17–18

The play moves so quickly through space and time that there is no sensation, while watching it, of passing time. Eleven years have passed since the opening scene of the play, if we are thinking of real history. Antony is now about fifty-three years old and his head may well be grizzled. The "boy Caesar" is now thirty-three years old. He is not really venerable, but he is certainly a boy no longer.

. . . the getting of a lawful race

Meanwhile, another ambassador, an officer named Thidias, approaches Cleopatra separately. Clearly, if she is to be induced to sacrifice Antony, it can be best done in Antony's absence. Cleopatra is eager to flatter Octavius into decent terms, both for herself and Antony, and it must be admitted that what historical evidence we have gives us no clear sign that she dreamed of deserting Antony at any time.

However, even while she is fawning on Thidias and giving him her hand to kiss, Antony enters. In the midst of his disgrace and defeat, he finds it only too easy to believe he is being betrayed. He orders Thidias to be whipped and rages at Cleopatra for her immorality and for the other men in her life (surely this is something he knew all about to begin with). He cries out in self-pity:

> *Have I my pillow left unpressed in Rome,*
> *Forborne the getting of a lawful race,*
> *And by a gem of women, to be abused*
> *By one that looks on feeders?*
>> —Act III, scene xiii, lines 106–9

To those who know only as much of Antony and Cleopatra as they read in this play it would come as a surprise to know that Antony did indeed beget a lawful race (that is, legitimate children). He had two sons by Fulvia.

The "gem of women" must be a reference to Octavia, but there, too, Shakespeare is bending history. In the play Antony's connection with Octavia seems fleeting, but in actual history, he spent a couple of years with her in Athens and their relationship was long enough and real enough to produce two daughters.

. . . the hill of Basan . . .

Half mad with frustration, Antony taunts Cleopatra with her infidelities to him (in advance yet, for the examples he cites came about before they had met in Tarsus) until he makes himself a cuckold in his own eyes, crying out:

> *O, that I were*
> *Upon the hill of Basan to outroar*
> *The horned herd!*
>
> —Act III, scene xiii, lines 126–28

Basan is the biblical Bashan, an area of pasturage renowned for its fat cows and strong bulls. Thus, the psalmist describes his troubles metaphorically in this way: "Many bulls have compassed me: strong bulls of Bashan have beset me round" (Psalms 22:12). Since bulls are horned, the reference to cuckoldry is clear (see page I–84).

But the reference is biblical. It is conceivable that a cultivated Roman of the times might have come across a Greek translation of the Hebrew Bible and have read it out of curiosity or interest—but to suppose that the non-intellectual Antony would do so is out of the question.

. . . the old ruffian . . .

Cleopatra manages to calm down Antony at last and bring him to what senses remain in him.

Octavius Caesar's army is now just outside Alexandria and Antony decides to meet him in one last land fight. In fact, he even—as a gesture—offers to meet Octavius in single combat.

Octavius meets this challenge with characteristic contempt. He says to Maecenas:

> *My messenger*
> *He hath whipped with rods; dares me to personal combat.*
> *Caesar to Antony: let the old ruffian know*
> *I have many other ways to die; meantime*
> *Laugh at his challenge.*
>
> —Act IV, scene i, lines 2–6

Actually, though one could not guess it from the play, eleven months have passed since the Battle of Actium. Octavius Caesar did not swoop down on Egypt at once. That could wait, for Antony and Cleopatra were helplessly penned up there.

Octavius first founded the city of Nicopolis ("City of Victory") near the site of the battle. Then he had to spend time reorganizing the affairs of the Eastern provinces that had been Antony's domain and were now his. (Egypt, be it remembered, had never, till then, been a Roman province, but was in theory an independent kingdom.)

Then he had to return to Rome to take care of pressing matters there. It was only in July 30 B.C. that he could sail his army to Egypt itself. By that time Cleopatra was thirty-nine.

Antony and Cleopatra had spent the eleven-month respite in luxury as though they knew their time was limited and were determined to make the most of what was left. But now Octavius Caesar had come and the time for the final battle was at hand.

. . . the god Hercules . . .

The eve of the last battle is a strange one. The soldiers hear mysterious music in the air and underground, moving away into the distance. One soldier guesses at the meaning:

> *'Tis the god Hercules, whom Antony loved,*
> *Now leaves him.*
>
> —Act IV, scene iii, lines 15–16

This eerie tale is told by Plutarch and is the kind of legend that arises after the fact.

It is, of course, rather late in the day for Hercules to leave poor Antony. Hercules had clearly abandoned him on the eve of Actium.

. . . send his treasure after . . .

Nor is it only Hercules that abandons Antony. The common soldier who had advised a land battle at Actium now meets Antony again. If that land battle had been fought, he says:

> *The kings that have revolted, and the soldier*
> *That has this morning left thee, would have still*
> *Followèd thy heels.*
>
> —Act IV, scene v, lines 4–6

Thus it is that Antony discovers that the rough and faithful Enobarbus has at last deserted him and gone over to Octavius Caesar's camp. But Antony, in adversity, always rises to heights of strength and nobility he cannot possibly reach in prosperity. He realizes that not Enobarbus' wickedness but his own follies have driven the soldier away. He is thinking perhaps that after his own desertion at Actium, no soldier owes him loyalty, and he says:

> *O, my fortunes have*
> *Corrupted honest men!*
>
> —Act IV, scene v, lines 16–17

And, having learned that Enobarbus has crept away so secretly as to have been unable to take with him his personal belongings and the money he has earned in the course of his labors, Antony says to his aide-de-camp:

> *Go, Eros, send his treasure after; do it,*
> *Detain no jot, I charge thee.*
>
> —Act IV, scene v, lines 12–13

. . . alone the villain . . .

Shakespeare found the tale of this princely gesture in Plutarch and it is believable in Antony. He was lost, anyway, and it was the kind of quixotic gesture a man noble by fits would make. If it had been Octavius Caesar, we might suppose it to have been done out of a desire to punish the deserter, for punishment it most certainly turns out to be.

Enobarbus is already suffering over his betrayal, and realizes that the tardy converts to Octavius Caesar's cause are not truly trusted and are certainly not honored, but live in a kind of contemptible twilight. In the midst of his misgivings, he hears his property has been sent after him. Stupefied, he bursts out in agony:

> *I am alone the villain of the earth,*
> *And feel I am so most.*
>
> —Act IV, scene vi, lines 30–34

They are beaten . . .

In the last battle, despite everything, the advantage falls to Antony once more. He and his soldiers fight like madmen and his officer, Eros, rushes in to say:

They are beaten, sir, and our advantage serves
For a fair victory.

—Act IV, scene vii, lines 11–12

But, alas, this is one of Shakespeare's few inventions of the play. There was no victory at this point. There wasn't even a true battle. Antony's remnant of an army gave in almost at once and Antony was penned up in Alexandria.

What Shakespeare wanted was one last unexpected uplift; one last illusion; one last hope of escape from the doom the lovers had madly woven about themselves; perhaps one sight of might-have-been for the land battle at Actium that had never come.

O, Antony

The victory serves also to add the last unbearable pang to Enobarbus' agony. Had those faithful to Antony had the courage and will to fight and win while he himself had slunk away, a coward traitor? He staggers into the night, crying:

> *O, Antony,*
> *Nobler than my revolt is infamous,*
> *Forgive me in thine own particular,*
> *But let the world rank me in register*
> *A master-leaver and a fugitive.*
> *O, Antony! O, Antony!*

—Act IV, scene ix, lines 18–23

And so, asking forgiveness from Antony alone, and content to have all the world besides scorn him, he dies. Yet he does not have his wish, for with Shakespeare's deathless music pleading his case, who can scorn him? No one!

Again, Shakespeare follows his sources in having Enobarbus die of heartbreak. From a historical standpoint, it is hard to believe in such a death, but here, as in so many cases, it is far better to romanticize with Shakespeare than be flat with history.

There is a sequel to the story that Shakespeare doesn't hint at, but one that should be mentioned if only to soften a little our regret at Enobarbus' fate.

Enobarbus had a son, Lucius Domitius Ahenobarbus, who in later years served Octavius Caesar and who did well. This Lucius eventually married Antonia, who was Mark Antony's elder daughter by Octavia. They had a son, Gnaeus Domitius Ahenobarbus (Enobarbus' grandson and namesake), who thus had both Enobarbus and Antony for grandfathers.

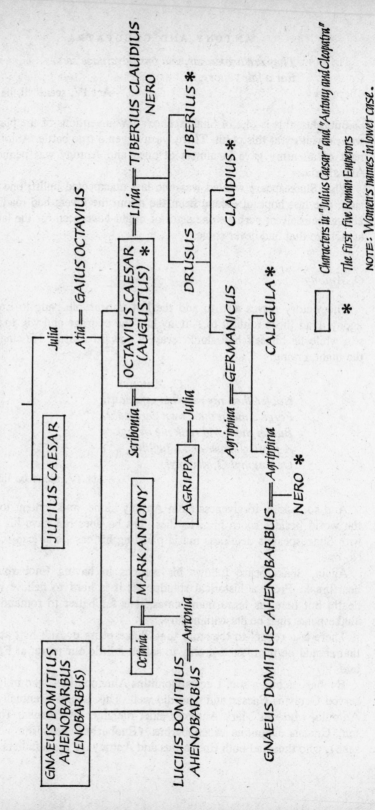

ANTONY and CLEOPATRA

The JULIAN–CLAUDIAN HOUSE

Characters in "Julius Caesar" and "Antony and Cleopatra"

☐ The First Five Roman Emperors

NOTE: Women's names in lower case.

JULIUS CAESAR

Julia

Atia = GAIUS OCTAVIUS

OCTAVIUS CAESAR (AUGUSTUS) ✱ = Livia = TIBERIUS CLAUDIUS NERO

TIBERIUS ✱

DRUSUS

CLAUDIUS ✱

Scribonia

Julia

AGRIPPA

Agrippina = GERMANICUS

CALIGULA ✱

MARK ANTONY

Octavia = Antonia

GNAEUS DOMITIUS AHENOBARBUS (ENOBARBUS)

LUCIUS DOMITIUS AHENOBARBUS

GNAEUS DOMITIUS AHENOBARBUS = Agrippina

NERO ✱

The younger Ahenobarbus married Agrippina, a great-granddaughter of Octavius Caesar and a great-granddaughter of Livia, the wife of Octavius Caesar, by her earlier marriage. Their son, the great-grandson of Antony and the great-grandson of Enobarbus, as well as the great-great-grandson of both Livia and Octavius Caesar himself, became the fifth Roman emperor in A.D. 54, eighty-four years after Enobarbus' death.

Could Enobarbus have suspected in his wildest dreams that a descendant of his would one day rule all Rome?

It is rather a shame to spoil the story by identifying this fifth emperor, the last of the house which Julius Caesar first brought to mastery in Rome, and who combined in himself the heritage of Octavius Caesar, his wife Livia, his sister Octavia, his enemy Antony, and his defected enemy, Enobarbus, but I must. The emperor was the infamous Nero, whose real name was Lucius Domitius Ahenobarbus.

All is lost

And now Shakespeare returns to history and lets Antony's forces betray him. Antony enters, shouting:

> *All is lost!*
> *This foul Egyptian hath betrayed me:*
> *My fleet hath yielded to the foe, and yonder*
> *They cast their caps up and carouse together*
> *Like friends long lost. Triple-turned whore! 'Tis thou*
> *Hast sold me to this novice . . .*
> —Act IV, scene xii, lines 9–14

Antony is almost mad in his frustration, and when Cleopatra enters, he yells at her those words most designed to hurt her, exulting in the possibility that she may be taken by Octavius Caesar to grace his triumph.

The shirt of Nessus . . .

Cleopatra rushes off, appalled by Antony's fury, and in deadly fear that he may even forestall Octavius Caesar's victory and kill her with his own hands. This possibility is made clear to the audience by Antony's rage-filled mythological allusion, when he cries:

> *The shirt of Nessus is upon me; teach me,*
> *Alcides, thou mine ancestor, thy rage.*
> *Let me lodge Lichas on the horns o'th'moon.*
> —Act IV, scene xii, lines 43–45

Alcides is, of course, Hercules (see page I–70). Hercules was the personification of blind strength, and since such strength can often be misapplied, several tales were told of what Hercules did in his mad rages. In one of these madnesses, he killed six of his own children and it was in penance for this that he was condemned to perform his twelve labors. Such madness Antony feels to be coming over himself.

The specific reference is to an event late in Hercules' life, when he took his last wife, Deianeira. At one time the two were crossing a river in flood. Nessus, a centaur (half man, half horse), offered to carry Deianeira across while Hercules swam. The arrangement was accepted, but, coming to the other side, the centaur galloped off with Deianeira and tried to rape her. The angry Hercules shot down the centaur with one of those arrows which had been dipped in the deadly poison of the Hydra's (see page I–237) blood.

As Nessus lay dying, he told Deianeira that if she saved some of his blood and placed it on Hercules' shirt, it would be an infallible way of assuring his fidelity. While he wore the shirt, he would love only her. Deianeira believed him.

Eventually, when Hercules began to wander, Deianeira remembered Nessus' advice and sent him a bloodstained shirt by Lichas, one of his attendants.

Hercules put it on (not noticing the blood, apparently) and at once the poison it carried from his own arrow began to burn into him with agonizing pain. He writhed in anguish, but the shirt had grown to his body and could not be removed. He seized Lichas as madness came over him, throwing him high into the air with all the might of his superhuman muscles. Lichas fell into the sea and was changed into a rock, while Hercules himself died in torture. Deianeira, at hearing the news, killed herself.

It was this "shirt of Nessus" that Antony felt himself to be wearing, and a like agony that he felt within himself. In his grief and rage he is ready to kill Cleopatra:

> The witch shall die:
> To the young Roman boy she hath sold me . . .
> —Act IV, scene xii, lines 47–48

The "young Roman boy" is now thirty-three, remember.

. . . the boar of Thessaly

Cleopatra is in the last extreme of panic. She knows that it is because of her that Antony has frittered away everything, and there is no doubt in her mind that he intends to kill her. She cries out to her ladies:

> *O, he's more mad*
> *Than Telamon for his shield; the boar of Thessaly*
> *Was never so embossed.*
>
> —Act IV, scene xiii, lines 1–3

Cleopatra matches Antony's example of mythological rage and madness (Hercules) with two examples of her own; making, as it happens, a mistake in each case.

It was not Telamon, but Telamon's son, Ajax (see page I–110), that went mad. After the death of Achilles under the walls of Troy, the question arose as to who was to inherit his divinely wrought armor, and the choice narrowed to the mighty-thewed Ajax and the shrewd and cunning Ulysses (see page I–92). We might suppose the Greeks reasoned that Ajax's muscles could kill only one Trojan at a time but that Ulysses' shrewd policy might yet win the war altogether. (And it did, for it was Ulysses who finally conceived the stratagem of the wooden horse—see page I–188.) So the armor went to Ulysses.

Now, finally, Ajax's long-suffering and unsubtle heart broke and he went mad. He planned to revenge himself on the leaders of the Greek army, and mistaking a herd of sheep for men, he lunged among them with his sword, screaming imprecations. When he recovered from his rage and found himself surrounded by slaughtered beasts, he realized that he had but made himself ridiculous—so he killed himself.

As for the boar of Thessaly who was so embossed (that is, foaming at the mouth with fury), he was a huge mad creature sent to Calydon to ravage the countryside because the Calydonians had neglected to make proper sacrifices to Diana (Artemis). But Calydon was in Aetolia, not Thessaly.

The sevenfold shield . . .

Cleopatra feels that the only way of saving her life (and this is straight from Plutarch and is not Shakespeare's dramatic invention) is to send news to Antony that she has died with his name upon her lips. Her feeling is that he would then realize she had not betrayed him and she could safely come back to life so that together they might plan their next move.

But she miscalculated the effect of the news on Antony. In the midst of his raving for her death, the news is brought to him that she is already dead, and instantly his rage vanishes.

The full swell of the orchestra ceases sharply and leaves behind the soft wail of one lonely flute, as Mark Antony turns to his aide and says:

> *Unarm, Eros. The long day's task is done,*
> *And we must sleep.*
>
> —Act IV, scene xiv, lines 35–36

He scorns the armor he is removing, for it cannot protect him from this new blow. He says:

> *The sevenfold shield of Ajax cannot keep*
> *The battery from my heart.*
>
> —Act IV, scene xiv, lines 38–39

Again a reference to Ajax; this time to his famous shield, which Homer describes in connection with the duel of that hero with Hector. It was a huge shield, covering Ajax from neck to ankles, made of seven separate layers of tough oxhide and covered with bronze. It was so heavy that none but Ajax (or Achilles) could wield it, and so strong that a spear driven by the full fury of Hector's arm could penetrate but six of the layers.

. . . souls do couch on flowers . . .

Antony plans suicide and dreams that in death he and Cleopatra will be reunited. He imagines them in Elysium (see page I–13) and says:

> *. . . stay for me.*
> *Where souls do couch on flowers, we'll hand in hand,*
> *And with our sprightly port make the ghosts gaze:*
> *Dido and her Aeneas shall want troops,*
> *And all the haunt be ours.*
>
> —Act IV, scene xiv, lines 50–54

I am dying, Egypt . . .

But even Antony's last act betrays him. He cannot have himself killed by his men. Eros kills himself rather than Antony. (That is in Plutarch and Shakespeare is not forced to make it up.) In desperation, Antony falls on his own sword, but does not aim correctly. He is badly wounded and dying, but still alive.

Now comes a messenger from Cleopatra, who, too late, fears the effect of the news of her death. She has locked herself, for safety, in her own tomb. (It was the custom of Egyptian monarchs to build, while alive, their own resting places after death—the pyramids having represented that custom at its most incredibly extreme. Shakespeare refers to Cleopatra's tomb as the "monument," and, of course, it served that purpose too.)

The dying Antony is brought to the tomb, carried on the shoulders of his guard. Cleopatra watches from a high window. She dares not open the doors to the tomb, for once Antony is dead, it seems entirely reasonable that his soldiers will kill her. From the courtyard, Antony, never more in love, calls out:

> *I am dying, Egypt, dying; only*
> *I here importune death awhile, until*
> *Of many thousand kisses the poor last*
> *I lay upon thy lips.*
>
> —Act IV, scene xv, lines 18–21

Cleopatra and her women draw Antony up to the window on a stretcher. (Plutarch describes the effort it took to do so and how Cleopatra, with the strength of despair, managed.) The lovers are together one last moment and the kiss that Antony asked for is given.

And then he dies, fourteen years after the death of Julius Caesar had embarked him on that wild course during which he had held the world in his hands, and had thrown it away.

. . . eternal in our triumph

The news of Antony's death reaches Octavius Caesar, who bursts into tears.

Could Octavius, that cold politician, that efficient machine who never made a serious mistake, be so soft at the death of the man he had been fully determined to execute? Or was his sorrow a calculated device to blunt the sympathy of men for Antony?

It is clearly Shakespeare's intent to argue the latter, for as Octavius Caesar's speech grows more and more emotional and eloquent, an Egyptian arrives with a message from Cleopatra and Octavius turns off the flow at once and is all business, saying:

> *But I will tell you at some meeter season.*
> *The business of this man looks out of him;*
> *We'll hear him what he says.*
>
> —Act V, scene i, lines 48–51

Octavius Caesar learns that Cleopatra is still locked in her tomb and is sending to him to find out his terms. He is all sharpness now. His victory has been partially blunted by Antony's suicide, for in Roman terms a suicide under such conditions is a noble action and gains the dead man sympathy (which Octavius had to neutralize as far as possible by ostentatious tears and praise—as Antony had done over the corpse of Brutus, see page I–315).

But there still remains Cleopatra. It is now in the highest degree necessary to keep her from killing herself. He sends her comforting words by her messenger and then sends Proculeius, one of his own men, to her, telling him:

> . . . *give her what comforts*
> *The quality of her passion shall require,*
> *Lest, in her greatness, by some mortal stroke*
> *She do defeat us. For her life in Rome*
> *Would be eternal in our triumph.*
>
> —Act V, scene i, lines 62–66

. . . *conquered Egypt* . . .

Proculeius reaches Cleopatra and asks her terms for surrender. She states them, saying:

> . . . *if he* [Octavius] *please*
> *To give me conquered Egypt for my son,*
> *He gives me so much of mine own as I*
> *Will kneel to him with thanks.*
>
> —Act V, scene ii, lines 18–21

She is offering to abdicate and asking that her son be recognized as King of Egypt so that the land will remain independent to some extent. She doesn't say which son, but presumably she means Caesarion, who is now seventeen years old and who is coruler with her as Ptolemy XIV.

Naturally, this is an entirely unacceptable request from Octavius Caesar's standpoint. With the son of Cleopatra on the throne, or even alive as a private citizen, he would always be the focus for revolts. What Octavius Caesar intended, and what he did, was to annex Egypt, not only as a Roman province, but as a personal possession with he himself getting all the revenues, as though he were a king of Egypt.

This meant potential rivals would have to be put out of the way. Caesarion was too dangerous to be left alive, and in the aftermath of Octavius Caesar's victory, he was executed. The same fate was waiting for Antony's older son by Fulvia. Two of the children of Antony and Cleopatra were allowed to live and were brought up by none other than Octavia, who, in this, showed herself nobly forgiving. (It is also possible that Octavia had loved Antony and had felt a certain guilt in having been used by her brother as one more weapon with which to defeat him.)

The daughter of Mark Antony and Cleopatra, Cleopatra Selene, was eventually married to Juba of Numidia, the son of a king (also named

Juba) who had died at the Battle of Thapsus (see page I–281) fighting against Julius Caesar. The younger Juba had been given a complete Roman education and in 25 B.C. was made King of Mauretania, located where the present-day Morocco is to be found. Thus a younger Cleopatra became an African queen.

The two had a son—the grandson of Antony and Cleopatra—who was called Ptolemy of Mauretania. He was the very last of the Ptolemies. He reigned quietly till A.D. 40, when he was called to Rome and there, seventy years after the suicide of Mark Antony, was put to death by the mad emperor Caligula, for no better reason than that he had accumulated wealth which the Emperor felt he would like to confiscate for his own use.

But all that lay in the future. At the moment, Cleopatra is asking that Egypt be left to be ruled by her son, and Proculeius answers in soft words, for he knows that Roman soldiers are quietly surrounding the tomb and forcing the doors.

Suddenly Cleopatra is seized from behind and the dagger she attempts to draw is wrested from her. It is clear that she will not be allowed to commit suicide. All means for doing so will be taken from her and she will be watched. All she has left, it seems, are her memories:

> *I dreamt there was an Emperor Antony.*
> *O, such another sleep, that I might see*
> *But such another man.*
>
> —Act V, scene ii, lines 76–78

He words me . . .

Octavius himself arrives; smooth, gentle, and gracious. In Plutarch, Cleopatra is described as being far from herself; her hair torn, her face scratched and puffy. Still, she is Cleopatra; pushing forty perhaps, but the creature of charm who could have her will of the greatest of Romans. Why not Octavius Caesar as well?

But Octavius is immune. He is cold and unimpassioned. He pushes aside the list of possessions she hands him and is ummoved when Cleopatra's secretary, currying the favor of the victor, reveals that Cleopatra, even at this great crisis, has thoughtfully listed less than half her assets. (After all, why should this disturb Octavius? He plans to take all Egypt.)

His last words to her are:

> *Feed and sleep:*
> *Our care and pity is so much upon you*
> *That we remain your friend; and so adieu.*
>
> —Act V, scene ii, lines 187–89

When she tries to prostrate herself before him, he will not allow it. But as soon as he leaves, Cleopatra looks after him bitterly and says:

> *He words me, girls, he words me, that I should not*
> *Be noble to myself!*
>
> —Act V, scene ii, lines 191–92

She knows certainly that what Octavius has in mind for her is his own triumph. If she had any doubts in the matter, one of Octavius' officers, Cornelius Dolabella (according to Plutarch, and followed in this by Shakespeare), sends her secret information to this effect.

Sadly, Cleopatra pictures to her ladies the triumph in such a way as to make it plain to the audience (not Roman, and therefore not necessarily understanding the virtues of suicide) that death is preferable. As a climax she describes the comic plays that will be written about them:

> *Antony*
> *Shall be brought drunken forth, and I shall see*
> *Some squeaking Cleopatra boy my greatness*
> *I'th'posture of a whore.*
>
> —Act V, scene ii, lines 218–21

It is almost as though Shakespeare is preening himself here. After all, he has written the play and in it, Antony is far more than a mere drunkard and Cleopatra far more than a mere whore. The magic of Shakespeare converts them at last to ideal lovers and it is as such, thanks to him, that they will live forever.

. . . *the pretty worm of Nilus* . . .

Now must come the suicide.

Actually, the method used is a mystery. The Roman guards left behind by Octavius Caesar were surely impressed with the fact that Cleopatra must be kept alive. Cleopatra must therefore have succeeded in hiding something small and unnoticeable, prepared for such a contingency.

Her body was found virtually unmarked except for what seemed to be a puncture or two on her arm. It had to be poison then, but administered how? Was it the puncture of a poisoned needle which she had kept hidden in her hair? Or was it a poison snake?

The poison snake is much more unlikely and is, indeed, rather implausible, but it is exceedingly dramatic and, whether true or not, is accepted by all who have ever heard of Cleopatra. If they have heard only one thing of her, it is her method of suicide by snake.

She prepares for that suicide as though she were meeting her lover once again, and indeed, she expects to, in Elysium. She demands that she be dressed in her most splendid gowns as on that occasion when she met Antony for the first time:

> Show me, my women, like a queen: go fetch
> My best attires. I am again for Cydnus,
> To meet Mark Antony.
>
> —Act V, scene ii, lines 227–29

A peasant is brought in now with the gift of a basket of figs for her. It is this, partly, which makes the tale of the poison snake implausible. Would anyone have been allowed in to see her under the circumstances? Would he have failed to undergo a search if he were passed through? Is it conceivable that the basket of figs would have been unexamined?

Yet that is the tale that Plutarch reports as one possibility. He also talks of poisoned needles and poisoned razors.

Cleopatra asks the peasant:

> Hast thou the pretty worm of Nilus there,
> That kills and pains not?
>
> —Act V, scene ii, lines 243–44

He does! The "pretty worm" is the asp, or Egyptian cobra, whose venom works quickly and painlessly. What's more, the creature was worshiped, as so many dangerous animals were in Egypt, and the coiled head of the cobra was worn on the headdress of the Pharaohs. A death by cobra bite was a royal death; it was rather like being bitten by a god.

Cleopatra is now ready. She says to her ladies in waiting:

> Give me my robe, put on my crown, I have
> Immortal longings in me. Now no more
> The juice of Egypt's grape shall moist this lip.
> Yare, yare, good Iras; quick: methinks I hear
> Antony call: I see him rouse himself
> To praise my noble act. I hear him mock
> The luck of Caesar, which the gods give men
> To excuse their after wrath. Husband, I come:
>
> —Act V, scene ii, lines 280–87

And yet not all is pure love of Antony. There is some relish in feeling that she is depriving Octavius of his final victory. For as the asp is biting her, she says to it:

> *O couldst thou speak,*
> *That I might hear thee call great Caesar ass*
> *Unpolicied!*
>
> —Act V, scene ii, lines 306–8

It is well done . . .

Cleopatra dies. Her lady in waiting Iras is already dead of heartbreak, and Charmian (whom early in the play the soothsayer had predicted would outlive her mistress) is applying the asp to her own arm. In come the Roman soldiers, but too late.

Gaping at the dead Cleopatra, they get the significance of it at once. One of the soldiers cries:

> *. . . All's not well: Caesar's beguiled.*
>
> —Act V, scene ii, line 323

Then, when the same soldier angrily asks Charmian whether this sort of thing was well done, she answers proudly, just before dying:

> *It is well done, and fitting for a princess*
> *Descended of so many royal kings.*
>
> —Act V, scene ii, lines 326–27

. . . an aspic's trail . . .

Octavius arrives to witness the defeat of what he planned as his crowning victory. They puzzle out the manner of her suicide. There is a swelling and a spot of blood on Cleopatra's breast and the soldier who had questioned Charmian now says:

> *This is an aspic's trail; and these fig leaves*
> *Have slime upon them . . .*
>
> —Act V, scene ii, lines 350–51

It is an old superstition that snakes are slimy. They are not. Some snakelike sea creatures are slimy—lampreys, eels, salamanders. Snakes, however, are perfectly dry to the touch.

. . . another Antony

It falls to the cold Octavius to give Cleopatra her final epitaph. Even he is moved as he gazes at her dead body as she lies there—Cleopatra still. He says:

> . . . she looks like sleep,
> As she would catch another Antony
> In her strong toil of grace.
>
> —Act V, scene ii, lines 345–47

Nor is he vindictive. He says:

> Take up her bed,
> And bear her women from the monument.
> She shall be buried by her Antony.
>
> —Act V, scene ii, lines 355–57

. . . then to Rome

And now the world calls the one survivor and victor of all the turbulent events of the play. He says:

> Our army shall
> In solemn show attend this funeral,
> And then to Rome.
>
> —Act V, scene ii, lines 362–64

The civil wars that have lasted fifty years are over. The next year, 29 B.C., Octavius Caesar ordered the closing of the temple of Janus, indicating that Rome was at peace, the first time that had happened in over two hundred years. Then, in 27 B.C., he accepted the title of Augustus, by which he is best known to history.

From 27 B.C. Augustus reigned for forty-one years, establishing a new kind of government, the Roman Empire, and serving as its first and by all odds the greatest of its emperors. So firm was the government he established and so honored was it in the memory of man that though the last Roman Emperor in Italy abdicated in A.D 476, another ruler calling himself Roman Emperor continued to reign in Constantinople. The Constantinopolitan line, which used the title of Roman Emperor to the end, endured till 1453, and even after it was gone there was still a Roman Emperor in Vienna—a line that continued till 1806.

And even after that was gone there were emperors. In the German language, these were called Kaisers and in the Slavic languages tsars—both distortions of Caesar, the family name of Julius and Octavius. The last Russian tsar resigned his throne in 1917, the last German Kaiser in 1918, the last Bulgarian tsar in 1946.

It is interesting that 1946 is exactly two thousand years after 44 B.C., the year in which Julius Caesar was assassinated. For that length of time not one year passed in which somewhere in the world there wasn't someone calling himself by a form of "Caesar" as title (as all the Roman emperors did).

13

The Tragedy of

TITUS ANDRONICUS

O<small>F THE</small> four plays and one narrative history which are set in Rome, *Titus Andronicus* is the only one that does not deal with accepted Roman history or legend. It is utter fiction. Not one character in it, not one event, is to be found in history.

What's more, *Titus Andronicus* is the bloodiest and most gruesome of Shakespeare's plays, and the one in which the horror seems present entirely for the sake of horror.

Indeed, *Titus Andronicus* is so unpleasant a play that most critics would be delighted to be able to believe it was not written by Shakespeare. They cannot do so, however. There are contemporary references to *Titus Andronicus* as a Shakespearean tragedy, which also place the time of its writing at about 1593. It is an early play but by no means the earliest, and Shakespeare could surely have done better than *Titus Andronicus* by this time.

Apparently, what Shakespeare was doing was experimenting with Senecan tragedy (see page I–270). These blood-and-thunder plays written about horrible crimes and horrible revenges were immensely popular in Elizabethan times. Thomas Kyd, for instance, had written such a drama, *The Spanish Tragedy,* shortly before Shakespeare had begun his dramatic career, and had scored an immense success.

Shakespeare had no objection to success and was perfectly willing to adjust himself to popular taste. In *Titus Andronicus* he therefore gave full vent to blood, cruelty, disaster, and revenge. Indeed, he went so far that one can almost wonder if he weren't deliberately pushing matters to the limit in order to express his disgust of the whole genre.

. . . the imperial diadem of Rome

The play opens in Rome, with the Romans in the process of selecting a new Emperor.

The two candidates for the throne are the two sons of the old Emperor; Saturninus, the older, and Bassianus, the younger. Both are clamoring

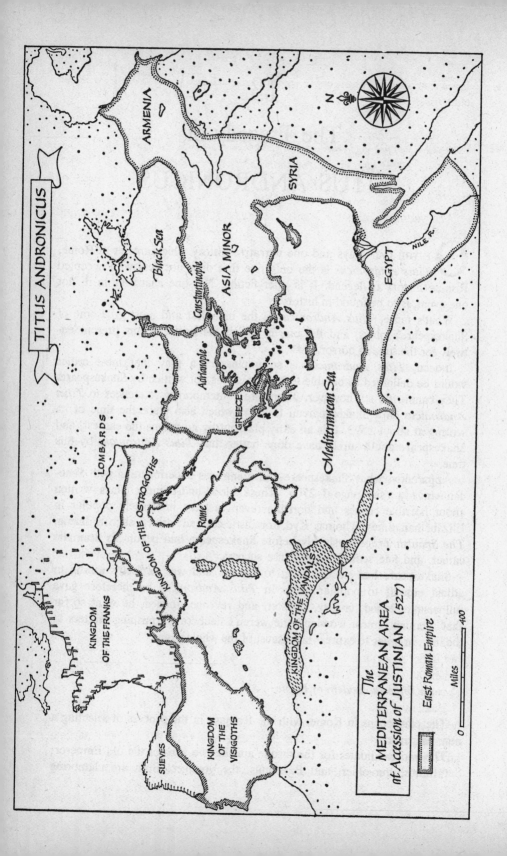

TITUS ANDRONICUS

The
MEDITERRANEAN AREA
at Accession of JUSTINIAN (527)

ARMENIA

SYRIA

EGYPT

NILE R.

Black Sea

ASIA MINOR

Constantinople

Adrianople

GREECE

Mediterranean Sea

LOMBARDS

KINGDOM OF THE OSTROGOTHS

Rome

KINGDOM OF THE VANDALS

KINGDOM OF THE FRANKS

SUEVES

KINGDOM OF THE VISIGOTHS

☐ East Roman Empire

Miles
0   400

for acceptance by the people. Saturninus stresses the fact that he is the elder:

> *I am his first-born son that was the last*
> *That ware the imperial diadem of Rome;*
> *Then let my father's honors live in me.*
> —Act I, scene i, lines 5–7

The younger son, with a lesser claim, is forced to be more emotional. He begins:

> *If ever Bassianus, Caesar's son,*
> *Were gracious in the eyes of royal Rome,*
> —Act I, scene i, lines 10–11

Who the Emperor was who was "the last that ware the imperial diadem of Rome" is never stated.

To be sure, Bassianus calls himself "Caesar's son," but this is not a reference to Julius Caesar (see page I–253) or Octavius Caesar (see page I–292). All Roman emperors were called "Caesar," for that was one of the royal titles (see page I–390).

In fact, the identity of the just-dead Roman Emperor couldn't possibly be determined, for the entire play is a weird amalgamation of different periods of Roman history. There is a panoply of senators, tribunes, and common Romans on stage, as though it were of the stern period of the Roman Republic, as in *Coriolanus*. On the other hand, we have emperors, of a later period, and barbarian invaders of a still later period.

The names of the sons have some points of interest. The only important Saturninus in real Roman history was a radical politician who was killed about 100 B.C. in the years when the Roman Republic began the public disorders that were eventually to kill it. As for Bassianus, the name of the younger son, that is to be found among the names of three of the emperors of the dynasty of Septimius Severus, who ruled in the early third century.

The elder son of Septimius Severus was Bassianus. He succeeded on his father's death in 211. Bassianus did not rule under that name but was universally called "Caracalla," a nickname derived from the long cloak (*caracalla*) he habitually wore.

Bassianus had a younger brother, Geta, who was supposed to have inherited the emperorship along with him. The two brothers were deadly enemies, however, and by 212 Bassianus had killed Geta under particularly cruel circumstances.

Thus, the competition between Saturninus and Bassianus in the play seems to reflect, faintly, the competition between Bassianus and Geta in history.

In one respect, in fact, the time of Caracalla might be thought to be the latest period in which the play could be set, for it treats of a thoroughly pagan Rome. There is no sign of Christianity in the play, yet after Caracalla's time, the growth of Christianity would have made the new religion impossible to ignore.

There are, however, other aspects of the play that make the time of Caracalla far too early.

As it happens, there is in existence a tale called *The Tragical History of Titus Andronicus,* of which the only known copy was published about a century and a half after Shakespeare's play was written. That copy may, however, be a reprint and the original may have appeared early enough to serve as Shakespeare's source.

In the booklet the time is set in the reign of Theodosius, by whom is probably meant the most famous Emperor of that name, Theodosius I. He ruled from 379 to 395, nearly two centuries after Caracalla.

When Theodosius died, he left behind two sons, but these, unlike the sons of Septimius Severus (or those in the play), did not compete for the throne. They inherited the co-emperorship in peace, with the elder, Arcadius, ruling the Eastern half from Constantinople, and the younger, Honorius, ruling the Western half from Rome.

To be sure, by the time Theodosius was Emperor, Rome was thoroughly Christian and Theodosius himself was particularly pious in this respect, so that the paganism of the play would then become an anachronism. (On the other hand, considering the horrible events that take place in it, the existence of Christianity would be embarrassing.)

. . . surnamèd Pius

It turns out that there are factions in Rome who want neither son of the old Emperor, but who turn instead to a valiant general. The announcement is made by Marcus Andronicus the tribune, who happens to be a brother of that general. He says:

> *Know that the people of Rome, for whom we stand*
> *A special party, have by common voice,*
> *Chosen Andronicus, surnamèd Pius*
> *For many good and great deserts to Rome.*
>
> —Act I, scene i, lines 20–23

Andronicus is the Titus Andronicus of the title. The surname of "Pius" was sometimes used in Roman history to indicate a man who was devout and who honored his parents and his gods. The most famous case of such a usage is that of Emperor Antoninus Pius, who reigned from 138 to 161 and whose reign saw the Roman Empire at its most peaceful.

. . . the barbarous Goths

The special claim of Titus Andronicus to the gratitude of Rome lay in the wars he had been fighting. Marcus says:

> He by the senate is accited home
> From weary wars against the barbarous Goths.
> —Act I, scene i, lines 27–28

Furthermore, the war has been going on a long time, as Marcus further explains:

> Ten years are spent since first he undertook
> This cause of Rome, and chastisèd with arms
> Our enemies' pride:
> —Act I, scene i, lines 31–33

The Goths were a group of Germanic tribes who began raiding the Roman Empire about the middle of the third century, not long after the time of Caracalla. They were badly defeated in 269 by the Roman Emperor Claudius II, who called himself Claudius Gothicus in consequence, but who died the year after.

The Gothic menace lightened for a century thereafter. In 375, however, a group of these Goths (of tribes known as Visigoths) were driven into the Roman Empire by the Huns. Within the border of the Empire, they defeated the Romans in a great battle at Adrianople in 378. Theodosius, whom we have mentioned earlier, then ascended the Roman throne and managed to contain the Gothic menace by diplomacy and judicious bribery, rather than by military victories.

After Theodosius' death, the Visigoths raided Italy and took Rome itself in 410. They were not defeated at this time but wandered out of Italy of their own accord and finally set up a kingdom in southern France that eventually expanded into and over all Spain. In 489 another branch of the Gothic nation, the Ostrogoths, invaded Italy and set up a kingdom there.

Up to this point, there isn't much hope of finding any Roman that can serve as an inspiration for Titus Andronicus. Nowhere is there a general who fought long wars against the Goths and won. We must look still later in time.

In the prose story *The Tragical History of Titus Andronicus,* the Goths are said to have invaded Italy under their king "Tottilius."

Actually there was a king of the Ostrogoths, of nearly that name, who fought in Italy. He was Totila, who ruled from 541 to 552.

Here is what happened. Although the Germanic tribes had settled the Western provinces of the Roman Empire, the Eastern provinces remained intact and were ruled from Constantinople. In 527 Justinian became Roman Emperor in Constantinople and was determined to reconquer the West. In 535 he sent his great general, Belisarius, to Italy, and with that began a twenty-year (not a mere ten-year) war of Roman and Goth, in which the Romans were eventually victorious.

Belisarius won initial victories, but the Goths rallied when Totila became king. Belisarius was recalled and replaced with another general, Narses (a eunuch, the only one of importance in military history), who finally defeated Totila in 552 and completed the conquest of Italy in 556. In the *Tragical History* Titus Andronicus was a governor of Greece and came from Greece to rescue Italy, and that fits too.

Again, the name "Andronicus" is best known in history as that of several emperors who ruled in Constantinople, so that the very name of Titus Andronicus focuses our attention on the Eastern part of the Roman Empire. Finally, both Belisarius and Narses were ill requited by ungrateful emperors, and the tale of *Titus Andronicus* tells how the general of the title is ill requited by an ungrateful Emperor.

We can suppose then that *Titus Andronicus* was inspired by the events of the time of Belisarius and Narses, but none of the events in the play actually match the events in history.

Half of the number . . .

The two royal brothers retire before the awesome name of the victorious general.

In comes Titus Andronicus with a coffin and draws sad attention to his family's sufferings in the wars:

> . . . *of five and twenty valiant sons,*
> *Half of the number that King Priam had,*
> *Behold the poor remains, alive and dead!*
> —Act I, scene i, lines 79–81

Priam is, of course, the King of Troy (see page I–79) whom legend credited with fifty sons. Of Titus' twenty-five sons, no less than twenty have died in the course of the ten-year war with the Goths. The twenty-first is brought back dead in his coffin from the latest battle, while the last four living sons attend it sorrowfully.

Also with them are Tamora, the captured Queen of the Goths, and her three sons.

. . . the dreadful shore of Styx

Andronicus' first care is to bury the dead son with due pagan rites. He reproaches himself for being so slow to do it:

> *Titus, unkind and careless of thine own,*
> *Why suffer'st thou thy sons, unburied yet,*
> *To hover on the dreadful shore of Styx?*
> —Act I, scene i, lines 86–88

The Styx is the river that marks the boundary of Hades. The shades of dead men cannot cross that river till they have been buried with the proper ritual, and must till then hover disconsolately on its shore.

. . . Scythia . . .

Andronicus' sons demand that a human sacrifice be dedicated on the occasion of the funeral of their dead brother so that his soul may rest in peace. (An example of why the play cannot be placed in a Christian setting.)

Titus Andronicus orders Alarbus, the oldest son of Tamora, Queen of the Goths, to be so sacrificed. Tamora pleads against it in a speech that can't help but appeal to us, but the stern Titus insists, not out of cruelty but out of what he conceives to be religious devotion.

Chiron, Tamora's youngest son, cries out:

> *Was never Scythia half so barbarous.*
> —Act I, scene i, line 131

When Greece was at its height, the Scythians were a nomadic people who lived on the plains north of the Black Sea. The Greeks knew little about them, but knew the area they inhabited to be tremendous and their numbers large. They were for some reason considered the epitome of barbarousness by the Greeks, and their name, so maligned, has been used in that fashion ever since.

. . . the Thracian tyrant . . .

Tamora's remaining son, Demetrius, sounds a darker note:

> *The selfsame gods that armed the Queen of Troy*
> *With opportunity of sharp revenge*
> *Upon the Thracian tyrant in his tent*
> *May favor Tamora, the Queen of Goths,*
>
> —Act I, scene i, lines 136–39

The Trojan Queen is Hecuba (see page I–85), who had sent her youngest son, Polydorus, for safekeeping to the court of the Thracian king, Polymnestor. After the fall of Troy, when all of Hecuba's other children were killed (save Helenus), Polymnestor was persuaded by the Greeks to kill Polydorus too.

Hecuba discovered this and persuaded Polymnestor to visit destroyed Troy by promising to reveal to him a treasure in its ruins. He came to Troy with his two sons and, according to the tale, Hecuba in a fit of despairing fury managed to stab his two sons to death and tear out Polymnestor's eyes.

Nevertheless, the sacrifice takes place and Lucius, the oldest of Titus' remaining sons, announces the result in triumphant goriness:

> *Alarbus' limbs are lopped,*
> *And entrails feed the sacrificing fires,*
>
> —Act I, scene i, lines 143–44

With that, the tale of double revenge begins—first Tamora's and then Titus'. And Demetrius' allusion to Hecuba indicates the crude and brutal bloodiness of what is ahead.

. . . to Solon's happiness

Titus' twenty-first son is thus buried and his brother, Marcus, points out (prophetically) that it is safer to be dead:

> *. . . safer triumph is this funeral pomp,*
> *That hath aspired to Solon's happiness.*
>
> —Act I, scene i, lines 176–77

This refers to the tale (probably apocryphal) of the visit of the great Athenian lawgiver, Solon, to the Asia Minor kingdom of Lydia. The rich king of Lydia, Croesus, displayed his treasures to Solon and then asked the Greek if this was not happiness indeed. Solon replied, sternly, "Call no man happy till he is dead." In other words, while there is life there is the possibility of disaster.

Of course, the disasters come. Croesus is defeated by Cyrus the Persian, his country is taken away, his throne is lost, and he himself is placed at the stake to be burned to death. Then he remembers Solon's remark and calls out the Athenian's name. The curious Cyrus asks the details and, on hearing the story, spares Croesus' life.

. . . the sacred Pantheon . . .

The throne is offered Titus Andronicus, who refuses it on the ground that he is too old. The sons of the old Emperor now show signs of breaking into rivalry again, but Andronicus ends it by speaking for Saturninus, the elder. He calls him:

> Lord Saturnine; whose virtues will, I hope,
> Reflect on Rome as Titan's rays on Earth,
> —Act I, scene i, lines 225–26

Titan is, of course, one of the names for the sun (see page I–11).

Saturninus is promptly crowned and as promptly shows his gratitude:

> Titus, to advance
> Thy name and honorable family,
> Lavinia will I make my empress.
> Rome's royal mistress, mistress of my heart,
> And in the sacred Pantheon her espouse.
> —Act I, scene i, lines 238–42

Lavinia is Titus' daughter, noble and virtuous. Her name recalls a Lavinia of Roman legend, the daughter of Latinus, who was king of that region in Italy where Rome was later to be founded. The Trojan hero Aeneas, coming to Italy from fallen Troy (see page I–20), married Lavinia and founded the city of Lavinium, named in her honor. Lavinium was the parent city of Alba Longa and that, in turn, was the parent city of Rome.

A pantheon ("all gods") is any building dedicated to the gods generally. The Pantheon is in Rome, a structure first built under the sponsorship of Agrippa (see page I–340), the general and son-in-law of Octavius Caesar, in 27 B.C. It was rebuilt in its present form about A.D. 120 by the Emperor Hadrian. It is the one Roman building that remains in perfect preservation and it is still a place of worship, having been consecrated a Christian church in 609. In the time of Belisarius, then, it was in its last century as a pagan temple (though by that time there were virtually no pagans left in Italy).

. . . the stately Phoebe . . .

All seems well and then, with the suddenness of a summer thunderstorm, everything falls apart.

Bassianus, the new Emperor's younger brother, sets up a cry that Lavinia is his and begins to carry her away. Lavinia's four brothers are on Bassianus' side in this—apparently there is a recognized betrothal here, although no hint of that was given earlier—and so is Lavinia's uncle, Marcus.

Only Titus Andronicus stands out against them in rigid observance of his honor, for he has formally given Lavinia to Saturninus.

Titus dashes after his sons and kills Mutius, one of them. This is the twenty-second son of Titus to die.

Saturninus, however, orders Andronicus to make no further attempt to get Lavinia back. He has suddenly fallen in love with Tamora anyway and prefers to have the Gothic Queen as his wife. He describes her as:

> . . . lovely Tamora, Queen of Goths,
> That like the stately Phoebe 'mongst her nymphs
> Dost overshine the gallant'st dames of Rome,
>
> —Act I, scene i, lines 316–18

This comparison to Phoebe (see page I–12), goddess of the moon (with alternate names like Selene, Diana, and Artemis), seems odd. Tamora is no young maid who might aptly be compared to the virginal goddess, but is the widowed mother of three grown sons.

Nevertheless, Saturninus prepares to marry her at once:

> Sith priest and holy water are so near,
> And tapers burn so bright and everything
> In readiness for Hymenaeus stand,
>
> —Act I, scene i, lines 324–26

Hymenaeus is a longer form of Hymen, god of marriage (see page I–55).

. . . wise Laertes' son

Titus Andronicus, defied by his family and snubbed by the Emperor who owes him everything, suddenly finds himself alone and dishonored, only minutes after he had been offered the imperial crown itself.

Yet Titus sticks to honor. He is even unwilling to have his dead son buried in the family tomb because he died opposing Titus' conception of proper obedience to the Emperor. Marcus, however, argues:

> *The Greeks upon advice did bury Ajax*
> *That slew himself; and wise Laertes' son*
> *Did graciously plead for his funerals:*
> —Act I, scene i, lines 380–82

Ajax and Ulysses contended for the armor of Achilles after the latter's death (see page I–110). When Ulysses received the award, Ajax went mad and killed himself. Marcus points out that the Greeks, despite the dishonor of Ajax's last deeds, his madness and suicide, finally decided to give him honorable burial in view of the greatness of his earlier deeds. Ulysses himself (who is "Laertes' son") argued in favor of that.

Given this precedent, Titus allows the burial of his twenty-second son.

Other reconciliations are also made. Tamora, the new Empress, plays the role of peacemaker, reconciling the Emperor Saturninus with his younger brother, Bassianus (now married to Lavinia), and with his general, Titus Andronicus. (Nevertheless, she promises her new husband, in an aside, to take proper revenge on them all in due time.)

Titus Andronicus accepts the new peace and suggests a great hunt for the next day.

. . . Prometheus tied to Caucasus

All now leave the stage after the single action-packed scene of the first act, and one person alone remains to begin the second act, a person who has been on stage most of the first act but who till now has not spoken a single line. It is Aaron the Moor. Behind his existence is some complicated background.

The ancient Greeks could not help but notice that the inhabitants of the southern shores of the Mediterranean were somewhat darker in complexion than they themselves were. There would be a tendency to call the inhabitants of northern Africa "the dark ones."

The Greek word for "dark" is *mauros,* and this name came to be applied to north Africans. In Latin the word became *maurus* and this was the origin, in particular, of the name of a kingdom on the northwestern shoulder of the African continent, which came to be called Mauretania— the kingdom over which Cleopatra's daughter ruled in Augustus' time (see page I–385).

From the Latin *maurus,* came the French *Maures,* the Spanish *Moros* and the English "Moors." In the eighth century armies from north Africa (now Moslem in religion) invaded Spain and southern France. In the ninth century they invaded Sicily and Italy. Europeans came to know the Moors with a discomforting intimacy.

(There was a tendency for the Spaniards, who did not evict the Moors till nearly eight centuries had passed after their first invasion, to apply the name to all Moslems. In 1565 they occupied the Philippine Islands and were astonished to find tribes in the southern islands who were Moslems. Two centuries before the Spaniards came, Moslem traders had been visiting the islands and Moslem missionaries had converted the natives. The Spaniards called these southern Filipinos Moros, and the name is retained even today.)

In the fifteenth century, the Portuguese mariners, exploring down the coasts of west Africa, brought back black slaves and there began a new version of the abominable practice of human slavery. Since it was customary to call Africans "Moors," this new variety of African was called "black Moors" or "blackamoors." And then, to save syllables, they might still be called simply "Moors."

Aaron, in this play, though called a Moor, is distinctly a blackamoor, as we can tell from numerous illusions. The likelihood of a black being present in the Italy of Belisarius' time is not entirely zero. After all, the power of the East Roman Emperor, Justinian, extended far up the Nile. Why he should be associated with the Gothic armies is more puzzling—but then there is no question of any historical accuracy. He is introduced merely as a convenient villain.

A "Moor" would make a wonderful villain and an inhuman one at that. To the Elizabethans, the strange and therefore repulsive features of a black face and the habit of equating blackness with the devil made blacks a natural stereotype for villainy. (Such irrational thinking on the part of whites has caused innumerable blacks innumerable separate agonies then and since.)

Aaron ruminates on Tamora's sudden climb to the peak but is not disturbed thereby. Her rise is his as well, and he tells himself to:

> *fit thy thoughts*
> *To mount aloft with thy imperial mistress,*
> *And mount her pitch, whom thou in triumph long*
> *Hast prisoner held, fettered in amorous chains,*
> *And faster bound to Aaron's charming eyes*
> *Than is Prometheus tied to Caucasus.*
>
> —Act II, scene i, lines 12–17

Prometheus was a Titan who stole fire from the sun and gave it to poor shivering mortals, in defiance of a decree of Zeus. In punishment Zeus chained him with divine, unbreakable fetters to Mount Caucasus (which Greeks imagined to be somewhere east of the Black Sea, and which gave its name to the Caucasian range of mountains which is really there.)

The fact that Tamora is so in love with Aaron mirrors another convention that was found in the literature of the time. Whites seemed to imagine that black men had some unusual power of attraction over white women; perhaps because of their supposedly more primitive "animal" nature and therefore their supposedly more powerful sexual prowess.

. . . this Semiramis . . .

Aaron goes on to glory in the prospect of what will come. He expects

> To wanton with this queen,
> This goddess, this Semiramis, this nymph,
> This siren, that will charm Rome's Saturnine
> And see his shipwrack and his commonweal's.
> —Act II, scene i, lines 21–24

In 810 B.C. a queen, Sammu-rammat, ruled the kingdom of Assyria. She didn't rule either long or effectively, and Assyria was, at the time, rather weak. In the next century, however, Assyria rose to world power and dominated western Asia with its fearful and ruthless armies.

The dim memory that mighty and terrifying Assyria was once ruled by a woman seemed to impress the Greeks, for they distorted Sammu-rammat to Semiramis and began to weave legends around her. She was supposed to have been a great conquering monarch, who founded Babylon, established a huge empire, reigned forty-two years, and even tried to conquer India.

As if this were not enough to render her colorful, the Greeks also imagined her to be a monster of lust and luxury with numerous lovers and insatiable desires, so that the name "Semiramis" has come to be applied to any lustful woman in high place.

. . . Vulcan's badge

Aaron's soliloquy is interrupted by Tamora's two remaining sons, Chiron and Demetrius, who have suddenly decided, each one of them, to fall in love with Lavinia and are now quarreling over it. Aaron reminds them that she is the wife of Bassianus, the Emperor's brother. This does not bother Demetrius, who says:

Though Bassianus be the Emperor's brother,
Better than he have worn Vulcan's badge.

—Act II, scene i, lines 88–89

This is a reference to Vulcan's cuckoldry, thanks to the love affair of his wife, Venus, with Mars (see page I–11).

Aaron thinks the quarrel is foolish. Why don't they both enjoy Lavinia in turn? To do this, persuasion will not be enough, for, as he says:

Lucrece was not more chaste
Than this Lavinia,

—Act II, scene i, lines 108–9

Lucrece, of course, is the Roman matron who was dealt with in *The Rape of Lucrece* (see page I–205), and is Shakespeare's favorite symbol of chastity. (*The Rape of Lucrece* was written at just about the time *Titus Andronicus* was. Might it be that this line set Shakespeare to thinking of the poem, or was it that the poem was running on in his mind and inspired this line?)

There are other ways than persuasion to win Lavinia, however. Coolly, Aaron points out that in the course of the next day's hunt, they might ambush her and rape her in turn. The two Gothic princes agree enthusiastically.

Saturn is dominator . . .

Time moves on and the hunt starts. During its course, Aaron finds a spot in the forest where he may hide a bag of gold for a nefarious purpose that is still in the future.

Tamora comes upon him and urges him on to dalliance such as

The wandering prince and Dido once enjoyed,

—Act II, scene iii, line 22

This is another reference to Dido and Aeneas (see page I–20), a favorite mythical standby of Shakespeare's.

Aaron, however, has more important business at hand. He says:

Madam, though Venus govern your desires,
Saturn is dominator over mine:

—Act II, scene iii, lines 30–31

Astrologically speaking, each person is born under the domination of a particular planet which determines the major component of his or her personality. The nature of the influence of Venus is obvious.

Saturn is, of all the planets visible to the unaided eye, the farthest from Earth and therefore the most slowly moving among the stars. To be born under Saturn then is to be as heavy, grave, and gloomy as that slow-moving planet; to be "saturnine," in short.

His Philomel . . .

Aaron goes on to explain why he is so grave and gloomy. Dire thoughts of revenge are in his mind and he refers to:

> *My fleece of woolly hair that now uncurls*
> *Even as an adder when she doth unroll*
> *To do some fatal execution?*
> —Act II, scene iii, lines 34–36

Mention of his "fleece of woolly hair" shows clearly that Shakespeare has in mind a black African and not the swarthy but non-black Moors of north Africa.

Aaron goes on to specifics, indicating that he has set in motion a horrible fate for Lavinia. He says:

> *This is the day of doom for Bassianus:*
> *His Philomel must lose her tongue today,*
> —Act II, scene iii, lines 42–43

One of the more gruesome Greek myths deals with two sisters: Philomela and Procne, who were the daughters of a king of Athens. The latter was given in marriage to Tereus, the King of Thrace. Tereus, however, fell in love with Philomela, his sister-in-law, and, luring her to his court, raped her. Then, in order to prevent her from telling his crime, he cut her tongue out and hid her among his slaves.

The phrase "lose her tongue" can therefore be a metaphoric reference to rape. It turns out to be a literal forecast in this play.

. . . as was Actaeon's . . .

Aaron gives Tamora a letter to be used later in the development of his plan and leaves.

At this point, Bassianus and Lavinia enter. All are at the hunt, of course, and Tamora, in her hunting costume, is sardonically likened to Diana, the goddess of the hunt, by Bassianus. Tamora is offended at what she considers to be their spying and says:

> Had I the power that some say Dian had
> Thy temples should be planted presently
> With horns, as was Actaeon's, and the hounds
> Should drive upon thy new-transformèd limbs,
>
> —Act II, scene iii, lines 61–64

Actaeon was a hunter in the Greek myths, who, in the course of a hunt, came inadvertently upon Diana bathing. Admiring, he stopped to watch. When he was caught at his peeping by Diana's nymphs, the indignant goddess turned him into a stag so that his own hounds ran him down and killed him.

The reference to the horns on Bassianus' head undoubtedly has the secondary purpose of referring to the planned rape of his wife.

. . . your swart Cimmerian

Bassianus and Lavinia strike back by implying that Tamora has been surprised at something far less innocent than bathing and speak openly of her liaison with Aaron. Bassianus says:

> Believe me, Queen, your swart Cimmerian
> Doth make your honor of his body's hue,
>
> —Act II, scene iii, lines 72–73

The Scythians, who lived north of the Black Sea (see page I–397), arrived there only in 700 B.C. Before that, the land was populated by those whom Homer named the Cimmerians. (Crimea, the peninsula jutting into the northern rim of the Black Sea, is thought to derive its name from them.)

The Cimmerian regions were mistily distant to the Greeks of Homer's time and strange legends arose concerning them. They were supposed to live in a land of eternal mist and gloom where the sun never shone. (One wonders if explorers brought back tales of the polar regions.)

As a result, one speaks of "Cimmerian darkness" as expressing the ultimate in darkness. Aaron is a "Cimmerian" not because he comes from the Far North, but because his skin is so dark.

. . . Cocytus' misty mouth

But now the cruel machinations of Aaron begin to work.

Tamora's two sons, Chiron and Demetrius, enter. Tamora tells them that she has been lured to the spot by Bassianus and Lavinia for evil purposes. The two Gothic princes promptly stab Bassianus, hide his body in a deep pit, and drag Lavinia offstage to rape her, each in turn, with Tamora egging them on fiendishly. She refuses the girl's pleas for mercy, reminding her of how Titus Andronicus had refused her own pleas for mercy for her oldest son.

She leaves and Aaron enters, guiding Quintus and Martius, two of Andronicus' three remaining sons. Martius slips into the pit in which Bassianus' body is hidden and while Quintus leans over anxiously to find out if he is hurt, Aaron slips away.

Martius discovers the body of Bassianus and is horrified. He says:

> So pale did shine the moon on Pyramus,
> When he by night lay bathed in maiden blood.
> O brother, help me with thy fainting hand—
> If fear hath made thee faint, as me it hath—
> Out of this fell devouring receptacle
> As hateful as Cocytus' misty mouth.
>
> —Act II, scene iii, lines 231-36

Pyramus was an ill-fated lover in the ancient tale, who died by moonlight (see page I-23). Cocytus is one of the five rivers of the underworld and its name means "wailing." It is meant to symbolize the sorrow of death.

A craftier Tereus . . .

The horrors continue. Aaron brings the Emperor Saturninus on the scene and Quintus and Martius are found with Bassianus' body. The forged letter, prepared by Aaron, is produced to make it seem that the two had bribed a huntsman to kill Bassianus. The bribe in the shape of the bag of gold Aaron had planted on the scene is also produced.

Titus' sons, having been effectively framed, are dragged off to imprisonment at once.

All leave and Tamora's sons now emerge. They have raped Lavinia and have cut out her tongue to prevent her telling. They have, however, gone the old Greek myth one better, for they have cut off her hands as well. Chiron says, with sadistic humor:

> Write down thy mind, bewray thy meaning so,
> And if thy stumps will let thee play the scribe.
>
> —Act II, scene iv, lines 3-4

The princes leave, and Marcus, the brother of Titus Andronicus, comes upon the scene and discovers Lavinia. He grasps the meaning of the sight at once and says:

> Fair Philomela, why she but lost her tongue,
> And in a tedious sampler sewed her mind:
> But lovely niece, that mean is cut from thee;
> A craftier Tereus, cousin, hast thou met,
> And he hath cut those pretty fingers off,
> That could have better sewed than Philomel.
>
> —Act II, scene iv, lines 38–43

In the Greek myth, Philomela had had her tongue cut out and been placed in the slaves' quarters. She could use her hands to reveal her secret, however, for she prepared a tapestry in which she wove the legend, "Philomela is among the slaves." This was delivered to her sister, Procne, who took instant action, liberating Philomela and preparing revenge.

By cutting off Lavinia's hands, the villainous princes had deprived her of Philomela's chance.

Marcus Andronicus finds it hard to believe anyone could have mangled so fair a person as Lavinia. Concerning the malefactor, Marcus says that

> . . . had he heard the heavenly harmony
> Which that sweet tongue hath made,
> He would have dropped his knife, and fell asleep
> As Cerberus at the Thracian poet's feet.
>
> —Act II, scene iv, lines 48–51

Orpheus, the sweet-singing minstrel from Thrace ("the Thracian poet"), descended into the underworld in order to win back his dead love, Eurydice (see page I–47). On approaching Cerberus (see page I–101), the three-headed hellhound who guarded the entrance, he sang so soft and sweet a lullaby that even that horrible creature fell asleep and let him pass unharmed.

. . . Tarquin and his queen

Unimaginable miseries now heap themselves on Titus Andronicus. His two sons, Quintus and Martius, are being led to execution and no one will hear his pleas on their behalf. His one remaining son, Lucius, has tried to rescue his brothers by force, has failed, and is sentenced to exile. Marcus then brings him the mutilated Lavinia and Titus breaks into fresh woe.

All is interrupted by Aaron, who brings the news that if one of the

Andronici, Titus, Marcus, or Lucius, will sacrifice a hand, that hand would be accepted as an exchange for the lives of Titus' two sons, who would then be returned free. After an argument over which Andronicus should make the sacrifice, Titus wins out and his hand is struck off.

This is but to add to the sorrows of Titus, however, for his stricken hand is soon returned and with it the heads of his two sons, who had been executed anyway. Of all Titus' children, there now remain only Lucius and the mutilated Lavinia.

Tamora has had ample revenge for the loss of her son and now it is Titus who begins to plan revenge. So does Lucius, still under sentence of exile. Alone on the stage, he plans to go abroad and raise an army against Rome, saying to his absent father, in soliloquy:

> *If Lucius live, he will requite your wrongs,*
> *And make proud Saturnine and his empress*
> *Beg at the gates, like Tarquin and his queen.*
> —Act III, scene i, lines 296–98

Tarquin was the last king of ancient Rome, who was expelled from Rome in 509 B.C. (see page I–211). He had occasion to stand at the gates of Rome in an attempt to get the throne back, and failed. To be sure, he didn't beg in the usual sense of the word. He had an army at his back.

The idea of revenge by means of an outside army fits in just a little with the time of Belisarius and Narses. Belisarius himself never attempted revenge against the ungrateful Emperor Justinian, even though legend has him reduced, toward the end of his life, to begging in the streets. (The legend has no basis in truth, however.)

Belisarius' successor, Narses, is a different matter. He ruled Italy into extreme old age, and after Justinian's death, when Narses was more than ninety years old, the aged general was ordered home. According to the legend (probably not true) his recall was accompanied by an insulting message. He was told that since he was a eunuch, he should return and confine himself to spinning wool with the palace maidens.

The insulted Narses said, "I will spin them such a skein as they will not easily unravel" and invited the barbarous Lombards to invade Italy—which they did most effectively.

. . . *Cornelia never with more care*

The play now shifts to the Andronicus house. For the first time, a grandson of Titus appears. He is a son of Lucius and is also named Lucius.

Young Lucius enters, carrying books and running. Mute Lavinia is running after him. The boy is frightened but Titus and Marcus catch and com-

fort him, assuring him that Lavinia means him no harm, and loves him.
Titus says:

> Ah, boy, Cornelia never with more care
> Read to her sons than she hath read to thee
> Sweet poetry and Tully's Orator.
>
> —Act IV, scene i, lines 12–14

The Cornelia referred to was a daughter of Publius Cornelius Scipio,
the Roman general who finally defeated Hannibal in 202 B.C. Cornelia
was considered the model of the virtuous Roman matron, chaste, honorable, and loving—and utterly devoted to her two sons.

These two sons received the finest education available at the time. So
proud was she of them that when another Roman matron, on a visit, displayed her jewelry and asked to see Cornelia's, the latter merely pointed
to her sons. "These are my jewels," she said.

As for Tully, that is a name by which the great Roman orator Marcus
Tullius Cicero (see page I-268) is sometimes known in English. One of
his famous works was *De Oratore* (*Concerning the Orator*), and it is to
this that Titus refers.

. . . Ovid's METAMORPHOSES

But Lavinia stirs the books that young Lucius has let fall, concentrating
on one, which the boy identifies for his grandfather:

> Grandsire, 'tis Ovid's Metamorphoses:
> My mother gave it me.
>
> —Act IV, scene i, lines 42–43

One of the myths contained in *Metamorphoses* (see page I-8), which
deals with tales of transformations of human beings into other forms, is
that of Philomela and Procne, for in the end, Philomela is turned into a
nightingale and Procne into a swallow. Lavinia wants to find that tale in
order to have Titus and Marcus understand that her mutilation was the
result of a rape.

Clearly, this shows haste on Shakespeare's part. After all, Marcus has
guessed as much when he first encountered Lavinia after the mutilation.
He then said:

> But, sure, some Tereus hath deflowered thee,
> And, lest thou shouldst detect him, cut thy tongue.
>
> —Act II, scene iv, lines 26–27

It now occurs to Marcus that a person can write with a stick in the sand by holding that stick in his mouth and guiding it with his wrists. Hands are not required at all. Lavinia uses this method to reveal that Chiron and Demetrius are the guilty ones. Now Titus is certain against whom he must plan revenge.

. . . not Enceladus

Apparently considerable time has elapsed since the beginning of the play, for Tamora is about to have a baby and it is to be presumed that the Emperor Saturninus is the father. However, events have miscarried. It is Aaron, not Saturninus who is the father, and this is shown all too plainly in that the baby is a black infant.

Naturally, this fact must be hidden, or Tamora's infidelity will be plain even to Saturninus and she will be destroyed. The Nurse who attended Tamora brings the baby to Aaron, with instructions from Tamora to kill it and destroy the evidence.

But Aaron, in this one respect, departs from the line of flat villainy. He becomes a proud father and in words that strangely fore-echo the pride of the black activists of the 1960s, cries out to the Nurse, who is expressing disgust at the child:

> Zounds, ye whore! Is black so base a hue?
> Sweet blowze, you are a beauteous blossom, sure.
> —Act IV, scene ii, lines 71–72

When Chiron and Demetrius, who are also present, offer to kill their baby half brother to secure their mother's safety, Aaron draws his sword fiercely, saying:

> I tell you, younglings, not Enceladus,
> With all his threat'ning band of Typhon's brood,
> Nor great Alcides, nor the god of war,
> Shall seize this prey out of his father's hands.
> —Act IV, scene ii, lines 93–96

Enceladus was one of a brood of tremendous giants (with serpents for legs) which were brought forth by Mother Earth, who was annoyed to see Jupiter (Zeus) and his fellow gods destroy the Titans, for the Titans had been her children.

The giants, under Enceladus' leadership, fought the gods in a battle which, in the versions that reach us, seem to be described as a burlesque of Homer—almost a comic retelling of a myth, with grotesque exaggerations. For instance, Enceladus is killed by Athena, who throws a huge mountain at him; a mountain that flattens him and becomes the island of Sicily.

Aaron's remark makes it seem that Enceladus and the other giants are the offspring of Typhon, but this is not so. Typhon was born after the defeat of the giants and was the greatest and most fearful monster of all. Typhon engaged Jupiter in a great duel and was almost victor, for he cut out and hid the sinews of Jupiter's hands and feet and paralyzed the great god. It wasn't till Mercury (Hermes), the god of thieves, stole back the sinews and restored Jupiter's powers of movement that Typhon was finally killed by the lightning bolts of the king of the gods.

After the mention of Enceladus and Typhon, to go on to Alcides (Hercules) and the god of war (Mars) seems distinct anticlimax.

The Gothic princes wilt before Aaron's fury and ask him what he means to do. His first act is to kill the Nurse, thus reducing, by one, the number of those who know the secret. He then prepares to change the baby for a white one who will be made heir to the throne while Aaron will secretly raise his own black baby to become a warrior.

. . . one of Taurus' horns

In preparing his revenge, Titus feigns madness, meanwhile, in order to throw Saturninus and Tamora off the scent and lull them into a false security. Titus' madness (and surely he has suffered enough to make the onset of madness plausible) consists of a wild search for justice through Heaven and Hell. He cries out:

> I'll dive into the burning lake below,
> And pull her [justice] out of Acheron by the heels.
> —Act IV, scene iii, lines 44–45

The Acheron is another of the rivers of Hades. (Two others, Styx and Cocytus, have already been mentioned in this play.)

Titus goes on to bemoan the physical shortcomings of the Andronici, in the face of so huge an undertaking as the search for justice. He says to his brother:

> Marcus, we are but shrubs, no cedars we,
> No big-boned men framed of the Cyclops' size.
> —Act IV, scene iii, lines 46–47

The Cyclopes were one-eyed giants who forged the lightning for Jupiter. They were also a race of giants who lived on Sicily in the time of the Trojan

War. At least Ulysses, on his return from Troy, falls in with one of them in particular, Polyphemus, and defeats him—one of the best-known events in the *Odyssey*.

The main thrust of the search for justice, however, consists in shooting arrows into the sky with letters attached; letters that plead with the gods for justice. Titus has all the Andronici helping him in this respect. He advances his own apparent madness by pretending to see the effects of the action in the constellations, which he describes as though having literal existence.

He exclaims to young Lucius:

> *Good boy, in Virgo's lap; give it Pallas.*
> —Act IV, scene iii, line 65

To Publius, the son of Marcus, he says:

> *Publius, Publius, what hast thou done!*
> *See, see, thou hast shot off one of Taurus' horns.*
> —Act IV, scene iii, lines 69–70

Virgo (the Maiden) and Taurus (the Bull) are both included among the signs of the zodiac. Very likely most of Shakespeare's audience did suspect that the imaginary creatures pieced out in the sky by the imaginary lines connecting stars existed there in literal truth. The humor lay in the thought that man-hurled arrows could reach them. (Pallas, by the way, is an alternate name for the Greek goddess Athena.)

Marcus keeps the play at madness going. He says to Titus:

> *. . . When Publius shot,*
> *The bull being galled, gave Aries such a knock*
> *That down fell both the Ram's horns in the court,*
> *And who should find them but the Empress' villain?* [Aaron]
> *She* [Tamora] *laughed, and told the Moor he should not choose*
> *But give them to his master for a present.*
> —Act IV, scene iii, lines 71–76

Aries (the Ram) is also a constellation of the zodiac. It neighbors Taurus so that one can well imagine the Bull charging the Ram. It enables Marcus to get off a kind of joke beloved by the Elizabethans, concerning the cuckolding of the Emperor.

. . . as ever Coriolanus did

If it is Titus' plan to lull the Emperor and Empress into total security, it falls short. Saturninus is furious at the letters of appeal to the heavens, since they end in Rome's streets where they are found by the people, who grow to sympathize with the ill-treated Titus.

The Emperor is further irritated by a Clown (a lowborn person, that is) who delivers a message to him from Titus. The Emperor forthwith orders the Clown hanged.

He prepares to go further and have Titus arrested, when a messenger arrives to say that a Gothic army is at the gates of Rome:

> *They hither march amain, under conduct*
> *Of Lucius, son to old Andronicus;*
> *Who threats, in course of this revenge, to do*
> *As much as ever Coriolanus did.*
>
> —Act IV, scene iv, lines 66–69

Coriolanus was a legendary figure in early Roman history who, out of revenge for what he considered mistreatment, raised an enemy army, placed himself at its head, and laid siege to Rome. Fifteen years after Shakespeare wrote *Titus Andronicus* he wrote *Coriolanus* about the earlier event (see page I–245).

Tamora, however, promises to make Lucius into a Coriolanus indeed. Coriolanus withdrew without taking Rome because his mother begged him to (see page I–250). Now Tamora intends to try to persuade Titus to beg his son to withdraw. (She is not aware that Titus has discovered the full extent of the villainy of her sons.)

. . . worse than Procne . . .

The scene shifts to the outskirts of Rome, where Lucius is leading the Gothic army to the city's walls. A Goth has captured Aaron, who has been trying to find a place of safety for his baby. Lucius, when Aaron is brought to him, threatens to hang father and child, and, to save the baby, Aaron confesses all.

Meanwhile, Tamora has worked out her plan to persuade Titus to call off his son. She proposes to take advantage of his madness by disguising herself as Revenge and her two sons as Rape and Murder (that is, as spirits specifically designed to avenge those two crimes).

In her guise as Revenge, Tamora promises to make mad Titus quits with all his enemies and asks him, in turn, to send for his son, Lucius, to attend a feast which Titus will give. It will then be Revenge's part (supposedly) to bring in the Emperor, the Empress, and the Empress' sons for Titus to wreak vengeance upon. (Actually, it is Tamora's plan, once she has Lucius with Titus, to have both killed, and then somehow to arrange to have the leaderless Goths dispersed.)

Titus pretends to fall in with this plan and sends Marcus to invite Lucius to the feast.

But then, when Revenge turns to leave, Titus insists on keeping Rape and Murder. Otherwise, he says, he will call back Marcus and leave things as they were. Tamora orders her sons to humor him and leaves by herself.

Once Tamora is gone, Titus instantly calls his friends and orders Rape and Murder tied up. They announce themselves to be the Empress' sons, hoping this will awe their assailants, but Titus merely orders them gagged. He then tells them what he intends to do by way of revenge, saying:

> For worse than Philomel you used my daughter,
> And worse than Procne I will be revenged.
> —Act V, scene ii, lines 195–96

When Procne discovered what her husband, Tereus, had done to Philomela, she took a horrible revenge. She killed Itys, the young son of Tereus and herself, boiled his flesh, and fed it to Tereus.

This Titus intended to surpass. They had cut off not only the tongue but the hands of Lavinia. In return, Titus intended to have their mother feed on not one, but two sons.

With that, he cuts the throats of Chiron and Demetrius, catching the blood in a basin held by Lavinia.

. . . rash Virginius

The feast begins now. All are present (even Aaron and his baby). Titus, dressed as a cook, poses the Emperor a question:

> Was it well done of rash Virginius
> To slay his daughter with his own right hand,
> Because she was enforced, stained, and deflow'red?
> —Act V, scene iii, lines 36–38

Virginius was a plebeian soldier who, according to legend, lived about 450 B.C. (a generation after Coriolanus). His beautiful daughter, Virginia, attracted the attention of Appius Claudius, a patrician who was then the most powerful man in Rome. Appius Claudius planned to seize the girl by having false witnesses testify that the girl was actually the daughter of one of his slaves and was therefore also his slave.

The distracted Virginius, seeing no way of stopping Appius Claudius, suddenly stabbed his daughter to death in the midst of the trial, proclaiming that only through death could he save her honor.

Titus Andronicus states the situation erroneously, by the way. Virginius' daughter was not "enforced, stained, and deflow'red." She was merely threatened with that.

Saturninus says that Virginius was justified in his action, whereupon Titus promptly stabs Lavinia to death. When Saturninus angrily demands the reason for that action, Titus says she has been raped by Chiron and Demetrius, and that they in turn have been killed and baked into a pie which the Empress is at that moment eating.

Titus then stabs and kills Tamora; at which the Emperor Saturninus stabs and kills Titus; at which Lucius stabs and kills Saturninus.

. . . what Sinon . . .

A Roman Lord now asks Lucius what has brought Rome to this civil war and assassination:

> Tell us what Sinon hath bewitched our ears,
> Or who hath brought the fatal engine in
> That gives our Troy, our Rome, the civil wound
> —Act V, scene iii, lines 85–87

Sinon is the Greek who persuaded the Trojans to allow entry to the wooden horse ("the fatal engine") and made the final sack of the city possible (see page I–210).

I do repent . . .

Lucius and Marcus, between them, now tell all the wrongs done the Andronici by the Emperor, the Empress, her sons, and Aaron. They even show Aaron's baby as proof of another kind of wickedness.

The appalled Romans hail Lucius as the new Emperor and call in Aaron for punishment. Lucius orders that he be buried breast-deep in the earth and allowed to starve to death.

Even now, Aaron refuses to crawl, and one can't help but feel a kind of sneaking admiration for his defiance. He says, ferociously, after having heard his doom:

I am no baby, I, that with base prayers
I should repent the evils I have done:
Ten thousand worse than ever yet I did
Would I perform, if I might have my will:
If one good deed in all my life I did,
I do repent it from my very soul.

—Act V, scene iii, lines 185–90

It is a fitly grisly speech to end a grisly play that opens with:

(1) the dead body of one of Titus' sons, then continues with
(2) the sacrifice of Tamora's son, Alarbus, by Lucius,
(3) the stabbing of Mutius by his father, Titus,
(4) the stabbing of Bassianus by Chiron and Demetrius,
(5) the rape and mutilation of Lavinia by Chiron and Demetrius,
(6) the mutilation of Titus by Aaron,
(7) the execution of Martius and
(8) Quintus, by order of the Emperor,
(9) the stabbing of the Nurse by Aaron,
(10) the hanging of a Clown for small offense by Saturninus' order,
(11) the throat-cutting of Chiron and
(12) Demetrius by Titus,
(13) the unwitting cannibalism of Tamora,
(14) the stabbing of Lavinia by Titus,
(15) the stabbing of Tamora by Titus,
(16) the stabbing of Titus by Saturninus,
(17) the stabbing of Saturninus by Lucius, and finally,
(18) the projected death by slow starvation of Aaron.

PART III

Italian

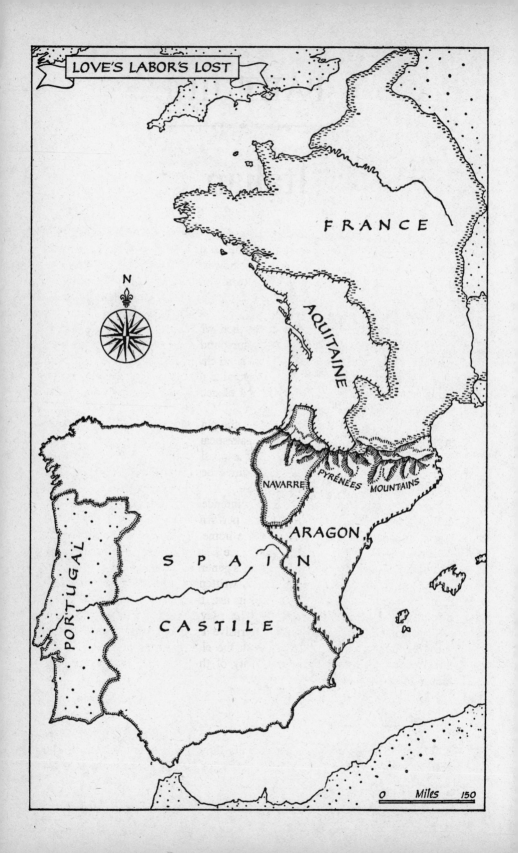

14

LOVE'S LABOR'S LOST

THERE ARE fifteen of Shakespeare's plays which deal with English history or English legend. If I adhered to strict chronological sequence, these would follow here. If I did that, however, the division between the two volumes of this book would fall inconveniently in the middle of those plays. I am consequently leaving the fifteen English plays to make up *in toto* the second volume.

We will conclude this first volume then with a dozen romances which are placed in Renaissance Italy and surrounding regions, and which are, for Shakespeare, contemporary. There is no clear historical background and even where some reference can be pinpointed to this or that year, this is not significant and will not do as a method of deciding the order in which the plays should be presented.

In this final part of the volume, then, the plays that remain will be placed in the order in which (it is thought) Shakespeare wrote them.

And of these *Love's Labor's Lost* is possibly the earliest. Along with *The Comedy of Errors* it has sometimes been dated as early as 1588, though dates as late as 1593 are possible.

The play doesn't seem to have been intended for wide public popularity, and may have been written for private performance. One possibility is that it was intended for a celebration at the home of the Earl of Southampton (see page I-3). If so, the play must have been an astounding success, for Southampton then became Shakespeare's generous patron.

If *Love's Labor's Lost* were indeed written primarily for the entertainment of a coterie of men interested in art, that would explain the overelaboration of much of the style. The play was a satire on pedantry, and its complicated verbiage and intrusive Latinity would appeal to the sense of humor of the educated. Both the elaborateness and the Latinity have tended to diminish the popularity of the play considerably in later times.

Navarre shall be . . .

The play opens with a King and his three companions on stage. The King is announcing his decision to retire for three years (along with his companions) to a sober and austere study of philosophy. He is very optimistic about the effect this will have, for he says:

> *Navarre shall be the wonder of the world;*
> *Our court shall be a little academe,*
>
> —Act I, scene i, lines 12–13

The speaker is, according to the cast of characters, Ferdinand, King of
Navarre.

Navarre does not exist as an independent kingdom on our maps today
(or on the maps of Shakespeare's time, for that matter), and most people
would be at a loss to point out where it might ever have existed. It is not a
mythical land, however; it is no Ruritania. It once did exist indeed, and in
medieval times it constituted a sizable region about the western end of the
Pyrenees. Mostly, it lay to the south and west of that range in what is now
north-central Spain, but some of its territory lay to the north in what is
now southwestern France.

Through the Middle Ages, it maintained an increasingly precarious independence between France on the north and the growing strength of the
other Christian kingdoms of the Spanish peninsula. In 1474 Aragon and
Castile (the two most important of those kingdoms) were bound together
when Ferdinand, Crown Prince of Aragon, married Isabella, Queen of
Castile. In 1479 Ferdinand succeeded to the crown of Aragon, and under
the united rule of himself and Isabella, modern Spain was formed. (The two
monarchs were the parents of Catherine, the ill-fated first wife of Henry
VIII, see page II-754.)

Navarre could not stand against the union of the kingdoms. The portion
of Navarre south of the Pyrenees was occupied by Ferdinand in 1512
and made an integral part of the Spanish crown in 1515.

The part of the kingdom north of the Pyrenees was under the rule of
Catherine de Foix, who married Jean d'Albret (a descendant of the Constable of France, who had died at the Battle of Agincourt, see page
II-475). Jean d'Albret called himself King of Navarre and his son succeeded to the title, as Henry II of Navarre, in 1517, when his mother died.

Naturally, Ferdinand of Spain claimed the rule of all Navarre, but in
order to establish that claim he would have had to fight France, which held
the actual control of northern Navarre. This Ferdinand never tried to do,
and Henry II remained titular King of Navarre. That is, he had the title
but no more; in actual fact, he was merely a French nobleman and had
none of the power of an independent monarch.

Henry II married Margaret (or Marguerite, in the French spelling),
who was sister to King Francis I (see page II-747). She is consequently
known in history books as Margaret of Navarre, and it was she who, before

this marriage, had been thought of by Wolsey as a possible second wife for Henry VIII (see page II–69).

Henry had a daughter, Jeanne d'Albret, who was Queen of Navarre from 1562 to 1572. Her son was another Henry, who in 1572 became Henry III of Navarre, but is known to history simply as Henry of Navarre because, first, he was by far the most important ruler Navarre ever had, and second, because in his time the King of France was also Henry III and to use the same Roman numeral for both would lead to confusion.

Through his father, Henry of Navarre was a member of the family of Bourbon, which, through a solid line of male ancestors, was descended from a younger son of King Louis IX (see page II–457) who had died in 1270. Now, three centuries later, only one male descendant remained of the older lines and he was Henry III of France, who became king in 1574. If Henry III died without surviving sons (and he was a homosexual who never had children), Henry IV (who was thoroughly and spectacularly heterosexual) was the next in line to the throne.

This would not ordinarily have made much of a stir except that France had been involved in a religious civil war for a dozen years, one in which a sizable and militant Protestant minority was stanchly withstanding the Catholic majority. As it happened, Henry of Navarre was a Protestant and, in view of his position as prospective heir to the throne, the leader of the Protestant faction. There were many Frenchmen, on the other hand, determined that no Protestant should ever be King of France, regardless of his descent.

This standoff was the situation when *Love's Labor's Lost* was written. England, as it happened, had just defeated the Spanish Armada in 1588, and had heroically foiled a vast Spanish-Catholic attempt to subvert the Protestant character of the island kingdom. England was consequently all on fire with the picture of itself as the Protestant David hacking down the great Catholic Goliath of Spain. Since Spain was the chief support of the French Catholics against the possible succession of Henry of Navarre, there was much warmth and admiration for Henry in England.

It would be natural, then, for Shakespeare to write a play in which the King of Navarre was a hero and in which he was presented in the most favorable light. In order to make the situation not too pointed and topical, it was inadvisable to use the name "Henry," so he used "Ferdinand" instead. This was a favorite name during the Italian Renaissance and might have been inspired by the fact that Ferdinand II of Spain had taken over southern Navarre.

In early 1589 Henry III of France was assassinated by a fanatic monk who felt the King wasn't Catholic enough, and Henry of Navarre succeeded to the throne as Henry IV of France. Unfortunately for the new king, the title he gained was not accepted by the Catholic party and he remained king only over his own minority. The Catholics controlled much of France, including the all-important city of Paris, and the civil war grew fiercer. Henry IV was a good general and won important victories, but against the sheer weight of Catholic intransigence he could not prevail.

In 1591 the Earl of Essex, the great friend of Southampton and Shakespeare, even led an army in support of Henry of Navarre, but Essex was a poor soldier and failed in this, as in all his military efforts (see page II–508).

Finally, in 1593, Henry of Navarre, with a sigh and a shrug, agreed to turn Catholic. Then, and only then, did Paris accept him. Henry entered the capital, was hailed as king, was eventually crowned, and became Henry IV in truth. ("Paris is worth a mass," said Henry.)

Of course, this made him a traitor to the Protestant cause and Englishmen must have reflected sardonically over the proverbial (to them) faithlessness of the French nature. It is doubtful if *Love's Labor's Lost* could possibly have been written in its present form after 1593, for that reason.

. . . Berowne, Dumaine, and Longaville

No action in the play has any but the very faintest and most distant association with the real Henry of Navarre, of course, but Shakespeare continues to use reality as the source of inspiration for names at least.

Thus, the King turns to the three with him and says:

> *You three, Berowne, Dumaine, and Longaville,*
> *Have sworn for three years' term to live with me,*
> *My fellow scholars . . .*
> —Act I, scene i, lines 15–17

The name Berowne may have been inspired by Armand de Gontaut, Baron de Biron, who was a close associate of Henry of Navarre and who in 1589 gained the leadership of his armies. He won victories for Henry and was killed in battle in 1592.

Biron had been closely associated with the expeditionary force led by Essex. This made Biron specially popular in England and it is not surprising that Shakespeare makes Berowne the most attractive person in the play.

Longaville is a version of Longueville and there was a Duc de Longueville also among Henry's generals.

Dumaine is not so easy to place. That name may have been inspired by Charles, Duc de Mayenne, who was associated with Henry IV, but not as a friend. Mayenne was the leader of the Catholic opposition to Henry. To be sure, after Henry's conversion Mayenne was reconciled to the King and from 1596 on remained completely loyal to him. This, however, certainly took place well after the play was written.

The French king's daughter . . .

Berowne is the one companion who doesn't think the King's plan will work. He doubts that they can successfully make themselves strict and austere philosophers for three years. He particularly doubts they can really forswear female company, as the King plans to have them do. In fact, that would be impossible, for Berowne says:

> *This article, my liege, yourself must break;*
> *For well you know here comes in embassy*
> *The French king's daughter with yourself to speak,*
> *A maid of grace and complete majesty,*
> > —Act I, scene i, lines 132–35

This too has a glancing resemblance to the real-life career of Henry of Navarre. In 1572 young Henry (only nineteen at the time) was married to Marguerite de Valois (also nineteen). At that time Henry III's older brother, Charles IX, was still on the throne (he didn't die till 1574) and Marguerite was sister to both of them. All three of them, Henry III, Charles IX, and Marguerite (plus an earlier short-lived monarch, Francis II), were children of King Henry II of France, who had died in 1559.

The continuing religious civil war made the marriage no idyll, but in 1578 there was a well-publicized visit of Marguerite (along with her mother, Catherine de' Medici) to the court of Navarre. It may well have been this visit which was in Shakespeare's mind.

If the visit was intended to improve the state of the marriage, by the way, it failed miserably. Henry was interested in many ladies and Marguerite bore him no children. Finally, in 1599, their marriage was annulled and Henry was able to marry again and beget an heir to the throne. This, however, was well after *Love's Labor's Lost* was written.

. . . surrender up of Aquitaine

And why was the French princess coming? Berowne says that the embassy is

> *About surrender up of Aquitaine*
> *To her decrepit, sick, and bed-rid father.*
> > —Act I, scene i, lines 136–37

The matter of Aquitaine is pure invention, of course. Even at its most powerful, Navarre never controlled that large section of southern France called Aquitaine (see page II–209). The name, however, would be a familiar one to Englishmen if only because Eleanor of Aquitaine was one of the most famous of English queens.

The real Marguerite de Valois had no living father at the time of her marriage to Henry. She had been only six years old when her father died. However, the French royal family, at the time the play was written, seemed indeed decrepit, sick, and bed-rid. In 1588 Henry III of France had reigned fourteen years and though only thirty-seven was prematurely aged, and exhausted by the crises of the time and his personal excesses. Two older brothers had reigned briefly and died, one at sixteen and one at twenty-four. A younger brother was already dead at thirty, and none of the brothers left descendants.

. . . Armado hight

It seems that the Princess must be greeted and entertained despite all ascetic arrangements. The cynical Berowne, delighted, inquires if there is any other and more reliable entertainment allowed the scholars than the occasional visit of a princess.

The King informs him that there is an eccentric and euphuistic Spaniard at the court who can be very entertaining, albeit unconsciously so. He refers to him as:

> This child of fancy, that Armado hight [is named],
> —Act I, scene i, line 169

If the play were written in the aftermath of the great defeat of the Spanish fleet in 1588, a Spaniard would be a natural butt for the play, and his name, Armado (Don Adriano de Armado in full, according to the cast of characters), is a none too subtle recall of the defeated Armada.

There has been a tendency for some people to find satirical representations in all the characters of this play. If it were written for a small "in group" rather than for the general public, it might well contain "in jokes" against the personal enemies of the group in the audience.

Thus, the Earl of Essex had become Queen Elizabeth's favorite in the very years of the Armada (and this play) after her previous favorite, the Earl of Leicester, died. Essex's great rival was Sir Walter Raleigh, who had been Leicester's protégé and whose nose had been put out of joint by the handsome Essex's greater success with the Queen. Some people therefore think that Armado was intended as a satire on Raleigh for the amusement of the Essex coterie. However, there seems little one can point to in what Armado says or does that has "Raleigh" written on it. (There are other candidates for the role of real-life Armado too, but none are really convincing.)

Boy, what sign . . .

Armado at once enters the plot, indirectly, to lend humor to it. He has spied a country bumpkin, Costard, making love to a young country girl, Jaquenetta, in defiance of the published edict against association with womankind, and has reported the matter to the authorities. Costard is arrested by Constable Dull and is turned over to the custody of Armado.

It turns out, of course, that Armado is himself in love with Jaquenetta, and he displays this in the approved manner of the puling stage lover. He uses his page as a sounding board for his melancholy and says:

> *Boy, what sign is it when a man of great spirit grows melancholy?*
> —Act I, scene ii, lines 1–2

The page is of the smallest possible size and is named Moth (pronounced "mote" in Shakespeare's day with the obvious pun). It is his function to be witty in Shakespearean fashion, so he answers:

> *A great sign, sir, that he will look sad.*
> —Act I, scene ii, line 3

Some people have attempted to equate Moth with Thomas Nashe, a pamphleteer who was contemporary with Shakespeare and who engaged in battles of wits in polemical style with other controversialists. He was coarse, pretentious, and arrogant.

By those who think this, Armado is equated with Gabriel Harvey, another controversialist of the time who was an opponent of Nashe's. The Armado-Moth quibbling might therefore be taken to represent, with satiric inadequacy, the Homeric polemics of Harvey and Nashe.

Samson, master . . .

Armado pictures himself as a warlike hero unmanned for love and demands of Moth that he give him examples of great men in love:

> *. . . and, sweet my child, let them be men of good repute and carriage* [bearing].
> —Act I, scene ii, lines 68–69

Moth had already named Hercules as an example, and rightly, for he was described in the numerous myths that clustered about his name to have lain with innumerable women. Once, according to legend, he lay with fifty women in one night, impregnated them all, and ended by having fifty sons—a feat far greater, really, than all his twelve usual labors put together.

At the mention of "good repute and carriage," Moth adds, however:

> *Samson, master—he was a man of good carriage, great carriage, for he carried the town-gates on his back like a porter, and he was in love.*
>
> —Act I, scene ii, lines 70–72

The twist on the word "carriage," from carrying oneself to carrying external objects, refers to a time when Samson was visiting a harlot in Gaza. The Philistines, knowing the town gates were locked, waited for morning to deal with him, but Samson rose at midnight "and took the doors of the gate of the city, and the two posts, and went away with them, bar and all, and put them upon his shoulders, and carried them up to the top of an hill" (Judges 16:3) so that he got away when his enemies confidently thought he was trapped. At the time of this feat he was in love (if you can dignify the relation between himself and the woman by that word).

Later on, Armado meets Jaquenetta, confesses his love to the unimpressed girl, and soliloquizes afterward on the great men of the past who had been in love. To Hercules and Samson, he adds one more, saying:

> . . . *yet was Solomon so seduced, and he had a very good wit.*
>
> —Act I, scene ii, lines 172–73

The biblical writers felt that Solomon's numerous wives seduced him away from perfect love of God. "And he had seven hundred wives, princesses, and three hundred concubines: and his wives turned away his heart. For it came to pass, when Solomon was old, that his wives turned away his heart after other gods" (1 Kings 11:3–4).

. . . the Duke Alencon's . . .

The Princess arrives and she has with her, symmetrically enough, three ladies: Maria, Katherine, and Rosaline.

The symmetry proves even neater when each of the ladies evinces an interest in one of the King's followers, each different lady with a different man. What's more, each has met her man before. With Maria it's Longaville, with Katherine it's Dumaine, and with Rosaline it's Berowne. Thus, Katherine says of Dumaine:

I saw him at the Duke Alencon's once;
And much too little of that good I saw

—Act II, scene i, lines 61–62

If we stick to the time of Henry of Navarre, there was a Duc d'Alençon who was well known to the English of the time. He was the fourth and youngest of the four sons of Henry II, and he had watched his three older brothers become kings of France, one after the other: Francis II, Charles IX, and Henry III. He died in 1584, while his brother Henry was reigning.

Alençon was known to the English as a persistent wooer of Queen Elizabeth I, which was rather pathetic, for Alençon was quite worthless and Elizabeth (one of the most remarkable women in history) could not have endured him an hour. However, Elizabeth was incapable of a clear no at any time, but had a genius for temporization, so that the poor simpleton pursued the golden prize uselessly from 1579 to 1582.

. . . in Brabant once

When the King and his followers arrive to receive the ladies, the men are as intrigued by the women as vice versa, and, as luck would have it, each man is interested in the particular woman who is interested in him.

It works out beautifully, for Berowne (the wittiest of the men) is at once involved with Rosaline (the wittiest of the women), and, eager to break the ice, he uses a device not unknown today, when he says to her:

Did not I dance with you in Brabant once?

—Act II, scene i, line 114

Brabant was a duchy located in what is now central Belgium. In the time of Shakespeare it was part of the Spanish dominion in what was then known as the Spanish Netherlands.

As it turns out, the two had indeed danced together in Brabant, and there follows a typical Shakespearean game of wordplay.

. . . Charles his father

There is some business to be done, of course—the matter of Aquitaine. The King of Navarre does not wish to return it to France until he is paid a sum that the King of France owes him for expenses incurred by Navarre's father. The Princess, however, claims payment has already been made and orders her male attendant, Boyet, to produce the receipts, saying:

Boyet, you can produce acquittances
For such a sum from special officers
Of Charles his father.

—Act II, scene i, lines 160–62

The father of the real Henry of Navarre was not named Charles. His name was Anthony, Duc de Vendôme.

On the other hand, Henry of Navarre had an uncle, the younger brother of his father, who *was* a Charles. He was Charles de Bourbon and was a cardinal. He was a Catholic, of course, and the next in line for the throne after Henry of Navarre, if the latter died without surviving sons. Indeed, when Henry III was assassinated in 1589 and Henry of Navarre declared himself the new king as Henry IV, the intransigent Catholics proclaimed Charles instead and called him Charles X. However, Charles was already in his middle sixties and he died in 1590.

There were other Charleses too in the Bourbon ancestry. The most famous Bourbon of all, prior to Henry of Navarre himself, was Charles, Duc de Bourbon and Constable of France. He was made Constable (that is, commander of the armies) in 1515 under King Francis I, but achieved his greatest fame by quarreling with the King and defecting to the national enemy, the Emperor Charles V (see page II–747) in 1523. The Constable died, while still fighting against his King, in 1527, sixty years before his distant cousin, Henry of Navarre, succeeded to the throne.

. . . Dan Cupid

The receipts the Princess speaks of are not actually on hand. They are on the way, however, and must be waited for.

This means that business can be temporarily forgotten and the gentlemen and ladies can continue their business of pairing off and indulging in their wit duels. Berowne is particularly chagrined at finding himself in love and at being beaten by:

This senior-junior, giant-dwarf, Dan Cupid,

—Act III, scene i, line 182

The term "Dan Cupid" does not signify that Cupid's first name was conceived to be Daniel. Rather, it means "Lord Cupid." The Latin word for "Lord" is *Dominus*. This is shortened to "Don" by the Spaniards and, in turn, distorted to "Dan" by the English.

In his disgust, Berowne inveighs against women and tries, but fails, to dismiss them with hard words. He even scouts their morality, saying:

> *. . . by heaven, one that will do the deed,*
> *Though Argus were her eunuch and her guard!*
>> —Act III, scene i, lines 200–1

The reference is to Argus Panoptes ("all eyes"), who had a hundred eyes set all over his body. At any given moment only fifty of them slept, so that there were always fifty awake. Juno set Argus to watching Io, the illicit love of her straying husband, Jupiter.

The only way Jupiter could rescue Io (in heifer's disguise at the time) was to send Mercury to tell Argus a droning tale that put all hundred eyes to sleep at once. Mercury then killed him and all Juno could do was save the hundred eyes and put them in the tail of the peacock, a bird sacred to her.

. . . king Cophetua . . .

Berowne, despite his brave words, finds that love drives him to write a letter to Rosaline (strictly against the King's rules) and to have it delivered to her secretly by Costard the clown. Armado, however, is also using Costard as delivery boy, sending a letter by way of the clown to Jaquenetta.

When Costard tries to deliver the letter to Rosaline, the Princess seizes it and behold, it turns out to be Armado's letter. She opens it and finds that the Spaniard is writing most grandiloquently to the peasant girl. He makes comparisons that are flattering to himself, if little likely to delight the girl, for he says:

> *The magnanimous and most illustrate king Cophetua set eye*
> *upon the pernicious and indubitate beggar Zenelophon,*
>> —Act IV, scene i, lines 65–68

King Cophetua, the hero of a ballad, was a completely fictional personage. He was an immensely rich king of Africa who disdained all womankind till he accidentally saw a beggar maid from his window. He had to have her, married her, and lived with her long and happily. The name given the beggar maid may have been Penelope to begin with. It varies from version to version of the story, however, and Zenelophon is a name as good as another.

As evidence for the very popular thesis that "love conquers all," the ballad grew famous and was particularly close to the hearts of any girl that dreamed of marrying above her station someday.

It is impossible to help but notice now and then that Armado is extraordinarily like Don Quixote in his consistent overestimate of himself and in his insistence on imagining himself a superhuman storybook hero. He ends the letter with some doggerel which begins:

> *Thus dost thou hear the Nemean lion roar*
> *'Gainst thee, thou lamb . . .*
>
> —Act IV, scene i, lines 90–91

Armado represents himself as the Nemean lion (see page I–58) while Jaquenetta is the lamb. (And remember that Don Quixote tried to fight a lion in the cage and called himself, in consequence, "Knight of the Lions.")

There is something rather pleasant in the thought that Shakespeare might be borrowing from Miguel de Cervantes, the Spanish author of the Don Quixote saga, since Cervantes was almost an exact contemporary of Shakespeare's (the former was three years younger and both died in the same year) and by all odds one of the few writers, on the basis of *Don Quixote* alone, worthy of being mentioned in the same breath with Shakespeare.

There is only one catch, but that is a fatal one. The first part of *Don Quixote* was published in 1605, a dozen years at least *after Love's Labor's Lost* was written.

When the Princess wonders about the identity of the man who wrote the unintentionally amusing letter, Boyet tells her he is:

> *A phantasime, a Monarcho, and one that makes sport*
> *To the prince and his book-mates.*
>
> —Act IV, scene i, lines 101–2

A "phantasime" is a man with a wild imagination (fantasy), and Monarcho was a harmless Italian madman who was tolerated at Elizabeth's court becuse he was found to be amusing, and who had died perhaps ten years before the play was written.

One can't help remembering that in the second part of *Don Quixote*, published in 1615, there is a long section in which the mad knight is humored by a kindly Duke and Duchess who keep him at their estate for the fun he affords them.

Could it be in reverse? Could Cervantes have come across *Love's Labor's Lost* and turned a small suggestion into a towering work of genius? I have never seen this stated even as a conjecture but I can't help wondering.

. . . King Pepin of France . . .

Boyet playfully rallies Rosaline on the letter Berowne has sent her, a letter she hasn't seen yet because of Costard's mix-up. She counters with:

Shall I come upon thee with an old saying that was a man
when King Pepin of France was a little boy . . .
                                    —Act IV, scene i, lines 121–23

King Pepin (see page I–455) reigned in France in the eighth century, over eight hundred years before Shakespeare's time, and he was apparently considered the epitome of the dead-and-gone in French idiom.

Dictynna . . .

The next scene introduces Holofernes, a most unbearable pedant, whose speech consists half of Latin and who spends all his time nit-picking the English language. He is a satire on what learning can come to if it is carried to extremes without even a modicum of good sense to go along with all the education.

Those who look for personal satire in *Love's Labor's Lost* suspect Holofernes to represent a gibe against John Florio, the London-born son of a Protestant refugee from Italy. Florio was a linguist who spent his life translating foreign works into English, notably Montaigne's *Essays,* and who compiled Italian-English dictionaries, collections of proverbs, grammars, etc. He was intensely learned and was probably pedantic enough to make it seem that Holofernes was a satiric reference to him.

Another possibility is Thomas Harriot, an English mathematician who was Raleigh's scientific adviser on an expedition to the New World (a position which would be alone sufficient to make him instant anathema to the Essex coterie, including Shakespeare). Harriot wrote a book on the voyage which was published in 1588 and which was pedantic enough, perhaps, to inspire the satire.

Holofernes is a pedant from his very name onward, for the name, though biblical, is not one that many would think of using. It occurs only in the apocryphal (but very popular) Book of Judith, accepted as canonical by the Catholics but by neither Jews nor Protestants. It deals with an invasion of Judea by an army of Assyrians under a general named Holofernes. The general was hoodwinked and assassinated by the Jewish heroine Judith, and as a villainous name it would scarcely be used except to signify someone who would find pleasure in obscure and unusual allusions.

Thus, Constable Dull tries to trap Holofernes with a riddle which he thinks is impossible to puzzle out—to wit, what was a month old when Cain was born, is still alive, but is not yet five weeks old. The answer is, of course, "the moon," since when it is four weeks old it starts all over again with another "new moon."

Holofernes knows the answer and gives it at once, but naturally would not dream of saying "the moon" or even using the more common classical terms such as "Diana," "Selene," "Artemis," or "Cynthia." Instead, he picks the most obscure allusion possible and says:

> Dictynna, good man Dull.
>
> —Act IV, scene ii, line 37

Dictynna was undoubtedly one of the many local names for the moon goddess which then had to be woven into the general body of myths worked out by the old Greek poets. It was said that one of the companions of Diana, the goddess of the hunt, who was often considered a personification of the moon, was Britomartis, who hid from the unwanted love of King Minos of Crete. Britomartis finally threw herself into the sea in desperation and was rescued in a fisherman's net. Thereafter, she was given the name "Dictynna" from a Greek word for "net." Her association with Diana was used to explain the fact that Dictynna could be used as a personification of the moon.

Of course, Dull can make nothing of the answer and Holofernes has to explain it.

Again, he quotes a Latin line and falls into ecstasies over it, saying:

> Ah, good old Mantuan
>
> —Act IV, scene ii, lines 95–96

Now, the greatest of all the Latin poets, Vergil, who wrote the *Aeneid,* was born near Mantua and was frequently referred to as "the Mantuan." A reader might be forgiven if he supposed at first that Holofernes was quoting from the *Aeneid* and rhapsodizing over Vergil.

He is not, however. He is referring to Battista Spagnoli, an obscure Italian Renaissance poet, who used "Mantuan" as his pen name.

Ovidius Naso . . .

Jaquenetta brings Holofernes a poem delivered her by Costard and supposedly intended for her. It is the letter, however, written by Berowne in the form of an eloquent sonnet and intended for Rosaline. Jaquenetta can make nothing of its high-flown style.

Nathaniel the Curate, a humble admirer of Holofernes, is also present, and he reads it. Holofernes criticizes the reading at once, of course, and falls into admiration of the Roman poet Ovid (see page I-8). Quite irrelevantly, he makes use of the poet's name to make a ridiculous metaphor, saying:

Ovidius Naso was the man; and why indeed "Naso" but
for smelling out odoriferous flowers of fancy . . .

—Act IV, scene ii, lines 125–27

"Naso," you see comes from *nasus*, the Latin word for "nose."

. . . as mad as Ajax . . .

In another part of the park, Berowne is still trying to write love poetry
and still berating himself for it, saying:

By the Lord, this love is as mad as Ajax: it kills sheep; it
kills me—I a sheep.

—Act IV, scene iii, lines 6–7

This refers to the tragic death of Ajax in madness and frustration, killing
sheep under the hallucinatory belief they are his enemies (see page
I–110).

. . . critic Timon . . .

He hears someone coming and hides. It is the King, who reads aloud
a lovesick sonnet to the Princess, then hides as Longaville comes in to read
aloud a lovesick sonnet to Maria, then hides as Dumaine comes in to
read aloud a lovesick sonnet to Katherine.

Each one is in love against their original intention and each moves in a
simultaneous and symmetrical way. Each one in turn steps forward to announce his discovery of the next and then Berowne steps forward to berate
them all in most hypocritical fashion considering his own activity. He affects to bemoan the conversion of serious scholars into moaning lovers
and says:

O me, with what strict patience have I sat,
To see a king transformèd to a gnat!
To see great Hercules whipping a gig [top],
And profound Solomon to tune a jig,
And Nestor play at push-pin with the boys,
And critic Timon laugh at idle toys!

—Act IV, scene iii, lines 164–69

The contrasts he cites are extreme ones. He pictures Hercules, the epitome of strength and heroism, and Solomon and Nestor, bywords for wisdom in Greek and Hebrew literature, respectively, engage in childish

occupations. (This is like serious Navarrese scholars writing love poems.)

As for "critic Timon," this is Timon the misanthrope concerning whom Shakespeare was to try to write a play, *Timon of Athens* (see page I–133) fifteen years later.

. . . the school of night

But, of course, in the midst of Berowne's self-righteous scoldings, in come Jaquenetta and Costard with Berowne's letter, which they still don't understand. Berowne, to his chagrin and embarrassment, must admit that he too has been writing sonnets.

The others are very naturally quite anxious to turn the tables and they make unsparing (and, by our standards, unchivalrous) fun of Rosaline, who is Berowne's love. Rosaline is a brunet at a time when it was conventional to consider blondness beauty.

The King sneers at Rosaline's blackness (meaning her hair, of course, and not her skin). Loyally, Berowne insists that he considers blackness a sign of beauty, but the King says:

> *O paradox! Black is the badge of hell,*
> *The hue of dungeons, and the school of night;*
> —Act IV, scene iii, lines 253–54

The phrase "school of night" is a puzzler. Some people think it is a misprint and that what is meant is that black is the "shade" of night.

On the other hand, some think "school" is what is really meant and that this is another of Shakespeare's partisan references. This may have referred to a group of amateur scholars who gathered together in a secret group to study the new astronomy that had arisen out of Copernicus' book in 1543, which held that the Earth moved round the sun and not vice versa.

Shakespeare never accepted this and, in fact, his view of science is always strictly conservative and medieval. The Copernican view was widely held to be against the Bible and religion, and therefore atheistic. The group of scholars would be, then, according to their enemies, a "school of night"; that is, one where devilish doctrines were taught.

Raleigh was supposed to patronize this wicked school, which, of course, gave the Essex faction a handle with which to strike at him.

. . . the true Promethean fire

Berowne survives the teasing and launches into a long and eloquent defense of love. Once again, he blames the King and the others for even trying to abolish love so that they might study undisturbed. Constant study will wither, while love will supply true inspiration. He says:

> From women's eyes this doctrine I derive:
> They are the ground, the books, the academes,
> From whence doth spring the true Promethean fire.
>
> —Act IV, scene iii, lines 301–3

The phrase "Promethean fire" harks back to Prometheus (the name means "forethought"), who was considered, in the Greek myths, to be one of the Titans, the race of divine beings who ruled the universe before Zeus and his relatives (the Olympians) won that rule by force.

In the war between the Titans and the Olympians, Prometheus foresaw that the latter would win and he was careful to avoid joining the other Titans or to do anything that would offend Zeus. He was therefore allowed to retain his freedom when the other Titans were condemned to Tartarus.

Nevertheless, Prometheus was still a Titan and he could not wholeheartedly be a friend of the Olympians. Recently created mankind did not have the secret of fire—which was deliberately withheld by Zeus. Prometheus therefore stole fire from the sun and brought it down to man.

Zeus punished Prometheus for this by chaining him to a crag in the Caucasus where an eagle (or a vulture) gnawed at his liver all day long. The liver regenerated at night so as to be ready for fresh torture the next day.

It is possible to consider Prometheus the embodiment of man's forethought or ingenuity—personified "inventiveness." The fire he brought man might be, symbolically, the light of insight and inspiration and that is what Berowne would mean by "the true Promethean fire."

Berowne's defense of love is in the tradition of courtly love that was developed in southern France in the mid-twelfth century and was associated with the troubadours. Eleanor of Aquitaine (see page II–209) was one of the first great patrons of such notions.

Courtly love had little to do with real passion or with sex but rather presented love as a kind of game to amuse an idle aristocracy, a game which consisted of complex rules of behavior, of love poetry, of exchanges of wit, of idealization of women—of everything but actual contact.

So Berowne speaks in grandiloquent phrases of love as an act of heroic aspiring to idealized woman, saying:

> For valor, is not Love a Hercules,
> Still climbing trees in the Hesperides?
> Subtle as Sphinx;
>
> —Act IV, scene iii, lines 339–41

For his eleventh labor, Hercules had to obtain golden apples from the garden of the Hesperides. The Hesperides were three nymphs who were descendants of Hesperus, the evening star. The name is from the Greek word for "west," since the evening star is always visible in the west after sunset. The Hesperides are thus the individuals to whom the garden belongs, but Shakespeare takes it to be a region in which the garden is located. Of course, Hercules must climb the tree if he is to get the apples, and the valor consists of doing so despite the fact that it is guarded by a fearsome dragon.

The Sphinx, in Greek mythology, was a monster with the body of a lion and the head of a woman. It was most notable for propounding riddles (hence it was "subtle"), which it forced those it met to answer. It killed those who could not answer correctly. Oedipus, on his way to Thebes, was faced with the riddle "What has sometimes two feet, sometimes three, sometimes four, and is weakest when it has most?" Oedipus at once answered, "Man, for he crawls on all fours as a baby, walks on two feet in youth, and needs a cane in old age." The Sphinx, in chagrin, killed herself.

Love's Labor's Lost is Shakespeare's tribute, then, to courtly love, and this speech is the clearest expression of it.

Berowne is convincing. The men decide to lay aside subterfuge, forget their resolutions, and woo the women.

Priscian . . .

Meanwhile Nathaniel the Curate and Holofernes the Pedant are discussing Armado. Holofernes finds fault with Armado, particularly in his fantastic manner of speech (as though Holofernes himself were not infinitely worse). Nathaniel drinks in the other's every word (writing down particularly good ones in his notebook). Nathaniel even tries a little Latin of his own, which Holofernes immediately corrects, saying:

> *Priscian a little scratched.*
>
> —Act V, scene i, lines 31–32

Priscian is the usual English name for Priscianus Caesariensis, a Latin grammarian at Constantinople about A.D. 500. His book on Latin grammar was the final authority through the Middle Ages, and it was common to say "to break Priscian's head" in characterizing any mistake in Latin. In this case the mistake is so minor (a single letter) that Holofernes is satisfied to say that Priscian was merely scratched.

. . . honorificabilitudinitatibus

Armado, Moth, and Costard come onstage. Holofernes and the Spaniard are immediately involved in complicated badinage and Moth comments ironically at their ability to use long words and involved phrases. Costard, with equal irony, wonders why Armado, who is so familiar with long words, doesn't swallow the diminutive Moth. He says:

> *I marvel thy master hath not eaten thee for a word; for thou art not so long by the head as honorificabilitudinitatibus.*
> —Act V, scene i, lines 42–44

This is the longest word in Shakespeare but it is not really used as a word, merely given as an example of a long word. It is Latin, of course, and is the ablative plural of a word meaning "honorableness." It has twenty-seven letters and is thought to be the longest word in Latin and, therefore, the longest word in English—at least in Shakespeare's time. Nowadays, it is "antidisestablishmentarianism" which is usually cited as longest, with twenty-eight letters. (It means the doctrine of opposition to the disestablishment of the Anglican Church and came into prominence in the nineteenth century.)

Actually, it is only those whose knowledge is limited to what are called the humanities who fall for this hoary old chestnut. In German, it is customary to run words together to make long compound words far longer than any in ordinary Latin or English. Since organic chemistry was almost entirely a German monopoly in the nineteenth century, the habit has persisted in naming organic chemicals, even in English. The intricate structure of organic chemicals requires an intricate naming system and there is, for instance, a chemical called "betadimethylaminobenzaldehyde," which is twenty-nine letters long and which is far from the longest possible.

. . . the Nine Worthies

Apparently the King is planning an entertainment that evening for the Princess. He has consulted Armado on what it should consist of and he, in turn, consults Holofernes. Holofernes makes an instant decision:

> *Sir, you shall present before her the Nine Worthies.*
> —Act V, scene i, lines 118–19

The Nine Worthies (see page II–401) are usually given as Hector, Alexander, Julius Caesar, Joshua, David, Judas Maccabeus, Arthur, Charlemagne, and Godfrey Bouillon.

· Holofernes does not go by this standard list, apparently. He starts assigning the different worthies to the people present and after mentioning Joshua and Judas Maccabeus, he says:

> . . . *this swain, because of his great limb or joint, shall pass*
> *Pompey the Great . . .*
>
> —Act V, scene i, lines 128–30

We can only suppose that Pompey the Great is substituted for Julius Caesar, and if this is so, it is a great mistake, for Caesar was far the greater man (see page I–257).

Saint Denis . . .

The last scene in *Love's Labor's Lost* is the longest in the play and, for that matter, in Shakespeare. It begins with the ladies coming together to talk about the fact that they have all received love tokens from the men. Boyet arrives to say he has overheard the men speaking and they have decided to woo the ladies in earnest.

The Princess says, lightly:

> *Saint Denis to Saint Cupid!*
>
> —Act V, scene ii, line 87

It is to be a merry war between the sexes in the tradition of courtly love. The men come to woo and the French ladies will resist. Saint Denis, the patron saint of France (see page II–515), will be opposed to the assaults of love, here represented as Saint Cupid.

Like Muscovites or Russians . . .

Boyet tells the ladies that the gentlemen will come to them in exotic costume, for they

> . . . *are apparelled thus—*
> *Like Muscovites or Russians . . .*
>
> —Act V, scene ii, lines 120–21

In Shakespeare's time, Russians were exotic and popular in England because of Chancellor's voyage (see page I–640).

The ladies therefore decide to wear masks and to switch their characteristic ribboned decorations ("favors") with one another, so that each man might think the wrong girl his and court at cross-purposes. This is done and the ladies utterly thwart the men first when they are disguised as Russians and then in their own persons.

Berowne in particular is forced, in frustration, to forswear the complexities of courtly love, at which the ladies win every time, and vows to be an honest lover henceforward. He says:

> Henceforth my wooing mind shall be expressed
> In russet yeas and honest kersey noes.
> —Act V, scene ii, lines 413–16

Russet and kersey are the color and material of homemade peasant clothing and Shakespeare thus expresses (as he usually does in his plays) his opinion of the superiority of plain Englishness over foreign ways and customs.

Whose club killed Cerberus . . .

But it is time now for the masque of the Nine Worthies to be presented by the various eccentrics of the play.

Costard comes in with a sonorous Pompey the Great. Nathaniel is a hesitant and easily rattled Alexander the Great, and then in come Holofernes and Moth as Judas Maccabeus and Hercules respectively. Holofernes speaks first for Moth with the expected scraps of Latin, saying:

> Great Hercules is presented by this imp
> Whose club killed Cerberus, that three-headed canus;
> And when he was a babe, a child, a shrimp,
> Thus did he strangle serpents in his manus.
> —Act V, scene ii, lines 586–89

The trite Latin rhyme of canus (dog) and manus (hand) reduces pedantry to its most foolish.

Hercules' twelfth and climactic labor was that of bringing into the upper world the three-headed hound Cerberus (see page I–101), who guarded the entrance to the underworld. He did not kill it, but brought it up alive as proof of the successful completion of the labor, then returned it.

When Hercules was a year old, according to legend, the jealous Juno (who was angry because Hercules was the offspring of one of Jupiter's many extramarital ventures) sent two serpents to kill him in the cradle. The infant Hercules seized each serpent in one of his baby fists and strangled it. The diminutive page is therefore not so ridiculous a representation of Hercules as might be thought. He represents Hercules, the Heroic Babe.

Dead . . .

The rest of the masque of the Nine Worthies is reduced to a shambles. Holofernes, trying to make the Judas Maccabeus speech for himself, is teased into silence. Armado, who comes next as Hector, can make no more headway.

Costard is urged on by Berowne to accuse Armado of making Jaquenetta pregnant, and for a minute the audience is made to think there will be a mock duel between the two, but all is interrupted by the arrival of a messenger. He comes with news of the Princess' father, the King of France. The Princess guesses at once:

> *Dead, for my life!*
> —Act V, scene ii, line 721

Henry III was stabbed on August 1, 1589, and died the next day. This may have nothing to do with the play at all, for there is a good chance it was written before then.

The French King's death, in the play, is a convenient device to end the developing and increasingly intense game of courtly love before it is forced to graduate into something else. The unreal world of the Navarrese court is forced to face reality, for the Princess must return to Paris to face the difficulties of a succession.

The men insist that though the game is over, their love is real. The ladies order them to remain austere, as they had originally planned to do, for one year anyway and if, at the end, they are still in love, that love will be returned.

And so love's labor is lost—for a year. Yet the audience may suppose that the year will pass and that love will then win.

15

THE TAMING OF THE SHREW

THE TAMING OF THE SHREW, written, possibly, in 1593 or 1594, is a play within a play. At least it starts out so with what Shakespeare calls an "Induction" ("Introduction") representing the frame within which the play proper is presented.

. . . Richard Conqueror

The Induction begins with Christopher Sly, more than half drunk, being thrown out of an alehouse by an irate landlady who demands money for the glasses he has broken; money he refuses to pay.

With the owlish gravity of drunkenness, he rejects the names she calls him. He says:

> . . . the Slys are no rogues. Look in the chronicles: we came in with Richard Conqueror.
>
> —Induction, scene i, lines 3–4

Christopher Sly is, as he says later, a tinker, a profession lost to the modern world. A tinker was a solderer and repairer of kettles, pots, and other such household metalware, the name of the profession coming from the tink-tink of a small hammer against the utensil.

It did not take much capital or much intelligence to be a tinker, and while tinkers acted as though they were general handy men, they usually couldn't go much beyond solder or a nail, so that we now have the verb "to tinker," meaning "to fiddle with, rather unskillfully."

Tinkers could scarcely make a living if they sat in one place and waited for neighbors' kettles to come apart. They were usually itinerant, carrying their few tools on their backs and going from village to village. They were distrusted, as strangers usually are, and perhaps a number of them used the tinker's equipment only as a blind and were really beggars, or even smalltime thieves and con men. At any rate, tinkers were traditionally considered rascals and rogues.

Christopher Sly, then, being a tinker, and showing himself in costume

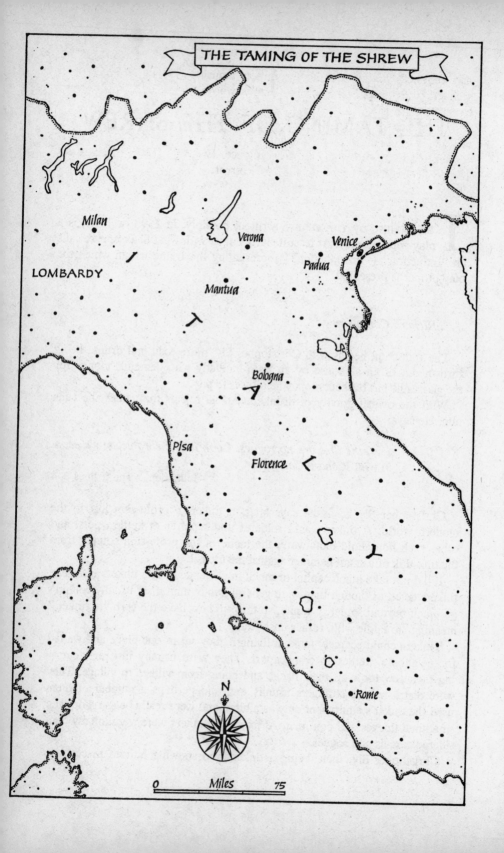

THE TAMING OF THE SHREW

Milan

LOMBARDY

Verona

Mantua

Venice

Padua

Bologna

Pisa

Florence

Rome

N

0   Miles   75

and action to be an utter no-account, is amusing in claiming to be descended from one of the Norman barons who conquered England in the eleventh century.

What's more, Sly's amalgamation of William the Conqueror and Richard the Lion-Hearted (the latter was the great-great-grandson of the former) helps the humor with the audience. Even the least sophisticated of the Elizabethans would surely catch the error.

. . . for Semiramis

Christopher Sly falls into a drunken slumber, just as a Lord and his hunting party come on the scene. Finding Sly, it occurs to the Lord to play an elaborate practical joke. They are to take Sly, dress him in fine clothes, and, when he wakes, convince him that he is a great nobleman who for many years has been mad and thought himself a pauper.

This is done, and in the second scene of the Induction, Sly, awakening with a call for small beer, finds himself attended by a variety of obsequious servants who wait on him with the greatest tenderness and with a wealth of classical allusions. The Lord himself plays a role as servant and says respectfully:

> . . . wilt thou sleep? We'll have thee to a couch
> Softer and sweeter than the lustful bed
> On purpose trimmed up for Semiramis.
> —Induction, scene ii, lines 37–39

Semiramis is the legendary Queen of Assyria who had become a byword, among the Greeks, for luxury (see page I–403).

Adonis painted . . .

Among other things, they offer Sly a choice of paintings dealing with mythological subjects. Thus, one servant says:

> . . . We will fetch thee straight
> Adonis painted by a running brook
> And Cytherea all in sedges hid,
> —Induction, scene ii, lines 49–51

This refers to the myth of Venus and Adonis, concerning which Shakespeare had written a long poem a year or two before he wrote this play (see page I–5).

Cytherea is an alternate name for Venus, derived from the fact that an important seat of her worship was the island of Cythera, just off the southeastern corner of Greece.

We'll show thee Io . . .

The Lord offers a second choice:

> *We'll show thee Io as she was a maid*
> *And how she was beguilèd and surprised.*
>   —Induction, scene ii, lines 54–55

Io was a daughter of the river god Inachus in the Greek myths, and Jupiter fell in love with her. The myth has nothing to say about how Io was "beguilèd and surprised," though Jupiter used guile on other young ladies, notably Europa (see page I–44). The myth concentrates instead on the manner in which Jupiter's jealous wife, Juno, persecuted Io afterward (see page I–86).

. . . Daphne roaming . . .

A third choice is presented:

> *Or Daphne roaming through a thorny wood,*
> *Scratching her legs that one shall swear she bleeds,*
> *And at that sight shall sad Apollo weep,*
>   —Induction, scene ii, lines 57–59

Daphne was a nymph sworn to virginity whom Apollo loved. She rejected his advances and fled from him when he tried to seize her. He pursued and would have caught her, but at the last minute, her mother, Gaea (the earth goddess), turned her into a laurel tree.

Little by little, then, Sly is convinced that after all he is a lord. He even begins to speak in blank verse instead of the usual prose. And to cap the climax, a play is presented for his edification, and it is this play which is what we usually think of as *The Taming of the Shrew.*

. . . fair Padua . . .

The play within a play opens with two young men, Lucentio and his servant Tranio, entering. Lucentio summarizes the situation:

Tranio, since for the great desire I had
To see fair Padua, nursery of arts,
I am arrived for fruitful Lombardy,

—Act I, scene i, lines 1–3

Padua is a city in northeastern Italy a little over twenty miles west of Venice and noted for its university.

Medieval Italy was, in fact, famous for its universities, for learning had taken new root there while it was still all but dead in the countries beyond the Alps. The first medieval university was established in Bologna, eighty miles southwest of Venice, in 1088. It specialized in the study of Roman law and remained the great center of legal studies for centuries afterward.

Bologna had its quarrels and problems and, on occasion, its schisms. In 1222 a group of its professors and students broke away and established a competing university at Padua, and it was this which made that city the "nursery of arts." It, as well as Bologna, supported a great law school and the two were great rivals.

Padua was an independent city-state through the Middle Ages but in 1405 it was absorbed into the territory of the Venetian republic and was still part of it in Shakespeare's time (and remained so till 1797). Padua was not actually part of Lombardy in the medieval or modern sense. Lombardy is located in northwestern Italy with Milan as its chief city, and even at its closest approach, Lombardy is fifty miles west of Padua.

This, however, is not as bad as it sounds. In the eighth century all of northern Italy was under the control of the Lombards and the term might therefore be used in a poetic sense for northern Italy generally. (Nevertheless, Shakespeare may well have been a little hazy on the fine points of Italian geography. This shows up more clearly elsewhere.)

Pisa . . .

Lucentio has come to Padua for an education, but he pauses also to announce his birthplace:

Pisa, renownèd for grave citizens,
Gave me my being . . .

—Act I, scene i, lines 10–11

Pisa is located on the western coast of Italy, about 140 miles southwest of Padua. During the Middle Ages it was for a time a great commercial city, the rival of Genoa and Venice. It was at its height between 1050 and 1250, and in 1173 it built what is now its leading feature, a bell tower that, through some flaw in its foundation, settled out of the vertical. It is the Leaning Tower of Pisa.

Toward the end of the thirteenth century Pisa was defeated in a long war with Genoa and began a steady decline. In 1406 it was captured by the forces of the city of Florence, forty-five miles to its east, and remained under Florentine domination through Shakespeare's time (and, indeed, until 1860). In fact, Lucentio describes himself as:

> *Vincentio's son, brought up in Florence,*
> —Act I, scene i, line 14

Florence, the home city of Dante, was the very epitome of Renaissance culture. It was the Athens of Italy, and one would boast of being brought up there as one might boast of having been brought up in Athens in ancient times or in Paris in modern times.

As Ovid . . .

Tranio is a little nervous at Lucentio's grandiloquent speech, for he views with some concern the prospect of a close course of study. He says:

> *Let's be no stoics nor no stocks, I pray,*
> *Or so devote to Aristotle's checks*
> *As* [to make] *Ovid be an outcast quite abjured.*
> —Act I, scene i, lines 31–33

Tranio's distaste for Stoics (see page I–305) or for Aristotle (see page I–104) is not so puzzling in a merry young man.

As for Ovid, whom he prefers, his best-known work is his *Metamorphoses* (see page I–8). However, a more notorious piece of work was his *Ars Amatoria* (*The Art of Love*), which gave, in witty and amusing style, a course in seduction for young men.

Ovid insisted it was intended to deal only with the relations of young men and women of easy virtue, but it could easily be applied to anyone, of course, and the Emperor Augustus, a very moral man, was outraged at its publication. It was one of the reasons why Ovid was banished to a far corner of the Empire a few years later.

It is undoubtedly *The Art of Love* of which Tranio is thinking, and he is urging Lucentio not to be so wrapped up in his studies as to forget to have a little fun now and then.

. . . hear Minerva speak

Tranio need not have worried. Lucentio is, actually, all on the side of Ovid too, and something comes up at once to prove it.

A rich merchant of Padua, Baptista, comes on the scene with his two daughters, Katherina (or, for short, Kate) and Bianca. Trailing him are two other men also, the aged Gremio and the younger Hortensio.

Both Gremio and Hortensio are clamoring for the hand of Bianca, the younger daughter, a gentle girl, who stands with eyes cast down and rarely speaks. (Her very name means "white," as though to emphasize her colorlessness.)

Baptista will have none of this, however. He will not allow Bianca to marry until the elder sister, Kate, is married. The two suitors can have their chance at her. If one marries her the other may woo Bianca.

But it turns out at once that Kate is a furious shrew, whose every word is a threat, whose eyes flash fire, and who is ready at a moment's notice to commit mayhem. The two suitors climb over each other in an attempt to get away from her.

Tranio and Lucentio are watching from the sidelines. Tranio is amazed at the shrewishness of Kate, but Lucentio has eyes only for the gentle Bianca. When Bianca humbly accepts her father's delay of her marriage, Lucentio is ravished with her modest words. He says to Tranio:

> Hark, Tranio, thou mayst hear Minerva speak.
> —Act I, scene i, line 84

Minerva was the Roman goddess of wisdom (her very name may be related to *mens*, meaning "mind") and is the analogue of the Greek Athena.

. . . love-in-idleness

Baptista and his daughters go off, but not till after the father mentions in passing that he is looking for a music teacher for Bianca.

Gremio and Hortensio look after them in chagrin and decide that the only way they can manage to pursue their suit of Bianca is to find some madman, somehow, who will be willing to marry Katherina. After all, Baptista is enormously rich, so that Katherina (considering her shrewishness and the difficulty of getting rid of her) would command a huge dowry.

They leave too, and Lucentio comes out of his wide-eyed trance to find himself deeply in love at first sight with Bianca. He says to Tranio:

> But see, while idly I stood looking on,
> I found the effect of love-in-idleness.
> —Act I, scene i, lines 150–51

Love-in-idleness is the pansy, which was thought in Elizabethan nature folklore to have the effect of a love potion (see page I-34). Lucentio decides to be utterly frank about his feelings and plans, for he says to Tranio:

> Thou art to me as secret and as dear
> As Anna to the Queen of Carthage was,
>
> —Act I, scene i, lines 153–54

Anna was the sister of Dido (see page I-20) and her confidante. Lucentio goes on to say:

> . . . I saw sweet beauty in her face,
> Such as the daughter of Agenor had,
> That made great Jove to humble him to her hand
> When with his knees he kissed the Cretan strond.
>
> —Act I, scene i, lines 166–70

Agenor was a mythical king of Tyre and his daughter was Europa, for whose sake Zeus (Jupiter, or Jove) turned himself into a bull and with her swam to Crete (see page I-44).

Love gives Lucentio an idea. He will impersonate a schoolmaster and get the post teaching Bianca. While he is doing this, his servant, Tranio, can pretend to be Lucentio, performing the educational and social tasks that the real Lucentio ought to be doing (and concerning which his father, Vincentio, back in Pisa, will expect to hear of now and then).

. . . Would 'twere done

At the end of the first scene, attention is suddenly drawn to Christopher Sly, the tinker, sitting in the balcony. He is dreadfully bored, but doesn't like to say so. When the page, who is pretending to be his wife, asks how he likes it, he says:

> 'Tis a very excellent piece of work, madam lady. Would 'twere done!
>
> —Act I, scene i, lines 252–53

But Christopher Sly is done, for we hear no more of him ever. From this point on, the play within a play is the play itself, while Christopher Sly, the Lord who fools him, and all the play-acting servants vanish from the scene.

It's possible that Shakespeare simply forgot about them. Shakespeare had, apparently, borrowed the device from an earlier anonymous play,

The Taming of a Shrew ("a" rather than "the"), which used the play within a play technique. It may be, however, that Shakespeare got so interested in the play about the shrew that he grew impatient with the outer frame as merely serving to get in his way and dropped it.

Why, then, did he not go back and cross out the Induction and these few lines at the end of the first scene? In this connection, we must take into account the legend that Shakespeare prided himself on never revising.

Another possibility is that Shakespeare did keep the frame but that the later parts were omitted by accident from the particular copy that survived and was used as the basis for the first collection of his plays.

Verona, for a while . . .

The second scene opens with the entrance of Petruchio, the hero of the play. He says:

> *Verona, for a while I take my leave*
> *To see my friends in Padua . . .*
> —Act I, scene ii, lines 1–2

Verona is another city of northern Italy and is located some forty miles west of Padua. In Shakespeare's time, Verona, like Padua, was part of the Venetian republic.

. . . Florentius' love

Petruchio is accompanied by his servant, Grumio, and together they are on the doorstep of Hortensio's house, Hortensio being one of the friends Petruchio has come to see.

There is a contretemps at once, one designed to show that Petruchio is as great a shrew in his way as Katherina is in hers. He orders Grumio to knock at the gate, but Grumio takes him to mean to strike Petruchio himself, and refuses. There is a loud clamor, at which Hortensio opens the door.

Petruchio and Hortensio embrace each other and the former explains that he has come to Padua to seek his fortune. Hortensio at once has the notion of suggesting that Petruchio marry Katherina but, remembering her shrewishness, hesitates to play so foul a trick on a friend.

Petruchio, however, urges him on. He is after money and that is the only requirement he has. Aside from that:

Be she as foul as was Florentius' love,
As old as Sibyl, and as curst and shrewd
As Socrates' Xanthippe or a worse,
She moves me not . . .

—Act I, scene ii, lines 68–71

Florentius is the name of a knight in *Confessio Amantis* by John Gower (see page I–181). The plot is one in which a knight is forced to marry a horrible old hag who has helped him in time of need and who requires the marriage as recompense. The reward to the knight for keeping his word is that the hag turns into a beautiful maiden after the marriage.

"Sibyl" is from the Greek *sibylla,* their name for a priestess attached to a shrine or temple who had the ability to utter prophecies. Such a woman would fall into real or pretended fits (which may have been drug-induced) and would utter incoherent sounds which a priest would then interpret in the form of carefully ambiguous sentences.

Sibyls were supposed to attain great ages, for after all, an old woman, with her great experience, might more plausibly be expected to have arcane knowledge than a young one. Besides, prior to the nineteenth century, births of common people were not registered and individuals who lived to their seventies were rare. A wrinkled old crone was an unusual and somewhat frightening sight and it was easy to believe she had strange powers (of a sibyl in ancient times, of a witch in later times) and had lived for a century and more.

A mythic explanation is that Sibylla, beloved by Apollo, offered to give herself to him in return for the gift of prophecy and for as many years of life as the grains of sand which she could hold in her hand. When Apollo granted the wish and Sibylla reneged on her own promise, the angry god pointed out that the girl had asked for years of life and not for youth and allowed her to grow older and older and older.

As for Xanthippe, she was Socrates' wife, and the tales told of her show her to have been a scolding shrew. To be sure, any impartial person would have to admit she had some justification, since Socrates neglected his family to wander about the market place, talking philosophy and teaching rich noblemen without pay, so that his family was always in want. Nevertheless, people aren't impartial. Since Socrates is thought of as the wisest of men and as a kind of pagan saint, Xanthippe is frowned upon for complaining.

Fair Leda's daughter . . .

The complications grow. Petruchio insists he will woo and win Katherina for her money, quite without regard for her shrewishness. Whereupon it occurs to Hortensio (as earlier it had occurred, independently, to Lucentio) to disguise himself as a teacher and be brought to the house under the patronage of Petruchio. If Petruchio offers to woo Katherina, surely the delighted Baptista will accept his protégé for the post of teacher and Hortensio would then be on the inside track with Bianca.

At this point, though, in comes Gremio, with no one other than the disguised Lucentio. Gremio is going to sponsor the disguised Lucentio for the post of teacher, planning to have the man plead Gremio's cause with Bianca. Then in comes Tranio, in fancy clothes, disguised as his master, Lucentio. He too is heading for Baptista's house to woo Bianca.

When Gremio and Hortensio object, the disguised Tranio says grandly:

> Fair Leda's daughter had a thousand wooers;
> Then well one more may fair Bianca have.
> And so she shall. Lucentio shall make one,
> Though Paris came in hope to speed alone.
> —Act I, scene ii, lines 243–46

Leda was a queen of Sparta with whom Jupiter fell in love. He visited her in the shape of a swan with the result that eventually Leda laid an egg, out of which Helen was hatched. Helen, as the very epitome of womanly beauty, naturally had many wooers (see page I-90), but was eventually snatched away by Paris.

There are thus four men now after Bianca. There is 1) Gremio; 2) Hortensio, soon to be disguised as a teacher; 3) Lucentio, already disguised as a teacher; and 4) Tranio, disguised as Lucentio.

All understand though that everything depends on how Petruchio fares with Katherina, and Gremio says, gloomily, that that task is liable to be harder than Hercules' twelve labors put together.

. . . dance barefoot . . .

In Baptista's house, meanwhile, Katherina the Shrew is cruelly baiting her younger sister, Bianca, whose hands she has bound. Katherina is demanding to know which of Bianca's many suitors the younger girl likes best, and one may easily suppose that Kate is annoyed at the ease with which Bianca gains love, while she herself remains with no one.

This is made the clearer when Baptista comes in, rescues Bianca, and scolds Katherina. Katherina at once accuses Baptista of favoritism:

> Nay, now I see
> She is your treasure, she must have a husband;
> I must dance barefoot on her wedding day,
> And, for your love to her, lead apes in hell.
> —Act II, scene i, lines 31–34

To dance barefoot on the wedding day symbolizes the humiliation of an older unmarried sister on the occasion of a younger sister's marriage. Leading apes in hell is the traditional fate of women who die spinsters.

Shakespeare seems to be making it quite clear that Katherina is a girl who desperately wants love and who doesn't know how to go about getting it. She lacks the natural charm that is so often visible in a quiet, simpering girl, and the fascination that goes with a spirited temper is somewhat less obvious.

Shakespeare does not give us the early history of Katherina, but it is not difficult to suppose that her temper was nothing out of the ordinary till a younger sister came along. A quieter little girl, a younger, the baby of the family, would draw the attention of the father, and with every sign of favoritism, Kate would grow wilder in her indignation and Baptista would cling all the more closely to the little one.

There is no sign that Baptista is actually cruel to Kate, and he *is* trying to get her a husband, but he cannot conceal the fact that he likes Bianca better, so that the vicious cycle continues till Katherina is virtually mad for lack of love and in becoming so has made it impossible for herself to receive love even if it were offered—or almost impossible.

. . . in Mantua

Now the pack of suitors enters Baptista's house. Petruchio tackles his Hercules' labor at once, announcing himself in affable fashion, and stating that he has come to woo Katherina, of whose mild and sweet behavior he has heard a great deal. While Baptista stands there gasping at this novel description of his older daughter, Petruchio blandly introduces Hortensio in disguise, urging his acceptance as a music teacher. Petruchio says of his disguised friend:

> *His name is Litio, born in Mantua.*
>
> —Act II, scene i, line 60

Thus, another north Italian city is mentioned. Mantua is sixty miles southwest of Padua.

. . . at Rheims . . .

Old Gremio has his ax to grind too. He wants his teacher (the disguised Lucentio) in the house for his own purposes (though he hasn't an inkling that his candidate for the post fully intends to double-cross him). Gremio introduces the disguised Lucentio under the name of Cambio.

Since the disguised Hortensio has been put forward as a specialist in music and mathematics, Gremio avoids those subjects in order to get his man hired as well. He introduces him, saying:

> . . . this young scholar that hath been long studying at
> Rheims—as cunning in Greek, Latin, and other languages, as
> the other in music and mathematics.
>> —Act II, scene i, lines 79–82

Rheims (Reims) is not an Italian, but a French city, and is located five hundred miles northwest of Padua. Its distance and its foreignness may serve to give the disguised Lucentio an exotic cachet that would be particularly valued in a teacher. Reims is chiefly noted for the fact that the kings of France were traditionally crowned there (see page II–539).

Tranio also introduces himself as Lucentio, thus (presumably) making it easier for the real Lucentio to avoid discovery and allowing a two-pronged attack on Bianca. The real Lucentio would win her love for his person, and Tranio, in the guise of Lucentio, would win her father's official permission.

. . . my super-dainty Kate

Meanwhile, Petruchio asks permission to woo Katherina at once, pleading haste. Hortensio, who has gone inside to teach the girls music, comes flying out with the lute broken over his head, thanks to Katherina's shrewish temper. Petruchio isn't fazed at all. As soon as Katherina enters, breathing fire, he is at her at once, insisting on calling her only by the familiar version of her name. He says:

> . . . you are called plain Kate,
> And bonny Kate, and sometimes Kate the curst.
> But, Kate, the prettiest Kate in Christendom,
> Kate of Kate Hall, my super-dainty Kate,
> For dainties are all Kates . . .
>> —Act II, scene i, lines 185–89

In Shakespeare's time "cates" were delicacies, luxury foods, and, of course, Petruchio is playing the pun for all it is worth.

. . . a second Grissel

Katherina hears herself praised in a fashion she has never experienced before, but, alas, she cannot accept it. Nothing will convince her that she is not being ridiculed, so she fights it off, in the old, old way, making it impossible for herself to receive what she most longs to receive.

But Petruchio is patient, and when after a long battle of wits, she is no less shrewish than she was at the beginning, he simply praises her to her father and announces success. He says to Baptista:

> . . . she's not froward but modest as the dove.
> She is not hot but temperate as the morn;
> For patience she will prove a second Grissel
> And Roman Lucrece for her chastity.
> And to conclude, we have 'greed so well together
> That upon Sunday is the wedding day.
> —Act II, scene i, lines 286–91

Grissel is a variant form of Griselda, the heroine of the last tale in Boccaccio's *Decameron,* a tale picked up by Chaucer and included in his *Canterbury Tales.* The tale is of an Italian nobleman who marries a beautiful and virtuous lowborn maiden named Griselda, whom he proceeds to test. He pretends to kill the two children she bears him, pretends to tire of her and marry a younger woman, and so on. Through a set of unbelievable trials, Griselda remains unbelievably patient and is finally rewarded by being restored to her own in full with her children about her. Griselda has ever since been a byword for patience.

Lucrece is Shakespeare's favorite pattern of chastity (see page I–205).

. . . unto Venice

Katherina protests vociferously against the notion of marriage and those who hear this are amused. Petruchio is, however, perfectly calm. Ignoring Kate's shrewish anger, he says:

> . . . I will unto Venice
> To buy apparel 'gainst the wedding day.
> —Act II, scene i, lines 307–8

Venice was the richest of the Italian cities. As a great trading center, it was bound to have merchandise from all over the world and therefore a wonderful selection of clothes.

. . . "supposed Vincentio"

With Katherina taken care of, Bianca must be disposed of. Hortensio is still playing his role as teacher, which leaves Gremio and the disguised Tranio (playing the role of Lucentio) as two official suitors who happen to be on the spot. Baptista offers to give Bianca to whichever of these two can offer more.

The two start bidding. Since Tranio is not really bidding on his own, he can easily raise the other's bid every time until Gremio is forced out of the competition. On the other hand, Gremio controls his own wealth, whereas Tranio, pretending to be Lucentio, has nothing at all unless his father confirms the bid.

Baptista therefore says that Tranio (the supposed Lucentio) can have Bianca if his father will guarantee what Tranio has promised; otherwise Gremio can have her.

This leaves Tranio rather in a fix. Since he's not really Lucentio, he can't really deal with Lucentio's father, Vincentio. Well then, there will have to be still another imposture:

> *I see no reason but supposed Lucentio*
> *Must get a father, called "supposed Vincentio."*
> —Act II, scene i, lines 400–1

Indoors, meanwhile, the disguised Lucentio and the disguised Hortensio are both teaching Bianca and actually whispering love messages in competition. It becomes clear that Bianca prefers Lucentio.

To me she's married . . .

Petruchio now puts in his plan to tame Katherina. He is deliberately late for the wedding and when he does come, it is in an impossible costume. He was supposed to have gone to Venice for gorgeous clothing, but he arrives in old, unmatched clothes and riding a horse so old and sick it can barely move.

The gathered wedding guests are horrified. Surely he cannot mean to let Katherina see him so, let alone marry him so. But he says:

> *Good sooth, even thus; therefore ha' done with words.*
> *To me she's married, not unto my clothes.*
> —Act III, scene ii, lines 116–17

It is the key to Petruchio's scheme. Katherina must accept him for whatever he is and even for whatever he pretends to be; but she must *accept.*

He continues his mad behavior at the wedding, which takes place offstage and which Gremio describes for the audience. Petruchio swears his acceptance of Katherina, strikes the priest, throws wine at the sexton, and kisses the bride with a sound like a cannon report.

Once they are back from the church, Petruchio announces he must go away at once, with Katherina. All beg him to stay for the wedding feast. He refuses. Katherina begs. He still refuses.

Whereupon Katherina falls into a fury and orders the wedding feast to proceed. Petruchio agrees, but it must proceed without them. He seizes Katherina and says fiercely to the assembled guests:

> I will be master of what is mine own.
> She is my goods, my chattels; she is my house,
> My household stuff, my field, my barn,
> My horse, my ox, my ass, my anything,
> And here she stands. Touch her whoever dare.
>
> —Act III, scene ii, lines 229–33

There is a glancing reference here to the tenth commandment, which begins "Thou shalt not covet" (see Exodus 21:17) and in listing the examples of objects belonging to a neighbor that must not be coveted, ends with "nor his ox, nor his ass, nor anything that is thy neighbour's."

There is a strong temptation for males watching the play to feel pleased with Petruchio at this point, but our better natures must assert themselves. This bald assertion of male superiority that treats women as commodities, as animals, as objects, is quite out of line with modern thinking.

It is quite common to excuse Shakespeare by saying that such male domination was taken for granted in Elizabethan society and that Shakespeare was just echoing his time—but Shakespeare does not take this attitude in any other play. Shakespeare's heroines are, if anything, wiser, more capable, and better than his heroes. We can reasonably assume, then, that Petruchio is doing more than merely express a common attitude toward women—this is all part of his plan and nothing deeper than that.

. . . in her own humor

Petruchio brings Katherina to his country house. He has been in a shrewish rage all the way, according to his servant, Grumio, who arrives there first. When Petruchio comes onstage, he continues to seem mad with passion. Kate can't rest, eat, or sleep for his yelling and discontent with everything.

This, however, merely continues the role he has been playing since the day of his wooing. The servants who know him aren't fooled. One says:

> He kills her in her own humor.
>
> —Act IV, scene i, line 174

And Petruchio himself, in a soliloquy, tells the audience:

> *Thus have I politicly* [calculatedly] *begun my reign,*
> *And 'tis my hope to end successfully.*
> —Act IV, scene i, lines 182–83

Of course, Petruchio has the money for which he married Katherina. But he wants, we may suppose, a quiet, loving wife too, and it is for this he plans his course of action.

. . . the Art to Love

Meanwhile Lucentio's wooing progresses wonderfully well. In his guise as a schoolmaster teaching Latin, he says:

> *I read that I profess, the Art to Love.*
> —Act IV, scene ii, line 8

This is Ovid's book which had been indirectly hinted at by Tranio at the very start of the play. The disguised Lucentio says he not only reads *The Art to Love,* he practices it, and Bianca demurely says she hopes he's good at it.

Hortensio, in his guise as Litio the music teacher, is outraged at Bianca's open preference for someone who seems a lowborn rascal, and abandons her, saying he will go marry a widow who has long been after him.

. . . as far as Rome

But while Bianca is accepting the real Lucentio, Tranio (the false Lucentio) must find a false Vincentio to win over Bianca's father. At last an old Pedant who looks the part comes onstage and Tranio stops him and asks if he is traveling on. The Pedant says:

> *. . . up farther and as far as Rome,*
> *And so to Tripoli if God lend me life.*
> —Act IV, scene ii, lines 75–76

It is a longish journey he plans. It is 250 miles overland due south from Padua to Rome, and then 600 miles across the sea to Tripoli, which is on the north African coast.

When asked where he is from, he answers:

Of Mantua.

—Act IV, scene ii, line 77

Mantua is sixty miles west of Padua, so that if he has come to Padua from Mantua on his way to Rome, he has gone at right angles to his proper course. But then, he may not have come directly from Mantua.

In any case, Tranio at once invents a proclamation in Padua, announcing death to all Mantuans in the city because of some high political quarrel, and offers to save the Pedant's life by allowing him to pose as a Pisan; that is, as Vincentio. The Pedant gratefully accepts.

. . . perfect love

Katherina is slowly wearing down from lack of food and sleep. She is trying to beg food from Petruchio's servant, Grumio, saying that she is

> *. . . starved for meat, giddy for lack of sleep,*
> *With oaths kept waking and with brawling fed.*
> *And that which spites me more than all these wants,*
> *He does it under name of perfect love.*

—Act IV, scene iii, lines 9–12

Surely, this is a key passage. He is wearing her down and forcing her to accept whatever she is offered, not out of cruelty, but in order to force her eventually to accept the one important thing—love.

It is precisely this which is hardest for her to accept, for, as she says, she is more annoyed at being offered love than at being denied food and sleep. And it is precisely love which she *must* accept.

. . . what o'clock I say it is

For all her begging, though, Katherina continues to get no food. What's more, Petruchio promises her clothes but when the haberdasher and tailor arrive, he is utterly discontented with what they offer. Although Katherina cries out that she likes them, he will have none of them, and when Katherina protests, he calmly pretends she is agreeing with him.

They make ready to go to Padua and visit Katherina's father without new clothes, but in exactly what they are wearing. Petruchio casually says it is seven o'clock and Kate tells him, politely enough, that it is two. Whereupon Petruchio falls into a passion:

I will not go today, and ere I do,
It shall be what o'clock I say it is.

> —Act IV, scene iii, lines 192–93

That is what Petruchio is after. He must train Katherina to accept as true whatever he says, however ridiculous it must seem to her.

. . . moon or star . . .

The Pedant in the guise of old Vincentio goes through the matter of the dowry with old Baptista in very satisfactory fashion, and while the fathers are thus engaged, the real Lucentio makes ready to elope with Bianca.

Meanwhile Petruchio and Katherina (along with Hortensio) are on the road to Padua. Petruchio comments on the brightness of the moon. Katherina points out it is the sun. Whereupon Petruchio falls into a rage again, and says:

Now by my mother's son, and that's myself,
It shall be moon or star or what I list,
Or ere I journey to your father's house.

> —Act IV, scene v, lines 6–8

Finally Katherina breaks down and says, wearily:

Forward, I pray, since we have come so far,
And be it moon or sun or what you please.
And if you please to call it a rush-candle,
Henceforth I vow it shall be so for me.

> —Act IV, scene v, lines 12–15

Petruchio puts her through her paces, making her say first that the object in the sky is the moon, then the sun. When they meet an old man, he has Katherina greet him first as a young maiden and then apologize and greet him as an old man. Katherina follows the flicking of Petruchio's whip perfectly, accepting whatever he says as true.

And that prepares her to accept the one thing he has constantly been saying from the moment he met her—*that he loves her*.

Thus, by bending Katherina to his will, Petruchio has used a temporary brutality to force the girl to accept what most in the world she has longed to accept—the love of a man. Now, and now only, she can be content.

. . . kiss me, Kate . . .

The old man that Petruchio and Katherina have met happens to be Vincentio, the *real* Vincentio, coming to Padua to see his son. Once he gets there, he goes nearly mad with frustration, for the Pedant claims *he* is Vincentio and Tranio claims he is Lucentio, so that the true Vincentio can't make himself believed.

He is saved only by the appearance of the real Lucentio, who is now married to Bianca. Baptista is a little annoyed at the ruse that has kept him from giving Bianca to Gremio, but the real Vincentio approves the match and the two fathers will now settle everything.

There is another wedding feast and when Katherina wants to join the happy throng, Petruchio says:

> *First kiss me, Kate, and we will.*
>
> —Act V, scene i, line 142

Katherina begins to object, for they are in the middle of the street in broad daylight. Petruchio, however, frowns, and Katherina hastily kisses him as nicely as you please. Petruchio says:

> *Is not this well? Come my sweet Kate.*
>
> —Act V, scene i, line 149

Of course, it is well. By the kiss, Katherina shows that she has accepted love. It is the triumph of Petruchio, a triumph for love and not for brutality, and Cole Porter did well to name his own musical version of the play *Kiss me, Kate.*

. . . she cannot come

At the wedding feast all is gay, and Petruchio, in perfect good humor now, has to withstand a number of quips about being married to a shrew. He waits till the women are gone and proposes a wager. The three newly married men, Lucentio, Hortensio, and himself, are each to send, separately, for their wives. The man with the most obedient wife wins a hundred crowns.

Lucentio sends first, in perfect confidence. The answer comes back by way of a servant:

> *Sir, my mistress sends you word*
> *That she is busy and she cannot come.*
>
> —Act V, scene ii, lines 79–80

The widow whom Hortensio has married does even worse; for the word comes back:

> *She says you have some goodly jest in hand.*
> *She will not come. She bids you come to her.*
>
> —Act V, scene ii, lines 91–92

It is not really surprising that sweet Bianca doesn't come. Why should she? She has spent her whole life being sweet Bianca, and simpering and exuding charm, for only one purpose—to catch a man (first her father, then her husband). Well, her catching days are over, at least for a while, and now she means to relax. Wouldn't anyone after a lifetime of work?

The same for the widow, doubly, since she has had to work a second time to catch a second husband.

I command . . .

Lucentio in sending for his wife had told his servant to "bid your mistress." Hortensio, after Bianca's failure, had said "entreat" instead. Petruchio scorns all softness. He says:

> *Sirrah Grumio, go to your mistress; say*
> *I command her come to me.*
>
> —Act V, scene ii, lines 95–96

And to everyone's surprise, she does come, in perfect obedience. And again, why not? She had not labored to win love. It had been Petruchio who had labored to give love, and she has every reason to be grateful.

At his command, Katherina goes back to bring in the other two wives, and the gentle Bianca, when she hears about the lost wager, says to Lucentio:

> *The more fool you for laying* [betting] *on my duty.*
>
> —Act V, scene ii, line 129

Who's the shrew now?

Petruchio orders Kate to deliver the women a long lecture on the duty they owe their husband and she does, saying in part:

> *I am ashamed that women are so simple*
> *To offer war where they should kneel for peace,*
>
> —Act V, scene ii, lines 161–62

It may seem that this final speech is one long irony and that what Katherina has learned has been to show a false acquiescence so that she can rule her husband by pretending to be ruled by him. (In the movie version with Richard Burton and Elizabeth Taylor, this interpretation is implied in the very last post-speech action.)

Yet it is not necessary to suppose this. It doesn't matter who "rules." Petruchio and Katherina are in love and as long as love exists, "ruler" and "ruled" lose their meaning. Petruchio looked only for money, and got love too. Katherina looked for nothing and got love. It is a completely happy ending.

16

THE TWO GENTLEMEN OF

VERONA

O F SHAKESPEARE'S early comedies, *The Two Gentlemen of Verona*, written about 1594, is perhaps the most forgettable. It is so weak, in fact, that some critics think it may have been written as early as 1590 or else that the version we now have is a mangled copy of the real play.

Shakespeare may have used as his source material for the play an unfinished romance, *Diana Enamorada,* written in Spanish by a Portugal-born poet, Jorge de Montemayor, in 1542. The only difficulty with that suggestion is that the romance was not translated into English until 1598, some four years after *The Two Gentlemen of Verona* was written. We might speculate that Shakespeare saw the English translation in manuscript or that he saw the French translation, which had appeared in 1578.

Verona, where the play opens, is a city in north-central Italy. It is a favorite setting for Renaissance comedy and was briefly mentioned in *The Taming of the Shrew* as the home town of Petruchio (see page I-451). It is also the home town of the two friends who are protagonists in this play.

. . . young Leander . . .

The play opens with the two gentlemen of Verona on the scene. They are Valentine and Proteus. The latter name is significant. In Greek mythology, Proteus was an infinitely changeable sea deity (see page II-655), and much of the action in this play is produced by the changeable character of the Proteus we now meet.

Valentine and Proteus, it seems, are about to part. Valentine is setting off on his travels, for in Shakespeare's time, a period of travel in youth was considered an essential part of the education of a young man.

Proteus, however, prefers to remain at home in Verona, for he is in love with a young lady and will not leave her. Valentine teases Proteus, saying that the latter is so lovesick that even in praying, he will do so . . .

> *. . . on some shallow story of deep love:*
> *How young Leander crossed the Hellespont.*
> —Act I, scene i, lines 21–22

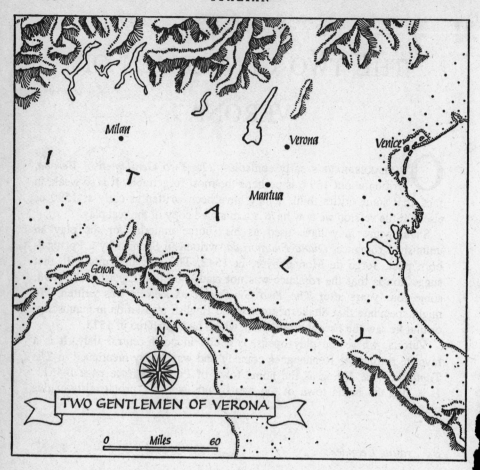

TWO GENTLEMEN OF VERONA

0   Miles   60

The Hellespont (better known today as the Dardanelles) is a narrow strait, about forty miles long, separating Turkey and Greece, and it forms part of the waterway connecting the Black Sea with the Mediterranean. At its narrowest it is only three fourths of a mile wide. On the European side in ancient times was the Greek city of Sestos, where a beautiful young girl, Hero, served as priestess of Aphrodite, according to a tale that was told in antiquity and that has never lost its popularity. On the Asian side, in the Greek city of Abydos, lived a handsome youth named Leander.

Hero and Leander met at a festival and fell instantly in love. Thereafter, every night Leander swam the Hellespont to be with Hero, guided by a light she placed in her window. One stormy night, the light was blown out and Leander lost his way and was drowned. When his dead body was washed ashore, the grief-stricken Hero plunged into the waters to her own death.

The tale is a favorite of Shakespeare's. He mentions it several times.

To Milan . . .

But Valentine must leave and the two friends cannot talk long. Valentine says:

> *Once more adieu! My father at the road*
> *Expects my coming, there to see me shipped.*
>   —Act I, scene i, lines 53–54

Verona isn't a seaport, to be sure. It is sixty-five miles from the sea. Perhaps Valentine means to travel overland to Venice and take ship there; or to travel to the sea by way of the Adige River, on which Verona is located. That depends, of course, on where he is going, and he tells us quickly, for he says to Proteus:

> *To Milan let me hear from thee by letters*
> *Of thy success in love . . .*
>   —Act I, scene i, lines 57–58

But Milan is not a seaport either (it is seventy-five miles north of Genoa) and cannot be reached directly by sea. One has the vision of Valentine traveling sixty-five miles to Venice, taking ship all around Italy to Genoa, a voyage of about one thousand four hundred miles, and then traveling seventy-five miles overland to Milan.

This is scarcely necessary, since in actual fact Milan is only ninety miles due west of Verona over undoubtedly well-traveled roads. One can argue, of course, that there were ways of traveling from Verona to Milan by inland waterways, but it is much more likely that Shakespeare simply didn't bother checking his geography. Nor need he have really. The audience wouldn't care and the actual cities have nothing to do with the story. It might just as well have been London and Amsterdam with an appropriate sea voyage between.

Attends the Emperor . . .

With Valentine gone, Proteus turns his attention to his love for Julia, who, it quickly turns out, returns his love fully and is coy only out of maidenly modesty (and, perhaps, design too, to make herself more dearly valued).

And yet Proteus' stay in Verona does not entirely please his father, Antonio, who wants *his* son educated too. He discusses the matter with Panthino, who is listed as his servant in the cast of characters, and Panthino is all in favor of sending Proteus on his travels. He says:

I think your lordship is not ignorant
How his companion, youthful Valentine,
Attends the Emperor in his royal court.

—Act I, scene iii, lines 25–27

Through the most famous part of its history, in the fifteenth century, Milan was an independent duchy and the Duke of Milan was one of the best-known princes in Italy. There were two famous lines of these dukes, Visconti and Sforza, and indeed it is the Duke of Milan (unnamed) who is an important character in the play. Why, then, this reference to the Emperor?

To be sure, Milan had an imperial past. In the fourth century it, rather than Rome, was the place of residence of the Roman emperors in the West, and it was from Milan, for instance, that the Roman Emperor Constantine I issued his edict establishing official toleration of Christianity in 313.

More likely to have influenced Shakespeare's thinking, however, was the fact that in 1535 Milan lost its independence and became part of the wide-spreading dominions of Emperor Charles V (see page II-747). Shakespeare may have associated Milan with the Empire so thoroughly that he spoke of the Emperor when he meant to refer to the situation as it had been a century earlier and speak of the Duke. (Or else the term "Emperor" is just another fault in the mangled copy of the original play on which alone our present version is based.)

And so, impressed by Valentine's success at the court of Milan, Antonio decides to send his son, Proteus, there too, and Proteus, to his chagrin (for he has just learned of Julia's love for him), finds he must go.

Now begin the complications. In Milan Valentine has fallen deeply in love with Silvia, the daughter of the Duke of Milan. She is presented as a paragon of beauty and virtue. Also in love with her is Thurio, much inferior to Valentine in looks and character, but who the Duke has destined to be her husband. As for Silvia, there is soon no doubt it is Valentine she loves.

Into this triangle comes Proteus, who has taken an emotional leave of Julia and has exchanged rings with her as tokens of love. As soon as Proteus meets Silvia, however, he demonstrates his right to his name. He changes completely, falling in love with Silvia on the instant, forgetting his Julia, and at once planning to betray his friend.

Valentine intends to use a rope ladder to get to Silvia's window and elope with her. He confides this to Proteus, who promptly passes the information on to the Duke. The Duke therefore confronts Valentine, who is on his way to the elopement, and has no trouble at all in catching him out. In a rage, the Duke banishes Valentine from his court, leaving the field that much clearer for the perfidious Proteus.

. . . with a codpiece . . .

Meanwhile, Julia, left behind in Verona by Proteus, can endure her loneliness no longer. She determines to travel to Milan to see him, and to avoid the troubles that might come to an unattended maiden on a voyage such as that, she decides to dress like a man.

This is a convention used by Shakespeare in several of his plays (though first, chronologically, in this one), and to us it carries no conviction at all. The audience is invariably amused that the hero cannot see that under the male clothing a female lies barely concealed, and gains but a poor notion of the hero's powers of observation. However, a convention is a convention (like the one in the movies whereby whenever two lovers in isolation begin a love duet, the sound of an orchestra appears out of nowhere). Besides, in Shakespeare's time female parts were played by boys, and to have a boy-Julia dress up like a man was much more convincing than to have a girl-Julia do so. In fact, it was when the boy-Julia was playing Julia as a girl that he may have been least convincing.

In this play, at any rate, Shakespeare does manage to point out some of the difficulties of trying to switch outward appearances. Julia's maid, Lucetta, who disapproves of her mistress' plan, asks coldly how to make the breeches, and when Julia tells her to make them any way she pleases, Lucetta answers:

> *You must needs have them with a codpiece, madam.*
> —Act II, scene vii, line 53

A codpiece was a baglike affair, covering the opening in the front of the breeches. It was, in effect, a container for the penis and was quite fashionable in the fifteenth and sixteenth centuries. There was a tendency to fill it out with stuffing of one sort or another, partly as protection, and partly to make the organ seem more prominent than it was (much in the way that ladies' brassieres are tampered with in our own times). They might also be decorated or prinked out for the same purpose.

Naturally, the maidenly Julia is shocked at the mention of the object, but Lucetta says:

> *A round hose, madam, now's not worth a pin,*
> *Unless you have a codpiece to stick pins on.*
> —Act II, scene vii, lines 55–56

The reference to the codpiece as a pincushion is Lucetta's wry way of saying that Julia will have nothing inside to interfere with that use. It may also be a sardonic reference to men who use so much stuffing that pins may safely be stuck in it.

Despite Lucetta's discouragement, Julia remains firm in her determination to make the trip.

. . . from Mantua . . .

Valentine, traveling sadly away from Milan, falls in with a group of outlaws in a forest through which he is passing. Valentine points out he has no money and pretends he has been banished for having killed a man in a duel.

The fact that he has no money spoils him as a victim; the fact that he has killed a man commends him as a comrade; and the fact that he is handsome seems to have an effect also. The Third Outlaw says:

> By the bare scalp of Robin Hood's fat friar,
> This fellow were a king for our wild faction!
> —Act IV, scene i, lines 36–37

Any mention of outlaws would instantly remind an English audience of Robin Hood, and Shakespeare is usually very responsive to his audience. The "fat friar" is, of course, Friar Tuck, who scarcely needs further words to an American audience either.

The outlaws then introduce themselves to Valentine, for it seems that many of them are gentlemen who have been outlawed for some little prank or other which are common to hot-blooded young men of high birth. As the Second Outlaw says, in what seems to be an aggrieved tone, concerning his own outlawry:

> And I from Mantua, for a gentleman
> Who, in my mood, I stabbed unto the heart.
> —Act IV, scene i, lines 50–51

Mantua was briefly mentioned in *The Taming of the Shrew* as the home town of the Pedant (see page II–454). It is about twenty-five miles southwest of Verona and in Shakespeare's time (and for nearly five centuries before) it was an independent duchy.

. . . at Pentecost

Meanwhile, Proteus continues to betray everyone in sight. Having abandoned Julia and having treated Valentine most despicably, he is now prepared to double-cross Thurio. Under the pretense of pushing the latter's suit with Silvia, Proteus woos her for himself, singing for her the lovely ballad "Who is Silvia?"

Julia, in her male disguise, has come in time to hear it and understands at once the extent of Proteus' duplicity. She also hears Silvia nobly remain faithful to her Valentine and scorn Proteus as a traitor. Silvia urges Proteus to return to Julia (of whom she has apparently heard).

Silvia plans to flee from Milan and make her way to Valentine, wherever he is, while Julia decides to carry her plan one step further by attempting to gain employment with Proteus as his servant, under the name of Sebastian.

Proteus does indeed employ her and at once uses her as his go-between with Silvia. Sebastian and Silvia fall to discussing Julia, and Silvia wants to know how tall she is. Sebastian says:

> *About my stature: for, at Pentecost,*
> *When all our pageants of delight were played,*
> *Our youth got me to play the woman's part,*
> *And I was trimmed in Madam Julia's gown,*
> *Which servèd me as fit, by all men's judgments*
> *As if the garment had been made for me.*
>
> —Act IV, scene iv, lines 158–63

Pentecost was originally a Jewish harvest festival ("Shabuoth") celebrated seven weeks after Passover. (The Hebrew word means "weeks.") Its celebration came on the fiftieth day counting from the first day of Passover. For that reason it received the name Pentecost, which is from a Greek word meaning "fiftieth."

Pentecost gained a special Christian significance becase it was on that day, the first celebration after the crucifixion of Jesus, that the apostles received the inspiration of the Holy Spirit. Thus, in Acts 2:1–4, it says: "And when the day of Pentecost was fully come, they were all with one accord in one place. And suddenly there came a sound from heaven as of a rushing mighty wind, and it filled all the house where they were sitting. And there appeared unto them cloven tongues like as of fire, and it sat upon each of them. And they were all filled with the Holy Ghost, and began to speak with other tongues, as the Spirit gave them utterance."

Consequently, Pentecost remained an important Christian holiday and was celebrated on the seventh Sunday after Easter.

Easter and Pentecost were favored times for baptisms, but in England and other parts of northern Europe Pentecost was the more often used because it came in a warmer season of the year (late May or early June). Since the newly baptized generally wore white for a week to signify the new-washed purity of their souls, Pentecost is commonly called Whitsunday ("White Sunday") in England. Some speculate that this is really

"Wit Sunday" ("Wisdom Sunday") celebrating the time when spiritual wisdom rained down upon the apostles.

Naturally, Pentecost was a joyous holiday and was celebrated with dances, plays, and other outdoor amusements.

. . . Ariadne passioning

Julia describes her Pentecost role, saying:

> . . . I did play a lamentable part.
> Madam, 'twas Ariadne passioning
> For Theseus' perjury and unjust flight,
>   —Act IV, scene iv, lines 166–68

Julia, in her guise as Sebastian, is thinking of herself, of course, for she is much in Ariadne's position (see page I–31).

. . . Silvia I give thee

But now the action speeds up bewilderingly.

Silvia flees Milan to seek for Valentine. Her father, the Duke, and also Thurio and Proteus leave in pursuit of her while Julia follows Proteus.

Silvia is captured by the outlaws and is rescued by Proteus, but she still refuses to listen to his protestations of love (which Valentine overhears, so that he learns the truth at last).

The desperate Proteus threatens rape and then, finally, Valentine confronts his false friend. After Valentine's tongue-lashing, Proteus tearfully repents and at once Valentine forgives him. Valentine does more than that, in fact. He says:

> . . . that my love may appear plain and free,
> All that was mine in Silvia I give thee.
>   —Act V, scene iv, lines 82–83

Most critics find it utterly beyond the bounds of reason to suppose that Valentine should on an instant forgive an all-but-unforgivable falseness in his friend and then abandon his love to him as well—to say nothing of the insult offered Silvia in treating her as though she were a sack of wheat to be bartered. Some suspect a corrupt text, an ill-remembered denouement, a cut version.

Any of these possibilities may be so for all we know, and yet it might also be argued that Shakespeare meant it exactly as it stands. There is some reason to suspect that Shakespeare may have had homosexual tendencies (see page I-4), but there are no outright homosexuals in his plays except for Patroclus in *Troilus and Cressida* (see page I-98), and that was enforced by the Greek tale. Nevertheless, there are a number of cases in the romances in which friendship between males is suspiciously close and in which the language used between them is suspiciously ardent. The case of Valentine and Proteus is one of them and it is just possible to argue that Shakespeare was trying to maintain that affection between males was a higher and stronger emotion than that between the opposite sexes.

When Proteus gives up Silvia after being reproached by Valentine and then asks forgiveness, he is implicitly abandoning the lesser love (female) for the greater (male), and what can Valentine do but reciprocate and hand the lesser love back?

Fortunately for heterosexual sensibilities, this does not happen. When Valentine makes his offer, "Sebastian" swoons. Her true identity is discovered and the repentant Proteus is thus reunited with his ever true Julia.

The Duke and Thurio are also captured by the outlaws and Thurio shows himself to be a coward, while Valentine's bravery is conspicuous. The Duke of Milan therefore consents to have Valentine marry Silvia. Even the outlaws are forgiven and are taken into the employ of the Duke. All is happy as the curtain descends.

ROMEO AND JULIET

• Verona

Mantua

ITALY

N

Siena

0   Miles   60

17

The Tragedy of

ROMEO AND JULIET

I N *Romeo and Juliet* Shakespeare dramatized a love tale that was well known and much wept over by young people before his time. The nub of the tale, that of two young lovers unnecessarily dying for love through misunderstandings and family feuding, is not a very difficult thing to invent, and examples date back to ancient times.

The tale of Pyramus and Thisbe, for instance, which Shakespeare burlesques in *A Midsummer Night's Dream* (see page I–48), has such a plot. Indeed, both *Romeo and Juliet* and *A Midsummer Night's Dream* were written at about the same time (1595 probably) and there are some who suggest that in the version of the Pyramus and Thisbe legend presented by the Athenian laborers, Shakespeare was deliberately satirizing his own just-completed *Romeo and Juliet.* (For myself, I find this difficult to believe.)

The first version of a plot which is specifically that of *Romeo and Juliet* appeared in a collection of romances, *Il Novellino* published in Italian in 1476 by Masuccio Salernitano. It was adapted and, in the process, made into something considerably closer to the Shakespearean version (down to the names of the characters) by Luigi da Porto in or about 1530.

The first important English version of the story was in the form of a long narrative poem, *The Tragical History of Romeus and Juliet,* published in 1562 by the English translator Arthur Brooke. It was Brooke's poem that Shakespeare used as his direct source, following it quite closely, but adding (needless to say) master touches of his own.

In fair Verona . . .

The play opens with a "Chorus," who explains the subject matter, beginning:

> *Two households, both alike in dignity,*
> *In fair Verona, where we lay our scene,*
> *From ancient grudge break to new mutiny,*

—Prologue, lines 1–3

Verona (see page I–451) is mentioned in *The Taming of the Shrew* and is the place in which *The Two Gentlemen of Verona* opens. The city first appears as the scene of the Romeo and Juliet story in Da Porto's version. The earlier Salernitano version placed the tale in Siena, 150 miles south of Verona.

The actual scene does not matter, of course. The play is not historical and it is not confined to any particular city. It could just as easily, with very minor modifications, have taken place in England, and in the contemporary musical *West Side Story* it is transferred, fairly intact, to the New York of today.

Nevertheless, if we consider Verona, we find that in the play it is treated as an independent principality, something which it was in history only between 1260 and 1387.

That period would well fit the vision of an Italian city split by the rivalry of internal factions led by competing noble families, whose enmity resulted in street fighting with private armies of retainers and sympathizers.

Most Italian cities of the time contained those who favored a strong and centralized secular government under the German Emperor (Ghibellines) and others who favored a congeries of independent city-states under the moral leadership of the Pope (Guelphs). Families lined up on this side or that and feuded in consequence, or sometimes they had feuds for other reasons and lined up on opposite sides in consequence.

In Florence, for instance, the most famous city of Renaissance Italy, there arose about 1300 a deadly feud between the two families of the Cerchi and the Donati. It began over some trivial incident but gradually each side drew to itself others, so that the Cerchi headed the "Bianca" (White) faction, which was Ghibelline, while the Donati headed the "Nera" (Black) faction, which was Guelf. The whole city was torn in two by them and for nearly half a century its history was determined by the ups and downs of what had begun as a family feud.

Shakespeare does not give the nature of the feud between the Veronese households, and there is no indication that it is political in nature.

. . . the house of Montague . . .

The play opens on a Sunday (from internal evidence), with two retainers of the Capulet faction coming onstage. They are indistinguishable from comic English servingmen (as are all Shakespeare's comic lower-class characters, regardless of the supposed nationality of the upper-class ones) and are given the most un-Italian names of Sampson and Gregory.

They boast to each other of their desperate bravery and Sampson says:

> *A dog of the house of Montague moves me.*
>
> —Act I, scene i, line 8

The Montagues are one of the feuding families, and the Capulets the other. In Da Porto's version, the two quarreling households of Verona are given the names of Montecchi and Capelletti, but for English audiences the very similar Montague and Capulet would be more congenial to the ear.

Put up your swords . . .

The two Capulet retainers deliberately provoke two others of the Montague faction who enter later. The Montague retainers are ready to be provoked and there is suddenly swordplay.

One of the leaders of the Montagues, Benvolio, enters now and runs forward, anxious to stop the proceedings. He cries out:

> Part, fools!
> Put up your swords. You know not what you do.
> —Act I, scene i, lines 66–67

Throughout, Benvolio endeavors to make peace, to end the feud or at least to keep it blanketed. This is evident in his very name, which is Shakespeare's invention since the equivalent character in Brooke's poem is not named. "Benvolio" means "good will."

Benvolio's attempt at conciliation is only one of several indications in the play that the family feud is dying. It is possible to argue that it could easily be ended altogether by some sensible and decisive act of placation on one side or the other. The fact that this does not happen adds to the eventual tragedy.

Turn thee, Benvolio . . .

Indeed, the chief reason that the feud is not ended appears immediately. Hard upon Benvolio's entry comes the evil genius of the play, Tybalt, of the house of Capulet. Furiously, he cries out to the peacemaking Benvolio:

> What, art thou drawn among these heartless [cowardly] hinds?
> Turn thee, Benvolio; look upon thy death.
> —Act I, scene i, lines 68–69

Benvolio protests that he is merely using his sword to break up the fight and keep the peace, but Tybalt will have none of it:

What, drawn, and talk of peace? I hate the word
As I hate hell, all Montagues, and thee.

—Act I, scene i, lines 72–73

This is the clearest expression in the play of the irrational psychology of all that is meant by "feuding." It is almost the only expression. It is Tybalt, the only irrational hater among the leaders of the factions, who prevents the triumph of reason.

In Da Porto's tale, the corresponding character is Thebaldo, but it is a happy stroke to change it to Tybalt. It brings on thoughts of the folk tale of "Reynard the Fox" (see page I–153), in which Tibert was the name of the cat. A common version of this was Tybalt, so that to the Elizabethan audience, the very use of the name at once brings up the picture of this particular Capulet as a quarrelsome and vicious tomcat.

Your lives shall pay . . .

The fight, forced on Benvolio by Tybalt, continues to expand. Other members of the faction arrive, including even Capulet and Montague themselves, the aged heads of the family (whose wives sternly refuse to let them fight), until finally the Prince of Verona himself appears on the scene.

He is, quite understandably, exasperated at this disorder in the streets. There have been three such incidents and his patience is at an end. He says, angrily:

If ever you disturb our streets again,
Your lives shall pay the forfeit of the peace.

—Act I, scene i, lines 99–100

The name of the Prince is given as Escalus. No Veronese prince of that name is known, but, interestingly enough, Verona was ruled from 1227 to 1259 by Ezzelino da Romano. That may be no more than coincidence.

. . . Dian's wit

When the streets are cleared, Lady Montague expresses her relief that her son, Romeo, was not involved. It turns out that Romeo has taken to mooning sadly about in a fashion which, to Elizabethan audiences, marks the conventional symptoms of unrequited love. Romeo is no sooner spoken of than he appears in the guise of the romantic lover.

The older Montagues are puzzled by Romeo's behavior and Benvolio volunteers to discover the cause. The task is easy, for Romeo admits to unrequited love at once. Romeo says of the girl he loves:

> She'll not be hit
> With Cupid's arrow. She hath Dian's wit,
> —Act I, scene i, lines 211–12

Romeo does not name her at this point and, indeed, she never appears in the play.

Romeo's moan is that the girl he loves insists on chastity. She has "Dian's wit" and Diana is the Roman goddess of the hunt (analogous to the Greek Artemis, a virgin goddess sworn to chastity).

Benvolio therefore gives Romeo the very sensible advice to find someone else, but Romeo rejects that advice scornfully. (It is the sad fact that whereas Benvolio is always sensible, Romeo is always romantic, and that too helps bring on the catastrophe.)

. . . to keep the peace

On the other side, Capulet is talking with Count Paris, a kinsman of Prince Escalus. Their talk at first is of the feud and here it seems quite obvious that there is little real interest in keeping it alive. Capulet says:

> . . . 'tis not hard, I think,
> For men so old as we [he and Montague] to keep the peace.
> —Act I, scene ii, lines 2–3

Paris agrees and says:

> Of honorable reckoning are you both,
> And pity 'tis you lived at odds so long.
> —Act I, scene ii, lines 4–5

What more do we need to see that only a face-saving formula is needed and the feud will be gladly abandoned.

. . . fourteen years

But Capulet has more on his mind than the peace, and so has Paris. Capulet has a lovely daughter and Paris would like to marry her. It would be a good match and Capulet is eager for it. He is held back by only one thought. Perhaps the girl is too young. He says:

> *My child is yet a stranger in the world,*
> *She hath not seen the change of fourteen years;*
> > —Act I, scene ii, lines 8–9

He is speaking of Juliet, the heroine of the play, and as is stated and emphasized on several occasions, she is not quite fourteen! Her very name is a diminutive, for Juliet means "little Julia." (There was a Julia in *The Two Gentlemen of Verona* who was also a sweet and plucky girl of that city, though she could scarcely have been as young as Juliet.)

In Elizabethan times, of course, life went more quickly. Girls became marriageable more quickly, were made mothers more quickly, and died more quickly. Nevertheless, fourteen is rather young. Shakespeare does not bother giving the ages of any of the heroines of his other early plays; only in this one does he make an exception, and for no obvious reason, he emphasizes it strenuously. —Perhaps there *is* a reason.

My fair niece Rosaline . . .

Circumstances now begin to complicate matters. Even while Capulet is talking to Paris, he is making preparations for a feast that very night. He gives the list of invited guests to a servant and tells him to go through Verona and invite them all.

But as the fates would have it, the servant who receives this order is illiterate and has no chance to explain that fact to the hasty Capulet.

And, as the fates would further have it, in come Romeo and Benvolio, still discussing the former's romantic love affair, and it is to Romeo that the servant applies for help in reading off the names of the invited guests. Romeo obliges and, included on the list are:

> *Mercutio and his brother Valentine;*
> *Mine uncle Capulet, his wife and daughters;*
> *My fair niece Rosaline; Livia;*
> *Signior Valentio and his cousin Tybalt;*
> > —Act I, scene ii, lines 69–72

It is Rosaline with whom Romeo is in love, and this means that Rosaline, as the niece of Capulet, is shown to be a member of the opposing faction.

Yet this does not seem to bother anybody at all. To be sure, Romeo has not mentioned her name; to do so would ill fit his mood of romantic melancholy. Yet he doesn't keep it entirely secret, either, for he has apparently imparted the identity of his loved one to Benvolio since the close of the first scene. Thus, Benvolio says to Romeo:

At this same ancient feast of Capulet's
Sups the fair Rosaline whom thou so lov'st;
—Act I, scene ii, lines 85–86

Can it be that Rosaline has turned down Romeo because of the feud between their families? There is no mention of any such thing. Romeo has stated that Rosaline has sworn herself to indiscriminate chastity.

Is there any sign of danger at all in this love affair of Romeo's that crosses the lines of the feud? No one makes any mention of it. Even the cautious Benvolio does not seem to remark danger in it. In fact, Benvolio, still anxious to wean Romeo away from a useless love that makes him unhappy, advises him to attend the ball, saying:

> *Go thither, and with unattainted eye*
> *Compare her face with some that I shall show,*
> *And I will make thee think thy swan a crow.*
> —Act I, scene ii, lines 88–90

So unimportant is the feud, in other words, that even the cautious Benvolio sees no danger in walking right into the center and hotbed of the Capulet faction.

. . . Lammas Eve . . .

It is time to introduce Juliet now. Lady Capulet wishes to broach the subject of marriage to her, but with her also is Juliet's garrulous old Nurse, who had a daughter Juliet's age, for she says, referring to Juliet:

> *Susan and she (God rest all Christian souls!)*
> *Were of an age.*
> —Act I, scene iii, lines 18–19

If the Nurse were to serve as surrogate breast feeder for Juliet, she would have to have had a child of her own shortly before. More important, this leads to talk of Juliet's age once more. The Nurse says:

> *I'll lay fourteen of my teeth—*
> *And yet to my teen* [sorrow] *be it spoken, I have but four—*
> *She's not fourteen.*
> —Act I, scene iii, lines 12–14

The Nurse then launches into an irrelevant tale of Juliet's childhood that begins

> . . . of all days in the year,
> Come Lammas Eve at night shall she be fourteen.
>
> —Act I, scene iii, lines 16–17

Lammas Day is August 1. In early English times it was the day of a harvest festival, and the fruits of the field, symbolized by half loaves of bread, were consecrated at mass. The Anglo-Saxon term for half loaf was "hlafmaesse" and this was distorted to "Lammas."

Earlier the Nurse had asked Lady Capulet how long it was to Lammastide and had been answered:

> A fortnight and odd days.
>
> —Act I, scene iii, line 15

We can therefore place the beginning of the play at about July 13. It is summer and the hot weather is referred to later in the play.

There must be some reason why Shakespeare harps so on Juliet's age.

> . . . since the earthquake . . .

The Nurse has another way of dating Juliet's age, too, for she remembers the circumstances of the weaning. She says:

> 'Tis since the earthquake now eleven years;
> And she was weaned . . .
>
> —Act I, scene iii, lines 23–24

This verse has sometimes been given special significance, for in 1580 there was a notable earthquake felt in London. The argument is therefore presented that this was referred to at this point and that the play was consequently written in 1591. This seems awfully thin, however, and most critics do not accept the reasoning at all.

The garrulous Nurse is finally persuaded to be silent and Lady Capulet begins to talk Juliet into marriage. She takes the opportunity at once to stymie any objections as to age, by saying:

> By my count,
> I was your mother much upon these years
> That you are now a maid.
>
> —Act I, scene iii, lines 71–73

Apparently, then, Lady Capulet is herself some twenty-eight years old. Juliet, however, seems unmoved by the thoughts of marriage and Lady

Capulet tells her that Paris will be at the banquet that night and she can look him over and decide whether she can love him.

. . . 'tis no wit . . .

In the next scene it is later in the day and the Capulet feast will soon begin. In the street outside come Romeo and Benvolio, who plan to attend in masks.

This seems to give an impression that it is dangerous for the Montagues to invade the Capulet feast, but the presence of masks does not necessarily prove it. Masking at feasts was common and masked dances are featured in *Henry VIII* (see page II–761) and *Love's Labor's Lost* (see page I–440), for instance. Masks afforded young men and ladies a chance to flirt in semiconcealment.

To weaken the case for danger, Romeo does no more than wear a mask. He makes no attempt to disguise his voice, for instance, and is, in point of fact, readily recognized at the feast, as will soon be apparent.

To be sure, Romeo does express reservations about going. He says:

> . . . *we mean well in going to this masque,*
> *But 'tis no wit to go.*
> —Act I, scene iv, lines 48–49

But when asked why, he can only say:

> *I dreamt a dream tonight* [last night].
> —Act I, scene iv, line 50

If the feud were really alive and deadly, he could easily have said that it was "no wit to go" because discovery would mean death. To fall back on a dream, a mere presentiment of evil, shows how little importance Romeo attaches to the feud.

. . . Queen Mab . . .

With Romeo and Benvolio is a friend, Mercutio, who is of neither faction and is friendly with both, for he has been invited to the feast. He is, it appears, a relative of Prince Escalus.

Mercutio is, in essence, Shakespeare's invention. Da Porto had a minor character named Marcuccio, but Shakespeare took that and touched it with his own special gold even down to the small change in the name. Mercutio suggests Mercury, the winged messenger of the gods, who flits through the air with superhuman speed. Mercutio is mercurial, with a flashing wit that never leaves him.

Mercutio does not seem to think of the feud as a deadly thing either. He makes no attempt to dissuade the Montagues from going, as he might well have done if there were real danger. Rather, he is intent on rallying Romeo out of his melancholy and is so anxious to have him come to the feast that he eagerly turns dream presentiments into nonsense by advancing his own theory on the origin of dreams as the product of a tricky elf. He says:

> O, then I see Queen Mab hath been with you.
> She is the fairies' midwife, and she comes
> In shape no bigger than an agate stone
> —Act I, scene iv, lines 53–55

Queen Mab is out of Celtic mythology. The pagan Irish had a goddess named Meadhbh, who was the ruler of a group of the "little people." This may have contributed to the notion of Queen Mab.

Queen Mab need not be considered a fairy queen in the sense that Titania was in *A Midsummer Night's Dream* (see page I–26). She is the fairies' "midwife"; that is, she helps men and women give birth to dreams, and this is no task for a queen.

Here, in all likelihood, "Queen" is used in its original sense of "woman" and to speak of "Queen Mab" would be something like speaking of "Dame Mab" or "Mistress Mab." The word "queen" early split into two forms: one of them, "quean," degenerated to mean a degraded woman, a harlot; the other, "queen," rose to mean an elevated woman, the wife of a king. "Queen," in its ordinary original sense, neither depressed nor elevated, vanished altogether.

Mercutio's speech about Queen Mab presents the view that dreams are not messages of fate but the product of the routine thoughts of the day. Lovers dream of love, courtiers of curtsies, lawyers of fees; soldiers of war and drink, and so on. This is one of many examples of Shakespeare's modern-sounding rationalism.

Thus, when Romeo tries to stem the flow of Mercutio's brilliance and says:

> Peace, peace, Mercutio, peace!
> Thou talk'st of nothing.
> —Act I, scene iv, lines 95–96

Mercutio answers at once, with stabbing relevance:

> True, I talk of dreams.
> —Act I, scene iv, line 96

. . . a Montague, our foe

Within the mansion the feast is in full progress. The masked dancers are enjoying themselves and Romeo sees Juliet for the first time. He falls immediately and hopelessly in love and completely vindicates Benvolio's promise that Romeo had but to look at other women to forget Rosaline. Romeo says:

> *Did my heart love till now: Forswear it, sight!*
> *For I ne'er saw true beauty till this night.*
> > —Act I, scene v, lines 54–55

But his voice is overheard and instantly recognized—and by Tybalt, the *only* person of consequence in either faction who takes the feud seriously. He flares into mad rage at once and is prepared to kill. He says:

> *This, by his voice, should be a Montague.*
> *Fetch me my rapier, boy.*
> > —Act I, scene v, lines 56–57

Capulet is at once aware that Tybalt is in a passion and demands the reason. Tybalt says:

> *Uncle, this is a Montague, our foe,*
> *A villain . . .*
> > —Act I, scene v, lines 63–64

Capulet is not moved in the slightest. He recognizes Romeo at once and says to Tybalt:

> *. . . let him alone.*
> *'A bears him like a portly* [respectable] *gentleman,*
> *And, to say truth, Verona brags of him*
> *To be a virtuous and well-governed youth.*
> > —Act I, scene v, lines 67–70

Surely the feud is as good as dead when the leader of one side can speak so of the son and heir of the leader of the other side. Capulet speaks so highly of Romeo, in fact, that one could almost imagine that a prospective match between Montague's son and Capulet's daughter would be a capital way of ending the feud.

Then, when Tybalt objects to Capulet's tame endurance of the presence of a Montague, the old man isn't in the least shamed into taking a stronger stand. On the contrary, he turns savagely on Tybalt, crying:

You are a saucy boy. Is't so, indeed?
This trick may chance to scathe [harm] *you.*

—Act I, scene v, lines 85–86

Tybalt, trembling with frustrated rage, is forced to withdraw.

. . . my only hate

Meanwhile, Romeo has made his way to Juliet, who is as instantly struck
with him as he by her. In fifteen lines he reaches the stage of kissing her.
He must leave soon after and Juliet inquires his name of the Nurse. She
finds out he is Romeo, the son of Montague, and says at once, dramatically:

My only love, sprung from my only hate!

—Act I, scene v, line 140

It turns out later in the play that she was particularly close to her cousin
Tybalt. We can imagine, without too much trouble, young Juliet listening
with awe and admiration to the tales told her by her paranoid cousin; of
fights with the Montagues, of their disgraceful defeats and treacherous victories. Tybalt would surely have poured into her ears all the sick preoccupation with the feud that filled his own wrathful heart.

And she would have absorbed it all. That may well be the point of
Shakespeare's stressing Juliet's extreme youth. She was young enough to
absorb the feud in its full romanticism without any admixture of disillusionment that would have come with experience.

. . . King Cophetua . . .

Although Romeo has left the feast, he cannot really leave. He must have
another sight of Juliet if he can. Slipping away from his companions, he
climbs the wall bounding the Capulet estate and finds himself in the
orchard.

Benvolio and Mercutio come seeking him, and Mercutio in mockery
calls after him with all the clichés of lovers' tales. He asks of the hiding
Romeo just one word about Venus or Cupid as a sign of his whereabouts,
defining Cupid, ironically, as:

. . . he that shot so true
When King Cophetua loved the beggar maid!

—Act II, scene i, lines 13–14

This is another reference (see page I–431) to the famous tale of the happy love of a socially ill-assorted couple.

But Romeo remains in hiding, and Benvolio and Mercutio shrug and leave. Surely if the feud were alive and dangerous, they would never have left Romeo alone in the very center of enemy territory. Instead, they seem not a bit concerned.

. . . refuse thy name

Romeo's patience is rewarded, for Juliet (as lovesick as he) comes out on her balcony to sigh romantically.

Romeo, spying her, indulges in a long soliloquy in which he praises her beauty in the most extravagant terms, but never once mentions the fact that she is a Capulet. It does not seem to concern him that she is of the opposing faction any more than it concerned him that Rosaline was. But then, Romeo is not fourteen and he is old enough to know the feud is really on its last legs.

Not so Juliet. She speaks at last and all her talk is of the feud. She says:

> O Romeo, Romeo! Wherefore art thou Romeo?   *means "why"*
> Deny thy father and refuse thy name;
> Or, if thou wilt not, be but sworn my love,
> And I'll no longer be a Capulet.
> —Act II, scene ii, lines 33–36

It is irritating in the extreme that the first line of this passage, taken by itself, is so often treated in popular quotation as though Juliet were saying "Where are you, Romeo?" and were looking for him. Not only does it show a pitiful ignorance of the meaning of the archaic word "wherefore," but it ruins a key point in the plot development. "Wherefore" means "why," and Juliet is asking the absent Romeo why he is a Montague. Oh, if only he weren't.

All she can talk about is his name. She says:

> 'Tis but thy name that is my enemy.
> Thou art thyself, though [you were] not a Montague.
> What's Montague? It is nor hand, nor foot,
> Nor arm, nor face. O, be some other name
> Belonging to a man.
> What's in a name? That which we call a rose
> By any other name would smell as sweet.
> —Act II, scene ii, lines 38–44

What can Romeo be thinking as he hears this? We might speculate that left to himself he might have approached his father and urged him to talk to Capulet, under a flag of truce if necessary, and try to arrange a reconciliating marriage. It is so easy to feel that this would work. Who but Tybalt shows any signs of anything but weariness with the feud, and he could be beaten into submission. To be sure, marriage had been spoken of with Paris, but nothing had yet been committed.

However, Romeo may well have recognized the romanticism of the young girl who feels the thrill of loving the family enemy; who loves the risk and danger and sadness of it; and perhaps he would not dream of throwing cold water on that feeling. So he makes himself known and dramatically denounces his name, saying:

> *I take thee at thy word.*
> *Call me but love, and I'll be new baptized;*
> *Henceforth I never will be Romeo.*
>
> —Act II, scene ii, lines 49–51

Thus he commits himself to the full gamut of romantic folderol as seen through the eyes of a dramatic fourteen-year-old, and the catastrophe is under way.

. . . the place death . . .

Juliet is astonished at Romeo's sudden presence and makes the most of it in terms of the romantic version of the feud. She berates Romeo for having taken chances, saying:

> *The orchard walls are high and hard to climb,*
> *And the place death, considering who thou art,*
> *If any of my kinsmen find thee here.*
>
> —Act II, scene ii, lines 63–65

Exaggeration, we might easily guess. To be sure, if Tybalt had made his appearance at this moment there would have been trouble. We can suspect, however, that if anyone but Tybalt had appeared, Romeo would have gotten away with nothing but some hard words. In fact, the subject of marriage might have been broached.

Is it possible that even Juliet considered the feud and its consequences only as an afterthought? Her first fear was that he might have hurt himself falling off the wall.

Romeo accepts Juliet's insistence on the danger of death, perhaps recognizing that it is part of his appeal to her and glad to take advantage of that. Still, he doesn't really seem to take it seriously, for he says:

Alack, there lies more peril in thine eye
Than twenty of their swords!
—Act II, scene ii, lines 71–72

With all that done, the two get down to the serious business of expressing their love.

Thy purpose marriage . . .

From words of love, they pass quickly to the thought of marriage. Juliet
says:

If that thy bent of love be honorable,
Thy purpose marriage, send me word tomorrow,
By one that I'll procure to come to thee,
—Act II, scene ii, lines 143–45

If Romeo had had the rational plan of trying to work a marriage settlement in an aboveboard fashion to the advantage of everyone, he abandons
it. If romantic little Juliet wants secret messages, and clandestine word,
and even an exciting forbidden marriage—then she shall have them.

The meeting comes to an end with Monday's dawn nearly upon the two.
Romeo, thoroughly happy, says:

Hence will I to my ghostly [spiritual] *friar's close cell,*
His help to crave and my dear hap [good luck] *to tell.*
—Act II, scene ii, lines 188–89

With luck, the friar can arrange the secret marriage that Juliet longs for.

. . . the powerful grace . . .

The scene shifts at once to the cell of Friar Laurence ("Fra Lorenzo" in
Da Porto's version) early Monday morning. He is an alchemist as well as a
friar and is gathering herbs in order to extract their juices for his experi-
ments, saying:

O, mickle [much] *is the powerful grace that lies*
In plants, herbs, stones, and their true qualities;
For naught so vile that on the earth doth live
But to the earth some special good doth give;
—Act II, scene iii, lines 15–18

Here is expressed the medieval view that all creation is made for the express good of man; that everything on earth has some property that makes it valuable to man.

. . . your households' rancor . . .

Romeo comes to the friar with his tale of love and Friar Laurence is more than a little confused at this sudden change from Rosaline to Juliet and clucks disapprovingly over the whole matter. He decides, however, to go along with the secret marriage for a clearly expressed reason; saying:

> *In one respect I'll thy assistant be;*
> *For this alliance may so happy prove*
> *To turn your households' rancor to pure love.*
>
> —Act II, scene iii, lines 90–92

Friar Laurence obviously considers the feud to be dying and a marital alliance, he judges, will end it altogether. He seems, however, to prefer the indirect and hidden approach to the direct one; he is as romantic as Juliet.

. . . Prince of Cats . . .

It is broad day now and Benvolio and Mercutio have still not found Romeo. Meanwhile Tybalt, angered over the incident at the feast, has sent a formal challenge to Romeo. The two friends aren't worried, sure that Romeo can take care of himself. Mercutio thinks very little of Tybalt as a swordsman, characterizing him as

> *More than Prince of Cats. O, he's the courageous captain of*
> *compliments. He fights as you sing pricksong—keeps time,*
> *distance, and proportion . . .*
>
> —Act II, scene iv, lines 19–22

The "Prince of Cats" is a jeer at Tybalt's name, of course. The mockery is aimed at that favorite butt of Shakespeare's—the French or Italian way of doing things (in this case, scientific fencing) as opposed to the wholesome English fashion of simply dealing out good thwacks.

Laura, to his lady . . .

And now at last Romeo appears, and Mercutio fully expects him to begin again with his whining lovesickness. He mimics him in advance:

Now is he for the numbers that Petrarch flowed in.
Laura, to his lady, was a kitchen wench . . .
                              —Act II, scene iv, lines 40–42

Petrarch (Francesco Petrarca in Italian) was an Italian poet whose work may be thought of as sparking the Renaissance. He was born in 1304 and in 1327 met a lady known to us as "Laura." Who she was in actuality is not certain.

Though he did much work in Latin, he is best known for his collection of Italian sonnets, odes, and other poems written between 1330 and 1360. These poems deal with his love for Laura, and through that love, deal with many other matters. Because of this, Petrarch and Laura are one of the great pairs of lovers of history, though the love may have been an ideal one only.

. . . you ratcatcher . . .

But how things have changed! Romeo is no longer a mewling wretch, but is lively and sparkling, quite ready to engage Mercutio in a game of wits and to give as good as he gets, so that the latter is delighted that Romeo is himself again.

The Nurse then comes on the scene. Mercutio is, with some difficulty, shoved offstage and Romeo tells her that all has been arranged for Friar Laurence to marry them that very afternoon. The Nurse goes off with the news and plans also to get Juliet a rope ladder that she can lower to Romeo that night, so that he might climb to her room and enjoy the fruits of love.

We might imagine that on the next day, once Juliet has had her romantic marriage and all it involves, Romeo will confront his father with the fact, and old Montague will in turn confront the Capulets. All, we hope, will be well—if only Romeo can stay out of trouble till then.

But it is still Monday afternoon, midsummer, and very hot. Tempers may be short and Benvolio (still promenading with Mercutio) feels it will be well to go in. With characteristic caution he wishes to avoid meeting an irritated Tybalt, brooding over the crashing of the party the night before. Mercutio refuses to take this seriously.

At this point, however, in comes Tybalt, inquiring after Romeo. Mercutio baits him while Benvolio anxiously tries to keep the whole matter under control.

But now Romeo enters, already married to Juliet, although no one knows it but bride, groom, and friar. Tybalt challenges him with an insult and Romeo, aware of their present relationship, of which Tybalt is not, patiently endures the insult and refuses to fight.

So far all is well. Romeo has done the sensible thing, even if it was not a particularly heroic one.

And now the secrecy, Juliet's romantic secrecy, does its fell work. If Mercutio had known of Romeo's marriage he would have understood and stood aside. He did not know and finds he cannot endure Romeo's tame acceptance of insult. If Romeo will accept the grace, Mercutio will wipe it out on his behalf. He cries out to Tybalt:

> *Tybalt, you ratcatcher, will you walk?*
>
> —Act III, scene i, line 76

"Ratcatcher" is one more reference to Tybalt the cat, and Mercutio is inviting the other to walk to some quiet place where they may fight without interruption.

Tybalt hesitates. His quarrel is not with Mercutio. He asks Mercutio what he wants and the latter says, lightly:

> *Good King of Cats, nothing but one of your nine lives.*
>
> —Act III, scene i, lines 78–79

It is an old fable that a cat has nine lives, and there is something to it. A cat is careful, sly, equipped with needlelike claws for a fight and soft pads for stealth. It can climb a tree and land on its feet when it falls. It will escape sure death for other animals eight times out of nine.

. . . both your houses

All might still be well. Mercutio, we may well expect, is the better swordsman and will kill Tybalt. Mercutio is not a member of either faction and so is not included in the ban against street fighting. With Tybalt dead, the chief upholder of the feud will be gone. It will be all the easier to reconcile the factions.

All Romeo need do now is stand aside.

But Romeo cannot. Mercutio is his loved friend, Tybalt his new relative. He wants neither hurt so he tries to get between and stop them. At which point, in one flash, all goes wrong. Tybalt's sword passes under Romeo's arm and Mercutio is blocked from parrying. Badly wounded, Mercutio recognizes the fact that the quarrel was not really his, after all, and says so in a phrase that has entered the language:

> *I am hurt.*
> *A plague o' both your houses.*
>
> —Act III, scene i, lines 91–92

. . . fortune's fool

Mercutio makes his last bitter jests and <u>hobbles off to die.</u>

Yet still things are not utterly lost. Romeo has lost a dear friend but it was by no willing action of his own. He had tried for the best, endeavored to make peace. It was Tybalt who was the murderer and it is he who may be executed for it and again the feud will be made up the easier, perhaps, for Tybalt's end.

Yet Romeo cannot leave it at that, not even for Juliet. Mercutio died in his quarrel and he has no choice. Wildly, <u>he challenges Tybalt and kills</u> him—and by then all the noise has roused the citizens.

Romeo is half amazed at all that has happened in a matter of a few minutes, for now he must get out of the city at once or, by the Prince's decree, *he* will be executed.

It is *still* less than twenty-four hours since he met Juliet and already he has not only gained her, but lost her as well. No wonder he cries out in agony:

> *O, I am fortune's fool!*
>
> —Act III, scene i, line 138

Yet a little chink of hope remains. When the Prince arrives, Benvolio tells the tale of what has happened with objective accuracy. Despite the clamors of the Capulet faction, the Prince believes Benvolio (and perhaps remembers that the dead Tybalt had killed his own kinsman) and does not place the death penalty on Romeo after all. He merely banishes him.

While banishment seems bad enough under the circumstances, a sentence of banishment can be unsaid, while an execution is final.

. . . Phoebus' lodging . . .

Meanwhile, toward sunset, Juliet is waiting with unbearable impatience for the coming of night, of Romeo, of love. She says:

> *Gallop apace, you fiery-footed steeds,*
> *Toward Phoebus' lodging! Such a wagoner*
> *As Phaëton would whip you to the west*
> *And bring in cloudy night immediately.*
>
> —Act III, scene ii, lines 1–4

The sun is pictured here in the fashion of the Greek myth, as a blazing chariot conducted by golden horses, traveling toward the west where they can move behind the horizon and rest till it is time for the next day's journey across the sky. The horizon is therefore Phoebus' (the god of the sun) place of lodging. Phaëton is the son of the sun god, whose ill-fated attempt to drive the horses of the sun chariot nearly led to disaster (see page II–297).

But then in comes the Nurse with the rope ladder—and with news, as well, of Tybalt's death.

Juliet is heartbroken, for she loved Tybalt. Her greater love for Romeo wins out, however, and she weeps over the rope ladder that was to have carried her husband to her, then goes to her room where she hopes to die.

But that is more than the Nurse can bear. She can still help. She assures Juliet she knows where Romeo is hiding and will get him to come to his wife and comfort her.

. . . pass to Mantua

Romeo, in Friar Laurence's cell, is completely broken. Overwhelmed with horror at the thought of banishment, he will not listen to the friar's consolation. Even when the Nurse comes, asking him to go to Juliet, he can think only of suicide.

It is only with the greatest difficulty that the friar finally manages to make him understand that banishment is not necessarily the end, saying:

> *Go get thee to thy love, as was decreed,*
> *Ascend her chamber, hence and comfort her.*
> *But look thou stay not till the watch be set,*
> *For then thou canst not pass to Mantua,*
> *Where thou shalt live till we can find a time*
> *To blaze* [announce] *your marriage, reconcile your friends,*
> *Beg pardon of the Prince, and call thee back*
>
> —Act III, scene iii, lines 146–52

Mantua (see page I–454) is only twenty miles south of Verona, not really very far, though to Romeo it might well have seemed an infinite distance under the circumstances.

The chink of hope remains, but oh, how different from what it would have been if Mercutio had not been ignorant of Romeo's marriage.

For even that chink of hope to remain, however, time is needed as Friar Laurence says, and, alas, time disappears.

Thursday let it be . . .

Old Capulet is perturbed at Juliet's misery and attributes it entirely to the death of Tybalt. He says to Paris:

Look you, she loved her kinsman Tybalt dearly,
—Act III, scene iv, line 3

Yes indeed, and this is the best evidence we have that she may well have picked up her fatal notions of the feud from him.

Thinking to console his daughter, Capulet decides to let her marry Paris at once after all. He asks the day and Paris says:

Monday, my lord.
—Act III, scene iv, line 18

This fixes the time sequence for all the play. Capulet considers that and says:

Monday! Ha, ha! Well, Wednesday is too soon.
A [on] Thursday let it be . . .
—Act III, scene iv, lines 19–20

He doesn't know that Juliet is already married, of course.

No warmth, no breath . . .

Unsuspecting this new gruesome development, Juliet receives Romeo late Monday night. The night after their meeting and their great balcony scene, they spend in connubial love. At dawn on Tuesday they must separate and Romeo gets out of town safely.

But then Juliet learns of her prospective marriage to Paris and of course refuses firmly. Old Capulet promptly flies into a passion and makes it plain that she will marry Paris whether she wishes to or not.

Juliet can find no one to help her. Capulet threatens to disown her. Lady Capulet turns away. Even the Nurse, in desperation, can only advise Juliet to marry Paris and commit bigamy.

Juliet can think of no alternative but to fly to Friar Laurence.

At this point the friar might have shown courage. He might have gone to the Capulets with the truth and endeavored to protect himself and Juliet with his priestly robes. Under the circumstances, there would have been great risk, but there were no reasonable alternatives.

Friar Laurence turns to an unreasonable one. As romantic as Juliet, he tries a complicated plan of indirection. He gives Juliet a mysterious drug he has prepared himself. He tells her to take it the night of the next day (Wednesday) and it will put her into a cataleptic trance. He says:

. . . no pulse
Shall keep his native progress, but surcease;
No warmth, no breath, shall testify thou livest;

—Act IV, scene i, lines 96–98

This trance will last forty-two hours, that is, through Thursday and Friday. The Capulets, thinking she is dead, will place her in the family tomb. Romeo will be there by Friday night, and when she wakes he will carry her off to Mantua.

This drug is, of course, an element of fantasy, for no drug is known (even today) that can safely counterfeit death so accurately over so long a time.

. . . mandrakes torn out of the earth

For the first time in the play, there is a sizable gap in time. Some thirty-six hours are skipped over and it is Wednesday night. Juliet suddenly submits to her father's plans (to his relief and pleasure) and has now prepared herself, supposedly, for a wedding the next morning. She sends out the Nurse so that she may sleep alone, and as she prepares to take the friar's drug, she is beset with quite understandable fears.

What if it kills her? Or, worse still, what if it wears off too soon and she comes to in the tomb before Romeo is there to claim her? What if she is surrounded by the effluvium of death, the gibbering of ghosts, and, in general, by

. . . loathsome smells,
And shrieks like mandrakes torn out of the earth,
That living mortals, hearing them, run mad—

—Act IV, scene iii, lines 46–48

The mandrake is a herb with a large, fleshy root that is usually forked in such proportions as to give it a resemblance to a partly formed man. About this fancied resemblance a number of superstitions arose.

Since the root looked like a man it would, supposedly, help in the formation of one, and mandrakes were therefore thought to have the ability to make women fecund. This superstition (a worthless one, of course) is sanctioned by the Bible, where Jacob's second wife, Rachel, who is barren, begs for the mandrakes gathered by the son of his first wife, her sister Leah (Genesis 30:14).

It was also thought that because mandrakes looked like little men they ought to share some of the qualities of men—feel pain, for instance, and cry out if wounded. From this arose the tale that if a mandrake were uprooted, it would emit a bloodcurdling shriek—so horrible a shriek as to madden or even kill those who heard it.

Since mandrakes were desired for the ability to increase fecundity, and for other valuable properties assigned to them, it was necessary to pull them up anyway. What was sometimes done was to tie the top of the herb to a dog. From a distance, stones could be thrown at the dog, and in running away, he would pull out the mandrake, which could then be reclaimed.

. . . the infectious pestilence . . .

The first part of Friar Laurence's plan works well. Juliet does take the potion and falls into a cataleptic trance. In the midst of the preparations for the wedding on Thursday morning, the Nurse finds her apparently dead. Juliet is carried to the tomb with heartbreaking lamentation.

But there is another part of the plan. Romeo must be informed of all this and be ready to return to carry off Juliet on Friday. To carry this message to Romeo, Friar Laurence has sent off a friend, Friar John.

Romeo gets a message indeed, but it is from a servant of his who comes spurring hard from Verona with the tale that Juliet is dead and entombed. Romeo, stricken, has no thought but to reach Juliet's corpse and kill himself there. For the purpose he buys poison.

As for Friar John, however, he fails to reach Romeo. Before leaving he had sought the company of another friar, who had been visiting the sick, and both fell in with "searchers," that is, health officers, seeking to prevent spread of infection.

Friar John tells Friar Laurence that:

> . . . the searchers of the town,
> Suspecting that we both were in a house
> Where the infectious pestilence did reign,
> Sealed up the doors, and would not let us forth,
>
> —Act V, scene ii, lines 8–11

He could neither leave town nor send the message. Friar Laurence, thunderstruck, now realizes he must hasten to the tomb so that Juliet will not waken alone and so that he can explain matters. Meanwhile, he sends another message.

The care of the "searchers" and their assiduity in applying quarantine is easily understood. In 1347 an "infectious pestilence" reached Europe. This was the infamous Black Death, the most frightening epidemic in world history. It is supposed to have killed some twenty-five million people in Europe in the space of three years, and quarantine was the only countermeasure the frightened continent knew.

Saint Francis . . .

On Friday all converge on the tomb. Paris arrives first to grieve over his
lost bride. Then comes Romeo, intent on suicide. They fight and Paris is
killed. Romeo then lays himself down next to Juliet, takes the poison, and
dies. It is less than five days since he first laid eyes on his tragic love.

Only then does Friar Laurence finally come—a few minutes too late to
prevent this further development of the catastrophe. He comes in muttering:

> *Saint Francis be my speed* [help]!
>
> —Act V, scene iii, line 121

St. Francis (Giovanni Francesco Bernardone) was born in Assisi in
1182, and after the usual life of a gay, but not particularly immoral, young
man of the upper classes, he experienced a conversion to a saintly life.
About 1202 he began to embrace a life of poverty and gathered disciples
about him who were dedicated to preaching humbly and making their way
through life by reliance on free-will offerings of the pious. This was the beginning of the Franciscan order. Presumably Friar Laurence belonged to it.

. . . kill your joys with love

Friar Laurence finds Paris and Romeo both dead, and even as he tries to
absorb this, Juliet wakes. The friar tries to persuade her to come with him
so that he might bestow her in a nunnery, but with Romeo dead, she does
not want to live and will not budge. The friar thinks he hears a noise and
has one last chance at a boldness that might save the last pitiful remnant—
Juliet's life. He misses that, too, and flees in fear of being discovered.

Left alone, Juliet kills herself with Romeo's dagger.

The watch, drawn by all the disturbance, now gathers, and so does the
town: Montague, Capulet, the Prince. Little by little, the whole story comes
out and the Prince sorrowfully states the moral:

> *Where be these enemies? Capulet, Montague,*
> *See what a scourge is laid upon your hate,*
> *That heaven finds means to kill your joys with love.*
> *And I, for winking at your discords too,*
> *Have lost a brace of kinsmen. All are punished.*
>
> —Act V, scene iii, lines 291–95

The mutual grief ends the feud; as it might, so easily, have ended days
earlier in mutual joy.

18

THE MERCHANT OF VENICE

THE MERCHANT OF VENICE, written in 1596 or 1597, lays its scene in what is surely one of the most remarkable cities in history. It is a city which at its peak was richer and more powerful than almost any full-sized nation of its time. It was queen of the sea and a barrier against the formidable Turks.

This city, Venice, which was like an Italian Athens born after its time, or an Italian Amsterdam born before, had its birth at the time of the invasion of Italy by Attila the Hun in 452. Fleeing Italians hid in the lagoons offshore along the northern Adriatic and about this colony as the nucleus Venice arose.

While the Franks, the Byzantines, the Lombards, and the papacy all struggled for control over Italy, Venice, under skillful leadership, managed to gain for itself a steadily increasing independence and, through trade, a steadily increasing prosperity.

Venetian prosperity and power climbed steeply during the period of the Crusades, since it, along with several other Italian cities, had the ships to carry the Crusaders and their supplies—and charged healthily for it. By 1203 Venice could blackmail a group of Crusaders into attacking the Byzantine Empire first. In 1204 the Crusaders took Constantinople itself and the Byzantine Empire was divided as loot, with a considerable share going to Venice, which thus became a major Mediterranean power.

Venice embarked on a long struggle with Genoa, a port on the other side of the Italian boot, and by 1380 had won completely. The war made her aware of her need for continental territories to assure herself of food supplies despite the ups and downs of naval warfare. She spread out into nearby Italy and by 1420 northeastern Italy was hers from the Adriatic nearly to Lake Como.

The fifteenth century, however, saw her pass her peak. The Turk captured Constantinople in 1453 and it became less easy to trade with the East. The Portuguese explorers circled Africa by 1497 and, as it grew possible to bypass the Mediterranean, the Venetian stranglehold on trade with the East further diminished.

Then, in the sixteenth century, France, Spain, and the Empire began to

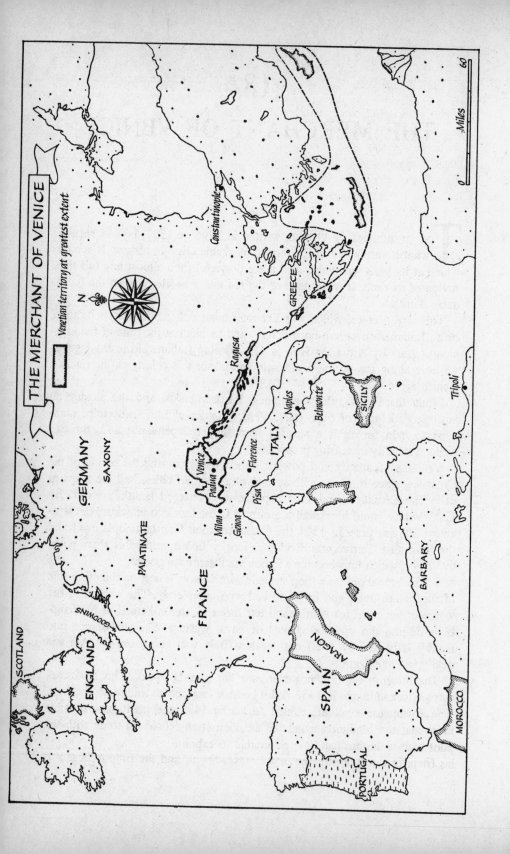

use Italy as a battleground and the entire peninsula, including Venice, was reduced to misery.

But even in Shakespeare's time, although Venice was no longer what she had been, she remained a romantic land, with the trappings of empire still about herself—an efficient, stable, and long-established government over wealthy merchants and skillful seamen with territory and bases here and there in the Mediterranean. What's more, Shakespeare's century saw Venice reach its artistic heights. Titian and Tintoretto were sixteenth-century Venetians, for instance.

Then too, even in decline, Venice remained Europe's shield against the Turks throughout Shakespeare's lifetime and for several decades after his death.

. . . why I am so sad

The play opens with Antonio on stage. He is the "merchant" of the title and he is in conversation with two friends, Salerio and Solanio. Antonio says:

> In sooth I know not why I am so sad.
> It wearies me, you say it wearies you;
> —Act I, scene i, lines 1–2

The sadness is never explicitly explained in the play and it may be accepted as simply setting a mood. Antonio, after all, is to spend much of the play in a position of great danger.

However, it is possible to speculate that there is a more specific cause of sadness, one which Shakespeare does not care to elaborate upon. As will appear soon enough, Antonio has a male friend to whom he is devoted with a self-sacrificial intensity that is almost unbelievable. This friend, we are soon to find out, is about to woo a young lady in the hope of marrying her.

Antonio may very easily be meant by Shakespeare to represent the nobility of homosexual love, something he hints at in several plays (as, for instance, in The Two Gentlemen of Verona, see page I–473) without quite daring to be specific about it.

Well then, if Antonio's friend has, in the eagerness of his new plans involving a lady, grown more distant, is not this reason enough for the poor man to be sad—and yet be unable to explain it, without disgrace, to his friends?

. . . your argosies . . .

His friends, however, have a more prosaic explanation. Salerio suggests that he is nervous over the state of his business affairs, saying:

> *Your mind is tossing on the ocean,*
> *There where your argosies with portly sail—*
>
>   —Act I, scene i, lines 8–9

The word "argosies" harks back to a city founded on the eastern shore of the Adriatic in the seventh century by refugees, as Venice had similarly been founded two centuries earlier. In this case, the founders were Greeks who were being pushed out of the interior by invading Slavs. The new city was named Ragusium, better known to us in the Italian version of the name, Ragusa.

Ragusa was, for a time, a flourishing trading city, much like Venice itself, or like Genoa and Pisa. Ragusa was particularly known for its large merchant ships, which were called *ragusea*. In English the first two letters were transposed and the word became "argosy."

It is clear from these opening exchanges, then, that Antonio is an extremely wealthy merchant, but one whose business involves extreme risk. Antonio, however, pooh-poohs the chances of these risks coming to pass.

. . . two-headed Janus

But if Antonio is not worried about business and is merely irrationally sad, then, says Solanio with a touch of impatience, he might just as well be irrationally merry. Solanio says:

> *. . . Now by two-headed Janus,*
> *Nature hath framed strange fellows in her time:*
> *Some that will evermore peep through their eyes*
> *And laugh like parrots at a bagpiper,*
> *And other of such vinegar aspect*
> *That they'll not show their teeth in way of smile*
> *Though Nestor swear the jest be laughable.*
>
>   —Act I, scene i, lines 50–56

In other words, some people are, by simple temperament, happy; others sad.

As for Janus, he is the most familiar of the purely Roman (that is, non-Greek) gods. He was the god of doorways and therefore the god of going in and going out. (The word "janitor" is derived from his name.) It is an easy extension from that to seeing in him the god of beginnings and endings, of comings and goings (and January, the beginning of the year, is named in his honor.)

In the Roman forum Janus was honored with a temple whose gates were open in time of war and closed in time of peace. Rome's military history was such that for seven centuries they were hardly ever closed.

Though on Roman representations he is shown with two identical faces in opposite directions, it is possible to improve on that. Since he is the god of beginnings and endings, he might be imagined to have one face turned toward the past and the other toward the future.

It could easily be imagined that the past-viewing face was cheerful, since the pains of the past were over, while the forward-viewing face was sad, since there was uncertainty as to what the pains of the future might be—hence the figure of speech in Solanio's statement.

. . . let my liver rather heat . . .

Three other friends of Antonio enter: Bassanio, Gratiano, and Lorenzo, while Salerio and Solanio leave.

Gratiano also notes Antonio's sadness and he too advocates merriment for its own sake. He says to Antonio:

> *Let me play the fool!*
> *With mirth and laughter let old wrinkles come,*
> *And let my liver rather heat with wine*
> *Than my heart cool with mortifying groans.*
> —Act I, scene i, lines 79–82

The link between liver and wine might seem at first blush to indicate that Shakespeare had a prescient knowledge of the connection physicians would eventually draw between cirrhosis of the liver and alcoholism.

Nothing of the sort. The liver is the largest gland in the body, weighing three or four pounds in man and being correspondingly large in other mammals. It is easy to equate size and importance and to argue that the liver is so large because it has a peculiarly important function and must therefore serve as the seat of life and of the emotions. (The similarity between "liver" and "live" is not accidental.)

Contributing to this also is the fact that ancient priests, looking for prognostications of things to come, would often study the liver of animals sacrificed to the gods. This is natural, since the liver is so large and varies so in detail from animal to animal that it is particularly easy to study. Yet it is not the ease that can be advanced as a reason, so special importance must be insisted upon instead.

In Belmont . . .

It is Bassanio with whom Antonio is in love and the strength of the latter's affection is quickly shown. Bassanio has been living beyond his means
and is deeply in debt. He has been forced to borrow and says, frankly:

> *. . . To you, Antonio,*
> *I owe the most in money and in love,*
>
> —Act I, scene i, lines 130–31

But Antonio is willing to continue the support. He says earnestly to
Bassanio:

> *. . . be assured*
> *My purse, my person, my extremest means*
> *Lie all unlocked to your occasions* [needs].
>
> —Act I, scene i, lines 137–39

Surely the attachment on Antonio's side can only be love in its fullest
sense. Yet it may be one-sided. Bassanio's affection may be nothing more
than friendship, for he seems to have no hesitation in attempting to draw
on Antonio's support for a competing love.

Bassanio explains that he may be in a position to repay all he has borrowed if only Antonio will be willing to invest a bit more. He says:

> *In Belmont is a lady richly left;*
>
> —Act I, scene i, line 161

In short, Bassanio knows of a rich heiress and if he can marry her,
he can pay off all his debts. All he needs is enough money to appear a
respectable suitor; he cannot go as a beggar.

(The beginning of Bassanio's speech makes him sound like a fortune
hunter, but the play will amply show that he wants the woman for herself
and that the money is secondary. He stresses the money now because he
wants to explain that he will be able to pay off his debt to Antonio, and
not that he is greedy for wealth for himself.)

As for Belmont, that may well be a fictitious name for the estate left
to the heiress. In the Italian tale from which this portion of the plot is derived, the place is Belmonte, and there is a Belmonte in Italy, on the western shore of the Italian toe, a little over five hundred miles south of Venice.
Probably there is no connection, and as far as the play is concerned, it
doesn't matter where Belmont is, but it is interesting that a Belmonte exists.

Her name is Portia . . .

Bassanio has seen the lady and knows her to be beautiful and virtuous. He says:

> *Her name is Portia, nothing undervalued*
> *To Cato's daughter, Brutus' Portia;*
>> —Act I, scene i, lines 165–66

Brutus' Portia—that is, his wife—appears as a pattern of Roman virtue in *Julius Caesar* (see page I-281), a play Shakespeare wrote some two years after *The Merchant of Venice*.

. . . Colchos' strond

Bassanio goes on in his lyrical praise of Portia to say:

> *. . . her sunny locks*
> *Hang on her temples like a golden fleece,*
> *Which makes her seat of Belmont Colchos' strond,*
> *And many Jasons come in quest of her.*
>> —Act I, scene i, lines 169–72

The tale of the Golden Fleece is one of the most famous in Greek mythology. Two children, the son and daughter of a king of Thebes, had a wicked stepmother. With the help of the gods they were whisked away from Thebes on the back of a winged ram with a golden fleece (see page I-541). The ram flew them to what must have seemed the end of the world to the very early Greeks—the easternmost shore of the Black Sea.

On the way, the girl, Helle, fell off and drowned in one of the narrow waterways between the Aegean and the Black seas, a waterway known as the "Hellespont" in consequence. The boy, however, was carried safely to the kingdom of Colchis (called Colchos in this Shakespearean passage). The King of Colchis, Aeetes, sacrificed the ram and suspended the Golden Fleece from a tree, leaving it under the guard of a never sleeping dragon.

To attain that Golden Fleece and bring it back to Greece was a worthy aim for an adventurer, and Jason, an exiled Thessalian prince, undertook the quest. With a fifty-oared ship, the *Argo,* and a crew of heroes, he penetrated the Black Sea and won the Fleece.

. . . the County Palatine

When Bassanio is done explaining, Antonio promptly offers to finance the project in a characteristic burst of selflessness. With that done the scene shifts at once to Belmont, where we meet Portia and her companion, Nerissa.

It seems that Portia's father, in dying, has left three caskets behind, one of gold, one of silver, and one of lead. Each suitor must choose one of the caskets, and only he who picks the correct casket, the one with Portia's portrait inside, can marry her. If the suitor loses, he must swear to leave at once and never to reveal which casket he had chosen.

There are many suitors come to take their chances and Portia has an opportunity to display her mocking wit at their expense (and Shakespeare has a chance to air his prejudices).

Nerissa mentions a prince of Naples first and he is dismissed by Portia at once as interested only in horses and horsemanship. Nerissa then says:

> *Then is there the County Palatine.*
>
> —Act I, scene ii, line 44

In the early Middle Ages a "count palatine" was a high official who served in the King's household; that is, in the palace. Eventually, the title came to be inherited only as a title and without any special householdly duties.

In only one case did the title remain prominent, and that was in connection with a tract of land along the middle Rhine River whose ruler remained the Count Palatine. The territory was therefore known as the "Palatinate." Its capital was at Heidelberg.

In Shakespeare's time the Palatinate was a center of German Calvinism, a form of religion which was similar to English Puritanism. In 1592, just a few years before *The Merchant of Venice* was written, Frederick IV succeeded to the title. He was a sincere Calvinist (he was called "Frederick the Upright"), which meant he was grave and solemn to a degree.

It was perhaps with that in mind that Shakespeare has Portia say with respect to him:

> *He hears merry tales and smiles not; I fear he will prove the weeping philosopher when he grows old, being so full of unmannerly sadness in his youth.*
>
> —Act I, scene ii, lines 46–49

There was a "weeping philosopher"; he was Heraclitus of Ephesus, who lived about 500 B.C. and whose gloomy view of life caused him to weep over the follies of mankind. (There was also a "laughing philosopher," Democritus of Abdera, who lived about 400 B.C. and whose cheerful disposition enabled him to laugh over the follies of mankind.)

. . . every man in no man . . .

A reference to a French suitor has Portia say:

> *Why, he hath a horse better than the Neapolitan's, a better*
> *bad habit of frowning than the Count Palatine; he is every*
> *man in no man. If a throstle sing, he falls straight a-cap'ring;*
> —Act I, scene ii, lines 57–60

This is, in part, the old stereotype of the Frenchman—a frivolous person without strong convictions who takes on the coloring of his surroundings. In this case, Shakespeare may even have a specific case in mind.

In 1593, just three years before *The Merchant of Venice* was written, the French Protestant leader Henry of Navarre (pictured so favorably in *Love's Labor's Lost,* see page I–423) accepted Catholicism to establish himself as King Henry IV. To English Protestants this was a perfect case of French lack of principle.

. . . his behavior everywhere

An English suitor does not escape Portia's sharp tongue either. Concerning him, she says:

> *How oddly he is suited* [outfitted]! *I think he bought his*
> *doublet in Italy, his round hose in France, his bonnet in*
> *Germany, and his behavior everywhere.*
> —Act I, scene ii, lines 72–75

This is the old complaint of the conservative nationalistic Englishman (of whom Shakespeare is so often a spokesman) that the younger generation is mad for foreign novelties and has nothing but contempt for the traditions of their own land. (This view is not confined to England or to the sixteenth century.)

. . . borrowed a box of the ear . . .

The mention of a Scotsman brings forth an expression of contempt from Portia, who says:

> *. . . he hath a neighborly charity in him, for he borrowed a box of the ear of the Englishman and swore he would pay him again when he was able. I think the Frenchman became his surety . . .*
>
> —Act I, scene ii, lines 78–81

Scotland was, like France, one of England's traditional enemies. Since Scotland was much weaker than France it was regularly beaten, so that Shakespeare can indulge in a rather cheap vaunt over an enemy that was often defeated but never accepted defeat.

As a matter of fact, the sixteenth century saw England inflict two disastrous boxes of the ear upon Scotland. In 1513 England defeated Scotland in the Battle of Flodden Field (see page II–746), and then again, in 1542, at the Battle of Solway Moss.

Shakespeare's reference to the Frenchman becoming the Scotsman's surety refers to the traditional friendship between France and Scotland. France was always ready to support Scotland financially in her wars against England, but was never able to support her by direct military force.

. . . the Duke of Saxony's nephew

Then Nerissa asks about another:

> *How like you the young German, the Duke of Saxony's nephew?*
>
> —Act I, scene ii, lines 83–84

To which Portia replies:

> *Very vilely in the morning when he is sober, and most vilely in the afternoon when he is drunk.*
>
> —Act I, scene ii, lines 85–86

This was no more than a matter of making fun of the proverbial German habit of drunkenness, but Shakespeare hit closer than he knew. The Elector of Saxony (a title unique to Germany, which Shakespeare converts into the more familiar "duke") had, at the time *The Merchant of Venice* was written, a younger brother who was then about twelve years old, and who grew up to be a notorious drunkard.

. . . as old as Sibylla . . .

However, none of these suitors will even try the casket test. They are there only to serve as butts for Portia's jokes, and now Nerissa reports they are leaving. Portia is relieved, but she insists she will marry only in accordance with the casket test just the same:

> *If I live to be as old as Sibylla, I will die as chaste as Diana unless I be obtained by the manner of my father's will.*
> —Act I, scene ii, lines 105–7

Sibylla's age was proverbial (see page I–452) and Shakespeare makes use of that in several plays.

. . . the Marquis of Montferrat

But now we get down to business. Nerissa asks:

> *Do you not remember, lady, in your father's time, a Venetian, a scholar and a soldier, that came hither in company of the Marquis of Montferrat?*
> —Act I, scene ii, lines 111–13

The marquisate of Montferrat was an independent state in Shakespeare's time located just north of Genoa. In 1587 Vicenzo I became marquis. His immediate predecessors had been enlightened rulers who had patronized art and literature and were therefore looked upon with great favor by artists and writers. Vicenzo himself helped deliver the great poet Torquato Tasso from the insane asylum to which he had been sent as a result of his paranoid mania.

Nevertheless, Vicenzo was a most extravagant and wasteful ruler, and at the time *The Merchant of Venice* was written, these proclivities of his were quite clear. If Bassanio was his friend and had been forced to keep up with him, no wonder he managed to go through so much of Antonio's fortune.

It was undoubtedly on this earlier visit that Bassanio had seen Portia and discovered her beauty and virtue. She had not been unaffected either, for on the mere mention of him she grows excited. But new suitors are coming and the scene reaches its end.

Three thousand ducats . . .

Back in Venice, there is the problem of financing Bassanio. Antonio's ready cash is tied up in his merchant vessels, so the young man must borrow the actual money elsewhere. Antonio, however, is willing to act as guarantor of the loan. (Otherwise, Bassanio would lack the credit to borrow anything at all.)

The third scene of the play opens, then, with Bassanio in conversation with a prospective source of money. The man of whom the loan is being requested says musingly (for it is a large sum):

> *Three thousand ducats—well.*
>
> —Act I, scene iii, line 1

In the Middle Ages there were few regions with a sufficiently reliable supply of silver to issue good coins. Venice was one of the exceptions. Her rich trade brought precious metals to her gates and it paid her to use them in producing good coins of full weight and honest value. The reputation of Venice lay behind the coins and merchants from all over Europe and the Mediterranean lands were anxious to accept those coins—which was to the benefit of Venetian trade.

These coins were put out by the Duchy of Venice, a state which in the Italian language was the "Ducato di Venezia," so that the coins were called *ducati* or, in English, "ducats." Good coins, also called ducats, were put out by the Duchy of Apulia in southern Italy.

In either case, three thousand ducats was a huge sum for the time. Bassanio was not skimping.

The person to whom Bassanio is talking is not an ordinary Venetian. We can picture him (and he is usually presented on the stage) as a tall man with a beak of a nose, a long black beard, curly sideburns, a skull cap, and a long black coat. He is, in short, a Jew, and his name is Shylock.

Shylock is not a Jewish name; there was never a Jew named Shylock that anyone has heard of; the name is an invention of Shakespeare's which has entered the common language (because of the power of the characterization of the man) to represent any grasping, greedy, hard-hearted creditor. I have heard Jews themselves use the word with exactly this meaning, referring back to Shakespeare's character.

Where did Shakespeare get the name? There is a Hebrew word *shalakh,* which appears twice in the Bible (Leviticus 11:17 and Deuteronomy 14:17). In both places, birds of prey are being listed as unfit articles of diet for Jews. No one knows exactly what bird is meant by *shalakh,* but the usual translation into English gives it as "cormorant."

The cormorant is a sea bird which eats fish so voraciously that the word has come to mean personified greed and voraciousness. Shakespeare apparently is using a form of the Hebrew word both as name and characterization of the Jewish moneylender.

. . . upon the Rialto . . .

Shylock hesitates. The loan is a large one but Antonio, who is being offered as surety, has a good reputation for honest business dealing and is known to be wealthy enough to cover the sum. And still Shylock hesitates, for Antonio's ventures are thinly spread and he is at the moment in a period of unusual risk. Shylock says of Antonio:

> *. . . he hath an argosy bound to Tripolis, another to the Indies; I understand, moreover, upon the Rialto, he hath a third at Mexico, a fourth for England—and other ventures he hath, squand'red abroad.*
>
> —Act I, scene iii, lines 17–21

Of the places listed by Shylock, the least familiar is Tripolis. This word means "three cities" in Greek and any city built up out of the union of three towns is liable to be given that name. As an example there is one in northern Africa, which is better known to us by the Italian version of the name, Tripoli. It is the capital of the modern kingdom of Libya.

There is also a second Tripolis on the eastern shore of the Mediterranean, in what is now Lebanon. It is the second largest city of that nation nowadays, and is better known to the west as Tripoli. Its Arabic name is Tarabulus.

Which Tripoli Antonio's argosy was bound for, whether the one on the southern or the eastern shore of the Mediterranean, we have no way of telling.

Shylock heard his news "upon the Rialto," a phrase that needed no explanation for the audience of the play.

In 1590, some seven years before *The Merchant of Venice* was written, the Venetians built a magnificent marble bridge across the Grand Canal, their chief waterway. The Latin *rivus altus* means "deep stream," and a bridge crossing the stream would very likely adopt its name. The Italian version of the phrase is "Rialto."

The Rialto bridge was lined with a row of shops on either side and with a broad footpath between. It became a busy commercial center and Venetian merchants and traders would gather there to exchange news and gossip.

. . . your prophet the Nazarite . . .

Despite his misgivings, Shylock thinks Antonio is good surety for the loan. Bassanio, eager to help Shylock come to a favorable decision, invites him to dinner, and Shylock draws back at once:

> *Yes, to smell pork, to eat of the habitation which your prophet the Nazarite conjured the devil into!*
>   —Act I, scene iii, lines 31–33

So far the exchange between Bassanio and Shylock has indicated nothing of the religious difference; it might have been any two men discussing a business deal. But now, with the mention of eating, comes the first clear stamp of Jewishness upon Shylock. He won't eat pork!

The Jewish abhorrence of pork is based on biblical statutes. The eleventh chapter of the Book of Leviticus states that only those beasts that have a cloven hoof and that chew the cud are ritually clean and may be eaten and sacrificed. As one example of a beast that is not ritually clean, the seventh and eighth verses say: "And the swine, though he divide the hoof, and be cloven-footed, yet he cheweth not the cud; he is unclean to you. Of their flesh shall ye not eat, and their carcase shall ye not touch."

Many other creatures are listed as unclean in the chapter; such as the camel, the hare, the owl, the cormorant, the shellfish, and so on.

It is the pig, though, that stands out. Most of the other creatures forbidden to Jews were not a customary part of the diet of Gentiles either. Pork, on the other hand, was a favored dish of Gentiles, and for Jews to have so extreme an abhorrence of it seemed most peculiar.

It became a hallmark of the difference between Jew and Gentile. When Antiochus IV of the Seleucid Empire tried to eradicate Judaism in the second century B.C., he insisted that Jews eat pork as the best way of indicating they had abandoned their religion (and a number of Jews suffered martyrdom rather than comply). In medieval Europe too the value of a conversion from Judaism was judged by the eagerness with which the erstwhile Jew ate pork.

Shylock, in his comment on pork, does not, however, refer to the Old Testament prohibition. The Elizabethan audience would not have been familiar with that. The dietary laws of the Mosaic Code had, in the Christian view, been superseded through a vision St. Peter had had (as is described in Chapter 10 of the Book of Acts) and the Leviticus chapter was therefore a dead letter.

Instead, Shylock is made to express his disgust by means of a reference to the New Testament. The reference is to a wonder tale concerning Jesus which describes how at one time he evicted many devils from a man possessed and sent them into a herd of swine. The version in Matthew states

(8:32) that the devils "went into the herd of swine and, behold, the whole herd of swine ran violently down a steep place into the sea, and perished in the waters."

Presumably, Shylock scorns pork as evil-haunted, and feels swine to be a fit habitation for demons and therefore most unfit food for men. And, of course, we might also view the passage as a mocking reference by Shylock to the kind of childish and superstitious tales (in his view) that made up the Christian religion.

In actual fact, a Jew of the time would have been careful to avoid mocking at Christianity or to refer sneeringly to "your prophet the Nazarite," out of consideration for his own safety in a hostile world. Shakespeare, however, was intent on constructing a villain, and how better to do so than to have him sneer at what the audience held sacred.

It is also important to remember that neither Shakespeare nor his audience had any firsthand knowledge of how Jews talked or acted anyway. The Jews had been driven out of England by Edward I in 1290, and save for a few special exceptions, they were still absent from the land in Shakespeare's time. They were not allowed to return, in fact, until the time of Oliver Cromwell, forty years after Shakespeare's death.

. . . a fawning publican . . .

Now Antonio enters and Shylock views him with instant hate. He says, aside:

> How like a fawning publican he looks.
> I hate him for he is a Christian;
>
> —Act I, scene iii, lines 38–39

The word "publican" occurs on a number of occasions in the New Testament, where it is used for those who collected taxes on behalf of the Roman masters of Judea. A tax collector is never popular and one who collects on behalf of an occupying power is doubly damned. "Publican" was therefore a term of opprobrium among the Jews of Roman times. The word is frequently coupled with "sinners," so that when the Pharisees wished to express their disapproval of Jesus, they pointed out that he ate "with publicans and sinners" (as in Matthew 9:11, for instance).

Certainly Antonio cannot possibly be considered a publican and it is very likely that an actual Jew would not so glibly have used a term that does not occur in the Old Testament. But Shakespeare's audience knew "publican" as a word associated with the only Jews they really knew, those spoken of in the New Testament, and as a word of opprobrium besides.

Thus, the very use of the word, whether sensible or not, indicated Shylock's Jewishness, and that is what Shakespeare wanted it to do.

Shylock's next remark about hating Christians further emphasizes his unrelieved villainy to a good Christian audience. They are not likely to reflect that the Jews of Shakespeare's time had little to associate with their Christian neighbors but abuse, blows, and worse and could scarcely be expected to love them for it. (As Israel Zangwill, the English-Jewish writer, is supposed to have said with sardonic bitterness in the last years of the nineteenth century: "The Jews are a frightened people. Nineteen centuries of Christian love have broken down their nerves.")

And yet the Christians were but victims of their training too. Each Christian knew of Jews from the New Testament tales that were repeated in church week in and week out. The Jews had rejected Jesus and demanded the crucifixion. The Jews had opposed and persecuted the apostles. In the time of the Crusades, tales arose that Jews poisoned wells and sacrificed Christian children as part of the celebration of the Passover.

Furthermore, added to all these abstractions, there was in England a contemporary case of an actual Jew of alleged enormous villainy. Queen Elizabeth I had had as her personal physician one Roderigo Lopez. He first accepted the post in 1586.

Lopez was of Portuguese origin, which made him a foreigner, and he had once been a Jew, which made him worse than a foreigner. To be sure, he was converted to Christianity, but born Christians generally suspected the sincerity of a Jew's conversion.

In 1594 Lopez came under suspicion of trying to poison the Queen in return for Spanish bribes. It is the modern opinion that he was innocent, and certainly Queen Elizabeth seemed to believe he was innocent. The Earl of Essex (of whom Shakespeare was a devoted follower) held a strong belief in Lopez' guilt and forced a trial. A Portuguese ex-Jew could scarcely expect a very objective or fair trial, and Lopez was convicted and then executed before a huge crowd under conditions of utmost brutality.

The execution made the whole question of Jewish villainy very topical, and a play entitled *The Jew of Malta* was promptly revived. This play, first produced in 1589, had been written by Christopher Marlowe (who had died in 1593) and dealt with the flamboyant and monstrous villainy of a Jew. The revival was enormously successful.

Shakespeare, who always had his finger on the popular pulse, and who was nothing if not a "commercial" writer, at once realized the value of writing a play of his own about a villainous Jew, and *The Merchant of Venice* was the result.

The rate of usance . . .

But Shakespeare is Shakespeare; he cannot make his Jew a simple straw man of unreasoning villainy. Shylock must have rational motives, and he says, in further explanation of his hatred of Antonio:

> *He lends out money gratis, and brings down*
> *The rate of usance here with us in Venice.*
> —Act I, scene iii, lines 41–42

"Usance" represents the "use" of money, and closely allied to it is the word "usury." In early times money was usually lent as a gesture of friendship or charity, to relieve distress; and it would seem a most ignoble act to take back more than was lent. To charge "usance" (or "interest") was strongly condemned by the ethical teachings of Judaism. In Exodus 22:25 God is described as saying: "If thou lend money to any of my people that is poor by thee, thou shalt not be to him as an usurer, neither shalt thou lay upon him usury."

In a more complicated society, however, money is lent not necessarily to friends, but to strangers; and not to those who are in personal need, but to those who need ready money to begin a course of action that will eventually (it is hoped) lead to profit. The money is hired for business purposes and the hire should be paid for. Naturally the rate of payment should be greater if the risk of loss is greater.

The medieval church did not distinguish between lending out of charity and lending out of business need, and interest on both were alike forbidden.

The Jews, however, might interpret the Exodus verse as applying to "my people" (i.e., Jews) only. Lending at interest to non-Jews would therefore be permissible. Furthermore, Jews in Christian countries found themselves locked out of one type of employment after another, until very little was left them but the profession of moneylending, which was (in theory) forbidden to Christians.

Thus was set up the sort of vicious cycle that is constantly used to plague minorities of any kind. Jews were forced into becoming usurers and then the fact that they were usurers was used to prove how villainous and hateful they were.

To make matters still more ironical, Christians were by no means as virtuous in the matter as theory had it. The church's strictures could not stand up against economic needs. Christian usurers arose in northern Italy to the point where the term "Lombard" (see page I-447) became synonymous in England with "pawnbroker" or "moneylender." In fact, it was because Italian moneylenders came to England in the thirteenth century that Edward I was able to do without Jews and could expel them from the nation.

. . . once upon the hip

Shylock broods on the wrongs he and his have suffered, and he mutters:

> *If I can catch him once upon the hip* [at a disadvantage],
> *I will feed fat the ancient grudge I bear him.*
> *He hates our sacred nation . . .*
>
> —Act I, scene iii, lines 43–45

The hatred is thus mutual (and in a passage shortly to come Antonio makes it clear that it is). The villainy is not, however. To the Christian audience, Shylock's hatred of Christians is a mark of dark and malignant villainy, but Antonio's hatred of Jews is very natural and even praiseworthy. Undoubtedly, if the audience consisted entirely of Jews, the view would be precisely reversed—and no more rational.

This double standard in viewing the ethical behavior of oneself and one's enemy is common to almost all men and is the despair of the few.

The skillful shepherd . . .

Antonio and Bassanio are anxious for a definite reply from Shylock, but Shylock delays as he considers how best he might turn Antonio's need to his advantage.

Shylock is stung, too, by Antonio's scornful hint that ordinarily he does not lend or borrow at interest. Shylock feels it necessary to prove that shrewd bargaining is not sinful.

He turns to the Old Testament and cites the case of Jacob, who agreed with his uncle, Laban, to herd his sheep and goats and take for his own pay only those lambs and kids who were born streaked, spotted, or otherwise not of solid color.

Ordinarily these would have made up a tiny minority of the young (which was why Laban agreed to the bargain), but Jacob peeled wands in such a way as to give them a striped appearance and placed them where the ewes would see them during the act of mating. Shylock says:

> *The skillful shepherd pilled me certain wands,*
> *And in the doing of the deed of kind* [mating]
> *He stuck them up before the fulsome ewes,*

THE MERCHANT OF VENICE

> *Who then conceiving, did in eaning* [lambing] *time*
> *Fall parti-colored lambs, and those were Jacob's.*
> *This was a way to thrive, and he was blest;*
> *And thrift is blessing if men steal it not.*
>
> —Act I, scene iii, lines 81–87

The story is a reasonably accurate rendition of the second half of the thirtieth chapter of Genesis. The belief that the characteristics of the young can be influenced by the nature of the environment during conception and pregnancy is part of the folklore of the ages, but it lacks any real foundation. No reputable biologist accepts this view, nor can real evidence be cited for it, and even the authority of the Bible is insufficient to put it across.

If the biblical tale were true and if the young animals were born as described, it would have had to be the result of a miracle and not of any natural event brought about by Jacob.

... cite Scripture ...

The case of Jacob is a poor one to support usury (something Antonio quickly points out), and a real Jew could easily have found better arguments. However, the use of the Jacob tale is to condemn Shylock to the audience rather than to support him. Since he is made to quote, with approval, a shady act of business on the part of Jacob, the audience can nod to each other and say "Jews were always like that from the very beginning."

But to avoid some of the blame appearing to stick to the Bible rather than to Shylock (for Shakespeare never knowingly sought trouble with the authorities) Antonio is made to remark in an aside to Bassanio:

> *The devil can cite Scripture for his purpose.*
>
> —Act I, scene iii, line 95

This is not merely a metaphorical reference to Shylock, but is a direct derivation from a biblical tale. Matthew tells of Jesus being tested in the desert by the devil, who tries to persuade Jesus to display miraculous powers for prideful self-aggrandizement.

Thus, the devil takes Jesus to the top of the Temple in Jerusalem and urges him to jump off in order that he might display the protection that angels would afford him. The devil accompanies his urging with a quotation from the Old Testament, saying: ". . . for it is written, He shall give his angels charge concerning thee: and in their hands they shall bear thee up, lest at any time thou dash thy foot against a stone." (This is from Matthew 4:6 and the quotation is from Psalms 91:11–12.)

. . . my Jewish gaberdine

As Shylock continues to be pressed, his politeness suddenly snaps
and his hatred peeps forth. Bitterly, he begins:

> *Signior Antonio, many a time and oft*
> *In the Rialto you have rated* [reviled] *me*
> *About my moneys and my usances.*
> *Still* [Always] *have I borne it with a patient shrug.*
> *For suff'rance* [patience] *is the badge of all our tribe.*
> *You call me misbeliever, cutthroat dog,*
> *And spit upon my Jewish gaberdine,*
>
> —Act I, scene iii, lines 103–9

The Jewish gaberdine was a long, coarse cloak of the kind pilgrims wore
in humility, to show that they were approaching some shrine as sinners
hoping to be forgiven. In many places, Jews were forced to wear some
distinctive garb of humiliating nature that had the double duty of indicating to the world what sinners they were and at the same time warning
Christians from afar, so that they need not be sullied by showing Jews
any kindness or courtesy.

Indeed, in the very city of Venice in which this play is laid, and in 1516,
some eighty years before the play was written, the authorities went further.
It was decided to herd the Jews into a special quarter which could be ef-
ficiently isolated. In part, this was a further development of the idea that
Jews should not pollute Christians with their presence; and in part there
was a kind of humanity behind it, since the Jews were safer in their own
section and could be more easily protected by the authorities against looting and lynching. (They could also be more easily massacred en masse if
the authorities chose to look the other way.)

For the purpose, the Venetians chose an island on which an iron
foundry (*gheto* in Italian) must once have stood, for that was the name of
the island. It was established as the Jewish quarter and "ghetto," with an
additional "t," has gone ringing down history ever since as the name for
any Jewish quarter anywhere and, in very recent times, for any city area
occupied largely by any minority group.

Again, a vicious cycle was established. The Jews were forced to dress
differently and live separately and were then hated for being different and
exclusive.

. . . an equal pound of your fair flesh . . .

Shylock's point is that he can scarcely be expected to lend money to someone who has treated him with such scorn and hatred. If Antonio had, at this point, been diplomatic, the loan might have been made in ordinary fashion and that would have been that. Instead, however, Antonio answers cruelly:

> *I am as like to call thee so* [dog] *again,*
> *To spit on thee again, to spurn thee too.*
>> —Act I, scene iii, lines 127–28

This is utterly out of character for Antonio, who throughout the play is shown to be the soul of courtesy, gentleness, and love, and in the end has mercy even on Shylock. But Shakespeare needs a motive for Shylock's behavior in this play, and Antonio's harshness now, when Shylock all but begs for some sort of Christian remorse for the cruelty shown him, turns his persecuted heart to stone.

He agrees to make the loan but only on a queer condition, saying:

> *If you repay me not on such a day,*
> *In such a place, such sum or sums as are*
> *Expressed in the condition, let the forfeit*
> *Be nominated for an equal pound*
> *Of your fair flesh, to be cut off and taken*
> *In what part of your body pleaseth me.*
>> —Act I, scene iii, lines 142–48

On the surface, there is some generosity being shown here. Shylock is lending money *without interest*. If he is repaid on time, he will take only the three thousand ducats he is lending, no more. And if the money is not repaid, there is a forfeit of a pound of flesh, no money at all.

Shylock suggests this as a kind of merry jest, but it is clear that he is playing a long shot. He has already expressed his doubts of the safety of Antonio's manifold sea ventures, and *if* something should happen to them, by means of the forfeit he can kill Antonio. If the ships come home safe, he loses interest, of course, but after Antonio's remarks, the loss of interest is worth the slender chance of killing him legally.

Bassanio and Antonio both realize this, and Bassanio, in horror, refuses the deal. Antonio, however, convinced that his ships will return, insists on agreeing to the terms.

It is from this passage and from those following in the play that the phrase "pound of flesh" has entered the language as meaning the wringing out of the last bit of a bargain, however harsh and brutal the consequences.

. . . my complexion

The Shylock and Portia scenes now alternate. Back in Belmont, a new suitor arrives, the Prince of Morocco, who begins:

> *Mislike me not for my complexion,*
> *The shadowed livery of the burnished sun,*
> *To whom I am a neighbor and near bred.*
>
> —Act II, scene i, lines 1–3

There is nothing here to indicate that the Prince of Morocco is anything more than a Moor, that is, a swarthy member of the "white race." However, Shakespeare's emphasis on his complexion induces us to think that he was imagined as a black, for Shakespeare confused Moors and blacks, as in *Titus Andronicus* (see page I–402).

. . . Sultan Solyman

As Morocco prepares to take the test of the casket, he can't resist boasting a little. He swears he would dare anything to win Portia:

> *By this scimitar*
> *That slew the Sophy, and a Persian prince*
> *That won three fields of Sultan Solyman,*
>
> —Act II, scene i, lines 24–26

"Sultan Solyman" is Suleiman I the Magnificent, under whom the empire of the Ottoman Turks reached the peak of its glory. He reigned from 1520 to 1566 and during that reign he was the strongest ruler in Europe, far greater in war and peace than the contemporary Christian monarchs: Henry VIII, Charles V, and Francis I (see page II–747), whose names make so much greater noise in the West-oriented chronicles of our historians.

During the early part of his reign Suleiman led the Ottoman armies deep into Europe. In 1526 he destroyed the Hungarian army at the Battle of Mohács and absorbed most of Hungary into his realm. In 1529 he reached the peak of his fortunes when he actually laid siege to Vienna (which, however, he did not succeed in taking).

Suleiman might have done even better against Europe, had he not also had to face eastward and battle the Persians, who, although Moslems, were of a different sect. Between 1548 and 1555 there was strenuous war between Suleiman and the Persians; a war which was won by Suleiman, but not by a very great margin. There were further wars between the Ottoman

Empire and the Persians after Suleiman's death. Indeed, one was in progress at the time *The Merchant of Venice* was being written, so that Morocco's reference was topical.

From Morocco's words we might suppose he fought as an Ottoman ally, for it was Persians he claims to have beaten. When Morocco says he "slew the Sophy," he is referring to the Shah of Persia.

In the sixteenth century Persia was undergoing one of its periods of greatness under the rule of a family descended from one Safi-al-Din, who had lived in the thirteenth century. The family was called the Safavids, and this became "Sophy" in English.

The first ruler of the Safavid line was Ismail I, who came to the throne in 1501. In 1587 Abbas I became shah. He was the greatest of the line and is sometimes called Abbas the Great. He labored to reform and revitalize the Persian army and make it more fit to defend the land against the Ottoman Turks. In this he had some help, for in 1598 an English mission arrived in Persia to negotiate a treaty against the common Turkish enemy.

Thus, at the time that *The Merchant of Venice* was written, references to Persia and the Sophy were easily understood.

Nevertheless, Morocco, despite his vauntings, realizes that the casket choice means that luck, not valor, will give the victory. He says:

> *If Hercules and Lichas play at dice*
> *Which is the better man, the greater throw*
> *May turn by fortune from the weaker hand.*
> *So is Alcides beaten by his page.*
> —Act II, scene i, lines 32–35

Lichas is the attendant of Hercules (or Alcides, see page I–70), and, as it happens, he comes to a bad end (see page I–380).

. . . thou a merry devil

Before we come to Morocco's casket choice, however, it is back to Venice and a distant glimpse of Shylock's home life. Onto the stage comes Launcelot Gobbo, Shylock's Christian house servant. Launcelot is considering leaving Shylock, for as a good Christian, he has qualms about serving a Jew.

Eventually, after an encounter with his blind father, Launcelot enters the service of Bassanio. He announces this change of service to Shylock's daughter (who makes her first appearance). She says:

I am sorry thou wilt leave my father so;
Our house is hell, and thou a merry devil
Didst rob it of some taste of tediousness.

—Act II, scene iii, lines 1–3

There is, of course, nothing to indicate that Shylock is cruel to his daughter or anything but a good family man (although he is later shown to be puritanical and intent on keeping his daughter from participating in foolish merrymaking). Nevertheless, the audience would readily assume that a Jew's home would be bound to be hellish.

Jessica is beautiful and lacks all the stigmata associated by Elizabethan audiences with Jews. Thus, Launcelot weeps at leaving her, even though she is as Jewish as Shylock.

This is, of course, an old convention. The villainous Jew (or Moslem, or Indian chief, or Chinese mandarin) very frequently has a beautiful daughter who falls in love with the handsome Christian and betrays her people for his sake to the cheers of the audience. In modern action tales, the beautiful Russian girl can hardly wait to fall in love with the handsome American spy and switch sides. (The audience would consider it unspeakably horrible if the situation were reversed, however.)

The name "Jessica" by the way, is not likely to strike modern readers as particularly Jewish, yet is much more so than "Shylock." Toward the end of the eleventh chapter of Genesis, the sister of the wife of Abraham's brother, Nahor, is given as Iscah. It is of this name that Jessica is a form.

Become a Christian . . .

That Jessica is in love with a Christian appears at once, for she loves Lorenzo, who has already appeared as a friend of Antonio's. Jessica says in a soliloquy after bidding Launcelot goodbye:

Alack, what heinous sin is it in me
To be ashamed to be my father's child!
But though I am a daughter to his blood,
I am not to his manners. O Lorenzo,
If thou keep promise, I shall end this strife,
Become a Christian and thy loving wife!

—Act II, scene iii, lines 16–21

This demonstrates that medieval prejudice against the Jew was, in theory at least, religious rather than racial. If the Jew were to consent to become a Christian he would then be accepted into the Christian community on an equal basis.

Actually, this was by no means always so. In Spain and Portugal in the fifteenth century, extreme pressures forced the conversion of many Jews, who were then nevertheless discriminated against by those who took to calling themselves "Old Christians." The converts were called "marranos" ("swine"), and no matter how they attempted to be Christian they were forever suspected of being secretly Jewish.

. . . Black Monday . . .

The opportunity for Jessica to run off with Lorenzo soon appears. Shylock has been invited to dinner with Bassanio, and he is going despite the fact that he will "smell pork." This means Jessica will be left alone.

Launcelot Gobbo, who has carried the invitation from his new master to his old, promises there will be entertainment (to Shylock's further discomfort, for he is puritanical in his outlook—another proof of villainy to a theatergoing audience). Launcelot says:

> I will not say you shall see a masque, but if you do, it was
> not for nothing that my nose fell a-bleeding on Black Monday
> last at six o'clock i' th' morning,
> —Act II, scene v, lines 22–25

This is a satire against the habit of finding a premonition in everything. After all, what can a nosebleed "on Black Monday last" have to do with a masque tonight?

The adjective "black" is sometimes used to commemorate some particularly disastrous occurrence. This particular case dates back to 1360, some two and a quarter centuries before *The Merchant of Venice* was written. At that time Edward III, who had won two great victories in France (see page II-257), settled down in March to lay siege to Paris itself.

The army was reduced in numbers as the result of the previous winter's campaigning and was in want of provisions besides. It was not equipped to withstand a really bad siege of weather, but it was hoped that with spring well under way and the French badly demoralized the siege would not last long.

How wrong they were! On Monday, April 14, 1360, the day after Easter Sunday, a tremendous hailstorm struck the English camp. The fierce wind and unseasonable cold, the hail and the darkness all combined to strike a superstitious fear into the hearts of those who survived the horrible day.

The siege was lifted and Edward himself was sufficiently disheartened to decide on peace. This was signed on May 8 and the rest of Edward's long reign was an inglorious anticlimax. England was not to regain the upper hand in France until the reign of Henry V and the Battle of Agincourt (see page II–498) a half century later.

This Black Monday of 1360 left enough impression on English minds to give the name to Easter Monday ever after.

. . . Hagar's offspring . . .

But Launcelot is doing more than bringing Bassanio's invitation to Shylock. He is also bringing a secret message from Lorenzo to Jessica, arranging for the elopement, and he cannot resist hinting to her of this in phrases that Shylock imperfectly overhears. Shylock says sharply to Jessica:

> What says that fool of Hagar's offspring, ha?
>
> —Act II, scene vi, line 43

Sarah, the wife of Abraham and the ancestress of the Jews, had a handmaiden named Hagar. Since Sarah herself was barren, she gave the handmaiden to Abraham in order that he might have a son by her. This, indeed, came to pass and Hagar's son was named Ishmael.

When, years later, Sarah herself bore Abraham a son, Isaac, it was this younger son who was designated as Abraham's heir. Ishmael and his mother, Hagar, were evicted from the family and sent away in order that there be no dispute over the inheritance.

Thus, one might metaphorically speak of Hagar's offspring, Ishmael, as representing those who did not really inherit the covenant God made with Abraham and over whom the mantle of the true religion did not fall. Shylock would use such a term as a contemptuous designation for any Christian.

Jessica quiets her father's suspicions and, as soon as he is gone, she disguises herself as a boy and joins Lorenzo, taking with her a good supply of her father's money.

That she should escape from her father and elope with a lover, anyone would be ready to excuse since we are all sympathetic with the drives of love. That she should also steal from her father is a less sympathetic action in modern eyes. However, to Elizabethan audiences, stealing from a Jew was not really stealing.

The Hyrcanian deserts . . .

Meanwhile the Prince of Morocco, back in Belmont, must choose among the three caskets. The gold casket bears a legend that says:

"Who chooseth me shall gain what many men desire."
—Act II, scene vii, line 37

Morocco does not hesitate. Surely this can only refer to Portia, for as he says:

The Hyrcanian deserts and the vasty wilds
Of wide Arabia are as throughfares now
For princes to come view fair Portia.
—Act II, scene vii, lines 41–43

Regions are named which are as distant and unattainable as can be imagined. Arabia is an utterly unknown desert to Christians of Shakespeare's time, and the original home of the feared Moslems.

As for Hyrcania, that was the name of the region south of the Caspian Sea (which was therefore called the Hyrcanian Sea in Roman times). Hyrcania reached its period of greatest prominence in the time of the Parthian Empire during the first and second centuries. Parthia was then the great enemy of Rome and its Hyrcanian heartland was never reached by Roman armies.

So Morocco chooses the golden casket and finds a skull inside. Apparently many men desire gold and, in searching out their heart's desire, find death instead. He loses and must leave forthwith.

. . . he shall pay for this

In Venice, Jessica's elopement has been carried through. Shylock has discovered the loss of his daughter, together with the money and jewels she has stolen, and is distracted.

He suspects Lorenzo and is sure that he is escaping by way of the ship that is taking Bassanio (along with his friend, Gratiano) to Belmont. A search of the ship reveals nothing, but Shylock is nevertheless convinced that Antonio, the friend of Lorenzo, is at the bottom of it.

Solanio tells the tale, mimicking the distracted Shylock, who has gone raging through Venice crying for justice against those who stole his daughter and his ducats. The boys of Venice run after him, mocking, and Solanio himself thinks it is all terribly funny, and so, no doubt, did the Elizabethan audience.

The modern audience, if Shylock is played properly as the tragic character he is, is very likely to find it not funny at all, and to find themselves sympathizing with Shylock instead.

Solanio does say one thing rather uneasily:

Let good Antonio look he keep his day,
Or he shall pay for this.

—Act II, scene viii, lines 25–26

The forfeit of the pound of flesh had been set in a moment of extreme irritation on Shylock's part. If it had come to the touch it is conceivable that Shylock might have relented. But now, maddened by the conspiracy to rob him of possessions and daughter by the very men (as he was convinced) to whom he had supplied necessary money, he could scarcely be expected to want anything but revenge—revenge to the uttermost. And while the thought of the kind of revenge he anticipates is not something we can sympathize with, it is something we can understand if we can bring ourselves to occupy his shoes for a moment in imagination.

The Prince of Aragon . . .

And in Belmont there comes another suitor. Nerissa announces him to Portia:

The Prince of Aragon hath ta'en his oath,
And comes to his elections presently.

—Act II, scene ix, lines 2–3

Aragon was the name of a region on the Spanish side of the central Pyrenees to begin with. It was ruled by the kings of Navarre (see page I–422), but in 1035 Sancho III of Navarre left Aragon to his third son, separating it from his kingdom. Independent Aragon then expanded southward at the expense of the Moors, who at that time controlled much of Spain.

By the middle of the fifteenth century Aragon occupied the easternmost fourth of what is now Spain. Most of the rest was occupied by the kingdom of Castile. In 1469 the heir of Castile was an eighteen-year-old girl named Isabella, while the heir of Aragon was a seventeen-year-old boy named Ferdinand. It seemed natural to arrange a marriage. In 1474 the girl became Isabella I, Queen of Castile, while her husband ruled jointly with her as Ferdinand V, King of Castile. In 1479 the old King of Aragon died and Isabella's husband also became Ferdinand II of Aragon.

The two lands were united to form modern Spain and were never separated again. The union was followed by the final defeat of the southern remnant of the Moors in 1492. In that same year Christopher Columbus' first voyage laid the foundation for Spain's vast overseas empire and made her the first true world power.

Although Aragon thus vanished from the map as an independent power a century before *The Merchant of Venice* was written, its name remained green in the minds of Englishmen. Ferdinand and Isabella had a daughter who became a famous and, in her time, popular queen of England—Catherine (or Katherine) of Aragon (see page II–754).

The Prince of Aragon is displayed as a far less attractive character than Morocco. For one thing, he is proud, but then this was taken as a national characteristic of the Spanish stereotype. And, no doubt, the happy accident that Aragon resembles "arrogant" helped Shakespeare choose the title.

The Prince of Aragon dismisses the leaden casket at once since lead is beneath his dignity. The golden casket offers him what many men desire and that is not for him either, since he is not satisfied with what "many" men desire. He is special. The silver casket has a legend, reading:

silver   *"Who chooseth me shall get as much as he deserves."*

                                   —Act II, scene ix, line 35

Aragon recognizes no limits to his own deserts and chooses it. He finds it contains the caricature of a fool's head. Only a fool, in other words, places too high a value on his own deserving, and Aragon loses too.

. . . the Goodwins . . .

But now things suddenly turn black for Antonio. Even when Solanio had been mocking Shylock's grief-stricken outcries two scenes earlier, his friend Salerio had spoken of rumors concerning lost merchant vessels. Now the news is more specific and more damaging. Salerio reports to Solanio the news that

> . . . *Antonio hath a ship of rich lading wracked on the narrow seas—the Goodwins I think they call the place—a very dangerous flat, and fatal* . . .
>
>   —Act III, scene i, lines 2–5

The "narrow seas" is the English Channel, or perhaps the Strait of Dover (only two dozen miles wide) in particular. It would seem to us that a Venetian would be more likely to refer to the strait between Italy and Sicily or Spain and Africa as the "narrow seas," but to the English audience of the play, the phrase would have only one meaning.

The "Goodwins" are the Goodwin Sands, seven miles east of the southeastern tip of England. These are a ten-mile-long stretch of treacherous shoals, where the sands are actually partly exposed at low tide.

. . . I am a Jew . . .

Shylock enters, sorrow-laden and bitter. The two Venetians jeer at him, but when they ask about news concerning Antonio, it is clear that matters are worse and worse. Shylock is now grimly intent on his bargain and he echoes Solanio's earlier remark when he says of Antonio:

> *Let him look to his bond. He was wont to call me usurer.*
> *Let him look to his bond.*
>
> > —Act III, scene i, lines 44–45

When Salerio, rather shaken out of his mockery, asks what use Shylock will find in a piece of human flesh, Shylock bursts out into a moving defense of himself and his fellows. It would almost seem that Shakespeare, driven by the force of his own genius and the necessity of creating a well-rounded character at all costs, gives Shylock—all against the playwright's own will, one might think—a tragic dignity and puts words in his mouth that the mocking Venetians can find no words to answer.

What does he want with the pound of flesh? Shylock grinds out:

[handwritten margin note: Shylock's statement]

> *To bait fish withal. If it will feed nothing else, it will feed my revenge. He hath disgraced me, and hind'red me half a million, laughed at my losses, mocked at my gains, scorned my nation, thwarted my bargains, cooled my friends, heated mine enemies—and what's his reason? I am a Jew. Hath not a Jew eyes? Hath not a Jew hands, organs, dimensions, senses, affections, passions?—fed with the same food, hurt with the same weapons, subject to the same diseases, healed by the same means, warmed and cooled by the same winter and summer as a Christian is? If you prick us, do we not bleed? If you tickle us, do we not laugh? If you poison us, do we not die? And if you wrong us, shall we not revenge? If we are like you in the rest, we will resemble you in that. If a Jew wrong a Christian, what is his [the Christian's theoretical] humility? Revenge! If a Christian wrong a Jew, what should his sufferance [patience] be by Christian example? Why revenge! The villainy you teach me I will execute, and it shall go hard but I will better the instruction.*
>
> > —Act III, scene i, lines 50–69

Remember this is a Jew's defense as placed in his mouth by someone not friendly to Jews. It is not, therefore, the most effective defense a Jew can make. Even so, the points are clear. Shylock does not claim to be better than a Christian. He merely claims to be no worse, and even in the context of the play, that gives him a great deal of room. Everyone in the play humiliates and torments him without conscience or remorse and nowhere and at no time do they consider it wrong. Even the saintly Antonio sees no wrong here.

Shylock, at least, recognizes villainy when he sees it. He admits his own plan to be villainous. His defense is that it has been taught him by Christians. In recognizing the villainy, he rises, in a way, an ethical notch above his tormenters.

How now, Tubal . . .

Solanio and Salerio leave the stage with another sneer, but with no attempt at a real answer. Another Jew enters. Shylock greets him at once with feverish anxiety:

> How now, Tubal! What news from Genoa?
> Hast thou found my daughter?
> —Act III, scene i, lines 75–76

Tubal is no more a personal Jewish name than Shylock is. The name is to be found in the listing of nations in the tenth chapter of Genesis, where in the second verse it is written, "The sons of Japheth; Gomer, and Magog, and Madai, and Javan, and Tubal, and Meshech, and Tiras." These are taken to be the names of tribes and regions rather than of true individuals.

The one place where Tubal occurs in a context familiar to the casual biblical reader is in Genesis 4:22, which reads, "And Zillah, she also bare Tubal-cain, an instructor of every artificer in brass and iron."

According to biblical legend, then, Tubal-cain was the first metallurgist. But even here the name means "smith of Tubal," a region in eastern Asia Minor (one suspects from Assyrian records) famous for its metal production.

Tubal has brought no definite news of Jessica's whereabouts, but has evidence that she gave one of Shylock's jeweled rings to a sailor in exchange for a monkey. Shylock groans in agony and says:

> Thou torturest me, Tubal. It was my turquoise; I had it of
> Leah when I was a bachelor. I would not have given it for a
> wilderness of monkeys.
> —Act III, scene i, lines 113–16

Shylock's frustrated outcry is undoubtedly designed to get a laugh, and the Elizabethan audience undoubtedly obliged. For us, however, this is surely a remarkably touching moment. Could Shylock, this monster of evil, so love his dead wife and honor her memory? Could there be a spark of love in his harsh heart? Was he a human being?

And what of Jessica, with whom the audience is expected to be completely in sympathy? The ring was her mother's. Was she so completely dead to family affection as to part with it for so trivial and unworthy an exchange? What might this tell us of the effect of conversion from Judaism to Christianity—and does anyone in the audience think of that?

And at the very time Shylock's heart is ground by the loss of his wife's ring, he hears that Antonio is losing everything through a succession of shipwrecks. More than ever now, he must have his pound of flesh of the man who has abused him so much and who (he surely believes) has arranged the elopement of his wicked daughter.

. . . a swanlike end

Meanwhile Bassanio and Gratiano have arrived in Belmont. Portia is desperately in love with Bassanio and does not want him to choose, fearing he will guess wrong and be forced to leave. He, however, wants to choose, for he cannot bear the suspense. He advances to the test and Portia, in agony, says:

> Let music sound while he doth make his choice;
> Then if he lose he makes a swanlike end,
>
> —Act III, scene ii, lines 43–44

From classical times it was believed that swans sang before they died. Apparently it seemed natural to suppose that a bird so dignified, graceful, and austerely beautiful ought to be admirable in everything. So many birds were remarkable for the sweetness of their song that if the beautiful swan was mute, surely it could only be because it was saving something supremely wonderful for some divine climax. When better could this climax come than at its death?

This was prettified by legend makers. The swan was felt to be sacred to Apollo and to be filled with his spirit of song at the approach of death, glorying in translation, perhaps, to a better world.

This symbolism of a glorious afterlife, which many of the ancients longed for and which became part of Christian dogma, must have kept the legend going despite the fact that no one ever heard a swan sing at any time. "Swan song" is still used for the last work of a creative artist of any sort.

. . . young Alcides . . .

Portia feels Bassanio is going to fight the demon of chance for her hand and compares him to

> *. . . young Alcides, when he did redeem*
> *The virgin tribute paid by howling Troy*
> *To the sea monster.*
> —Act III, scene ii, lines 53–57

The reference is to the rescue of Hesione (see page I–403).

Hard food for Midas . . .

Portia has self-righteously declared she cannot give Bassanio any hints, but the music she orders played contains hints just the same. The song urges him to judge not by his eyes alone.

Bassanio gets the point and at once begins to ruminate on the way in which objects that are fair without may be worth nothing within. Apostrophizing the golden casket, he says:

> *. . . Therefore then, thou gaudy gold,* refuses The gold casket
> *Hard food for Midas, I will none of thee;*
> —Act III, scene ii, lines 101–2

In Greek legend Midas was a king of Phrygia—a land in western Asia Minor that existed prior to 700 B.C. and was then destroyed by nomadic invaders from the east. It did have kings named Mita, which could easily become Midas in Greek.

Phrygia, which gathered its wealth from over a large territory and concentrated it in the royal palace, must have seemed powerful and rich to the tiny city-states of Greece, who were in those days sunk in a Dark Age. Naturally, the wealth of King Midas became legendary.

The story that arose was that Midas had come across the drunken Silenus, a favorite of the wine god, Dionysus. Midas treated Silenus well and in return Dionysus offered him anything he might wish. Greedily, Midas asked that anything he touched be turned to gold. This worked well for a while, until he tried to eat. His food turned to gold as he touched it and Midas realized that the "golden touch" meant starvation. He had to beg Dionysus to relieve him of the dangerous gift.

This legend has always been popular among those who, lacking wealth, find in it the consolation of knowing that "money isn't everything," and

Bassanio, in scorning gold, gives it the most unfavorable allusion he can think of. It was merely "hard food for Midas."

In speed to Padua . . .

Bassanio chooses the leaden casket as the one least subject to dissimulation without, and, of course, it contains Portia's portrait. The two may now marry and are in transports of delight. Portia gives Bassanio a ring which he must never part with and the young man swears he will surrender it only with his life. Gratiano chimes in to say he has fallen in love with, and will now marry, Portia's lady in waiting, Nerissa. She gives Gratiano a ring, also.

At the height of their happiness, Lorenzo, Jessica, and Salerio arrive from Venice with the news that Antonio, beggared by the wreckage of his fleets, was unable to meet his debt to Shylock, who is now demanding his pound of flesh.

Portia hastens to send Bassanio back to Venice, placing her entire fortune at his disposal so that he might buy off Shylock. For herself, she has additional plans. She gives a message to a servant, saying:

> Take this same letter,
> And use thou all th'endeavor of a man
> In speed to Padua. See thou render this
> Into my cousin's hands, Doctor Bellario;
> —Act III, scene iv, lines 47–50

Portia's cousin Bellario is apparently a professor of law at the University of Padua (see page I–447), and her plan involves him and, as she quickly explains to Nerissa, their masquerading as men. (This is a favorite device in the romances of the period. Shakespeare has already used it in *The Two Gentlemen of Verona,* see page I–469, and in this play, Jessica has already made use of the masquerade. Thus, all three female characters in *The Merchant of Venice* appear, at one time or another, in the costume of a man.)

. . . the sins of the father . . .

With Portia and Nerissa gone, Lorenzo and Jessica are in charge at Belmont, and with them, of course, is Launcelot Gobbo, who affects to be unimpressed by Jessica's conversion. He refers to an Old Testament text to make his point when he says:

> . . . *look you the sins of the father are to be laid upon the*
> *children.*
> —Act III, scene v, lines 1–2

This is taken from the Ten Commandments themselves. As part of the second commandment, God is quoted as saying: ". . . I the Lord thy God am a jealous God, visiting the iniquity of the fathers upon the children unto the third and fourth generation of them that hate me" (Exodus 21:5).

This is actually a rather primitive view, which is altered in the course of the Old Testament itself. The prophet Ezekiel, writing in the time of the Babylonian Exile, quotes God as saying: "Yet say ye, Why? doth not the son bear the iniquity of the father? When the son hath done that which is lawful and right, and hath kept all my statutes, and hath done them, he shall surely live. The soul that sinneth, it shall die. The son shall not bear the iniquity of the father, neither shall the father bear the iniquity of the son: the righteousness of the righteous shall be upon him, and the wickedness of the wicked shall be upon him" (Ezekiel 18:19–20).

Nevertheless, the harsher and more primitive verses of the Old Testament seem always the better known to Christians (perhaps for the greater contrast they make with the New).

. . . Charybdis your mother . . .

Of course, Launcelot admits, it may be that Jessica's mother was unfaithful and that Jessica is not truly the daughter of Shylock. Jessica points out that then her mother's sin of infidelity would be visited upon herself and Launcelot agrees and says:

> *Thus when I shun Scylla your father, I fall into*
> *Charybdis your mother. Well, you are gone both ways.*
> —Act III, scene v, lines 15–17

Scylla and Charybdis were a pair of deadly dangers which in Homer's *Odyssey* are described as being on either side of a narrow strait. The strait in question is generally accepted as being the Strait of Messina between Italy and Sicily—which is two and a half miles wide at its narrowest.

Scylla is described as a monster on the Italian side of the strait. It has twelve legs and six heads. Each head is on a long neck and is armed with a triple row of teeth. (It is almost impossible to resist the temptation that this is the distorted description of a large octopus with its sucker-studded tentacles.) The heads bark like so many puppies and during the confused yelping, the necks dart forth, with each head snatching at a sailor on any ship that passes beneath.

Charybdis was the personification of a whirlpool on the Sicilian side of the strait, which three times a day sucked down the waters and then threw them up again.

Odysseus had to pass the strait twice. First, with a full ship, he chanced Scylla and lost six men. The next time, alone on a raft, he passed across Charybdis, seizing a branch overhead when the raft was sucked down and waiting for its return before proceeding.

To be "between Scylla and Charybdis" is the classical way of saying "between the devil and the deep sea." The statement "avoiding Scylla, he fell into Charybdis" was used by the Roman poet Horace, whom Launcelot is here paraphrasing.

. . . saved by my husband . . .

Jessica, however, counters all Launcelot's misgivings with a reference to the New Testament, saying:

> *I shall be saved by my husband. He hath made me a Christian.*
>
> —Act III, scene v, lines 18–19

St. Paul in his first epistle to the Corinthians says ". . . the unbelieving husband is sanctified by the wife, and the unbelieving wife is sanctified by the husband: else were your children unclean . . ." (1 Corinthians 7:14).

All this may be mere persiflage, but one is at least entitled to wonder if the cautious Shakespeare is trying to save himself trouble. Anticipating the reactions of those displeased at making a heroine of a Jew's daughter, he places their arguments in the mouth of the clown and answers them.

. . . hope for mercy . . .   Act IV

In Venice, Antonio must stand trial. All of Venice, from the Duke himself on downward, are on Antonio's side; all plead with Shylock not to insist on the forfeit. Shylock does insist, however. What's more, he will not accept money in place of the pound of flesh. He wants his revenge, not money.

The Duke says:

> *How shalt thou hope for mercy, rend'ring none?*
>
> —Act IV, scene i, line 88

Here is another New Testament reference, for it is an echo of the Sermon on the Mount, where Jesus says: "Blessed are the merciful: for they shall obtain mercy" (Matthew 5:7).

Shylock does not bother to defend himself directly; nor does he hypocritically pretend to be merciful. Instead, he faces down the angry crowd of Christians in the courtroom with a neat poniarding of *their* hypocrisy. Scornfully, he says:

> *You have among you many a purchased slave,*
> *Which like your asses and your dogs and mules*
> *You use in abject and in slavish parts,*
> *Because you bought them.*
> > —Act IV, scene i, lines 90–93

Shylock has bought human flesh as the Venetians have and has done it at three thousand ducats a pound, a far greater price than any Venetian paid for his. If Shylock is expected to give up what he has bought, why are not the Venetians expected to give up their purchases? (The argument is not foolproof. Shylock is being offered a huge sum to give up his pound; and his purchase means death for a man, as the purchase of an entire body does not. Nevertheless, the point of hypocrisy is made.)

. . . opinion with Pythagoras

The Duke can see no way out of the Shylock-imposed dilemma, unless Bellario, the renowned lawyer from Padua (Portia's cousin), has some helpful opinion to offer. While they wait for a message, Shylock gets his knife ready and Gratiano bitterly berates him, saying:

> *Thou almost mak'st me waver in my faith,*
> *To hold opinion with Pythagoras*
> *That souls of men infuse themselves*
> *Into the trunks of men. Thy currish spirit*
> *Governed a wolf who, hanged for human slaughter,*
> > —Act IV, scene i, lines 130–34

Pythagoras, an ancient Greek philosopher of the sixth century B.C., believed in the transmigration of souls. There is a famous story that he once stopped an animal from being beaten because he insisted he recognized the voice of a dead friend. (I wonder if that might not have been merely a humane device to stop the beating of an animal.)

Clearly, such transmigration is counter to Christian doctrine, and for Gratiano to accept it would mean that he had wavered in his faith.

The reference to a hanged wolf may well have referred to Lopez (see page I–514), whose very name is related to the Spanish word for wolf.

The quality of mercy . . .

Now Portia's plan reveals itself. The message from Bellario comes, brought by Nerissa in man's costume. Bellario cannot come himself but sends a young lawyer, Balthasar, in his place. Balthasar is, of course, Portia in disguise.

Portia too calls for mercy and says Shylock must be merciful. Shylock demands where in the law it says he *must* be merciful and Portia retreats, but in doing so delivers one of the most famous speeches in all of Shakespeare, one which begins:

> The quality of mercy is not strained [forced];
> It droppeth as the gentle rain from heaven
> Upon the place beneath . . .
>
> —Act IV, scene i, lines 183–85

It is true, then, that one is not compelled to be merciful, but mercy doesn't require compulsion. One is merciful simply because it is so wonderful to oneself and to others to be merciful.

Wrest once the law . . .

Shylock nevertheless refuses. He insists on the letter of the law and nothing else, crying:

> I crave the law,
>
> —Act IV, scene i, line 205

Bassanio desperately offers ten times the original loan, and if that fails, he urges the young judge to

> Wrest once the law to your authority.
> To do a great right, do a little wrong,
>
> —Act IV, scene i, lines 214–15

In a sense, this reflects a great philosophic struggle between Jew and Christian (as interpreted through Christian thought) between the letter and the spirit. In the New Testament the orthodox Pharisees are pictured as insisting on the letter of the law, while the more liberal Jesus is willing to bend the letter if that means retaining the spirit.

St. Paul makes this specific by saying that God ". . . hath made us able ministers of the new testament; not of the letter, but of the spirit: for the letter killeth, but the spirit giveth life" (2 Corinthians 3:6).

A Daniel come to judgment . . .

But it is not so easy to bend the law. Venice is a commercial, trading city and must deal with a wide variety of foreigners with other customs and beliefs. Venetian law, like Venetian money, must inspire confidence and it cannot unless it is equitable and just and never bent to personal advantage.

Portia points out that to palter with the law would set bad precedents, and Shylock cries out exultantly:

> *A Daniel come to judgment! Yea, a Daniel!*
> *O wise young judge, how I do honor thee!*
>   —Act IV, scene i, lines 222–23

Daniel, in the biblical Book of Daniel, is a wise interpreter of dreams, but the reference here is to Daniel's role in the apocryphal book of The History of Susanna.

The heroine of the book, Susanna, a chaste wife, is lusted after by two wicked elders. Her virtue was proof against their ancient charms and they conspired to accuse her of adultery to punish her. They stated they had seen her intimate with a young man and the court condemned Susanna to death.

At this point Daniel, a young man at the time, entered the story (just as "Balthasar" did). He demanded the right to cross-examine the elders separately before the council. He asked each the name of the tree under which he had seen the criminal intimacy take place. Not having concerted this part of the story, they named different trees and it was plain that they were lying. Susanna was freed and the elders executed.

Of course, since Susanna is an apocryphal book and not part of the Bible in the Jewish tradition, Shylock would not be apt to refer to it in reality.

. . . the stock of Barabbas

It seems that all is lost for Antonio. Shylock even refuses to pay the expense of a surgeon to help Antonio after the operation, because that is not part of the agreement (something which loses any sympathy any Elizabethan might possibly have for him).

Antonio makes a last touching speech that so moves Bassanio that he says (and, one can only believe, sincerely) that he would gladly deliver his new wife to Shylock's ruthless clutches if only that would save Antonio (and here Shakespeare's feeling of the utter nobility of male affection and its greater strength than that between man and woman shines through). Gratiano chimes in with a similar wish, and both Portia and Nerissa, in their male disguises, cannot hide the fact that such gestures sit rather poorly with them.

As for Shylock, the strong family man, he finds these remarks revolting and says:

> *These be the Christian husbands! I have a daughter;*
> *Would any of the stock of Barabbas*
> *Had been her husband, rather than a Christian!*
> —Act IV, scene i, lines 294–96

There is scarcely a name that rings so unpleasantly in Christian ears as "Barabbas." In the New Testament, it is the name of a prisoner who was slated for execution when Jesus was. Because it was the time of Passover, Pontius Pilate offered to free a prisoner and put it up to the populace: ". . . Whom will ye that I release unto you? Barabbas, or Jesus . . ." (Matthew 27:17). Since the populace demanded the release of Barabbas, Jesus was led out to crucifixion.

Matthew merely describes Barabbas as "a notable prisoner" (Matthew 27:16), but Mark says that Barabbas "lay bound with them that had made insurrection with him, who had committed murder in the insurrection" (Mark 15:7). Barabbas, in other words, had been taken after having participated in a rebellion against Rome. In the nationalistic spirit of the times one can see that to the Jewish masses Barabbas may have been a hero, but to the Christians of later times, he was a murderer whose life was unjustly traded for that of Jesus.

Marlowe in his *The Jew of Malta* called his Jew Barabbas, so that his villainy would be expressed in his very name. Shylock's remark can thus be interpreted as being a wish that Jessica had married even the worst kind of Jew (or, from the Christian standpoint, any Jew) rather than any Christian. (It is an odd point in favor of Shylock, and one rarely remarked upon, that despite what his daughter has done to him, he regrets her marriage because of his belief that a Christian would make an unkind husband. It would seem he still loves his daughter.)

Again, since Barabbas is a name that does not occur in the Old Testament, Shylock, in reality, would not have made the reference.

. . . become a Christian

Shylock is ready to take his pound of flesh when suddenly Portia stops him. She turns his insistence of the letter of the law against him. There is no mention of blood in the bond and therefore Shylock must take his pound of flesh without spilling one drop of Christian blood. What's more, he must take exactly a pound, neither the tiniest fraction more or less.

It is a legal quibble, but under the circumstances, it has its logic.

Shylock finds himself caught and offers to take the three-times payment Bassanio has offered. Bassanio is willing, but Portia grimly insists on the letter of the law. Shylock asks for his bare principal, but Portia insists on the letter. Shylock offers to abandon the money altogether and even that cannot be done, for in planning to take the pound of flesh he was a foreigner seeking the life of a Venetian, and as such, half of all his goods is forfeit to Antonio and half to the state.

(Actually, if we were arguing law, then, in the existence of a statute against a foreigner seeking the life of a Venetian, the agreement to accept a pound of flesh as forfeit for non-payment of a loan to a foreigner was illegal to begin with.)

Antonio now displays his magnanimity most impressively. That half of Shylock's fortune that is to go to the state he urges be returned to Shylock on the payment of a mere fine (a suggestion first made by the Duke). That half that is to go to Antonio himself, he would turn over to Shylock's daughter, Jessica, and her Christian husband, on Shylock's death.

But then one thing more is added, which sits less well with a modern audience than with an Elizabethan one. In return for all this, Antonio sets a condition:

> *. . . that for this favor*
> *He presently* [immediately] *become a Christian;*
> —Act IV, scene i, lines 385–86

The notion of forced conversion to Christianity was often justified by a verse in Luke. In a parable told in that Gospel, a man giving a feast found that his guests refused his invitation. He therefore sent his servants out to find strangers to attend the feast, and, if necessary, to make them attend by force. "And the lord said unto the servant, Go out into the highways and hedges, and compel them to come in, that my house may be filled" (Luke 14:23).

And indeed, Christians have converted Jews and pagans at the point of a sword. (So have Moslems and, to be truthful, on at least one occasion,

Jews. In the second century B.C. the Maccabean King of Judea, John Hyrcanus I, conquered the Idumeans, a non-Jewish people who lived to the south of Judea, and forced them to accept Judaism.)

The present Western liberal tradition considers such forced conversions in any direction to be abhorrent, but the Elizabethans would not find it so. To force a Jew to turn Christian was, in their view, a crowning mercy, since it rescued him from the certainty of hell and placed him on the route to salvation. Many in the Elizabethan audience may well have thought Antonio was being entirely too softhearted, and it is not impossible to suppose that Shakespeare himself wanted to do Shylock this favor out of a sneaking affection for this full-rounded villain he had managed to create. After all, Marlowe had given *his* Jew in *The Jew of Malta* an unrepentant and horrible death.

. . . renew old Aeson

After the tension of the trial, there is a final act of idyllic happiness back in Belmont, where Lorenzo and Jessica are continuing their blissful honeymoon. The night is glorious and they hymn it alternately in classical allusion to sad and tragic loves, as a delicious contrast to their own happy one.

Lorenzo says:

> . . . *in such a night*
> *Troilus methinks mounted the Troyan walls,*
> *And sighed his soul toward the Grecian tents*
> *Where Cressid lay that night.*

> —Act V, scene i, lines 3–6

The tale of Troilus and Cressida was handled by Shakespeare five years after the writing of *The Merchant of Venice* (see page I–71 ff).

Jessica responds:

> *In such a night*
> *Did Thisbe fearfully o'ertrip the dew,*
> *And saw the lion's shadow ere himself,*
> *And ran dismayed away.*

> —Act V, scene i, lines 6–9

Shakespeare had treated the tale of Pyramus and Thisbe, in burlesque form, a year or two earlier in *A Midsummer Night's Dream* (see page I–48).

Lorenzo says:

In such a night
Stood Dido with a willow in her hand
Upon the wild sea banks, and waft her love
To come again to Carthage.

—Act V, scene i, lines 9–12

The sad tale of Dido and Aeneas (see page I–20) is one of Shakespeare's favorites.

But then Jessica comes up with an allusion that doesn't fit at all. She says:

In such a night
Medea gathered the enchanted herbs
That did renew old Aeson.

—Act V, scene i, lines 12–14

Medea was the archetype of the powerful witch in Grecian myth, a woman of passionate desires who would stop at no crime to gratify them. She was the daughter of Aeetes, to whose guardianship the Golden Fleece (see page I–161) was entrusted. When Jason and his companions came searching for it, she fell in love with Jason and betrayed her father. She returned to Jason's kingdom with him and, according to one tale, restored the youth of Jason's old father, Aeson, by the use of her enchantments.

Medea might be included in the list of tragic loves because Jason tired of her eventually and abandoned her. In rage, she killed her own children by the faithless Jason. Still, it is odd that Jessica should refer to the tale of a woman who betrayed her father for her lover and who was regarded not as a heroine by the Greeks but as a villainess, and who came to so bad an end besides. Might we argue that Shakespeare's sneaking sympathy for Shylock shows itself here yet again?

. . . like an angel sings

Lorenzo and Jessica are interrupted by messengers reporting that Portia and Nerissa on one hand and Bassanio and Gratiano on the other are returning. (They are arriving separately; the young men don't know even yet that their wives were at the trial in masculine guise.) Yet Lorenzo cannot bear to leave the night. He says:

Sit, Jessica. Look how the floor of heaven
Is thick inlaid with patens of bright gold.
There's not the smallest orb which thou behold'st

But in his motion like an angel sings,
Still [always] quiring to the young-eyed cherubins;
Such harmony is in immortal souls,
But whilst this muddy vesture of decay
Doth grossly close it in, we cannot hear it.

—Act V, scene i, lines 58–65

This notion of the "music of the spheres" (see page I–199), first advanced by Pythagoras, was still extant in Shakespeare's time. The great German astronomer Johann Kepler tried to figure out the exact notes being sounded by the various planets. This was done just about the time Shakespeare was writing *The Merchant of Venice*. Could Shakespeare have heard about it and could he have been inspired by it to write this lyrical passage?

. . . sleeps with Endymion

Portia, returning, is also captivated by the night, saying:

. . . the moon sleeps with Endymion,
And would not be awaked.

—Act V, scene i, lines 109–10

Endymion, in the Greek myths, was a handsome prince who, asleep in a cave one night, was spied by Selene, goddess of the moon. Ravished by his beauty, she descended to the cave and kissed the sleeping youth. She wanted no more and, throwing him into a magic, eternal slumber, she returned night after night to kiss him and sleep awhile by his side.

. . . like Argus

Portia has returned home before her husband and gives orders that no one is to reveal the fact she has been away at all. She is ready for the last complication of the play. The rings

After Antonio had been saved, Bassanio, in gratitude, had offered the young judge (whom he did not recognize to be his wife) some reward. She would take nothing but the ring which Portia had given him and which he had sworn not to surrender. Reluctantly, Bassanio (recognizing his debt to Antonio) gave up the ring. Doubling the fun, Nerissa made Gratiano give up his ring too.

(Surely one must see the contrast with Shylock, who would not have given up his wife's ring for anything.)

When Bassanio and Gratiano come, bringing Antonio with them, the women at once ask for the rings. Naturally, they refuse to believe their husbands' explanations and pretend to be sure the rings were given to other women.

Portia, in particular, swears that if Bassanio did give her ring to some man, as he says, then she would take that man for her bedmate. She says:

> *Watch me like Argus.*
> *If you do not, if I be left alone—*
> *Now by mine honor which is yet mine own,*
> *I'll have that doctor for mine bedfellow.*
> > —Act V, scene i, lines 230–33

(Of course she will. If she is alone, she will sleep with herself as the only person in the bed.)

Argus was a giant in Greek mythology, whose special monstrous attribute was a hundred eyes, some of which were always open (see page I–86).

But then, before the quarrel can grow more fierce than suffices to amuse the audience, the truth is revealed, Lorenzo and Jessica learn they will be Shylock's heirs, and all ends in a blaze of happiness.

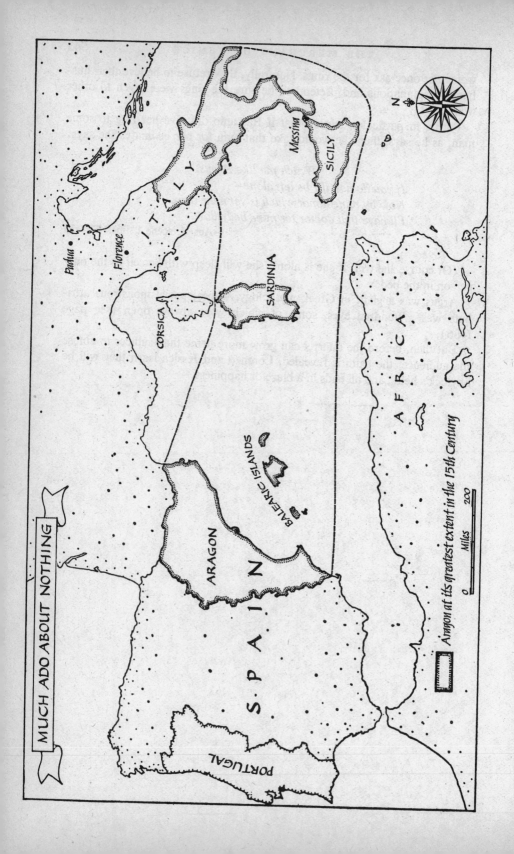

MUCH ADO ABOUT NOTHING

N

PORTUGAL

S P A I N

ARAGON

BALEARIC ISLANDS

CORSICA

SARDINIA

AFRICA

Padua

Florence

I T A L Y

Messina

SICILY

Aragon at its greatest extent in the 15th Century

0   200
Miles

19

MUCH ADO ABOUT NOTHING

MUCH ADO ABOUT NOTHING is among the pleasantest of Shakespeare's plays. It was written about 1599 and is the first of a cluster of three comedies, written in the space of a year or so, that represent Shakespeare's comic genius at its height.

. . . Don Pedro of Aragon . . .

The play opens with Leonato, the governor of Messina, speaking with a Messenger who has just brought him a letter. Leonato says:

> *I learn in this letter that Don Pedro of Aragon comes this night to Messina.*
>
> —Act I, scene i, lines 1–2

Messina is one of the principal cities of the island of Sicily. It is located in the northeastern corner of that triangular island just at the narrow strait that separates Sicily from Italy. As for Aragon, that is a medieval kingdom that was located in eastern Spain (see page I–526).

But what was Don Pedro of Aragon doing in Sicily?

Well, through much of the Middle Ages Sicily had been ruled by the German emperors. In 1266, however, it fell into the hands of the French dynasty of Anjou.

In 1282 the Sicilians grew tired of this Angevin rule. On March 30, just as the church bells were ringing for the sunset prayers called vespers, the Sicilians rose in concert and killed every Frenchman they could find. This event, the "Sicilian Vespers," ended Angevin rule on the island.

The last German ruler of Sicily, prior to the advent of the Angevins, had had only one surviving child, a daughter. She had married the King of Aragon, and the Sicilians considered this Aragonese King to be the natural successor to the crown. They invited him to come to Sicily. He did so and by 1285 had established himself firmly as ruler of Sicily, beginning a dynasty that was to continue for over five hundred years.

The Aragonese King who took over in Sicily was Pedro III (also known as Pedro the Great). Naturally, he was not the Don Pedro of Aragon who figures in *Much Ado About Nothing,* a play which is completely and entirely unhistorical. Undoubtedly, however, it was his name that floated into Shakespeare's mind when he needed one for the prince.

. . . a young Florentine . . .

It is quickly established that there has been a battle which Don Pedro has won and which has been practically bloodless. Leonato says:

> *I find here that Don Pedro hath bestowed much honor on a young Florentine called Claudio.*
>
> —Act I, scene i, lines 9–11

Florence was the leading city of Renaissance Italy, the medieval analogue of ancient Athens. Shakespeare never set the scene of one of his plays in that city, but he knew its reputation and worth. Simply by making Claudio a Florentine he was informing the audience that the man was intelligent and gallant.

. . . of Padua

Leonato has a daughter, Hero, beautiful and shy, and a niece named Beatrice, merry and impudent. The latter is trying to make herself heard and finally manages to say:

> *I pray you, is Signior Mountanto returned from the wars or no?*
>
> —Act I, scene i, lines 29–30

Mountanto is the name of a style of fencing thrust and the implication is that the gentleman in question is a great swashbuckler, presumably a phony, whose valor is all talk.

The Messenger doesn't know whom she means and her cousin, Hero, must identify him, saying:

> *My cousin means Signior Benedick of Padua.*
>
> —Act I, scene i, line 34

Padua is the scene of much of the action of *The Taming of the Shrew* (see page I–447).

The Messenger assures the company that Benedick is alive and well, and Beatrice breaks out at once in a flood of slander against him. Leonato feels it necessary to explain this away and says to the Messenger:

> *You must not, sir, mistake my niece. There is a kind of merry war betwixt Signior Benedick and her. They never meet but there's a skirmish of wit between them.*
>
> —Act I, scene i, lines 58–61

And indeed, it is this "merry war" that is the heart of the play and that will keep it alive and popular forever.

. . . *my dear Lady Disdain* . . .

In come the warriors, including Don Pedro, Claudio, and Benedick. There is a gracious and good-humored conversation with Leonato in the course of which Benedick carefully manages to fail to see Beatrice.

Finally, Beatrice is forced to address him and says:

> *I wonder that you will still* [always] *be talking, Signior Benedick; nobody marks* [listens to] *you.*
>
> —Act I, scene i, lines 112–13

Whereupon in the most lordly way possible, Benedick turns, looks at the lady with a vague surprise, and says:

> *What, my dear Lady Disdain! Are you yet living?*
>
> —Act I, scene i, lines 114–15

And the battle is joined.

. . . *the Prince your brother* . . .

But not quite all is merry. Among the party is a sour-visaged gentleman who has thus far said nothing. Leonato greets him too, and says:

> *Let me bid you welcome, my lord; being reconciled to the Prince your brother, I owe you all duty.*
>
> —Act I, scene i, lines 149–51

He is speaking to Don John, the Prince's illegitimate brother, who has apparently been in rebellion against Don Pedro. In fact, that was what the battle was about. Don John lost, apparently ignominiously, with Claudio particularly notable on the winning side, and the loser has had to reconcile himself with his brother. No wonder he looks so sour.

Nothing of this is historical, but Shakespeare may well have thought of the name because King Philip II of Spain (who died only a year or so before *Much Ado About Nothing* was written and who had ruled Sicily) had happened to have an illegitimate brother widely known as Don John of Austria.

The historical Don John was, to be sure, nothing at all like the Don John of the play and had never rebelled against his brother. In fact, the historical Don John is best known for his victory over the Turks at the Battle of Lepanto and then for his death, not long afterward, at the age of thirty-one in 1578.

. . . possessed with a fury . . .

Claudio has fallen in love with Hero and as is natural for a lover, he wants his friend, Benedick, to praise her. Benedick, a very sensible young man, refuses to be poetic about it. He says:

> There's her cousin, and she were not possessed with a fury, exceeds her as much in beauty as the first of May doth the last of December.

> —Act I, scene i, lines 184–86

The Furies were creatures of Greek legend who were vengeful spirits that pursued those guilty of great crimes, and were probably personifications of the madness that stemmed from guilt and remorse. It is clear, though, that despite Benedick's unkind characterization of Beatrice he is very much struck by her—and we might guess that Beatrice wouldn't take so much trouble to tongue-lash Benedick if she weren't equally struck by him.

In short, the two are in love and everyone in the play and in the audience knows it—except for Beatrice and Benedick themselves.

. . . called Adam

Don Pedro is on Claudio's side, however, and the two of them then proceed to tease Benedick over his confirmed bachelorhood. They assure him he will fall in love and marry someday, and Benedick swears mightily that he won't, saying:

If I do, hang me in a bottle like a cat and shoot at me; and he that hits me, let him be clapped on the shoulder and called Adam.
—Act I, scene i, lines 248–50

The reference is to a north English ballad, famous in Shakespeare's time, concerning three master archers who lived in a forest in the extreme north of England. These were Clym of the Clough, William of Cloudesly, and Adam Bell, and any of the three might be used as a way of signifying a champion archer. In this case, it is Adam who gets the nod.

". . . *Benedick the married man*"

Finally, Benedick's protestations reach a climax and succeed in adding a word to the language. He says that if he ever gets married, they can make a sign on which he is to be caricatured and

> *let them signify under my sign "Here you may see Benedick the married man."*
—Act I, scene i, lines 257–58

"Benedick" is but a slightly corrupt form of "Benedict," and either is now used with a small letter (a benedict) to signify sometimes a bachelor, sometimes a married man. The most appropriate use, however, is for a long-time bachelor who is newly married.

. . . *his quiver in Venice*

Benedick's companions are not impressed and feel that he will pay for his scorning of love. Don Pedro warns him laughingly:

> . . . *if Cupid have not spent all his quiver in Venice, thou wilt quake for this shortly.*
—Act I, scene i, lines 261–62

Venice, as a great trading center (see page I–499), would be crowded with sailors from all lands, eager for the use of women after the Spartan life aboard ship, and the city would therefore be considered a center of sexual license.

. . . born under Saturn . . .

All is going along marvelously well. Don Pedro promises to use his influence to see to it that Claudio and Hero get married. Leonato learns of it and is delighted.

There is only one exception. Don John, the defeated brother, is miserable. His companion, Conrade, tries to cheer him up, but fails. Don John is even surprised that Conrade should try. He says:

> *I wonder that thou being (as thou say'st thou art) born under Saturn, goest about to apply a moral medicine . . .*
> —Act I, scene iii, lines 10–12

In astrological thinking, each person is considered as having been born under the influence of a particular planet, which governs his personality in some fashion related to its own properties.

Mercury is the fastest moving of the planets, and to be "mercurial" is to be gay, volatile, and changeable.

Venus, named for the goddess of love, is related to "venereal," which can mean loving or lustful. The word has fallen out of use because of its association with diseases such as syphilis.

Mars, the ruddy planet named for the god of war, has an obvious connection with "martial."

Jupiter (Jove) is the second brightest of the planets and is named for the chief of the gods. It is considered most fortunate to be born under it and to be "jovial" is to be merry, good-natured, and sociable.

Saturn is considered to produce effects opposite to those of Jupiter. It is the slowest moving of the planets and is named for a particularly ancient god. Those born under his influence are therefore "saturnine," that is, grave, gloomy, and slow. Don John himself is portrayed as a saturnine individual.

The name "Conrade" has a connection with Sicily, by the way. The last of the German emperors to rule as King of Sicily was Conrad IV, who reigned from 1250 to 1254. His son, Conradin, attempted to retain hold over Sicily but was defeated and beheaded in 1268 by Charles of Anjou, who set up the Angevin dynasty that was to end fourteen years later in the Sicilian Vespers.

But another of Don John's companions, Borachio, comes in with the news that a match is being arranged between Claudio and Hero. Don John brightens. He feels a particular hate for Claudio, who was so prominent in the battle that defeated Don John, and if some mischief can be worked up at the young man's expense, so much the better.

. . . apes into hell

Leonato is planning a masked dance that night as an amusement for the royal company he is hosting, and during the preparations, Beatrice is her usual merry self, as busily denying she will have a husband as Benedick had earlier been denying he would have a wife. She even looks forward, with some cheer, to the traditional punishment Elizabethans imagined for old maids. She will not marry and

> *Therefore I will even take sixpence in earnest of the berrord and lead his apes into hell.*
>
> —Act II, scene i, lines 39–41

The "berrord" is the "bearward" or animal keeper. She will accept a coin from him as wages and do a job for him, which is to lead his apes into hell (see page I–454).

. . . Philemon's roof . . .

Don Pedro intends to take the occasion of the masked ball to smooth Claudio's path to Hero. He will dance with Hero, pretending to be Claudio. Drawing her to one side, and speaking more gallantly than Claudio himself might be able to, he will win her love for his friend.

When Don Pedro dances with Hero, she naturally tries to find out who is under the mask, and he says:

> *My visor is Philemon's roof; within the house is Jove.*
>
> —Act II, scene i, lines 95–96

This refers to a tale told in Ovid's *Metamorphoses* (see page I–8).

Jupiter (Jove) and Mercury once traveled through Asia Minor in disguise to test the hospitality of its inhabitants. They were treated discourteously everywhere until they came to the lowly cottage of an old, poor couple, Philemon and Baucis. Their welcome there was so hospitable that they offered to grant the couple whatever their wish might be. Their only wish was that they might die together, without warning, at the same moment, so that neither should know one moment of the pain of living without the other. It was granted.

Don Pedro, in referring to himself as Jove, may be tempted at the moment to speak for himself rather than for Claudio. Indeed, Don John, for sheer mischief, will take the occasion soon to get the news to Claudio that Don Pedro had indeed spoken for himself (though, in the end, he did not).

. . . the "Hundred Merry Tales" . . .

Benedick dances with Beatrice at the ball and, under the cover of ano-nymity, tells her of certain anonymous slanders he has heard concerning her. She repeats the information and guesses the informer, saying:

> *That I was disdainful, and that I had my good wit out of the "Hundred Merry Tales." Well, this was Signior Benedick that said so.*
>
> —Act II, scene i, lines 128–30

The "Hundred Merry Tales" was a popular, and therefore well-worn, collection of funny stories, most of them coarse. It would be equivalent, in modern terms, to saying that she had gotten her witty sayings out of Joe Miller's joke book.

It was a deadly thing to say to Beatrice and in vengeance (she probably knew very well with whom she was dancing) she floods Benedick with cruel remarks which he cannot counter.

. . . the infernal Ate . . .

Benedick has so much the worse of it on this occasion that after the dance he boils over with frustration, and says to Don Pedro concerning Beatrice:

> *She would have made Hercules have turned spit, yea, and have cleft his club to make the fire too. Come, talk not of her. You shall find her the infernal Ate in good apparel.*
>
> —Act II, scene i, lines 250–54

She is such a shrew, in other words, that even Hercules would bow be-fore her in fear.

As a matter of fact, the image is not too far removed from one of the legends concerning Hercules. As a punishment for some crime, Hercules was condemned to serve Omphale, Queen of Libya, for three years. She chose to have him do the woman's work about the house, spinning, clean-ing, making beds, while she wore his lion's skin and carried his club.

As for Ate, she is the Greek goddess of vengeance and mischief, who created so much trouble even among the gods that she was cast out of heaven and condemned to live on earth, where, Benedick implies, she has taken on the likeness of Beatrice.

. . . the great Cham's beard . . .

And when Beatrice enters, Benedick bounds to his feet at once and demands to be sent away. He says to Don Pedro melodramatically:

> *Will your Grace command me any service to the world's end?*
> *I will go on the slightest errand now to the Antipodes that*
> *you can devise to send me on; I will fetch you a toothpicker*
> *now from the furthest inch of Asia; bring you the length of*
> *Prester John's foot; fetch you a hair off the great Cham's*
> *beard; do you any embassage to the Pygmies—rather than*
> *hold three words' conference with this harpy.*
> —Act II, scene i, lines 261–69

The Antipodes ("with the feet pointed opposite") is a term invented by the Greeks. When their philosophers worked out the fact that the earth was spherical, there appeared at once the odd and paradoxical situation that people might live on the other side of the earth, with their feet pointed upward (from the standpoint of the Greeks).

Since the temperature rose as one went south, some Greek philosophers suggested there was a burning zone about the equator that men could not pass and that the world of the Antipodes (the Southern Hemisphere) could never be reached.

(By Shakespeare's time this was shown to be false, but the Antipodes remained as a symbol of the distant and unattainable.)

Prester John ("John the Priest") was a mythical monarch whose existence was widely accepted in the later Middle Ages. He was supposed to be a Christian king of immense power, with wide dominions in Asia, a king who had conquered the pagan regions and converted them to Christianity (hence his title).

There were indeed Christians in the Far East. These were the Nestorian Christians, a heretical sect that had been driven out of the East Roman Empire in the fifth century and had found haven in Persia and beyond. They penetrated to central Asia and China and, for a while in the twelfth century, were influential among the Mongol tribes who were gaining power.

In 1145 a Syrian bishop, Hugh of Gebal, brought the tale to the papal court. He spoke of a great Christian monarch in the East, thus combining a Mongol conqueror (who was not a Christian) with the Nestorians (who were not kings). In 1177 Pope Alexander III wrote a letter to this supposed Prester John, suggesting an alliance against the Moslems. The messenger carrying the letter never returned and nothing is known of his fate. Nevertheless, people continued to believe in the myth of a great Christian empire somewhere beyond the horizon.

In 1206 the greatest of the Mongols took the name of Genghis Khan, and he proved a Prester John indeed, though not a Christian one. For a bloody and unbelievable half century the Mongols expanded with unheard-of speed and built the largest continuous land empire the world had yet seen. In 1240 they even penetrated central Europe, defeating all armies sent against them.

Under Kublai Khan, the grandson of Genghis Khan, they reached their height. In the late thirteenth century the Italian traveler Marco Polo spent seventeen years at the court of Kublai Khan and thereafter wrote an immensely popular account of his travels. The memory of the Khans (or Chams) remained green, therefore, and it is the beard of the Mongol ruler which Benedick offers to pluck (though by Shakespeare's time only remnants of the Mongol Empire remained).

The Pygmies were a dwarfish race first mentioned in Homer's *Iliad*, and were reputed to live south of Egypt (see page I–63). The Harpies, in Greek legend, were originally symbols of the storm wind, but they were eventually pictured as winged birds of prey with women's heads. They were described as horrible, filthy creatures that snatched food away from men's tables, soiling and fouling what they could not take.

. . . like favorites

Having said all this, Benedick stalks off in a huff, to Beatrice's amusement. The rest of the group are happy too, as it quickly turns out that Don Pedro has wooed on his friend's behalf, and successfully. Soon there will be a wedding between Claudio and Hero.

Don Pedro, having listened to Benedick and Beatrice berate each other, suddenly thinks it would be delightful to trick them into falling in love. It is quite obvious to everyone that they are actually in love and it is just necessary to find some face-saving way of getting each to admit it.

Don Pedro, Leonato, and Claudio therefore seize an opportunity when Benedick is within earshot, to pretend they don't know they are being overheard, and to begin a long, circumstantial tale about Beatrice being in love with Benedick and being afraid to show it. They say that she may die of it.

Benedick is quite incredulous at first, but the three are most convincing, and, in his heart, he *wants* to believe, of course. So it comes about that he decides he can't very well let the poor girl die and he might as well save her life by loving her.

Next, Beatrice must get the same treatment. Hero and a lady in waiting, Ursula, will talk in the garden and Beatrice will be lured there to overhear them. Hero gives directions, saying that the talk will be in a shady place where the plants

Forbid the sun to enter—like favorites,
Made proud by princes, that advance their pride,
Against that power that bred it.

—Act III, scene i, lines 9–11

Considering the year in which the play was written, this sounds like an unmistakable reference to the Earl of Essex (see page I–120), who had been the favorite of Queen Elizabeth and who was now falling out of favor and taking it hard. Soon he was to attempt rebellion against the Queen and be beheaded for his pains.

Shakespeare was patronized by Essex and was surely sympathetic to him (see page I–119). In fact, there is every reason to suppose he did not forgive Elizabeth for executing the Earl, and when Queen Elizabeth died he remained mute, something spitefully noted by the poet Henry Chettle, who wrote an elegy in the dead monarch's honor.

And yet here is this passage in *Much Ado About Nothing*. We might suppose that Shakespeare, not one to risk his neck, or his living either, fearful that his connection with Essex might bring harm down upon his head, inserted this passage as an indication of disapproval of Essex. Such an indication might place him on the right side and out of trouble.

The girls' stratagem works and Beatrice is tricked into love out of pity, just as Benedick was.

. . . they that touch pitch . . .

Everything is going better and better, but there is Don John even yet. His earlier bit of mischief had miscarried and he wants something more effective. His companion, Borachio, has an idea. Why not frame Hero? He can arrange things so that he himself will woo Hero's lady in waiting Margaret at Hero's window. Don Pedro and Claudio will be allowed to overhear and be made to believe that Hero is a creature of light behavior who bestows her favors on anyone.

This vile plot is carried through offstage and works, but almost at once the nemesis of the plotters appears in the shape of comic constables, who mangle the English language with every sentence.

Their chief is Dogberry, epitome of the cowardly policeman who is willing to make an arrest only if there is no risk in it. Thus, when asked by a watchman whether they may arrest any thieves they encounter, Dogberry prudently says:

Truly, by your office you may; but I think they that touch
pitch will be defiled . . .

—Act III, scene iii, lines 57–58

The proverb is biblical; at least it occurs in the apocryphal Book of Ecclesiasticus (13:1), where it is written: "He that toucheth pitch shall be defiled therewith," an analogy that warns against evil companionship.

. . . a true drunkard . . .

Two newly sworn watchmen remain behind and almost at once Conrade and Borachio enter. Borachio, having successfully carried through the plot, is bubbling over with glee because he has earned a thousand ducats from Don John as a result. Borachio says to Conrade:

> *Stand thee close then under this penthouse for it drizzles rain, and I will, like a true drunkard, utter all to thee.*
>
> —Act III, scene iii, lines 104–6

It is to be presumed that Don John's companions are Aragonese and speak Spanish. Shakespeare makes no point of it in the play but Borachio's reference to himself as a drunkard is interesting, since the Spanish word *borracho* means just that.

. . . god Bel's priests . . .

Borachio is triumphant over the ease with which appearance was mistaken for reality (Margaret at the window for Hero). Through him, Shakespeare strikes out at one of his favorite targets—changing fashion. Borachio denounces fashion for making mankind ridiculous:

> *Sometimes fashioning them like Pharaoh's soldiers in the reechy [grimy] painting, sometimes like god Bel's priests in the old church window, sometimes like the shaven Hercules in the smirched worm-eaten tapestry . . .*
>
> —Act III, scene iii, lines 134–38

The new fashions only succeed, in other words, in making men look like one variety or another of ancient figures so that those fashions don't even have the virtue of being really new.

The reference to "Bel's priests" brings in another apocryphal book of the Bible. In this case it is Bel and the Dragon, in which the prophet Daniel proved to King Cyrus of Persia that the idol Bel was merely an inanimate object. The priests of Bel pretended that the idol consumed food and wine brought to it by the faithful each day, and Daniel showed that it was the priests themselves who ate and drank.

. . . Count Comfect . . .

The watchmen abandon Dogberry's caution and, like valiant men, promptly arrest Conrade and Borachio. Dogberry and his chief assistant, the aged Verges, go to Leonato to acquaint him with the conspiracy against his daughter. Between their wordiness and Leonato's haste to be on with the wedding preparations, communication fails and the plot, which ought to have been scotched, is not.

At the wedding ceremony, Claudio, in the most brutal manner, scornfully refuses to accept Hero, accusing her of immorality. Sadly, Don Pedro confirms this.

Leonato is half convinced, Benedick is puzzled and confused, and Hero faints. Beatrice, of course, is instantly and entirely on the side of Hero.

The Friar, who had been performing the marriage ceremony, suggests (very much in the manner of Friar Laurence in *Romeo and Juliet*) that the family pretend Hero is dead till the matter can be straightened out. Her supposed death will produce remorse in Claudio and Don Pedro and make them the readier to accept her innocence if the evidence points to it; while if she turns out to be really guilty, her supposed death would hide her shame and make it easier to have her quietly put in a nunnery.

Beatrice, furious, is in no mood, however, for lengthy investigations. She wants direct action. Poor Benedick, confessing his love for her, can scarcely get two words out at a time. Beatrice rages her contempt for Don Pedro and Claudio. She says:

> *Princes and counties! Surely, a princely testimony, a goodly*
> *count. Count Comfect; a sweet gallant surely!*
> —Act IV, scene i, lines 313–15

"Comfect" is candy (as in our modern "confectionary"), and Beatrice is sneering at the faint manliness of those who could treat a young girl so cruelly.

Beatrice has only one small demand of Benedict; that he kill Claudio. Benedick doesn't want to, but he cannot stand against Beatrice's impetuous fire; gloomily, he goes off to challenge Claudio.

. . . a calf's head and a capon . . .

Quietly Benedick challenges Claudio to a duel, out of the hearing of Don Pedro. Claudio, however, can scarcely take his old, bantering friend seriously. He insists on thinking it is some sort of joke and says to Don Pedro (who has overheard the conversation imperfectly and asks if Claudio is being invited to dinner):

> *. . . he hath bid me to a calf's head and a capon; the which*
> *if I do not carve most curiously, say my knife's naught. Shall*
> *I not find a woodcock, too?*

—Act V, scene i, lines 153–56

They are all items of food; but calves, capons, and woodcocks are all common symbols of stupidity too. Claudio is still wondering if Benedick is advancing some stupid joke. But Benedick insists on being grim, and stalks off after insulting Claudio unmistakably and formally leaving the service of Don Pedro.

The plot is breaking down, however. Not only does Benedick inform Don Pedro that his brother, Don John, has fled Messina (a suspicious act made necessary, presumably, by the arrest of Conrade and Borachio), but the foolish Dogberry has managed to extract a confession from the villains.

When the truth is out, Don Pedro and Claudio are prostrate with remorse and guilt. Leonato demands a simple recompense; that Claudio marry a niece of his that looks very much like the supposedly dead Hero. In deep contrition, Claudio agrees at once, and, of course, the "niece" turns out to be Hero herself. All are reconciled, right down to Claudio and Benedick.

. . . all Europa . . .

Now it is Benedick's turn. He will marry soon and subject himself to the dangers of the horns of cuckoldry after all. Claudio laughingly says:

> *Tush, fear not, man! We'll tip thy horns with gold,*
> *And all Europa shall rejoice at thee,*
> *As once Europa did at lusty Jove*
> *When he would play the noble beast in love.*

—Act V, scene iv, lines 44–47

There is a play on words here between Europa, meaning the continent of Europe, and Europa, the princess whom Jove loved in the shape of a bull (see page I-44).

. . . in a consumption

It comes out now that both Beatrice and Benedick had fallen in love because each had been told the other was lovesick, but it no longer matters. Benedick saves face by saying:

Come, I will have thee; but, by this light, I take thee for pity.
—Act V, scene iv, lines 92–93

And Beatrice answers (as usual) with interest:

> . . . *by this good day, I yield upon great persuasion, and partly to save your life, for I was told you were in a consumption.*
>
> —Act V, scene iv, lines 94–96

With that, they kiss and are clearly blissfully happy. And we may presume that the marriage will stay happy too. No doubt the "merry war" between them will continue and Beatrice' sharp tongue will continue to have the better of it, but what of that?

After all, "Beatrice" means "she who makes happy" and "Benedick" means "blessed," and Shakespeare could not have chosen those names accidentally. Beatrice will make Benedick happy and he will be blessed in her.

The play ends with the news that Don John has been caught, but punishment is deferred for the next day. Nothing will interfere with the gaiety of the end.

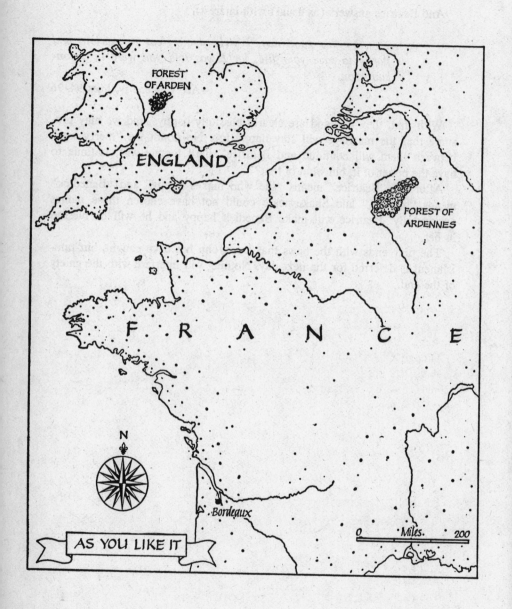

FOREST
OF ARDEN

ENGLAND

FOREST OF
ARDENNES

F R A N C E

N

Bordeaux

0   Miles.   200

AS YOU LIKE IT

20

AS YOU LIKE IT

A S YOU LIKE IT seems to have been written about 1599, a little after *Much Ado About Nothing,* and is therefore the second of the cluster of Shakespeare's three joyous comedies.

In this second comedy, much of the action takes place in an idealized pastoral setting, something very popular in the period. The plot Shakespeare obtained from a pastoral romance, *Rosalynd,* published in 1590 by the English poet Thomas Lodge, and improved it beyond measure.

. . . eat husks with them . . .

The story opens with Orlando and the old servant, Adam, onstage. Orlando is the youngest of three sons. His dead father has left him but a small sum for himself and has placed his bringing up in charge of the oldest brother, Oliver.

Though Oliver supports the middle brother in school, he is (for some reason Shakespeare does not bother to explain) a jealous tyrant to his youngest brother, keeping him deliberately in idleness and penury. When Oliver comes onstage, young Orlando says to him bitterly:

> *Shall I keep your hogs and eat husks with them? What prodigal portion have I spent that I should come to such penury?*
> —Act I, scene i, lines 36–38

This is a reference to the famous parable of the prodigal son in the Gospel of St. Luke (see page II–368).

. . . the old Duke . . .

The two brothers nearly come to blows and Orlando demands the small sum coming to him so that he might leave. Oliver agrees, with ill grace, but it is in his mind to be rid of Orlando forever and without paying him any money either.

Charles, a wrestler at the court of the Duke, is there to speak to Oliver, and it is this wrestler who is to be the means whereby Oliver will carry out his plan. Charles, asked after court news, says:

> There's no news at the court, sir, but the old news. That is, the old Duke is banished by his younger brother, the new Duke . . .

>> —Act I, scene i, lines 96–98

Who these dukes might be, and over what region they might rule, Shakespeare does not say and, certainly, does not care. In Lodge's pastoral romance, the dead father of the young hero was called Sir John of Bordeaux. That would make the scene the southwestern section of France. And indeed, the wrestler (here called Charles) is, in the source romance, serving at the court of Torismund, King of France. There was once a Torismund, who ruled the Germanic tribe of the Visigoths in 451, and that tribe did, indeed, control at that time southwestern France.

In Shakespeare's version, the father of Oliver and Orlando is Rowland de Boys. "Rowland" is a form of "Roland" and that name is best known as that of a Frankish warrior who died at the Battle of Roncesvalles in 778, which was fought in the Pyrenees about 130 miles south of Bordeaux. This is reminiscent of the time and place of Torismund.

That, however, is as far as it goes. The King of France is changed by Shakespeare into a Duke who is not further characterized or even named. (He is called Duke Senior in the play.) The usurping younger brother is named Frederick.

. . . the Forest of Arden . . .

Charles goes on to say of the exiled Duke:

> They say he is already in the Forest of Arden, and a many merry men with him; and there they live like the old Robin Hood of England. They say many young gentlemen flock to him every day, and fleet the time carelessly as they did in the golden world.

>> —Act I, scene i, lines 111–15

If we imagine a French setting, the Forest of Arden would be the wooded region of Ardennes, straddling the modern boundary between France and southern Belgium. There is, however, an actual Forest of Arden just north of Shakespeare's birthplace, Stratford-on-Avon, and the dramatist must surely have had this at least partly in mind.

In the Forest of Arden, Duke Senior and his men are living the life of happy outlaws, in the midst of nature, eating the game they capture and not having a care in the world. This is the bucolic bliss that is conventional in pastorals, for it is common for people trapped in the hurly-burly of the crowded haunts of men to imagine (wrongly) that there is some special delight in a simple life that existed in the "good old days."

This vain imagining even made its way into many mythologies. The early Greek poet Hesiod pictured the human race as having degenerated through successive ages, each worse than the one before. The first period was the "golden age," in which men lived without care, eating acorns, honey, and milk, free of hunger and pain; to these men death was only a falling asleep. It is to this that Charles refers as "the golden world."

To the English audience, the best-known example of happy outlaws in the forest was that of Robin Hood and his band of merry men. He was originally a peasant outlaw fighting against the Norman overlords, but with time he was polished up and made more acceptable to the aristocracy. By Shakespeare's time he had been transmuted into a Norman nobleman, Robert, Earl of Huntingdon, who was unjustly dispossessed and outlawed. The resemblance between this version of Robin Hood and the case of Duke Senior makes Charles's reference a natural one.

. . . the little wit . . .

Charles has come to warn Oliver that it is rumored his youngest brother, Orlando, will try to wrestle him. Charles gives troubled warning that he will be forced to hurt Orlando. Oliver, however, callously urges Charles to kill Orlando rather than merely hurt him.

The scene then shifts to the court, where we find the two charming young cousins, Rosalind and Celia. Rosalind is the daughter of the exiled Duke, and Celia the daughter of the usurping one. Rosalind is kept at court, despite her father's exile, because Celia loves her so.

Celia endeavors to keep her cousin cheerful and in this is helped by the court fool, who is named Touchstone. This is a particularly significant name, for a touchstone is a hard, flinty rock upon which a soft metal like gold will leave a rubbed-off mark if drawn across it. Pure gold and gold alloyed with varying amounts of copper can be used to make reference marks of different shades of yellow, orange, and red. If an unknown gold alloy is then rubbed across the touchstone, the mark it leaves, when compared with the standards, will reveal the amount of the copper content. As a result, "touchstone" has come to mean any criterion or standard against which the qualities of something may be tested.

To have a fool named Touchstone, then, is to indicate that it is by the encounter with the wit of a fool that the wisdom of a man may be judged.

Thus, when cautioned about the too great freedom of his remarks, Touchstone says to the girls:

> *The more pity that fools may not speak wisely what wise men do foolishly.*

> —Act I, scene ii, lines 83–84

To this, Celia responds:

> *By my troth, thou sayest true, for since the little wit that fools have was silenced, the little foolery that wise men have makes a great show.*

> —Act I, scene ii, lines 85–87

This remark has nothing to do with anything in the play and it would seem that Shakespeare was seizing the opportunity to make a cutting reference to some contemporary event. The satiric writing of Elizabethan times had grown more and more scurrilous until those jabbed at by it managed to push the government into banning such satires on June 1, 1599. Censorship, nevertheless, is almost invariably a greater evil than those it tries to cure, and Shakespeare expresses his disapproval of it here.

. . . is humorous

The young ladies learn of the wrestling matches and of the apparent invincibility of Charles. Orlando is now there to take his turn at the wrestling, and both girls, but especially Rosalind, are greatly taken with his youth and good looks.

All try to persuade Orlando not to wrestle, but he insists, and to everyone's surprise throws Charles and badly hurts him. Duke Frederick wants to know the young victor's name and is put out to find he is a son of Sir Rowland de Boys, an old enemy of his.

Later a courtier comes back to warn Orlando to leave quickly:

> *. . . such is now the Duke's condition*
> *That he misconsters* [misconstrues] *all that you have done.*
> *The Duke is humorous.*

> —Act I, scene ii, lines 254–56

The word "humorous" refers to the humors (or body fluids) of the old Greek physicians (see page I–582), which were supposed to control the temperament. To say the Duke is "humorous" is to say that he is a creature of moods and his present mood, apparently, is a dangerous one.

. . . call me Ganymede

The Duke is moody indeed, for he turns against Rosalind also. Having kept her at court ever since her father was exiled, he now bids her leave at once on pain of death, and insists on it despite Celia's wild protests.

After the Duke stalks offstage, Celia insists that she will flee with Rosalind and that together they will seek Duke Senior in the Forest of Arden. Rosalind is disturbed at the thought of two girls wandering through the wilderness and she suggests that she, at least, dress as a man (Shakespeare's favorite device in his romances).

Rosalind even takes a name for herself in her guise as man, saying to Celia:

> *I'll have no worse a name than Jove's own page,*
> *And therefore look you call me Ganymede.*
>
> —Act I, scene iii, lines 122–23

Ganymede, in the Greek myths, was a beautiful Trojan prince (see page I-67) with whom Jupiter (Zeus) fell in love. Since Ganymede was the object of homosexual love, the name is appropriate for a young man who, being really a young lady, is bound to look and behave like an effeminate.

Celia also chooses a new name, saying to Rosalind that it will be

> *Something that hath a reference to my state:*
> *No longer Celia, but Aliena.*
>
> —Act I, scene iii, lines 125–26

"Aliena" is Latin and is a feminine form of the word meaning "stranger." Celia has become alienated from her father.

The two girls decide to take Touchstone with them, and leave.

. . . the penalty of Adam

In the second act the scene shifts to the Forest of Arden, where Duke Senior is contentedly lecturing his followers on the advantages of the simple life:

> *Here feel we not the penalty of Adam;*
>
> —Act II, scene i, line 5

For his sin in eating the forbidden fruit, Adam was expelled from the Garden of Eden, where food was always at hand, and was condemned to work for his bread: "In the sweat of thy face shalt thou eat bread" (Genesis 3:19). Here in the Forest of Arden, however, Duke Senior and his men are living on the bounty of the earth and the Garden of Eden (another version of Charles the wrestler's "golden world") is returned.

. . . like the toad . . .

Duke Senior finds that the cruel fate of exile has turned to good, and says:

> Sweet are the uses of adversity,
> Which, like the toad, ugly and venomous,
> Wears yet a precious jewel in his head;
>
> —Act II, scene i, lines 12–14

Toads are ugly indeed, though beneficial (rather than venomous) insofar as they eat insects and help keep the numbers of those creatures under control. There existed a legend, however, that there were stony concretions in toads' heads that could be used to warn against the presence of poison if set in a ring. They did so by changing color. Such a "toadstone" was also thought to reduce the pain and decrease the swelling that followed the bite or sting of a poisonous animal. Needless to say, despite Shakespeare, there is no such thing as a toadstone.

. . . caters for the sparrow

But if Duke Senior is contented, poor Orlando certainly is not. Having been warned away from court, he arrives back home only to discover that his oldest brother, Oliver, plans to kill him outright. The warning is brought to Orlando by old Adam, who urges him to leave and offers him his own life savings of five hundred crowns. Adam (who, according to tradition, was played on the stage by Shakespeare himself) says:

> Take that, and he that doth the ravens feed,
> Yea, providently caters for the sparrow,
> Be comfort to my age.
>
> —Act II, scene iii, lines 43–45

This is a reference to Jesus' statements "Are not five sparrows sold for two farthings, and not one of them is forgotten before God?" (Luke 12:6) and "Consider the ravens: for they neither sow nor reap; which neither have storehouse nor barn; and God feedeth them" (Luke 12:24).

But Orlando will not abandon old Adam and together they leave home and wander off toward the forest, as earlier Rosalind, Celia, and Touchstone had done.

. . . the first-born of Egypt

Not everyone in Arden is enamored of the life. One of the Duke Senior's entourage is Jaques, whose affectation it is to be melancholy and to be cynical about everything. He sneers at a beautiful song sung by his fellow courtier Amiens, then says:

> I'll go sleep, if I can; if I cannot, I'll rail against all the first-born of Egypt.
>
> —Act II, scene v, lines 54–55

A possible meaning for Jaques' remark rests in the fact that the first-born of Egypt were the victims of the tenth plague brought down upon them by God through Moses. "And it came to pass, that at midnight the Lord smote all the firstborn in the land of Egypt, from the firstborn of Pharaoh that sat on his throne unto the firstborn of the captive that was in the dungeon; and all the firstborn of cattle" (Exodus 12:29).

It was after this climactic visitation that the Hebrew slaves were finally allowed to leave the country and to make their way into the wilderness. It could be that Jaques is using the phrase "all the first-born of Egypt" to symbolize the events that led to the exile of Duke Senior, and it is this against which he intends to rail.

. . . the lean and slippered pantaloon

Orlando suddenly bursts in on Duke Senior, Jaques, and the others in wild desperation. Old Adam is too weak with hunger to go farther and Orlando demands food with sword drawn.

Duke Senior speaks to him gently, and Orlando, realizing he is with friends, goes off to get Adam. When the Duke uses this event to show that there are more tragic scenes on earth than their own, Jaques falls to moralizing on the general uselessness of life and of man's pilgrimage in it. Life, he says, is in seven stages that end in nothing. By the sixth, man is well advanced in age:

> . . . The sixth age shifts
> Into the lean and slippered pantaloon,
> With spectacles on nose . . .
>
> —Act II, scene vii, lines 157–59

In Shakespeare's time there had arisen the custom in Italy of having traveling bands of actors give plays in different towns. These bands developed stock characters in standard masks and costumes, and one of the most popular of the stock characters was called Pantaleone.

The name means "all lion," signifying great bravery (and is Pantaloon in its English version). Naturally it would seem funny to have "all lion," a lecherous, miserly coward, always being outwitted by the young lovers. His characteristic appearance was sufficiently well known to make it unnecessary for Jaques to do more than mention the name.

Pantaloon was always dressed in baggy trousers, by the way, which came to be called pantaloons in their turn, or, for short, "pants."

Atalanta's better part

The pastoral life in the Forest of Arden now engulfs our various characters. Touchstone matches wits with the shepherd, Corin, and easily wins. Orlando, with time now to think of the love he has conceived for Rosalind on the occasion of his wrestling match, writes verses concerning her and hangs them on the trees in approved pastoral fashion.

Rosalind in her disguise as Ganymede finds them. Celia finds them too and is reading one which describes Rosalind as made up of:

> Helen's cheek, but not her heart,
>   Cleopatra's majesty,
> Atalanta's better part,
>   Sad Lucretia's modesty.

> —Act III, scene ii, lines 145–48

Three of these four ladies are subjects of Shakespearean plays or poems: Helen in *Troilus and Cressida*, Cleopatra in *Antony and Cleopatra* and Lucretia in *The Rape of Lucrece*.

As for Atalanta, she was a beautiful girl whose hand was sought by many but who had vowed to live a virgin. She therefore insisted that no one marry her unless he beat her in a foot race and that if he was himself beaten his head was to be chopped off. This frightened many, and the few who risked the race were beaten by the fleet-footed Atalanta and were killed.

Finally, a youth named Hippomenes prayed to Aphrodite and was given three golden apples. He raced Atalanta and each time she began to forge ahead he threw one of the golden apples before her. Being a woman, each time she paused to pick it up and, thanks to the time she lost, Hippomenes won.

The reference in the poem, then, is that Rosalind has Atalanta's "better part," the beauty which drew so many to court her, but not the cruelty which killed those who wooed and failed to beat her. Atalanta was a by-word for fleetness. Thus, later on Jaques speaks scornfully of Orlando's retorts to his own ill-natured remarks, saying:

> *You have a nimble wit. I think 'twas made of Atalanta's heels.*
> —Act III, scene ii, lines 273–74

. . . an Irish rat . . .

Rosalind is very pleased at all this, but affects indifference, saying:

> *I was never so berhymed since Pythagoras' time that*
> *I was an Irish rat . . .*
> —Act III, scene ii, lines 175–76

It was Pythagoras' doctrine of the transmigration of souls (see page I–535) that is here being referred to. By it, Rosalind's soul might once have inhabited the body of an Irish rat.

But what has that to do with rhyming? Well, the Celtic bards of Wales and Ireland were past masters at weaving curses into their improvised poetry. They could use such deadly verses to kill rats and other vermin. Therefore an Irish rat would be most "berhymed."

. . . Gargantua's mouth . . .

But Celia knows who has written the verses and finally reveals that it is none other than Orlando. The excited Rosalind instantly demands to know everything about it and him and wants all the answers immediately. To which Celia, laughing, says:

> *You must borrow me Gargantua's mouth first . . .*
> —Act III, scene ii, line 223

Gargantua was a giant of folklore, who was apparently first famous for his enormous appetite, since the name comes from *garganta*, which is Spanish for gullet. He became best known as a character in a famous sat-ire named for him by the French humorist François Rabelais. That book was first published in 1535.

. . . *Jove's tree* . . .

Celia says she saw Orlando under an oak tree and Rosalind says:

> *It may well be called Jove's tree when it drops forth such fruit.*
> —Act III, scene ii, lines 234–35

The oak tree is sacred to Jupiter. Indeed, the most ancient oracle in Greece was an oak tree in Dodona, in Epirus, two hundred miles northwest of Athens. Plates and other objects of brass were suspended from the branches and these struck together when the wind blew. The sounds were then interpreted by the priests of the shrine and were delivered as oracles.

Rosalind, in her boy's disguise, manages to find Orlando and cleverly persuades him that if he is to be a truly good lover, he must practice. She offers to play Rosalind and allow him to woo her in that fashion. (It may possibly have given Shakespeare pleasure to present scenes that were so vividly homosexual and yet done in such a way as to be inoffensive.)

. . . *honest Ovid* . . .

Touchstone also has fallen in love, and with a goat-herding girl named Audrey. He says to her:

> *I am here with thee and thy goats, as the most capricious poet, honest Ovid, was among the Goths.*
> —Act III, scene iii, lines 6–8

Ovid had fallen into disgrace with the Emperor Augustus (see page I–389) perhaps because his erotic books spoiled Augustus' efforts to improve the morals of Rome, or because the poet assisted Augustus' dissolute granddaughter, Julia, in some particularly disgraceful intrigue.

Ovid was therefore exiled to the Black Sea town of Tomi (the present-day port of Constanta in Romania). It was far in the backwoods, among a rustic and backward peasantry, eight hundred miles from Rome. Ovid spent the last nine years of his life there, sending a stream of weepy, self-pitying letters to his family at Rome hoping they would persuade the Emperor to remit the punishment. He never did.

The inhabitants of Tomi were not Goths, but two centuries later the Goths (a Germanic tribe from the Baltic) had reached the Danube River. Tomi was therefore "among the Goths" in anticipation.

Not only does Touchstone pun on "goats" and "Goths," but he also calls Ovid capricious, a word which is derived from the Latin *caper,* meaning goat.

Dead shepherd . . .

Still another set of lovers is Silvius and Phebe, the conventional shepherd and shepherdess of pastoral tales. In this case, Silvius is desperately in love with Phebe, but Phebe answers only with scorn.

Rosalind (as Ganymede) undertakes to right matters by scolding Phebe for being so cruel. She only makes matters worse, however, for to Rosalind's horror, Phebe is attracted to her at once in her boy's disguise. When Rosalind leaves, Phebe sighs:

> *Dead shepherd, now I find thy saw of might,*
> *"Who ever loved that loved not at first sight?"*
> —Act III, scene v, lines 81–82

The line is a quotation from the poem *Hero and Leander* written by Christopher Marlowe. The poem was published in 1598, a year or so before *As You Like It* was written, but Marlowe himself had been killed in a tavern brawl in 1593 at the age of twenty-nine. Hence the reference to the "dead shepherd."

. . . his brains dashed out . . .

Orlando, as agreed, courts Rosalind in her disguise of Ganymede, pretending (and he thinks it is only pretense) that she is Rosalind. Rosalind deliberately eggs him on to avowals of love by pretending great cynicism in the matter. She scouts the notion that lovers would die if refused, saying:

> *Troilus had his brains dashed out with a Grecian club; yet*
> *he did what he could to die before,*
> —Act IV, scene i, lines 92–94

Troilus, having been betrayed by his love (see page I–119), had ample reason to die of that, if men could. Yet he managed to live long enough to be killed in battle. Actually, though, he was killed by Achilles' spear and not by anyone's club.

Rosalind also sneers at the Hero and Leander tale (see page I–466), saying of Leander:

> *. . . he went but forth to wash him in the Hellespont, and*
> *being taken with the cramp, was drowned; and the foolish*
> *chroniclers of that age found it was "Hero of Sestos."*
> —Act IV, scene i, lines 97–100

. . . Caesar's thrasonical brag . . .

Now Orlando's older brother, Oliver, enters the picture again. Duke Frederick, suspecting that his daughter and her cousin had run off with Orlando, orders Oliver to find his brother on pain of his own death.

In the forest, Oliver, sleeping, is threatened by a lioness. Orlando comes upon his brother and the beast and is tempted to leave Oliver to his fate. He cannot bring himself to do this, however, so he attacks the lioness and Oliver, awaking, witnesses the rescue. The older brother repents his earlier wickedness and is a changed character from this moment.

He meets Celia and Ganymede and tells his story. He and Celia immediately fall in love. Rosalind/Ganymede later tells this to Orlando, saying:

> *There was never anything so sudden but the fight of two rams*
> *and Caesar's thrasonical brag of "I came, saw, and overcame."*
> —Act V, scene ii, lines 29–31

Caesar's deliberately brief report of his battle in Asia Minor in 47 B.C. (see page II–64) was intended to display a soldierly character, since military men were supposed to be men of action and not of words. There is nevertheless a certain affectation in the way in which Caesar sought the fewest syllables.

Rosalind's characterization of it as a "thrasonical brag" makes use of too many syllables, on the other hand. "Thrasonical" means "bragging." The word comes from Thraso, a bragging soldier in *The Eunuch,* a play by the Roman dramatist Terence. That in turn comes from a Greek word meaning "overbold," which we may be sure Thraso pretended to be but was not.

Hymen from heaven . . .

Now Rosalind begins to arrange everything. She makes Phebe promise to marry Silvius if it turns out she really cannot have "Ganymede." She then retires and returns in her natural woman's guise, led by none other than Hymen, the god of marriage (see page I–55), who says:

> *Good Duke, receive thy daughter;*
> *Hymen from heaven brought her,*
> —Act V, scene iv, lines 111–12

The characters now pair off: Orlando with Rosalind, Oliver with Celia, Silvius with Phebe, and Touchstone with Audrey.

Only one thing is left to make everything right and that is supplied by the sudden appearance of Orlando's remaining brother, the one in the middle. He brings the news that Duke Frederick, leading a large army against Duke Senior, has met an old hermit and has been converted to the religious life. Duke Senior may thus consider himself restored to his title, and all ends happily.

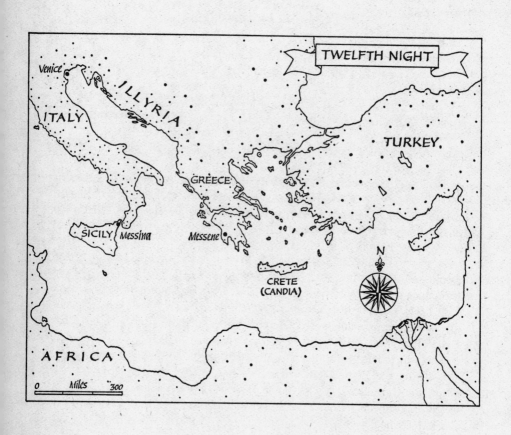

21

TWELFTH NIGHT,

or, What You Will

TWELFTH NIGHT is the twelfth day after Christmas—January 6. This is the traditional anniversary of the day on which the infant Jesus was viewed by the Magi and therefore the first manifestation of Jesus to the Gentiles. The day is also called Epiphany, from a Greek word meaning "manifestation."

There is no biblical justification for this particular date or for any fixed number of days after the birth of Jesus for the appearance of the Magi. Nevertheless, it did afford the people in medieval times the chance of a twelve-day celebration following Christmas (hence the popular carol, "The Twelve Days of Christmas").

Twelfth Night was in some ways the climax of the festive period. In connection with this, a lawyers' guild seems to have commissioned Shakespeare in 1600 to write them an amusing play for Twelfth Night 1601. He did so and the play was called *Twelfth Night* after the occasion and not because of anything in the play itself.

It was the third of Shakespeare's joyous comedies, all written at the turning of the century, and he apparently viewed them as trifles designed for amusement only. His titles show it: *Much Ado About Nothing* and *As You Like It.* Even this third play, usually called *Twelfth Night,* has a subtitle which perhaps more effectively describes Shakespeare's feeling—*What You Will.*

This was the last warm comedy Shakespeare was to write for many years. The shadows closed in and for a decade he wrote somber tragedies and bitter non-tragedies (scarcely comedies). Why this should have been so, we can only speculate. One tempting thought is that it was the execution of Essex (see page I-120), which took place just after *Twelfth Night* was completed, that darkened the light for Shakespeare.

. . . the food of love . . .

The setting of the play is Illyria.

In actual geography, Illyria is the coastal district of what we now call Yugoslavia and makes up the eastern shores of the Adriatic Sea, just across from Italy. It never made up a prominent part of the civilized ancient world, though in the fourth century it contributed a series of great Roman emperors: Claudius II, Aurelian, Diocletian, and Constantine I.

In the seventh century invading Slavs occupied Illyria and in the fourteenth century it fell into the grip of the Ottoman Turks. In Shakespeare's time what had once been Illyria and then became Serbia was still part of the Ottoman Empire. Parts of its coast, however, were controlled by Venice, and were Italian in culture.

Still, we need not be overconcerned with actual geography. Shakespeare's Illyria, like his seacoast of Bohemia in *The Winter's Tale* and his Forest of Arden in *As You Like It,* really exists nowhere but in the play.

It is the Duke of Illyria who speaks first. He is, apparently, lovesick, and says:

> If music be the food of love, play on,
> Give me excess of it, that, surfeiting,
> The appetite may sicken, and so die.

> —Act I, scene i, lines 1–3

The Duke's name is Orsino, which is derived from the Latin word for "bear" and is therefore most inappropriate for the overcultivated, overrefined Duke of this play. However, at the time the play was being written, Queen Elizabeth I of England was expecting an Italian visitor, Don Virginio Orsino, Duke of Bracciano (a town twenty miles northwest of Rome). Perhaps Shakespeare was offering the name as a delicate compliment to the Italian guest.

. . . fell and cruel hounds

The Duke is apparently hopelessly in love with Olivia, a rich noblewoman of Illyria, and cannot be diverted from his sentimental melancholy. When it is suggested that he hunt the hart (that is, stag) he breaks into a self-pitying play upon the word, saying that when he saw Olivia:

> That instant was I turned into a hart,
> And my desires, like fell and cruel hounds,
> E'er since pursue me.

> —Act I, scene i, lines 22–24

This is a reference to the tale of Actaeon (see page I–406), who was turned into a stag by the angry Diana and was then killed by his own hounds.

. . . like Arion . . .

Meanwhile, on the Illyrian seacoast, Viola, a young lady, appears. With her are a ship's captain and his sailors. They have just survived a wreck in which the girl's twin brother has apparently been lost.

Viola is heartsick over her brother's death, but the Captain says he saw her brother tie himself

> *To a strong mast that lived upon the sea;*
> *Where, like Arion on the dolphin's back,*
> *I saw him hold acquaintance with the waves*
> *So long as I could see.*
> —Act I, scene ii, lines 14–17

Arion is a character out of Greek legend. He was a master musician at the court of Periander, tyrant of Corinth, about 600 B.C. He traveled to Sicily to compete in a musical contest, winning the prize and many rich gifts.

On the ship back to Corinth, the sailors decided to kill Arion and appropriate those gifts. He asked permission only to play and sing one last time and, having done so, jumped into the sea and the ship sailed on.

The music had, however, attracted a school of dolphins, and on the back of one of these, Arion was brought to Corinth faster than the ship could be rowed. At Corinth, Arion told his story and when the ship arrived, Periander had the sailors executed.

Be you his eunuch . . .

Viola is heartened by the news, but there is still the problem of what she is to do next. As an unattended maiden, she would be in great danger, so once again Shakespeare uses the device of a girl dressed in a man's clothes. As a man, she decides to seek employment in Duke Orsino's service. The Captain approves and says:

> *Be you his eunuch, and your mute I'll be;*
> —Act I, scene ii, line 62

This is a stab at realism. A girl dressed in men's clothing would, in real life, give herself away with her hairless cheeks, her shrill voice, and her mincing ways. All these would fit a eunuch.

Eunuchs were common in the East, and even in the West were valued in Italy for their high singing voices. The use of eunuchs in the papal choir was continued well into the nineteenth century. Nevertheless, Viola as a eunuch would not be fitted for the romantic role she is to have in the play, and the device of eunuch and mute is dropped at once and there is no mention of either at any later point in the play.

. . . born under Taurus

The next scene is in the house of Olivia, the unresponsive object of Orsino's affection.

In the house we meet Sir Toby Belch, Olivia's uncle, who sponges off her and off anyone else he can find. "Toby" is a diminutive of "Tobias" and "Belch" is descriptive of his tippling habits. With him is Maria, one of Olivia's women, and entering the scene almost immediately is Sir Andrew Aguecheek. (The name indicates his cheek has the habit of trembling, as though with ague or chills, but actually out of fear.) He is there because Sir Toby is encouraging him to court Olivia, meanwhile helping himself to the money the poor fellow has.

Toby makes merciless fun of Sir Andrew, who never penetrates any mockery at his own expense. Thus, when Andrew boasts of his dancing ability, Toby encourages him to caper about, saying:

> *What shall we do else? Were we not born under Taurus?*
> —Act I, scene iii, lines 134–35

This is a reference to the zodiac, so important to the pseudo science of astrology. There are twelve signs (constellations or star configurations) in the zodiac, which girdles the sky, and the sun spends one month in each of them.

Apparently Sir Toby and Sir Andrew were both born in the month (April 20 to May 21) when the sun was in Taurus the Bull and were therefore born "under Taurus." Each sign is supposed to have a vast number of significances and is, as an example, supposed to govern a particular part of the body. When Andrew suggests that Taurus presides over sides and heart, Toby says:

> *No, sir; it is legs and thighs. Let me see thee caper.*
> —Act I, scene iii, lines 137–38

Naturally, if Taurus presides over legs and thighs, those born under Taurus must be great dancers.

. . . what says Quinapalus . . .

Also at Olivia's house is a Clown named Feste, which is very much like the Italian word for "holiday" and may be an oblique reference to the fact that the play was written to celebrate a holiday.

He has been absent without leave, and he is warned by Maria that he may be discharged. The Clown must therefore win over Olivia and he muses over methods for doing so, saying to himself:

> For what says Quinapalus? "Better a witty fool than a foolish wit."
>
> —Act I, scene v, lines 34–35

It is useless to try to find Quinapalus in a reference book; the name is invented. The Clown apparently has had an education and it is his particular comic device to speak in pseudo-learned jargon. (This would appeal particularly to the lawyers who had commissioned the play.)

. . . such a barren rascal

The Clown does indeed amuse Olivia and win her forgiveness, but one member of her staff remains untouched. He is Malvolio (his name means "ill will," the opposite of Benvolio, see page I–477, in *Romeo and Juliet*), who is Olivia's capable steward and hard-working business manager.

Malvolio is humorless, austere, proud, and easily angered. The Clown's wit does not amuse him; it merely offends. He says:

> I marvel your ladyship takes delight in such a barren rascal.
>
> —Act I, scene v, lines 82–83

Malvolio is Shakespeare's notion of a Puritan, and, indeed, he is referred to as one later in the play.

The Protestant Reformation, which began to affect England in the reign of Henry VIII (see page II–783), settled down at last into a typical English compromise under Elizabeth I. There remained those men of Protestant persuasion, however, who were dissatisfied with the compromise and demanded that the English church be purified of those remnants of Catholicism which it possessed.

These demanders of purification came to be called Puritans, and they grew more prominent throughout Elizabeth's reign, although she remained strong enough to refuse to give in to them even when they gained control of Parliament.

The Puritans were self-consciously virtuous men who were equally conscious of the vices of those who disagreed with them. Stalwartly against serious forms of immorality, vice, and crime, Puritans tended to be just as stalwartly against trivial forms of these same things. By wasting their efforts on inconsequentials, they antagonized many who would have been willing to join the assault on important issues. Furthermore, their pride in virtue was such that anyone was delighted when a Puritan was caught in sin, and it became easy to equate Puritanism with cant and hypocrisy.

Indeed, Olivia's retort to Malvolio's complaint about the Clown is a reflection of the common attitude toward the Puritan. She says:

> O, you are sick of self-love, Malvolio, and taste with a distempered appetite.
>
> —Act I, scene v, lines 90–91

Shakespeare, as a professional dramatist and actor, had a specific grudge against Puritans, since they denounced the theater as a haunt of sin and vice and an encouragement to idleness. It was their intention to close down the theaters if they could, and a professional dramatist and actor like Shakespeare could scarcely be expected to show Puritanism anything but hostility in consequence.

. . . Sebastian of Messaline . . .

Meanwhile Viola has taken employment with Orsino under the name of Cesario and promptly falls in love with the Duke. As for Orsino, he takes a liking to the "young man" and uses him to carry a message to Olivia.

Viola/Cesario carries the message to Olivia but in such a way as to make the Duke something less than impressive. Olivia is, however, favorably impressed with the "young man" and begins to show an affection which Viola/Cesario naturally finds horrifying.

While that happens, Viola's twin brother, Sebastian, turns out to have survived the wreck after all. He has clung to the mast till picked up by another ship, whose captain, Antonio, takes a strong liking to the young man. Antonio's attitude is, in fact, even more marked than that of the other Antonio (in *The Merchant of Venice*) toward Bassanio, and is more clearly homosexual.

Once both are on the Illyrian coast, Sebastian abandons a pseudonym he has been using (why, we are not told) and identifies himself, saying:

> You must know of me then, Antonio, my name is Sebastian, which I called Roderigo. My father was that Sebastian of Messaline whom I know you have heard of.
>
> —Act II, scene i, lines 16–19

It is useless to search for Messaline. There is no such place. Either Shakespeare negligently made up a name or else, more likely, it is a printer's error that has been preserved ever since (because actually it makes no difference).

If it is a misprint there are two possibilities for what the place may have been. It may have been Messene, a Greek city in the southwestern Peloponnesus, about 360 miles southeast of the Illyrian coast; or Messina in Sicily, an almost equal distance southwest of it, and the scene of the action in *Much Ado About Nothing* (see page I–545).

Sebastian takes his leave of Antonio, for he is bound for Orsino's court, where (unknown to him) his sister is. The court is dangerous for Antonio, who has gained the Duke's enmity, but his affection for Sebastian is so strong that he follows him anyway.

. . . the four elements

The scene shifts to Olivia's house again, where late at night Sir Toby and his friends are having a rousing time. Sir Toby engages in mock-scholarly arguments with the foolish Sir Andrew, saying:

> *Does not our lives consist of the four elements?*
> —Act II, scene iii, lines 9–10

The ancient Greek philosophers sought to find out the basic substance ("element") out of which the earth was constructed. Different philosophers had different candidates for the post, and Empedocles of Acragas finally suggested, about 450 B.C., that there was more than one. Four, altogether, were named: earth, water, air, and fire, and out of these all the earth was constructed. A century later Aristotle adopted this view and fixed it in human thought for two thousand years.

The view did not begin to go out of fashion till half a century after Shakespeare's death, and we still today speak of the "raging of the elements" when we talk of wind and water being lashed to fury by a storm over the ocean.

Malvolio comes in at length, to scold them for the noise they are making, and Sir Toby answers him with spirit, in the fashion that all fun-loving, but not really wicked, people might use to counter the self-righteous. He says to Malvolio:

> *Dost thou think, because thou art virtuous, there shall be no*
> *cakes and ale?*
> —Act II, scene iii, lines 114–15

It is after he leaves that Maria says of him:

> *Marry, sir, sometimes he is a kind of Puritan.*
> —Act II, scene iii, line 140

. . . Penthesilea

Maria describes the most prominent component of Malvolio's character to be a monstrous self-pride and suggests that they work up a plan to take advantage of that. She will imitate Olivia's handwriting and drop notes in places where he can find them so that he will be misled into thinking Olivia is in love with him. He will then, Maria is sure, promptly make a most enormous ass of himself.

Toby is absolutely delighted, and when she leaves, he calls after her:

> *Good night, Penthesilea.*
>
> —Act II, scene iii, line 177

Penthesilea in the Greek legends was an Amazon. According to some of the tales, she was the younger sister of Hippolyta, whom Theseus had married (see page I–18). It was Penthesilea who killed Hippolyta in the Amazonian war of revenge against Theseus, and afterward she joined the Trojans in their war against the Greeks and was killed in turn by Achilles.

Clearly, an Amazon is bound to be a large and muscular woman, and Penthesilea particularly so, since she fought with credit against Achilles himself. But Maria, it is clear in several places in the play, is a particularly small girl, which gives Toby's remark its humor.

. . . green and yellow melancholy

Duke Orsino, who intends to continue to use Viola/Cesario as his messenger to Olivia, talks of love to the "young man." Viola/Cesario sadly tells her love to Orsino, pretending it is her sister she is speaking of, and saying:

> *She never told her love,*
> *But let concealment, like a worm i'th'bud,*
> *Feed on her damask cheek. She pined in thought,*
> *And, with a green and yellow melancholy,*
> *She sat like Patience on a monument,*
> *Smiling at grief.*
>
> —Act II, scene iv, lines 111–16

There is a glancing reference here to the doctrine of the four humors, first advanced by the school of Greek physicians who followed the famous Hippocrates of Cos (of the fifth century B.C.).

They believed that there were four fluids, or "humors," in the body:

phlegm, blood (*sanguis* in Latin), bile (*chole* in Greek), and black bile (*melanchole* in Greek).

Bile is the secretion of the liver and there is only one variety, a greenish-yellow fluid. On standing, it grows much darker and becomes almost black; hence the distinction between bile and black bile.

The Greek physicians elaborated the theory that the predominance of one fluid over the other resulted in a particular type of temperament or "humor" (see page II–424). There were people who were phlegmatic, sanguine, choleric, or melancholic.

The expression "green and yellow melancholy" refers to the fact that bile was supposedly predominant in the melancholic, though Shakespeare is thinking of ordinary bile, rather than black bile.

. . . *a bearbaiting* . . .

At Olivia's house, the plot to catch Malvolio progresses. A new character enters, Fabian. He is another of Olivia's servants and he too has a grudge against Malvolio. He says:

> *You know he brought me out o'favor with my lady about a bearbaiting here.*
> —Act II, scene v, lines 6–7

In bearbaiting, a bear is tied to a stake, and sometimes muzzled. Dogs are then set on it and the "sport" consists in watching the maddened bear slowly tortured to death, usually killing a few dogs on the way. It was very popular in the time of Elizabeth I, and in 1575 thirteen bears were baited with the Queen an interested spectator. This "amusement" was not finally outlawed in England till 1835.

Apparently Fabian had organized a bearbaiting, and Malvolio had complained of it to Olivia, whose soft heart had been touched and who had been angry with Fabian in consequence.

This is a reflection of the fact that the Puritans, to their great credit, strove to have bearbaiting made illegal. (There were, however, not wanting those who said, cynically, that Puritans were against bearbaiting not because it gave pain to the bear but because it gave pleasure to the spectators.)

. . . *Jezebel*

Malvolio now enters the trap. The letter has been planted in the garden, and the plotters hide in a tree watching Malvolio. The steward is so lost in self-conceit that he dreams of marriage with Olivia and begins to assume the airs of a great lord. Sir Toby is almost choked with indignation, and Sir Andrew, imitating Toby, cries out:

> *Fie on him, Jezebel.*
> —Act II, scene v, line 41

Jezebel was the idolatrous Queen of Israel, wife of wicked King Ahab. She is a byword for pride. When her son (the successor of Ahab) was killed by the revolutionary general Jehu, she met the murderer in her palace as a queen should. Though facing death, she dressed herself like a queen and taunted Jehu with a past revolution that had failed. Or, as the Bible puts it (2 Kings 9:30–31), "And when Jehu was come to Jezreel, Jezebel heard of it, and she painted her face, and tired her head, and looked out at a window. And as Jehu entered in at the gate, she said, Had Zimri peace, who slew his master?"

Of course, Sir Andrew's use of the name is inappropriate from the standpoint of sex; for a man, however proud, can scarcely be a Jezebel; and his simplicity is designed to raise a laugh in the audience.

. . . the impressure her Lucrece . . .

Malvolio eventually spies the letter, picks it up, and examines it. The handwriting on the outside seems Olivia's and the seal which closes the fold has Olivia's imprint. Malvolio describes it as:

> *. . . the impressure her Lucrece, with which she uses to seal.*
> —Act II, scene v, lines 94–95

A person of quality would use a particular stamp (perhaps engraved on a ring) to impress the drop of wax sealing a letter, as further indication of ownership and guard against forgery. Olivia uses a representation of the Roman matron Lucretia, concerning whom (see page I–205) Shakespeare had written *The Rape of Lucrece* some six or seven years before. Of course, Maria had made use of her mistress' seal.

. . . from the Sophy

Malvolio interprets the letter exactly as pleases his self-love. It advises him to do just the sort of thing Maria knows Olivia loathes. He is told to smile constantly, to be haughtier and surlier than ever, to talk politics, cultivate eccentricity, wear yellow stockings, and be cross-gartered. He swears to do it all, and when he leaves, Fabian, in the tree, half dead with suppressed laughter, says:

> *I will not give my part of this sport for a pension of thousands*
> *to be paid from the Sophy.*
>> —Act II, scene v, lines 181–82

The "Sophy" is the title given in England to the Persian Shah (see page I–521). In 1599, not long before *Twelfth Night* was written, Sir Anthony Shirley came back from Persia, laden with gifts from the Shah for his role in helping reorganize the Persian army. This remark of Fabian's, therefore, is a topical reference.

As for Toby, he is so delighted with the working out of the plan that he offers to follow Maria

> *To the gates of Tartar, thou most excellent devil of wit.*
>> —Act II, scene v, lines 207–8

By Tartar is meant Tartarus, the level below Hades where evil souls were tortured for their sins (see page I–13).

Cressida was a beggar

Viola/Cesario has come to Olivia's for another interview on behalf of the Duke. She exchanges wit with the Clown and then gives him a coin. The Clown promptly asks, in literary style, for another:

> *I would play Lord Pandarus of Phrygia, sir, to bring a Cres-*
> *sida to this Troilus.*
>> —Act III, scene i, lines 52–53

This refers to the famous tale Shakespeare was soon to put to use in his own *Troilus and Cressida.* Viola/Cesario gets the allusion and commends the begging, whereupon the Clown instantly points out that:

> *Cressida was a beggar.*
>> —Act III, scene i, line 56

A late sequel to the medieval tale explained how Cressida was punished for betraying Troilus. She was stricken with leprosy and became a diseased beggar. Shakespeare did not use this part of the tale in his own treatment (see page I–124), but this line is evidence enough that he knew of it.

. . . music from the spheres

In the second interview, Olivia is bolder than in the first. She says, when Viola/Cesario speaks of the Duke:

> *I bade you never speak again of him;*
> *But, would you undertake another suit,*
> *I had rather hear you to solicit that*
> *Than music from the spheres.*
>
> —Act III, scene i, lines 109–12

This is another Shakespearean reference to the Pythagorean doctrine of the music of the spheres (see page I–199). Despite Olivia's invitation to speak for himself, Viola/Cesario has no option but to flee.

. . . a Dutchman's beard . . .

Olivia's love for Viola/Cesario does not go unnoticed, however. The foolish Sir Andrew is not so foolish as to fail to see it, and, petulantly, he decides his own suit is useless and prepares to leave.

Toby and Fabian, unwilling to let go their profitable gull, try to argue him out of this first sensible decision he has made. They assure him that Olivia is only trying to make him jealous and that Sir Andrew is losing out only because he isn't a daring enough lover. Sir Toby says:

> *. . . you are now sailed into the North of my lady's opinion,*
> *where you will hang like an icicle on a Dutchman's beard un-*
> *less you do redeem it by some laudable attempt either of valor*
> *or policy.*
>
> —Act III, scene ii, lines 26–30

To sail into the north of a lady's opinion is a clear metaphor representing her growing coldness. It is also a topical reference. Between 1594 and 1597 there was the most spectacular attempt man had yet seen to explore the Arctic regions. The Dutch explorer Willem Barents had sailed northeastward, discovering Spitsbergen in 1596 and exploring the coasts of the large Siberian islands of Novaya Zemlya. He spent the winter of 1596–97 in the Arctic, the first non-Eskimo to do so. He died in 1597 on his return voyage and in his honor that stretch of water lying between Spitsbergen and Novaya Zemlya is known as the Barents Sea. There is no doubt but that the "Dutchman" in Sir Toby's speech is a reference to Barents.

. . . be a Brownist . . .

Given the choice between valor and policy, Sir Andrew (equally pathetic in both) chooses valor as the manlier. He says:

> *I had as lief be a Brownist as a politician.*
> —Act III, scene ii, lines 32–33

This is another sneer at Puritanism. The Brownists were followers of Robert Browne, who was such an extreme Puritan he felt he had to leave the Church of England altogether. He founded an independent church in 1580 and in 1582 went off into exile to the Netherlands.

The Brownists were to form an interesting part of American history. Some of them, who had made a new home for themselves in Dutch exile, felt they could not maintain their English identity there and determined to establish a colony in the New World. In 1620, four years after Shakespeare's death, they sailed westward and landed in Plymouth, becoming America's revered Pilgrim Fathers.

. . . the bed of Ware . . .

Pleased with Sir Andrew's decision to be valiant, Sir Toby mischievously urges him on to write a challenge to Viola/Cesario. He tells him to write

> *. . . as many lies as will lie in thy sheet of paper, although the sheet were big enough for the bed of Ware in England . . .*
> —Act III, scene ii, lines 47–49

Ware was a market town about twenty miles north of London which in Shakespeare's time was famous for a huge bed, eleven feet square, reportedly capable of allowing twelve people to sleep on it at once. It was in several different inns in the vicinity at one time or another and in 1931 finally came into the possession of the Victoria and Albert Museum in London.

. . . the augmentation of the Indies

This new practical joke has scarcely been placed under way when the old one regarding Malvolio reaches a climax. Maria comes in to say that Malvolio has fulfilled all the requests of the letter; yellow stockings, cross-garterings, and all, down to the perpetual smiling:

He does smile his face into more lines than is in the new map
with the augmentation of the Indies.

—Act III, scene ii, lines 78–80

Mariners were particularly interested in marking a rhumb line on a map that would indicate the shortest distance from one point to another. On the globe, such a line would be a curve spiraling northward or southward.

In 1568 the Flemish geographer Gerhard Kremer (better known by the Latinized version of his last name, Mercator) put out a map of the world plotted in such a way that the rhumb lines were straight. Maps for navigation based on Mercator's scheme could be easily marked with rhumb lines, and many of them were therefore put in, crossing and crisscrossing.

What's more, the sixteenth-century explorations had led to an increasingly detailed knowledge of the Americas ("The Indies"), and about the time that *Twelfth Night* was being written, a new map, with numerous rhumb lines, was published, showing the New World in far greater and more accurate detail than had ever been shown before. This added detail was the "augmentation of the Indies."

. . . Jove, not I . . .

Maria tells Olivia that Malvolio seems to be raving, and when he appears on the scene, grotesquely clothed and quoting meaningfully from the letter, Olivia, flabbergasted, can only think he really is mad.

Malvolio is so far gone in self-delusion, however, that he interprets everything in the light of Olivia's supposed love for him, and in the midst of his triumphing, he remembers to be pious, saying:

Well, Jove, not I, is the doer of this, and he is to be thanked.
—Act III, scene iv, lines 87–88

This is undoubtedly intended to mock Puritan sanctimoniousness, and, just as undoubtedly, the real Malvolio would have said "God" or "the Lord" or "the Almighty." Growing Puritan strength, however, in later years clamped down on references to God on the stage, and this form of ridiculous censorship led to the foolish substitution of "Jove."

. . . Legion himself . . .

Sir Toby comes fussing in, full of mock concern over Malvolio's madness, and saying:

If all the devils of hell be drawn in little, and Legion himself
possessed him, yet I'll speak to him.
—Act III, scene iv, lines 89–92

This is a reference to one of the examples of demonic possession in the
New Testament. When Jesus asks the name of the "unclean spirit" pos-
sessing a man, that spirit answers "My name is Legion: for we are many"
(Mark 5:9).

. . . like cockatrices

Toby baits Malvolio with his supposed madness and when the latter
rushes off in a fury, Toby arranges to have him placed in a dark room because of his supposed madness, so that the practical joke may continue.

Meanwhile the affair of Sir Andrew and Viola/Cesario is developing
further. Sir Andrew has written a cautiously phrased and clearly cowardly
letter. Sir Toby accepts it gravely, but does not deliver it. He intends to
deliver a challenge verbally, enormously exaggerating Sir Andrew's fire-
eating propensities. He will then report with equal exaggeration to Sir Andrew, concerning what a raging fury Viola/Cesario is in. He says:

This will so fright them both that they will kill one another
by the look, like cockatrices.
—Act III, scene iv, lines 203–4

The cockatrice is the fabulous serpent which can kill by his mere glance
(see page I-150).

. . . in Lethe steep

There now begins a series of mistakings very like those in *The Comedy*
of Errors, complicated by difference in sex.

Antonio, the captain who has befriended Sebastian, has given him a
purse of money to use, then follows him to keep an eye on him and guard
him.

Meanwhile, Viola/Cesario, coming for another interview with Olivia, is
waylaid by Sir Toby, who delivers Sir Andrew's challenge. The frightened
Viola/Cesario finds he must fight the frightened Sir Andrew, but before
anything can happen, Antonio comes charging in.

Assuming that Viola/Cesario is Sebastian, he is about to begin a fight
in good earnest, when the Duke's officers come in to arrest him on the
old charge of piracy. Antonio must ask Viola/Cesario to return his bag of

money, for a fine may save his life. Naturally, Viola/Cesario knows nothing about the money, and Antonio is greatly upset over this seeming perfidy as he is dragged away.

And Sebastian too has his share of the confusion. Olivia encounters him, thinks he is Viola/Cesario, and begins to speak of love. Sebastian finds this entirely to his liking and says:

> . . . *I am mad, or else this is a dream.*
> *Let fancy still* [always] *my sense in Lethe steep;*
> *If it be thus to dream, still* [always] *let me sleep!*
>
> —Act IV, scene i, lines 61–63

Lethe was the name of one of the rivers of Hades, according to Greek mythology. All spirits were forced to drink of it, for it had the property of inducing forgetfulness so that past life on earth vanished from memory and only the spirit world remained. Sebastian is wishing, then, to forget his past existence and to live only in the present one, in which beautiful loving women appear from nowhere.

. . . King Gorboduc . . .

But the Malvolio affair is not yet done. Malvolio is now locked in a dark room and Sir Toby plans a further torment. He will have the Clown personify a curate, "Sir Topas," who will pretend to examine Malvolio.

The Clown demonstrates his skill at the part by talking a little learned-sounding gibberish. He says:

> . . . *as the old hermit of Prague, that never saw pen and ink, very wittily said to a niece of King Gorboduc, "That that is is."*
>
> —Act IV, scene ii, lines 13–16

Gorboduc was a legendary king of early Britain, and in 1562 he was the subject of a play written by Thomas Norton and Thomas Sackville. In this play, Gorboduc divided his kingdom between two sons, Ferrex and Porrex, and civil war followed. It was the first blank-verse tragedy published in England and began the cycle of drama that culminated so rapidly in the Shakespearean climax.

. . . the Egyptians in their fog

The Clown now begins the discussion with Malvolio through the closed door and is merciless. He insists the room in which Malvolio has been locked is not dark and that it is only the latter's mad imagination that makes it seem dark. The Clown says:

> . . . there is no darkness but ignorance, in which thou art more puzzled than the Egyptians in their fog.
>> —Act IV, scene ii, lines 43–45

The "fog" spoken of here is the ninth plague brought down on Egypt by Moses prior to the Exodus. It is mentioned in Exodus 1:22–23: "And Moses stretched forth his hand toward heaven; and there was a thick darkness in all the land of Egypt three days: They saw not one another, neither rose any from his place for three days."

. . . the opinion of Pythagoras . . .

Malvolio, maintaining his sanity firmly, offers to answer any questions. The Clown asks:

> What is the opinion of Pythagoras concerning wild fowl?
>> —Act IV, scene ii, lines 51–52

Malvolio answers:

> That the soul of our grandam might happily inhabit a bird.
>> —Act IV, scene ii, lines 53–54

This is another Shakespearean reference to the Pythagorean theory of transmigration of souls (see page I–535), and is a perfectly correct answer.

. . . from Candy

By now Duke Orsino has grown tired of sending to Olivia fruitlessly and decides to go himself. When he reaches Olivia's house, he is met by his officers, who bring the sea captain Antonio to judgment.

The first officer says:

> Orsino, this is that Antonio
> That took the Phoenix and her fraught [cargo] from Candy;
> And this is he that did the Tiger board
> When your young nephew Titus lost his leg.
>> —Act V, scene i, lines 60–63

There is an unobvious reference here to the island of Crete. Crete has been a Greek-speaking island throughout history and in the early Middle Ages the largest city upon it was named Herakleon. In 826 Crete was captured by Moslems, who built a fortress on the site of the city and called it Khandax.

In 1204 the Venetians took the island and to them Khandax became Candia (and to the English, Candy). Since Candia was the largest city in Crete, it gave the name to the entire island. (Within the last century the island has become Greek again, taken back its own name, and its largest city is back almost to what it was—Iraklion).

In Shakespeare's time Venice and the Ottoman Turks were in a state of chronic warfare over the eastern islands, including Crete, and so there is this vague reference to some sort of battle in which Crete is named.

. . . th'Egyptian thief . . .

Mix-ups continue. Antonio denies he was a pirate but claims his deeds to have been lawful acts of war. However, he accuses Viola/Cesario of ingratitude and the latter desperately denies knowledge of what the captain is talking about.

To make matters worse, Olivia enters. She has married the delighted Sebastian and now thinks Viola/Cesario is he and claims her lovingly. Orsino, seeing that his servant has won the heart he himself could not, is furious and is almost moved to murder. He says:

> *Why should I not, had I the heart to do it,*
> *Like to th'Egyptian thief at point of death,*
> *Kill what I love?*

> *—Act V, scene i, lines 117–19*

"Th'Egyptian thief" is a character in a romance, *Ethiopica,* by Heliodorus, a Greek author of the third century B.C. It is the earliest Greek romance that has survived and follows a pair of lovers, Theagenes and Charicleia, through innumerable adventures. At one point an Egyptian bandit, Thyamis, kidnaps Charicleia, whom he hopelessly loves, and when he is besieged, he tries to kill her in the darkness so that if he cannot have her, no one else can. He misses his mark, Charicleia survives, and the story reaches a happy ending.

It was translated into English in 1569 and was popular enough to ensure that Shakespeare's audience would get the allusion without trouble.

. . . a bloody coxcomb . . .

Olivia claims Viola/Cesario as her husband and the mix-up is growing dangerous for the latter, when in comes a bleeding Sir Andrew. He and Sir Toby have mistaken Sebastian for Viola/Cesario and attacked him. They were well banged as a result. As the sniveling Sir Andrew says:

> *H'as broke my head across, and has given Sir Toby a bloody coxcomb too.*
> —Act V, scene i, lines 175–76

The coxcomb, from the object worn on a fool's head (see page II-17), gradually came to be a familiar appellation for the head.

Toby comes on the scene too, bleeding and deeply humiliated. Then comes Sebastian, and his appearance solves the entire mix-up at once. Even Antonio understands, and we can be sure he will not be seriously punished.

I'll be revenged . . .

The Duke now discovers that Viola/Cesario is a girl and that she loves him. He asks to see her in her woman's clothing and she replies that that clothing is with the Captain who brought her on shore and he is in prison through the action of Malvolio. (This is the first mention of any such thing. The reason for Malvolio's action is not explained, nor for Viola's failure to do anything about it. It is clearly an afterthought.)

Nevertheless, it gives an excuse to bring in Malvolio. The joke at his expense is explained and all agree he has been ill used. He is not mollified, however, but instead goes snarling off, his last words being:

> *I'll be revenged on the whole pack of you!*
> —Act V, scene i, line 380

To be sure, Olivia expresses her sympathy again after he leaves and the Duke sends after to have him pacified and brought back, but that last line stands.

If Malvolio represents Puritanism, Shakespeare's insight was not wrong. Puritans *were* revenged on the theater. They continued to grow stronger until, under their leadership, Parliament rose in revolt against King Charles I in 1642. After years of fighting, the Puritans and their allies won a final victory in 1648 and the King was executed in 1649. Malvolio, in the person of Oliver Cromwell, controlled England and the theaters were closed down.

In 1660, to be sure, with Cromwell dead, the son of Charles I was brought back from exile and was made King Charles II. There followed a time of gaiety and frivolity and the stage was given over to "Restoration comedy"—mere froth and not even an echo of Shakespeare.

22

ALL'S WELL THAT ENDS WELL

ALL'S WELL THAT ENDS WELL was written about 1602. Though it ends happily and is therefore technically a comedy, it lacks a carefree fun and happiness of the previous comedies. It is, indeed, rather an unpleasant play, like *Troilus and Cressida* (see page I-71), which was written shortly before.

. . . my son . . .

The play opens with a group of people dressed in mourning onstage. The first to speak is the Countess of Rousillon, who has recently lost her husband (hence the mourning). She has fresh cause for sorrow, too, and says:

> *In delivering my son from me I bury a second husband.*
> —Act I, scene i, lines 1–2

What's happening is that her son, Bertram, the young Count of Rousillon, is going to Paris to be brought up at the court of the King of France and his mother hates to part with him.

Rousillon is treated in this play as part of France, and indeed (as Rousillon—the French use two *s*'s), so it is—today. It is located just north of the Pyrenees at their eastern edge adjacent to the Mediterranean Sea. Its chief city is Perpignan.

Through much of its history, however, it was *not* part of France. While the Pyrenees are the general boundary between France and Spain, Rousillon was, from 1172 on, part of the kingdom of Aragon (see page I-526), located just south of the mountains.

It was not till 1450 that France was sufficiently united and sufficiently free of the English menace (see page II-562) to turn its attention to the spread of Spanish power across the mountain range. King Louis XI of France (see page II-651) sent expeditions southward and Rousillon became French in 1465. In 1493, however, Louis' son, Charles VIII, more interested in invading Italy, handed Rousillon back to Aragon to win Aragonese good will for his venture.

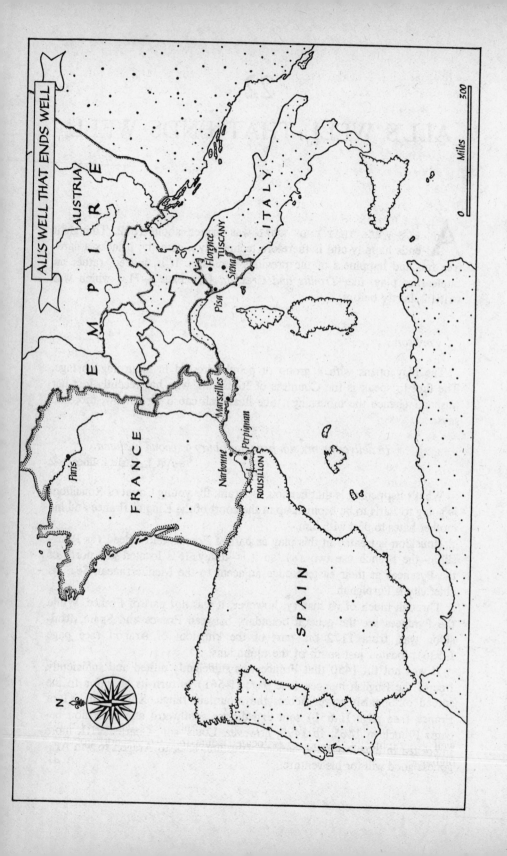

By that time Aragon had formed a union with Castile, and modern Spain had taken shape. Spain was at the height of its power then and held on to Rousillon till 1659, at which time it became permanently French.

Thus, when *All's Well That Ends Well* was written, Rousillon was Spanish, not French. Shakespeare obtained his plot from one of the tales in the *Decameron* by Boccaccio, which dealt with Beltram of Rossiglione. But the *Decameron* was published in 1353 and at that time Rossiglione (which, presumably, is Rousillon) was Aragonese, not French, and yet Boccaccio portrayed Beltram as a Frenchman.

Not that it's important, of course, for as far as the play is concerned, Rousillon might have been any other name—an imaginary one, for that matter.

. . . the King . . .

An elderly lord, Lafew, reassures the Countess, saying:

> *You shall find of the King a husband, madam; you, sir, a father.*
> —Act I, scene i, lines 7–8

It is useless to try to find out who the King of France is. No actual King of France unmistakably fits the events in the play, and he is not named either in this play or in the *Decameron* source.

It turns out that the King is suffering from a lingering, chronic disease and that cure is despaired of. One medieval French king who did suffer from a lingering, chronic disease was Charles VI (see page II–464), who reigned from 1380 to 1422 and was mentally ill most of the time. There is no other comparison, however, and we might as well accept the fact that the King, as well as everything else in the play, is fictional.

. . . Gerard de Narbon

The Countess regrets the death of a physician so skilled that he might surely have cured the King. She tells Lafew:

> *He was famous sir, in his profession, and it was his great right to be so: Gerard de Narbon.*
> —Act I, scene i, lines 28–29

He was, in other words, of the city of Narbonne, and this, at least, fits well geographically. Narbonne is located some thirty miles north of Perpignan.

. . . but Bertram's

Gerard de Narbon has left behind a beautiful and virtuous daughter, who is in the Countess' care. When all leave the stage, she remains and says:

> *. . . my imagination*
> *Carries no favor in't but Bertram's.*
> *I am undone; there is no living, none,*
> *If Bertram be away . . .*
>
> —Act I, scene i, lines 88–91

This is the major complication of the play. Helena, the doctor's daughter, loves Bertram, the young Count of Rousillon, and therefore loves "above her station." The doctor, however skilled, is of menial position, while Bertram is, of course, a nobleman.

. . . a notorious liar

Helena's soliloquy is interrupted by the entrance of Parolles, Bertram's favorite companion. Parolles professes to be a fierce warrior, dresses and talks the part, but does not fool Helena. She says, aside:

> *I love him [Parolles] for his [Bertram's] sake,*
> *And yet I know him a notorious liar,*
> *Think him a great way fool, solely a coward;*
>
> —Act I, scene i, lines 105–7

As a matter of fact, everyone who meets Parolles sees through him at once and knows him to be all talk (his very name is related to the French word for "words"). Only Bertram is deceived and takes him for genuine, which seems to be clear evidence that Bertram is rather a fool.

Under Mars . . .

Helena and Parolles engage in conversation and when Helena refers to the star under which he was born, he replies, swaggeringly:

> *Under Mars, ay.*
>
> —Act I, scene i, line 199

He claims in this way to have an inborn martial personality (see page I-404). Helena says, dryly, however:

When he [Mars] was retrograde . . .
—Act I, scene i, line 203

Mars' path across the sky is generally from west to east against the background of the stars. Periodically, however, it changes direction and moves from east to west. It is then moving backward or "retrograde." The ancient Greeks labored to account for such retrograde motion but it wasn't till Copernicus elaborated the heliocentric view with the sun at the center of the solar system that the situation was made clear. Periodically, the earth in *its* orbit overtakes Mars and it is then that the planet seems to move backward.

Helena, by use of the term, indicates that if Parolles is born under Mars, he nevertheless moves backward and retreats hastily in battle.

The Florentines and Senoys . . .

The second scene opens in the King's palace in Paris. The King is involved in statecraft, saying:

> *The Florentines and Senoys are by th'ears,*
> *Have fought with equal fortune, and continue*
> *A braving war.*
> —Act I, scene ii, lines 1–3

Florence was the great city of the Italian Renaissance (see page I-448) and the "Senoys" are natives of Siena, a city about thirty miles south of Florence. For centuries Siena and Florence were rivals, and down nearly to Boccaccio's time, the fight remained fairly equal.

Siena, however, was already declining when the *Decameron* was written and it came more and more under the Florentine shadow. In 1557 Florence finally gained political control of Siena and the latter's history as an independent city-state came to an end.

. . . our cousin Austria

The King goes on to say:

> *We here receive it*
> *A certainty, vouched from our cousin Austria,*
> *With caution, that the Florentine will move us*
> *For speedy aid; wherein our dearest friend*

Prejudicates the business, and would seem
To have us make denial.

—Act II, scene i, lines 4–9

Again there is no use in searching history for any specific event that would mirror this.

In the sixteenth century there was a great rivalry between Francis I of France and the Emperor Charles V (see page II–747), the core of whose dominions within the Empire was Austria. Francis and Charles fought over Italy all through their reigns, with Charles having the better of it most of the time.

With this in mind, we can perhaps interpret the King's speech in terms of practical politics as follows. Austria has warned France that if she interferes in Italy and supports Florence, Austria will come to the aid of Siena in order to preserve the balance of power. France then adopts the prudent path of neutrality.

The Tuscan service . . .

Yet if France cannot openly intervene, there is another method open to her. She can send "volunteers" (a device known to and used by nations in our own times). The King says:

> *Yet, for our gentlemen that mean to see*
> *The Tuscan service, freely have they leave*
> *To stand on either part.*

—Act II, scene i, lines 12–14

The region in which Florence and Siena are located was known as Etruria in ancient times, and was inhabited by the Etruscans. The regional name was distorted to Tuscany (Toscana in Italian) in the Middle Ages.

Through the Middle Ages Tuscany did not form a separate and united political entity but was broken up among several city-states, of which Florence, Pisa, and Siena were the most important. In 1557, however, with the absorption of Siena, Florence came to be in control of the entire region. Cosimo I, Duke of Florence, was awarded the higher title of Grand Duke of Tuscany in 1569 by Pope Pius V. In Shakespeare's time, then, Tuscany was on the map.

. . . King Pippen . . .

And while the court is involved with the Tuscan wars, Helena arrives.

She hopes to cure the King with some of her dead father's remedies and she also hopes to see Bertram. She carries with her the best wishes of the old Countess, who loves the girl and doesn't seem to be disturbed by the thought of a *mésalliance*.

Lafew is at court to introduce Helena. He asks the King if he wants to be cured, but the King has so often been disappointed that he has given up and answers, crossly, in the negative. Lafew says:

> *O, will you eat*
> *No grapes, my royal fox?*
> —Act II, scene i, lines 71–72

The reference is, of course, to Aesop's famous fable of the fox who could not reach the grapes and who consoled himself with the thought that he did not want them anyway, since they were probably sour.

Lafew assures the King that he can indeed get the grapes and that there is indeed a cure. He describes the cure as something

> *. . . whose simple touch*
> *Is powerful to araise King Pippen, nay,*
> *To give great Charlemain a pen in's hand,*
> *And write to her a love-line.*
> —Act II, scene i, lines 77–80

It can raise, in Lafew's hyperbole, the long dead Charlemagne, and his father Pepin (Pippen) the Short (see page II–455).

Lafew then brings in Helena and leaves her with the King, saying as he himself departs:

> *I am Cressid's uncle,*
> *That dare leave two together.*
> —Act II, scene i, lines 99–100

Cressid's uncle was Pandarus, who served as go-between for her and Troilus (see page I–79) and was thus the original pander. Lafew's "pandering" is, of course, of quite another kind.

Moist Hesperus . . .

Helena promises the King a quick recovery. In fact, he will be well

> *Ere twice in murk and occidental damp*
> *Moist Hesperus hath quenched her sleepy lamp,*
> —Act II, scene i, lines 165–66

Hesperus (see page I–187) is the evening star. It sets in the western ocean (hence "occidental damp" and "moist") and it sets up to three hours after the sun, so that her light is a "sleepy lamp."

. . . Galen and Paracelsus

The medicine works precisely as Helena had promised and the King is quickly made well. All, even Lafew, are astonished, since all the other physicians had been utterly helpless. Even the worthless Parolles agrees, saying:

> So I say—both of Galen and Paracelsus.
> —Act II, scene iii, line 11

Galen was a Greek physician who settled in Rome in 164. He wrote many books on medicine, which were excellent for their time. They survived the fall of ancient civilization and were considered the last word on the subject throughout the Middle Ages.

The first physician to argue strenuously against blind acceptance of Galen and in favor of a new regime of mineral medicines as opposed to the old use of herbs was Theophrastus von Hohenheim, better known by his self-adopted nickname of Paracelsus. He lived from 1493 to 1541 and from Shakespeare's point of view would have been a "modern" physician.

What Parolles is saying, then, is that the King had been given up by all physicians of both the old school and the new.

. . . Saint Jaques' pilgrim . . .

The King is naturally grateful to Helena and offers her, as a reward, marriage with any of the noblemen at court. She chooses Bertram, who starts back in revulsion and horror at the thought of marrying a lowborn girl.

The King insists, however, and Bertram is forced into marriage. As soon as that is done, however, the young man determines to make it a dead letter. He orders Helena back to Rousillon without taking her to bed or even kissing her.

She goes submissively, and when she arrives, she has only a letter to show Bertram's mother, the Countess. He says he is off to the Tuscan wars and will never return as long as he is burdened with a wife he cannot accept. Nor will he ever accept her until she can produce his ring, which he will not give her, and show him a child begotten by him, for which he will give her no opportunity.

The old Countess is horrified. She is all on Helena's side, as is everyone else in the play (and in the audience) except for Parolles and, of course, Bertram himself.

But Helena begins to put into action a plan of her own. She departs from Rousillon in secret, leaving behind a letter that starts:

> *I am Saint Jaques' pilgrim, thither gone.*
> —Act III, scene iv, line 4

St. Jaques is James the Apostle, the son of Zebedee. According to a tradition which has no biblical backing whatever, he visited Spain and preached the gospel there. As a result, he is accepted now as the patron saint of Spain. He must, however, have returned to Judea, for the Bible records his death there at the order of Herod Agrippa I (Acts 12:1–2).

Tradition then takes over again and has his dead body miraculously whisked to Spain, where it finally came to rest in a shrine at Compostela, a city in the northwestern corner of Spain, about six hundred miles west of Perpignan. If Helena goes there she is traveling in the direction opposite to that Bertram has taken. She is going west into farthest Spain, he east to Tuscany.

"James" is the English version of a Hebrew name of which "Jacob" is the Old Testament version. In Spanish it is Iago, and St. James is Santiago. The city in which the bones were thought to rest is Santiago de Compostela.

. . . his despiteful Juno . . .

Helena asks the Countess to write and tell Bertram she is gone so that he can come safely home from the wars. She scolds herself, saying:

> *His taken* [undertaken] *labors bid him* [Bertram] *me forgive;*
> *I, his despiteful Juno, sent him forth*
> *From courtly friends with camping foes to live,*
> —Act III, scene iv, lines 12–14

Hercules, who was Jupiter's son by a mortal woman, naturally incurred the wrath of Juno (Hera), who was Jupiter's lawful wife. It was her enmity that visited him with periodic bouts of madness and condemned him to perform twelve labors for an unworthy cousin. Analogously, Helena considers the mere fact of her own existence to be condemning Bertram to warlike labors.

. . . the palmers . . .

As a matter of fact, though, Helena is not quite as unselfish as she is presenting herself to be. She does not go to the shrine at all but sneaks off to Florence in disguise as a pilgrim, hoping that she may yet win her reluctant husband. There she stops to ask:

> *Where do the palmers lodge, I do beseech you?*
> —Act III, scene v, line 35

A pilgrim who had visited the Holy Land was privileged to wear palm leaves as a token he had done so (it is a plant native to Palestine) and was therefore called a "palmer."

Helena asks the question of an old Widow, who offers her lodgings. The Widow has a beautiful and virtuous daughter, Diana, and it quickly turns out that Bertram (who is doing very well in Florence and is now a cavalry officer) is busily engaged in trying to seduce the girl.

Helena reveals her identity and persuades the two women to let her take Diana's place so that Bertram will sleep with her unknowingly, thinking she is Diana.

Diana agrees and cajoles Bertram into giving her his ring (the one he wrote in his letter that Helena would have to display before he would accept her as wife) and offers him an assignation provided he promises to stay only an hour and to refrain from speaking to her during that time. She promises to give him another ring in exchange for his after he has slept with her. So eager is he to win her that he agrees.

Helena then arranges to have herself reported as having reached Santiago de Compostela and to have died there.

. . . he parallels Nessus

Parolles, meanwhile, has won the contempt of all the officers, and they scheme to maneuver him into betraying his real character. Parolles has been sent out on a dangerous mission for which, out of sheer stupid braggadocio, he has volunteered. He is captured by his own colleagues and is blindfolded.

Pretending to be foreigners of strange speech, they question him through a mock interpreter. At the merest hint of torture, he tells everything he knows and reviles the very men who (unknown to him) are holding him prisoner. He even defames Bertram.

Thus, of one officer, he says:

> *. . . for rapes and ravishments he parallels Nessus.*
> —Act IV, scene iii, line 264

Nessus was the centaur who tried to rape Hercules' wife, Deianeira (see page I-380).

When he has completely unmasked himself for the coward he is, his blindfold is removed and he realizes that he is ruined. He decides to make the best of it, however, and later, in fact, he enters the service of the kindly Lafew and does well enough.

. . . at Marseilles . . .

With Helena's reported death, Bertram can return to Rousillon, but first he wants to go through with the seduction of Diana. This takes place offstage, but we gather that Helena has safely substituted herself. Bertram has kept the bargain, stayed an hour, refrained from speaking, and accepted the ring (Helena's ring, which she, in turn, had received from the King of France). And Helena has the ring Bertram gave Diana.

Helena is therefore also ready to return, taking the Widow and Diana with her. She intends to see the King and says to her companions:

> I duly am informed
> His Grace is at Marseilles, to which place
> We have convenient convoy.
>
> —Act IV, scene iv, lines 8–10

Marseilles is the great French port on the Mediterranean, about 280 miles west of Florence and 140 miles northeast of Roussillon. If Helena goes to Marseilles, she is two thirds of the way home.

She is counting on the King's continuing gratitude, for she says her services were such that

> . . . gratitude
> Through flinty Tartar's bosom would peep forth,
> And answer thanks
>
> —Act IV, scene iv, lines 6–8

In the thirteenth century Mongol tribes from central Asia swept westward and penetrated deep into Europe, reaching almost to the Adriatic in 1240. This gave Europe a scare from which it didn't recover for a long time.

The Mongols called themselves Tatars, but to the Europeans this became Tartars (from Tartarus, see page I-40). The Tatars, considered as creatures from hell, were naturally considered the epitome of heartlessness, and Helena felt that even they would feel gratitude for services such as hers.

All's well that ends well . . .

Helena has gone through a great deal and there is more yet to go through, but she keeps up her spirits with a stouthearted:

> *All's well that ends well; still the fine's the crown.*
> —Act IV, scene iv, line 35

The word "fine," from the French *fin,* means "end" here. Helena is saying that the nature of the end crowns the work, making it success or failure. This so summarizes the play—which, from Helena's point of view, is nothing but misery all the way to very nearly the end—that it has become the title of the play.

Yet is it possible the play once had a different title?

An English clergyman, Francis Meres, wrote a book in 1598 in which he compared contemporary English authors with classical and Italian ones, and, in the process, he listed Shakespeare's plays. He included one named *Love's Labor's Won.* This is the only play ever attributed to Shakespeare that we have no record of under the title mentioned. Either it's a lost play or we have it under a different title.

If the latter, it must be one that isn't mentioned by Meres under its own title and one that had already been written by 1598. One possibility is *The Taming of the Shrew,* in which Petruchio must labor hard indeed to establish love between himself and Katherina (see page I–462). There is, however, a reference in a 1603 account book to both *The Taming of the Shrew* and *Love's Labor's Won.*

The most popular theory, therefore, is that it refers to *All's Well That Ends Well* and to Helena's hard labor to win Bertram. But, alas, that means that the play would have had to be written several years before it was.

It's a problem that may never be solved completely, but I would like to suggest a possibility I have not seen advanced. Shakespeare may perhaps have written *Love's Labor's Won* in, say, 1597, and because it was a failure, rewrote it extensively and produced it as *All's Well That Ends Well,* with no record of the earlier version except for the casual mention of Meres, writing between the two.

. . . no great Nebuchadnezzar . . .

There is an interval before the resolution in the last act in which the Countess has the last of several confrontations with a Clown. None of these serves to advance the plot, but each is intended as comic relief. In this last, the Clown mentions "grace" and promptly expands it into wordplay by saying to Lafew:

I am no great Nebuchadnezzar, sir; I have not much skill in grace.
—Act IV, scene v, lines 21–22

This equates "grace" and "grass," and Nebuchadnezzar is brought in because according to the biblical account (Daniel 4:28–37) he was punished for his arrogance by being stricken with a madness that drove him out into the fields and caused him to eat grass for seven years.

The Black Prince . . .

The Clown also refers to the devil as having an English name, for he is

The Black Prince, sir, alias the prince of darkness, alias the devil.
—Act IV, scene v, lines 43–44

It is quite appropriate to speak of the devil as the "prince of darkness," for our modern conception of the devil comes, in part, from the Persian notion of a dualistic cosmic order in which the forces of light and good under Ahura Mazda fight a continuing giant battle against the forces of darkness and evil under Ahriman.

And a prince of darkness would naturally be a Black Prince like the famous eldest son of Edward III (see page II–260).

Plutus himself . . .

Bertram has now come back to Rousillon. When Helena reaches Marseilles, she finds that the King has gone to Rousillon and she follows. All are now converging on Rousillon for the climax.

Bertram is generally blamed by all for his treatment of Helena, but since Helena is dead, the slate is washed clean and preparations are made for a second marriage, to none other than Lafew's daughter.

A token must be given to the new bride and Bertram hands over the ring which he had (as he thought) obtained from Diana. It is really Helena's ring, however, which she obtained from the King; and the King recognizes it. Despite Bertram's denial, the King is firm in that recognition, saying:

Plutus himself
That knows the tinct and multiplying med'cine,
Hath not in nature's mystery more science [knowledge]
Than I have in this ring. 'Twas mine, 'twas Helen's,
—Act V, scene iii, lines 101–4

Plutus was the god of wealth, and was equated with gold in particular. It was believed in medieval times that there was some substance which could be used to turn less valuable metals into gold and this was called "the philosopher's stone." This same substance could also cure any disease and was "the elixir of life." Though medieval alchemists never found this substance, they were sure it existed in the earth, else how was the gold in its bowels formed?

Plutus, therefore, can be spoken of as knowing the medicine (a reference to the elixir of life) that produces gold, so that it was a "multiplying med'cine" because it multiplies the earth's store of gold.

. . . ever, ever dearly

The King begins to suspect that Bertram got the ring by foul play, that Helena was murdered. Bertram is arrested and suddenly Diana enters, claiming Bertram as her husband.

Desperately, Bertram tries to blacken Diana as a camp follower of the army in Tuscany, and the growing confusion is only straightened out when Helena appears, alive after all.

She shows Bertram's ring, and refers to the fact that she is now pregnant with Bertram's child. She has fulfilled Bertram's conditions and he must now accept her as his wife. Bertram cries out to the King:

> If she, my liege, can make me know this clearly,
> I'll love her dearly, ever, ever dearly.
>
> —Act V, scene iii, lines 315–16

Those are his last words in the play, and all's well that ends well.

23

The Tragedy of OTHELLO

the Moor of Venice

O F THE plays included in this section, *Othello* is the only one to represent a major Shakespearean tragedy which will bear comparison to such plays as *Hamlet, Macbeth,* and *King Lear*. It seems to have been written in 1603, after *Hamlet* and before the other two.

Othello is remarkable in that its hero is a "Moor." To Shakespeare a Moor was not clearly distinguished from a black and, given the parochial feeling of Europeans of the time (and, to a large extent, since) concerning men who differed in religion (Moors) or skin color (blacks), these would serve as natural villains, with their mere difference sufficient to account for their villainy. In *Titus Andronicus* Aaron the Moor (see page I–401) is a villain of this sort, and in *The Merchant of Venice* the Prince of Morocco (see page I–520), while a valiant soldier, is scorned by Portia, who derides the color of his skin.

In *Othello*, however, the Moor is pictured in another fashion, as an exotic figure who exerts a powerful sexual attraction over a white girl, partly because of the wide difference between him and the men she is accustomed to. This is not so uncommon a thing. In the early 1920s Rudolph Valentino played the title role in the motion picture *The Sheik* and caused millions of women to swoon in ecstasy, despite (or possibly because of) the fact that he was a "Moor" and must be a Mohammedan.

The Moor, as an exotic and therefore romantic figure, was used by an Italian writer of tales, Giovanni Battista Giraldi, who wrote under the name of Cynthius. A hundred of his stories were collected into a book called *Gli Hecatommithi* (*The Hundred Tales*) and published in 1565. One of these stories begins: "There once lived in Venice a Moor, who was very valiant and of a handsome person . . ." No reason is given for a Moor living in Venice; no discussion as to his religion is brought out. What was needed for the story, apparently, was someone at once romantic and of a passionate southern nature.

This story was taken by Shakespeare, who kept close to many of the details of the plot.

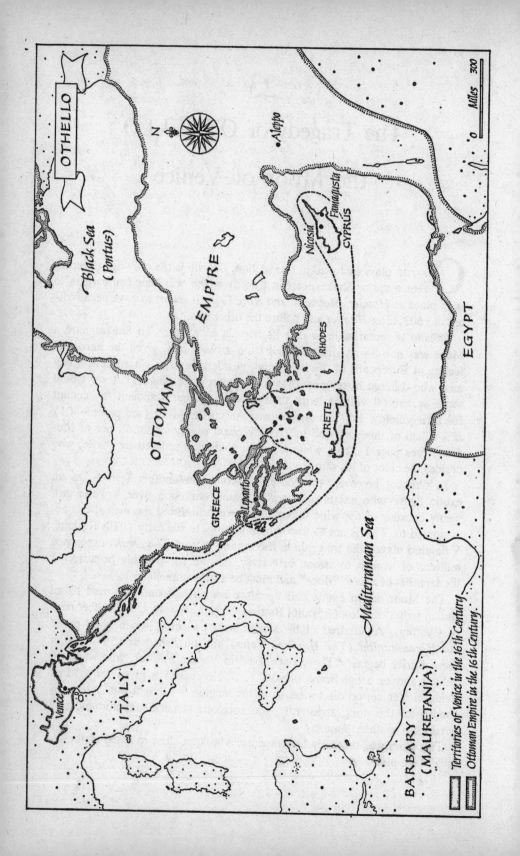

. . . a Florentine

The play opens in the city of Venice (see page I–499) late at night. Two Venetians are having an earnest discussion over some point that is not immediately apparent. One of them, Roderigo, is rather petulant over what he feels to be a double cross on the part of the other, Iago.

Iago insists that he is not double-crossing, that he does indeed hate a person who is not yet identified. He gives his reasons. Influential men, it seems, have asked the unnamed to make Iago his lieutenant and have been refused. Another has been chosen for the post and he is

> *Forsooth, a great arithmetician,*
> *One Michael Cassio, a Florentine,*
> *(A fellow almost damned in a fair wife)*
> *That never set a squadron in the field,*
> —Act I, scene i, lines 16–19

Iago is almost sick with anger at having been passed over for such a one. Cassio is an "arithmetician," that is, one who studied the art of war out of books, instead of in actual battle. And he is a Florentine rather than a Venetian, and Florence, in Shakespeare's time, was renowned for trade, rather than war.

The reference here to Cassio's "fair wife" is a puzzling one. This wife does not appear in the play nor is she ever referred to again. In the Cynthius original, the character who is equivalent to Cassio does have a wife and perhaps Shakespeare intended to use her at first. If he did, he abandoned the idea and did not bother to correct the line.

At Rhodes, at Cyprus . . .

Iago goes on, with gathering anger:

> *And I, of whom his eyes had seen the proof*
> *At Rhodes, at Cyprus, and on other grounds*
> *Christian and heathen, must be belee'd and calmed*
> —Act I, scene i, lines 25–27

When Venice gained territories in the eastern Mediterranean (see page I–592) she took on burdens as well, and the greatest of these was the task of opposing the Ottoman Turks, who became dominant in the Balkan peninsula and the eastern Mediterranean in the course of the fourteenth century.

Rhodes, an island off the southeast shores of Asia Minor, was under the rule of Italian adventurers after the Crusaders' conquest of parts of the East. It remained under Western control for nearly three centuries while Turkish power spread over Asia Minor and into the Balkans.

In 1480 the Turkish sultan, Mohammed II, laid siege to Rhodes and was beaten off. In 1522 the later sultan, Suleiman I the Magnificent (see page I–520), finally took it.

Cyprus is a larger island, near the eastern end of the Mediterranean. It too was captured by Crusaders, but in 1489 it came under the control of Venice. Venice's expansion over some of the shores and islands of the eastern Mediterranean involved her in wars with the Turks, and over the space of two and a half centuries there were to be five of these.

The fourth of these wars was fought from 1570 to 1573. This was after Cynthius had written the tale Shakespeare used as model. It took place in Shakespeare's boyhood, however, and it may possibly have been in his mind as he wrote.

. . . his Moorship's ancient

Still referring to Cassio, Iago says, bitterly:

> He, in good time, must his lieutenant be,
> And I—God bless the mark!—his Moorship's ancient.
> —Act I, scene i, lines 29–30

Clearly now we are talking about Othello, the Moor of Venice, and Iago's scorn is seen in the twisting of "Worship" into "Moorship." An "ancient" is what we now call an "ensign" (see page II–398), a lesser position than that of lieutenant even in our own navy. We can be sure Iago is not the man to take this lying down.

. . . the thick-lips . . .

Roderigo comments discontentedly upon how everything seems to be going well for the Moor:

> What a full fortune does the thick-lips owe [possess]
> If he can carry't thus!
> —Act I, scene i, lines 63–64

As we are soon to find out, what is bothering Roderigo is that the Moor is doing very well in his courtship of Desdemona, the lovely daughter of

Brabantio, one of Venice's most powerful and wealthy senators. Roderigo would like to have Desdemona for himself.

The use of the term "thick-lips" is the first indication that Shakespeare is talking about a true black, rather than merely a Moor of north Africa, who, despite a swarthy complexion, would not be a black. (In Cynthius' story, on the other hand, there is no indication whatsoever that the Moor was a black.)

There are other such references. Thus, Iago's first impulse of revenge is to warn Brabantio in the coarsest possible way, so as to ensure he will take frantic action against the Moor. Before Brabantio's house they call and yell till the senator comes to the window. Then Iago shouts out his warning:

> Zounds, sir, y'are robbed! For shame. Put on your gown!
> Your heart is burst, you have lost half your soul
> Even now, now, very now, an old black ram
> Is tupping your white ewe.
>
> —Act I, scene i, lines 83–86

It is to Othello, of course, that Iago refers with the phrase "old black ram."

. . . a Barbary horse . . .

When Brabantio proves hard to persuade that his daughter has eloped with Othello, Iago, impatient of his incredulity, says:

> Because we come to do you service and you think we are ruffians, you'll have your daughter covered with a Barbary horse . . .
>
> —Act I, scene i, lines 106–9

To the ancient Greeks, all who did not speak Greek were "barbarians," and when Rome came to dominate the Mediterranean that was modified to include those who did not speak Greek or Latin. Since the most prominent barbarians in the last centuries of the Roman Empire were the German-speaking tribesmen to the north, the word came to take on a derogatory tinge and to mean "uncivilized" and "brutal" as well as merely "foreign."

The Italians of the Renaissance period, having rediscovered the Greco-Roman pagan past, picked up the habit. To them, the Europeans north of the Alps and the Africans south of the Mediterranean were barbarians. All Europe could agree with respect to the Africans anyway, and north

Africa came to be called "Barbary." The people of north Africa are still called Berbers today, and that is but another form of the word.

Iago, in referring to Othello as a "Barbary horse," is now using Moor in its more correct sense, with reference to northern Africa rather than black Africa.

. . . to the Sagittary . . .

Brabantio is finally persuaded to search through the house to see if his daughter is at home, and while he is doing so, Iago takes his leave so as not to be identified. Roderigo is to carry on himself and Iago leaves him instructions as to how to guide the search. He says:

> Lead to the Sagittary the raised search;
> And there will I be with him.
>
> —Act I, scene i, lines 155–56

"Sagittary" might be the name of the inn at which Othello is lodging, but there is no clear indication of it. "Sagittary" is the equivalent of the Latin *sagittarius* ("archer") and it is just possible that the name is that of an arsenal where weapons of war are stored. Venice did indeed have a famous one, and Othello, who is pictured in the play as Venice's most capable general, might well be engaged in inspection and stocktaking, even during his honeymoon.

. . . the Signiory

Brabantio, unable to find his daughter, rouses his family and friends to take revenge on Othello.

Meanwhile, Iago has reached Othello again and (with an appearance of bluff honesty) warns him of Brabantio's hostility. Othello, who has indeed eloped with and married Desdemona, shrugs it off, saying:

> Let him do his spite.
> My services which I have done the Signiory
> Shall out-tongue his complaints.
>
> —Act I, scene ii, lines 16–18

The Signiory is the ruling body of Venice. It comes from the same Latin root as "senior" or "senator," so that the name signifies it is a body of elders who put their experience and wisdom to the task of ruling the state.

The government of Venice was, in many ways, the admiration of Europe.

Although originally fairly democratic, it became a closed oligarchy about 1200. From then on for six hundred years a few great families ran the state according to a rigid ideal of duty. (Of course they took, as their reward, the lion's share of the city's wealth for themselves.) In all this time there was but one dangerous revolt against the oligarchy—in 1310—and that was firmly crushed.

Other states might have their extravagant royal families, their court intrigue, civil wars, broils, disruptions; Venice went on in the even tenor of its ways, trading, fighting, prospering, and making all its decisions in the cold light of self-interest.

It is not surprising, then, that Shakespeare in this play portrays the government of Venice to be unemotional and coldly rational at all times.

By Janus . . .

Othello calmly awaits the coming of Brabantio and his party. When a group of men enter with torches, it seems at first this must be they, but Iago, peering toward them, says:

> By Janus, I think no.
>
> —Act I, scene ii, line 32

Since Janus is commonly represented with two heads (see page I–502) and since the entire play is a demonstration of the two-facedness of Iago, it is entirely proper that he swear by Janus.

The Duke . . .

The party that has entered turns out to be under the leadership of Cassio, Othello's new lieutenant. Cassio says to Othello:

> The Duke does greet you, general;
> And he requires your haste-post haste appearance
> Even on the instant.
>
> —Act I, scene ii, lines 35–37

The north Italian word for "duke" is "doge," and this form of the word is associated primarily with Venice (though Genoa also had its doges).

The first Doge of Venice assumed the position possibly as early as 697. The last Doge stepped down in 1797, when Napoleon cavalierly put an end to the Venetian republic. There had been a continuous line of doges for eleven centuries, a most amazing record.

The most unusual doge on the whole list is Enrico Dandolo, who assumed the position in 1192 at the age of eighty-four. Not only was he old, but he was blind as well, yet in 1203 (when he was ninety-five!) he was the indomitable leader of the Crusaders' expedition against Constantinople and carried that expedition through to victory.

In later centuries, though, the Doge was pretty much a figurehead and it was the impersonal oligarchy, the Signiory, that ran the republic.

. . . the sooty bosom

Before Othello can answer the summons, Brabantio and his party arrive. Angrily, Brabantio accuses Othello of having used enchantment, as otherwise his daughter couldn't possibly have

> Run from her guardage to the sooty bosom
> Of such a thing as thou—to fear, not to delight.
> —Act I, scene ii, lines 69–70

Again a reference to Othello as a black. Othello, noble, powerful, accomplished, high in all men's regard, would be a good match for the girl but for his skin color. Yet it is interesting that Brabantio makes no mention of religion. Nor is the matter of religion mentioned anywhere in the play.

And yet if we take *Othello* seriously and don't dismiss it as simply a romance in which we need not peer too closely at the details, we must suppose that Othello was born a Mohammedan. It is inconceivable that the Venetians would trust a Mohammedan to lead their armed forces against the Mohammedan Turks; we must therefore further assume that Othello was a converted Christian.

. . . the general enemy Ottoman

For a while it seems that fighting will break out, but Othello preserves a magnificent calm and, in any case, Brabantio too has been summoned to the Signiory.

In the council chamber, the Signiory is gravely considering the news that a Turkish fleet is at sea, with its destination uncertain. Calmly, they weigh what evidence they have and decide the Turks are aiming for Cyprus.

When Othello enters, the Duke says:

> Valiant Othello, we must straight [immediately] employ you
> Against the general enemy Ottoman.
> —Act I, scene iii, lines 48–49

There have been numerous tribes of Turks who have made their mark in history, and those against whom the Crusaders fought in the twelfth century were the Seljuk Turks.

Two centuries later a group of Turks under Osman I (or Othman, in Arabic) began to win successes. The particular Turks under this ruler and under his successors were called Osmanli Turks or, more commonly, though incorrectly, Ottoman Turks. It was under the Ottoman rule that Turkish power reached its heights.

Under Orkhan I, the son of Osman I, all of Asia Minor was taken, and in 1345 Orkhan took advantage of a civil war among the Byzantines to cross over the Dardanelles. Thus the Turk entered Europe, never to leave.

In 1453 the Ottoman Turks took Constantinople and by Shakespeare's time they ruled a vast empire covering western Asia, northern Africa, and southeastern Europe. It had passed its peak at the time *Othello* was written but so slightly that the decline was not yet visible, and it still seemed (and was) the most powerful state in Europe.

The Anthropophagi . . .

It is only after speaking to Othello that the Duke notices Brabantio, who instantly pours forth his tale of anger and woe, accusing the Moor once again of having used enchantment.

Othello offers to send for Desdemona so that she might bear witness herself and meanwhile gives his own account. He has often been a guest at Brabantio's house, he says, and at his host's request would tell of his adventurous life and the strange things he has seen:

> . . . *of the Cannibals that each other eat,*
> *The Anthropophagi, and men whose heads*
> *Grew beneath their shoulders.*
> —Act I, scene iii, lines 142–44

"Anthropophagi" is Greek for "man-eaters." The word "cannibal" came into use only after Columbus' voyage, when man-eating habits were discovered among a group of Indians inhabiting the smaller islands of what are now called the West Indies. One of the names given them was "Caniba," and from that came "cannibal."

Actually, Shakespeare is taking a little bit out of Pliny here.

Gaius Plinius Secundus (the full name of the writer commonly called Pliny the Elder) was a Roman scholar who lived in the first century A.D. He was a prolific writer who tried to prepare a one-man encyclopedia of human knowledge culled from all the writers he could get hold of. In A.D 77 he published a thirty-seven-volume book called *Natural History* which digested two thousand ancient books and which was translated into English in 1601 (just two years before *Othello* was written) by Philemon Holland.

Pliny accepted rumors and travelers' tales and much of what he included was a farrago of legend and distortion, but all was so wondrous and interesting that the volumes survived the vicissitudes that followed the fall of the ancient world when other, more serious volumes did not.

Othello explains how Desdemona listened to his tales and came first to admire him and then to love him. Desdemona arrives and bears out Othello's tale, and Brabantio must give in. But in doing so, he sardonically warns that since Desdemona has proven capable of deceiving her father, she might deceive her husband as well.

H'as done my office

All leave but Roderigo and Iago. Roderigo is in despair, for Othello seems to have won utterly. Iago, on the other hand, is not concerned. He has contempt for women and it seems to him that Desdemona cannot long remain in love with an old Moor. All Roderigo has to do is go to Cyprus with plenty of money (which, of course, Iago intends to charm into his own pockets) and wait his chance.

Then when Roderigo leaves too, Iago ruminates on the Moor and on his own plans for revenge, saying:

> *I hate the Moor*
> *And it is thought abroad that 'twixt my sheets*
> *H'as done my office. I know not if't be true,*
> *But I, for mere suspicion in that kind,*
> *Will do, as if for surety.*
> —Act I, scene iii, lines 377–81

This must be nonsense. From all we can guess about Othello from the picture Shakespeare paints, he is not this sort of man. But Iago, intent on revenge, is busy working up his sense of grievance and will seize upon anything to do so. The revenge must involve Cassio as well. He says:

> *Cassio's a proper* [handsome] *man. Let me see now:*
> *To get his place . . .*
> —Act I, scene iii, lines 383–84

And he gets his idea.

. . . Our wars are done

The scene shifts to Cyprus, where Montano, the Venetian governor, is awaiting events. There has been a great storm, which two Gentlemen on watch have witnessed. That tempest has, however, also served to abort the Turkish menace. A Third Gentlemen enters and says:

> *News, lads! Our wars are done.*
> *The desperate tempest hath so banged the Turks*
> *That their designment* [intention] *halts.*
> —Act II, scene i, lines 20–22

There is no further mention of military matters and Othello has no chance to display his quality as a general. That is too bad, for thirty years before the play was written there had been a Venetian-Turkish war that would have offered a good model for a battle.

In 1570, when Shakespeare was six years old, Turkish forces had indeed invaded Cyprus, as in *Othello* they had merely threatened to do.

Venice, which controlled the island at the time, felt she could not face Turkey alone. She appealed for help to the Pope, who in turn appealed to the most dedicated of all the Catholic monarchs in Europe, Philip II of Spain.

While the Christian forces of Europe were slowly gathering for the counterattack, the Turks were advancing in Cyprus and were steadily beating back the Venetians. Nicosia, in the center of the island (and the capital of modern Cyprus), was taken on September 9, 1570, while Famagusta on the eastern shore was under siege. Turkish vessels penetrated the Adriatic.

It wasn't till the summer of 1571 that the Christian fleet was ready to sail and challenge the Turks. The fleet was put under the command of Don John of Austria, an illegitimate half brother of Philip II.

Famagusta had fallen, meanwhile, and in October 1571 the Turkish fleet was concentrated near a city on the northern shore of the Gulf of Corinth, a city which to Italian traders was known as Lepanto. It was six hundred miles northwest of Cyprus and seven hundred miles southeast of Venice itself.

On October 7, 1571, the allied fleet reached Lepanto and attacked the Turks in the last great battle to be fought with galleys, that is, by large ships driven by banks of oars. There were nearly 500 ships on both sides carrying over 60,000 soldiers in addition to the oarsmen. The Venetian ships distinguished themselves in the fighting that followed, and, in the end, it was a great Christian victory. About 50 Turkish galleys were destroyed and 117 captured. Thousands of Christian slaves were liberated, and the news that the invincible Turks had been catastrophically defeated electrified Europe.

And yet Shakespeare did not make use of such an event. He might have allowed Othello to defeat the Turks offstage and gain a Lepanto-like victory as easily as he allowed the storm to do the job.

But then Lepanto must surely have seemed less glorious in England than elsewhere. It was a victory for Philip II of Spain, who was England's great enemy in Shakespeare's time. In 1588, only seventeen years after Lepanto, he had launched a huge Armada against England. The English defeated it and what was left of the Spanish fleet was destroyed in a storm.

It was the storm that defeated Philip II, rather than the earlier battle that gave him victory, that may have been in Shakespeare's mind.

King Stephen . . .

One by one the Venetians arrive at Cyprus, having weathered the storm. First Cassio, then Desdemona, Iago, and Roderigo, and finally Othello. Othello, completely happy to be with his Desdemona, to have Cyprus safe, and the Turks gone, proclaims a holiday.

Now it is up to Iago to use that holiday as an excuse to get Cassio drunk —the first step in his plan.

Iago sets up a drinking party. Cassio protests he has a weak head for liquor but Iago will not listen. In no time there is drinking, comic songs, and foolish prattle. At one point, Iago sings a song that begins:

> *King Stephen was and a worthy peer;*
> *His breeches cost him but a crown;*
>
> > —Act II, scene iii, lines 86–87

It is a nonsense song, brought to Iago's mind by talk of England, and England did indeed have a King Stephen.

In 1135 King Henry I died, leaving as an heir a single daughter named Matilda. The nobility did not approve of a woman ruler, however, and turned to the old King's nephew, Stephen.

Stephen was crowned and kept his throne till his death in 1154. His reign, however, was a disastrous one. There was almost continuous civil war, first with Matilda and then with her son, Henry. Scotland took advantage of England's troubles to extend her sway southward, and the English nobility grew turbulent and independent of the crown.

And yet Stephen was a genial, good-natured man who was popular with the people, especially the Londoners, and might well have inspired good-natured comic songs in his honor.

. . . as many mouths as Hydra . . .

And now the plot begins to work. Cassio, quickly drunk, staggers away. Iago had earlier arranged with Roderigo to have him pick a fight with Cassio, and meanwhile he tells Montano, with apparent reluctance and great concern, that Cassio is often drunk.

Roderigo comes running back, with Cassio in clamorous pursuit. Montano tries to restrain Cassio and in no time they are fighting and Montano is wounded. Iago sends Roderigo to set the alarm bell ringing and soon Othello, roused from bed, is on the scene.

Othello wants to know what happened and Iago tells him accurately, omitting only the fact that he himself had arranged everything. Othello has no choice but to discharge Cassio.

Yet Iago's game is not over; it is merely beginning. Cassio's discharge is well and good and now Iago may become lieutenant in his place. By now, though, Iago is after bigger game and cannot be stopped.

Critics have often maintained that Iago lacks real motive for his villainy and continues out of "motiveless malignity." It seems to me, however, that this simply isn't so. To many people there is a fierce delight in pulling strings, in the feeling of power that comes out of making others into marionettes whom one can manipulate at will.

The excellent results of Iago's maneuvering, so far, had whetted his appetite for more of the same, and we might suppose that by this time Iago could even forget his own wrongs in the sheer delight of watching himself twitch those about him into annihilation.

Thus, he twitches another string and encourages Cassio to hope for rehabilitation. But poor Cassio is too abashed to approach Othello. He says:

> *I will ask him for my place again: he shall tell me I am a*
> *drunkard. Had I as many mouths as Hydra, such an answer*
> *would stop them all.*
>
> —Act II, scene iii, lines 302–4

The Hydra is the many-headed monster whom Hercules slew in the second of his twelve labors (see page I–237).

Iago, however, has the cure for Cassio's pessimism and pulls another string. All Cassio need do is ask Desdemona to intercede with Othello, and he can reach Desdemona through her lady in waiting, Emilia, who happens to be Iago's wife. With the dawn of hope, Cassio agrees to try.

. . . the green-eyed monster . . .

The plan begins well. Cassio sees Emilia and then Desdemona, and the latter agrees to intercede with Othello.

As Cassio leaves Desdemona, however, Iago and Othello arrive on the scene and Iago, looking after Cassio, mutters:

> Ha! I like not that.
>
> —Act III, scene iii, line 34

He won't explain himself, but it is enough to insert the first uncertainty into Othello's mind concerning Desdemona and Cassio. Then, when Desdemona begins to plead for Cassio, that can but increase the uncertainty.

After Desdemona leaves, Iago, with infinite cleverness, manages to fire Othello into jealousy by the very manner in which he himself refuses to say anything. The very show of reluctance on Iago's part gives Othello the greater room for imagining the worse, and Iago warns him in terms that but feed his fear, saying:

> O, beware, my lord, of jealousy!
> It is the green-eyed monster, which doth mock
> The meat it feeds on.
>
> —Act III, scene iii, lines 165–67

Because of these verses, the expression "green-eyed monster" has become a common metaphor signifying jealousy and its mundane meaning is lost. The "green-eyed monster" is obviously the cat, which plays with the mouse it catches, releasing it only to catch it again, over and over. In the same way, jealousy torments the one who experiences it, for he cannot ever be made secure. Every proof to the contrary releases him only briefly, till some new incident rouses the jealousy again.

. . . her jesses . . .

Othello understands the torments of jealousy and he will not sit still to be a prey to it. He will have the matter put to the test, either to be proven or disproven. Afer Iago has left, he muses:

> If I do prove her haggard,
> Though that her jesses were my dear heartstrings,
> I'd whistle her off and let her down the wind
>
> —Act III, scene iii, lines 259–61

The language used here is that of falconry. In medieval times it was an aristocratic sport to train falcons, hawks, and other birds of prey to hunt game, and, like every other specialized activity, it developed its own vocabulary.

A haggard is an untamed hawk; one that is caught after it is adult so that any taming is superficial and so that there always remains a tendency to revert to the wild. Jesses are small leather straps around the hawk's leg which are usually supplied with a ring that can be attached to the glove on the hawker's hand. To whistle her off would be to let her go.

Actually, though, Othello is already convinced of Desdemona's infidelity. When she comes in to call him gaily to dinner, she sees something is wrong and asks if anything ails him. He answers, ominously:

> *I have a pain upon my forehead, here.*
> —Act III, scene iii, line 283

He touches his forehead, and to the Elizabethan audience, any reference to the forehead means the horns that sprout there and signify cuckoldry.

The innocent Desdemona offers him her handkerchief to bind his head but he pushes it roughly away and it falls to the ground unnoticed by her.

. . . *poppy nor mandragora*

The handkerchief is a very special one, a gift to Desdemona from Othello. Now it lies there and Emilia picks it up. Her husband, Iago, had often asked her to steal it for him (we are not told why) and now she can give it to him.

Iago is elated on receiving it. He sees how he can use it in his plan. When Othello enters, Iago muses with grim satisfaction on the perturbed appearance of the general. He says to himself, concerning Othello:

> *Not poppy nor mandragora,*
> *Nor all the drowsy syrups of the world,*
> *Shall ever medicine thee to that sweet sleep*
> *Which thou owedst* [possessed] *yesterday.*
> —Act III, scene iii, lines 327–30

There has always been a use for the equivalent of tranquilizers, for there have always been tensions. Before the days of modern chemistry, tranquilizing herbs were found in nature, and of these the chief was a certain species of poppy which was originally grown along the shores of the eastern Mediterranean for the sake of its edible seeds.

Undoubtedly, other parts of the plant were nibbled on and it must have been noticed that nibbling the fruit eased small pains and discomforts, reduced tension, and encouraged sleep. It was eventually discovered that one could express juice from the fruit and use that as a sedative. The Greek word *opion* is a diminutive form of the word for juice, and in Latin that becomes *opium*.

One wonders if the famous lotus-eaters in the *Odyssey,* who ate of the lotus and wished nothing more than to dream away their lives in tranquil content, were not really poppy-eaters.

There is a less exaggerated mention in the *Odyssey* of a tranquilizing drug. When Helen and Menelaus are hosts to Telemachus (the son of Ulysses) in Sparta, they serve wine to which Helen adds a drug "that banishes all care, sorrow, and ill humor." A little opium might do that too. In Greek, the name of the drug Helen uses is *nepenthes,* meaning "no sorrow."

As for mandragora, that is an older form of mandrake (see page I–336).

. . . the Pontic Sea

Othello's state of mind has brought Iago himself to danger, for in his present frenzy, he demands proof or he will have Iago's life. Without flinching, Iago makes up the necessary lie. He says he once shared a bed with Cassio, who talked in his sleep and revealed his affair with Desdemona. He then adds the climactic bit when he says that the handkerchief Othello gave Desdemona is now in the possession of Cassio.

That does it. Othello is reduced to such a pitch of mad fury that he cries for blood. Coolly, Iago urges Othello to be patient and his intentness on revenge may vanish. But Othello says:

> *Never, Iago. Like to the Pontic Sea,*
> *Whose icy current and compulsive course*
> *Nev'r keeps retiring ebb, but keeps due on*
> *To the Propontic and the Hellespont,*
> *Even so my bloody thoughts, with violent pace,*
> *Shall nev'r look back, nev'r ebb to humble love,*
> —Act III, scene iii, lines 450–57

The "Pontic Sea" is the Black Sea, which is connected to the Mediterranean through narrow straits. At its southwest corner is the Bosporus, about twenty miles long and no more than half a mile wide at its narrowest. It runs just about north and south and at its southern end widens out into a small body of water which we call the Sea of Marmara. (The ancient Greeks called it the "Propontis," meaning "before the Pontus," since a Greek traveler leaving the Aegean Sea must travel through the Propontis before getting to the Pontus.)

The Propontis narrows to a second strait, the Dardanelles, or, to the Greeks, the Hellespont (see page I–466).

The Mediterranean Sea, into which the Hellespont opens, is a warm sea. The sun beats down upon it and sometimes the hot, dry winds blow northward out of the Sahara Desert. Much water is lost by evaporation and only a small part of it is replaced by river water. Only one major river flows into the Mediterranean and that is the Nile; and after its long trip through desert regions not as much water is delivered into the Mediterranean by the Nile as one might suppose from the length of the river. The other rivers that flow into the Mediterranean—the Ebro, Rhone, Po, Tiber —don't count for much, despite their historic associations.

The result is that if the Mediterranean were existing in isolation it would gradually dry and shrink to a smaller size than it is.

It is quite otherwise with the Black Sea, which is distinctly cooler than the Mediterranean and free of the Saharan winds. There is less evaporation, to begin with. This smaller amount of evaporation is more than made up for by the giant rivers that flow into it—the Danube, Dniester, Bug, Dnieper, and Don.

If the Black Sea existed in isolation, it would overflow.

The result is that the waters of the Black Sea pass constantly through the straits and pour ceaselessly into the Mediterranean without ever any ebb to this steady flow, and it is to this that Othello refers. (Water is also constantly pouring into the Mediterranean Sea from the Atlantic Ocean through the Strait of Gibraltar.)

. . . my lieutenant

Othello intends death now, as soon as the case is proved. He orders Iago to arrange the assassination of Cassio. Iago now has everything he wants. Cassio has been amply paid back for daring to move over his head— to the death. Othello has been destroyed; the noble general he once was he can never be again.

There remains Desdemona. She has not offended Iago. He seems to have a momentary qualm about her. When Othello orders him to kill Cassio, Iago says:

> 'Tis done at your request.
> But let her live.
>
> —Act III, scene iii, lines 471–72

Yet the immediate effect of this is to drive Othello further into his maddened rage, so that he cries out:

> Damn her, lewd minx! O, damn her! Damn her!
> Come, go with me apart. I will withdraw
> To furnish me with some swift means of death
> For the fair devil. Now art thou my lieutenant.
>
> —Act III, scene iii, lines 472–75

We might even imagine that Iago's soft request for mercy was designed to provoke this anger; that without any personal hatred for Desdemona at all, he nevertheless enjoyed pushing the buttons.

A sibyl . . .

Desdemona has by now realized she has lost her handkerchief and is very disturbed. Othello (testing whether she has given it to Cassio, as Iago said) asks for it, and the nervous Desdemona, forced to admit she doesn't have it on her person, is afraid to say she has lost it. Othello harshly warns her that the handkerchief is important; it has magic properties and is a love charm:

> *A sibyl that had numbered in the world*
> *The sun to course two hundred compasses,*
> *In her prophetic fury sewed the work;*
>
> —Act III, scene iv, lines 70–72

The aged sibyl is an image used often by Shakespeare (see page I-452), and we may well believe that Othello accepts the truth of sibyls as he does of Pliny's wonders.

Still Desdemona can't produce the handkerchief and still she fearfully denies it is lost. Othello stalks off in a rage.

. . . would prove a crocodile

Iago now sets about supplying the last touch. He has planted the handkerchief in Cassio's chambers. Cassio finds it, likes it, and gives it to his mistress, Bianca (a courtesan), to copy over so that he will have a similar handkerchief after he returns this one to its rightful owner, whoever that might be.

Iago then finds occasion to draw Cassio aside, with Othello watching from a place where he can see but not hear. Iago teases Cassio with the great love Bianca has for him. Cassio preens and smirks with the usual male self-satisfaction over such matters and Othello can only assume (in his fevered state) that he is laughing over his amour with Desdemona.

And then Bianca enters and throws the handkerchief back at Cassio, for she has decided it must belong to another one of his girlfriends. Of course, Othello recognizes it at once and the case is proven for him. The handkerchief he gave to Desdemona, she gave to Cassio, who thinks so little of it he passes it on to a courtesan. Othello is ready to kill Desdemona.

But the outside world intervenes. A deputation of important Venetian officials has arrived under the leadership of one Ludovico. They bring a message recalling Othello to Venice now that the war danger is gone and appointing Cassio as his successor.

Othello greets them with the necessary ceremony but is so far gone in his jealous madness that he cannot put a good face on matters even for the sake of the Venetian deputation. When Desdemona innocently tries to speak in Cassio's favor to the Venetians, Othello strikes her.

The horrified Ludovico upbraids Othello and exclaims at the sight of the weeping Desdemona. But the raving Othello says:

> *O devil, devil!*
> *If that the earth could teem with woman's tears,*
> *Each drop she falls would prove a crocodile.*
> —Act IV, scene i, lines 244–46

In other words, if tears falling to earth could act as semen to make the earth pregnant and bring forth life, Desdemona's tears would cause it to bring forth crocodiles.

This refers to a well-known legend concerning crocodiles. (Othello is a veritable compendium of legends.) Crocodiles were supposed to moan and sigh, so that passers-by might think human beings in distress were somewhere nearby. If any were softhearted enough, or curious enough, to turn aside in search of them, the crocodile's jaws snapped shut, and it would then continue to weep even while eating.

The story is quite untrue, but the phrase "crocodile tears" has entered the language to represent any form of hypocritical grief. The implication is that Desdemona's modesty and virtue are tissues of hypocrisy. The irony, of course, is that the play is filled with crocodile tears; they are all Iago's and Othello doesn't see them.

. . . into Mauritania . . .

When Othello stalks off, Ludovico wonders if he is sane, and Iago seizes the opportunity to encourage that thought of possible insanity without actually committing himself to it.

But by now Iago has almost more strings in his hand than he can properly handle. Thus, when Othello takes himself to Desdemona's chamber to give her a bitter tongue-lashing, Emilia openly wonders if Othello might not be the victim of malicious slander. Then too, Roderigo has been gulled and robbed by Iago to the point where he can take no more. He threatens to talk to Desdemona directly and request the return of his jewels.

We can be pretty sure that Desdemona has never received any jewels but that Iago, as go-between, has kept them. Iago, therefore, must begin to shut mouths.

He begins by promising Roderigo that he will have Desdemona the very next night if he can manage to keep Othello on the island that long. Iago explains that Othello has been recalled and ordered to a distant country (another lie). This is to force Roderigo to act, for it will seem to him that Desdemona is about to move utterly beyond his grasp. Iago says:

> . . . *he* [Othello] *goes into Mauritania and taketh away with him the fair Desdemona, unless his abode be lingered here by some accident;*
>
> —Act IV, scene ii, lines 224–26

Mauritania was the name given in ancient times to the northwest shoulder of Africa, the region now called Morocco. It may be used here as a vague term, meaning "land of the Moors," that is, north Africa generally.

Iago arranges to have Roderigo attempt to find occasion to kill Cassio, since the death of Othello's appointed successor would force the Moor to remain on the island for a while. (From Iago's standpoint, this will get rid of the hated Cassio, and Othello has ordered him to do that; and he will find occasion, we can well imagine, to take care of Roderigo too.)

. . . *that Promethean heat*

Matters now rush to their horrible climax. It is night and Desdemona, in almost unbearable depression, goes to bed.

Cassio, returning from time spent with his ladylove, is set upon by Roderigo. They fight and both are wounded. Men come running, and Iago, finding that Cassio is not dead, makes the best of matters by killing Roderigo and shutting his mouth at least.

While that is going on, Othello is trying to do his part. He comes upon Desdemona sleeping and even now finds he still hesitates. He looks from the candle he carries to the sleeping woman and says:

> *If I quench thee, thou flaming minister,*
> *I can again thy former light restore,*
> *Should I repent me; but once put out thy light,*
> *Thou cunning'st pattern of excelling nature,*
> *I know not where is that Promethean heat*
> *That can thy light relume.*
>
> —Act V, scene ii, lines 8–13

Prometheus, in the Greek myths, had first made man the gift of fire, stealing it from the sun (see page I–437). A later myth also made him the creator of man. He was supposed to have made clay models into which he breathed life.

Othello's reference to "Promethean heat" is therefore a double-barreled allusion. It refers to Prometheus' connection with the sun's fire; not just ordinary fire but a special kind. Secondly, it refers to Prometheus' ability to infuse cold and lifeless clay with the warmth of a living human body; and that ability Othello lacks.

. . . the very error of the moon

Othello no longer raves. He goes about the task of killing with a cold sorrow. Desdemona wakes and Othello accuses her of having given the handkerchief to Cassio. He will not accept her denial but tells her Cassio is dead (he assumes Iago has done his work properly), and Desdemona's terror at that news seems to him to be the final admission.

He strangles her with her pillow and even while he is forcing his weight down on her fragile neck, there is a clamor at the door. Emilia demands entrance. Othello closes the bed curtains and lets her in. Emilia has come to tell of the deadly fight between Roderigo and Cassio.

Othello says calmly:

> It is the very error of the moon.
> She comes more nearer earth than she was wont
> And makes men mad.
>
> —Act V, scene ii, lines 108–10

It has always been tempting to think that changes in the heavens bring about analogous changes on the earth (something that is the basis of the pseudo science of astrology). The regular changes of the moon from new to full and back again would seem to imply that certain passions or foibles of men would wax and wane in sympathy.

In particular, mental abnormalities would wax with the moon, and there are the well-known legends that men turn into werewolves under the full moon, that witchcraft is most dangerous then, and so on. Spells of madness would vary with the moon's phases too by this line of thought, and the very word "lunatic" is derived from the Latin word for the moon.

And of course, if the moon approached more closely to the earth than usual, its effects would be multiplied.

. . . towards his feet . . .

But now Othello finds out Cassio is not killed, merely wounded. That staggers him.

A faint cry from the bed reveals that Desdemona is not quite dead, either. She lives only long enough to try one last time to shield Othello, and weakly claims she killed herself.

Othello, trying desperately to cling to the certainty that he did the right thing, boldly proclaims he killed her for her infidelity, and now Emilia comes into her own. She shrieks her utter faith in Desdemona's virtue.

Others, including Iago, come bursting in in response to Emilia's cries and find Desdemona dead. Iago must admit he told Othello of Desdemona's unfaithfulness, and now comes his doom. The matter of the handkerchief comes up and Emilia reveals the truth. She had found the handkerchief and given it to Iago.

Then—too late, too late—Othello understands. He tries to kill Iago, who evades him, stabs Emilia, and runs.

Emilia dies, but Iago is brought back a prisoner. Othello looks at him through the hellish mist that now surrounds him and says, brokenly:

> *I look down towards his feet—but that's a fable.*
> —Act V, scene ii, line 282

This takes us back to one of the more joyous aspects of the pagan religions of the Greeks and Romans. They peopled the woods and wilds with spirits representing the free, animal fertility of life. The Greek satyrs and the Roman fauns were pictured as men with goats' horns and hindquarters, possibly because goats were always pictured as lustful animals. (Then too, goats may well have been the first creatures to be domesticated for meat and milk and it was important that they be lustful and multiply.) The most important of the satyrs was Pan himself.

The sexually strait-laced Jews (and, later, Christians) viewed all fertility deities with disapproval and suspicion, and to the Jews the satyrs (or similar creatures in Eastern cults) were *sairrim,* which the King James Bible translates as "devils." They tempted mankind to sin.

The devil, Satan, is usually pictured, even today, with horns, tail, and other goatish characteristics. He is still a satyr or, in particular, Pan. Medieval legends had it that the devil could take on many undevilish disguises, but that he could not abandon all his marks. Whatever he did, there remained one trace of goatishness; that is, a goat's cloven hoof. Hence the expression "to show the cloven hoof," meaning to reveal the hidden evil in one's character.

Othello looks toward Iago's feet to see the cloven hoof that would indicate the devil and interrupts himself mournfully with his "—but that's a fable."

He has learned! Till now he has believed the fables from Pliny, he has believed in magic handkerchiefs and sibyls, in crocodiles and moon-bred lunacy—and, of course, in Iago too.

Now, for the first time, he has discovered the necessity of skepticism—far too late.

Demand me nothing . . .

As all of Iago's lies and trickeries are exposed, the confused Othello wants to know but one thing. Why did Iago do it? The audience wants to know too, since the revenge went far beyond anything necessary to punish Iago's grievances. But Iago says:

> Demand me nothing. What you know, you know.
> From this time forth I never will speak word.
> > —Act V, scene ii, lines 299–300

Ludovico threatens to make him talk under torture, but it seems reasonable to suppose that no torture will make Iago talk. This failure to say why has irritated many, but, in my opinion, it should not. Iago's pleasure at manipulating lives was intense and it is something we can all understand, for, in a much milder way, it is present in all men—and yet it is not something that can be easily explained.

. . . the base Judean . . .

Now it is only necessary to take Othello back to Venice so that he might be tried for murder.

Othello, however, has one last thing to say. With an effort, he manages to pull himself together into almost the man he once was and speaks once more, a little in self-pity, much more in self-hate. He asks them all to tell the tale honestly, saying:

> Then must you speak
> Of one that loved not wisely, but too well;
> Of one not easily jealous, but, being wrought,
> Perplexed in the extreme; of one whose hand,
> Like the base Judean, threw a pearl away
> Richer than all his tribe . . .
> > —Act V, scene ii, lines 339–44

In many editions of the play, the phrase "like the base Judean" is made to read "like the base Indian." It seems to me that "Judean" is much the more preferable. If "Indian" is used, the allusion is obscure; if "Judean" is used, it is brilliantly apparent.

In Matthew 13:45–46, Jesus is reported as saying "Again, the kingdom of heaven is like unto a merchant man, seeking goodly pearls: Who, when he had found one pearl of great price, went and sold all that he had, and bought it."

It is easy to envision Jesus (who, in the Christian view, represented the kingdom of heaven) as being the pearl of great price more valuable than all else in the world besides. The Jews, in rejecting Jesus as the Messiah, would then be pictured as throwing away the pearl of great price. In particular, Judas, who betrayed Jesus, would be the "base Judean."

From this point of view, the extent of Othello's self-hatred is clear. He compares his murder of Desdemona with the crucifixion of Jesus, and himself with Judas.

. . . in Aleppo once

Othello goes on to say:

> And say besides that in Aleppo once,
> Where a malignant and a turbaned Turk
> Beat a Venetian and traduced the state,
> I took by th' throat the circumcised dog
> And smote him—thus.

—Act V, scene ii, lines 348–52

With the last word, before anyone can stop him, Othello stabs himself, falls upon Desdemona in a final kiss, and dies.

This last pathetic passage cannot be taken literally. Aleppo is a city in what is now northwestern Syria, and (except for a brief period in 969) it has been Moslem for over thirteen centuries. If Othello killed a Turk in Aleppo, he was killing him in the midst of a city of Turks and it is not likely he would have got away alive.

He must mean something else . . .

The Moslems and Jews were marked off from the Christians by being circumcised; that is, a flap of skin at the end of the penis was removed. "Uncircumcised dog" was a common derogatory phrase for Christians among the Moslems, indicating that they were outside the pale of the true religion. Othello's use of the reverse phrase in his last agony is like a return to his origins.

After all, if Othello was Moslem originally, conversion to Christianity in later life could not utterly wipe out the tricks of speech he had learned as a young man. Furthermore, he would still be circumcised; baptism may cause one to be born again in the spiritual sense, but it cannot grow a new foreskin.

Othello therefore pictures himself as having returned to his origins, of having forgotten the Christian virtues of forgiveness, of having become "a malignant and a turbaned Turk." He beat a Venetian (Desdemona). He also traduced (defamed) himself; robbing himself of his own fame and reputation by his actions; and insofar as he was the representative of the state in Cyprus, he traduced the state.

So he took by the throat "the circumcised dog" (himself) and killed him.

O Spartan dog

It is the end. The destruction has been complete, and Iago's plot has worked itself out to the final bit. That Iago himself is trapped and is to be destroyed by torture must seem quite irrelevant to him. The victory is his.

Ludovico says to Iago bitterly:

> *O Spartan dog,*
> *More fell than anguish, hunger, or the sea!*
> *Look on the tragic loading of this bed.*
> *This is thy work.*
>
> —Act V, scene ii, lines 357–60

A "Spartan dog" is a bloodhound, one that is trained to hunt and kill, and therefore a cruel and bloodthirsty person.

But does Ludovico expect Iago's conscience to be touched? It is precisely "the tragic loading of this bed" that is his victory, and one can imagine that Iago, wounded and pinioned and with the certainty of agonizing torture awaiting him, must, as he looks upon the bed, smile.

So the play ends—and the manner of its ending reflects history too, in a way, for all that the play is utter fiction from beginning to end.

The Battle of Lepanto, however much of a glorious victory it seemed to Europeans, and however much of a psychological boost it gave them, had no military value. Within a year the Turks had replaced their losses and were as powerful as ever at sea. The Christian allies, having won their victory, quarreled among themselves and did nothing more. The Venetians were left to face the Turks alone. The war on Cyprus continued to go against them, and in 1573 the Venetians yielded and ceded Cyprus to the Turks, who were to keep it for three centuries.

And so, just as Othello's coming to Cyprus may be compared to the victory at Lepanto, so his death seems to signify the valuelessness of that victory and the ultimate loss of Cyprus to the enemy.

24

MEASURE FOR MEASURE

IN THIS PLAY, written in 1604, Shakespeare takes the opportunity to study the relationship of justice and mercy. He had done so in *The Merchant of Venice*, but there he had not been consistent. Portia had demanded mercy of Shylock, but when the tables were turned she did not show it (see page I–539).

We all favor mercy for those with whom we sympathize, but are not nearly as keen when mercy is sought for those we hate. In this play Shakespeare carries through the notion of mercy to ultimate consistency, and in offering mercy to the villain makes many critics unhappy. In presenting an unpleasant situation so that the offering of mercy becomes hard indeed, more critics are made unhappy. The result is that Shakespeare's great play of mercy is usually considered one of his unpleasant comedies, like *All's Well That Ends Well*.

... any in Vienna ...

The setting of the play is in Austria. This setting Shakespeare takes over from a tale by Cynthius; a tale from the same collection, in fact, from which he had a year earlier or less taken the plot for *Othello* (see page I–609).

Cynthius' tale begins with the Emperor Maximian appointing a new judge over the city of Innsbruck. There was a real Emperor Maximian who ruled over the Roman Empire, along with Diocletian, from 286 to 305, but there is no indication that the play takes place in Roman times.

The name may have been inspired to Cynthius by the fact that two Holy Roman emperors named Maximilian ruled in the sixteenth century. The first, Maximilian I, ruled from 1493 to 1519, and the second, Maximilian II, became Emperor in 1564. He was on the throne when Cynthius' collection was published in 1565.

The two Maximilians, like all the emperors after 1438, were members of the House of Habsburg, who ruled, specifically, as archdukes of Austria.

Shakespeare shifts the scene from Innsbruck, a provincial town in west-

MEASURE FOR MEASURE

Archangel

RUSSIA

POLAND

THE EMPIRE

BOHEMIA

AUSTRIA

Vienna

HUNGARY

FRANCE

Innsbruck

ITALY

N

0   Miles   300

ern Austria, to Vienna, the capital, but he is writing a Renaissance romance, and all the characters have Italian names. Thus, the Archduke of Austria and presumably Holy Roman Emperor (but referred to only as "Duke" in the play) is Vincentio.

The Duke is planning to retire for a while from the tasks of government and intends to appoint a deputy to wield his powers. He suggests his candidate to an aged lord, Escalus, who approves and says:

> *If any in Vienna be of worth*
> *To undergo such ample grace and honor*
> *It is Lord Angelo.*
>
> —Act I, scene i, lines 22–24

Angelo is given the post, though he is reluctant, and the Duke then leaves in great haste.

. . . the King of Hungary . . .

The scene then shifts to a Viennese street, where we are introduced to Lucio, who is listed in the cast of characters as "a fantastic." He is fantastic in costume and conversation, in other words; he is avant-garde, ahead of the fashion, a gay man about town.

He is talking to two unnamed Gentlemen and says:

> *If the Duke, with the other dukes, come not to composition*
> *with the King of Hungary, why then all the dukes fall upon*
> *the King.*
>
> —Act I, scene ii, lines 1–3

Nothing further is mentioned of this, of any threat of war, of the King of Hungary; nor is there any hint as to who "the other dukes" might be.

Hungary is Austria's eastern neighbor. Through the Middle Ages it was an extensive and often powerful kingdom which was, however, weakened by the existence of a turbulent aristocracy whose quarrels among themselves worked to the ruin of all.

Hungary had reached its height a little over a century before *Measure for Measure* was written, when, from 1458 to 1490, Mathias Corvinus ruled. He temporarily broke the power of the Hungarian nobility, spread his power northward over Slovakia and Silesia, and in 1485 even conquered Vienna. He made Vienna his capital and ruled over Austria.

Corvinus died in 1490 and his weak successor gave up the earlier conquests and let the nobility gradually regain their power. The real disaster, however, came in 1526, when the Ottoman Turks (see page I–520) in-

vaded Hungary and destroyed the Hungarian army at the Battle of Mohács.
By 1540 the major part of Hungary had been made part of the Ottoman
Empire and the western fringe was taken over by the Austrian Duke,
Ferdinand I.

. . . nineteen zodiacs . . .

The talk shifts almost at once to internal affairs. It seems that a wave
of puritanism is sweeping over Vienna and a moral crackdown is in process.
Older laws against sexual immorality, which had been allowed to lapse,
are now being drawn noose-tight and houses of prostitution in the suburbs
are being closed down.

What's more, a young nobleman, Claudio, is being haled off to prison for
moral offenses. He is engaged to Juliet, but the marriage had been delayed
while the matter of a dowry was being negotiated and meanwhile Juliet
has managed to get pregnant.

The Duke's deputy, Angelo, a man of rigid and unassailable virtue
(his very name means "angel"), is applying the law against unmarried intercourse to the extreme and Claudio will be slated for execution.

Claudio, in this deep trouble, stops to talk to his friend Lucio and complains of being thus struck down by penalties:

> Which have, like unscoured armor, hung by th'wall
> So long, that nineteen zodiacs have gone round
> And none of them been worn . . .
>
> —Act I, scene ii, lines 168–74

The sun travels once around the zodiac in one year. Nineteen zodiacs
are therefore nineteen years.

Lucio advises Claudio to appeal to the Duke, but the Duke is not to
be found. Claudio therefore asks Lucio to hasten to a nunnery where his
(Claudio's) sister is about to take her vows. Perhaps she will plead with
Angelo on his behalf and win him over.

. . . to Poland

But the Duke has not really left after all. He wishes to observe affairs
while remaining unobserved, see how the moral reform will work out, and
so on. The Duke explains this to a monk, Friar Thomas, saying that even
Angelo, his deputy, doesn't know the truth:

> *. . . he supposes me traveled to Poland;*
> *For so I have strewed it in the common ear,*
> —Act I, scene iii, lines 13–15

In Shakespeare's time Poland was much larger than it is today. It bordered on Austria (and what had once been Hungary) to the northeast, and included large sections of what is now the Soviet Union. It extended from the Baltic to the Black Sea and was almost at the peak of its territorial expansion. But the aristocracy in Poland, as in Hungary, was uncontrollable and kept the central government weak.

. . . snow-broth . . .

Lucio reaches Isabella (Claudio's sister) at the nunnery. She has not yet made her final vows and she may speak to him. He tells her of Claudio's situation. Claudio cannot make amends by marrying the girl he has made pregnant because Angelo is intent on setting an example. Lucio has no great hopes that Angelo can be swerved from this, for the man is icily virtuous. Lucio describes Angelo as

> *a man whose blood*
> *Is very snow-broth . . .*
> —Act I, scene iv, lines 57–59

The implication is that he cannot feel the stirrings of passion and cannot sympathize with those who do. Under the lash of virtue he would insist upon a rigid justice that would be as cruel as anything vice would demand.

Yet, as a last resort, Lucio urges Isabella to go to Angelo and plead with him. He might be softened by a girl's request.

The chances of success are slim, however, for in the next scene Angelo is shown in conversation with Escalus and he insists on the letter of the law firmly. Strict justice and nothing but justice is what he demands, and he gives orders that Claudio be executed the next morning at 9 A.M.

. . . at Hallowmas . . .

The gravity of the developing situation with respect to Claudio is lightened by a scene in which a comic constable, Elbow, has arrested Pompey, who works as servant in a brothel, and Froth, who has been a customer there. Both are brought before Angelo and Escalus for judgment.

When Pompey begins to testify, however, he does so with a long-windedness that weaves round and round the point without ever coming to it. It drags in even the exact time of the death of Froth's father. Pompey says:

> Was't not at Hallowmas, Master Froth?
> —Act II, scene i, lines 123–24

Froth answers with grave precision:

> All-hallond Eve.
> —Act II, scene i, line 125

"Hallowmas," which is also "All Hallows' Day," is a day set aside for the celebration of all the saints generally, known and unknown, and it is also known as "All Saints' Day." The celebration is on November 1, which happens, by no great coincidence, to be an important pastoral holiday of the ancient Celts. Many of the ancient customs of the earlier pagan holiday have come down to us, transfigured by Christian disapproval, and have given us a mélange of witches and hobgoblins.

The night, naturally, is the best time for the spirits of darkness, and since in ancient times (among the Jews, for instance) the twenty-four-hour day included the sunlit period plus the night before, rather than the night after, it was the night of October 31 that was witch time. This is the "All-hallond Eve" that Froth refers to, or "All Hallows' Eve" or "All Saints' Eve," or, as it is best known today, Halloween.

. . . a night in Russia

Angelo, whose virtue leaves him no room for humor, leaves in disgust, allowing Escalus to render judgment, and saying:

> This will last out a night in Russia,
> When nights are longest there.
> —Act II, scene i, lines 133–34

In Shakespeare's time Russia was just impinging on west European consciousness (see page I–154). At that time Russian territory had already reached the Arctic Ocean, and in 1553 an English trade mission under Richard Chancellor reached that nation through the one port that was open to the sea powers of the West—Archangel, on the Arctic shore.

It was this which gave England the notion of Russia as an essentially Arctic nation; a notion that was never quite wiped out of European consciousness. There were parts of Russia that were farther south than any part of England, even in the sixteenth century, before still further expansion southward had taken place. What counted, though, was the latitude of Archangel, which is only a hundred miles south of the Arctic Circle. "When nights are longest there" (in December and January) they are over twenty-three-hours long—though much of that time is twilit.

. . . a shrewd Caesar . . .

The mild Escalus, left to deal with Pompey and Froth, lets them go but warns them not to be picked up again, for he does not wish to see them before him once more. He says to Pompey:

> If I do, Pompey, I shall beat you to your tent, and prove a
> shrewd Caesar to you;
> > —Act II, scene i, lines 247–49

The reference is, of course, to the Roman general Pompey and his defeat by Julius Caesar (see page I–257).

As mercy does

Claudio's moment of execution is approaching, and now his sister, Isabella, comes to plead for his life. Yet she is as strictly virtuous as Angelo and has no great sympathy for her brother's sexual offense. She says (very Angelo-like):

> There is a vice that most I do abhor,
> And most desire should meet the blow of justice,
> > —Act II, scene ii, lines 29–30

Naturally, her cold plea doesn't touch Angelo and she is at once ready to give up. Lucio, however (who is the pattern of goodhearted vice throughout the play and makes a good contrast to the two examples of marble-hearted virtue), urges her to plead more passionately.

Fired at last, Isabella turns to the only legitimate pleas that can turn aside justice:

> No ceremony that to great ones 'longs,
> Not the king's crown, nor the deputed sword,
> The marshal's truncheon, nor the judge's robe,
> Become them with one half so good a grace
> As mercy does.
> > —Act II, scene ii, lines 59–63

Thus is the conflict of the play set forth clearly: justice versus mercy.

And as Isabella grows more eloquent, Angelo begins to thaw—but not out of mercy. He is attracted not so much by the reasoning as by the reasoner. He asks Isabella to return the next morning, and when he is left alone, he discovers to his surprise that he too has finally felt the stirrings of passion.

. . . but to die . . .

At the second meeting between Isabella and Angelo, Angelo is ready to offer the mercy that Isabella has begged, but only at the price of Isabella herself. It is now Isabella's turn to be unbendingly virtuous. She refuses the price even if that means her brother must die, doing so without hesitation, and marches off to inform her brother of that fact.

Claudio is horrified at the news Isabella brings him and, at first impulse, agrees that it is better for himself to die than for his sister to lose her virtue. But then he begins to think about death and he quails, saying:

> *Ay, but to die, and go we know not where,*
> *To lie in cold obstruction and to rot,*
> *This sensible warm motion to become*
> *A kneaded clod; and the delighted spirit*
> *To bathe in fiery floods, or to reside*
> *In thrilling region of thick-ribbèd ice;*
> *To be imprisoned in the viewless winds,*
> *And blown with restless violence round about*
> *The pendant world; or to be worse than worst*
> *Of those that lawless and incertain thought*
> *Imagine howling—'tis too horrible!*
> *The weariest and most loathed worldly life*
> *That age, ache, penury, and imprisonment*
> *Can lay on nature is a paradise*
> *To what we fear of death.*

—Act III, scene i, lines 118–32

This sounds a great deal like the various descriptions of the sufferings of the damned in hell in Dante's *Divine Comedy*.

So Claudio asks his sister to sacrifice her virtue for him. We might expect from Isabella the mercy she had requested so movingly of Angelo. She might not give in to Claudio, but she might at least sympathize with his fear of death and forgive him his human weakness. She does not. As rigid and extreme as Angelo (before lust intervened), Isabella shrieks out at her brother:

Die, perish! Might but my bending down
Reprieve thee from thy fate, it should proceed.
I'll pray a thousand prayers for thy death,
No word to save thee.
—Act III, scene i, lines 144–47

. . . Mariana, the sister of Frederick . . .

But the Duke, disguised as a friar, has overheard the colloquy between brother and sister in the jail, and now he begins to take countermeasures. He insists on speaking to Isabella before she leaves and says to her:

Have you not heard speak of Mariana, the sister of Frederick,
the great soldier who miscarried at sea?
—Act III, scene i, lines 212–14

There is no indication that this reference to Frederick implies any real person. We might point out, though, that there were a number of Fredericks involved in German and Austrian history. One of them, Frederick I Barbarossa, was Holy Roman Emperor from 1152 to 1190 and he was indeed a great warrior, the strongest of the medieval emperors. In his old age, when almost seventy, he joined the Third Crusade (the one in which Richard the Lion-Heart was involved, see page II–219) and in Asia Minor drowned in a river while bathing. This is close to having "miscarried at sea."

It turns out that this Mariana had been betrothed to Angelo, but when her brother was wrecked at sea, her dowry was lost and Angelo promptly and coldly broke the marriage contract (about par for his kind of virtue).

The Duke now proposes the exact device used by Helena in *All's Well That Ends Well,* which Shakespeare had written a year or two earlier. Isabella is to pretend to accede to Angelo and to insist that he stay with her only briefly and in silence. It will then be arranged to have Mariana substitute for Isabella. Angelo will pardon Claudio as payment, then be forced to marry Mariana when the truth is revealed.

. . . Pygmalion's images . . .

Pompey now comes onstage again. Once more he is arrested on the old charge of running a house of prostitution and this time there will be no mercy. When Lucio enters, Pompey recognizes an old customer and friend and asks for him to intercede. Lucio, however, is quite heartless and makes a mere joke of it, saying:

How now, noble Pompey! What, at the wheels of Caesar?
Art thou led in triumph? What, is there none of Pygmalion's
images, newly made woman, to be had now, for putting the
hand in the pocket and extracting it clutched?

—Act III, scene ii, lines 44–48

Again there is the reference to Pompey and Caesar that, earlier, Escalus had used. Of course, Pompey was never led in triumph behind Caesar's chariot, for he died before that could be. And even if he had not died, it was not the custom of Roman generals to be awarded a triumph for their victories over other Roman generals. The metaphor is colorful, but inaccurate.

Pygmalion is a mythical character, whose story is told in Ovid's *Metamorphoses*. He was a King of Cyprus who had carved a statue so beautiful that he fell in love with it. He prayed to Aphrodite to give him a wife resembling the statue and she did better. She had the statue come to life, and Pygmalion did indeed marry her.

Lucio's reference to "newly made woman" plays on words bawdily, referring both to Pygmalion's come-to-life statue and to prostitutes who have just completed a turn. In the latter sense, they would have money that Pompey could make use of in order to bribe his way to freedom.

. . . the Emperor of Russia

The Duke/Friar is also onstage and Lucio lingers to talk to him, not recognizing him as Duke, of course. Lucio quotes some rumors, saying of the Duke:

Some say he is with the Emperor of Russia,

—Act III, scene ii, line 89

In 1472 Ivan III, till then Grand Duke of Muscovy, married Sophia, niece of the last Byzantine Emperor. Ivan thereupon claimed the throne of the Empire (now defunct, actually) for himself and assumed the title of Tsar ("Caesar"). In Western Europe this title was translated into "Emperor," and Russia remained under a tsar-emperor for nearly four and a half centuries.

Lucio, out of sheer high spirits and a mischievous desire to shock a holy man, goes on to repeat all sorts of slanders against the Duke. When the Friar makes plain his indignation over this, Lucio increases his slanders, accusing the Duke of unbridled lust, drunkenness, and ignorance.

. . . come Philip and Jacob . . .

Lucio goes off laughing, but he has tried to be funny at a very unfortunate time for himself. Mistress Overdone, the proprietress of a bawdy-house, is also being arrested, and she believes it was Lucio who bore witness against her. She therefore accuses Lucio, in turn, to Escalus. It seems that he has had a child by one of the prostitutes of her house. She says:

> *Mistress Kate Keepdown was with child by him in the Duke's time; he promised her marriage; his child is a year and a quarter old, come Philip and Jacob; I have kept it myself . . .*
> —Act III, scene ii, lines 202–5

St. Philip and St. James, two of the apostles, are together commemorated on May 1. The Hebrew name of James is Jacob. "Come Philip and Jacob" therefore means "next May 1."

A Bohemian born . . .

The plot to deceive Angelo is completed. Mariana is introduced; it is explained to her what she must do and she agrees.

But Angelo, once he has slept with Mariana (thinking she was Isabella), fears the discovery of the sin. If he pardons Claudio, everyone will be astonished and ready to believe something unusual has happened. If Isabella talks, her tale would be accepted. If, however, Claudio is executed, who would then believe Isabella's story?

Therefore, even as the Duke/Friar waits for notice of Claudio's reprieve, a letter to the Provost (the keeper of the prison) arrives from Angelo, ordering the execution of Claudio and, in addition, of someone named Barnardine.

The Duke/Friar asks who Barnardine is and the Provost replies:

> *A Bohemian born, but here nursed up and bred;*
> —Act IV, scene ii, lines 133–34

Bohemia (now part of modern Czechoslovakia) is the westernmost Slavic region of Europe. The fourteenth century was its golden age and its King, Charles I, was Holy Roman Emperor from 1347 to 1378. Bohemia declined after that, chiefly through internal religious strife.

After 1462 Bohemia was ruled by Hungary, and when the latter country was defeated by the Turks, Bohemia was taken over by the Austrian

House of Habsburg. Bohemia remained Austrian through Shakespeare's life and for three centuries afterward.

. . . pluck out his eyes

Barnardine, it seems, has been in prison for nine years for murder and now, all reprieves having been exhausted and his crime thoroughly proved, is ready for death. The Duke/Friar considers having his head sent to Angelo in place of Claudio's. It turns out, though, that a prisoner has died that morning of fever and he happens to resemble Claudio. It is that head which will be sent to Angelo, and Barnardine as well as Claudio will remain unexecuted.

Yet when Isabella comes to receive her reprieved brother, the Duke/Friar tells her that her brother has been executed. Her instant cry is for revenge as she shrieks:

> *O, I will to him and pluck out his eyes!*
> —Act IV, scene iii, line 121

Some critics are appalled at the Duke's needless cruelty in hiding from Isabella the fact that her brother has been saved. The Duke's action seems reasonable to me, however. He was present when Isabella cruelly turned on her death-fearing brother and excoriated him, saying she would pray for his death. Well, now she had what she prayed for. That might teach her a little something about justice and mercy and she would later have an opportunity to learn a little more. (Besides, one is entitled to wonder whether she is more outraged at the death of her brother or at the fact that her sacrificed virtue—which Angelo thought he had—was so little valued by him.)

". . . death for death"

Now begins a charade arranged by the Duke. He returns to Vienna in his own guise and is so greeted. Isabella (following the instructions of the Friar, not knowing him to be the Duke) accuses Angelo of having insisted on her body as the price of her brother and then having had the brother executed anyway. Angelo denies everything and the Duke affects to believe him and orders Isabella punished.

Mariana joins in the accusation against Angelo and the whole story comes out, but still Angelo denies and still the Duke refuses to accept the accusation.

It turns out that a Friar has urged the women to make the accusation and the question turns to him. Lucio, out of sheer love of mischief, accuses the Friar of having slandered the Duke, putting his own words into the Friar's mouth.

The Duke retires, returns as Friar, and he too is ordered arrested. Lucio abuses him quite gratuitously and pulls off the Friar's hood. All freeze in astonishment as the Duke's face is revealed.

And now the Duke speaks in earnest for the first time since his return. It is his task to represent mercy and his first words are to pardon Escalus the harsh words he addressed to the Friar, not knowing that behind the cowl was the Duke.

Angelo has no choice now but to confess his guilt and ask for death. The Duke, however, is in no hurry for that. First there is a kind justice (not a cruel one) to be done Mariana. She must be given the social status that goes with marriage. Angelo and Mariana are therefore taken offstage to be married.

Isabella asks forgiveness for having, unknowingly, treated the Duke as less than a Duke and she receives pardon freely.

And then Angelo, returning as a married man, must hear sentence passed against him. The Duke offers him his own kind of justice and suggests that mercy itself would demand merciless justice, and would cry out:

> "*An Angelo for Claudio, death for death!*"
> *Haste still* [always] *pays haste, and leisure answers leisure;*
> *Like doth quit like, and Measure still for Measure.*
> —Act V, scene i, lines 412–14

It is the cry of rigid return of damage for damage and is usually recognized as among the primitive ethics of early religious development. It reminds one of the passage in the Old Testament which says: "And if a man cause a blemish in his neighbour; as he hath done, so shall it be done to him; Breach for breach, eye for eye, tooth for tooth" (Leviticus 24:19–20). In a way, of course, this was an attempt at limitation of revenge. If one man knocked out another's tooth, revenge must not take the form of killing, but satisfy itself with no more than knocking out a tooth in return. Nevertheless, the doctrine of "eye for eye, tooth for tooth" sounds barbaric to those who make no such fetish of exact justice.

It is usually thought that the Old Testament doctrine quoted above was repudiated by the New Testament, for Jesus says in the Sermon on the Mount: "Ye have heard that it hath been said, An eye for an eye, and a tooth for a tooth: But I say unto you, That ye resist not evil" (Matthew 5:38–39).

But then later in the same sermon, Jesus says: "Judge not, that ye be not judged. For with what judgment ye judge, ye shall be judged; and with what measure ye mete, it shall be measured to you again" (Matthew 7:1–2).

This latter passage may refer to divine judgment, but it can be applied to human judgments; and whether divine or human, it is eye for eye and tooth for tooth all over again.

It is the New Testament passage which the play counters, for it is the New Testament passage that gives the play its title.

Let him not die

Mariana pleads for Angelo's life, but he is her husband and she loves him. It is easy for her to want mercy for the man. What about Isabella?

To Isabella, Angelo is nothing but a villain. He tried to rob her of both her virginity and her brother, and as far as she knows, the brother is indeed lost. She has no reason to want mercy, every reason to want revenge. Mariana pleads with her and slowly Isabella kneels. She says to the Duke:

> *I partly think*
> *A due sincerity governed his deeds,*
> *Till he did look on me. Since it is so,*
> *Let him not die.*

> —Act V, scene i, lines 448–51

That is why it was necessary for the Duke not to reveal to Isabella that her brother lived. She had to forgive Angelo at the worst. She had to learn mercy at last.

Angelo is therefore pardoned and for this many critics (as savage as Angelo) condemn the play, because they want to see the man hanged. Yet is it only for those with whom we sympathize that mercy is to be sought? If that is so, then what credit is there in mercy and why should we have expected Shylock to show mercy for an Antonio with whom he did not sympathize, or for Angelo to show mercy for a Claudio with whom he did not sympathize? It is precisely to those whom we hate that we must show mercy if the word is to have meaning at all.

Thy slanders I forgive . . .

But the Duke has one more person to teach—himself. After pardons are granted all round, even to the wicked murderer, Barnardine, the Duke finds there is one person he cannot pardon—the one who has sinned directly against himself. This is Lucio, who has slandered him.

The Duke orders Lucio to marry the prostitute on whom he has fathered a child and, afterward, to be whipped and hanged.

Lucio seems to be more dismayed at the disgrace of the marriage than at the rest and manages to be witty even at this last moment. Whereupon the Duke, with an effort, manages to be merciful on his own account too. He says:

> *Upon mine honor, thou shalt marry her.*
> *Thy slanders I forgive; and therewithal*
> *Remit thy other forfeits.*
>
> —Act V, scene i, lines 521–23

Then, in his last speech, the Duke indicates pretty clearly that he intends to marry Isabella, and thus ends the play.

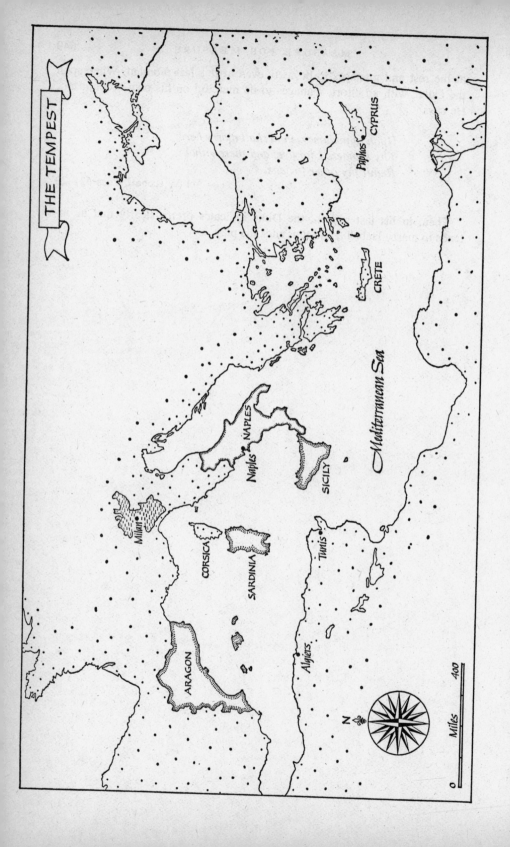

THE TEMPEST

CYPRUS

Paphos

CRETE

Mediterranean Sea

NAPLES

Naples

SICILY

Milan

CORSICA

SARDINIA

Tunis

ARAGON

Algiers

N

Miles

0   400

25

THE TEMPEST

A LTHOUGH *The Tempest* is usually found first in editions presenting the collected works of Shakespeare, it is actually the last play to be written entirely by Shakespeare, its date being 1611. His only work afterward consisted of his contributions to Fletcher's plays *Henry VIII* (see page II–743) and *The Two Noble Kinsmen* (see page I–53).

In a way, it is pleasing that Shakespeare ended with *The Tempest*, for this marks a return to his sunny comedies written over a decade earlier. We may be glad that the great man ended his career on an upbeat.

What's more, *The Tempest* is Shakespeare's complete creation too, for it is one play in which he apparently made up his own plot.

Good boatswain . . .

The play opens with a ship struggling against a tempest. On board are a group of Italian noblemen, for here, as in so many of his other romances, Shakespeare uses Italy as the home of romance.

The crew is desperately trying to save the ship when the Italian aristocrats emerge from below. One speaks, saying:

> *Good boatswain, have care. Where's the master? Play the men.*
> —Act I, scene i, lines 9–10

The speaker is Alonso, King of Naples, and with him on the ship is his brother, Sebastian, and his son, Ferdinand. The kingdom of Naples was from about 1100 down to 1860 the political unit making up the southern half of the Italian peninsula, with Sicily usually (but not always) included. Its capital was the city of Naples.

Alonso is not a typically Italian name. It is a Spanish one, a variant of Alfonso. Both Sebastian and Ferdinand are names best known in history as belonging to Spanish and Portuguese monarchs, rather than to Italians. This is not surprising, for Naples in Shakespeare's time was closely connected with Spain.

In 1420 Naples was under the rule of the aging Queen Joanna II, who had no heirs and who feared that the French would seize her kingdom. Nearby Sicily was under the rule of Alfonso V of Aragon (see page I–545) and she made him heir to her rule. She changed her mind afterward, but Alfonso V had no mind to retire. After she died in 1435, he began a long struggle to fix himself on the Neapolitan throne. By 1443 he had succeeded and made Naples the capital of his entire dominion, including Aragon itself. He reigned as Alfonso I of Naples.

Aragon continued to rule Naples until 1479, when Aragon and Castile formed a dynastic union that gave rise to modern Spain. The united Spanish kingdom continued to rule Naples through Shakespeare's time and beyond. At the time *The Tempest* was written, Naples was ruled by a viceroy serving the Spanish King, Philip III.

In thinking of Naples, then, Shakespeare automatically thinks Spanish even when he treats it as an independent kingdom. (In *Othello*, such characters as Roderigo and Iago have Spanish names even though they are supposedly Venetians.)

. . . the Duke of Milan . . .

Despite the royalty on board, the ship is apparently sinking and must be abandoned.

The events do not go unobserved, however. There is an island nearby —not one that can be pinned down on a map—but one that exists only in this tale. All we can say is that it ought to be located somewhere between Italy and the African shore.

Two individuals are all the truly human inhabitants the island of the play has: a man, Prospero, and his daughter, Miranda.

The daughter is terribly perturbed over the ship, which is being destroyed in the tempest, but Prospero calms her and assures her that no harm will be done. He says it is now time, at last, to tell her of their past and how they came to be on the island.

> *Twelve year since, Miranda, twelve year since,*
> *Thy father was the Duke of Milan and*
> *A prince of power.*

> —Act I, scene ii, lines 53–55

Milan is a duchy in northern Italy (see page I–447).

. . . rapt in secret studies

Prospero, as Duke, had little interest in governing and left the actual

conduct of affairs to his brother, Antonio, while he himself was concerned
with scholarship:

> *The government I cast upon my brother*
> *And to my state grew stranger, being transported*
> *And rapt in secret studies.*
> > —Act I, scene ii, lines 75–77

In the Middle Ages there were two kinds of studies: that of theology
and related philosophy, which was considered the highest goal of reason;
and that of the secular knowledge of the world.

The latter was suspect for a number of reasons. It had its roots in the
pagan learning of the Greeks, for one thing. For another, the secular
scholars (notably the alchemists) actually cultivated an air of mysticism
that reinforced vague beliefs that they consorted with spirits and practiced magic. Naturally, the general public would fear such scholars and
suspect that there was much more to their work than they could possibly
admit.

And indeed, it becomes clear that Prospero's "secret studies" did indeed involve magic, that he could command spirits and control portions of
the universe.

This King of Naples . . .

Prospero's preoccupation with his books and studies allowed his brother,
Antonio, to intrigue for the throne. Antonio came to an understanding
with Alonso of Naples (the same who was on the ship caught in the tempest).

Prospero says:

> *This King of Naples, being an enemy*
> *To me inveterate, hearkens to my brother's suit;*
> > —Act I, scene ii, lines 121–22

The King of Naples therefore sent an army to Milan. Antonio treacherously opened the city gates so that Milan was taken and then ruled as
new Duke, but tributary to Naples.

Though *The Tempest* is fictional throughout, there is an echo of history
here. In 1535 the last native Duke of Milan, Francesco Maria Sforza, died
without heirs. The duchy was taken over by Emperor Charles V (see

page II–747), who in 1540 gave it to his son, who was later to be Philip II of Spain. Milan remained Spanish throughout Shakespeare's life and for nearly a century beyond. And since Naples had been Spanish before that, it is almost as though Naples had taken Milan.

As it happens, Antonio, the usurper, is also on the sinking ship, along with the King of Naples.

. . . a cherubin

Once the *coup d'état* had been effected, Prospero and Miranda were taken away, placed on a small ship, and set afloat on the Mediterranean. Fortunately, a sympathetic Neapolitan lord, Gonzalo, made it possible for them to survive the ordeal by secretly giving them clothing and other necessaries and, most of all, a number of the most valuable books from Prospero's library. And, as it happens, Gonzalo is also on the ship.

Miranda is affected by the tale but, in her gentle sympathy, does not think of her own danger then but only of the added trouble she must have been to her father. He denies that she was any trouble. Rather the reverse, for she was

> *O, a cherubin*
> *Thou wast that did preserve me!*

> —Act I, scene ii, lines 152–53

A cherub is a creature mentioned in the Bible. From the wording in some places, it would seem to represent the storm blast. Thus, in Psalms 18:10 it is written: "And he [the Lord] rode upon a cherub and did fly: yea, he did fly upon the wings of the wind."

The cherub is nowhere described in the Bible except for the indication that it had wings. It may have been represented as a fearsome creature along the lines of the eagle-winged, man-headed bulls that were so characteristic a feature of Assyrian sculpture.

Whatever its origins, however, the cherub came to be considered as an infant angel and took the place in Christian art of the cupids of pagan art. It is in the sense of infant angel that Shakespeare uses the word here.

Incidentally, the Hebrew plural is, characteristically, indicated by an "-im" suffix, so that one can speak of one cherub, but two cherubim. Such a plural is utterly foreign to English, of course, and the tendency is to consider cherubim (or cherubin) as a singular and then speak of cherubims or cherubins if the plural is needed. Shakespeare uses such a false singular here.

. . . my Ariel . . .

Having completed his tale, Prospero makes Miranda sleep by his magical art and proceeds about the more serious business of the day. He calls to him the chief spirit at his command:

> *Come away* [here], *servant, come! I am ready now.*
> *Approach, my Ariel! Come!*
> —Act I, scene ii, lines 187–88

Ariel is a spirit of the air, wild and free, and untainted by any form of earthiness or earth-bound humanity.

The name has a biblical sound. In Isaiah 29:1 the prophet says: "Woe to Ariel, to Ariel, the city where David dwelt!" The word means "lion of God" or possibly "hearth of God" and is meant as a poetic synonym for Jerusalem.

Yet it sounds like the name of a spirit or angel, since all the angelic names in the Bible and the Apocrypha end in the suffix "-el" (God), as Gabriel, Rafael, Azrael, and Uriel. The first part of the name, "Ari-" sounds like "airy," which makes it fitting for an airy spirit.

The name Ariel is also to be found in the heavens through a queer concatenation of events.

In 1787 the German-English astronomer William Herschel discovered two satellites of the planet Uranus (which he had discovered a few years earlier) and broke with the long-established custom of naming bodies of the solar system after Greek and Roman deities. Instead, he called them Titania and Oberon (see page I–28).

In 1851 the English astronomer William Lassell discovered two more satellites, closer to the planet, and went along with the spirit names. He called the new satellites Ariel and Umbriel.

These two spirits are from the poem *The Rape of the Lock* by the English poet Alexander Pope, published in 1712. In the poem, Ariel is the name given to a sylph who guards Belinda, the heroine. (It seems quite reasonable to suppose that Pope borrowed the name from Shakespeare.) Umbriel, on the other hand, is a melancholy spirit, always sighing and weeping, with a name suggested by the fact that *umbra* is Latin for "shadow." Umbriel is always in the shadows and the name occurs nowhere else in literature.

Nevertheless, so much better known is *The Tempest* than *The Rape of the Lock* that the satellite Ariel is much more likely to be associated with the former than with the latter.

Thus, in 1948, when the Dutch-American astronomer Gerard P. Kuiper discovered a fifth satellite of Uranus, closer (and smaller) than any of the others, he automatically allowed Ariel to suggest another name from *The Tempest* and the new satellite he named "Miranda."

I flamed amazement . . .

When Ariel arrives, it appears that the tempest is no true tempest but an appearance raised by magical arts, designed to frighten the men on the ship and set the stage for Prospero's plan to set all things to rights. Ariel explains how he carried out his task of creating panic:

> Now on the beak,
> Now in the waist, the deck, in every cabin,
> I flamed amazement. Sometime I'd divide
> And burn in many places;

—Act I, scene ii, lines 196–99

Ariel was, in other words, converting himself into "St. Elmo's fire." This is the glow produced on dark, stormy nights by gathering static electricity, which is discharged from pointed objects. Such a discharge, if vigorous enough, will produce a glow.

It will appear on the points of masts or spars, for instance. If one glow is seen it is called "Helena" (in reference to Helen of Troy) and if it divides in two it is "Castor and Pollux" (the twin brothers of Helen).

There is no St. Elmo. The name is thought to be a corruption of "St. Erasmus," the patron saint of Mediterranean sailors. The glow was thought to be the visible sign of the saint guarding them during the storm.

. . . the still-vexed Bermoothes . . .

Ariel carefully explains that no one has been hurt, although they have been separated: the King's son brought to shore alone; the other royalty brought to another place; the ship itself taken safe to harbor; and the rest of the fleet sent sadly on its way thinking they had seen the flagship, with the King on board, wrecked.

Ariel describes the place where he has bestowed the ship, saying:

> Safely in harbor
> Is the King's ship; in the deep nook where once
> Thou call'dst me up at midnight to fetch dew
> From the still-vexed [always stormy] Bermoothes . . .

—Act I, scene ii, lines 226–29

The Bermoothes are the Bermudas, a group of small islands which, all together, are no larger than Manhattan. They had come dramatically into the news shortly before *The Tempest* was written.

In 1607 the English had made their first permanent settlement in what is now the United States, at Jamestown in Virginia. The settlement barely managed to survive its first few years and it required periodic infusions of new colonists and supplies from England to keep going. In 1609 a fleet of nine ships sailed westward to supply Jamestown.

A storm hit them off the Bermudas and the flagship, carrying the admiral and the new governor of Virginia, was separated from the rest. The remaining eight ships made it to Jamestown; the flagship did not and was given up for lost.

Apparently, though, it had managed to come ashore in the Bermudas and there its passengers and crew managed to eke a living until they could build two small boats that carried them west across the six hundred miles that separated them from the mainland. They showed up in Jamestown nearly a year after the storm and it was as though they had come back from the dead.

It was a sensation and the tale of the adventure filled England to the point where Shakespeare calls the islands "still-vexed" because of the association with the storm that wrecked the flagship, though the Bermudas are not more stormy than other places. The description of the Bermudas by those who were stranded there so long was most favorable and Prospero's magic island seems modeled on the reports of Bermuda (which has remained British territory ever since).

In fact, there seems no question but that the tale of this shipwreck inspired Shakespeare to write *The Tempest*. There is a storm that separates the flagship from the fleet. Men are lost and yet not lost but are saved in almost miraculous fashion after spending time on an almost magical island. All Shakespeare had to do was add an Italian-style romance.

The foul witch Sycorax . . .

Pleased with himself, Ariel reminds Prospero that the long term of service he has rendered draws to a close and that he has been promised his freedom. Prospero, who is working out his climactic scheme, and needs only another day, is irritated, and reminds Ariel from what misery he had been rescued.

Prospero says:

> *Hast thou forgot*
> *The foul witch Sycorax, who with age and envy*
> *Was grown into a hoop?*
>
> —Act I, scene ii, lines 257–59

The name is an invention of Shakespeare's, though it may have arisen out of the combination of Greek words for "pig" and "crow." Prospero asks Ariel where Sycorax was born and the spirit answers:

> *Sir, in Argier.*

—Act I, scene ii, line 260

Argier is a distorted version of Algiers, a city on the southern shore of the Mediterranean, 650 miles southwest of Naples. It had been founded in 950 as a Moslem town and has remained Moslem ever since. To the Christians of Europe, a Moslem town would seem like a natural birthplace for a witch.

Algiers had, besides, made the news in the sixteenth century. In 1545 Emperor Charles V had sent a fleet to Algiers, hoping to capture it. That fleet had been dispersed by a storm and the attempt ended in disaster. It was easy for good Christians to suppose that the diabolical Moslems had raised the storm by means of witchcraft and so it would seem natural to associate Sycorax with that city.

Sycorax was so evil a witch, however, as to have been banished even from Algiers. She was taken to the island that later became Prospero's and was left there.

She was a powerful witch and when Ariel would not obey her wicked commands, she imprisoned the spirit in a pine tree for twelve years. She died in that interval and Ariel might have remained imprisoned forever, had not Prospero arrived and freed him. It was in gratitude for this that Ariel was serving Prospero.

. . . Caliban her son

When Sycorax died, however, she left something behind. She had been pregnant when brought to the island and had borne a child upon it whom Prospero describes as

> *A freckled whelp, hagborn, not honored with*
> *A human shape.*

—Act I, scene ii, lines 283–84

Ariel answers:

> *Yes, Caliban her son.*

—Act I, scene ii, line 284

This Caliban, the offspring of a witch and, presumably, one of the devils that served her, is a semihuman monster, earthy, dull, and savage. The name has entered the language to mean any brutal and debased person.

The name is Shakespeare's invention but it may be guessed that it was suggested by "cannibal," a word which had been made prominent by explorations of the New World (see page I–617).

. . . my dam's god, Setebos

Caliban is called forth to do some labor and appears, railing and cursing, misshapen and monstrous. He complains that it was his island before Prospero came and that now he has been enslaved, but Prospero insists that they had tried to treat him with humanity and kindness and that in response he had tried to rape Miranda.

Caliban, however he may wish to rebel, must do as he is told. He says:

> I must obey. His art is of such pow'r
> It would control my dam's god, Setebos,
> And make a vassal of him.
> —Act I, scene ii, lines 372–74

Setebos was a god worshiped by the Patagonians of southern South America. He was first mentioned by Ferdinand Magellan, whose expedition in 1519–22 was the first to circumnavigate the world. Setebos then appeared in English in a book called *History of Travel* by Robert Eden, published in 1577. Apparently Shakespeare saw it there and thus another aspect of the New World entered the play.

. . . the King of Tunis

Prospero's plans continue to progress. Ariel leads Ferdinand, the young son of the King of Naples, to the cell. Ferdinand is in deep grief for his father, who, he is certain, is dead. Nevertheless, upon first sight of Miranda he falls head over heels in love. For her part, Miranda, who never saw a young man before, is equally smitten. Prospero is delighted, but, to test the youth, pretends anger and keeps them apart.

On another part of the island, the rest of the party is sunk in grief over the loss of Ferdinand. (These multiple griefs are part of the revenge Prospero is taking.) Gonzalo, the kindhearted old lord, is desperately trying to cheer up the King with cheerful conversation. They have their lives, he points out, and the island seems fruitful and comfortable. Besides, there are other blessings to be counted, for he says:

*Methinks our garments are now as fresh as when we put them
on first in Afric, at the marriage of the King's fair daughter
Claribel to the King of Tunis.*

—Act II, scene i, lines 71–74

This tells us what the trip was all about. A royal party has crossed the
Mediterranean from Naples to Tunis and it was on the return voyage that
the tempest brought them to this island.

Tunis is at the point where Africa approaches most closely to Italy. It is
only 90 miles west of Sicily and but 350 miles southwest of Naples.

From the eighth century on, Tunis and the country surrounding it had
been Moslem, and this area is still Moslem today. It seems unlikely that
Shakespeare would be describing the marriage of a Christian princess to a
Moslem king.

But then, in 1535, the Holy Roman Emperor, Charles V, had sent a
naval expedition against Tunis (as ten years later he was to send one against
Algiers). This earlier expedition had been successful and Tunis was taken
with great slaughter. It was not a permanent conquest and did not in the
least affect the Moslem character of the city, but it made a great stir and,
presumably, Tunis emerged out of the shadows as the result of that victorious impingement of Christendom upon it.

. . . of Carthage . . .

The mention of Claribel causes everyone to praise her and to say that
Tunis had never had so fair a queen. But Gonzalo brings up Dido (see page
I-20) as a possible competitor. Adrian (one of the courtiers present) ob-
jects and says:

She [Dido] *was of Carthage, not of Tunis.*

—Act II, scene i, line 85

To which Gonzalo replies with equanimity:

This Tunis, sir, was Carthage.

—Act II, scene i, line 86

This statement is almost true.

Carthage was originally a Phoenician colony which had been utterly
destroyed (after three wars) by Rome in 146 B.C. A new city was founded
on the same site in 44 B.C. at the orders of Julius Caesar and was given the
same name. The new Roman city was settled by Romans and Romanized

Africans, however, and had nothing in common with the older Phoenician colony but the name and the site.

Roman Carthage flourished until 698, when it was finally taken by the Arabs. With that, it died a second time and this time forever, but Tunis, a dozen miles westward along the seashore, became great in its place. Tunis is *near* the site of Carthage, but, strictly speaking, it is wrong to say, as Gonzalo does, that it *is* Carthage. In fact, Tunis (then called "Tunes") existed as a distinct and separate town when Roman Carthage was at its height.

. . . the miraculous harp

Antonio, the usurping King of Naples, comments on the fact that Gonzalo has, in a moment, re-created the vanished city of Carthage. He says:

His word is more than the miraculous harp.
> —Act II, scene i, lines 89–90

This is a reference to the Greek myth of Amphion and Zethus, twin brothers, whose father had been ruler of Thebes but had been deposed and killed by a younger brother. (Odd that Antonio should make such a reference.) Amphion and Zethus captured Thebes from their usurping uncle and wished to fortify it against a counterattack. They therefore built a stone wall around the city. Zethus carried the stones and piled them near the wall while Amphion, playing a magic lyre (or harp), made the pile of stones move of their own accord into the wall.

The conversation continues until Ariel enters and causes all but Sebastian and Antonio to fall asleep.

Antonio, the wicked usurping brother of Prospero, takes the opportunity to urge Sebastian to kill *his* brother and become King of Naples in his place. Sebastian allows himself to be tempted, but when they draw their swords to kill the King, Ariel wakes all the sleepers and Sebastian and Antonio must pretend they had heard wild beasts and had drawn their swords for that reason. (Thwarted ambition is presumably another part of Prospero's revenge.)

. . . this mooncalf . . .

Meanwhile another pair of individuals are to be found wandering on the island. Trinculo, the King's jester, has escaped and is wandering aimlessly. So has Stephano, the King's butler.

Caliban sees Trinculo approaching and, in terrible fright, pretends he is dead. Trinculo finds him, doesn't know what to make of the half-human monster, but crawls under his garment to stay out of the last dregs of the tempest.

Stephano, who has salvaged some bottles of liquor, is carrying one and is drunk. He comes across the Caliban-Trinculo combination and views it as a monster with four legs and two voices. When Trinculo calls his name, Stephano is terrified and says:

> . . . This is a devil, and no monster. I will leave him;
> I have no long spoon.
>
> —Act II, scene ii, lines 102–3

Stephano refers to the proverb which is usually quoted, now, as "Who sups with the devil must needs have a long spoon."

But Trinculo identifies himself before Stephano is out of earshot. Stephano returns, pulls Trinculo out from under Caliban's garment, and says:

> Thou art very Trinculo indeed! How cam'st thou to be the siege [excrement] of this mooncalf? Can he vent Trinculos?
>
> —Act II, scene ii, lines 110–12

A mooncalf is the name given to the occasional deformed calf born of a cow, because this was thought to be due to the malign influence of the moon (see page I–629). Eventually, the expression came to be used for any monstrous form of life.

Stephano gives Caliban a drink and the grateful Caliban (who has never tasted liquor before) wishes to worship Stephano as a god, and suggests to him that he kill Prospero and become king of the island, making Miranda his queen. Stephano thinks this is a good idea and all three troop off on this errand. There is obviously no danger, though, for Ariel is (invisibly) on guard.

. . . the phoenix' throne . . .

Prospero, meanwhile, has put Ferdinand to work moving logs, and though the young prince is engaged in a demeaning manual labor, he loves it because it gives him a chance to be near Miranda. And Miranda, when she enters, cannot bear to see him working, and tries to carry the logs for him. The love grows with every second and Prospero, overhearing, is happy indeed.

The situation is not quite so pleasant for the King and his party. Gonzalo is half dead with walking; and Sebastian and Antonio are still plotting the assassination. Suddenly, though, a banquet is set before them through Prospero's magic.

They are astonished, and Sebastian says, in stupefaction:

> Now I will believe
> That there are unicorns; that in Arabia
> There is one tree, the phoenix' throne; one phoenix
> At this hour reigning there.
>
> —Act III, scene iii, lines 21–24

Sebastian compares the incredible sight they have seen with two other incredibles: the unicorn and the phoenix.

The unicorn is generally pictured as a horselike creature with a single spiral horn on its forehead. Belief in this creature originated from three sources.

First, the Bible speaks of unicorns. This, however, is a mistranslation of the Hebrew *re'em,* which is the aurochs or wild ox. The Assyrians showed these in bas-relief in profile so that only one horn showed. In the Greek translation of the Bible, *re'em* therefore became *monokeros* (one-horn) and in Latin *unicornis* (one-horn).

Second, there were dim tales of actual creatures with a single hornlike structure. These were the rhinoceroses, rumors of which reached Europe from India (the earliest report on record being contained in the writings of the Greek physician Ctesias about 400 B.C.).

Finally, there was the narwhal, a species of whale in which a single tooth (not a horn) formed a long, tapering spiral. These were brought back by sailors and called horns of unicorns, for as such they could be sold for fabulous sums for their supposed efficacy against poisoning. The effect of this was to make the horn of the unicorn appear in illustrations as though it was a transplanted narwhal tusk.

The phoenix is more fabulous still and had its origins, perhaps, as an Egyptian solar myth. The Egyptians used a calendar in which the year was considered to be exactly 365 days long (instead of 365¼). The extra quarter-day was ignored and the individual days crept ahead of the seasons from year to year, therefore, until they had made a complete circuit in 1461 Egyptian years (or 1460 actual years). In other words, if a particular star were directly overhead at midnight on New Year's Day, it would not be overhead at midnight on New Year's Day for 1461 more years. This length of time was called the Sothic cycle because the Egyptians used Sirius as their reference star and in their language this star was called Sothis.

Perhaps this 1461-year cycle of the sun versus the Egyptian calendar was mythologized into a long-lived flaming bird which, after 1461 years, died and gave rise to a new bird like itself.

If so, the Greeks, who used a Babylonian calendar and not an Egyptian one and who therefore knew nothing of the Sothic cycle, altered the length of time to a rounder number—500 years is often mentioned. The bird is called the phoenix (from a word meaning "red-purple," as a hang-over perhaps from the Egyptian notion of a flaming sunlike bird).

There were all sorts of accretions to the myth—the nature of the flaming pyre in which the bird consumes itself, the details of the birth of the new bird, and so on. The place where the death and rebirth takes place also varies; some place the site, significantly enough, at Heliopolis, the Egyptian city at which the sun god was worshiped. Others place it in Arabia or India (on the basis that the farther east, the more wonderful).

There is only one phoenix at a time (as there is only one sun), and it seemed reasonable to suppose that if the phoenix immolated itself on a palm tree, it would be a palm tree as unique as itself. The Arabian desert is barren, so one can imagine it containing a single tree, the one on which the phoenix dies and is reborn.

. . . the figure of this harpy . . .

Before the bemused and grateful travelers can eat, Ariel appears in horrible shape and the feast is taken away. Ariel denounces the malefactors for their treatment of Prospero. (The frustration of desire is another punishment and Alonso begins to feel remorse at his treatment of Prospero and to fear that the loss of his son is punishment therefor.)

Prospero is pleased with Ariel's action and says:

> Bravely the figure of this harpy hast thou
> Performed, my Ariel . . .
>
> —Act III, scene iii, lines 83–84

The Harpies were originally spirits personifying the storm winds—rather like the cherubs. The Greeks finally personified them as hag-headed birds, with long talons and horrible screeches. Sometimes they were described as carrying off individuals.

The most famous myth concerning them, however, involves Phineus, a soothsayer in eastern Thrace who incurred the anger of the gods. He was blinded and condemned to eternal hunger, for whenever food was placed on the table, Harpies would descend shrieking, snatching away some and fouling the rest. The Harpies were driven away at last by Jason and his men (see page I-505).

The fame of the myth fixed this particular picture of the Harpy and made it appropriate for Ariel to assume the guise of one when the feast was snatched away from the Neapolitan King and his followers.

Ceres, most bounteous lady . . .

But Ferdinand's ordeal is over. Prospero is satisfied with him and tells him that he may marry his daughter. To make up for the pain caused him, Prospero puts on a spirit show for the happy couple. The classical goddesses are brought down to bless them.

Iris comes in first, calling on another:

> *Ceres, most bounteous lady, thy rich leas*
> *Of wheat, rye, barley, fetches, oats, and peas;*
>
> —Act IV, scene i, lines 60–61

Ceres (the Roman version of the Greek goddess Demeter) is the personification of the cultivated and fruitful soil, and all the food it produces. (We get our word "cereal" from her name.) She is naturally one whose blessing will ensure a fruitful marriage. After having enumerated Ceres' products, Iris says:

> *—the queen o'th'sky,*
> *Whose wat'ry arch and messenger am I,*
> *Bids thee leave these, and with her sovereign grace,*
> *Here on this grass plot, in this very place,*
> *To come and sport; her peacocks fly amain.*
>
> —Act IV, scene i, lines 70–74

The "queen o'th'sky" would be Juno, of course (the Greek Hera), who is that because she is the wife of Jupiter (Zeus). Juno was considered by the Romans to have marriage and motherhood as her prime concern; she was the idealized wife. It was her place, therefore, to preside over the festivities on this occasion. The peacock was considered particularly sacred to her and these birds were supposed to draw her chariot.

Iris is the personification of the rainbow. Since the rainbow, though clearly in the heavens, seems to arch down to earth, it is easy to imagine it as a bridge linking heaven and earth, and one along which a messenger can travel. The bridge and the messenger become one and Iris is pictured here as serving Juno, in particular. The "wat'ry arch" is, of course, the rainbow, which appears after a rain, when the air is full of water droplets.

The rainbow attribute of Iris is indicated by Ceres' first words when she enters:

> *Hail, many-colored messenger . . .*
>
> —Act IV, scene i, line 76

. . . dusky Dis . . .

Ceres has one reservation about attending the festivities. She says to Iris:

> *Tell me, heavenly bow,*
> *If Venus or her son, as thou dost know,*
> *Do now attend the Queen? Since they did plot*
> *The means that dusky Dis my daughter got,*
> *Her and her blind boy's scandaled company*
> *I have forsworn.*

> —Act IV, scene i, lines 86–91

Dis is one of the Roman equivalents of the Greek god of the underworld, Pluto. Pluto seized Persephone, the daughter of Demeter (Ceres), and took her to the underworld to be his queen. Demeter located her only after a weary search and even then could only arrange to have her returned for part of each year. It is only in that part that Demeter allows the earth to bear crops; while Persephone is underground the earth lies blasted and cold. (This is an obvious way of mythologizing the cycle of summer and winter, see page I–5.)

Pluto would not have fallen in love with Persephone had he not been wounded by the arrows of blind Eros (Cupid), the son of Aphrodite (Venus), which is why Ceres holds her grudge.

. . . towards Paphos . . .

Actually, Venus and her son have no place at the celebration. They are the personification of erotic love and Prospero has made it plain that Miranda is to remain a virgin until the marriage rites are fully performed. Iris says, therefore, of Venus:

> *I met her Deity*
> *Cutting the clouds towards Paphos, and her son*
> *Dove-drawn with her.*

> —Act IV, scene i, lines 92–94

Paphos (see page I–15) was a city where Venus (Aphrodite) was particularly venerated.

. . . they may prosperous be

Juno now enters and says to Ceres:

> *Go with me*
> *To bless this twain, that they may prosperous be*
> *And honored in their issue.*
>
> —Act IV, scene i, lines 103–5

This "wedding masque," which occupies so much of the play, may have been deliberately inserted to apply to a real wedding at which *The Tempest* was to be shown; or else, since the wedding masque was there, the play was thought particularly appropriate for such a celebration.

At any rate, *The Tempest* seems to have had one of its early productions in the winter of 1612–13 as part of the festive preparations for the marriage of Elizabeth, the daughter of King James I, with Frederick V of the Palatinate (son of the Frederick IV who was ridiculed by Portia in *The Merchant of Venice,* see page I–506).

The two were married in February 1613, both bride and bridegroom being seventeen years old. Juno's statement that they be "honored in their issue" came true, as it happened. The couple had thirteen children.

. . . called Naiades . . .

Juno and Ceres sing, and with that done, a dance must be next. For that purpose, Iris makes a new call:

> *You nymphs, called Naiades, of the wandring brooks,*
> *With your sedged crowns and ever-harmless looks,*
> *Leave your crisp channels, and on this green land*
> *Answer your summons . . .*
>
> —Act IV, scene i, lines 128–31

The nymphs were the spirits of wild nature, pictured as beautiful young women. (The very word means "young woman.") These came in a number of varieties. The nymphs of the mountains were "oreads," those of the trees were "dryads," and those of the rivers and streams (whom Iris has called) are "naiads."

Properly speaking, if the nymphs were called, satyrs ought also to have been called, for they were the male counterpart, masculine spirits of the wild. However, the nymph-satyr association is an almost entirely erotic one (see page I–630), which we memorialize these days by the use of "nymphomania" and "satyriasis" as medical terms, and that would have been unsuitable for the celebration Prospero designed for the young people.

Instead, harvestmen are called, and a chaste pastoral dance is staged.

. . . the great globe itself

At the conclusion of the dance, Prospero bethinks himself that Caliban, Stephano, and Trinculo are plotting to kill him and realizes he must get back to business. He ends the masque and when the young couple look troubled, he says:

> These our actors,
> As I foretold you, were all spirits and
> Are melted into air, into thin air;
> And, like the baseless fabric of this vision,
> The cloud-capped towers, the gorgeous palaces,
> The solemn temples, the great globe itself,
> Yea, all which it inherit, shall dissolve,
> And, like this insubstantial pageant faded,
> Leave not a rack behind. We are such stuff
> As dreams are made on, and our little life
> Is rounded with a sleep.
>
> —Act IV, scene i, lines 148–58

This is a surprisingly somber speech for what is, essentially, a happy play, especially since it comes at a particularly happy time for Prospero, who sees the best part of his plan coming to such lovely fruition.

It is almost irresistibly tempting to think Shakespeare is talking to himself at this point. At the time Shakespeare wrote *The Tempest* he was forty-seven years old, the prime of middle age by our standards, but quite old in his time. He may have felt the infirmity of the years creeping up on him and he may have been thinking more and more of death. As a matter of fact, he had only five more years left to live, for he died in 1616 at the age of only fifty-two.

These beautiful lines, then, may have been his thoughtful salute to his own inevitable death and to the end of all the "insubstantial pageants" he had invented.

It might also be viewed (without Shakespeare possibly being able to know) as an extraordinary prediction of the future life of the young couple whose real-life forthcoming nuptials were being celebrated. Young Elizabeth and Frederick, who were entering so happily into princely marriage and life, were to experience tragedy soon.

In 1619 Frederick was elected King of the Protestant nation of Bohemia (see page I-148), which was revolting against Catholic Austria. He was still only twenty-three and he could not resist the advance in title from Elector to King. This was the beginning of the Thirty Years' War, but one year of it was enough for poor Frederick. He was defeated at the Battle of the White Mountain near Prague on November 8, 1620 (four years after Shakespeare's death), and he spent the rest of his life as a landless refugee, living on a pension granted him by the Protestant Netherlands. He died in 1632.

His wife, Elizabeth, lived on long enough to see her brother, Charles I, defeated by revolting Englishmen and executed in 1649. She did not return to England till 1661, when her nephew had become King as Charles II. She died the year after. For Frederick and Elizabeth, a short-lived happiness had indeed dissolved and left not a rack (cloud) behind.

And yet Juno's blessing did not go for nought (and here as elsewhere, see pages I-593 and II-192, Shakespeare's intuition led him into the making of true predictions). Frederick and Elizabeth were "honored in their issue." Not only did they have thirteen children, but one of them, Sophia, was the mother of the man who eventually became King George I of England. All the monarchs of England since 1714 have been descendants of Elizabeth and Frederick.

I'll break my staff

Caliban and the others do not prove to be hard to handle. Ariel has already lured them on through thorns and swamps, and when they reach Prospero's cell, spirits in the shape of dogs are set to snarling at them and drive them away.

It remains only to settle matters with the King and the others, who, after the tantalizing episode of the banquet that came and then vanished, have been kept charmed into motionlessness till Prospero be ready for them.

Ariel is sorry for them and expresses his sympathy, and if Prospero has been meditating any final cruelty against his enemies he abandons it. He, a human, cannot be less kind than the inhuman Ariel.

Prospero announces that he will be satisfied to inflict no further punishment provided only the criminals are penitent. He has accomplished all he wants and it is no longer important to him that he possess his magic powers. There will be one last item to round out all and then, he says:

> I'll break my staff,
> Bury it certain fathoms in the earth,
> And deeper than did ever plummet sound
> I'll drown my book.

—Act V, scene i, lines 54–57

Many critics seem to think that this is Shakespeare's farewell to his art. He is saying he will write no more and will no longer practice the matchless magic of his literary genius. (This is, in my opinion, too sentimental an interpretation and I doubt it. For one thing, a compulsive writer like Shakespeare couldn't deliberately plan to give up writing while he was capable of holding a pen—on this one point I claim to be an authority. For another, he did continue to write in actual fact, engaging in two collaborative efforts with Fletcher: *Henry VIII* and *The Two Noble Kinsmen.*)

. . . brave new world

Point by point, all is brought to a conclusion. The King and the others are brought in and are scolded and forgiven; while Gonzalo, at least, is praised and thanked. Prospero reveals his identity and takes back his dukedom.

What's more, Ferdinand (whom Alonso and the rest thought dead) is revealed, playing chess with Miranda—to Alonso's great joy.

Miranda, herself, is wide-eyed at all these men. She had never imagined there could be so many and she cries out in naïve astonishment:

> *O, wonder!*
> *How many goodly creatures are there here!*
> *How beauteous mankind is! O brave* [splendid] *new world*
> *That has such people in't!*

—Act V, scene i, lines 181–84

The glad exclamation of Miranda has been made into part of our language in the form of a bitter sarcasm by Aldous Huxley, who in 1932 published his book *Brave New World,* which pictures a future society that has been completely saturated with scientific technology but at the loss of all the human values we hold dear.

And now the crew of the ship arrive with the amazing news that despite all appearance, the vessel is in perfect shape and that not a man has been lost. Caliban, Stephano, and Trinculo also enter and are forgiven as having been sufficiently punished.

All are to go aboard the ship, which Ariel shall speed so that it will rejoin the fleet, and then he, himself, will be free at last.

It is a happy ending in which not one person, not one, not even the most villainous one, Antonio, comes to any physical harm. It is as though Shakespeare in his last complete play could not leave the boards without everyone entirely happy.

Volume Two

THE ENGLISH PLAYS

Contents

IV. English

PART IV

English

KING LEAR

N

HUMBER R.

ALBANY

BRITA

Z

IRELAND

WALES

Leicester

Gloucester

KENT

SARUM PLAIN

Salisbury

Dover

Camelot?

CORNWALL

GAUL
(FRANCE)

EARLY BRITAIN

———— Suggested line of
division between Cornwall and Albany

0   Miles   100

26

The Tragedy of

KING LEAR

SHAKESPEARE wrote fifteen plays which, in one way or another, involve English history. Four of these are laid in the relatively dim time prior to the Norman conquest in 1066, and the one which deals with the oldest and the most purely legendary events is *King Lear*.

Indeed, the original Lear was myth, rather than legend, for he was a god. In the Celtic mythology, Lear (Lir or Ler to the Irish and Llyr to the Welsh) was the god of the sea. The best-known legend concerning him involved his four children, who were transformed into swans by a wicked stepmother.

The original mythical tale of Lear and his children had nothing at all to do with the version that reaches us through Shakespeare, but it did make the name "Lear" famous to the generations of children who were told the tales, and if they forgot all else they did remember that the tale had something to do with Lear's children.

About 1135 Lear made his first appearance as a presumably historical character. This was in the *Historia Regum Britanniae* (*Story of the British Kings*) by Geoffrey of Monmouth.

At the time Geoffrey wrote, the Celtic people of Britain had been driven back steadily for over six centuries and were now confined to Wales. Even there, Anglo-Norman influence was gradually becoming paramount (and, indeed, a century and a half later England carried through the final and permanent conquest of Wales).

There is always interest in what seems to be a dying culture, and Geoffrey, who lived on the Welsh border and was probably of Celtic descent, possessed that interest. Perhaps it was only natural for him to want to compensate for its dwindling present by emphasizing its great past. To do this, he made heavy use of legendary and mythic material, producing a history that is very largely fictional, although it was taken for sober fact through the Middle Ages. If there are grains of truth lying behind Geoffrey's fantasies we can no longer be sure what they are.

It was in Geoffrey's book, for instance, that the dim tales of King Arthur first made their literary appearance. The original of Arthur was probably a leader of the Celtic armies who defeated the Saxon invaders and temporarily halted their advance.

Geoffrey brought Lear out of the myths too, making him a king of all Britain in a period much earlier than that of Arthur. Lear was supposed to have founded "Lear-cester" and made it his capital. This is the city now called Leicester, in England's mid-regions about ninety-five miles northwest of London. (Actually, the only connection between Leicester and Lear lies in the accident of their starting with the same letter.)

Geoffrey tells a story of Lear's children and of their cruel ingratitude and fixed this new version of the legend into human consciousness forever. In Shakespeare's own time it appeared in new forms; in *The Faerie Queene,* the long epic poem written by Edmund Spenser in 1590, for instance. It appeared in play form under the title of *The True Chronicle History of King Lear,* which was first presented in 1594 and apparently was revived in 1605.

William Camden, an English historian, wrote a popular history of the British Isles in 1586, and rang an interesting change on the legend. Rather than attributing it to the Celtic king, Lear, he made the central character Ine, a Saxon king, who reigned from 688 to 726.

When Shakespeare decided to do his version of the Lear story, he turned to a history written by Raphael Holinshed for his source material. (He had used this history for many of his plays.)

Holinshed had published *Chronicles of England, Scotland and Ireland* in two volumes in 1577 and it proved an enormously popular work. Holinshed was rather uncritical in his acceptance of earlier works and his early chapters accepted much of what he found in Geoffrey of Monmouth. This included the story of Lear, which was in this way inherited by Shakespeare.

According to Holinshed, Lear reigned at the time when Joash was King of Judah. This would make his time about 800 B.C. This does us no good, for our actual historical knowledge of the political history of the British Isles of this period (or of any period up to the invasion of Julius Caesar in 55 B.C.) is exactly nothing.

If we accept 800 B.C. as the time of Lear, however (just for the fun of it), that would make it deal with events earlier than those of any of the Roman plays. If we consider it in connection with the Greek plays, it would come about halfway between *Troilus and Cressida* and *Timon of Athens.*

. . . the Duke of Albany than Cornwall

The play opens in the palace of King Lear, but with no indication of where it might be located—Leicester or elsewhere. Two noblemen are on the scene and one says:

> *I thought the King had more affected the Duke of Albany than Cornwall.*

> —Act I, scene i, lines 1–2

The title "Duke" is an anachronism, of course. It originated as *dux* ("leader") in the time of the Roman Empire when it was a title used for the leader of a troop of armed men. The title was taken over by the Germanic kingdoms that succeeded the Roman Empire and gradually came to be applied only to noblemen of the highest rank, particularly in France, where the word appeared as *duc*.

It was only in the fourteenth century, when the English King was trying to establish himself as King of France too, that the French title was imported into England.

Nevertheless, the anachronism is a useful one. No doubt the high nobility of the Celtic tribes had some Celtic title, but of what purpose would it have been to use it? The title was the equivalent of the familiar "Duke" and as the Celtic people of Lear's time are made to speak Shakespearean English they may as well make use of Shakespearean titles.

Cornwall and Albany, the duchies mentioned in the first speech of the play, fit its era in a way, for both regions of Britain have important Celtic associations.

As the Celts retreated step by step westward before the advancing Saxons from the east, they were eventually isolated in the two western peninsulas, Wales and Cornwall (which were sometimes distinguished as North Wales and West Wales, respectively).

The peninsula of Cornwall narrows steadily so that it has the flaring shape of a horn, with the narrow mouthpiece pointing out to sea. The Celtic word for horn is *corn*, so that "Cornwall" might be considered as signifying "horn-shaped Wales."

Once that meaning of the name was forgotten in later centuries, the myth-makers invented a hero named Corineus, who conquered the peninsula by killing a giant, and for whom it was then supposedly named.

Cornwall, smaller and narrower than Wales itself, offered less chance for its Celtic inhabitants to resist the English. In 815 the last of it was finally conquered by Egbert, the Saxon King of Wessex.

But what about Albany? This is from a Latin word for "white" and is sometimes given to a district of high mountains, the tops of which are white with snow even in the summer. In ancient times, for instance, a region at the eastern end of the Caucasian mountain range, bordering the Caspian Sea, was known to the Romans as Albania.

Again, the mountainous section of the Balkans, immediately opposite the heel of Italy, known as Epirus to the ancient Greeks, is called Albania today by English-speaking people. It is now a sovereign state and its own people call it "Shqipni."

Finally, the Highlands region of northern Scotland (Celtic to this day), with its rugged hills, was also called Albania in ancient times, and the name lingers on to this day as a poetic term for the region. In Holinshed, Albania is said to include not merely the Scottish Highlands, but all the lands north of the Humber River, which would mean that "Albany" would include northern England and all of Scotland under its sway (though in King Lear's time, to be sure, neither "England" nor "Scotland" would have meaning).

The character who delivers the first lines of the play is the Earl of Kent. ("Earl" is a title of Saxon origin and it remained the highest the English possessed till the introduction of the Frenchified "Duke.") Kent is the southeasternmost English shire. It is the section of England closest to the Continent and therefore particularly subject to invasion. The Romans landed in Kent when they launched their invasions and called the region Cantium from the name given themselves by the tribe which inhabited it. This became "Kent" to the English, but the historic city of Canterbury in that shire preserves the older form of the name.

Neither the Duke of Albany nor the Duke of Cornwall are given a proper name anywhere in the play; each is known only by his title. In Holinshed, Albany's name is Maglanus and Cornwall's name is Henninus. The Earl of Kent has no proper name either, but he is not in Holinshed; he is Shakespeare's creation.

. . . the division of the kingdom . . .

Apparently, the question of whether the King was fonder of ("more affected") one Duke or the other is important. The person to whom the Earl of Kent is speaking replies:

> *. . . now, in the division of the kingdom, it appears not which of the dukes he values most . . .*
>
> —Act I, scene i, lines 3–5

The dukes are, we see, to be among the King's heirs; so the matter of affection is relevant.

The person who answers Kent in this way is the Earl of Gloucester. He plays no part in the pre-Shakespearean version of the story, but heads a subplot that is introduced by Shakespeare. The subplot is inspired by a passage in *Arcadia,* a pastoral romance written in 1581 by the English poet Sir Philip Sidney. The tale, as told by Sidney (in overelaborate and, by modern standards, most tedious style), is set in Asia Minor, with such regions mentioned as Galatia, Paphlagonia, and Phrygia.

Shakespeare transported the tale to pre-Roman Britain and used it to set off and reinforce the King Lear story.

But why did he pick "Earl of Gloucester" as the title for the man who, in Sidney's original romance, was the Prince of Paphlagonia? There's no way of asking Shakespeare, of course, but we can speculate.

The first Earl of Gloucester in actual history was Robert, a son of King Henry I of England. He lived from 1090 to 1145 and played a prominent role in the civil war that followed the death of Henry I. He was the chief supporter of Henry's daughter, Matilda, against the claims of Henry's nephew, Stephen.

But since Robert of Gloucester was Henry's son, why was he not himself the claimant of the throne? Ah, it so happens he was Henry's bastard son and therefore unqualified to succeed. The Gloucester subplot is intimately concerned with the matter of a bastard son and perhaps that is why "Earl of Gloucester" suggested itself to Shakespeare.

. . . I have a son . . .

The fact of bastardy turns up at once. Gloucester is attended by a youth who turns out to be his bastard son, Edmund. He has been abroad (presumably being educated, for in Shakespeare's time traveling and studying on the Continent was the preferred manner of giving noble English youngsters a liberal education) and has now returned. Gloucester therefore introduces him to Kent with several gross jokes on the matter of Edmund's illegitimacy.

It seems unlike Gloucester, as his character is later revealed, to speak in this coarse way, but Shakespeare has much to do in this crowded play, and it is necessary for the sake of the plot to establish Edmund's relationship to his father forcefully and at once.

Gloucester goes on to say:

> But I have a son, sir, by order of law, some year elder than
> this . . .
> —Act I, scene i, lines 19–20

This older and legitimate son (the father's heir on both counts) will be introduced later as Edgar. The names of both sons are anachronistic in a play that involves pre-Roman Britain. Neither Edmund nor Edgar is a Celtic name. Both are Saxon names. In Shakespeare's time, however, Saxon names were sufficiently archaic in sound to give *King Lear* its ancient flavor. Whether Saxon or Celtic made (and makes) no real difference.

. . . the lords of France and Burgundy . . .

In sweep King Lear and his court. Included are the Duke of Albany and the Duke of Cornwall, whom Kent had mentioned. Present also are Lear's three daughters, who, in order of decreasing age, are Goneril, Regan, and Cordelia. (In Holinshed, the oldest daughter is Gonorilla and the youngest Cordeilla.)

Lear has no sons, and he plans to have his daughters his heirs. Since the Duke of Albany is married to Goneril, and the Duke of Cornwall to Regan, they will profit by this.

As for Cordelia, she is unmarried but there are two suitors for her hand. The autocratic Lear mentions them as he enters, with a cavalier snap of his fingers at Gloucester. He says:

> Attend the lords of France and Burgundy, Gloucester.
>
> —Act I, scene i, lines 35–36

In the time of pre-Roman Britain there was, of course, neither a France nor a Burgundy. The region which later came to be known by those names made up a land named Gaul. Indeed, Holinshed, in his *Chronicles,* mentions only one suitor, Aganippus, who was "one of the princes of Gallia (which now is called France)." He also says there were twelve princes in the Gaul of the time.

This makes sense. Gaul was divided into tribal areas and the Gauls themselves were as Celtic as the Britons, with a language that did not differ too greatly.

Shakespeare, however, refuses to complicate his story by introducing a tribal Gallic situation with which his audience would be unfamiliar. It was easier to speak of France.

As for Burgundy, it was a large section of eastern France that in the fourteenth and fifteenth centuries was under the semi-independent rule of princes related to the French royal house. Burgundy played an important part in the wars of the fifteenth century between England and France. Although it was finally reabsorbed by France in 1477, its memory remained green in England. Shakespeare could use the title freely.

. . . divided in three . . .

Now Lear reveals his plans. He is an old man and he wants relief from his duties. He says:

> Know that we have divided
> In three our kingdom; and 'tis our fast intent
> To shake all cares and business from our age,
> Conferring them on younger strengths, while we
> Unburthened crawl toward death.
>
> —Act I, scene i, lines 39–43

In short, Lear will abdicate in order that his last few years might be spent in restful quiet.

The unforced and voluntary abdication of a monarch, for no other reason than that he wishes to divest himself of the onerous burden of government, is most unusual. By far the vast majority of monarchs have clung insistently to their rule, however old, tired, and diseased they may become and however taxing and difficult the demands made on them.

One of the few who did freely abdicate was Ine, King of the West Saxons. In 726 he left the throne in order that he might spend the remainder of his life in religious devotions. He began a pilgrimage to Rome but, alas, he had waited too long and died before he reached his goal. Perhaps it was this abdication that induced William Camden to switch the Lear story to Ine in his history book.

Two other really outstanding examples of voluntary abdication can be found in history. In 305 the all-powerful Roman Emperor Diocletian, after a successful twenty-one-year reign, abdicated and spent the final eight years of his life in happy retirement. And in 1554 the Holy Roman Emperor Charles V, after a thirty-five-year reign during which he was the most powerful ruler in Christian Europe, divided his kingdom and retired to a monastery where he spent the last bit of his life in peace.

It was, perhaps, the example of Charles V, still fresh in the minds of men, that lent some plausibility to the tale of Lear. Without it, the notion of abdication might have given the play a weird divorce from reality. (In Holinshed, Lear does not actually abdicate. He merely makes arrangements for a division of his kingdom after his death—and his sons-in-law grow tired of waiting.)

The mysteries of Hecate . . .

It falls into Lear's head at this point, before announcing the division of the kingdom, to draw from his daughters a public confession of their love for him. Somehow this seems typical of the aged king, who has had adulation for so many years without yet having had his fill of it. He loves the flattery that comes of kingship and displays that love so openly, we cannot help but wonder how he can possibly bear to part with it. And, of course, it is just the fact that he cannot that breeds the catastrophe.

Goneril and Regan play the game smoothly, inform their father of their deep love in grandiloquent style, and Lear is satisfied.

Cordelia, the youngest daughter, cannot do so. She cannot force herself into this degrading flattery. She attempts to avoid answering and when pursued, she says, essentially, that she loves Lear as a child ought to love a parent. But this is not what the childish Lear wants and at once his terribly short temper flares and explodes in the violent overreaction that is characteristic of him. He disowns Cordelia completely:

> For, by the sacred radiance of the sun,
> The mysteries of Hecate and the night,

By all the operation of the orbs
From whom we do exist and cease to be
Here I disclaim all my paternal care,

—Act I, scene i, lines 111–15

Shakespeare avoids the anachronism of having any reference to Christianity in the play and yet he has no way of making use of the Celtic mythology. The Romans effectively wiped out the Druids, who made up the Celtic priesthood, and used as their excuse the claim that the religion was a particularly dark and evil one. (The real reason, undoubtedly, was that the Druids were organizers of a national resistance to the Romans.) What little the Romans spared was wiped out by Christianity later.

As a result, the Druid beliefs are virtually unknown to us and we have only the impression (probably mistaken) that they involved gruesome and bloody rites.

Shakespeare is therefore satisfied to have Lear speak in terms of a generalized worship of the heavenly bodies, which is rather sound thinking on his part. His mention of Hecate, with her underworld associations (see page I–50), is a concession to the general impression of the dark aspects of Druidism.

The barbarous Scythian

Lear in his unreasoning reaction goes to the extremes of saying:

The barbarous Scythian,
Or he that makes his generation messes
To gorge his appetite, shall to my bosom
Be as well neighbored, pitied, and relieved,
As thou my sometime daughter.

—Act I, scene i, lines 118–22

Lear talks of parents who eat their children—"makes his generation messes"; he will soon have occasion to talk of children who eat their parents. He speaks of Scythians, who, since the time of the ancient Greeks, have been the epitome of barbarism.

At the supposed time of Lear, however, the Scythians have not yet arrived at their later home north of the Black Sea, and would not for another century. And, of course, when they arrived, they might be barbarous but no more so than the Britons of the time.

. . . the Dragon and his wrath

Cordelia is silent under the blow, but the blunt and honest Kent tries to intervene. Lear, in autocratic fury, cuts him off at once:

> *Peace, Kent!*
> *Come not between the Dragon and his wrath.*
> > —Act I, scene i, lines 123–24

This is a legitimate piece of Celtic imagery. The early Celtic tribes in Britain used the figure of a dragon on the standards they took into war. The war leader was Pendragon ("head of the dragon"); that is, he was at the head of those who carried the dragon standard. Several of the early Celtic kings of legend had the title, and the best known to us is Uther Pendragon, the father of King Arthur.

Here Lear makes use of the dragon to symbolize the kingship.

. . . by Apollo . . .

In his rage, Lear divides what would have been Cordelia's portion between Goneril and Regan. Kent again tries to intervene, and persists even when Lear threatens severe punishment and begins to swear by the gods. Kent retorts at once:

> *Now by Apollo, King,*
> *Thou swear'st thy gods in vain.*
> > —Act I, scene i, lines 162–63

Roman gods are as anachronistic in pre-Roman Britain as the Christian God would have been, but what can Shakespeare do? The only "false gods" known to the audience, aside from the idols mentioned in the Bible, are the Roman gods. Later in the play, Jupiter and Juno are sworn by.

. . . slenderly known himself

Lear goes his headstrong way. He banishes honest Kent and, with many an insult, offers dowerless Cordelia to France or Burgundy. Burgundy refuses her but France takes her out of love.

The final details of the arrangement are made. While Lear resigns his powers, he keeps the name of King plus a hundred knights as his personal retinue. He plans to live with his two daughters in alternation, a month with each.

The company now disperses and Goneril and Regan, the two elder daughters, are left onstage to consider the situation. It is not to their liking and we might sympathize with them. So far, we have no reason to find fault with them. They expressed their love for their father in hypocritical manner, to be sure, but they were forced to do that. Were they to court Cordelia's fate?

What's more, they are now to be forced to deal with an erratic old monarch who has always been uncomfortably autocratic and who may now be growing senile. Goneril says:

> You see how full of changes his age is.

> —Act I, scene i, line 290

Regan agrees:

> 'Tis the infirmity of his age; yet he hath ever but slenderly known himself.

> —Act I, scene i, lines 295–96

He has, in other words, even in the fullness of his mental powers, taken too seriously the flattery accorded him and believed himself to be as wise and as prudent as all insisted he was. (The time would come when Lear would recognize this fault of his most bitterly—and learn better.)

Thou, Nature . . .

The scene now shifts to Gloucester's castle, the location of which is also not stated. It might be in the city of Gloucester, which is located about a hundred miles west of London. The use of the name is anachronistic, of course, for Gloucester was founded in Roman times during the reign of the Emperor Nerva, about A.D. 97.

In the castle, Edmund, the bastard son, stands with a letter. He says:

> Thou, Nature, art my goddess; to thy law
> My services are bound.

> —Act I, scene ii, lines 1–2

There was the feeling in Shakespeare's time that the existence of society altered the quality of human life. In a "state of nature," men lived without rules other than their own wants and desires, and were savages. The development of a social organization, on the other hand, involved the acceptance of rules designed to protect men in general against the selfish desires of any one among them. This view reached a thoroughgoing expression in a book called *Leviathan* by the English philosopher Thomas Hobbes, who published it in 1651, a generation after Shakespeare's death.

(It was also possible to take the alternate view. One could say that in a state of nature, man was good and kind. It was only with the development of a social organization that men began to hanker after power, office, wealth, and mastery. This view, however, did not reach prominence till the eighteenth century, and it was the French philosopher Jean Jacques Rousseau who, through his book *The Social Contract*, published in 1762, was its greatest spokesman.)

Edmund in accepting Nature as his goddess is throwing off all the artificial shackles imposed by society. In doing so, he throws off the social rules that distinguish between legitimate sons and illegitimate ones, or between older sons and younger sons. It is he who can take who has the right, and Edmund means to inherit his father's lands and titles according to the natural law that gives it to the stronger and shrewder. He has worked up a scheme to make that possible.

These late eclipses . . .

Gloucester now enters, perturbed and unsettled by the events at the court. At once he sees the letter which Edmund, with deliberate clumsiness, tries to hide from him. Gloucester insists on reading it and it turns out to be from Edgar, the legitimate son; in veiled, but not *too* veiled, language Edgar invites Edmund to join him in the assassination of their father so they might share the inheritance without waiting any longer for death.

The audience is quite aware that Edmund has forged the letter and that Edgar is innocent, but Gloucester is not.

Gloucester is reluctant to believe the worst of Edgar (he is no monster of instant anger as Lear is) and urges Edmund to devise some system of testing his half brother. He then goes on to brood:

> *These late eclipses in the sun and moon portend no good to us.*
>
> —Act I, scene ii, lines 112–13

This represents the early belief (see page I-96) that any irregular occurrence in the heavens is a divine sign foretelling disastrous events.

There is an additional importance to the speech, however, which rests not in itself, but in the hint it may give as to the time of writing of the play.

The first performance seems to have been given on December 26, 1606, so obviously it was written before that. In the previous year, 1605, there was an eclipse of the moon in September and an eclipse of the sun (visible in England) in October. This was followed, within months, by the appearance of a pamphlet deducing all kinds of horrible possibilities from these eclipses.

It is likely then that the play was still being written in early 1606 and Shakespeare had time to put in the speech given by Gloucester at this point, who lists the miseries that can be portended by such eclipses, perhaps in imitation of the pamphlet.

. . . the Dragon's Tail . . .

Gloucester then leaves and his last speech is mockingly commented upon by Edmund, who clearly disbelieves utterly in astrology and in the influences of the heavens. Shakespeare may have intended this to further damn Edmund as an atheist and cynic, but fashions have changed and the bastard's rational comments force the modern audience to approve of what he says most heartily as an eloquent indictment of the follies of astrology.
Edmund begins:

> This is the excellent foppery of the world, that when we are sick in fortune, often [through] the surfeits of our own behavior, we make guilty of our disasters the sun, the moon, and stars . . .
>
> —Act I, scene ii, lines 128–31

He goes on to give a specific example, mocking astrological patter:

> My father compounded with my mother under the Dragon's Tail, and my nativity was under Ursa Major, so that it follows I am rough and lecherous. Fut! I should have been that I am, had the maidenliest star in the firmament twinkled on my bastardizing.
>
> —Act I, scene ii, lines 139–44

The Dragon's Tail is a reference to the constellation of Draco, a winding string of moderately bright stars in the neighborhood of the north celestial pole. Ursa Major ("Great Bear"), which is also near the pole, includes the well-known stars of the Big Dipper.

Astrologically this is meaningless, since these constellations are not part of the zodiac and it is through the zodiac that the paths of the sun, moon, and planets make their way. No doubt the meaninglessness would not disturb Edmund at all, since his remarks have an inner consistency of their own. "The Dragon's Tail" has a bawdy connotation that fits "compounded" and "Ursa Major" implies a rough, bearlike nature.

. . . Tom o' Bedlam

Edgar, who is Edmund's legitimate half brother, is approaching, however, and Edmund must prepare to play a new part. He says:

> My cue is villainous melancholy, with a sigh like Tom o' Bedlam.
>
> —Act I, scene ii, lines 146–47

"Bedlam" is a corruption of "Bethlehem," of all things. In 1402 the hospital of St. Mary of Bethlehem in London began to be used as a lunatic asylum. It was notorious enough to give rise to the custom of calling a lunatic or an asylum for such a "bethlehem" or "bedlam" in colloquial language.

In the days before modern programs for taking care of the mentally ill had been developed, a lunatic asylum was full of the wailing and shrieking of the mad, so that "bedlam" came to mean any scene of wild uproar.

"Tom" is among the common names of Englishmen, and is frequently used (just as much today as in older times) in connection with some concept involving masses of men—as in "Tom, Dick, and Harry," or "Tommy Atkins" for the faceless infantryman, or even "tomcat" for the male cat.

For some reason, the word "Tom" was associated with men of less than normal intelligence, so that one could speak of "Tom fool" and refer to silly nonsense as "tomfoolery" or "tommyrot." Similarly, one could speak of a madman, particularly one who was not violent enough to be hospitalized or who had been discharged as sufficiently harmless, as "Tom o' Bedlam."

Edmund's use of the phrase "Tom o' Bedlam" as Edgar comes on the scene is a dramatic forecast of what is to come. That future begins to be molded as Edmund easily convinces the ingenuous Edgar that their father, Gloucester, is enraged with the latter. Edgar, utterly confused by this unexpected turn of events, is persuaded to agree to go armed for his own safety.

. . . his Fool

Meanwhile King Lear has taken up his month's residency with his oldest daughter Goneril and is at the palace (the location not specified) of her husband, the Duke of Albany. As the daughters had suspected, the old man, having doffed the mantle of royalty, cannot doff the arrogancies that pertain to it.

Goneril has just received news of an incident (one of many, undoubtedly) from Oswald, her obsequious steward. She says:

> *Did my father strike my gentleman for chiding of his Fool?*
> —Act I, scene iii, lines 1–2

The institution of the court fool (or jester) is typical of western Europe of the Middle Ages, and it arises out of the early Christian attitude toward madness. In pagan times the madman was felt to be touched by the divine and was treated with awe and respect (a feeling that plays its part in *Hamlet,* for instance, see page II–106).

To the early Christians, on the other hand, thanks in part to the tales of possession in the New Testament, madmen were felt to be infested with demons as a result of their sins. In that case, where mad antics were not extreme enough to inspire fear or disgust, they merely amused. In Shakespearean London, and for a considerable length of time afterward, it was considered fun to visit Bethlehem Hospital and watch the madmen, very much as we today go to see a zoo, except that the animals are much better treated and much more sympathetically viewed than the madmen were.

If a madman were sufficiently harmless and amusing—if, for instance, he could make "witless" remarks that were nevertheless humorous—he might be kept for the purpose by a family that was sufficiently well off to afford to feed a useless mouth. Naturally, a shrewd but poor fellow could see that if he but pretended to be slightly mad and took care to be pungently clever, he might get a good job.

The court fool became a standard part of the palace scene, then, and was the analogue of the modern television set, for ideally, he could do comic songs and dances, make witty comments, do sight gags, and so on. It was anachronistic to introduce one into pre-Roman Britain, but the audience would scarcely worry about that. In Shakespeare's time the court fool still flourished, though they were to vanish from the scene within a generation of his death.

Naturally, such a fool could say and do things an ordinary man could not possibly get away with (see page I–107). Behind the protection of his own madness and the amusement of his royal patron, he could mock arrogant lords and stately bishops and cast aspersions on all the sacred cows.

Any fool (not as mad as he seemed, usually, and someone who might well be the most intelligent member of the court) would find it hard to resist puncturing the emptiest heads, and if those heads lacked a sense of humor (as they naturally would), the fool would make himself extremely unpopular.

Goneril, as it will appear, is not fond of the Fool herself and she is exasperated at the disruption introduced by her father. And we can still sympathize with her. Divided authority is always troublesome and a captious father is not easy to take.

She decides to put her father in his place and orders Oswald to put on an air of insolence to the King. What's more, she will consult Regan so they can present a united front to the troublesome old man.

. . . Here's my coxcomb

The Earl of Kent, banished by Lear for defending Cordelia, returns now, in disguise, and talks himself into a position as Lear's servant. Lear does not recognize him but appreciates the manner in which he trips up Oswald the Steward when the latter begins to carry out Goneril's orders by slighting the King. The King, in this scene, acts with typical haste, pride, and arrogance. There is still a lot to be said for the daughter's point of view.

When Lear hires Kent and gives him an advance of money to close the bargain, the Fool enters and says:

> Let me hire him too. Here's my coxcomb.
> —Act I, scene iv, line 97

Licensed fools had standardized costumes, of which one noticeable item was the hat, which had sewn to it a piece of serrated red cloth to represent a cockscomb. The cock, after all, is a stupid creature filled with a foolish pride and given to making senseless sounds, so that there seems a resemblance between cock and fool.

The hat is, therefore, a "cockscomb," or, as universally spelled, a coxcomb. The term has come to be shifted from the appurtenance of a fool to the fool himself. A stupid man, particularly one who is vain and arrogant, is a coxcomb.

The Fool, in fact, performs a double function in offering Kent his coxcomb. Not only is he mock-purchasing Kent's services; he is also expressing an opinion, as he makes clear when he says to Kent:

> If thou follow him, thou must needs wear my coxcomb.
> —Act I, scene iv, lines 105–6

The Fool ("fool" though he is) is wise enough to see Lear's true position as one who cannot possibly reward a follower, for he no longer has anything to give or keep now that he has given his kingdom away. It is more than Lear can see—yet.

. . . one in motley . . .

The special costume of a court fool serves two purposes. First, it is a silly costume which is designed to stir laughter in itself and make the task of the fool the easier. Second, it advertises his function and makes it plain to anyone within sight that he is a privileged character.

Naturally, a costume intended to catch the eye at once must be conspicuous. In addition to the coxcomb, therefore, the Fool wears a costume of rough varicolored wool, so that he is a mélange of patched colors. This is called "motley," and the word itself is the badge of the fool.

The Fool uses the word in a little verse he improvises as part of his grim remarks on the folly of Lear's division of the kingdom. (It is virtually his one subject—a mournful bell tolling a single note.)

He points out there are sweet (amusing) fools and bitter (stupid) fools. Pointing first to himself and then to Lear, he says:

> *The sweet and bitter fool*
> *Will presently appear;*
> *The one in motley here,*
> *The other found out there.*

> —Act I, scene iv, lines 148–51

Lear, frowning, demands to know if he is being called a fool. The Fool replies caustically:

> *All thy other titles thou hast given away; that thou wast born with.*

> —Act I, scene iv, lines 153–54

And Kent says, ruefully:

> *This is not altogether fool, my lord.*

> —Act I, scene iv, line 155

That, of course, is the great secret of the successful fool—that he is no fool at all.

. . . Epicurism and lust

Goneril enters, further enraged at the treatment of her steward, Oswald. She scolds Lear, with all the arrogance one would expect of a daughter of that old autocrat, showing none of the respect due a parent. Angrily, she indicts the King's hundred knights as a disorderly rabble. She says:

> *. . . this our court, infected with their manners,*
> *Shows like a riotous inn. Epicurism and lust*

Makes it more like a tavern or a brothel
Than a graced palace.
                              —Act I, scene iv, lines 249–52

"Epicurism" is a reference to the teachings of the Greek philosopher Epicurus (see page I–311) and the self-indulgence it seems to justify.

Reason is, to some extent, on Goneril's side. Undoubtedly, Lear's hundred knights, owing obedience only to the King, are hard to control, particularly since the arrogant old King is sure to back them uncritically in any crisis. It is not what Goneril says that puts her in the wrong, but the harsh and cruel way in which she says it.

. . . I am guiltless . . .

Albany, Goneril's husband, enters and is clearly at sea. He does not know what the quarrel is all about and, mild-mannered man that he is, scarcely knows what he can do. Seeing that Lear is enraged, he can only say:

> *My lord, I am guiltless, as I am ignorant*
> *Of what hath moved you.*
>   —Act I, scene iv, lines 280–81

Albany's role in this play represents a departure from Holinshed. In the *Chronicles,* the sisters' husbands, Albany and Cornwall, are equally opposed to Lear and, in the end, are equally defeated by a French army.

Shakespeare, in his treatment, does not wish a French victory and finds it convenient to have a Celtic hero. Either Albany or Cornwall would have done, but Shakespeare chooses Albany and we can find a good reason for that choice.

Since Albany, as a region, represents the Scottish Highlands, it was at first a Scottish title. The first Duke of Albany was Robert Stewart, who was regent of Scotland and who received the title in 1398.

In Shakespeare's lifetime the title "Duke of Albany" was held by James VI of Scotland, who in 1600 passed it on to his infant son, Charles. In 1603 James VI became James I of Great Britain, so that the title had been held by Shakespeare's King and was now held by one of the royal princes.

Since that was so, Shakespeare would scarcely have liked to equate the title with villainy. If the play were truly historic, his hands would have been tied, but since it was legendary and it would make no difference if Albany were made virtuous rather than villainous, Shakespeare made the change and no doubt King James was gratified.

Cornwall remained doubly villainous, as though the villainy of two men had to be concentrated in him, but in Shakespeare's time there was no contemporary Duke of Cornwall to take umbrage.

(In 1660 the title of "Duke of Albany" was passed on to King James's youngest grandson, who was later to reign as James II. The young man was also Duke of York, and when the Dutch colony of New Amsterdam was captured by a fleet under his leadership, New Amsterdam was renamed New York in his honor, and Fort Orange, a town up the Hudson River was, for the same reason, renamed Albany.)

. . . a serpent's tooth . . .

But if Goneril goes too far in her anger, Lear goes even further in his reaction. His own immense and tyrannical pride maintains itself unabated and he at once curses Goneril with almost unendurable venom. That curse reaches a climax in a passage that contains one of Shakespeare's most familiar gifts to the language. The curse calls down the dreadful punishment of sterility on his oldest daughter, but

> If she must teem,
> Create her child of spleen, that it may live
> And be a thwart disnatured torment to her.
> Let it stamp wrinkles in her brow of youth,
> With cadent tears fret channels in her cheeks,
> Turn all her mother's pains and benefits
> To laughter and contempt, that she may feel
> How sharper than a serpent's tooth it is
> To have a thankless child.
>
> —Act I, scene iv, lines 288–96

A parent's curse is a fearful thing, particularly to an audience that lives in a time that still imparts a quasi-magical power to such things. While Goneril has been disrespectful to her father, Lear's reaction is disproportionate. After all, he has not had cause till this moment to complain of Goneril.

The balance, then, is still against Lear by any dispassionate weighing of the events of the play thus far.

. . . more knave . . .

Lear, virtually incoherent with fury, prepares to leave for Regan's palace. As he does so, Goneril says sharply to the frightened Fool, whose dislike she amply returns:

You, sir, more knave than fool, after your master!
—Act I, scene iv, line 321

The word "knave" is homologous with the German *Knabe,* meaning "boy," and did originally mean merely that. It came to be applied to a young male servant in particular and then, because it was taken for granted by the upper classes that servants were all dishonest, to any tricky or deceitful person.

The phrase "more knave than fool" has become a cliché, more because of its use here than for any other reason, though it has appeared earlier, even as long before as Roman times, for a phrase very like it is to be found in Cicero's writings.

. . . the seven stars . . .

Lear sends Kent ahead with a letter to Regan. The King is confident that Regan will treat him kindly.

The Fool, on the other hand, sick at heart with the knowledge that Regan is very like Goneril, tries to keep up Lear's spirits with a string of patter. Lear only half listens, his mind full of self-pity and, worse for himself, beginning to suspect that Cordelia was wronged.

The Fool says:

. . . The reason why the seven stars are no moe [more] *than seven is a pretty reason.*
—Act I, scene v, lines 35–37

The "seven stars" are the Pleiades, the most striking cluster of stars visible to the naked eye. In Greek mythology, the Pleiades were seven sisters who, in life, were chased by a hunter. They were rescued by the gods, who changed them into doves, then placed them in the heavens.

Ordinarily, Lear would have let the Fool triumph with this musty old riddle, but in his absent-mindedness he automatically gives the answer, saying:

Because they were not eight.
—Act I, scene v, line 38

But the Fool is not so easily topped. He responds at once with a bitter:

Yes indeed. Thou wouldst make a good Fool.
—Act I, scene v, line 39

The noble Duke my master

The second act opens at Gloucester's castle. Curan, a courtier, meets with Edmund and imparts some news, saying:

> *I have been with your father and given him notice that the Duke of Cornwall and Regan his duchess will be here with him this night.*

—Act II, scene i, lines 2–5

Nowhere in the play is the division of the kingdom between Albany and Cornwall described geographically. (After all, the details don't matter to the plot.) Since Albany is the region in the northern part of the island of Britain and Cornwall is in the southwest, we might suppose that the southwestern half of what is now England and Wales would be added to Cornwall's holdings and the northeastern half to Albany's.

If so, Gloucester's estates would be in Cornwall's portion of the kingdom. (The city of Gloucester is about 130 miles from the modern boundary of Cornwall.) This is made plain by Gloucester's comment with respect to this:

> *The noble Duke my master,*
> *My worthy arch and patron, comes tonight.*

—Act II, scene i, lines 60–61

It was, of course, the duty of any person to stand ready to entertain his overlord as guest at a moment's notice, and however onerous the sudden and unexpected visit might be, Gloucester could only accept it as an honor.

. . . likely wars . . .

Curan has another piece of news too, or rather a rumor which he puts in the form of a question:

> *Have you heard of no likely wars toward, 'twixt the Dukes of Cornwall and Albany?*

—Act II, scene i, lines 11–12

It is by no means unusual that those who divide a kingdom later quarrel over the division, each trying to obtain more or, if possible, all. In fact, it is so far from unusual that one might almost consider it inevitable.

This further strengthens the hint that there will not be a united front against Lear (as there is in Holinshed). Shakespeare continues to prepare a noble role for Albany.

And yet we cannot hope for too much from Albany too soon. He is no match for his firm and strong-minded queen. Indeed, after the quarrel scene between Lear and Goneril, Albany had tried to reason with his wife. Goneril had snapped out:

> *Pray you, content.*
>
> —Act I, scene iv, line 320

And with that, Albany fell silent. Yet it must be remembered that it was Goneril who had inherited half the kingdom. Albany shared it only by virtue of marriage. He was merely prince consort, so to speak, and conscious of a certain weakness in his position.

. . . *make thee capable*

Edmund is pleased over the coming of Cornwall and Regan. It will enable him to arrange Edgar's supposed criminality before more important eyes than he had expected.

Edgar is going armed, at his brother's advice. At a moment when Gloucester is almost upon them, Edmund insists that Edgar fly because he has been accused of treason against Cornwall and even hints that Cornwall's rapid approach bears some connection with that.

He urges Edgar to draw and stage a mock fight so that Edmund will not be accused of complicity in the escape.

Edgar, confused and not understanding at all what is happening, finds himself fleeing for his life, while Edmund remains behind to inflict a flesh wound on himself. Edmund then damns Edgar as a traitor and would-be parricide to his father. Gloucester is thoroughly taken in. He will have Edgar pursued and, when found, executed. As for Edmund, he says:

> . . . *of my land*
> *Loyal and natural boy, I'll work the means*
> *To make thee capable.*
>
> —Act II, scene i, lines 85–87

Edmund's original goal of gaining the inheritance has been attained, then, for Gloucester has just promised that. The scheming son can aspire to still more, however. Cornwall and Regan have arrived and have already gained knowledge of Edgar's supposed crimes and escape. Cornwall says:

For you, Edmund,
Whose virtue and obedience doth this instant
So much commend itself, you shall be ours.

—Act II, scene i, lines 115–17

. . . *the riotous knights*

Actually, Cornwall and Regan have come to Gloucester's because they know that there is conflict at Goneril's and they do not wish to have Lear troubling them.

Presumably, Goneril and Regan are rivals and would eventually squabble over the kingdom in line with the rumors of wars " 'twixt the Dukes of Cornwall and Albany." For the nonce, however, they have a common enemy in Lear, or at least a common problem in the handling of the cantankerous old man, and they pull together in this.

Regan is even careful to turn the incident concerning Edgar to her own uses when she says:

Was he [Edgar] *not companion with the riotous knights*
That tended upon my father?

—Act II, scene i, lines 96–97

Edmund hastens to assure her this is so, and she now has another case in point to use against her father, should that become necessary.

. . . *Vanity the puppet* . . .

Kent appears on the scene now with letters from Lear to Regan. Simultaneously, Oswald appears with letters from Goneril to Regan. Kent, burning with anger against Oswald and his errand, advances on him with an almost lyrical string of complicated insults that reaches its climax when he says of Oswald that he is

. . . *nothing but the composition* [mixture] *of a knave, beggar, coward, pander, and the son and heir of a mongrel bitch* . . .

—Act II, scene ii, lines 20–22

The confused Oswald tries only to avoid the other's rage, but Kent insists on a sword fight, crying:

Draw, you rascal. You come with letters against the King, and take Vanity the puppet's part against the royalty of her father.

—Act II, scene ii, lines 36–38

Kent is anachronistically drawing here on the morality plays which became popular in western Europe about 1400. These were allegories following the progress of Man to Salvation through and across the difficulties created by temptations from without and weakness from within. Various abstractions were presented in human form and one of these would be Vanity, portrayed as a haughty lady in fine array.

Kent expresses his contempt for Goneril by comparing her with the evil Vanity, compounded of nothing but arrogance and self-love, and empties her further by picturing her as the same abstraction lowered a step by being presented as a puppet show.

. . . whoreson zed . . .

The noise of Kent's onslaught and Oswald's screaming brings out Cornwall, Regan, and Gloucester, who demand to know the matter. When Oswald tries to speak, Kent breaks out again, yelling at him:

> *Thou whoreson zed, thou unnecessary letter!*
> —Act II, scene ii, line 65

"Zed" is the letter which in the United States is usually called "zee." It is a respectable and well-used letter in the Greek alphabet (where it is called "zeta," a name from which "zed" is derived). It did not, however, occur in the original Latin alphabet. It was a late acquisition, along with *x* (the Greek *xi*), and was used only for words of Greek derivation.

The letter *z* still stands at the very end of the Latin alphabet we use today in English and is used less frequently than any other letter but its companion, *x*. Because *z* would occur only in rather fancy words and not in the simple vocabulary of the common man, it would seem an unnecessary letter.

"Whoreson," by the way, a common Shakespearean adjective of patronization or contempt, is but a short way of saying "son of a whore" and, therefore, "bastard."

. . . Sarum Plain

When Oswald essays a superior smile, Kent's choler rises still further and he says:

> *Smile you my speeches, as I were a fool?*
> *Goose, if I had you upon Sarum Plain,*
> *I'd drive ye cackling home to Camelot.*
> —Act II, scene ii, lines 84–86

What the metaphoric point of the passage may be is not known, though there must have been some meaning to the Elizabethan audience. The reference has the advantage, though, of reaching into the Celtic past.

Sarum Plain is a region seventy-five miles west of London and forty miles south of Gloucester; it receives its name from the town of Sarum ("Sarbiodonum" in the period when Britain was part of the Roman Empire) on its southern edge. Sarum is usually called "Old Sarum" because only ruins remain, while another town, two miles south, took its place as "New Sarum" in the thirteenth century. New Sarum is now better known as Salisbury and Sarum Plain as Salisbury Plain.

Camelot is the legendary capital of King Arthur and is therefore also associated with Celtic Britain. The exact site of Camelot (or whatever town or fortress Camelot harks back to) is not known, but speculations concerning it involve the southwestern corner of England and the general area of Salisbury Plain and its environs.

You stubborn ancient knave . . .

Kent's anger makes it impossible for him to be tactful and he ends by irritating and offending the none too patient Cornwall. Stocks are sent for and Kent is pinned within them by wrists and ankles. It was a disgraceful punishment, used only for offenders of low degree, and was therefore a deliberate insult offered to King Lear, whose servant Kent announced himself to be.

In calling for the stocks, Cornwall says to Kent:

> *You stubborn ancient knave, you reverent braggart,*
> *We'll teach you.*
>
> —Act II, scene ii, lines 128–29

Here, and in a couple of other references, the impression is given that Kent is old. Yet when Kent first appeared before King Lear in disguise, and was asked his age, he replied:

> *Not so young, sir, to love a woman for singing, nor so old to*
> *dote on her for anything. I have years on my back forty-eight.*
> —Act I, scene iv, lines 38–40

In our own society, an age of forty-eight does not make a man old.* It did, however, in Shakespeare's time, when the life expectancy was consid-

---

* The author of this book, as it happens, has, at the time of this writing, years on his back forty-eight, and he repels any suggestion of being ancient and reverent with scorn and contumely.

erably less than it is now and when the quality of diet and medical treatment was much worse than it is now. People whom we would today call middle-aged would be in Shakespeare's time in far poorer physical shape (on the average) and far more past the median age of the society.

This disparity between what is considered old now and was considered old then shows up elsewhere in Shakespeare's plays too (see page II–263, for instance).

. . . Poor Tom

Edgar, Gloucester's legitimate son, is even worse off than Kent. Edgar has been proclaimed outlaw, to be freely killed by any who meet him, and everyone is seeking him. He must assume some disguise until the search is given over and it occurs to him to pretend to be a type of pathetic individual who is all too common in the [Shakespearean] countryside. He says:

> The country gives me proof and precedent
> Of Bedlam beggars . . .
> > —Act II, scene iii, lines 13–14

A Bedlam beggar is a mild madman, or one of retarded mentality, who is not hospitalized, but cannot take his place in society, either, and therefore must subsist by begging.

It is a dreadful and humiliating disguise, but it is one which few would study carefully or expect to find a young aristocrat behind. (Besides, it gives Shakespeare a chance to intensify further the pathos and horror of several scenes ahead and to illustrate further, most meaningfully, some points concerning the human condition.) Then too, as a Bedlam beggar, Edgar will at least live; as himself, he knows, he will surely die, and soon.

Bitterly, Edgar begins to whine out an imitation of the Bedlam beggar's self-pitying cry for alms:

> . . . Poor Turlygod, Poor Tom
> That's something yet: Edgar I nothing am.
> > —Act II, scene iii, lines 20–21

"Poor Tom" is a reference to the common phrase "Tom o'Bedlam" (see page II–15), by which these beggars were known. "Turlygod" is probably an example of the incoherencies which characterized the poor whirling brains of these creatures, and which were imitated by those who used the appearance of idiocy to make richer the pickings of beggary.

Hysterica passio . . .

Lear arrives at Gloucester's castle (having found his second daughter even in her retreat) and the first thing he sees is his faithful servant in the stocks. This visible insult, in a place to which he was flying as his last refuge, rocks him to the point where he begins to feel his sanity giving way. He says:

> *Hysterica passio, down, thou climbing sorrow,*
> *Thy element's below . . .*
>
> —Act II, scene iv, lines 56–57

"Hysterica passio" means "affliction of the womb." The womb was thought, in ancient times (quite wrongly), to be the origin of uncontrollable emotion, whence "hysteria." This arose perhaps from the notion that women were more emotional than men, so that the epitome of the condition was to be found in an organ characteristic of women rather than men.

Lear feels himself to be losing control, with a lower organ (the womb) rising to take charge of the brain.

What follows next can only place new tensions on the old man. It is only with difficulty he obtains an interview with Regan, and once she arrives and Lear turns to her for sympathy, she makes it coldly plain that she is on Goneril's side.

Goneril herself arrives, and the old King, still raging at his older daughter, is pushed from one to the other, each turning the screw a bit further in limiting his privileges until finally it is clear to him that he is to be left with nothing.

Even now he tries to assert himself as the old and terrible autocratic King. He thunders:

> *I will have such revenges on you both*
> *That all the world shall—I will do such things—*
> *What they are, yet I know not; but they shall be*
> *The terrors of the earth.*
>
> —Act II, scene iv, lines 278–81

Until now, there has been little choice between Lear and his daughters. All were haughty, arrogant, and ruthless in using power when they had it. But now Lear has lost his power and the daughters have it; Lear is old and his daughters are young.

To be sure, Lear is now in Cordelia's position and is being treated no worse by his daughters than she was (with less reason) treated by him.

But Cordelia found a husband in France at once and Lear can turn to nothing.

It is at this point that we begin to pity the old King, and Shakespeare sees to it that we do when he makes Lear begin to break down. The King tries not to suffer the unbearable humiliation of weeping before his stony-faced daughters and he must turn to the only person present who is on his side, his poor, helpless Fool, and say, pathetically:

> O Fool, I shall go mad.
>
> —Act II, scene iv, line 285

From this point on Shakespeare does not allow our new-won pity to flag for a moment. Steadily, in fact, it is intensified.

A wild storm is approaching and Regan mutters that she will allow Lear to remain in the palace, but only by himself. Not one follower can accompany him.

Lear, unwilling to accept so contemptuous an offer, calls blindly for his horse and leaves, not knowing where he's going and utterly heedless of the coming storm. Kent, who has been freed by now, goes anxiously in search of him.

. . . from France . . .

The third act opens with the storm in full fury and with Kent searching for the King. He comes upon one of the King's followers and tells him of the gathering friction between Albany and Cornwall. Kent has been receiving letters from Cordelia, too (he mentioned one of them while he was in the stocks), and he has still more important information. He says:

> But, true it is, from France there comes a power
> Into this scattered kingdom,
>
> —Act III, scene i, lines 30–31

In Holinshed, King Lear is described as fleeing to France because of his ill-treatment; of there being graciously received by his youngest daughter. In Shakespeare's version, however, Cordelia does not wait to be appealed to. Hearing of Lear's misfortunes, she sets forth at once to the rescue.

Apparently, the rescuing forces will be landing soon, for Kent wants to send the latest news to them by way of the follower to whom he is speaking. He says:

> If on my credit you dare build so far
> To make your speed to Dover, you shall find
> Some that will thank you . . .
>
> —Act III, scene i, lines 35–37

Dover, on the southeastern tip of England, is the port closest to France. It is only twenty-two miles across the Channel to Calais, the French city on the opposite shore, so that Dover is a logical point of entry for the French forces.

. . . the realm of Albion

Kent finds Lear, quite mad now, and raving into the teeth of the storm, with the poor, shivering Fool at his heels. It is only with great difficulty that Kent persuades the King to let himself be led toward a miserable hovel where they may have some shelter from the rain and wind.

As they move toward the hovel, the Fool pauses to repeat a doggerel prophecy to the audience. Such obscure prophecies in limping rhyme were common enough in those days. In fact, an excellent example is the largely meaningless verses put together by the French mystic Michel de Notredame, better known to us as Nostradamus. These verses, published in 1555, leaped to fame when one of them seemed (undoubtedly by accident) to prophesy accurately the rather unusual death of King Henry II of France in 1559. (Henry died in a tournament accident while he was wearing a golden helmet, and the verse spoke of a king dying in a "golden cage.")

The most famous English example is a Mother Shipton, a prophetess who is supposed to have lived at about the same time as Nostradamus, though there is no clear reference to her prior to 1641. Her maundering couplets have been interpreted as prophesying all kinds of modern inventions, like the steam engine, for instance. They also predicted the end of the world in 1881.

The Fool's couplets mock such prophecies by listing four conditions that are always true, and then six that can never come true, and concluding that when all these come to pass

> Then shall the realm of Albion
> Come to great confusion.

—Act III, scene ii, lines 91–92

"Albion" is a poetic name for England and is derived, like "Albany," from the Latin word for "white." The name may have arisen because of the white cliffs of Dover, appearing on the horizon to visitors from Gaul. (Of course, legends offer far more foolish explanations—for instance, that the island of Britain was first discovered and ruled by the mythical Albion, the supposed son of Neptune.)

. . . Merlin shall make . . .

The Fool concludes by saying:

> *This prophecy Merlin shall make, for I live before his time.*
> —Act III, scene ii, lines 95–96

Merlin is the magician who plays so important a role in the Arthurian legends and in Celtic tales generally. If Holinshed's dating of Lear's reign were correct, Merlin would have lived no less than thirteen centuries after the Fool.

It is very unusual for Shakespeare to call attention to an anachronism for the sake of a laugh, but he is deliberately releasing the unbearable tension of the storm scene, before tightening it once more to an even higher level.

. . . a letter this night . . .

Even while Lear is battling the storm, kindly Gloucester, within the haven of his castle, is perturbed. He had objected to Kent's being placed in the stocks, and now he has apparently spoken on behalf of the King. This has served only to bring down Cornwall's savage displeasure upon him.

But there is even more reason than sympathetic humanity alone to favor the King. There could well be political necessity too. Gloucester discusses the matter with his supposedly loyal son, Edmund, saying:

> *There is division between the Dukes, and a worse matter than that. I have received a letter this night—'tis dangerous to be spoken—I have locked the letter in my closet. These injuries the King now bears will be revenged home; there is part of a power already footed; we must incline to the King . . .*
> —Act III, scene iii, lines 8–14

It is not hard to follow what must be going on in Gloucester's mind, quite apart from affection and pity for Lear. If a French invasion strikes a Britain rent by civil war, the invaders may well win and Lear will be restored to his throne. Lear, always easy to enrage, and always hasty and impulsive in action, will remember that it was in Gloucester's castle that he was humiliated and turned out of doors. Gloucester, despite his innocence, might well have to suffer as a result, unless he takes active measures to demonstrate that he is on the King's side.

He proposes therefore to go out in search of the King while "loyal" Edmund remains behind to preoccupy Cornwall and Regan and keep them from noticing that he is gone.

The diabolical Edmund, however, sees a better trick than that. If he informs Cornwall of his father's act of mercy and shows him the letter his father has received, Gloucester will be proven a clear traitor, at least to the Duke. Gloucester will then be deprived of his lands and Edmund will come at once into his inheritance.

. . . Take physic, pomp

The play now returns to Lear, who, with Kent and the Fool, has reached the hovel.

The old, raging, tyrannical King is beginning to change. He is still pitying himself and berating his daughters, but some light is dawning. He is beginning to interpret the universe in terms other than himself.

When Kent tries to make Lear enter the hovel, the old King insists the Fool enter first. The Fool, in this instance, signifies poverty and weakness generally, and the old King, even though he is now at the lowest ebb of his life, manages to realize there are, and always have been, people worse off than himself. He says:

> Poor naked wretches, wheresoe'er you are,
> That bide the pelting of this pitiless storm,
> How shall your houseless heads and unfed sides,
> Your looped and windowed raggedness, defend you
> From seasons such as these? O, I have ta'en
> Too little care of this! Take physic, pomp;
> Expose thyself to feel what wretches feel,
> That thou mayst shake the superflux to them,
> And show the heavens more just.
>
> —Act III, scene iv, lines 28–36

This speech marks the turning point of the play, the beginning of Lear's redemption through suffering.

. . . pelican daughters

The hovel into which they are entering is not untenanted, however. In it is Edgar, playing the role of Poor Tom, the Bedlam beggar, and also seeking shelter from the storm.

Edgar dares not (out of caution, shame, or both) abandon his disguise,

even for the half-drowned individuals who now enter. He speaks wildly
and goes into his begging routine:

> Do Poor Tom some charity, whom the foul fiend vexes.
> —Act III, scene iv, lines 59–60

This is, of course, the early Christian view of madness—the result of
possession by a devil.

King Lear can scarcely, in his own madness, grasp what Poor Tom is
all about. To his own confused mind, the nearly naked Poor Tom must
have been brought to his miserable pass by his daughters. This brings Lear
to his own case and he broods:

>   . . . 'twas this flesh begot
> Those pelican daughters.
> —Act III, scene iv, lines 74–75

Pelicans mash up fish in their large bill, then open them and allow their
young to feed on the material. The young in their eagerness push the
fleshy bag of the bill against the adult's chest. To careless observers, it
seems that the young are tearing at the body of the parent bird and (the
legend arose) feeding on its blood.

Lear thinks of the daughters as, symbolically, feeding on him; the reverse of the reference he made (of parents eating their children) in his
denunciation of Cordelia (see page II–10).

. . . out-paramoured the Turk . . .

Edgar has no choice but to continue his begging routine. When questioned about his past life by Lear, he recites the sins that account for the
punishment of demonic possession that has driven him mad. He says:

> . . . Wine loved I deeply, dice dearly; and in woman out-
> paramoured the Turk. False of heart, light of ear, bloody of
> hand; hog in sloth, fox in stealth, wolf in greediness, dog in
> madness, lion in prey . . .
> —Act III, scene iv, lines 91–95

There is a casual anachronism in the mention of the "Turk." The Turks
did not enter history till some sixteen centuries after the supposed time of
Lear. In Shakespeare's time, however, they were at the very peak of their
power and the "Turk," that is, the Sultan who reigned at Istanbul (Constantinople), was the most dreaded monarch in Europe. Yet to the average
Christian what must have been most impressive about the Sultan was not

his wide dominions, his absolute power of life and death, but the size of his harem. There could have been few who did not secretly (or not so secretly) envy the Sultan his unparalleled opportunities, and to "out-paramour the Turk" is to express the very limit of lust.

Having listed his sins, Poor Tom piously proceeds to go through the ritual of repentance:

> *Keep thy foot out of brothels, thy hand out of plackets, thy pen from lenders' books, and defy the foul fiend.*
>
> —Act III, scene iv, lines 97–99

This ritual of I-have-been-a-sinner-but-I-have-repented is well calculated to elicit coins from passers-by and is still used with great effect at revival meetings and at such secular organizations as Alcoholics Anonymous.

Lear, however, is touched chiefly by the demonstration of how much lower it is possible to be than he has himself become. From bewailing the loss of the vast social swathing of the kingship, he begins to realize that he is still, even now, a product of an artificial society. He begins to tear his clothes off, saying to Poor Tom:

> *. . . Thou art the thing itself; unaccommodated man is no more but such a poor, bare, forked animal as thou art.*
>
> —Act III, scene iv, lines 108–10

. . . Flibbertigibbet

There is an interruption before Lear can carry out his design to become an unaccommodated man. Gloucester enters with a torch; he has found Lear.

It is to Gloucester most of all that Edgar must not reveal himself. At the sight of his father, therefore, Edgar turns his madness up a notch and cries out, in his Poor Tom character:

> *This is the foul fiend Flibbertigibbet.*
>
> —Act III, scene iv, line 117

Flibbertigibbet is a name that is to be found in a book of demonology called *A Declaration of Egregious Popish Impostures,* written by an English prelate named Samuel Harsnett.

In this book Harsnett inveighed against Jesuits and gave names to numerous demons, Flibbertigibbet among them. For this task he needed nothing more than an active and morbid imagination, and that he had.

In the course of the play, Poor Tom mentions other demonic names:

Smulkin, Modo, Mahu, Hoppedance, Obidicut, and so on. All are from Harsnett's book. Harsnett's book was published in 1603, so it would appear that *King Lear* could not possibly have been written earlier than this date.

Lear is fascinated by Poor Tom's maunderings. He can scarcely find time to listen to Gloucester's offer of better shelter and of food and water. Lear shakes off Gloucester and says:

> *First let me talk with this philosopher.*
> *What is the cause of thunder?*
>
> —Act III, scene iv, lines 157–58

In Shakespeare's time "philosopher" bore the flavor that "scientist" does now. (The word "scientist" was not invented until the nineteenth century.) That is why Lear, inspired by the still rumbling storm, asks the question concerning thunder, hoping presumably for a scientific answer.

When Kent joins his pleadings to Gloucester's, Lear says stubbornly:

> *I'll talk a word with this same learnèd Theban.*
> *What is your study?*
>
> —Act III, scene iv, lines 160–61

Until the century after Shakespeare's death, science (or philosophy, if you will) was associated almost exclusively with the ancient Greeks. The term "Theban," that is, a native of the Greek city of Thebes, would automatically imply "philosopher."

Or would it? Is it possible Lear is being ironic? The Athenians, who were the epitome of Greek culture and philosophy, considered the Thebans, their neighbors to the northwest, to be dull and stupid. The term "learnèd Theban" would be a contradiction in terms to them.

But Lear does not seem to be in a mocking mood. He is continuing to grow more human. As he took care of the Fool's protection before his own, so he now will not consent to be taken better care of until Poor Tom is taken along too. Gloucester and Kent are forced to agree to this and when they do, Lear applies to Poor Tom the best of all possible philosophic names by saying:

> *Come, good Athenian.*
>
> —Act III, scene iv, line 183

Child Rowland . . .

Through all this, Edgar, in agony, must continue the pretense of madness, which it is dangerous to abandon. As they leave the hovel to end the scene, he puts together ill-assorted pieces of doggerel:

> *Child Rowland to the dark tower came;*
> *His word was still, "Fie, foh, and fum,*
> *I smell the blood of a British man."*
>
> —Act III, scene iv, lines 185–87

Child Rowland (or Roland) is a hero of an old Scottish ballad. (The word "child" is used here with the force of a title. It is applied to a youth of good birth who has not yet attained knighthood.) From such references as are preserved, it would seem that the ballad tells of a young lad, guided by Merlin, seeking in Elf-land his kidnapped sister and gaining her through great peril. The actual ballad is lost and Poor Tom may here be reciting the first line. If so, it is the only line that still exists.

(Robert Browning wrote a Gothic poem entitled "Child Roland to the Dark Tower Came" inspired by this line in *King Lear,* but this poem has no connection with the old ballad.)

From the heroic old ballad, "Poor Tom" passes to the stock exclamation attributed to villainous giants on the track of a hiding hero. Shakespeare at least avoids the anachronism of having the last line end in "the blood of an Englishman," as it is frequently given now. Englishmen did not exist in the time of Lear and came into being only after the Anglo-Saxon invasion of the island of Britain in the fifth century.

. . . Earl of Gloucester . . .

While Gloucester is carrying out his errand of mercy, Edmund is carrying out his own base betrayal. He reveals the letter to Cornwall, showing that Gloucester is concealing knowledge of an invasion from France. He gets his reward, for Cornwall says grimly:

> . . . *it hath made thee Earl of Gloucester. Seek out where thy father is, that he may be ready for our apprehension.*
>
> —Act III, scene v, lines 18–20

Yet Edmund is not an utterly heartless child; he is not quite a Goneril or a Regan. He is eager for advancement, even over his father's fall, and yet it chokes him a little—for he says in an aside:

> *I will persever in my course of loyalty* [to Cornwall] *though the conflict be sore between that and my blood.*
>
> —Act III, scene v, lines 22–24

This is an important line, for it reveals a rudimentary flaw in Edmund's villainy that will play a significant part in the denouement of the play.

. . . to bed at noon

Gloucester manages to get all the poor fugitives, the King, the Fool, Edgar, and Kent, into a farmhouse near his castle, a better refuge than the miserable hovel.

He leaves and the mad King then conducts an imaginary trial of Goneril and Regan in so affecting a manner that Edgar has difficulty keeping up his pretense of being Poor Tom. At the close of the trial, Lear imagines himself to be in his bed and speaks of eating in the morning. At that, the Fool says, wearily:

> *And I'll go to bed at noon.*
> —Act III, scene vi, line 84

Those are the Fool's last words in the play. He appears no more after this scene, nor is he referred to. We can suppose that he has fulfilled his dramatic purpose of harping on Lear's folly and of playing counterpoint to Lear's mad raging in the storm, and now he is discarded.

We can also suppose that, worn out and exhausted by cold, rain, and fear, he knows he will soon die even though he is young in years ("go to bed at noon"). Yet it is hard that Shakespeare didn't see fit (or, more likely, carelessly neglected) to grant him a single line as epitaph from Lear.

When Gloucester returns, he is more anxious than ever. He has heard talk of a plan to kill the King (presumably to prevent his being used as a rallying point about which to mobilize those in opposition to the new regime of the dukes). He has arranged a litter and an escort to bring the King to Dover and safety.

. . . The army of France . . .

By now, news of the French invasion has reached Cornwall too. He says to Goneril:

> *Post speedily to my Lord your husband; show him this letter.*
> *The army of France is landed.*
> —Act III, scene vii, lines 1–3

If there has been growing rivalry between Albany and Cornwall, the latter apparently expects it will disappear in a common front against the common enemy. Certainly, Goneril is on the side of the Duke and Duchess of Cornwall and she may reasonably be expected to have the deciding influence over her easygoing husband.

Edmund is sent along with Goneril. This serves two functions, one positive and one negative. First, it makes possible a scene between Edmund and Goneril that advances the plot. Second, it makes it possible for Edmund to be absent in the course of what follows immediately—for Gloucester is about to be punished. We might reasonably guess that Edmund did not anticipate the exact nature of the punishment and might, if he had been present, have attempted to interfere.

. . . pluck me by the beard

Gloucester is captured and dragged in not long after his false son has left. He is tied to a chair in his own castle while his "guests" amuse themselves grimly by insulting him. Regan tweaks hairs from his beard and Gloucester says with indignation:

> By the kind gods. 'tis most ignobly done
> To pluck me by the beard.

> —Act III, scene vii, lines 36–37

We have lost the old regard for the beard. In many cultures, a beard was the sign of manly dignity and of virility; it was when the beard appeared that a boy became (sexually) a man. In such cultures, shaving was unthinkable; it would have been equivalent, in a way, to castration.

Among the ancient Jews, there was a biblical injunction forbidding them to shave or trim their beards in any way. ("Ye shall not round the corners of your heads, neither shalt thou mar the corners of thy beard," Leviticus 19:27.) To be forcibly shaven was to be unbearably shamed. When King David sent ambassadors to the Ammonites, the Ammonites forcibly shaved off the ambassadors' beards on one side of the face as a gesture of defiance, and that was cause enough in itself for war (see 2 Samuel 10:4–6).

Even in much later times, it was the height of disrespect to touch the beard of a man—for that bore much the same forbidden intimacy that a touch of the genitals would possess. That is the meaning of the phrase "to beard an enemy"; that is, to defy him by touching his beard and proving him to be impotent to avenge the insult. To seize the beard firmly was even more insulting, and to pull out hairs, by adding pain, adds an unspeakable dimension to the insult.

To an Elizabethan audience, seeing the play for the first time, we might well imagine that sharp intake of breath, that shudder of horror, at seeing this young woman wantonly insulting, in this indescribable way, an old man in his own house. We ourselves watch this incident stonily; a shaven society is unmoved.

. . . Edgar was abused

The horror increases rapidly. Gloucester is forced to confess he has sent King Lear to Dover and it is clear he has knowledge of the French invasion.

Cornwall, in a passion, decides to gouge out Gloucester's eyes (onstage!) and orders his servants to hold the chair steady. When one eye has been gouged out, one of the servants in desperation snatches a sword to stop so wicked a deed. In the fight, Cornwall is wounded, but Regan stabs the goodhearted servant from behind and kills him. Gloucester's other eye is then gouged out.

When blind Gloucester warns of Edmund's vengeance, Regan has the vile pleasure of telling him that it was Edmund who betrayed him.

Gloucester now understands all that has happened and says, in heartbreak:

> O my follies! Then Edgar was abused.
> Kind gods, forgive me that, and prosper him.
> —Act III, scene vii, lines 92–93

Cornwall must be led away, for his wound is a bad one. He has no time for Gloucester now and orders him turned out. An old and loyal tenant of his (identified in the play as "Old Man") guides him, bemoaning the fact that poor Gloucester cannot see his way. With infinite pathos, Gloucester recognizes the existence of different kinds of blindness and says:

> I have no way and therefore want no eyes;
> I stumbled when I saw.
> —Act IV, scene i, lines 18–19

There is a cliff . . .

Blind Gloucester, more grief-stricken for Edgar's sake than for his own, is seen by that same Edgar in his guise as Poor Tom. Aware of his father's blindness and evident misery, he has no thought for his own wrongs. He says bitterly:

> . . . the worst is not
> So long as we can say "This is the worst."
> —Act IV, scene i, lines 27–28

As long as breath exists, in other words, there remains the possibility of still greater misery.

Gloucester's own despair expresses itself in even grislier fashion, for he muses:

> As flies to wanton boys, are we to th'gods,
> They kill us for their sport.

—Act IV, scene i, lines 36–37

The Old Man identifies Poor Tom to Gloucester. Gloucester at once sees in Poor Tom a perfect guide, for a sane man might get into trouble with cruel Cornwall for succoring the blinded "traitor." Surely a Bedlam beggar is immune to punishment.

Edgar, overcome by grief, scarcely able to play his role, must nevertheless do so, while the servant is there, at least. So he continues babbling of devils.

Gloucester asks Edgar to lead him to Dover. All roads lead to Dover now, where the forces of France await. Gloucester has, however, a special purpose. He says:

> There is a cliff whose high and bending head
> Looks fearfully to the confinèd deep:
> Bring me but to the very brim of it,

—Act IV, scene i, lines 75–77

He is referring, of course, to the famous white cliffs of Dover, and his intention is suicide.

. . . This kiss . . .

Meanwhile Goneril and Edmund are hastening to the Duke of Albany to bid him join Cornwall in the war against France. They are met by Oswald, who tells them, in confusion, that Albany seems not at all perturbed by the French invasion. Goneril sees at once that her husband cannot be relied on and sends Edmund back to Cornwall with a warning to that effect.

She does so in a way that sheds new light on Goneril, for she tells Edmund:

> Decline your head. This kiss, if it durst speak,
> Would stretch thy spirits up into the air:

—Act IV, scene ii, lines 22–23

It is clear that Goneril is in love with Edmund. There has been no previous hint to this effect in the dialogue of the play, though Edmund's effect on Goneril could be made plain, easily enough, in the course of the "business."

It is important to realize that Edmund is extremely handsome. That point is made clear in the very opening dialogue of the play, between Gloucester and Kent. When Gloucester introduces Edmund with a rather leering reference to the illicit intercourse that produced him, Kent answers courteously:

> *I cannot wish the fault undone, the issue of it being so proper* [handsome].
>
> —Act I, scene i, lines 17–18

Milk-livered man

After Edmund leaves, Goneril faces Albany and outfaces him too. She is not in the least perturbed by Albany's exclamations against her wicked treatment of her father. She says to him, in contempt:

> *Milk-livered man!*
>
> —Act IV, scene ii, line 50

The liver is taken as the seat of the emotions. A liver rich with blood would inspire a man with noble and manly emotions. A red-livered man, then, would be aggressive and courageous. On the contrary, a liver with a deficiency of blood could rouse no such emotions; it would belong to a shrinker and coward. The usual expression is "lily-livered"; that is, white for lack of blood. "Milk-livered" does the same and carries the connotation of babyhood as well.

This linking of the liver with the emotions is wrong, of course, but it is no more wrong than our contemporary placing of the heart in this role. It is just as wrong to speak of "stouthearted" men, or "fainthearted" ones.

A Messenger arrives now, however, to inform them that Cornwall has died of the wound given him by his rebelling servant. This does not bother Goneril unduly from the standpoint of pity or sympathy, of which she has none. In fact, Cornwall's death removes a rival and makes more possible her own eventual rule with her husband (whoever he may be) over a united Britain.

However, Regan is now a widow, and Edmund is speeding toward her at Goneril's own command. As a widow, Regan would have an unfair advantage in any competition for the handsome Edmund. Cornwall's death means, therefore, the initiation of a sharp rivalry between the two sisters, each a dangerous, deadly combatant.

. . . so suddenly gone back . . .

Kent has now reached Dover. He finds the army there, but not its leader. He asks someone identified only as "Gentleman":

> *Why the King of France is so suddenly gone back, know you*
> *no reason?*
>
> —Act IV, scene iii, lines 1–2

The Gentleman explains, rather vaguely, that it is due to internal problems in France itself.

It is rather clumsy to have the King of France come and then go before he actually appears on the stage. This may be an expression of Shakespeare's anti-French feelings. In Holinshed, the French army invades Britain and defeats the British forces, and Shakespeare may well have had difficulty accepting that. He removed the French King at the last minute in the most economical way possible (he hated rewriting, according to Ben Jonson) and converted the political situation into more nearly a civil war.

The British pow'rs . . .

The entire drama is now converging on Dover. Cordelia reappears at the head of the invading army (which is now led by a British princess so that its foreignness need not be so prominent and so offensive to the audience). The native British forces are also approaching, however. A Messenger arrives to tell Cordelia:

> *The British pow'rs are marching hitherward.*
>
> —Act IV, scene iv, line 21

But if they are doing so, it is not in perfect unison. The Duke of Albany is clearly disaffected. When Regan (still at Gloucester's castle) asks Oswald for news and, specifically, if Albany is at the head of his forces, Oswald replies:

> *Madam, with much ado:*
> *Your sister is the better soldier.*
>
> —Act IV, scene vi, lines 2–3

But there is disaffection between the sisters too. Oswald (Goneril's steward) is at Gloucester's castle only because he is carrying a letter from Goneril to Edmund, and Regan is clearly jealous. She gives Oswald a letter of her own to Edmund, which now Oswald must carry toward Dover. Regan also instructs Oswald to kill blind old Gloucester if he should meet him.

. . . henceforth I'll bear

Gloucester has reached Dover too, led by Edgar. Edgar still hides his identity, apparently fearing what the effect on his father's tottering reason would be of any sudden revelation. He can no longer maintain his role as Poor Tom, however, and has begun to speak in stately blank verse. The blind Gloucester says, in confusion:

> *Methinks thy voice is altered, and thou speak'st*
> *In better phrase and matter than thou didst.*
> —Act IV, scene vi, lines 7–8

Edgar pushes that aside and begins to describe the cliff to which he claims to have led Gloucester, doing so in thrillingly effective terms while Gloucester is still standing on a featureless plain. Edgar's purpose in doing so, he explains in an aside to the audience:

> *Why I do trifle thus with his despair*
> *Is done to cure it.*
> —Act IV, scene vi, lines 33–34

The scheme works. Gloucester attempts to hurl himself from the imaginary cliff and falls forward to the ground. Edgar approaches in the guise of another man and convinces his blind father that he had been led to the brow of the cliff by a demon and had been saved by divine intervention. Gloucester, whose early comments on eclipses have revealed him to be a superstitious man, accepts this, and realizes he cannot hasten death in defiance of fate. He says resignedly:

> *. . . henceforth I'll bear*
> *Affliction till it do cry out itself*
> *"Enough, enough," and die.*
> —Act IV, scene vi, lines 75–77

. . . the rain came . . .

King Lear is at Dover too, still mad at least part of the time, and, in his lucid intervals, refusing to see Cordelia out of his deep shame. He has now apparently gotten away from those guarding him and is wandering about garlanded in flowers.

He is still learning to know himself. He has come to recognize what flattery is, for he says:

> They flattered me like a dog, and told me I had white hairs in my beard ere the black ones were there.
>
> —Act IV, scene vi, lines 97–99

He was told he had the wisdom of age, in other words, before he had outgrown the folly of youth. But he had found the limits of those powers which flattery would hold limitless. He says:

> When the rain came to wet me once and the wind to make me chatter; when the thunder would not peace at my bidding; there I found 'em . . .
>
> —Act IV, scene vi, lines 101–4

Lear, in his aimless wanderings, has come upon Gloucester and Edgar. Gloucester recognizes the King's voice and asks if it is not the King. Lear draws himself up and says, regally, in a phrase that has entered the language:

> Ay, every inch a king.
>
> —Act IV, scene vi, line 109

But he is not the king he once was. He goes through a bitter charade of dispensing justice, to show how royal he is, but he knows now he cannot give true justice, for he does not know the hearts of men. He can see, now, the injustices suffered by mankind generally, and not by himself only. He says:

> Through tattered clothes small vices do appear;
> Robes and furred gowns hide all. Plate sin with gold,
> And the strong lance of justice hurtless breaks;
> Arm it in rags, a pygmy's straw does pierce it.
>
> —Act IV, scene vi, lines 166–69

. . . the English party

Those who are trying to guard the King enter now, but Lear madly tries to evade them, and they run offstage.

Edgar, knowing that a battle will soon be fought in the vicinity, tries to lead his blind father to safety. Now that his father is resigned to life, Edgar might have revealed himself, but he had been interrupted by Lear's arrival before and, much more seriously, by a second interruption now.

Oswald enters, and, seeing Gloucester, is ready to kill him to please Regan. Edgar intervenes, however, assuming the guise of a rustic and speaking in a thick peasant dialect. They fight and Oswald falls.

With his last breath, Oswald proves faithful, at least, to those he served. He says to the supposed peasant:

> *If ever thou wilt thrive, bury my body,*
> *And give the letters which thou find'st about me*
> *To Edmund Earl of Gloucester; seek him out*
> *Upon the English party.*
>
> —Act IV, scene vi, lines 251–54

Here is the inevitable anachronism. Somewhere in the play there has to be a slip, with the use of the word "English," and here it is. There were no English in Britain in Lear's supposed time, nor would there be for thirteen centuries. The word is changed to "British" in some editions of the play, but it is "English" in the oldest printed version.

Edgar opens the letters he finds on Oswald's body. (All's fair in love and war.) The one from Goneril to Edmund urges the latter to seize some opportunity to kill Albany and offers him her hand thereafter. The bastard son has risen to heir, then to the earldom, and might yet become King of all Britain.

. . . a very foolish fond old man

Lear has been caught by those who have tried to guard him. He sleeps now and Cordelia faces him at last, half afraid to wake him and yet hoping he might be restored to sanity by this sleep. She thinks of the wild storm into which he had been pitilessly expelled and says, movingly:

> *Mine enemy's dog,*
> *Though he had bit me, should have stood that night*
> *Against my fire . . .*
>
> —Act IV, scene vii, lines 36–38

And when Lear wakes, she kneels to him in recognition of his royalty. But Lear knows himself now; he knows himself entirely; and he will not be the king of old. He tries to kneel to her, and when she prevents him, he says:

> *Pray, do not mock me:*
> *I am a very foolish fond old man,*

> *Fourscore and upward, not an hour more nor less;*
> *And, to deal plainly,*
> *I fear I am not in my perfect mind.*
>
> —Act IV, scene vii, lines 59–63

Then, when he is perfectly sure he is really speaking to his youngest daughter, Cordelia, he says:

> *I pray, weep not.*
> *If you have poison for me, I will drink it.*
> *I know you do not love me; for your sisters*
> *Have, as I do remember, done me wrong.*
> *You have some cause, they have not.*
>
> —Act IV, scene vii, lines 71–75a

And all the wronged and weeping Cordelia can say is:

> *No cause, no cause.*
>
> —Act IV, scene vii, line 75b

The whole reconciliation scene is done in the simplest language, with scarcely a poetic flight, scarcely a polysyllable, yet nowhere in Shakespeare, and, I believe, nowhere in literature, is the human heart so skillfully and ruthlessly torn in sympathy with what it sees and hears.

The enemy's in view . . .

The battle is about to begin. Edmund now leads the forces of the dead Duke of Cornwall, and Regan jealously sues for his love.

The Duke of Albany arrives with Goneril, and he, for one, makes his motive plain:

> *. . . for this business,*
> *It touches us, as France invades our land*
>
> —Act V, scene i, lines 24–25

He is patriotically resisting a foreign invasion even though he admits the enemy cause is just.

Edgar, still in disguise, approaches Albany privately and gives him the letter he had obtained from Oswald's corpse, urging him to read it later. Albany agrees.

As Edgar leaves, Edmund returns, saying:

The enemy's in view: draw up your powers.
Here is the guess of their true strength and forces
By diligent discovery.
—Act V, scene i, lines 51–53

King Lear hath lost . . .

Edgar places his father in a position of safety, but after the battle he comes rushing back, crying:

Away, old man; give me thy hand; away!
King Lear hath lost, he and his daughter ta'en:
—Act V, scene ii, lines 5–6

When Gloucester seems to yearn for death again, and voices a preference for staying and dying rather than flying, Edgar says:

Men must endure
Their going hence, even as their coming hither:
Ripeness is all. Come on.
—Act V, scene ii, lines 9–11

This battle was described by Holinshed as a victory for Lear, Cordelia, and the French. Shakespeare changes that for his deeper purposes, but it seems certain that to have the French defeated suited his nationalistic prejudices in any case.

. . . let's away to prison

The captured Cordelia wishes to see her sisters, presumably to plead for her father's release. Lear, however, refuses. He has learned what is important in life at last and he says:

No, no, no, no! Come, let's away to prison:
We two alone will sing like birds i'th'cage:
When thou dost ask me blessing, I'll kneel down
And ask of thee forgiveness; so we'll live,
And pray, and sing, and tell old tales, and laugh
At gilded butterflies, and hear poor rogues
Talk of court news; and we'll talk with them too,
Who loses and who wins, who's in, who's out;
And take upon's the mystery of things,
As if we were God's spies: and we'll wear out,

In a walled prison, packs and sects of great ones
That ebb and flow by th'moon.

—Act V, scene iii, lines 8–19

One might argue that this makes up to Lear for all that has passed. If Lear had divided the kingdom and died, or if his daughters had been content to wait for him to die and had treated him with reasonable patience till then, he would never have been more than he was at the beginning, a foolish raging tyrant, full of the professions of love, and ignorant of love.

But through all his misery and calamity, he has ended with a few moments of utter happiness, and those few are worth all his life besides.

As for the loss of liberty and all else, what does it matter? Lear says:

Upon such sacrifices, my Cordelia,
The gods themselves throw incense.

—Act V, scene iii, lines 20–21

On capital treason . . .

Edmund has more than imprisonment in mind. He fully intends to be King of Britain and for that purpose other candidates for the crown must be disposed of. In particular, Lear and Cordelia must be killed. He has stated this intention in a soliloquy before the battle and now he sends an officer to do the job. When Albany enters and demands the prisoners, Edmund smoothly puts him off.

Regan and Goneril fall to quarreling over who is to have Edmund. Regan has an advantage in that she is not burdened with a husband, and she announces Edmund as her new lord.

Albany, however, interrupts. He has read the letter Edgar brought him and he stops all proceedings with the firm cry of:

Edmund, I arrest thee
On capital treason; and in thy attaint
This gilded serpent.

—Act V, scene iii, lines 83–85

Goneril, who is "this gilded serpent," is indifferent. As she says a little later on:

. . . the laws are mine, not thine:
Who can arraign me for 't?

—Act V, scene iii, lines 160–61

Impenitent to the last, she is unperturbed by the revelation of her intention to have her husband murdered. It is she who is sovereign of her part of Britain and Albany has power only as her husband. What can he do?

Her mind is much more on Regan, the sister-competitor who would have Edmund. Regan isn't well and when she groans that she is sick, Goneril says, grimly:

> *If not, I'll ne'er trust medicine.*
> —Act V, scene iii, line 97

A bit of poisoning is quite in her line.

The gods are just . . .

But Edmund has the right of trial by combat. If no one will appear to fight him, Albany will do so. That, however, is not necessary; a champion does appear. It is Edgar, disguised still, but by a full suit of armor this time.

The two fight and Edmund is beaten down. Regan has already been led away, and now Goneril, seeing Edmund at the mercy of his adversary, rushes off in despair and distraction.

Edmund, wounded and dying, knows that all ambition is over. Unlike Goneril, he is not evil for the mere sake of evil. With ambition gone, the good in him begins to show.

Edgar identifies himself, and says somberly:

> *The gods are just, and of our pleasant vices*
> *Make instruments to plague us:*
> *The dark and vicious place where thee he* [Gloucester] *got*
> *Cost him his eyes.*
> —Act V, scene iii, lines 172–75

And Edmund can only respond, humbly:

> *Th' hast spoken right, 'tis true;*
> *The wheel is come full circle; I am here.*
> —Act V, scene iii, lines 175–76

Yet the illegitimate son has one moment of dying triumph. The dead bodies of Regan and Goneril are brought in, and Edmund cannot help but exult:

> *Yet Edmund was beloved:*
> *The one the other poisoned for my sake,*
> *And after slew herself.*
> —Act V, scene iii, lines 241–43

It can very easily be argued that it was not ambition in itself that spurred Edmund on. He was illegitimate and therefore snubbed and despised all his life for a fault that was not his. He was searching for love and he found it at last. It was a grisly and fatal love, but with it he too could die happy.

Burst smilingly

Edgar tells the tale of his travels with his blind father and brings that tale to its end. Just before he had armed himself for the encounter with Edmund, and not sure he would survive, he finally revealed himself to old Gloucester. And Edgar then says:

> But his flawed heart—
> Alack, too weak the conflict to support—
> 'Twixt two extremes of passion, joy and grief,
> Burst smilingly.

> —Act V, scene iii, lines 198–201

Edmund is onstage and hears this. He had had his father's love, at any rate. He says so in his initial soliloquy in the second scene of the play:

> Our father's love is to the bastard Edmund
> As to th' legitimate . . .

> —Act I, scene ii, lines 17–18

Edmund may not have been satisfied with that love, for no land went with it—the entire inheritance would naturally go to the legitimate one— but he did not entirely forget it either. He was absent when Gloucester lost his eyes and perhaps he heard it first from Edgar's account and felt remorse.

At least he now says, when Edgar's tale is concluded:

> This speech of yours hath moved me,
> And shall perchance do good . . .

> —Act V, scene iii, lines 201–2

And Edmund tries, for, when nearly at the last gasp, he manages to warn Albany that he has sent a man to kill Lear and Cordelia and that there might still be time to save them.

. . . Her voice was ever soft

But Edmund's attempt is, in part, too late. His officer had hanged Cordelia, but Lear, in a last superhuman effort, had killed him. Lear is now released, but Cordelia is dead and the old King comes in with his daughter in his arms. He cannot bring himself to believe she is dead and, for the remaining few moments of his life, tries to convince himself she is not. He says:

> Cordelia, Cordelia, stay a little. Ha,
> What is't thou say'st? Her voice was ever soft,
> Gentle and low, an excellent thing in woman.
> —Act V, scene iii, lines 273–75

. . . my poor fool . . .

Lear is all but oblivious to his surroundings. For a moment he recognizes Kent, and Kent tries to explain that he had loyally remained with him during his misfortunes. Kent says:

> . . . Where is your servant Caius?
> —Act V, scene iii, line 285

That apparently was the name Kent used in his disguise, a name, however, that is not mentioned elsewhere in the play.

Lear pays little attention to this and is oblivious to the news of Edmund's death. He concentrates only on Cordelia, moaning:

> And my poor fool is hanged: no, no, no life?
> —Act V, scene iii, line 307

It would seem that "poor fool" is a sad term of affection for Cordelia. We might long to have it apply to the Fool, so that there could be one mention of him anyway from Lear's lips, even if it is only to hear that he was hanged, but we can't in good conscience do so. It would be impossible for Lear to think of anything but Cordelia now. And with his last breath, he thinks she lives:

> Do you see this? Look on her. Look, her lips,
> Look there, look there.
> —Act V, scene iii, lines 312–13

And here he dies—perhaps happily.

This ending of *Lear* can easily be viewed as the cruelest and most unbearable in Shakespeare. Why could not Edmund have spoken a moment sooner and Cordelia been saved? Shakespeare had every excuse to do so, for in Holinshed, Cordelia's forces had won the victory and placed Lear back on the throne for a final two years as ruler.

But that would have placed the whole meaning of the play out of focus. The happy ending in Holinshed is not that Cordelia had lived, but that Lear had been restored and had died at last in her arms.

The happy ending in Shakespeare is Lear's regeneration and it is to make it perfectly clear that that is the happy ending that nothing else must be allowed to compete with it.

27

CYMBELINE

With *Cymbeline* Shakespeare moves from the outright legendary time of *King Lear* (which he had written four years earlier) to a period when Britain first dimly appears in the light of history, thanks to the coming of the Romans.

The Romans made their first appearance in Britain in 55 B.C., when Julius Caesar, who was then busy conquering Gaul, launched the first of two raids against the northern island. Those raids did not lead to permanent Roman occupation, and for nearly an additional century Britain remained entirely under native rule. It was during this century that there existed a British chieftain named Cunobelin or, in the Shakespearean version, Cymbeline.

With Roman rule strengthening and deepening just across the Channel in Gaul, Britain was coming increasingly under Roman influence, economically at least. Trade with Gaul made Britain increasingly aware of Roman civilization and increasingly dependent upon it. The southern tribes of Britain (over whom Cymbeline ruled—for he was by no means King of a united Britain) began to go so far as to place Latin inscriptions on their coins.

Holinshed (see page II-4), whose scrappy information on Cymbeline was surely noted by Shakespeare, says that monarch began his reign in 33 B.C. and reigned for thirty-five years, that is, till A.D. 2. This is almost certainly too early, for the Roman sources we have make it seem that Cymbeline died only shortly before the permanent Roman occupation of Britain. We might guess, then, that Cymbeline ruled, roughly speaking, from A.D. 5 to A.D. 40.

If so, the time of *Cymbeline,* when compared with that of the Roman plays, is only slightly after *Antony and Cleopatra* and some five centuries before *Titus Andronicus.*

. . . his wife's sole son . . .

Except for Cymbeline himself, there is nothing in the play, no person and no event, which can be equated with any part of actual history. The play must therefore be treated as pure romance.

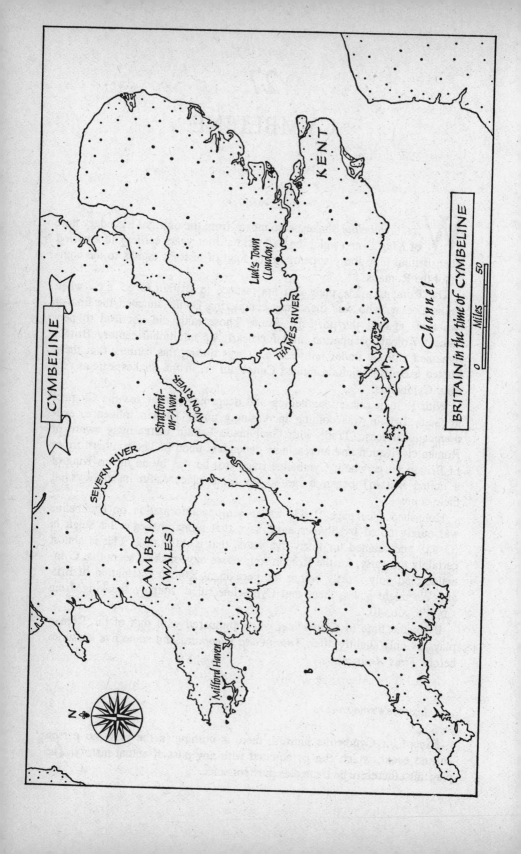

CYMBELINE

KENT

Channel

Lud's Town
(London)

THAMES RIVER

Stratford-
on-Avon

AVON RIVER

SEVERN RIVER

CAMBRIA
(WALES)

Milford Haven

N

BRITAIN in the time of CYMBELINE

0   Miles   50

It begins with a rather complicated situation (and indeed, the plotting in *Cymbeline* is denser than in any other play). Cymbeline had three children, two sons and a daughter. The two sons were stolen in infancy and were never heard of again. That left the daughter, Imogen, heir to the throne.

Cymbeline's wife, the mother of Imogen, was dead and the King had married again. The second wife was a beautiful widow with great influence over her husband. By her earlier marriage, the new Queen had a son, Cloten, and for him Cymbeline had particular plans.

The play opens in Cymbeline's court (place not specified) and two Gentlemen are discussing the situation. The First Gentleman is explaining it to the Second and says:

> *His daughter, and the heir of's kingdom, whom*
> *He purposed to his wife's sole son—a widow*
> *That late he married—hath referred herself*
> *Unto a poor but worthy gentleman. She's wedded,*
> *Her husband banished, she imprisoned.*
> —Act I, scene i, lines 4–8

Cymbeline's motivation is not hard to follow. In a semibarbarous tribal society, a woman could scarcely be expected to rule unless she had some strong man as husband—some man, moreover, who was the social equal of the turbulent nobility he expected to rule. The man Imogen had actually married was unsuited, because he was poor and because (as we soon find out) he had filled a rather menial position at the court.

The widow who had become Cymbeline's new Queen was, however, of high social position, and so was her son, Cloten. If Cloten married Imogen, the two together could rule without dispute and the succession would be settled. Cymbeline was getting on in years and his final duty to the state was exactly that—to arrange a peaceful succession. No wonder he was annoyed at Imogen's action.

It is interesting to speculate that Shakespeare may have been inspired to set up this particular part of the plot by the actual historical situation involving the Roman Emperor Augustus (the Octavius Caesar of *Antony and Cleopatra*, see page I–292), who in this play is treated as a contemporary of Cymbeline.

Augustus too had no sons of his own to inherit the rule. Augustus too by an early marriage had a single daughter, Julia. Augustus too then married a beautiful girl, Livia, and she was a divorcée (not a widow) with a son by her first marriage. (She was also pregnant with what turned out to be a second son.)

Julia, the daughter of Augustus, had been married to Agrippa (see page I–340) and had a number of children, including two sons. Her husband died in 12 B.C., however, and that left only a pair of infant grandsons to succeed if Augustus should die suddenly. Augustus therefore had Julia marry his stepson Tiberius, as Cymbeline would have wanted Imogen to marry Cloten.

Of course, there were differences between the play and the historical analogy. In history, it was the stepson who was unwilling to make the marriage; in the play, the daughter. In history, the device was successful, for by the time Augustus died in A.D. 14, his young grandsons were also dead, and Tiberius succeeded to the Imperial throne in peace. In the play, Cymbeline's plan has failed even before the action has begun.

... with Cassibelan

The Second Gentleman is interested in just who it is that Imogen has married, and he is told:

> His father
> Was called Sicilius, who did join his honor
> Against the Romans with Cassibelan,
>
> —Act I, scene i, lines 28–30

Cassibelan is known to us, through Caesar's writings, as Cassivellaunus. He ruled over the district immediately north of the Thames River in the time of Caesar's second raid into Britain (54 B.C.). Cassibelan resisted the invader strongly.

Sicilius is an oddly Roman name for a British fighter in an age which had barely yet encountered Roman culture, but he is, of course, an entirely fictitious character, and Shakespeare has a penchant for using Roman and Italian names for his invented men and women even when this is entirely inappropriate. (The name Cloten, used for the Queen's son, is, however, an appropriate one. A legendary King of Britain, who had supposedly ruled about five centuries before Cymbeline, was named Cloten.)

Sicilius received a second Roman name as a result of his service in the Roman wars. He was called Leonatus ("lion-born").

Sicilius' two sons died in battle against the Romans and Sicilius himself then died of grief at a time when his wife was pregnant. She gave birth after her husband's death, and, as the First Gentleman explains:

> The King he takes the babe
> To his protection, calls him Posthumus Leonatus,
> Breeds him and makes him of his bedchamber.
>
> —Act I, scene i, lines 40–42

Posthumus is a Latin name meaning "last." A child born after the death of a father is a posthumous child, since he is the last the father can possibly have of a particular woman. The Romans often used Posthumus as the name for a child born after the death of the father. When Augustus' daughter, Julia, was left a widow by Agrippa's death, she was pregnant. A son was eventually born who was thus named Agrippa Posthumus, and here is another echo of the Augustan family situation in *Cymbeline*.

. . . *in Rome* . . .

With the family circumstances explained, the action of the play begins. The Queen enters with Imogen and Posthumus, toward whom she is feigning sympathy and friendship. Posthumus, newly exiled, is taking sad leave of his bride, Imogen, and is telling her where he may be reached by letter:

> *My residence, in Rome at one Philario's*
> *Who to my father was a friend . . .*
> > —Act I, scene i, lines 97–98

Men of consequence who were exiled from homes in the kingdoms on the outskirts of the Roman realm would naturally gravitate toward Rome. It was after all the seat of power, and a decree of the Senate or, later, of the Emperor, could do much to restore the exile to his homeland, or even place him on a throne.

Where the historical Cymbeline was concerned, a son of his (not a son-in-law), named Adminius, was in fact sent into exile for some reason, about A.D. 40.

. . . *in Britain*

The play shifts its scene to Rome, but the shift is not only in space, but in time as well. Suddenly, we are not in the Rome of the early emperors at all, but in the Rome of Renaissance Italy some fourteen hundred years later. The very name "Philario" at whose house Posthumus will stay is Italian rather than Roman, and the play continues to mingle bits of Augustan Rome with bits of Renaissance Italy to the end.

The Italian portion of the action that is now taken up by Shakespeare is from one of the tales of the *Decameron* by Giovanni Boccaccio, and Shakespeare was too negligent, or lazy, to try to convert the tale to a Roman setting.

In Rome, Philario and some friends are talking of Posthumus. One of those friends says:

> *Believe it, sir, I have seen him in Britain.*
> > —Act I, scene iv, line 1

The speaker's name is Iachimo and that name is one of the numerous versions of Jacob (an equivalent English version is James). Iachimo is a medieval Italian name, not a Roman one.

Another gentleman at the table, who is identified as "Frenchman," says:

> *I have seen him in France.*
>
> —Act I, scene iv, line 11

There were no France and no Frenchmen in Cymbeline's time, of course. The directions that precede this scene say also that "a Dutchman and a Spaniard are present," though neither of these speaks. The presence of a Spaniard is possible, if by that we mean a member of one of the Celtic tribes that then inhabited the peninsula called "Hispania" by the Romans. A Dutchman, however, is as impossible as a Frenchman.

When Posthumus arrives, the Frenchman greets him by recalling a prior meeting:

> *Sir, we have known together in Orleans.*
>
> —Act I, scene iv, line 36

A town did exist at the site of modern Orléans even in the time of Cymbeline. This Gallic town was captured and destroyed by Julius Caesar in 52 B.C. It was later rebuilt by the Romans and given the name of Aurelianum, of which "Orléans" is a corruption.

Yet despite Shakespeare's casual anachronisms in this scene, he does not make the mistake of calling Posthumus an Englishman. When Posthumus enters, Philario says:

> *Here comes the Briton.*
>
> —Act I, scene iv, line 29

. . . th' Arabian bird . . .

Posthumus no sooner arrives but he falls into a discussion of the relative intensities of virtue of the women of different nations and begins to boast about the fidelity of his own Imogen. (This is similar to the tragic boasting of Collatinus at the siege of Ardea, see page I–205.)

Iachimo undertakes to prove that Imogen's vaunted fidelity can easily be broken. All he asks is a letter of introduction from Posthumus to give him entry and wagers a large sum against Posthumus' diamond ring (given him by Imogen) that he will bring back proof of intercourse with her.

The bet is taken and Iachimo travels to Britain. As soon as he sees

Imogen, however, his heart misgives him. Her beauty and evident nobility daunt him and he soliloquizes:

> *If she be furnished with a mind so rare,*
> *She is alone th'Arabian bird, and I*
> *Have lost the wager.*
>
> —Act I, scene vi, lines 16–18

The phoenix was, in legend, an Arabian bird. There was only one phoenix in existence and, after a long life of five hundred years or so, it reproduced itself by building a nest of spices to which it set fire. It died in the flames, singing melodiously, and out of the ashes a new phoenix was born. (Is this a symbol of the one and only sun, which sets in flames only to rise afresh the next morning? For another theory, see page I–663.)

The phoenix is a symbol of uniqueness and it is in this respect that Iachimo compares Imogen to it, for he has a cynical view of the commonness of feminine virtue.

. . . like the Parthian . . .

Iachimo intends the assault just the same, and if the direct approach fails, he will try deceit. He says:

> *Arm me, audacity, from head to foot,*
> *Or like the Parthian I shall flying fight—*
>
> —Act I, scene vi, lines 19–20

The Parthian cavalry (see page I–61) was particularly noted for its habit of swarming in to attack, then go racing away. If pursued, the Parthian horsemen would rise in their saddles, even as they were galloping, turn, and let loose a last volley of arrows. This "Parthian shot" could do great damage and the Parthians may have used the entire maneuver as an indirect device to lure the enemy into a wild and undisciplined pursuit.

. . . for the Emperor

Iachimo's direct assault does fail. He pretends that Posthumus is leading a life of extreme lechery in Rome and suggests that Imogen reply in kind. Imogen refuses to believe the report and repels the suggestion indignantly. Iachimo at once pretends he has only been testing her and shifts ground. He says:

Some dozen Romans of us and your lord—
The best feather of our wing—have mingled sums
To buy a present for the Emperor;

> —Act I, scene vi, lines 185–87

To Shakespeare, following Holinshed's dating of Cymbeline's rule, the Roman Emperor mentioned here is Augustus. Indeed, Cymbeline would have, by Holinshed's dating, have died twelve years before Augustus.

By the more likely later dating of Cymbeline's rule, however, the later years of his reign (in which time the play is set) would be found in the reign of Augustus' stepson, Tiberius, who died in 37, or even in the reign of Augustus' great-grandson, Caligula, who died in 41.

Our Tarquin . . .

Iachimo pretends that the plate and jewels bought for the Emperor are in a large trunk and asks permission to keep the trunk in Imogen's bedroom for safekeeping for one night before he leaves to return to Rome the next day.

Imogen agrees and the trunk is duly delivered. It does not contain jewels, however. That night, when Imogen is sleeping, the trunk opens and Iachimo himself steps out and advances to the bed, saying:

> *Our Tarquin thus*
> *Did softly press the rushes ere he wakened*
> *The chastity he wounded. Cytherea,*
> *How bravely thou becom'st thy bed . . .*

> —Act II, scene ii, lines 12–15

This is a reference to the tale of the rape of the Roman matron Lucretia by Sextus Tarquinius (see page I–206). Cytherea is one of the names of Venus (see page I–162).

. . . the Gordian knot . . .

Iachimo is no Tarquin, however. He makes no attempt to rape Imogen; he wants only to win the bet. He notes the details of the room and takes off Imogen's bracelet as physical proof that he has been with her. The bracelet comes off easily, or, as Iachimo says:

> *As slippery as the Gordian knot was hard.*

> —Act II, scene ii, line 34

The tale of the Gordian knot dates far back. The Greeks had a legend that during a period of internal unrest in the Phrygian kingdom in Asia Minor in the ninth century B.C., an oracle declared that the proper person to select as next king would soon arrive in a wagon. Gordius, a peasant, did arrive in this fashion and was at once declared king. Gordius dedicated his wagon to Jupiter (Zeus) after fastening its pole to the yoke by a very intricate knot of bark with the ends hidden inside.

The legend arose that anyone who could untie this "Gordian knot" would conquer all the East, but for centuries attempts to untie it failed, so that "Gordian knot" came to be used for any difficult or even insoluble problem. Finally, in 333 B.C., Alexander the Great, passing through the old Phrygian capital (called Gordium), solved the problem neatly. He cut the knot with his sword and went on to conquer all the East.

The tale of Tereus . . .

Iachimo even took pains to note what it was Imogen was reading at the time of falling asleep:

> *She hath been reading late*
> *The tale of Tereus. Here the leaf's turned down*
> *Where Philomel gave up.*
> —Act II, scene ii, lines 44–46

Apparently she is reading Ovid's *Metamorphoses* (see page I-8), which was written during the reign of Augustus and would, by Shakespeare's conception of the time of the play, have been a current best seller. The book was one of Shakespeare's favorites and the tale of Tereus inspired *Titus Andronicus,* see page I-405.

A clock then strikes (the same anachronism found in *Julius Caesar,* see page I-280) and Iachimo leaves.

. . . Julius Caesar smiled . . .

Meanwhile there is trouble brewing between the Roman Empire and the island of Britain. The tribute paid by Britain is in arrears and Augustus has sent an ambassador to demand its payment. Philario tells this to Posthumus and gives it as his opinion the Britons will pay rather than fight. Posthumus stoutly insists there will be war, saying:

> *Our countrymen*
> *Are men more ordered than when Julius Caesar*
> *Smiled at their lack of skill but found their courage*
> *Worthy his frowning at.*
> —Act II, scene iv, lines 20–23

Caesar had become aware of the island of Britain in the course of his conquest of Gaul, for he discovered that the Gauls were obtaining help from their fellow Celts on the island. He felt it necessary to do something to discourage the Britons, yet did not like to commit too great a force while leaving a still restless Gaul at his back. He therefore planned a quick raid.

In August 55 B C. he ferried two legions (ten thousand men) across what we now call the Strait of Dover and landed them on the Kentish coast. It did not turn out to be easy. The Britons (as Shakespeare has Post-humus say) did not fight with the discipline of the Roman legions, but they fought with reckless courage, as all the Celtic enemies of Rome did.

After three weeks, Caesar was glad enough to take his men back to Gaul, with an embarrassing number of casualties and nothing much to show for it. To avoid a serious loss of face, he had to plan a second and considerably larger invasion the next year.

Proud Cleopatra . . .

The conversation is interrupted because of the return of Iachimo, who claims to have won his bet. Posthumus is incredulous, so Iachimo begins to describe Imogen's bedroom:

> *—it was hanged*
> *With tapestry of silk and silver; the story*
> *Proud Cleopatra, when she met her Roman*
> *And Cydnus swelled above the banks, . . .*
>
>   —Act II, scene iv, lines 68–71

This refers to the first meeting of Antony and Cleopatra at Tarsus on the Cydnus River (see page I–343). This had taken place about forty years before the play's period by Holinshed's reckoning; eighty years before by ours.

This and further details convince Posthumus. In shame and despair, he strips the diamond ring from his finger and hands it over, crying:

> *It is a basilisk unto mine eye*
> *Kills me to look on't . . .*
>
>   —Act II, scene iv, lines 107–8

The basilisk is the fabulous serpent which kills with its glance (see page I–150).

... *old Saturn*

The shamed Posthumus, left to himself, is in agony over Imogen's supposed infidelity, made worse by his memory of her apparent virtue—which now seems to him to have been but hypocrisy. He says:

> *Me of my lawful pleasure she restrained*
> *And prayed me oft forbearance—did it with*
> *A pudency* [modesty] *so rosy, the sweet view on't*
> *Might well have warmed old Saturn.*
>
> —Act II, scene v, lines 9–12

Saturn (the Latin version of the Greek Cronos) was the chief of the Titans (see page I-11) and the father of Jupiter (Zeus). The thought of a god who was still older than the chief of the gods naturally gave to Saturn/Cronos the picture of ancientness.

What's more, Saturn (Cronos) must originally have been an agricultural deity who was pictured with a sickle. There was confusion with "Chronos," the Greek personification of Time, who mowed down everything eventually. Saturn (Cronos) therefore came to be "Father Time" as well, and more ancient than ever.

Imogen is thus pictured as being capable of inspiring the very oldest with a feeling of sexual desire.

... *granted Rome a tribute*

The Roman ambassador, Caius Lucius (quite unhistorical), arrives at Cymbeline's court and demands the lapsed tribute, saying:

> *Cassibelan thine uncle,*
> *Famous in Caesar's praises no whit less*
> *Than in his feats deserving it, for him* [Caesar]
> *And his succession granted Rome a tribute,*
> *Yearly three thousand pounds, which by thee lately*
> *Is left untendered.*
>
> —Act III, scene i, lines 5–10

This was the result of Caesar's second invasion, in 54 B.C. This time he crossed the Channel with a fleet of eight hundred ships and no less than five legions, including two thousand cavalry. He drove the Britons back step by step to the Thames, where Cassivellaunus (Cassibelan) took up the fight. He fought most resolutely, practicing a scorched-earth policy when he retreated and trying to persuade the southern tribes to burn the Roman ships. His skill and perseverance did not avail against Julius Caesar in the end, and he was forced to capitulate.

. . . *"Came and saw and overcame"* . . .

This was by no means a disgraceful defeat for the Britons. As Cymbeline's Queen points out:

> *A kind of conquest*
> *Caesar made here, but made not here his brag*
> *Of "Came and saw and overcame." With shame,*
> *The first that ever touched him, he was carried*
> *From off our coast, twice beaten.*
>
> —Act III, scene i, lines 22–26

Julius Caesar, it seems, had marched into Asia Minor in 47 B.C., after his short stay in Alexandria (see page I–321). In Asia Minor an army had been raised against him by Pharnaces, ruler of Pontus, a land which for forty years had been grimly fighting Rome. Pontus' strength had reached the vanishing point, however, and at the Battle of Zela (a town on the western border of Pontus) Pharnaces' army broke and fled almost at once.

Julius Caesar then sent a brief message to Rome, designed to show the rapidity of his victory: *Veni, vidi, vici.* The usual translation is "I came, I saw, I conquered," but Shakespeare's "Came and saw and overcame" is just as good. (I have invented a rather lame translation of my own to catch the alliteration as well: "Went, watched, won.")

Cymbeline's Queen is, however, being a bit boastful herself. Caesar was beaten off the first time with some shame, but the second invasion was a clear victory for him, if not an easy one. Still, he did not remain on the island, though he did arrange for a formal annual tribute. Yet things might have gone worse for Britain if Caesar had not been reluctant to try to support a permanent force in the island with Gaul still not securely in Roman hands. It would be different a century later.

. . . *Lud's Town* . . .

The Queen goes on to say that Caesar might easily have been entirely overthrown, especially at one point when a storm had wrecked some of his shipping. (This took place in the course of the first raid, actually.) When that happened, Cassibelan

Made Lud's Town with rejoicing fires bright
And Britons strut with courage.

—Act III, scene i, lines 32–33

"Lud's Town" is London, so called because the legend makers who contrived the early history of Britain spoke of a King Lud who, presumably, founded a town on the site of present-day London. This is stated by Geoffrey of Monmouth (see page II–3), who makes Lud a brother of Cassivellaunus and his predecessor, so that London would, by that account, have been founded about 66 B.C.

Actually, the first knowledge we have of London is as a fortification founded by the Romans in their conquest of the island soon after Cymbeline's death, a full century after the supposed founding by Lud. Nor is there any actual reason outside the legend-filled chronicles of Geoffrey and others of his sort to suppose there was ever a king named Lud (like Lear, he may have originated as a Celtic deity) or that London was originally called "Lud's Town."

. . . that Mulmutius . . .

Cymbeline cites Britain's proud and ancient history:

Our ancestor was that Mulmutius which
Ordained our laws—

—Act III, scene i, lines 55–56

According to the legends, Mulmutius was the sixteenth King of Britain, reigning about 400 B.C., and he was the first to have established a law code. He was the son of Cloten, whose name Cymbeline's stepson bore.

Cymbeline goes on to make Mulmutius even more ancient still, by saying:

Mulmutius made our laws,
Who was the first of Britain which did put
His brows within a golden crown and called
Himself a king.

—Act III, scene i, lines 59–62

This would make Mulmutius prior to Lear, hence earlier than 800 B.C. and certainly earlier than the founding of Rome. Cymbeline may be boasting here that Britain has had kings, and therefore civilization, longer than Rome.

. . . the Pannonians and Dalmatians . . .

Cymbeline feels no real enmity to the Romans, however, despite this friction now between them. He says to the ambassador, Caius Lucius:

> *Thou art welcome, Caius.*
> *Thy Caesar knighted me; my youth I spent*
> *Much under him;*
>
> —Act III, scene i, lines 69–71

This is mentioned in Holinshed, and, of course, the Caesar referred to here is Augustus, not Julius.

While it is unlikely that Cymbeline was knighted by Augustus in anything like the medieval sense, it was customary for the Romans to hand out meaningless honors to client kings. It pleased the kings and kept them faithful to Roman interests. Cymbeline did maintain friendly relations with Rome throughout his reign, and Rome's gimcrack honors doubtlessly played a role.

In the play, though, Cymbeline does not preserve the peace but plans to continue withholding the tribute. This is not wild chauvinism; he feels he can get away with it:

> *I am perfect*
> *That the Pannonians and Dalmatians for*
> *Their liberties are now in arms, a precedent*
> *Which not to read would show the Britons cold.*
>
> —Act III, scene i, lines 73–76

The Pannonians were tribes inhabiting that section of modern Hungary west of the Danube. The Dalmatians were tribes inhabiting the interior of modern Yugoslavia. They were indeed fighting Rome.

This was Augustus' fault. He was a man of peace, no brilliant warrior like his great-uncle Julius. Having obtained rule over the entire Empire by his defeat of Mark Antony (see page I-370), his chief concern was to find some easily defensible boundary behind which the Empire could settle down to a permanent peace.

To do this he felt he had to have the broad Danube River as Rome's boundary on the north. To reach that river, Augustus had to institute a naked war of aggression against the independent tribes that still lived to the south of that river. By 9 B.C. the Roman legions had reached the Danube all along the line and it did indeed become the boundary of the Empire, a boundary that was to remain reasonably intact for four centuries.

However, the tough Pannonian and Dalmatian tribes did not accept Roman occupation easily. In the latter years of Augustus' reign, they kept rebelling and it was necessary for Roman troops to do the job over several times. As a matter of fact, it was the necessity of pacifying the frontier that kept Augustus and his successor, Tiberius, from ever dreaming of overseas adventures. For that reason, the tribes of Britain were safe whether they paid tribute or not.

It was only after the death of Tiberius that Rome's Continental boundaries were quiet enough to make feasible an invasion across the Channel and permanent occupation of Britain.

. . . in Cambria . . .

While war threatens between Rome and Britain, the maddened Posthumus can think only of revenge. He has instructed Pisanio, his loyal servant, to give Imogen a letter he has sent; a letter which will send her on a wild-goose chase. In the course of that chase, he plans to kill her.

The appalled and bewildered Pisanio gives the letter to Imogen. It tells her that Posthumus has secretly returned to a corner of Britain to see her again, despite the sentence of death hanging over him if he is found in that country. He says:

> *. . . Take notice that I am in Cambria at Milford Haven . . .*
> —Act III, scene ii, lines 43–44

"Cambria" is that portion of Britain now known as Wales. Wales did not exist by that name till well after the Anglo-Saxon invasion, four centuries after Cymbeline's time. The word "Wales" is from an Old English term meaning "foreigner."

The Welsh themselves call their land "Cymru"—that is, the land of the "Cymry" ("fellow countrymen")—and it is this Cymru which was Latinized as Cambria.

Milford Haven is an excellent harbor in the southwest corner of Wales. A town by that name now exists on the northern shore of that harbor.

The heir of Cymbeline . . .

The scene now shifts to Wales, toward which Imogen and Pisanio are traveling. There we meet an old man and two stalwart young men. It is no surprise to anyone used to romances that the two young men are the lost sons of Cymbeline, stolen as infants. The old man describes himself as a loyal British soldier who had been falsely accused of treason and convicted. His property had been taken from him and himself sent into banishment. In revenge, he tells the audience, he kidnapped the King's sons before leaving the court and had brought them up in the wilderness. He speaks of the elder:

> *This Polydore,*
> *The heir of Cymbeline and Britain, who*
> *The King his father called Guiderius . . .*

>   —Act III, scene iii, lines 86–88

He also identifies the younger:

>   *. . . the younger brother Cadwal,*
> *Once Arviragus . . .*

>   —Act III, scene iii, lines 95–96

Guiderius and Arviragus are the names of Cymbeline's sons as given in Holinshed, and Guiderius, the elder, is said to have succeeded Cymbeline. There is nothing about the kidnapping of the sons and their life as outlaws, of course; that is pure romance.

And as a matter of fact, Guiderius and Arviragus may be inventions of later legend makers anyway; concocted to fill in historical gaps.

From Roman records, we have several other names applied to Cymbeline's sons. There was Caractacus (the Latin version of the British name Caradoc), who was to fight the Romans doggedly and heroically for seven years. A second son, Togodumnus, died in battle against the Romans, and a third son, Adminius (see page II–57), was a traitor.

As for the false names given the brothers by the exiled soldier, Polydore is a Greek name, but Cadwal is Celtic enough. There was a historical man by that name (also written Caedwalla or Cadwallader). He was a Welsh war leader who defeated the English King of Northumbria in 633 and laid northern England waste in the last major offensive of the Welsh against the invading Anglo-Saxons. Cadwallader was also the name of a Welsh prince in the mid-twelfth century.

The old warrior has taken a new name for himself also:

> *Myself, Belarius, that am Morgan called,*
> *They take for natural father.*

>   —Act III, scene iii, lines 106–7

Morgan is also a Celtic name, still popular among the Welsh. Yet the best-known Morgan in Celtic legend is a woman—Morgan le Fay, the enchantress sister of King Arthur, and the malevolent cause of most of the troubles that crop up in that legend.

. . . Sinon's weeping

The scene shifts back to Pisanio and Imogen, who have now arrived in Wales. The time has come when Pisanio must either obey his master and kill Imogen, or disobey. He chooses the latter course and shows Imogen the order to kill her sent by Posthumus.

Poor Imogen is thunderstruck and fears that Posthumus' action will undermine the reputation of handsome men generally, for:

> True honest men, being heard [to speak] like false Aeneas,
> Were in his time thought false, and Sinon's weeping
> Did scandal many a holy tear . . .
> —Act III, scene iv, lines 59–61

Aeneas' falseness in connection with Dido (see page I–20) and Sinon's in connection with the Trojan horse (see page I–210) were favorite references of Shakespeare's.

Pisanio promises to send Posthumus false word that he has killed Imogen and he urges the girl to don man's disguise and remain in Milford Haven, where the Roman army will soon arrive, and perhaps Posthumus with them.

He also gives her some medicine to use in case of stomach upset. He had received the medicine early in the play from the Queen and what he doesn't know is that the Queen thought it was poison. And what the Queen doesn't know is that Cornelius, the physician, mistrusting her, didn't give her real poison but only a temporary sleeping draught.

Pisanio then returns to court to avoid suspicion in connection with Imogen's disappearance.

. . . crossed the Severn

Lucius, the Roman ambassador, accompanied by Cymbeline and the British court, is also traveling westward toward Milford Haven. Cymbeline has gone as far as he can, but sends some men along as further escort, saying:

> Leave not the worthy Lucius, good my lords,
> Till he have crossed the Severn.
> —Act III, scene v, lines 16–17

The mouth of the Severn River is at the boundary between England and Wales. It is the longest river in England, some 210 miles long. To the Romans it was the Sabrina River, and both the English name, Severn, and the Welsh name, Hafren, are versions of that.

Its chief tributary is the Avon River, which joins it from the east some twenty miles from the Severn's mouth. On the Avon, about twenty-five miles upstream from that junction, is the town of Stratford-on-Avon, a town immortalized as the place of Shakespeare's birth.

Fidele, sir . . .

Imogen, in her man's disguise, comes across the cave home of Belarius and his two supposed sons (her own full brothers). No one is there, for they are out hunting, and, very hungry, she enters and eats. The hunters return, find her eating, are struck with "his" beauty, and all are suddenly friends. (There is something very like the movie *Snow White and the Seven Dwarfs* in this scene.) The young men ask her name and she says:

> *Fidele, sir. I have a kinsman who*
> *Is bound for Italy; he embarked at Milford;*
>
> —Act III, scene vi, lines 60–61

Thus, she accounts for her westward journey. The name she chooses, Fidele, is from the Latin *fidelis* ("faithful"), thus advertising the virtue which Posthumus mistakenly denies her.

Thersites' body . . .

A brief scene makes it clear that Fidele has joined her brothers and their supposed father in an idyllic existence.

Along comes the serpent, however, in the shape of Cloten. He has forced Pisanio to tell of Imogen's whereabouts and he has conceived the clever notion of putting on Posthumus' clothes and raping Imogen while wearing them, to avenge Imogen's earlier slights of his courtship.

He encounters Guiderius (his stepbrother), however, and there is first a quarrel and then a fight. Cloten is killed and Guiderius cuts off his head and throws it in the stream.

Meanwhile, Fidele is back in the cave, suffering from a stomach upset. She takes the medicine given her by Pisanio and falls into a deathlike trance.

The brothers find her, think her dead, and are heartbroken. They must give her all due burial rites and must do the same for Cloten, who, after all, is a prince. They approach the latter task with bad grace, however, and Guiderius says, resignedly:

> *Pray you fetch him hither.*
> *Thersites' body is as good as Ajax'*
> *When neither is alive.*
>
> —Act IV, scene ii, lines 251–53

Thersites was the very symbol of the vituperative and dishonorable soldier (see page I–93), while Ajax was second only to Achilles as the Greek champion at Troy (see page I–86).

His foot Mercurial . . .

After singing dirges over the bodies and strewing flowers over them, Belarius and the brothers leave.

Imogen wakes, sees the body next to her, and judging by the clothes, thinks it is Posthumus. She says:

> *I know the shape of's leg; this is his hand,*
> *His foot Mercurial, his Martial thigh,*
> *The brawns of Hercules; but his Jovial face—*
> > —Act IV, scene ii, lines 309–11

The "foot Mercurial" in Imogen's fevered description refers to Posthumus' fleetness, since Mercury, with his winged feet, was the speedy messenger of the gods. The thigh was like that of Mars, the muscles like those of Hercules; but the face, as majestic as that of Jove (Jupiter), was gone.

She can only think that everything Pisanio had told her was a lie intended to lure the unsuspecting Posthumus into the clutches of Cloten. She shrieks at the absent Pisanio:

> *All curses madded Hecuba gave the Greeks,*
> *And mine to boot, be darted on thee!*
> > —Act IV, scene ii, lines 313–14

Hecuba, the aged Queen of the Trojans (see page I–85), was the very symbol of maddening misfortune.

Siena's brother

Meanwhile, the Roman invasion is on the way. Lucius, the Roman ambassador, asks after reinforcements from Rome and is told by a Captain:

> *. . . they come*
> *Under the conduct of bold Iachimo,*
> *Siena's brother.*
> > —Act IV, scene ii, lines 339–41

This is another switch to Renaissance Italy, for Iachimo is described as the brother of the Duke of Siena. Siena is a city 120 miles northwest of Rome. To speak of its Duke would have meaning in the Renaissance but certainly not in Augustan Rome.

Another anachronism comes immediately after when Lucius comes upon

Imogen, still cradling the headless corpse, and asks the identity of the dead body. Imogen hides the truth by answering:

> Richard du Champ.
>
> —Act IV, scene ii, line 377

This is an excellent Norman-French name, but one that did not become possible till nearly a thousand years after the time of Cymbeline.

Lucius is instantly attracted to Imogen, who is still in her disguise as the youth Fidele, and "he" enters Lucius' service as his page.

The Roman legions . . .

The war begins. A Lord reaches Cymbeline and interrupts his concern over Cloten's disappearance to tell him:

> The Roman legions, all from Gallia drawn,
> Are landed on your coast,
>
> —Act IV, scene iii, lines 24–25

Actually, there was no Roman invasion of Britain in Cymbeline's time. There was a threat of one, no more, in connection with the flight of Cymbeline's son, Adminius, to Rome (see page I–57).

Adminius requested help of Caligula (Rome's third Emperor, who, unlike the first two, was young and mad) so that he might be placed on the British throne.

In general, Rome helped those who requested such help because in this way the great city gained another puppet whose land was eventually absorbed. In this case, though, Caligula did nothing more than send an army to the Channel coast of Gaul. It seemed to him that an attempt to cross the Channel would involve risks not worth the gains, and perhaps he wasn't entirely mad at that moment. Later historians, uniformly unsympathetic to Caligula, say he told his army to gather sea shells and consider those the spoils of war.

It was after the death of both Cymbeline and Caligula that the real invasion came.

Stand, stand . . .

Posthumus has received word that Imogen has been killed and now he repents his action bitterly, even though he still thinks she has been unfaithful. To punish himself, he has come to Britain and plans to dress like a peasant and fight the Romans till he is killed.

The battle between the Romans and Britons that now begins is fought in Wales, in the near vicinity of Belarius' cave. Posthumus, in peasant disguise, beats Iachimo in single combat and disarms him. Iachimo, feeling the disgrace of being beaten by a peasant, considers it a punishment for his betrayal of Imogen and repents his action.

The battle turns against the British and Cymbeline is captured. At this moment, however, Belarius, Guiderius, and Arviragus join the fight on the British side, in a narrow lane where a few stalwart men can defy an army. Belarius cries out:

> Stand, stand! We have th'advantage of the ground.
> The lane is guarded. Nothing routs us but
> The villainy of our fears.
>
> —Act V, scene ii, lines 11–13

Posthumus, in his peasant costume, joins them. They rescue Cymbeline, hearten the fleeing Britons, and turn the tide of battle, for now Lucius and Iachimo appear and state the Romans have lost.

Apparently, Shakespeare got the idea for this bit of the play from a passage in Holinshed, concerning a Danish invasion of Scotland in 976. When the Scots army was falling back, a Scottish farmer, Hay, and his two sons defended a narrow lane in just the way Belarius and his sons are described as doing here. The Scots were heartened, and the Danes began to imagine Scottish reinforcements had arrived, so that the battle went to the Scots at last.

. . . thou Thunder-master . . .

At the end of the battle, Lucius is taken. Posthumus is also captured, claiming to be a Roman and therefore slated for execution—something he feels is deserved. In prison, however, Posthumus sleeps and dreams. In his dream, his dead family—father, mother, two brothers—all appear, protesting to Jupiter over Posthumus' undeserved miseries.

Sicilius, Posthumus' father, says:

> No more, thou Thunder-master, show thy spite on mortal flies.
> With Mars fall out, with Juno chide, that thy adulteries
> Rates and revenges.
>
> —Act V, scene iv, lines 30–32

The "Thunder-master" is Jupiter (Zeus), whose weapon is the thunderbolt. Sicilius is urging Jupiter to pick on someone his own size, and, as a matter of fact, the Greek myths are ample evidence that Jupiter did do so on occasion.

For instance, he quarrels briefly with Mars (Ares) in the *Iliad*. After Mars has been wounded by Diomedes, the war god goes complaining to Jupiter, who says, "Renegade, be off, or else stop whining! I dislike you more than all the rest of my family put together."

And, of course, Juno (Hera) is notorious for her jealousy of Jupiter's numerous illicit amours. Many myths show her scolding him for them and following his loves and their children with grim persecution (see page I-24).

Lucina . . .

Posthumus' mother wails that the gods were against her son from the beginning:

> *Lucina lent not me her aid, but took me in my throes,*
> *That from me was Posthumus ripped,*
>
> —Act V, scene iv, lines 37–38

Lucina was the Roman goddess of childbirth and was eventually considered one of the aspects of Juno, who as queen of heaven and wife of Jupiter presided over all the facets of wife- and motherhood. As a result, the goddess of childbirth was often called Juno Lucina, and Posthumus' mother is pointing out that she died in childbirth.

Jupiter himself makes an appearance and is annoyed at the complaints against his management:

> *Poor shadows of Elysium, hence, and rest*
> *Upon your never-withering banks of flow'rs.*
>
> —Act V, scene iv, lines 67–68

Elysium is the paradise of the Greek myths (see page I-13). Jupiter assures them he will take care of Posthumus:

> *Our Jovial star reigned at his birth, and in*
> *Our temple was he married.*
>
> —Act V, scene iv, lines 75–76

The "Jovial star" is the planet Jupiter, considered by astrologers to be a fortunate planet under which to be born.

Augustus lives . . .

Jupiter leaves a tablet on Posthumus' breast which remains there when the sleeper wakes. It contains a not very subtle forecast of the future. Before Posthumus can be led to the gallows, he is called before the King.

It is the last scene of the play now and that last scene becomes a series of disclosures. First, the Queen is reported dead, partly of grief over the disappearance of her son. Before dying, she confesses that she had married for power, not love, that she had planned evil against Imogen and against Cymbeline himself, hoping to make Cloten king.

Lucius next enters as a prisoner of war, but warns that one battle will not end the matter. He says:

> *Augustus lives to think on't . . .*
> —Act V, scene v, line 82

There is an echo here of a battle that Augustus *did* live to think about. While no real battle was lost by the Romans in Britain in Augustus' lifetime, one was lost in Germany. Under a rather incapable Roman general, Publius Quintilius Varus, three legions were led into the dark forests of Germany and there they were ambushed and destroyed in A.D. 9 by the German tribesmen.

No such defeat had battered down a Roman army in more than two centuries. Augustus was prostrated with grief. He could "think on't" but he could not avenge; he simply could not replace the three legions at that time without placing an unacceptable tax burden on the Empire. The story is that Augustus could only beat his head against his palace walls crying "Varus, Varus, give me back my legions!"

. . . our wonted tribute . . .

But disclosures continue, one after the other. Imogen, still as Fidele, asks where Iachimo got the diamond ring he is wearing, and Iachimo reveals the story of his vile deceit. Following this, Posthumus and Imogen are reunited (but not before Posthumus in one last misfortune strikes Imogen while she is in her disguise). The true identity of Guiderius and Arviragus is then revealed.

Even Lucius is freed and the war ends in a feast of love, for Cymbeline says to Lucius:

> *Although the victor, we submit to Caesar*
> *And to the Roman empire, promising*
> *To pay our wonted tribute . . .*
> —Act V, scene v, lines 460–62

In this way, Shakespeare makes it seem that while Britain became part of the Roman Empire, it did so by defeating the Romans and taking on the yoke voluntarily. Ridiculous, to be sure, but nothing is too ridiculous to swallow if it flatters national pride.

According to Holinshed, once Cymbeline was dead and Guiderius King, the tribute was stopped again and war began once more.

Actually, the sons of Cymbeline do seem to have been more anti-Roman than their father. At least the Romans said they were, and with a new Emperor, Claudius, at the helm, they launched an invasion in 43 under Aulus Plautius.

Some forty thousand Romans landed in southeastern England, rapidly subduing the area south of the Thames, killing off some of Cunobelinus' (Cymbeline's) sons, and leaving one, Caractacus, to carry on the fight.

Caractacus fought bravely for some years, then fled to what is now southern Wales, carrying on the fight among the hills until 51, when he was finally captured and sent to Rome as a prisoner. His family went with him and they were all well treated by Claudius, who was not at all a bad Emperor.

With this begins the history of Roman Britain, a more or less prosperous time for the island, compared with what went before and after; a time that endured for three and a half centuries.

28

The Tragedy of

HAMLET

Prince of Denmark

Read Bks to Class

ROMAN rule over Britain came to an end in 410, when the last legions left the island. Germanic tribes were tearing at the western provinces of the Empire and Roman soldiers could no longer be supported in Britain.

Before the end of the century, pagan Germanic tribes—Jutes, Saxons, and Angles, from what is now the North Sea coast of Germany and Denmark—invaded the eastern and southern coasts of Britain. For two centuries they fought the Celts, and little by little, Britain, the island of such legendary kings as Lear and such dimly historical ones as Cymbeline, was converted into Anglo-Saxon England.

England never made up all the island, however. The northern third came to be known as Scotland, and this retained much of the original Celtic flavor, despite cultural infiltration from the south. The western peninsula of Wales also remained Celtic, and, in fact, remained independent till the thirteenth century.

By 600 England had reached almost its present extent, and the next four and a half centuries—till the crucial year of 1066, when the island fell to Norman conquerors from across the Channel—makes up the period of Anglo-Saxon England.

Two of Shakespeare's plays are set late in this period, but in neither case is the setting in England itself. Rather, the plays are set just beyond the English borders in lands intimately connected with England.

The events in the two plays are roughly contemporary, but one is considerably less historical than the other, and we will consider that less historical one first.

That play is *Hamlet,* which, by all odds, is Shakespeare's best known and most popular play. Its scene we know from the title itself, when that is given in full: *The Tragedy of Hamlet, Prince of Denmark*. In the play, Denmark is pictured as a martial and imperial nation.

This is strange to us, to whom Denmark is the epitome of the peaceful, civilized little state that minds its own business, does not annoy its neighbors, and has achieved a kind of society that is very largely stable, healthy, and pacific.

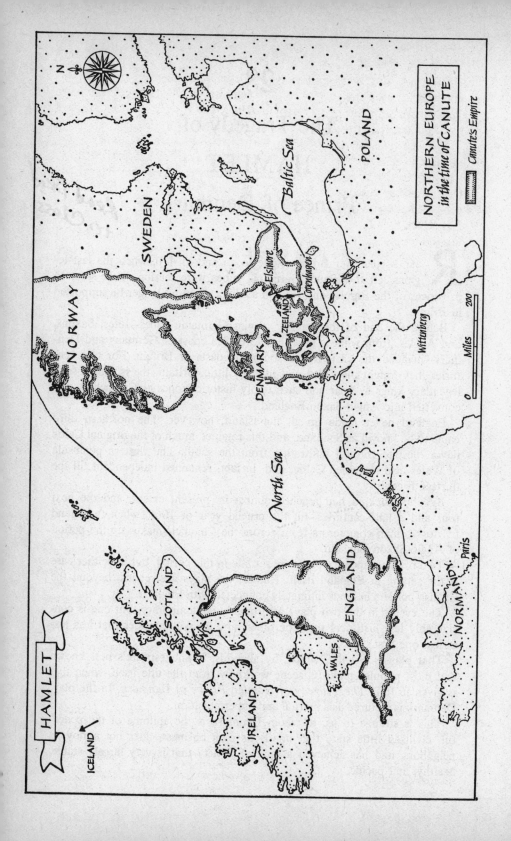

HAMLET

ICELAND

NORWAY

SWEDEN

SCOTLAND

IRELAND

WALES

ENGLAND

NORMANDY

Paris

North Sea

DENMARK

ZEELAND

Elsinore

Copenhagen

Baltic Sea

POLAND

Wittenberg

N

0   200

Miles

NORTHERN EUROPE
in the time of CANUTE

Canute's Empire

And indeed, the recent history of Denmark is most peaceful. It was involved in the Napoleonic wars, it fought against Prussia and Austria in 1864, it was invaded by Germany in 1940, but in every case its role was strictly defensive. It was a victim, not a participant.

The last time Denmark deliberately entered a war of her own accord, in the role of aggressor, was in 1700. In that year its king, Frederick IV, who had just ascended the throne the year before, joined with Poland and Russia against Sweden. Sweden was then ruled by the half-mad military genius Charles XII, who was only eighteen years old at the time. Charles XII struck like lightning and Denmark was out of the war, neatly defeated, in a matter of a few months. Never again did she attack a neighbor.

But Shakespeare wrote *Hamlet* about 1600 or 1601, at which time Denmark was still an imperial nation. From Copenhagen, the Danish King, who at the time was Christian IV, ruled not only over Denmark, but over certain German duchies to Denmark's south, over all of Norway and portions of what is now southern Sweden, and even over such polar islands as Iceland and Greenland. It had not been long before that that Denmark had ruled all Sweden; Sweden had not gained complete independence until 1523.

Nor is it the Denmark of Shakespeare's time that appears in *Hamlet*— but a far older Denmark, even bloodier and more threatening and aggressive.

Denmark had entered European history about 800, when it, along with Norway, was the home base of Viking raiders who made life hell for the inhabitants of the British Isles and the Frankish kingdoms on the Continent.

About 950 Denmark began to succumb to Christianity, but that did not, at first, soften its imperialism much. Its aggressions began to take on a national character, however, and to be more than the feats of freebooting pirates. One of its first great kings, Sven I (called Forked-beard, because he wore one), established Danish rule over Norway, reduced Sweden to impotence, and invaded England. He died almost immediately after the initial success of his English invasion, but under his son Canute the Danish Empire reached its height. From 1014 to 1035 Canute was supreme in northern Europe.

After Canute's death, England broke away (though ruled for a few years by his sons), but Denmark continued its expansionist policies in other directions.

The history of Denmark, Norway, and Sweden during the Viking period before the time of Sven I is shrouded in darkness. We have nothing but legendary material within which we have the usual difficulty in picking out kernels of truth, and in which we scarcely know how to recognize a kernel of truth even if we come across one.

The legendary material reaches us in a book written about 1200 by a Danish historian, Saxo Grammaticus, whose history of Denmark comes down to 1186. It is a Danish analogue of such British histories as that of Geoffrey of Monmouth (see page II–3), and gives an account of some sixty legendary Danish kings, some of whom can be equated with mythical Norse gods.

Included in Saxo Grammaticus' tales is a bloody one concerning a prince he called Amlethus. It includes a dead father and a usurping uncle, and Amlethus must feign madness while plotting a revenge he finally achieves.

There is no sign whatever of any historical basis of the story, and it may have had its origin in dim tales of Viking feuds. Nevertheless, Saxo Grammaticus was close to the greatest imperial period of Danish history, and the atmosphere of Canute's empire seems to have crept into his version of the old legendary tale.

At least, as the tale worked its way through the centuries, ending at last in Shakespeare's *Hamlet,* the flavor of the period of Canute still lingered, so that while *Hamlet* contains not one clearly historical character or event, comparisons can still be made with actual events in the eleventh century, and we might set the time of *Hamlet* as 1050.

Who's there

The play opens on the battlements of a gloomy castle, where, from the start, an atmosphere of uneasy brooding is established. Two sentries approach each other and each is nervous and suspicious. One of them, Barnardo, on hearing the other's footsteps, is all tension at once and calls out:

> *Who's there?*
>
> *a play set in Denmark?*
>
> —Act I, scene i, line 1

But the other, Francisco (here is an example of Shakespeare's penchant for Italian or Roman names even under the most inappropriate circumstances), is just as suspicious, and demands:

> *Nay, answer me. Stand and unfold yourself.*
>
> —Act I, scene i, line 2

The castle is that of the King of Denmark and is located in Elsinore. This town, known to the Danes themselves as Helsingør, is located in the northeast corner of the island of Sjaelland (Zealand in the English spelling).

Sjaelland is an island of respectable size, being about as large as Rhode Island and Delaware put together, and is located in the Baltic Sea between continental Denmark and Sweden. Indeed, Elsinore is at the point of closest approach to Sweden. The strait separating it from the Swedish city of Hälsingborg is only three miles wide.

The island of Sjaelland is the core of Denmark for all that it is not part of the continent. Over one fourth of the Danes live on this island, and its present capital (and largest city), Copenhagen, is located on it. Copenhagen is on the eastern shore of the island, about twenty-five miles south of Elsinore, and is also on the eastern limit of Danish dominion. To the east, it is separated by fifteen miles of water from the important Swedish city of Malmö.

It may seem odd that Denmark's capital is at the easternmost border of the nation, for generally (though not always) a capital city is centrally located. This, however, is usually true when the city is founded, and tradition may keep it in the same location even after the changes of history place it in a strongly eccentric position. (Thus, when Washington, D.C., was made the American capital in 1800, it was centrally located as far as the original thirteen states were concerned, but now that the United States has grown westward, it is located far on the nation's eastern edge.)

Copenhagen was established as Denmark's capital about 1170. (This, by the way, fits the 1050 date of the play's events. The court is at Elsinore because Copenhagen is not yet the capital.) In those centuries both Elsinore and Copenhagen were centrally located, for southernmost Sweden was in Danish hands, so that the island of Sjaelland lay between *two* pieces of continental Denmark. In fact, southernmost Sweden was still part of Denmark in Shakespeare's time and was not given up by Denmark till 1658, nearly half a century after Shakespeare's death.

The actual setting visualized by Shakespeare seems to have been Kronborg Castle in Elsinore. This was by no means an ancient edifice in his time. It had been constructed in 1580, only twenty years before *Hamlet* was written, by Frederick II, the father of the Danish King reigning at the time of writing.

The castle still stands and Shakespeare's play has made it world-famous. In fact, *Hamlet* is played in its courtyard occasionally.

. . . like the king . . .

It is midnight and Francisco, having been relieved, exits. Another sentry, Marcellus, with a friend, Horatio, joins Barnardo, and the three gather round, talking in whispers.

The cause of the nervousness appears at once. Barnardo and Marcellus have seen a Ghost and are trying to convince the skeptical Horatio of the fact. The task is not hard, for they have barely begun when the Ghost appears again.

It is important, even crucial, to think of the Ghost not as we think of ghosts generally, but as the men of Shakespeare's time thought of them. We are all familiar with the play (even in the unlikely case that we have never read it or seen it), and we think of the apparition as "the ghost of Hamlet's father."

But it was no such thing to the Elizabethan audience. The Ghost is a spirit that can take on any shape for any purpose. The most that can be said is that it *looks* like Hamlet's father, that it has taken on the *shape* of Hamlet's father. What it *really* is, no one can say.

Shakespeare makes that plain at every step. When it appears to the three men, Barnardo describes it as:

> *In the same figure like the king that's dead.*
>
> —Act I, scene i, line 41

Then, nudging Horatio, who's staring openmouthed, he says:

> *Looks 'a not like the king?*
>
> —Act I, scene i, line 43

Then, when Horatio finally finds his tongue and (as the best-educated of the three) addresses the Ghost in stately syllables, he says the same thing in more complicated fashion:

> *What art thou that usurp'st this time of night,*
> *Together with that fair and warlike form*
> *In which the majesty of buried Denmark*
> *Did sometimes march?*
>
> —Act I, scene i, lines 46–49

"Usurp" is to take without right. The Ghost was a supernatural visitation and by ordinary natural law the place and time should have been free of it. In that sense, it usurped the time of night, and, in addition, it usurped the appearance of the dead King. Horatio seems to feel that it is not really the ghost of the dead King but merely a spirit who assumes that appearance for purposes of its own. In fact, Horatio is questioning the spirit as to its real identity.

If we don't understand this clearly, then we don't really understand the play.

. . . the ambitious Norway . . .

The Ghost disappears without speaking, and the three men, badly shaken, marvel over the accuracy of its likeness. Horatio says:

> *Such was the very armor he had on*
> *When he the ambitious Norway combated:*
> *So frowned he once, when, in an angry parle,*
> *He smote the sledded Polacks on the ice.*
>
> —Act I, scene i, lines 60–63

Norway had indeed been part of the Danish Empire of Sven and Canute, and it is tempting to see in the martial deeds ascribed to the dead King a reflection of those historical Danish conquerors.

As for Poland, the land of the "sledded Polacks," it emerged as a nation in the tenth century under Miszko I, who ruled from 960 to 992. Under his successor Boleslav I, a contemporary of Sven and Canute, Poland even became an expansionist nation, conquering eastern Pomerania on the south Baltic coast. Northward across the Baltic was the southern coast of Sweden, which was then Danish territory. Poland and Denmark were thus neighbors.

After the death of Boleslav in 1025, the tide of Polish conquest receded. In 1031 Canute took eastern Pomerania from Poland, so that the reference to smiting the Polacks reflects history accurately enough.

But "on the ice"? A battle of Poles and Danes in eastern Pomerania need not be on the ice, but it is interesting to speculate that perhaps Shakespeare had heard of such a battle in the east.

Denmark in the generations following Canute had carried on wars against the eastern pagans (a kind of crusade), and a century later this task was taken over by the Germans. The armed German bands, known as the "Teutonic Knights," formed about 1200 and gradually took over the southern shores of the Baltic Sea, displacing the Danes. By 1237 they controlled the lands we now speak of as Estonia, Latvia, and Lithuania (which, since 1940, have been part of the Soviet Union).

From this as their base they planned to expand eastward into the Russian lands themselves, for those were being thrown into utter ruin by the irresistible advance of the Mongols. Only the lands of Novgorod in northwestern Russia had remained free of direct Mongol domination (at the price of heavy tribute), and it was Novgorod that adjoined the new dominions of the Teutonic Knights.

At that time, Novgorod was led by Prince Alexander. In 1240 he defeated the Swedes on the Neva River (near the site of modern Leningrad) and gained the name of Alexander Nevski as a result. In April 1242 he met an army of invading Teutonic Knights on the melting ice of Lake Peipus, which now lies on the boundary between Estonia and Russia. The ice broke under the heavily armored German horsemen and their army was destroyed. The Russians won an overwhelming victory and put a final term to the eastward ambitions of the Teutonic Knights.

This, the most famous battle on the ice in history, was between Germans and Russians, rather than between Danes and Poles, and it had been a victory for the Eastern power, not the Western, but it is the picture that inevitably arises in connection with the passage quoted above.

. . . young Fortinbras

Horatio goes on to wonder if perhaps the ghostly visitation is an omen of troubled times to come. One can see his reasoning. The old King had conquered the Norwegians (as Sven and Canute had in actual history), but there was a movement afoot among the Norwegians to break free again (as there had been in actual history, by the time of Canute's death in 1035).

Horatio describes the present situation:

> *Now, sir, young Fortinbras*
> *Of unimprovèd mettle hot and full,*
> *Hath in the skirts of Norway here and there*
> *Sharked up a list of lawless resolutes,*
> *For food and diet, to some enterprise*
> *That hath a stomach in't; which is no other,*
> *As it doth well appear unto our state,*
> *But to recover of us by strong hand*
> *And terms compulsatory, those foresaid lands*
> *So by his father lost;*
>
> —Act I, scene i, lines 95–104

The King of Norway, whom the old King of Denmark had defeated, was named Fortinbras. It was his son, also named Fortinbras, who was trying to reverse the earlier decision, now that the old Danish King had died. There is no historical King of Norway by the name of Fortinbras. The name is French and means "strong-in-arm." It was customary for the early Scandinavian kings to be known by some distinguishing characteristic. There was Sven Forked-beard himself, for instance, and his father was Harold Bluetooth. There was also an Eric Bloodaxe, a Harold Hardrada ("severe ruler"), and so on. A king with the surname of Strong-in-arm isn't so farfetched.

In actual history, though, Canute of Denmark had taken Norway from Olaf II. Olaf had accepted Christianity and had worked to ensure the general conversion of the Norwegians. As a result he is known as Olaf the Saint, having been canonized in 1164, and is the patron saint of Norway. But he was defeated by Canute anyway and died in a final battle in 1030.

In 1035, after Canute's death, the son of Olaf did indeed try to regain Norway. The son's name was Magnus.

. . . *the mightiest Julius* . . .

Barnardo agrees that this may be the significance of the Ghost. It portends war for Denmark and it wears the form of the old King as a way of foretelling that war—the war brought on in response to that King's conquests.

Horatio concurs in this analysis of the situation and draws an analogy from history:

In the most high and palmy state of Rome,
A little ere the mightiest Julius fell,
The graves stood tenantless, and the sheeted dead
Did squeak and gibber in the Roman streets;
—Act I, scene i, lines 113–16

This is a reference to the legends that arose concerning the night before the assassination of Julius Caesar. Shakespeare had used those legends in his play *Julius Caesar* (see page I–273), which he had written a year before *Hamlet*.

Horatio refers not only to ghostly manifestations, but to more normal astronomical ones in connection with the assassination, for he goes on to say:

. . . *the moist star,* Moon
Upon whose influence Neptune's empire stands,
Was sick almost to doomsday with eclipse.
—Act I, scene i, lines 118–20

The "moist star" is the moon, which is neither a star nor moist. In ancient times, however, the term "star" could be used for any shining heavenly object, and Shakespeare, as always, is steeped in ancient learning and is oblivious to the new astronomy burgeoning in his day. The moon is "moist" not in itself but in that it affects the oceans ("Neptune's empire"). The moon causes the tides, in other words.

There was, however, no lunar eclipse on the night before the assassination. Caesar's

. . . *the trumpet to the morn*

The Ghost momentarily returns and again Horatio speaks to it, attempting to persuade it to reveal something of the country's fate that it might be useful to know. It is about to speak when the sound of a cockcrow is heard and it disappears. Horatio says:

I have heard,
The cock, that is the trumpet to the morn,
Doth with his lofty and shrill-sounding throat
Awake the god of day, and at his warning,
Whether in sea or fire, in earth or air,
Th'extravagant and erring spirit hies
To his confine;

a well-known superstition

—Act I, scene i, lines 149–55

This is a well-known superstition and, like many superstitions, makes most sense when it is taken in context. Before modern times, the night was without the glaring artificial illumination that destroys it today; it was dark indeed. In that darkness, it was easy to imagine supernatural visitations, when every dead tree might be a monster and any vanishing owl a ghost. Since these sights were not seen by day, it could well be reasoned that ghosts and spirits vanished with the onset of day.

Then, prior to modern times, the mechanical clock did not exist and the periods of nighttime could be distinguished only crudely. It was enough to be able to divide the night into three or four "watches" (a word taken from the practice of leaving sentries on watch, each taking part of the night in turn). For instance, we might speak of the early portion of the night, the middle portion, the later portion, and then the actual coming of the morning.

Naturally, men would be anxious for morning, especially in the long winter nights, and would welcome any sure sign of its approach. The crow of the rooster would be a sign early seized on and it could be used to mark the latest portion of the night. Thus, in the Bible, when it is described how all-unknown the time of the Second Coming is, the watches of the night are mentioned: "Watch ye therefore: for ye know not when the master of the house cometh, at even, or at midnight, or at the cockcrowing, or in the morning" (Mark 13:35).

And if spirits vanish with the day, the crowing cock is a natural signal for them. Within its context it all makes sense.

In fact, Marcellus offers a refinement of the legend by stating that on Christmas Eve the cock crows all night long so that no spirit dare budge abroad. Horatio is the epitome of rationality (he doesn't actually say the cock's crow is a signal for spirits to depart; he merely says "I have heard" it was so) and now he replies courteously, but cautiously, to Marcellus' eager credulity:

> So have I heard and do in part believe it.
> —Act I, scene i, line 165

But it is morning and Horatio suggests that this matter of the Ghost be imparted to Prince Hamlet. If the Ghost takes on the appearance of the old King, he may be most willing to speak to that old King's son.

. . . our dear brother's death

With this first mention of Prince Hamlet, the hero of the play, the scene shifts to the court, where the new King and his Queen sit. The King speaks and at once describes the situation:

Though yet of Hamlet our dear brother's death
The memory be green . . .

—Act I, scene ii, lines 1–2

The old King's name had been Hamlet. Father and son were named alike here in Denmark, as in Norway. To distinguish them I will refer to the old King as the "elder Hamlet."

The reigning King of Denmark, who has succeeded the elder Hamlet, and who now speaks, is Claudius. Shakespeare has chosen an aristocratic Roman name for the purpose. (It was the name of a patrician family in the time of the Republic and one from which several of the early emperors were descended—including Claudius, the fourth Emperor, under whom Britain was conquered in the years following Cymbeline's death.)

In Saxo Grammaticus' original tale, the new King was named Feng, and perhaps Shakespeare did well to change that.

Apparently, from these first words of Claudius, the elder Hamlet has died quite recently, and the new King is the elder Hamlet's brother. (The word "brother" might be used in a general sense, indicating merely a close relative, an associate, or a good friend, but in this case, the play makes it clear enough that the new King is actually the younger brother, in the strictest sense of the word, of the old.)

One point which the play does not make clear is why the younger brother succeeded to the throne rather than the elder Hamlet's son. We are used to thinking, these days, that a dead king is automatically succeeded by his oldest son, but the notion of automatic succession according to strict order of family connection is a rather recent notion, and prevails in a rather restricted portion of the world. Modern audiences can easily be confused by this and lose some of the significance of the play.

In many parts of the world, and in Europe too, in the early Middle Ages the king was generally chosen from the royal family but not necessarily according to any strict order of relationship. It was more important to select a mature member of the family, skilled in war and leadership, than to choose the most nearly direct descendant. In that era of short life and violent death, it was common for a dead king to be survived by an infant son who could not possibly be the kind of king a nation needed in a barbaric age. A younger brother of the dead king was a much more logical choice.

Of course, when the young prince grew to maturity he might well consider himself to have a reasonable right to the throne and he might choose to fight for it. The king (uncle to the prince) might be well aware of this possibility and might choose to have the young child put out of the way in one manner or another—execution, imprisonment, banishment. This sort of thing happened frequently enough to make the "wicked uncle" a kind of stock character in adventure stories, second only to the "wicked stepmother."

The Elizabethan audience would know this well. The notion of legitimacy in English and French history had brought on wars and civil wars. The notion of the "wicked uncle" was also well known, for among the English kings, John had been a wicked uncle to the "rightful king," the young Arthur of Brittany, and Richard III had been a wicked uncle to the "rightful king," the young Edward V. Both events had been immortalized in plays Shakespeare had already written: *King John* and *Richard III*.

The Elizabethan audience would therefore well understand that a king's brother might succeed to the throne to the exclusion of the king's son. They would also understand quite well, without being told, that the son would be in mortal danger. Shakespeare did not have to explain this, and since he doesn't and times have changed, modern audiences may be insufficiently aware of this point.

. . . now our Queen

Generally, though, the son who is excluded from the throne is quite young—like the twelve-year-old Arthur of Brittany, or the thirteen-year-old Edward V. The excluded Prince Hamlet, however, is not a child at all. Why, then, did he fail to succeed? That point is never made explicitly clear —but we can guess. Claudius goes on to say:

> . . . *our sometime sister, now our Queen,*
> *Th'imperial jointress to this warlike state,*
> *Have we, as 'twere, with a defeated joy,*
> *With an auspicious and a dropping eye,*
> *With mirth in funeral, and with dirge in marriage,*
> *In equal scale weighing delight and dole,*
> *Taken to wife.*

> —Act I, scene ii, lines 8–14

The elder Hamlet's wife, Gertrude, (Prince Hamlet's mother) has married the new King, her erstwhile brother-in-law.

This has significance. It is a practical act of statecraft. Where a succession is not utterly undisputed, it can be bolstered by any connection with a previous reign, particularly where the previous reign was popular or well established. A new king might pretend he was the adopted son of the old king, or he might marry the old king's daughter. Or he might marry the old king's wife, assuming she were still young enough to beget an heir. (In that age of early and common death in childbirth, there was a considerable turnover in royal wives and surviving queens were often quite young.)

In the original story, as given by Saxo Grammaticus, the brother-successor marries the queen of the brother-predecessor, and in the time Saxo was writing, this would have been a rather ordinary thing to do. In fact, we can cite a case in actual history that involves Canute, whose historical existence hovers so over the background events in *Hamlet*.

When Canute became England's King in 1016, he barred the throne to the young sons of the earlier native king, Ethelred II. To lend an air of continuity to the government and to reconcile the English somewhat to the existence of a Danish king, Canute therefore married Emma, the widow of Ethelred.

This is not to say that the tale of Ethelred, Canute, and Emma directly influenced Shakespeare, or even Saxo Grammaticus, but it is the sort of thing that went on in the eleventh century. What seems to us a kind of involuted and upsetting family relationship was not at all uncommon in the time in which the play is set and seemed less uncommon to Elizabethan audiences, who were closer to that time, than to ourselves.

To Norway . . .

Having announced the succession and the marriage (for the benefit of the audience), King Claudius turns to matters of state. He sends two messengers, Cornelius and Voltemand, to Norway with a message. He says:

> *. . . we have here writ*
> *To Norway, uncle of young Fortinbras—*
> *Who, impotent and bedrid, scarcely hears*
> *Of this his nephew's purpose—to suppress*
> *His further gait herein . . .*
>
> —Act I, scene ii, lines 27–31

[handwritten margin note:] Norway analogous to Denmark

The situation in Norway is curiously analogous to that in Denmark. In Norway, the elder Fortinbras has been succeeded by a younger brother (not named), as in Denmark the elder Hamlet has been succeeded by a younger brother, Claudius. In Norway, a son of the older brother, named like his father, Fortinbras, is excluded from the succession, while in Denmark, a son of the older brother, named like his father, Hamlet, is also excluded from the succession. The younger Fortinbras, however, is occupying himself in foreign wars, while the younger Hamlet will have a different part to play.

. . . to thy father

Claudius then turns to Laertes, the son of a valued courtier. (Here we have a Greek name, for Laertes, in the Greek legends, is the name of the father of Ulysses.) King Claudius knows that Laertes has some request and he urges him to speak freely without fear of being denied. He says:

The head is not more native to the heart,
The hand more instrumental to the mouth,
Than is the throne of Denmark to thy father.

—Act I, scene ii, lines 47–49

This extravagant expression of affection for Laertes' father (who, as it turns out, is named Polonius) is odd. There is nothing in the play that justifies it directly. Polonius is presented as a tedious old bore who is always wrong and whose advice, when followed, leads to disaster. Why, then, should the shrewd Claudius value him so highly?

The logical presumption is that Polonius had been of great use to Claudius in matters of which we are not told; perhaps in helping the new King gain his throne. Did he maneuver the nobles into supporting the brother rather than the son? Did he persuade the widowed Queen to marry her brother-in-law? We can only guess.

If anything like this is true, though, it would explain the strong dislike that Prince Hamlet holds for the old courtier; a dislike that is otherwise not easily explained.

The Elizabethan audience, much more accustomed to the intrigues of royal succession than we are, might be expected to catch on to this sort of thing as a matter of course.

. . . return to France

Laertes' request is a simple one. He has been abroad, being educated. He returned, as a loyal subject, to attend the coronation, but now that that is done he asks:

My dread lord,
Your leave and favor to return to France,

—Act I, scene ii, lines 50–51

anachronism

The University of Paris was the most famous educational institution of western Europe in the later Middle Ages and it is to be assumed that that is where Laertes was being educated. To be sure, it had its formal beginnings only about 1150 at the earliest—a full century after the time suggested for *Hamlet,* but that is a minor anachronism as Shakespearean anachronisms go.

. . . thy nighted color . . .

Claudius grants permission to Laertes and next turns to the figure who until now has maintained himself as a somber, silent reproach on the gay spectacle, for he is clad in garb of deepest mourning.

The Elizabethan audience does not need to be told that between King Claudius and Prince Hamlet there can only be enmity, that the very existence of one is a deadly danger to the other. They address each other with freezing, calculated politeness.

The Queen throws herself between. Her name is Gertrude and that, at least, is Teutonic and is a form of Saxo Grammaticus' original "Gerutha." She is wife to one and mother to the other and loves each. She urges friendship, saying to her son:

> Good Hamlet, cast thy nighted color off,
> And let thine eye look like a friend on Denmark.
>
> —Act I, scene ii, lines 68–69

A modern audience might be appalled by her insensitivity. Young Hamlet had loved his father and was wearing mourning in his memory. Not much time had passed since the father's death; how could she urge him to remove it?

Well, to be sure, Gertrude is not very bright. She shows herself throughout the play to be a rather shallow person, not very clear on what is going on and unaware of the consequences of her actions.

Still, there might be more. The royal marriage had interrupted the mourning and there comes a time when an ostentatious reminder of the old King becomes an insult to the new. Hamlet is the natural opponent of the succession and if he continues to wear mourning it is clear enough that he feels there is no joy in the new King. It amounts almost to a claim for the throne on his own behalf. All of this would be plain to Claudius and to the Elizabethan audience (wise in the ways of disputed succession) as well.

Gertrude, sure that this open enmity is bound to lead to the death of either husband or son, or both, sees no way out but to urge her son to put off his mourning.

. . . the most immediate to our throne

Hamlet insists on the mourning, describing it in terms of deep grief for his father and thus, by implication, disowning any political significance.

Claudius, we may well suspect, doesn't believe this at all. He joins his voice to urge the end of the mourning costume and even offers a bribe:

> . . . think of us
> As of a father, for let the world take note
> You are the most immediate to our throne.
>
> —Act I, scene ii, lines 107–9

He clearly and openly declares Hamlet as his heir. If, then, Hamlet will allow Claudius to reign quietly, he may count on the succession next time round. The point is, though, can Claudius be believed? Hamlet makes it plain enough, as the play goes on, that in his opinion Claudius cannot.

. . . school in Wittenberg

Claudius combines the carrot with a touch of the stick. Like Laertes, Hamlet has been out of the country, receiving an education. Unlike Laertes, he is not to be allowed to return, for Claudius says:

> For your intent
> In going back to school in Wittenberg,
> It is most retrograde to our desire,
> And we beseech you, bend you to remain
> Here in the cheer and comfort of our eye,
>
> —Act I, scene ii, lines 112–16

It sounds like love, but almost anyone could see through that. Once outside the country, Hamlet may intrigue, gain foreign allies, raise armies. At court, he will be in sight of his suspicious uncle and stepfather, and in his grasp too.

An education at Wittenberg is much more anachronistic than one at Paris. Wittenberg is a German city about fifty-five miles southwest of Berlin and a little over three hundred miles south of Elsinore. The University of Wittenberg, where, presumably, Hamlet has been studying, was not founded till 1502.

City and university grew famous because in 1508, only six years after its founding, a young monk, Martin Luther, was called to teach in it and accepted. It was there that Luther evolved the tenets of what is now called Lutheranism. It was to the doors of a church in Wittenberg that in 1517 he nailed his list of ninety-five theses on which he challenged debate, an act which initiated the Protestant Reformation.

The University of Wittenberg became the intellectual center of Lutheranism, and, in a way, this makes it fitting that Hamlet is being educated there, for the Denmark of Shakespeare's day (in common with the rest of Scandinavia) turned Lutheran. The Reformation was introduced into Denmark under the royal sponsorship of King Christian III in 1536.

This passage might also be helpful in explaining something about the succession. After all, Prince Hamlet is not too young to be king and he is (as is explained on two occasions later in the play) popular with the people. Why was he passed over?

One answer is that he was not there; he was not on the spot when the succession was decided. The elder Hamlet had, as is made plain later in the play, died quite suddenly and unexpectedly, and Prince Hamlet was far away in Wittenberg at the time. The news of his father's death would have had to reach the Prince (and we can imagine that Claudius would have done what he could to delay it) and then the Prince would have had to make his way to Elsinore.

It would all take time, and when he arrived, he found the succession settled—against him.

Hyperion to a satyr

The Queen adds her pleas to the King's, asking Hamlet to stay at court. Hamlet, under no illusions, knowing that if he does not stay voluntarily he will be kept by force, grants a cold and formal obedience, which the King accepts with a fulsomeness that can easily be considered sarcastic.

The court departs and Hamlet is left alone to vent his rage. He finds the new King a completely unworthy successor to the old. He compares the two in extreme terms, saying of his father:

> So excellent a king, that was to this
> Hyperion to a satyr,
> —Act I, scene ii, lines 139–40

Hyperion was the Titan god of the sun (see page I–11). A satyr was a fertility spirit of the woodlands, with the horns, hoofs, and hindquarters of a goat. The reference to the satyr is significant since the most remarkable property of the satyr in the legends was (as is befitting his position as a fertility spirit) his insatiable sexual desire.

We may assume that Hamlet is scarcely objective here. He hates Claudius and can see no good in him, but nothing we see of Claudius in the play *directly* matches Hamlet's low opinion. In fact, if we accept Hamlet's estimate of Claudius, the play loses much of its point.

Like Niobe, all tears . . .

But Hamlet is angry with his mother as well. She had seemed so in love with his father, had mourned so at his death—

> . . . she followed my poor father's body
> Like Niobe, all tears . . .
> —Act I, scene ii, lines 148–49

Niobe was one of the more pathetic characters in Greek myth. She had six sons and six daughters and boasted her superiority to the goddess Latona (Leto), who had only one son and one daughter. Of course, Latona's children happened to be the god Apollo and the goddess Diana (see page I–130), and they avenged the slur on their mother by shooting down Niobe's children with their divine arrows. Niobe wept endlessly at their deaths until, in belated compassion, the gods turned her into stone—a stone which still welled water.

A little month . . .

Hamlet is angered at the fact that his mother has married again, and we can understand that. It is very common to have a child consider a dead parent betrayed when the surviving parent marries again. We need not think it was such an unlikely thing to happen, though, just because Hamlet thinks the new husband so inferior to the old. It is quite possible that Gertrude, still beautiful, might have thought quite differently.

The elder Hamlet was a warlike king with all the martial virtues, and there is nothing in the play to cause one to suspect that he was not far more at home in a suit of armor than in the marriage bed. Claudius, as a "satyr," may very well have been a much better lover than the elder Hamlet, and much more adept at flattering and pleasing shallow Gertrude too. It is easy indeed to suppose that Gertrude was sure she had made a better bargain the second time round.

What is most significant, though, is to pay attention to just what it is that bothers Hamlet about the marriage. He says:

> . . . within a month—
> Let me not think on't; frailty, thy name is woman—
> A little month . . .
>
> —Act I, scene ii, lines 145–47

He's angry also at the fact that it was the marriage of a sister-in-law and brother-in-law. This was incestuous, according to the strict rules of the church in such matters. However, state reasons often made it necessary for royalty to make marriages that would be considered incestuous under ordinary conditions, and the church was usually indulgent in such cases.

Yet even in the matter of incest, what bothers Hamlet is another aspect of it:

> . . . O, most wicked speed, to post
> With such dexterity to incestuous sheets!
>
> —Act I, scene ii, lines 156–57

It is the *haste* with which the marriage took place, the rapidity. That's what bothers him really, for he comes back to it again and again.

Now, this preoccupation of Hamlet with the wickedness of his mother's marriage is taken by many critics to signify Hamlet's unconscious love for his mother. They find a Freudian explanation for the events of the play and think Hamlet is striking at Claudius in resentment at the stranger entering his mother's bed.

This theory falls apart if we remember that it is not the marriage itself that bothers Hamlet most, but its *haste*. What does the haste signify?

Just this. We can imagine Hamlet spurring madly toward Elsinore from Wittenberg, anxious to arrive there in time to put in his claim for the throne. And when he gets there, perhaps merely a matter of a couple of weeks after his father's death, he finds that Claudius has already announced his forthcoming marriage to Gertrude and that this marriage, with the feeling of continuity it provides to the previous reign, is all that is needed to sway the support of the nobility (whose voice is crucial in choosing the king) toward Claudius.

Had Gertrude waited, Hamlet would have been there and probably gained the throne. After that, she would probably have been free to marry Claudius, if she had so desired, with no complaint or objection from Hamlet.

It had not been the marriage, then, that had foiled Hamlet, but the *haste* of it. When he arrived, he found he could do nothing but accept the verdict and attend the actual marriage—and wear mourning as a gesture of defiance.

And if the marriage had been arranged in haste by Polonius, that would be more than enough to explain Hamlet's attitude toward the old courtier.

Would not Gertrude have realized that by her act she was excluding her son from the throne? Perhaps not. One can imagine that she would be flattered at being so desired by the new King and perhaps pleased with the thought of remaining Queen (she could not have remained Queen if her son became King, but only Queen Mother, which is not the same thing at all) and, on top of that, it may never have occurred to her that her son would be annoyed. After all, he would still be next in line to the throne, wouldn't he?

But Hamlet would most certainly be annoyed, and horribly annoyed too. We have evidence for that from the history of Canute.

When Canute married Emma, the widow of the previous King, that action excluded Emma's children from the succession. Indeed, after Canute's death, his own children inherited (one of them Emma's) to the exclusion of the older children by the previous marriage. Seven years after Canute's death, one of those older children finally succeeded to the throne in 1042. He was Edward the Confessor.

Edward, as his name implies, was a pious king, and was, in fact, eventually sainted. He was mild and gentle and yet he managed to work up a profound dislike for the mother who had kept him from the throne. Once he became King he placed his mother in a nunnery and, what's more, kept her there the rest of her life.

Shouldn't Hamlet, who is precisely in the Confessor's position, and who is no saint, also feel most unkindly toward his mother's action? What need of an Oedipus complex, then? It is not unconscious love that explains his actions, but a very conscious and reasonable hate.

Perchance 'twill walk . . .

To cap off Hamlet's depression over the manner in which he has lost the succession is his feeling that he is boxed in; there is nothing he can do to change the situation. He says:

> But break my heart, for I must hold my tongue.
>> —Act I, scene ii, line 159

And it is precisely at this moment of despair that Horatio, Marcellus, and Barnardo enter. Hamlet is astonished to see Horatio, a schoolmate from Wittenberg, but as soon as the amenities are over, Horatio retails the news of the Ghost to Hamlet.

Hamlet is thunderstruck, questions them carefully, with his agile mind working at top speed. Finally, he agrees to come to the battlements, saying:

> I will watch tonight.
> Perchance 'twill walk again.
>> —Act I, scene ii, lines 242–43

(This reminds one of a piece of theatrical slang. "The ghost walks" means that salaries are about to be paid. One tale to account for the origin of the phrase involves an actor who was playing the Ghost in a production of *Hamlet*. Displeased with the lack of pay, he went on strike and refused, at the last moment, to do his bit. The harassed manager was forced to hand over immediate payment and the word went out: "The ghost walks.")

Hamlet's mood changes from despair to one of keenly watchful waiting. What the Ghost signifies he cannot say, but any change is bound to give him an opening. He says:

> All is not well.
> I doubt some foul play. Would the night were come!
> Till then sit still, my soul.
>> —Act I, scene ii, lines 255–57

. . . his will is not his own

The scene now shifts to the house of Polonius, the courtier. Laertes, his son, is making ready for his journey to Paris. With him is his sister, Ophelia, with whom, apparently, Hamlet is in love. (The reasons for Hamlet's dislike for Polonius must be deep indeed, considering that the old man is the father of his beloved Ophelia.)

Laertes warns his sister not to take Hamlet too seriously. Even if the prince is sincere in his affection, he may be helpless to do anything about it. He explains:

> *His greatness weighed, his will is not his own.*
> *For he himself is subject to his birth.*
> *He may not, as unvalued persons do,*
> *Carve for himself; for on his choice depends*
> *The safety and health of this whole state;*
> *And therefore must his choice be circumscribed*
> —Act I, scene iii, lines 17–22

This is a careful explanation of something Ophelia ought surely to understand, and of something, for that matter, that the Elizabethan audience could well take for granted.

Yet what then? Does it not apply to a King's marriage as much as to a Prince's? Is this not an indication that the marriage of Claudius and Gertrude, however much a love match it might be, was first and foremost a matter of state? And if so, is it reasonable to suppose that Hamlet, however noble a stance he may take with regard to the marriage, is not aware of the state reason for it—and most resentfully.

. . . a borrower nor a lender . . .

In comes Polonius to send his son off with a very well-known set of sententious maxims that Laertes bears with admirable patience, and which includes literature's greatest gift to the small of heart, for Polonius says, among other things:

> *Neither a borrower nor a lender be,*
> *For loan oft loses both itself and friend,*
> *And borrowing dulls the edge of husbandry* [thrift].
> —Act I, scene iii, lines 75–77

How many skinflints who know not one other verse in Shakespeare are letter-perfect in this, to use at the first sign of another's need!

When Laertes has gone, Polonius questions Ophelia as to her brother's words. Ophelia, a submissive daughter, admits they concerned Hamlet, whereupon Polonius independently warns her against the Prince and orders her to withdraw from him.

More honored in the breach . . .

It is night again, and now Hamlet has joined Horatio and Marcellus on the battlements. While they wait, there is the sound of trumpets and cannon, and Horatio, startled, asks the significance. Either Horatio is not a native Dane or he has been too long abroad, for Hamlet must explain that the King is feasting and that every time he drinks, trumpets, drums, and cannon make their joyful noise in celebration. It is a custom, Hamlet says, and goes on to say:

> *But to my mind, though I am native here*
> *And to the manner born, it is a custom*
> *More honored in the breach than the observance.*
> *This heavy-headed revel east and west*
> *Makes us traduced and taxed of other nations.*
> *They clepe [call] us drunkards . . .*
>
> —Act I, scene iv, lines 14–19

The phrase "more honored in the breach than the observance" means Hamlet considers it more honorable to break the custom than to keep it. He disapproves of the King's revelry apparently out of a general dislike for drinking bouts and out of a determined distaste for anything Claudius does.

It is important to notice that Hamlet refers to Danes generally as earning a reputation for drunkenness and not to Claudius specifically. It is common in productions of *Hamlet* to show Claudius as half drunk much of the time, but this is utterly unfair and spoils the significance of many of the events in the play.

There is nothing in what we see of Claudius in the play to make us think he is a drunkard. Rather, he is shown always as a shrewd and careful monarch, an opponent who taxes Hamlet to the full.

. . . goblin damned

And now the Ghost makes its appearance once again. Hamlet is staggered, but nevertheless advances boldly, saying:

Be thou a spirit of health or goblin damned,
Bring with thee airs from heaven or blasts from hell,
Be thy intents wicked or charitable,
Thou com'st in such a questionable shape
That I will speak to thee. I'll call thee Hamlet,
King, father, royal Dane. O, answer me!

—Act I, scene iv, lines 40–45

It is clear that Hamlet himself hasn't the slightest idea of the real nature of the apparition. It could be anything. All he knows is that the thing, whatever it is, has assumed the shape of his father, and because of that he will speak to it and accept that shape if that will make it speak to him in turn. He does not say the Ghost *is* his father. He says "I'll *call* thee Hamlet."

The Ghost beckons Hamlet away as though to some place where they can talk privately, and Horatio is in agony over that. He too is uncertain over the nature of the Ghost and says to Hamlet:

What if it tempt you toward the flood, my lord,
Or to the dreadful summit of the cliff
That beetles o'er his base into the sea,
And there assume some other horrible form,
Which might deprive your sovereignty of reason
And draw you into madness?

—Act I, scene iv, lines 69–74

But Hamlet will not be held back. Perhaps he is thinking that whatever the Ghost's intentions, the chance that something will come of it that will offer him a way out of checkmate is worth the risk. He says:

My fate cries out
And makes each petty artery in this body
As hardy as the Nemean lion's nerve.

—Act I, scene iv, lines 81–83

(The reference is to the beast whose slaying represented the first labor of Hercules. It was an enormous lion of superstrength that infested the valley of Nemea, see page I-58.)

Hamlet breaks away, dashing after the Ghost, and the others can only toil after while Marcellus says in mournful words that have become a common part of the language:

Something is rotten in the state of Denmark.

—Act I, scene iv, line 90

. . . sweep to my revenge

Alone with Hamlet on the battlements, the Ghost finally speaks, and identifies itself as being what it appears to be:

> *I am thy father's spirit*
>
> —Act I, scene v, line 9

He then goes on to say what it is he has come for, what it is he wants of Hamlet. Speaking of himself in the third person, he says:

> *Revenge his foul and most unnatural murder.*
>
> —Act I, scene v, line 25

Hamlet, horrified, demands the details, saying:

> *Haste me to know't, that I, with wings as swift*
> *As meditation or the thoughts of love,*
> *May sweep to my revenge.*
>
> —Act I, scene v, lines 29–31

This is the first indication that *Hamlet* is, in essence, a play about revenge. In its earliest form, as a tale sung by bards and dealing with crime and revenge among the Vikings, there could have been little subtlety about it. A ruler is killed and the son of the dead man manages to kill the murderer. The accent would be on heroic feats of arms, the son fighting against odds.

By the time of Saxo Grammaticus, the son must use cunning, but there is still no mystery. The murder is open and known.

In the 1580s a version of *Hamlet*, earlier than Shakespeare's, appeared on the English stage. It is forever lost and we know of it only through casual references. The author of this *Ur-Hamlet* (the prefix is German and means "early" or "original") may have been Thomas Kyd, who died in 1595 at the age of only twenty-eight.

Kyd had a penchant for melodrama and for tragedies in the style of Seneca (see page I-270). His most popular play, *The Spanish Tragedy*, was published in 1594 and had ghosts in it which permeated and spurred on a tale of revenge. If Kyd wrote *Ur-Hamlet* too, it may have been the play on which he sharpened his teeth for the later *Spanish Tragedy*. It was in that *Ur-Hamlet* that the Ghost was introduced and where the original murder had to be made secret and hidden, or there would have been nothing for the Ghost to reveal.

This product of Kyd's youth must have been terribly overdone. What references we have to it speak of it contemptuously as a piece of blood and bombast. The English dramatist Thomas Lodge wrote in 1596 of a ghost crying like an oysterwife, "Hamlet, revenge!"

Shakespeare kept the Ghost and the revenge motif but must have added enormous subtleties that the *Ur-Hamlet* did not have.

Notice that at this first mention of revenge, Hamlet (a fiery and impulsive individual who seems irresolute only to those who, in my opinion, miss the point of the play) at once promises to achieve it as swiftly as thought. He will find that he cannot, and one point made by the play is that revenge is difficult, and that *useful* revenge may be impossible.

. . . that adulterate beast

The Ghost now tells its story. The official tale of the elder Hamlet's death was that he had been stung by a serpent. The Ghost says, however:

> *But know, thou noble youth,*
> *The serpent that did sting thy father's life*
> *Now wears his crown.*
> —Act I, scene v, lines 38–40

It is Claudius, then, who is the murderer—the wicked uncle. The Ghost makes that specific and says:

> *Ay, that incestuous, that adulterate beast,*
> *With witchcraft of his wits, with traitorous gifts—*
> *O wicked wit and gifts, that have the power*
> *So to seduce!—won to his shameful lust*
> *The will of my most seeming-virtuous queen.*
> —Act I, scene v, lines 42–46

The Ghost speaks not only of incest but of adultery as well. And indeed, in 1576 a French writer, François de Belleforest, wrote a version of the Hamlet story from the Saxo Grammaticus original in which Gertrude commits adultery with Claudius while the elder Hamlet is still alive. The same implication is present here in this passage and in a few other places in the play. For the most part, though, Shakespeare ignores this matter and is intent on keeping the duel entirely between Claudius and Hamlet.

Indeed, the Ghost goes out of its way to keep Gertrude out of it. He says:

> *Taint not thy mind, nor let thy soul contrive*
> *Against thy mother aught. Leave her to heaven*

> *And to those thorns that in her bosom lodge*
> *To prick and sting her.*

> —Act I, scene v, lines 85–88

The Ghost cannot explain why Gertrude should have preferred Claudius to the elder Hamlet, except through sheer perversity. He says:

> *. . . lust, though to a radiant angel linked,*
> *Will sate itself in a celestial bed*
> *And prey on garbage.*

> —Act I, scene vi, lines 55–57

I can't help but think that this is intended to be ironic and that properly played (except that it would interfere with the intention of the scene) should elicit at least a snicker. The Ghost of the elder Hamlet is describing himself as a radiant angel and we may be excused for suspecting him of lack of objectivity. As for Claudius being "garbage," he at least possessed "witchcraft of his wits." A charming, laughing, witty younger brother may be garbage to an older brother who imagines himself to be a radiant angel—but that same younger brother can look pretty good to a frustrated woman.

> *. . . one may smile, and smile . . .*

But dawn is coming and the Ghost must leave. Hamlet is left alone to plan the revenge. Shakespeare doesn't give us the line of thought in full detail but we can speculate on what it might be—taking into account what follows.

To begin with, Hamlet does not in the least doubt the Ghost, at least not at that moment. It is fair to suppose that the Ghost spoke in such a way as to convince Hamlet completely that it was indeed the spirit of his father speaking. Hamlet says as much to Horatio shortly afterward:

> *Touching this vision here,*
> *It is an honest ghost, that let me tell you.*

> —Act I, scene v, lines 137–38

Nor does Hamlet doubt that Claudius killed his father. He has ample reason to hate Claudius for having seized the succession from under his own nose and he needs little persuasion to believe anything evil about him. In fact, when the Ghost first reveals Claudius as the murderer, Hamlet breaks out:

O my prophetic soul!

My uncle?

—Act I, scene v, lines 40–41

He had the feeling! He knew it all along!

But if Hamlet is sure the Ghost is truthful, and if he is sure his uncle has indeed murdered his father, and if he has promised revenge swift as thought— Why doesn't he do it?

Why doesn't he seize some opportunity, when he is close to his uncle, or when he can maneuver himself close, to out with a dagger and bring him down?

It is the question one always asks about Hamlet. He is pictured as irresolute, as a man who thinks but cannot act, and very complicated reasons (sometimes involutedly Freudian) are presented as explanations.

But I don't think the reasons are complicated at all. If Hamlet wants only revenge for the sake of revenge; if he wants only to pay back his father's murderer at whatever cost to himself; then, yes, execute Claudius as soon as the King's body is within reach of his dagger.

That, however, is not all that Hamlet wants (if we go by any of a dozen little hints in the play). He wants also to be King. If he were to stab Claudius under conditions that would lead to his own immediate seizure and execution at the hands of horrified soldiers and courtiers, that would not suit him at all. Even if he managed to kill Claudius and get away whole, how could he then persuade the Danish nobility to make him King?

One cannot openly kill one's way to the throne. Perhaps one could in Viking times, but not in Shakespeare's. Even Claudius did not succeed by open murder. He killed the elder Hamlet secretly, and those who then made him King (including, presumably, Gertrude) did not know of the murder.

Hamlet can undoubtedly drive the King off the throne and secure his own succession if he can reveal the truth about his father's death. He could then kill Claudius, or have him executed, and do so most righteously. Even if he kills Claudius first, he might excuse the deed and gain the throne if he can reveal Claudius to have been a regicide and himself to be an avenger rather than a murderer.

But how can he do that? How can he prove Claudius to be a murderer?

Hamlet has no evidence of the murder except what the Ghost has told him, and who would believe that? That the Ghost exists at all would be backed by the word of three common soldiers, whom no one would believe, and Horatio, whose word *would* carry weight. But who would bear witness as to what the Ghost had said? No one. The Ghost had spoken only to Hamlet and no one else had heard the tale. And who could bear witness that the Ghost is an honest one and not an evil, lying spirit? No one again. Hamlet could say so, but he is an interested party.

Now if Claudius were a drunken boor, an inefficient king, a dark tyrant, the question might not arise. The court might be so pleased at having gotten rid of him that they would accept any tale, however unlikely, as a cover to make the murder seem a righteous execution.

But it is the very nub of the matter that Claudius is a *popular* king. He has the gift of charm, by the Ghost's own admission, and could win Gertrude by that gift. He is shown to us throughout the play as a capable and intelligent king and, except for what he has had to do to get and keep the crown, even a likable one. Later in the play, to be specific, he wins over Laertes at a dangerous moment by a display of courage and intelligence, mingled with his charm.

Can such a king be killed and can that murder be excused through some cock-and-bull story told by a ghost?

If it is thoughts like these that go through Hamlet's mind, he must recognize that he cannot kill Claudius outright and gain the throne, simply because Claudius *seems* to be such a pleasant and likable fellow. And it is here that the thoughts I have been postulating must reach the surface, for Hamlet says, in frustration:

> *O villain, villain, smiling, damnèd villain!*
> *My tables—meet it is I set it down*
> *That one may smile, and smile, and be a villain.*
>
> —Act I, scene v, lines 106–8

Claudius is a villain and should be killed, but he is a smiling villain and therefore dangerous to kill. (Without some sort of analysis following Hamlet's line of thought in this fashion, the passage about the "smiling, damnèd villain" sounds like a non sequitur.)

Hamlet grimly writes the thought down for emphasis. He knows himself. He is not the irresolute Hamlet so many of us imagine; he is the impulsive, overeager Hamlet he shows himself to be on several occasions in the play. He makes a notation to impress the fact on his own mind that he must *not* be overhasty—not if he wants the throne.

. . . more things in heaven and earth . . .

What Hamlet needs is time—time to work out what to do and to do it so cautiously as not to raise the suspicions of Claudius. Furthermore, he has a new appreciation of his own dangers. Claudius might object to Hamlet merely on the ground that Hamlet has a grievance, and that produces danger enough for the young Prince. But if Claudius is a murderer and expects the Prince to become an avenging demon if he ever finds out, he must be ten times as suspicious, ten times as uneasy, and Hamlet's life is therefore ten times as insecure.

Horatio and Marcellus finally come up to Hamlet after the Ghost is gone, and for a while the Prince speaks almost at random—his mind is desperately working out expedients and he must keep off his friends with only an un-occupied part of it, so to speak.

Once he has sorted matters out, however, he moves rapidly. First, he swears Horatio and Marcellus to secrecy. Obviously, if Claudius discovers that Hamlet has been in conversation with the Ghost of his dead father, he will know that Hamlet has learned the truth and will strike out at once.

The rational Horatio swears, but still finds it very difficult to believe what is happening. Hamlet dismisses those doubts with a most famous pair of lines, saying:

> There are more things in heaven and earth, Horatio,
> Than are dreamt of in your philosophy.
> > —Act I, scene v, lines 166–67

"Your philosophy" (where "your" does not refer to Horatio personally, but is used as an impersonal pronoun) is, in this case, what we would now call "science." (The word "science" did not come to be used in its modern sense till the nineteenth century.)

These two lines have been used for three and a half centuries to beat down what has been conceived to be scientific dogmatism and have usually been so used by mystics of one sort or another.

Nevertheless, scientists are perfectly aware of the truth of these lines—without it there would, in fact, be no need for scientific research—and search humbly for just those things that might as yet be undreamed of. It is the mystics who, for their part, do not search but think they "know"—by revelation, intuition, or other non-rational fashion—and it is they who are usually the arrogant ones.

. . . an antic disposition . . .

Hamlet has bethought himself now of the necessary delaying tactic. He makes Horatio and Marcellus swear never to refer to what has just occurred, no matter how Hamlet himself acts. Hamlet warns them that his own actions may seem odd:

> (As I perchance hereafter shall think meet
> To put an antic disposition on),
> > —Act I, scene v, lines 171–72

There is no reason to speculate as to whether Hamlet was *really* mad or only pretending. Of course, he was pretending. He says so. Nor is there any mystery as to why he was pretending. It was an extremely sensible thing to do, if we remember to interpret the event not in accordance with the prejudices of our time, or even Shakespeare's, but of the considerably earlier time of Saxo Grammaticus' chronicle, from which Shakespeare inherited the madness.

In pagan times a madman was thought to be touched with the divine (see page II–16) and was respected and even feared a little. If Hamlet were mad, any action which in a sane man might have seemed a suspicious move against Claudius' safety might be dismissed as a senseless antic. Furthermore, Claudius would find it difficult to take any action against a mad Hamlet under any circumstances, for the gods would then be displeased and evil might befall the entire nation.

We might wonder if Shakespeare could get away with a device that belonged in pagan times. (In Christian times madmen were thought to be possessed by malevolent evil as a punishment for sin, and far from being sacrosanct, were sometimes tormented most hideously.) Undoubtedly he could, for there was one well-known instance of just such a strategy in what Shakespeare and the men of his time considered sober history. This was the case of Lucius Junius Brutus, who in the time of King Tarquin pretended to suffer from a harmless form of madness (see page I–210) to keep himself from being executed by the suspicious tyrant. Then, when the time came, Brutus threw off the mask and helped establish the Roman Republic.

It is for this reason that Hamlet feels he has to play mad—to gain time and security so that he might devise some plan to make himself king.

Naturally, all this would be a hard job. Hamlet would not relish the role of madman; nor did he see any easy way of handling the shrewd and popular Claudius. He says, gloomily:

> The time is out of joint. O cursed spite,
> That ever I was born to set it right!

> —Act I, scene v, lines 188–89

. . . the very ecstasy of love

Some time elapses between the first and second act, and during that interval Hamlet apparently labors to establish himself as a madman. The act must be complete, for he can trust no one but Horatio (and perhaps not even him, were it not that he had been part of the affair with the Ghost).

In particular, Hamlet must beware of Ophelia, not for her own sake (for she is quite an artless girl, no more shrewd and worldly-wise than Queen Gertrude), but because her father is Claudius' closest adviser and because she herself is completely under her father's thumb. What's more, Hamlet is really in love with the girl and therefore particularly vulnerable there. It is easy to reason in this way that Hamlet must establish himself as mad to Ophelia most of all—and this is exactly what he does.

The scene is not presented onstage and we see it only through Ophelia's eyes when she runs to her father to describe Hamlet's deliberately mad behavior when he seeks her out. Polonius instantly reaches the wrong conclusion. He blames it on the fact that he had ordered Ophelia to be less friendly with Hamlet and that Hamlet had reacted desperately. He says:

> Come, go with me. I will go seek the King.
> This is the very ecstasy of love,
>
> —Act II, scene i, lines 101–2

. . . aught to us unknown . . .

Claudius has, of course, also been shown ample signs of Hamlet's madness, but he is no fool. Next to Hamlet himself, Claudius is the most intelligent individual in the play, and he doesn't believe the madness. It is easy to guess from the events in the play that he suspects the madness to be exactly what it is, a ruse behind which some plot against himself can be matured.

But Claudius needs evidence of that. It isn't generally pointed out that Claudius' predicament in this play is exactly that of Hamlet. Hamlet wants to kill the King, but the King wants to kill Hamlet. Neither is safe as long as the other is alive. But the King, as well as Hamlet, cannot take the simple road and simply kill. The King is but new on the throne and can scarcely yet feel secure; to kill the son of the preceding King would easily raise enough hostility against himself to hurl him from the throne. Just as Hamlet needs to do more than merely kill the King, but must gain the throne too, so the King needs to do more than merely kill Hamlet, but must keep the throne too.

Claudius needs an excuse to hallow the murder (just as Hamlet does). If Claudius can show that Hamlet is merely pretending madness as a cover for treason, he will be able to execute Hamlet safely—just as, if Hamlet can prove that Claudius killed his brother, and Hamlet's father, he will be able to kill Claudius safely.

We must not look upon the play as a case of Hamlet stalking the King—but as one of Hamlet and the King stalking each other. The suspense arises out of the question of which one will find an opening first.

In the second scene of the second act, Claudius is looking for the opening most strenuously. He has a perfectly innocent reason for endeavoring to investigate Hamlet's madness, since it is only natural that a loving stepfather would search out means of helping a dear stepson.

To this end, he calls to court Rosencrantz and Guildenstern, who are also students at Wittenberg and, like Horatio, good friends of the Prince. Claudius explains the fact of Hamlet's madness and urges them:

> . . . by your companies
> To draw him on to pleasures, and to gather
> So much as from occasion you may glean,
> Where aught to us unknown afflicts him thus,
> That opened lies within our remedy.

> —Act II, scene ii, lines 14–18

There is a chance, after all, that Hamlet, if he is only pretending as Claudius thinks, may be sufficiently off his guard to reveal his plans to his old schoolmates and try to get them to join his party. At the very least, he may reveal himself to be not mad. Even the admission of pretense, without anything more, would give color to the theory of conspiracy.

Rosencrantz and Guildenstern agree to serve as spies. We may reasonably assume that they are not novices at court intrigue and that they may guess, even without Claudius having told them so specifically, that Hamlet is in a position to aspire to the throne and that Claudius wants this aspiration nipped. This they are presumably most eager to do, for if they are useful to the King in so secret a matter so closely touching him, they may well be rewarded most handsomely.

Hamlet himself, toward the close of the play, at a time when Rosencrantz and Guildenstern are on the point of coming to a bad end, refuses to show any regret for them, though it is he who has manipulated that bad end. He says:

> Why, man, they did make love to this employment.
> They are not near my conscience . . .

> —Act V, scene ii, lines 57–58

. . . well ended

The ambassadors from Norway return (another indication of the time lapse between Act I and Act II) and that crisis at least is over. The King of Norway has forced young Fortinbras to end his projected war against Denmark. Fortinbras will march against Poland instead and seeks safe-conduct through Denmark.

Polonius comments on the results:

> This business is well ended.

> —Act II, scene ii, line 85

This does show Claudius as an efficient and capable king. In the crisis with Norway, he has prepared busily for war yet he has not neglected diplomacy, and has managed that with such skill and address as to achieve his ends without a shot fired or a man lost.

There is no reason that we can see why anyone in Denmark should hate him except Hamlet—which is exactly what makes Hamlet's task so difficult.

. . . I'll loose my daughter . . .

But now Polonius approaches the King on the subject that really affects the latter most. In fact, when Polonius announces the arrival of the ambassadors and also says that he has discovered the cause of Hamlet's lunacy, the King instantly leaps on the second:

> *O, speak of that! That do I long to hear.*
> —Act II, scene ii, line 50

He recognizes Hamlet as a far more immediate danger to himself than Norway is. Polonius, of course, insists on the ambassadors first, since he is far too dull to understand the King's alarm, and the King must give way.

Even after the ambassadors are dismissed, Polonius approaches the matter of Hamlet only with incredible long-windedness. The Queen is irritated, but the King, who must be in an absolute agony of impatience, nevertheless endures it with his unfailing charm.

Finally, Polonius comes out with his theory that Hamlet has gone mad for love.

Claudius is horribly disappointed, surely, that Polonius has come up with this, for he is certain that something much more important must be hiding behind the madness. Yet he can't jump without evidence. All he can do is gently express his doubts. He says:

> *Do you think 'tis this?*
> —Act II, scene ii, line 151

When Polonius is volubly certain it is, Claudius says, patiently:

> *How may we try it further?*
> —Act II, scene ii, line 159

Polonius has a suggestion at once. Hamlet has the habit of walking in the room in which they then are. Polonius offers to take advantage of the habit:

At such a time I'll loose my daughter to him.
Be you and I behind an arras then.
Mark the encounter.

—Act II, scene ii, lines 162–64

The King agrees. After all, Hamlet may be off his guard with Ophelia and may reveal what the King wants revealed whether Polonius' theory is right or not.

. . . method in't

Hamlet comes walking in at this point, reading. There is nothing in the play which specifically indicates he has overheard anything at this point, but it helps to make sense of what follows if we suppose he becomes aware of Polonius' plan. It makes sense to suppose that as Claudius and Polonius are earnestly talking, Hamlet approaches the entrance to the room, overhears them, listens, and does not actually enter until they are done talking.

Once Hamlet enters, Polonius volunteers to tackle him on the spot, for Polonius has a great opinion of his own shrewdness.

Hamlet, on the other hand, has a great dislike for Polonius (for possible reasons I have mentioned earlier), and if he has overheard the old man's plan to use his daughter as a tool, he can scarcely fail to dislike him even more.

Hamlet therefore engages in a grim duel with Polonius. Hamlet's words seem, on the surface, to mirror madness, and yet there is an inner consistency to them that puzzles Polonius.

Hamlet can scarcely enjoy his role as madman and it must give him some relief to be able to stab at his enemies under the cover of that madness, while they, in turn, so concentrate on the madness that they scarcely realize they are being stabbed.

Thus, Hamlet makes veiled references to Polonius' daughter, saying abruptly:

Let her not walk i'th'sun.

—Act II, scene ii, line 185

Whatever meanings may be attached to the warning—and Hamlet himself follows it with a ribald warning—it might also be taken to imply a plea that Polonius not use the girl as bait. If we accept the possibility that Hamlet has overheard Polonius' plan, it may well be that he wishes to spare Ophelia the hurt he must otherwise do her.

Naturally, Polonius is quite blind to this and Hamlet goes on to describe what is contained in the book he is reading:

. . . the satirical rogue says here that old men have gray

*beards, that their faces are wrinkled, their eyes purging thick
amber and plum-tree gum, and that they have a plentiful lack
of wit . . .*

—Act II, scene ii, lines 198–201

It is impossible to doubt that this is aimed at Polonius directly. It would
seem a despairing groan at Polonius' folly (his "plentiful lack of wit") in
persisting in using his poor daughter as a weapon.

Polonius, utterly confused by words that seem mad and yet seem to
have some meaning he doesn't quite grasp, makes the famous remark:

Though this be madness, yet there is method in't.

—Act II, scene ii, lines 207–8

. . . your ambition . . .

When Polonius, foiled, leaves, Rosencrantz and Guildenstern enter.
Hamlet is unfeignedly delighted to see them, and almost at once, they begin a kind of collegiate wordplay.

Then Hamlet, unable to hide his bitterness and perhaps not entirely on
his guard with schoolmates, refers to Denmark as a prison. When Rosencrantz denies it, Hamlet says:

*Why, then, 'tis none to you, for there is nothing either good or
bad but thinking makes it so. To me it is a prison.*

—Act II, scene ii, lines 256–57

Rosencrantz sees his opening. So far there would seem no madness in
Hamlet and his discontent with Denmark can mean only one thing. It is
only necessary to get him to state it. He says:

*Why then your ambition makes it one. 'Tis too narrow for
your mind.*

—Act II, scene ii, lines 256–57

But of course the clever Hamlet is not the man to be maneuvered so
easily. We might argue that the word "ambition" is a red flag to him. Instantly, he shifts in the direction of madness, countering the accusation that
Denmark is "too narrow" for him with a bit of bathos:

*O God, I could be bounded in a nutshell and count myself a
king of infinite space, were it not that I have bad dreams.*

—Act II, scene ii, lines 258–60

If the false friends had let that go, Hamlet might have been lulled into security, but Guildenstern presses the matter eagerly, saying:

> *Which dreams indeed are ambition . . .*
>
> —Act II, scene ii, line 261

By the needless repetition of the word, Hamlet suspects exactly what they are after and how they came to Denmark. He forces them to admit that they have been sent for by the King. Once that is clear, their last chance of discovering anything from him is gone.

. . . Hercules and his load . . .

But Rosencrantz and Guildenstern have news to give too. A party of actors is arriving at Elsinore to amuse the court, and Hamlet is very interested. Partly this helps to display Hamlet as the Renaissance man, interested in everything, capable at everything, and partly it is Shakespeare's chance to make some "in comments" on the theatrical world of his time. Thus, at one point, Hamlet asks:

> *Do the boys carry it away?*
>
> —Act II, scene ii, line 368

This refers to companies of child actors, who were becoming popular and offering serious competition to the adult actors. Rosencrantz answers:

> *Ay, that they do, my lord—Hercules and his load too.*
>
> —Act II, scene ii, lines 369–70

In the course of his eleventh labor—getting the golden apples of the Hesperides—Hercules enlisted the aid of Atlas, the giant Titan who held up the sky (see page I–336). Atlas actually obtained the apples while Hercules temporarily relieved him of his load. In later years, when Atlas was visualized as supporting the earth rather than the sky on his shoulder, it was natural to think of Hercules as relieving Atlas of that load.

Rosencrantz's remark can be taken as a metaphorical way of showing how completely the boys "carry it away."

On the other hand, the Globe Theatre, in which Shakespeare's plays were being presented at the time *Hamlet* was being written, had as its sign a picture of Hercules supporting the globe of the earth (hence "Globe Theatre"), and Rosencrantz's remark may also be an oblique reference to the fact that even the Globe Theatre is not immune to the inroads of the new fashions.

. . . Roscius was an actor . . .

Polonius now enters once more with the news of the actual arrival of the players. Hamlet, who had been acting sane enough when the drama was being discussed, at once shifts into madman full gear. He begins a mad chatter about actors:

> *When Roscius was an actor in Rome—*
> —Act II, scene ii, lines 399–400

Quintus Roscius was a famous comic actor in Rome in the first century B.C. Cicero himself did not feel it beneath him to take lessons in elocution and delivery from the actor. When Roscius was sued for a large sum in 76 B.C., Cicero defended him with a speech that became famous. Roscius was even raised to a rank roughly equivalent to the British knighthood by Sulla, who was dictator of Rome from 82 to 79 B.C.

Polonius ignores Hamlet and plows on bravely in his praise of the actors who have arrived. They are so versatile, he says, that:

> *Seneca cannot be too heavy, nor Plautus too light.*
> —Act II, scene ii, lines 409–10

Seneca (see page I–270) was the writer of blood-and-thunder tragedies. Titus Maccius Plautus, on the other hand, of the third century B.C., was the Roman master of bawdy slapstick comedy. One can't help but wonder if Shakespeare might not have been slipping in a bit of praise for his own versatility, for he had himself written plays in both the style of Seneca at his heaviest (*Titus Andronicus*) and Plautus at his lightest (*The Comedy of Errors*).

O Jeptha . . .

Hamlet responds, mockingly, with a scrap of what seems to be a well-known ballad of Shakespeare's time:

> *O Jeptha, judge of Israel, what a treasure hadst thou!*
> —Act II, scene ii, lines 412–13

The reference is to Jephthah, a military leader ("judge") of an Israelite army. During a battle against the Ammonites, he swore to sacrifice the first living thing that emerged to greet him on his return home, if the battle were won. He gained the victory and when he returned, out came his daughter to greet him. He kept his vow and had her killed on the altar (Judges 11:30–40).

It is a horrible story and, perhaps because of its horror, has always been a favorite tale from the Bible.

Hamlet, it would seem, is bitterly mocking Polonius, who would sacrifice his own daughter in his foolish attempt to catch Hamlet.

When Hamlet sings a few more lines to the effect that Jephthah loved his only daughter, Polonius admits the comparison by saying that he too has a daughter he loves, and Hamlet answers, grimly:

> *Nay, that follows not.*

> —Act II, scene ii, line 422

This whole colloquy makes sense best if we assume that Hamlet has indeed overheard the plan of the King and Polonius. He implies that Polonius cannot really love his daughter if he is going to use her as a degraded pawn against the man she loves.

. . . the hellish Pyrrhus

But Hamlet has an idea now; an idea that must have come to him the instant he heard the actors were coming to Elsinore. He knows them well; he is a connoisseur of the drama; and he knows they were once capable enough for his purposes. But time has passed. Are they still as skillful as he remembers them to be?

He must test them. He demands one of them recite a speech, therefore; a speech that will require much emotion and even suggests the one he wants. It is taken from a play in which Aeneas is telling Dido (see page I-20) of the fall of Troy. This in itself gives room for much emotion, and Hamlet suggests the most tear-jerking episode of all—the death of old King Priam (see page I-209). Hamlet identifies the speech by reciting an early passage himself, ending with:

> *With eyes like carbuncles, the hellish Pyrrhus*
> *Old grandsire Priam seeks.*

> —Act II, scene ii, lines 474–75

Pyrrhus, the son of Achilles (see page I-115), is associated with the most atrocious events of the sack.

The Player takes up the speech, spending some thirty lines on the description of the killing of Priam. Polonius very rightly interrupts:

> *This is too long.*

> —Act II, scene ii, line 509

But Hamlet, in an agony of impatience, cuts him off. He is not interested in the speech itself, but in the quality of its execution. He says:

. . . Say on; come to Hecuba.

—Act II, scene ii, line 512

Hecuba, the wife of Priam, goes through almost unimaginable misfortune in the course of the Trojan debacle (see page I–398).

The actor goes on to recite lines concerning the unfortunate queen, and Polonius remarks in wonder that the actor has actually begun to affect himself in self-induced agony.

> *Look, whe'r* [whether] *he has not turned his color, and has tears in's eyes.*

—Act II, scene ii, lines 530–31

O, vengeance

Hamlet's pretense of madness and his long wait for the moment when he might act must surely be in the highest degree frustrating. Far from being the irresolute person he is usually supposed to be, he seems to have the greatest difficulty controlling himself. When the players leave and he is alone on the stage, that control wavers. He is bitter that an actor can allow himself to weep over Hecuba's long-dead woes, whereas Hamlet himself must dissemble and do nothing more than play mad while his uncle keeps the winnings.

He berates himself in a rising crescendo of self-accusation:

> *Am I a coward?*
> *Who calls me villain? Breaks my pate across?*
> *Plucks off my beard and blows it in my face?*
> *Tweaks me by the nose? Gives me the lie i'th'throat*
> *As deep as to the lungs? Who does me this?*
> *Ha, 'swounds, I should take it, for it cannot be*
> *But I am pigeon-livered and lack gall*
> *To make oppression bitter, or ere this*
> *I should ha' fatted all the region kites*
> *With this slave's offal. Bloody, bawdy villain!*
> *Remorseless, treacherous, lecherous, kindless villain!*
> *O, vengeance!*

—Act II, scene ii, lines 582–93

The play's the thing

But at the last moment, in that wild cry for vengeance, he grasps at himself and steadies. There is a pause and he says quietly:

Why, what an ass am I!

—Act II, scene ii, line 594

It is back to business. He needs evidence, evidence that does not depend upon the uncertain word of a mysterious Ghost, evidence clear and open to all; and it may be that the necessary material is at hand. Hamlet mutters to himself:

> *About, my brains.*
> *Hum—*
> *I have heard that guilty creatures sitting at a play*
> *Have by the very cunning of the scene*
> *Been struck so to the soul that presently*
> *They have proclaimed their malefactions.*

—Act II, scene ii, lines 599–604

Hamlet may well be thinking of the Greek tale concerning the cranes of Ibycus (see page I–198), when murderers did cry out their guilt under the emotional pressures of a moving play. And Hamlet has already prepared just such a situation. Having made certain that the Player could deliver a speech movingly, he arranged to have a particular play, *The Murder of Gonzago,* presented, then said to the Player:

> *You could for a need study a speech of some dozen or sixteen*
> *lines which I would set down and insert in't, could you not?*

—Act II, scene ii, lines 550–53

The device will serve a secondary purpose too. Hamlet is still troubled occasionally by a certain perfunctory doubt concerning the Ghost. His ambition forces him to believe and yet he is intelligent enough to know he may be helping to deceive himself. He says:

> *The spirit that I have seen*
> *May be a devil, and the devil hath power*
> *T'assume a pleasing shape . . .*

—Act II, scene ii, lines 610–12

For both reasons then—to satisfy others and to satisfy himself—Hamlet must proceed. He ends the long scene by coming to a firm decision:

> *The play's the thing*
> *Wherein I'll catch the conscience of the King.*

—Act II, scene ii, lines 616–17

. . . my most painted word

Rosencrantz and Guildenstern report to the King and Queen. They have failed (through their own heavyhandedness) and have gained nothing from Hamlet. All they can say is that Hamlet seems interested in a play which he hopes the King and Queen will attend. The King at once agrees. Anything Hamlet does may offer a clue to his intentions, and he cannot afford to lose that clue.

The next attempt, though (Rosencrantz and Guildenstern having failed), is to involve Ophelia. She is placed in the appropriate spot and Polonius busily orders her to read a devotional book to make her presence there look innocent. He proceeds to pontificate on the emptiness of outward show and the King speaks in a sad aside:

> *O, 'tis too true.*
> *How smart a lash that speech doth give my conscience!*
> *The harlot's cheek, beautied with plast'ring art,*
> *Is not more ugly to the thing that helps it*
> *Than is my deed to my most painted word.*
> *O heavy burden!*
>
> —Act III, scene i, lines 49–54

This speech reveals to the audience, for the first time, that the King is really guilty and that the Ghost is an honest spirit indeed. Then too, it shows that the King *does* have a conscience. The play could scarcely "catch the conscience of the King" if Claudius were actually a monstrous villain. One can imagine Goneril (see page I–48) easily sitting through a play describing her own crimes in detail without turning a hair and blandly denying everything if accused. It is important to know that Claudius is not that sort of person so that we will know that Hamlet's stratagem has a point to it.

To be, or not to be . . .

Ophelia is placed. The Queen is sent away while the King and Polonius hide. Hamlet enters, musing, with the soliloquy that is the most famous speech in all of Shakespeare spoken at this point. It begins:

> *To be, or not to be: that is the question:*
> *Whether 'tis nobler in the mind to suffer*
> *The slings and arrows of outrageous fortune,*
> *Or to take arms against a sea of troubles,*
> *And by opposing end them.*
>
> —Act III, scene i, lines 56–60

It seems to be a meditation on suicide, and Hamlet feels that everyone would kill himself and escape this miserable world, if only he were sure that some unknown and more frightful horror did not await him in the afterworld.

Can it be that Hamlet is contemplating suicide? Or wishing that the dread of hellfire did not prevent him from contemplating it?

It is difficult to believe that, for Hamlet labors very hard throughout the play to avoid death. Suicide is a sin, but if he is executed by Claudius, then he is quit of the world without suicide. Why then does Hamlet avoid death even by the extreme and possibly shameful action of pretending madness?

It is possible to argue that it is this and not suicide in the abstract which is bothering him. He has two choices as far as action is concerned. He can act directly, kill the King, and take the consequences, which would surely be death for himself. He would in this way "take arms against a sea of troubles, and by opposing end them."

On the other hand, he can dissemble, feign madness, lay his plots, and meanwhile take no action against those who have wronged him. Here he "suffers [submits to, without retaliation] the slings and arrows of outrageous fortune."

And he is not certain which choice is the nobler, which is more fitting for himself. And since the choice of direct action is virtual suicide for himself, he is lured into the thought of suicide in the abstract.

In the end, he is rather shamefaced about it. Suspecting that heroism would require direct action even at the cost of death, he knows also that he wants the crown and must take the route to that crown even at the price of heroism. He concludes:

> *Thus conscience* [inner calculation] *does make cowards of us all,*
> *And thus the native hue of resolution*
> *Is sicklied o'er with the pale cast of thought,*
> *And enterprises of great pitch and moment*
> *With this regard their currents turn awry,*
> *And lose the name of action.*
>
> —Act III, scene i, lines 83–88

. . . *proud, revengeful, ambitious* . . .

But now Hamlet is aware of Ophelia's presence; she is apparently at her prayers. Hamlet is not fooled by this. He knows that Claudius and Polonius are in hiding and eavesdropping, probably because he overheard them at the time the plot was first proposed, or possibly because he becomes aware of them now through some incautious movement on their part.

To blunt this maneuver, Hamlet knows he must play the role of madness intensely, which means being cruel to Ophelia. He can't help that and yet he regrets it too. His first words on seeing her (and knowing that she is but a helpless tool) are a tender:

> Nymph, in thy orisons
> Be all my sins remembered.
> —Act III, scene i, lines 89–90

It is tempting to believe that Hamlet includes here among his sins the one that he is about to commit—pitiless cruelty toward a young and innocent girl.

The fact that he must speak harshly to Ophelia must surely infuriate him even further against the two calculating men who are forcing him to do so. Bitterly, he baits them as earlier he had baited Polonius alone. Therefore, in the midst of his remarks to Ophelia, hard and lewd—the sort of thing the gentlemanly Hamlet could never say if he were sane (or so he hopes the King and Polonius will think)—he blurts out:

> I am myself indifferent honest, but yet I could accuse me of
> such things that it were better my mother had not borne me:
> I am very proud, revengeful, ambitious . . .
> —Act III, scene i, lines 122–25

Of course he is. He has the pride of a prince who will take nothing less than the throne, and the ambition of one too. And that he is revengeful is the central point of the play. Furthermore, it is literally true that he feels it were better his mother had not borne him—for his mother. If his plans go through, the Queen may live but she will no longer be Queen, and she will be disgraced.

It is in this same speech that he begins ordering Ophelia to a nunnery in a crescendo of cruel sarcasm. But is it Ophelia he plans to send to a nunnery, or is it his mother, Queen Gertrude? (Remember that Edward the Confessor sent his mother, Emma, to a nunnery once he had gained the throne.)

Hamlet flings himself out of the room, and the naïve Ophelia, sure he is mad, mourns for him in beautifully phrased sorrow.

. . . to England

Hamlet, however, has overreached himself, for he has underestimated Claudius. It must have given him some satisfaction to tell Claudius exactly what he intended to do, assuming that Claudius would pay no attention to a madman's words. It must have made Hamlet feel less ashamed that he had forsaken the very "name of action" in order ignominiously to "suffer the slings and arrows of outrageous fortune." At least he could threaten.

But the King, emerging from hiding, is not fooled. He never has thought Hamlet was mad and he clearly takes the Prince's words about "proud, revengeful, ambitious" at face value. He says:

> . . . what he spake, though it lacked form a little,
> Was not like madness. There's something in his soul
> O'er which his melancholy sits on brood,
> And I do doubt the hatch and the disclose
> Will be some danger . . .
>
> —Act III, scene i, lines 166–70

Claudius must take action and he makes his decision; a decision he reveals, at this moment, only in part:

> . . . he shall with speed to England
> For the demand of our neglected tribute.
>
> —Act III, scene i, lines 172–73

This connection of Denmark and England again places Hamlet back in the Canute era.

England had been paying tribute to Danish raiders ever since 991, well before the land had actually been conquered by Sven Forked-beard. Such tribute was called the "Danegeld," and altogether about 160,000 tons of silver were handed over to the Danes.

Naturally, after Sven Forked-beard conquered England, there was no further tribute as such, for the Danes controlled all the land. This control continued till the death of Canute's second son, Hardecanute, in 1042. After that, Denmark and England parted company forever; nor was Denmark ever in a position to blackmail England again. If we consider the events of *Hamlet* as taking place in 1050, it is quite accurate to speak of "our neglected tribute." It stayed neglected too.

. . . out-herods Herod . . .

Foolish Polonius still adheres to the Ophelia theory of Hamlet's madness and suggests that Queen Gertrude tackle Hamlet and find out the truth (with Polonius eavesdropping—he is a great eavesdropper). The King wearily agrees but he has no illusions and knows what he must do.

Meanwhile, Hamlet, unaware that he has overreached himself, is instructing the players in the method of making the play they are to produce most effective. He wants King Claudius to be hit hard and therefore the play must be as natural as possible. A ridiculous or postured artificiality would ruin the impact, and he advises them strongly against bombastic overacting. He says, with energy:

> *I would have such a fellow whipped for o'erdoing*
> *Termagant. It out-herods Herod. Pray you avoid it.*
> —Act III, scene ii, lines 13–15

Hamlet is here harking back to the mystery plays, which were adaptations of biblical stories, usually of the life of Jesus, put on in the Middle Ages for a largely illiterate populace. To attract the lower classes and to keep their attention one had to introduce elements of suspense and humor, with the result that ranting villains and broad farce were included.

Naturally, a most obvious villain was King Herod (see page I–325), who, in the biblical tale, tried to kill the infant Jesus. He was always represented as a vicious tyrant, making fearful faces and yelling at the top of his voice.

Another natural villain would be some Moslem, for Islam was the perennial (and usually victorious) enemy of medieval Christendom. The west Europeans knew virtually nothing of Moslem theology and they imagined that the Moslems must worship some idol. They invented an idolatrous god called "Tervagant" (a name quickly distorted to "Termagant"), who howled as madly as Herod.

Observe my uncle

The players, rather wearily, but patiently, assure Hamlet that they know their craft, but the Prince anxiously continues to instruct them.

Hamlet then calls Horatio to himself (the one man he dares trust) and begins a sugared flattery. The modest Horatio tries to stop him, but Hamlet says:

> *Nay, do not think I flatter.*
> *For what advancement may I hope from thee,*
> *That no revenue hast but thy good spirits*
> *To feed and clothe thee?*
> —Act III, scene ii, lines 58–61

Hamlet is being less than honest here, but he is also being a shrewd politician. There *is* advancement he hopes from Horatio. He hopes to make Horatio a crucial witness, one who will stick to his story against possible pressure. That may well be the reason for the rather gratuitous mention of Horatio's poverty. If he *does* stick to the story and Hamlet becomes king, he may well hope the poverty will cease.

The flattery done, Hamlet gets to the point:

There is a play tonight before the King.
One scene of it comes near the circumstance
Which I have told thee, of my father's death.
I prithee, when thou seest that act afoot,
Even with the very comment of thy soul
Observe my uncle.

—Act III, scene ii, lines 77–82

If now the King gives himself away (as Hamlet is probably sure he will), Horatio will be able to bear witness that Hamlet knew of the crime from the Ghost, that he held back cautiously and honorably until he had better evidence, that he deliberately set up the play to get that evidence, and got it. With such witness from Horatio available, Hamlet could freely kill the King and achieve the succession as a hero-son and the instrument of a vengeful God.

. . . the chameleon's dish . . .

But while Horatio may watch closely and remain unobserved, Hamlet cannot. He knows he will constantly be observed and that means he must maintain his pretended madness; at least just a little longer. When the King and the court begin to enter, he says hurriedly to Horatio:

They are coming to the play: I must be idle;
Get you a place.

—Act III, scene ii, lines 92–93

Yet he cannot prevent himself from playing at word games with the hated Claudius. Claudius asks, with formal politeness:

How fares our cousin Hamlet?

—Act III, scene ii, line 94

"Cousin," we must remember, was used by Elizabethans to mean "relative" in general, or even someone who was merely a colleague or a close friend. (Its shortened form, "coz," is found frequently in the plays.)

The question is meant "How are you?" but Hamlet deliberately takes it to mean "On what do you dine?" and answers:

Excellent, i'faith, of the chameleon's dish; I eat the air,
promise-crammed; you cannot feed capons so.

—Act III, scene ii, lines 95–97

The answer, being off the point, and seeming nonsensical, supports

Hamlet's supposed madness, and yet at the same time it makes a great deal of sense. (It is with this nonsense-sense that Hamlet amuses himself and makes up to himself the disgraceful part which, in his own eyes, he is forced to play.)

The chameleon is a slow-moving, slow-living lizard that does not require much food to maintain life and is therefore never as busily eating as warm-blooded, fast-living mammals are. Furthermore, when a chameleon does eat, it is with the fast flick of a long tongue that unerringly spears an insect and is back in an eye-blink. One could watch a chameleon, on and off, for a long time without catching it in that momentary feeding. For that reason, the tale rose that the chameleon did not eat at all in the ordinary sense, but lived on air.

Hamlet, then, claimed he was being forced to live on air; on promises that were only breath emerging from the mouth and nothing more substantial. Surely, he must be referring to the King's statement earlier in the play that he would make Hamlet his heir. Perhaps Claudius had not done so officially yet, using the madness as an excuse; or perhaps Hamlet was sure that the King was intent on finding some excuse to kill him. In any case, Hamlet knew he would never fatten (like a capon) on such promises, and his remark is intended as an insult to Claudius.

. . . the galled jade . . .

The play within a play begins with a dumb show that presents the plot and shows the circumstances of a murder (presumably to be dealt with in the play) which is just like that described by the Ghost. There is no real sense to the dumb show, for it robs the succeeding play of its suspense and, what's worse, gives all away to Claudius. If the King sees it, he either stops the play at once on some pretext or is warned and steels himself to show no emotion when the play actually takes place. If I were producing *Hamlet*, I would omit the dumb show, even if I didn't omit anything else.

The play itself begins in pompous rhymed verse (which Shakespeare deliberately writes in inferior style to make it seem like a play in comparison to the "reality" of *Hamlet*) and advances, at once, certain allusions that must strike viciously home.

Thus, in the play, the Player King and the Player Queen have been married thirty years; the Player King is not well and fears he may die, but hopes his wife will live on and marry happily a second time. The Player Queen, however, rejects the thought:

> *Such love must needs be treason in my breast.*
> *In second husband let me be accurst!*
> *None wed the second but who killed the first.*
> —Act III, scene ii, lines 184–86

And Hamlet, who has taken a place with Ophelia to be able to see the King's face, says to himself:

> *That's wormwood.*
>
> —Act III, scene ii, line 187

One can imagine him saying that with satisfaction, pleased at the application to his mother. But the Queen watches unmoved, either too hardened to respond or, much more likely, too shallow to be touched. Hamlet has to ask her directly what she thinks, and she answers with a very famous (and invariably misquoted) line:

> *The lady doth protest too much, methinks.*
>
> —Act III, scene ii, line 236

She may be referring to the penchant of inferior dramatists to overdo their efforts in misleading the audience, until their very insistence in pointing in one direction guarantees the actual movement in the other.

But the King is growing uneasy. The references are too close to home, and he lacks the Queen's naïveté. He says to Hamlet (who is, after all, sponsoring the play):

> *Have you heard the argument* [plot]? *Is there no offense in't?*
>
> —Act III, scene ii, lines 238–39

The fact that the King is unaware of the plot means he has not seen the dumb show. Why keep it in the play then?

Grimly, Hamlet assures the King that only the guilty need fear:

> *'Tis a knavish piece of work, but what of that? Your Majesty, and we that have free souls, it touches us not. Let the galled jade winch* [wince]; *our withers are unwrung.*
>
> —Act III, scene ii, lines 246–48

Claudius is far too intelligent not to understand the menace underlying Hamlet's words, yet he dare not do anything at the moment. Hamlet may be bluffing and Claudius delays reaction.

. . . the ghost's word . . .

The crucial scene is now approaching. Lucianus, the nephew of Gonzago, the Player King, is about to kill Gonzago in exactly the fashion that Claudius killed the elder Hamlet.

Hamlet, almost beside himself with tension, can't stand the delay. When Lucianus attempts to increase suspense by a little "mugging" to show villainy, Hamlet cries out:

> Begin, murderer. Leave thy damnable faces and begin.
>> —Act III, scene ii, lines 258–59

Lucianus speaks, then pours poison in Gonzago's ear. Claudius is obviously affected, and Hamlet adds a commentary to thrust the matter home:

> You shall see anon how the murderer gets the love of Gonzago's wife.
>> —Act III, scene ii, lines 269–70

It is all Claudius can take. Extremely upset, he rises. The play is brought to an abrupt end as he leaves hurriedly.

All rush out after him, and Hamlet, left alone on the stage with Horatio, is filled with triumph; half mad with it, in good faith. Having expressed his jubilation, however, he is practical enough to make sure he has his witness:

> O good Horatio, I'll take the ghost's word for a thousand pound. Didst perceive?
>> —Act III, scene ii, lines 292–93

Horatio saw. Not only that, but the whole court saw the King's action, and when the matter is explained to them they will be able to have no doubt whatever as to the King's guilt. Hamlet can now kill the King at will.

. . . I lack advancement

What Claudius has suspected he now knows for certainty. Hamlet, somehow, is aware of the truth and can use it with deadly effect. Claudius must know his own life hangs by a thread.

The Queen, who apparently does not know the truth, can only see that Claudius is terribly disturbed and fears for her son. (And rightly so, for at this point Claudius *must* react. It is clearly a matter of life and death for him.)

The Queen sends for her son, then, in an effort to make peace between him and his stepfather, totally unaware that that is quite impossible. Rosencrantz and Guildenstern come with the message, and Hamlet, very sure of himself now, merely amuses himself with them.

They are still trying to find out what lies behind his madness, and Hamlet says, ironically:

> *Sir, I lack advancement.*
> —Act III, scene ii, line 347

Rosencrantz points out that Hamlet is the heir to the throne, but Hamlet says:

> *Ay, sir, but "while the grass grows"* . . .
> —Act III, scene ii, line 351

He does not complete the proverb, since it is well known to the audience. It is "While the grass grows, the horse starves," meaning you can't live on promises for the future, which can easily amount to nothing. Here is another reference to what he had earlier called "the chameleon's dish."

Hamlet's mocking of Rosencrantz and Guildenstern grows sharper, too, for he has little to fear now. The game is his and he tells the two false friends quite openly that they will get nothing out of him.

The soul of Nero . . .

Polonius now enters to repeat Gertrude's command that Hamlet come to her. Hamlet cannot resist one last bit of foolery with the foolish Polonius, then agrees to come. He has a moment to himself in which to soliloquize:

> *Soft, now to my mother.*
> *O heart, lose not thy nature; let not ever*
> *The soul of Nero enter this firm bosom.*
> *Let me be cruel, not unnatural;*
> *I will speak daggers to her, but use none.*
> —Act III, scene ii, lines 400–4

Here again we see that Hamlet's tendency is not irresolution, but the reverse. He must at every step fight off the temptation to action on enraged impulse.

He can feel that his anger and resentment toward his mother, whose hasty marriage has deprived him of the crown and forced him into this long unnatural course of intrigue, may drive him into a moment of hot-blooded action; even to sudden matricide.

Nero, who was Roman Emperor from 54 to 68, was a tyrannical monster, whose most sensational misdeed was that of ordering the execution of his own mother, Agrippina, in 59. (The story is that she asked the assassins to strike at the womb that bore so unnatural a son.)

Agrippina was, to be sure, a wicked woman whose interference in Nero's rule was most exasperating, but it is difficult for men to find any excuse at all for matricide. When Nero visited Greece in 67, he tried to gain entrance to the Eleusinian Mysteries, but was refused because he had killed his mother, and such was the popular horror of the crime that Nero, absolute tyrant that he was, was forced to back down.

It was this that Hamlet must at all costs now avoid. The most he could do to his mother, even if it turned out she was an active accomplice to his father's murder—which she was not—would be to put her in a nunnery. If he killed his mother, or had her killed, on whatever excuse, he would surely be barred from the succession by a horrified populace that would feel the whole nation would be cursed on his account if he were king.

. . . the primal eldest curse . . .

The King *must* now get Hamlet out of the court and to England at once, and he arranges for Rosencrantz and Guildenstern to go with the prince. Clearly, they will be his jailers to make sure he goes where he is supposed to go.

Polonius enters to tell the King that Hamlet is on the way to his mother and that he, Polonius, will play the spy once more and report to the King.

And then the King, alone on the stage, kneels to pray. His remorse is great, for, as he says:

> O, my offense is rank, it smells to heaven;
> It hath the primal eldest curse upon't,
> A brother's murder.
>
> —Act III, scene iii, lines 36–38

The horror of the memory of Cain lies on Claudius. The first crime committed by man against man was that of Cain, and it was the murder of his brother Abel. For it, Cain received a curse—"And now art thou cursed from the earth . . ." (Genesis 4:11)—and this "primal eldest curse" outside Eden, Claudius feels, rests on him now.

Yet he knows not how to gain forgiveness, since, however much he regrets the murder, he cannot give up the fruits and, indeed, will commit other crimes to avoid giving them up.

. . . hire and salary . . .

Even as he prays, or tries to pray, Hamlet, on his way to the Queen, comes upon him.

Hamlet's sword is out and he can kill the King. It will even be best to do it now, for he can say that immediately upon having received confirmation of the King's guilt, rage so blinded him that he could not wait for formal condemnation.

His plan has worked magnificently. One sword thrust and he will have all—both revenge and the throne.

But Hamlet's passion interferes!

The King is praying; to kill him now in such a holy occupation would send him to heaven. Hamlet muses:

> *A villain kills my father, and for that*
> *I, his sole son, do this same villain send*
> *To heaven.*
> *Why, this is hire and salary, not revenge.*
>
> —Act III, scene iii, lines 76–79

Thus, Hamlet refrains from the deed. He will wait until the King is at some profane activity.

And thus Hamlet overreaches himself at the moment of triumph. Having won the game, having all in his hand, he grasps for more than he needs or has any right to ask. He wants Claudius not only killed, but damned. One might argue that damnation is God's business and not Hamlet's and that, having aspired to play the role of God, Hamlet has gone too far and has earned punishment.

The irony is that the King is unable to pray anyway, and had Hamlet struck, Claudius would have been damned as well as killed. The King rises from his knees, saying:

> *My words fly up, my thoughts remain below.*
> *Words without thoughts never to heaven go.*
>
> —Act III, scene iii, lines 97–98

. . . Is it the King

Hamlet finally reaches his mother. From his new position, he can speak to her openly at last and he begins with such self-confident firmness that she fears (remember, he has labored hard to convince her that he is mad, and she herself is, in any case, not very intelligent) he will murder her. She calls for help.

Polonius, eavesdropping from behind the curtain, is also sure that Hamlet will kill his mother. (After all, Hamlet has deliberately played the madman with Polonius more intensively than with anyone else.) The old courtier calls for help from behind the curtain, and now at last Hamlet gives way. The passionate need for action which he has held back all this time breaks through.

He is sure that the King has followed him up the stairs and is now the one who is eavesdropping. The King is engaged in no holy action now, if this is so, and Hamlet's sword flashes. Polonius falls dead and the Queen groans:

> *O me, what hast thou done?*
>
> —Act III, scene iv, line 26

Hamlet, a little rueful at having lost control, says:

> *Nay, I know not. Is it the King?*
>
> —Act III, scene iv, line 27

He lifts the curtain, finds it isn't, and says, in frustration:

> *Thou wretched, rash, intruding fool, farewell!*
> *I took thee for thy better.*
>
> —Act III, scene iv, lines 32–33

. . . the precious diadem stole

For a while, inertia carries Hamlet onward. He has come to the point of being able to lecture his mother and he cannot give up that chance, merely in order to meet a drastically changed situation. Not immediately, anyway. So he goes on to lecture his mother nearly past the point where her endurance breaks.

Again there is the emphasis on the godlike virtues of the dead elder Hamlet:

> *See what a grace was seated on this brow:*
> *Hyperion's curls, the front of Jove himself,*
> *An eye like Mars, to threaten and command,*
> *A station like the herald Mercury*
>
> —Act III, scene iv, lines 56–59

And in contrast there is Claudius, for whom Hamlet cannot find words bad enough. He denounces, most eloquently, the vileness of the sexual passion he imagines existing between Gertrude and Claudius, but as his anger mounts with his own words, he approaches closer to what sits most near his heart. He says of Claudius:

> *A murderer and a villain,*
> *A slave that is not twentieth part the tithe* [tenth]
> *Of your precedent lord, a vice of kings,*

A cutpurse of the empire and the rule,
That from a shelf the precious diadem stole
And put it in his pocket—

—Act III, scene iv, lines 97–102

There we have it. Hamlet rises in this scene to his own particular climax. First there is mention of Claudius' crime of fratricide, then (worse) his crime of lust and adultery with the Queen, and then (still worse) his crime of having stolen the succession. Shakespeare could scarcely have meant this listing of crimes to be anything but a crescendo, biting deeper and deeper toward the core, and, clearly, what bothers Hamlet most is the loss of the crown.

The Queen cannot stop Hamlet, who is in a choking rage at that loss. He says of Claudius:

A king of shreds and patches—

—Act III, scene iv, line 103

At this point, the Ghost enters for one last time. Hamlet, in his anger, has forgotten reality, and the Ghost has come to bring him back to that. Polonius is dead and he must take action now. He cannot lose himself in a pointless rating of his mother, who has gone far past the point where her limited intelligence can accept what he is saying anyway.

. . . mad in craft

With an effort, Hamlet grasps hold of himself, and sees now the ruin that faces him. All that he has gained by the play within a play he has lost by his impulsive and unlucky thrust at Polonius. Had he killed the King at prayer, all would have been well. By holding off to make sure of damnation as well, he had given himself time to kill Polonius and come to grief.

For now the King has a handle with which to strike back at Hamlet. Whatever Hamlet might claim concerning the King's earlier crime would now go unheard as the King would sorrowfully point out that nothing a madman could say need be listened to. And indeed, how could the court fail to consider him a madman? He had an excuse to kill the King, but none to kill Polonius. Indeed, if he tries to make it appear that he is not mad at all, then the killing of Polonius becomes a crime for which his imprisonment or execution might well be called for.

Hamlet says, in chagrin:

For this same lord [Polonius],
I do repent; but heaven hath pleased it so,

To punish me with this . . .

—Act III, scene iv, lines 173–75

Perhaps he recognizes his sin in having desired the damnation of Claudius, when all he could rightly ask for was his death.

Now he must return to playing mad, just when he thought he would no longer have to and just when (with that thought in mind) he has revealed to his mother that he is quite sane. He knows he cannot rely on his mother's good sense, for she has none. He can only hope. As impressively as he can, he orders her not to reveal his secret. The King must *not*, he says:

> *Make you to ravel all this matter out,*
> *That I essentially am not in madness,*
> *But mad in craft.*

—Act III, scene iv, lines 187–89

. . . to England . . .

That will at least gain time, but Hamlet has no illusions about the great loss he has suffered. Claudius is thoroughly on his guard now and cannot be taken by surprise. Furthermore, Hamlet must now face Claudius' reaction and somehow counter it. He says to the Queen:

> *I must to England; you know that?*

—Act III, scene iv, line 201

Nor does Hamlet doubt that there is worse in store for him than mere rustication abroad. He says:

> *There's letters sealed, and my two school-fellows,*
> *Whom I will trust as I will adders fanged,*
> *They bear the mandate;*

—Act III, scene iv, lines 203–5

It is no great trick, under the circumstances, for Hamlet to guess the content of the letters. The King cannot possibly be safe till Hamlet is dead. England's King, though no longer subject to Denmark, will not care to affront the latter nation lightly. Undoubtedly, the letter will contain a request that the King of England imprison or execute Hamlet.

There is a similar incident in Homer's *Iliad*. There the hero Bellerophon rouses the enmity of his host's wife by refusing her amorous invitation. The angered wife accuses Bellerophon to her husband of attempting to rape her. (There is a similarity here with the tale of Joseph and Potiphar's wife—Genesis 39:7–20.) The husband, unwilling to stain his hands with a guest's blood, thus violating the sacred laws of hospitality, sends Beller-ophon with a letter in cipher to the friendly King of Lycia. The letter, when deciphered, was a request that Bellerophon be executed. (Bellerophon, however, escaped.)

Suspecting the contents of the letter, then, Hamlet is grimly determined to circumvent it.

It had been so with us . . .

The King now comes to the Queen and each is less than honest with the other. The Queen describes Hamlet as having killed Polonius in a fit of madness, to which the King replies:

> *It had been so with us, had we been there.*
> *His liberty is full of threats to all,*
>
> —Act IV, scene i, lines 13–14

It is his excuse, for Gertrude's benefit, for sending Hamlet away. It will give him time, he implies, to excuse Hamlet and prevent public demand for his punishment. The Queen does not say that Hamlet is really sane and would indeed have killed the King had he been there (but Claudius is shrewd enough to know that without being told). On the other hand, the King does not say he really intends to have Hamlet killed, and the Queen is by no means shrewd enough to penetrate that hidden intention.

Undoubtedly, the King wants to have Hamlet dead more than anything else in the world. Yet he must still be cautious. As he says to some of the court a little later:

> *How dangerous is it that this man goes loose!*
> *Yet must not we put the strong law on him:*
> *He's loved of the distracted multitude.*
>
> —Act IV, scene iii, lines 2–4

It is plain, here, that Claudius suffers the same difficulty Hamlet does. Hamlet wants to kill the King *and* get the throne too. The King wants to kill Hamlet *and* keep the throne too. It is the matter of the throne that makes direct action impossible for either one; neither dare risk losing the popularity he possesses by an act of brutal murder.

. . . thy cicatrice . . .

Hamlet hides Polonius' body and strenuously plays mad again to deprive Claudius of the chance of direct action. The body is recovered at length, however, and Hamlet is made ready to go to England.

It must be done hastily, and Claudius muses:

> *And, England, if my love thou hold'st at aught—*
> *As my great power thereof may give thee sense,*
> *Since yet thy cicatrice looks raw and red*
> *After the Danish sword, and thy free awe*
> *Pays homage to us—thou mayst not coldly set*
> *Our sovereign process, which imports at full*
> *By letters congruing to that effect*
> *The present death of Hamlet.*
> —Act IV, scene iii, lines 58–65

The audience is thus told of Claudius' plan. The reference to the Danish sword fits the great raids of the Danes on England in the tenth century and of the Danish conquest of England in the early eleventh century. (Furthermore, Claudius' harsh reference to the Danish sword makes certain the fact that Shakespeare's English audience will not be lured into sympathy with him.)

. . . thinking too precisely . . .

On his way to the ship that will carry them to England, Hamlet meets the army of young Fortinbras crossing Denmark (with permission) on its way to Poland. Hamlet asks a Captain, an officer in Fortinbras' army, where they go. The Captain replies:

> *We go to gain a little patch of ground*
> *That hath in it no profit but the name.*
> *To pay five ducats, five, I would not farm it,*
> —Act IV, scene iv, lines 18–20

Yet the Poles will defend it and thousands of men may die over it. (Shakespeare here, as in many places in his plays, makes plain his sardonic contempt and distaste for the whole apparatus of war and national glory, though he is condemned by the audience and the times to insert much chauvinism in his writing.)

Hamlet is abashed, for here is an example of the dichotomy he has brooded over in his famous soliloquy. Fortinbras, his Norwegian analogue, is interested only "in the name of action." He "takes arms against a sea of troubles" even for the sake of nothing of worth, but merely so that he might act.

Yet Hamlet himself does not act directly, but always plans circuitously in order to gain everything. It is his "conscience that doth make cowards of us all." Or, on this occasion, he puts the blame on:

> . . . *some craven scruple*
> *Of thinking too precisely on th'event . . .*
> —Act IV, scene iv, lines 40–41

And yet his plots have miscarried anyway and he is being led off to exile and possibly to death. He is through with intricate plotting and cries out in agony:

> *O, from this time forth,*
> *My thoughts be bloody, or be nothing worth!*
> —Act IV, scene iv, lines 65–66

. . . a baker's daughter . . .

The death of Polonius has done more than wreck Hamlet's plan at the instant of victory; it has driven Ophelia mad with grief, to the horror of the King and Queen.

Ophelia's speech is distracted, but was more significant to the Elizabethan audience than it is now to us. She says, at one point:

> *They say the owl was a baker's daughter. Lord, we know what we are, but know not what we may be.*
> —Act IV, scene v, lines 42–44

The statement that we don't know what the future holds for us is true enough, and certainly true enough for Ophelia, who had had no suspicion her father would be murdered, but what has it to do with the owl and the baker's daughter?

There is an old English legend to the effect that Jesus, in the guise of a beggar, came to a baker's shop to ask for some food. The baker put some dough into the oven to make a loaf of bread for the supposed beggar, but the baker's daughter, overcome with niggardliness, decided that the gift was too great and cut the dough in half. She was promptly turned into an owl as punishment, a drastic example of one who knew what she was but did not know what she would become.

. . . where are my Switzers . . .

Claudius mourns the gathering troubles, for Polonius had been hastily buried to avoid rousing trouble, and the very trouble they had tried to avoid has come as a result—the people are restless. And besides Ophelia's madness, there is her brother's rage. Laertes has hastened home from France and is rousing the people against the court. (The ease with which popularity can be lost and public opinion made to veer makes it clear that both Claudius and Hamlet are entirely right in trying to effect their respective ends in as cautious and circumspect a manner as possible.)

There is a noise at the door and the King cries out:

> *Attend, where are my Switzers? Let them guard the door.*
> *What is the matter?*
>
> —Act IV, scene v, lines 97–98

Here is an interesting anachronism.

The district of Schwyz, secure in the Alps, formed a federation with two neighboring districts in 1291 which became the nucleus of the nation still called Schweiz in German, but Switzerland in English.

Neighboring Austria claimed sovereignty over the districts (or cantons), but in 1315 at Morgarten, on the edge of Schwyz territory, the army of Duke Leopold I of Austria was badly beaten by the tough Swiss infantry-men. The cantons retained their independence and other neighboring cantons joined them. In 1386 and 1388 the Swiss won two more victories and began to gain a reputation for being hard and steady infantrymen, invincible in their own mountains.

This reputation was enormously enhanced when, from 1474 to 1477, the Swiss fought against Charles the Bold of Burgundy, who had a European-wide reputation as a warrior, and beat him utterly. They defeated him in three battles and killed him in the last.

After that the Swiss were everywhere in demand. Their mountainous soil could not support them in luxury and their greatest export became soldiers who would serve loyally for pay. They were trained in the difficult art of pike-warfare (it is not easy to handle a long and heavy pike) and every contending army had its corps of Swiss.

It was not until 1515 that the spell was broken. In that year, the French army under its King, Francis I, won a great battle at Marignano in northwestern Italy over the Swiss and Venetians. For the first time, those steady pikemen had been defeated, and never again were they to have quite such a hold over the military imagination.

Even so, it remained customary for kings to hire a company of Swiss mercenaries as personal guards. They were steady, and loyal only to the King (while he paid them), and since they shared no common feelings with the people of the land, they could not be corrupted by factional or revolutionary sentiments. When in 1792 King Louis XVI of France was attacked at the palace of the Tuileries by French revolutionaries, the Swiss guards were slaughtered to a man as they loyally tried to resist in an utterly hopeless cause.

Pope Julius II instituted a Swiss guard just prior to the Battle of Marignano, and the Pope has been guarded by one down to this very day, though its function now is purely ceremonial.

It is natural, then, for Shakespeare, writing in 1600, to give Claudius a Swiss guard too, though at the time of the events in the play, not only were there no such guards in existence, but Switzerland itself had not yet become a nation.

. . . life-rend'ring pelican

Laertes is at the palace gates at the head of an angry mob. Laertes himself bursts in and advances angrily at Claudius, crying:

> *O thou vile King,*
> *Give me my father.*
> —Act IV, scene v, lines 115–16

Clearly, he believes Polonius has been executed at Claudius' command, despite all (we suspect) that Claudius owed to his courtier. Laertes makes no subtle plans. Unlike Hamlet's, his response bears "the name of action." He raises a rebellion and tackles the King directly.

Ah, but before we make invidious comparisons against Hamlet, there are two points to make.

First, the people know that Polonius was killed and many suspect that Claudius was responsible. They did not know the elder Hamlet was killed and it was Hamlet's task to convince them of that fact and to convince them, further, that Claudius was the murderer. It was the convincing and not the revenge that was difficult.

Secondly, Laertes wants nothing beyond revenge, whereas Hamlet wants revenge and the throne. It is the desire for the throne that introduces the endless complications. (If we interpret Hamlet's actions as being the result of a desire for revenge *only,* then the play is and must remain an unanswerable puzzle.)

Claudius shows himself at his best in facing Laertes. The King (no drunkard, no weak libertine) is fearless and shrewd. He remains calm, speaks softly, and forces Laertes to listen. He denies having been responsible for Polonius' death and asks Laertes if, in revenge, he wants to destroy his father's friends as well as his enemies.

Laertes insists he is only after the guilty. To his father's friends he will be a friend:

> *To his good friends thus wide I'll ope my arms*
> *And like the kind life-rend'ring pelican*
> *Repast them with my blood.*
> —Act IV, scene v, lines 145–47

The pelican was widely considered in ancient times as a creature that fed its young on its own blood.

In medieval times this was taken further. Natural history in those days was often distorted into moralistic fables supposed to illustrate biblical points, as though all the universe existed only for the sake of preaching simplistic sermons to mankind. Thus, the young pelican was supposed to anger the male parent who killed them. The young remained dead for three days, at which time the female parent sat on them and poured her own blood on them, reviving them.

This allegory of the death and resurrection of Jesus helped make the mistaken belief about the pelican popular, hence Laertes' metaphor.

There's rosemary . . .

Mad Ophelia comes in at this moment. She has gathered flowers and herbs and distributes them:

> There's rosemary, that's for remembrance. Pray you, remember. And there is pansies, that's for thoughts.
> —Act IV, scene v, lines 174–76

She is speaking the language of flowers. In a society closer to nature than our own, it was easy to make each flower significant of something and to use it for lovers' messages or for quasi-superstitious purposes. Rosemary was symbolic of fidelity in love because its fragrance lingered over long periods. Its existence was therefore not forgotten. Pansies symbolized thought by their very name, which comes from *pensée*, the French word for "thought."

As to other flowers Ophelia mentions, together with some of her odd turns of phrase, the significance is disputed.

. . . a gentleman of Normandy

The sight of his sister enrages Laertes further and Claudius has a hard job controlling him. In private (away from the Queen) he reveals Hamlet as the murderer and explains why he couldn't take action against him directly. The Queen loves Hamlet and the King (who really appears to love Gertrude over and above the fact that the marriage was useful to him and helped him gain the crown) does not wish to alienate her by imprisoning or executing her son. Then too, there is the perpetual fear of public opinion (which hampers both Claudius and Hamlet in their respective plots). Claudius refers to this when he says:

> *The other motive*
> *Why to a public count* [trial] *I might not go*
> *Is the great love the general gender bear him,*
>
> —Act IV, scene vii, lines 16–18

Claudius is about to tell him, however, that he has arranged to have Hamlet killed in England, when a messenger arrives with word that Hamlet is not in England at all but is back in Denmark.

Claudius thinks quickly. He doesn't want civil war; he wants a quiet murder that will look like accident, with the responsibility (and risk) falling on Laertes if anything goes wrong.

He recalls something he had heard from France, saying:

> *Two months since*
> *Here was a gentleman of Normandy.*
>
> —Act IV, scene vii, lines 81–82

The mention of Normandy is *not* an anachronism. While the Danish raids were laying England prostrate, similar raids were devastating the northern coast of France. In 911, nearly a century and a half before the time of the events in *Hamlet,* a Viking raider named Hrolf had forced the French King, Charles III (the Fat), to cede a district on the Channel coast to himself and his followers. This became known as Nortmannia ("Northman-land") and then Normandy.

In 1050, at the time of the events in *Hamlet,* Normandy was a powerful, centralized, well-governed duchy under the remarkable Duke William II (the Bastard). Normandy was then a great power, for its Duke was stronger than the King of France and at least on a par with the King of Denmark. (Sixteen years later, in fact, William was to conquer England and become King William I, the Conqueror.)

The Normans in the century and a half since Hrolf's time had been completely absorbed into French civilization and now spoke a French dialect. Their Viking origins were virtually forgotten, but it is interesting to speculate that the Norman visitor whom Claudius mentions might have come, at least in part, to visit the land of his ancestors.

With this contagion . . .

Claudius recalls that the Norman had spoken of Laertes' skill as a swordsman and that Hamlet had been made jealous thereby. Hamlet would surely be eager to measure his skill against Laertes and Laertes can use a friendly fencing match as a device to kill him. Matters can be so arranged that while Hamlet is using a foil with the usual guarded point, Laertes can

"accidentally" be using one with an unguarded point and thus "accidentally" kill his father's murderer.

Laertes eagerly agrees and carries the treachery one step further. He
will not only use an unguarded point; he will make use of a very virulent
poison he happens to own.

> I'll touch my point
> With this contagion, that, if I gall him slightly,
> It may be death.
>> —Act IV, scene vii, lines 146–48

In other words, the home thrust will not be necessary, if it cannot be
managed against Hamlet's swordplay. A scratch will be enough.—And here
Laertes loses our sympathy. His revenge might be justifiable according to
the standards of the time, but surely not through a cowardly act of
treachery.

Yet even this is not enough. What if Laertes doesn't manage even to
scratch Hamlet? Claudius plans to prepare a poisoned drink as well and if
Hamlet comes out of the duel victorious and unscratched, the drink after
exertion will kill him.

Almost as though to punish Laertes for his planned treachery, or perhaps to screw his sorrow to the notch where he will not repent, the news
comes that Ophelia is drowned. She fell into a brook, whether through
madness or design, and made no attempt to escape.

. . . three and twenty years

Hamlet is not only back in Denmark. He is at Elsinore, with Horatio,
and comes across gravediggers preparing a grave. At one point, the gravedigger throws up a skull and tells Hamlet that he recognizes it. He says:

> Here's a skull now hath lien you i'th'earth three and twenty
> years.
>> —Act V, scene i, lines 174–75

It turns out to be the skull of Yorick, the court jester of the elder Hamlet. Hamlet is startled. He turns to Horatio and, holding the skull, says:

> Alas, poor Yorick! I knew him, Horatio, a fellow of infinite
> jest, of most excellent fancy. He hath borne me on his back a
> thousand times.
>> —Act V, scene i, lines 185–88

Hamlet remembers Yorick and so he could not have been an utter infant at the time of the jester's death. It wouldn't be too unreasonable to suppose him to be seven years old at the time—and if the jester were twenty-three years dead, Hamlet would be thirty.

This by no means represented youth in Hamlet's time (or in Shakespeare's time either). If Hamlet were really thirty, it would explain his utter discontent with Claudius' act of making him heir to the throne. The life expectancy of a thirty-year-old was not really very great. By the time Claudius was dead, Hamlet himself would not, in the course of nature, expect a very much longer life himself. Is he to have the throne for a poor few years?

However, it must be admitted that a thirty-year-old Hamlet doesn't fit the rest of the play. Queen Gertrude would be in her late forties at least and that is a bit too old for her, perhaps. Then too, how explain the fact that a thirty-year-old Hamlet is still a schoolboy at Wittenberg and still, in that age of early marriages, unmarried. It would be much more comfortable to imagine a twenty-year-old Hamlet, and that could be managed very simply if the gravedigger had merely mentioned the skull of Yorick had lain in the ground thirteen years rather than twenty-three.

. . . old Pelion . . .

The funeral party now arrives. The court attends, but the ritual is clearly limited and Hamlet realizes it must be a suicide who is being interred. It is Ophelia who is being buried, and the suspicion is, indeed, that she has killed herself. Laertes is furious at the priestly decision to stint the rites. He says:

> *Lay her i'th'earth,*
> *And from her fair and unpolluted flesh*
> *May violets spring! I tell thee, churlish priest,*
> *A minst'ring angel shall my sister be*
> *When thou liest howling!*
>
> —Act V, scene i, lines 240–44

And Gertrude strews flowers on the open grave with a phrase that has become so common a cliché that few remember any longer that Shakespeare said it first, or the occasion on which it was said:

> *Sweets to the sweet! Farewell!*
>
> —Act V, scene i, line 245

Laertes, overcome with grief, now jumps into the grave and in grandiloquent phrases demands he be covered too:

Now pile your dust upon the quick and dead
Till of this flat a mountain you have made
T'o'ertop old Pelion or the skyish head
Of blue Olympus.
—Act V, scene i, lines 253–56

A Greek myth tells of two young giants, Otus and Ephialtes, who grew six feet in height every year and one and a half feet in breadth. At the age of nine, being fifty-four feet tall and thirteen and a half feet broad, they decided to attack and defeat the gods. They planned to assault Mount Olympus (see page I–105), and to do so they decided to pile Mount Pelion on Mount Ossa.

Mount Ossa is 25 miles southeast of Mount Olympus and is 1.2 miles high. Mount Pelion is 30 miles farther southeast still and is 1.0 mile high. If Pelion is piled on Mount Ossa, a platform higher than Mount Olympus (itself 1.8 miles high) would be formed and the two giants could then aim their missiles downward with greater effect. However, the gods, with superior weapons, killed them before they could attempt the feat.

Pelion and Ossa, and even Olympus, are not really terribly high mountains, but the familiarity of this myth has placed them in literature as symbols of great height and they are so used here.

. . . the burning zone

Hamlet, who has been overhearing all this, is for the first time aware of Ophelia's death. Distracted, he comes forth to announce his own love for the lost Ophelia and bitterly mimics Laertes' braggadocio, mentioning the third mountain, which Laertes had omitted:

And if thou prate of mountains, let them throw
Millions of acres on us, till our ground
Singeing his pate against the burning zone,
Make Ossa like a wart! Nay, an thou'lt mouth,
I'll rant as well as thou.
—Act V, scene i, lines 282–86

It was part of the Aristotelian picture of the world that it consisted of the "elements" in layers. At the center of the universe was the solid earth; about that a sphere of water (not quite complete, so that dry land stuck through); about that a sphere of air; about that a sphere of fire (occasionally visible in the form of lightning); and finally the heavenly spheres of the planets and stars.

Hamlet here imagines that a mountain can be piled so high as to rise entirely through the sphere of air and into the sphere of fire.

. . . our deep plots do pall . . .

Laertes is kept from attacking Hamlet on the spot, partly by the Queen's anxious pleas that Hamlet is mad, and partly by the King's careful reminder that there is the fencing match yet to come.

Hamlet leaves them and reaches the castle with Horatio. He is a soberer Hamlet, much quieter than he was. He must be brooding about that unlucky sword stroke of his that not only spoiled his plot, but made him a deadly enemy in Laertes and lost him his lovely Ophelia.

He is about to tell Horatio how he managed to escape from the death awaiting him in England. It was entirely a matter of improvisation and luck, quite different from the long, careful plotting in Elsinore. Yet the improvisation had succeeded where all his carefulness had earlier failed. He can only find refuge in fatalism, saying:

> *Our indiscretion sometime serves us well*
> *When our deep plots do pall* [fail], *and that should learn us*
> *There's a divinity that shapes our ends,*
> *Rough-hew them how we will.*
>
> —Act V, scene ii, lines 8–11

From now on, it seems, Hamlet will involve himself in no subtlety. He will merely wait his chance, trusting it will come.

. . . th'election and my hopes

Hamlet tells how, unable to sleep aboard ship, and aware of danger, he crept to the cabin of Rosencrantz and Guildenstern and stole the letter they carried. He opened it, found that the King of England was being asked to execute Hamlet. He copied over a new letter, asking the English King to execute the bearers of the letter, sealed it with his father's seal (which he happened to be carrying), and put the new letter in place of the old.

A pirate ship then attacked (as Horatio had earlier been told in a letter from Hamlet) and Hamlet alone was captured. He managed to persuade the pirates to take him back to Denmark and here he was, now, while Rosencrantz and Guildenstern went on to their deaths.

Hamlet now lists his grievances against King Claudius:

> *He that hath killed my king, and whored my mother,*
> *Popped in between th'election and my hopes,*
> *Thrown out his angle for my proper life,*
>
> —Act V, scene ii, lines 64–66

This is the only time in the entire play that Hamlet openly admits that he had had "hopes" for the succession and that it is a grievance to him that he was outmaneuvered in this respect by Claudius.

Again, as in the scene with his mother after the killing of Polonius, he lists his grievances in order of what must be mounting outrage, and again the order is the same: the murder of the King and (worse) the marriage of his mother and (still worse) his own loss of the throne. This time he adds a fourth matter which has arisen since the scene with his mother and which is obviously worst of all: Claudius had tried to have him killed.

. . . the fall of a sparrow . . .

Horatio points out that if Hamlet still wants vengeance and the throne, he must allow for the fact that the news of the death of Rosencrantz and Guildenstern will alert Claudius to exactly what has happened. There isn't much time during which Hamlet can count on confusion and uncertainty keeping Claudius off guard again. Hamlet agrees that there isn't much time:

> *It will be short; the interim's mine*
>
> —Act V, scene ii, line 73

And yet Hamlet is in no haste. He is through plotting, for his plots have brought nothing but disaster on his head. When a messenger arrives suggesting that Hamlet engage in swordplay with Laertes, with King Claudius betting on victory for Hamlet, he wearily agrees.

He has earlier been keen indeed in guessing the King's plot in connection with the trip to England, but now he worries about nothing. The matter of fencing with someone whom he knows now to be a deadly enemy seems to give him no qualms. He assures Horatio that he has been practicing swordplay and will win, yet goes on:

> *But thou wouldst not think how ill all's here about my heart.*
> *But it is no matter.*
>
> —Act V, scene ii, lines 213–14

He may be thinking of Ophelia and wondering if her loss is not a heavy price to pay even for the throne—which he has not yet gained. Horatio, however, assumes Hamlet is suffering some presentiments of evil concerning the duel and therefore urges him to refuse the challenge. Hamlet shrugs this off. He is placing all his hopes on the "divinity that shapes our ends." To the suggestion he back away, he says:

> *Not a whit, we defy augury. There is special providence in the*

fall of a sparrow. If it be now, 'tis not to come; if it be not to come, it will be now, if it be not now, yet it will come. The readiness is all.

—Act V, scene ii, lines 220–24

The reference is to Jesus' assurance of divine care to his apostles: "Are not two sparrows sold for a farthing? and one of them shall not fall on the ground without your Father" (Matthew 10:29).

Why, then, should Hamlet have sought so earnestly to force events to his liking? God will do so in His own time and it will be Hamlet's task merely to be ready when that time comes.

. . . poor Hamlet's enemy

And now the fencing match!

Laertes and Hamlet ceremoniously greet each other and Hamlet gracefully begs pardon, placing the blame for Polonius' death on his own madness, and says:

If't be so,
Hamlet is of the faction that is wronged;
His madness is poor Hamlet's enemy.

—Act V, scene ii, lines 238–40

This sounds rather dishonest of Hamlet. He knows he was never mad. And yet it is still necessary for him to play at madness; and it was the game of madness that guided events up to the point where he thrust blindly through the curtain. In that sense it was indeed the necessary pretense of madness that was "poor Hamlet's enemy." And in addition, at the very moment when Polonius was killed, when Hamlet was in the mood of exalted triumph at the success of the play within a play, when he was finally in a position to talk to his mother in a way he had long wanted to—perhaps at that very moment he was mad indeed.

. . . the King's to blame

The fencing then starts. Laertes carefully picks the poisoned blade while Hamlet takes the first that comes to hand. His only question is a careless:

These foils have all a length?

—Act V, scene ii, line 266

Hamlet has the best of it at first, and the Queen drinks to his victory. Despite Claudius' convulsive attempt to stop her, she makes use of the cup of poison which he has prepared for Hamlet.

In a final exchange, Laertes manages to wound Hamlet, and, as the play is usually presented, Hamlet, suddenly aware that Laertes is fighting with an unguarded sword-point, forces a change in weapons and wounds Laertes in his turn.

The Queen collapses, crying she is poisoned. Laertes falls too, and in contrition admits what has been done, crying to Hamlet:

> *Thy mother's poisoned.*
> *I can no more. The King, the King's to blame.*
> —Act V, scene ii, lines 320–21

Hamlet has what he said he would get. Without making plans, without laying plots, divinity has shaped his ends. The King is accursed before the entire court of the vilest crimes, under conditions where it is impossible to disbelieve the accusation.

For Hamlet "readiness is all," and he is ready.

He kills the King.

. . . an antique Roman . . .

But it has all worked out with one fatal flaw. Hamlet has been poisoned. He is dying too. He has achieved his revenge, but not the succession after all.

Hamlet, feeling himself weakening, asks Horatio to report the events correctly, lest any rumors spread that Hamlet had acted any way but honorably. (Perhaps he is still worried that people may not consider it noble of him to have taken so devious a route to revenge when he was pretending madness and managing "to suffer the slings and arrows of outrageous fortune.")

Horatio, however, does not wish to survive. Seizing what is left of the poisoned wine, he says:

> *I am more an antique Roman than a Dane.*
> *Here's yet some liquor left.*
> —Act V, scene ii, lines 342–43

Under Christian law, suicide is a sin. Life came from God and belonged to God. The deliberate ending of life is murder, even where the life is the murderer's own.

Not so among the pre-Christian Romans. To them (as to the Japanese before World War II) it was an honorable gesture to prefer death to disgrace.

Perhaps the most impressive case was that of Cato the Younger, who, when his army was defeated by Julius Caesar, killed himself rather than survive the end of his country's freedom (see page I–281).

Hamlet, with his last dying strength, wrests the poison from Horatio. Hamlet has lost life and succession but he must at least save his honor. Claudius had been popular; might there not be some who would insist he was innocent and that Hamlet had killed him out of pure thwarted ambition? Horatio must bear witness to the truth:

> If thou didst ever hold me in thy heart
> Absent thee from felicity awhile,
> And in this harsh world draw thy breath in pain,
> To tell my story.

> —Act V, scene ii, lines 347–50

On Fortinbras . . .

And now come outsiders. Fortinbras of Norway returns victorious from Poland. Ambassadors arrive from England. But Hamlet's eyes are closing, his voice fading. He says:

> I cannot live to hear the news from England,
> But I do prophesy th'election lights
> On Fortinbras. He has my dying voice.

> —Act V, scene ii, lines 355–57

Hamlet was apparently the only child of the elder Hamlet, and Claudius has no children. From anything we can tell from the play, the Danish royal family has been utterly wiped out with Hamlet's death, and yet Denmark must have a king. Young Fortinbras of Norway is of a kindred nation and has proved himself a capable warrior. It is reasonable to pass the scepter on to him.

Actually, there is an echo of Canute's time in this too. When Canute's second son, Hardecanute, died in 1042, the Danish royal line of Canute died out. Hardecanute, aware that this might happen, arranged to have the kingship pass to Magnus of Norway, who earlier in this chapter (see page II–84) was pointed out as playing a role analogous to that of young Fortinbras in *Hamlet*.

Magnus the Good ruled as King of both Norway and Denmark from 1042 to 1047.

And thus ends this play of ironic revenge, with the announcement that the English King has executed Rosencrantz and Guildenstern, and with

Horatio preparing to tell the story to Fortinbras. And we may conclude with Horatio's touching words to Hamlet, as the Prince dies:

> *Now cracks a noble heart. Good night, sweet Prince,*
> *And flights of angels sing thee to thy rest.*
>
> —Act V, scene ii, lines 360–61

29

The Tragedy of

MACBETH

O N MARCH 24, 1603, Queen Elizabeth I of England died, leaving no children behind. (Indeed, she had never married.) Her aunt, Margaret Tudor, the older sister of Elizabeth's father, Henry VIII, had married James IV of Scotland. Their son reigned over Scotland as James V during much of the reign of Henry VIII in England. James V was thus first cousin to Elizabeth I.

James V died in 1542, only thirty years old, even before Elizabeth I started to reign. He left behind a six-day-old daughter who was to be the famous Mary, Queen of Scots. Mary was forced to abdicate in 1567 by her rebellious nobles, and her infant son (then thirteen months old) was named King in her place.

This son, who reigned as James VI, was the great-great-grandson of Henry VII of England (through two female ancestors), where Elizabeth was the granddaughter of Henry VII. James VI was still King of Scotland when Elizabeth I died. He was her nearest surviving relative and he succeeded to the throne, becoming James I of Great Britain and Ireland.

In 1589 James VI had married Anne of Denmark, the daughter of Frederick II of Denmark, who had died the year before, and the elder sister of the new King, Christian IV (who was destined to reign for the phenomenal length of sixty years).

In 1606 Christian IV came to visit his brother-in-law, James I of Great Britain, and it is thought that Shakespeare wrote the play *Macbeth* in honor of this occasion.

It was made to order for the purpose, with all of Shakespeare's skill. It is, for instance, a play dealing with early Scottish history, the only one of Shakespeare's plays to be devoted to that theme, and this is clearly done in honor of James's Scottish origins.

[. . . *Enter Three Witches*]

Shakespeare catered further to the tastes of the new monarch by saturating the play with witchcraft, and *Macbeth* is the only play in which this is done.

Early modern times were the heyday of the witch-hunting mania. Nor

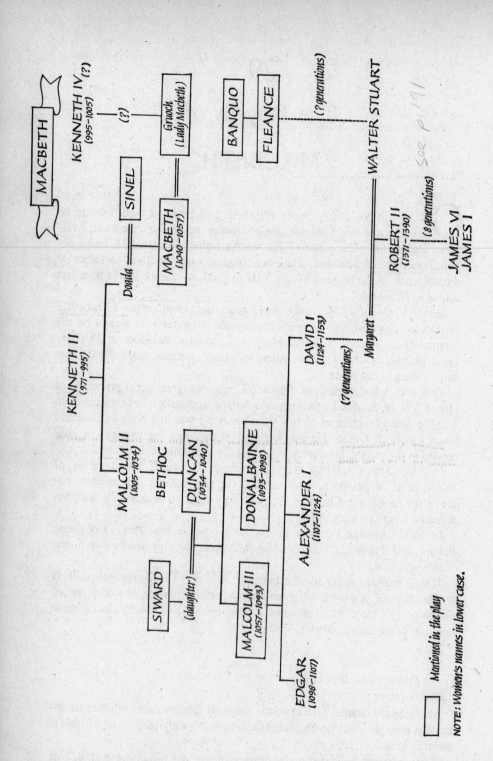

MACBETH

KENNETH IV (995–1005) (?)

(?)

Gruoch (Lady Macbeth)

SINEL

MACBETH (1040–1057)

BANQUO

FLEANCE

(? generations)

WALTER STUART

Donada

KENNETH II (971–995)

ROBERT II (1371–1390)

(8 generations) See p. 191

JAMES VI JAMES I

MALCOLM II (1005–1034)

BETHOC

DUNCAN (1034–1040)

DAVID I (1124–1153)

Margaret

(7 generations)

DONALBAINE (1093–1098)

ALEXANDER I (1107–1124)

SIWARD

(daughter)

MALCOLM III (1057–1093)

EDGAR (1098–1107)

☐ Mentioned in the play

NOTE: Women's names in lower case.

was it all madness. There were still remnants of pre-Christian beliefs and ritual here and there among the peasantry of western Europe, and undoubtedly there were some people who tried to cultivate magic powers and who believed themselves really to be what other people called witches.

Some of these were caught and treated as dangerous sinners who really did have the magical powers they thought they had. Along with them, numerous old women were tortured and murdered for no other crime but that of being old, ugly, and accused. The usual excuse for it was the terrible verse in the Bible which reads, "Thou shalt not suffer a witch to live" (Exodus 22:18).

As it happened, James I had pretensions to scholarship. He wrote books, discoursed learnedly on theology, had decided opinions which he strongly maintained, and in general wore people out with his pompous pedantry. He could scarcely fail to have a high opinion of himself, after all, for who was there to argue with him and prove him wrong? Another king might feel free to do so, perhaps, and Henry IV of France (much the abler man) said of James, very sarcastically, "He is the wisest fool in Christendom," and the general feeling is that Henry was right.

This does not mean he was all fool, however. Much of his learning was quite genuine, and in 1604 he wrote *A Counterblast to Tobacco* (anonymously), in which he denounced the new habit of tobacco smoking in harsh terms—yet terms with which a modern non-smoker can heartily agree and which, in the light of modern medical discoveries, would seem to be justified.

James I considered himself a particular expert on the matter of witchcraft. In 1597 he had written a book called *Demonology*, in which he advocated, among other things, the severest measures against witches.

Naturally, if James I was interested in witches, Shakespeare was going to give him witches. Nor did he have to make them up. He found them involved, in the sources he consulted, in the story of an early Scottish king, Macbeth. In fact, it is possible that one reason he chose this particular passage of Scottish history was because it allowed him to make use of witches.

Consequently *Macbeth* starts, mysteriously, in "an open place" in Scotland, and the very first stage direction is:

[*Thunder and lightning. Enter Three Witches.*]
—Act I, scene i

On they come; mysterious, grotesque, foreboding. One can well imagine James I sitting back with satisfaction and casting a pleased look at his royal brother-in-law. He will be able to study the stage witches and after the play is over he will surely proceed to explain to poor Christian at most tedious length all the places where Shakespeare proved he didn't really understand about witches.

. . . Graymalkin

This first appearance of the witches (aside from pleasing James) serves merely to fix the atmosphere. They have only come together to decide when the really crucial next meeting is to take place. From the rapid question-and-answer, we learn that there is a battle in progress and that they plan to meet with someone named Macbeth.

Having said that, they must leave at once, for they are called. The First Witch cries out:

> *I come, Graymalkin.*
>
> —Act I, scene i, line 8

The Second Witch says:

> *Paddock calls.*
>
> —Act I, scene i, line 9

Witches were thought to have sold their souls to the devil and, in return, to have received evil spirits as companions and servants. The Latin word for servant is *famulus*. A spirit who acts as a servant is therefore a "familiar spirit," or simply a "familiar."

These familiars were thought to take the shape of animals so that they might exist in the neighborhood of the witch without being detected. A cat was one favorite shape of this sort (based, perhaps, on no other reason than that old ladies who had survived their families and were forced to live on in isolation found cats to be quiet and agreeable company. If old ladies, being old, are witches, then their cats are their familiars).

Graymalkin is apparently a favorite name for a gray cat, "malkin" being a diminutive of the then popular name Matilda.

The Second Witch has a familiar in the shape of a toad (the apparently natural habitat of an evil spirit, since it is a squat and ugly creature). An obsolete name for a toad is "paddock."

What bloody man . . .

The witches chant a final couplet and whirl off the stage, but we need not wonder long what is happening. The matter of the battle is made plain at once when onto the stage comes an aged King and his court. A bleeding soldier follows and the King says:

> *What bloody man is that? He can report,*
> *As seemeth by his plight, of the revolt*
> *The newest state.*
>
> —Act I, scene ii, lines 1–3

The King who asks the question is Duncan I, who became King in 1034. At this time Scotland was just forming as a nation. Until some two centuries before, it had been populated by a collection of tribes who had found security in their wild hills against the Romans, who ruled the southern part of the island till 410 (see page II–76), and the Saxons, who began to flood into that southern part later in the century (see page II–77).

By 800, however, the northern section of the island of Britain had lost its security, for danger came directly from the eastern and northern seas in the form of the Viking raids (see page II–79). England and Ireland suffered as badly.

Much of the northernmost areas of Scotland became Viking and remained so for a long time, while the Scots in the southern sections began to huddle together in self-defense. In 840 the nucleus of a nation called "Scotland" was formed, but for a long time the title of King was bandied back and forth, most bloodily, by several families, and Scottish history remains very dim.

It is only with Duncan that Scottish history begins to gain some firmness and the kingship settles down to a single dynasty. There remained dynastic disputes and always and perpetually war with England on the south, but all the kings of Scotland from this point on (with the one exception that is the theme of this play) were descendants of Duncan.

We know virtually nothing of Duncan I save that he reigned. Holinshed (see page II–4), who was Shakespeare's source, speaks of him as "soft and gentle of nature." He does not mention his age, but it is very likely he was fairly young. He had succeeded his grandfather, Malcolm II (1005–34), to the throne. Even if Malcolm II had attained the age of seventy (a great age for the time) at his death, it would be fair to suppose that his grandson, Duncan, would then be about thirty at the time of his accession. He reigned only six years, so that in the last year of his reign, 1040, when the play opens, he would be only thirty-six. Another piece of evidence in favor of his youth is that he had two sons at the time of his death, of whom the older was only nine.

Nevertheless, Shakespeare makes him an old man. Partly this serves to increase the horror of the crime that brings his reign to a bloody close. Partly, too, it may have been done to avoid offending King James I. James's own father, Henry, Lord Darnley, had met a similar bloody end, and it was widely believed that James's mother had been involved in the deed. It would be the height of folly to remind James of this. Lord Darnley had been only twenty-two years old when he died, however, and if Duncan was made an aged, white-bearded king, the similarity would be minimized.

(Since *Macbeth* covers the period from 1040 to 1057, the events in this play are contemporaneous with those in *Hamlet*.)

'Gainst my captivity

The bloody man is recognized by one of those who attend the King and who now says:

> This is the sergeant
> Who like a good and hardy soldier fought
> 'Gainst my captivity.

> —Act I, scene ii, lines 3–5

The speaker is Malcolm, the elder son of Duncan. He was born about 1031 and would therefore have been some nine years old at the time *Macbeth* opens. By the end of the play he would be twenty-six years old and perfectly capable of acting the role assigned to him in the last act. Shakespeare does not allow the dramatic time within the play to equal the actual historical time. It is his intention, in fact, to push through the play in a whirlwind of activity, making very little time seem to pass. For that reason, he has none of the characters age in the play, and Malcolm is as old at the beginning as he is at the end.

Malcolm has a younger brother, Donalbain (Donald Bane, or Donald the Bonny; that is, Handsome), who is on the scene but does not speak.

Duncan and Malcolm are both treated with great gentleness in the play and made to seem very attractive, partly because James I traced one line of his descent from them. He was eighteen generations removed from Duncan I, in a genealogy that included three women; and, of course, seventeen from Malcolm.

Donalbain is neglected almost entirely. He speaks seven lines in the entire play. Partly this is because he did, in actuality, have only a minor part to play in the events of this play. Partly, too, we can suspect it is because he is not represented among the ancestors of King James.

The merciless Macdonwald

The sergeant, who is referred to as "Captain" in the cast of characters of the Signet edition, describes the battle:

> The merciless Macdonwald—
> Worthy to be a rebel for to that
> The multiplying villainies of nature
> Do swarm upon him—from the Western Isles
> Of kerns and gallowglasses is supplied;

> —Act I, scene ii, lines 9–13

The Scottish realm, so recently united by Duncan and his immediate predecessors, is by no means firmly knit. Various individual chieftains would wish to preserve their independence or even to take over the central monarchy for what little that was actually worth in those days. The Western Isles are off the northwestern coast of Scotland and are better known these days as the Hebrides, a distortion of an old name used by the Greek geographers. They came under Viking domination about 900, and indeed, the Vikings controlled the northernmost sections of Scotland (the Highlands) altogether; not only at the time of the play, but for two centuries after Duncan's time.

The "kerns and gallowglasses" (names given to Irish soldiers, light-armed and heavy-armed respectively) came from the Hebrides and, according to Holinshed, from Ireland too—which had also been under strong Viking domination until nearly this time.

Macdonwald, then, is fighting with Viking help, against the new Scottish kingdom of the Lowlands which threatens to destroy Viking domination of the north—and which eventually did.

. . . brave Macbeth . . .

At first, according to the Captain's account, the battle seemed to be in Macdonwald's favor:

> . . . Fortune, on his damned quarrel smiling,
> Showed like a rebel's whore: but all's too weak:
> For brave Macbeth—well he deserves that name—
> Disdaining Fortune, with his brandished steel,
> Which smoked with bloody execution,
> Like valor's minion carved out his passage
> Till he faced the slave;
>
> —Act I, scene ii, lines 14–20

Macbeth, then, so fleetingly mentioned by the witches in the first scene, is the loyalist general, fighting on behalf of his sovereign, Duncan.

Actually, Macbeth is more than just a general. He seems to have been a grandson of Kenneth II (971–95), the father of Malcolm II; perhaps his mother was a sister of the latter king. Since Duncan was a grandson of Malcolm II, Macbeth would be the first cousin (once removed) of the reigning King. The chances are that, historically, Macbeth was older than the King, forty years of age perhaps, though in the play Macbeth is shown as a fighter in the prime of his strength, while Duncan is an aged man.

The relationship between Macbeth and Duncan is made plain enough in the play. When Duncan hears the Captain tell of Macbeth's chopping his way to Macdonwald and killing him, he cries out:

O valiant cousin!

—Act I, scene ii, line 24

It might be argued that in Shakespeare the term "cousin" can be used as a general term for honored friend as well as for relative. On the other hand, later in the play, Macbeth says specifically:

. . . I am his kinsman and his subject,

—Act I, scene vii, line 13

The fact of the relationship is important. Macbeth, as Duncan's cousin, was of the royal family, and in those days there was no fixed system of "legitimacy" whereby one member of the royal family had definite and universally agreed upon precedence over another for the throne (see page II-164).

Ideally, the strongest and most competent member of the royal family should be on the throne. Duncan was soft and gentle, but he was also negligent and inefficient. He was not a king for those hard times, and under him, Scotland experienced rebellion and anarchy. This displeased Macbeth. As Holinshed says, ". . . Makbeth speaking much against the King's softness, and overmuch slackness in punishing offenders . . ."

We can perhaps sympathize with Macbeth. It was Duncan's incapacity that allowed Macdonwald's rebellion and it was then Macbeth who had to risk his life in incredible exertions to make good Duncan's failure. It might well have occurred to many, comparing Duncan's inertia and Macbeth's overflowing energy, that the wrong cousin was on the throne. (And it may have occurred to Macbeth himself too.)

None of this, of course, is to be found in Shakespeare's play, where the right of Duncan (the ancestor of James I) is unquestioned, while Macbeth (who is not in the line of ancestry) is granted no shadow of legitimate claim to the kingship.

. . . the Norweyan lord . . .

Macbeth's superiority in arms showed the brighter in the aftermath of the victorious battle against Macdonwald, for the rebel's death did not end matters. No sooner had that battle ended, reported the Captain:

> *But the Norweyan lord, surveying vantage,*
> *With furbished arms and new supplies of men,*
> *Began a fresh assault.*

—Act I, scene ii, lines 31–33

According to Holinshed, this is "Sueno king of Norway." This might be

Sven II of Denmark, who became king in 1047, and who began a new Danish dynasty after the extinction of the line of Canute and the temporary sway of Magnus I of Norway (see page II–84). If so, the use of his name would be a little anachronistic, though in later years he made two futile attempts to attack England, which was then in the strong grasp of William the Conqueror.

It may well have been a Danish rather than a Norwegian invasion of Scotland that Macbeth had to deal with at that time, whatever the name of the leader of the invading army. If so, though, Shakespeare was certainly careful to leave it Norwegian. After all, with Christian IV of Denmark, the royal brother-in-law, in the audience, mention of a Danish defeat would have been unpolitic.

Perhaps this Norwegian invasion was not really a second battle, but rather part of the first battle delayed. Macdonwald, fighting with Viking help, may have been defeated by the skillful maneuvering of Macbeth, who, acting with admirable celerity, encountered Macdonwald before he could join with his Norwegian allies. Having defeated him, he then turned on the Norwegians.

. . . Macbeth and Banquo

Disturbed at the news of the fresh invasion, Duncan asks:

> Dismayed not this
> Our captains, Macbeth and Banquo?
> —Act I, scene ii, lines 33–34

This is the first mention of Banquo in the play. He is mentioned in Holinshed, but there is reason to think he is not a historical personage. He seems, rather, to have been invented for a political purpose.

James I of England belonged to the house of Stuart. The first Stuart to reign over Scotland was Robert II, who began his reign in 1371.

Robert II succeeded to the throne because his mother was the younger sister of the preceding King of Scotland, David II. It was through his mother that Robert II (and therefore James I) could count himself a scion of the old kings of Scotland, dating back to Duncan and beyond. Through his father, he was merely a descendant of Walter FitzAlan, a Norman baron who had been made steward of the Scottish King David I (who had reigned three quarters of a century after Duncan).

For the house of Stuart, in the male line, to go back no further than David I, and to be represented then by an immigrant from England (Scotland's age-long enemy) who had a non-military position from which the name itself was drawn, was humiliating. (To be sure, a steward was a higher position than it now sounds. In medieval times the king's steward was the overseer of his estate and of all domestic ceremonies—a virtual "secretary of the interior.")

Consequently, the legend of Banquo was originated. It was from him that the house of Stuart was supposed to be descended. Banquo was presented as of good Scottish stock, dating back to Duncan's time. What's more, he was a general, fighting valiantly and victoriously. This produced a much better aura about the Stuart line than Walter FitzAlan did.

By Holinshed's time the myth of Banquo had been fixed, and he is mentioned in the chronicle. However, Holinshed was writing in Elizabeth's time and he had no reason to be overly gentle with Banquo, who doesn't come out very well. For Shakespeare things were different. Since James I considered himself a descendant of Banquo as well as of Duncan, Banquo had to be handled with kid gloves, and was.

. . . another Golgotha

The Captain laughs off any possibility of Macbeth and Banquo being frightened. He himself has left the battle, because of his wounds, while it was still undecided, but the generals were raining blows on the enemy as though

> . . . they meant to bathe in reeking wounds,
> Or memorize another Golgotha,
>
> —Act I, scene ii, lines 39–40

Golgotha ("place of a skull") was the name of the site on which Jesus was crucified (see Matthew 27:33), and it had a most dolorous infamy in consequence. The Captain implies that Macbeth seemed to be dealing out so much slaughter as to seem ambitious to make the field tragic enough to be as horribly infamous as Golgotha.

. . . Thane of Ross

The Captain is weakening and cannot complete his story. He is led away to have his wounds attended to. Two newcomers arrive, however, and Malcolm identifies one of them:

> The worthy Thane of Ross.
>
> —Act I, scene ii, line 45

"Thane" is from a word that means a "follower" or "servant." The King's immediate followers or servants are his nobles, and the word became a title of nobility, equivalent to "earl."

Ross is a section of northern Scotland and its use is probably an anachronism here. Ross seems still to have been under Viking control at this
time, and the first Earl of Ross was not appointed till more than a century
after Duncan's reign.

Entering with Ross is the Thane of Angus (the name of a county in
east-central Scotland) and already with the King is the Thane of Lennox.
These titles are also anachronistic, well known in later times but not in
Duncan's.

The Thane of Cawdor . . .

The King asks where Ross came from and the latter answers:

> *From Fife, great King;*
> *Where the Norweyan banners flout the sky*
> —Act I, scene ii, lines 48–49

Fife is a county in southeastern Scotland, just across the Firth of Forth
from Edinburgh. The Viking forces landing there are striking at the very
heart of Scotland. What's more, they are receiving assistance from a Scottish turncoat:

> *Norway himself, with terrible numbers,*
> *Assisted by that most disloyal traitor*
> *The Thane of Cawdor, began a dismal conflict;*
> *Till that Bellona's bridegroom, lapped in proof,*
> *Confronted him . . .*
> —Act I, scene ii, lines 51–55

Cawdor is a small town in northern Scotland, about ten miles east of
the city of Inverness. It was probably at the northern limits of the territory
controlled by Duncan. To the north were the Vikings.

The Thane of Cawdor, feeling, probably, that the Vikings would win,
was on their side. He was not actually on the battlefield, for it later turns
out that Macbeth (who fought on that battlefield) was not aware of the
Thane's treason. Apparently, he had helped the Vikings with supplies,
men, or, at the very least, information—and the King's officials had learned
of it.

Bellona was the Roman goddess of war, considered sometimes to be the
wife of Mars. Bellona's bridegroom would, therefore, be Mars, and the
name is flatteringly applied here to Macbeth, for he wins the second
battle as well as the first. The Norwegians are defeated and are forced to
pay reparations.

As for the traitorous Thane of Cawdor, who now finds he has backed the wrong horse after all, Duncan pronounces his sentence, saying:

> *No more that Thane of Cawdor shall deceive*
> *Our bosom interest: go pronounce his present death,*
> *And with his former title greet Macbeth.*
> 　　　　　　　　　　　　—Act I, scene ii, lines 63–65

To his own titles, estates, and revenues, in other words, Macbeth will find added those of Cawdor.

The weird sisters . . .

The scene now shifts back to the three witches. They are on a blasted heath; on a wasteland, that is, a plot of ground uninhabited and uncultivated.

For some thirty lines they engage in witch-ish mumbo jumbo, and talk of killing swine and putting curses on sailors. It has nothing to do with the play, or, for that matter, with the witches. It is merely there for atmosphere, and, undoubtedly, to please King James.

But then there is the sudden sound of a drum and the witches know Macbeth is coming. They quickly recite a charm:

> *The weird sisters, hand in hand,*
> *Posters of the sea and land,*
> *Thus do go about, about:*
> 　　　　　　　　　　　　—Act I, scene iii, lines 32–34

The name Shakespeare has them call themselves, "the weird sisters" (by which name Holinshed also refers to them), suffices in itself to show that they are more than mere witches.

The word "weird" has come to mean "uncanny," "eerie," "gruesome-looking," partly because of its use right here in this play—but that is not its original meaning at all. It is from the Anglo-Saxon word "wyrd," meaning "fate."

The weird sisters are the three beings who determine fate. They are what were called in Nordic mythology the Norns. Originally, there may have been one Norn (Fate), but the tendency was to make three of them, representing the Past, Present, and Future. (The Greeks also had three.)

The Norns were the arbiters of destiny, from whose decisions there was no appeal, and before whom even the gods were helpless. They were the embodiment of What Was, What Is, and, most fearsome of all, What Will Be.

It was these awesome creatures of ineluctable Necessity—and not just old crones, stirring caldrons and cackling—who were awaiting Macbeth.

. . . to Forres

Macbeth and Banquo come on the scene now and Banquo asks:

> How far is't called to Forres?
>
> —Act I, scene iii, line 39

The two generals are traveling alone and they are far to the north of the site of the recent battle against the Vikings. Forres is about ninety miles north of Fife and some twenty miles east of Cawdor.

Apparently, in the aftermath of the battle, the King and his court traveled north to deal with the Thane of Cawdor. According to Holinshed, Cawdor was tried and condemned at Forres. The Scottish court was in any case forced to spend some time at Forres along the northern marches to oversee the chronic warfare with the Vikings in the Highlands.

Presumably, Macbeth and Banquo were called northward to attend the King at Forres and, when almost there, encountered the weird sisters on the heath.

. . . that shalt be King . . .

Each of the weird sisters in turn hails Macbeth:

> [First] *All hail, Macbeth! Hail to thee, Thane of Glamis!*
> [Second] *All hail, Macbeth! Hail to thee, Thane of Cawdor!*
> [Third] *All hail, Macbeth, that shalt be King hereafter!*
>
> —Act I, scene iii, lines 48–50

The division is a neat one. The First Witch speaks of What Was: Macbeth was Thane of Glamis. (Glamis is a town in Angus County, ten miles north of Dundee.) The Second Witch speaks of What Is: Macbeth is now Thane of Cawdor, though he is not yet aware of that fact and isn't even aware, apparently, of the discovery of the treachery of the previous thane of that title. The Third Witch speaks, of course, of What Will Be.

Why do the weird sisters confront Macbeth thus? The prophecy of future kingship is self-fulfilling. If the play is taken at its surface value, it is only the fact that the Third Witch put the matter of the kingship into Macbeth's head that leads to all the later action. If so, the witches can be looked at as demons whose only motive is to maneuver Macbeth's soul to damnation.

Or do the weird sisters merely symbolize in dramatic outward form the dark thoughts reverberating within Macbeth's head? His victories may have sharpened his own feeling that the wrong cousin is on the throne. He may be playing with the thought of making himself King, and the witches are a way of making that plain to the audience.

But Shakespeare didn't create the matter of the three witches; they are to be found in Holinshed, so we can't look upon them as merely the products of a great dramatist's technique.

After Holinshed describes the encounter of the weird sisters with Macbeth and Banquo, in terms that Shakespeare adheres to closely, that chronicler says, "But afterwards the common opinion was, that these women were either the weird sisters, that is (as ye would say) the goddesses of destiny, or else some nymphs or fairies, endued with knowledge of prophecy by their necromantical science."

Apparently, then, there had arisen a strong tradition, which first Holinshed and then Shakespeare adopted, that Macbeth had indeed met with something supernatural. How did such a tradition arise? It might have been pure invention, or, perhaps, we might speculate as follows:

In the sixth century Ireland underwent a kind of renaissance that endured until the Vikings came along in the ninth century and reduced the island to barbarism. During the sixth-to-ninth-century golden age, Irish monks spread their doctrines all over the British Isles and into the European continent itself. It was Christianity, but not quite the Christianity of Rome; there were differences in detail.

Rome fought against this "Celtic Christianity" and ultimately prevailed. In 664 at the Synod of Whitby, England turned officially from Celtic Christianity to Roman Christianity. Celtic Christianity even retreated from Ireland itself.

Indeed, Celticism found, as its last stronghold, Scotland. Down to Duncan's reign it still maintained itself stubbornly. We know very little of the detail of that struggle, for when Roman Christianity triumphed, it wiped out the very memory of what it considered devilish cults and heresies.

It was after Macbeth's time that Roman Christianity won its final victory and Celticism died at last. The Scottish church may have looked back on Macbeth as one of the last representatives of the old Celticism and might have considered him in league with vague old magical and pagan practices. Can it be that dim tales of his league with the powers of darkness (only his Celticism, really) crystallized at last into the tale of the witches?

Thou shalt get kings . . .

While Macbeth stands stunned by what has happened, Banquo (less imaginative than his fellow general) seems to think he has encountered carnival magicians. He asks if they have prophecies for him. The Third Witch, What Will Be, makes the dark sayings of her sisters plain when she says:

Thou shalt get kings, though thou be none.
—Act I, scene iii, line 67

This is a reference to the legend that Banquo is the ancestor of the Stuart line. (One can imagine that at that first showing of *Macbeth,* the Third Witch manages to indicate royal James as she declaims the line.)

By Sinel's death . . .

But now Macbeth has found his tongue, and expresses his bewilderment:

> *By Sinel's death I know I am Thane of Glamis;*
> *But how of Cawdor? The Thane of Cawdor lives,*
> *A prosperous gentleman . . .*
—Act I, scene iii, lines 71–73

Sinel was Macbeth's father and had been the previous Thane of Glamis. To that title Macbeth succeeded automatically on his father's death.

But even as Macbeth asks for more information, the weird sisters vanish, and hard on the heels of that vanishing come Ross and Angus, searching for the generals. They bring a message from the King, and Macbeth learns for the first time of Cawdor's treason and the fact that he, himself, has succeeded to the title.

At once, the amazed Macbeth realizes that the weird sisters have told one truth at least. And the thought enters his mind that he really may be King.

Whose horrid image . . .

For Macbeth to become King, Duncan must cease being King, and one direct way to bring that about is for Macbeth to kill Duncan. The thought is a very easy one in a land that was as yet barely troubled by civilization, and Scotland up to that point had gone through an unending series of tribal wars in which one thane or another was intent on killing whoever it was that called himself King in order that he himself might take his turn at the title. Macdonwald had only been the latest of many.

Yet Macbeth does not find it an easy thought at all. He soliloquizes:

> *. . . why do I yield to that suggestion*
> *Whose horrid image doth unfix my hair*
> *And make my seated heart knock at my ribs,*
> *Against the use of nature?*
—Act I, scene iii, lines 134–37

Macbeth's strong reaction against the thought of killing Duncan must be understood in terms of Shakespeare's time, not Macbeth's.

In feudal times (and Macbeth's Scotland was certainly feudal) the King was merely the first among equals. In many cases, the King was not as strong as some of his chief vassals, and disobedience to the King on the part of those vassals, or even outright rebellion, was much more the rule than the exception.

In early modern times, as feudalism began to break down, the King came to be something more than he had been. Instead of being chosen by the nobles generally (as is the situation in *Macbeth* and in *Hamlet,* see page II-156) the principles of "legitimacy" were developed. Each new king became king by the rigid succession of birth, even if he were a tyrant, an incompetent, or a moron.

Such a legitimate king was, in effect, chosen by God, since it was God who allowed him to be born in the right fashion to make his kingship inevitable. The King's rights were then obtained from God and he was accountable to no one else. This was the doctrine of the "divine right of kings."

To kill a king in any society which believed in the divine right of kings was to commit the highest form of sacrilege. The killing was of God's deputy and, therefore, in a way, of God himself.

In England, the doctrine of divine right was never as popular or as effective as it became on parts of the Continent. Through much of its history, England had a Parliament which insisted more and more on participating firmly, and even decisively, in governmental decisions, and which felt that the King was responsible to the gentry of the nation as well as to God.

The moment when divine right and consequent absolutism reached its peak in England was under Henry VIII, who ruled from 1509 to 1547 and who combined an indomitable will and a ferocious cruelty with an uncommon knack for earning popularity with his subjects. His second daughter, Elizabeth I, who reigned from 1558 to 1603, had the same knack of popularity and was much less cruel. Though both Henry and Elizabeth acted as though they were accountable only to God, they didn't make much of a fuss about it.

James I was of another sort altogether. He was a Scotsman and personally repulsive in his habits (even by Elizabethan standards), with no knack for earning popularity at all among a population who didn't like his birth, his accent, or his personality. Yet he prided himself on being a scholar and therefore insisted on airing his theories of government, and on loudly preaching the doctrine of the divine right of kings.

Perhaps one can scarcely blame him, for the times were dangerous ones for kings. The Protestant Reformation had begun in 1517 and the nations of Europe drew into irreconcilable camps, Catholics on one side and Protestants on the other. A number of the nations (England among them) were partly Catholic and partly Protestant, so that the danger of civil war was added to that of foreign war.

In the maddened emotions of this period, it became increasingly possible to have people think the killing of kings to be justified, and even praiseworthy, if the King were of the wrong religion in the eyes of the killer.

James I's own mother, Mary, Queen of Scots, was executed in 1587, for religious as well as political reasons. Then in 1589 the French King, Henry III, was stabbed to death by a fanatical monk, Jacques Clément, who felt that the King was "soft" on Protestantism.

With *Macbeth* being played before James I, with the matter of regicide very much in the air, and with James's viewpoints on the divine right of kings well known, it behooved Shakespeare to make the possible killing of Duncan a much more horrifying matter than, in fact, it probably would have been considered in Macbeth's time.

. . . chance may crown me

Macbeth, with early seventeenth-century awe, recoils, then, from regicide, and thinks of the alternative. He continues his soliloquy:

> *If chance will have me King, why, chance may crown me,*
> *Without my stir.*
>
> —Act I, scene iii, lines 143–44

Why not? Chance (or better, Fate) had made him Thane of Cawdor without his stir. And there isn't really such a great gap between Macbeth and the kingship. A bit earlier, in response to the statement of the Third Witch, Macbeth had said:

> *. . . to be King*
> *Stands not within the prospect of belief,*
> —Act I, scene iii, lines 73–74

That, however, is an exaggeration. In later centuries, when the principles of legitimacy were accepted, the fact that Duncan had two sons in good health would make it seem that the kingship was not likely to pass to a collateral line. In Macbeth's time, this simply was not so.

In that age of brief lives and violent death, Duncan might die at any time, in battle or of disease, even if he were as young as he was in reality; and much more so if he were as old as Shakespeare presents him as being. Once Duncan is dead, a successor would have to be chosen from the royal family. The two sons were, in actual historical fact, mere children, and Macbeth was not only a member of the royal family, but a great and victorious general. It would be certain that Macbeth would be chosen successor. It would be easy, then, for Chance to crown him without his stir.

Thinking of that, perhaps, Macbeth tries to shake off his pensiveness and joins the others (who are more or less patiently waiting for him) on the final stage of the journey toward Forres, where are the King and the court.

The Prince of Cumberland

At Forres, the former Thane of Cawdor has been executed and the King greets Macbeth with joy and praise. Macbeth is rather studied and mechanical in his protestations of devotion.

And then the King, happy in the double victory over traitors at home and Vikings abroad, feels it is time to consider the state as secure and to give thought to a successor. He says:

> We will establish our estate upon
> Our eldest, Malcolm, whom we name hereafter
> The Prince of Cumberland:

—Act I, scene iv, lines 37–39

Cumberland is one of the northernmost counties of England itself, but it did not form an undoubted part of England till its conquest by William II Rufus, son of William the Conqueror, in 1092, half a century after Duncan's time. Before that it was more or less under Scottish control.

The Prince of Cumberland would be a title worn by the heir to the Scottish throne, equivalent to Prince of Wales in the English system. Indeed, by "establish our estate" Duncan means what would more directly be expressed as "settle the succession."

This is a thunderbolt to Macbeth. The wishes of a previous king (particularly a popular one) would have an important effect on popular opinion and even on the feelings of the nobility. If everyone grew used to thinking of Malcolm as heir to the throne, he was very likely to succeed automatically on Duncan's death.

Suddenly, it is far less likely that Chance would crown Macbeth without his stir. If Macbeth wants to be King, he will have to stir, somehow. He soliloquizes:

> The Prince of Cumberland! That is a step
> On which I must fall down, or else o'erleap,
> For in my way it lies.

—Act I, scene iv, lines 48–50

. . . to Inverness

But it is time for celebration and happiness. The King plans to visit

Macbeth's castle so that he and his great general may feast together and grow ever more friendly and loving. He says to Macbeth:

> From hence to Inverness,
> And bind us further to you.
>
> —Act I, scene iv, lines 42–43

Inverness is fifty miles west of Forres and it is here where Macbeth's castle is located, and where his wife, Lady Macbeth, is to be found.

. . . unsex me here

Macbeth has already sent a letter to his wife, and she enters, in the next scene, reading it, for her first appearance in the play. She is known to us (in the play) only as Lady Macbeth, which is perhaps just as well, since the name of the wife of the historic Macbeth was the uncommonly uneuphonious one of Gruoch.

Lady Macbeth's reaction to the tale of what the weird sisters have said is not at all like that of Macbeth himself. Not for her the hesitations. She springs at once to the conclusion that the way to the throne must be cleared by instant action. She soliloquizes:

> Come, you spirits
> That tend on mortal thoughts, unsex me here,
> And fill me, from the crown to the toe, top-full
> Of direst cruelty!
>
> —Act I, scene v, lines 41–44

Passages such as this one have made it common to think of Lady Macbeth as the very epitome of feminine ferocity—and yet Shakespeare wrongs her.

According to some of the fragmentary versions of early Scottish history that reach us, Lady Macbeth was the granddaughter of Kenneth IV, a Scottish king who was of a family that was rival to the one from which Duncan was descended. Indeed, Kenneth IV died in battle against Malcolm II, Duncan's grandfather.

In the primitive clan society of early Scotland, the real Lady Macbeth would have felt she had a blood feud with Duncan. (Her own husband, Macbeth, was the son of a sister of Malcolm II and might be considered as not inheriting the blood guilt in Lady Macbeth's eyes.) Under those circumstances, Lady Macbeth might, and probably did, encourage her able husband to rebel against the feckless King.

And this is what actually happened. If Macbeth, encouraged by his wife, aspired to the throne, he did so in the approved Scottish fashion of the time. He raised an army and rebelled.

Thus, Holinshed says: "he [Macbeth] slew the king at Enverns [Inverness], or (as some say) at Botgosuane, in the sixth year of his [Duncan's] reign." Holinshed does not say "murdered," he says "slew," and that is a word which would fit death in battle. Botgosuane, by the way, is a place some thirty miles northeast of Inverness.

Such a rebellion and such a death in battle of the King would not serve Shakespeare's purposes, for he wanted a play of horror, witchcraft, and despair. Looking for something more grisly, he came across a short account in Holinshed of the assassination of a Scottish king, Duff, by one of his nobles, Donwald. Donwald was not anxious to assassinate the King, but he was encouraged to do so by his wife. Donwald ended by doing the deed at a time when the King was his guest and asleep.

Shakespeare transplanted the deed bodily from Donwald to Macbeth, saddling the latter forever with a crime he probably would never have dreamed of committing. What's more, he made Lady Macbeth bear the blame of Lady Donwald through all the centuries.

It is indeed a fearful example of the power of the pen to alter the truth itself if it is wielded with sufficient genius. There are many other examples in Shakespeare, with the case of Richard III perhaps even more pitiable than that of Macbeth.

. . . as his host

Returning to Shakespeare's Macbeth, we find him with his conscience still clamoring.

Duncan has arrived at Macbeth's castle, has been greeted by Lady Macbeth, and is now at dinner. Macbeth, however, half sick with uncertainty and worry, has left the table, and is muttering to himself all the arguments against the deed. There is, after all, a third factor, older than either kingly divinity or feudal duty, to be considered; and one that is in some ways more fearful. Macbeth argues against the deed by saying:

> First, as I am his kinsman and his subject,
> Strong both against the deed; then, as his host
> Who should against his murderer shut the door,
> Not bear the knife myself.
>
> —Act I, scene vii, lines 13–16

The sacred duties of hospitality date back to dim prehistory. In ages when effective communities were no larger than villages or tribes, travelers were forced to depend on the hospitality of strangers, and in sheer self-interest, custom imposed stringent rules to prevent the abuse of such strangers. (After all, the host of today may be the traveler of tomorrow.) To be hospitable was strictly enjoined, and to harm a guest or allow harm to come to him was a terrible crime.

Thus, when Lot in Sodom entertained strangers (who were angels, though he did not know that), the men of the city offered those strangers violence. Lot, according to the sacred duty of hospitality, offered to sacrifice his daughters to the mob, rather than allow them to touch his guests (Genesis 19:1–8).

Thus, the guilt is piled high on Macbeth and horror is heaped on horror. The man he thinks of murdering is his feudal lord, his King, his cousin, and his guest. He is, moreover, old, weak, and virtuous, and to top it all off, he is to be killed treacherously, while asleep.

. . . the poor cat . . .

Lady Macbeth comes out from the feast, searching impatiently for her husband and fearful that his odd actions will bring on suspicion.

The two make a remarkably natural and even likable (except for the nature of the deed they are planning) couple. They argue, but they act as a team and protect each other. It is clear that they are in love and that their marriage is a successful one.

But now at this moment in the play, Lady Macbeth must infuse her own resolution into her wavering husband. When Macbeth begins to talk of abandoning the plan, she asks if he wishes to

> . . . live a coward in thine own esteem,
> Letting "I dare not" wait upon "I would,"
> Like the poor cat i'th'adage?
>
> —Act I, scene vii, lines 43–45

The lines are frequently quoted to describe irresolution, picturing someone who lets "I dare not" follow instantly (that is, "wait upon") every time he expresses the desire "I would." The adage to which Lady Macbeth refers is, however, rarely known by those who quote the lines.

It is a medieval Latin proverb that can be translated "The cat loves fish, but does not wish to wet its foot." By Shakespeare's time it was so well known through its use by Chaucer as not to require actual quoting. The picture of the cat, yearning for fish, advancing its paw, then drawing it back at the first touch of water, over and over, is clear enough in Lady Macbeth's hard voice, so that Macbeth can only writhe and say:

> Prithee, peace!
> I dare do all that may become a man;
> Who dares do more is none.
>
> —Act I, scene vii, lines 45–47

I have given suck . . .

But Lady Macbeth goes on remorselessly, saying:

> *I have given suck, and know*
> *How tender 'tis to love the babe that milks me:*
> *I would, while it was smiling in my face,*
> *Have plucked my nipple from his boneless gums,*
> *And dashed the brains out, had I so sworn as you*
> *Have done to this.*
>
> —Act I, scene vii, lines 54–59

Macbeth has no surviving children in this play, or in history, it would appear. We must assume, then, that Lady Macbeth had a baby that died young, or, perhaps, had had a child by a previous marriage. And indeed, after Macbeth's death, a stepson of his, Lulach, did attempt to carry on the dynasty.

What's more, Lady Macbeth seems to be of an age, still, where more children are considered possible, for Macbeth, awed by her ferocious determination, says:

> *Bring forth men-children only;*
> *For thy undaunted mettle should compose*
> *Nothing but males.*
>
> —Act I, scene vii, lines 72–74

. . . Pale Hecate's offerings . . .

It is now night; a horrible night. Banquo and his son, Fleance, appear in the castle courtyard, announce it to be past midnight and the King asleep. Macbeth appears and Banquo gives him a last present from the monarch, saying:

> *This diamond he greets your wife withal,*
> *By the name of most kind hostess . . .*
>
> —Act II, scene i, lines 15–16

The crime against hospitality is thus underlined.

Left alone, Macbeth's burning imagination presents him with a hallucinated dagger, and he describes the ghastly night as follows:

> *Now o'er the one half-world*
> *Nature seems dead, and wicked dreams abuse*
> *The curtained sleep; witchcraft celebrates*

Pale Hecate's offerings; and withered murder,
Alarumed by his sentinel, the wolf,
Whose howl's his watch, thus with his stealthy pace,
With Tarquin's ravishing strides, towards his design
Moves like a ghost.
>   —Act II, scene i, lines 49–56

The pictures crowd each other—death, bad dreams, witchcraft, murder, howling wolves, ghosts. Hecate is a mythic underworld goddess (see page I–50) and in later times had come to be considered a kind of queen of witches, so that she fits into the atmosphere of this play. The advance of murder is compared to that of Tarquin, who raped the virtuous Lucretia (see page I–205).

His soliloquy done, Macbeth hastens into the castle to commit the murder.

This is carried through offstage, but the words of Macbeth and Lady Macbeth as they come from and go to Duncan's bedchamber are most effective witness to the deed.

Lady Macbeth has effectively done her part. She has drugged the servants who are supposed to be guarding the King and she has made sure the door to his chamber is unlocked.

Finally, the murder is done and Macbeth comes in, panting and wild-eyed, still carrying the daggers dripping blood, and almost incoherent with the horror of it all.

. . . Sleep no more

Macbeth, who has had such difficulty overcoming his scruples in the first place, now feels his conscience will never give him rest. He says, in a kind of self-loathing:

Methought I heard a voice cry, "Sleep no more!
Macbeth does murder sleep"—the innocent sleep,
Sleep that knits up the raveled sleave of care,
The death of each day's life, sore labor's bath,
Balm of hurt minds, great nature's second course,
Chief nourisher in life's feast—
>   —Act II, scene ii, lines 34–39

Lady Macbeth, with anger, tells him to stop being childish and to wash the blood from his hands, but he can only stare at the blood and say:

Will all great Neptune's ocean wash this blood
Clean from my hand? No, this my hand will rather

The multitudinous seas incarnadine,
Making the green one red.

—Act II, scene ii, lines 59–62

But the daggers, which Macbeth has foolishly brought with him, must be returned to the bedchamber. When Macbeth flatly refuses to return to the scene of the crime, the indomitable Lady Macbeth does so. After all, it is necessary to put blood on the drugged servants and leave the blood-caked daggers near them, to make it seem they are guilty of the crime.

. . . a new Gorgon

But now there comes a knocking. Someone is trying to gain entrance into the castle. Macbeth and his wife must quickly get into their night-clothes so they can go to the door as though innocently roused from sleep.

The men at the door, who are finally let in (by a drunken porter whose talkative delay gives Macbeth and Lady Macbeth time to get ready), are Lennox, whom we have met before, and Macduff, whom we have not. Macduff is the Thane of Fife, and he has been ordered by the King to call for him early in the morning so that they might proceed on their way.

Macbeth arrives, completely master of himself, and casually points out the way to the King's chamber. Macduff leaves, but soon returns, distraught. He has discovered the bloody corpse of the King and cries out:

Approach the chamber, and destroy your sight
With a new Gorgon:

—Act II, scene iii, lines 73–74

The Gorgons of Greek mythology were three in number and were fearsome examples of the monsters fathered by the Greek imagination. They were winged creatures with glaring eyes, huge teeth, protruding tongues, and, most remarkable, writhing serpents in place of hair. (Could this have been inspired by the sight of octopuses or sea anemones?) So horrible were the Gorgons that the mere sight of them turned men into stone, and Macduff is implying that the sight of the dead King would be just so horrible.

. . . my fury

Macbeth and his wife carry it off well. No one can possibly suspect them. Indeed, when Duncan's son, Malcolm, inquires in horror the name of the murderer, Lennox gives the obvious explanation:

Those of his chamber, as it seemed, had done 't

—Act II, scene iii, line 103

As Lennox goes on to say, the servants were smeared with blood, so were their daggers, and they themselves could make no satisfactory defense. And at this point Macbeth makes a self-serving remark, hoping to draw the fangs of what might otherwise become a suspicious incident afterward. He says:

> *O, yet I do repent me of my fury,*
> *That I did kill them.*
>
> —Act II, scene iii, lines 108–9

Obviously dead men tell no tales. The live servants on questioning might have made their innocence clear; dead servants could not.

But Macbeth's clever insertion of the statement at this point where it might be least questioned does not after all go unnoticed. Macduff turns on him at once, asking:

> *Wherefore did you so?*
>
> —Act II, scene iii, line 109

It is easy to understand Macduff's annoyance. Even granted that the servants were the murderers, they could scarcely have done the deed on their own account. They had nothing to gain and could only have been bribed to do it by someone else who *did* have something to gain. It would have been important to question the servants thoroughly (and, in those days, with the help of a bit of torture) to find out who had hired them to do the deed.

It might (who knows) even have occurred to Macduff that if the servants had committed the murder, they would scarcely have remained on the scene waiting for capture. That anomaly too (which might even be reflected in Lennox's statement that the servants were the murderers "as it seemed," a distinct qualification) deserved question.

As it is, Macbeth's action had destroyed vital evidence.

Nervously, Macbeth tries to explain and Lady Macbeth shrewdly creates a diversion by pretending to faint. Nevertheless, the harm is done. Macduff's suspicion has been aroused; and it will persist.

. . . to avoid the aim . . .

It is the King's sons who are most in danger. At this point, suspicion could light more easily on them than on anyone else. They stand most to gain from the death of the King, for the older will succeed (he has just been proclaimed Prince of Cumberland and might have decided he could not wait even a day for the crown) and the younger, if an accomplice, will receive high office.

Of course, they know they did not do it, but that introduces another danger of quite another sort. If someone else killed Duncan, or hired the servants to kill Duncan, then surely it must be in order to gain the crown. And if so, Malcolm and Donalbain will have to be killed too, and that portion of the deed of murder might yet come. Malcolm says:

> *This murderous shaft that's shot*
> *Hath not yet lighted, and our safest way*
> *Is to avoid the aim. Therefore to horse;*
> *And let us not be dainty of leave-taking,*
> *But shift away.*

> —Act II, scene iii, lines 143–47

In actual historical fact, as stated before, Malcolm and Donalbain were mere children. After the lost battle in which Duncan was killed (in history), the youngsters were taken away by the remnants of the defeated forces. In the play, where they are made much older, and where their father is assassinated rather than defeated in battle, the situation is a flight rather than a retreat.

. . . to England

The fleeing sons could expect asylum and good treatment abroad. Abroad they would represent a "rightful heir" to the throne; they could be used to stir up dissension at home for the benefit of the neighboring nation that was serving as their host. The neighboring nation might even invade, using the "rightful heir" as a cover that would make the invasion seem a noble act of restitution rather than simple aggression.

Malcolm says:

> *I'll to England.*

> —Act II, scene iii, line 139

Donalbain says:

> *To Ireland, I; our separated fortune*
> *Shall keep us both the safer.*

> —Act II, scene iii, lines 140–41

According to Holinshed, Malcolm received in England "most friendly entertainment," while Donalbain in Ireland "was tenderly cherished."

The fact of the exile proved in the long run to be of great importance to Scottish history (as we shall see), and even the respective places of exile, England for Malcolm and Ireland for Donalbain, were to be important.

. . . gone to Scone

The flight of Malcolm and Donalbain plays into Macbeth's hands. The nobility has gathered, apparently, to consider the situation, and Macduff, who has attended, emerges from the castle with the news. Ross, who was not at the meeting, asks the formal decision as to who had done the murder. Macduff answers somberly:

> *Those that Macbeth hath slain.*
> —Act II, scene iv, line 23

The killing of the servants sticks in Macduff's throat. There is an edge of sarcasm to the comment, surely. Ross asks the motive of the killing and Macduff responds with what is now the accepted theory:

> *They were suborned:*
> *Malcolm and Donalbain, the king's two sons,*
> *Are stol'n away and fled, which puts upon them*
> *Suspicion of the deed.*
> —Act II, scene iv, lines 24–27

Ross says:

> *Then 'tis most like*
> *The sovereignty will fall upon Macbeth.*
> —Act II, scene iv, lines 29–30

Why not? Macbeth is, after all, the outstanding member of the royal family remaining in Scotland. Macduff says:

> *He is already named, and gone to Scone*
> *To be invested.*
> —Act II, scene iv, lines 31–32

Scone is a place about two miles north of Perth and thirty miles north of Edinburgh. It was the traditional place where Scottish kings were crowned, and legend traces this back to the eighth century, or three centuries before Macbeth's time.

More solidly, the matter of Scone takes us back to Kenneth I, who ruled over the tribes of Scots who had entered the land from northern Ireland. Kenneth, the Scots leader, forced his domination over the tribes of Picts, who had inhabited the land through Roman times, and it was with this amalgamation of the two Celtic peoples that the history of Scotland as we know it starts, about 846.

Scone was the old Pictish capital, and Kenneth adopted it as a gesture of conciliation. He brought to it the great "Stone of Scone." Very likely, this was a pre-Christian object of worship, but it was Christianized and the monks gave out that this was the very stone that Jacob had slept on in Canaan when he dreamed of angels making their way between heaven and earth. ("And Jacob rose up early in the morning, and took the stone that he had put for his pillows and set it up for a pillar, and poured oil upon the top of it"—Genesis 28:18.)

The Scottish kings were crowned while sitting on it, until Edward I of England seized it in 1296 and carried it back to London. Ever since then the Stone of Scone has been under the coronation throne in Westminster and English kings have been crowned on it. Scone continued to be the place of coronation for Scottish kings, even without the Stone, right down to the time of James VI, whose elevation to the throne of England as James I ended Scotland's history as an independent nation.

. . . play'dst most foully . . .

All seems to be going perfectly for Macbeth. As the Third Witch had predicted, he has become King. Yet there are flaws in the picture. Macduff clearly does not accept the official version. When Ross asks if he is going to Scone, he answers:

> No, cousin, I'll to Fife.

> —Act II, scene iv, line 36

This is a clear sign of disapproval. It is also reasonable to suppose that by refusing to attend the coronation, he will avoid taking some sort of oath to Macbeth as his King. That would leave the way clear to a future rebellion against Macbeth without the necessity of having qualms about feudal honor.

Nor is Macduff the only one to suspect. Banquo shares a certain knowledge with Macbeth that others do not have. He was on the scene when the weird sisters spoke.

He appears at Forres, where the old Thane of Cawdor had been executed and near where the weird sisters had appeared. The city is now King Macbeth's capital. Banquo, alone on the stage, broods about it:

> Thou hast it now: King, Cawdor, Glamis, all,
> As the weird women promised, and I fear
> Thou play'dst most foully for't.

> —Act III, scene i, lines 1–3

Holinshed makes Banquo an accomplice. He says: "At length, therefore, communicating his [Macbeth's] purposed intent with his trusty friends, amongst whom Banquho was the chiefest, upon confidence of their promised aid, he slew the king . . ."

This certainly doesn't sound like a secret, treacherous assassination, where one tells as few people as possible (no one, best of all) and needs little aid. This is what would happen if an armed rebellion is planned and if allies are sought who might bring contingents of troops to the side of the rebellion.

Armed rebellion was, of course, a standard method of procedure in medieval times, and even in England down through the fifteenth century, as many other Shakespearean plays attest. It would not seriously hurt Banquo's reputation to know he had taken part in one, especially if it were victorious.

Once Shakespeare had converted the death of Duncan into a cowardly murder in defiance of the laws of hospitality, though, Banquo had to be kept out of it. After all, Banquo's supposed descendant, James I, was in the audience.

In the play, then, Banquo is allowed no knowledge of Macbeth's plot and can only suspect that he had "play'dst most foully for't." Yet this concession to the audience sits rather uneasily upon the play. If Macduff, with no knowledge of the weird sisters, can suspect Macbeth so actively as to refuse his presence at the coronation, then for Banquo, with his knowledge, to have nothing more than a vague fear is for him to be naïve almost to the point of imbecility.

. . . my oracles as well

For the sake of the drama, Shakespeare vastly condenses the time span of the play. The historic Macbeth had a fairly long reign of seventeen years. The first ten years, said Holinshed, were peaceful and were, we may reasonably assume, an improvement over Duncan's short, incompetent, and rebellion-filled reign. Holinshed says:

"Makbeth, after the departure thus of Duncane's sons, used great liberality towards the nobles of the realm, thereby to win their favor, and when he saw that no man went about to trouble him, he set his whole intention to maintain justice, and to punish all enormities and abuses, which had chanced through the feeble and slothful administration of Duncane. . . . He made many wholesome laws and statutes for the public weal of his subjects."

But later in his reign, says Holinshed, "the prick of conscience (as it chanceth ever in tyrants, and such as attain to any estate by unrighteous means) caused him ever to fear, lest he should be served of the same cup, as he had ministered to his predecessor."

Of course, we need not suppose that Macbeth's growing suspicion, which made him react with increasing cruelty against any possibility of disloyalty or rebellion, was entirely due to "the prick of conscience." We might find a more mundane reason in the fact that after ten years, Duncan's exiled sons had reached man's estate and were intriguing day and night for Macbeth's fall.

Shakespeare, in the play, skips the ten years of peace, prosperity, and justice as though they had never been. From the coronation at the end of Act II, he proceeds at once to Macbeth's latter years as a suspicious tyrant at the beginning of Act III.

Macbeth's fear that he will be served as he has served points logically to Banquo first of all. Banquo also had his promises from the weird sisters. They had told him that though he would not himself be King, his posterity would gain the kingship.

What's more, Banquo has not forgotten that. In the soliloquy which opens the third act, he says:

> . . . *it was said*
> *It should not stand in thy posterity,*
> *But that myself should be the root and father*
> *Of many kings. If there come truth from them—*
> *As upon thee, Macbeth, their speeches shine—*
> *Why, by the verities on thee made good,*
> *May they not be my oracles as well*
> *And set me up in hope?*
>
> —Act III, scene i, lines 3–10

. . . *strange invention*

But Macbeth now enters. He was a brave general in Act I; a treacherous assassin in Act II; and now, in Act III, he is the suspicious tyrant.

But then, even in the play, the suspicions that torment the new King are not presented as groundless. Macbeth says to Banquo, in the course of the conversation that follows Banquo's opening soliloquy:

> *We hear our bloody cousins are bestowed*
> *In England and in Ireland, not confessing*
> *Their cruel parricide, filling their hearers*
> *With strange invention.*
>
> —Act III, scene i, lines 29–32

In the shortened time span of the play this seems to follow not long after the flight of Malcolm and Donalbain, and their intrigue abroad seems to have begun at once. In actual history, some ten years have elapsed, and it is the fact that the children have grown into young men capable of leading armies that now makes them dangerous.

My genius . . .

But it is Banquo who is the immediate danger. A little later in the scene, when Banquo has left, Macbeth muses about him, saying:

> *There is none but he*
> *Whose being I do fear: and under him*
> *My genius is rebuked, as it is said*
> *Mark Antony's was by Caesar.*
>
> —Act III, scene i, lines 54–57

The relationship of Mark Antony's genius (that is, his guardian spirit) to that of Octavius Caesar is mentioned in *Antony and Cleopatra,* the play which Shakespeare wrote immediately after *Macbeth* and which was probably revolving in his mind as he wrote this passage.

There seems no reason for Macbeth to take this attitude toward Banquo. Just before this passage, he says of him:

> *. . . in his royalty of nature reigns that*
> *Which would be feared. 'Tis much he dares;*
> *And, to that dauntless temper of his mind,*
> *He hath a wisdom that doth guide his valor*
> *To act in safety.*
>
> —Act III, scene i, lines 50–54

Yet there is absolutely nothing in the play to justify these words. Banquo's part has been an entirely passive one. It is Macduff who displays a wise suspicion and a courageous opposition; Banquo's suspicions, which should be much more firmly based than Macduff's, don't prevent him from remaining at Macbeth's side. It would seem, rather, that he is as ambitious as Macbeth and sees in Duncan's death nothing more than a step forward to the gaining of the crown for his posterity.

It is easy to suppose that Shakespeare is ladling out this undeserved praise to Banquo for the sake of Banquo's descendant in the audience.

For Banquo's issue . . .

Macbeth, for his own safety, then, would have Banquo dead. He cannot openly have Banquo executed, for he has no good cause, and to do the deed without cause would offend and frighten the other noblemen of the realm and would make them all the more liable to listen to the blandishments of Duncan's exiled sons.

Macbeth would have to use the same tactics he used for Duncan—the secret assassination—and to make that possible he questions Banquo on his movements that night.

The King is planning a banquet, but Banquo must take care of an errand first and will be riding through the early part of the night. Macbeth asks, still apparently offhand:

> *Goes Fleance with you?*
>
> —Act III, scene i, line 35

Fleance will indeed be going with Banquo, and this is important, for if Macbeth is to abort the prediction that Banquo's posterity will sit on the throne then Fleance, Banquo's only son, must die too.

If he does not do so, as Macbeth says later, after Banquo's departure:

> *For Banquo's issue have I filed* [defiled] *my mind;*
> *For them the gracious Duncan have I murdered;*
>
> —Act III, scene i, lines 65–66

And yet, as in almost every point where Banquo is involved in the play, there arise questions. There is the straightforward story of Duncan, Macbeth, and the vengeance of Duncan's sons, which is not seriously distorted by Shakespeare's conversion of Duncan's death in battle into Duncan's death by assassination. To it, however, is added the Stuart-manufactured legend of Banquo, and it doesn't really fit. Even Shakespeare can't make it fit.

Why should Macbeth be so upset over the possibility that Banquo's posterity will succeed to the throne? Macbeth has no children of his own and therefore there is none of his posterity to be cheated. The throne must go to someone, and if Macbeth leaves no successor why not to Banquo's descendants as to any other?

To be sure, Macbeth has a stepson, but he is not mentioned in the play. To be sure, Macbeth may still be hoping for children of his own, but that is not mentioned in the play either. In short, there is no reason at all given in the play why Macbeth should possibly resent the throne's going to the posterity of his friend and ally Banquo.

We can only suppose that where the necessity of absolute consistency in the play and the necessity of pleasing King James are at variance, prudent Shakespeare decides to please the King. He makes Banquo an undeserved hero (undeserved even by what we find in the play itself) and makes a great, though unnecessary, point concerning Banquo's posterity, among whom James I includes himself.

Nought's had . . .

Macbeth makes arrangements with two desperadoes to take care of

Banquo and then returns to the palace to rejoin his wife. Both he and Lady Macbeth are undergoing a degeneration of character.

Lady Macbeth had arranged for the killing of Duncan without a qualm, but now in the aftermath, things are beginning to go wrong. She says:

> *Nought's had, all's spent,*
> *Where our desire is got without content:*
>
> —Act III, scene ii, lines 4–5

She has achieved the pinnacle of her ambition and finds that she cannot now rest. It is as difficult to remain there as to get there and she is condemned to everlasting struggle. Her resolution is beginning to weaken, and it will continue to weaken till it destroys her.

As for Macbeth, the matter is reversed. He too recognizes the difficulties of his new position and the uselessness of having struggled for it. He can even envy the dead Duncan, saying:

> *Duncan is in his grave;*
> *After life's fitful fever he sleeps well.*
> *Treason has done his worst; nor steel, nor poison,*
> *Malice domestic, foreign levy, nothing,*
> *Can touch him further.*
>
> —Act III, scene ii, lines 22–26

But stress is hardening Macbeth, not softening him. He had been all qualms in the killing of Duncan, but is much less so now. Indeed, he doesn't even feel it necessary to tell his wife of what he plans in connection with Banquo. He says:

> *Be innocent of the knowledge, dearest chuck,*
> *Till thou applaud the deed.*
>
> —Act III, scene ii, lines 45–46

It is almost as though he recognizes the entry of weakness into his wife and feels it safer to act alone henceforth.

. . . Fleance is 'scaped

Banquo returns, with Fleance, from his afternoon ride and is walking toward the palace and the banquet which Macbeth is giving when he is set upon by the assassins and killed.

One of the murderers reports to Macbeth as the feast begins, and says:

> *Most royal sir, Fleance is 'scaped.*
>
> —Act III, scene iv, line 21

The plan has failed in essence, therefore, for the prediction of the weird sisters has not been aborted, and Banquo's posterity may still (and, according to the legends of later times, did) survive to rule over Scotland.

As at all points connected with the Banquo subplot, there are puzzles. When Banquo was killed, Fleance fled and presumably left Scotland, though Shakespeare does not say so. In fact, after the scene of Banquo's murder, Fleance is never mentioned again in the play; he has served his purpose of representing the posterity that is to come. Holinshed, who accepts the Banquo-Fleance legend, says that he fled to Wales.

But why flee at all? Presumably he knew nothing of Macbeth's guilt, for Banquo (for all we can tell from the play) kept his doubts to himself and acted the part of loyal subject to his erstwhile cogeneral. If Banquo is killed by mysterious footpads, why should Fleance assume they were assassins hired by Macbeth? Why does he not, on fleeing from those murderers, make his way to the palace—if not immediately, then eventually—and demand that Macbeth find the murderers of his father and punish them? That would, of course, place him in the power of Macbeth, and he would not then live long.

Shakespeare does not bother to explain this point. In the rush and fury of a dramatic production, many loose ends can be left with impunity. Holinshed, who is writing sober history, must explain it and does so quite feebly. He says that after Banquo's murder, Fleance, "having some inkling (by the admonition of some friends which he had in the court) how his life was sought no less than his father's," fled the country.

And where does Fleance go? To England, to join Malcolm? To Ireland, to join Donalbain? Surely either son would have welcomed a recruit that bore the important name of Banquo's son. No, he went to Wales, and is no more heard of. He does not participate in the final battle of revenge against Macbeth, even though his father's final words as he falls under the daggers of the assassins are:

> Fly, good Fleance, fly, fly, fly!
> Thou mayst revenge.
>
> —Act III, scene iii, lines 17–18

There are no difficulties, of course, if it is remembered that Banquo and Fleance never existed and that they are pasted onto the story through Stuart insistence, while Shakespeare emphasizes them the more to please his King.

. . . th'Hyrcan tiger

There follows a very dramatic scene at the banquet. Before Banquo had left Macbeth to go off on his fatal trip, Macbeth had said to him:

Fail not our feast.

—Act III, scene i, line 27

He knew full well, of course, that it was his intention that Banquo never return. The unsuspecting Banquo answers, however:

My lord, I will not.

—Act III, scene i, line 28

Now Banquo, though dead, keeps his word, and his ghost appears at the feast, throwing Macbeth into a frenzy of horror, which the others cannot understand, for only Macbeth can see the apparition.

He cries to it at one point:

Approach thou like the rugged Russian bear,
The armed rhinoceros, or th'Hyrcan tiger;
Take any shape but that [Banquo], *and my firm nerves*
Shall never tremble.

—Act III, scene iv, lines 101–4

The "Hyrcan tiger" is the tiger from Hyrcania, which is a region bordering the Caspian Sea on the southeast. Indeed, the Caspian Sea was called the "Hyrcanum Mare" in ancient times.

It is interesting that Macbeth does not treat the apparition as necessarily the ghost of Banquo, in the sense that we would speak of it nowadays—a spirit belonging to no one else, with its bloody wounds gaping. To Macbeth it is an evil spirit from hell which chooses for some purpose of its own to take on the shape of the murdered Banquo and might just as easily have taken on any other. Macbeth is daring it to do just that, to take on any other, however horrible, for it is only the dead Banquo at this particular moment that is capable of unmanning him. (Macbeth's attitude toward the ghost of Banquo is precisely that of Hamlet and Horatio toward the ghost of the elder Hamlet, see page II–82.)

The appearance of the ghost breaks up the feast, and Lady Macbeth is forced to ask the guests to leave in a phrase that has entered the language. She says:

Stand not upon the order of your going,
But go at once.

—Act III, scene iv, lines 120–21

In other words, they must not waste time trying to file out in strict order of precedence, with those of greater social status going first.

. . . Macduff denies his person

And even here the Banquo subplot seems an intrusion. As soon as the guests have left, Macbeth is himself and can discuss with Lady Macbeth the state of the nation without the slightest qualms. It is as though the episode with the ghost had never been.

Macbeth's concern, even with Banquo dead, is the nobility in general. They have shown a constant tendency to revolt during Duncan's reign and they may do so again. Macbeth must keep all of them under surveillance and, as he says to Lady Macbeth:

> *There's not a one of them but in his house*
> *I keep a servant fee'd.*
>
> —Act III, scene iv, lines 132–33

One nobleman in particular rouses his keenest suspicion. He says to Lady Macbeth:

> *How say'st thou, that Macduff denies his person*
> *At our great bidding?*
>
> —Act III, scene iv, lines 128–29

Because Shakespeare has dropped Macbeth's ten good years, this seems as though the reference is to Macduff's failure to be present at the coronation, and one can even reasonably suppose that the feast just concluded was intended to celebrate that coronation.

In Holinshed, it was not by absence at the coronation or immediately thereafter that Macduff roused the royal suspicion. It couldn't be, since for ten years after that coronation Macduff lived peacefully in Scotland. Holinshed's story is that about 1050 Macbeth decided to build a better and more elaborate royal palace, and demanded that the various members of the nobility fulfill their feudal duties by contributing money and labor to the project. When it was the turn of Macduff, he sent laborers and money, but did not appear himself, as the others had done, because he mistrusted Macbeth. It was this absence that goaded Macbeth to the stern action which Shakespeare will describe.

By the worst means . . .

With Banquo dead and with Macduff due to be taken care of next, Macbeth feels the need of guidance. On the heath near Forres, the weird sisters searched him out and, in a way, forced evil upon him against his will. Now,

however, he has been corrupted to the point where he intends to seek them
out and voluntarily snatch at evil. He says:

> *I will tomorrow*
> *And betimes I will, to the weird sisters:*
> *More shall they speak, for now I am bent to know*
> *By the worst means the worst.*
> —Act III, scene iv, lines 133–36

This mention of the weird sisters leads into a short scene in which they
appear again. This time Hecate, the witch queen, appears also, and in jig-
ging rhyme scolds the weird sisters for dealing with Macbeth without her.
There is a song and they are gone.

This seems to be an interpolation by some hand other than Shakespeare's. A younger contemporary of Shakespeare, Thomas Middleton,
wrote a play called *The Witch* in 1610, in which Hecate was a character
and in which two songs appear which are to be found one in this scene, and
the other two scenes later. Some suggest that there was an attempt by Middleton to prepare a musical version of *Macbeth* and that the Hecate scenes
are a remnant of that.

In fact, the version of *Macbeth* which we now possess may not be the
original but may be one which was somewhat cut to fit into the musical
format. (After all, songs and dances take up time.) One reason for thinking
so is that *Macbeth* is comparatively short. It is only three fifths the length
of *Hamlet*.

On the other hand, there are no obvious gaps in the plot to make us suspect cutting, except possibly for the appearance of a Third Murderer at the
last minute on the occasion of Banquo's assassination. Originally, Macbeth
had made arrangements with two assassins, and the appearance of a third
for no apparent reason and fulfilling no apparent function is puzzling. There
have been a number of attempts to explain it, and it is conceivable that
some earlier scene explaining the existence of the Third Murderer is lost.

. . . the tyrant's feast . . .

The death of Banquo has indeed roused suspicions among the nobility.
The Thane of Lennox, speaking with an unnamed Lord, manages to voice
those suspicions. Banquo's murder, like Duncan's, has been blamed on an
escaped son, and Lennox cannot swallow that.

The unnamed Lord may have arrived in Scotland from abroad, for he
seems to have information concerning affairs in England. Lennox asks him
concerning the whereabouts of Macduff, who seems a living warning
against being too frank in talk these days:

> . . . for from broad words, and 'cause he failed
> His presence at the tyrant's feast, I hear,
> Macduff lives in disgrace.
>
> —Act III, scene vi, lines 21–23

Both Lennox and the Lord he is addressing refer to Macbeth as a tyrant, but this does not necessarily mean that Macbeth was extraordinarily cruel. In the original Greek sense, the word was used to describe one who had seized the throne without possessing it by right of birth. Such a usurper was a tyrant even if he ruled justly and mildly. But, of course, Macbeth was now becoming a tyrant in the modern sense as well.

. . . the most pious Edward . . .

The Lord begins to answer Lennox's question concerning Macduff with an account of the present doings of Malcolm:

> The son of Duncan
> From whom this tyrant holds the due of birth,
> Lives in the English court, and is received
> Of the most pious Edward with such grace
> That the malevolence of fortune nothing
> Takes from his high respect.
>
> —Act III, scene vi, lines 24–29

"The most pious Edward" was Edward the Confessor. He was the son of the Saxon King Ethelred the Unready and Emma, a princess of Normandy (see page II-89). He had been born about 1003, but when he was only eleven years old, his father (a most inept king) was hurled from the throne by a Danish invasion under Sven Forked-beard. Edward was carried off to Normandy, his mother's home, for safekeeping.

Sven died soon after his conquest, but his son Canute managed to seize England and to rule over it, very capably, for eighteen years. Canute married Emma, Ethelred's queen, and had a son by her, Hardecanute. When Canute died in 1035, Emma supported her young son by him, rather than her considerably older son by Ethelred. As it happened, it was Harold Harefoot (an illegitimate son of Canute) who succeeded. He died in 1040, however, and Hardecanute then became King of England.

It was just when Harold died and Hardecanute succeeded that Duncan was killed and that his son Malcolm was brought to England.

Hardecanute was the half brother of Emma's son by Ethelred. That other son, Edward, was still in Normandy. Hardecanute, feeling the relationship, and realizing perhaps that he would leave no successors, invited Edward back to England. When Hardecanute died in 1042 at the age of twenty-three, Edward succeeded to the throne, twenty-eight years after his father had lost it.

Edward was a weak king, whose reign brought disaster to England. The young Duke of Normandy (William the Bastard, who a quarter century later gained the much to be preferred name of William the Conqueror) was a cousin, and Edward considered him the logical successor to the throne, though this was quite unacceptable to the Saxon aristocracy. What's more, Edward had taken a vow of chastity and meant it, so he would have no children to dispute the possibility of a Norman succession.

Edward's vow of chastity was an indication of his interest in the religious life. So was his nickname "the Confessor," which attested to the regularity of his attendance of religious services. He was greatly esteemed for his piety even in his lifetime, and after his death, when (very largely because of him) England was conquered by Normandy and its Saxon population reduced to a subject race, his reign was looked back upon as a kind of "good old days" and his piety was enlarged to saintliness. In 1161, indeed, not quite a century after his death, he was canonized.

It is to be expected, aside from Edward's saintliness, that he would be hospitable to the young Scottish prince. For one thing, he could scarcely help seeing in Malcolm's exile from Scotland an echo of his own long exile from England. For another, practical politics always made it convenient to support a pretender to the throne of a neighboring kingdom.

. . . warlike Siward

The Lord proceeds with his account. Macduff, it seems, has also gone to England (and Macbeth, who apparently is not yet aware of this, is thus too late to visit on Macduff the fate of Banquo). The Lord says:

> . . . *Thither* [to England] *Macduff*
> *Is gone to pray the holy King* [Edward], *upon his aid*
> *To wake Northumberland and warlike Siward;*
> *That by the help of these, with Him above*
> *To ratify the work, we may again*
> *Give to our tables meat, sleep to our nights,*
> —Act III, scene vi, lines 29–34

Despite the praise given to Edward, it is clear what a weak king he is. In the confusion of a century of Danish invasion, the Saxon nobility had become quite independent and the English nation was a congeries of quarreling lords. (This greatly helped that nation fall to the well-governed and united Norman duchy a decade later.)

If the anti-Macbeth faction of Scotland wanted help from England, they could not get it directly from Edward, who was very largely a figurehead. They had to get it from one or more of the feudal lords and use Edward only for what he was worth as an intercessor with these same lords.

In this case, the logical choice was Siward, the Earl of Northumberland. In asking Siward for help, the anti-Macbeth faction was making a very practical choice.

For one thing, there was a matter of relationship. Shakespeare says nothing of it in the play, but according to Holinshed, Duncan had been married to the daughter of Siward, and Malcolm, the exiled Scottish prince, was therefore the grandson of the Northumbrian earl.

Quite apart from that, there was a matter of practical politics. Northumberland was the northernmost county of England, abutting on the Scottish border, and there was a long record of border raiding between the lords of southern Scotland and those of northern England. An Earl of Northumberland would therefore be only too ready to meddle in internal Scottish politics in the hope of salvaging good for himself. In this case, the good that Northumberland would hope to salvage for himself was all too obvious.

Northumberland was what was left of the older kingdom of Northumbria, which had included all the region from the Humber River to the Firth of Forth; that is, roughly from York to Edinburgh.

The northern portion of Northumbria, then called "Bernicia," had been ceded to Scotland by Edgar I of England in 970. The reasons for the cession are dim, but it seems not to have been the result of any military defeat for England. It seems rather to have been something in the nature of an attempt to come to a permanent accommodation with Scotland in order that the two lands might live forever in peace. It worked on a short-term basis, anyway, for Edgar's thirty-one-year reign was sufficiently free of military troubles to gain him the name, in the chronicles, of "Edgar the Peaceful."

However, one can scarcely expect that the lords of northern England would be entirely reconciled to the loss of Bernicia. The earls of Northumberland would surely be on the constant watch for the opportunity to regain it. Siward, if he agreed to help Malcolm, might well have had in mind Bernicia (which to the Scots had become "Lothian") in return.

This cannot appear in Shakespeare's play, of course, for there the opposing forces are divorced from practical politics and are rather representative of the eternal struggle of Good versus Evil, with Siward, in this case, on the side of the Good.

Siward, who is portrayed in this play as a plain and heroic soldier in the best English tradition, was, however, a most unlikely example of partisan-on-the-side-of-Good. He was of Danish extraction and he had become earl in 1041 through the simple expedient of murdering his wife's uncle, who had been the previous earl. Siward, in short, had actually committed the kind of crime that Macbeth had not, in actual historical fact, committed.

Thanks to Shakespeare's bow to English nationalism and to the family pride of James I, the role of Good and Bad was neatly inverted for all time.

. . . none of woman born

It is time now for Macbeth's projected visit to the weird sisters, and they come onstage again in the opening of the fourth act. They are brewing charms while listing a most grisly account of the ingredients they use as Shakespeare once more caters to the witch-hunting pedantry of James I. There is also the second intrusion of Hecate with a song, and then Macbeth comes.

The weird sisters are quite willing to tell him what he wants to know in a series of visions. The first one is that of an armed head, signifying war, who says:

> Macbeth! Macbeth! Macbeth! Beware Macduff!
> Beware the Thane of Fife. Dismiss me: enough.
> —Act IV, scene i, lines 71–72

As on the occasion of the first meeting with the weird sisters, the first piece of information is not really informative. Then they had greeted Macbeth as Thane of Glamis, to begin with; and he had known he was that. Now they tell him to beware Macduff, and he is already planning to kill him.

The second vision is in the form of a bloody child, who says:

> Be bloody, bold, and resolute! Laugh to scorn
> The pow'r of man, for none of woman born
> Shall harm Macbeth.
> —Act IV, scene i, lines 79–81

The phrase "none of woman born" is a common metaphor for "no one," since who can there be who has not had a mother? Macbeth certainly accepts this interpretation of the statement, for his first remark is an exultant:

> Then live, Macduff: what need I fear of thee?
> —Act IV, scene i, line 82

Macbeth is inured to blood by now, however, and he quickly decides to kill Macduff anyhow just to make sure.

And yet the phrase "none of woman born" can be used in a more special way to mean no one who has been born of woman *in the usual way;* that is, by emerging through the vaginal canal. In that case, the woman would actively have borne the child; she would have given it birth. If the child were taken out of the mother's body in any other way, as by what we now call Caesarean section, for instance, the child would still have a mother but he would not have been born of that woman.

Caesarean sections in which the child lived could not have been common prior to the birth of modern surgery and antisepsis, but they were not unheard of either. Julius Caesar was supposed to have been born by Caesarean section, and indeed, the name of the operation recalls that fact.

Macbeth, in his relief at the nature of the statement by the second apparition, does not take careful note of the circumstances surrounding it. The weird sisters cannot tell outright falsehoods; they can only deceive. The fact that the statement concerning "none of woman born" is made by a bloody child indicates the truth, for a child crudely taken directly out of the mother's abdomen would be bloody.

Nor does Macbeth note the inconsistency of the first two statements. After all, if none of woman born can harm him, why has he been warned to beware Macduff?

Here we have the significance of the well-known speech by Banquo, which is made shortly after Macbeth has met the weird sisters for the first time. When Macbeth is greeted as the Thane of Cawdor, it seems that part of what the weird sisters have told him is true. The suspicious Banquo warns him, however, that:

> *The instruments of darkness tell us truths,*
> *Win us with honest trifles, to betray's*
> *In deepest consequence.*

> —Act I, scene iii, lines 124–26

It is exactly this which is happening now.

Great Birnam Wood . . .

A third apparition is that of a crowned child with a tree in his hand, who says:

> *Macbeth shall never vanquished be until*
> *Great Birnam Wood to high Dunsinane Hill*
> *Shall come against him.*

> —Act IV, scene i, lines 92–94a

Dunsinane Hill is a crag a thousand feet high that is part of the Sidlaw Hills that run between Perth and Dundee in east-central Scotland. Birnam is a town about a dozen miles north of Perth, and the wood is the forested region between.

Again Macbeth jubilantly accepts the statement literally, saying:

> *That will never be.*
> *Who can impress the forest, bid the tree*
> *Unfix his earth-bound root?*
>
> —Act IV, scene i, lines 94b–96

Once more, he does not pay attention to the apparition itself. The crowned child is clearly meant to represent Malcolm, and the tree in his hand clearly shows how the wood will be made to *appear* to come to Dunsinane.

. . . *the eighth appears* . . .

At this point, really, Macbeth has what he wants, and by the internal logic of the play, should leave. However, Shakespeare never for a moment forgets his royal audience and he wants a display for James. He therefore has Macbeth ask if Banquo's descendants shall ever reign.

This the weird sisters gladly answer by means of an apparition consisting of a line of kings marching across the stage, with Banquo's bloody ghost marching along with them to indicate them to be his.

Macbeth writhes at seeing them and finds their numbers unbearable. He cries out:

> *Another yet! A seventh! I'll see no more.*
> *And yet the eighth appears, who bears a glass*
> *Which shows me many more; and some I see*
> *That twofold balls and treble scepters carry:*
>
> —Act IV, scene i, lines 118–21

This line of kings refers to the Stuart dynasty, which traced its descent from Banquo. They are:

(1) Robert II (1371–90)
(2) Robert III (1390–1406)
(3) James I (1406–37)
(4) James II (1437–60)
(5) James III (1460–88)
(6) James IV (1488–1513)
(7) James V (1513–42)
(8) James VI (1567–1625)

As you see, there are indeed eight, but there is a gap between the last two. No king is listed for the period between 1542 and 1567. In that interval there was a queen, Mary, who was the daughter of James V and the mother of James VI (James I of Great Britain). She was, however, executed by the order of Queen Elizabeth I after a long imprisonment in England. James VI, her son, never did anything about getting her released, nor did he protest her execution, for he preferred to stay on his good behavior in the hope of a peaceful succession to the English throne as the nearest relative of Elizabeth.

In 1603, at Elizabeth's death, James VI did indeed succeed to the throne, gaining it from the executioner of his mother, as he might not have done if he had made a fuss at that time. One might argue that by guaranteeing a peaceful succession, the craven behavior of James VI served England well. Since Shakespeare viewed a disputed succession with horror (as can be seen from the number of plays that revolve about this matter and the way in which he treats the subject in those plays), he might have taken this view. In that case, with James VI (now James I of Great Britain) in the audience, why risk any unpleasantness by any reference to Mary, Queen of Scots—and so such reference is omitted.

It is James, himself, the King who sat watching, who was the "eighth king" of the apparition, and it was he who, in the play, held up the glass in which Macbeth saw "many more."

Shakespeare had no way of knowing at the time the play was written that such a prophecy would come true, and it represents mere flattery of the reigning monarch. Indeed, for a time, it looked as though the prophecy would prove most spectacularly untrue. In 1649 Charles I of Great Britain, the son and successor of James I, had his head cut off by his erstwhile subjects, and for some years Great Britain remained without a king.

In 1660, however, Charles II, the son of the executed Charles I, was restored, and there has been no serious break since. Seventeen monarchs (thirteen kings and four queens) have reigned in Great Britain after James I, and every single one of them has been a descendant of James I. The present British Queen, Elizabeth II, is a twelfth-generation descendant of James I.

The fact that some of the future monarchs shown in the glass held by the eighth King wore "treble scepters" was meant to indicate that they would be kings not only of England, but of Scotland and Ireland as well; they would be kings of Great Britain, in other words. And this too proved true. James I was the first of this kind, but all his reigning descendants to this day remain sovereign over Scotland and over part of Ireland at least.

Into his power . . .

It is now that Macbeth discovers that Macduff has actually left for England. The nature of his errand cannot be in doubt, and Macduff has been so incautious as to leave his family behind. Macbeth orders them all slain and those orders are carried out.

The news of the slaughter of his family has not reached Macduff, however, when that nobleman meets with Malcolm (the elder son of Duncan) before the palace of the English King.

Malcolm greets Macduff with suspicion and reserve. It may be that Macduff's purpose is but to entice him to Scotland, there to be killed. If we turn to history, such a view would by no means be paranoid. About twenty years earlier something very much like that had happened, so that we can scarcely blame Malcolm for saying:

> Devilish Macbeth
> By many of these trains hath sought to win me
> Into his power . . .
> —Act IV, scene iii, lines 117–19

What had happened twenty years before (and Shakespeare does not bother to mention it, although the tale was undoubtedly well known to this audience) came at a time when King Edward the Confessor was still an exile in Normandy. After the death of Canute in 1035, his illegitimate son, Harold, sat insecurely on the throne and wanted to eliminate possible competitors about whom the discontented might rally.

Letters reached Normandy, therefore, purporting to come from Saxon nationalists anxious to overthrow the Danish King. Edward refused to take the bait, but he had a younger brother, Alfred, who did. Alfred raised a fleet and sailed to England, where he was greeted with apparent friendliness by those who seemed sympathetic to his cause. Once off guard, however, he and his men were easily killed.

It is only with great difficulty, then, that Macduff manages to convince Malcolm of his sincerity. Malcolm deliberately accuses himself of a variety of crimes, feeling that if Macduff is interested only in luring him back to Scotland, he will accept all crimes. When Macduff falls away in disgust instead, Malcolm accepts him joyfully to his side and tells him that an invasion of Scotland by Siward of Northumbria is even then being planned.

'Tis called the evil

At this point there comes an interruption that has nothing to do with the play, but a great deal with James I in the audience.

A Doctor emerges from the palace and Malcolm asks if King Edward is coming out. The Doctor says:

> Ay, sir. There are a crew of wretched souls
> That stay his cure: their malady convinces [defies]
> The great assay of art; but at his touch,
> Such sanctity hath heaven given his hand,
> They presently amend.
> —Act IV, scene iii, lines 141–45

Macduff asks in wonder what the disease might be that is the despair of physicians yet which the English King can cure with a touch. Malcolm explains:

> *'Tis called the evil:*
> *A most miraculous work in this good King,*
> *Which often since my here-remain in England*
> *I have seen him do. How he solicits heaven,*
> *Himself best knows: but strangely-visited people,*
> *All swoll'n and ulcerous, pitiful to the eye,*
> *The mere despair of surgery, he cures,*
> *Hanging a golden stamp about their necks,*
> *Put on with holy prayers: and 'tis spoken,*
> *To the succeeding royalty he leaves*
> *The healing benediction.*

—Act IV, scene iii, lines 146–56

The disease here spoken of as "the evil," or sometimes more specifically as "the King's evil," is scrofula, a tuberculous swelling of the lymph glands of the neck, with a variety of unsightly side effects.

For some reason, it came to be believed that the touch of a king could heal the condition. The practice was first commonly followed in France, and in England the first practitioner was Edward the Confessor, who brought the practice from Normandy.

The custom of touching for the evil continued, on and off, in later centuries, and reached a new peak of popularity with James I and his immediate successors. So pleased was James I at becoming King of England that he simply had to practice touching for the evil, since by that time the procedure was associated with the King of England particularly. By touching successfully (and what Englishman would publicly dare deny he had been helped by the royal touch) he could prove himself a legitimate English monarch.

This whole episode is simply dragged in, for Edward does not actually appear and the practice of touching has nothing to do with the play at all in any way. Indeed, it all mounts to the climactic sentence that "'tis spoken, to the succeeding royalty he leaves the healing benediction." This can apply directly to James and one can only wonder if the actor playing Malcolm did not look directly at James as he said this and perhaps make some sort of respectful bow—and if James did not then smile fatuously and lean over to explain to his Danish brother-in-law.

Actually, considering that James was a physically dirty individual of appalling personal habits, his touch was much more likely to give disease than cure it.

Once this interlude on the King's evil is completed, Shakespeare returns to the play. Ross has just arrived from Scotland with the news of the taking of Macduff's castle and the slaughter of his family. This further exacerbates general hatred of Macbeth and all are now furiously ready to join Siward's army and march into Scotland.

Out, damned spot . . .

Macbeth has fortified himself against the invasion at Dunsinane Hill, protected by stone walls, by a still loyal force of Scotsmen, by his own fury, and by his reliance on the prophecies of the weird sisters.

Lady Macbeth, however, has broken under the strain and walks in her sleep. Watched by a doctor and one of her waiting women, she not only walks, but talks, reliving the lurid past in broken snatches.

In bitter irony, she, who had once contemptuously told her husband to wash Duncan's blood off his hands, has nightmares in which she cannot wash the blood off her own. Rubbing her hands in despair, she cries in her sleep:

> *Out, damned spot! Out, I say!*
>
> —Act V, scene i, line 38

A little later, she says:

> *What, will these hands ne'er be clean?*
>
> —Act V, scene i, line 46

And, finally:

> *Here's the smell of the blood still. All the perfumes*
> *Of Arabia will not sweeten this little hand.*
>
> —Act V, scene i, lines 53–55

We ourselves don't usually think of Arabia as a source of perfumery; we are all too apt to think of it as desert merely. Southern Arabia, a reasonably fertile portion, was, however, the source of frankincense, and that burned itself into the European consciousness because of its mention in the Bible, particularly as one of the gifts brought to the infant Jesus by the wise men.

Lady Macbeth's breakdown has come only with the lapse of considerable time. In the play, we are prepared for this sharp change in the Queen by the fact that she has been absent from the stage for a long time— five scenes.

In actual history, seventeen years have passed since Duncan's death, and this passage of time is implied, if not specifically indicated, by Macbeth's depressed speech shortly after he appears at Dunsinane, while he is arming for the battle:

> *I have lived long enough. My way of life*
> *Is fall'n into the sear, the yellow leaf,*
> *And that which should accompany old age,*
> *As honor, love, obedience, troops of friends,*
> *I must not look to have . . .*
>
> —Act V, scene iii, lines 22–26

If Macbeth was in his early forties when Duncan died, as he may well have been, he would be pushing sixty in 1057, which is the year in which Siward, Malcolm, and Macduff were closing in on him. That is old enough on the medieval scale to make him speak justly of "the sear, the yellow leaf." (In the play, of course, despite this speech, he has not visibly aged and can still engage in harsh single combat.)

. . . the English epicures

Indeed, things are even worse for Macbeth than the play itself indicates. The present war, in actual history, is at least three years old and it has been going badly for Macbeth. Siward's invading force had already defeated Macbeth in 1054, although there is no reference to that in the play. Now Macbeth has been forced back into a kind of last stand.

What's more, many of the Scottish nobility have deserted him for the English, something which *is* pointed out in the play. The desperate Macbeth scorns that, however. He relies on the prophecies of the weird sisters still. He cannot be defeated till a forest moves and he cannot die at the hand of anyone born of woman. He says, grimly:

> *Then fly, false thanes,*
> *And mingle with the English epicures.*
> *The mind I sway by and the heart I bear*
> *Shall never sag with doubt nor shake with fear.*
>
> —Act V, scene iii, lines 7–10

The reference to "English epicures" is a reminder that throughout history England has been larger, more populous, milder, and more fertile than Scotland. England has always been more affluent, then, than cold, bare Scotland to the north. The impoverished Scots could console themselves by imagining that their harsh land toughened them, while England's smiling acres condemned its people to luxurious effeminacy. Not so, of course, but it made the Scots feel better to think so.

. . . Donalbain be with his brother

One person who might be with the invading English is not. Caithness, one of the deserting Scottish nobles, asks:

> *Who knows if Donalbain be with his brother?*
> —Act V, scene ii, line 7

He is not, and after this remark, he is no further mentioned. Actually, he had spent his exile in Ireland and had grown up as much under Celtic influence as Malcolm under English influence. Donalbain, to the end of his life, remained a leader of the retreating Celtic aspects of Scottish culture. He could scarcely join his brother when that brother was marching north surrounded by Englishmen and was himself virtually one of them.

Donalbain remained in exile as long as his brother dominated Scotland, which meant lingering on the outskirts of the land for some thirty-five *additional* years.

As for mythical Fleance, Banquo's son, he is nowhere mentioned. One might suppose that he would be eagerly marching with the invading army to avenge his father's murder, but he isn't. There is apparently a limit to how much can be invented for the Banquo-Fleance myth.

. . . a mind diseased

In the fury of his preparations, Macbeth is still concerned about his beloved wife. He finds time to ask about her health. The doctor (unwilling to go into detail about the sleepwalking and what has been revealed) says cautiously that she is not physically sick but mentally troubled. Macbeth says, desperately:

> *Cure her of that.*
> *Canst thou not minister to a mind diseased,*
> *Pluck from the memory a rooted sorrow,*
> *Raze out the written troubles of the brain,*
> *And with some sweet oblivious antidote*
> *Cleanse the stuffed bosom of that perilous stuff*
> *Which weighs upon the heart?*
> —Act V, scene iii, lines 39–45

It is one of the particularly remarkable passages in Shakespeare, for, of course, we of the twentieth century recognize that Macbeth is asking, and quite accurately, for a psychiatrist. The treatment might well be to help Lady Macbeth realize consciously those memories she was repressing so effectively that they could only burst forth when she was asleep. But the doctor, a man living well before the time of Freud, says resignedly:

> *Therein the patient*
> *Must minister to himself.*

> —Act V, scene iii, lines 45–46

. . . hew him down a bough

The invading army has by now penetrated past Perth and is marching upon the fortified castle at Dunsinane from the west. Siward asks the name of the forest the army is passing through and is told it is Birnam Wood. Malcolm then says:

> *Let every soldier hew him down a bough*
> *And bear't before him. Thereby shall we shadow*
> *The numbers of our host . . .*

> —Act V, scene iv, lines 4–6

The strategy is to make the invading force seem even larger than it is by making its actual number less clear. (There is always a tendency to magnify the enemy when one is in ignorance of the truth.)

This speech is also a concrete appearance of the third apparition of the weird sisters. Malcolm, the "crowned child," is holding a tree in his hand, or the bough of one, and so is every other soldier.

. . . sound and fury

Within the castle, Macbeth has more than mystic prophecies to spur him on. He has sound military reasons for anticipating victory. The English force, swollen by Scottish deserters, is too large to meet in open battle, but that is not necessary. His castle is prepared to face a long siege and he says, grimly:

> *Our castle's strength*
> *Will laugh a siege to scorn. Here let them lie*
> *Till famine and the ague eat them up.*

> —Act V, scene v, lines 2–4

In medieval times a siege was as hard on the besiegers as on the besieged. In a day when even elementary hygiene was unknown, disease among the idle, bored besiegers could be counted on. What's more, where the besiegers were made up of several different groups potentially hostile (as in this case, English and Scots), one could count on those groups falling out among themselves. It had happened often enough in history so that Macbeth might safely expect it.

There is no reason, then, to expect Macbeth necessarily to lose. Not yet. But then something happens that alters everything.

Macbeth's aide, Seyton, comes in with news, saying:

> *The Queen, my lord, is dead.*
>
> —Act V, scene v, line 16

That is all the information given the audience at this point, but the matter is probably worse than it sounds, for at the very end of the play, in its final speech, Malcolm refers to the

> *. . . fiendlike queen,*
> *Who, as 'tis thought, by self and violent hands*
> *Took off her life—*
>
> —Act V, scene viii, lines 69–71

Macbeth must face the fact that his beloved wife has killed herself.

He is a soldier, facing a crucial battle, and he tries first to accept the news in stoical fashion, after the fashion of Brutus in *Julius Caesar* on hearing of the death of Portia (see page I–305). Macbeth says:

> *She should* [would] *have died hereafter;*
> *There would have been a time for such a word.*
>
> —Act V, scene v, lines 17–18

Accepting the word "should" in its modern sense, it sounds as though Macbeth is callously and impatiently wishing that his wife had waited for a more convenient time to die. Reading it as "would," however, we see that he is trying to console himself with the thought that death is inevitable and that if she had not died now, she would have died at some later time. Soon or late, he would have had to accept this news.

But then, having tried to bear up, he breaks down. With his wife gone, there is nothing left to live for. All his crimes and remorse, all his reverses had not brought him to despair, but his wife's death does and he finds life meaningless—utterly without value. He reaches the despairing conclusion that:

> *Life's but a walking shadow, a poor player*
> *That struts and frets his hour upon the stage*
> *And then is heard no more. It is a tale*

Told by an idiot, full of sound and fury
Signifying nothing.

—Act V, scene v, lines 24–28

At this point, a Messenger comes in to report that a very strange thing has happened—Birnam Wood seems to have shaken loose and to be approaching Dunsinane.

Haggard Macbeth rather welcomes this than otherwise. There is no more talk of a siege. He had earlier doubted his capacity to defeat the invading force in open battle, but now that the prophecy of the weird sister is coming true and the condition for Macbeth's defeat has been met, Macbeth suddenly orders a sortie.

He is going to meet the enemy. Far from fearing death, he welcomes it, saying:

I 'gin to be aweary of the sun
And wish th'estate o'th'world were now undone.

—Act V, scene v, lines 49–50

. . . the Roman fool . . .

In the battle that follows, Macbeth kills Siward's son in single combat, but the invaders win generally and take the castle. It remains only to kill or capture Macbeth himself. Macbeth, however, is determined to sell his life dearly. He is defeated but he will not yet give in, and says:

Why should I play the Roman fool, and die
On mine own sword? Whiles I see lives, the gashes
Do better upon them.

—Act V, scene viii, lines 1–3

This contemptuous reference to "Roman fool" deals with the Roman penchant for suicide, notably, for instance, with the case of Mark Antony, who fell on his own sword when faced with final defeat (see page I-382). Shakespeare was blocking out *Antony and Cleopatra* in his mind at the time *Macbeth* was being written, so the reference comes naturally.

Untimely ripped

None in the invading host is more furiously active in seeking out Macbeth than is Macduff, who has a wife and children to avenge. When they finally meet, Macbeth taunts Macduff by saying that no man of woman born can harm him.

Whereupon Macduff, understanding the equivocation of the phrase at once, grates out:

> *Despair thy charm,*
> *And let the angel whom thou still hast served*
> *Tell thee, Macduff was from his mother's womb*
> *Untimely ripped.*
>
> —Act V, scene viii, lines 13–16

The use of the word "angel" sounds strange to modern ears, which associate angels with divine goodness. In the medieval view, however, Satan and all his cohorts were angels once, something of which Milton makes epic capital in his *Paradise Lost*. A fallen angel was a demon and it is to one of these fallen angels that Macduff refers.

As for himself, Macduff came to life by means of a Caesarean birth. We don't know the details. Did his mother die toward the end of her pregnancy and was the child "untimely ripped" from her for that reason? We don't know. Holinshed, who was Shakespeare's source, tells us no more about that than Shakespeare does.

At any rate, Macbeth now sees the significance of the nature of the apparition of the bloody child who spoke of "none of woman born" and understands Banquo's early warning about "honest trifles." He cries out:

> *. . . be these juggling fiends no more believed,*
> *That palter with us in a double sense;*
>
> —Act V, scene viii, lines 19–20

. . . Lay on, Macduff

For a moment, Macbeth refuses to fight, but when Macduff orders him then to surrender and be made a scorned and baited prisoner, he collects himself. His life is forfeit; he knows he cannot win; but he will go down like a soldier. Macbeth says:

> *Though Birnam Wood be come to Dunsinane,*
> *And thou opposed, being of no woman born,*
> *Yet I will try the last. Before my body*
> *I throw my warlike shield. Lay on, Macduff;*
> *And damned be him that first cries "Hold, enough!"*
>
> —Act V, scene viii, lines 30–34

These are Macbeth's last words. He is killed and gains, at last, the release of death.

. . . King of Scotland

Macduff, carrying Macbeth's head, greets Malcolm with the news and cries out to him:

> *Hail, King of Scotland!*
>
> —Act V, scene viii, line 59

All join and, indeed, Malcolm does become King of Scotland in 1057, seventeen years after the death of his father, Duncan, and having now reached the age of twenty-six. He was to have, on the whole, a long and a fortunate reign, remaining on the throne as Malcolm III Canmore for thirty-five years. Nor did he have to pay Siward with a province, for Siward died almost immediately after the final battle with Macbeth, and England was soon to be convulsed with the disorders following the death of Edward the Confessor in January 1066. Malcolm held on to Lothian and it remained Scottish right down to Shakespeare's time.

The Anglicization which Malcolm brought to Scotland can be seen in Malcolm's final speech, in which he says:

> *My thanes and kinsmen,*
> *Henceforth be earls, the first that ever Scotland*
> *In such an honor named.*
>
> —Act V, scene viii, lines 62–64

The Scottish title gave way to the English one as the old Celtic language gave way to Teutonic English, so that though Scotland remained politically independent, it became a cultural appanage of the southern kingdom.

The time was soon to come when Malcolm III was to return the favor of protection during exile. After William of Normandy (see page II-138) conquered England at the Battle of Hastings in the fall of 1066, two youngsters managed to make their way to Scotland. They were a brother and sister, Edgar and Margaret, grandchildren of Edmund Ironside, who had been a half brother of Edward the Confessor.

Malcolm protected these exiles as Edward the Confessor had protected him ten years before. Indeed, Malcolm married Margaret, so that the blood of the Saxon kings of England was preserved in the line of kings who ruled in Scotland.

Malcolm managed to maintain a precarious on-and-off peace with William of Normandy—now King William I (the Conqueror) of England—but became more daring when the Conqueror's son, William II Rufus, succeeded to the throne in 1087. In one last raid on northern England in 1093, Malcolm encountered an English army and was defeated and killed. With him died Edward, his eldest son by Margaret, who had been named in honor of the king who had once protected the exiled son of Duncan.

After Malcolm's death, his brother Donalbain, who had remained in exile throughout his brother's reign, managed to seize the throne, fifty-three years after the fateful death of his father, Duncan. Donalbain was supported by the Celtic party in Scotland and his reign represented a last, feeble resurgence of Celticism. After an extremely unquiet reign, he was deposed in 1098.

Three of Malcolm's sons by Margaret then ruled in succession: Edgar, Alexander I, and David I. It was from David I that all the succeeding kings of Scotland, even the Stuarts (including James I), descended. James I was of the sixteenth generation of descent from David I, and the present Queen of England, Elizabeth II, is of the twenty-eighth generation of descent.

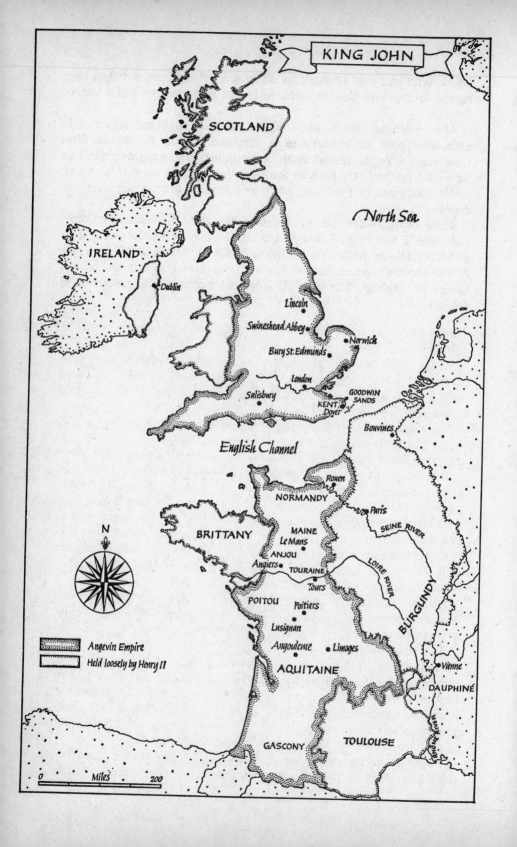

KING JOHN

SCOTLAND

North Sea

IRELAND

Dublin

Lincoln

Swineshead Abbey

Norwich

Bury St. Edmunds

London

Salisbury

GOODWIN
SANDS

KENT
Dover

Bouvines

English Channel

Rouen

NORMANDY

Paris

SEINE RIVER

N

BRITTANY

MAINE
Le Mans

ANJOU

Angiers

TOURAINE

Tours

LOIRE RIVER

BURGUNDY

POITOU

Poitiers

Lusignan

Angoulēme

Limoges

AQUITAINE

Vienne

DAUPHINÉ

GASCONY

TOULOUSE

RHÔNE RIVER

Angevin Empire

Held loosely by Henry II

0   Miles   200

30

The Life and Death of

KING JOHN

THE FOUR "English plays" I have dealt with so far all have their events taking place in the period before 1066. These events are largely legendary and what portions of the action are inspired by actual history are badly distorted.

In 1066 William of Normandy conquered England from the Saxons and the light of history began to shine more brightly on the land, and, indeed, on all of Europe. The barbarian invasions of Western Europe came to a halt at last, there was a rise in literacy and in culture, and the chronicles and histories of the time were better recorded.

In the 1590s Shakespeare wrote no less than nine historical plays dealing with this post-Conquest period of English history. Eight of these dealt with the troubled fifteenth century, with a central point involving the troubled successions to the throne.

Undoubtedly, this reflected the great problem of Shakespeare's own time. In the 1590s Queen Elizabeth I was in her sixties. She had refused to marry; she had no children; and death could be only a few years away.

If her death were followed by a disputed succession, England might once again experience the horrors of civil war, as she had experienced them in the past. Most thinking Englishmen were concerned about this and must have been uncomfortably aware that on any morning they might wake to find the great Queen dead and the nobility choosing up sides for a struggle.

Shakespeare's concern expressed itself in one play after another, dealing with the struggle for the throne, showing in pitiless clarity the ignominy of motive, act, and character such a struggle produced.

About 1596, though, when five of these fifteenth-century plays had been already written and three remained to be written, Shakespeare broke in with a play about King John in the early thirteenth century.

This came about, perhaps, because in 1591 there had appeared a play entitled *The Troublesome Reign of John, King of England* which had proven popular. More than once, Shakespeare had been able to try his own hand at a version of a popular play, always producing a better one that drove the earlier version into oblivion. He was the more tempted because here again was a plot that dealt with a disputed succession and the troubles in the form of civil war and foreign invasion that resulted.

To get the background, let us go back to King Henry II of England, who ruled from 1154 to 1189. He was, through his mother, a great-grandson

KING JOHN

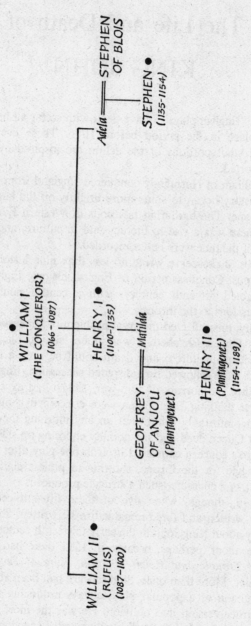

From WILLIAM the CONQUEROR to HENRY II

```
                    WILLIAM I ●
                 (THE CONQUEROR)
                    (1066-1087)

  WILLIAM II ●          HENRY I ●              Adela ══ STEPHEN
   (RUFUS)             (1100-1135)                      OF BLOIS
   (1087-1100)                                         │
                  GEOFFREY ══ Matilda            STEPHEN ●
                  OF ANJOU                       (1135-1154)
                 (Plantagenet)

                    HENRY II ●
                   (Plantagenet)
                    (1154-1189)
```

● Kings of England

NOTE: Only significant individuals are included.

Women's names in lower case.

of William the Conqueror, and he was, in his own right, a strong and competent king.

Altogether, Henry II had five sons. The oldest son, William, died in 1156 at the age of three, but the other four sons survived infancy. They were, in order of decreasing age, Henry, Richard, Geoffrey, and John. Two of these sons died during the lifetime of their father, Henry in 1184 and Geoffrey in 1186. Richard, the older of the two remaining sons, succeeded to the throne in 1189 as Richard I.

When Richard died in battle in 1199, his younger brother, John—the last living son of Henry II—succeeded. He was thirty-two years old at the time.

. . . what would France . . .

The play opens in 1199 with John fresh upon the throne. Immediately, he must face the hostility of France. This hostility had stretched back to the time of John's father, Henry II.

Henry II (and his sons after him) ruled over broader territories in France than the French King himself controlled, and for over half a century it was the overriding concern of the kings of France to regain some or all of this territory.

Through much of the reign of Henry II, the King of France had been Louis VII. Louis avoided meeting Henry II in actual battle but had intrigued against him skillfully and, toward the end of his reign, deliberately encouraged Henry's sons to revolt against him.

Louis died in 1180 and his son Philip II succeeded to the throne and to his father's policy. Philip had carried on war against Henry and Richard and when Richard died and was succeeded by John, Philip intended to continue his efforts.

The play opens then with the newly crowned King John facing Chatillion, the arrogant ambassador of his royal French foe, who now, at the age of thirty-four, has already been on the throne for nineteen years.

John says:

> Now say, Chatillion, what would France with us?
> —Act I, scene i, line 1

The borrowed majesty . . .

Haughtily, Chatillion says:

> Thus, after greeting, speaks the King of France
> In my behavior to the majesty,
> The borrowed majesty, of England here.
> —Act I, scene i, lines 2–4

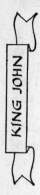

KING JOHN

From HENRY II to HENRY III

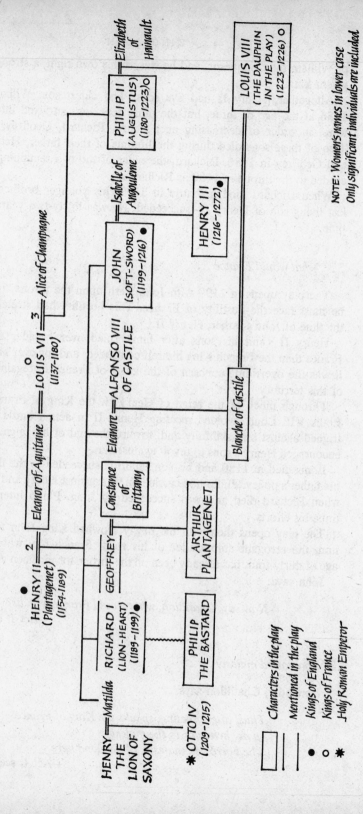

NOTE: Women's names in lower case
Only significant individuals are included

HENRY II ══ Matilda

RICHARD I
(LION-HEART)
(1189–1199) ●

HENRY ══ Matilda
THE
LION OF
SAXONY

OTTO IV
(1209–1215) ✻

PHILIP
THE BASTARD

HENRY II ══ Eleanor of Aquitaine ══ LOUIS VII ══ Alice of Champagne
(Plantagenet)   (1137–1180)
(1154–1189) ●   2   ○   3

GEOFFREY ══ Constance
                      of
                      Brittany

ARTHUR
PLANTAGENET

Eleanore ══ ALFONSO VIII
                      OF CASTILE

Blanche of Castile

JOHN ══ Isabelle of Angouleme
(SOFT-SWORD)
(1199–1216) ●

PHILIP II ══ Elizabeth
(AUGUSTUS) ○   of
(1180–1223)   Hainault

HENRY III
(1216–1272) ●

LOUIS VIII
(THE DAUPHIN
IN THE PLAY)
(1223–1226) ○

Characters in the play
Mentioned in the play

Kings of England
Kings of France
Holy Roman Emperor

● ○ ✻

Clearly, Philip of France is repudiating John's title to the throne of England. John's is a majesty that is only "borrowed" from its true holder. Chatillion is deliberately insulting the new English King, but John is no knight-errant. He is a devious man who can bear insults and accept defeats where this is necessary.

With him, however, is his mother, Queen Eleanor, who is quite another kind of person. She is on fire with resentment at once and responds harshly:

A strange beginning: "borrowed majesty"!
—Act I, scene i, line 5

Eleanor (or "Elinor," as Shakespeare spells it) is surely one of the most unusual women of the Middle Ages. Her father was William X, the Duke of Aquitaine, the rich and smiling country that makes up the southwestern quarter of France. In 1137 he died, leaving Eleanor behind as his only child. She was a fifteen-year-old beauty and the richest heiress in Europe. Because of the land she inherited she is known as Eleanor of Aquitaine in the history books.

Naturally, such an heiress could scarcely remain unmarried long. Louis the Young, heir to the throne of France, was a natural husband, for by the marriage Louis could add Aquitaine to the French territory which he already controlled directly. The marriage took place just three months after Eleanor had become duchess. One month after that (it was still 1137), Louis' father died and the young bridegroom became King Louis VII of France.

It was not, however, a happy marriage. Eleanor was gay, frivolous, and quite aware that she was a great heiress in her own right. She led a court of troubadours and pleasure seekers whom King Louis found distasteful.

Louis was a grave and serious person, very much involved in kingly duties. Undoubtedly he seemed like a wet blanket and spoilsport to his merry Queen; undoubtedly she seemed like a featherbrained ninny to her hard-working King.

What was worse was that though she bore two children to Louis, both were girls, and by French custom, neither could inherit the throne either for themselves or for their descendants. Louis wanted a son and Eleanor wasn't giving him one.

The final straw came in connection with a Crusade. Half a century earlier a Christian army had taken Jerusalem and the Holy Land, but now the Moslems were making a comeback. A Second Crusade was necessary, and in 1147 Louis VII volunteered to be one of the leaders.

Queen Eleanor, however, would hear of nothing but that she must go with her husband, complete with her court. The whole adventure was to be like a knightly romance, with beautiful ladies watching their gallant lovers winning the colorful tournaments which Eleanor no doubt pictured a Crusade to be.

It didn't work that way. The Second Crusade was a costly and humiliating fiasco and Louis VII was forced to return home, a complete failure, and totally estranged from his wife. In 1152 he divorced her even though that meant losing Aquitaine.

Eleanor was a good hater and the humiliation of the divorce was sufficient motive for her to make a quick second marriage that would be as harmful as possible to her ex-husband. She was thirty now, but still good-looking and, what was more important, still an heiress.

Ruling over the northwestern quarter of France was a gallant and intelligent nineteen-year-old youth, Henry of Anjou. His father had been Count of Anjou, but his mother was Matilda, who had been daughter of King Henry I of England. There were many who considered Matilda to be the rightful Queen of England, but she had been unable to establish that rule, and her cousin, Stephen, ruled instead.

(In a way, the death of King Henry I in 1135 had led to a true time of troubles thanks to the disputed succession, and one might wonder whether Shakespeare had ever been tempted to write a play dealing with it. However, if he had written of Matilda and Stephen, he would have had to picture an English queen who was eventually defeated and who was driven out of London by the aroused citizens. With Queen Elizabeth on the throne and with many in the land hating her for religious reasons, such a play might have found itself too easily viewed as treasonable, and if Shakespeare ever had the thought of writing one, he must have dismissed that thought quickly.)

Even though Stephen was England's King, he was growing old. One of his sons had died and the second had neither the ability nor the desire to succeed. Once Stephen died, it was certain Henry of Anjou would succeed to the throne.

Eleanor married Henry at once, as much to spite Louis VII as anything else, while Henry took this older woman to wife as much for the sake of Aquitaine as anything else. This second marriage of Eleanor took place only two months after her divorce from Louis VII.

Two years later Stephen died and Henry became King Henry II of England. England and his French dominions together made up Henry's "Angevin Empire," so called because Henry was of the line of Anjou. It was this Empire that Louis VII and his son, Philip II, strove to break up.

Eleanor did for Henry II what she had not been able to do for Louis VII; she supplied the English King with sons, and in the latter part of his reign he was surrounded by four of them.

They were scarcely a blessing to him, though. He was busy and could pay them little attention, so that they grew up quite mother-oriented. What's more, Eleanor's second marriage soon turned out to be as unhappy as the first, and out of her hatred for Henry, Eleanor encouraged her sons to rebel against their father.

The rebellion did not succeed and the sons had to flee to Louis VII for protection. Eleanor tried to join them, but Henry managed to capture her at least and imprisoned her for the rest of his reign.

The sons came crawling back to make their peace with their formidable father, but they continued to be a threat to him and to each other to the very end of Henry's life.

When Henry II died, on July 6, 1189, and Richard became King, his first action was to release his mother from imprisonment. She was sixty-seven years old now, but as firm and as formidable as ever. She devoted the remainder of her life to backing her two sons, and to my way of thinking (despite the inflated reputation of Richard, at least) she was more of a man than both sons put together.

When Richard died in 1199, Eleanor was seventy-seven years old, a tremendous age for that time, but she was still strong enough and energetic enough to canvass the English nobility and populace for oaths of allegiance that would settle John, her youngest and best-loved son, firmly on the throne.

Naturally she, much more than John, would react with instant resentment to the deliberately provocative phrase "borrowed majesty."

Arthur Plantagenet . . .

John quiets his mother, for he wants to hear what Chatillion has to say. Chatillion does not keep him waiting. He says:

> Philip of France, in right and true behalf
> Of thy deceased brother Geoffrey's son,
> Arthur Plantagenet, lays most lawful claim
> To this fair island . . .
>
> —Act I, scene i, lines 7–10

At this time, notions of "legitimacy" were beginning to rise in western Europe. That is, it was felt that the crown should not pass merely to some member of the royal family—preferably to some adult member with proven ability at fighting and administration (see page II-95)—but to the one who was next in line according to some definite system, regardless of age or capacity.

The system usually used was to have the eldest son inherit, followed by his heirs, and only when the eldest son had no heirs at all would the crown pass on his death to the second son and his heirs. Only by default of heirs to the second son would it pass to the third, and so on.

Prince William (first son) died at the age of three, naturally without heirs. Prince Henry (second son) also died without heirs. Prince Richard (third son) succeeded to the throne, therefore.

Even before Richard's succession, Prince Geoffrey (fourth son) had died without heirs, having been thrown from his horse while jousting, when only twenty-eight years old. It would seem then that when Richard died without heirs in 1199, the crown would pass to John, according to the strict tenets of legitimacy.

There was a catch. Geoffrey, the fourth son, was indeed childless at the time of his death, but at that time his wife was pregnant. In 1187 she was delivered of a posthumous baby boy, whom she named Arthur. By the strict tenets of legitimacy, Arthur, heir of the fourth son, had precedence over John, the fifth son, to the crown of England.

It is this right which Philip II of France is maintaining.

But why Arthur Plantagenet? What is the significance of that second name?

That began as a nickname of Geoffrey of Anjou, the father of Henry II. According to one story, Geoffrey made a pilgrimage to the Holy Land and donned lowly garb as a gesture of humility. He carried a sprig of broom, a common shrub, in his bonnet as another such gesture. Another legend has it that he planted broom shrubs to improve his hunting tracts. (The broom plant has long thin branches which can be tied in a bundle to a stick and used to sweep with. Such an instrument came to be called a "broom" eventually, no matter what it was made of.)

The broom plant is the *planta genista* in Latin and *planta genêt* in medieval French. Geoffrey, whether through his bonnet or his hunting, gained a nickname by this gesture and was called Geoffrey Plantagenet.

When Henry succeeded to the English throne as Henry II, he was often referred to as Henry Plantagenet, as though he had inherited his father's nickname. To some later historians it seemed a virtual family name, to be granted all the descendants of Henry II through the male line.

. . . Ireland, Poictiers . . .

Nor is it only England that is claimed by Philip on Arthur's behalf. The French dominions of the Angevin Empire are demanded as well. Chatillion lists some of the territories, saying the claim extends

> To Ireland, Poictiers, Anjou, Touraine, Maine,
> Desiring thee to lay aside the sword
> Which sways usurpingly these several titles,
> And put the same into young Arthur's hand,
> Thy nephew and right royal sovereign.
>
> —Act I, scene i, lines 11–15

Ireland had first been invaded by the English in 1169. Norman knights entered the western island on the pleas of some Irish chieftains who had been defeated by others. The Normans were quite successful and Henry II feared they might carve out independent Norman kingdoms that would make more trouble for England than the chaotic Irish tribal society could possibly make. Henry therefore brought an army into Ireland and established a section about Dublin as English-controlled territory.

In 1177 Henry II appointed his young son John (only ten years old at the time) as titular Lord of Ireland, in order to give him a title. When John tried to take personal charge of Ireland in 1185, he botched the job. John remained Lord of Ireland, off and on, during Richard's reign (losing it for a while because he intrigued against Richard during the latter's absence on a Crusade).

As for "Poictiers, Anjou, Touraine, Maine," there are four districts lying between Normandy and Aquitaine, all of them part of the empire built up by Henry II.

. . . ambitious Constance . . .

King John naturally refuses to accept the demands of Philip of France and Chatillion leaves with what amounts to a declaration of war.

After he is gone, old Eleanor of Aquitaine bursts out in fury:

> *What now, my son! Have I not ever said*
> *How that ambitious Constance would not cease*
> *Till she had kindled France and all the world*
> *Upon the right and party of her son?*
>
> —Act I, scene i, lines 31–34

The Constance here referred to is the Duchess of Brittany. Brittany itself is the northwesternmost peninsula of France, a region known as Armorica to the Romans. In the sixth century, when the island, Britain, was being overrun by Saxons, parties of Britons fled to the peninsula for safety and it was from that time that the peninsula came to be known as Brittany.

Throughout the Middle Ages Brittany retained a kind of precarious semi-independence, although it was frequently forced to pay tribute to the King of France or to the Duke of Normandy. In the eleventh century Normandy was at the peak of its power when its duke, William II, invaded and conquered England, and Brittany was subservient to him and to his successors.

It was part of the French dominions of Henry II, but of all his French provinces it was least tightly tied to him. When it tried to establish its real independence under its duke, Conan IV, Henry invaded Brittany and occupied much of its territory. Henry then saw a way of converting a loose connection into a tight dynastic union. Conan's only living child was a daughter, Constance. Henry arranged to have her marry his son Geoffrey, and on Conan's death, not long after, Geoffrey became Duke of Brittany.

When Geoffrey died, Constance ruled Brittany, and when her son was born, her ambitions for him were clearly evident in the very name she chose. She called him Arthur, the legendary hero of the Britons in their struggle against the Saxons. This was particularly appropriate as a name for the Duke of Brittany, the land to which so many Britons had fled.

At the time of Arthur's birth, there was only Richard standing closer to the throne, and there seemed a good possibility that Richard would have no children. That meant that Arthur might very well be King of England someday, and Constance put her full effort toward making sure of that. She was as ambitious in her way as Eleanor was in hers, and the stage was set for the battle of the queens on behalf of their sons.

. . . Cordelion . . .

The matter of high politics is interrupted at this point by a much lowlier matter; a disputed succession again, but this time to an ordinary bit of land. A sheriff brings in two brothers clamoring for judgment. The King asks their identities, and the older brother, Philip, replies that he is

> . . . eldest son,
> As I suppose, to Robert Faulconbridge,
> A soldier, by the honor-giving hand
> Of Cordelion knighted in the field.
>
> —Act I, scene i, lines 51–54

"Cordelion" is a variation of "Coeur-de-lion," meaning literally "heart-of-lion," the common nickname of King Richard I of England, elder brother and predecessor of King John.

It is proper that the nickname be in French, for the language of the court of the King of England had been Norman French since the time of the Conquest. Even in King Richard's time, over a century and a quarter after the Battle of Hastings, at which William of Normandy conquered England, the English King ruled more land in France than in England, considered himself more French than English, spoke French rather than English, and *was* French rather than English.

Richard grew up in Aquitaine, his mother's appanage, ruled over it throughout his youth, and considered it his home. He visited England only twice during his reign, both times briefly, and then only to collect money. He fought in France and he died in France.

Nevertheless, his nickname has been translated into English, so that he is "Richard Lion-Heart" or "Richard the Lion-Hearted," and he has, under that name, become a great English hero about whom numberless tales have been told.

He deserves the nickname, to be sure, since he loved to fight and he usually won. He was a born knight-errant, who enjoyed more than anything else the giving and taking of huge thwacks. On the other hand, he was larger than most men, better fed and better muscled, better trained and better outfitted. Why shouldn't he be brave then?

Also to his credit was the fact that he was a troubadour as well as a knight. He sang sweetly and composed verses as good as those any king might compose. What's more, he loved his mother.

There, however, his virtues end. Richard was a vain, faithless person, who was not very intelligent, and whose reign was one long disaster for England. He won battles and lost wars, and in his eternal quest for money with which to lose those wars, he would use any means, however ignoble. He sold land, offices, justice. He gave up his rights to Scotland for money. He squeezed the Jews and behaved in such a manner that anti-Semitic riots burst out all over England, one of the rare times such actions disgraced the land.

He was not even a manly person, except for his ability to fight. He lacked resolution and another nickname for him (not as well known as "Lion-Heart") was "Richard Yea-and-Nay," meaning he could easily be swayed to either side of a question and then swayed back again.

And yet because he played what seemed a heroic role in the Crusades, he is forgiven everything by Englishmen, and the picture of him in their minds is the utterly false one glamorously drawn in books such as Walter Scott's *Ivanhoe* and *The Talisman*. (And, of course, in all the legends that build up Richard, his brother John is made to stink by comparison. John was not actually a worthy man, to be sure, but except that he did not shine in personal combat, he was no worse than Richard.)

. . . perfect Richard . . .

The argument between the two brothers involves the accusation of bastardy. Both are the sons of Faulconbridge's wife, but the question is one of fatherhood. The younger son, Robert, insists that the older, Philip, was a bastard; that he was born while Faulconbridge was overseas on King Richard's business, while Richard remained in Faulconbridge's home, apparently on Faulconbridge's business.

King John and Queen Eleanor believe this even before it is explained. The Queen finds resemblances to her dead son in face and voice and King John says:

> Mine eye hath well examined his parts,
> And finds them perfect Richard . . .

> —Act I, scene i, lines 89–90

In short, the older son is accepted as the bastard of Richard I and is enthusiastically accepted as a grandson by Eleanor and as a nephew by John. (He is called Philip the Bastard in the cast of characters and his speeches are uniformly attributed to "Bastard.")

It seems queer that a bastard should so quickly and cheerfully be accepted by the legal members of a family.

To explain this, it must first be made clear that the situation, as described by Shakespeare, is completely unhistorical. A person named Philip is mentioned in passing as a bastard son of Richard I in Holinshed, but the actual existence of any son of Richard, legitimate or illegitimate, is in the highest degree unlikely.

It seems certain that, despite the fact that Richard was married to Berengaria of Navarre, he never had serious relations with any woman. He seems to have been a thoroughgoing homosexual, a fact glossed over by his later idolaters, but known perhaps to his contemporaries. Constance might not so eagerly have groomed her son for the kingship if she had not been utterly confident that Richard would have no children to leave the crown to.

But if we forget history and grant the existence of Philip, bastard son of Richard I, why is he introduced into the play and made so much of when Shakespeare is quite hard on bastards in other plays (notably in *King Lear*—see page II-12)? Indeed, Philip the Bastard is the hero of this play, if there is one.

For one thing, there is a precedent for a bastard, near-allied to a reigning king, who is honored by that king and who offers complete fidelity in return. This is the case of Jean Dunois, a bastard son of Louis of Orléans and therefore first cousin of Charles VII of France. Dunois was treated with honor by Charles when he was the beleaguered Dauphin in a land overrun by triumphant English and Dunois, in return, fought ably on Charles's behalf. It was he, with the help of Joan of Arc, who raised the siege of Orléans, so that there was double reason for calling him "Bastard of Orléans."

Secondly, Philip the Bastard is useful dramatically. King John is insufficiently heroic and King Richard would have made a better representative of England. Since Richard is dead, a mythical bastard is brought in who is presented in all respects as a kind of Richard brought back to life.

Thirdly, if Philip's existence is admitted, then, but for the fact of illegitimacy, he, and not either Arthur or John, would be the rightful King of England. We might well suppose that this point can be used to serve as a kind of climax to the play at the end.

Colbrand the giant . . .

John is ready to grant the Faulconbridge inheritance to Philip, despite his patent illegitimacy, but Eleanor urges him to join the court, exchanging his land for the chances of gaining honor and glory.

Philip does so gladly, and in doing so makes (to our modern tastes) brutal mockery of his brother's appearance, for his brother, the legitimate son, lacks the genes of large King Richard, and is lean and wizen by comparison.

Philip is dubbed Sir Richard Plantagenet by King John (though the title is never used in the play). The Bastard is then left alone on the stage and his soliloquy on vanity (carried out in a tone of mocking cynicism that is characteristic of him) is interrupted by the panting arrival of his mother. She is in hot pursuit of her younger son, whose aspersions on her honor (in claiming his older brother to be a bastard) she resents.

She asks the Bastard furiously as to the whereabouts of his brother, and he answers, still mocking:

> *My brother Robert? Old Sir Robert's son?*
> *Colbrand the giant, that same mighty man?*
> > —Act I, scene i, lines 224–25

Colbrand the giant is a character in the very popular romance *Guy of Warwick*. This was composed in the time of Henry II and eventually came to be accepted as authentic history, which, of course, it was not. Guy of Warwick is an English knight-errant who performs the usual knight-errantish deeds across Europe, fighting Saracens, opposing magicians, rescuing beautiful damsels, and slaying monsters.

Returning to England, he found that land under the heel of a Danish giant, Colbrand, who, at the head of the Danish forces, is collecting vast tribute. (There is something authentic here. In the tenth century England was indeed prostrate before Danish raids and did indeed have to pay out all the tribute it could scrape up.)

In Winchester, Sir Guy of Warwick fought in single combat with Colbrand, slew him, and delivered England from the Danish yoke. And for as long as the romance remained popular, Colbrand the giant remained a stock phrase to characterize anything vast and terrible. It is used here, of course, as humorous irony, for the thin Robert.

. . . Basilisco-like

Lady Faulconbridge is taken aback by the evident mockery of her, a mockery the Bastard quickly makes more explicit. She says, nervously:

> *What means this scorn, thou most untoward knave?*
> > —Act I, scene i, line 243

And he replies, with reference to his recent promotion to a title, based on his mother's dishonor:

> Knight, knight, good mother, Basilisco-like,
>
> —Act I, scene i, line 244

The reference is to a play by Thomas Kyd (see page II–100), *The Tragedy of Solyman and Perseda* (1588), in which one of the characters is a boastful knight named Basilisco. He is very proud of his title and would not have it omitted, so that in speaking of his name, he adds, "Knight, knight, good fellow, knight."

To which the "good fellow," implying that despite the title the character will not be denied, replies, "Knave, knave, good fellow, knave!"

Shakespeare has the Bastard reverse the progression and refer to the inspiration for it, sure that he would thus delight the audience by reference to a competitor.

Faced with the Bastard's calm assurance of his own illegitimacy, his mother breaks down and admits Richard to have been his father.

Before Angiers . . .

The second act shifts the scene to France, where the war between the Kings of England and France has begun. The real issue is whether the continental dominions of the Angevin Empire are to remain in the hands of the Plantagenets or are to revert into the hands of the King of France. The status of Prince Arthur is but a convenient pawn in this fundamental struggle, something that Arthur's mother, Constance, does not understand.

The current of war has carried Philip of France to the gates of one of the important cities of the Angevin Empire, and his first speech of the play begins:

> Before Angiers well met . . .
>
> —Act II, scene i, line 1

Angiers, or, in its modern French form, Angers, is a city about 170 miles southwest of Paris. It was the capital of the County of Anjou, ancestral home of the Angevin line.

. . . brave Austria

Philip has not come alone. His son is with him, and so is Arthur, on whose behalf he is supposedly fighting, as well as Arthur's mother, Constance. In addition, he has a foreign ally, and in his first speech it is he whom he is greeting:

> *Before Angiers well met, brave Austria.*
>
> —Act II, scene i, line 1

In Shakespeare's time Austria was a great power, but in the time of the play it was still a rather minor German duchy. It had been under the overlordship of Bavaria and had only broken free in 1156. It achieved its first prominence in European history as a result of an action of the very man referred to here as "brave Austria." (His speeches in the play are always marked as "Austria.")

The man addressed is, properly speaking, Leopold V, Margrave of Austria. (The title "margrave" is equivalent to that of "count.") Leopold had spread his sway over Styria to the south, and since Styria was a duchy, he advanced in title and became Leopold I, Duke of Austria.

Leopold went off to the Crusades and was part of the host that came to assist at the siege of Acre, a coastal city in the hands of the Moslems. In July 1191 the Christian army, with Richard the Lion-Heart its principal leader, took the city.

Leopold, who had after all participated in the siege, placed his standard on one of the battlements of the fallen city. Richard, seeing no point in giving credit to anyone else, ordered the standard removed and had it thrown to one side. Some say that when Leopold protested, Richard kicked him in the rear end and forced him into humiliating silence.

The English chroniclers seem to consider this an amusing and heroic action.

When it was time for Richard to go home, he realized there were going to be difficulties. He had managed to antagonize almost everyone in Europe and he lacked the army to force his way across the Continent against that antagonism. He decided to sneak across the Continent. He had his ship drawn ashore near Venice and off he went in disguise.

But Richard could not very well imitate a nobody. He was large, muscular, and haughty. Nothing he could do could prevent him from appearing what he was—an arrogant knight of high estate. It was only a matter of time before he would be identified, and as luck would have it, he was recognized at the worst possible time.

Near Vienna, in December 1192, he was surrounded by armed men who were clearly intent on holding this obviously important personage for ransom. Richard drew his sword and said he would surrender only to their leader. When that leader appeared, it turned out to be none other than Duke Leopold, who promptly imprisoned him.

Leopold was execrated in England for this action, of course. He was viewed as a base coward who had been rightly kicked in the butt as advance payment for his subsequent villainies.

He serves as a needed villain in this play, someone at whom the English audience can mock and sneer. King Philip of France won't do; for he was a most capable king who was to prove victorious. (He even came to be known, for his victories, as Philip Augustus, in memory of Rome's great first Emperor, see page II–55.)

Leopold, however, was another matter. He is greeted as "brave Austria," which is undoubtedly intended to draw hooting catcalls. He is a braggart who wears a lion skin but doesn't act the part, so that he is a transparently warped image of the lion-hearted Richard. And what is more, it is to the Bastard, the resurrected spirit of Richard, that the chief task of baiting and, eventually, killing Leopold is left.

There is only one catch to this whole thing. Leopold of Austria died in 1194, five years before the accession of King John. He cannot possibly play a role in John's time.

. . . came early to his grave

King Philip next introduces Austria to young Arthur, saying:

> *Arthur, that great forerunner of thy blood,*
> *Richard, that robbed the lion of his heart*
> *And fought the holy wars in Palestine,*
> *By this brave duke came early to his grave;*
> —Act II, scene i, lines 2–5

This (which serves to alert any dull-wit in Shakespeare's audience who doesn't know why Austria must be treated as a villain) makes it sound as though Richard died in Austrian imprisonment, but this is not so. In fact, he didn't even stay in Leopold's grasp long. The German Emperor Henry VI forced Leopold to disgorge his important prisoner and set him free at last for 150,000 marks, which had to be squeezed out of the sweat of Richard's subjects. Richard finally returned to England, safe and sound, in 1194.

How, then, did Richard die?

Well, having stayed in England just long enough to collect some money, Richard crossed the Channel into France and spent the remainder of his reign fighting King Philip.

In 1199 a peasant unearthed a crock of gold on the land of Guiomar, Viscount of Limoges, a territory in northern Aquitaine. Of course, Richard considered Aquitaine peculiarly his own, and as he always needed money, he promptly demanded the gold. The Viscount of Limoges was willing to grant part but not all.

Richard at once rode off to lay siege to a castle at Châlus, twenty miles southwest of Limoges, where the Viscount was holed up. The Viscount offered to surrender conditionally, but Richard refused conditions. While the King reconnoitered the walls, an arrow struck him in the left shoulder. Richard ordered an assault at once and the castle was taken. Only then did he bother to have the arrow extracted.

It was too late. The age was innocent of antibiotics or even of the notions of ordinary hygiene. The wound festered and turned gangrenous and Richard died on April 6, 1199.

He could not be said to have been killed by Guiomar of Limoges. He was killed by his own folly and his eagerness to fight over little causes.

Shakespeare combines the two men, Leopold of Austria and Guiomar of Limoges. The character called "brave Austria" here is listed in the cast of characters as Lymoges, Duke of Austria, and at one point later in the play he is addressed by Constance as Lymoges. The combination is grotesque but it gives Shakespeare a needed villain.

. . . the Lady Blanch of Spain

The combined forces of Philip and Austria make ready to lay siege to Angiers, when Chatillion arrives with news concerning John. The English King, he says, has raised an army and has invaded France:

> With him along is come the mother-queen
> An Ate, stirring him to blood and strife;
> With her her niece, the Lady Blanch of Spain;
> With them a bastard of the king's deceased;
> —Act II, scene i, lines 62–65

Ate is the Greek goddess of vengeance and mischief, and that certainly is a rather apt description for Eleanor of Aquitaine, who through her long life made ample trouble for her two husbands and for all those who crossed her.

The present fight is between her son John and her grandson Arthur, and in this she is entirely on the side of her son, while her attitude toward Arthur is such that one can scarcely recognize the grandmotherly relationship. For one thing, of course, she had scarcely ever as much as seen Arthur; for another, she hated Constance, her daughter-in-law, for if Arthur became King, Constance would become Queen Mother.

As for "Blanch of Spain," she was not Eleanor's niece, but King John's niece and therefore Eleanor's granddaughter. In addition to the five sons which Eleanor had borne Henry II, she bore three daughters as well (which, plus two daughters to Louis VII, gave her ten children altogether—an amazing number of childbirths to have survived in those days, especially when it left her time to make so much trouble besides.)

Eleanor's three daughters by Henry were, in order of age, Matilda, Eleanor, and Joan, and all married kings.

The middle daughter, Eleanor (namesake of the old Queen) was born in 1161, so that she was six years older than John. In 1170, when the younger Eleanor was still only nine years old, she was married to Alfonso VIII, King of Castile (a region then making up the north-central part of what is now Spain). About 1187 they had the daughter whom Shakespeare calls "Blanch of Spain," but who is known in history as "Blanche of Castile." She was eleven years old at the time of the accession of King John.

. . . great Alcides' shoes . . .

John and his forces appear and he and Philip at once engage in argument. Philip insists the rightful King of England is Arthur and John denies that Philip has any say in the matter.

Eleanor joins in on John's side and is answered at once by Constance. The two women are well matched in vitriolic temper and in articulate billingsgate, and when they begin tearing at each other, the men are forced to one side.

Austria tries to stop them and the instant he opens his mouth, the Bastard cries him down. This begins the constant baiting of Austria by the resurrected spirit of Richard, to the delight of the audience. The Bastard refers, for instance, to Austria's affectation in wearing a lion skin and says:

> *It lies as sightly on the back of him*
> *As great Alcides' shoes upon an ass.*
>
> —Act II, scene i, lines 143–44

Alcides is Hercules, of course (see page I–70). The Bastard is saying that a lion skin on Austria's back is like Hercules on an ass's back.

The canon of the law . . .

The men are not at their words long, however, when the quarrel breaks out once more between Constance and Eleanor, and the younger manages to outcry the older. Constance maintains that if Arthur is suffering wrongs and injuries, it is entirely owing to the wickedness of his grandmother. He is being punished not for his own, but for her sins:

> *Thy sins are visited in this poor child;*
> *The canon of the law is laid on him,*
> *Being but the second generation*
> *Removed from thy sin-conceiving womb.*
>
> —Act II, scene i, lines 179–82

Constance is referring to the Book of Exodus (21:5): "I the Lord thy God am a jealous God, visiting the iniquity of the fathers upon the children unto the third and fourth generation of them that hate me."

A will that bars the title . . .

King John, irritated by these caustic fleers at his beloved mother, cries out:

> *Bedlam, have done.*
> —Act II, scene i, line 183

By this anachronistic reference to the hospital of St. Mary of Bethlehem (Bedlam), see page II–15, he is calling Constance a lunatic.

Eleanor, however, strives to remove the argument from the level of personalities and brings in a matter of legality. She says to Constance scornfully:

> *Thou unadvisèd scold, I can produce*
> *A will that bars the title of thy son.*
> —Act II, scene i, lines 191–92

It seems that while Richard was alive and making ready to leave for the Holy Land (from where, conceivably, he might not return), he recognized Arthur as his heir. (Richard's actions toward the succession always seemed to be those of a man who knew that he himself would have no children.)

Arthur was only two years old at the time and it made sense to have the boy raised in England, in Normandy, or in Aquitaine—somewhere where he could be educated into considering himself an Angevin and a Plantagenet. The Bretons preferred, however, to keep the young child in Brittany.

In 1196 Richard was safely home from the Crusade, and he demanded that Arthur, now nine years old, be given up to him. The Bretons refused again. Rather than let their young duke become a Norman by upbringing, they turned him over for education to King Philip of France.

It was plain, then, that Arthur would have a French education and would become a thoroughgoing Frenchman. Richard considered Philip his archenemy and he could not face leaving his kingdom to a puppet of that same archenemy. He therefore disowned Arthur, naming John as his heir. John was still Richard's heir when Richard died. (John was at the deathbed.) It was undoubtedly this to which Eleanor was referring.

Of course, it remains a question whether a reigning king can alter the tenets of legitimacy to suit his own desires. Constance, however, does not raise this fine point. Instead, she answers, with equal contempt, that if Eleanor has a will, it is a forged one.

. . . to the walls

The discussion ends where it began—in absolute disagreement. Both armies try to enter the city of Angiers, but the citizens have something to say about that, and in response to the sound of a trumpet, one of them appears above, crying:

> *Who is it that hath warned us to the walls?*
> —Act II, scene i, line 201

In the Signet edition, the speaker is identified as "Hubert," and in the cast of characters, he is listed as "Hubert, a citizen of Angiers." Later in the play, Hubert plays a role which makes him clearly identified with a historical Hubert who can scarcely have been a citizen of Angiers. The Kittredge edition and the original printed version of the play identify the speaker simply as "Citizen," and in my opinion, this is what should be done.

Saint George . . .

The Citizen will admit only that side into Angiers which proves its right by victory in battle. The English and French forces prepare to fight, therefore, and the Bastard says:

> *Saint George, that swinged* [beat] *the dragon, and e'er since*
> *Sits on's horseback at mine hostess' door,*
> *Teach us some fence!*
> —Act II, scene i, lines 288–90

In medieval times a legend had grown popular concerning a Christian martyr, George, who lived in Palestine and who died in 303, during the last great Roman persecution of the Christians. He was canonized as St. George, and the event in his life which attracted most notice was his rescue of a maiden from the wicked jaws of a dragon—which he slew.

George may well have been a historical character, but it seems quite reasonable to suppose that the incident with the maiden and the dragon was a Christianization of the popular motif in such pagan myths as that of Perseus and Andromeda. In any case, the deed appealed to the Norman knights at the time of the Crusades. They liked a saint who played the knight, and St. George was popular with them.

Edward III, who reigned a century and a half after John, fancied himself a knight and adopted St. George as England's patron saint. The cry of "St. George" became a rallying cry in battle, and it would be expected that St. George would, by divine action, improve the English strokes in battle ("Teach us some fence").

Of course, the popularity of St. George led to numerous taverns adopting him as a name. The tavern signs up and down England would have him on horseback and full armor, on the point of sticking the dragon. Hence he "sits on's horseback at mine hostess' door"—though perhaps not as soon as in King John's time.

. . . the mutines of Jerusalem

The English and French forces fight a long and inconclusive battle and are each still refused admittance.

The Bastard then impatiently suggests that it is ridiculous to fight a battle for the spectator-sport pleasure of the people of Angiers. He says to the two kings:

> Do like the mutines of Jerusalem,
> Be friends awhile and both conjointly bend
> Your sharpest deeds of malice on this town.
> —Act II, scene i, lines 378–80

It is not often that quarreling factions forget their disputes and join against a common enemy, although that seems such a sensible thing to do. Very often, in history, one side or the other of the dispute, fearing loss, actually joins the common enemy.

An example of the more sensible attitude is that of the Jews of the first century. Though split into numerous factions by differences over detail in religion, they managed to combine when it came to fighting the Romans and from 67 to 70 held off the best armies the Romans could send in.

. . . Lewis the Dolphin . . .

The exasperated kings agree and prepare to combine forces and assail the stubborn city from separate directions, when the Citizen spokesman of Angiers anxiously suggests a compromise, with the essential point being a matrimonial one. He says:

> That daughter there of Spain, the Lady Blanch,
> Is near to England: look upon the years
> Of Lewis the Dolphin and that lovely maid.

If lusty love should go in quest of beauty,
Where should he find it purer than in Blanch?
                    —Act II, scene i, lines 423–27

The queer title, "the Dolphin," dates back to the house of the Count of Vienne, a city on the Rhone River. In 1133 Guigues Dauphin became count, bearing the title of Guigues IV. Why he was called Dauphin (the French word for "dolphin") is not known. Some think a dolphin was on his coat of arms or his battle standard. On the other hand, it may have been a personal name.

Succeeding counts all bore the name until it became virtually a title. The spreading territory ruled by Vienne on the east bank of the Rhone River came to be known as Dauphiné (the land of the Dolphin family, so to speak) in consequence.

Humbert II of Dauphiné, who began to rule in 1333, spent so much money on wars and other extravagances that he went virtually bankrupt. In 1349 he sold his kingdom to John, the oldest son of Philip VI of France. When John became King John II of France the very next year, he in turn made his oldest son the ruler of Dauphiné. The oldest son was, in other words, the Dauphin, and that remained the title of the heir to the French throne for five hundred years.

In that sense, Louis (who later resigned as Louis VIII) was Dauphin since he was the oldest son of Philip II of France. However, the time of the play is a century and a half before the title was transferred to France, so its use in connection with Louis is anachronistic. Although Shakespeare presents Louis as a man who, while young, is capable of taking part in warfare, he was actually born in 1187 and was only twelve years old at the time of the accession of King John, no older than Prince Arthur of Brittany and a year older than Blanche of Spain.

However, neither the youth of children nor disparity of ages is a bar in the case of dynastic marriages.

The compromise is agreed to. The marriage was, in actual history, arranged in May 1200 and quickly took place. Some land was ceded by John to the Dauphin (meaning to Philip) as a dowry, though not as much as Shakespeare indicates, and in return Philip recognizes John as King of England.

. . . Earl of Richmond . . .

This means that Prince Arthur is abandoned. John has offered him a sop, saying unctuously:

> *We will heal up all,*
> *For we'll create young Arthur Duke of Britain*

And Earl of Richmond . . .
> —Act II, scene i, lines 550–52

This, however, is nothing at all, for Arthur was already Duke of Brittany and no one disputed that. What's more, the Duke of Brittany traditionally held the title of Earl of Richmond as well, since the time of William's conquest of England a century and a half before. John was merely recognizing what existed and was granting nothing.

What John hypocritically offered, Philip hypocritically accepted on behalf of Arthur. Philip, after all, had upheld Arthur's cause in the first place only as far as it would serve to advance his own self-interest.

. . . break faith upon commodity

All depart and the Bastard is left alone on the stage to deliver a diatribe against this same self-interest, which he terms "commodity." He says:

> *Since kings break faith upon commodity,*
> *Gain, be my lord, for I will worship thee!*
> —Act II, scene i, lines 597–98

The Bastard's anger at the compromise cannot be understood without reference back to the earlier *The Troublesome Reign of John, King of England,* which served as inspiration for *King John.* In *The Troublesome Reign* it seems that Blanche had been promised to the Bastard. Faith had therefore been broken with the Bastard, who had looked forward to a beautiful and highborn bride. To have that snatched away because of the self-interest (commodity) of the kings would naturally infuriate him. Shakespeare, having removed the motivating wrong, neglected to moderate the fury.

A widow, husbandless . . .

During the negotiations between England and France over the marriage of Louis and Blanche, Constance has been absent, which is convenient, for had she been present, she would have raised an unbearable storm over the betrayal. She is, at the time, in King Philip's tent, anxiously awaiting the result of the battle.

The Earl of Salisbury is sent to tell her the results. He is William Longsword, a bastard son of Henry II, who during the reign of Richard I was given the hand of the heiress to the earldom of Salisbury so that he himself became the 3rd Earl. In some ways he may have helped form one of the models for the Bastard of the play. He was the illegitimate brother rather

than the son of Richard, and he was given the honors due a member of
the family.

At first Constance will not believe the news Salisbury brings her. She
insists he is only trying to frighten her, and she warns him that he will be
punished for that:

> For I am sick and capable of fears,
> Oppressed with wrongs, and therefore full of fears,
> A widow, husbandless, subject to fears,
> A woman naturally born to fears;
>
> —Act II, scene ii, lines 12–15

Here Shakespeare alters the historical state of affairs for the sake of
greater poignancy. Constance is a widow, yes, but she is by no means hus-
bandless. In those days, women who owned great estates did not stay
unmarried. They needed the protection of a man; and there were many
men who needed the estates.

It was not long after the death of Geoffrey, son of Henry II and father
of Prince Arthur, that Constance married Ranulf de Blundeville, Earl of
Chester. This marriage was annulled in 1199, the year in which King John
mounted the throne, and Constance married a third husband, Guy de
Thouars, who was still her husband at this time and for the remainder of
her life.

Her grief is magnificent, however, and she tears passion to tatters as it is
gradually borne in on her that Salisbury is telling the truth and that she and
her son are indeed betrayed.

. . . the holy legate . . .

Until now, Shakespeare has kept rather closely to actual chronology, and
the first two acts have dealt, more or less, with the events of the first couple
of years of John's reign. However, Shakespeare wants to unify the events
of the reign and bring them all down to his central purpose in writing the
play (discussing the results of a disputed succession) by making everything center about the matter of Prince Arthur.

Since the entire business with Arthur from beginning to end occupies
only the first third of John's reign, it becomes necessary for Shakespeare
to drag forward the later events and pile them into a kind of heap. It will
require considerable effort to sort out the chronology of the actual historical
events.

Thus, at the opening of the third act, King John is with King Philip in
the latter's tent and with them are the other important characters of the
play. The railing Constance has been impatiently turned away and the Bastard has been baiting Austria once more, when Philip suddenly says:

Here comes the holy legate of the Pope
—Act III, scene i, line 61

The appearance of this legate betokens the year 1211 and not 1200, as was the case a moment before. Eleven years have vanished (though later in the play some of the events in that eleven-year gap will be described as taking place *after* the legate's appearance). To explain the legate, we must do a little rapid recounting of history.

After the compromise of 1200, Philip sat back to wait his chance to break it under conditions favorable to himself.

King John knew that Philip was doing just this and did his best to organize his dominions for defense. For the purpose he needed to secure the communications between his provinces in the north of France and those in the south. The best way to do so (it seemed to him) was to arrange a marriage. He had obtained a divorce from his first wife and he decided that Isabella, the daughter of the Count of Angoulême, would make a good second wife. She was only thirteen at the time, but her family controlled strategic land between Anjou and Aquitaine, north and south.

John arranged matters quickly and married her in 1200. She was to remain John's Queen for the rest of his reign and was to be the mother of the next King of England.

Unfortunately for John, however, she had been betrothed to Hugh IX of Lusignan, a city fifty-five miles north of Angoulême. John tried to make it up to the offended nobleman, but Hugh IX would not be appeased. He had been a loyal comrade in arms of Richard the Lion-Heart, but now he felt wounded and mistreated and he turned to King Philip for redress. (By a curious turn of events, Isabella of Angoulême was to return to France in 1220, after John's death, when she was still in her early thirties. She was then to take as her second husband Hugh X of Lusignan, the son and successor of her old betrothed.)

Philip listened to the complaints of Hugh IX. As King of England, John was an independent sovereign, but as overlord of Normandy, Anjou, Aquitaine, and the rest, he was Philip's vassal, just as Hugh was John's vassal. According to the letter of the feudal law, Philip could judge a quarrel between a vassal and that vassal's vassal when the latter appealed. In order to do so, Philip summoned John to appear before him to answer the charges.

John would not, of course. His dignity as King of England made that impossible, and Philip knew he would not. When John failed to come, he was in contempt, and Philip could, again quite according to the letter of feudal law, declare John deprived of the lands he held as Philip's vassal.

Naturally, that meant nothing unless Philip was prepared to take them by force, but this was exactly what he planned to do. In 1202, two years after the marriage of the Dauphin with Blanche of Castile, the war started again. Philip ordered John deposed, once again recognized Arthur as rightful King of England, and called on all his French vassals (and all John's French vassals too) to join him against John.

The third and fourth acts of the play deal with that war, a war which placed John in dire need of money. Events made John so financially desperate, in fact, that he was forced to turn to the church for money. This the church would not yield willingly, and John proceeded to take it from them anyway, something which got John into a great deal of trouble, not only in his lifetime, but beyond.

Not only was the major portion of his reign occupied with a cankerous and eventually losing fight with the church, but after his death, the churchly chroniclers, who controlled events in retrospect since it was they who wrote history, commemorated their bitterness against John for this fight by blackening his character. He was not an admirable man by any means, but the chances are he was not nearly as black as the chroniclers made him appear.

When the legate arrived in 1211 (not 1200), it was in order that he might breathe new life into the church's end of the struggle and escalate the papal offensive against John.

. . . *from Pope Innocent* . . .

The legate identifies himself:

> *I Pandulph, of fair Milan cardinal*
> *And from Pope Innocent the legate here,*
>   —Act III, scene i, lines 64–65

It was John's misfortune (and all his life he was dogged with bad luck) to be dealing with the particular Pope with whom he had to deal. The papacy had been growing in strength since the beginning of the crusading movement, and reached its very apogee and peak of power when Lothair of Segni was elected Pope on January 8, 1198. He chose to reign under the name of Innocent III.

Innocent III was determined to assert the superiority of the church over the temporal power, not only in the case of John, but in that of every Western king. He was usually successful, for he had great ability and was a man of grim resolution.

. . . *Stephen Langton* . . .

Pandulph demands that John explain certain of his actions in defiance of the church (actions which have not been referred to or foreshadowed in the course of the play but which, of course, would be known to the educated members of the Elizabethan audience).

Pandulph asks of John:

> *Why thou against the church, our holy mother,*
> *So wilfully dost spurn; and force perforce*
> *Keep Stephen Langton, chosen Archbishop*
> *Of Canterbury, from that holy see:*
>> —Act III, scene i, lines 67–70

This particular problem had arisen in 1205, when Hubert Walter, the forty-third Archbishop of Canterbury, died. John saw this as a golden opportunity. He could appoint to the office some creature of his own who would co-operate with him and help tip some of the gold of the churchly coffers into the royal treasury.

This, however, Pope Innocent III would not consent to allow. He saw quite clearly what John's intention was and he therefore appointed his own candidate in the person of Stephen Langton.

On the face of it, Langton was an excellent choice. He was an Englishman, born in Lincolnshire, and he was a renowned scholar. In 1181, while still a young man, he went to Paris and spent a quarter of a century immersed in scholarship there. He was the first to divide the Old Testament books into the chapters we now find in our Bibles.

In Paris he met Lothair, the future Pope Innocent III, and eventually when Lothair became Pope, Langton became a cardinal.

John, however, was not concerned merely that the next Archbishop of Canterbury be an Englishman and a scholar. Langton, long a resident of France, had lost much of his Englishness and, as a friend of the Pope besides, would never co-operate with John in obtaining funds from the church to support a war against France. John *had* to oppose the appointment at whatever cost, and years of stalemate passed.

. . . no Italian priest

John quite angrily refuses to bend to Innocent's command. He says:

> *. . . no Italian priest*
> *Shall tithe or toll in our dominions;*
> *But as we, under God, are supreme head,*
> *So under Him that great supremacy*
> *Where we do reign, we will alone uphold*
> *Without th'assistance of a mortal hand:*
>> —Act III, scene i, lines 79–84

The historic King John might well have felt quite justified in resisting the papal demands. For well over a century, kings and emperors had been quarreling with popes over the right to appoint bishops.

Henry I, the great-grandfather of John, had quarreled with the Pope of his time over the very matter of the appointment of the Archbishop of Canterbury, and a compromise had then been reached in 1107, just a century before John's time, which had given the English King certain rights in such matters. Since then the papacy had grown stronger and Innocent III had no intention of being bound by compromises extorted from the weaker popes of the past. John, however, would naturally feel otherwise.

Yet the language of the speech, the contemptuous reference to the Pope as an "Italian priest" and to himself as "the supreme head," belongs to a later time. It is something Henry VIII might have said, three centuries after John's time, in turning the English church away from papal domination.

Shakespeare was writing *King John* a half century after Henry VIII had successfully accomplished this, and was writing for an English audience, turned mainly Protestant, who would look back on the quarrels with the papacy with their sympathies entirely for the crown. The remark concerning an "Italian priest" was a clear bid for the nationalist feelings of the audience, and indeed, at least part of the success of the Protestant Reformation in northern Europe was resentment over the great role played in the church by the men of southern Europe, and particularly by the men of Italy.

In fact, King John, whose character had been blackened in earlier days because of his opposition to the church, underwent a kind of renovation when England turned Protestant, precisely because of that opposition. It is for that reason that he comes off as well as he does in Shakespeare's play.

Shakespeare was, however, far less grossly anti-Catholic than much of his audience. *The Troublesome Reign of John, King of England,* from which Shakespeare seems to have drawn much of his inspiration for the play, was harshly anti-Catholic. Thus, in the earlier play, the Bastard at one point ransacks monasteries and finds a nun hidden in the abbot's room, a friar in the nun's room, and so on. This reflects the charges of immorality which were among the excuses used by Henry VIII in closing down the English monasteries a half century before the play was produced, and, of course, such scenes served also to titillate the prurient tastes of the audience.

Shakespeare scorns such grossness, but clearly makes Pandulph a villain, and insofar as John resists the power of the papacy, makes the King a hero.

. . . you blaspheme . . .

King Philip of France, listening to John's bold reply to Pandulph, says:

Brother of England, you blaspheme in this.
—Act III, scene i, line 87

There is a hypocrisy in this that the play does not make clear, for Philip II had had his own troubles with the church.

In 1193, six years before John became King of England, Philip II, who was then a widower, married Ingeborg, the sister of King Canute VI of Denmark. What went on during the wedding night no one knows, but whatever it was, it didn't suit Philip. The next morning he repudiated her and arranged to have an assembly of bishops annul the marriage. When Ingeborg refused to return to Denmark, Philip had her placed in a convent and three years later took another wife.

This behavior was utterly against the rules of the church, and the Danish King, whose sister had been thus insulted, appealed to Pope Celestine III (Innocent's predecessor).

Pope Celestine III ordered Philip to abandon his new wife and reinstate Ingeborg. Philip paid no attention to this at all. But then, in 1198, Celestine III died and Innocent III became Pope. Innocent was not the man to be played with.

In January 1200 he placed France under an interdict. That is, all public worship was ended in France. The churches were closed, the church bells no longer rang, the sacraments (except for baptism and extreme unction) were suspended. Thus, when Louis the Dauphin married Blanche of Castile, the rites had to be performed on territory ruled by John, for marriages could not be performed on French soil. It was a fearful weapon against a people to whom suspension of worship seemed like a license to the devil to take souls to hell. It placed a king under the powerful pressure of an affrighted public opinion to give in to the Pope.

By September 1200, then, Philip had to surrender and agree to take back Ingeborg. He didn't really; he kept her in a convent; but he had to grant her the title of Queen.

And it is this Philip who is presented here as clucking his tongue over John's defiance of Pandulph.

. . . curst and excommunicate

Despite Philip's warning, John remains truculent and defiant, saying:

> *Yet I alone, alone do me oppose*
> *Against the Pope, and count his friends my foes.*
> —Act III, scene i, lines 96–97

For John to say this at such a time and occasion was most impolitic, but it was ideal for the Protestant audience. It must have elicited cheers, and that would be the signal for Pandulph to assume to the role of archvillain indeed and to fulfill the very image of what Protestants must have imagined Catholic priests to be like—right down to the plotting of rebellion and regicide.

Pandulph is made to say:

> *Then, by the lawful power that I have,*
> *Thou shalt stand curst and excommunicate:*
> *And blessed shall he be that doth revolt*
> *From his allegiance to an heretic;*
> *And meritorious shall that hand be called,*
> *Canonized and worshipped as a saint,*
> *That takes away by any secret course*
> *Thy hateful life.*

—Act III, scene i, lines 98–105

In actual history, England and John were struck down by the weapons of the church even before the coming of Pandulph. Innocent III placed England under the interdict in March 1208. John, however, more unbending than Philip of France, refused to back down. By the use of force, he kept many priests at work, and maintained what he conceived to be his royal prerogative. For a year and a half he defied the interdict and it was only then that Innocent decided on a more specific thrust.

In November 1209 John was excommunicated. It was now no longer the kingdom generally that suffered but John personally. He was denied communion with the church. He could not attend mass or participate in any religious functions. His subjects were relieved of any duties they owed him and the Pope even went through the motions of deposing John and turning his kingdom over to Philip of France.

What must have interested Shakespeare's audience particularly was that a later pope applied similar weapons against Elizabeth I, who was England's Queen at the time *King John* was written. The papal weapons did not work, however, against a mainly Protestant land, especially since most English Catholics remained loyal to Queen and country even in the face of the papal stand.

But most of all the audience must have thrilled with horror at the open call to assassination, for in the 1590s it was widely believed by Protestants that monks and Jesuits preached assassination of prominent Protestants as a matter of policy.

To be sure, they could point to evidence. In 1584 William the Silent, the leader of the Dutch Protestant revolt against the arch-Catholic Philip II of Spain, had been assassinated by a Catholic in the Spanish King's pay. In 1589 Henry III, the Catholic King of France, had been assassinated by a monk who thought he was not Catholic enough. And in 1572 French Protestants had been slaughtered by the thousands on St. Bartholomew's

Day, on which occasion Philip II of Spain and Pope Gregory XIII gave forth with open expressions of delight. (It is said that on receiving news of the massacre, Philip II laughed out loud for the only time in his life.)

Under the force of Pandulph's curse and excommunication, Philip of France is pictured as being forced, reluctantly, to break his truce with John. The war resumes.

This is, of course, a perversion of history. To repeat, it was John's marriage to Isabella of Angoulême and his refusal to come before Philip for judgment that began the war again in 1202 (two years after the marriage of Louis and Blanche, and not immediately afterward as in the play). It was certainly not caused by troubles with the church, which were more the result of the war with France than the cause of them.

The perversion, however, serves its purpose. Not only does it condense history and place the entire length of the reign within the scope of the play, but it gives the play a more nationalist bias that makes it more suitable for the partisan ears of Englishmen.

In the case of John's marriage, he was clearly in the wrong and (technically at least) Philip was in the right, even though he might be hypocritically ignoring his own marital entanglements of the recent past. This is nothing on which to rest John's case, and Queen Isabella is nowhere mentioned or referred to in the play.

To rest the quarrel upon John's bold defiance of the Pope and on Philip's craven cowering beneath the papal thunders placed John entirely and heroically in the right to the Protestant Englishmen of the 1590s.

. . . Austria's head . . .

Once again, the English and French forces fall to battle in the vicinity of Angiers, and the Bastard enters with a private victory. He says:

> *Now, by my life, this day grows wondrous hot.*
> *Some airy devil hovers in the sky*
> *And pours down mischief. Austria's head lie there,*
> —Act III, scene ii, lines 1–3

The Bastard has, apparently, killed the Duke of Austria, and is usually presented as now wearing the lion skin (which may account for his sardonic remark about the day growing hotter—because of his added garment).

This apparently is inspired by the one comment Holinshed makes concerning a supposed bastard son of Richard. He says: "The same year [1199, that of Richard's death and John's accession], Philip, bastard son to King Richard, to whom his father had given the castle and honor of Cognac, killed the Viscount of Limoges, in revenge of his father's death. . . ."

For the dramatic purposes of the play, the Bastard has, by this kill, earned an even better title to be considered the reincarnation of Richard, and his wearing of the lion skin further symbolizes his position as heir of the tradition of the Lion-Heart.

Hubert, keep this boy

John enters with a victory of his own, for young Arthur is his captive. He says to a follower:

> Hubert, keep this boy.
>
> —Act III, scene ii, line 5

Since the Signet edition calls the Citizen of Angiers, in an earlier scene, Hubert, it would seem that that Citizen has suddenly become a trusted servant of John.

This is hard to accept. It is better to consider the man now termed Hubert as someone utterly distinct from the Angiers Citizen. Indeed, this present Hubert is a historical character, Hubert de Burgh, who was an important administrator under King John. Indeed, toward the end of the reign, he was promoted to the position of chief justiciar.

He had served John even before the latter's accession to the throne and was an important official at the time of the wars with France here described. He did indeed serve as jailer of Prince Arthur, the role he is described as having in the play.

My mother is assailèd . . .

John says further:

> Philip make up:
> My mother is assailèd in our tent,
> And ta'en, I fear.
>
> —Act III, scene ii, lines 5–7

The Philip here referred to is not the King of France, of course. John is addressing Philip Faulconbridge, the Bastard.

The reference to John's mother being assailed is a reminiscence of a real event that took place during the war over Isabella of Angoulême.

Eleanor, at one point in the fighting, had fled for safety to a castle at Mirebeau, a few miles south of Anjou. In 1203 an army marched to besiege that castle, one that was nominally led by Prince Arthur of Brittany, who was now fifteen years old, and a man by the standards of the time.

John, now as ever, a loyal and loving son to his mother, dropped everything to hasten to the relief of the castle (which was being besieged by his mother's grandson). On August 1 he won a victory there. He not only dispersed the French army but captured Hugh IX of Lusignan, the old betrothed of John's Queen. Most important of all, it was on this occasion (as in the play) that he captured Arthur. This victory represented the very peak of John's military career.

In the play, though, it is the Bastard who rescues the aged Queen Mother, for in response to John's fears for her safety, the Bastard says:

> *My lord, I rescued her;*
> *Her Highness is in safety, fear you not:*
> —Act III, scene ii, lines 7–8

Bell, book, and candle . . .

Now John announces he will hasten to England, for he will need more money to pursue the war. (It is the war which leads to desperation for money, which leads to the quarrel with the church, and not the quarrel which leads to the war as in the play.)

John sends the Bastard ahead to scrounge the necessary money by any means out of the church, and the Bastard says with grim joy:

> *Bell, book, and candle shall not drive me back*
> *When gold and silver becks me to come on.*
> —Act III, scene ii, lines 22–23

This is a reference to actions which symbolize the solemnity of excommunication, in a rite dating back to the eighth century. At the conclusion of the reading out of the excommunication, a bell is rung, a book is closed, and a lighted candle is put out. The ringing bell signifies that the act is public; all men are called to hear. The closing book signifies the words that lend the presiding bishop the power to perform the rite and is a clear enough symbol that the words of the churchly rituals are henceforth locked away from the excommunicated culprit. Finally, the candle is extinguished to signify that the light of the church is removed from the culprit.

The Bastard is saying that not even excommunication will keep him from rifling the treasures of the church. This should lead up to the scene in which (in the earlier play) he does ransack the chests of abbots and nuns and finds evidence of sexual misdemeanors, but Shakespeare will have nothing to do with that scene.

He is a very serpent . . .

Once the Bastard leaves, John has to face another problem. The question now is what to do with Arthur. Had the young man died in battle, John would have been triumphant. It would have been a fair death, and by that death John would have become the rightful King of England by every possible legal criterion.

But Arthur has been captured alive, and as long as he lives he will remain the center about which disaffection and rebellion might rally. Yet he is also in John's power and under these conditions an inconvenient prince might easily be dealt with.

Shakespeare pictures John as succumbing to the obvious temptation. He flatters Hubert, into whose charge he has put Arthur, makes vague promises of love, preference, and reward, then says:

> . . . *Hubert, throw thine eye*
> *On yon young boy; I'll tell thee what, my friend,*
> *He is a very serpent in my way,*
> *And wheresoe'er this foot of mine doth tread*
> *He lies before me: dost thou understand me?*
> *Thou art his keeper.*
>
> —Act III, scene ii, lines 69–74

Hubert understands, and undertakes to kill Arthur.

. . . O, amiable, lovely death

Yet if the convenience of the dispatch of Arthur is clear to John, it is clear to his enemies too, or to some of them at least.

It is clear to Constance of Brittany, for instance, the bereft mother, who fears the fate of her son in John's hands and rises to a height of grief that has no parallel in literature for sheer intensity of anguish. She hymns the death she wants for herself, for instance, as:

> *Death, death, O, amiable, lovely death!*
> *Thou odoriferous stench! sound rottenness!*
> *Arise forth from the couch of lasting night,*
> *Thou hate and terror to prosperity,*
> *And I will kiss thy detestable bones,*
>
> —Act III, scene iii, lines 25–29

It seems almost a shame to point out that this scene, in any form, is unhistorical. Constance had, in history, died in 1201, a year after the marriage of the Dauphin to Blanche of Castile and two years before the capture of Prince Arthur.

. . . the right of Lady Blanch . . .

Pandulph, the Pope's legate, also sees Arthur's danger, but his reaction is quite different from that of Constance, of course. He is shown as the typical Italian Jesuit of English Protestant imaginings, unmoved by emotion, oblivious to right and wrong, seeing only political advantage. Where Philip of France and Louis the Dauphin are in despair over the loss of the battle and Constance wails in tragic anguish over the loss of her son, Pandulph sees that actually John has lost.

He points out that John is sure to murder the captured Arthur, and when Louis the Dauphin asks what good that will do the French, Pandulph says:

> *You, in the right of Lady Blanch your wife,*
> *May then make all the claim that Arthur did.*
> > —Act III, scene iii, lines 142–43

Blanche is the daughter of John's older sister, and that might lend color to the claim. It would, however, be a feeble color. Descent through the daughters of Henry II would not, according to English usage, make someone eligible for the throne until all the line of the sons of Henry II was extinct. And while John was alive, that line was not extinct.

Moreover, it passed the bounds of likelihood (it would seem) that the English would be willing to accept a French prince as their king simply because he was married to the daughter of an English king.

Pandulph rebuts this point even before it is made, for he is sure the murder of Arthur will boomerang against John:

> *This act so evilly borne shall cool the hearts*
> *Of all his people, and freeze up their zeal,*
> > —Act III, scene iii, lines 149–50

Pandulph points out that under those conditions, Louis need merely invade England with a small force to have Englishmen rally round him by the thousands.

. . . with false reports

What actually happened to Arthur no one knows. All history can tell us is that after the Battle of Mirebeau, he was transferred to a prison tower in a fortified castle in the charge of Hubert de Burgh and was never heard of again. Presumably he died, and everyone took it for granted he was killed at John's orders before the year 1203 saw its end. Some even proposed that John did it with his own hands.

It isn't likely that John would have done it himself (there were plenty he could hire to do the job), but certainly no modern historian doubts that Arthur was killed. Considering the storm that arose after Arthur's disappearance, John would certainly have exhibited Arthur alive or if he were dead, revealed the true manner of that death, if his story would in the least have withstood investigation. The fact that he never offered a defense is the worst evidence against him.

Shakespeare, however, is anxious to make a case in John's favor. He is a King of England and an ancestor of Queen Elizabeth I, and it will not do to make him so villainous as to shame his descendants. (The only English King whom Shakespeare treats as a thorough villain is Richard III, and he is not among those from whom Elizabeth claims descent. Indeed, the villainy of Richard III makes Elizabeth's claim to the throne all the more secure, and so Shakespeare has no need to hold back in that case.)

According to Shakespeare's account in this play, then, John has ordered Hubert to kill the Prince, but later the order has been lessened to blinding. Hubert, however, cannot, in the pinch, carry out even the lesser sentence. In a most sentimental scene, Arthur pleads with Hubert, and the latter gives way and decides to spare him. To do so would ruin him with John, of course, and so he says to Arthur:

> *Your uncle must not know but you are dead.*
> *I'll fill these doggèd spies with false reports;*
> —Act IV, scene i, lines 128–29

So it would appear, according to Shakespeare's version, that though John originally ordered the death of Arthur, the killing was not carried through, nor was mutilation, and John turned out to be innocent of Arthur's blood.

. . . once again crowned

The scene shifts to London, where John has gone through the ceremony of a coronation a second time and says:

> *Here once again we sit, once again crowned,*
> *And looked upon, I hope, with cheerful eyes.*
> —Act IV, scene ii, lines 1–2

The second coronation has involved a renewed oath of allegiance from the various nobles of the realm. There can be two purposes in this second coronation. By forcing these oaths after the excommunication, John can keep his vassals from maintaining that their oaths at the initial coronation in 1199 had been voided by excommunication. They have, after all, sworn new ones.

Secondly, by now Arthur should be dead, and there would be none to dispute John's claim to the throne. If the first coronation was invalid, Arthur being alive, the second coronation would be valid, Arthur being dead. And it was wise to have the second coronation take place before the news of Arthur's passing became current.

Was once superfluous . . .

The lords are not blind, however, and they are disturbed at the possible purposes of the second coronation. One of them, Pembroke, says, sullenly:

> This "once again," but that your Highness pleased
> Was once superfluous . . .
>
> —Act IV, scene ii, lines 3–4

In other words, the second coronation was one too many and was carried through only at the whim of the King.

Pembroke was William Marshal, 1st Earl of Pembroke. He had been born in 1146, was one of England's foremost soldiers under Richard the Lion-Heart, and had helped run England while Richard was away on the Crusade. In John's early years he was leading armies in England and France continually and was always a staunch supporter of the King.

This theme of superfluity is taken up by Salisbury, who talks of it in the best-known passage of the play (which contains one of the most frequently misquoted phrases in Shakespeare). Salisbury says, with reference to a second coronation added to a first that was ample:

> To gild refinèd gold, to paint the lily,
> To throw a perfume on the violet,
> To smooth the ice, or add another hue
> Unto the rainbow, or with taper-light
> To seek the beauteous eye of heaven to garnish
> Is wasteful and ridiculous excess.
>
> —Act IV, scene ii, lines 11–16

People almost invariably quote the phrase as "to gild the lily," although it makes much more sense to deride the gilding of gold.

. . . Arthur is deceased . . .

John tries to placate the troubled lords, but the true reason for their concern comes out at once. They fear John's intentions toward Arthur. They point out that since John's hold on the throne is secure, he ought to release Arthur.

At this point Hubert enters, and John, assuming Arthur is dead, readily grants the request and ostentatiously orders Hubert to set Arthur free. Then, when he gets Hubert's (false) report concerning Arthur's death, he turns and says blandly:

> *We cannot hold mortality's strong hand.*
> *Good lords, although my will to give is living,*
> *The suit which you demand is gone and dead.*
> *He tells us Arthur is deceased tonight.*
>
> —Act IV, scene ii, lines 82–85

The lords, who knew very well that Arthur in prison was very likely to experience a convenient death, did not for a moment accept John's implication that that death was natural. Horrified and angered, they withdraw. Pandulph's prediction is coming true.

Where is my mother's care

Almost at once, a Messenger enters with news of a distracting nature from France. A French army, larger than ever before, is now making war on England.

And as a matter of fact, Arthur's capture at Mirebeau marked the turning point of John's fortunes. Once Arthur disappeared into captivity, reports of his death at once began to circulate and the results were devastating for John.

Brittany was incensed at the apparent murder of its prince. Its chief bishop accused John openly of having engineered the murder, and King Philip did his best to broadcast the accusation. John's French vassals began to fall away in droves. The killing of the Prince was a crime that, in their eyes, would be sure to draw down the curse of heaven, and they did not want to be in the way when lightning struck.

Philip's armies, heartened by a sense of right, penetrated the Angevin dominions, and John's forces, correspondingly disheartened, were driven back and back.

At the news of Philip's successes, John is astounded that they could have been carried through without his having been warned in time by his mother. He says:

> *Where is my mother's care,*
> *That such an army could be drawn in France*
> *And she not hear of it?*
> —Act IV, scene ii, lines 117–19

But the Messenger says:

> *My liege, her ear*
> *Is stopped with dust: the first of April died*
> *Your noble mother:*
> —Act IV, scene ii, lines 119–21

This was April 1, 1204. Eleanor of Aquitaine had died at last, some eighty-two years old, active to the last. It had been her marriage with Henry II a half century before that had created the Angevin Empire, and she had lived just long enough to see it being destroyed under the last of her sons.

The Messenger adds:

> *. . . and, as I hear, my lord,*
> *The Lady Constance in a frenzy died*
> *Three days before . . .*
> —Act IV, scene ii, lines 121–23

This is a dramatic juxtaposition, but of course Constance had really died three years before.

. . . the streets of Pomfret . . .

Philip's forces continued victorious after Eleanor's death, and on June 24, 1204, they took Rouen, capital of Normandy. Normandy was the original home of the line of kings that now ruled England; now it was French again, not quite a century and a half after William of Normandy had conquered England.

With the loss of Rouen, John was driven from northern France altogether (though he retained parts of Aquitaine), and he could do nothing but lay slow plans for reconquest. It was now that he really had to rifle English churchly coffers for money, for he had not only lost French provinces, but also the revenues of those provinces.

The Bastard returns from his money collections and brings with him tales of a disturbed populace. He says:

> . . . here's a prophet that I brought with me
> From forth the streets of Pomfret, whom I found
> With many hundreds treading on his heels,
> To whom he sung, in rude harsh-sounding rhymes,
> That ere the next Ascension-day at noon,
> Your Highness should deliver up your crown.
>
> —Act IV, scene ii, lines 147–52

Pomfret is a slurred form of Pontefract, a city in southern Yorkshire, some thirty miles southwest of York. William the Conqueror, during a campaign of devastation designed to break the Saxon resistance in the north, broke down an old Roman bridge in the vicinity in 1069. The town therefore received the name of Pontefract ("broken bridge"). It is best known for its castle, where Richard II was to meet his death nearly two centuries later (see page II–312).

Ascension Day is the fortieth day after Easter and commemorates the tale told in Acts of the Apostles (1:3,9) to the effect that Jesus remained with the apostles for forty days after the Resurrection and then "he was taken up; and a cloud received him out of their sight."

. . . many thousand warlike French

The prophecy is not harmful in itself, but it can work to break morale, to give the people cause for despair and even revolt, so that they might readily yield to some foreign enemy. It is thus a possibly self-fulfilling prophecy.

Indeed, Hubert reports the news of fear and unrest among the populace. He tells the King concerning the English people:

> Young Arthur's death is common in their mouths,
> And, when they talk of him, they shake their heads
> And whisper one another in the ear,
>
> —Act IV, scene ii, lines 187–89

Hubert also brings other news, saying the people

> Told of a many thousand warlike French,
> That were embattailèd and ranked in Kent.
>
> —Act IV, scene ii, lines 199–200

Louis the Dauphin did indeed lead an army to the invasion of England (as, in the play, he was urged to do by Pandulph), and he won sufficient success in doing so to cause him to be called by the vainglorious title of

"Louis the Lion-Heart" since he was doing in England what Richard I had done in France.

Louis' invasion, however, did not take place till 1216 (by which time he was twenty-eight), a round dozen years after Arthur's death. Its occasion was not the death of the young Prince but John's troubles with his own rebelling nobility. Nor did the nobles rebel over Prince Arthur, but over John's financial exactions. They forced the King to sign the Magna Carta in 1215, granting them certain rights and limiting the royal powers.

Shakespeare doesn't mention the Magna Carta anywhere in *King John,* and this is sometimes considered an odd and curious fact.

It is not in the least odd or curious. To us today, the issuing of the Magna Carta is the most important event in King John's reign because it was such a meaningful early step toward the establishment of a limited monarchy in England and the eventual birth of a form of democratic government which we in the United States were to inherit. However, it was by no means important in Shakespeare's time, when England had just been through a century of unusually strong central government by strong-willed monarchs, and when Parliament was comparatively weak and unimportant.

Within a generation of Shakespeare's death, the situation was to change. Parliament was to grow strong, rebel, and cut off a king's head, but that was half a century in the future. In the 1590s, the memory of the Magna Carta was dim indeed.

Besides, even if it had been strong, Shakespeare might still have ignored it. The whole point of the play, as Shakespeare presents it, is the quarrel over the succession, and all else is subordinated to it. It is his intention to show that the death of Arthur was the wrong way to settle that quarrel, and he must show how evil followed it. Therefore, the French invasion must come hard on that death and not after the Magna Carta—something which would only obscure the point Shakespeare was trying to make.

. . . my uncle's spirit . . .

John, aware now of what a terrible mistake he has made, turns in whining indignation on Hubert for having followed orders. Hubert is forced to reveal that he has not really killed the Prince, and for a while John thinks joyfully that all may be mended.

But what is Shakespeare to do with the Prince? It is all very well to say that John's order to kill him was not carried out, so that John was innocent. The fact is that Arthur never emerged from prison. *Something* must have happened to him.

Shakespeare presents him, therefore, as attempting to escape by leaping from the tower. He is killed in the process, and can just manage to say, after jumping:

O me! my uncle's spirit is in these stones!
Heaven take my soul, and England keep my bones!

—Act IV, scene iii, lines 9–10

So Arthur's death is accidental after all.
But who will believe it? No one. Not even the characters in the play.

. . . toward Bury . . .

Pembroke, Salisbury, and Bigot, the English lords who had been at
John's second coronation, come across Arthur's body and are certain he
was murdered by Hubert at John's orders. They will not believe Hubert's
denials, and though the ever faithful Bastard tries to prevent them, they
throw off their allegiance of John. Lord Bigot cries:

Away toward Bury, to the Dolphin there!

—Act IV, scene iii, line 114

This is Bury St. Edmunds, a town in Suffolk, sixty miles northeast of
London. The Dauphin's invading army is clearly making terrifying progress.
Bury was particularly associated with the opposition to King John on the
part of the lords, since it was there in November 1214 that the lords had
taken an oath to persevere in their demands for what became the Magna
Carta and to compel King John to accept their terms.

Thus have I yielded . . .

The circling disasters have forced John to surrender in some directions
so that he might survive in others. He gives in to Pope Innocent III. The
fifth act opens with John making his submission to Pandulph, giving him
his crown:

Thus have I yielded up into your hand
The circle of my glory.

—Act V, scene i, lines 1–2

The submission took place in 1213, well before the Dauphin's invasion.
Indeed, it took place precisely so that John could free his hands for an
invasion of France.

John had in 1213 almost completed his plans to invade France and reconquer the French provinces he had lost nearly a decade before. It was
for this very purpose that he had scrabbled so hard for money that he had
driven himself into excommunication. Now he dared not take an army over-

seas while he was excommunicate. The army would too easily be induced to desert and a rebellion could too easily be raised behind his back at home.

John therefore agreed to allow Stephen Langton to assume his post as Archbishop of Canterbury, and in return, Langton lifted the excommunication from John's head. For this, John agreed to hand over his kingdom to the Pope, ruling thereafter only as a papal vassal. It was a great humiliation for John, but it had its value. John paid the Pope an annual tribute of a thousand marks and that was the full extent of the papal overlordship. And John received a benefit in return for this very light tribute. Since England was now the territory of the church, Philip of France could scarcely invade it without considerable trouble with Rome.

And yet, however meaningless the transfer of the crown was, John had given it up, in a manner of speaking, and he had done so by Ascension Day, as the prophet from Pomfret had predicted.

Once the quarrel with the Pope was settled, John made ready to invade France, in conjunction with the German Emperor Otto IV. Otto was the son of John's elder sister Matilda, so that he was John's nephew.

On July 27, 1214, the army of Otto IV, with English contingents, met the army of Philip II at Bouvines, a village ten miles southeast of Lille. It was a confused battle in which the knights made the air resound with the clash of metal upon metal. At one point, Philip II was seized and pulled off his horse. He was so well protected by his armor, however, that the enemy could find no chink through which to kill him before he was rescued.

In the end, the result of the mutual battering was that the Emperor's forces were driven from the field. The victory of Philip II was complete and the Battle of Bouvines proved one of the decisive engagements of the Middle Ages.

John lost his last hope of retrieving the Angevin Empire and gained the nickname of "John Softsword." All his rapacity and connivery had alienated his nobles and he had not even the chance of vindicating his plans by a great victory. The loss of this battle helped strengthen the cause of the lords and helped lead to the Magna Carta. The confusions of that time led to the invasion of Louis the Dauphin.

Shakespeare does not mention the Battle of Bouvines any more than he does the Magna Carta. His anti-French animus never allows him to admit that the French can win a battle—except by treachery or witchcraft.

. . . the French lay down their arms

Once John has submitted, Pandulph becomes all English in his sympathies. He has encouraged Louis previously, but now he says:

> Upon your oath of service to the Pope,
> Go I to make the French lay down their arms.
> —Act V, scene i, lines 23–24

In 1213, actually, Pandulph did serve England by preventing a French invasion, even going so far as to threaten Philip with excommunication if he tried it.

This just meant, however, that John was free to organize an invasion of France, the one that ended disastrously at Bouvines. We can well imagine that Philip was furious at a papal policy that kept him from invading England but did not stop England from invading France. After Bouvines, Philip sent the Dauphin into England, uncaring whether it was papal territory or not.

Pandulph couldn't stop that invasion, but King John was sufficiently beholden to him to be willing to appoint him Bishop of Norwich in 916. For several years after John's death, Pandulph remained one of the most influential persons in the English government. He returned to Italy in 1220, but after he died in Rome in 1226, his body was taken to Norwich for burial.

. . . London hath received

Pandulph cannot stop the furious Dauphin, and the Bastard enters to report further French progress. He says:

> All Kent hath yielded—nothing there holds out
> But Dover Castle—London hath received,
> Like a kind host, the Dolphin and his powers.
> —Act V, scene i, lines 30–32

This represents the extent to which John had alienated his own people in the course of his single-minded and futile attempt to reconquer the lost French provinces.

Louis had landed in Kent (having actually been invited to invade by some of the English barons annoyed at John's attempts to repudiate the Magna Carta) on May 30, 1216. Only three days later, on June 2, Louis entered London, which offered no resistance.

Then, on July 16, 1216, Pope Innocent III, whose strong hand John still hoped might force the Dauphin back, died.

With the Pope dead, with the Dauphin in London, with the English nobility flocking to the enemy, with a Scottish army threatening invasion from the north, John's fortunes hit bottom.

This fever . . .

Only the Bastard remains (in the play) true to the spirit of Richard. He is a hero, never daunted by odds, always ready to fight in the bluff fashion beloved of English nationalists. He carries on the battle against Louis the Dauphin and the defecting English lords, crying out to the latter:

> *You bloody Neroes, ripping up the womb*
> *Of your dear mother England, blush for shame.*
> —Act V, scene ii, lines 152–53

Nero had his mother killed, but to be fair about it, it was his mother's idea (see page II–126) that she be stabbed in the womb.

John, however, cannot last much longer. Battle between the loyal forces and the Dauphin begins, but during its course, when Hubert asks him how he is, he replies:

> *This fever, that hath troubled me so long,*
> *Lies heavy on me: O, my heart is sick!*
> —Act V, scene iii, lines 3–4

This is the first indication we have that John is ill. But now he must leave the field. He sends a message to the Bastard, who is leading John's army, telling him where he is going. John says:

> *Tell him, toward Swinstead, to the abbey there.*
> —Act V, scene iii, line 8

This is some sort of error. It is not Swinstead. What is meant is Swineshead Abbey, in Lincolnshire, twenty-five miles southeast of Lincoln itself.

. . . on Goodwin sands

Though John is sinking fast, he has some good news to support him. The Dauphin's hoped-for reinforcements will not arrive. A Messenger says:

> *Be of good comfort, for the great supply*
> *That was expected by the Dolphin here,*
> *Are wracked three nights ago on Goodwin sands.*
> —Act V, scene iii, lines 9–11

The Goodwin sands are dangerous shoals, ten miles long, lying about five miles off the southeastern tip of England. There is a tale that they at one time jutted above the sea, from which they were protected by a wall. After the time of William's conquest, the story goes, the wall was neglected, fell into ruin, and the islands were inundated in a storm in 1100 that beat them down into mere shoals. The tale is dramatic but is probably an invention.

. . . poisoned by a monk

The battle ends in, apparently, a narrow French victory. The Bastard goes to find the King and finds Hubert instead. Hubert tells him:

> The King, I fear, is poisoned by a monk:
> I left him almost speechless . . .
>
> —Act V, scene vi, lines 23–24

Indeed, John died of the fever on the night of October 18, 1216, at the age of forty-nine, with his French dominions mostly gone and his own England half in control of a foreign army.

There was a story, popular in later years, to the effect that he had been poisoned by a monk. This would naturally go well with Shakespeare's Protestant audience. In actual fact, it is probable John died a natural death. Natural deaths were common enough in those days.

. . . Prince Henry in their company

Hubert has further news for the Bastard. He says:

> The lords are all come back,
> And brought Prince Henry in their company,
> At whose request the King hath pardoned them,
> And they are all about his Majesty.
>
> —Act V, scene vi, lines 33–36

Shakespeare has had to manage this clumsily. The English nobility had defected, according to his reading of history, because of Arthur's death. How, then, could they come back when Arthur was still dead?

Shakespeare's tale is that Louis the Dauphin, for no clear reason (except, perhaps, that he was a vile Frenchman, which was reason enough for Shakespeare's audience), had decided to kill all the English lords on his side once he had won his victory, and was so imprudent as to let his resolve be known. A French lord who was one-quarter English (which made him a fellow with decent impulses, of course) warned the English lords, who at once returned to John.

This is ridiculous. What really happened was that John died, thus removing the one person whom the nobility would not deal with. Had John continued to live, it is at least possible that the French would have won a complete victory, with incalculable consequences in history.

As it was, in place of John there was now a nine-year-old boy who ruled as Henry III and who was crowned on October 28, 1216. He held sway, to begin with, only over a section of western and southwestern England, all the rest being held by Louis or by rebel barons.

Still, with Henry III crowned, the rebels had a change of heart. The new King, as a child, would be popular with the people, and with a child-king the barons might expect to retain the rights they had recently won. Indeed, those around the young King, particularly Hubert de Burgh, were careful to reissue the Magna Carta, and it was that which chiefly acted as a magnet to bring back the rebels. Since Shakespeare did not use the Magna Carta, he could not use that as the motivation.

. . . with all submission . . .

John's son, Henry, has made no appearance in the play at all, until John is on his deathbed. In part, this makes sense, for Henry wasn't born till 1207, four years after Arthur's death.

Young Henry's sudden appearance now allows Shakespeare an important scene. Once more, as in the case of Prince Arthur, a young prince claims the throne according to strict legitimacy. Once more there is an older relative who might claim the throne instead. As John had been to Arthur so was the Bastard to young Henry. To be sure, the Bastard was illegitimate and so could not, in theory, inherit. However, he was a tried and loyal soldier, the son of Richard the Lion-Heart, even if illegitimate, and undoubtedly in this great crisis that England faced, many would have welcomed him on the throne rather than a nine-year-old boy. (Of course, we are accepting Shakespeare's picture of the moment and must ignore the fact that in actual history, the Bastard did not exist.)

Shakespeare has the Bastard show the proper way to react to a disputed succession. Forgetful of his own possible claim, the Bastard labors only to unite England and avoid civil war.

As soon as John dies, the Bastard kneels before the young prince and says:

> . . . happily may your sweet self put on
> The lineal state and glory of the land!
> To whom, with all submission, on my knee,
> I do bequeath my faithful services
> And true subjection everlastingly.
>   —Act V, scene vii, lines 101–5

This England never did . . .

Meanwhile the report arrives to the effect that Pandulph has persuaded the Dauphin to make an honorable offer of peace, and the Bastard delivers the rousing finale of the play, a finale filled with the pride of a nation that a few years back had defeated the huge fleet of the Spanish Armada. He says:

> *This England never did, nor never shall,*
> *Lie at the proud foot of a conqueror*
> *But when it first did help to wound itself.*
> *Now these her princes are come home again,*
> *Come the three corners of the world in arms,*
> *And we shall shock them! Naught shall make us rue*
> *If England to itself do rest but true!*

—Act V, scene vii, lines 112–18

Thus the play ends, with the audience undoubtedly cheering.

But it had its truth too. The French, and such of the English as remained with them, were badly defeated at Lincoln in 1217. That restored almost all of England to the control of Henry III and to those who ruled in his name. Louis the Dauphin was left with little more than London.

Blanche of Castile on the French shore tried to raise a fleet which would sail to England with reinforcements and provisions to help her husband. Hubert de Burgh, however, collected ships of his own, met the French fleet en route, and destroyed most of it.

That left Louis helpless, and he agreed to leave England on receipt of a payment of ten thousand marks from Henry.

Seven and a half centuries have passed since then, and from that day to this, London has never again seen a foreign army within its city limits.

31

The Tragedy of

KING RICHARD THE SECOND

AT THE close of *King John,* the young Prince Henry is succeeding to the throne as Henry III, and the year is 1216. At the start of *Richard II,* it is 1398, nearly two centuries later, and in order to understand the historical setting of the latter play it is necessary to go over some of the events that took place in that gap.

Henry III, who was nine years old when he ascended the throne, remained King for fifty-six years, dying in 1272. He was succeeded by his son, Edward I, who in 1307 was succeeded by his son, Edward II, who in 1327 was succeeded by his son, Edward III.

This century that followed the death of King John saw England preoccupied with itself and its immediate neighbors on the British Isles. It was a period of virtual isolationism for the land. This is not to say it was a period of absolute peace. Under Edward I, in particular, English armies were fully employed. Wales was conquered and Scotland was almost conquered.

The once great dominions in France, however, had continued to shrink, and the expansive days of the Angevin Empire were almost forgotten. When Edward III came to the throne in 1327, what was left was chiefly a section of territory along the southwestern shores of France, bordering on the Bay of Biscay, with Bordeaux as its chief city. That still remained of the inheritance of Eleanor of Aquitaine (see page II–210).

Edward III came to the throne at the age of fifteen, but he had already spent two years as Duke of Aquitaine, ruling over the shrunken English territory around Bordeaux. This gave him a French orientation and perhaps made him see himself as a new Richard the Lion-Heart (see page II–207), who had once, as a youth, ruled over Aquitaine too.

For the first few years, young Edward could only dream. He was dominated by his mother and her lover, Mortimer, but in 1330 the new King seized power in his own name and at once made up his mind to rule in knightly fashion.

Edward III always saw himself as a knight. He was as romantic as Richard I in his notions and just as apt to see his role entirely as conquering warrior. He strengthened England's grip over Wales and Scotland (a grip that had weakened during the reign of the preceding King, Edward II). Then he turned his eyes to France.

Edward III remembered that he was a direct descendant of Henry II.

He was the great-great-great-grandson of Henry II, and filling the gap completely were four kings. Eventually, Edward took to symbolizing that solidly male, solidly royal descent by calling himself Edward Plantagenet (see page II–212). Edward's sons and their sons continued to call themselves Plantagenets.

As long as French dominions remained under English control, there was bound to be enmity between the two nations. Philip Augustus of France (see page II–243) had destroyed the Angevin Empire, but the region about Bordeaux remained, and in order to regain this, the French were always willing to intrigue against the English. They supported the Scots, for instance.

Edward, in return, supported the cities in Flanders and the Netherlands who wished to engage in their commercial ventures without interference from the French King and who were therefore willing to turn to the English King.

In 1328 there occurred a most significant event. King Charles IV of France died and left behind him no sons, no brothers, and no nephews. However, he did have a living sister, Isabella, and this Isabella was none other than the mother of young Edward III, who at that time had been on the throne for but a year. By English custom, Edward III would have inherited the French crown.

The alarmed French did not, however, want an English king ruling over them. There was a so-called "Salic law" dating back to the days of the Frankish tribes who had asserted their rule over Roman Gaul, which was supposed to forbid the inheritance of the kingship by a female or by the descendant of a female. It had never been called into play, however, for this was the first time in French history that a king had died without either a son or a brother to succeed him.

It was now applied and the throne passed to a first cousin of Charles IV, Philip of Valois. He was further removed by blood than Edward III, but unlike the latter, Philip traced his descent from the royal line through males only, and he assumed the throne as Philip VI.

Edward at first recognized Philip's title, but as the quarrel between England and France over the Flemish trade sharpened, the English King decided to take a drastic step. In 1337 he declared himself rightful King of France (a title the British monarch retains to this day) and began to make preparations for an invasion of that land in order to make good that title by force. This began what is known in history as the Hundred Years' War.

Actually, this title is an overstatement. The Hundred Years' War was not a single war but a series of wars interspersed by periods (sometimes lengthy ones) of peace. From beginning to end, though, the English effort to conquer France lasted a hundred and fourteen years.

France was much larger, richer, and more populous than England, yet England came surprisingly close to making good its conquest. There were reasons for this. England had cut new military teeth in her wars against

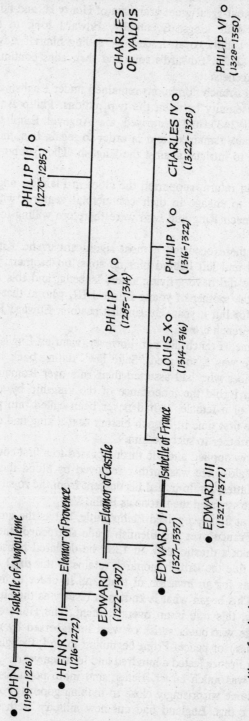

From JOHN to EDWARD III

the Scots and the Welsh and had developed a fearsome weapon in the long-bow, which she borrowed from the Welsh. The weapon looked simple but it was not. To use it properly, it had to be pulled with a force of a hundred pounds; and this required strong muscles and long training.

The French, on the other hand, were torn apart by unruly, undisciplined nobles who could not learn, for a long time, how to fight united in battle, and who considered the bow a plebeian weapon anyway, fit only for cowards and commoners. (And it should be remembered that through the period of greatest English conquests, France was torn by civil war.)

Edward's first great stroke of fortune came on June 24, 1340, when, after several unsuccessful attempts to invade France, his ships defeated and virtually destroyed the French fleet off Sluys on the coast of what is now the Netherlands. This gave England control of the Channel (an advantage she was to keep through most of history since) and finally made it possible for Edward to ship an army into France.

By this time an invasion had become an absolute necessity, for Edward had gone bankrupt in his unsuccessful attempts till then and had had to repudiate his debts. Only in France could he gather the loot that would make him solvent again.

In 1346, therefore, he abandoned the cautious use of Continental allies (never entirely trustworthy) and attacked France directly, sending an English army into Normandy. This army almost reached Paris before the French King could gather his forces for the defense.

Edward now scurried northeastward with a French force four times the size of his own in pursuit. The English turned at Crécy, near the mouth of the Somme River, in a patch of land which had been English-controlled for half a century. There the first great land battle of the Hundred Years' War was fought in August 1346. The French army, badly led and wildly disorganized, was cut to pieces by the smoothly functioning English bowmen.

Edward moved on to Calais, a hundred miles north, and took it after a year-long siege in August 1347. Calais was just across the Channel from Dover, and the sea gap there was only twenty-five miles. These victories set up a kind of mystique among the English, an illusion that one Englishman could defeat ten Frenchmen. For a long time this was of great psychological help to the English, but in the long run it lured them on to attempt too much and to lose all.

After the fall of Calais, the war marked time. In 1350 Philip VI died, and his son, John II, succeeded to the throne. John was as steeped in knightly tradition as Edward III was, but lacked any trace of generalship. On top of that, the vast and deadly plague called the Black Death was weakening and disorganizing France. (It also wreaked havoc in England, but not quite as badly.)

England saw its chance to resume aggressive warfare, therefore, with the main thrusts pointing inward from her old base at Bordeaux in the

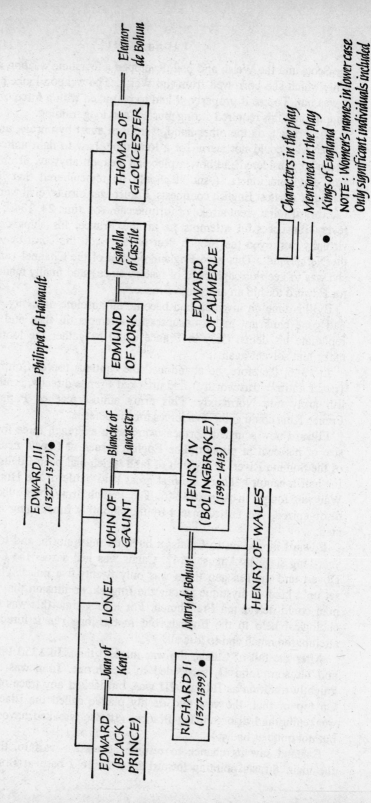

RICHARD II

From EDWARD III to HENRY IV

EDWARD III === Philippa of Hainault
(1327–1377) ●

EDWARD
(BLACK
PRINCE) === Joan of Kent

LIONEL

JOHN OF
GAUNT === Blanche of Lancaster

EDMUND
OF YORK === Isabella
of Castile

THOMAS OF
GLOUCESTER === Eleanor
de Bohun

RICHARD II
(1377–1399) ●

HENRY IV
(BOLINGBROKE) ●
(1399–1413) === Mary de Bohun

EDWARD
OF AUMERLE

HENRY OF WALES

Characters in the play

Mentioned in the play

Kings of England

●

NOTE : Women's names in lower case
Only significant individuals included

southwest and her new base at Calais in the northeast. In September 1356, just ten years after Crécy, a battle just like it was fought at Poitiers in west-central France. Again the French outnumbered the English. Again the French were disorganized and unprepared for English archery. The heavily armored Frenchmen were maneuvered into ambush on marshy ground. They were mired down and captured like so many beached whales, with their King, John II, taken also and carried off prisoner to England.

Anxious to regain his freedom, John gave in to English demands and in October 1360 signed the Treaty of Calais, ending the first portion of the Hundred Years' War. Edward received a considerable enlargement of his territories in southwestern France, and in return gave up his claim to the French throne.

The victory was, however, more apparent than real. England was weakened by her war effort, and even more by her own encounter with the Black Death, and could not maintain her newly won position. In 1364 Charles V, the capable son of John II, ascended the French throne and, with the help of his general, Bertrand du Guesclin, gradually nibbled away at English holdings, reducing them steadily.

As for Edward III, he could do nothing to reverse the downhill slide. He was not really a great king except for the victories he had won in the field, and now he left the fighting to his sons and gradually sank into premature senility. He died in 1377, having reigned fifty years.

Edward III fathered many sons, as Henry II, his great predecessor, had done. And Edward's sons, like Henry's (see page II–212), gave occasion for quarrels over the succession. Since Edward's sons and their descendants play their roles in eight of Shakespeare's plays, beginning with *Richard II*, let us list them in order of decreasing age:

(1) Edward of Woodstock
(2) William of Hatfield (died young)
(3) Lionel of Antwerp
(4) John of Gaunt
(5) Edmund of Langley
(6) Thomas of Woodstock
(7) William of Windsor (died young)

Edward, the oldest, born in 1330, was heir to the crown. In 1337 he was made Duke of Cornwall—the first duke ever to be created in England. ("Duke" was a French title, and the English had hitherto been content with the native title of "Earl." This Frenchification of title was a sign of Edward's view of himself as a King of France as well as of England.) Then, in 1343, young Edward was proclaimed Prince of Wales, the title usually granted, sooner or later, to the oldest son of a reigning king.

Edward of Wales's adult life was entirely that of a warrior-knight, and though, like his father, he was inept at anything but battle, he was idolized by the English for his victories, just as his father was. The story eventually arose that he wore black armor, so that he was called "the Black Prince." It is by that name only that he is now universally known, though its first recorded use did not occur till nearly a century after his death.

At the Battle of Crécy, the Black Prince, still only sixteen years old, was head of the right wing of the army. At one point, the story goes, the right wing seemed in trouble and an anxious English officer suggested that the King send it reinforcements. Surveying the situation, Edward III responded like a knight rather than a general, and said, "Nonsense! Let the boy win his spurs!"

Win them the boy did, and in 1355 the Black Prince was sent to France with an independent command. It was his army (more French than English, by the way) that met the French army near Poitiers. It was the Black Prince, then, who won the second great English land victory of the Hundred Years' War, and it was he who captured King John II of France.

After the signing of the Treaty of Calais, the enlarged English dominions in southwestern France were put under the rule of the Black Prince, and a rare mess he made of it. He maintained an expensive court, taxed heavily, made no attempt to win the favor of his subjects, and in general turned the natives fiercely anti-English and made it that much easier for Charles V and Du Guesclin to win back lost French ground little by little.

Perhaps the Black Prince recognized that he could only do well in battle, for in 1367 he quite gratuitously interfered with a dynastic struggle going on in Spain between two claimants to the throne. He interfered on the side of Pedro (known as "the Cruel") and placed him in control of the country. Once his princely Blackness had left, however, Pedro was quickly overthrown. The Black Prince was further rewarded with broken health, for sickness assailed him in Spain and from it he never recovered.

He returned to England in 1371 and, after a long illness, died in 1376, one year before his father. His younger brother, Lionel, had died even earlier, in 1368.

At the time of the death of Edward III, then, only three of his seven sons remained alive. These were the fourth son, John of Gaunt (aged thirty-seven), the fifth son, Edmund of Langley (aged thirty-six), and the sixth son, Thomas of Woodstock (aged twenty-two).

In an older time, one of these sons would have succeeded, but by now the principle of legitimacy (see page II-164) was thoroughly established. None of the younger sons could inherit until the line of the oldest son was extinct. The Black Prince might be dead but he had left behind him a surviving son.

The son was named Richard, and it is no surprise at all that a man like the Black Prince would hark back to the Lion-Heart. Richard had been born on January 6, 1367, at Bordeaux, and was therefore known as Richard of Bordeaux. He was nine years old when his father died, and a few months later, in November 1376, his grandfather Edward III proclaimed the boy Prince of Wales, which amounted to recognizing him as heir to the throne.

When Edward III died on June 21, 1377, the ten-year-old Prince of Wales became King Richard II of England without trouble.

Nevertheless, a ten-year-old cannot rule, and the new King's uncles were the important powers in the land.

The existence of a boy-king was particularly unfortunate at this time, for England was in trouble. The war in France continued to sputter now and then, enough to produce large expense without victory. The heavy taxation this made necessary, combined with the havoc of the Black Death, drove the English peasantry into revolt—one of the few peasant revolts in English history.

In May and June 1381 there were local uprisings all over England. One group of rebels under a leader named Wat Tyler actually occupied London for four days. King Richard himself, only fourteen years old, faced them fearlessly, and at a crucial point, when Wat Tyler was suddenly stabbed to death and it seemed the mob would get out of control, the King rode into their midst and offered to be their leader. This brave act prevented bloodshed in London and the peasant revolt elsewhere was put down forcefully but far less bloodily than similar revolts on the Continent. It was the greatest act of the King's reign.

Nevertheless, he was still a boy, and his uncles still remained the real rulers. This, in fact, continued through most of Richard's reign, even after he had long passed the age when he was capable, according to custom, of ruling by himself.

It was only in the last few years of his reign that Richard II finally managed to shake free, and it is with those last few years that Shakespeare's play deals. And even so, when the play begins, King Richard is speaking to an uncle.

Old John of Gaunt . . .

The play opens in 1398 in Windsor Castle on the Thames, about twenty miles west of the center of London. It had been an austere fortress (first built by William the Conqueror in 1070) until Edward III had converted it into a residential palace.

Since that time it has become so associated with English royalty that when the royal house wanted a new non-German name during the excitement of World War I (they had inherited a German name from Prince Albert, the German consort of Queen Victoria), they chose "Windsor." When Edward VIII abdicated in 1936, he became "Duke of Windsor."

Richard II is thirty-one years old when the play opens but has tasted real power for only a year or so. He is making up for the long years under his uncles' domination and he addresses one of them with the regal haughtiness of a proud King, beginning:

> Old John of Gaunt, time-honored Lancaster,
>
> —Act I, scene i, line 1

John was the fourth son of Edward III and the oldest son to survive his father. Two centuries before it might well have been he who would have succeeded to the throne (as John II), but times had changed.

John was born in 1340, not long after Edward III had first attempted an invasion of France at the beginning of the Hundred Years' War. The royal family had accompanied the King and the army, and it was in the city of Ghent (in what is now Belgium, but was then the County of Flanders) that he was born. He is known by his birthplace as John of Ghent, or, in the Shakespearean spelling, John of Gaunt.

John of Gaunt receives very favorable treatment at the hands of Shakespeare, partly because he was the ancestor of the monarchs who were on the English throne during the dramatist's lifetime. In 1595, when *Richard II* was written, Elizabeth I was the English Queen, and she was the great-great-great-great-granddaughter of John of Gaunt.

In real life, John of Gaunt seems to have been a man of mediocre ability, saved from obscurity only by the fact that he was a king's son.

In the last years of Edward's reign, with the King senile and the Black Prince an invalid, the leadership of the smoldering war in France fell to John of Gaunt. In 1373 he led an army out of Calais and marched it across the width of France to Bordeaux. The French, in no mood to fight another grand battle, faded before him, so that he accomplished nothing except to lose half his army through attrition.

Returning to England, he tried to organize a parliamentary party in opposition to one organized by the Black Prince. He was, however, no more successful in politics than in war. Even though the death of the Black Prince left John of Gaunt temporarily supreme in his influence over the senile King, the death of the King soon afterward robbed him of that influence again.

—Except money. He had an unfailing touch for wealth. He married for money, as did everyone in those days when they could. In 1359 John of Gaunt married Blanche, the daughter of Henry, 1st Duke of Lancaster. When Henry died, leaving no sons, John of Gaunt was granted the title and inherited the vast revenues attached thereto. He became John of Lancaster and it was by this name that he was known to his contemporaries. Thus, Richard in the first line of the play calls him not only "John of Gaunt" but "Lancaster" as well.

John of Gaunt, as Duke of Lancaster, drew revenue from perhaps one third of all England and became the richest of all the King's subjects, and yet that did not help make up for his personal mediocrity and political ineptitude.

In the intrigue and infighting that surrounded the throne of the young King, John of Gaunt felt himself terribly outclassed and seized, with relief, at a chance for leaving England.

The excuse was a dynastic one. John of Gaunt's first wife, the heiress of Lancaster, had died in 1369, and John had not waited long to make another advantageous marriage. In 1371 he married Constance of Castile, the daughter of Pedro the Cruel, whom the Black Prince had placed on the Castilian throne. (Castile was then the largest Christian kingdom on the Spanish peninsula.)

Pedro, however, had been defeated and killed in 1369, and in the 1380s the son of Pedro's illegitimate brother ruled Castile as John I. John of Gaunt claimed that he himself was the rightful King of Castile since he was Pedro's son-in-law. Off he went in 1385 on an expedition to Spain. No doubt he saw himself repeating the grand successes of his father, Edward III, in his invasion (for similar reasons) of France.

If so, he was wrong. His expedition was one great big flop. John of Gaunt was defeated by John I and had to sign an agreement giving up his claim to the Castilian throne.

He got money, though, in compensation—as always, he grew rich even as he failed. What's more, his young daughter by his Spanish wife married King John's son, who later ruled as Henry III. In 1406 John of Gaunt's grandson was to rule Castile as John II, but Gaunt was not to live long enough to see that day.

When John of Gaunt returned to England in 1389, he found the situation worse than he had left it, and, as always, he was himself helpless to handle matters or to prevent the catastrophe that followed.

He could only survive it, and now, in 1398, he faced his nephew, who had emerged from all the difficulties surprisingly triumphant and who intended to make himself absolute king of his realm.

John of Gaunt, now aged, could not stop that, either. Of course, we must not overestimate Gaunt's age. The famous first line of the play makes it sound as though John of Gaunt were aged indeed, and so he was by the standards of his time and Shakespeare's. It was a time, we must remember, when life expectancy was thirty-five at best and anyone over forty was getting on in years. (Shakespeare himself died at fifty-two.)

Nevertheless, Gaunt was not particularly old by our own standards. At the time he stood before King Richard, he was only fifty-eight years old.

. . . Henry Hereford . . .

John of Gaunt has been called before the King to present his son, who has become involved in a dispute so severe that it requires a royal judgment. Richard says:

> *Hast thou according to thy oath and band* [bond]
> *Brought hither Henry Hereford, thy bold son,*
>
> —Act I, scene i, lines 2–3

Henry, the oldest son of John of Gaunt, was born April 3, 1366, at Bolingbroke Castle in Lincolnshire. He was therefore known as Henry of Bolingbroke and is referred to throughout this play as "Bolingbroke." He is first cousin to the King and a year older than he.

In 1386, when John of Gaunt was leaving for Spain, Bolingbroke married Mary de Bohun, an heiress. Bolingbroke had, quite obviously, his father's aptitude for getting his hands on money. Bolingbroke was, however, a much more capable politician than his father, and while John of Gaunt was in Spain, his son played a surprisingly important role in the events taking place in England.

These events centered about Thomas of Woodstock, the sixth son of Edward III, and the youngest of the three sons that survived the death of that king. Thomas of Woodstock was the most forceful of Edward's sons, next to the Black Prince himself. Though he was fifteen years younger than John of Gaunt and not much more than a boy himself at the time of Edward's death, it was Thomas who became the power behind the throne. (He was called Thomas of Woodstock, by the way, because he had been born in 1355 in the same castle where the Black Prince had been born.)

Like John of Gaunt, Thomas of Woodstock had married an heiress. She was Eleanor de Bohun, whose father, the Earl of Hereford, had died without a male heir and had left her half his rich estate. Eleanor was sister of Mary de Bohun, who later married Bolingbroke. Thomas of Woodstock and Henry Bolingbroke were not only uncle and nephew, therefore, but brothers-in-law as well.

Thomas of Woodstock had been one of those most active in suppressing the peasants' revolt. He had also led a last great raid out of Calais and into France in 1380. Like all such efforts since Poitiers, it had been most impressive but had achieved very little.

Nevertheless, it was Thomas' energy that dominated most of Richard's reign, and it was chiefly to get away from Thomas that John of Gaunt made his way to Spain.

While Gaunt was absent, Thomas was supreme and was virtually the uncrowned King of England. In 1385 he forced the young King (now eighteen and quite capable, in his own eyes, of ruling without supervision) to create him Duke of Gloucester. Uncle Thomas thus became Thomas of Gloucester, and it is as "Gloucester" that he is referred to in *Richard II*.

By 1386 the battle lines were clearly drawn. The young King was increasingly conscious of the semidivine aura about a legitimate king. It was

God who had made him only surviving son of the oldest son of Edward III, and domineering uncles, who were merely younger brothers of that king, must not interfere. The manner in which he, Richard, had ridden into a wild and hostile mob, who had fallen away from him and had dared not touch the Lord's Anointed, must have convinced him forever that he was apart from other men. But Thomas of Woodstock was *not* convinced of that.

In fact, Thomas organized Parliament about an antimonarchical stand, and when King Richard offered to rebel against his uncle's domination, Thomas openly threatened to bring about the King's deposition.

But Richard II had been building a party of his own, gathering men about him who would stand with him against Thomas of Gloucester. In August 1387 he decided to strike out for independence. He moved to have Thomas of Gloucester and the chief men of the antimonarchical party accused of treason.

The move was premature, however. Thomas of Gloucester and his allies at once "appealed" (that is, accused) the King's friends of treason. Thomas of Gloucester and the other noblemen who were the movers of this counterstep came to be known as the "lords appellant" in consequence.

In the tug of war that followed, it was the lords appellant who turned out to have the power on their side. The King had to call a Parliament which was dragooned into convicting the King's friends and executing some of them. Richard was left friendless and helpless and Thomas was in control to a greater extent than ever.

Henry Bolingbroke, during the course of this battle between royal nephew and powerful uncle, stood on the side of the uncle, who was his own uncle as well as his brother-in-law. Bolingbroke was one of the lords apellant, in other words.

Thomas of Gloucester undoubtedly found him a shrewd and valuable ally. After all, if John of Gaunt died in Spain, Bolingbroke would inherit all the wealth and power of Lancaster. This, however, was a case of two heads being worse than one. Thomas was a hothead who was prepared actually to depose Richard, but if he did so, the question arose as to who would then be king.

Undoubtedly, Thomas would have liked to be king, but Bolingbroke made it quite clear that John of Gaunt, as oldest surviving son of Edward III, was the logical next in line, and that he himself, as the oldest son of John of Gaunt, was in line thereafter. Thomas of Gloucester must have seen no great advantage in substituting for the weak King the firm, shrewd Bolingbroke. So Richard was saved and the vengeance fell chiefly on his supporters rather than on himself.

Richard II had learned one lesson anyway. He needed not only a party of his own, but a large party, larger than any his hated uncle could build, and one that would strike with overwhelming force when it did strike. For years, therefore, he labored to build up another group of allies, a veritable private army.

What's more, he labored with success (for he had great charm when he chose to exert it) to win over as many as possible of the lords appellant and their adherents, leaving Thomas of Gloucester and his chief allies increasingly isolated. In particular, Richard wooed and won Bolingbroke, who deserted his uncle when the final crunch came.

Thomas of Gloucester, grown careless with success, and badly under-estimating the young King, was caught off guard and began a countermove too late. In the summer of 1397, alarmed by the King's rising strength, Thomas began another attempt to procure the deposition of Richard, but he had lost his allies. John of Gaunt (strengthened in his stand by his son, no doubt) opposed the move and it failed.

King Richard could now strike. He visited Thomas of Gloucester's castle in September 1397 and had him suddenly arrested and sent out of the country, to Calais. Gloucester's chief allies were also arrested and were eventually either executed or banished.

Richard was now supreme and could reward those who had stood with him. Bolingbroke was given his father-in-law's title of Hereford. What's more, where the father-in-law had been merely an earl, Bolingbroke be-came Duke of Hereford, and it is as "Henry Hereford" that Richard first refers to him in the quoted passage above.

Bolingbroke's position with the King was not as firm, however, as their alliance in 1397 might make it appear. Gratitude is a short-lived com-modity in politics, and Bolingbroke was too near the throne to be treated with anything but suspicion.

Richard had no sons of his own and he planned to leave the throne, according to the strict tenets of legitimacy, to the descendants of Lionel, third son of Edward III (since he himself was the last of the line of the first son and there were no heirs to the second).

The heirs of Lionel, however, could not compare in wealth, prestige, and importance with the fourth son, John of Gaunt, and his son Bolingbroke. Richard must have known that shrewd, ambitious Bolingbroke had an eye on the throne despite the fact that he was not really next in line; Boling-broke had shown that plainly in his earlier alliance with Thomas of Glouces-ter. Richard II had to watch Bolingbroke warily, therefore, and deal with him promptly when and if he grew clearly dangerous.

. . . the Duke of Norfolk . . .

That point of danger may now have come, and Richard may well feel himself to be in a delicate position. He demands of John of Gaunt whether he has brought his son

Here to make good the boist'rous late appeal
Which then our leisure would not let us hear,
Against the Duke of Norfolk, Thomas Mowbray?
—Act I, scene i, lines 4–6

Thomas Mowbray, born in 1366, was just Bolingbroke's age. He had been a companion of the King (one year younger than himself) when both were young, and was made Earl of Nottingham in 1383.

But then Mowbray began a career of changing sides. He grew jealous of another favorite of the King's and, out of pique, joined the party of Thomas of Gloucester against the King and became one of the lords appellant. He was not an extremist, however, and when the question of deposing the King came up, he threw his influence on the side of the milder line of action, that of merely bringing the King's favorites to trial.

Afterward, Richard wooed Mowbray as he wooed Bolingbroke, and was successful there too. Once again Mowbray became a close companion of the King. Indeed, when Richard swooped suddenly down upon Thomas of Gloucester and put him under arrest, it was in Mowbray's care that he placed his uncle. It was Mowbray who carried Gloucester off to prison in Calais and who served as his jailer there. Mowbray, like Bolingbroke, was promoted for his services, and became Duke of Norfolk.

But now what was to be done with Thomas of Gloucester? He was, after all, a son of Edward III, and he could not be disposed of out of hand. He simply could not. He had to be tried for treason and Parliament gathered for that purpose. And it proved to be too late, for word came from Calais that, behold, Thomas of Gloucester had died.

Now it was certainly possible for people to die suddenly in those days. The smallest fever or infection could kill in a time when medical knowledge was nearly nil, and diseases were easily caught in a time when the appreciation of hygiene was likewise nearly nil.

Still, the death of Gloucester at this juncture was so politically convenient for Richard (who might not have been able to make out a good case for treason, considering that Gloucester had been popular with Parliament) that the whispers at once started that the troublesome uncle had quietly been murdered at his nephew's orders—just as once Arthur of Brittany, in similar circumstances, had been quietly murdered at his uncle's orders (see page II–239).

As these whispers and rumors grew, Mowbray began to feel himself in a most uncomfortable position. He had been Gloucester's jailer. If Gloucester had been murdered, it must have been Mowbray who had given the immediate order. If this were shown to be so, Mowbray might have to face execution himself.

Richard was in an equally uncomfortable position, for Mowbray's only conceivable defense would be that he had been ordered to take the action by the King. And if that came out, then Richard would find himself in the difficult position of King John, who lost northern France partly because of the obloquy that fell upon him through Arthur's death.

Mowbray could not help but realize that his danger came not only from the King's enemies, who hated him for his deed (if the deed had actually been committed—history is not certain), but from the King himself. After all, dead men tell no tales, and a dead Mowbray could scarcely accuse the King.

Mowbray began to fear for his safety and looked about for some way of making himself secure. He needed allies and Bolingbroke seemed a natural one. He and Bolingbroke were the last of the lords appellant still alive and were therefore in equal danger. He therefore approached Bolingbroke.

It turned out Mowbray had calculated wrongly. Bolingbroke was determined to play for high stakes. Mowbray had tipped his hand and Bolingbroke seized the advantage at once. To begin with, he went to King Richard, reported Mowbray's conversation, and accused him of treason. Desperately, Mowbray was forced to deny the charge and to call Bolingbroke a liar.

. . . sacrificing Abel's . . .

Richard is in an extraordinarily ticklish position. He is forced to call the two noblemen before him and hear their mutual accusations, yet more than anything else he wants the quarrel ended. He wants the matter of the death of Thomas of Gloucester left unexplored and even unmentioned.

But that is precisely what Bolingbroke does not want. He wants the matter brought up. The clouds of suspicion that would be raised could do nothing but harm Richard, and if they harmed Richard they would have to help Bolingbroke.

Therefore, after the mutual accusations and counteraccusations between Bolingbroke and Mowbray have been carried through, the former comes to the point. He not only accuses Mowbray of misusing certain public funds, but adds solemnly:

> . . . he [Mowbray] *did plot the Duke of Gloucester's death,*
> *Suggest his soon-believing adversaries,*
> *And, consequently, like a traitor coward,*
> *Sluiced out his [Gloucester's] innocent soul through streams*
>   *of blood;*
> *Which blood, like sacrificing Abel's cries*
> *Even from the tongueless caverns of the earth*
> *To me for justice and rough chastisement:*
>   —Act I, scene i, lines 100–6

The murder of Gloucester is compared to that of Abel, whose sacrifices of the firstlings of his flocks were found acceptable by God, and who was slain by his elder brother Cain, whose sacrifices were not accepted. God, in rebuking the murderer, says, "the voice of thy brother's blood crieth unto me from the ground" (Genesis 4:10).

The comparison limps, though, if it is intended to apply to a murder by Mowbray, who had no close relationship to Thomas of Gloucester. On the other hand, if Mowbray were acting under orders from King Richard, the matter was altogether different. Gloucester would have been killed by the son of his older brother and the comparison becomes close indeed.

One can imagine Bolingbroke looking at Mowbray in the course of his accusing speech and then, when he reaches the terrible phrase "like sacrificing Abel's," turning to stare directly at the King. Richard must surely wince at the allusion, and he mutters uneasily:

> *How high a pitch his resolution soars!*
> —Act I, scene i, line 109

. . . to fetch his Queen

Mowbray does his best to avoid the dangerous topic, hoping perhaps to show his loyalty to the King and to ensure his future safety. He denies killing Thomas of Gloucester in a few brief and rather unconvincing words. He is more circumstantial in denying the lesser charge, that he has stolen public funds.

Part, he insists, he paid out as required, and part he kept as payment of a debt owed him by Richard:

> *The other part reserved I by consent,*
> *For that my sovereign liege was in my debt*
> *Upon remainder of a dear account,*
> *Since last I went to France to fetch his Queen.*
> —Act I, scene i, lines 128–31

Richard had married twice. In January 1382, when he was only fifteen, he married Anne of Bohemia, who was sixteen. She was daughter of the King of Bohemia, who had reigned as Charles IV, Holy Roman Emperor, and who had died four years before. It turned out to be a love match and Anne proved to be a popular Queen. When Richard, in a fit of petulance, deprived London of its privileges after the city had refused him a loan, it was her intercession that won pardon.

She died of the plague in 1394 when she was only twenty-eight. (In that same year, Bolingbroke's wife died also. She was only twenty-four. Life was short in those days.)

Richard II went into deep and, apparently, sincere mourning, but kings cannot long remain in mourning, especially if they have no heirs. Besides, a marriage can be a useful stroke of international policy.

The war in France had been sputtering on despite the Treaty of Calais, but by 1388 it had died out almost entirely. Richard desperately wanted that truce to continue, for he had neither the money nor the inclination to carry on the war. What better way of ensuring continued peace than by taking a French bride.

The French King, Charles V, the great enemy of the Black Prince, had died in 1380 and had been succeeded by his son, Charles VI. In 1397 the daughter of the new King, Isabella, was seven years old, and it was she that Richard married as his second wife. It would be some years before she could bear him an heir to the throne, but Richard was still reasonably young and could wait.

Mowbray had played a part in the negotiations that led to the marriage and was clearly claiming gratitude from Richard for this. And, in a way, Richard did have much to be grateful for. It was after this French marriage that Richard had Thomas of Gloucester arrested. He might not have had the courage to do so if he did not know that France was friendly at the moment and would make no move to embarrass him.

And yet the French marriage was unpopular. In this period of history, French marriages were always unpopular in England; it was consorting with the enemy, and English xenophobes were prompt to blame anything that went wrong afterward on French influence.

Some maintained that once Richard had made a French marriage he grew interested in French manners and vices, picked up French ideas of absolute monarchy, and, in short, was corrupted away from his earlier English virtue. This is nonsense. Richard's penchant for absolutism was long-standing, and he needed no seven-year-old French girl to put the notion into his head.

. . . Coventry upon Saint Lambert's day

Desperately, Richard tries to get the two disputants to end their quarrel now, before irreparable damage is done to his position. He fails, however. Bolingbroke is intent on carrying through his scheme to shake the throne, while Mowbray does not dare let the accusation of murder stand without some resolution of the dispute.

Richard is forced, therefore, to take the path called for by the laws of chivalry and to set up a trial by combat. In a way, he was making the best of it, for the complicated and punctilious code of chivalry could bring on many delays and Richard might have time to work out some method of procedure that would extricate him from this dismal mess he was in.

The mutual accusations of Bolingbroke and Mowbray were made in

January 1398, only four months after the death of Thomas of Gloucester. The inevitable delays of the chivalric code put off the trial by combat eight months more. Shakespeare does not specify this delay or make a point of it. In his histories, it is always important to hasten the action, and he does so now. He has Richard say to the two disputants:

> Be ready, as your lives shall answer it,
> At Coventry upon Saint Lambert's day.
>
> —Act I, scene i, lines 198–99

There is no indication of how long a time lapse this involves.

Coventry is a town in Warwickshire which was the site for the best-known single event in the history of Saxon England. About 1050 Coventry was in that portion of central England then known as Mercia. The wife of the Earl of Mercia was Godgifu, a name which was later smoothed down to Godiva. She urged her husband, out of her own softheartedness, to lower the taxes on Coventry. He finally said he would if she would ride through the market place naked. She took him at his word, riding through the market place on horseback with no clothes on, but with her long hair covering her adequately.

In the fourteenth century Coventry became part of the estates of the Black Prince. It passed on to Richard II and became a royal residence. Parliament sat there at least two times.

It was common in medieval times to identify days by the names of saints. The medieval church had a large number of saints who were specially noted on one particular day or another, usually because that was the anniversary of their martyrdom. Lambert was a native of what is now the Netherlands and lived in the seventh century. His day is September 17, so the trial by combat at Coventry is set for September 17, 1398.

. . . thy sometimes brother's wife

The time lapse between the quarrel before the King and the meeting at Coventry is filled in by Shakespeare with a scene in John of Gaunt's London house, to which the distraught Duchess of Gloucester has come, grieving for her murdered husband.

Shakespeare makes no specific mention of the Duchess' age, but somehow the impression is given that she is old; that she is of Gaunt's generation. Actually, though, Thomas of Gloucester was only forty-two when he died or was murdered. His wife was only thirty-one at the time and is only a year older at the time of this scene.

The Duchess tries to rouse Gaunt to some sort of action, but John will not be roused. Eloquently, she points out that if an assassination of a prince of the realm goes unavenged, other princes may with impunity be killed.

But John knows that Richard II is the real murderer and he cannot nerve himself to turn against his King. He can only council patience, saying:

> God's is the quarrel; for God's substitute,
> His deputy anointed in His sight,
> Hath caused his [Gloucester's] death . . .
>
> —Act I, scene ii, lines 37–39

Here is the semidivinity admitted of a king by grace of God, a king "who can do no wrong." This is exactly the sort of absolutism which Richard II is indeed trying to establish, but which never really took firm root in England, though it did so in other parts of the world.

Frustrated, the Duchess can only say:

> Farewell, old Gaunt; thy sometimes brother's wife
> With her companion, Grief, must end her life.
>
> —Act I, scene ii, lines 54–55

She does, too, for she dies the next year, aged thirty-three. Through most of history the life expectancy of the female (treated as a drudge and subjected to the terrible dangers of frequent childbirth) has been even shorter than that of the male. It is only in contemporary times, when medicine has removed the dangers of childbirth, that the natural fitness of women has reflected itself in a several-years-longer life expectancy than is true of men.

. . . good old York . . .

Before the Duchess leaves, however, she says:

> Commend me to thy brother, Edmund York.
>
> —Act I, scene ii, line 62

She wants York to visit her, but then, in an access of renewed grief, bemoans the uselessness of such a visit to her castle:

> Alack; and what shall good old York there see
> But empty lodgings and unfurnished walls,
>
> —Act I, scene ii, lines 67–68

Edmund, the fifth son of Edward III, was the only one of the brothers of John of Gaunt who was still alive. He was born at King's Langley in Herefordshire on June 5, 1341, and was therefore Edmund of Langley.

He accompanied the English forces in France and Spain but won no particular distinction. He married Isabella, a younger daughter of Pedro the

Cruel. After John of Gaunt had married Constance, the two brothers found themselves married to two sisters.

Edmund was a mild-mannered, weak man who did not take much part in the strenuous infighting about Richard. He remained on good terms with his royal nephew and in 1385 was created Duke of York. He is fifty-seven years old at the time of this scene, only a year younger than "old John of Gaunt," and therefore "good old York." (He was the only one of the seven sons of Edward III fated to live beyond his sixtieth birthday.)

My Lord Aumerle . . .

Now we move on to Coventry, where the preparations are being made for the single combat. Overseeing the formalities is the Lord Marshal, who says:

> *My Lord Aumerle, is Harry Hereford armed?*
>
> —Act I, scene iii, line 1

Aumerle is Edward, the son of Edmund of York. By birth, Aumerle is Edward of Norwich, for that was where he was born, and he became Earl of Rutland in 1390. He was only seventeen at the time of that promotion.

Edward of Norwich remained firmly on the side of Richard throughout —so firmly, in fact, that when his uncle Thomas of Gloucester was murdered, Edward was awarded much of the dead man's estates and was created Duke of Albemarle (named for a district in Normandy). Albemarle is slurred to Aumerle in this play. Aumerle is still only twenty-five years old at the time of this scene.

. . . his warder down

The lists are prepared with great ceremony, which Shakespeare reports in copious detail. But then, when the two combatants, Bolingbroke and Mowbray, face each other, lances couched, the Marshal cries:

> *Stay, the King hath thrown his warder down.*
>
> —Act I, scene iii, line 118

King Richard by this action stops the proceedings cold and, without the combat having taken place at all, goes on to give his verdict. It is an odd one, in which both parties are declared guilty and both are sent into exile; Bolingbroke for ten years and Mowbray for life.

The pair of exile verdicts are not puzzling in themselves. Richard was wary of both men. Mowbray knew too much and Bolingbroke dared too much, and the King would be rid of both. Exile on the plea that only so can the peace be kept (for a duel to the death will only rouse desire for vengeance against the victor, whichever he might be) is the logical solution.

Bolingbroke's exile is the shorter because he is the grandson of Edward III and the son of John of Gaunt, and must be treated more gingerly. Indeed, Bolingbroke's ten years are reduced to six as a sop to Gaunt. Still, that is only froth. Once Bolingbroke is out of the country it will be easy enough to prevent his return. Undoubtedly this is Richard's thought.

But why did Richard wait till the last minute? Had Richard pronounced the double exile at the moment the quarrel was brought before him, he might have gained the image of a strong king careful of the nation's peace. Why then set up a holiday atmosphere and a pitch of excitement that attracted the attention of all England during an eight-month wait, and then —only then—puncture the whole thing?

This, mind you, is not a Shakespearean invention intended to serve a dramatic purpose. It really happened this way, according to Holinshed.

Was it that Richard was irresolute and that not until the last minute could he bring himself to pronounce sentence? Or was it the reverse? Was it Richard's vanity, his sense of divinity, that made him enjoy playing the role of a god—letting everything come to a magnificent climax and then, with an almost negligent gesture, crushing it all?

Whether irresolution or vanity, the move was a bad one for Richard. It created tremendous sympathy for both Bolingbroke and Mowbray, and whether men got the impression that Richard was weak or tyrannical, the impression of him was a bad one.

My native English . . .

Shakespeare is careful to build up the anti-Richard feeling in the audience (to match that which was being built up in the nation) by presenting both exiles with pathetic speeches. Mowbray, thinking of perpetual exile, says:

> The language I have learnt these forty years,
> My native English, now I must forgo,
> And now my tongue's use is to me no more
> Than an unstringèd viol or a harp.
>
> —Act I, scene iii, lines 160–63

Actually Mowbray was only thirty-two years old, not forty, but the rest is true enough. The picture is of a man, speaking only English, who must spend the rest of his life wandering through lands where only other languages are spoken. It is hard for Englishmen and Americans to gather the full horror of such a sentence now, when the language is spoken by hundreds of millions the world over, and when there is almost no place on earth where one cannot find *someone* who understands English.

In the time of Richard II, English was a language spoken by three million Englishmen only. Few foreigners bothered to learn so minor and out-of-the-way a language. Men of culture were much better off with French or Italian—to say nothing of Latin. And in Shakespeare's time, the situation was little better.

. . . the frosty Caucasus

As for Bolingbroke, he must listen to old Gaunt's sententious consolations, to the effect that the exile is to imagine he is on a voluntary tour and that everything is happy, happy. Bolingbroke responds bitterly concerning the insufficiency of imagination:

> *O, who can hold a fire in his hand*
> *By thinking of the frosty Caucasus?*
> —Act I, scene iii, lines 293–94

The Caucasus was the name of a mountain in Greek mythology, one that was placed on the eastern edge of their known world, on the eastern shores of the Black Sea—where a whole range of peaks are now known as the Caucasian Mountains in consequence. Mount Caucasus was imagined to be higher and therefore colder than any other mountain on earth, and it can be used, poetically, to symbolize ultimate cold.

. . . Bushy, Bagot here and Green

Aumerle has seen his cousin, Bolingbroke, off on his way to banishment and returns to Richard to report that dangerous man safely out of the way. Richard, listening somberly, now admits his deepest suspicions of Bolingbroke. The exiled cousin had designs on the throne and was preparing the way to that throne by courting popularity. Richard says:

> *Ourself and Bushy, Bagot here and Green,*
> *Observed his courtship to the common people,*
> —Act I, scene iv, lines 23–24

To understand the identity and position of Bushy, Bagot, and Green, we must remember that Richard II, in common with many kings of the late medieval and early modern periods, was engaged in one long attempt to assert the royal power over that of the aristocracy—the proud dukes and earls whose income was equal to that of the king or higher, and who fought constantly for the equivalent of kingly power for themselves.

The power of the higher nobility dated back to feudal times and they were jealous of that power and would not yield an inch. To the king, therefore (that is, to any king who was even slightly above the stage of a moron), the nobles were uncomfortable and even intolerable as advisers. They were too proud, too harsh, too fond of their own way, and too ready to intrigue and betray if thwarted.

It was natural for Richard II, and for many another king both before and after, to seek for advisers among the lesser nobility or the middle class. Such men had no power of their own and therefore had to be intensely loyal to the king, for they had nowhere else to turn.

Such king's men would naturally be despised and resented by the high nobility. Feeling this enmity, the king's men or "favorites" would do their best to enrich themselves or otherwise gain power in order that they might not be utterly lost should the king die. The king might, in turn, be willing to grant favors, titles, wealth to those who were loyal to him.

Among the high nobility there would, of course, be all the more resentment against favorites who received rewards. The lords would cry out that the favorites were rifling the realm.

Moreover, the favorites would be a convenient target. The king, as the Lord's anointed, is relatively immune from blame. The favorites, however, can be blamed for everything, and in particular, for misleading and corrupting the king. And by aiming at the favorites, it is rather easy to strike the king himself. The lords appellant had struck at Richard's favorites earlier in his reign and in doing so had kept Richard himself helpless for a decade.

Sir John Bushy, Sir John Bagot, and Sir Henry Green, all mentioned in this passage, had originally been hangers-on of the party of Thomas of Gloucester. Richard II had won them over as he had won over such greater men as Bolingbroke and Mowbray.

With Bushy, Bagot, and Green, however, there was no need for Richard to feel any uneasiness. They were country gentry with no power of their own and with full awareness of the hostility of the higher nobility. Only in King Richard could they find safety, let alone power, and only to King Richard would they be loyal.

. . . the rebels which stand out in Ireland

At the moment, Richard II seems to be riding high. He has, with a strong hand, taken care of the internal enemy and overcome the dangers that would come of questioning the death of Gloucester. He could now turn against external enemies. Green says, concerning Bolingbroke and his efforts to court popularity:

Well, he is gone, and with him go these thoughts.
Now for the rebels which stand out in Ireland;
—Act I, scene iv, lines 37–38

Ireland's long history is almost uniformly tragic, and with respect to that sad island, England, beginning with Henry II's invasion (see page II-213), is almost uniformly the villain.

The eastern portion of the island, centering about Dublin, was under an uneasy English control, though most of the island remained wild and free for centuries. In fact, in the two centuries that followed Henry II, English domination grew weaker as English efforts were all too often directed elsewhere. Edward III, for instance, was so busily concerned with France that he could only left-handedly deal with Ireland.

By the time Richard II came to the throne, the English settlers in Ireland were forced to pay tribute to the native clan leaders to the west.

Richard II did not rejoice in war and did everything he could to remain at peace, yet public opinion (particularly that of the nobility, which saw in war a chance for loot and "glory") drove him in the direction of war.

He had to fight Scotland, for instance, which continued to receive support, supplies, and money from France, and which used them to raid England's northern counties. In 1385 Richard had therefore led an English army northward and burned Edinburgh, but on the whole the expedition turned out to be an expensive failure, ending in stalemate.

The chronic rebellion in Ireland offered Richard another chance, and he was forced to take it. In 1394 he led a sizable army into Ireland. Here he made no attempt to settle matters by brute force. Making use of what was always his strongest card, he tried diplomacy, flattery, and charm. He won over many of the Irish chieftains with fancy titles and with grants of land, and concentrated on the pacification of Mac Murrough, chieftain of Leinster, that section of Ireland immediately outside the English-controlled area.

This too was achieved, at least on paper, when Mac Murrough, with most of the Irish clans won away from him, was forced to yield. In 1395 Richard II came back from Ireland with his army intact and his aims apparently accomplished. He found himself welcomed as a conquering hero. It was an unusual experience for the King and it must have given him quite a false notion of how easy an Irish campaign might be.

But it had not lasted. While Richard had been gathering power into his own hands in England, Mac Murrough of Leinster had taken advantage of the royal preoccupation by tearing up the paper he had signed and placing himself in opposition to the English again. He even engineered the assassination of the English viceroy, Roger de Mortimer, in 1398.

This could not be endured and Richard II was going to have to go back to Ireland to straighten out affairs again. With Mowbray and Bolingbroke both gone, there seemed no reason why he could not do so. In fact, an impressively victorious Irish campaign would rouse the English out of any dumps into which they might have fallen over the exile verdicts and any uneasiness they might feel over the fate of Thomas of Gloucester.

. . . to farm our royal realm

There was one difficulty, however. Wars are expensive, always expensive, and medieval kings were forever in difficulty when it came to raising funds anyway. According to the feudal system, the money went to the feudal lords and the King only received revenues from his own royal estates and from certain perquisites such as customs dues. To get more he had to go begging to the nobility or the merchants, and both could be niggardly enough. It was usually quite difficult to get enough money for ordinary expenditures, considering the scale of lavish living most monarchs felt it necessary to assume if they were to impress their subjects and other monarchs with their power. To get special funds for war was very nearly impossible. (Very often, the money had to come by finding some rich subject a traitor and confiscating his estates, or by winning a victory and looting the enemy.)

Richard had no defeated enemy to loot and, at the moment, no traitorous estate to confiscate. He had to take other action, and says:

> We are enforced to farm our royal realm,
>
> —Act I, scene iv, line 45

This is, he must lease those estates belonging directly to the crown, as well as other royal sources of revenue, granting them for a fixed number of years in return for an immediate cash grant. It was rather like borrowing from the bank at a high rate of interest. Richard would obtain money right at the moment when he needs it, but the revenues he has leased out, added up over the years, would be much greater than the spot cash he has received. In the long run, then, the King loses a great deal (unless he makes it up by victory), while those leasing the revenues make huge profits.

Naturally, Richard would grant the leases to those he favors, and equally naturally, those who had no share in the profits would be horrified at the procedure.

The lining of his coffers . . .

Nor does Richard fail to see other possible sources of revenue.

Bushy enters with the grave news that John of Gaunt has suddenly fallen sick and has sent for Richard, begging the King to come to him. Richard rejoices at the news. He openly hopes for Gaunt's quick death, again with

an eye to the Irish war, for some of the Lancastrian wealth can then be
taken by the crown. He says:

> *The lining of his coffers shall make coats*
> *To deck our soldiers for these Irish wars.*
>
> —Act I, scene iv, lines 61–62

Actually, John of Gaunt did not fall sick until four months after the non-
duel between Mowbray and Bolingbroke.

. . . fashions in proud Italy

The scene shifts to the London palace in which John of Gaunt lies dying. At his bedside is his last remaining brother, Edmund of York. Both are
in deep depression over the heedless follies of Richard—his extravagances,
and most of all his leasing of lands and revenues to his favorites.

York blames the evil influences to which Richard's youth is subject, and,
as is true in every period of history, decries the frivolity of the younger generation and their tendency to follow foreign innovations in place of the
good old-fashioned customs of the past. (It is what we now call the "generation gap.")

Richard, says York, will not bend his ear to good council:

> *No, it is stopped with other flattering sounds:*
> *As praises—of whose taste [even] the wise are fond—*
> *Lascivious meters, to whose venom sound*
> *The open ear of youth doth always listen;*
> *Report of fashions in proud Italy*
> *Whose manners still our tardy-apish nation*
> *Limps after in base imitation.*
>
> —Act II, scene i, lines 17–23

The reference to Italy is anachronistic and is more nearly an expression
of Shakespeare's own nationalism rather than of York's in 1399.

In the fourteenth century, during the reign of Edward III, Italy was indeed exploding with a burst of intellectual activity. Their artists and writers
were suddenly looking at the Greek and Latin past with new eyes and began to model their own work on classic models. They called their time a
period of rebirth (the "Renaissance"). The centuries between the time of
the ancients and this new time of rebirth they called the "Middle Ages."

Slowly, the Renaissance culture spread out from Italy, north and west,
almost hypnotizing other nations with its glories. It was not, however, till
the sixteenth century that it reached England. It was in Shakespeare's time,

not in Richard's, that Italian art, literature, music, fashions—the whole Italian way of thought—captivated the English.

The Italian touch was priceless, for it stimulated England into a blaze of genius of an intensity it had never seen before and was never to see again. And of this golden age of English culture, Shakespeare himself was the brightest ornament.

Yet men are never comfortable with cultural change, even when they themselves typify it and profit by it. There were many items in the new Italian influence which were indeed disturbing to what we would today call the Establishment. Shakespeare's contemporary, the Italian scientist Galileo, was upsetting the Ptolemaic and Aristotelian view of the universe, and Machiavelli was introducing a new kind of politics divorced from medieval notions of chivalry and feudal honor. (Shakespeare never accepted these innovations, and his plays remain firmly on the side of the old.) Besides, sixteenth-century England was moving away from Catholic Christianity, and Italy, as the center of the papacy, had come to seem a dangerous land of evil to Englishmen.

In 1595, then, when Shakespeare was writing and producing this play, older men were indeed shaking their heads and moaning at the spreading of Italian ways and the vulnerability of the thoughtless young to foreign corruption. Shakespeare merely transferred this contemporary view to the time of Richard's reign two centuries before.

This royal throne of kings . . .

Gaunt replies in a memorable speech. Richard is destroying England by his policies, he says. England, invincible to foreign attack by virtue of its happy position as an island, is dying from within. His panegyric to England in the course of this speech is the most lyrical bit of Shakespearean patriotism, for Gaunt describes England as:

> *This royal throne of kings, this scept'red isle,*
> *This earth of majesty, this seat of Mars,*
> *This other Eden, demi-paradise,*
> *This fortress built by Nature for herself*
> *Against infection and the hand of war,*
> *This happy breed of men, this little world,*
> *This precious stone set in the silver sea*
> *Which serves it in the office of a wall,*
> *Or as a moat defensive to a house,*
> *Against the envy of less happier lands,*
> *This blessed plot, this earth, this realm, this England,*
>
> —Act II, scene i, lines 40–50

Yet this too is somewhat anachronistic. The description is of an England blessedly isolated and on the defensive, but in Gaunt's time, the English philosophy of war was entirely offensive. In the past half century, English armies had won heady victories over France and had interfered effectively in Spanish affairs. Before that, they had roved even farther afield. John of Gaunt points that out in this same speech, saying that English kings are:

> Renowned for their deeds as far from home,
> For Christian service and true chivalry,
> As is the sepulcher in stubborn Jewry
> Of the world's ransom, blessed Mary's son,
> —Act II, scene i, lines 53–56

The reference is, of course, to Richard the Lion-Heart, who led an army to the Holy Land and fought his way nearly to Jerusalem (see page II–219).

Then why the defensive note in Gaunt's panegyric, the emphasis on England behind an oceanic moat beating off the invasions of men from "less happier lands"?

Gaunt's speech applies not at all to the time of Gaunt's death, but to the time in which Richard II was first produced.

In 1595 all Englishmen had a fresh and glorious memory of victory. Only seven years before, in 1588, a vast armada of ships had swept northward from Spain, intent on crushing England. It would have seemed to any impartial observer that Spain, the greatest military power in Europe at the time, would surely defeat England, which was then, at best, a second-rate power, and which was, moreover, apparently on the brink of civil war.

Yet England's smaller but nimbler ships, and her daring sea-hardened captains (like Sir Francis Drake), aided by the chance intervention of storms at sea, smashed the Armada and, almost at a stroke, made England a great power.

It is easy to imagine the pride that must have swept the nation, the feeling of invincibility that burgeoned. England indeed must have seemed to her population to be an impregnable island guarded by supermen in superships. John of Gaunt's speech, when delivered, must have brought the audience screaming to its feet. Gaunt goes on to say that this glorious England is being ruined from within by Richard's policies:

> That England that was wont to conquer others
> Hath made a shameful conquest of itself.
> —Act II, scene i, lines 65–66

That, surely, must have lost Richard any sympathy anyone in the audience may have had for him.

. . . old Lancaster hath spent

Present in this scene between John of Gaunt and Edmund of York (but not speaking through the first part of the scene) is also the Earl of Northumberland, the scion of a proud and ancient family called the Percys.

A William de Percy crossed the Channel with William the Conqueror in 1066 and was given great lands in northern England. His family had remained there ever since, and upon them had devolved the task of fending off the periodic raids of the Scots, and of conducting raids of their own.

The Percy family, hardened in this border warfare, felt itself virtual lords of the north, for they were generally little beholden to any help from the central government. This attitude of theirs is of crucial importance to the events of this time.

A Henry Percy had fought at Crécy with Edward III, and it was his son, another Henry Percy, who was raised in rank to an earldom and who is the "Northumberland" (the most northern of the English counties and the most exposed to Scottish depredation) of this play.

Richard now enters, and John of Gaunt finally speaks plainly to him, accusing him of extravagance and foolish fiscal policies. The King, infuriated, threatens his dying uncle, who, secure in the knowledge of approaching death, taunts him, at last, with having murdered Thomas of Gloucester.

Northumberland helps Gaunt out of the room and comes back almost immediately with the news that the old man has died. Northumberland says:

> *His [Gaunt's] tongue is now a stringless instrument;*
> *Words, life and all, old Lancaster hath spent.*
> —Act II, scene i, lines 149–50

This death took place, in actual fact, on February 3, 1399. By that time Bolingbroke had been in exile four and a half months.

. . . plate, coin, revenues, and movables

Coldly, Richard greets the news of Gaunt's death. His concern is with his projected Irish expedition, and he still needs money for that. He therefore haughtily announces:

> *Towards our assistance we do seize to us*
> *The plate, coin, revenues, and movables*
> *Whereof our uncle Gaunt did stand possessed.*
> —Act II, scene i, lines 161–63

This is an act of enormous significance. John of Gaunt, as Duke of Lancaster, had the broadest estates and the largest revenues in England. Once he was dead, his son, Bolingbroke, automatically became Henry of Lancaster and all those estates and revenues were his. That right could not be taken away except for high treason and there was no accusation of that in his banishment.

To confiscate those estates was illegal, but Bolingbroke was far away in exile and the Lancastrian revenues were more than Richard could, at that moment, resist.

. . . the last of noble Edward's sons

Edmund of York is now moved to object to this crime, for his is an unusual privilege. As he says:

> I am the last of noble Edward's sons,
>
> —Act II, scene i, line 171

(He is destined to live on three more years in that position.)

York lists all of Richard's acts of injustice that he has patiently endured, and includes one which is not otherwise mentioned in the play, for he speaks of:

> . . . the prevention of poor Bolingbroke
> About his marriage . . .
>
> —Act II, scene i, lines 167–68

This seems to refer to events in France, where Bolingbroke has been ever since his exile.

In France, Bolingbroke is by no means a nonentity, but is an honored guest at the French court for obvious reasons. He is near the succession to the throne and in case of renewed war between England and France, Bolingbroke could be an important French weapon. He could be used to start a civil war within England by being encouraged to claim the throne.

For Bolingbroke's part, French friendship was obviously valuable, since with French help he might recover what he had lost and even gain the throne itself. A marital alliance that would knit Bolingbroke to the French royal family might be to the advantage of both. Bolingbroke was a widower and therefore available, and he began to negotiate a marriage contract with a cousin of the French King.

Naturally, it was to Richard's interest to keep this from happening; to keep Bolingbroke from too close a connection with the French throne. Richard therefore sent an envoy hastily to France, demanding that the marriage not be permitted to go through, and negotiations were accordingly broken off. That was "the prevention of poor Bolingbroke about his marriage."

This would only serve to sharpen the enmity between the two cousins. The projected marriage would make it clear to Richard that Bolingbroke was plotting to gain French help, while Bolingbroke would see that Richard had an unrelenting eye upon him.

. . . a thousand dangers on your head

Edmund of York goes on to say that this final act of injustice, this seizing of Lancastrian wealth and the disinheriting of Bolingbroke, goes too far. He warns Richard that by this act:

> *You pluck a thousand dangers on your head,*
> *You lose a thousand well-disposèd hearts,*
>
> —Act II, scene i, lines 205–6

This was something Richard might have seen for himself. He had, after all, touched the "pocket nerve" at last. All kinds of tyranny might be endured as long as money, property, revenues are held sacred. But now, if Richard could act thus in the case of the greatest nobleman in the kingdom, casually disinheriting him without accusation of treason (let alone conviction), what other nobleman would feel safe? Richard was striking at the security of every lord in the realm and was begging for treason.

. . . to the Earl of Wiltshire . . .

But Richard has reached the heights of megalomania and can no longer see clearly. His faith in the kingship and the apparent success of all his strokes has blinded him to any possibility of failure. Ignoring York's remonstrances, he puts the matter of the seizing of Lancastrian wealth into action at once, saying:

> *Go, Bushy, to the Earl of Wiltshire straight;*
> *Bid him repair to us to Ely House,*
> *To see this business.*
>
> —Act II, scene i, lines 215–17

The reference is to the 1st Earl of Wiltshire, William le Scrope, who had been raised to the earldom by Richard in 1397. In 1398 he was made treasurer of England and it would be he who would have to take charge of the paper work required to transfer the holdings of Lancaster to the throne.

This Wiltshire did, apparently without a murmur, though both he and his father had served John of Gaunt. His father, Richard le Scrope (1st Baron Scrope of Bolton) had served as Chancellor—the King's chief administrator—from 1378 to 1382, but having tried to stem Richard's extravagance, had been dismissed.

. . . Lord Governor of England

Now at last, Richard is ready to go to Ireland. Shakespeare's compression of time makes it appear that he leaves almost immediately upon Gaunt's death, but of course some time must elapse, if only to organize the necessary financial matters. In actual fact, Richard did not leave for Ireland till the end of May 1399, nearly four months after the death of his uncle.

He had to leave someone in charge, and the choice was an inevitable one:

> *And we create in absence of ourself*
> *Our uncle York Lord Governor of England,*
> —Act II, scene i, lines 219–20

Edmund of York, next to the King himself, was now the most exalted in the land, the only surviving son of Edward III. His word was most likely to carry weight by its sheer authority, least likely to be questioned.

But he was old, weak, and irresolute, and everyone knew it. If there were no emergency during Richard's absence, York would do. If there were a sudden burst of trouble, however, he would be helpless. It was something anyone ought to have been able to foresee, but Richard was too caught up in his own glory to suspect that anything might possibly go wrong.

. . . eight tall ships . . .

Richard leaves the stage now, but Henry of Northumberland remains behind, with two lesser noblemen, Ross and Willoughby. Northumberland is disturbed. He has, till now, been on Richard's side, but the act of sequestering the Lancastrian estate bothers him. He feels insecure and sounds out the others, who soon show themselves to be equally upset.

Undoubtedly, Richard's act had given Bolingbroke his opportunity, and the latter had seized upon it at once. Bolingbroke, disinherited as well as banished, and for no clear fault, was now wronged past endurance, and in his wrongs, many noblemen saw their own possible future if they did not act.

Bolingbroke entered into cautious (and treasonable, if he failed) diplomacy with various lords after John of Gaunt's death and came to an agreement with Northumberland. By the time Richard left for Ireland, negotiations were complete and the moment of opportunity had come, for the King was gone from the land and the Lord Governor he had left behind (Edmund of York) was a deputy of straw.

In the play it all seems to happen at once—John of Gaunt's death, the King's departure for Ireland, Bolingbroke's move. Actually, as I said, John of Gaunt died in February and the King departed in May. Bolingbroke made his move at the beginning of July 1399.

What Bolingbroke needed in the way of help was ships, for the sea lay between him and England. He did not want the ships from the French King directly since it would hurt his cause to seem to be an enemy agent. The solution to the dilemma is made plain at once, however, when Northumberland begins to reveal his secret to the clearly sympathetic Ross and Willoughby. He says:

> . . . I have from le Port Blanc, a bay
> In Brittaine [Brittany], received intelligence
>> —Act II, scene i, lines 277–78

Not hated France, but the Duke of Brittany would do the job.

In the days of King John, Brittany had been part of the Angevin Empire (see page II–210). But it had been Arthur of Brittany, the land's boy-duke, who had aspired to the English throne and who had been killed by John. Thereafter, John and his English forces were driven out of northern France and a new line of dukes, of French origins and sympathies, began to rule over Brittany. Bertrand du Guesclin, the French hero of the early decades of the Hundred Years' War, was a Breton.

Nevertheless, when the fortunes of war clearly turned against France, Brittany bethought itself and attempted to remain neutral in the struggle. This gave Brittany a rather favorable image as far as Englishmen were concerned. The Breton duke, John V, who held the duchy in 1399, displayed great friendship to Bolingbroke and was willing to lend him ships. These ships Bolingbroke could accept without compromising his cause.

Northumberland, then, after listing the men of note who accompany Bolingbroke, tells the others:

> All these well furnished by the Duke of Brittaine
> With eight tall ships, three thousand men of war,
> Are making hither with all due expedience,
>> —Act II, scene i, lines 285–87

. . . in post to Ravenspurgh

Bolingbroke is making for a northern port on England's east coast, where he can join with Northumberland and the other lords of the region and where Richard (in Ireland, which lies off England's west coast) would have most trouble to move an army to counter the invasion.

Northumberland urges his listeners to spur northward to meet the returning Bolingbroke:

> *Away with me in post* [haste] *to Ravenspurgh;*
> —Act II, scene i, line 296

Ravenspurgh, or Ravenspur, as it is usually spelled in gazetteers, is (or rather was) a town on the spit of land jutting out to sea north of the Humber. It no longer exists. Its site was swept away by the sea about a century after Bolingbroke's landing.

And thus, at the beginning of July 1399, only ten months after his sentence of exile, five months after his father's death, and perhaps six weeks after Richard had left for Ireland, Bolingbroke returned in arms to England.

. . . young Henry Percy

Shakespeare continues to compress time and make events follow one another rapidly. Richard has just left and already the Queen is bewailing his absence and giving voice to apprehensions which will not be calmed:

> *Some unborn sorrow ripe in Fortune's womb*
> *Is coming towards me . . .*
> —Act II, scene ii, lines 10–11

The Queen is Isabella of France, who at this point is, in actual historical fact, only ten years old. Shakespeare finds it necessary, however, for dramatic purposes, to have her speak and be addressed as a grown woman.

And no sooner does the Queen express her fears, when Green rushes in with the news of Bolingbroke's landing, following so hard after Richard's leaving (in the play, not in reality) that for a moment, Green hopes to catch the King before he has left.

It is too late. The King is gone and disaffected lords are already flocking to Bolingbroke's standard. Green lists them, including among others:

> *The Lord Northumberland, his son, young Henry Percy,*
> —Act II, scene ii, line 53

This is the first mention of Northumberland's son, who in the next play of the series is to be one of the chief characters.

Henry Percy was born in 1364, so that he was three years older than Bolingbroke. At this moment in history, when Bolingbroke was landing at Ravenspurgh, Henry Percy was thirty-five years old, which for those times was well into middle age. He could by no stretch of fancy be described, in actual fact, as "young Henry Percy."

But Shakespeare knew what he was doing. As he made the Queen older to make this scene and a couple of others more effective, so he made Henry Percy younger because he is destined yet to play an important role as a young fire-eater, with the accent on the youth.

(Henry Percy's father, Northumberland, is fifty-seven by the way, an old man only two years younger than "old John of Gaunt" and only one year older than "good old York." However, to keep the illusion of Henry Percy's youth, the old age of his father is never referred to in this play.)

Such was the precocity of life in those days that Henry Percy, at the time of Bolingbroke's landing, had already had twenty years experience as a warrior, for he had been taking active part in battle from the age of fourteen. He had for quite a while now been in charge of the border warfare with Scotland and was so keen at this task, so forward and aggressive, that he gained the nickname "Hotspur"—that is, someone who was all on fire to spur on his horse and charge the enemy. It is the nickname one would give a rash person with no control over his temper, and it is in that fashion that Shakespeare will picture Henry Percy in the next play. In this play his speeches are assigned to "Percy" and in the next to "Hotspur." The two are the same person, and for this play I will speak of "Henry Percy."

Henry Percy was at one point captured by the Scots and released only after the payment of a heavy ransom. Toward this ransom, King Richard contributed three thousand pounds, a huge sum in those days. Ordinarily, one might suppose that Percy owed the King considerable gratitude for this, quite apart from the usual call of allegiance of a subject to his king. However, gratitude was not a common motivating force in politics in those days, any more than it is nowadays, and Henry Percy joined his father at once—in favor of Bolingbroke and against Richard.

. . . the Earl of Worcester

The Queen demands to know why Northumberland and the rest have not been declared traitors. Green replies:

> We have: whereupon the Earl of Worcester
> Hath broken his staff, resigned his stewardship,
> And all the household servants fled with him
> To Bolingbroke.
>
> —Act II, scene ii, lines 58–61

This habit of calling people by their highest titles can be obscuring. The Earl of Worcester held the post of Lord Steward, the highest officer over the King's personal household, empowered by the staff of office he carried to give all commands. Why should he betray the King?

It becomes less mysterious when it is explained that the Earl of Worcester's actual name was Thomas Percy and that he was Northumberland's younger brother. Rather than name his brother and nephew traitors, he joined their company. (In actual fact, though, he did not break the staff till a month after Bolingbroke's landing, when the rebellion was clearly succeeding. Worcester was the last of the Percys to switch from Richard to Bolingbroke.)

. . . presently at Berkeley

Things continue to grow worse. The Duke of York, who is in charge of the kingdom, is totally incompetent to handle the situation. He is confused, despairing, and far too old to be vigorous (though he is actually only a year older than Northumberland).

York recognizes that the north is lost. All its nobility is flocking to Bolingbroke. The stand must be made in the west, where Bolingbroke might be held off until Richard returns with his forces from Ireland. York says, therefore:

> . . . Gentlemen, go muster up your men,
> And meet me presently at Berkeley.
> —Act II, scene ii, lines 117–18

The town of Berkeley is only ten miles from the border of Wales. Its castle, in which York plans to make his stand, is remarkably ill-omened, however. It was here, only seventy years before, that the King's great-grandfather, Edward II, was brutally murdered after his deposition.

. . . straight to Bristow Castle

The favorites now begin to disperse. Conditions look bad and they know well they will themselves be the first targets of the rebels. They must find some sort of safety at once. Green says:

> Well, I will for refuge straight to Bristow Castle.
> The Earl of Wiltshire is already there.
> —Act II, scene ii, lines 134–35

Bristow is an older name for Bristol, a city about twenty miles south of Berkeley and, at that time, the largest city in the west of England. If that does not hold, nothing will.

Bushy goes with Green, but Bagot finds even Bristol not safe enough. He will feel secure only in the royal presence. He says:

> . . . *I will to Ireland to his Majesty.*
>
> —Act II, scene ii, line 140

As a result he will live longer than the others.

From Ravenspurgh to Cotshall . . .

Clearly, everything hinges on Richard. If he returns quickly, if he takes speedy and firm action, then the mere fact that he is King may win for him. There is respect for the title and a dislike for the name of traitor. A king is divinely ordained and rebellion against him is not only a crime but a sin, and the medieval mind knew that well. However much the lords might hold out against Richard, the smallest indication of firm action on his part might cause defection among the ordinary soldiers serving under the rebels.

The rebelling lords therefore had to move quickly and win as much as possible as soon as possible. By the time Richard returned, the rebellion would have to be clearly victorious. They therefore raced southwestward while Richard was still in Ireland, and Edmund of York weakly tried to gather forces in the west.

Without meeting any resistance to speak of and with their forces strengthening, the rebels sped on, and Northumberland, who is with Bolingbroke, speaks of the distance they have marched.

> *But I bethink me what a weary way*
> *From Ravenspurgh to Cotshall . . .*
>
> —Act II, scene iii, lines 8–9

What Shakespeare refers to here as "Cotshall" are the Cotswold Hills, a low, rolling region that makes up much of Gloucestershire. The distance traversed from Ravenspurgh to reach Gloucester and the neighborhood of Berkeley, where Edmund of York is to be found, is 175 miles as the crow flies.

To be sure, Northumberland mentions the distance only to indulge in gross flattery, implying that Bolingbroke's pleasant conversation has made the long way short. He is feathering his nest, expecting Bolingbroke to be king and hoping to reap rich payment for his services.

. . . tender, raw, and young

Nor does Northumberland think of himself only. The to-be-king must be made to feel in debt to Northumberland's son and heir also. When that son, Henry Percy, arrives from reconnoitering Berkeley Castle, Northumberland introduces him to Bolingbroke, and Percy at once plays the necessary part, saying:

> *My gracious lord, I tender you my service,*
> *Such as it is, being tender, raw, and young,*
> *Which elder days shall ripen . . .*
> —Act II, scene iii, lines 41–43

The picture is of a teen-age stripling standing there, an untried fledgling, rather than a middle-aged veteran of two decades of ferocious fighting. That distortion will be extraordinarily useful in the next play in chronological sequence, which Shakespeare was to write two years later.

. . . that young Mars of men

Percy's report makes it clear that Edmund of York does not have the force to resist and the rebels can therefore move on boldly. On July 26, 1399, Bolingbroke's army lays siege to Berkeley Castle—less than a month after his landing at Ravenspurgh.

When Edmund of York appears, he can only bluster, wishing he were a younger man:

> *Were I but now the lord of such hot youth*
> *As when brave Gaunt, thy father, and myself*
> *Rescued the Black Prince, that young Mars of men,*
> *From forth the ranks of many thousand French,*
> —Act II, scene iii, lines 98–101

This is typical English bombast of Shakespearean times, with its implication that a few Englishmen are a match for large numbers of French. Actually, there is no record of John of Gaunt and Edmund of York ever rescuing the Black Prince in this fashion.

Bolingbroke speaks meekly to his uncle, insists he comes only for his lost revenues and title. He wants only what is his own. Those around him support him and York confesses he feels Bolingbroke was ill used in this respect and quickly talks himself into abandoning any attempt at resistance.

York declares himself a neutral, or tries to, but this is not quite enough for Bolingbroke, who wants this last surviving son of Edward III committed with all his prestige to the rebel cause. He insists that York accompany the rebel army to Bristol, where the favorites are, and to this York in the end must agree.

My lord of Salisbury . . .

But what of Richard II? Storms had kept ships from moving from England to Ireland (even the stars fought against Richard) and a crucial three weeks passed after Bolingbroke's landing before the news reached the King—three weeks in which the rebel forces had gathered and the march southwestward had taken place.

Once the news did arrive, Richard was overwhelmed. He had convinced himself of his own untouchability and he was not prepared for disillusionment. In fact, everything had been going wrong for him even before the news about Bolingbroke had reached him.

The rough Irish tribesmen were showing no signs of being overawed by the kingly majesty. Richard followed Mac Murrough into the bogs but never caught him. The King merely tired his own men while pursuing a phantom and was forced back into Dublin, quite conscious of having been made to look foolish. It left him in a deep depression and it was while in this state that the news of Bolingbroke's invasion reached him.

He sent one of his loyal followers, John Montacute, 3rd Earl of Salisbury (who was *not* a descendant of William Longsword, the "Salisbury" of *King John,* see page II–227), eastward across St. George's Channel into north Wales, there to raise an army. The King himself was supposed to follow soon, but he could not bring himself to stir. Where speed was essential if even a last hope was to be preserved, Richard lingered on eighteen fatal days more in Ireland. One wonders if he simply could not bring himself to face the facts.

The delay ruined everything. Salisbury had gathered a Welsh army, forty thousand strong, but where was news from Richard? In a case of such do-or-die emergency, the only logical reason for failure to hear from him was that he was dead—either killed in battle, drowned at sea, or perished of disease. The illogical reason—that he was just wasting time—occurred to no one.

So the Welsh Captain, who leads Salisbury's gathered army, says:

> *My Lord of Salisbury, we have stayed ten days,*
> *And hardly keep our countrymen together,*
> *And yet we hear no tidings from the King;*
> *Therefore we will disperse ourselves. Farewell.*
>
> —Act II, scene iv, lines 1–4

Salisbury pleads for further delay but is refused. The Welsh Captain explains that all sorts of unfavorable omens abound and the soldiers will not linger. (The English were fond of picturing the Welsh as terribly superstitious.)

. . . a royal bed

While Salisbury loses his army, the rebel forces have reached and taken Bristol. Bushy and Green are captured and led to their execution. To justify that execution, Bolingbroke accuses them of having misled and perverted King Richard. Among other things, Bolingbroke says:

> *You have in manner with your sinful hours*
> *Made a divorce betwixt his queen and him,*
> *Broke the possession of a royal bed,*
> —Act III, scene i, lines 11–13

There is a strong implication here of homosexuality between the King and the favorites. When a young king is close to young male favorites, such a scandal is always readily believed by some—and sometimes it is true.

There is the case of Edward II, father of Edward III and great-grandfather of Richard II. Edward II, like Richard II, was a weak and extravagant king. He too had favorites who were unpopular with the nobility. He too was rebelled against. In the case of Edward II, however, the connection with the favorites was definitely homosexual. His Queen was indeed neglected and resentful over the fact, and it was she, therefore, who was the heart and soul of the conspiracy that destroyed him.

Just three years before *Richard II* was written, another historical play, *Edward II* by Christopher Marlowe, had been produced. Perhaps Shakespeare could not resist adding this note of sexual scandal as a way of helping his own play compete with the earlier one.

If so, it is a false note. The supposedly mistreated Queen is only ten years old, remember, so there was scarcely a "royal bed" to dispute the possession of. Nor can the reference be turned back to Richard's first wife, Anne of Bohemia, with whom, all sources agree, Richard was deeply in love and by whom he was deeply beloved.

To fight with Glendower . . .

Bolingbroke sees to the execution of Bushy and Green and orders good treatment for Richard's Queen. There is next the Welsh army under Salisbury to consider, since Bolingbroke does not yet know that it has melted away. He says:

> *. . . Come, Lords, away*
> *To fight with Glendower and his complices;*
> —Act III, scene i, lines 42–43

Wales had maintained the Celtic resistance to first the Saxons and then the Normans for eight centuries. The last independent Prince of Wales was Llewelyn ab Gruffydd, who ruled north Wales in the time of Edward I. Edward warred against Llewelyn, forced him to submit, and annexed Wales to the English crown in 1277. (Thereafter the title "Prince of Wales" was routinely given to the oldest son of the English King. The first to receive this title was Edward I's young son, the future, and ill-fated, Edward II.)

There began a long series of attempts by the Welsh to regain their independence. Llewelyn himself revolted and was killed in 1282. That didn't end matters, however. The Welsh continued to wait for a rescuer, someone who would drive the hated English from the wild Welsh hills.

Such a one seemed to have been found in Owen Glendower, a Welshman who boasted a tenuous connection with the old princely line and who seemed to have a charismatic hold over his countrymen.

It is he who was probably the Welsh Captain who addressed Salisbury in the previous scene. Bolingbroke, in speaking of Salisbury's Welsh army, would naturally speak of fighting Glendower rather than Richard, for that would make his actions seem part of a patriotic national war rather than a treasonable civil one.

. . . the balm off from an anointed king

Finally, in August 1399, Richard comes to shore in northern Wales near where he conceives Salisbury's army to be encamped. He has been in Ireland for ten weeks. It was a fatal ten weeks. He had left England at what seemed the peak of his power, an absolute king no one dared gainsay; he returned to find himself with neither an army nor subjects.

From this point on Richard suffers an uninterrupted flow of disaster and humiliation, and his character changes. He is no longer the headstrong young King, displaying his absolutism stubbornly against all advice. He has become a poet, singing his way to death in some of the most melodious speeches Shakespeare ever wrote. Having deliberately lost Richard every shred of audience sympathy, Shakespeare now deliberately wins it back, until at the end, the audience is surely weeping for the same Richard they had been heartily angry with in the first half of the play.

To begin with, though, Richard still has his illusions. He still thinks the aura of kingship will win for him, that Bolingbroke's initial victories were possible only because the King was away from England. He says:

> Not all the water in the rough rude sea
> Can wash the balm off from an anointed king;
>
> —Act III, scene ii, lines 54–55

The anointing oil ("balm") used at the coronation was a symbol of the

divine grace that made him King and that could not be reversed by man—
he believes.

But quickly he begins to unbelieve as he learns the scope of the disaster. Salisbury appears, but without his army; that had broken up and dispersed the day before. The news arrives that Bristol is taken and Bushy, Green, and Wiltshire executed. And the Duke of York, Richard's last hope, is gone over to Bolingbroke too.

By as much as Richard had a false idea of his glory before, so now is he cast into useless despair. A more practical man might have weighed matters and done what he could with the hand he had been dealt. Richard might have fled overseas, hoping, like Bolingbroke, to get aid, and return. He did no such thing. He could think of no better action than to scurry off with Lord Aumerle and a few others about him to the doubtful security of the walls of Flint Castle nearby.

. . . the death of kings

Richard's despair is his undoing. Shakespeare depicts him as already anticipating the very worst even before he flees to Flint Castle. There is not only deposition but death in his mind, as he explains in a moving speech that includes the lines:

> *For God's sake let us sit upon the ground*
> *And tell sad stories of the death of kings:*
> —Act III, scene ii, lines 155–56

His despair may be realistic but it is not the act of a leader who must inspire faith and not require sympathy.

Furthermore, he lacks a realistic appraisal of the situation. With all his paeans to death, he avoids it and accepts humiliation in exchange for life. This is the last thing he should do. In a similar situation, Cleopatra (see page I-388) accepts death as a means of depriving Octavius Caesar of his greatest victory. Richard is in a better position than Cleopatra, for Richard is the legitimate King of England. Everyone admits that, even Bolingbroke. For Bolingbroke to succeed requires some very ticklish negotiation in which Richard himself must co-operate.

Richard, stronger and less despairing, might have defeated Bolingbroke by refusing to co-operate, if only by accepting the death he apparently longs for.

. . . Bolingbroke on both his knees . . .

If Richard does not truly understand the situation, Bolingbroke does.

Bolingbroke has discovered that the Welsh army is dispersed and that Richard is penned up in Flint Castle.

He takes his army there and surrounds the castle, but what next? If Bolingbroke wishes to be king, it is not enough to defeat Richard. He must get Richard alive, bring him to London, and carry through all the negotiations that would make Bolingbroke's own accession completely legal. If Richard dies resisting capture, or if he must be dragged to London by obvious force and refusing to co-operate in any way, Bolingbroke may still make himself king but most Englishmen would refuse to accept him as *legitimate* king. His reign would then be precarious and he would face revolt after revolt.

Bolingbroke tries hard, therefore, to allay Richard's fears and suspicions. He pictures himself as a suppliant only, returning to recover his own and nothing more. He sends Northumberland to carry a message to the walls of Flint Castle, telling him:

> . . . *thus deliver:*
> *Henry Bolingbroke*
> *On both his knees doth kiss King Richard's hand,*
> *And sends allegiance and true faith of heart*
> *To his most royal person; hither come*
> *Even at his feet to lay my arms and power,*
> *Provided that my banishment repealed,*
> *And lands restored again be freely granted;*
>
> —Act III, scene iii, lines 33–40

Northumberland delivers the message and Richard, in utter humiliation, grants the request. The banishment is lifted, the Lancastrian estates restored; and now Bolingbroke is Henry of Lancaster.

To be sure, Richard knows what a strong king would have done (supposing a strong king would have allowed himself to get into Richard's situation). Richard says to Aumerle after having given in:

> *Shall we call back Northumberland, and send*
> *Defiance to the traitor and so die?*
>
> —Act III, scene iii, lines 128–29

Aumerle councils against that, urging Richard to play for time. It is useless advice.

Richard takes the advice, but if he cannot bring himself to risk and accept death rather than humiliation, he nevertheless pampers himself with all the joys of self-pity. He says he will change his kingdom:

> . . . *for a little grave*
> *A little, little grave, an obscure grave;*

Or I'll be buried in the King's highway,
Some way of common trade, where subjects' feet
May hourly trample on their sovereign's head;
For on my heart they tread now whilst I live,
—Act III, scene iii, lines 152–57

There is something infinitely non-heroic about this speech by a King who had so short a while before been so absolute. Yet Aumerle weeps at it and surely so must the audience.

And yet if all Richard wants is a grave, why did he not accept one and defeat his enemy in the act?

. . . glist'ring Phaethon

But Bolingbroke cannot be sure Richard will not resist and deliberately invite death. As long as Richard is up there on the castle walls, Bolingbroke is not entirely safe. Richard must be in his hands, surrounded by his armed men, his life guarded and kept safe; for Richard, alive, well, and unharmed, will be needed in London if Bolingbroke is to become king in fact as well as in name.

Northumberland therefore returns with a new request. Would Richard come down to the courtyard so that Bolingbroke can speak to him face to face?

It seems so small and reasonable a request, but actually it is a call for complete surrender. Richard has his last free choice and makes it. He surrenders and descends, saying:

Down, down I come, like glist'ring Phaethon,
Wanting the manage of unruly jades.
—Act III, scene iii, lines 177–78

The figure is perfect! Phaethon, in the Greek myths, was the son of Helios, the sun god. Laughed at by his friends for claiming this relationship, Phaethon played on Helios' paternal fondness and obtained permission to take in charge the golden chariot of the sun and drive its divine horses over their daily course.

The steeds, however, missing the firm, familiar control of Helios, went wild. The sun moved out of its course, swooping toward the earth, burning a broad swath across Africa and permanently darkening its natives. (In this fashion, the Greek mythmakers accounted for the Sahara Desert and for Black pigmentation.) Finally, to prevent the earth generally from being destroyed, Jupiter loosed his thunderbolt, struck Phaethon, and hurled him, dying, down to earth.

And so it was with Richard. He was the son of the Black Prince and

the grandson of Edward III, both of whom were dominating personalities
who controlled the English aristocracy in their lifetimes. Richard, however,
when he was put in control of the golden chariot of the English throne,
could not, in the end, manage the "unruly jades" who were the aristocracy,
and with Bolingbroke administering the lightning bolt, down, down he
came, like glist'ring Phaethon.

Richard is quite aware he has surrendered. He knows what is coming
next too. He says:

> For do we must what force will have us do.
> Set on towards London, cousin, is it so?
> —Act III, scene iii, lines 205–6

. . . the balance of great Bolingbroke

At London, Richard is to be tried before Parliament and there is no
doubt as to how that trial will go.

The Queen, who is in honorable detention at the Duke of York's palace,
hears the very gardeners discussing the matter, and they are certain that
Richard faces doom. She challenges them angrily, refusing to believe this
possible, and says:

> Thou, old Adam's likeness, set to dress this garden,
> How dares thy harsh rude tongue sound this unpleasing news?
> —Act III, scene iv, lines 73–74

A gardener is a man of Adam's original profession, of course, since
"the Lord God took the man [Adam] and put him into the garden of
Eden to dress it and to keep it" (Genesis 2:15).

The gardener answers her with a careful explanation of the facts of
power politics:

> King Richard he is in the mighty hold
> Of Bolingbroke. Their fortunes both are weighed:
> In your lord's scale is nothing but himself
> And some few vanities that make him light;
> But in the balance of great Bolingbroke
> Besides himself are all the English peers,
> And with that odds he weighs King Richard down.
> —Act III, scene iv, lines 83–89

The Queen can do nothing but resolve to hasten to London, there to
see the King perhaps.

As far as Callice . . .

In London, Parliament has been called into action on September 13, 1399 (just four days short of the anniversary of the non-duel between Bolingbroke and Mowbray). It was called in the name of Richard II—who was still legally King and was treated so.

The trial begins with the probing of the dire event that has set Richard's downfall into motion—the murder of Thomas of Woodstock, Duke of Gloucester.

Bagot, the last remaining member of Richard's coterie of favorites, is questioned, and he puts the blame squarely on Aumerle. Speaking to him, he says:

> *I heard you say, "Is not my arm of length,*
> *That reacheth from the restful English court*
> *As far as Callice to mine uncle's head?"*
> —Act IV, scene i, lines 11–13

Bagot is accusing Aumerle of having gloried in giving the order, at court, that sent couriers speeding to Callice (Calais) to direct Mowbray to have Thomas of Gloucester murdered.

Calais, after having been taken by Edward III in 1347, remained continually in English hands throughout the Hundred Years' War, serving always as an armed camp, easily supplied across a narrow stretch of sea. From it English raiding parties could swoop into France at will.

Even after the end of the Hundred Years' War, when France was almost completely cleared of English forces, Calais was the exception. England maintained its hold on that nearest scrap of its onetime broad conquests.

It was not until 1558, when Queen Mary I led England into a foolish war on behalf of her husband, King Philip II of Spain, that Calais was lost by the English. The humiliation of that loss of the final bit of French territory was such that Queen Mary mourned, "When I die, Calais shall be found written on my heart."

. . . banished Norfolk . . .

There follows a scene of bombastic charge and countercharge. Aumerle denies having ordered Gloucester's death. Others accuse him; some defend him. The practical Bolingbroke suggests that the matter be settled by recalling Thomas Mowbray, Duke of Norfolk, who had been Gloucester's jailer and with whom Bolingbroke himself had nearly fought over this very matter a year before.

The Bishop of Carlisle, however, one of the few left with the courage to support Richard openly, announces it is too late to recall Mowbray:

> *Many a time hath banished Norfolk fought*
> *For Jesu Christ in glorious Christian field,*
> *Streaming the ensign of the Christian cross*
> *Against black pagans, Turks, and Saracens;*
> *And, toiled with works of war, retired himself*
> *To Italy, and there at Venice gave*
> *His body to that pleasant country's earth,*

> —Act IV, scene i, lines 92–98

Mowbray did, upon his banishment, make a pilgrimage to the Holy Land. The picture of him as another Lion-Heart fighting the Saracens is, however, sheer romance. The Crusades had been over for a full century, and there were no Christian armies fighting in the Holy Land and would not be for over five centuries more.

After his pilgrimage, Mowbray retired to Venice and died there on September 22, 1399, nine days after the opening of the Parliament. His lifelong banishment had lasted just one year, and Bolingbroke was left the last surviving of all the lords appellant.

. . . good old Abraham

There is nothing, of course, that may so safely be honored as a dead adversary, and Bolingbroke, who did his best to disgrace and kill Mowbray while the latter was alive, can now afford to make an impressive show of being affected. He says of his dead enemy:

> *Sweet peace conduct his sweet soul to the bosom*
> *Of good old Abraham.*

> —Act IV, scene i, lines 103–4

The expression "Abraham's bosom" dates back to the ancient Greek custom of eating with the right hand while reclining on the left elbow. An honored guest would sit at the right of the host, and when the guest reclined leftward, his head would be near the host's chest. His head was, so to speak, in the bosom of his host. To be "in the host's bosom" was, therefore, to be in the place of honor.

In the Gospel of St. Luke, there is the parable of the rich man and the beggar Lazarus. After both died, the rich man was taken off to hell while the beggar went to heaven. Or as Luke tells it, adopting the Greek idiom (for he himself was, in all likelihood, a Greek and not a Jew), "the beggar died, and was carried by the angels into Abraham's bosom" (Luke 16:22).

The picture, properly conceived, is that of Lazarus the beggar becoming an honored guest in heaven, and of sitting on the right hand of Abraham himself at the heavenly banquets.

In societies which did not eat reclining, "Abraham's bosom" did not have this clear significance. Rather, it became synonymous with heaven—as it is here.

. . . Henry, fourth of that name

The dispute over Thomas of Gloucester (which, in actual history, stretched over days of debate) did its work. Bolingbroke wasn't interested in actually establishing the guilt, jury-fashion, or having Aumerle (his cousin, and the only son of the only living son of Edward III) executed. It was enough to stir up the mud so as to spatter Richard with strong suspicion of that dark crime. Richard was sufficiently blackened to make his deposition possible.

Richard himself must have thought so. Conscious of his own guilt and unbearably pressed by those who imprisoned him, he finally agreed to surrender the crown and accept Bolingbroke as heir.

Edmund of York brings the news and advises Bolingbroke to:

> Ascend his throne, descending now from him,
> And long live Henry, fourth of that name!
> —Act IV, scene i, lines 111–12

Eagerly, Bolingbroke accepts the crown, and from this point on he might be termed "Henry IV." Throughout the rest of the play, however, his speeches are still attributed to Bolingbroke.

The blood of English . . .

There is not, however, universal acclamation of this. One man, the Bishop of Carlisle, is still brave enough to speak. Boldly, he denounces the parliamentary procedures as illegal, since subjects were passing judgment on their King with the King not even present, thus denying him the legal rights of any common criminal.

So much is historical, but Shakespeare adds to it by putting a hindsight prophecy into Carlisle's mouth. Carlisle says:

> My Lord of Hereford here, whom you call king,
> Is a foul traitor to proud Hereford's king;
> And if you crown him, let me prophesy

The blood of English shall manure the ground,
And future ages groan for this foul act;

— Act IV, scene i, lines 134–38

He was right, of course. Hindsight prophecies always are.

Richard's deposition, despite all Bolingbroke's painstaking legalisms, was *still* an intolerable blow at legitimacy. Once Bolingbroke was made King by act of Parliament instead of by act of God through line of birth, it did not take long for even the dullest-witted lord to see that almost anyone else could be made king in that same way. There began, therefore, a full century of striving for a throne that could so easily be seized, and the blood of English *did* manure the ground.

My Lord of Westminster . . .

The Bishop of Carlisle is arrested for his bold statement. Northumberland says:

Of capital treason we arrest you here.
My Lord of Westminster, be it your charge
To keep him safely till his day of trial.

— Act IV, scene i, lines 151–53

"My Lord of Westminster" is the abbot of Westminster Abbey. The Abbey is the most famous of all English churches. It is near the Houses of Parliament and English monarchs are crowned there. Many monarchs as well as many of their famous subjects are buried there too.

. . . proceed without suspicion

Yet Bolingbroke's cautious soul is stirred by Carlisle's speech. He knows that the consent of Parliament is a shifty sort of thing to base the kingship on and that men could easily claim afterward that there had been trickery involved.

It was not enough to say that Richard had agreed to hand over the crown. He must stand before Parliament in person, and with his own hand and tongue, in the full sight and hearing of everyone, do so. Bolingbroke says:

Fetch hither Richard, that in common view
He may surrender; so we shall proceed
Without suspicion.

— Act IV, scene i, lines 155–57

Richard comes and meekly does as he is asked to do. In beautiful lines, he yields the crown and gives it to Bolingbroke. He even finally learns the truth about himself. No more does he dream of a kingly aura; no more does he imagine there is some unwashable balm that bathes him. In fact, he says:

> With mine own tears I wash away my balm,
> > —Act IV, scene i, line 206

So Judas did . . .

And yet has Richard *really* given up, or, deprived of everything, is he trying to lead from weakness? Whatever he has done he has clearly done under duress, and all can be disavowed. What he needs are backers, and how many of those who now stand there watching him stripped of royalty might be induced to change sides—out of pity or out of fear or out of both?

Is there perhaps some lingering nervousness about treating a legitimate king so? If Richard is King by grace of God, then is there not a blasphemy in the attempt to undo what God has done?

Even as Richard is in the process of giving up his crown, he tries to activate just this fear by making the comparison with another trial nearly fourteen centuries before. He points out that those who now turn pitilessly on him once honored and flattered him. He says:

> Did they not sometime cry "All hail" to me?
> So Judas did to Christ: but he in twelve
> Found truth in all but one; I in twelve thousand, none.
> > —Act IV, scene i, lines 169–71

The reference is to the moment when Judas betrayed Jesus to the authorities and did so while still pretending to be a loyal disciple. "And forthwith he [Judas] came to Jesus, and said Hail, master, and kissed him" (Matthew 26:49). It was with that "Judas kiss" that he identified the one who was to be arrested, and Richard implies a similar treason, but more widespread, in his own case.

He attempts to cast fear into the hearts of those who might be watching and telling themselves that they are taking no active part and are therefore innocent. He says:

> . . . some of you, with Pilate, wash your hands,
> Showing an outward pity: yet you Pilates
> Have here delivered me to my sour cross,
> And water cannot wash away your sin.
> > —Act IV, scene i, lines 238–41

Pontius Pilate, the Roman procurator of Judea, when forced to condemn Jesus, regretted the judgment (according to Matthew) and attempted to evade responsibility: "he [Pilate] took water, and washed his hands before the multitude, saying, I am innocent of the blood of this just person" (Matthew 27:29). It did not help Pilate; he went down in history with infamy on his name.

. . . worthily deposed

Bolingbroke is not so blind that he does not see the danger. It must not be made to appear that Richard is being forcibly stripped of his crown simply because Bolingbroke is ambitious. It must be clear to the nation that Richard has forfeited the crown, and that Bolingbroke has become King simply because, as next in line, he has a duty to step into the empty throne. But how can Richard have forfeited the crown? Why—by having committed a series of crimes that have made him unworthy to be God's anointed?

And to prove that that is so, he must openly confess to those crimes.

Thus, when Richard has given up the crown and asks if there is more he must do, Northumberland says:

> No more, but that you read
> These accusations, and these grievous crimes,
> Committed by your person and your followers,
> Against the state and profit of this land:
> That by confessing them, the souls of men
> May deem that you are worthily deposed.
>
> —Act IV, scene i, lines 221–26

And here, at last, Richard balks. Up to this point, everything that has been done can be undone. If he confesses to the crimes listed on the paper, he will be beyond the point of no return.

As Richard tries to avoid that ultimate loss, Northumberland twists and turns with him, presenting the paper again, and yet again, with an increasingly impatient "My lord—."

To which the King, or ex-King now, in the agony of knowledge that he is no longer lord, cries out in a phrase that has, ever since the play was produced, characterized the historical Northumberland in the minds of man:

> No lord of thine, thou haught, insulting man,
>
> —Act IV, scene i, line 253

Finally, Bolingbroke himself can stand it no more and orders Northumberland to desist, whereupon Northumberland says bluntly:

The Commons will not then be satisfied.
            —Act IV, scene i, line 271

But Richard gets away with it. Out of the total disaster, he has salvaged one crumb; he has refused to admit to any wrongdoing, and Bolingbroke's title to the throne is therefore flawed. This does Richard no personal good in the end, but it helps make Bolingbroke's reign a laborious time of civil conflict, and perhaps Richard would consider that better than nothing if he could know.

In any case, Bolingbroke could wait no longer. The parliamentary sessions designed to make the transfer of power completely legal had lasted two and a half weeks, in actuality, and that was enough.

. . . to the Tower

Bolingbroke ends the proceedings by ordering Richard led away. He says:

> *Go some of you, convey him to the Tower.*
>   —Act IV, scene i, line 316

The Tower of London was a royal residence (remaining so right down through Shakespeare's time). It housed many of the governmental functions, such as the mint and the archives—even the royal menagerie at times. It was also used to imprison men of rank. This is not surprising, for there were no prisons in the modern sense in medieval England and few places where anyone could be kept in reasonable security from attempts at rescue other than within the fortress-castles themselves.

Our coronation . . .

And with Richard gone, Bolingbroke says:

> *On Wednesday next we solemnly set down*
> *Our coronation . . .*
>   —Act IV, scene i, line 318

The deposition of Richard II took place on September 30, 1399. Richard had reigned for twenty-two years, most of that time without power. This deposition in September came two years and nine days after the September death of Thomas of Gloucester and one year and twelve days after the September non-duel between Bolingbroke and Mowbray.

. . . a merry day

Richard did not entirely miscalculate. The plotting against the new King began at once—in a matter of weeks at the most. Shakespeare, with his dramatic time compression, has it begin at the instant of deposition.

There remains Aumerle, for instance, who even now is loyal to Richard. He and the Bishop of Carlisle, and others too, are ready to take extreme action to restore Richard. In this they are joined by the Abbot of Westminster.

The Abbot says, cautiously:

> *Come home with me to supper: I will lay*
> *A plot shall show us all a merry day.*
>
> —Act IV, scene i, lines 333–34

. . . Julius Caesar's ill-erected Tower

Richard's Queen, having come to London, waits grief-stricken, hoping to see him on his way to detention. She says:

> *This way the King will come, this is the way*
> *To Julius Caesar's ill-erected Tower,*
>
> —Act V, scene i, lines 1–2

The Tower of London, the most famous non-ecclesiastical building in England, was not, despite legend, first built by Julius Caesar. Caesar's two raids into England in 55 and 54 B.C. were merely raids (see page II-62), and he left little behind but a memory.

Julius Caesar was, however, one of the most renowned men in history and England was proud of the connection, even if it was only to memorialize and magnify the defeat.

The oldest portions of the Tower were actually begun after another and even more significant conquest. When William, Duke of Normandy, took England in 1066 and became "William the Conqueror," he began at once to construct a fortification just outside London, a place where a Norman garrison might be stationed to overawe the city in case it had any notion of rebelling. This fortification grew into the Tower.

Despite the Queen's reference to the "ill-erected Tower"—that is, to a tower erected for ill purposes—it had not yet gained the dreadful reputation in Richard II's time that it was to have by Shakespeare's own time, and in that sense the remark is an anachronism. It was only a century after the time of this play that kings and queens began to die in the Tower.

You must to Pomfret . . .

But even the Tower of London is not enough; it is too close to the center of things. Bolingbroke is too much the realist not to expect conspiracies, so Richard must be removed, taken farther away, pushed toward the horizon, where he might possibly fall from the minds of men. Consequently the emotional leave-taking of Richard and his Queen, when they meet on the road to the Tower, is interrupted by the arrival of the ex-King's nemesis, Northumberland.

That rough man says:

> *My lord, the mind of Bolingbroke is changed:*
> *You must to Pomfret, not unto the Tower.*
>   —Act V, scene i, lines 51–52

Pomfret, or Pontefract (see page II-244), had a castle that was almost as old as the Tower of London, for it was begun in 1069, three years after the Conquest, by a Norman knight named Ilbert de Lacy. (In those years, the Normans put up their frowning castles all over England as a way of holding down the countryside, a tactic that worked admirably well from their standpoint.)

Angrily, Richard makes a hindsight prophecy, predicting that Northumberland and Bolingbroke, united against him now, will yet fall out:

> *. . . Thou shalt think*
> *Though he divide the realm and give thee half,*
> *It is too little, helping him to all;*
> *He shall think that thou which knowest the way*
> *To plant unrightful kings, wilt know again,*
> *Being ne'er so little urged another way,*
> *To pluck him headlong from the usurped throne.*
>   —Act V, scene i, lines 59–65

Of course, that is what does happen, and an astute observer can see that it is inevitable. We might even suppose that Richard at this point in the play can hope that it will happen soon and that in the course of that falling out, he may yet retrieve his throne.

In actual historical fact, Richard did not leave for Pomfret immediately after the deposition. He remained in the Tower for nearly a month, leaving for Pomfret on October 28, 1399.

As for Isabella, Richard's Queen, she remained in England two years more, returning to France in 1401. She had spent five years in England, and was still only twelve years old on her return to France. But she was also still the daughter of the King of France. She married again, to Charles of Orléans, Count of Angoulême, and died in 1409 at the age of twenty.

. . . call him Rutland . . .

The scene shifts now to the palace of Edmund of York, who is telling, with a wealth of sad emotion, how Richard and Bolingbroke arrived in London, the former to disgrace, the latter to acclaim.

This involves an anachronism. The Duchess of York, Isabella of Castile, had died in 1393, five years before the deposition. Insofar as she plays a part in this last act, she is strictly Shakespeare's invention.

In comes Aumerle, and his mother greets him by that name. York says stiffly:

> . . . Aumerle that was,
> But that is lost for being Richard's friend;
> And, madam, you must call him Rutland now.
> I am in Parliament pledge for his truth
> And lasting fealty to the new-made king.
>
> —Act V, scene ii, lines 41–45

Aumerle had been promoted to his dukedom after the death of Gloucester. That has now been stripped from him and he is back to his earlier title of Rutland, a mere earldom. The speeches he is given in this last act are, however, still attributed to "Aumerle."

Aumerle's demotion was, on the whole, a light punishment, and might have been more severe if Bolingbroke were not endeavoring to make as few enemies as possible in the course of the difficult transition period.

Yet a second offense could scarcely be expected to win equally light punishment, and York quickly discovers that Aumerle/Rutland is involved in a conspiracy being set up by the Abbot of Westminster and that it plans on nothing less than the assassination of the new King. (This discovery, in actual fact, took place in January 1400, about three months after Richard's deposition.)

The seriousness of the situation is plain to Edmund of York, since he is the guarantor of his son's loyalty and will therefore be himself considered equally guilty. Hastily, he gets ready to spur to Bolingbroke to warn him of the plot and clear himself. The distracted Duchess, who can think only of her son and not of plots, urges Rutland to make all haste to Bolingbroke in order to confess and be forgiven before he can be accused. The two men leave on a mad race to the court, with the Duchess planning to hasten there herself.

. . . my unthrifty son

Meanwhile, at court, where everyone is getting ready for a grand tournament and celebration at Oxford in honor of the new reign (a celebration which was to be the occasion on which the conspirators planned to kidnap and assassinate Bolingbroke), the new King is worried over something quite other than conspiracies:

> *Can no man tell me of my unthrifty son?*
> *'Tis full three months since I did see him last,*
> *If any plague hang over us, 'tis he.*
> —Act V, scene iii, lines 1–3

Bitterly, Bolingbroke states that his son is a habitué of taverns and consults with loose and lowborn companions.

Henry's "unthrifty son" is another Henry, born in the castle at Monmouth (on the border of southeastern Wales) on September 16, 1387. Mary de Bohun was his mother and Eleanor de Bohun, Duchess of Gloucester (see page II–264), was both his aunt and great-aunt.

When Bolingbroke was exiled in 1398, young Henry of Monmouth remained in England, in Richard's own care. By all reports, Richard treated him well. The boy was even knighted on the occasion of the ill-fated expedition into Ireland.

In October 1399, mere weeks after Bolingbroke had become King, young Henry was created Prince of Wales. Bolingbroke was anxious, after all, to establish not merely himself on the throne, but his line as well, and by making the young boy Prince of Wales, he was establishing him as heir to the throne.

In January 1400 the Prince of Wales was only a little over twelve years old. He could scarcely be a very great habitué of taverns or a very effective consort of thieves and highwaymen.

Shakespeare is here indulging, however, in a dramatic irony that would be well appreciated by every man in the audience. Henry of Monmouth, as they would all know, was fated to become Henry V, England's most heroic king, its most perfect throned knight, the victor of her most fortunate battle, and the monarch ideal of English history. This is the person over whom Bolingbroke's concern hovers.

Henry of Monmouth was apparently a rather gay young man as Prince of Wales (and why not?), and later legend exaggerated this youthful ebullience into a kind of dissolute recklessness in order to make more wonderful and glorious the sudden conversion of a wastrel princeling into a knightly king. Shakespeare makes full use of this tale, and expounds it in the next three plays of this series.

He lays the groundwork now, making the prince older than he really is, as earlier he had made Henry Percy considerably younger than he really was, in order that, by making the two of an age, he could prepare a dramatic contrast.

. . . unto the stews

Indeed, it is none other than Henry Percy who now tells the King that he has seen the Prince and told him of the coming celebration at Oxford. When Bolingbroke asks what the Prince answered, Percy says:

> His answer was, he would unto the stews,
> And from the commonest creature pluck a glove,
> And wear it as a favor . . .

—Act V, scene iii, lines 16–18

One can scarcely think of a sharper gesture of contempt than to fight under the banner of a common prostitute (a "stews" is a brothel), for it mocked the rules of courtly love that held a true knight should fight for an idealized lady.

We might speculate as to why the young Prince is pictured as so contemptuous of a celebration in honor of his own father's accession to the throne, an accession that probably would (and eventually did) bring the Prince to the throne in turn.

The hostility between King and Prince, which shows itself here, and which is carried on in the next two plays, may be only the natural unfriendliness between a man in high position and his destined successor. After all, the successor waits for promotion through death, and every king must wonder what his heir is thinking and whether the princely ears might not prick up at every kingly cough. It is almost traditional in English history, particularly, that the King and the Prince of Wales be enemies.

But is there anything in this particular case of Henry Bolingbroke and Henry of Monmouth that goes beyond the stock rivalry of the monarch and his heir?

Could it be that the young Prince had loved Richard, who undeniably had charm and who had been good to the boy? Perhaps the Prince was distressed at Richard's deposition and imprisonment. Bolingbroke says he hasn't seen his son for three months. That period of time might have been plucked out of thin air by Shakespeare, but it does represent, even if only by coincidence, the time lapse since Richard's deposition.

The Prince may never have recovered from the manner in which his father had achieved the throne, may never have learned to value his own title, since he considered it tainted. There is nothing specifically to indicate this except, possibly, for one significant speech three plays later, but it is an interesting possibility.

In this passage, concerning the Prince of Wales and the stews, Shakespeare sets up the first contrast between that young rake and Henry Percy; a contrast he will use with considerable effect in the next play.

It is Henry Percy, gallant, eager after honor, a budding warrior, who accosts Henry of Wales. And it is Henry of Wales who gives this flip, disgraceful, and even disgusting reply. But it will all come out right in the end.

. . . strong and bold conspiracy

But now in comes Aumerle/Rutland, breathless, eager to confess his crime, demanding forgiveness for something intended but not yet committed. Following fast comes Edmund of York furiously demanding death for his treasonable son. And after him comes the Duchess, pleading for life for that same son. All three surround Bolingbroke.

To us, today, Edmund of York's wild attempts to ensure the death of his only son and heir seem disgusting, especially in a man who, till then, had been so weak, and who had betrayed his own king.

However, in the medieval code, loyalty to one's liege was the supreme secular virtue and the equivalent of modern loyalty to the nation. I presume we would react differently to a modern play in which a father accuses his son and sacrifices him to justice where that son is preparing to betray the United States to a wartime enemy.

In the end, Aumerle is forgiven once more, but the fact of the conspiracy disturbs Bolingbroke. He bursts out:

> *O heinous, strong and bold conspiracy!*
> —Act V, scene iii, line 58

What to do? The conspiracy aimed at the reinstatement of Richard. Although far away at Pomfret Castle, Richard still served as the center of disaffection and would serve as the center of more, even if this one were aborted and if Richard himself did nothing.

It would be best if Richard were to die, but would he be so obliging as to do so? Of course, Richard might be quietly killed, but if that were to happen, Bolingbroke would be handing a propaganda weapon to his enemies, the same one that Richard handed out in the killing of Thomas of Gloucester, or John had in the killing of Arthur of Brittany. What, then, to do?

Have I no friend . . .

There is a tradition that Bolingbroke made use of a device reported on several occasions in history. That is, he was supposed to have made some ruminating remark in a moment of passion where men could overhear, in the hope that they would act on that remark. They could then be disowned when they had done their work.

Such a remark is reported to have been made at table by Bolingbroke, according to Holinshed, and Shakespeare follows that report. One of the King's attendants, Sir Pierce Exton (who does not appear in the play before this point) overhears it and, coming onstage, immediately upon the conclusion of the scene with Rutland and his parents, says to a friend:

> Didst thou not mark the King, what words he spake?
> "Have I no friend will rid me of this living fear?"
>
> —Act V, scene iv, lines 1–2

Exton is sure that Bolingbroke was referring to Richard II and that the friend who rid him of the ex-King would greatly profit by the deed. Off he hastens, then, to Pomfret Castle with a band of hired killers.

Actually, there is no real evidence in favor of this. There is only Holinshed's weak statement that "One writer, which seemeth to have great knowledge of King Richard's doings, saith that . . ."

The remark of Bolingbroke, "Have I no friend will rid me of this living fear?" could well have been borrowed from the well-known tale concerning the earlier king, Henry II (see page II–205). In 1170 he had made such a remark in connection with his bitter enemy, Thomas Becket, Archbishop of Canterbury, who was then slain in his own cathedral by four of the King's knights.

Taste of it first . . .

The real cause of Richard's death remains a mystery. He may have been killed, of course, at Bolingbroke's orders, but one good possibility is that he died of starvation. He may have been deliberately starved (that leaves no marks for suspicious eyes searching for evidence of murder and can be represented as a wasting illness) or perhaps he starved himself, either out of a desire to avoid lingering out a life of imprisonment or out of a morbid fear of poison.

There is an indication of this last in the scene in Pomfret Castle that follows, a scene that is Richard's last appearance in the play. The keeper brings Richard a meal and Richard says:

> Taste of it first, as thou art wont to do.
>
> —Act V, scene v, line 99

But the meal goes uneaten. In Shakespeare's version, it is now that Exton and his crew break in and Richard is killed. This takes place at the beginning of February 1400, some four months after Richard's deposition.

Our town of Ciceter . . .

Meanwhile, the conspirators, finding that Aumerle does not join them, suspect they have been betrayed. They abandon their attempt to kidnap Bolingbroke and in desperation (for they will surely be executed if caught, for the intention alone) gather their men for a fight.

They fall back to the west, where half a year before the earlier forces loyal to Richard had tried to make their stand, and a battle develops.

None of this is described in the play, but immediately after Richard's death, the scene shifts back to Windsor Castle and Bolingbroke reports the progress of that battle. He says:

> . . . *the latest news we hear*
> *Is that the rebels have consumed with fire*
> *Our town of Ciceter in Gloucestershire,*
> —Act V, scene vi, lines 1–3

Ciceter is the slurred form of Cirencester, a town twenty miles east of Berkeley, where Edmund of York had once tried to resist Bolingbroke.

Northumberland, however, quickly arrives with the news that the rebels have been defeated and their military leaders executed. This includes the Earl of Salisbury, who the previous summer had tried to hold the Welsh army together for Richard. The Abbot of Westminster also dies, but the Bishop of Carlisle is merely ordered into seclusion (though he died soon after).

. . . a voyage to the Holy Land

Now that the last armed partisans of Richard are dead, there is only Richard himself, and his role is finished too, for Exton brings in the coffin containing the dead ex-King. (The body must be viewed, else there will be no way of preventing imposters from claiming they are the supposedly dead King and being followed by many loyal but misled men. It has happened many times in history both before and after the time of Richard II.)

Thus is Bolingbroke's triumph and Richard's fall complete, and yet there remains one thing to be done. It must not appear that Bolingbroke desired the death, or Richard might still win in the very act of dying.

Bolingbroke therefore turns on Exton in execration, and when the murderer protests that he but took the King at his word, Bolingbroke says:

> *They love not poison that do poison need,*
> *Nor do I thee . . .*
> —Act V, scene vi, lines 38–39

This Machiavellian doctrine may be well understood by the men of the court, learned in power politics, but there are the common people, to whom the murder of a king, even a deposed king, is a horrible crime.

Guilty or innocent, then, Bolingbroke must do penance. He must make a show of grief, of having loved the ex-King. He must bury him with full honor, and then do even more, for he says:

> *I'll make a voyage to the Holy Land,*
> *To wash this blood off from my guilty hand,*
> —Act V, scene vi, lines 49–50

He never does this, partly because he never has the opportunity. The guilt he has incurred and his uncertain claim to the crown keep him facing further conspiracies.

But this final reference to the Holy Land fits in with another reference to the Holy Land with which the next play, *Henry IV, Part One,* begins, so that the two melt together with scarcely a seam.

32

The History of

HENRY IV, PART ONE

IN 1597, two years after *Richard II* had been presented, *Henry IV, Part One* was written. Its action follows almost immediately upon that of the former play. *Richard II* closed with the death of Richard II (see page II–312) in February 1400. *Henry IV, Part One* opens a little over two years later, in June 1402, in the King's palace in London.

The King is Henry IV, who in *Richard II* was Henry of Bolingbroke, Duke of Hereford, and later (after the death of his father, John of Gaunt) the Duke of Lancaster. In the previous play, his speeches were labeled "Bolingbroke." Now they are labeled "King."

In *Richard II*, Bolingbroke was pictured as a young man, dominating and forceful. Now he is pictured as an old man, tired and worn. Actually, he was still only thirty-six years old when the play opens, but this is actually middle age by medieval standards.

In addition, Henry IV suffered some chronic disease through most of his reign. This grew gradually worse and made him seem older than he was. The disease involved skin lesions as its most notable symptom and many at the time considered it to be leprosy striking him in divine punishment for his crime of taking the throne from the legitimate king, Richard II. It seems very doubtful that this was so, however, and some suggest syphilis instead, though at this time that disease had not yet become prominent in Europe. It may have been something as common and as undramatic as psoriasis.

But even if Henry IV were in complete health, he might well have sunk under the cares of state, for during much of his reign he was occupied with the suppression of revolt, and of wars with the Welsh and Scots, who seized on the confusion of civil war among the English to advance their own national ambitions.

. . . to the sepulcher of Christ

Henry strikes the theme of his reign in the first line of the play:

So shaken we are, so wan with care,

—Act I, scene i, line 1

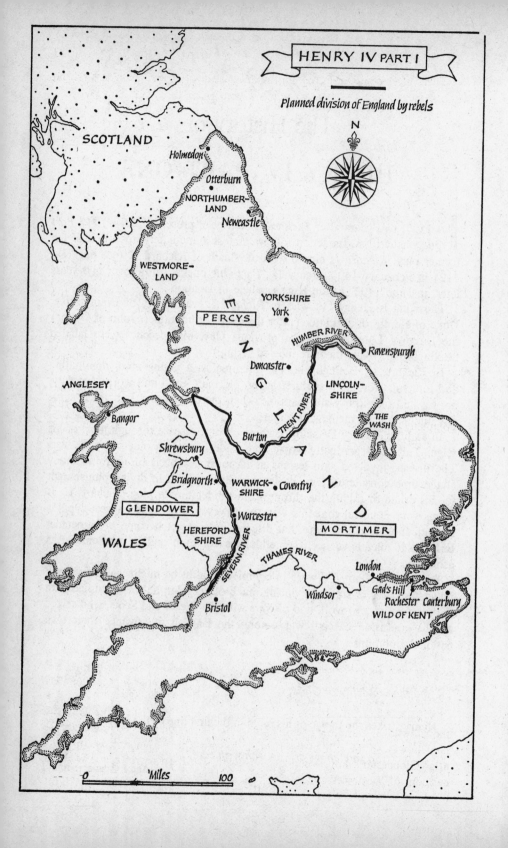

HENRY IV PART I

Planned division of England by rebels

N

SCOTLAND

Holmedon

Otterburn

NORTHUMBER-
LAND

Newcastle

WESTMORE-
LAND

YORKSHIRE

PERCYS

York

HUMBER RIVER

Ravenspurgh

Doncaster

LINCOLN-
SHIRE

ANGLESEY

THE
WASH

Bangor

TRENT RIVER

Burton

E N G L A N D

Shrewsbury

Bridgnorth

WARWICK-
SHIRE

Coventry

GLENDOWER

Worcester

MORTIMER

HEREFORD-
SHIRE

WALES

SEVERN RIVER

THAMES RIVER

London

Windsor

Gad's Hill

Rochester Canterbury

WILD OF KENT

Bristol

0   'Miles   100

Then, after bemoaning the continuing disputes that embroil the land, he hopes for respite so that he might embark on an expedition that was a longed-for ambition of his:

> . . . Therefore, friends,
> As far as to the sepulcher of Christ—
> Whose soldier now, under whose blessed cross
> We are impressed and engaged to fight—
> Forthwith a power of English shall we levy,
> Whose arms were molded in their mother's womb
> To chase these pagans in those holy fields
>
> —Act I, scene i, lines 18–24

Henry had promised to go to the Holy Land to do penance for the death of Richard II (see page II–314) at the close of Richard II, and he is still trying.

It is a forlorn hope and it is quite certain that if he really had attempted to lead a Crusade, it would have led only to disaster, for the Ottoman Empire, which was at that time the principal Moslem power, was far stronger than any army any Western power could send against it.

Yet one can understand Henry's longing to do something to convince the nation that he was in God's good grace, something to make his rule completely legitimate. Not only would that put an end to civil war, but it would ensure the safety of his line, for it would mean that his son and his son's son would be legitimate kings in their turn.

. . . my gentle cousin Westmoreland

Having made this resolve, King Henry turns to the nobleman at his side, and says:

> . . . Then let me hear
> Of you, my gentle cousin Westmoreland,
> What yesternight our council did decree
> In forwarding this dear expedience.
>
> —Act I, scene i, lines 30–33

The man addressed here is Ralph Neville, 1st Earl of Westmoreland. He had originally been a follower of Thomas of Gloucester (see page II–264) and had been knighted in 1380 by that nobleman.

Young Neville showed a masterly ability to choose the winner. When the showdown came between Thomas of Gloucester and King Richard II, Neville was on the side of the King and against his earlier patron. In 1397, after Gloucester's imprisonment and death, Neville was rewarded with the earldom of Westmoreland.

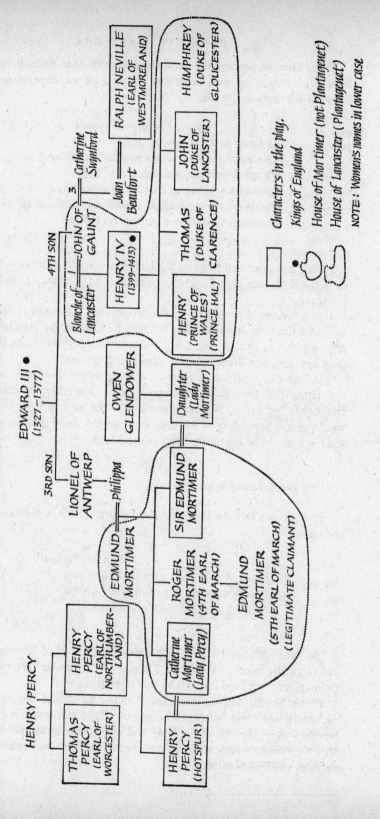

HENRY IV PART I and HENRY IV PART II

LANCASTER vs. MORTIMER

EDWARD III ●
(1327–1377)

3RD SON
LIONEL OF ANTWERP

4TH SON
JOHN OF GAUNT

3RD SON line:
LIONEL OF ANTWERP
EDMUND MORTIMER ══ Philippa
— ROGER MORTIMER (4TH EARL OF MARCH)
— SIR EDMUND MORTIMER ══ Daughter (Lady Mortimer) ── OWEN GLENDOWER
— Catherine Mortimer (Lady Percy) ══ HENRY PERCY (HOTSPUR)
EDMUND MORTIMER (5TH EARL OF MARCH) (LEGITIMATE CLAIMANT)

4TH SON line:
JOHN OF GAUNT
══ 1 Blanche of Lancaster
══ 3 Catherine Swynford
══ Joan Beaufort ── RALPH NEVILLE (EARL OF WESTMORELAND)

HENRY IV (1399–1413) ●
— HENRY (PRINCE OF WALES) (PRINCE HAL)
— THOMAS (DUKE OF CLARENCE)
— JOHN (DUKE OF LANCASTER)
— HUMPHREY (DUKE OF GLOUCESTER)

HENRY PERCY line:
HENRY PERCY
— HENRY PERCY (EARL OF NORTHUMBERLAND)
— THOMAS PERCY (EARL OF WORCESTER)
— HENRY PERCY (HOTSPUR) ══ Catherine Mortimer (Lady Percy)

Legend

□ Characters in the play.

● Kings of England

(outline) House of Mortimer (not Plantagenet)

(outline) House of Lancaster (Plantagenet)

NOTE: Women's names in lower case

Meanwhile, he had further advanced his hopes by a marriage to a daughter of the wealthy John of Gaunt, Duke of Lancaster.

John of Gaunt had had, in addition to his legitimate offspring, several children by his mistress, Catherine Swynford. He later married Catherine and legitimized those children. It was one of these legitimized children— Joan Beaufort—that Ralph Neville married.

This made him brother-in-law (or half brother-in-law) to Henry Bolingbroke, who was John of Gaunt's oldest son by his legitimate wife. When Bolingbroke became King Henry IV, Ralph Neville of Westmoreland became the King's "gentle cousin," for "cousin" in Shakespearean terms was a general term for any relative.

What's more, when Bolingbroke had landed in England and began his rebellion against Richard II (see page II–287), Westmoreland quickly chose the winning side again and once again profited. Under King Henry, he was put in charge of the western frontier and supervised the fighting against the Welsh.

. . . the noble Mortimer

Westmoreland, listening to this useless talk of the Holy Land, quashes it at once. Yes, the question of a Crusade was being discussed, but then came news of a serious defeat in the west:

> . . . the noble Mortimer
> Leading the men of Herefordshire to fight
> Against the irregular and wild Glendower,
> Was by the rude hands of that Welshman taken,
> A thousand of his people butchered;
> —Act I, scene i, lines 38–42

Who is "the noble Mortimer"? To straighten that out and see the significance of his capture, let us go back to Edward III and his seven sons (see page II–259).

The first was Edward, the Black Prince, and it was his son who became King Richard II. The fourth son was John of Gaunt, and it was his son, Bolingbroke, who succeeded Richard II and reigned as Henry IV.

But, according to the tenets of strict legitimacy, once Richard II was dead, the next king should be drawn from the line of the second son of Edward III. Failing that, the line of the third son should follow. Only failing that, too, could Henry IV be considered legitimate king.

Edward's second son was William of Hatfield, who died a boy, leaving no descendants of any kind. Edward's third son was Lionel of Antwerp, Duke of Clarence. Lionel died in 1368, but by then he had reached the age of thirty, had married, and had had a child. It was a daughter, named Philippa.

Philippa married Edmund Mortimer, 3rd Earl of March. ("March" means "borderland" and the name is applied to districts on the Welsh border.) Edmund Mortimer died in Ireland in 1381.

By that time, though, he had a son, Roger Mortimer, who became the 4th Earl of March. This fourth earl, who succeeded while Richard II was still King, was, in point of fact, the heir to the throne if Richard should die without children. March was, through his mother, the grandson of the third son of Edward III; Bolingbroke was only the son of the fourth son of Edward III.

Richard II recognized the 4th Earl of March as his heir and made him his deputy in Ireland after the first and relatively successful royal expedition to Ireland (see page II–277). But then in 1398 Roger Mortimer was assassinated and that was the immediate occasion for Richard's second, and thoroughly disastrous, expedition to Ireland (see page II–292).

Roger Mortimer had, however, left a son, Edmund Mortimer, 5th Earl of March, and him Richard at once recognized as next in line to the throne. However, Richard was deposed the next year by Bolingbroke, who took the throne for himself without regard to young Edmund of March, who was great-grandson of third son, Lionel—but who was only eight years old.

At eight, the "rightful heir" was not dangerous, but he could be used as a puppet by older men who could rebel in the sacred name of legitimacy. Besides, he would grow older. The cautious Henry IV therefore placed the Earl of March and a younger brother in strict custody and kept them thus throughout the reign.

But then, who was this Mortimer who had been defeated by the Welsh? It was Sir Edmund Mortimer, an uncle of the 5th Earl of March and not himself the legitimate heir. He is at best third in line, after nephew Edmund and his younger brother Roger.

Holinshed, from whom Shakespeare obtains much historical information for this play, confuses the two Edmund Mortimers, uncle and nephew, and thinks it is the uncle, leading the armies, who is the rightful heir to the throne (as though Henry IV were such a madman as to give an army to the rightful heir).

Shakespeare, following Holinshed, makes the same mistake and throughout *Henry IV, Part One* has his characters act as though the legitimate heir to the throne has been captured by the Welsh.

As for Glendower, he was pictured as heading Welsh forces during the time, two years before, when Bolingbroke had rebelled against Richard II (see page II–294).

Glendower had had an English education, and his serious rebellion against the English began in September 1400, after Henry IV had been King for half a year, partly because of personal feuds with a neighboring English lord and partly because the confusion inherent in the beginning of the reign of a king considered a usurper by many offered him troubled water to fish in.

Glendower's rebellion did best in south Wales. His capture of Mortimer, which took place on June 22, 1402, not only enhanced his prestige but gave him an opportunity for meddling in internal English politics.

. . . the gallant Hotspur. . .

Westmoreland has further news, not quite so bad and yet not good either, for it concerns a battle in progress, with no clear knowledge as yet as to its outcome. This second battle is on the Scottish border. Westmoreland says:

> On Holy-rood Day the gallant Hotspur there,
> Young Harry Percy, and brave Archibald,
> That ever-valiant and approved Scot,
> At Holmedon met . . .
> —Act I, scene i, lines 52–55

Holy-Rood Day (Holy-Cross Day, for "rood" is the Anglo-Saxon equivalent of the Latin-derived "cross") is September 14. The day celebrates the anniversary of the return of the Holy Cross (upon which Jesus was crucified) to Jerusalem by the East Roman Emperor Heraclius. This took place in 627, after Heraclius had defeated the Persians, who had captured Jerusalem and taken the Cross thirteen years earlier. (Seven years later the Moslem Arabs took Jerusalem and the Cross was lost forever, so that the celebration of Heraclius' feat was really a rather hollow one.)

This battle with the Scots took place, indeed, after the battle with the Welsh, but nearly three months after. For dramatic purposes, Shakespeare compresses time so as to make it seem that they took place almost together.

Harry Percy, who led the English side in this battle with the Scots, played a small part in *Richard II*. He is the son of Northumberland, who in *Richard II* was the most prominent of Bolingbroke's partisans.

In *Richard II*, Harry Percy was presented as a young man, a teen-age stripling. Now, two years later, he is depicted as a seasoned warrior, though still young, and is given his nickname "Hotspur" (see page II–288). In the interval between the plays he had led the campaign against Glendower and had cleared north Wales of the insurgents (though leaving the Welshman strong in south Wales).

However, he had been fighting long before then, for he was, in actual fact, no young man at all, but thirty-eight years old, two years older than the King himself.

Seventeen years before, Hotspur had been engaged in another battle on the Scottish border which had gone down in legend. The battle involved the earls of Douglas, who dominated the south of medieval Scotland as the Percys dominated the north of medieval England. The two families engaged in border warfare with scant regard for the central government on either side.

In 1388 James, 2nd Earl of Douglas, invaded England and besieged Newcastle (about forty miles south of the border) for three days. He captured Hotspur's battle flag and Hotspur, to retrieve this blow to his military reputation, forced a battle at Otterburn near the border. The Scots won again and Hotspur was captured—but Douglas was killed. This battle inspired (in a badly distorted way) a well-known ballad, "Chevy Chase."

Hotspur was released on payment of a heavy ransom, much of which was contributed by Richard II, whom Hotspur repaid rather foully ten years later.

James was succeeded by a bastard son, Archibald, the 3rd Earl of Douglas. He died at the end of 1400, and was succeeded by his son, another Archibald, the 4th Earl. It is the 4th Earl of Douglas who is "brave Archibald."

The 4th Earl of Douglas invaded England in 1402 and at Holmedon (Humbleton) in Northumberland met the same Hotspur who had once fought against his grandfather. (Naturally, Shakespeare cannot make use of this interesting fact, since it would wreck the basic interest of the play, which depends on making Hotspur and the Prince of Wales approximately the same age. Hotspur's age may be supposed to be in the early twenties, as far as this play is concerned.)

Sir Walter Blunt . . .

Westmoreland's news of an uncertain battle is capped by the King himself, however, for a new messenger has just arrived and has brought later news. The King introduces the messenger, saying:

> Here is a dear, a true industrious friend,
> Sir Walter Blunt, new lighted from his horse,
> —Act I, scene i, lines 62–63

Blunt (his name was actually Blount) is a veteran soldier, who had been with the Black Prince on his victorious foray into Spain thirty-five years before (see page II–260) and had also accompanied John of Gaunt on his much less fortunate Spanish venture (see page II–263). Now he was serving the son as loyally as he had served the father.

Mordake, Earl of Fife . . .

The news Blunt brings is good. Hotspur has won a great victory.

Hotspur did it, actually, by the cool use of archery from long distance, while the Scots vainly tried to charge into close quarters, with no archers of their own to cover. It was as though two armies were fighting today and only one had air support. It was a slaughter and the Scots lost ten thousand against very few English. (Even allowing for inevitable exaggeration by the victors, it was a slaughter.)

What was most important was that a number of high-ranking Scots noblemen were captured. The King lists them:

> *. . . Of prisoners, Hotspur took*
> *Mordake, Earl of Fife and eldest son*
> *To beaten Douglas, and the Earl of Athol,*
> *Of Murray, Angus, and Menteith.*
> —Act I, scene i, lines 70–73

Of these, the most important is the first mentioned, Mordake (or Murdoch, as we would spell it today), Earl of Fife. He was the son of Robert Stuart, 1st Duke of Albany (and *not* the son of Douglas).

This actually makes him a still higher prize, for Robert Stuart's older brother, John, had been reigning as King of Scotland since 1390, under the name of Robert III. The King was old and incapacitated, so that Robert Stuart, the younger brother, was the regent and the actual ruler.

Hotspur had thus captured the son of the regent of Scotland and the nephew of the reigning King.

. . . my young Harry

The joy of the victory and the great honor it brings Hotspur forces a sad thought to the mind of the King. When Westmoreland joins in the praise of Hotspur, the King says:

> *Yea, there thou mak'st me sad, and mak'st me sin*
> *In envy that my Lord Northumberland*
> *Should be the father to so blest a son:*
> *A son who is the theme of honor's tongue,*
> *Who is sweet fortune's minion and her pride;*
> *Whilst I, by looking on the praise of him,*
> *See riot and dishonor stain the brow*
> *Of my young Harry . . .*
> —Act I, scene i, lines 78–85a

Here is the central conflict of the play. A kind of twin character is presented, both named Harry, both of an age. One is all good: martial, honorseeking, brave, and knightly to a fault. The other is all bad: dissolute, disregarding his position, the friend of blackguards.

It is in order to set up this conflict that Shakespeare has taken nearly twenty years off Hotspur's age. What's more, he has had to add a few years to the Prince's age (the King's "young Harry," who is the Prince of Wales), for at the time of the Battle of Holmedon, the King's son was, in actual fact, only fifteen years old.

Yet, even at this young age, the Prince of Wales has already been campaigning in north Wales. With whom? Why, with Hotspur himself. In real history, in other words, Hotspur has taken the young Prince campaigning with him and has undoubtedly been like a father to him; he was old enough.

But, however much they made a kind of father-and-son pair in history, they make a brother-and-brother pair in Shakespeare, and so effective is this play under the lash of Shakespeare's transcendent genius, that history is forever thrust out of the arena.

Shakespeare has immortalized the rakehell Prince as he has immortalized the gallant young Hotspur, and no possible debunking in this book or any other can wipe out the Shakespearean picture and replace it with what is, after all, merely truth.

. . . mine Percy, his Plantagenet

The sorrowing King can only wish that it could turn out somehow that matters had been reversed. He says:

> . . . O that it could be proved
> That some night-tripping fairy had exchanged
> In cradle clothes our children where they lay,
> And called mine Percy, his Plantagenet!
>
> —Act I, scene i, lines 85b–88

Edward III had been a Plantagenet by virtue of his descent from Henry II through an unbroken line of males (see page II–212). All the descendants of Edward III, through the male line only, were Plantagenets too. The Prince of Wales was the son of the son of the son of Edward III and was therefore a Plantagenet.

. . . young Percy's pride

But then King Henry turns away from his self-pity and approaches something more important—the insubordination of Hotspur. The gallant young man had taken an important prisoner, and prisoners were valuable, for they could be ransomed for large sums. (Hotspur himself, remember, had been captured and ransomed at a high price after the Battle of Otterburn.)

The King says indignantly to Westmoreland:

> . . . *What think you, coz,*
> *Of this young Percy's pride? The prisoners*
> *Which he in this adventure hath surprised* [captured]
> *To his own use he keeps, and sends me word*
> *I shall have none but Mordake, Earl of Fife.*
> —Act I, scene i, lines 90–94

The King apparently feels that a victory by any Englishman was a victory for England and that any prisoners taken were therefore the King's (today we would say "the national government's") and not the general's.

This, however, Hotspur refuses to allow. The ancient practice of the border armies was to make personal profit of the prisoners, and he was not going to be denied his ransoms, which were earned at the peril of his life.

Indeed, this is an example of the kind of quarrel that was bound to arise in a land whose King had come to the throne in the fashion that Henry IV had. The nobles (including Henry IV himself, then Bolingbroke) had rebelled against Richard II's arrogation of too much power to tax and control. The Percys had been foremost in this rebellion and without them Henry could not have reached the throne. Having fought for freedom from centralized "tyranny" (for "states' rights," to use our own nearly equivalent term), the Percys naturally felt they ought to have it and that Henry IV, whom they had helped to the throne in that cause, should certainly not be the one to deny them.

Henry IV, however, once in power, could see no way of conducting the affairs of the kingdom but in the very way Richard II did. He had to increase his powers and get money wherever he could, for he needed money as badly as ever Richard did.

The quarrel was irreconcilable but it must be said that consistency seemed to be on the side of the Percys. Indeed, Hotspur might fairly argue that he was proposing a generous compromise against his own best interest. Mordake, whom he was proposing to surrender to the King, was the most important prisoner he had, and was likely to bring the highest ransom. The King, in rejecting that offer and demanding all, must have seemed simply a greedy tyrant to the Percys.

(Shakespeare followed Holinshed in this matter of the prisoners, by the way, and Holinshed may be wrong. There is reason to think that, in actuality, King Henry grudgingly conceded the point. But if he did so, it didn't change matters. The quarrel between centralization and decentralization was irrepressible and if it was patched over here, it would simply break out there.)

. . . his uncle's teaching . . .

Westmoreland, on hearing the news of the quarrel over the prisoners, considers Hotspur too young to be the true instigator. There are older, more conspiratorial heads behind it. He says, wrathfully:

> This is his uncle's teaching, this is Worcester,
> Malevolent to you in all aspects,
>
> —Act I, scene i, lines 95–96

Worcester was Sir Thomas Percy, Earl of Worcester, who had broken with Richard II rather late in the day (see page II–288). He was the younger brother of the Duke of Northumberland and therefore the uncle of Hotspur.

The fact that he hesitated before joining the rest of the Percys in the rebellion against Richard II may well have meant that he was inclined toward Richard or that he disliked or distrusted Bolingbroke (or both) and that he abandoned the former for the latter only when it became unsafe to do otherwise. It would therefore be quite credible that he should be the readiest of the Percys to consider a rebellion against the new King.

As it turns out, Westmoreland's suspicions of Worcester are quite correct, but we cannot expect the former to attempt to smooth matters over in any case. Westmoreland was of the Neville family, after all, and they are a northern family who had long been enemies of the Percys. Westmoreland would be only too eager to see them in trouble.

Now, Hal . . .

The King decides to call the Percys to his palace at Windsor for a conference on the matter, and so ends the first scene, filled with matters of state, with battles lost and won, with warriors and rebels, with anger and danger. That done, Shakespeare switches to the London lodgings of the Prince of Wales.

Here, however, as King Henry had indicated, is no Hotspur; no knight of storybook honor and valor. Instead, we have a gay and thoroughly human youngster, with his boon companion, a grossly fat, dissolute, white-haired old villain, who, without a single saving grace but his wit, manages to be so entirely lovable as to win his way not only into the Prince's heart, but into the audience's as well.

The fat old man is Sir John Falstaff, and though he is not a historical character, but is an almost whole-cloth creation of Shakespeare's, he is more real to the reader in his gross humanity than anyone else in the play.

He bursts into the scene at once, speaking even before the Prince does:

> *Now, Hal, what time of day is it, lad?*
>
> —Act I, scene ii, line 1

(Because Falstaff consistently calls the Prince by this ultrashort nickname, one less formal, even, than Harry, the Prince is best known in this play as "Prince Hal.")

Now what sparked Shakespeare in the direction of this fat wonder?

One of Shakespeare's sources for *Henry IV, Part One* was a play by an anonymous writer entitled *The Famous Victories of Henry V*, which covered the ground in this play and in the two following, *Henry IV, Part Two* and *Henry V*, but was shorter than any one of these. *The Famous Victories* contained the legend of Prince Hal's wild youth and his sudden reformation at his coronation.

In *The Famous Victories* are the germs of some of the events in Shakespeare's plays, but one has only to read the episodes of the earlier play and the corresponding episodes in Shakespeare to see, with amazement, how much can be done with how little, in the hands of a genius.

In *The Famous Victories,* one of the Prince's companions was Sir John ("Jockey") Oldcastle, and Shakespeare borrowed that name, but nothing else. The John Oldcastle of the older play had not a scrap of wit or of anything worth remembering; whereas Shakespeare's John Oldcastle was and remains one of the greatest comic creations of all time.

Well then, who was John Oldcastle? Is there anyone by that name who was indeed a companion of the Prince and who was turned away after the Prince had become King (which, as we shall see, was the affecting and tragic climax of Falstaff's life)?

There was, as it happens, a Sir John Oldcastle in history, and he was indeed a friend of Prince Hal. He was not, however, an old man, nor was he fat or dissolute. He was no more than ten years older than the Prince and twenty-five years old, perhaps, at the time of Hotspur's victory over the Scots. He was an able warrior who took part in Hotspur's expedition into north Wales, and it was at that time that he grew friendly with the young Prince of Wales, who was also present on that expedition.

Oldcastle kept Hal's friendship throughout the period that he was Prince of Wales and, what's more, continued to keep it after Hal became King Henry V.

In 1408 (six years after the opening events of *Henry IV, Part One* and while Hal was still Prince of Wales) Oldcastle married an heiress of the wealthy Cobham family and eventually could be styled Lord Cobham. He had every right to look forward to honored old age or to an honored death in battle.

There was but one flaw. He was unorthodox in his religion.

Some thirty years before *Henry IV, Part One*'s opening events, an English religious reformer, John Wycliffe, had developed a doctrine very much like those developed by the moderate Protestants a century and a half later. Despite the opposition of the orthodox, Wycliffe lived out his life in safety and died a natural death in peace in 1384, because of the protection afforded him by none other than John of Gaunt, the father of Henry IV.

Wycliffe left behind disciples called "Lollards" (from a Dutch word meaning "mumbler," applied to them derisively because they were always mumbling prayers). The church authorities strenuously opposed Lollardism, and Henry IV, whose flawed title made it expedient for him to gather friends anywhere he could, turned against those whom his father had protected.

The Lollards found their converts chiefly among the lower classes, so the movement was fairly easy to oppress and, eventually, suppress, but some few noblemen were converted. One of these was Sir John Oldcastle. What is more, he was a convinced and dedicated Lollard who was determined to keep his faith to the death.

By the time Hal became King Henry V, the oppression of Lollardism had reached the point where Oldcastle's life was in danger. Henry V, who did not want to harm the friend of his youth, but who could not resist church pressures forever (particularly since he needed church funds for his own aggressive designs against France), personally appealed to Oldcastle to submit and to renounce his heresy.

Oldcastle refused and was eventually condemned as a heretic in September of 1413. The King granted him a forty-day stay of execution, hoping he would reconsider. He didn't; he escaped instead, and tried to raise a rebellion. Part of its aim was the kidnapping of the King.

The uprising was pitifully inept and failed, but Oldcastle escaped again and wandered the Welsh hills for nearly four years before he was finally captured. At last, on December 14, 1417, he was executed in the fashion of the time; that is, as a heretic, he was suspended over a slow fire and gradually roasted to death. Henry V could not save him.

Why was Sir John Oldcastle, brave warrior, earnest reformer, and martyr, so scurrilously treated in *The Famous Victories?* He was a heretic, wasn't he? And a traitor too? And the author of the play was, as the play itself shows, an untalented scribbler incapable of rising above the stereotype.

The Cobhams, however, were still a noble and influential family in Shakespeare's time. They might ignore the existence of Sir John Oldcastle in *The Famous Victories,* where he played a small role in a poor play unworthy of notice.

When Shakespeare's play was put on the stage, though, and became an instant hit, with Sir John Oldcastle the very center of its fun, the Cobhams roared with anger. In addition, England was now largely Protestant and Oldcastle was viewed as a proto-Protestant and martyr, so that the Cobhams were not alone in their indignation. Shakespeare, for all his genius, had a strong commercial sense. He was not going to do anything really unpopular, so he instantly agreed to change the name and made that change before the printed version of the play appeared.

The change in the name did no good at all for the Lord Cobham of Shakespeare's time. His political opponents promptly dubbed him "Sir John Falstaff."

But having erased Oldcastle's name, where did Shakespeare come upon Falstaff?

Well, Prince Hal, after he became King, had another associate, Sir John Fastolfe, who fought with him in France and bore himself well in many battles. There was one occasion, though, when he was accused of cowardice. It was a wrongful accusation and he eventually justified himself. However, in Shakespeare's early play *Henry VI, Part One,* Fastolfe briefly appears as a cowardly runaway.

What more did Shakespeare need? Here was an associate of Prince Hal who proved cowardly. He altered a few letters in the name and so was born Sir John Falstaff.

. . . old sack . . .

Falstaff and Prince Hal engage in a battle of wits, which is, as always in the play, a standoff. The Prince is constantly on the attack, for Falstaff is a marvelous target (both literally and figuratively); yet Falstaff can nimbly dodge any blow and turn it back again.

Much of the flavor of these exchanges has dimmed with time and obsolescence, however, to say nothing of changes in fashion as far as what is and isn't considered funny. Matters of obsolescence can be corrected in footnotes and commentary, but this cannot restore spontaneity of appreciation, of course. Still, as examples, Prince Hal's first comments to Falstaff begin:

> *Thou art so fat-witted with drinking of old sack . . .*
> —Act I, scene ii, lines 2–3

It is clear from the context that sack is a kind of alcoholic drink, yet it is not one that is familiar to us today, even though it is so closely associated with Falstaff that we can scarcely think of one without the other. It is simply any dry wine, which is *vin sec* in French, with "sack" as an Anglicization of the French *sec.* Sack came to be associated in particular with the dry wines of southern Europe, such as the white sherry of Spain.

Then again, Falstaff begins at one point:

> *Marry, then, sweet wag . . .*
>
> —Act I, scene ii, line 23

"Marry" is a common Elizabethan interjection that we don't use nowadays and that seems to make no sense. Why "marry"? It is an oath, a shortened form of "By the Virgin Mary" (just as "dear me" is supposed to be from the Italian *dio mio,* or "my God"). Oaths have a way of sterilizing themselves in order that they might enter respectable society.

. . . my old lad of the castle

One particular thrust and riposte has more than ordinary interest. Falstaff wickedly deflects some of Prince Hal's jabs by bringing in one of the tavern women as a non sequitur, saying:

> *. . . is not my hostess of the tavern a most sweet wench?*
>
> —Act I, scene ii, lines 41–42

Prince Hal, twisting agilely, says:

> *As the honey of Hybla, my old lad of the castle—and is not a buff jerkin a most sweet robe of durance?*
>
> —Act I, scene ii, lines 43–45

Hybla is proverbial for the sweetness of its honey, so Hal is agreeing with Falstaff in most equable fashion—but the sting follows immediately. "The Castle" was a well-known London brothel and Falstaff's propensities are thus hinted at. The play on words would have been perfect if the original name of the character, Oldcastle, had been kept. This play on words now remains as a mere fossil trace, so to speak, of that name. Shakespeare didn't change this passage, either because of negligence or because he couldn't bear to give up the joke.

And then Hal stings Falstaff still harder by bringing in a buff jerkin as a balancing non sequitur. "Durance" means durability but it also means imprisonment. Prince Hal might be innocently commending the good wearing qualities of a garment, but since sheriff's officers wore these buff jerkins (tan leather jackets), he might also be implying that Falstaff would eventually end in prison, if nothing worse.

Falstaff takes it in its worse sense and is jarred out of his good humor. He says, irritably:

> *. . . What a plague have I to do with a buff jerkin?*
>
> —Act I, scene ii, lines 47–48

To this, Prince Hal retorts at once with a balancing:

> *Why, what a pox have I to do with my hostess of the tavern?*
> —Act I, scene ii, lines 49–50

The "pox" is, of course, syphilis; an indication of what might occur to those who have to do with my hostess of the tavern or other such light wenches. The mention is anachronistic, though not as anachronistic as in *Troilus and Cressida* (see page I-106).

Prince Hal's scornful denial of having anything to do with "my hostess of the tavern" is to be noted. Shakespeare is careful of the dignity of the future hero-king.

Hal does indeed consort with low companions, but he does and says nothing really disgraceful. He participates in a robbery, as we shall see, but only as part of a practical joke, and he makes amends for it. He drinks, to be sure, but is never shown the worse for liquor, let alone actually drunk. Most of all, he is never tarred with sexual immorality. Shakespeare never shows him as anything worse than a young man with a keen sense of humor and a liking for horseplay. A little worse than this, perhaps, is the fact that for the sake of amusement, he will tolerate rather disgraceful behavior on the part of those who amuse him.

. . . wisdom cries out . . .

But Prince Hal's toleration is not something that makes him blind to wicked behavior. Rather he uses it as a butt for irony. We might speculate that he relishes Falstaff even more for the excellent target he makes than for the wit of his rejoinders.

Thus, Falstaff begins to talk lugubriously of reforming (as he does periodically) and says, in mock sorrow, that a dignified old lord had scolded him in the open street (presumably for corrupting the Prince). Falstaff had not listened. He says, sighing:

> *. . . and yet he talked wisely, and in the street too.*
> —Act I, scene ii, lines 90–91

Prince Hal seizes upon the expression at once to deliver a devastating biblical jab, saying:

> *Thou didst well, for wisdom cries out in the streets, and no*
> *man regards it.*
> —Act I, scene ii, lines 92–93

This is a reference to a verse in the Book of Proverbs, which reads:

"Wisdom crieth without; she uttereth her voice in the streets" (Proverbs 1:20).

The irony in that "Thou didst well" lies in what follows that verse in the Bible, and what follows must be well known to Falstaff, who is both educated and intelligent. It is a warning that since personified Wisdom has cried out and was disregarded she would in turn desert those who had not heeded her in their hour of need. Personified Wisdom says, "I also will laugh at your calamity; I will mock when your fear cometh."

The comment might therefore be regarded as a threat to Falstaff from the Prince; a threat which, in the end, is carried out.

The disconcerted Falstaff manages to return to his protestations of reform, but when the Prince suddenly suggests a bit of purse snatching, avid old Falstaff is ready at once. The Prince laughs and Falstaff says of purse snatching in a tone of wounded dignity:

> Why, Hal, 'tis my vocation, Hal. 'Tis no sin for a man to labor in his vocation.
>
> —Act I, scene ii, lines 108–9

And of course, Prince Hal must laugh and own defeat when faced with so wildly and madly inadequate a defense. For the fun of watching Falstaff squirm out of anything, he will forgive him everything—or almost everything.

. . . at Gad's Hill . . .

Yet the reference to purse snatching gets the audience ready for something serious. If there is one definite item in the tales of Prince Hal's wildness (one that is included as the opening episode in *The Famous Victories of Henry V*), it is the legend that Prince Hal was involved in a piece of highway robbery.

Shakespeare cannot do without it—it is too much a part of the story as known to everyone (like Washington and the cherry tree)—but he transmutes it beyond recognition. Falstaff, fencing verbally with the Prince, is looking forward to some more serious action. There is a plan for a robbery on foot and Falstaff means to get a share of the loot.

Poins, another one of the Prince's low companions, enters and announces that arrangements have been indeed made for the robbery. He says:

> . . . tomorrow morning, by four o'clock early [4 A.M.], at Gad's Hill! There are pilgrims going to Canterbury with rich offerings, and traders riding to London with fat purses. I have vizards [masks] for you all; you have horses for yourselves.

Gadshill lies tonight in Rochester. I have bespoke [reserved]
supper tomorrow night in Eastcheap.
                              —Act I, scene ii, lines 128–34

Canterbury lies fifty miles southeast of London, and is the spiritual
center of England, as London is the temporal center. Between pious pilgrims carrying offerings to Canterbury and rich merchants carrying money
to London, the road between is a gold mine for highwaymen. Poins
is promising they can complete the job and be back in Eastcheap (a lower-
class district in London) having a good supper by night, and the richer for
much loot.

About halfway between Canterbury and London is the town of Rochester, where Gadshill (another of the worthless crew with whom the Prince
amuses himself) has arranged all the necessary details and where he is
staying.

The similarity between Gadshill, the man, and Gad's Hill, the place
where the robbery is planned, is confusing, but the first is derived from
the second. In *The Famous Victories* there is a character called "the Thief,"
whose name is Cutbert Cutter, but who is nicknamed "Gad's Hill," presumably because that is his favored spot for thievery.

Gad's Hill (or Gadshill) itself is a low hill about three miles northwest
of Rochester, where, presumably, highwaymen can command a prospect
of the road in either direction, and which was notorious for the robberies
committed there. (Its greatest fame, next to the fictional events upon
it described in this play, is the fact that it was the home of the English
novelist Charles Dickens in his later years. He died in Gadshill in 1870.)

. . . Not I . . .

Yet although legend makes Prince Hal a participant in the robbery,
Shakespeare softens the blow. When Falstaff invites Prince Hal to be a
member of the gang, Hal says indignantly:

Who, I rob? I a thief? Not I, by my faith.
                              —Act I, scene ii, line 142

And despite a momentary temptation to waver, he holds fast to his refusal to be a thief, though he makes no attempt to sway the others against
the action.

Poins, however, takes an opportunity to speak to Prince Hal alone and
induces him to take part in a practical joke. Falstaff and the others will
indeed be allowed to hold up merchants and steal their money, but then
Poins and the Prince, masked beyond recognition, will rob the robbers in

their turn. The hope is that later that evening, Falstaff will be sure to tell monstrous lies to explain matters and will be trapped in them.

In this way, Prince Hal participates in the robbery only out of an irrepressible desire to play a practical joke, and this is a weakness which men are quite apt to excuse.

I know you all . . .

Yet still Shakespeare seems nervous. He simply cannot allow Prince Hal, the future hero-king, to be too base to begin with, despite all the legends in the world. He must supply him with a motive for his undignified behavior, and one that sounds as noble as possible.

Therefore, when Falstaff and Poins are gone and he is alone on the stage, he looks after them thoughtfully and says:

> *I know you all, and will awhile uphold*
> *The unyoked humor of your idleness.*
> *Yet herein will I imitate the sun,*
> *Who doth permit the base contagious clouds*
> *To smother up his beauty from the world,*
> *That, when he please again to be himself,*
> *Being wanted, he may be more wond'red at*
>
> —Act I, scene ii, lines 199–205

Prince Hal is pictured as not serious in his tomfoolery, as aware all along of his own greatness, and indeed, as following a deliberate design of increasing that greatness by its contrast with his earlier follies.

This may have gone over with an Elizabethan audience to whom Henry V was a half-divine memory, but it rings completely false to us. It is out of character for the Prince, and indeed, if it were to be taken seriously, it would lessen our regard for him. To play the fool out of high spirits and youthful zest can be endearing; to do so out of deep political calculation is repellent.

However, the speech need not be taken as a real part of the play itself. It is Shakespeare speaking to the audience, assuring them that Prince Hal is really going to be the hero-king someday and that they need not be disturbed at the Gad's Hill incident.

Needless to say, there is nothing at all in the legend of Prince Hal to indicate that he was roistering out of deep policy.

The scourge of greatness . . .

Back the scene shifts now to high politics. At Windsor Castle, the King is confronting the Percys in anger over the matter of the prisoners being withheld from him. He has reached the point, as the scene opens, where he is using threats.

Worcester replies for the Percys and does so intransigently:

> *Our house, my sovereign liege, little deserves*
> *The scourge of greatness to be used on it—*
> *And that same greatness too which our own hands*
> *Have holp to make so portly.*
>
> —Act I, scene iii, lines 10–13

This is the claim of the Percys to gratitude for their part in placing Henry IV on the throne, a claim they make on several occasions through the play—yet it is this very claim that places them under a permanent pall of suspicion as far as the King is concerned.

The King will not yield to any suggestion that he owes gratitude, for such suggestions are dangerous. The mere act of yielding to subjects for any reason will but give them occasion to ask for more, if that yielding is thought to represent something due those subjects. (In modern terms, we might say that Henry IV appreciated the futility and dangers of attempting "appeasement.")

This harks back to the prophecy of Richard II in *Richard II,* when on the occasion of the deposed King's last meeting with Northumberland, Shakespeare has Richard warn the arrogant nobleman that the time will come when he will feel any reward too little while the new King will fear that a man who could rebel against one king would easily rebel against another as well (see page II–307).

And indeed, King Henry, quite aware that Worcester's attitude verges on the flatly rebellious, orders him out of the royal presence.

This villainous saltpeter . . .

Northumberland, however, having vainly tried to stop Worcester in his defiance, now hastens to conciliate the angry King. He declares the report of Hotspur's withholding of the prisoners to have been exaggerated, and Hotspur himself attempts to justify himself in a famous speech that begins:

> *My liege, I did deny no prisoners,*
> *But I remember, when the fight was done,*
> *When I was dry with rage and extreme toil,*
> *Breathless and faint, leaning upon my sword,*
> *Came there a certain lord, neat and trimly dressed,*
> *Fresh as a bridegroom . . .*
>
> —Act I, scene iii, lines 28–33

This courtly fop (whose identity it would be wonderful to know if it were not that the whole incident is fictitious), appearing on the scene of the battle, prattles on in so foolish a manner, according to Hotspur, as to induce wild irritation in the wearied fighter. (Of course, Hotspur is shown throughout the play as a person prone to irritation, and from the description of this event, we can scarcely blame him in this particular case.)

As one example of the stupidities uttered by the courtier, Hotspur quotes him as saying:

> . . . that it was great pity, so it was,
> This villainous saltpeter should be digged
> Out of the bowels of the harmless earth,
> Which many a good tall fellow had destroyed
> So cowardly, and but for these vile guns,
> He would himself have been a soldier.
>
> —Act I, scene iii, lines 58–63

Gunpowder is a mixture of charcoal, sulfur, and potassium nitrate (the last bearing the common name of "saltpeter"). Of the three components, saltpeter is the least common and the most difficult to obtain. It is therefore the bottleneck in gunpowder manufacture and that is why the fop regrets its being mined.

Gunpowder was known to the Chinese long before it came into use in Europe, and there are occasional examples of European knowledge of it in the thirteenth century. Roger Bacon, the English scholar, makes references in 1268 to something that might well be gunpowder. (This was in the time when China and eastern Europe were united into one vast Mongol Empire and travelers from Europe were reaching the Far East by a long overland journey. Perhaps vague word of gunpowder was brought back.)

The first European actually to design a metal cylinder from which a projectile might be hurled by an explosion of gunpowder was a German monk and alchemist, Berthold Schwarz. This first cannon may have been constructed in 1313.

Cannons, to begin with, were clumsy, ineffectual, and far more dangerous to the persons firing them than to the persons being aimed at. They were used for the first time in actual warfare at the Battle of Crécy in 1346 by Edward III (see page II–257) and then by that monarch again the next year at the siege of Calais. At both battles, they served mostly for show and psychological effect, however, and it was many decades before they could be of real use.

In 1402, at the time of the Battle of Holmedon, cannon were still a rarity. Hotspur won the battle with his archers and no cannon were used. As for small handguns, they hadn't even been devised yet. The fop's complaint about saltpeter is therefore anachronistic.

By Shakespeare's time, however, two centuries later, it had already be-

The fact that Edmund Mortimer had married Glendower's daughter would certainly tend to give some color to the King's outraged (and, to the Percys, outrageous) accusation of the captive as a traitor. However, Shakespeare's compression of events is here unfair to Mortimer.

Mortimer had been captured in June and Hotspur had taken his prisoners in September 1402. For three months Mortimer had already languished in captivity and no move had been made to ransom him. Even after the prisoners were taken, there was no move, and the King, in trying to take the prisoners for himself, was actually preventing the ransom.

One can scarcely blame Mortimer, then, for buying his own freedom at the price of marrying Glendower's daughter in December, after fully half a year of imprisonment. It might even be natural to expect him to remember after that lapse of time that it was not the ungrateful Henry but his own young nephew who was the rightful King of England.

. . . the gentle Severn . . .

Indignantly, Hotspur denies the imputation of treason against his brother-in-law, using as evidence a single combat between Mortimer and Glendower. He says:

> . . . on the gentle Severn's sedgy bank,
> In single opposition hand to hand,
> He did confound the best part of an hour
> In changing hardiment with great Glendower.
> —Act I, scene iii, lines 97–100

The Severn (see page II–69) rises in central Wales and flows east then north through eastern Wales, where the battle between Mortimer and Glendower took place. It crosses into western England, then turns southward and flows into Bristol Channel.

The account of the fight on the Severn seems altogether unlikely. Hotspur describes a single combat between generals, which takes place often in knightly romances and epic tales, but virtually never in sober history. He includes details—like three stops by mutual agreement for rest and drink —which are to be found in the tales of King Arthur rather than in legitimate chronicles.

King Henry is not influenced by Hotspur's glowing account. He dismisses the tale as myth, saying that Mortimer wouldn't dare meet Glendower in single combat. He ends the argument by a flat demand for the prisoners and a flat refusal to ransom Mortimer, on pain of strong reprisal otherwise. Indeed, he forbids any further mention of Mortimer; then he leaves.

. . . the next of blood

Hotspur, staring after the King, goes almost mad with rage. He thinks at once of rebellion:

> *. . . I will lift the downtrod Mortimer*
> *As high in the air as this unthankful king,*
> *As this ingrate and cank'red Bolingbroke.*
>
> —Act I, scene iii, lines 133–35

As though the displacement were already made, as though Mortimer were on the King's throne and Henry deposed, Hotspur gives the latter his name of Bolingbroke (see page II–264), by which he was most commonly known before he was King.

Worcester now returns, understands the situation at once, and sets about fanning Hotspur's flame and turning it to use. When Hotspur angrily describes the King's refusal to ransom Mortimer, Worcester responds coolly:

> *I cannot blame him. Was not he* [Mortimer] *proclaimed*
> *By Richard that dead is, the next of blood?*
>
> —Act I, scene iii, lines 143–44

Here again is Holinshed's error. The young Earl of March, Mortimer's nephew, was so proclaimed. Still, if we accept Shakespeare's version, what Worcester is doing is reminding Hotspur that in yearning to depose Henry for Mortimer's sake, he is no rebel striving to uplift a relative, but a loyal subject fighting for the true King.

And now, for policy's sake, Northumberland begins to make a great reversal. In *Richard II* he was pictured as the most eager of those who wished for Richard's deposition (see page II–304). Now he responds to Worcester's statement with a piece of canting piety, saying:

> *He was, I heard the proclamation:*
> *And then it was when the unhappy king*
> *(Whose wrongs in us God pardon!) did set forth*
> *Upon his Irish expedition;*
>
> —Act I, scene iii, lines 145–48

. . . this canker Bolingbroke

Both Worcester and Northumberland are dangling the bait before Hotspur. They are old men; it is Hotspur who has the energy to carry through a violent action. They must take advantage of his anger at the King and not allow him to cool down. Hence the careful explanation that Hotspur's brother-in-law is the true heir and their snuffling sorrow for Richard.

Hotspur (who conveniently forgets that he was himself thoroughly involved in Richard's deposition) takes the bait and berates his father and uncle for their deeds, professing himself appalled

> *That men of your nobility and power*
> *Did gage* [pledge] *them both in an unjust behalf*
> *(As both of you, God pardon it, have done)*
> *To put down Richard, that sweet lovely rose,*
> *And plant this thorn, this canker Bolingbroke?*
>
> —Act I, scene iii, lines 170–74

Having taken the bait, Hotspur is now ready for instant action, without thought or preparation, impelled only by his hot rage.

To pluck bright honor . . .

Worcester stops him at once. He wants Hotspur's enthusiasm, his bravery, his ability to fight a battle. He does not want him trying to plan, but wants him rather to be guided by wiser heads—like Worcester's own. Worcester begins therefore to unfold the conspiracy against the King, a conspiracy which he has already set afoot.

Hotspur, however, having been hotly spurred to emotion, is not so easily stopped. At the first mention of a plot, he at once sees battles, victory, the toppling of a king, the setting up of another, all redounding to his own honor—and he goes off into a paean in praise of honor:

> *By heaven, methinks it were an easy leap*
> *To pluck bright honor from the pale-faced moon,*
> *Or dive into the bottom of the deep,*
> *Where fathom line could never touch the ground,*
> *And pluck up drowned honor by the locks,*
>
> —Act I, scene iii, lines 199–203

This is Hotspur at his most one-sided extreme. Nothing exists for him but "honor," and it is important to realize that what he means by "honor" is a reputation for daring, warlike deeds. To win that reputation he would jump to the moon or dive into the abyss. It is the psychology of the "college try," the drive for the winning touchdown at all costs.

It is admirable, in a way, and it is admired, and our hearts beat faster as Hotspur declaims—and yet it is schoolboyish. There is more to life than touchdowns, and the push for the personal touchdown may lose the team its game. There are times when great ends must come before the Hotspur version of "honor," and this Hotspur never learns.

Lest the audience mistake the schoolboyishness of Hotspur in their admiration for his speech about honor, Shakespeare has Hotspur follow it immediately by a description of the schoolboy tricks he will play on the King:

> He said he would not ransom Mortimer,
> Forbade my tongue to speak of Mortimer,
> But I will find him when he lies asleep,
> And in his ear I'll hollo "Mortimer."
> Nay, I'll have a starling shall be taught to speak
> Nothing but "Mortimer," and give it him
>
> —Act I, scene iii, lines 218–23

Hotspur still keeps his schoolboyish attractiveness, of course, but how does this compare with Prince Hal? It is the comparison of Hotspur and Prince Hal that is the core of the play, and we surely feel that the Prince, however convivial he might be with Falstaff, would never meet a high crisis with the kind of low comedy Hotspur has just offered.

. . . sword-and-buckler Prince of Wales

Nor does Shakespeare rely on the audience keeping Prince Hal in mind at this point without help. Hotspur passes on at once to a mention of the Prince—for the first time in this play. He makes the mention with utmost contempt, saying:

> And that same sword-and-buckler Prince of Wales,
> But that I think his father loves him not
> And would be glad he met with some mischance,
> I would have him poisonèd with a pot of ale.
>
> —Act I, scene iii, lines 228–31

Part of the contempt lies in the adjective "sword-and-buckler," the typical weapons of the lower classes—which makes it a sneering reference to Prince Hal's well-known penchant for low associates.

Nor does Hotspur offer to fight the Prince; it would stain his honor to take up a gentleman's weapons against such a dishonorable wretch. It would be enough to poison him, and not even with a glass of wine (a gentleman's drink), but with the low-class pot of ale.

. . . a candy deal of courtesy

Worcester has borne patiently with Hotspur's ravings, but they show no signs of stopping. When he and Northumberland try to dam the flood they have themselves initiated, Hotspur breaks away, and in such a fury that he can scarcely speak, recalls the King's softly insinuating courtesies when first they met, on the occasion of the beginning of the revolt against Richard (see page II–291). Hotspur says:

> *Why, what a candy deal of courtesy*
> *This fawning greyhound then did proffer me!*
> *"Look when his infant fortune came to age,"*
> *And "gentle Harry Percy," and "kind cousin"—*
> *O, the devil take such cozeners* [deceivers]!
> > —Act I, scene iii, lines 248–52

Hotspur, who is incapable of the use of smooth diplomacy, is all the more furious that he should have been made the object of it and been (as he thinks) gulled by it.

The Archbishop

But now Hotspur runs down at last and Worcester has the chance to outline his plot.

The Scottish prisoners are to be given back to the Scots without ransom on conditions that the Douglas power join them in their revolt. Mortimer will, of course, also join them with the power of Glendower at his back.

It is not enough, however.

If the Percys go to war in alliance with Scotland and Wales, national tempers will be stirred against them. Patriotic dislike of Scotland and Wales was dangerously strong. What was needed was some English figurehead of unimpeachable loyalty on their side and this Worcester has also prepared. It will be up to Northumberland to supply one. He . . .

> *Shall secretly into the bosom creep*
> *Of that same noble prelate well-beloved,*
> *The Archbishop.*
> > —Act I, scene iii, lines 263–65

Hotspur assumes at once the Archbishop of York is meant, and Worcester says:

> *. . . True; who bears hard*
> *His brother's death at Bristow, the Lord Scroop.*
> > —Act I, scene iii, lines 267–68

Here once more Shakespeare, misled by Holinshed, makes a mistake, but rather a minor one.

The two "brothers" here referred to are William le Scrope and Richard le Scrope, for since both are the sons of the 1st Baron Scrope, they would certainly seem to be brothers.

However, there are two 1st Baron Scropes. One is Richard, 1st Baron Scrope of Bolton, and the other is Henry, 1st Baron Scrope of Masham, and the two are merely first cousins.

William le Scrope is the son of Scrope of Bolton, and it is William who became Earl of Wiltshire (see page II–284) and who was captured at Bristow (Bristol) by the forces of Bolingbroke and executed.

Richard le Scrope is the son of Scrope of Masham, and Richard became Archbishop of York in 1398, in the last year of the reign of Richard II.

The Archbishop of York is thus the second cousin, not the brother, of "the Lord Scroop."

Undoubtedly, grief and resentment over the death of a second cousin is not likely to be as deep and painful as grief and resentment over the death of a brother. And the Archbishop did desert that second cousin to the extent of supporting the rebellion of Bolingbroke. Nevertheless, the family connection did exist, and whatever the motive, the Archbishop was talked into considering joining the plot. It was clear he would make an admirable front man.

With the plot detailed, Worcester leaves to join Mortimer and Glendower. Clearly mistrusting Hotspur's strategic insight, his last warning is:

> . . . No further go in this
> Than I by letters shall direct your course.
>
> —Act I, scene iii, lines 289–90

Charles' wain . . .

The scene shifts to Rochester, where the robbery at Gad's Hill is being prepared. Into the innyard comes a carrier (the equivalent of today's truck driver) anxious to get his horse saddled so that his load of merchandise might move with the break of day. He sets the time by saying:

> . . . And it be not four by the day [4 A.M.] I'll be hanged. Charles' wain is over the new chimney, and yet our horse not packed.
>
> —Act II, scene i, lines 1–3

It was at 4 A.M. that the gang was to meet at Gad's Hill, so it will soon be time for the robbery.

Charles' Wain is the seven stars we usually refer to as the Big Dipper. It looks like a big dipper, to be sure, but to rustic eyes it also looks like a country cart ("wain" is an alternate form of "wagon") with a long pole to which the horse is to be hitched.

The "Charles" in Charles' Wain is a reference to Charlemagne ("Charles the Great"), who ruled over western Europe from 768 to 814 and was the most renowned of all the Western medieval kings.

Why was the wain that of Charlemagne? Nobody knows. There are theories. One, for instance, is that the nearby star, Arcturus, was considered to be the horse drawing the wagon; Arcturus was confounded with Arturus (King Arthur) and King Arthur with Charlemagne. So it ends with Charles drawing the wagon, which therefore becomes Charles' Wain.

The Big Dipper is close enough to the polestar so that in the latitude of England it never sets. It circles the polestar and is always above the horizon, so that it can be seen at any time of any clear night. Its exact position varies with the time of night, and to those who use no other clock and are frequently astir in the night, as are the carriers, its exact position ("over the new chimney") will tell them the time.

. . . the Wild of Kent . . .

After some back and forth banter between the carrier and another who joins him, Gadshill enters. It is he who is arranging the robbery, and an informant assures him that the earlier information still holds good:

> . . . there's a franklin in the Wild of Kent hath brought three hundred marks with him in gold . . .
> —Act II, scene i, lines 56–58

A franklin is a free farmer. (The word "frank" is an old word for "free," hence a person who is frank is as honest and open as a freeman is expected to be, not lying and underhanded like a slave—a distinction made by freemen, of course.) A free farmer had much more chance to prosper than did the serfs, who were bound to the land and to some lord (rather like what we would call "sharecroppers"). A franklin therefore came to mean a prosperous farmer.

"Wild" is more commonly spelled "weald" nowadays. The word is akin to the German *Wald* and refers to a forest. There was, in older times, a well-forested region in Kent, Surrey, and Sussex, the area southeast and south of London. This has long since been cleared, of course, but the term still refers to the plain between the North Downs and the South Downs, two low ranges of hills in southeastern England.

A mark was a coin equivalent in value to thirteen shillings and four-pence, so that three hundred of them were equal to two hundred pounds, a tremendous sum in those days.

. . . Saint Nicholas . . .

Gadshill's informant knows what Gadshill is planning and makes grim mention of the gallows, adding,

. . . I know thou worshippest Saint Nicholas . . .
—Act II, scene i, lines 66–67

St. Nicholas was the patron saint of travelers, and since travelers were the chosen prey of highwaymen, the latter worshiped him in the sense that they hoped he would send them many travelers. In fact, "St. Nicholas' clerks" was a slang term for highwaymen, and in the immediately preceding speech, Gadshill says of the franklin and those accompanying him:

. . . if they meet not with Saint Nicholas' clerks, I'll give thee this neck.

—Act II, scene i, lines 63–64

This usage of the name of good St. Nicholas would seem all the more inappropriate these days, for another version of the name, by way of the Dutch "Sant Nikolaas," is "Santa Claus."

. . . other Troyans . . .

Gadshill's response to the other's gibe concerning the gallows is a confident

There are other Troyans that thou dream'st not of, the which for sport sake are content to do the profession some grace; that would (if matters be looked into) for their own credit sake make all whole.

—Act II, scene i, lines 71–75

The reference to Troyans (Trojans) harks back to the old legends of the siege of Troy (see page I–73). The classical legends depicted them as bravely defending their city, and later legends had them the ancestors of the Romans and the British. With all this favorable notice, the word came to mean "a good fellow" or "a fine chap."

Gadshill's reference is, of course, to Prince Hal.

And now the robbery goes off exactly as planned. Falstaff and the rest (minus Poins and Prince Hal) wait for the merchants and attack them when they come (the whole being carried through in broad farce, particularly at the expense of Falstaff's fatness).

Once Falstaff has the gold, however, Prince Hal and Poins, thoroughly disguised, fall upon the thieves, two against four, and easily obtain the gold. Falstaff is forced to run clumping away, despite his fat.

. . . the ninth of the next month . . .

Hotspur has his much greater plot in action as well, but as is to be expected, it is moving more slowly, for much must be done. In Hotspur's castle in Northumberland, Hotspur is trying to gather together the different forces that might make part of the conspiracy. He comes onstage, reading a letter from an unnamed nobleman who has been approached. The letter writer is cautiously refusing to join the uprising but is trying to make the refusal a very polite one (just in case the Percys win out after all).

Hotspur is, however, characteristically enraged and interrupts his reading with animadversions on the writer's character and courage, and with outcries of firm confidence in the plot. When the letter writer mentions danger, Hotspur cries out:

> *. . . I tell you, my lord fool, out of this nettle, danger, we pluck this flower, safety.*
> —Act II, scene iii, lines 9–10

As evidence of the excellence of the plot, Hotspur runs over the list of those involved for the benefit of the letter writer, who cannot hear (and perhaps for his own benefit as well), and says:

> *Have I not all their letters to meet me in arms by the ninth of the next month, and are they not some of them set forward already?*
> —Act II, scene iii, lines 26–29

Since the army will be gathered on the "ninth of the next month" and since the rebellion came out in the open in July 1403, it is now June 1403. It is just a year since the defeat of Mortimer by Glendower, the event which opened the play.

Hotspur's musing has him all on fire to get on with the affair and he prepares to leave, scarcely paying attention to his wife, Catherine, who nags anxiously at him to find out what he is doing and where he is going. She guesses close to the mark when she says:

> *I fear my brother Mortimer doth stir about his title and hath sent for you to line his enterprise . . .*
> —Act II, scene iii, lines 81–83

This is a clear reminder of the relationship between Hotspur and the captive Mortimer, something that is at least part of the motive for the conspiracy.

. . . the king of courtesy . . .

The contrast continues. While Hotspur is engaged in foolhardy but romantic knight-errantry, Prince Hal is whiling away his time in a tavern in Eastcheap. He tells Poins, with great delight, that he has made friends with tapsters. The tapsters say, he reports:

> . . . that, though I be but Prince of Wales, yet I am the king of courtesy and tell me flatly I am no proud Jack like Falstaff, but a Corinthian, a lad of mettle, a good boy (by the Lord, so they call me!) and when I am King of England I shall command all the good lads in Eastcheap.
>
> —Act II, scene iv, lines 9–15

Prince Hal, it can be seen, is the pink of courtesy toward those beneath him (though he is not above making a little good-natured fun of the poor tapsters and does so in a passage that follows). Falstaff may stand upon his knighthood and hold himself aloof from the workingman, but not the Prince.

They are fascinated by his graciousness and call him a "Corinthian" in approval. Corinth was the leading commercial city of Greece at various times in its history (see page I–171) and was a haunt of traders and sailors, who brought in wealth and demanded pleasure and relaxation after the rigors and dangers of sea voyage. Corinth was therefore notorious as the home of skillful prostitutes and gay life—the Paris of Greece. In Shakespeare's time and for several centuries more, a "Corinthian" was a pleasure seeker, a gay blade.

. . . not yet of Percy's mind . . .

Yet Prince Hal is not unaware of Hotspur. In fact, he mentions him and describes him in such a way as to burlesque the earlier scene between Hotspur and his wife.

After exhausting himself with laughter over the tapsters, the Prince says (ruefully, perhaps, as though knowing that to others Hotspur's ways may seem nobler):

> I am not yet of Percy's mind, the Hotspur of the North; he that kills me some six or seven dozen of Scots at a breakfast,

washes his hands, and says to his wife, "Fie upon this quiet life! I want work." "O my sweet Harry," says she, "how many hast thou killed today?" "Give my roan horse a drench," says he, and answers, "Some fourteen," an hour after, "a trifle, a trifle."

—Act II, scene iv, lines 102-9

For the first time the contrast between the two men is put into a less conventional light. Hotspur's chivalry and "honor" becomes a kind of grotesque preoccupation with killing for no reason but to kill. His concern is first for his horse, who is necessary to him for his killing, only later for his wife, who is not.

Coming as it does, immediately after the Prince's foolery with the tapsters, we see the contrast particularly clearly. Prince Hal forgets matters of importance in his preoccupation with laughing, but Hotspur forgets matters of importance in his preoccupation with killing. Brought down to this, in the absence of the trappings of battle and with the enlightenment of Prince Hal's sarcasm, we may catch a glimpse of the fact that laughter is perhaps a better reason for which to neglect business than murder is, and that he who delights his "inferiors" is perhaps more to be admired than he who kills them.

. . . beware instinct . . .

Now enters Falstaff, ferociously upset over the miscarrying of the robbery. They had the money, after all, and then it was taken away from them, all because the Prince and Poins were not with them to stand against those who had robbed the robbers.

As he sits there, fuming and muttering, Prince Hal asks, with a straight face, for the details. Falstaff begins at once to embroider, and to multiply the number of those by whom he had been attacked.

Having given him all the rope necessary, the Prince confronts Falstaff with the truth; that he and Poins, but two in number, easily took the money from Falstaff and three others.

Now what can Falstaff say?

This is the climax of the jest. Perpetrating the practical joke was fun and listening to Falstaff lie was fun, but surely best of all would be watching Falstaff squirm out of the hole he had talked himself into. The Prince was probably certain that Falstaff's endless ingenuity would meet the challenge most amusingly.

And as for Falstaff, it is quite possible that even in the course of his lying, his quick wit worked out the truth, and that he made his lies all the worse in order to make his escape the more spectacular.

Now it comes. Falstaff, faced with the truth, says:

> *By the Lord, I knew ye as well as he that made ye. Why, hear*
> *you, my masters. Was it for me to kill the heir apparent?*
> *Should I turn upon the true prince? Why, thou knowest I am*
> *as valiant as Hercules, but beware instinct. The lion will not*
> *touch the true prince.*

> —Act II, scene iv, lines 268–73

This was an age when the study of zoology was largely the creation of moral myths to edify mankind. The entire world of life seemed nothing more than a schoolroom to educate sinful man. The lion was the king of beasts and therefore, out of the brotherhood of kingship, would not harm a king of men.

. . . a true prince

But Falstaff is not just a figure of fun. We can very easily argue that he can give as good as he gets, and certainly he has been bamboozled most cruelly. He has been mocked, mistreated, forced to walk when his horse was hidden, forced to hand over his ill-gotten gains, forced to flee, and now he was being mocked and derided.

Was there not to be at least some residuum of hard feeling as a result? And though Falstaff could not openly show his displeasure against the Prince of Wales, was there no secret way his wit could find to show it? Surely, he knew Hal well enough to know what might really be bothering him.

Shakespeare nowhere says so in this play, but we might fairly argue that Prince Hal has never really reconciled himself to the manner in which his father attained the throne (see page II–304). Secretly, he may consider his father a usurper and himself merely the heir to a usurped crown. He can scarcely value either his own title or his own position, and it is just this, perhaps, that causes him to pass his time in wasting and roistering. Why behave like a Prince of Wales when, in his heart, he doesn't really feel he is one?

And if that is so, and if Falstaff knows this feeling of Hal's or shrewdly suspects it, it would be precisely on this sore that his wit would land, in return for his own humiliation.

He has already described Prince Hal, in a voice and face that surely seems all respect, as a "true prince." Now he jabs harder and, while remaining in a position in which no one can find the slightest trace of lack of respect, manages to flay the Prince when he says:

> *I shall think the better of myself, and thee, during my life—I*
> *for a valiant lion, and thou for a true prince.*

> —Act II, scene iv, lines 274–76

Falstaff is saying that his own instinctive shying away from a fight with Prince Hal is overpowering evidence in favor of himself as a lion and Hal as a true prince. But is this not like saying that there is some doubt that Hal is a true prince and that evidence like this is needed to set such doubts at rest? Worse yet, it is notorious that Falstaff is *not* a valiant lion. By equating the two characteristics, is Falstaff not hinting that it is notorious that Hal is *not* a true prince?

And even if this is the furthest thing from Falstaff's mind, would the sensitive Prince Hal not interpret the speech in this fashion and be unable to answer since the doubts as to his own legitimacy cannot be put into words before his future subjects? He must suffer grimly in silence, and from this view, Falstaff has turned the tables neatly.

. . . made Lucifer cuckold . . .

And now the harsh world intrudes on this gayest of all Shakespearean scenes. A nobleman has come from court to summon Prince Hal. Carelessly, the Prince sends Falstaff to turn him away, but Falstaff returns with grim news. The conspiracy is now in the open; Hotspur's army is in the field.

Falstaff lists the enemies, and in listing Glendower, he identifies him, indirectly, as

> . . . *he of Wales that gave Amamon the bastinado, and made Lucifer cuckold, and swore the devil his true liegeman . . .*
> —Act II, scene iv, lines 337–39

In other words, Glendower has overpowered the various devils (Amaimon is the name of one of the chief devils of hell in medieval demonology, which named hordes of them—see page II-34) and made them his servants. This is a claim Glendower himself makes later in the play.

. . . kills a sparrow flying

When Falstaff lists the Scotsman, Douglas, it is his skill as a horseman that seems to be most impressive. Falstaff describes him as:

> . . . *that sprightly Scot of Scots, Douglas, that runs a-horseback up a hill perpendicular—*
> —Act II, scene iv, lines 343–45

Prince Hal chimes in, setting up Falstaff for a riposte:

He that rides at high speed and with his pistol kills a sparrow
flying.

—Act II, scene iv, lines 346–47

Falstaff eagerly gives him the straight line:

You have hit it.

—Act II, scene iv, line 348

And Prince Hal answers at once:

So did he never the sparrow.

—Act II, scene iv, line 349

Once again, Prince Hal punctures the pretensions of chivalry. The picture of a doughty knight, utter master of his horse and with an unerring
eye making impossible shots with easy grace, is suddenly shattered. (The
fact that the pistol didn't come into use till about twenty years after the
time of this scene and that the use of the word is anachronistic is not very
important.)

. . . some of thy instinct

Hal's dry joke also serves the purpose of showing the audience that he
is utterly unafraid at this news.

And yet he must be affected. The rebellion must clearly have, as one of
its justifications, the claim that Henry IV is not the rightful King and that
Hal is therefore not a true prince. Falstaff's jibe is thus repeated and made
infinitely stronger by the news.

That Hal may well be brooding about this comes at once. Falstaff, teasing again, asks the Prince if he isn't horribly afraid at hearing this news.
Prince Hal answers with a bitter return jab:

Not a whit, i' faith. I lack some of thy instinct.

—Act II, scene iv, line 372

He has not forgotten Falstaff's remark.

. . . in King Cambyses' vein

But Hal can scarcely turn his anger full upon Falstaff, for if Falstaff is
jabbing at him, it is not Falstaff's fault that the situation exists to be jabbed

at. Rather it is Hal's father who is at fault; it is King Henry who usurped the crown and crushed his young son under a burden of guilt.

If this is so, we can understand why, for the rest of the scene, Prince Hal engages in what would otherwise seem an utterly heartless parody of his father, who is now engaged in the crisis of his thus far brief reign.

Falstaff warns Prince Hal that he will get a dressing down when he comes to his father, and they decide to practice an answer. Falstaff himself will play the angry King, and he says:

> . . . *I must speak in passion, and I will do it in King Cambyses' vein.*
>
> —Act II, scene iv, lines 386–87

Cambyses was King of the Persian Empire from 529 to 522 B.C. His great feat was the conquest of Egypt and the addition of that land to his realm. Herodotus tells the tale in his great history, written nearly a century later, but, getting his information from Egyptian priests, who could scarcely have been sympathetic to the Persian monarch, the Greek historian presents Cambyses as a raging and blasphemous madman.

The first important piece of historical drama in Elizabethan times was devoted to this ancient king. It was *The Life of Cambises, King of Percia,* written by Thomas Preston and put on the boards in 1569. It was a bombastic piece filled with murder and bloodshed and proved a popular success.

Naturally, Cambyses was shown in the play as raging madly across the stage, and his name became one of the bywords for monstrously overacting. Shakespeare was not too proud to present such tales of blood and gore himself, notably in *Titus Andronicus* (see page I–391), but by 1597 he had matured and was ready enough to poke fun at the practice, caring nothing for the fact that the Cambyses to which Falstaff refers is a character in a play not written till a century and a half after Falstaff was dead.

. . . I do not only marvel . . .

Nor is it only ranting passion that Shakespeare aims to satirize. Falstaff begins to speak in intricately balanced sentences:

> *Harry, I do not only marvel where thou spendest thy time, but also how thou art accompanied. For though the camomile, the more it is trodden on, the faster it grows, so youth the more it is wasted, the sooner it wears.*
>
> —Act II, scene iv, lines 398–402

The style is derived from a book written by an English courtier named John Lyly. The book was *Euphues, the Anatomy of Wit,* published in

1578, when the author was only twenty-four. It was a didactic book aimed at the reform of education and manners, but its contents were unimportant compared to its style. Lyly perfected the balanced sentence; each in two parts of similar length and contrasting contents. He made use of exotic words and farfetched similes often drawn from nature.

Indeed, his style was so tortured and overwritten that it removed the language from the common folk. Only the well-educated could write in his manner or understand it once it was written. It therefore appealed to snobs and for a while had a fantastic run of popularity as those who did not understand it nevertheless pretended to do so in order to be in the swim.

By the 1590s, however, opposition and ridicule began to make themselves felt. A writer like Shakespeare, who aimed for all men and not for the superelegant few, naturally found euphuism (as the style was called) abhorrent, and this is one of the places where he laughs at it with deadly effect. (He gibes at it also in *Love's Labor's Lost,* see page I–426.)

. . . banish plump Jack . . .

But Falstaff suddenly turns from his euphuism into a panegyric (in the King's name) on himself. In annoyance, Prince Hal stops him and offers to play the King himself.

Doing so, he turns the tables on Falstaff and (in the King's name) begins to berate Falstaff in colorful style. But Falstaff is perfectly master of the situation. With scarcely the skip of a heartbeat, he seizes the floor and (in the Prince's name, this time) launches into another panegyric of himself, ending:

> . . . *for sweet Jack Falstaff, kind Jack Falstaff, true Jack Falstaff, valiant Jack Falstaff, and therefore more valiant being, as he is, old Jack Falstaff, banish not him thy Harry's company, banish not him thy Harry's company, banish plump Jack, and banish all the world.*
>
> —Act II, scene iv, lines 475–80

In the excitement of this peroration, Prince Hal's response is pushed into the background. But it is a somber and serious one and it reflects, perhaps, the Prince's pain over Falstaff's gibing at his status as a true prince. In response to the plea not to banish Falstaff, Prince Hal says:

> *I do, I will.*
>
> —Act II, scene iv, line 481

It is a grim portent of the climax of Falstaff's life.

. . . all to the wars . . .

But the fun is interrupted once again. This time the sheriff and his watch are at the door in search of the robbers of Gad's Hill. At least one of the robbers, Falstaff, is unmistakable, and the sheriff is searching for a man of huge fatness. If Falstaff is seen, he is as good as convicted, and highway robbery was, at the time, a capital offense. It was not a fine that Falstaff was risking, or even imprisonment, but the halter and the noose.

Yet either Falstaff is not quite the coward he is usually considered or else he has utter faith in the Prince. He faces the sheriff's entry calmly and at Prince Hal's direction retires behind a curtain and actually goes to sleep there while the Prince fends off the sheriff with ambiguities that hide the truth without actually being outright lies.

But once the sheriff is gone, the fun is over. Prince Hal searches the sleeping man's pockets to see what smiles might be gained at the expense of the contents (a restaurant bill), but then he turns serious. Looking at the sleeping Falstaff, he says to Peto (another of the low crew):

> *I'll to the court in the morning. We must all to the wars, and thy place shall be honorable. I'll procure this fat rogue a charge of foot, and I know his death will be a march of twelve score* [paces]. *The money shall be paid back again with advantage* [interest].
>
> —Act II, scene iv, lines 545–50

The reference to the repayment of money with interest promises to clear up the last trace of guilt on the Prince's part as far as the robbery is concerned. Not only did he not take direct part in it, but he will return the money with additional payment to make up for the bodily fear and the inconvenience which the merchants incurred.

I can call spirits . . .

Once again, back to Hotspur. Two scenes before, he had left his Northumberland castle. The lengthy scene between Prince Hal and Falstaff has given him time to reach Wales and now he is in the very lair of the redoubtable Glendower. With him there is Mortimer, earlier a prisoner of Glendower and now the Welshman's ally and son-in-law. With him also is Worcester, the brains of the conspiracy.

Hotspur is impatient. To him, Glendower in particular is a weird and alien figure. Hotspur can be poetic enough in the cause of his monomania, honor, but on all other subjects he is prosaic and literal. Besides, he has led armies against the Welsh, who were, in their turn, led by the very man who now faces him across the table, and this can scarcely make him comfortable.

Glendower, for his part, has kept his hold over his Welshmen by impressing them with the notion that he has supernatural powers, and apparently he means to do the same in the case of his new English allies.

Thus, when Hotspur tries to flatter Glendower by describing the King's fear of him, Glendower responds with ponderous gravity:

> *I cannot blame him. At my nativity*
> *The front* [face] *of heaven was full of fiery shapes*
> *Of burning cressets* [beacons], *and at my birth*
> *The frame and huge foundation of the earth*
> *Shakèd like a coward.*
>
> —Act III, scene i, lines 12–16

This is another expression of the common belief that the heavenly bodies have nothing to do but act as gentlemen ushers announcing various events taking place (or about to take place) on our own insignificant earth (see page I-96).

Hotspur takes our modern view of the matter (like Edmund in *King Lear*—see page II-14) and says:

> *Why, so it would have done at the same season if your moth-*
> *er's cat had but kittened, though yourself had never been born.*
> —Act III, scene i, lines 17–19

With rising anger, Glendower states his claims to supernatural powers over and over, while Hotspur stubbornly continues to sneer. This reaches a peak in a famous exchange indeed. Glendower says, impressively:

> *I can call spirits from the vasty deep.*
> —Act III, scene i, line 52

And Hotspur answers at once:

> *Why, so can I, or so can any man;*
> *But will they come when you do call for them?*
> —Act III, scene i, lines 53–54

However much sensible men applaud this answer and are grateful to Hotspur for making it, and quote him in season and out, it was a dreadful remark to make on this occasion. It was Glendower he was speaking to, and without Glendower the rebellion would not succeed. Was this a time to cross him? Why not take him at his own evaluation as long as his friendship was necessary?

In this again is the contrast between Hotspur and Prince Hal. The Prince is courteous even to tapsters from whom he has nothing to gain; Hotspur is rude even to Glendower, from whom he has everything to gain.

Into three limits . . .

Mortimer, angry at Hotspur's folly, manages to call him off, and turns the meeting to its purpose—an agreement on the division of the kingdom after the conspirators have won a victory over King Henry. (This is a case of dividing the bearskin before the bear is killed, but it is necessary, for none of the parties will fight unless they are satisfied in advance they will not be cheated afterward.)

They hunch over a map and Mortimer indicates the division:

> *The Archdeacon hath divided it*
> *Into three limits very equally.*
> *England, from Trent and Severn hitherto,*
> *By south and east is to my part assigned;*
> *All westward, Wales beyond the Severn shore,*
> *And all the fertile land within that bound,*
> *To Owen Glendower; and, dear coz, to you*
> *The remnant northward lying off from Trent.*
> *—Act III, scene i, lines 71–78*

The Archdeacon here referred to is the Archdeacon of Bangor (a town on the northwestern shore of Wales just across the narrow strait from the island of Anglesey). Presumably the Archdeacon was chosen as a learned man and a neutral who would be fair to all three.

The division is a reasonable one, if a division there must be. Glendower, getting all the land west of the Severn, gets not only the region now recognized as Wales but good English areas including all of Herefordshire and parts of Shropshire and Worcestershire.

If the Percys get the land north of the Trent, then they have all of northern England down as far as Nottingham and Derby. They come as close as a hundred miles to London in places.

The rest of England, south of the Trent and east of Severn, is the part that Mortimer (or rather, his nephew, Edmund of March) will reign over as King. It would be more populous and wealthy than either of the other portions and it might be supposed that both Glendower and Hotspur would swear to some sort of surface allegiance to Mortimer. Still, the conditions of the rebellion are such and the services of Glendower and Hotspur of that sort as to make any control over them impossible. There would be, essentially, three independent kingdoms: England, Wales, and (to use the Anglo-Saxon name for the old northern kingdom) Northumbria.

Such a situation could not be stable, of course. Inevitably there would be friction; inevitably warfare and blood. England would descend into anarchy, perhaps for generations, conceivably for centuries.

Shakespeare's audience would be bound to listen with indignation to any plan to divide England in three. If they had up to this point admired Hotspur for his bravery and gallantry, they could scarcely admire him any further. It may well be to encourage the audience to lose that admiration more thoroughly that Shakespeare has Hotspur act so childishly in this scene.

A huge half-moon . . .

Thus, even while Mortimer and Glendower pass on to the next order of business—when and where the different armies shall meet to form a united front against the King—Hotspur breaks into a pout over the map, which he has continued studying. He says, sulkily:

> Methinks my moiety north from Burton here,
> In quantity equals not one of yours.
> See how this river comes me cranking in
> And cuts me from the best of all my land
> A huge half-moon, a monstrous cantle [section] out.
> —Act III, scene i, lines 95–99

The Burton referred to here is Burton-on-Trent, a town near the southernmost point reached by the curving Trent River. From Burton, the Trent River runs east toward Nottingham, then swings north into the Humber. If the Trent River were to continue eastward, it would enter the Wash, and Lincolnshire would be included in Hotspur's portion rather than in Mortimer's. It is this which Hotspur bemoans, and he actually suggests damming the river in such a way as to make it flow east.

But then Glendower, whose portion is not affected by the Trent one way or another, suddenly objects (even though Worcester and Mortimer are humoring Hotspur in this impossible project just to keep him from going out of control). Again Glendower and Hotspur are at it, to the endangerment of the whole project.

. . . the dreamer Merlin . . .

When the two separate at last and Glendower leaves, the others are free to turn on Hotspur. Mortimer instantly scolds him for baiting the Welshman, and Hotspur replies defensively:

> *I cannot choose. Sometime he angers me*
> *With telling me of the moldwarp and the ant,*
> *Of the dreamer Merlin and his prophecies,*
> *And of a dragon . . .*
>
> —Act III, scene i, lines 147–50

Merlin, the ancient sage of the Welsh myths (and a prominent part of the King Arthur legend), was a figure of hope to the late medieval Welshmen, longing as they did for some way of recovering their lost independence. Many prophecies were attributed to him and naturally they were interpreted in such a way as to give the Welsh hope.

According to Holinshed, one of the prophecies current in Wales at this time was to the effect that the kingdom of the moldwarp (mole) would be divided by a dragon, lion, and wolf. To interpret this one, it was necessary to suppose that King Henry was the devious mole, having won the crown by his underground maneuvering. The dragon was clearly Glendower, for it was a creature much associated with Wales and early Celtic legends. The lion was who else but Hotspur, while Mortimer could just as well be the wolf as anything else.

No doubt it was this that Glendower was regaling Hotspur with, along with a good deal more of mystical matter, and it was this that Hotspur couldn't abide.

Defect of manners . . .

Despite the harm Hotspur is clearly doing, Mortimer labors to flatter him and keep him in good humor.

Not so Worcester. It is he who has set the conspiracy in motion, and he has said very little while Hotspur was playing the fool. Now he bursts out in anger against Hotspur's tactlessness:

> *You must needs learn, lord, to amend this fault.*
> *Though sometimes it show greatness, courage, blood—*
> *And that's the dearest grace it renders you—*
> *Yet oftentimes it doth present harsh rage,*
> *Defect of manners, want of government,*
> *Pride, haughtiness, opinion, and disdain;*
>
> —Act III, scene i, lines 179–84

Thus are Hotspur's faults clearly outlined to the audience just in case they have not picked them up for themselves out of the action. The contrast with Prince Hal continues to swing toward the Prince's side.

. . . at Shrewsbury

But the conspiracy is in motion and the meeting place has already been assigned. Mortimer had said, earlier:

> *Tomorrow, cousin Percy, you and I*
> *And my good Lord of Worcester will set forth*
> *To meet your father and the Scottish power,*
> *As is appointed us, at Shrewsbury.*
> *My father Glendower is not ready yet,*
> *Nor shall we need his help these fourteen days.*
> —Act III, scene i, lines 82–87

Shrewsbury is the chief town of Shropshire, on the upper Severn, ten miles east of the Welsh border. It controls the roads into northern Wales and the Percys can wait there in reasonable security, with their backs toward Wales, until Glendower joins them. Then they can advance.

After a scene in which Mortimer's Welsh wife (Glendower's daughter) sings and there is a little comic relief from Hotspur and his wife (Hotspur is always at his most engaging when he is making broad love to his wife—he is the slap-on-the-rump type) it is time to leave. Off they all ride and the rebel army is in the field.

. . . thy younger brother . . .

Back in London, meanwhile, King Henry and Prince Hal confront each other in earnest, much as the play acting with Falstaff had presaged. In fact, the King almost sounds like Falstaff as he deplores the Prince's taste for low company. At one point he says:

> *Thy place in council thou hast rudely lost,*
> *Which by thy younger brother is supplied,*
> —Act III, scene ii, lines 32–33

This is anachronistic. At the time of Hotspur's rebellion, Prince Hal was, in actuality, not yet sixteen, and had no voice in the government. It was not until 1409, six years after the rebellion, that he demanded and received a place on the council. By that time his father was ailing and the Prince moved naturally into political opposition.

It is easy to account for this. There is the normal rebellion of a son against parental authority, and the desire for a man soon to be king to begin organizing the kingdom in his own fashion. As for Henry IV, he, knowing he had not long to live, apparently feared the possibility that the Prince might be tempted to seize the throne before it was properly his— and the King's obvious hostility further alienated the son.

For a time, in fact, the King forced the Prince of Wales out of his position and replaced him with a younger brother, as indicated in the verses quoted above. It was the King's hostility, however, and not the Prince's dereliction of duty that brought about the change. What's more, the popularity of the Prince forced the King to restore him to his position.

And who was the younger brother?

Mary de Bohun (see page II-264) had been the wife of Henry IV (then Henry Bolingbroke) for a dozen years before her death in 1394. In that time she gave birth to six children, including four sons. Prince Hal was the oldest of the four, of course. The second, one year younger, was Thomas, who eventually became the Duke of Clarence. It was Thomas of Clarence who replaced Prince Hal on the council for a short time in 1412 when he was twenty-four and Prince Hal twenty-five.

The legends that make Prince Hal wild and dissolute would naturally have it that he was relieved of his council post because of his behavior. In fact, a favorite story is that he struck the Chief Justice of England when that functionary was trying to arrest one of the rakehells whom the Prince had befriended and protected. The Prince was himself arrested in consequence and placed in confinement.

This is almost certainly not so. The legend cannot be traced back further than the sixteenth century and it is probably mere embroidery on the earlier legends—making a good story better. This incident is included in *The Famous Victories,* but Shakespeare does not use it directly, probably because it would present Prince Hal in entirely too gross and bad a light. Shakespeare does refer to this later in the series of plays, though, when it can be used to present the Prince in a noble light.

. . . I did pluck allegiance . . .

The King continues to scold Prince Hal, assuring him that by making himself common to every Englishman he will weary them. He holds himself up as an example, explaining how cleverly he won the affection of the people by keeping himself carefully aloof so that the occasional sight of him was impressive—while King Richard bored the populace by being forever in view.

And on those occasions when the people did see him, Henry played up to them. Now, remembering those days, he tells his son:

> *. . . I stole all courtesy from heaven,*
> *And dressed myself in such humility*
> *That I did pluck allegiance from men's hearts,*
> *Loud shouts and salutations from their mouths*
> *Even in the presence of the crownèd King.*
>
> —Act III, scene ii, lines 50–54

Here, clearly, the King proves himself to be incredibly undiplomatic. How can he impress his sensitive son by this open admission that he stole the kingdom and by seeming to glory in the baseness of the theft? If we are correct in interpreting Prince Hal's actions as brought about by his unhappiness over the ambiguity of his title and position, then how must he feel when his father's every word casts mud upon that same title and position?

Prince Hal can only withdraw into himself, and when his father's long, self-serving speech ends, he says coldly:

> *I shall hereafter, my thrice-gracious lord,*
> *Be more myself.*
>
> —Act III, scene ii, lines 92–93

Is there irony in the adjective "thrice-gracious"?

And what is "myself"? If Hal is not really a true prince in his own estimation or by his father's words, why should he act like one? Why not be "more myself," that is, a mere subject, and enjoy himself like one? The remark might be interpreted as a grim promise to be even more dissolute.

. . . no more in debt to years . . .

But then the King finds the proper key to Prince Hal's soul. He compares the Prince to Hotspur, pointing out that in deeds Hotspur has a better claim to the throne than Prince Hal does. He describes Hotspur as being one who:

> *. . . being no more in debt to years than thou,*
> *Leads ancient lords and reverend bishops on*
> *To bloody battles and to bruising arms.*
>
> —Act III, scene ii, lines 103–5

Having said this, he then goes on to picture Prince Hal as stooping to the utmost in degradation. Wondering helplessly why he bothers to reason with Hal at all, King Henry says, in a moving speech:

> *Why, Harry, do I tell thee of my foes,*
> *Which art my nearest and dearest enemy?*

Thou that art like enough, through vassal fear,
Base inclination, and the start of spleen,
To fight against me under Percy's pay,
To dog his heels and curtsy at his frowns,
To show how much thou art degenerate.

—Act III, scene ii, lines 122–28

Prince Hal cannot withstand that. True prince or not, whatever his status, he is no coward and no degenerate. In an impassioned and stirring speech, he promises that he will yet make his father proud of him:

I will redeem all this on Percy's head
And, in the closing of some glorious day,
Be bold to tell you that I am your son,

—Act III, scene ii, lines 132–34

So warlike does Prince Hal sound now, so like Hotspur himself and so like what a Prince of Wales should be, that the King joyfully cries out:

A hundred thousand rebels die in this!
Thou shalt have charge and sovereign trust herein.

—Act III, scene ii, lines 160–61

. . . my son, Lord John of Lancaster

But the time of battle is at hand. Interrupting the conversation between father and son is Walter Blunt, who comes in with the news:

. . . Douglas and the English rebels met
The eleventh of this month at Shrewsbury.

—Act III, scene ii, lines 165–66

The date indicated is July 11, 1403.
But the King has already taken his countermeasures. He says to Prince Hal:

The Earl of Westmoreland set forth today;
With him my son, Lord John of Lancaster:
For this advertisement is five days old.
On Wednesday next, Harry, you shall set forward;
On Thursday we ourselves will march. Our meeting
Is Bridgenorth.

—Act III, scene ii, lines 170–75

Westmoreland is the real general, and the mention of John of Lancaster has little historical significance. John is the third son of Henry IV and is two years younger than Prince Hal. John was born on June 20, 1389, and had just turned fourteen, actually, when Hotspur raised his rebellion. He too is made some ten years older by Shakespeare.

Bridgenorth, the assigned place of meeting of the royal forces, is on the Severn River, twenty miles downstream from Shrewsbury.

. . . paid back again

Another scene with Falstaff follows, but now the Prince comes in only at the end, for he can find little time for idle amusements.

Remember that after Prince Hal had turned away the sheriff's men and found Falstaff sleeping behind the curtain he had gone through Falstaff's pockets for a lark. Now Falstaff claims pickpockets have relieved him of great, but fictitious, valuables, and a broadly farcical quarrel proceeds between himself and the landlady, Mistress Quickly, complete with ribald allusions.

When the Prince enters, he keeps the two at each other for a while for the fun of it, but when Falstaff finally asks about the situation as far as the Gad's Hill robbery is concerned, Prince Hal says:

> . . . I must still be good angel to thee. The money is paid back again.
>
> —Act III, scene iii, lines 183–84

Prince Hal's hands are thus cleaned of the one really serious fault Shakespeare can bear to have him commit.

Hal goes on to say that he has procured Falstaff a charge of foot. That is, Falstaff can sign up a group of infantrymen for service in the war and he can lead them as its officer. This is a post of considerable honor for Falstaff.

. . . so dangerous and dear a trust

Hotspur, Worcester, and Douglas the Scot are in camp now near Shrewsbury. So far all has gone like clockwork for them and they are supremely confident.

But now comes the beginning of a check. A Messenger comes with letters from Hotspur's father, the Earl of Northumberland. The Earl is sick, it would appear. Nor can his army come under a deputy, for as Hotspur says, scanning the letter:

> *. . . nor did he think it meet*
> *To lay so dangerous and dear a trust*
> *On any soul removed but on his own.*
> > —Act IV, scene i, lines 33–35

This is a severe blow. Northumberland's men are needed to make the army large enough to withstand the King's forces. What is much worse is that men were sure to think the illness was a feigned one; that Northumberland quailed at the last moment and lacked the courage to place himself firmly on the side of open rebellion. Naturally, if Hotspur's soldiers felt that Northumberland thought it safer to be ill than to fight, the heart would go out of them and they would fight half defeated to begin with.

Worcester, clear-thinking, sees this. Probably if he had guided the army, it would now have retreated, waiting some other chance for battle. Hotspur thinks otherwise, however. Anxious always to fight, he counters Worcester's warning of the psychological damage the defection has brought them with a psychological counterattack, saying:

> *I rather of his absence make this use:*
> *It lends a luster and more great opinion,*
> *A larger dare to our great enterprise*
> *Than if the Earl were here;*
> > —Act IV, scene i, lines 75–78

Given Hotspur's character, he feels the fewer his allies, the greater his own share of glory and "honor" if he wins. The thought of this but spurs him on, and thinking that his entire army thinks as he does, he imagines they will all fight with great vigor for this reason.

(Yet it must be added that the time will come when Prince Hal is himself King and is about to face a much larger and much more unequal battle—and in a much greater speech he will reason just as Hotspur does here. But Prince Hal will have better reason to do so and he will win; for he is the greater man.)

. . . like feathered Mercury

More bad news arrives, brought by Sir Richard Vernon, a partisan on the side of the Percys. The royal army, he says, is marching toward them with breathless speed. Westmoreland, John of Lancaster, the King himself are all leading contingents that are converging upon the rebel forces.

But there is a personal contrast, one that fills this play, that must be taken care of. Hotspur shrugs these enemies, even the King, all aside, and demands:

> . . . Where is his son,
> The nimble-footed madcap Prince of Wales,
> And his comrades, that daffed the world aside
> And bid it pass?
>
> —Act IV, scene i, lines 93–96

Now for the first time the comparison changes. Until now, whenever Hotspur and Prince Hal have been directly compared, it has always been glory and honor for the first, contempt and disgrace for the second. But now it is another story. Vernon has seen Prince Hal not in the tavern but in the field, and he says:

> I saw young Harry with his beaver [helmet] on,
> His cushes [thigh-armor] on his thighs, gallantly armed,
> Rise from the ground like feathered Mercury,
> And vaulted with such ease into his seat
> As if an angel dropped down from the clouds
> To turn and wind a fiery Pegasus
> And witch the world with noble horsemanship.
>
> —Act IV, scene i, lines 103–9

Mercury, the messenger of the gods, is routinely pictured with small wings at his ankles, symbolizing the speed with which he can move. Prince Hal bounds into his saddle as though he, like Mercury, can fly.

His horse too shares in this metaphor, for he is compared to Pegasus, the famous winged horse of Greek mythology.

This description Hotspur cannot face. Earlier, Prince Hal, goaded by his father's contempt, promised to meet Hotspur in single combat and by victory earn his right to be called the King's son. Now, in balancing contrast, Hotspur, goaded by Vernon's description, cries:

> . . . Come, let me taste my horse,
> Who is to bear me like a thunderbolt
> Against the bosom of the Prince of Wales.
> Harry to Harry shall, hot horse to horse,
> Meet, and ne'er part till one drop down a corse.
>
> —Act IV, scene i, lines 118–22

He cannot draw his power . . .

Hotspur can hardly wait for battle now. There remains still one of the rebel contingents to come, and Hotspur longs for it so that the battle may start without further delay. He says:

O that Glendower were come!

— Act IV, scene i, line 123

This brings down the worst blow of all, for Vernon says:

> *. . . There is more news.*
> *I learned in Worcester, as I rode along,*
> *He cannot draw his power this fourteen days.*

— Act IV, scene i, lines 123–25

It would be dramatically interesting if it could be shown that Glendower was pouting because of Hotspur's insults earlier in the play. It could then be seen just how Hotspur's character impeded the conspiracy—but there is no clear hint of that.

In actual fact, Glendower's failure was the consequence of competent action on the part of the royal army. They had moved quickly, more quickly than the rebels counted on, and took Shrewsbury before Hotspur's army could enter. With Shrewsbury in the King's hands, Hotspur was cut off from Glendower. Hotspur now had to fight his battle in an attempt to smash the royal army or, failing that, at least to take Shrewsbury and pave the way for joining Glendower, and do so under heavy disadvantage—or not fight at all.

Yet not to fight at all at this point would be to risk the melting away of his army, disheartened at being outmaneuvered, and might make of Hotspur a hunted fugitive sure to be captured and executed—a most dishonorable end.

. . . as ragged as Lazarus . . .

At least some of the royal forces are not yet at Shrewsbury, however, at least in the Shakespearean view. Falstaff is encountered near Coventry in a long soliloquy that shows him at his very worst, and in a situation where the audience must find it hard indeed to feel anything but disgust.

He has received over three hundred pounds with which to hire 150 soldiers he is to lead into battle. He carefully chooses substantial men who desperately don't want to be in the army and who can bribe their way out of a forced enlistment. Thus, he obtains additional money and ends by enlisting men from the very dregs of society.

Falstaff describes them contemptuously in an address to the audience as:

> *. . . slaves as ragged as Lazarus . . .*

— Act IV, scene ii, line 25

This harks back to the very famous parable in Luke about Lazarus, a beggar who waited for crumbs at the gate of a rich man's mansion. After both died, Lazarus went to heaven and the rich man to hell.

It is easy to see that this parable would be much cherished by the vast majority of the poor and oppressed, since it holds out the promise of redress after death and, even more, the anticipation of seeing one's oppressors punished. Consequently, Lazarus, from the frequent references to the parable, became the archetype of misery and pauperdom on earth.

Another reference to the parable, and to its other side, is found earlier in the play. When Falstaff is making elaborate fun of the fiery face of his alcoholic servant, Bardolph, Falstaff says:

> *I never see thy face but I think upon hellfire and Dives that lived in purple; for there he is in his robes, burning, burning.*
> —Act III, scene iii, lines 32–34

The rich man in the parable is given no proper name, but in the Latin version of the Bible he is *dives,* which simply means "rich man." It was easy for those who knew little Latin to suppose that Dives was the proper name of the hell-bound individual.

Falstaff, in describing the miserable wretches he has recruited, uses another biblical reference when he says:

> *. . . you would think that I had a hundred and fifty tattered prodigals lately come from swine-keeping, from eating draff and husks.*
> —Act IV, scene ii, lines 34–36

Here we have another famous parable from Luke: that of the prodigal son, reduced to misery by his own folly, and then taken back and forgiven. (Naturally, the promise of forgiveness is a source of consolation to all men, so that the parable became popular indeed.)

At the depth of the prodigal's misery he is forced to keep swine for a bare living (a terrible fate for a Jew, who considers swine unclean) and is so famished that he envies the swine their food. The popular version of the parable has him actually eat the draff, or pig swill, but what the Bible says is "And he would fain have filled his belly with the husks that the swine did eat" (Luke 15:16). It does not say that he actually ate them.

It is impossible to find excuses for Falstaff in this action of his, which is personally immoral and nationally treasonable, except the very feeble one that others did the same. Yet perhaps that is what Shakespeare had in mind. In many places in his plays Shakespeare manages to show his distaste for war, and here he bitterly satirizes the kind of corruption which war makes common, the general erosion of human values which it brings about.

At the close of the soliloquy, Falstaff encounters Prince Hal and Westmoreland on their way to the gathering of the royal forces. Falstaff says to the Prince:

> *How now, mad wag? What a devil dost thou in Warwickshire?*
> —Act IV, scene ii, lines 51–52

They are still some fifty miles east of Shrewsbury, though Westmoreland says his army is there already.

The number of the King . . .

Outside Shrewsbury, Hotspur's incontinent rage and lack of self-control (spurred on, perhaps, by his peevish anger at the fact that the despised Prince of Wales is showing knightly qualities after all) are still working against himself and his allies.

Hotspur wants to attack at once, and in this he is backed by that other border fighter, Douglas. Vernon and Worcester, with more common sense, urge caution—some of the cavalry have just arrived and are tired. Some have not even arrived. Finally, Worcester says desperately:

> *The number of the King exceedeth ours.*
> *For God's sake, cousin, stay till all come in.*
> —Act IV, scene iii, lines 28–29

Hotspur manages to restrain himself, but barely. When Blunt arrives with an offer to negotiate, Hotspur responds with a long list of his grievances and then grudgingly asks for a chance to ponder the matter overnight.

. . . the fortune of ten thousand men

The scene switches to the palace of the Archbishop of York, in the city of York. He is sending messages in all directions in the greatest haste, for as he says to the man who will carry them:

> *Tomorrow, good Sir Michael, is a day*
> *Wherein the fortune of ten thousand men*
> *Must bide the touch . . .*
> —Act IV, scene iv, lines 8–10

A touchstone is a dark, hard rock upon which the soft metal gold will rub off where it touches and leave a mark. The marks made by pure gold and by gold to which varying amounts of copper have been added differs in color. A sample of unknown gold alloy can be marked across the touch-stone and the color compared to standards. In this way the composition of the gold alloy can be determined.

A touchstone has thus come to mean anything that can be used as a test. The fortune of ten thousand men must bide the "touch," that is, will be tested by the battle to see which side will be victorious, which defeated.

It is now the day before the Battle of Shrewsbury, or July 20, 1403, and the Archbishop is making preparations for strengthening himself against the King in case his ally, Hotspur, is defeated in the battle.

. . . crush our old limbs . . .

The scene shifts back to the King's camp near Shrewsbury. It is sunrise and Hotspur has had his night to think things over. He has sent Worcester and Vernon to the King to see what can be done to achieve a peaceful set-tlement. (He has, as is later made clear, accepted Westmoreland in their place as a surety for the safe return of these negotiators.)

The King greets Worcester, the brains behind the rebellion, most coldly and says:

> . . . *You have deceived our trust*
> *And made us doff our easy robes of peace*
> *To crush our old limbs in ungentle steel.*
>
> —Act V, scene i, lines 11–13

Since Prince Hal is made ten years older than he really is, for dramatic purposes, his father must be made older too. The vision here is of an old man come tottering out to war, but as a matter of historical fact, the King is actually only thirty-seven years old at this point and is over twenty years *younger* than is Worcester, whom he is now addressing with such self-pity.

. . . that oath at Doncaster

Worcester repeats (as Hotspur had in an earlier scene) the Percy litany: how the King had returned from exile with a handful of men; how the Percys had saved him by taking up his cause; how without them he could not have succeeded. Something new is added, however. Worcester says, self-righteously:

> . . . *You swore to us,*
> *And you did swear that oath at Doncaster,*
> *That you did nothing purpose 'gainst the state,*
> *Nor claim no further than your new-fall'n right*

The seat of Gaunt, dukedom of Lancaster.
                                    —Act V, scene i, lines 41–45

Doncaster is a town in southern Yorkshire, forty-five miles west of
Ravenspurgh, where the King (then Bolingbroke) had landed.

Undoubtedly Bolingbroke did so swear in order not to frighten off possible allies who might be reluctant to come out openly in favor of an actual
deposition of Richard II. Once the rebellion gained rapid success, however, it was inevitable that the goals be made higher, and certainly, both
in history and in Shakespeare, the Percys were not behindhand in helping
Bolingbroke to the throne once the path there turned out to be a smooth
one.

But now, when the Percys have broken with the new King, they remember the oath and use it to show that Henry had unrightfully usurped
the throne. That too is to be expected in practical politics; the King dismisses the whole argument lightly.

. . . a truant been to chivalry

But Prince Hal answers. He is now going to fulfill the promise he made
his father on the occasion of their reconciliation. He praises Hotspur to
Worcester and says in frank self-criticism:

> For my part, I may speak it to my shame,
> I have a truant been to chivalry;
> And so I hear he [Hotspur] doth account me too.
>   —Act V, scene i, lines 93–95

The Prince then challenges Hotspur to single combat as a way of deciding the battle, rising thus from the depths of Falstaffian frivolity to the
heights of Hotspurian "honor."

The King is satisfied with the offer, but will not risk his heir. He offers
instead to grant full amnesty to all the rebels, even to Worcester, if they
will all lay down their arms.

Can honor set to a leg

Worcester leaves, but there is no surety that the offer of amnesty will
be accepted. It is necessary that the King's forces prepare for momentary
battle, in case the offer is not accepted.

Falstaff, who has been on the scene all this time with occasional bits of
comic relief, now betrays nervousness; a nervousness with which Prince
Hal refuses to sympathize.

Falstaff, then left alone on the stage, muses on the nature of "honor" as earlier in the play Hotspur had done, but to much different effect. He says, in part:

> *Can honor set to a leg? No. Or an arm? No. Or take away the*
> *grief of a wound? No. Honor hath no skill in surgery then?*
> *No. What is honor? A word . . .*
>
> —Act V, scene i, lines 131–34

Remember that honor is not to be taken in a broad sense to mean virtue, integrity, honesty, or any of the great moral attributes of mankind. To the Hotspurs of the world, it means merely military prowess and nothing more; it means the reputation of winning in battle and facing the enemy with no show of fear. It is the honor of the pugilist, of the western gunfighter, and —at its worst—of the gangster.

It is this honor which Falstaff derides, pointing out its essential emptiness. It is almost unavoidable to feel embarrassed at Falstaff's "cowardly" downgrading of honor, but as the centuries have passed and as wars have grown steadily more terrible, the Falstaffian view is making sense to more and more men. In fact, we have now reached the point where it would seem that the safety of the human race itself depends on dismissing this kind of "honor" as a mere word.

. . . so sweet a hope

Worcester dares not carry news of the King's offered amnesty to Hotspur. He cannot trust the King. Even if the amnesty is given and accepted, the Percys will all live at the edge of a volcano. The King will always suspect them, never trust them, and sooner or later find an occasion to destroy them.

Yet Hotspur the impulsive is perfectly capable of veering from extreme to extreme and may swing from intransigent violence to a sudden snatch at "honorable" peace.

Consequently, Worcester talks Vernon into helping him misrepresent the King's statement, and Hotspur is told there are to be no terms and that the battle must be fought. Worcester does add, however, that Prince Hal has challenged him to single combat.

At once Hotspur is interested. He wants the details, saying:

> . . . *Tell me, tell me,*
> *How showed his tasking* [challenging]*? Seemed it in con-*
> *tempt?*
>
> —Act V, scene ii, lines 49–50

But again Hotspur must be disappointed, for the Prince's manner of challenge is praised in highest terms. Vernon speaks highly of the Prince's bearing and behavior, and says of him:

> *If he outlive the envy of this day,*
> *England did never owe* [own] *so sweet a hope,*
> *So much misconstrued in his wantonness.*
>
> —Act V, scene ii, lines 66–68

In angry frustration, Hotspur can only promise, once again, that he will kill the Prince.

. . . all his wardrobe . . .

The Battle of Shrewsbury was fought in medieval style, with the King himself in the forefront of his forces. This was necessary, for the King was the rallying point and inspiration, and when he charged forward with the cream of his forces serving as his bodyguard, the rest of the army would follow in excitement and achieve the necessary breakthrough.

This was also a great risk. The death of the King would automatically mean the end of the battle with the Percys the victors. When the word went around that the King had fallen, the heart would go out of his army.

It was not unheard-of strategy, therefore, to prepare several soldiers (presumably volunteers) with the royal insignia, to draw the enemy fire, so to speak. It was done on this occasion.

The battle began with the Percy archers repeating the stand they had made at Holmedon ten months before. The royal forces began to fall as the Scots had done on the earlier occasion. The King had numbers on his side, however. Leading fresh forces into the battle in a violent charge, he drove the rebels back.

Shakespeare, who never displays much understanding of battle tactics, confines himself to describing single combats. The rebels bent all their efforts on bringing down the King, and according to Holinshed, Douglas the Scot was particularly active here. Shakespeare follows this. Douglas has killed three men in the King's regalia, including Blunt.

With Blunt dead at his feet, Douglas thinks the battle won. Hotspur, who knows the real King well, disabuses the Scot, who, annoyed at the false Kings in the fight, says in exasperation:

> *Now, by my sword, I will kill all his coats;*
> *I'll murder all his wardrobe, piece by piece,*
> *Until I meet the King.*
>
> —Act V, scene iii, lines 26–28

. . . they are peppered

Falstaff is shown on the battlefield too. His charge of infantrymen has been destroyed, though he himself remains unscratched. In fact, Falstaff has deliberately led his men into the hottest portion of the fight precisely in order to kill them off. He says:

> *I have led my rag-of-muffins where they are peppered.*
> —Act V, scene iii, lines 36–37

This seems senseless until one realizes that officers who did this could sometimes manage to draw the dead soldiers' pay for themselves before the statistics caught up with them, and presumably Falstaff plans to do this. Falstaff says:

> *There's not three of my hundred and fifty left alive, and they are for the town's end, to beg during life.*
> —Act V, scene iii, lines 37–39

This lends an even bitterer point to the comment he had just made on coming across the dead body of Sir Walter Blunt, when he said:

> *There's honor for you!*
> —Act V, scene iii, lines 32–33

Military renown, it would seem, leads to disregarded death if one is noble, and if one is a common man, to wounds, disablement, and the dubious privilege of begging for one's livelihood from those who have stayed home and avoided "honor." Advocates of military glory get scant encouragement from Shakespeare really, despite a few resounding speeches here and there.

. . . to jest and dally . . .

Prince Hal, without his sword (it is presumably lost in the heat of battle), enters at this point. He tries to borrow Falstaff's sword or his pistol. Falstaff won't yield his sword and his pistol case has a bottle of sack in it. The Prince hurls the bottle at Falstaff, saying impatiently:

> *What, is it a time to jest and dally now?*
> —Act V, scene iii, line 55

Falstaff is always Falstaff, just as Hotspur is always Hotspur, but the

Prince can play either role as suits the occasion, and on the battlefield, he must be Hotspur and not Falstaff.

. . . thou bleedest too much

In actual history, Prince Hal, even though merely a sixteen-year-old, was on the field and fought well. He was wounded by an arrow in the face (fortunately not much more than a scratch) and refused to retire, insisting that the wound was insufficiently serious and that his retirement would dishearten the soldiers.

Shakespeare keeps the wound and the incident. He has the King concerned over the wound. He says to the Prince:

> I prithee, Harry, withdraw thyself, thou bleedest too much.
> —Act V, scene iv, line 1

The Prince refuses:

> . . . God forbid a shallow scratch should drive
> The Prince of Wales from such a field as this,
> —Act V, scene iv, lines 10–11

. . . another counterfeit

Douglas, still searching for the King, comes upon the real one at last, but now he is suspicious. He approaches cautiously, saying:

> I fear thou art another counterfeit;
> And yet, in faith, thou bearest thee like a king.
> —Act V, scene iv, lines 34–35

These two lines represent the turning point of the battle and, in a way, of Henry's reign. Beyond the literal meaning of the lines, one can see the nation's fear that King Henry is but a counterfeit—that he is not the legitimate heir to the crown, so his rule cannot thrive.

But now we have Douglas' word that he acts like a king and looks like one. And, in fact, this is what he proved when he took a firm stand against rebels and won over them.

The King does not retreat before Douglas, as one might suppose he ought to not only because his life is more important to the cause than any knightly gesture could be, but because the King is represented by Shakespeare as an old man, and Douglas as a skilled and almost irresistible warrior.

In actual fact, though, the King was young enough at Shrewsbury to take active part in the fight, and according to Holinshed (who cited stories that were perhaps exaggerated by flatterers), he killed thirty-six men with his own hands. What's more, Holinshed reports that the King did indeed fight with Douglas and was beaten down, but rescued.

Holinshed does not mention the rescuer, but it was probably those who were charged with the King's safety, and who came roaring in as soon as they saw him in trouble. Naturally, Douglas would be forced to retreat.

Shakespeare, however, now begins to produce the climax of the play, using details which are not to be found in Holinshed or anywhere else. It is the Prince of Wales himself who rushes in when the King is about to be slain by Douglas; it is the Prince who, singlehanded, beats back the doughty Douglas and forces him to flee.

The King, rising again, says to his son:

> *Thou hast redeemed thy lost opinion,*
> *And showed thou mak'st some tender of my life,*
> *In this fair rescue thou hast brought to me.*
>
> —Act V, scene iv, lines 47–49

Thus, the King atones for his earlier picture of the Prince fighting against his father in Percy's pay, and the Prince is just human enough to rub it in a bit:

> *O God, they did me too much injury*
> *That ever said I heark'ned for your death.*
> *If it were so, I might have let alone*
> *The insulting hand of Douglas over you,*
>
> —Act V, scene iv, lines 50–53

. . . those proud titles . . .

There remains one thing, and one thing only. The two Harrys, Hotspur and the Prince, must meet. Each has sworn to slay the other.

And now they do meet, issue their formal challenges, and begin the duel toward which all the play from the very start has been heading. Falstaff enters too, cheering on his Prince, so that the Prince out-Hotspurs Hotspur with his Falstaff-self looking on.

The fight ends, as it must, in the Prince's victory, and Hotspur falls. But he is Hotspur to the last and says:

> *I better brook the loss of brittle life*
> *Than those proud titles thou hast won of me.*
>
> —Act V, scene iv, lines 77–78

In Hotspur's sense, "honor" passes from loser to victor. It is the same logic that makes the winner of a prizefight the Heavyweight Champion of the World even though the loser had won a dozen previous fights and the winner just this one. And it is the title of champion that Hotspur bewails the loss of, not life itself.

What's more, it is the same "sword-and-buckler Prince of Wales" that has won all. The turnabout is complete.

Poor Jack, farewell

But even while the Prince and Hotspur were fighting, Douglas entered and fought with Falstaff, who could escape only by falling down and pretending to be dead.

Prince Hal, leaving Hotspur's body, now stumbles over Falstaff's, and is struck with regret:

> *What old acquaintance? Could not all this flesh*
> *Keep in a little life? Poor Jack, farewell!*
> *I could have better spared a better man.*
> > —Act V, scene iv, lines 101–3

It might have made dramatic sense to have had Falstaff really dead here. It would have represented the final death of Prince Hal's gay, misspent ways. In bidding farewell to Falstaff, Hal might have been saying good-bye to youth and carefree joy, and might have taken up the role of Hotspur for the rest of his life.

Yet perhaps not. Prince Hal, in Shakespeare's drawing, never became entirely Hotspur even at the height of his career as hero-king. He never accepted honor as quite the all in all, but remained always human, always well rounded.

. . . a long hour by Shrewsbury clock

This would seem to be made plain in a final bit of symbolism. Once the Prince has left, Falstaff rises cautiously to his feet, spies Hotspur's corpse, stabs it, and impudently carries it off to claim a reward for having killed the chief rebel.

He encounters the two royal brothers, Prince Hal and John of Lancaster, who both stare in astonishment at seeing Falstaff alive.

The Prince protests that he himself killed Percy, but Falstaff calmly insists that he and Percy were both down and out of breath as a result of their respective encounters with Douglas and the Prince:

> *. . . but we rose both at an instant and fought a long hour
> by Shrewsbury clock.*
>
> —Act V, scene iv, lines 145–46

Prince Hal, amused as always by Falstaff's ways, lets the matter drop. He is not the glutton for honor that Hotspur was, after all, and he is willing to have Falstaff try to see how much of it he can make stick to himself. Besides, it fits actual history to have Hal not too clearly the slayer of Hotspur.

Hotspur was indeed killed at the Battle of Shrewsbury on July 21, 1403, but his death came at the hands of an unknown man. There is no historical foundation for the Prince of Wales as the slayer. Even Holinshed does not say the Prince killed Hotspur. Shakespeare states it out of dramatic necessity, but he has the Prince make no effort to ensure his own clear credit, so as to account for the lack of historical evidence since.

Falstaff leaves the stage, for the last time in this play, with the body of Hotspur on his back. The two extremes of Hal's personality thus meet and blend together physically at last, as they do (we are expected to understand) in the Prince himself.

. . . the day is ours

The death of Hotspur means the end of the battle. Once the word of his death was spread about, the disheartened rebels could only seek safety in flight. The Prince says:

> *The trumpet sounds retreat; the day is ours.*
>
> —Act V, scene iv, line 157

Worcester and Vernon are taken and delivered up to execution at once. (In actual fact, they were executed two days after the battle.) Douglas was captured alive, having fallen and hurt himself badly when trying to get away from the scene of battle. But he was a Scot and not an English traitor and he was released without ransom.

That was a good stroke of policy, actually. Hotspur had released his Scottish prisoners to induce them to fight on his side, and the King released Douglas in return for his neutrality and that of those Scots he could influence thereafter.

The battle might be won, however, but the rebellion was not over. The King himself makes that plain in his final speech of the play:

> *You, son John, and my cousin Westmoreland,*
> *Towards York shall bend you with your dearest speed*
> *To meet Northumberland and the prelate Scroop,*

Who, as we hear, are busily in arms.
Myself and you, son Harry, will towards Wales
To fight with Glendower and the Earl of March.
—Act V, scene v, lines 35–40

So the play ends only in the sense that the Prince versus Hotspur confrontation has reached a final, satisfying climax. The larger tale goes on, without a break, into the next play in the series, *Henry IV, Part Two.*

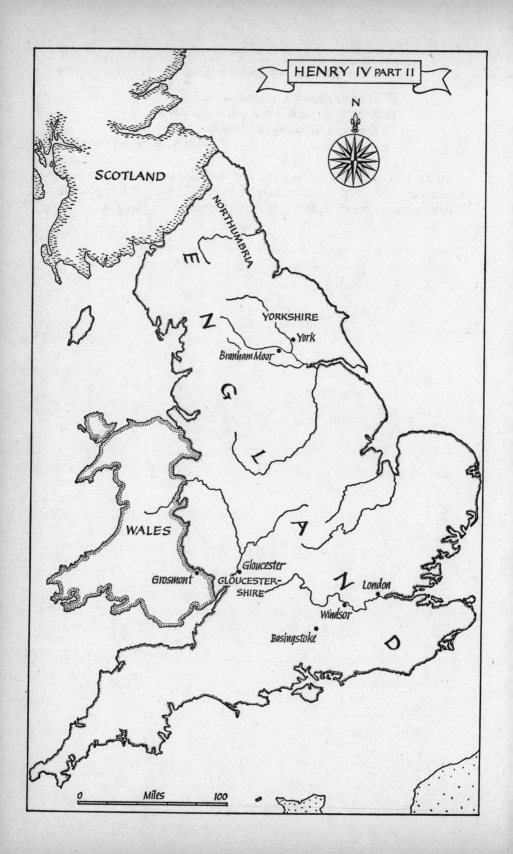

33

The History of

HENRY IV, PART TWO

T HE PLAY *Henry IV, Part Two* presents an interesting problem. Is it
a play that is really separate and distinct from *Henry IV, Part One?*
Or are the two to be taken together as one long, ten-act play—which is too
long to be played in one evening and is therefore divided into two plays of
normal length for convenience' sake.

To me it seems they are two separate plays and that the second exists
by accident. This is the way I see it:

According to the legends that had grown up in later times, Henry of
Monmouth, Prince of Wales ("Prince Hal") had been a madcap, riotous
youth, given to low companions, and even engaging in highway robbery. He
had, however, reformed under the stress of emergency, fought and killed
the rebellious Sir Henry Percy ("Hotspur"). He then reconciled himself
with his father, King Henry IV, succeeded to the throne as the hero-king
Henry V, broke away from his evil companions and banished them from
his presence.

This would make a beautifully tight plot for a single play, and *Henry IV,
Part One* is almost that play. It contains Hotspur, gallant and rebellious. It
contains Prince Hal, gay and wild; with Falstaff, that great comic invention, as his companion. Prince Hal does indeed reform, is indeed reconciled
with his father, becomes a gallant, gleaming knight, meets Hotspur on the
battlefield and kills him.

So far, so good. It only remains for Shakespeare to travel quickly from
the Battle of Shrewsbury (July 21, 1403) to the death of the King (March
20, 1413) and follow it by the triumphant coronation of the new King,
Henry V.

To be sure, there is a ten-year gap between the battle and the coronation,
but dramatic necessity could easily close the gap and no one in the audience
would complain.

Yet Shakespeare did not carry the play to its natural end. Having reached
the triumphant conclusion of the Battle of Shrewsbury, he holds back. He
not only ends the play at that point but makes a sequel inevitable, for in
the King's final speech in that play there is talk of further battles against
additional rebels in Yorkshire and in Wales.

But why? With the legend almost completed, why hold back and become
involved in five more acts of *Henry IV, Part Two,* acts which prove rather

impoverished in incident when compared with the crowded and wonderful events of *Henry IV, Part One.*

Let us speculate! Suppose Shakespeare had been writing *Henry IV, Part One* with the intention of making a complete whole of it (simply *Henry IV*) and, in the process, had invented Sir John Falstaff (see page II–327).

By the middle of the play, Shakespeare realized he had something bigger than he had quite expected to have. He sensed that Falstaff was going to make a tremendous hit and he was human enough to want to milk the character for all it was worth. So he decided, midstream, to make Falstaff carry two plays rather than one. He ended the original play after the Battle of Shrewsbury and decided to write a sequel.

If this was what happened, events proved Shakespeare right. *Henry IV, Part One* was an instant smash hit and Falstaff was the most successful item in it. Shakespeare could now bring the fat man back for five more acts of fun with the enthusiastic approval of the audience. So he got to work on *Henry IV, Part Two* almost immediately after the production of *Henry IV, Part One,* and by 1598 it was ready to be played.

It wasn't entirely easy, though. The non-Falstaff portions of the play had little of dramatic value to carry the play. There were new rebellions against Henry IV, to be sure, but they were pitifully poor as compared with the earlier one that had featured such bravura characters as Hotspur and Glendower.

Then too, even Falstaff himself introduced a problem. The structure of *Henry IV, Part One* had been too neat. The Prince of Wales had already reformed in that play and had become a knightly hero; he had already reconciled himself to his father. What could happen, then, in the Second Part?

Boldly, Shakespeare unreformed Prince Hal. Once again he had to be made to go through the mill. Once more he had to be scolded by the King, once more he had to repent and reform, once more he had to be accepted in a joyous reconciliation. What with this and the new set of rebellions, *Henry IV, Part Two* became an inferior repetition of *Henry IV, Part One,* but it was necessary if the incomparable Falstaff was to be brought back, and that meant it was worth the price.

. . . a bloody field by Shrewsbury

The events of *Henry IV, Part Two* begin immediately after those at the closing of *Henry IV, Part One.* The First Part had ended with the Battle of Shrewsbury and the Second begins with the report of the battle.

Shakespeare ties the two together by having a special introduction (or, to use the Shakespearean equivalent, "induction"). For the purpose, Rumor is personified, a human figure painted all over with tongues. He says:

I run before King Harry's victory,
Who in a bloody field by Shrewsbury
Hath beaten down young Hotspur and his troops,
—Induction, lines 23–25

It is not, however, the truth that Rumor brings. Rather the reverse. The news that is first being spread abroad is that it is the King who has been defeated and Hotspur who is victorious—that Douglas has slain the King and Hotspur has killed the Prince of Wales.

This might easily have actually characterized the first reports, quite apart from the dramatic possibilities it laid open for the first scene of the play. The early stages of the Battle of Shrewsbury did indeed seem to be in favor of Hotspur and his archers, despite their smaller numbers. Douglas the Scot did indeed work miracles of valor on the rebel side and at one time he did indeed strike down the King (see page II–376).

Presumably, messengers, eager to be the first with good news in order that they might reap the rewards that go to bearers of good tidings, would take off at once, under the assumption that what was so well begun would soon be well ended and that further delay would merely lose them the chance of being first.

. . . old Northumberland

Rumor says, therefore:

This have I rumored through the peasant towns
Between that royal field of Shrewsbury
And this worm-eaten hold of ragged stone,
Where Hotspur's father, old Northumberland,
Lies crafty-sick.
—Induction, lines 33–37

This is the third play in which Henry Percy, 1st Earl of Northumberland, appears. In *Richard II* he was the leader of the lords who deserted Richard for the rebel Bolingbroke; the one who more than anyone else worked to depose Richard and make Bolingbroke his successor as Henry IV.

In *Henry IV, Part One* he was the titular head of the Percy family, which broke away from Henry IV and tried to overturn him as well.

Northumberland is indeed quite old, being sixty-one at the time of the Battle of Shrewsbury, an advanced age for those times particularly.

The real head and brains of the Percy conspiracy had been Northumberland's slightly younger brother, Thomas Percy, Earl of Worcester. Worcester had been with Hotspur every step of the way down to that final battle at Shrewsbury, where Worcester had been captured and executed. Northumberland, however, had flinched at the end, and had not led his forces to join his son, using sickness as an excuse. The absence of Northumberland's forces had been an important factor in assuring Hotspur's defeat.

There is no clear indication in *Henry IV, Part One* that Northumberland's sickness was not real, except that his refusal even to send an army under a deputy was suspicious. Here in the Induction, however, the use of the phrase "crafty-sick" makes it clear indeed that, in Shakespeare's view, Northumberland was merely feigning sickness in a most poltroonish attempt to avoid trouble even at the expense of his son's life.

Northumberland's unheroic act served its purpose in actual historical fact. Northumberland claimed he was innocent of rebellion, and King Henry, impelled by practical reasons in the aftermath of Shrewsbury, allowed Northumberland to live and even to retain his title and estates.

Since Caesar's fortunes

The first to reach Northumberland is one who was not at the battle but who claims to have spoken with someone who was. Northumberland greets him anxiously:

> *What news, Lord Bardolph?*

> —Act I, scene i, line 7

The messenger is Thomas, 5th Baron Bardolph. He was involved in the rebellion from the start. He is a historical character, but unfortunately Shakespeare had already used the name Bardolph for Falstaff's alcoholic companion in *Henry IV, Part One*. He must retain the character, and so there are two Bardolphs in this play. Northumberland's ally must be distinguished by having his speeches assigned to "Lord Bardolph," while Falstaff's companion has his speeches assigned simply to "Bardolph."

Lord Bardolph's message is precisely that which Rumor had described —all of triumph and victory. He says:

> *O, such a day,*
> *So fought, so followed, and so fairly won,*
> *Came not till now to dignify the times*
> *Since Caesar's fortunes!*

> —Act I, scene i, lines 20–23

Throughout medieval times, ancient Rome was thought of as the Empire par excellence, and continued to be so regarded as late as the eighteenth century, when the English historian Edward Gibbon thought it represented the peak of human history. And of all the Roman generals, Julius Caesar (see page I–253) was the most famous. To say a victory is the greatest since Caesar's time is to give it praise indeed.

But then comes Travers, another rebel partisan, who did not see the battle either, but who had received news that was not at all like that reported by Lord Bardolph.

For a while the issue is in doubt, but then comes Morton, a third messenger. He was actually at Shrewsbury, so that his news, at last, is first-hand, but his manner tells all before he opens his mouth.

Northumberland, looking at him, says in despair:

> *Even such a man, so faint, so spiritless,*
> *So dull, so dead in look, so woebegone,*
> *Drew Priam's curtain in the dead of night,*
> *And would have told him half his Troy was burnt,*
> *But Priam found the fire ere he his tongue*
> *And I my Percy's death ere thou report'st it.*
>
> —Act I, scene i, lines 70–75

The reference is, of course, to the ten-year siege of Troy, the city ruled by aged Priam, and to its final destruction (see page I–209).

A speedy power . . .

Morton finally tells the news accurately and in full. He concludes:

> *The sum of all*
> *Is that the King hath won, and hath sent out*
> *A speedy power to encounter you, my lord,*
> *Under the conduct of young Lancaster*
> *And Westmoreland.*
>
> —Act I, scene i, lines 131–35

Lancaster is Prince John, Duke of Lancaster (see page II–364), third son of the King, while the Earl of Westmoreland (see page II–317) is the general of the royal armies.

This passage knits this play to the previous one, for in *Henry IV, Part One* the King's last speech includes the order sending Lancaster and Westmoreland to the north against Northumberland and his allies.

Shakespeare thus skips over the actual capitulation and pardon of Northumberland in the aftermath of the Battle of Shrewsbury. It was not until two years later (1405) that Northumberland renewed the rebellion, taking heart from the fact that the King's rule was in continuing trouble, since Glendower was still a source of infinite bother in Wales and since the French were making successful raids on the southern English coast. (Indeed, it was these problems in west and south that must surely have induced King Henry to pretend that he believed Northumberland's protestations of innocence, since he could scarcely enjoy the prospect of still more war in the north.)

Shakespeare ignores this two-year gap and has the new rebellion follow almost immediately upon the old one.

The gentle Archbishop of York . . .

Despite the defeat at Shrewsbury, the new rebellion has its possibilities. Morton goes on to say to Northumberland:

> *. . . my most noble lord,*
> *I hear for certain, and dare speak the truth:*
> *The gentle Archbishop of York is up*
> *With well-appointed pow'rs.*

—Act I, scene i, lines 187–90

The Archbishop of York was from the first considered to be an important adjunct to the Percy rebellion (see page II–344). He was popular, and, as a high ecclesiastic, would help convince the public of the rightness of the Percys' cause.

He had not taken part in the Battle of Shrewsbury, but there is a scene in *Henry IV, Part One* which shows him working to raise an army in case Hotspur is defeated (see page II–369).

Northumberland is also told of the Archbishop's skillful use of propaganda:

> *He's followed both with body and with mind,*
> *And doth enlarge his rising with the blood*
> *Of fair King Richard, scraped from Pomfret stones;*
> *Derives from heaven his quarrel and his cause;*

—Act I, scene i, lines 203–6

Thus, the ghost of Richard, slain, according to belief, at Pomfret Castle five years before (see page II–312), continues to haunt his successor. Henry's title, despite the victory at Shrewsbury, is still tainted, is still of doubtful legitimacy, and rebels rise at every hand to contest his dubious right to the throne.

. . . witty in myself . . .

Now, in the second scene, Falstaff appears. He is the reason for this play and immediately after the serious tone is set (and undoubtedly the audience was impatient enough to have that over and done) he waddles onto the scene in as broadly farcical a manner as possible.

He has received some honor for his dubious deeds at the Battle of Shrewsbury (where, for one thing, he loudly claimed the honor of having killed Hotspur, see page II–377) and on the strength of that he is putting on all the airs of a great nobleman.

Prince Hal has given him a page to accentuate Falstaff's new role, but the Prince does so in his own style, giving him a particularly small one (so that he is always played by the smallest and youngest child who can be made to recite the lines).

Undoubtedly the laughter breaks out the moment the fat man struts on-stage with the tiny Page mimicking him behind, and continues for as long as the actor playing Falstaff can manage to keep it going. After a quick exchange with the page, in which Falstaff has the worst of it (undoubtedly to renewed laughter), Falstaff proceeds to describe his own value as a character:

> *Men of all sorts take a pride to gird* [mock] *at me. The brain of this foolish compounded clay, man, is not able to invent anything that intends to laughter more than I invent or is invented on me. I am not only witty in myself, but the cause that wit is in other men.*
>
> —Act I, scene ii, lines 6–11

Shakespeare is boasting here, glorying in the success of the character he has invented and saying quite openly that no one could do better.

. . . A whoreson Achitophel

But Falstaff can't be allowed to associate with the Prince quite as freely and as often as was the case in *Henry IV, Part One*. To be sure, the Prince must have occasion for a new reconciliation with the King, but after Shrewsbury and the slaying of Hotspur, he can never be altogether Falstaffian again. He is allowed in *Henry IV, Part Two* just one scene, *one*, with Falstaff, on anything like the old terms.

For the rest, then, Falstaff must be played off, scene after scene, against individuals other than the Prince.

Thus, when Falstaff grandly asks after some satin he has ordered from a merchant, the little Page calmly punctures his pretensions by replying that the merchant does not consider Falstaff's credit good and thinks very little of Bardolph as security either. The humiliated Falstaff can only burst out in a denunciation of the merchant:

*Let him be damned, like the glutton! Pray God his tongue be
hotter! A whoreson Achitophel!*

—Act I, scene ii, lines 36–37

Falstaff, like many an ungodly man, makes frequent use of biblical allusions. The damned "glutton" is Dives (see page II–368), the rich man
who went to hell and who suffered from a heated tongue in consequence.
Luke describes him as begging to have Lazarus, the beggar in Paradise,
"dip the tip of his finger in water, and cool my tongue; for I am tormented
in this flame" (Luke 16:24).

As for Achitophel (Ahitophel in the King James version), he was a
wise counselor of David who abandoned the old king and joined the conspiracy mounted by Absalom, David's son. The conspiracy failed and
Ahitophel committed suicide by hanging himself. His name is therefore a
resoundingly sonorous symbol for a traitor; and a traitor who comes to a
bad end at that.

. . . the nobleman that committed the Prince . . .

But now a worthier foil for Falstaff arrives when the Lord Chief Justice
comes onstage (Sir William Gascoigne in actual history, though Shakespeare
doesn't use his name). He is the highest symbol of law in the land, and he
plays a famous role in the legend that surrounds Prince Hal's wild youth.

The story, which first became current in 1531, about a century after Hal's
death, is given in some detail in *The Famous Victories of Henry V* (see page
II–327) and is the most effective portion of this miserable play from which
Shakespeare drew part of his inspiration. According to the tale, the Chief
Justice had arrested one of the Prince's lowborn associates. The Prince de-
manded his release, a demand which the Chief Justice, with careful respect,
refused to grant. Beside himself with rage, the Prince thereupon struck the
Chief Justice.

Still respectful, the Chief Justice explained that as a human being he
accepted the blow from the Prince, but that as an official he represented the
King's majesty, so that the blow upon him was a blow against the King. He
therefore arrested the Prince and had him taken to jail.

Although Shakespeare did not include this episode in *Henry IV, Part
One* (feeling probably that it presented the Prince in too bad a light), he
relied on the audience knowing all about it so that one casual reference
was sufficient. When the Chief Justice enters, the Page says to Falstaff:

*Sir, here comes the nobleman that committed the Prince for
striking him about Bardolph.*

—Act I, scene ii, lines 57–58

. . . in question for the robb'ry

The Lord Chief Justice spies Falstaff and inquires about him. He has reason to take note of the man, for there is still the highway robbery at Gad's Hill (see page II–346). Even though the Prince paid back all the money (see page II–355), a felonious assault is a felonious assault, and in those times, that particular crime was a hanging matter.

The matter was never really threshed out and the Lord Chief Justice is disturbed about it. Speaking to his servant, who identifies Falstaff, the Lord Chief Justice inquires:

> *He that was in question for the robb'ry?*
> —Act I, scene ii, lines 62–63

. . . discomfort from Wales

Falstaff proceeds to do everything he can to avoid the subject. He affects to mistake the Chief Justice's servant for a beggar, then, when the Chief Justice himself approaches, becomes full of concern for the latter's age. As a last resort he begins to talk off the subject, saying:

> *. . . I hear his Majesty is returned with some discomfort from Wales.*
> —Act I, scene ii, lines 107–8

In that same last speech in *Henry IV, Part One* in which the King ordered Lancaster and Westmoreland to the north, he stated that he himself and the Prince of Wales would lead a portion of the army into Wales. This they did, but without notable success. Glendower's guerrilla tactics were a match for the English, all the more so since he received help from the French. In 1404 he actually concluded a treaty with France, which recognized him as "Owen, Prince of Wales," and in 1405 he won a considerable victory at Grosmont on the southern Welsh border.

It was as a result of this battle that Henry IV was forced to return "with some discomfort from Wales." It was also the result of this battle that encouraged Northumberland and the Archbishop of York to move into open opposition again.

Falstaff's reference to the Welsh expedition is an indication of the actual two-year lapse between the rebellions of Hotspur and Northumberland. Otherwise, one might wonder how, so soon after Shrewsbury, the King had time to march into Wales and return, either with comfort or discomfort.

Your day's service . . .

The Chief Justice tries manfully to force Falstaff to the point. He reminds Falstaff that he did not appear before the court when called and is technically in contempt. He says, however:

> *Your day's service at Shrewsbury hath a little gilded over your night's exploit on Gad's Hill. You may thank th'unquiet time for your quiet o'erposting* [getting away with] *that action.*
> —Act I, scene ii, lines 153–56

Thus are *Henry IV, Part One* and *Henry IV, Part Two* knit together at the Falstaff level as well as at the Northumberland level.

The Chief Justice also warns Falstaff against future misbehavior and against continuing to mislead the Prince of Wales. Falstaff shows no signs of doing anything but joking, so the Chief Justice is forced to give up, saying:

> *Well, the King hath severed you and Prince Harry. I hear you are going with Lord John of Lancaster against the Archbishop and the Earl of Northumberland.*
> —Act I, scene ii, lines 211–14

Thus, lip service is paid to the Prince's reformation in Part One, but it can be seen that the Prince's separation from his low companions is not yet voluntary. Rather, the King has brought it about by taking the Prince into Wales and sending Falstaff to the north, and has in this way "severed" them. The separation is not entire and there will still be room for the final one, which will come of the Prince's own volition in good time.

. . . Lord Marshal . . .

In the rebel camp, meanwhile, the Archbishop has outlined his plans and then says:

> *And, my most noble friends, I pray you all,*
> *Speak plainly your opinions of our hopes.*
> *And first, Lord Marshal, what say you to it?*
> —Act I, scene iii, lines 2–4

The person addressed here is Thomas Mowbray, the son of the Thomas Mowbray, Duke of Norfolk, whose quarrel with Bolingbroke (later Henry IV) fills the first act of *Richard II* (see page II–268).

The younger Thomas was born in 1386 and had been only twelve years old at the time of his father's non-duel; thirteen when his father died in Venice.

He had inherited some, but not all, of the titles and honors of his father. His father had once been the Earl of Nottingham and to this young Thomas had succeeded, so that he was 3rd Earl of Nottingham. His father had been created marshal of England for life and this too the son had inherited, so that he could be called Lord Marshal.

Nevertheless, it was only natural that he retain a certain enmity against the great adversary of his father, an adversary who now reigned as King of England. The fact that he was never granted his father's highest title of Duke of Norfolk, or the revenues that went with it, could only have exacerbated his anger.

Mowbray of Nottingham therefore joined Northumberland and the Archbishop against the King. He and two lesser rebels, Lord Hastings and Lord Bardolph, agree that their forces are too small unless they can count on the certain help of Northumberland. That is, they will be too small if the King turns against them in full force.

However, they rely on the King being unable to do this. After all, he has other problems in addition to the rebellion in the north. Hastings says:

> . . . his divisions, as the times do brawl,
> Are in three heads: one power against the French,
> And one against Glendower, perforce a third
> Must take up us. So is the infirm king
> In three divided . . .
>
> —Act I, scene iii, lines 70–74

So the Archbishop decides to press on with the rebellion, using the memory of Richard II to the full as a propaganda device.

Nevertheless, a successful rebellion cannot be raised against a usurping king with no more than a memory to counter him. The previous king, now dead, cannot be raised to life to resume the throne. A new king, presumably legitimate, must be waiting in the wings for the moment when the usurper is overthrown, and this was indeed the case here.

In actual history, the Archbishop raised the rebellion on behalf of the young 5th Earl of March (see page II-320), who was legitimate heir to the throne through his descent from Lionel, third son of Edward III. The 5th Earl had been Henry's prisoner ever since the beginning of his reign, but now he had been temporarily freed through a ruse, and for a very fugitive moment it seemed the rebels might have a "true king" to rally round. Young March was quickly retaken, however, by Henry.

But none of this appears in this play, for Shakespeare, misled by Holinshed, knows nothing of the young imprisoned earl. He thinks the legitimate King is the earl's uncle, Sir Edmund Mortimer (see page II–320), who is still alive and still with Glendower in Wales.

. . . near at hand

Falstaff, who is supposed to raise a troop of men (as in *Henry IV, Part One*) and join the royal forces moving northward, is in no hurry to do so. His immediate concern is trouble in the tavern. He has been sponging on Mistress Quickly, the hostess of the tavern, and she wants the sum he owes her before he leaves for the army. For that reason she has called in the minions of the law.

A broadly farcical battle takes place between Falstaff and Bardolph on one side and the constables and Mistress Quickly on the other, with Mistress Quickly by far the most formidable of the lot, with respect to both her voice and her arm.

The Lord Chief Justice enters to break up the fray. Falstaff addresses him with his usual inextinguishable effrontery, but is ordered to satisfy the woman. This Falstaff does, but not in the way the Chief Justice intended. He does not pay her at all, but wheedles the foolish woman into agreeing to advance him additional funds.

But while this goes on, a Messenger arrives, announcing to the Lord Chief Justice:

> *The King, my lord, and Harry Prince of Wales*
> *Are near at hand.*

> —Act II, scene i, lines 138–39

When asked exactly where they are, the Messenger says:

> *At Basingstoke, my lord.*

> —Act II, scene i, line 175

Basingstoke is forty-five miles west of London. The purpose for their return is to reinforce the armies marching north against the rebels there. The Messenger says:

> *. . . Fifteen hundred foot, five hundred horse,*
> *Are marched up to my Lord of Lancaster,*
> *Against Northumberland and the Archbishop.*

> —Act II, scene i, lines 179–81

The rebels, it seems, will not be able to rely quite as much as they had thought upon the division of the King's forces.

. . . exceeding weary

But the arrival of the King's forces in the vicinity of London enables the Prince of Wales to push on to London for a breather and for some relaxation after the old fashion.

He enters his London establishment with Poins (one of his lowborn companions, but the least disreputable of them, and in this play the only one of those companions to be his regular associate). His first words in this play are:

> *Before God, I am exceeding weary.*
> > —Act II, scene ii, line 1

He should well be weary, having been posting hard from Wales, but the line may also be taken to indicate that the madcap Prince of *Henry IV, Part One* is forever gone. He may call forth an echo of the old times for the sake of justifying this second play (which is really justified only by Falstaff's presence), but it is only an echo. He wants a drink, but is rather embarrassed (he would not have been embarrassed before Shrewsbury) at the plebeian nature of his wants. He says:

> *Doth it not show vilely in me to desire small beer?*
> > —Act II, scene ii, lines 5–6

He continues an idle conversation and Poins half mockingly scolds him for it, saying:

> *Tell me, how many good young princes would do so, their fathers being so sick as yours at this time is?*
> > —Act II, scene ii, lines 29–31

Thus, we see Prince Hal unreformed. Here he is with his low companion, drinking small beer, engaged in unedifying conversation, even though his father is sick. And yet the unreformation is inserted only in order to make it possible for Prince Hal to go through a reconciliation scene, eventually, with his dying father. Shakespeare draws in the unreformation as lightly as ever he can, and the Prince's noble nature is allowed to shine through quite clearly. Thus, he says now at the mention of his father's sickness:

> *. . . I tell thee, my heart bleeds inwardly that my father is so sick.*
> > —Act II, scene ii, lines 46–48

Why, then, does he not show his concern? As he explains to Poins, the

sight of an heir apparent doleful over the fact that he might soon succeed
to the throne would strike everyone as a piece of hypocrisy, and the Prince
does not wish to be thought a hypocrite.

. . . *Althaea's dream* . . .

Bardolph enters now with Falstaff's page and at once there are the inevitable jokes concerning the former's fiery complexion. Even the Page
joins in, with the most high-flown allusion of all, saying:

> *Away, you rascally Althaea's dream, away!*
> > —Act II, scene ii, line 86

In amusement, the Prince asks why the Page uses the phrase, and the
boy says:

> *Marry, my lord, Althaea dreamed she was delivered of a fire-
> brand, and therefore I call him her dream.*
> > —Act II, scene ii, lines 88–90

This, as it happens, is a mistake. It was not Althaea who dreamed she
was delivered of a firebrand but Hecuba, the Queen of Troy (see page
I–104). The dream came at the time of the birth of her son Paris, who was
fated to start the Trojan War, which would end in the burning of the city.

Shakespeare must know this, for four years later, when he wrote
Troilus and Cressida, he had Paris referred to by his madly prophetical sister, Cassandra, as "our firebrand brother" (see page I–104).

Can it be, then, that Shakespeare is trying to raise a laugh from his
audience by the Page's misallusion? If so, would he not have the Prince
(who could not possibly be allowed to show signs of lack of intelligence or
classical education) make some sort of amused and oblique reference to
this? Instead, the Prince tips the Page for an interesting metaphor, as
though it were entirely correct.

It must be a slip of Shakespeare's pen, one which he never corrected
because of his aversion to rewriting and reconsidering.

Who, then, was Althaea? What was the situation that made this supposed slip of the pen an easy one to commit?

Althaea was Queen of Calydon, a city in the Aetolian section of northern Greece. When her son, Meleager, was a week old, the Fates appeared
to her and told her her son would live only so long as a particular brand in
the fireplace would remain unburned. Althaea snatched the brand from
its place at once and preserved it carefully thereafter. Meleager grew to
manhood and flourished until one day, in a quarrel, he killed his two uncles,

Althaea's brothers. In a fit of rage, Althaea threw the brand in the fire, and when it was completely burned Meleager died.

A dramatic enough story, after all, and it is quite understandable that in the heat of turning out the play, Shakespeare for a moment confused the two mythological tales of firebrands.

. . . from Japhet

Bardolph has arrived in order to bring a letter from Falstaff, who has heard the Prince is in town. It is a haughty letter, befitting Falstaff's new sense of importance after Shrewsbury, and begins with a grandiloquent notice of his own title of "knight."

Poins jests ironically at this, comparing Falstaff's pride to those who have a distant relationship to the royal family and are always managing to bring it up. The Prince agrees, saying of such people, with resignation:

> . . . they will be kin to us, or they will fetch it from Japhet.
> —Act II, scene ii, lines 117–18

Japhet (Japheth in the King James version) was one of the three sons of Noah. In the tenth chapter of the Book of Genesis, the descendants of each of the three sons are listed. Several of the peoples of southwestern Asia (the Israelites, the Assyrians, the Phoenicians) are the descendants of Shem, while several of the peoples of northeastern Africa (the Egyptians and Libyans) are descendants of Ham; hence Semites and Hamites respectively.

From Japheth are descended a number of individuals, and the Bible says: "By these were the isles of the Gentiles divided . . ." (Genesis 10:5). It is usually taken to mean that the men of Europe are descended from Japheth. Therefore, any two Englishmen are related at least to the extent of being equally descended from Japheth.

Ephesians . . .

The Prince goes on to read Falstaff's letter, which is impossibly conceited and, though brief, is long enough to slander Poins. The amused Prince wants to know where Falstaff is staying these days and what company he is keeping. The Page answers the last part of the inquiry by saying:

> Ephesians, my lord, of the old church.
> —Act II, scene ii, line 149

Ephesus, that great merchant city of Roman times (see page I-170), was as renowned for its luxury as Corinth (see page I–171) had been. "Ephesian," like "Corinthian," came to be used in Elizabethan times for any roistering gay blade.

Ephesus was also one of the cities where St. Paul spent considerable time. He founded a church there and later wrote it a letter (Epistle to the Ephesians) which is included in the New Testament. He warned the church members against those among them who did not meet the strict qualification of Christian fellowship. He says: ". . . fornication, and all uncleanness, or covetousness, let it not be once named among you. . . . Neither filthiness, nor foolish talking, nor jesting. . ." (Ephesians 5:3–4).

The Page intends, by his remark, to compare Falstaff's companions with those Ephesians of the old church against whom St. Paul was warning the godly.

. . . Jove's case

Prince Hal is eager to see Falstaff once again and Poins suggests they visit the tavern disguised as waiters. The Prince is a little embarrassed again (he has definitely grown more inhibited) and says:

> From a God to a bull? A heavy descension!
> It was Jove's case.
>
> —Act II, scene ii, lines 173–74

The Prince comforts himself with the thought that Jupiter (Jove) once condescended to become a bull in order to woo the Phoenician princess Europa. (Europa, fascinated by the beautiful and tame white bull that had clambered out of the sea, climbed onto its back. The bull at once leaped back into the sea and swam with her to Crete, where she bore Jupiter three sons.)

And speaking thick . . .

Meanwhile Northumberland is making ready to go to war despite the pleas of his wife and of his daughter-in-law, Catherine Mortimer (called "Lady Percy" in the cast of characters), who had been the wife of his son, Hotspur (see page II–288). Northumberland pleads that honor requires his presence, and his daughter-in-law demands passionately why honor had not brought him to Shrewsbury, where Hotspur had died while waiting vainly for his father.

She points out (with anxious exaggeration) that the Archbishop of York is strong enough to do without Northumberland, saying bitterly:

Had my sweet Harry [Hotspur] *had but half their numbers,*
Today might I, hanging on Hotspur's neck,
Have talked of Monmouth's grave.

—Act II, scene iii, lines 43–45

Monmouth is, of course, Prince Hal (Henry of Monmouth), from the city in which he was born (see page II–309).

In the course of her speech, Lady Percy describes Hotspur with idolatrous affection as the very image of knighthood, one whom all others imitated. She says:

And speaking thick, which nature made his blemish,
Became the accents of the valiant,
For those that could speak low and tardily
Would turn their own perfection to abuse
To seem like him.

—Act II, scene iii, lines 24–28

Apparently, by "speaking thick," Hotspur's widow meant that he spoke rapidly, the words crowding on one another and often outpacing his thought, so that he is forced to stammer or fumble for a word.

In the end, Northumberland is overpersuaded by his womenfolk and turns to caution again. For the second time he vilely betrays those who count on him. He cannot simply do nothing now, as he did in Hotspur's rebellion, and hope for a second amnesty. This time his complicity is too clear. He therefore plans to flee to Scotland.

. . . Mistress Tearsheet . . .

The scene shifts back to Eastcheap now, where Falstaff is planning to have a last carouse before going off to the wars. Things are being made ready and in charge is the waiter Francis, who wants to arrange for music. He says to another servant:

. . . see if thou canst find out Sneak's noise. Mistress Tearsheet would fain hear some music.

—Act II, scene iv, lines 11–12

Doll Tearsheet's function in the tavern is clearly that of a prostitute, her very name indicating her trade. In *Henry IV, Part One* there were ribald remarks tending to point up Falstaff's lechery, but there were no direct indications thereof, perhaps because Shakespeare was concerned not to stain the madcap Prince Hal with any sexual immorality.

Now, with the Prince making only a glancing appearance, it is safe to bring in the women, and Doll Tearsheet comes on somewhat the worse for liquor. Falstaff enters, bawling a ballad, and the two immediately set to brawling, for the humor cannot lie in any actual love passages between the fat man and the painted woman, but in the mutual screeching and caterwauling that must precede them.

. . . Ancient Pistol . . .

Just as the quarreling is about to turn to elephantine caresses, the servant enters and says to Falstaff:

> Sir, Ancient Pistol's below and would speak with you.
>
> —Act II, scene iv, lines 70–71

"Ancient" would seem to indicate age, but actually, it is here a corruption of "ensign." An ensign was a flag and it was also the flag-bearer, the soldier who carried the flag.

The ensign or ancient had a difficult task. In the days before uniforms, it was hard to tell friend from enemy in the heat of battle. Armies, or groups within armies, had to cluster about some easily visible mark and remain with it. This mark or sign was often the ensign.

Naturally, the flag-bearer must carry the flag into the thick of the battle and guard it with his life. He is the particular target of the enemy, for if the flag is taken, at least a portion of the forces under it are left in confusion. The loss of so prominent an object as a flag would become known to all the army, and would be a signal of defeat. It would dishearten many and make total loss of the battle more probable.

Consequently an ensign must be a bold and seasoned daredevil, and his position is one of renown. One would expect him to be of fiery speech and temper and so Ancient Pistol is. His very name testifies to his explosiveness. In fact, Doll Tearsheet's first words at hearing of his arrival (she has met him before, obviously) are:

> Hang him, swaggering rascal! Let him not come hither. It is the foul-mouthed'st rogue in England.
>
> —Act II, scene iv, lines 72–74

. . . pampered jades of Asia

The very word "swagger" puts Mistress Quickly into a cold sweat, and she tries to bar Pistol from the premises (though she is manifestly uncertain of the meaning of the word). She says:

If he swagger, let him not come here.
                                        —Act II, scene iv, line 75

It is, however, the essence of Ancient Pistol that though incredibly valorous (and therefore swaggering) in speech, he is incredibly cowardly in performance. He is like a caricature of Falstaff, an even greater braggart and an even greater poltroon.

Even the grandiloquence of his speech is not his own, for he is a perpetual quoter of bits and pieces of dramatic plays of Shakespeare's time; choosing always the most bombastic and fustian speeches, garbling them, misquoting them, and misapplying them.

Thus, when despite all his ferocious talk, Pistol is put down by the angry Doll Tearsheet, he finds refuge in a quotation from *Tamburlaine the Great* by Christopher Marlowe, which had appeared ten years before the production of *Henry IV, Part Two* and which had made a great hit.

Marlowe, born in 1564 and therefore precisely of an age with Shakespeare, is second only to Shakespeare in reputation as an Elizabethan dramatist.

Indeed, Marlowe was writing successful plays while Shakespeare was still but a struggling actor, eking out his income by patching up other people's work. Marlowe died in a tavern brawl in 1593, when he was only twenty-nine years old, and it is conceivable that had he lived a reasonably full life he might have matured further and given Shakespeare a real run for his money. Perhaps Shakespeare suspected this and took a little special pleasure in a chance to satirize one of Marlowe's most famous (and bombastic) speeches.

This takes place in Act II of *Tamburlaine the Great,* when Tamburlaine, the Mongol conqueror who was, in fact, a contemporary of Henry IV, enters Babylon in his final triumph. (Tamburlaine was known to history as Tamerlane or Timur-i-lenk, and Babylon ceased to exist some fifteen hundred years before his time, but why quibble?)

Tamburlaine's carriage is drawn by the kings he has conquered, so that their humiliation and his own exaltation are emphasized. He addresses the defeated monarchs as the "pampered jades of Asia." They are jades (cart horses) who had been pampered while kings.

And now Pistol, having been screeched at and manhandled by the women of the tavern, affects in his most ferocious accents to treat them as mere jades (a term which can be used for prostitutes also) compared to his own conquering self:

> . . . *Shall packhorses*
> *And hollow pampered jades of Asia,*
> *Which cannot go but thirty mile a day,*
> *Compare with Caesars, and with Cannibals,*
> *And Trojan Greeks?*
>   —Act II, scene iv, lines 167–71

He has it all wrong, of course, saying "Cannibals" for "Hannibals" and using that contradiction in terms "Trojan Greeks." The more sophisticated portion of the audience which would know the speech by heart would naturally laugh (as we do at any of the countless parodies of Hamlet's famous "To be or not to be" soliloquy).

. . . the seven stars

Pistol keeps referring with dark significance to his sword, referring to it as "Hiren"—apparently giving it the name "Irene," meaning "peace," as a kind of ironic joke, and punning also on "iron"—but is finally persuaded to lay it down.

Grandiloquently, he expresses his affection for Falstaff, saying:

> Sweet knight, I kiss thy neaf [fist]. What! We have seen the
> seven stars.
>
> —Act II, scene iv, lines 190–91

In the days before efficient night illumination, staying up after sunset was far less common than today, and only roisterers would be carousing into the dim hours of the night. To see the seven stars (the Pleiades) together is to have been boon drinking companions through much of the night, and Pistol boasts of this relationship of himself to Falstaff.

. . . Come, Atropos . . .

But the fight breaks out again and Pistol, suddenly furious, snatches up his sword once more, crying:

> . . . let grievous, ghastly, gaping wounds
> Untwine the Sisters Three! Come, Atropos, I say.
>
> —Act II, scene iv, lines 202–3

The Sisters Three are the Fates, who guide men's destinies (see page I–50). This guidance is described metaphorically in the Greek myths, where they are pictured as spinning the thread of man's life. To "untwine" them is to untwine the thread; that is, to bring death. Pistol calls on Atropos, therefore (her name means "unswerving"), whose task it is to snip the thread of each man's life as the right moment comes.

. . . the Nine Worthies

Falstaff is forced to take up his own sword and drive Pistol out. This is the only occasion on which Falstaff proves a successful fighting man, which shows clearly that Pistol is even lower on the scale than Falstaff.

Doll Tearsheet, grateful to Falstaff for taking her part, can now return to her own kind of fighting, and there is as close an approach to tenderness as is possible under the circumstances. She wipes the perspiration from Falstaff's face and coos at him:

> I' faith, I love thee. Thou art as valorous as Hector of Troy, worth five of Agamemnon, and ten times better than the Nine Worthies.
> —Act II, scene iv, lines 222–25

Hector and Agamemnon were opposing commanders in chief in the Trojan War (see page I–80), but the Nine Worthies are something more complicated. They are a collection of nine warriors drawn from history who are the subject of medieval hero tales. They are so drawn as to include three pagans (Hector, Alexander the Great, and Julius Caesar), three Jews (Joshua, David, and Judas Maccabeus), and three Christians (Arthur, Charlemagne, and Godfrey of Bouillon).

. . . before the wicked . . .

It is at this point that the Prince and Poins, in their waiter disguise, enter. Presumably, Doll sees and recognizes them (or perhaps she had been paid in advance and was part of the plot), for she instantly starts to question Falstaff about the two men. Falstaff, predictably, begins a comic description of the Prince and Poins that cannot help but insult them desperately. The Prince and Poins spring out and confront him, and the Prince demands an explanation. The Prince warns him not to pretend he knew Hal was there all along, as he had done after the affair of Gad's Hill.

Falstaff, however, scorns to use the same excuse twice. He insists that what he said was not meant as abuse at all but was said out of friendship and love of the Prince. He says to Poins:

> I dispraised him before the wicked, that the wicked might not fall in love with thee. In which doing, I have done the part of a careful friend and a true subject . . .
> —Act II, scene iv, lines 327–30

And so Falstaff gets away with it again.

But now a Messenger comes. The King is in London too, and the rest of the army must move northward at once. In Henry IV, Part One, when the news of Hotspur's rebellion first comes, that does not at the start move the Prince or interfere with his pleasure. Now, however, he says at once:

By heaven, Poins, I feel me much to blame,
So idly to profane the precious time,

> —Act II, scene iv, lines 370–71

He makes ready to leave at once:

Give me my sword and cloak. Falstaff, good night.

> —Act II, scene iv, line 375

That is his last farewell to Falstaff as his friend. The Prince's unreformation is the minimum required to keep Part Two moving.

. . . Earls of Surrey and of Warwick

The King is in his palace. It is deep night and he is in his nightclothes, but cares of state oppress him and he must deal with the rebellion. He calls a page and tells him:

Go, call the Earls of Surrey and of Warwick
But, ere they come, bid them o'erread these letters
And well consider of them.

> —Act III, scene i, lines 1–3

The two noblemen mentioned had similar histories. The Earl of Surrey was Thomas Fitzalan, the fifth of the family to bear the title. His father, Richard Fitzalan, had been the 4th Earl and had been the right-hand man of Thomas of Gloucester. When Richard II carried out his coup against Thomas of Gloucester in 1397 (see page II–266), Richard, Earl of Surrey, was taken and executed. The titles had been bestowed outside the Fitzalan family.

Once Henry IV deposed Richard II and became King, however, young Thomas Fitzalan was restored to the earldom. It is this 5th Earl of Surrey, twenty-four years old now, that the King summons.

Also on the side of Thomas of Gloucester against Richard II had been Thomas de Beauchamp, Earl of Warwick. He too had been taken by Richard II in the great coup of 1397, but he made abject submission and escaped actual execution. He was, however, imprisoned and he lost his estates. He died in 1401, a little over a year after the deposition of Richard II.

Richard de Beauchamp, the son of Thomas, was restored to the earldom, and it is he who is the Warwick referred to here. He was twenty-three at this time and had already served Henry IV well, having fought against Glendower in Wales and against Hotspur at Shrewsbury.

While waiting for these lords, the King muses on the fact that the poor and miserable probably sleep well at night, while he, a king, cannot sleep at all. It is the cares of state, of course, that keep him waking, and he ends the soliloquy with the famous lines:

> . . . *Then happy low, lie down!*
> *Uneasy lies the head that wears a crown.*
> —Act III, scene i, lines 30–31

. . . cousin Nevil . . .

When the earls come, Henry finds himself thinking of the odd twists taken by fate. Northumberland had once been chief of those who had striven to depose Richard II, and now he was rebelling in the name of that same dead and deposed king. He quotes Richard's last speech to Northumberland, in which he foretold exactly the change in situation that had actually taken place (see page II–307).

The King calls on witnesses to this fact and turns to Warwick, reminding him that he was there (although Warwick does not actually appear as a character in *Richard II*). Henry says to him:

> *You, cousin Nevil, as I may remember—*
> *When Richard, with his eye brimful of tears,*
> *Then checked and rated by Northumberland,*
> *Did speak these words, now proved a prophecy:*
> —Act III, scene i, lines 66–69

The reference to "cousin Nevil" is a mistake on Shakespeare's part. The Warwick being spoken to is, as aforesaid, Richard de Beauchamp. His son, however, who died in 1445, four decades after the events here being described, was the last of the Beauchamps. The title then passed to the Neville family, and one of them, Richard Neville, was the most famous Earl of Warwick in history. Shakespeare carelessly pushes the famous Neville family name forward in time and applies it to the wrong man.

The earls try to reassure the brooding King. Warwick, especially, tells him that the rebels are probably weaker than rumor makes them and that he has news that Glendower is dead (which, however, he isn't). The King lets himself be persuaded that it is only his own illness that is making him such prey to anxiety and, presumably, returns to bed.

. . . page to Thomas Mowbray . . .

New characters are now introduced. Falstaff, on his way northward, must pick up soldiers and for the purpose stops at a place in Gloucestershire where an old college friend of his, Robert Shallow, is now a justice of the peace.

Shallow, an old man, who has clearly led a quiet and shrinking life, now remembers the old college days as a time when he was a kind of colossal roisterer. His senile chuckles and leers over it all fool no one in the audience, of course.

Talking to his cousin, Silence, another justice of the peace and an even more insignificant creature than Shallow, he boasts of his comrade swashbucklers, of their acquaintanceship with all the prostitutes of the vicinity, and of his friendship with Falstaff. He says:

> Then was Jack Falstaff, now Sir John, a boy, and page to Thomas Mowbray, Duke of Norfolk.
>
> —Act III, scene ii, lines 25–27

This is an interesting sidelight on Falstaff as a youth, for except for Shallow's recollections, he exists in the minds of men only as an elderly winebibber. In fact, when the Lord Chief Justice, in the first act, called Falstaff old, Falstaff, in his reply, implied that he was never anything else. He said:

> My lord, I was born about three of the clock in the afternoon, with a white head and something a round belly.
>
> —Act I, scene ii, lines 194–96

Yet here Shallow talks of him as young Jack Falstaff, page.

This detail fits in with the notion that Prince Hal bitterly resented his father's deposition of Richard II, and that his own wild behavior was designed deliberately to spite his father. Thomas Mowbray of Norfolk had nearly fought a duel with King Henry in the days when the latter was only Bolingbroke (see page II–268). Does it not seem natural, then, that Prince Hal should choose as his disreputable companion a onetime page of that same old enemy of his father's?

On the other hand, Shakespeare is playing fast and loose with time. Nowhere does he say how old Falstaff is, but it seems reasonable to picture him as fifty at least, and possibly sixty, especially since Shallow, who is always pictured as a doddering old man, was a schoolmate of his. Even if Falstaff were only fifty, he would have been born in 1355, and that would have made him at least ten years older than Thomas Mowbray, whose page Shallow recalls him as being.

. . . *Sir Dagonet* . . .

Falstaff now arrives, recruiting his men for the fight as he did in *Henry*

IV, Part One (see page II–367), and again he is at his worst and his least sympathetic. He plays callously on the names of those brought before him by Shallow, makes heartless jokes, and releases the best of the men in return for small bribes, keeping the worst for the wars.

Shallow objects, but is easily overborne and is too interested, in any case, in talking about old college days, and giving himself away with nearly every line. Thus, in one of his reminiscences he says:

> . . . *I was then Sir Dagonet in Arthur's show* . . .
> —Act III, scene ii, lines 289–90

The vision might be of Shallow playing a doughty knight in a theatrical spectacle based on the Arthurian legend. Not so! Dagonet was King Arthur's fool, knighted as a royal jest. Shallow played in this remembered play precisely the part he plays in the real one we are watching.

Falstaff listens with patience, saying little, but finally utters his immortal summary of gay college days, saying:

> *We have heard the chimes at midnight, Master Shallow.*
> —Act III, scene ii, lines 220–21

This contains precisely the significance of Pistol's earlier comment on the "seven stars" (see page II–400).

Yet however much Falstaff may patronize Shallow and sneer at him behind his back, the fact remains that Shallow is well off, whereas Falstaff must live by his wits. Falstaff, when he is alone on the stage, soliloquizes enviously:

> *And now has he* [Shallow] *land and beeves.*
> —Act III, scene ii, lines 337–38

To a man like Falstaff, the situation seems to be made to order. When the battle is over, he will be back and lighten Shallow of the load of some of his wealth.

New-dated letters . . .

It is now June 1405. The armies led by the Archbishop of York and Thomas Mowbray (the son of the man for whom Falstaff had once been page, according to Shallow) now face the King's forces.

The Archbishop of York makes an announcement:

> *I must acquaint you that I have received*
> *New-dated letters from Northumberland,*
> —Act IV, scene i, lines 6–7

The letters contain, of course, Northumberland's encouragement and best hopes, but announce that he himself will not be there. In fact, he will be in Scotland. History repeats itself. As was the case just before Shrewsbury two years earlier (see page II-365), Northumberland flinches away from the confrontation and dooms the rebellion.

As before Shrewsbury, the royal forces offer an amnesty to the rebels. Thomas Mowbray argues against accepting the amnesty (just as Worcester had argued before Shrewsbury), but this time the hard line does *not* succeed.

The Archbishop of York decides to accept the amnesty.

I do arrest thee . . .

It was the Earl of Westmoreland who has brought the offer of amnesty. Once it is accepted, John of Lancaster, the King's son and Prince Hal's younger brother, comes onstage to scold the rebels and listen to their grievances. He says to the Archbishop:

> *My lord, these griefs shall be with speed redressed.*
> *Upon my soul, they shall. If this may please you,*
> *Discharge your powers unto their several counties,*
> *As we will ours.*

> —Act IV, scene ii, lines 59–62

The offer is accepted, and the rebels' army is dispersed. But as soon as Lord Hastings returns with the news that the rebels' army is gone, Westmoreland says:

> *Good tidings, my Lord Hastings, for the which*
> *I do arrest thee, traitor, of high treason.*
> *And you, Lord Archbishop, and you, Lord Mowbray,*
> *Of capital treason I attach you both.*

> —Act IV, scene ii, lines 106–9

The Archbishop, shocked, points out that John of Lancaster is breaking his word. Lancaster replies with a quibble. He had promised to redress their grievances, and he would do that by executing them. Once dead, they would have no further grievances.

In actual history, this vile betrayal was carried out by Westmoreland rather than Lancaster, who was only sixteen at the time. The rebels were handed over to the King when he arrived, taken to York, and there beheaded. The citizens of York were fined heavily for their support of the rebels (for the King, as always, was in need of money).

. . . the hook-nosed fellow of Rome . . .

With the battle over, or rather, never begun, Falstaff arrives just in time to capture Sir Coleville of the Dale, who has no intention of fighting in a lost cause and surrenders himself without a blow.

Prince John arrives and berates Falstaff for his tardiness. Impudently, Falstaff praises himself and says:

> *. . . here, travel-tainted as I am, have [I], in my pure and immaculate valor, taken Sir John Coleville of the Dale, a most furious knight and valorous enemy. But what of that? He saw me, and yielded, that I may justly say, with the hook-nosed fellow of Rome, "There, cousin, I came, saw, and overcame."*
>
> —Act IV, scene iii, lines 37–43

One can only laugh at Falstaff's nerve and at what must surely be Lancaster's frustrated impatience, for Coleville of the Dale shows no signs at all of any desperate fight. Yet Falstaff calmly compares himself to none other than Julius Caesar and to the famous phrase used by that general after the Battle of Zela (see page II–64).

. . . sober-blooded boy . . .

Coleville is taken off to York with the others to be executed. Holinshed does indeed mention a Sir John Coleville of the Dale as one of those executed, which gives Shakespeare the idea for this passage, but of course there is no mention of any particular person—let alone the fictitious Falstaff—capturing him.

Lancaster gives Falstaff permission to return to court by way of Gloucestershire (where Falstaff intends to fleece Shallow). Falstaff, left alone, broods about the young Prince John:

> *Good faith, this same young sober-blooded boy doth not love me, nor a man cannot make him laugh.*
>
> —Act IV, scene iii, lines 89–91

Falstaff does well to be disturbed. His ability to please Prince Hal rests exactly on the fact that he can make the Prince laugh. A man who does not laugh, a man without a sense of humor, is immune to Falstaff. The Lord Chief Justice is such a one and Prince John is another, and it makes Falstaff uneasy to be with such humorless individuals. There is no way he can get round them.

This encounter with Prince John may have a deeper-lying significance as well. It was he who, in 1417, twelve years after the execution of the rebels at York, brought Sir John Oldcastle, the Lollard leader, back to London for trial, and he was present at the execution, which consisted of roasting over a slow fire.

Since Falstaff was originally intended to be Oldcastle (see page II–327), it is no wonder that he shivers in the presence of the cold-eyed, humorless Prince John. It is the shadow of death by torture, touching him in his other incarnation.

. . . my son of Gloucester

The King is in Westminster Abbey meanwhile, awaiting news of battle. He continues to be pictured as older and sicker with each appearance, though he was still only thirty-eight when the Archbishop of York was executed.

He is sufficiently conscious of impending death to want to have his sons around him. In particular, he feels the need of the presence of his oldest son, his heir. He says:

> Humphrey, my son of Gloucester,
> Where is the Prince your brother?
>
> —Act IV, scene iv, lines 12–13

Humphrey was the youngest of the four sons of Henry IV. He was born in 1390 and was therefore only fifteen at the time of the non-battle with the Archbishop. The use of the term "Gloucester" is an anachronism. He did not receive that title till after his father's death.

Humphrey does not know where Prince Hal is, and the King asks:

> Is not his brother, Thomas of Clarence, with him?
>
> —Act IV, scene iv, line 16

Thomas of Clarence is the King's second son. He was referred to in *Henry IV, Part One,* though not by name, as the younger son who had taken Prince Hal's place on the council (see page II–361). But Hal is not with Thomas; in fact, Thomas is onstage and tells the King that his older brother is with Poins and other companions of that sort.

At once the King bemoans his heir's degeneracy, saying:

> Most subject is the fattest soil to weeds
> And he, the noble image of my youth,

Is overspread with them. Therefore my grief
Stretches itself beyond the hour of death.
—Act IV, scene iv, lines 54–57

He fears for England under an unworthy successor just as though the Shakespearean version of the Battle of Shrewsbury had never taken place and as though Prince Hal had not demonstrated his heroism and knightlihood—and even though Hal has displayed very little wildness in this play. But the long delay that enabled Shakespeare to bring back Falstaff for a reprise is almost over, and the tale of Prince Hal's wildness and reform is taken up again and this time will be brought to its proper climax and not, as in *Henry IV, Part One*, aborted.

. . . a great power of English and of Scots

Westmoreland enters now to bring the news that the Archbishop of York and his partisans have been taken. And that is not all. Another messenger arrives with further news, saying:

The Earl Northumberland and the Lord Bardolph
With a great power of English and of Scots
Are by the shrieve [sheriff] *of Yorkshire overthrown.*
—Act IV, scene iv, lines 97–99

Shakespeare is now beginning to compress time rapidly. It was not until 1407, two years after the end of the Archbishop of York, that Northumberland (still in his Scottish exile) grew sufficiently heartened by trouble in the north of England over taxation to make his own move at last.

He invaded England at the head of an army of Scots and rebels and fought, in 1408, at Branham Moor, a dozen miles southwest of York. He was sixty-six years old by then, a patriarchal age for the times, but he can have none of our sympathy.

In *Richard II* he betrayed Richard, then hounded him brutally; in *Henry IV, Part One* he betrayed first Henry IV, then his own son; and in *Henry IV, Part Two* he betrayed the Archbishop of York. It is almost a pleasure to record that, having cravenly refused to fight with others, when his presence might have meant victory, he finally chose to fight alone, and was defeated and killed.

The other opponents of Henry IV, who played so important a role in *Henry IV, Part One* and were so unimportant in *Henry IV, Part Two*, also met their end at last. Mortimer, who had been captured by Glendower and had gained his freedom by marrying the Welshman's daughter, died at some uncertain date, but probably in 1409, the year after Branham Moor.

Glendower himself continued a skillful guerrilla activity to the very end of the reign of Henry IV, but was never again a real danger to the throne. His forces were gradually pinched off and he himself reduced to a fugitive, but he was never actually captured. To the end, no Welshman would betray him. He died, of course, probably in 1416, but no one knows where or how, and though relentlessly hunted, he died breathing free air.

The river hath thrice flowed . . .

And now Shakespeare, having advanced the year from 1405 to 1408 in a few verses, advances it again to 1413 in another few verses, and the King lapses into his final illness. Hearing the news of Northumberland's defeat, he says:

> *And wherefore should these good news make me sick?*
>
> —Act IV, scene iv, line 102

The King is made as comfortable as possible, but despite cheering words, the worst is feared and supernatural portents are spoken of. Thomas of Clarence says:

> *The river hath thrice flowed, no ebb between;*
> *And the old folk, time's doting chronicles,*
> *Say it did so a little time before*
> *That our great-grandsire, Edward, sicked and died.*
>
> —Act IV, scene iv, lines 125–28

The great-grandsire referred to is, of course, Edward III (see page II–253), who had died in 1377, thirty-six years before the death of Henry IV. Holinshed records that this triple rise in the water of the Thames, with no fall between, took place in 1411, two years before the King's death. There is no Hotspur present to say that the Thames would have flooded in just the same way if any cat had died (see page II–356), or to say that in the two years between the flooding and the death of the King, uncounted thousands had died, and who was to say for which, if any, the flood had come.

Besides, Shakespeare improves on Holinshed, who mentions nothing about its having happened a previous time just before the death of Edward III.

Thy wish was father . . .

And now at last Prince Hal arrives and finds his father dying. He asks to sit alone with his father, who lies in bed in a restless sleep, the crown at his side.

Prince Hal apostrophizes the crown, scolding it for the unhappiness it brings kings, and thinking his father will never wake again, he tries it on. His father's tainted title and his own questionable status as "true prince" are perhaps still in his mind, for he feels he will be called on to protect his royal status. He says, determinedly, as he puts on the crown:

> . . . Lo, where it sits,
> Which God shall guard. And put the world's whole strength
> Into one giant arm, it shall not force
> This lineal honor from me.
> —Act IV, scene v, lines 42–45

The Prince leaves the room, still wearing the crown, and the King wakes to find it gone. The King supposes Hal cannot wait for his father's death, so eager is he to become king in his turn, and orders the heir brought before him.

The Earl of Warwick finds the Prince in the next room, weeping, and brings him back with the crown. The Prince explains he thought his father would not wake, and the King says sadly:

> Thy wish was father, Harry, to that thought,
> I stay too long by thee. I weary thee.
> —Act IV, scene v, lines 92–93

Even more sadly, he pictures England's future as he sees it, given his son's penchant for rascals and debauchees:

> Harry the Fifth is crowned. Up, vanity!
> Down, royal state! All you sage counselors, hence!
> And to the English court assemble now,
> From every region, apes of idleness!
> Now, neighbor confines [nations], purge you of your scum.
> Have you a ruffian that will swear, drink, dance,
> Revel the night, rob, murder, and commit
> The oldest sins the newest kind of ways?
> Be happy, he will trouble you no more.
> England shall double gild his treble guilt,
> England shall give him office, honor, might,
> —Act IV, scene v, lines 119–29

Shakespeare pays for making one play into two by having to repeat a scene in which the father majestically and fearfully indicts the son, yet he does it completely differently the second time, without losing any force. In the previous play, the King had pictured his son as being in Hotspur's pay and cowering before his frowns; now he pictures England as reduced to a carnival and haunt of sin.

The Prince is as crushed by the second image as he was by the first. He humbly assures his father of his respect and love in so sincere a way as to win the royal pardon the second time as he did the first. This time, though, it is, in effect, a deathbed reconciliation.

With foreign quarrels . . .

With the reconciliation complete, the King prepares to give the Prince his dying advice. The old King feels that the civil wars which had arisen out of the imperfect title might die out with a new king who would gain a throne by inheritance, and not by seizure. Yet there was the danger that noblemen might conspire out of nothing but boredom. So he says:

> *Therefore, my Harry,*
> *Be it thy course to busy giddy minds*
> *With foreign quarrels, that action, hence borne out,*
> *May waste the memory of the former days.*
>
> —Act IV, scene v, lines 212–15

This course of advocating a foreign war merely to solve domestic problems seems to us today to be completely immoral. Yet in older times, when war was virtually a gentleman's only trade, it would have seemed less so. And, as a matter of fact, Prince Hal followed his father's advice (as given by Shakespeare—who had the advantage of knowing what was going to happen) once he became King Henry V.

Lest we grow too self-righteous about this, we might as well remember that in 1861, when Lincoln became President and the United States was split into two halves that were on the point of war, the new Secretary of State, William Henry Seward, suggested to President Lincoln that the United States deliberately go to war with Great Britain in order to unite the land against a common enemy. This Lincoln refused to do and Seward settled down to become a rational governmental leader.

In that "Jerusalem" . . .

The King then asks of Warwick whether the room in Westminster Abbey in which he first sickened had a name. (It is an odd request, but Shakespeare needs it for dramatic effect.) The King is told that it is called the Jerusalem chamber. Whereupon the King says:

> *Even there my life must end.*
> *It hath been prophesied to me many years*
> *I should not die but "in Jerusalem,"*

Which vainly I supposed the Holy Land.
But bear me to that chamber; there I'll lie.
In that "Jerusalem" shall Harry die.

—Act IV, scene v, lines 235–40

These are the last words we hear from Henry IV, still talking of the Holy Land, as he did at the end of *Richard II*. He died on March 20, 1413, at the age of forty-six, worn out by sickness and toil, having reigned for fourteen years and having been the victim, even more than Richard II himself, of the day on which the crown changed hands.

And yet he was by no means a failure. Facing rebellion year after year, he defeated it year after year, never backing down, never despairing, and the result was that, through infinite toil, he passed on to his heir a united nation; strong enough, as that heir was to discover, to make astonishing conquests across the Channel.

. . . *in continual laughter* . . .

In Gloucestershire, Falstaff is with Justice Shallow again, busily preparing to fleece him, while Shallow lends himself to the process by being so anxious to curry favor with Falstaff, whom he conceives to be a great man at court.

As a matter of fact, Falstaff, not knowing the changes about to take place, conceives himself to be a great man. In fact, he looks to Shallow for more than money to continue that greatness by the one means that has never failed him. He says in a soliloquy, after Shallow has spent a scene being as senile and quavery as Shakespeare can make him:

> *I will devise matter enough out of this Shallow to keep Prince*
> *Harry in continual laughter . . .*
>
> —Act V, scene i, lines 80–82

That day, alas for Falstaff, will never come.

Not Amurath an Amurath . . .

At court Henry IV has died and Prince Hal is now Henry V. There is apprehension among many who (as in Henry IV's great speech, see page II–411) expect the new King to be as riotous now as he had been when a Prince, and who look with anxiety at the prospect of having to kowtow to men like Sir John Falstaff.

The Lord Chief Justice is particularly concerned, for he cannot help but remember that he once put the man who is now King Henry V in jail. He prepares for the worst and speaks of:

> . . . *the condition of the time,*
> *Which cannot look more hideously upon me*
> *Than I have drawn it in my fantasy.*
>
> —Act V, scene ii, lines 11–13

The three brothers of the new King (Thomas of Clarence, John of Lancaster, and Humphrey of Gloucester) enter, and Warwick wishes that the King were but as good as the worst of his three brothers. Thus, the audience is keyed up for the first appearance of wild Prince Hal as King Henry V.

He appears and is, at once, the hero-king of legend, unbelievably great and unbelievably human at the same time. He speaks to his brothers, who are waiting in anxiety as they try to guess what the new times will bring, and says:

> *Brothers, you mix your sadness with some fear.*
> *This is the English, not the Turkish court.*
> *Not Amurath an Amurath succeeds,*
> *But Harry Harry.*
>
> —Act V, scene ii, lines 46–49

Amurath, or better Murad, is the name of five Turkish sultans. Only one of them, however, had yet been on the Turkish throne at the time that Henry V became King of England. He was Murad I, who was the Turkish Sultan from 1362 to 1389, during the reigns of Edward III and Richard II. It was a time when the Ottoman Turks were advancing triumphantly in the Balkans, and indeed, the crowning battle was fought at Kossovo in what is now southern Yugoslavia in 1389. The Christian army of the Serbs, who then controlled the area, was utterly destroyed and the Balkans fell under a Turkish rule that was to last for five centuries. Murad I, however, died in the course of the battle.

The next sultan of that name, Murad II, did not ascend the throne until 1421, eight years after the succession of Henry V, so it is a little anachronistic to have Henry V, at the time of his succession, speaking of an Amurath succeeding an Amurath.

The third king of that name, Murad III, reigned, however, in Shakespeare's time. He became Sultan in 1574, when Shakespeare was ten years old, and he died in 1595, some two years before *Henry IV, Part Two* was produced. It is undoubtedly Murad III of whom Shakespeare was thinking when he had Henry V speak these words.

The Turkish sultans were born of a polygamous social system. When a sultan died, there were many sons who might succeed to the throne, and principles of legitimacy were never clearly established. In addition, the Turkish princes were particularly alien to each other (more so than English princes, for instance) in that they were born of different mothers. What's more, the mothers themselves intrigued mercilessly on behalf of their sons while the old sultan was yet alive. (We get a brief glimpse of this in the Bible, for instance, at the court of the dying King David, in the first two chapters of 1 Kings.)

Usually, the Turkish prince who managed to gain the throne had his various brothers executed at once lest they be the occasion for civil wars. In particular, when Murad III (Shakespeare's Amurath) succeeded to the throne in 1574, his very first act was to order the execution of five brothers. Such a deed undoubtedly rang through Christian Europe, which considered it as just the sort of unspeakable act of which the infidel Turks were capable.

It is this which is in Shakespeare's mind when he has Henry V reassure his brothers that it is not an Amurath who is becoming King but just good old Harry, and that they are therefore safe. Indeed, Henry V did treat his brothers well. It was he who raised his youngest brother Humphrey to the title of Duke of Gloucester in 1414, the year after his accession, though Humphrey is anachronistically called by that title in *Henry IV, Part Two*. Henry V also, in that same year, made John of Lancaster Duke of Bedford, and it is as Bedford that that brother is best known to history.

In return, Henry V's three brothers served him faithfully during his reign and the two survivors served his successor faithfully.

. . . still bear the balance . . .

Henry next deliberately baits the Lord Chief Justice, reminding him that he himself was once sent to jail by him. The Lord Chief Justice, expecting the worst in any case, has the courage to answer that if he is to be punished for upholding the King's law against the King's son, then let the new King be prepared to see his own son scorn him and his law someday.

Henry V, having heard what he hoped to hear, answers gravely:

> *You are right, Justice, and you weigh this well.*
> *Therefore still bear the balance and the sword.*
> *And I do wish your honors may increase,*
> *Till you do live to see a son of mine*
> *Offend you—and obey you—as I did.*
> —Act V, scene ii, lines 102–6

He then goes on humbly to ask the Lord Chief Justice to be his adviser and lend his grave experience to help a young king. Thus does the new King prove that his father's fears that he would drive away "all you sage counselors" were groundless. In fact, Henry V goes further. He not only demonstrates his virtue, he specifically renounces his vice:

> *The tide of blood in me*
> *Hath proudly flowed in vanity till now.*
> *Now doth it turn and ebb back to the sea,*
> *Where it shall mingle with the state of floods*
> *And flow henceforth in formal majesty.*
>
> —Act V, scene ii, lines 129–33

It remains only to put that high resolve to the test, and for that Falstaff, unknowingly, waits.

. . . thy tender lambkin . . .

Falstaff is still with Shallow in Gloucestershire, being feted in rustic splendor, when Pistol arrives with the news, breathless and wild. He cannot speak except in his fustian tragic metaphors and is continually being interrupted by the Gloucestershiremen, who cannot understand him and who throw him into a fury. Finally, he manages to choke it out:

> *Sir John, thy tender lambkin now is king.*
> *Harry the Fifth's the man. I speak the truth.*
>
> —Act V, scene iii, lines 118–19

All is at once confusion. Shallow's appointment as justice of the peace automatically expires with the old King's death and so does Silence's (who faints).

But Falstaff calls for his horse at once. He has no doubt that he is now to be the power behind the throne. He says:

> *Master Robert Shallow, choose what office thou wilt in the land, 'tis thine.*
>
> —Act V, scene iii, lines 124–26

Pistol and Bardolph are ecstatic, with visions of wealth and power in their heads, but Falstaff's own vision climbs to the heights:

> *I know the young king is sick for me. Let us take any man's horses; the laws of England are at my commandment. Blessed are they that have been my friends, and woe to my Lord Chief Justice!*
>
> —Act V, scene iii, lines 137–41

I know thee not, old man . . .

With a thousand pounds of Shallow's money, Falstaff rides madly to London. With him are his various satellites, including Shallow. It is coronation day, April 9, 1413, with Henry V about to pass in most solemn procession. Falstaff can hardly wait; his part-time sweetheart, Doll Tearsheet, has been taken off to prison on an accusation of murder, and he is certain he can save her.

Henry V passes in all state and Falstaff forces a public confrontation by calling out to him. The procession stops and the climax of the two *Henry IV* plays comes.

In measured tones, the King begins:

> *I know thee not, old man. Fall to thy prayers.*
> *How ill white hairs become a fool and jester!*
> *I have long dreamt of such a kind of man,*
> *So surfeit-swelled, so old, and so profane,*
> *But being awaked, I do despise my dream.*
> —Act V, scene v, lines 48–52

Falstaff is thus publicly repudiated and humiliated, forbidden to approach within ten miles of the King at any time. (Holinshed says, without detail, that the riotous friends of Hal's princehood were forbidden to approach closer than that distance.)

Uncounted numbers have regretted this speech. Loving Falstaff because he made them (as well as the Prince) laugh, the watchers and readers of the play have mourned the Prince's action and felt he was a coldhearted prig to turn against the man so publicly. I have, in the past, been firmly of that opinion myself.

Yet on further thought, it is wrong to blame Henry V. Accepting the Shakespearean situation, we must see that Falstaff had invited the public humiliation by accosting the new King publicly, and on the coronation day of all times. Henry V had somehow to wipe out of the public mind the vision of himself as a wild, riotous person. That image had been centered on Falstaff, and therefore, it was on the King's treatment of Falstaff that his public image rested.

Henry V could not bend in this respect; he could not move. If the conspiracies against the throne were to cease, he must be seen as anointed King, rightful King, true King. In order to lift the ever present stain of the deposition of Richard II he had to speak as King and not as man.

Orson Welles starred as Falstaff in a recent motion picture based on *Henry IV, Part One* and *Henry IV, Part Two,* and this scene, as portrayed there, struck me as perfect.

The man who had been Prince Hal and was now Henry V spoke without looking at Falstaff, and though his words were the words of the King of England, his face bore the anguish of Prince Hal. And as for Orson Welles's Falstaff, he bore the blinding shock of the rejection but on his face was pride too, pride that this wild young prince whom he had always thought he could wind about his finger had become a great man far beyond and outside his control.

Finally, it must also be remembered that even as King, Henry V was not heartless. He says to Falstaff:

> For competence of life I will allow you,
> That lack of means enforce you not to evils.
> And, as we hear you do reform yourselves,
> We will, according to your strengths and qualities,
> Give you advancement.
>
> —Act V, scene v, lines 67–71

Surely this is decent treatment.

As far as France

With that done, Shakespeare can now point to the future. Lancaster, pleased at this action of the King in repudiating Falstaff, now has no fears for the reign. He expects a heroic time:

> I will lay odds that, ere this year expire,
> We bear our civil swords and native fire
> As far as France.
>
> —Act V, scene vi, lines 106–8

It is a hindsight prophecy that is almost correct. Within a year, Henry V begins planning an invasion of France, but it is only after two years that the invasion actually begins.

. . . will continue the story . . .

The promise of another play is made explicit in the Epilogue, in which the speaker says:

> If you be not too much cloyed with fat meat, our humble
> author will continue the story, with Sir John in it, and make
> you merry with fair Katherine of France. Where, for anything
> I know, Falstaff shall die of a sweat, unless already 'a be killed

*with your hard opinions, for Oldcastle died martyr, and this
is not the man.*

—Epilogue, lines 26–32

Shakespeare betrays his nervousness here. There is still controversy over the fact that Falstaff was first named Oldcastle (see page II–327), thus offending the influential Cobham family and the extreme Protestants. They were probably the more offended because they were in opposition to the Essex faction (see page I–120), on whose side Shakespeare notoriously was. Shakespeare therefore makes a flat and explicit disclaimer of any connection between Falstaff and Oldcastle.

Nevertheless, despite the promise here, Falstaff does not appear in the continuation of the story, which is to be found in the play *Henry V*. Either Shakespeare wanted no more of the controversy with Cobham, or he was tired of Falstaff after ten acts, or he felt Falstaff's appearance in France would be anticlimactic after the tremendous repudiation scene.

Perhaps all three possibilities influenced him. As a matter of fact, however, Falstaff did appear in a third play (which we will take up next), though, according to legend, not at Shakespeare's own desire. It is indeed anticlimactic and even distressing that Falstaff does so.

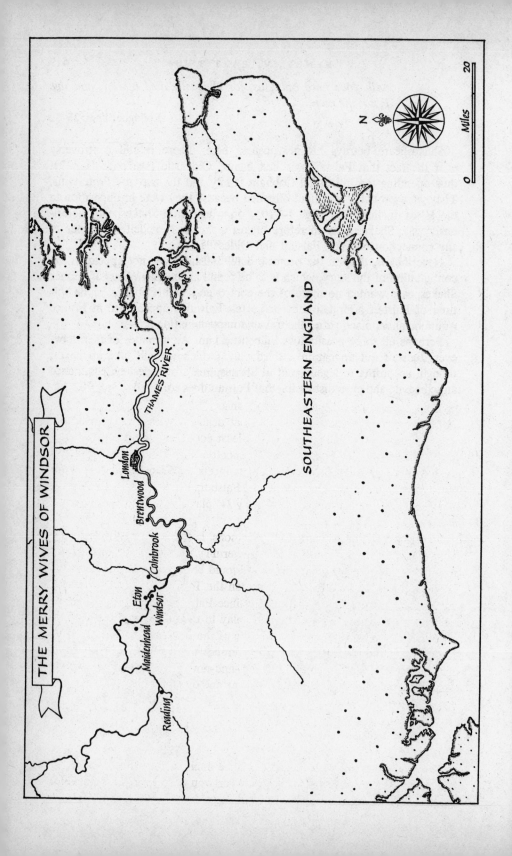

34

THE MERRY WIVES

OF WINDSOR

THERE is a story that Queen Elizabeth was so taken by the character of Falstaff in *Henry IV, Part One* and *Henry IV, Part Two* that she made it known she wanted very much to see Falstaff in love. The royal whim is a command and the story goes further that Shakespeare was required to complete the play (from a cold start) in two weeks.

Estimates as to the year in which this happened vary from 1597 (when *Henry IV, Part Two* was still being written) to 1601 (two years after its sequel *Henry V* was written).

There is no way of knowing whether this story of writing on command is true. The earliest reference to it we know of is a comment in 1702 by the English critic and dramatist John Dennis.

If it were true it would explain a great deal. It would explain why the play is almost entirely prose—by far the least poetic play written by Shakespeare. There was no time granted for poetry. Then too, the play shows great signs of haste, and a number of its facets are incomplete or flawed. Worst of all, the play is a slander on Falstaff, since there is nothing of the great comic genius of the two *Henry IV* plays in the fat fool we have in this one.

Or perhaps all this exists for other reasons, because the play was something that didn't work—and the tale concerning Elizabeth's command was invented to account for what otherwise would be puzzling in Shakespeare.

The scene is set in Windsor, a town on the Thames River, and the site of Windsor Castle (see page II-261). Since Falstaff is the central character, we would expect the events of the play to take place in the period of 1400 to 1413. There is, however, no sign of the period about it other than the names of the characters and *one* reference to Prince Hal. Aside from that it is actually Shakespeare's only here-and-now play, the only one whose events take place in Shakespeare's own time and own place.

. . . twenty Sir John Falstaffs . . .

The play starts off with the aged Justice Shallow tottering onstage. He had made a hit in *Henry IV, Part Two* (or would do so if, as is possible, the two plays are being written simultaneously) and here he is with his superannuated bravery, saying:

> *Sir Hugh, persuade me not; I will make a Star-chamber matter of it. If he were twenty Sir John Falstaffs, he shall not abuse Robert Shallow, Esquire.*
>
> —Act I, scene i, lines 1–4

In the first speech, then, there is mention of Falstaff, so that the audience can anticipate his appearance. In fact, we may even wonder whether the argument might not be over the thousand pounds that Falstaff obtained from Shallow toward the end of *Henry IV, Part Two* and then was unable to pay back because of his repudiation by the newly crowned Henry V.

Sir Hugh, it will turn out, is Sir Hugh Evans, a Welsh parson ("Sir" is a courtesy title for parsons), who will speak with a thick accent. (There is a successful character, Fluellen, in *Henry V* who also speaks with a thick Welsh accent. Whether Sir Hugh inspired Fluellen or vice versa depends on which play was written first, and this we do not know.)

The Star-chamber was a dreaded branch of the law since it dealt extra-legally in matters concerning which no specific law held. It consisted of judges without a jury. It could proceed on rumor; it could order torture; it was, to a considerable extent, irresponsible and much feared (hence the deadly threat in "I will make a Star-chamber matter of it"). It was abolished, and good riddance to it, in 1641, as part of the reforms initiated by the English parliamentary faction that had rebelled against Charles I.

The source of its name is uncertain, but the best guess seems to be that it met in a room in which the ceiling was decorated with stars.

. . . Justice of Peace . . .

Following Shallow is his cousin Slender, the faithful shadow and admirer of the old man. To be the admirer of so feeble a hero is to be the shadow of a shadow, and this role Slender fills, rather as did Silence in *Henry IV, Part Two*. Slender is the epitome of the country bumpkin.

After Shallow speaks, Slender worshipfully adds to the final words "Robert Shallow, Esquire" a formal title intended to make the man more formidable:

> *In the county of Gloucester, Justice of Peace, and Coram.*
>
> —Act I, scene i, lines 5–6

"Coram" is Slender's humorous (for the then audience) distortion of "Quoram," a term used for justices with special legal qualifications who were required to be present at the sessions of a court.

. . . Master Abraham . . .

Distorted versions of Shallow's greatness in the legal world rattle bravely between Slender and Shallow himself, but Evans, the Welshman, through his Welsh accent, labors to calm Shallow and make peace. He even introduces an interesting distraction.

George Page, a gentleman of Windsor, has, it seems, a pretty daughter, Anne, who brings with her a dowry of seven hundred pounds. Evans says:

> *It were a goot motion if we leave our pribbles and prabbles, and desire a marriage between Master Abraham and Mistress Anne Page.*
>
> —Act I, scene i, lines 54–56

This is a sensible diversion, since "Master Abraham" is Slender himself, and since Shallow's fury, it will soon turn out, depends upon the loss by Slender of a trifling sum of money, which the gain of seven hundred pounds would make negligible.

. . . Bardolph, Nym and Pistol . . .

Shallow and Slender are at once interested. Shallow is willing to see Mr. Page concerning the matter. They are actually standing before his door, and within his house, Falstaff himself is at present to be found.

When Falstaff appears, he is unrepentant, and insolently admits that he has committed various offenses against Shallow. (It is done without wit. The real Falstaff would have managed to turn it all into a laugh and have inveigled Shallow into apologizing.)

Falstaff then turns on Slender and demands his complaint. Slender indicates Falstaff's followers:

> *. . . your cony-catching rascals, Bardolph, Nym and Pistol. They carried me to the tavern and made me drunk, and afterward picked my pocket.*
>
> —Act I, scene i, lines 123–26

Bardolph has appeared with Falstaff in both *Henry IV, Part One* and *Henry IV, Part Two* and has a face greatly reddened by excessive drinking, which makes him an endless butt for Shakespearean wordplay. Pistol, who appears only in *Henry IV, Part Two* of those two plays, is the epitome of the swaggerer. He talks ferociously and grandiloquently but is, of course, an arrant coward.

Nym does not appear in either of the Henry IV plays, but does appear (along with Bardolph and Pistol) in *Henry V*. It is his comic bit to speak constantly of "humor" (the Shakespearean term for "temperament" or "personality").

It was a common device among the Elizabethans (and among dramatists of both earlier and later times) to extract humor out of having a man possess some overriding characteristic, like (to use contemporary examples) Jack Benny's cheapness or Bob Hope's feckless lechery. The word "humor" meaning "funniness" comes from the fun arising in the depiction of a "humor" meaning "outstanding temperamental characteristic."

. . . Mephistophilus

Each of the accused hangers-on of Falstaff draws his sword in indignation and answers in his own style. Bardolph uses a metaphor drawn from his concern for eating and drinking:

> *You Banbury cheese!*
>
> —Act I, scene i, line 127

Banbury is a town sixty-five miles northwest of London, noted in Shakespearean times as a stronghold of Puritanism, and therefore subjected by the anti-Puritan playwrights to considerable ridicule. A characteristic cheese produced in Banbury was only an inch thick, which did not affect its deliciousness, of course, but could be used as a handle to sneer at Puritan parsimony (though there was really no connection, since the cheeses antedated the Puritans). Bardolph's remark is a sneer at Slender's slenderness, for the name is descriptive of the man both physically and mentally.

Pistol, on the other hand, says:

> *How now, Mephistophilus!*
>
> —Act I, scene i, line 129

Pistol, as is characteristic of him, is drawing on the blood-and-thunder dramatics of the time and is referring to a character out of Christopher Marlowe's *The Tragedy of Dr. Faustus*, where Mephistophilus is the name of the devil who tempts Faust. It is a highly inappropriate comparison for Slender, but Pistol's dramatic quotations are always distorted, inappropriate, or both.

Nym says:

> *Slice, I say!* PAUCA PAUCA. *Slice! That's my humor.*
>
> —Act I, scene i, lines 131–32

Nym presents his humor as that of a man of action, not words. The phrase *"pauca"* is a short version of *pauca verba* (Latin for "few words").

When Slender, trembling, maintains his position, Pistol challenges him to a duel with the opening cry:

> *Ha, thou mountain-foreigner!*
>
> —Act I, scene i, line 157

A mountain-foreigner is a non-Englishman from the western hills; that is, a Welshman. The very word "Welsh" is from the Saxon *wealh,* meaning "foreigner."

. . . Scarlet and John

Pistol and Nym do most of the talking, so Falstaff turns to Bardolph for his statement, saying:

> *What say you, Scarlet and John?*
>
> —Act I, scene i, line 168

Will Scarlet and Little John were two of the prominent members of Robin Hood's band (who were known for robbing the rich, supposedly for the benefit of the poor). This reference to robber outlaws would seem to be a cynical indication that Falstaff knows his men for the petty thieves they are. Since Bardolph is Falstaff's right-hand man, he is compared to Little John, who plays the same role in connection with Robin Hood. And "Scarlet" is a none too subtle reference to Bardolph's fiery complexion.

Bardolph also denies the accusation—and that's it.

After 181 lines of the first scene of the play, Shakespeare wearies of trying to make it a play about Falstaff and his latter-day merry men, and drops the whole thing. The quarrel between Shallow and Slender on one side and Falstaff and his men on the other is never referred to again in the rest of the play.

Perhaps if Shakespeare had had time, he would have abandoned what he had written so far and made a new beginning; but if the tale is true that he was racing the clock, then any lines that filled space would have to do.

. . . Book of Songs and Sonnets . . .

Anne Page, the pretty young heroine of the seriously romantic portion of this play (a portion that is almost vanishingly small) enters briefly.

Slender, who sees Anne for the first time, is instantly struck into a kind of mooncalf love. He sighs and says:

> *I had rather than forty shillings I had my Book of Songs and Sonnets here.*
>
> —Act I, scene i, lines 191–92

This "Book of Songs and Sonnets" is commonly called *Tottel's Miscellany*. It was the first English anthology of poetry, and was compiled and published by Richard Tottel in 1557. Poor Slender, unless he can crib from the poems in this book, would be tongue-tied in the presence of Anne Page.

Slender asks his servant, Simple (who appears opportunely in order to be asked), where the book is. He is told:

> *. . . did you not lend it to Alice Shortcake upon Allhallowmas last, a fortnight afore Michaelmas?*
>
> —Act I, scene i, lines 196–98

Allhallowmas, or All Saints' Day, is celebrated on November 1. It is a day set aside for commemorating all saints generally, known and unknown.

Michaelmas is the festival in honor of St. Michael and all the angels. (St. Michael was the archangel who led the angels of light against Satan and his fallen hosts, according to the legends which are best known to us through their treatment in Milton's *Paradise Lost*.)

Michaelmas is on September 29, so Simple is saying that Slender lent the book on November 1, a fortnight before September 29, which was, of course, humorous to those in the audience who knew their church holidays. (We would preserve the fun if we had Simple say the book had been lent "on Christmas, two weeks before Thanksgiving." There is something to be said for cultural as well as linguistic translations.)

. . . Sackerson loose . . .

Alone with Anne Page and without any poetry to guide him, Slender is utterly lost. At one point he tries to impress Anne with his virile courage. He leads the subject round to bears, and having ascertained that Anne is afraid of bears, he says:

> *I have seen Sackerson loose twenty times, and have taken him by the chain;*
>
> —Act I, scene i, lines 284–86

Sackerson was a famous bear of Shakespeare's time, kept in Paris-

Garden just across the Thames from the center of London. He was a tame bear and taking him by the chain was a favorite amusement of children, especially since the bear was undoubtedly muzzled just in case it happened to forget it was tame.

. . . a region in Guiana . . .

Meanwhile, as it happens, Falstaff is desperately short of funds, and, in this play at least, there is no Prince Hal to lend him money. (Can the events in the play be taking place after Falstaff's repudiation by the Prince-become-King?) As a measure of economy, he fires Bardolph, who is promptly hired by the Host (owner) of the Garter Inn. Bardolph becomes a tapster, an ideal occupation for him, actually.

It falls into Falstaff's head, next, to replenish his finances by making love to Mistress Ford, the wife of a well-to-do middle-class citizen. In gratitude for his favors, she will (he thinks) make him gifts of money. To hedge his bets, Falstaff decides also to make love to Mistress Page (Anne Page's mother). She is also a possible source of money, for as Falstaff says:

> She bears the purse too. She is a region in Guiana, all gold and bounty.
> —Act I, scene iii, lines 67–68

Guiana is the name given to a section of the northern coast of South America, not noted, particularly, for its wealth. However, this is easily confused with Guinea, a name applied to the southern shore of the western bulge of northern Africa. (That name is derived from the land, whose people called it Ghana in ancient times, and who call it Ghana again since the various African regions gained their independence in the late 1950s and early 1960s—though the section of the Atlantic Ocean that washes its shores is still called the "Gulf of Guinea.")

The region now called Ghana was noted for its gold, and on this its ancient prosperity depended in great part. Indeed, when the English gained control of it, they called it the "Gold Coast." In 1663, well after Shakespeare's time, a gold coin was first stamped out of gold obtained from Guinea. Naturally, it was named the "guinea" and its value was finally fixed at twenty-one shillings (a pound plus a shilling). If this coin had been extant a century earlier, Shakespeare would most certainly not have confused Guinea and Guiana.

The guinea was no longer coined after 1813, but it continued to be used in professional fees because of its prestige—and of its extra shilling.

. . . Sir Pandarus of Troy . . .

Falstaff, in pursuit of this plan of his, has written the same letter to both Mistress Ford and Mistress Page and orders Nym to carry the letter to the former while Pistol acts as messenger to the latter.

In a most extraordinary attack of scruples both refuse to do anything as base as act the go-between. As Pistol says, grandly:

> *Shall I Sir Pandarus of Troy become,*
> *And by my side wear steel?*

> —Act I, scene iii, lines 75–76

Pandarus was the go-between in the Troilus and Cressida legend (concerning which Shakespeare was soon to write *Troilus and Cressida*) and gave rise to the word "pander" (see page I–113). We can sympathize with Pistol's feeling that the occupation of pimp is inconsistent with the dignity of a soldier's status, but we can be a little surprised that either he or Nym should find anything at all to which they cannot stoop.

The two henchmen quit Falstaff's service on the spot. Falstaff, undisturbed, sends the letters by his small page (presumably the one who is introduced in *Henry IV, Part Two*). There his speeches were identified as "Page" and he was nowhere given a name; here he is called Robin. (Naturally, since another character has the surname "Page.")

Falstaff leaves, and his resentful men, too proud to pander but not too proud to carry tales, decide to betray his plan to the husbands of the two ladies.

. . . Cain-colored beard

Meanwhile, Sir Hugh Evans, the Welsh parson, has decided on the need for a go-between to handle the love affair of Slender and Anne Page, which he is hopefully pushing. He has sent Simple (Slender's servant) to Mistress Quickly, who is servant to a physician, feeling that she will be the ideal go-between.

Mistress Quickly is the name given to the hostess of the Boar's Head Tavern in *Henry IV, Part One* and *Henry IV, Part Two*. In those plays, her tavern is clearly used as a house of prostitution, so that her role as go-between for lovers would be in character. In *The Merry Wives of Windsor*, however, she is a much more respectable person in occupation than the character of the same name in the earlier plays.

Mistress Quickly is willing to undertake the service (presumably she will be well paid for it), even though she doesn't know the man for whom she must labor and makes all sorts of false starts in trying to identify him. She asks if he has a large beard and Simple says:

> He hath but a little whey face, with a little yellow beard—a Cain-colored beard.
>
> —Act I, scene iv, lines 22–23

Cain, the slayer of Abel, and the world's first murderer according to the biblical story, was, for some reason, given a reddish-yellow beard in the tapestries dealing with biblical subjects. Judas, the betrayer of Jesus, was given the same color beard.

The juxtaposition is humorous here, of course, for anyone less likely than Slender to be driven by ungovernable passion into monstrous acts of violence or treason is hard to imagine.

. . . la grande affaire

The physician for whom Mistress Quickly is working is Dr. Caius, a Frenchman, whose accent is even heavier than Evans' and who is pictured as a comic stereotype—very fierce. His short temper will explode if he finds Mistress Quickly entertaining strange men in his absence, so that when she discovers he is coming home, she quickly shoves Simple into the closet.

Dr. Caius is apparently on his way to some great social affair at court. He says so, in French:

> Ma foi, il fait fort chaud. Je m'en vais a la Cour—la grande affaire.
>
> —Act I, scene iv, lines 51–52

This means "My word, it is very hot. I am going to the Court—the great affair." It is not translated in the play and nothing comes of it. It may have been thrown in just to color the characterization. Or it may have been an in-reference to something going on at the time the play was written.

It is just possible that Queen Elizabeth's hurry-up order for the play to be written (assuming this story is true) was not entirely because she couldn't wait to see Falstaff in love, but because she wanted some rollicking play to be staged on the occasion of some important—and imminent—ceremony at the court.

From other references later in the play, it may be deduced that the reference is to an installation of new appointees to the Order of the Garter. One such installation is known to have taken place in May 1597. This is quite early, almost impossibly early for the play, for it means that The Merry Wives of Windsor would have had to be written while Shakespeare was still working on Henry IV, Part Two.

Still, if this is so, then the assembled notables attending the installation (all of whom could undoubtedly speak French fluently) would surely find amusement in a comic Frenchman hastening off to go to the affair all were at that moment attending.

At the last minute, before Dr. Caius leaves, he remembers something he had forgotten and pulls open the closet door, unexpectedly revealing Simple. The furious Frenchman demands an explanation, and when it is given, it promptly turns out that Dr. Caius is himself a suitor for the hand of the lovely Anne Page. Naturally, he deeply resents the efforts of Sir Hugh to marry her off elsewhere.

Fuming, the Frenchman sits down to write a letter, then says to Simple:

> *You jack'nape, give-a dis letter to Sir Hugh. By gar, it is a shallenge.*
>
> —Act I, scene iv, lines 106–7

The stage is thus set for a comic duel between two competing fracturers of the English language.

When Dr. Caius stamps angrily off to court, in comes Fenton, a handsome young man who is also courting Anne Page (and of course, it is with him that the audience must side—to say nothing of Anne herself—as against the pip-squeak Slender and the firecracker Caius).

Mistress Quickly has already promised to help Slender and Caius and she will help Fenton too. It is all one to her, as long as she is paid, and Fenton pays her, saying:

> *Hold, there's money for thee; let me have thy voice in my behalf.*
>
> —Act I, scene iv, lines 153–54

. . . under Mount Pelion

By now, Mistress Page has received the letter from Falstaff, and as a respectable housewife ungiven to intrigue, she is thoroughly angered. She says:

> *What a Herod of Jewry is this! O wicked, wicked world.*
>
> —Act II, scene i, lines 20–21

By "Herod of Jewry" she merely means a villain (see page II–121).

Mistress Ford comes onstage with an identical letter and is identically indignant. Mistress Page, referring to Falstaff's size and the consequences of attempting to make love with him, says in anger:

I had rather be a giantess and lie under Mount Pelion.
—Act II, scene i, lines 77–78

According to the Greek myths, Zeus and the other Olympians defeated a race of monstrous giants early in earth's history. After the victory, the giants were placed, for safekeeping, under mountains designed to keep them penned forever. Thus, Enceladus, one of the leading giants, was placed under Mount Etna.

It is easy to suppose that the story arose from the need to account for the activity of volcanoes.

Mount Pelion played a part in another myth, which was, however, very like that of the revolt of the giants. In this second myth, two monstrous young men planned to assault Mount Olympus, the highest mountain in Greece and the home of the gods. To achieve a platform high enough, they were planning to pile Mount Pelion on Mount Ossa (see page II–141). Mistress Page fuses the two myths in her allusion.

Mistress Page and Mistress Ford, in their anger, determine to turn the tables on Falstaff; to lead him on, fruitlessly, until he is worn out. It is this determination of the two women to make Falstaff the butt of their merry plans (merry for themselves and the audience, if not for Falstaff) that makes them "The Merry Wives of Windsor."

. . . Sir Actaeon . . .

Nor are the two women the only ones to know of Falstaff's intentions. Nym and Pistol betray Falstaff, out of pique, and inform the husbands. Pistol says to them:

Prevent, or go thou,
Like Sir Actaeon he, with Ringwood at thy heels.
O, odious is the name.
—Act II, scene i, lines 116–18

Actaeon was a hunter, in Greek mythology, who caught sight of Diana (Artemis) bathing and stopped to watch. Diana, the virgin goddess of the hunt, was bitterly offended at this, and turned Actaeon into a stag so that he was torn to pieces by his own dogs. (Ringwood was a standard name for hounds in Elizabethan times.)

Because Actaeon wore the horns of a stag, and because the wearing of horns was symbolic of a husband of an unfaithful wife (see page I–84), Pistol is making use of the reference as a grandiloquent warning. At the last minute he finds himself too delicate to say the actual word, which is too "odious" for his refined sensibilities. The word, as everyone in the audience knows, is, of course, "cuckold."

. . . such a Cataian . . .

Page, a calm, sensible man, has no jealous fears and is incredulous. He says:

> *I will not believe such a Cataian . . .*
>
> —Act II, scene i, line 140

The use of "Cataian" (meaning a Chinaman) harks back several centuries before Shakespeare's time, to when a nomadic tribe, the "Khitan" or "Kitai," ruled northern China. They controlled the land from 907 to 1125, long enough to lend their name to it. The Mongols, under Genghis Khan, conquered the region in 1213, and before the end of the century, the Venetian traveler Marco Polo visited the land. The name of the old nomadic tribe, by then a century and a half gone, still lingered, and Marco Polo called north China "Cathay," so that in England a native of China became a "Cataian." Since xenophobia was even more widespread in medieval times than now, it was taken for granted that so exotic a creature as a Chinaman had to be a liar.

The present name of the land, China, comes from an even older line of rulers, the Ch'in dynasty, which controlled the land for less than half a century, from 259 to 210 B.C. The Ch'in emperor who ruled during most of this period was Chin Shih Huang Ti, a strong ruler under whom the Great Wall was built. Emperor Chin had all the historical books of the time burned in order to glorify his own reign by making it seem as though history began with him. He succeeded to the extent that his reign was the first to emerge from the obscurity of legend (in later times), and that gave China its name.

Unlike Page, Ford is pathologically jealous, and the news of Falstaff's plans throws him into a fever of rage. He decides to investigate the matter by dealing with Falstaff directly, under the disguise of a "Mr. Brooke."

. . . the world's mine oyster

Falstaff is waiting at the Garter Inn for news of his intrigue's success, and Pistol, having betrayed him, is unblushingly applying for a loan. Falstaff refuses,whereupon Pistol delivers the best-known lines of the play:

> *Why, then, the world's mine oyster,*
> *Which I with sword will open.*
>
> —Act II, scene ii, lines 2–3

The trade of mercenary soldier was common in most times and could be lucrative. Not only were you paid, if all went well, but you had the chance of loot in the sacking of cities and the taking of spoils. If all else failed, you could sack and loot your own side. Of course, you might be killed, but that was the occupational hazard of the position.

The phrase "the world's mine oyster" has become standard now for anyone who goes bravely out into life with nothing but native talent with which to wrest a fortune out of it.

. . . she-Mercury

Now comes Mistress Quickly, the ubiquitous go-between of this play, with messages to Falstaff from the merry wives. She goes about it with such circumstance that the impatient Falstaff cuts her short, saying:

> But what says she to me? Be brief, my good she-Mercury.
> —Act II, scene ii, lines 79–80

Mercury was, of course, the messenger of the gods (see page I–105), and a "she-Mercury" would then be any female messenger.

Thus prodded, Mrs. Quickly informs Falstaff that he has an assignation with Mistress Ford between ten and eleven in the morning, when Ford will be gone. Mistress Page also sends a letter promising an assignation at the first opportunity. Falstaff is delighted.

. . . a damned Epicurean rascal . . .

Ford enters now, disguised as Mr. Brooke, a stranger unknown to Falstaff. Intending to find out whether Falstaff will indeed succeed in making love to Mistress Ford, he spins Falstaff a tale that he himself is in love with the woman and cannot win her. He urges Falstaff to win her and inform Brooke, so that, with his own knowledge of this escapade, he can force her to his own will.

Falstaff falls in with this wholly improbable tale at once and assures Brooke that he already has an assignation, and genially slanders Ford for a cuckold.

He leaves and Ford is left behind, beside himself with rage, saying of Falstaff:

> What a damned Epicurean rascal is this!
> —Act II, scene ii, line 286

Epicurus was a Greek philosopher who founded a school in Athens in

306 B.C. He preached a practical, sensible philosophy that eschewed superstition (see page I–311), adopted a materialistic approach to life, proclaimed pleasure the chief goal of human existence, and defined the highest pleasure to be that achieved by moderation in those activities that
seemed pleasant.

Those who followed Epicurus in later centuries often abandoned the
key word "moderation," so that the teachings degenerated into hedonism,
the unrestrained search for pleasure. Epicureanism fell into disrepute and
the word slandered the founder of the philosophy by coming to stand for
a system of heedless pleasure, luxury, gluttony, and lust. Clearly, Ford
applies it to Falstaff in the most insulting possible way.

. . . Wittol

Poor Ford can only fume at the names applied to him in his real identity
by Falstaff: names which he feels he deserves and which he cannot bear.
The names of devils are not as ugly as those he has been called. He cries
out in agony:

> Amaimon sounds well; Lucifer, well; Barbason well; yet they
> are devils' additions, the names of fiends. But Cuckold!
> Wittol!

—Act II, scene ii, lines 295–98

Devils' names such as Amaimon and Barbason are among the numerous
inventions of medieval and early modern demonologists (see page II–34).
Thus, in 1584, a little over a dozen years before The Merry Wives of
Windsor was written, there appeared a work called The Discovery of
Witchcraft by Reginald Scot, which described an important devil called
"Marbas, alias Barbas." It is this which probably gave Shakespeare the
name "Barbason." As for Amaimon, he, in the medieval tales of demon-
ology, was supposed to rule over the eastern portion of hell.

All these old names of devils are now forgotten (and good riddance)
except for those which are mentioned in the Bible, and among these is
Lucifer. It appears at a point in the Book of Isaiah where the prophet
triumphs over falling Babylon and says, "How art thou fallen from heaven,
O Lucifer, son of the morning!" (Isaiah 14:12).

The Hebrew word here translated as "Lucifer" is helel. Literally, it means
"the Shining One," and is thought to refer to the planet Venus. The
planet Venus can appear in the sky either as a morning star in one half
of its orbit, or as an evening star in the other half. In its morning star
aspect, the Greeks called it phosphoros ("light-bringer") because it her-
alded the approach of dawn. In Latin this became lucifer. So helel became Lucifer.

The use of the term "Lucifer" in this verse in Isaiah was probably an ironic reflection on the pride of the Babylonian King, for whom "Morning Star" may have been among the flattering titles applied by sycophantic courtiers (much as Louis XIV of France loved to hear himself referred to as "the Sun King").

With time, however, these verses came to gain a more esoteric meaning. By New Testament times, the Jews had developed, in full detail, the legend that a band of angels had rebelled against God at the time of the creation of man and had been cast into hell in consequence. Isaiah's verse was re-interpreted as referring to this, so that to Christians, Lucifer became one of the names of the leader of those fallen angels.

The beautiful morning star, the *real* Lucifer, had indeed fallen from heaven.

But all these diabolical names did not sound as bad in Ford's ears as did "cuckold." And worse yet was "wittol."

This is a corruption of "witwall," a woodpecker which for some reason was associated with the cuckoo (the name of which gave rise to "cuckold"). The first syllable, "wit," is an old English word for "know." This some-how gave rise to the notion, then, that a wittol was a cuckold who knew his own condition.

After all, Ford was now in the position of becoming not only a cuckold but also a wittol; he was actually working to become a wittol out of sheer jealousy—rather to know than be uncertain.

. . . my Aesculapius . . .

And what of that challenge that Caius has sent to Sir Hugh? Apparently, the Host of the Garter has been asked to make the arrangements, and he has conceived the jest of giving each a different meeting place. Each, therefore, is waiting uselessly and thinking the other has dodged the match out of cowardice.

Caius has been waiting for quite a while, brimming over with impatience and anger, mouthing threats at the absent Evans, when the Host appears, pretending to be sure the duel is over. He says:

> Is he dead, my Ethiopian? Is he dead, my Francisco? Ha,
> bully? What says my Aesculapius? My Galen?
> —Act II, scene iii, lines 25–27

The Host is a bouncing fellow who repeats himself in slightly different ways, that being his badge of humor. Caius is an Ethiopian because he has a swarthy complexion (something typically French to the English of Elizabethan times). And, of course, Francisco is a humorous distortion of *français* for Frenchman.

Aesculapius and Galen are references to Caius' profession. Galen is the most famous physician of the Roman period (see page I–230). Aesculapius (or, in the Greek form, Asklepios) was a mythical son of Apollo and a great physician. He could even restore the dead to life, and when he was persuaded to do so, Jupiter was sufficiently angered at this interference with the natural order of things to kill him with a thunderbolt.

. . . in Hibocrates . . .

Meanwhile, though, Evans has been waiting in vain on the other side of Windsor. The Host has sent Page, Shallow, and Slender (who have been with him while he was teasing Caius) across-town to see how Evans is doing.

Evans, less ferocious than Caius, is nevertheless angry enough. Concerning Caius, he says:

> *He has no more knowledge in Hibocrates and Galen—and he is a knave besides . . .*
>
> —Act III, scene i, lines 62–63

Hippocrates, a Greek physician who was at the height of his career about 400 B.C., was the first rationalist teacher of medicine whom we know by name and is therefore called "the Father of Medicine." He established a school which continued for some centuries and of which the various writings were indiscriminately ascribed to Hippocrates himself. The famous Hippocratic oath, still sworn to by many medical students on graduation, is a product of that school.

Hippocrates and Galen were the two great physicians of antiquity and were considered the last word almost down to 1800. To accuse Caius of being ignorant of their teachings is a deadly medical insult.

. . . a Machiavel

The Host now appears with Caius in tow, and tells the two victims, in glee, of the joke he played on them, explaining that he valued both of them too much to allow them to come to harm. He is very proud of himself, saying:

> *Am I politic? Am I subtle? Am I a Machiavel?*
>
> —Act III, scene i, lines 95–96

Niccolò Machiavelli was a Florentine who, after faithfully serving his city, was deprived of office in the course of a political overturn in 1512. Forced into retirement, and saddened by the situation in Italy, which was then being ruined by invaders from the stronger nations beyond the Alps, he wrote his theories of political science in a book called *The Prince*.

In this book he described the principles he felt ought to guide rulers. Although himself a kindly and honest man, he recognized that in the harsh world of the time (and perhaps of any time) rulers had to be guided by realism and sometimes be harsh and cruel.

To foreigners, Machiavellian principles seemed typically Italian, featuring intrigue and subtle trickery, so that "Machiavellian" came to epitomize all that was scheming and underhanded. It still bears that meaning today.

When the stage clears and Evans and Caius are left alone together, however, it turns out they are by no means as pleased with the Host as he is with himself. They vow revenge.

. . . the wild Prince . . .

The question of Anne Page is taken up again. Even while other matters are going on, Slender has been sighing with "Ah, sweet Anne Page" and "Oh, sweet Anne Page." Now he actually has a dinner engagement with his fair dream girl, for Page himself approves of Slender as a husband for his daughter. Page owns, though, that Mrs. Page favors Slender's rival, the peppery Dr. Caius.

The Host asks what Page thinks of young Fenton, but Page turns him down firmly, saying:

> Not by my consent, I promise you. The gentleman is of no having. He kept company with the wild Prince and Poins; he is of too high a region;
>
> —Act III, scene ii, lines 67–69

Not only is Fenton a poor man (he "is of no having"), but he was part of the company that made *Henry IV, Part One* and *Henry IV, Part Two* so frolicsome. Such aristocratic wildness would sit quite poorly with a respectable middle-class burgher like Page.

This is the only reference in the play to Prince Hal and it serves but poorly to set the scene near 1400, for everything else in the play (even one quite specific reference to Queen Elizabeth, see page II–445) sets it near 1600.

. . . Jack-a-lent . . .

Mistress Quickly, in her dealings with Falstaff, had earlier persuaded the fat knight to lend Robin to Page, pretending that Page yearned for just such a boy attendant. Of course, the merry wives are really using him as a go-

between to arrange their own plans. They scheme to have Falstaff come to
Ford's house for his assignation with Mrs. Ford. They will then pretend that
Ford is coming, force Falstaff to hide in a large basket of filthy, smelly
linen, take him out of the house, and throw him into the ditch near the
Thames River.

The whole thing will be ruined if Falstaff catches wind of it, of course.
Mrs. Page says to Robin, therefore:

> *You little Jack-a-lent, have you been true to us?*
> —Act III, scene iii, lines 25–26

Robin is, of course, very gaudily dressed—an obvious comic device of
contrasting elaborate clothing with the small and insignificant body of the
boy. Because of his clothing, indeed, Robin resembles the gaudy puppet
used in pre-Lenten celebrations. Such a puppet is suspended by a rope and
all combine to strike at it with sticks till its outer wrappings break so that a
shower of goodies from within is made available for grabbing catch-as-
catch-can. Such a puppet is a "Jack-a-lent."

. . . *my heavenly jewel*

Robin earnestly swears that he has not given away the plot and apparently he hasn't, for Falstaff now enters with heavy flirtatiousness, quoting gallantly from a book of sonnets:

> *"Have I caught thee, my heavenly jewel?"*
> —Act III, scene iii, line 41

This is a quotation from one of the sonnets in *Astrophel and Stella,* a
collection of poems by Sir Philip Sidney written about 1584 or slightly
earlier. These were unsurpassed by the sonnets of any poet of the time,
except, of course, for those of Shakespeare himself.

. . . *like Bucklersbury . . .*

Mrs. Ford counterfeits bashfulness at this romantic approach and Falstaff affects plain talk, saying:

> *I cannot cog and say thou art this and that, like a many of*
> *these lisping hawthorn buds that come like women in men's*
> *apparel and smell like Bucklersbury in simple-time.*
> —Act III, scene iii, lines 68–71

Falstaff is no affected dandy, in other words. Simples are herbs with medicinal properties. Each herb was supposed to have one and only one particular medical value and hence it was a "simple" remedy. Many of the medicinal herbs have aromatic odors and the markets in which they are exposed for sale would therefore have delightful aromas (particularly when contrasted with the kind of smells common in the filthy, unwashed London of 1600).

Bucklersbury was the name of the London street where the herb-sellers and druggists of the time congregated. In the season when simples were for sale, their odors could be detected for blocks around.

Falstaff has not gone very far when young Robin arrives with his rehearsed account of Ford's coming—but then Mrs. Page arrives with the horrid news that Ford is *really* coming. Falstaff hides in the basket of dirty clothes (as the two women had planned all along) when Ford bursts in.

Page, Caius, and Evans are all with him trying to calm his jealous fury, but Ford *knows* Falstaff is there, thanks to the game he has played in the guise of Brooke, and will not be allayed. He is determined to expose his wife, but unwittingly lets the basket of clothes go by.

Naturally, he can't find Falstaff, and much crestfallen, he begins to think Falstaff was merely boasting in saying he had an assignation with Mrs. Ford. He can only apologize.

. . . the peaking cornuto . . .

The various plots advance. Anne Page continues to be the focus of Slender, Caius, and Fenton, with Page pushing the first, Mrs. Page the second, and Anne herself the third.

As for Falstaff, he is at the tavern brooding over his misfortune. He is very sorry for himself for having had his assignation interrupted, for having been buried under a pile of stinking clothes, and for having been nearly drowned in a ditch. Yet when Mistress Quickly comes, he is soon persuaded to try another assignation. (The women are not done making a fool of Falstaff, particularly since they overheard Ford say that he had learned of the first assignation from Falstaff's own lecherous boasting.)

But now Ford enters, once again disguised as Mr. Brooke, and anxious to know how it was Falstaff was not at the house. If Falstaff were to say that Mrs. Ford had refused him, that would be balm to the husband's jealous soul. But Falstaff doesn't say that at all. He was there, all right:

> . . . but the peaking cornuto her husband, Master Brooke, dwelling in a continual 'larum of jealousy, comes me in the instant of our encounter, after we had embraced, kissed, protested . . .
>
> —Act III, scene v, lines 69–73

"Cornuto" is from a Latin word meaning "horned" and is therefore another of the vast Elizabethan set of synonyms and circumlocutions for "cuckold."

Falstaff explains that he escaped in the basket of dirty clothes (which now Ford recollects having seen leaving) and also says that he has a second assignation for the next day. Now poor Ford is worse off than ever.

. . . the fat woman . . .

There is an interlude in which Evans, with his Welsh accent, gives William Page (the younger brother of Anne Page) a lesson in Latin with Mistress Quickly listening. Evans' accent and Mistress Quickly's naïveté combine to yield a number of ribald allusions, many of which are lost on us today, thanks to the constantly changing vocabulary of ribaldry.

But this interlude succeeds in allowing an impression of the passage of time, and we are ready for the second assignation. It goes exactly as the first did. Again, Ford comes raving toward the house to catch Falstaff. It's no use trying to use the dirty clothes dodge again, and it occurs to Mistress Ford to disguise him as a woman. She says:

> My maid's aunt, the fat woman of Brainford, has a gown above.
>
> —Act IV, scene ii, lines 71–72

Apparently, there was a grossly fat woman in Shakespeare's time who kept a tavern in Brentford (Brainford), a town on the Thames about halfway between Windsor and London—a town eventually engulfed by the expanding boundaries of the great city. Presumably she was renowned for her size and the audience would know whom Shakespeare meant and laugh at this hit as to Falstaff's fatness.

. . . the devil be shamed

Ford comes bursting into the house, with his friends trying to calm him down exactly as before. Mrs. Ford has deliberately directed that a basket of dirty clothes be carried out of the house, and Ford pounces on it with grim glee. He says:

> Now shall the devil be shamed.
>
> —Act IV, scene ii, lines 115–16

Shakespeare is here quoting from himself. In *Henry IV, Part One,* Hotspur, in his impatient colloquy with Owen Glendower, makes use of a proverbial phrase. When Glendower offers to teach him to command the devil, Hotspur offers to teach him, in turn, to shame the devil: "Tell truth and shame the devil" (see page II–288).

It may be that in having Ford announce that he will shame the devil (by revealing Falstaff under the dirty clothes and thus proclaiming truth) he is deliberately reminding the audience of that passage in *Henry IV, Part One* and attempting to tie this play in with the earlier one.

Ford's bitter cry proves useless, however. Though he throws the dirty clothes every which way, no Falstaff is revealed and it is Ford who is shamed.

At this point, Falstaff, disguised as the fat woman, is led out the door. Ford hates her anyway, as a witch, and in his mad frustration, he must beat someone. Seizing a cudgel, he beats the disguised Falstaff unmercifully out of the house, then searches every room and finds nothing.

. . . the Germans . . .

The Host has not yet been paid back by Evans and Caius for his practical joke at their expense. Now something comes up which may represent the Evans-Caius revenge, but it is hastily done and poorly knit into the texture of the play.

The Host is suddenly told by Bardolph:

> *Sir, the Germans desire to have three of your horses. The Duke himself will be tomorrow at court, and they are going to meet him.*
>
> —Act IV, scene iii, lines 1–3

Nothing earlier in the play has prepared the audience for this, nor are we told either now or later who the German Duke is. The usual conjecture is that it is a reference to Duke Frederick I of Württemberg, a duchy in southwest Germany in the corner between the Rhine and Danube rivers.

Frederick I was Duke when *The Merry Wives of Windsor* was written. (He died in 1608.) He was a most aggressive fellow, who had managed to free Württemberg from the overlordship of the Austrian Empire by persuading the Emperor to accept a large sum of money in return for freedom.

It was Frederick's ambition to be accepted into the very exclusive Order of the Garter. He made a plague of himself as he badgered Elizabeth on this point, and in the end, she sanctioned his election to the Order in 1597. He was not actually invested, however, despite his strenuous overtures, till after Elizabeth's death.

If *The Merry Wives of Windsor* really had its premiere on the occasion of the investiture of 1597, an investiture which Frederick did not attend, the whole passage may have been intended to poke fun at the unpopular German, who was, after all, a foreigner and a pest. Indeed, I wonder if it may be possible that the reason this portion of the plot is as incomplete and unsatisfactory as it is is that it was censored after the initial performance to avoid creating a minor international incident.

The Host is not troubled by these demands of the Germans. They have reserved the entire inn for a week and he plans to make them pay heavily.

. . . Herne the Hunter

By now Mistress Ford and Mistress Page have told their husbands the entire story and Ford really swears to turn over a new leaf. He will trust his wife henceforward. But meanwhile, is there one last trick they can play on Falstaff?

Mistress Page says:

> There is an old tale goes that Herne the Hunter
> Sometime a keeper here in Windsor Forest
> Doth all the wintertime, at still midnight,
> Walk round about an oak, with great ragg'd horns;
> —Act IV, scene iv, lines 27–30

This is a typical medieval legend, concerning a spirit that does petty harm to men, blasting trees, blighting cattle, and so on, rather like Puck in *A Midsummer Night's Dream* (see page I–29). Tales are invented to account for these wildwood spirits, and these appear in different nations in different ways. It is quite possible, though, that they are the remnants of pagan nature myths, driven underground by the coming of Christianity, and that Herne is what is left of some old god of the hunt who, for lack of worship, has turned bitter and spiteful.

It is Mrs. Page's suggestion that Falstaff be persuaded to disguise himself as Herne the Hunter and meet Mistress Ford under the oak tree. There he can be set upon by various children, disguised as elves and fairies, with Anne Page at their head as Fairy Queen. They will pinch and punish Falstaff for invading ground sacred to them.

Ford agrees to be disguised as Brooke one last time in order to inveigle Falstaff to go.

. . . at Eton

Page is particularly pleased with this plan, for it occurs to him to arrange to have Slender add something to the occasion. Anne Page will be in Fairy Queen disguise:

And in that tire [attire]
Shall Master Slender steal my Nan away,
And marry her at Eton.

—Act IV, scene iv, lines 72–74

Eton is a small town just across the Thames from Windsor, on the north bank. Eton is world-famous for its great boarding school, founded by Henry VI in 1440. A good percentage of England's ruling classes attended it.

. . . three Doctor Faustuses

But now horrible news suddenly reaches the Host. The Germans who have asked for the three horses have run off with them, without paying. As Bardolph says, they have:

. . . *set spurs and away, like three German devils, three Doctor Faustuses.*

—Act IV, scene v, lines 67–69

Here again is a reference to Christopher Marlowe's *Doctor Faustus*. It dealt with Faust's bargain with the devil and it was therefore easy for the ignorant to confuse Faust with the devil.

This may also be another slap at Frederick of Württemberg, the meaning of which has been pruned away, for Frederick had some sort of post horse trouble on a 1592 visit to England. There was, to be sure, later, a mix-up in which an important French diplomat had gotten into a quarrel over post horses. He didn't steal them but was accused of wanting to, and this created quite a scandal that may have still been fresh when *The Merry Wives of Windsor* was produced.

. . . of Readins, of Maidenhead, of Colebrook . . .

This whole to-do must have been arranged somehow by Evans and Caius as revenge against the Host, though this is never made plain, either because Shakespeare was too hurried and slipshod in preparing the play, or because the sense of the scene has been censored out.

In any case, Evans and Caius come in separately, with deliberately late warnings, in order that they might enjoy the Host's discomfiture. Thus, Evans says, in mock friendship:

There is a friend of mine come to town tells me there is three cozen-germans that has cozened all the hosts of Readins, of Maidenhead, of Colebrook, of horses and money.

—Act IV, scene v, lines 74–78

(A "cozen-german" is a "cheating German" and is a play on the word "cousin-german," which means "first cousin.")

Reading (Readins), Maidenhead, and Colnbrook (Colebrook) are all towns in the neighborhood of Windsor. Maidenhead is about ten miles upstream from Windsor on the Thames River, and Reading is about forty miles upstream. Colnbrook is not quite on the river but is a town ten miles due east of Windsor.

Thus, Evans and Caius are amply revenged and even Falstaff gets a chance to feel a little grim satisfaction at seeing someone else made the butt of a practical joke.

. . . Goliath with a weaver's beam

The plot continues to develop. Page plans to have Anne Page dressed in white so that she might be recognized by Slender, who will then steal her away. Mrs. Page plans to have her in green so that she may be recognized by Caius. Both have separately arranged this with Anne, who, however, means to fool both and slip away with Fenton.

Fenton promises the Host to make good the latter's loss over the post horses if the Host will serve as witness at the church so that he and Anne might get married.

And Mistress Quickly manages once again to persuade Falstaff to an assignation. When Ford, disguised as Brooke, appears, Falstaff promptly tells him all that has happened. He excuses his tame submission to being beaten by Ford because he, Falstaff, was disguised as a woman. Here we have the only faint tang of the real Falstaff in the play, when he goes on to explain that:

> . . . *in the shape of man, Master Brooke, I fear not Goliath with a weaver's beam,*

—Act V, scene i, lines 22–24

Goliath is, of course, the Philistine giant whom David slew. Goliath is described in the Bible as being six cubits and a span in height (over nine feet) and as having weapons that were correspondingly huge, for "the staff of his spear was like a weaver's beam" (1 Samuel 17:7).

. . . for the love of Leda

While the "fairies" lie in wait for him, Falstaff comes to Herne's oak at midnight, with the antlers on his head. It is a piece of dramatic irony. He had planned to plant horns on Ford's head, but here he wears them himself.

He consoles himself for this animal disguise by the thought of Jupiter (Zeus), who, though king of the gods, did not scorn to adopt animal disguise in the cause of love. (Prince Hal himself on one occasion solaces himself with such a thought too, see page II–396.) Falstaff says:

> Remember, Jove, thou wast a bull for thy Europa; love set on thy horns. O powerful love, that in some respects makes a beast a man; in some other, a man a beast. You were also, Jupiter, a swan for the love of Leda.
> —Act V, scene v, lines 3–7

The manner in which Jupiter turned himself into a bull in order to induce the Phoenician princess Europa to climb on his back so that he might swim off with her to Crete is referred to elsewhere in Shakespeare (see page I–44).

The case of Leda, Queen of Sparta, is almost as famous. Jupiter approached her in the shape of a swan and coupled with her in that fashion. The result was that Leda eventually laid two eggs, from which a total of four children were hatched. The most famous of the four was none other than Helen of Troy (see page I–76).

Our radiant Queen . . .

Mistress Ford comes; Falstaff is happy. Mistress Page also comes and Falstaff is not in the least taken aback; he is ready for both. But then they suddenly hear a noise and run away.

While Falstaff is for the third time deprived of joy, the "fairies" enter with Evans leading them, disguised as a satyr, and none other than Pistol in the role of Hobgoblin or Puck (see page I–29). Pistol addresses one of the fairies and, in a most un-Pistol-like speech, says:

> Cricket, to Windsor chimneys shalt thou leap.
> Where fires thou find'st unraked and hearths unswept,
> There pinch the maids as blue as bilberry.
> Our radiant Queen hates sluts and sluttery.
> —Act V, scene v, lines 46–49

There's no pretense here of any setting in the years shortly following 1400, with Fenton a companion of wild Prince Hal. "Our radiant Queen" is Elizabeth I, sitting in the audience and smiling at this reference to her belief in cleanliness and neatness.

. . . chairs of Order . . .

It is then time for the Fairy Queen to speak, but it is not Anne Page in this role, but rather Mrs. Quickly, who also gives the fairies orders for housewifery about the palace, saying:

> *The several chairs of Order look you scour*
> *With juice of balm and every precious flow'r.*
>
> —Act V, scene v, lines 64–65

These are the special seats in St. George's Chapel, Windsor, assigned to specific members of the Order of the Knights of the Garter, a very topical reference if the play is really part of the entertainment in the course of the festivities attendant upon the installation meeting of those Knights.

To make it clearer still, Mistress Quickly says:

> *And* HONI SOIT QUI MAL Y PENSE *write*
> *In emerald tufts, flow'rs purple, blue, and white.*
>
> —Act V, scene vi, lines 72–73

"Honi soit qui mal y pense" (meaning "Evil to him who evil thinks" or "Shame to him who thinks evil of it") is the motto of the Order of the Garter. It came about this way, according to legend.

About 1348 King Edward III was attending a court ball when Joan, Countess of Salisbury, somehow managed to lose her garter. This placed her in a ridiculous and embarrassing position, but the gallant King diverted attention by quickly picking up the garter and placing it on his own knee. And lest anyone draw some ribald conclusion from this, he said, "Honi soit qui mal y pense."

Edward III considered this a very knightly thing to do (and it was certainly most courteous of him), and so he established an order of knights in honor of the incident, the Most Noble Order of the Garter. It was made very exclusive, with only members of the royal family, some foreign royalty, and twenty-five knights from among the aristocracy. It is the highest order of knighthood in the world and very few commoners have ever been elected. One who was elected, in 1953, was Winston Churchill.

. . . I am made an ass

All this time, Falstaff, afraid of what the fairies might do in the way of charms and enchantments, has cowered and lain still. The fairies now pretend to discover him and begin to pinch him and beat him.

While this is happening, Slender steals away with someone in white who is *not* Anne Page; Caius steals away with someone in green who is *not* Anne Page; and Fenton steals away with Anne Page.

Ford comes in, crowing over Falstaff, and now, finally, Falstaff catches on. He says:

> *I do begin to perceive that I am made an ass.*
> —Act V, scene v, line 122

The Falstaff of the King Henry plays would certainly have discovered this much earlier in the game.

. . . *eat a posset* . . .

Yet when all have laughed their fill at Falstaff, they let it go. It is, after all, a merry play, and no one is permanently put down. Page says:

> *Yet be cheerful, knight. Thou shalt eat a posset tonight at my house.*
> —Act V, scene v, lines 173–74

A posset is a glass of hot milk, liberally laced with a strong alcoholic beverage, and Page plans to have a joke on his wife when he tells her how he has arranged to have Slender marry Anne.

But Slender shows up with a boy in tow. It was not Anne he had stolen. Mrs. Page explains that she has double-crossed Page by dressing Anne in green instead of white, but her glee is cut short when Caius arrives to reveal that he too has been stuck with a boy.

Then in come Fenton and Anne. They are married, and Falstaff manages a dry grin that in all this fooling of himself, the Pages have managed to be fooled as well.

But the Pages accept the matter in decent resignation and all return to celebrate with no hard feelings anywhere.

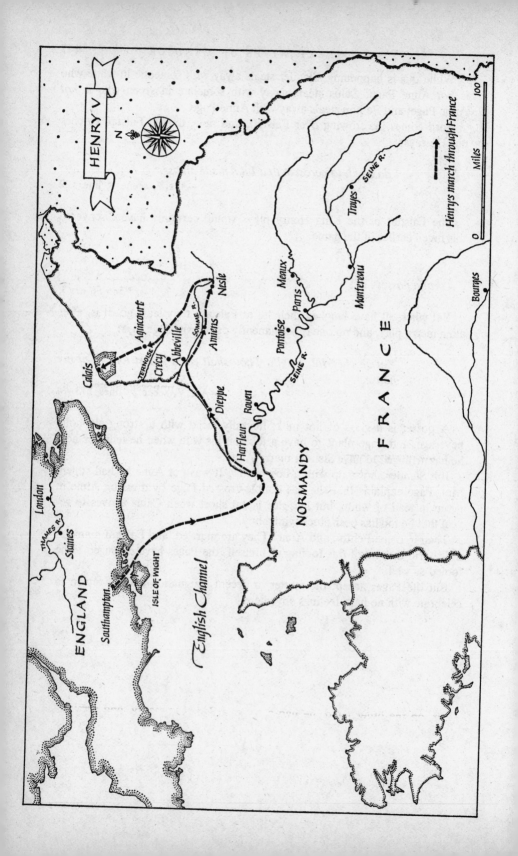

HENRY V

N

ENGLAND

London
THAMES R.
Staines
Southampton
ISLE OF WIGHT

English Channel

Calais
Agincourt
TERNOISE R.
Crecy
Abbeville
SOMME R.
Nesle
Amiens
Dieppe
Harfleur
Rouen

NORMANDY

FRANCE

Pontoise
SEINE R.
Paris
Meaux
Montereau
Troyes
SEINE R.
Bourges

Henry's march through France

0   Miles   100

35

The Life of

HENRY V

IMMEDIATELY after the completion of *Henry IV, Part Two*, Shakespeare went on to write *Henry V* in 1599.

The man for whom *Henry V* is named is the one who was Prince Hal, the madcap Prince of Wales, in the two *Henry IV* plays. Prince Hal is lovable and the closer we get to him, the more lovable he is. King Henry is merely admirable and, at that, more admirable from a distance.

Shakespeare's very attitude changes. He cannot write about a hero-king in quite the same way he did about a madcap prince. He even feels, or affects to feel, a little uneasy over the majesty of the theme. He must deal with the greatest land campaign the English had ever yet conducted and with the nation's greatest land victory, an almost impossible storybook victory, and he seems to feel it will strain even his own genius to do so.

. . . the warlike Harry . . .

If Shakespeare was not himself awed at the task, he might well have felt the audience would expect something impossible. Awaiting the tale of the great battle and of the hero-king who won it, they might expect some impossible pitch of grandeur.

Shakespeare begins, therefore, with an apologetic Prologue, deploring the insufficiency of the tools at his disposal and asking the audience to make up the difference in imagination:

> *Piece out our imperfections with your thoughts:*
> *Into a thousand parts divide one man*
> *And make imaginary puissance* [armies].
> *Think, when we talk of horses, that you see them*
> —Prologue, lines 23–26

If, on the other hand, he had a scene as large as reality, and armies as numerous:

> *Then should the warlike Harry, like himself,*
> *Assume the port of Mars, and at his heels*

> (*Leashed in, like hounds*) *should famine, sword, and fire*
> *Crouch for employment.*
>
> —Prologue, lines 5–8

Shakespeare tells us at once that we are to expect no Prince Hal in this play. "Warlike Harry" will be "like himself"; that is, an incarnation of Mars, the god of war.

In dealing with the events of this reign Shakespeare has the strongest temptation to be chauvinistic and jingoistic, for he will be dealing with total victory under the most amazing circumstances—and Shakespeare *is* chauvinistic and jingoistic. Yet even here, his essential pacifism and dislike of war (see page II–133) manages to break through. He might have described Henry V with glory and victory in his train, but he doesn't. It is "famine, sword, and fire" just waiting to be let loose.

. . . *in th'eleventh year* . . .

The play itself opens in the antechamber of the King's palace in London. The time is 1414, a year after the crowning of Henry V—the incident which ended *Henry IV, Part Two*.

There are two men onstage; they are high prelates, the Archbishop of Canterbury and the Bishop of Ely.

The Archbishop of Canterbury was, at this time, Henry Chicheley, the sixty-second of the line. He had just been appointed to the post on the death of his predecessor and was to remain Archbishop for twenty-nine years. He is terribly worried over internal politics, which seems at the moment to be threatening the church, and he says to the Bishop of Ely:

> *My lord, I'll tell you, that self* [same] *bill is urged*
> *Which in th'eleventh year of the last king's reign*
> *Was like* [likely], *and had indeed against us passed*
> *But that the scrambling* [disordered] *and unquiet time*
> *Did push it out of farther question.*
>
> —Act I, scene i, lines 1–5

The eleventh year of the last king's reign (that of Henry IV) was 1410, four years before the play opens. The bill in question, which had nearly passed then and was now being pushed in Parliament again, would have permitted the King to seize certain of the lands that had been willed to the church.

The temptation for such seizures was perpetual throughout western Europe. Left to itself, the church's holdings grew constantly larger, for it was common for men of property to will land or goods to the church, partly out of real piety and partly out of a shrewd feeling that such a gift would ease the pathway in the life to come and make up for a good deal of sinning. And although the church took, the church never had to yield in its turn, for it was immortal.

Consequently, more and more land was withdrawn from the possibility of normal taxation and a heavier and heavier burden was laid upon the steadily decreasing number of acres of secular territory that remained.

Eventually, the pressures always grew too great and on one pretext or another, churchly treasures were extracted or churchly land taken over. And naturally, the church always resisted.

The constant rebellions that had plagued Henry IV had made his need of money desperate. The church's property was hungered for, yet the very unsettlement of the time allowed the King no leisure to carry through, with parliamentary legality, what would have been a most ticklish process.

Now, with a new King and a period of quiet, the matter was being pushed again.

. . . th'offending Adam . . .

Both prelates agree, with somber uneasiness, that the bill, if passed, would be ruinous to the church. But how prevent it?

Meaningfully, the Archbishop of Canterbury turns to the character of the new King, pointing out how different he had proved himself from the wild Prince of Wales all had known. At the moment of coronation, says the Archbishop:

> *Consideration like an angel came*
> *And whipped th'offending Adam out of him,*
> *Leaving his body as a paradise*
> —Act I, scene i, lines 28–30

One of the best-known biblical stories is that of Adam and Eve, created in the paradisiacal Garden of Eden. By eating fruit forbidden them by God, they sinned and (together with the serpent who had tempted them) were punished.

Adam and Eve (and presumably the serpent too, though that is not mentioned) were driven out of the garden, which was left an unsullied paradise with their departure. And so, in the Archbishop's metaphoric hyperbole, was it with Henry V.

. . . Hydra-headed willfulness

The Archbishop goes on to say:

Never came reformation in a flood
With such a heady currance [fast current] *scouring faults;*
Nor never Hydra-headed willfulness
So soon did lose his seat—and all at once—
As in this king.

—Act I, scene i, lines 33–37

The Hydra was a monster out of Greek mythology, one that lived near the city of Argos. It was a horrible snake with nine heads, whose very breath was poisonous. Whenever a head was cut off, two new ones grew at once in its place, and one of its heads was immortal.

Hercules killed it. In order to do so, he had his attendant apply fire to the neck of each lopped-off head to prevent new growth. The immortal head he buried, still hissing and snapping, under a huge boulder.

Despite Hercules' victory, it is the horror of the Hydra that lingers in men's memories, and "Hydra-headed" remains an adjective to describe any situation that grows worse with every attempt at cure.

The Gordian knot . . .

The Archbishop goes on further, praising Henry V not only for his moral qualities, but for his intellectual ones as well. His grasp of theology and military matters, says the Archbishop, is unparalleled. And as for politics:

> *Turn him to any cause of policy,*
> *The Gordian knot of it he will unloose,*
> *Familiar as his garter . . .*

—Act I, scene i, lines 45–48

The reference to the Gordian knot is to a dramatic story involving Alexander the Great, one in which his solution to a hard problem was supposed to have ensured him a career of conquest (see page II–61).

Henry V, as it happened, was the closest approach to Alexander the Great that the English nation could boast. He was twenty-six when he became King (Alexander the Great had been twenty-one); he attacked a much larger nation and defeated greater armies than his own in as spectacular a style, on at least one occasion, as Alexander had done. And finally, Henry V was fated to die young at thirty-five as Alexander had done at thirty-three.

As touching France . . .

But how does all this affect the matter of the bill, the Bishop of Ely wants to know. The Archbishop of Canterbury explains at once:

> *. . . I have made an offer to his Majesty—*
> *Upon our spiritual Convocation,*
> *And in regard of causes now in hand,*
> *Which I have opened to his Grace at large,*
> *As touching France—to give a greater sum*
> *Than ever at one time the clergy yet*
> *Did to his predecessors part withal.*
>
> —Act I, scene i, lines 75–81

In short, the shrewd Archbishop has gauged King Henry's character. He is pious and would not willingly offend the church. He is anxious to achieve military glory and would be willing to have the church's blessing on an enterprise against France.

It is up to the Archbishop, then, to assure him that a war against France would be a just one and to offer him money with which to fight it. It would be less money by far than the church would have to surrender if the bill passes, so the church gains. On the other hand, Henry would have it free and clear without the necessity of pushing a bill through Parliament with all the uncertainties and enmities that that would give rise to, and without leaving behind him the dangerously embittered enmity of the always powerful church hierarchy.

Actually, modern historians do not think that the Archbishop of Canterbury was really the moving spirit behind Henry's foray into France, or that the churchman really deliberately fomented war to save church property. However, Holinshed in his history (see page II-4) places the blame on Canterbury, and Shakespeare, finding that there, adopts the view.

. . . the Law Salique . . .

The Archbishop, as he says, had actually begun to explain to Henry just why it was that he could rightfully claim the throne of France, when matters were interrupted by an embassy from that kingdom.

But now the scene shifts to Henry V and his court, in the throne room of the palace—and it turns out he wants to talk to the Archbishop after all, before he talks to the French ambassadors. Presumably he is not certain what answer to make to what they might have to say until he hears the Archbishop out. He says to the Archbishop:

> *My learnèd lord, we pray you to proceed,*
> *And justly and religiously unfold*
> *Why the Law Salique, that they have in France*
> *Or should or should not bar us in our claim.*
>
> —Act I, scene ii, lines 9–12

The Archbishop replies:

> *There is no bar*
> *To make against your Highness' claim to France*
> *But this which they produce from Pharamond:*
> *"In terram Salicam mulieres ne succedant";*
> *"No woman shall succeed in Salique land."*
>
> —Act I, scene ii, lines 35–39

Salic Law

The "Law Salique," or the "Salic law" in our more common phrase, played its part in the origins of the Hundred Years' War in the first years of the reign of Edward III nearly a century before (see page II–255). The Salic law is so called because it was first associated with the Salian Franks, that is, the Frankish tribe that lived along the Sala River (now called the Ijssel) in what is now the Netherlands.

This particular tribe first became prominent about 420, according to legend, under a certain King Pharamond, of whom nothing is known but the name. The grandson of Pharamond was named Merovaeus. He ruled from 448 to 458 and gave his name to the line of descendants that succeeded him, the so-called Merovingians. The grandson of Merovaeus was Clovis I, who succeeded to the leadership of the Salian Franks in 481. It is Clovis who is the first Frankish monarch to be an actual historical figure. By his time the Salian Franks had established themselves in a small region in northwestern Gaul. Under Clovis, they conquered wide areas, and by his death in 511, they controlled almost all of what we now call France.

It was in Clovis' reign that the laws of the Franks were first put in writing, and included among them was a restriction on the rights of inheritance of land through the female line. Not only could a daughter not inherit, but neither could the male descendant of a daughter.

Originally, it seems, this law was applied strictly to the inheritance of land, rather than to titles, but it was an easy step to extend it to the inheritance of the kingship. France adhered to this rule for fourteen centuries after Clovis. Other nations might have reigning queens, even great ones (think of Queen Elizabeth I of England, Queen Isabella of Castile, Queen Maria Theresa of Austria, Queen Catherine II of Russia), but France never did. What's more, from the tenth century on, she never allowed a man to ascend the throne who could not trace his ancestry to some past reigning king through males alone, without the intervention of a single female.

It was this Salic law, then, which barred King Henry from claiming the French throne, for he was forced to cite his descent from the French King Philip IV (who reigned from 1285 to 1314) by way of that king's daughter.

King Pepin . . .

It remains for the Archbishop to break down the validity of the Salic law, which he does at great length in a passage taken by Shakespeare from Holinshed.

The Archbishop maintains, for instance, that the Salic land is not France but a section of Germany (and so it is; for it is in the Netherlands, which in the time of Henry V was indeed part of Germany). He also says that the law was established by Charlemagne, three centuries after Clovis, and was applied to the Salian area which had been newly conquered by Charlemagne. In this he is a bit overzealous. The Salic law was always taken to apply to all the territory ruled by the Frankish monarchs.

The Archbishop then goes on to maintain that the Salic law, even if considered as applying to France, was, on several occasions, broken by the French themselves:

> *King Pepin, which deposed Childeric,*
> *Did, as heir general, being descended*
> *Of Blithild, which was daughter to King Clothair,*
> *Make claim and title to the crown of France.*
> —Act I, scene ii, lines 65–68

The Merovingian line, descending after Clovis' reign into blood and barbarism, had by 638 become a dreary series of short-lived monarchs without either the ability or the desire to rule, and completely under the domination of vigorous noblemen who called themselves "mayors of the palace."

In 741 Pepin the Short was Mayor of the Palace and he elevated a Merovingian puppet to the throne. This last of the Merovingians was Childeric III, sometimes called Childeric the Stupid.

Pepin grew tired of being king in everything but name and persuaded the Pope to give him legal title as well. In 751, therefore, with full papal blessing, Childeric was deposed and the Mayor of the Palace became Pepin I, King of the Franks. The new line was referred to as the Carolingians, from Pepin's father Charles (or Carolus, in Latin).

Pepin, in order to strengthen his legitimacy in the eyes of the populace, who had been ruled by Merovingians for two and a half centuries, traced his descent back to a previous King Clotaire (there were four Merovingians of that name) through the female line. It was easy to do that because descent through the female was not carefully recorded and was therefore the more easily faked.

It didn't matter, though, whether Pepin was of Merovingian descent or not. The point was he was accepted as King by the Pope and by medieval standards that took care of the matter. From a practical standpoint, that meant a new start was being made under conditions to which the Salic law didn't really apply.

Once Pepin was King, however, his descendants reigned in accordance with that law. Just as all the Merovingians were descended, through males only, from Pharamond; so all the Carolingians were descended, through males only, from Pepin I.

The Archbishop's citing of Pepin as a case in which the Salic law was broken is therefore worthless, really.

Hugh Capet also . . .

The Archbishop then goes on learnedly to the next case:

> Hugh Capet also—who usurped the crown
> Of Charles the Duke of Lorraine, sole heir male
> Of the true line and stock of Charles the Great—
>
> —Act I, scene ii, lines 69–71

Again it was a case of illegitimate succession.

The Carolingian line, stemming from Pepin I, reached a height of glory under his son, Charlemagne (Charles the Great), but then it too withered, and a line of young or incompetent (or both) kings ruled France. The last of these, Louis V (also called Louis the Do-Nothing), died in 986.

The only Carolingian left who was descended by way of males only from Pepin the Short was Charles of Lorraine, Louis's uncle. However, Charles of Lorraine ruled over a duchy that was under the control of a German king and the French nobility would have none of him. They decided to choose one of their own for King.

At the time, the most powerful French lord was Hugh Capet. He managed to get himself crowned King by the Archbishop of Reims, the highest prelate in France, and his rule was eventually recognized by the Pope.

. . . th'Lady Lingard

The Archbishop of Canterbury points out that Hugh Capet claimed descent from the Carolingians through the female line, saying that Hugh:

> Conveyed himself as heir to th'Lady Lingard,
> Daughter to Charlemain, who was the son

To Lewis the Emperor, and Lewis the son
Of Charles the Great.

—Act I, scene ii, lines 74–77

Here Shakespeare manages to speak of Charlemain (Charlemagne) and Charles the Great as though they were two different people.

Charlemain, the father of Lady Lingard according to this passage, is really Charles the Bald, who reigned over the territories of France from 840 to 877. He was the son of "Lewis the Emperor" (usually referred to in history books as "Louis the Pious") and the grandson of Charles the Great, the real Charlemagne.

Here the Archbishop is taking seriously what was undoubtedly a fraudulent claim by Hugh Capet intended to cover him with Carolingian legitimacy. Actually, Hugh's title to the crown was (like Pepin's) derived from the church and not from inheritance.

. . . Lewis the Tenth

The Archbishop then points out that:

> . . . *King Lewis the Tenth*
> *Who was sole heir to the usurper Capet,*
> *Could not keep quiet in his conscience*
> *Wearing the crown of France, till satisfied*
> *That fair Queen Isabel, his grandmother,*
> *Was lineal of the Lady Ermengard,*
> *Daughter to Charles the foresaid Duke of Lorraine.*

—Act I, scene ii, lines 77–83

"Lewis the Tenth" is taken directly from Holinshed, who says he is also known as "St. Louis," but that, of course, is really Louis IX. Actually, it doesn't matter if Louis IX chose to claim descent from the Carolingians through the female line. His actual right to the throne lay through his descent, by males only, from the church-blessed Hugh Capet.

Besides, the story may not be true at all. Louis didn't have a grandmother named Isabel. His father's mother was Elizabeth of Hainaut and his mother's mother was Berenguela of Castile.

The Archbishop concludes that since the kings of France inherit by virtue of descent through a female from Pharamond in two places (Pepin and Hugh Capet), they have no right to bar the claim of Henry V on the ground of female descent.

That, of course, would not be the French view at all. The Merovingians, as long as they lasted, ruled through male descent only, and so did the Carolingians.

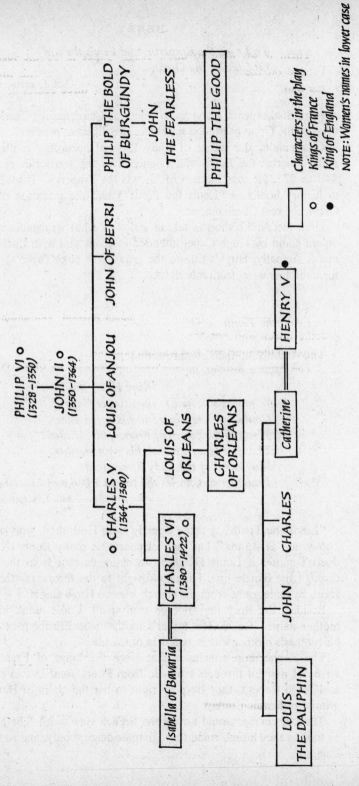

HENRY V

FRANCE after PHILIP VI

PHILIP VI o
(1328–1350)

JOHN II o
(1350–1364)

LOUIS OF ANJOU   JOHN OF BERRI   PHILIP THE BOLD
                                                OF BURGUNDY

                                                JOHN
                                                THE FEARLESS

                                                PHILIP THE GOOD

o CHARLES V
(1364–1380)

LOUIS OF
ORLEANS

CHARLES
OF ORLEANS

CHARLES VI o
(1380–1422)

Isabella of Bavaria   Catherine ——— HENRY V •

CHARLES

JOHN

LOUIS
THE DAUPHIN

Characters in the play
o Kings of France
• King of England

NOTE: Women's names in lower case

Then, if we were to allow Hugh Capet to be the legitimate King of France on the basis of papal approval and start with him, we find that the male descendants did not fail for over three centuries. Through eleven generations each king was succeeded by his oldest son: Hugh Capet by Robert II, Henry I, Philip I, Louis VI, Louis VII (see page II-207), Philip II (see page II-207), Louis VIII (see page II-226), Louis IX, Philip III, Philip IV, and Louis X in that order.

In 1316 Louis X died and the spell was broken. His son John had died just a few months earlier, leaving no descendants, and Louis was survived by only one daughter.

His younger brother, the second son of Philip IV, succeeded as Philip V, reigned six years, and died in 1322, being survived by two daughters only. He was succeeded by his younger brother, the third son of Philip IV, who reigned six years as Charles IV and then died in 1328, leaving one daughter.

There were no further sons of Philip IV to inherit. To be sure, Philip IV had a daughter Isabella. By English custom, she would now have become queen and her son would have succeeded her. By French custom, thanks to the Salic law, this was not possible.

The French instead, having used up the sons of Philip IV, turned to the line of his younger brother. That younger brother was Charles, Count of Valois, who had died in 1325 but had left a surviving son, Philip.

It was this Philip of Valois (see Genealogy page II-256) who ascended the French throne in 1328 as Philip VI. He was the grandson of Philip III and counted his descent from Hugh Capet through ten intervening individuals, all male.

But what of Isabella, the daughter of Philip IV? She had married Edward II, King of England, and her son had succeeded to the English throne in 1327 as Edward III.

Where Philip VI was grandson of Philip III, Edward III was grandson of Philip IV, a later king. Therefore, Edward III had the better claim to the French throne *except* that he was grandson through a daughter rather than through a son and the Salic law held him off. (Not only the Salic law, of course. The French people generally would far rather be ruled by a Frenchman than by an Englishman, and that was the more important fact in the end.)

Nevertheless, Edward III claimed the French throne. That was the legalistic justification for the first part of the Hundred Years' War, which included the great English victories of Crécy and Poitiers (see page II-257) and which finally dwindled down to a long but uneasy peace during the reigns of Richard II and Henry IV.

But now Henry V was on the throne and he was of a mind to take up once more the argument of Edward III.

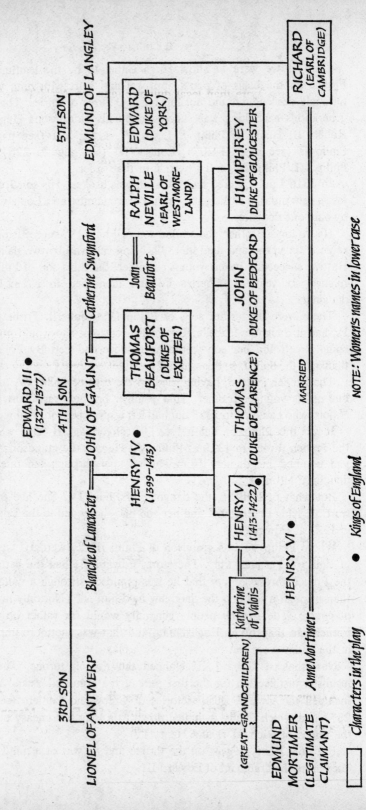

HENRY V

ENGLAND *after* EDWARD III

EDWARD III ●
(1327-1377)

3RD SON | 4TH SON | 5TH SON

LIONEL OF ANTWERP | JOHN OF GAUNT ══ *Blanche of Lancaster* | EDMUND OF LANGLEY

JOHN OF GAUNT ══ *Catherine Swynford*

(GREAT-GRANDCHILDREN)

EDMUND MORTIMER
(LEGITIMATE CLAIMANT)

Anne Mortimer ══ RICHARD (EARL OF CAMBRIDGE)

MARRIED

Katherine of Valois ══ HENRY V ●
(1413-1422)

HENRY IV ●
(1399-1413)

THOMAS (DUKE OF CLARENCE)

THOMAS BEAUFORT
(DUKE OF EXETER)

Joan Beaufort ══ RALPH NEVILLE (EARL OF WESTMORE-LAND)

JOHN DUKE OF BEDFORD

HUMPHREY DUKE OF GLOUCESTER

EDWARD (DUKE OF YORK)

HENRY VI ●

NOTE: *Women's names in lower case*

☐ *Characters in the play* ● *Kings of England*

. . . the Book of Numbers . . .

Henry wants more than legal quibbles, and the Archbishop is ready to quote God's law. He says:

> *. . . in the Book of Numbers is it writ:*
> *When the man dies, let the inheritance*
> *Descend unto the daughter.*
>
> —Act I, scene ii, lines 98–100

The reference is to Numbers 27:8, which reads: "If a man die, and have no son, then ye shall cause his inheritance to pass unto his daughter."

. . . your great-grandsire's tomb

The Archbishop then directs the King:

> *Go, my dread lord, to your great-grandsire's tomb,*
> *From whom you claim; invoke his warlike spirit,*
> *And your great-uncle's, Edward the Black Prince,*
> *Who on the French ground played a tragedy,*
> *Making defeat on the full power of France,*
> *Whiles his most mighty father on a hill*
> *Stood smiling . . .*
>
> —Act I, scene ii, lines 103–9

The reference is to an incident at the Battle of Crécy, when Edward III was so confident as to refuse to come to the aid of his son, the Black Prince, sure that the boy could take care of himself (see page II–260).

By reminding Henry of this most gallant episode (by the standards of the time), the Archbishop is trying to rouse Henry's fighting spirit. Yet Henry stands oddly irresolute and requires considerable urging by his courtiers. We may assume that Shakespeare is pleased to picture him as reluctant to go to war since that would mirror the dramatist's own distaste for this bloody pursuit.

Yet if this were real life rather than a play, we might imagine that something else was occupying Henry's mind and making him reluctant to go to war.

At this very time that Henry V was listening to the Archbishop of Canterbury, there lived Edmund Mortimer, 5th Earl of March (see page II–320), who was great-great-grandson of Edward III through the third son of that king while Henry V was great-grandson of Edward III merely through the fourth son.

To be sure, Edmund of March inherited through a woman, the daughter of that third son of Edward III, but since England did not recognize a Salic law and since Henry V would go to war rather than recognize it in France, how could he deny that March did not have a better claim than himself to the crowns of both countries?

The superior claim of March to the English crown was indirectly recognized by Henry IV, who had kept him in honorable imprisonment throughout his reign, and it was that superior claim which was partly the occasion of Hotspur's rebellion.

When Henry V came to the throne, he felt somewhat more secure than his father ever had, so he released Edmund of March. Still, he kept him under reasonably close watch all the time.

In this play, Henry V's precarious and doubtful claim to the throne (like his father's before him) is not emphasized. The emphasis is entirely on the war in France and on victory, victory, victory. But the matter of the disputed succession was to come up again in later decades and other plays of Shakespeare deal with that time.

Your brother kings . . .

Other members of the court support the Archbishop's suggestions. The first to speak is the Duke of Exeter:

> *Your brother kings and monarchs of the earth*
> *Do all expect that you should rouse yourself,*
>
> —Act I, scene ii, lines 122–23

The Duke of Exeter who speaks these lines is Thomas Beaufort, third and youngest son of John of Gaunt by his mistress Catherine Swynford. Since John of Gaunt is the grandfather of Henry V, Exeter is the King's half uncle. Exeter was a bastard by birth but John of Gaunt eventually married Catherine and had his children by her legitimized in 1397, two years before his death. They were debarred from the succession to the throne by Henry IV, John of Gaunt's oldest son by his first marriage, but they were all honored with high titles and positions.

Actually, though, Shakespeare (following Holinshed) anticipates a little here. Thomas Beaufort was only Earl of Dorset at this time. He did not become Duke of Exeter until 1416, two years later.

. . . your Grace hath cause . . .

The Earl of Westmoreland chimes in:

They know your Grace hath cause and means and might;
—Act I, scene ii, line 125

Westmoreland has played a role in the previous two plays, for he was the chief general of Henry IV. He had taken as his second wife Joan Beaufort, the sister of Thomas of Exeter, so that he was the King's uncle by marriage. Both he and Exeter are about fifty years old now.

The King of Scots . . .

And still King Henry is not ready to move. There is the question of Scotland. There has been perennial war with the Scots who occupy the northern third of the island of Great Britain for over a century now, since the time of Edward I (the grandfather of Edward III), and France has consistently supported the Scots. As a result, whenever the English were otherwise engaged, either in France or in civil war, the Scots were sure to invade the northern counties.

King Henry says as much, but the Archbishop, anxious not to let the French adventure be refused, pooh-poohs the Scottish danger. England can take care of herself, he insists, saying:

When all her chivalry hath been in France,
And she a mourning widow of her nobles,
She hath herself not only well defended
But taken and impounded as a stray
The King of Scots; whom she did send to France
To fill King Edward's fame with prisoner kings,
—Act I, scene ii, lines 157–62

The events described belong to the beginning of the reign of Edward III. In 1329, two years after Edward became King, David Bruce became King of Scotland, reigning as David II. He was only five years old at the time and his succession was displeasing to Edward, who was supporting another claimant to the throne, one who could be counted on to serve as an English puppet.

To put the puppet on the throne, Edward III sent an army toward Scotland, which met the Scottish forces at Halidon Hill, near the North Sea end of the border between the two nations. The English had archers and the Scots did not, so that when the Scots foolishly charged and exposed themselves, the English cut them down long-distance and won an utter victory on July 19, 1333, in very much the same way they were to do seventy years later in Hotspur's victory at Holmedon (see page II–322).

Young King David, still only nine years old, was taken to France by his loyal supporters and there Philip VI supported him for seven years. David II returned to Scotland only in 1341.

In 1346 Edward III had taken his army into France and it seemed quite likely at first that he would be defeated and destroyed. David II, therefore, seized the chance to lead a large army into England, penetrating seventy miles beyond the border, nearly to Durham. There, at a place called Neville's Cross, on October 17, 1346, he fought the English. The result was the same: English archers won over Scottish spearmen. David II was captured and kept imprisoned in England for ten years.

In the play, the Archbishop combines the two defeats, telescoping David's imprisonment after the second battle with the flight to France after the first and makes it appear that the Scottish King was sent prisoner to Edward III abroad. Nevertheless, the Archbishop makes his point as to the ineffectuality of Scottish aggression and urges King Henry to sail to France without overmuch worry concerning the northern border.

. . . not from the King

Now Henry is ready for the French ambassadors. They enter and he says:

> Now are we well prepared to know the pleasure
> Of our fair cousin Dauphin; for we hear
> Your greeting is from him, not from the King.
> —Act I, scene ii, lines 234–36

The King of France at this time was Charles VI. He had been reigning a full generation, for he had mounted the throne in 1380 when he was but twelve years old. He was the great-grandson of Philip VI, as Henry V was the great-grandson of Philip's great adversary, Edward III.

Charles VI was on the French throne during the reigns of Richard II and Henry IV, and France might well have recovered completely, in that period of English internal troubles, from the wounds inflicted earlier by Edward III and the Black Prince, had it not been for an unexpected disaster.

In April 1392 Charles VI fell ill of a fever, underwent convulsions, and suffered enough brain damage to make him a mental cripple. From then to the end of his life (a period of thirty years) he alternated between raving madness and a precarious sanity. He was called "Charles the Mad" and was incapable of really ruling, so that others had to act in his place. France was distracted and fell into protracted civil war of its own, so that the situation was made to order for the invasion of Henry V.

It is very likely, in fact, that the knowledge that France was in chaos was a more persuasive argument in favor of an English invasion than any amount of priestly exhortation from the Archbishop.

The madness of Charles VI is not referred to directly in this play (perhaps because the English monarchs of Shakespeare's day were descended from him and Queen Elizabeth I was his great-great-great-granddaughter). Nevertheless, the fact that the message is from the Dauphin, rather than from the King, is one indirect indication that the French King is incapable of ruling.

The best-known Dauphin of this period of French history is one who appears in connection with the story of Joan of Arc, whose own appearance is, as yet, fifteen years in the future. The Dauphin of the time of Joan of Arc was named Charles and he is *not* the Dauphin referred to at this point in *Henry V.*

The Dauphin who is sending this embassy to Henry is Louis, the oldest son of Charles VI, and he is referred to in the cast of characters as "Lewis, the Dauphin."

. . . our wilder days

Apparently, the Dauphin, Louis, is sending an answer to Henry's demand for sovereignty over the various provinces ruled by Edward III after his great victories and before the turmoil of the reigns of Richard II and Henry IV had frittered them away. This demand did not necessarily indicate that Henry V was planning an actual invasion; it might have served merely to indicate that he was not abandoning title to the lands and was reserving the right to take action if he wished.

At least, so the Dauphin interpreted the demand. He may have reasoned that Henry, on the basis of the tales of his younger days as Prince Hal, was pleasure-loving, and would not really care to immerse himself in the hardships of a campaign in France. To indicate his own contempt for the new English King, then, the Dauphin sent him a gift of tennis balls, a clear indication that he was to amuse himself in games and pleasures and forget about France.

Henry sees clearly what has misled the Dauphin. He says:

> . . . *we understand him well,*
> *How he comes o'er us with our wilder days,*
> *Not measuring what use we made of them.*
> —Act I, scene ii, lines 266–68

He then promises to respond to the tennis balls with cannon balls, and the decision is finally made for war.

. . . three corrupted men

The second act opens with the return of the Prologue, now entitled

Chorus, who, before each act, will fill in the events the audience must know.

The Chorus describes England preparing for war while France attempts to abort the threatened invasion by encouraging a continuation of the civil wars in England over the successsion. The French even try to arrange to have King Henry assassinated. The Chorus apostrophizes the England of Henry's time, saying:

> . . . *France hath in thee found out—*
> *A nest of hollow bosoms—which he fills*
> *With treacherous crowns; and three corrupted men—*
> *One, Richard Earl of Cambridge, and the second,*
> *Henry Lord Scroop of Masham, and the third,*
> *Sir Thomas Grey, knight, of Northumberland—*
> *Have for the gilt of France (O guilt indeed!)*
> *Confirmed conspiracy with fearful France,*
> *And by their hands this grace of kings must die,*
>
> —Act II, Chorus, lines 20–28

Who were these men?

Richard, Earl of Cambridge, was the younger son of Edmund, Duke of York, whom we met in *Richard II* as the weakling uncle of that king. Richard of Cambridge is therefore the younger brother of Aumerle, the friend of Richard II, who conspired against Henry IV soon after the latter became king (see page II–308).

Aumerle was demoted to the title of Earl of Rutland as a punishment for having remained friendly to Richard II too long. When old Edmund of York died in 1402, however (the year in which *Henry IV, Part One* opens), Rutland was allowed to succeed to his father's title and revenues and became Edward, Duke of York. He was also Earl of Cambridge, but about the time that *Henry V* opens, he had released that title to his younger brother, who became Richard, Earl of Cambridge.

Richard of Cambridge had a perfectly good reason to want the death of Henry V; one that required no French gold. He had married Anne Mortimer, younger sister of Edmund Mortimer, 5th Earl of March. It was Edmund of March who was "rightful" King, and if Henry V died without children (and he was unmarried at the time), then Edmund's right to the throne would be all the clearer. Then if Edmund died without heirs (as he eventually did), his sister, Anne, Richard's wife, would be next in line, and through her, Richard's son. (As a matter of fact, Richard's son would, in time to come, claim the kingdom, and Richard's grandson would one day rule it.)

And so, the dreadful turmoil of claims and counterclaims that had been set in motion with the deposition of Richard II continued into the reign of Henry V.

As for Henry Lord Scroop of Masham, he had family reasons for disliking Henry V. His uncle, Richard, had been the Archbishop of York who had risen against Henry IV and had been executed, a tale told in *Henry IV, Part Two* (see page II–406). Scroop of Masham's second cousin, once removed, had been the Earl of Wiltshire, who had been executed by Henry IV when, as Bolingbroke, he was taking over the throne (see page II–284). The Scroops owed a debt to the King's father, then, that they were willing to pay to the son.

The third conspirator, Sir Thomas Grey, is a minor figure, but it is interesting that he comes from Northumberland, the home territory of the Percys, who had raised two rebellions against Henry IV.

. . . Lieutenant Bardolph

We do not, however, with the opening of the second act, switch immediately to the King and to the conspiracy against him. There is first an interlude in London, among characters of the type with whom the King passed the time while he was Prince of Wales.

Two of them meet and one says:

> *Well met, Corporal Nym.*
> —Act II, scene i, line 1

This is the Nym of *The Merry Wives of Windsor* (see page II–424) complete with his "humors," his dark hints, and his affectation of desperate valor. We cannot say whether he was introduced in this play and carried over into *The Merry Wives of Windsor* or vice versa. It depends on which play was written first, and concerning that there is no definite decision.

Nym answers:

> *Good morrow, Lieutenant Bardolph.*
> —Act II, scene i, line 2

Bardolph (who has been promoted, it would seem, for he was only a corporal in *Henry IV, Part Two*) is rather remarkable for appearing in no fewer than four of Shakespeare's plays: *Henry IV, Part One, Henry IV, Part Two, The Merry Wives of Windsor,* and *Henry V*.

The rest of the group cannot say the same. Pistol is not in *Henry IV, Part One*, Prince Hal is not in *The Merry Wives of Windsor*, Falstaff is not in *Henry V*, and so on. Mistress Quickly is indeed in all four, but in *The Merry Wives of Windsor* her position and character are quite different from what they are in the other three plays, whereas Bardolph remains recognizably himself throughout.

It appears at once that Nym is at enmity with Pistol, for the latter has married Mistress Quickly, who had earlier been betrothed to Nym.

Nym is full of dark threats and when Pistol and his new wife enter there are many valorous words between the two enemies, but no action. They draw their swords, but when Bardolph threatens to kill whoever moves first, they both sheathe at once in obvious relief.

. . . He is very sick . . .

But where is Falstaff?

Falstaff's page hurries onstage with the news of him. He is the page who appears with Falstaff at the beginning of *Henry IV, Part Two,* the page given Falstaff by Prince Hal. He is also, presumably, the young page who is found in *The Merry Wives of Windsor* too. His speeches are assigned to "Page" in *Henry IV, Part Two,* to "Robin" in *The Merry Wives of Windsor,* and to "Boy" in *Henry V.*

The Boy says:

> Mine host Pistol, you must come to my master—and your hostess. He is very sick and would to bed.
>
> —Act II, scene i, lines 84–86

And Mistress Quickly, whose lines in this play are identified as "Hostess," responds anxiously:

> By my troth, he'll yield the crow a pudding one of these days. The King has killed his heart.
>
> —Act II, scene i, lines 90–91

At the end of *Henry IV, Part Two,* the Epilogue had promised to have Falstaff appear again in the next play, but Shakespeare has clearly changed his mind. Can it be that *The Merry Wives of Windsor* had already been written and that the unsuccessful version of Falstaff in that play had killed the character for Shakespeare?

. . . to trust these traitors

But before Falstaff's end is described, the scene shifts to Southampton, where the King's forces are gathering. Southampton is on the south-central coast of England, protected by the Isle of Wight against damage from storms or enemy attacks. The traitors, led by Richard of Cambridge, plan to kill the King here, before his forces can embark.

The plot is already known, however, and the King is holding his hand in

order that when he strikes it may be with full effect. This is, of course, a tactic that is not without its dangers, and the King's generals are nervous.
Bedford says:

> Fore God, his Grace is bold to trust these traitors.
> —Act II, scene ii, line 1

Bedford is the third son of Henry IV, one of the younger brothers of Henry V. He played his part in *Henry IV, Part Two,* where he was known by his earlier title and called "John of Lancaster." In 1414, however, as he was making ready for his French campaign, King Henry passed out a number of promotions and John of Lancaster became Duke of Bedford.

. . . his bedfellow

The King's generals also stand amazed at the self-assurance of the conspirators and at the way they manage to maintain the appearance of loyalty. What's more, one of them, at least, is a particular ingrate, for, as Exeter says:

> Nay, but the man that was his bedfellow,
> Whom he hath dulled and cloyed with gracious favors—
> That he should, for a foreign purse, so sell
> His Sovereign's life to death and treachery!
> —Act II, scene ii, lines 8–11

The reference is to Henry Scroop of Masham, who had been a good friend of the King's and who had been made treasurer by him and had been employed on diplomatic missions. One might wonder at the King's friendship with a Scroop of Masham, considering that two of the latter's relatives had been executed by the King's father, but this must be viewed in relation to the times. In the days when the King's officials were always drawn from the few noble families who were endlessly interrelated, it was impossible to find anyone who did not have some relative who at one time or another had been punished, demoted, exiled, or executed by the King or by his predecessor.

The reference to foreign gold here reinforces the comment in the Chorus. In actual fact, the conspirators were rebelling on behalf of the Mortimers, and if they took French gold, it was no more than the King's father had done when he rebelled against Richard II. Had Bolingbroke (later Henry IV) failed, he too would have been denounced as having been in French pay—and if the Mortimer faction had won out over either Henry IV or

Henry V, the accusation of foreign bribery would have been dropped. History, we must always remember, is written by the winners.

. . . with his lion gait . . .

King Henry sets his trap. He maneuvers the hypocritical conspirators into feigning superloyalty and demanding the punishment of some minor offender who had uttered drunken threats against the King.

Once that is done, Henry magnificently exposes their hypocrisy and all confess at once in terror. Eloquently, Henry berates them, saving his harshest words for his erstwhile friend and confidant, Scroop of Masham. The King says to Scroop of Masham:

> If that same demon that hath gulled thee thus
> Should with his lion gait walk the whole world,
> He might return to vasty Tartar back
> And tell the legions, "I can never win
> A soul so easy as that Englishman's."
>
> —Act II, scene ii, lines 121–25

The demon is Satan, of course, and his "lion gait" is a reference to Chapter 5, verse 8 in the First Epistle of Peter: ". . . your adversary the devil, as a roaring lion, walketh about, seeking whom he may devour."

Tartar is a shortened form of Tartarus, which in Greek mythology is a place of torture in the underworld.

So, with the traitors led off to execution and made into a public example, King Henry V is ready to embark. On August 11, 1415, the English ships set sail and Henry's willingness to stake all for the highest possible reward is expressed in the last line of the scene, in which the King says:

> No king of England, if not king of France!
>
> —Act II, scene ii, line 194

. . . to Staines

The men once attached to Falstaff are also planning to leave, and Hostess Quickly wishes to accompany her husband, Pistol, part way. She says:

> Prithee, honey-sweet husband, let me bring thee to Staines.
>
> —Act II, scene iii, lines 1–2

Staines is a town some twenty miles west of the center of London in the direction of Southampton.

. . . in Arthur's bosom . . .

But Pistol is sorrowing, for Falstaff is dead. We can detect that sorrow unmistakably even through the man's fustian oratory. As for Bardolph, he expresses his own sorrow in a direct simplicity that shows us well how Falstaff can inspire love despite his gross faults. Bardolph says:

> *Would I were with him, wheresome'er he is, either in heaven or in hell!*
> —Act II, scene iii, lines 7–8

Hostess Quickly retorts with spirit that Falstaff cannot be in hell. She says:

> *He's in Arthur's bosom, if ever man went to Arthur's bosom.*
> —Act II, scene iii, lines 9–10

The phrase "Arthur's bosom" is, of course, the Hostess' naïve error for "Abraham's bosom" (see page II–300). Among the less educated English, the one hero of past ages they would be sure to know about was King Arthur, and he would be confused with all past great men of importance.

. . . the Whore of Babylon

Falstaff comes to his death, then, with only his lowborn friends grieving for him, and his Prince Hal a majestic king now, setting forth upon a great adventure.

Hostess Quickly is questioned concerning the circumstances of Falstaff's death, and she says at one point:

> *'A did in some sort, indeed, handle women; but then he was rheumatic* [of wandering mind?], *and talked of the Whore of Babylon.*
> —Act II, scene iii, lines 38–40

The reference to the "Whore of Babylon" was good for another laugh in Shakespeare's time, for it again emphasized the simplicity of the Hostess, who took the Whore of Babylon to be a woman, perhaps some prostitute whom Falstaff had known and she herself had not.

Actually, the phrase is from the Book of Revelation, which (17:4–5) describes a woman: "And the woman was arrayed in purple and scarlet colour, and decked with gold and precious stones and pearls, having a golden cup in her hand full of abominations and filthiness of her fornications: And upon her forehead was a name written, MYSTERY, BABYLON THE GREAT, THE MOTHER OF HARLOTS AND ABOMINATIONS OF THE EARTH."

It is this symbolic vision which is referred to as the "Whore of Babylon," and the reference, at the time that Revelation was written, was to the Imperial Roman government. Rome was persecuting the early Christians and could not be mentioned directly for fear of consequences, but inveighing against Babylon (which had once dragged the Jews off into exile) was safe and the cover was transparent enough.

The sixteenth-century Protestants, rebelling against the Catholic Church, and in particular against the notion of papal supremacy, were quick to see the reference to Rome as a handy way of vilifying the papacy. Thus, Hostess Quickly not only raised a smile from the learned with her reference to the Whore of Babylon, but a snicker from the Protestant zealot as well.

. . . and of Orleans . . .

Now, for the first time, the French appear on the scene. King Charles VI (who is never shown insane) is perturbed at the news of the English invasion. Concerned that France be prepared for the onslaught, he apportions defense duties among the peers, saying:

> *Therefore the Dukes of Berri and of Bretagne,*
> *Of Brabant and of Orleans, shall make forth,*
> —Act II, scene iv, lines 4–5

Of these, the most significant name is that of Orléans, for that name was at the center of the disasters that followed the madness of the French King and laid the realm open to invasion.

Charles VI had a younger brother, Louis, with great ambition but little ability. In 1392 he was made Duke of Orléans, and it was just about that time that the King had his first attack of insanity. Someone had to take over the actual rule of the kingdom, and who better (in his own eyes) than the King's brother?

This was disputed. Charles VI had an uncle, Philip, the youngest of the three brothers of Charles V, the preceding King of France. When Charles V had become king, he had made his brother, Philip, the Duke of Burgundy, and this particular duke is commonly known as Philip the Bold.

Philip outlived his royal brother (with whom he got along well). During the years when Charles VI was too young to rule, Philip and his surviving brothers were the real powers of the kingdom. When the French King went mad and was as a child again, Philip saw no reason why he should not again be in control.

Thus, France broke up into two factions, headed by the King's brother,

Louis of Orléans, and the King's uncle, Philip of Burgundy, respectively. In 1401 the hostility between the two parties came almost to the point of open warfare. A peace between them was patched up but it was a most uneasy one, and on the whole it was Philip who remained in the ascendant.

Philip died in 1404 and was succeeded as Duke of Burgundy by his son John, popularly known as John the Fearless. He was first cousin to Louis of Orléans.

Louis of Orléans took advantage of Philip's death to seize power in the kingdom and, in particular, to keep control over the Dauphin. Louis bid for popularity by adopting a hawkish attitude toward England, which was then ruled by Henry IV (who was having his own troubles with the Percys). John the Fearless naturally came out in opposition, advocating an accommodation with England. The two French leaders patched up some sort of truce on November 20, 1407, but three days later, on November 23, Louis of Orléans was assassinated by bravoes in the pay of John the Fearless.

If by that move John thought he would seize control of France, he was wrong. It led to open civil war instead.

Louis of Orléans had left behind a son and heir, who was now known as Charles of Orléans. He was only thirteen years old at this time and a year before he had married none other than Isabella, the widow of Richard II of England (see page II-287). She was a daughter of Charles VI and therefore first cousin to her new husband; she was also five years older than he and died in 1409.

The new Duke of Orléans needed help and he found that help in the person of the wealthy and powerful Bernard VII, Count of Armagnac, whose daughter, Bonne, he married as his second wife in 1410. Thereafter, the party favorable to the Orléans faction was known as the Armagnacs, and when Henry V came to the English throne in 1413, France was bleeding to death in the continuing civil war between the Armagnacs and the Burgundians.

In 1414 the Armagnacs gained a temporary ascendancy and had the seven-year-old murder of Louis of Orléans officially condemned; for a while, John the Fearless found himself cut off from power. Angrily, John and the Burgundian territory he ruled (a sizable fraction of France) maintained a neutrality in the events that were to follow. Henry V was to be opposed by Armagnacs only when he invaded France; opposed by Armagnacs, moreover, who would be forever looking uneasily over their shoulders for fear of a stab in the back from the Burgundians.

It is Charles of Orléans, then, the head of the Armagnac party, who is one of the men assigned defense tasks by the King, and it is he who is to be one of the leaders of the army that is to oppose Henry V. Charles of Orléans was a poor general, but he was, surprisingly enough, a good poet, and by some he is considered to be the last of the troubadours.

Of the others mentioned, the Duke of Berri (or Berry) was John, the older brother of Philip the Bold and the last of the uncles of the mad King

Charles VI to survive. He was seventy-four years old at this time and had led a life of luxury at the expense of the peasants, whom he taxed ruthlessly and forced into revolt out of sheer desperation.

In the quarrels between the Armagnacs and the Burgundians, John of Berri had tried to play the role of mediator (as a quarter century before John of Gaunt had tried to do under similar conditions in England, see page II–263). Berri was not successful (anymore than Gaunt had been), and he tended to lean toward the side of the Armagnacs. However, at his age there was little he could really do, or wanted to do.

The Duke of Bretagne (Brittany) was John V "the Valiant." He had been on the side of Philip the Bold, but after the assassination of Louis of Orléans, John of Brittany turned against John the Fearless. Although he shifted toward the Armagnac faction, he did his best to maintain the traditional Breton neutrality in the war between England and France. His forces arrived at the battlefield too late to fight against Henry V, and one gets the impression that the lateness was deliberate.

The Duke of Brabant was Anthony, who was actually a brother of John the Fearless, so little could be expected of him in the way of resolute resistance against the English.

Indeed, of the four dukes mentioned, only Orléans could be counted on as wholeheartedly anti-English—and he was incompetent.

. . . the Roman Brutus

Shakespeare, as a patriotic Englishman, may be expected to magnify the fear of the French at the prospect of an English invasion, but they had a right to be uneasy. England might be much the smaller, poorer, and less populous kingdom, but France was in chaos and there was the disturbing memory of what had happened seventy years before at Crécy and Poitiers (see page II–257).

The French King refers to the earlier battles, but Louis the Dauphin shrugs off his father's fearfulness, maintaining that the English King Henry V is but a shallow person intent on pleasure.

This is vigorously rebutted by someone who is listed as "The Constable of France" in the cast of characters. He says, concerning King Henry:

> . . . you shall find his vanities forespent [used up]
> Were but the outside of the Roman Brutus
> Covering discretion with a coat of folly;
> —Act II, scene iv, lines 36–38

The Roman Brutus referred to is the Lucius Junius Brutus who lived in Rome in the early days described in The Rape of Lucrece (see page I–210), the one who hid his cleverness under a pretended stupidity.

But who was the Constable who said this and what is the meaning of the title?

Originally, the constable was an officer whose title, in Latin, was *comes stabuli* ("the stable official"). In the centuries when the heavily armored mounted knight was the chief force in battles, the condition of the horses was of vital importance. The constable might have been a stable official first, but the title came to be given to the commander of the cavalry and then to the commander in chief of the army.

The title reached its peak importance in France, and the Constable of France (the commander in chief of the French army) was at this time Charles D'Albret.

Even as the French talk, the Duke of Exeter comes from England bearing the demand that Charles VI resign the crown of France to Henry V. Charles VI does not answer at once, but asks time to think.

. . . *to Harfleur*

Again the Chorus appears, to open the third act. He says:

> *O do but think*
> *You stand upon the rivage* [shore], *and behold*
> *A city on th'inconstant billows dancing;*
> *For so appears this fleet majestical,*
> *Holding due course to Harfleur.*
> —Act III, Chorus, lines 13–17

Harfleur is a port at the mouth of the Seine River and there were a number of reasons for making for it. Henry V was conscious of the importance of sea power. England held Calais, and had done so for over half a century, since Edward III had taken it in 1347, so they controlled the eastern Channel. Harfleur was, at that time, the most important Channel port in the hands of France (though having been far overtaken by Le Havre, a couple of miles to the west, in the centuries since, Harfleur is an unimportant town now).

If Henry could take Harfleur as his first stroke, he would control all the Channel, could supply his forces in France at will, and would leave France without adequate means for striking back at England. Furthermore, since Harfleur was at the mouth of the Seine, it offered the possibility (if all broke just right) for a march up the Seine to Paris itself.

There may have been a psychological reason too. Harfleur was in Norman territory and it was in Normandy that the line of English kings of which Henry was a member had first risen to power and it was Normandy that represented England's oldest claim to French territory.

Having left Southampton on August 11, 1415, the English fleet crossed the Channel and arrived at Harfleur (120 miles to the southeast) on August 13.

Katherine his daughter . . .

Meanwhile, Exeter has brought word to Henry of King Charles's compromise offer. As the Chorus says:

> . . . *th'ambassador from the French comes back;*
> *Tells Harry that the King doth offer him*
> *Katherine his daughter, and with her to dowry*
> *Some petty and unprofitable dukedoms.*
> *The offer likes not;*

—Act III, Chorus, lines 28–32

The French King's offer has its points. The English King, whatever his estimate in his own eyes and those of his countrymen, was a minor personage in the eyes of the Europe of the time, and in no way to be compared with the King of France. English kings had, in the past, been proud to accept the social compliment of a French princess to wife.

Thus, Edward II, the father of conquering Edward III, had married Isabella, the daughter of Philip IV of France; and Richard II, the grandson of conquering Edward III, had married Isabella, the daughter of Charles VI.

Katherine (or Catherine) was the younger sister of Isabella and was only fourteen years old at this time—which made her eminently marriageable, nevertheless, according to royal customs of the time. If in addition France was offering dukedoms ("petty and unprofitable" or not), then, from her own point of view, she was making a most generous offer.

In fact, we might wonder about Shakespeare's characterization of the dukedoms as "petty and unprofitable." It sounds almost sarcastic. *Henry V* is a chauvinistic play, celebrating England's most renowned victory in war, and yet one can argue that Shakespeare's own hatred of war peeps through even here. The long argument of the Archbishop seems a device for demonstrating the tawdry origin of the war, and here we have Henry deliberately refusing a generous offer out of greed for all. Later on there will be other passages which might be interpreted as showing Henry in a less than favorable light, though very cautiously—so cautiously that the audience (especially a chauvinistic Elizabethan audience) might miss it all and give Shakespeare the dubious satisfaction of sneering at them in secret.

. . . the devilish cannon . . .

The Chorus indicates the start of hostilities, by saying:

> *. . . the nimble gunner*
> *With linstock now the devilish cannon touches,*
> *And down goes all before them.*
> —Act III, Chorus, lines 32–34

Artillery, which had been used at the Battle of Crécy as virtually nothing more than a dangerous toy to frighten horses and kill the gunners themselves, had made great strides in the seventy years since. Cannon were more reliable and cannon balls more destructive.

Gunpowder was still worthless in hand-to-hand fighting, for useful handguns had not been developed, but it could be used to batter a city's walls to far greater effect than ever a battering ram could be used, and with greater safety, by now, to the attacking soldiers.

. . . unto the breach . . .

Henry landed without resistance. The Constable chose the unheroic but wiser course of keeping the French forces at Rouen, fifty miles upriver, between the English and Paris, and leaving Harfleur to its fate. This inglorious policy was made necessary by France's financial chaos. The twenty-year squabbling that had accompanied the French King's madness had left the nation virtually bankrupt, and she had to fight the war cheaply.

D'Albret may well have reasoned, too, that Henry's force would be greatly weakened in the course of the siege and that there would be time enough to tackle him after a few months had passed.

He was not far wrong. Harfleur would not surrender and was put under siege on August 17, 1415. She was to stay under siege for five weeks, and during that time the English were to suffer considerably from disease.

Morale started slipping, too, since there is nothing so deadly in war as the dull boredom of a siege that seems to be getting nowhere. Henry was hard put to it to counter that slipping morale, as is indicated by his speech beginning:

> *Once more unto the breach, dear friends, once more;*
> *Or close the wall up with our English dead!*
> —Act III, scene i, lines 1–2

He is urging his forces to attack an opening forced in Harfleur's walls, inducing them to risk their lives with the time-honored technique of the general. That is, he tells them how brave and heroic they are in the hope that they will believe him and prove so.

That such feelings are not necessarily shared by all in the army Shake-

speare cannot resist making plain, for the speech is immediately followed
by a parody of its opening by Bardolph, who cries:

> *On, on, on, on, on, to the breach, to the breach!*
>
> —Act III, scene ii, lines 1–2

While saying this, he moves, we may be sure, very little.

Even the talk of charging is too much for Nym, who (giving Bardolph
his older title, perhaps through a Shakespearean oversight) says:

> *Pray thee, Corporal, stay; the knocks are too hot; and, for
> mine own part, I have not a case of lives.*
>
> —Act III, scene ii, lines 3–5

When a bolder officer enters to drive them on, Nym apparently runs
off, for he appears no more in the play. It is to be presumed he has deserted.
Bardolph and Pistol also leave the stage, though in their case the direction
must be toward the wall, for they will be heard from again.

Lingering behind is the Boy, Falstaff's old page, who has also gone to
the wars and who now delivers an ironical soliloquy on the character of the
three men he has accompanied. They are cowards and thieves. In particular, he says:

> *Nym and Bardolph are sworn brothers in filching . . .*
>
> —Act III, scene ii, lines 45–46

To be sure, soldiers are notorious for their taking ways, and were especially so in earlier times when they were treated as virtual slaves by their
officers and sometimes left to starve except for what they could loot. Nym
and Bardolph, however, and Pistol too, for that matter, are sneak thieves
virtually by profession. All were involved in the petty plundering of Slender
at the start of *The Merry Wives of Windsor* and Bardolph was party to the
highway robbery at Gad's Hill in *Henry IV, Part One.*

As for Nym, his very name is a reflection of *nehmen,* the German word
for "to take," and the related archaic English word "nim" or "nym," which
means "to steal."

. . . to the mines . . .

As an example of valiant men in the army (after all, Henry's troops did
not consist entirely of such miserable specimens as Bardolph, Nym, and
Pistol) Shakespeare introduces a scene involving four captains. These are
Gower, an Englishman; Fluellen, a Welshman; Jamy, a Scotsman; and
Macmorris, an Irishman.

The four nationalities are no accident, we may well believe. Shakespeare is trying to show the British Isles united under the English hero-king. Furthermore, it gives him a chance to extract humor from three different kinds of broken English (a type of humor that is unfortunately lost on us to a great extent, since the nature of dialects has changed since Shakespeare's time). It reminds us, in fact, of those dreary World War II motion pictures in which American soldiers bore nicknames such as Dakota, Texas, California, and Brooklyn—all in a single picture—to emphasize national unity.

Of the four, Fluellen the Welshman is the most interesting character. It is he who has just driven Bardolph and Pistol on to the breach and whose rough actions have forced cowardly Nym to desert.

He speaks with a thick Welsh dialect like that of Sir Hugh Evans in *The Merry Wives of Windsor*. What's more, he is a mass of crotchety eccentricities, such as wishing to refer learnedly to military history and to the ancient wars at every opportunity.

Though cranky and odd, Fluellen is, however, honest and brave. This is a reflection of Shakespeare's time, when the Welsh had adjusted themselves to English domination so that the English could afford to grant them their due, rather than a reflection of the time of Henry V, when the Welsh had lately been in rebellion and when the memory of Glendower (see page II–294) was fresh.

Gower begins the scene by addressing the Welshman, saying:

> *Captain Fluellen, you must come presently* [immediately] *to the mines; the Duke of Gloucester would speak with you.*
> —Act III, scene ii, lines 56–58

The Duke of Gloucester is King Henry's youngest brother, just raised to the dukedom before the French campaign began. He played a small role in *Henry IV, Part Two* (and was called Gloucester there—see page II–408—though at that time he had not yet received the title). I shall call him Humphrey of Gloucester to distinguish him from the Thomas of Gloucester referred to a number of times in connection with *Richard II*.

Humphrey of Gloucester commanded the English artillery and was also in charge of the mines. These were tunnels secretly dug under the walls so that a charge of gunpowder could be placed there and then set off, in the hope that a sizable section of the wall would then be weakened or even made to collapse (hence "undermined").

. . . the countermines

Fluellen scorns the mines, however, which he claims, pedantically, have not been properly dug. He says:

> *. . . for look you, th'athversary, you may discuss* [state] *unto the Duke, look you, is digt himself four yard under the countermines.*

> —Act III, scene ii, lines 62–65

Gunpowder was not all on one side. What Fluellen is saying is that the defending forces in Harfleur were digging mines of their own four yards beneath the English mines. The French mines were countermines. A proper charge in the lower tunnel would break down the upper one and bury the English miners, without damaging the walls significantly. This would be especially true if the defending forces managed to catch the English miners in a portion of the tunnel not yet directly under the wall.

And, as a matter of fact, the English, during the siege, twice tried to undermine the walls and were twice balked by countermines. The opposing miners actually fought small battles underground.

. . . he is an ass . . .

Gower explains that the mining procedures are under the charge of an Irishman, Captain Macmorris, and Fluellen bursts out:

> *By Cheshu* [Jesus], *he is an ass, as in the world! I will verify as much in his beard. He has no more directions in the true disciplines of the wars, look you, of the Roman disciplines, than is a puppy-dog.*

> —Act III, scene ii, lines 72–75

Macmorris enters in despair. The English miners have been ordered back by Gloucester and the Irishman insists that in just an hour he would have completed the job and blown up the wall.

Fluellen, however, chooses this moment to begin to needle the poor Irishman, of whose bravery there can be no doubt but who, we may suppose, lacks Fluellen's knowledge of military history. When Fluellen urges him to join in a discussion of some abstruse points of military science, Macmorris rightly refuses, insisting that this is not the time. And when Fluellen casually refers to Macmorris' "nation," Macmorris goes into a spasm of defensive anger.

It is clear that the Irishman is being made the butt by the other three and this, again, reflects the situation in Shakespeare's time. In 1597, just a year before *Henry V* was produced, the Irish had risen in rebellion, and they were still in rebellion at the time the audience was watching the first performance. The audience could therefore be expected to be anti-Irish and quite ready to laugh at an Irishman being made to look ridiculous.

. . . the wives of Jewry

The English army, weakening with disease, could easily die at Harfleur if the siege continued much longer, and Henry decided to storm the town. This meant, if the storm succeeded, that the town would be given over to an unrestrained sack. (It would be the promise of rape and loot that would encourage the soldiers in the dangerous task of storming a garrisoned wall, and the anger at their inevitably large casualties that would drive them on in revenge.)

Henry V threatens Harfleur with the consequences of such a sack. He cries out to the defenders on the wall:

> *. . . in a moment look to see*
> *The blind and bloody soldier with foul hand*
> *Defile the locks of your shrill-shrieking daughters;*
> *Your fathers taken by the silver beards,*
> *And their most reverend heads dashed to the walls;*
> *Your naked infants spitted upon pikes,*
> *Whiles the mad mothers with their howls confused*
> *Do break the clouds, as did the wives of Jewry*
> *At Herod's bloody-hunting slaughtermen.*
> *What say you? Will you yield, and this avoid?*
> *Or, guilty in defense, be thus destroyed?*
> —Act III, scene iii, lines 33–43

This is a dreadful passage to attribute to Henry V. We might suppose that this is only a war of nerves, a threat designed to frighten the Harfleurians into surrender, and that it isn't really meant.

And yet somehow we can see that this is another place in this play of pride and glory where Shakespeare's revulsion against war shows itself. War is something which makes even a king such as Henry V speak in such abominable terms as these. It makes the hero-king describe English soldiers as capable of utterly unspeakable atrocities. It makes him even willing to compare his men to those of Herod (see page I–325). That Judean monarch, according to Matthew 2:16, had ordered all the male children in Bethlehem under two years of age slaughtered in the hope that the infant Jesus would be among them. This is the so-called "Slaughter of the Innocents."

Worse yet, Henry V considers the Harfleurians to be "guilty in defense," implying that the whole burden of guilt for the vile acts he promises would rest on the victims themselves for having defended themselves too resolutely. As he says, a little earlier in the same speech:

What is't to me, when you yourselves are cause,

> *If your pure maidens fall into the hand*
> *Of hot and forcing violation?*

> —Act III, scene iii, lines 19–21

No matter how much we tell ourselves that this is strategy, that Henry doesn't mean it, it is bothersome. It is a line of reasoning always taken by the aggressor, most particularly by a brutal one. Hitler could not have done better, and by this line of reasoning Great Britain would have deserved all she would have received had the Nazis won the Battle of Britain and successfully invaded the too resolutely defended island.

We yield our town . . .

But if the English army was suffering, so were the defenders. The food supply was running low in Harfleur; the town had been dreadfully battered and many of its garrison killed. Worst of all, there seemed no sign of relief. Nowhere on the horizon was there a sign of the French army. The men of Harfleur had been abandoned.

Harfleur asked Henry for a five-day respite, till September 22, promising to surrender then if there were no signs of relief. Henry relied on the paralysis of the French and granted the delay, investing that much in the hope that it would make an expensive storming of the town unnecessary.

The investment proved worthwhile. There was no relief and Harfleur surrendered. Shakespeare skips the five-day interval, however, and has the surrender follow immediately on Henry V's threat. The Governor of Harfleur says from the wall:

> *We yield our town and lives to thy soft mercy.*

> —Act III, scene iii, line 48

On September 22, 1415, then, the town surrendered after a five-week siege and was occupied by the English quietly and without undue atrocity. The population was forced to leave, for the most part, so that the port could be taken over entirely by the English, and on September 23 Henry himself entered in pomp and state.

. . . retire to Calais

The victory had been a Pyrrhic one, however. Between the attrition of war, disease, and desertion, perhaps as little as only one third of Henry's original force of fighting men remained in fighting trim, and winter was coming on.

There were not wanting those who advised Henry to be content with the victory at Harfleur and to return to England to refit his army for a return the next year.

This, however, Henry could not do. To return with two thirds of his army gone and only one city to show for it would be impossible. Somehow he had to stay in France until he had something better to display.

Yet if he were to stay in France, it could not be at Harfleur. That would simply be asking the French forces to bestir themselves at last and put him under siege in his turn.

So King Henry says to his uncle, Exeter:

> *For us, dear uncle,*
> *The winter coming on, and sickness growing*
> *Upon our soldiers, we will retire to Calais.*
>
> —Act III, scene iii, lines 54–56

Calais was a strong English fortress, where his army could find safety and time to refurbish just as well as in England itself; and yet in Calais it could do so without being under English eyes and with the army's wounded state not so visible. Then, after a while, some further victories might be won that would make a return to England possible.

On October 8, 1415, then, Henry V's weakened and thinned-out army, made up of only fifteen thousand men, set forth on its march of 125 miles (as the crow flies) from Harfleur to Calais.

. . . the river Somme

The time taken by the march is filled in by Shakespeare with a short scene (entirely in French!) in which the young princess Katherine is trying to learn English from her old lady in waiting. The humor is intended for the educated among the audience, who understand French, and rests, in the end, on the fact that some perfectly good English words sound (to Katherine's ears) like French vulgarisms for sexual intercourse and for the vagina.

With that out of the way, we switch to the French gathered at Rouen, the chief city of Normandy. It is about fifty miles east of Harfleur and seventy miles northwest of Paris. The scene opens with King Charles saying:

> *'Tis certain he hath passed the river Somme.*
>
> —Act III, scene v, line 1

That remark, with "he" referring to King Henry, covers an eleven-day march that was a thorough horror. Henry had given strict orders that there was to be no looting, no destruction. This was not only humane; it was intelligent as well. The English army had to move quickly and it could not risk the disorder and delay that would follow if stragglers began to loot and the habit caught on. What's more, the marching columns were all too weak, and if an aroused peasantry began harassing it in revenge, it might be destroyed piecemeal.

Henry marched along the coast, taking the quickest route to Calais. The weather was, and remained, miserable, raining nearly constantly and turning raw and chilly at night. (It was, after all, October.) Dysentery and diarrhea continued to afflict the army.

Nevertheless, within three days they had traveled fifty miles and had reached the vicinity of Dieppe. They were nearly halfway to their goal.

Two days later, on October 13, 1415, they reached Abbeville, near the mouth of the Somme River (a stream that roughly paralleled the course of the Seine, but lying seventy miles to the northeast). Sixty miles beyond, due north, lay Calais and safety.

The French, however, were following a rational plan; an inglorious one, but rational. They were fading away before the English and letting the rigors of the march complete what the siege at Harfleur had begun. (It was the strategy of the Russians on the occasion of Napoleon's retreat from Moscow four hundred years later, and when such a strategy works, it works to perfection.)

Now, when the English reached the Somme, they found the bridges broken down, and a French army waiting on the other side.

If the English wanted to cross, they would have to swim the fast, cold current, and those who survived would have to fight as soon as they climbed the opposite bank.

That was impossible. The increasingly anxious Henry had to find another way of crossing and he began a march upstream to find it. This was the very worst part of the war. The food supplies gave out, yet the English army still dared not try to live off the country. They no longer had an assured goal, since they did not know where a ford might be found, and each day of march upstream took them farther and farther from Calais, leaving them weaker and weaker.

What's more, the English could be certain that the French on the other side of the river were gathering and growing stronger. The French army, indeed, kept pace with Henry, making no attempt to cross the river themselves. The French were content (at least so far) to let the river flow between the armies and to wait for the English invaders to sicken and die.

The English reached and passed Amiens, thirty miles upstream from Abbeville, and still there was no safe crossing point to be found. By October 18 they had reached Nesle, twenty-four miles farther still, and only then came the news that a ford had been discovered. They had to cross marshy ground to reach it, but by dismantling some houses they formed rough wooden flooring and that night they crossed the Somme.

It was this feat which King Charles is referring to, and there is no question but that the French had been caught napping. Undoubtedly, they felt the ford was not a practical one and they negligently allowed the army to cross while they were engaged elsewhere, or nowhere. Had they been alert enough to discover what was happening they could have attacked Henry in the midst of the crossing with his army divided in two by the river. They would then have surely crushed him.

The English were on the right side of the Somme River at last and the army was intact. Yet they were now over ninety miles from Calais. Five days of painful marching had but set them back by thirty miles and if that were not enough, a large French army lay between the bedraggled English host and safety.

Certainly anyone who could at this moment have considered Henry's situation would not have given a finger-snap for his chances of coming out alive. And if the French had kept their heads and had continued their cautious policy of avoiding battle, but had taken to small harassing actions instead, Henry would have been lost.

. . . isle of Albion

Unfortunately for the French, the rational strategy was an inglorious one as well, and they found it impossible to carry out. They were medieval knights. They were heavily armored, rode huge horses, carried thick lances. They faced a moth-eaten huddle of greatly outnumbered infantrymen and archers.

How could they avoid a battle under such circumstances? There was no risk in a battle. In their eyes, it was a "sure thing." The Constable, contemplating the situation now that Henry has crossed the Somme, sees battle and glorious victory as the obvious counter. He says to King Charles:

> *And if he be not fought withal, my lord,*
> *Let us not live in France; let us quit all*
> *And give our vineyards to a barbarous people.*
> —Act III, scene v, lines 2–4

The remaining French generals vie in decrying England and the English, to the undoubted delight of Shakespeare's audience, who know well what the upshot will be. With every vaunt and sneer of the French, the audience's anticipation of what is to come must grow keener (and Shakespeare will stretch out that anticipation as long as he can). The Duke of Bretagne (Brittany) is made to say:

> *. . . if they march along*
> *Unfought withal, but I will sell my dukedom*
> *To buy a slobb'ry and a dirty farm*
> *In that nook-shotten* [misshapen] *isle of Albion.*
> —Act III, scene v, lines 11–14

Albion is an old synonym for Great Britain, often used in poetry. There are various legends to account for its use, referring to some mythical individual named Albion (or Albia, if a woman), but surely this is unnecessary. It seems to come from the Latin word for "white," and anyone standing at Calais and seeing the white cliffs of Dover glimmering on the horizon would need no great imagination to call the island Albion, the "White Land."

(But despite this speech put into his mouth by Shakespeare, John of Brittany had no great stomach to get into the fight in real life and, as I said earlier, did not bring up his forces in time to have them at the battle.)

Charles Delabreth . . .

The French King sends a herald to Henry to ask him to surrender or, if that is refused, to challenge him to battle. He then calls the roll of the great French nobles, whom he urges to rise in their might and destroy the English army. He says:

> *Charles Delabreth* [D'Albret], *High Constable of France,*
> *You Dukes of Orleans, Bourbon, and of Berri,*
> *Alençon, Brabant, Bar, and Burgundy,*
> *Jacques Chatillon, Rambures, Vaudemont,*
> *Beaumont, Grandpré, Roussi, and Faulconbridge,*
> *Foix, Lestrale, Bouciqualt, and Charolois,*
>
> —Act III, scene v, lines 40–45

It is a sonorous and rolling list but it has a grim dramatic irony in it, for it is the list (taken from Holinshed) of those who in a short while are to be dead or captive as an outcome of the battle they are now demanding to fight.

One of the names on the list ought not be there. The Duke of Burgundy, hostile to the Armagnac party, who controlled the French King and Dauphin, was maintaining neutrality. However, Brabant is listed by Holinshed as a brother of Burgundy and the latter name must have caught Shakespeare's hasty eye, in connection with Brabant (and with Bar, which follows immediately after in Holinshed's list), so that all three, with the alliteration of *b*'s, appear together.

. . . from the bridge

Meanwhile, King Henry and his miserable host have been toiling northward, and by October 23, five days after the crossing of the Somme, they have worked their way fifty miles to a small stream called the Ternoise. They are now only forty miles from Calais.

The scene opens with Gower asking his Welsh comrade:

> *How now, Captain Fluellen, come you from the bridge?*
> —Act III, scene vi, lines 1–2

The bridge is one across the Ternoise, which the English army has captured and is crossing. Fluellen grandiloquently praises the fight in his own peculiar fashion, which is to compare everything to the ancient fighters. Exeter, who has led the army, is likened to Agamemnon (see page I–79) and a certain lower officer to Mark Antony (see page I–261).

It turns out that the second man referred to is none other than Pistol, who has, of course, imposed on the credulous Fluellen with his vaunting words rather than with any actual deeds.

. . . stol'n a pax . . .

Pistol comes on the scene, aware that he has impressed Fluellen, and presumes on that fact to ask a favor:

> *Fortune is Bardolph's foe, and frowns on him;*
> *For he hath stol'n a pax, and hangèd must 'a be—*
> *A damnèd death!*
> *Let gallows gape for dog; let man go free,*
> *And let not hemp his windpipe suffocate.*
> —Act III, scene vi, lines 40–44

Holinshed refers to such an incident involving an unnamed soldier. It took place on October 17, the day before the crossing of the Somme, and was intended to show the good order with which the English marched.

One pax was stolen—that is, a picture of the crucifixion which the people kissed during the mass. It was a thing of little intrinsic value but important, of course, to the local church from which it was taken. The soldier who stole it was hanged at the King's own order, nor did the army move till the execution was carried out.

The army could not help but be impressed by this, and, what is more important, the surrounding population could not help but be impressed either. Were it not that the population remained quiet, surely Henry's poor band would have been smothered.

Pistol is here requesting that Bardolph (whom Shakespeare makes the stealer of the pax) be gotten off through Fluellen's influence. Fluellen, however, can do nothing. He is an honest soldier who understands the reason for the King's command to refrain from looting, and the dire necessity that makes the execution irrevocable. He tells Pistol he could not interfere even if it were his own brother who was being executed. Thereupon Pistol insults Fluellen with an obscene gesture and leaves in a fury.

(We cannot help but be surprised at Pistol and rather pleased with him. He has taken trouble for a friend and on that friend's behalf has been willing to anger the redoubtable Fluellen. Good for Pistol!)

The King then enters, inquires as to the recent action, and is told by Fluellen that the only Englishman lost is the one who robbed the church. Fluellen describes Bardolph in such a way that we who know the two parts of *Henry IV* realize that the King must recognize the man. Yet Henry too can do nothing, for as he says, in explaining why it is necessary to forbid loot and execute looters without pity:

> . . . *when lenity and cruelty play for a kingdom, the gentler gamester is the soonest winner.*
>
> —Act III, scene vi, lines 117–19

And that is the end for poor Bardolph.

Montjoy

At this point the herald sent by King Charles reaches King Henry and delivers a lordly speech which, in essence, asks that the English either surrender or be destroyed.

Henry, having listened patiently, asks the herald's name and is answered:

> *Montjoy.*
>
> —Act III, scene vi, line 146

This is not really a name but a title. In ancient times a little mound that acted as a direction post on Roman roads was called "Mons Jovis" ("Mound of Jupiter"), since Jupiter was the god of hospitality and it is certainly a hospitable thing to direct a stranger.

The phrase, corrupted to *montjoie* in French and "montjoy" in English, was used for anything which could be used to direct. The heralds at tournaments, in directing the combatants, would use *montjoie* as their cry, and the phrase became the official title of the chief herald of France.

. . . on to Calais

Henry answers Montjoy with weary frankness:

> . . . *tell thy King, I do not seek him now,*
> *But could be willing to march on to Calais*
> *Without impeachment* [hindrance] . . .
>
> —Act III, scene vi, lines 148–50

Under the circumstances, this is perfectly reasonable, but Henry is cornered, and if the French insist, he will have to fight.

The French do insist, and a battle is now inevitable. The meeting place is at a small village called Agincourt, about five miles north of the Ternoise River. (On modern French maps the name will be found as Azincourt.)

. . . the pipe of Hermes

The French army has placed itself squarely across Henry's path to Calais. If Henry tries to advance he must collide with the French army and (in the French view) be destroyed. If Henry tries to retreat, his ragamuffin army will melt away altogether. If Henry tries to stay where he is, the French army will fall upon him.

It is now the night of October 24, 1415, and the French are supremely confident that the next day will be the last for Henry and his English army. In the French camp, then (to which the scene now shifts), all is optimism and impatience for the daylight.

The Dauphin, pictured by Shakespeare as a foolish fop, can do nothing but talk about his horse. He says:

> . . . the earth sings when he [his horse] touches it. The basest horn of his hoof is more musical than the pipe of Hermes.
>
> —Act III, scene vii, lines 16–18

This is one of the rare places where Shakespeare uses the Greek name of a god—Hermes. It is much more usual for him to call Hermes by the Latin equivalent, Mercury (see page I-9).

One of the feats told of Hermes' childhood was that he cut reeds at a river's edge and made of them the first shepherd's pipes. (This tale is also told of the nature god, Pan, so that such a device is sometimes called a "Panpipe" or "pipes of Pan.")

The Dauphin also says of his horse:

> It is a beast for Perseus:
>
> —Act III, scene vii, lines 20–21

The reference is to Pegasus (see page I-92), the winged horse of Greek myth. It was Bellerophon who rode Pegasus and the Dauphin would have done better to have used that name. However, there is also a connection between Pegasus and Perseus. Perseus had killed the monster, Medusa, and from her blood Pegasus sprang full-grown.

. . . brother Bedford

But what of the English camp?

It is quite different there. The Chorus comes onstage to open the fourth act by describing the somber English army watching the night's passing with apprehension.

King Henry is described as walking through the army, trying at every step to buoy up spirits with his own air of confidence. The result is immortalized in a famous line as Shakespeare has the Chorus say that to all the soldiers the King brought:

> *A little touch of Harry in the night.*
>
> —Act IV, Chorus, line 47

The fourth act proper opens with Henry making his progress through the army, beginning with his brothers. He says:

> *Gloucester, 'tis true that we are in great danger;*
> *The greater therefore should our courage be.*
> *Good morrow, brother Bedford.*
>
> —Act IV, scene i, lines 1–3

The Duke of Bedford (the King's middle brother) was not actually at the Battle of Agincourt. He was back in England, ruling in the King's place. It was the Duke of Clarence (the King's oldest brother) who was at the battle along with Gloucester (the King's youngest brother). The substitution of Bedford for Clarence may be a result of the influence of later events. Clarence died a few years later in France, while Bedford was to live on and become, next to King Henry himself, England's greatest champion in France. To those who know what is to come, Bedford's name would sound better than Clarence's in connection with Agincourt.

. . . Sir Thomas Erpingham

The King then moves on to greet an old officer, who is still fighting with the verve of a youngster. He says:

> *Good morrow, old Sir Thomas Erpingham:*
>
> —Act IV, scene i, line 13

Sir Thomas answers with gay gallantry. On the next day it is he who is to have the honor of giving the signal for the English to start fighting (to "open fire," as we would say today).

Upon Saint Davy's day

After that, King Henry meets Pistol. The King remains unrecognized, for he is muffled in a coat and passes himself off as a Welsh officer. (This is not altogether a lie, for Henry was born in Monmouth, a city that is on the very border of Wales and is often considered Welsh.)

Pistol, under the impression he is speaking to a countryman of Fluellen's, and still smarting from the latter's rebuff in the matter of poor Bardolph, says truculently to the King:

> Tell him [Fluellen] *I'll knock his leek about his pate*
> *Upon Saint Davy's day.*
> —Act IV, scene i, lines 54–55

St. David was a more or less legendary sixth-century Welsh priest who founded many churches through Wales. He became the patron saint of the land and David therefore became a common name among the Welsh. It was pronounced "Taffid" in their dialect and this was familiarized to "Taffy." "Taffy" came to signify a Welshman generally, as in the familiar nursery rhyme that begins (with English prejudice): "Taffy was a Welshman / Taffy was a thief . . ."

One tale told about St. David is that in 540, on the occasion of a battle between the Welsh and the Saxons, the Welsh, on David's advice, wore leeks in their caps in order that they might distinguish friend from foe. (Long afterward, armies adopted distinctive uniforms in order to achieve that same end.) The identification aided them in winning the victory. Presumably, leeks were chosen because the battle happened to take place in a field where leeks were growing.

It became customary, then, for Welshmen to wear leeks on St. David's feast day, which was March 1. It was their way of distinguishing themselves from the Saxons still, and of maintaining their national identity even under conditions where they had been under foreign control for centuries. The custom is precisely analogous to the more familiar situation (to ourselves in America) of the Irishmen wearing the representation of a shamrock on St. Patrick's Day.

To offer to knock off a Welshman's leek on St. David's Day is to insult not only him, but his very Welshness. It is hitting Fluellen at the very core of his being.

. . . in Pompey's camp . . .

Pistol leaves but the King remains on one side of the stage and can over-hear, without being observed, when Gower and Fluellen enter. As soon as Gower opens his mouth, Fluellen shushes him for making too much noise on the battlefield, lecturing him, as is his wont, on the ancient usages. He says:

> *If you would take the pains but to examine the wars of Pompey the Great, you shall find, I warrant you, that there is no tiddle taddle nor pibble pabble in Pompey's camp . . .*
> —Act V, scene i, lines 68–71

Pompey the Great is best known in history not for his victories but for his defeat by Julius Caesar (see page I–257). It is typical of Fluellen's pedantry that he should enlarge so on Pompey rather than on Caesar.

King Henry is rather impressed by Fluellen. He recognizes, as the audience must, that behind all those eccentricities is solid worth.

. . . if the cause be not good . . .

King Henry next encounters three common soldiers, John Bates, Alexander Court, and Michael Williams, all depressed and all fearful of what the dawning day will bring.

Michael Williams, the most outspoken of the three, even dares to wonder openly whether all they have gone through and are to go through is in a just cause. He says:

> *. . . if the cause be not good, the King himself hath a heavy reckoning to make, when all those legs and arms and heads, chopped off in a battle, shall join together at the latter day . . .*
> —Act IV, scene i, lines 136–39

At the day of judgment many of the dead soldiers will have been found, in other words, to have died in sin, and since they have died as a result of following the King's orders, the King is responsible for that.

The King (pretending to be a common soldier) argues otherwise, maintaining that each soldier is responsible for the state of his own soul and can lay the blame nowhere else.

Williams, still gloomy, apparently thinks the King would not be so ready to commit his men to battle if he were not sure of being ransomed himself, even if defeated and taken. When the King says that he has heard that the King would not let himself be ransomed (but, presumably, would fight to the end), Williams says, cynically:

> *Ay, he said so, to make us fight cheerfully; but when our throats are cut, he may be ransomed, and we ne'er the wiser.*
> —Act IV, scene i, lines 197–99

This was not altogether cynicism, either. At the Battle of Poitiers (see page II–259) French commoners died in droves, while French King John was taken into a very comfortable imprisonment pending his ransom.

It was, in fact, one of the horrors of medieval warfare that the noblemen who instigated and led the fighting were very rarely killed but were taken courteously, treated gently, and held for ransom (after all, it might be the captor's turn to be taken prisoner in the next battle), while the peasant, ill armed or unarmed, and fighting only because he would be killed if he didn't fight, was ruthlessly murdered. The peasant had no money to offer as ransom, you see.

The King (still as a common soldier) answers so vigorously that it comes to a quarrel. They can't fight now, of course, but they agree to fight at a more convenient time. They exchange gloves in token and agree to wear them in their caps as a gesture of defiance. Williams says angrily:

> *This will I also wear in my cap. If ever thou come to me and say, after tomorrow, "This is my glove," by this hand, I will take thee a box on the ear.*
> —Act IV, scene i, lines 218–21

Not today, O Lord

Despite his self-confident bearing with the men of the army, King Henry, once he is left alone, finds himself a prey to the agony of responsibility and self-doubt, and like his father before him (see page II–402) envies the lowborn, who can at least sleep while cares hound the King to wakefulness.

He then thinks of the possibility of divine punishment, and falls to prayer, saying:

> *Not today, O Lord,*
> *O, not today, think not upon the fault*
> *My father made in compassing the crown!*
> *I Richard's body have interred new,*
> *And on it have bestowed more contrite tears*
> *Than from it issued forced drops of blood.*
> —Act IV, scene i, lines 297–302

The theme of the four plays beginning with *Richard II* thus reaches its climax. If the Plantagenet line remains under its curse that followed the murder of Thomas of Gloucester (see page II–267), then the final blow might follow if Henry's army was destroyed and himself killed. That would plunge England into sure civil war once again and a resurgent and vengeful France might, this time, invade England during the chaos and serve it as Henry V was trying to serve France.

On the other hand, if Henry's army won free, might it not be an indication that the initial crime of the death of Thomas of Gloucester had finally been expiated, that England had been forgiven?

Henry's reburial of Richard, his tears of contrition and penitence, and (as he goes on to detail) his works of charity and piety on Richard's behalf might well be sincere regret, for there is good reason to suppose he loved Richard and sorrowed over his fall (see page II–309). It might also be an anxious supplication of heaven. And it might also be good politics. Open display of grief and penance might prevent the people of England from fearing heaven's hand against Henry and might hamper rebellious nobles who could otherwise use the ghost of Richard to raise revolt at home while Henry was absent in France.

. . . *full three-score thousand*

The sun rises now. The hosts oppose each other. The odds are most uneven. Westmoreland, speaking of the French, says:

> *Of fighting men they have full three-score thousand.*
> —Act IV, scene iii, line 3

And Exeter responds:

> *There's five to one; besides they all are fresh.*
> —Act IV, scene iii, line 4

In other words, twelve thousand English, worn out and bedraggled from a backbreaking march, are facing sixty thousand fresh Frenchmen. The odds may be exaggerated (and some English accounts go even further and make the odds ten to one) but the lowest estimate is that the French had a three-to-one advantage, and that is enough too.

. . . *good Salisbury* . . .

One English lord now makes his first appearance in the play. He makes a brave speech and as he leaves to take over his portion of the line, Bedford says:

> Farewell, good Salisbury, and good luck go with thee!
>> —Act IV, scene iii, line 11

Salisbury is Thomas Montacute, 4th Earl of Salisbury. He is the son of John of Salisbury, who tried to raise an army in Wales on behalf of Richard II (see page II–292) and then fought loyally for Richard to the end.

The earlier Salisbury had been a prominent Lollard (see page II–328) and had met his end in 1400 at the hands of an anti-Lollard mob. The younger Salisbury now fought loyally for the son of the man against whom his father had fought, and for the King who had destroyed Lollardy. Call it patriotism.

. . . the Feast of Crispian

The King enters just in time to hear Westmoreland wish that some of the soldiers uselessly in England were with them at the field, to reduce the odds. The King, overhearing, begins a wonderful speech in which he asks for not more men, but fewer, since with defeat, the fewer men the less harm to England, while with victory, the fewer men the greater honor to England. He says:

> . . . if it be a sin to covet honor
> I am the most offending soul alive.
>> —Act IV, scene iii, lines 28–29

Here Henry V is playing the role of Hotspur (see page II–341), but, as we shall see, with more rationality and patience.

The King goes on to say:

> This day is called the Feast of Crispian:
>> —Act IV, scene iii, line 40

According to a legend which can be traced back no further than the eighth century, Crispin and Crispian were two brothers, Christians, living in Rome. They fled the persecution of Christians begun under the Roman Emperor Diocletian. They traveled to Soissons in what was then Gaul (later France), and there they remained in hiding, supporting themselves as shoemakers. In 286 they were found and beheaded, presumably on October 25, which became their day of commemoration. They were the patron saints of shoemakers and their day was particularly celebrated in France. And it was on October 25, 1415, that the Battle of Agincourt was to be fought.

. . . we happy few . . .

In moving words, King Henry forecasts how in future years all who participate in the battle will recall with delight their part in it and ends with lines that are sheer magic:

> *We few, we happy few, we band of brothers;*
> *For he today that sheds his blood with me*
> *Shall be my brother; be he ne'er so vile,*
> *This day shall gentle his condition.*
> *And gentlemen in England, now abed,*
> *Shall think themselves accursed they were not here;*
> *And hold their manhoods cheap whiles any speaks*
> *That fought with us upon Saint Crispin's day.*
>
> —Act IV, scene ii, lines 60–67

Can Henry really have been so confident before a battle in which the odds were so enormously against him? Or is it a speech made up by a writer who has the advantage of hindsight? To be sure, Shakespeare didn't make up the essence of the speech (though he improved upon that essence wonderfully); it comes from Holinshed. Yet Holinshed was writing with hindsight too.

On the other hand, all evidence points to the fact that Henry V was a competent general. With the dawn he had a chance to study the field and the general conditions; he knew the nature of the French force and how he intended to counter them. Perhaps he honestly thought that, odds or no odds, he had a good chance to win. If so, it was not (as we shall see) without reason.

. . . the lion's skin

The Chief Herald of France again arrives to demand surrender. It is, in the view of the French, Henry's last chance to evade destruction. Henry answers with calm pride that they had better win their victory first before worrying about what to do with the supposedly beaten English. He says:

> *The man that once did sell the lion's skin*
> *While the beast lived, was killed with hunting him.*
>
> —Act IV, scene iii, lines 93–94

This is reminiscent of a reply made by King Ahab of Israel to a Syrian demand for surrender under similar circumstances to those at Agincourt.

Ahab said (1 Kings 20:11): "Tell him, Let not him that girdeth on his harness boast himself as he that putteth it off."

Henry goes on to say that even if his soldiers are killed, they will do mischief to France after death. He says of the prospective English corpses:

> . . . the sun shall greet them
> And draw their honors reeking up to heaven,
> Leaving their earthly parts to choke your clime,
> The smell whereof shall breed a plague in France.
>
> —Act IV, scene iii, lines 100–3

This is, again, a most unpleasant passage to wish upon the knightly King, and Shakespeare (we may assume) is once again voicing his own detestation of war and of its horrors.

The leading of the vaward

The Duke of York rushes in and says:

> My lord, most humbly on my knee I beg
> The leading of the vaward.
>
> —Act IV, scene iii, lines 130–31

This is the same man who, as Aumerle, had been friend to Richard II and conspirer against Henry IV fifteen years before (see page II–273). It was his younger brother, the Earl of Cambridge, who had conspired against Henry V just a few months earlier and who had been hanged in consequence.

Perhaps it is to prevent himself from moving into personal eclipse as a result of the deeds of himself and his brother that he now makes the grand gesture of offering to lead the foremost ranks against the French.

. . . both hanged . . .

The battle opens with a comic scene between a swaggering Pistol and a quivering French captive, as Pistol demands ransom, with neither able to understand the other's language.

The Boy (Falstaff's onetime page) must do the translating. Of course, the Boy can scarcely be a boy any longer. He was given to Falstaff immediately after the Battle of Shrewsbury, which was in 1403. It is now 1415. If the Boy had been eight years old when he walked behind Falstaff at the start of Henry IV, Part Two, he is twenty now.

However, Shakespeare is not bound by chronology and the Boy is still treated as too young to fight. He is, perhaps, twelve or thirteen.

The French soldier finally manages to make it plain he will pay ransom and he and Pistol go marching off. The Boy, remaining behind, says of Pistol in contempt:

> Bardolph and Nym had ten times more valor than this roaring devil i'th'old play that everyone may pare his nails with a wooden dagger; and they are both hanged; and so would this be, if he durst steal anything adventurously.
>
> —Act IV, scene iv, lines 72–77

We know that Bardolph was hanged for stealing that pax. This is the first word we have, though, that Nym was hanged too. We may presume it was for desertion.

The Boy goes on to say that he will stay with the luggage, which is being guarded by the boys only, all the men being off in fight. (The English numbers are too few to allow any to be detached for merely non-combat support.)

. . . tout est perdu

And then we switch suddenly to the French, who, from their earlier almost hysterical confidence, are suddenly in the depths of despair. The Duke of Orléans cries out to the Constable:

> O Seigneur! le jour est perdu, tout est perdu!
>
> —Act IV, scene v, line 2

That is: "O, sir! The day is lost, all is lost!"

What happened? How could the French lose, with all the odds so much in their favor?

To Shakespeare this is no problem, nor to the Elizabethan audience. After all, the French outnumbered the English only five to one, and it might be considered an article of faith to Englishmen in those times that one English soldier was at least as good as five miserable Frenchmen, so of course the English won.

We need not accept that for a moment. Even a modern Englishman would no longer accept that. The French are as brave fighters and soldiers as any in the world and have shown that to be true in more instances than is worth repeating. We need go no further than to say that in the end they drove every Englishman out of France.

Well then, what happened at Agincourt?

The answer is that the odds were not in French favor after all, not when all the factors were taken into account.

In the first place, the overconfident, poorly led French threw away the undeniable advantage they had possessed in numbers by choosing to fight on a front that was no more than a thousand yards wide, with either flank blocked off by dense woods. Only so many Frenchmen could be squeezed into those thousand yards, so that the English faced an actual front line little more numerous than themselves.

This still left the French with ample reserves, of course, but there was another matter.

The backbone of the French army was the armored knight. The large horse, covered with armor and bearing an armored knight on his back, represented a formidable mass when it charged, but could it charge? The ground had been damped down and turned to mud by the rainy spell that had made Henry's march such a horror, and the field was a quagmire. When the time came for the battle to start and for the French to advance, the line just stood there as the horses labored to lift their hoofs out of the clinging mud.

The English army, on the other hand, lacked horsemen and remained mobile. What's more, it consisted chiefly of archers, well trained in the use of the longbow. The lengthy, sturdy arrows shot out at tremendous speeds, could make their way through armor at surprisingly long distances. (Few of us know, nowadays, what the sight and sound of a large flight of long arrows is like. Perhaps the most dauntingly wonderful scene in the excellent motion picture made of this play by Sir Laurence Olivier is the one in which the arrows fly hissingly against the sky. It freezes the blood.)

The arrows landed among the thick ranks of the French, spreading destruction and confusion among soldiers who could hardly move. When French chaos was at its height, Henry ordered his footmen forward with ax and sword. It was a slaughterhouse in which the French didn't have a chance.

Even if the French had managed to charge—which they never did—it would probably have done them little good. Henry had surrounded his archers with stakes, blunt ends buried firmly in the ground, hard and sharpened ends upward. A charge would have broken when the first horses were impaled.

Could Henry V have foreseen the course of the battle?

Why not? Was it difficult to see the narrow breadth of the battlefield and the muddy nature of the ground? Was it hard to calculate the result of a battle between skilled archers and heavy, unmaneuverable horsemen? Remember that Henry had the advantage of remembering the one-sided archery victories of the English against the Scots in the last couple of decades (see page II–322).

It is not surprising, then, that Henry maintained his confidence despite the odds that were apparently against his army. It is not even surprising that he could state that he preferred fewer men to more—for his victory was sure even with fewer men, and the greater the odds against him the more psychologically devastating would the victory be.

And indeed, Agincourt became the most celebrated victory in English history, right down to the Battle of Britain in 1940. It would be years before the French could emerge from the psychological disaster they suffered and dare fight the English without feeling half defeated to begin with.

The noble Earl of Suffolk . . .

The English casualties were few—and included only two titled noblemen. One was the Duke of York, who had earlier demanded the honor of leading the van. King Henry asks for him and Exeter tells him York is dead:

> . . . and by his bloody side,
> Yoke-fellow to his honor-owing wounds,
> The noble Earl of Suffolk also lies.

> —Act IV, scene vi, lines 8–10

Thus ends the life of Aumerle of *Richard II.* As for the Earl of Suffolk, Holinshed lists him as a casualty, but beyond that I can find nothing more concerning him.

. . . kill his prisoners

The very extent of the victory at Agincourt was embarrassing to the English in one respect. They were encumbered with prisoners whom the various captors were holding for ransom. When it seemed to the English leaders that the French were rallying or that new contingents were reaching the field, the English had to rid themselves of the encumbrance that they might fight. They were too few in number to set aside a contingent large enough to guard the prisoners and make sure these would not escape and rejoin the French.

King Henry therefore gave a lamentable order, saying:

> The French have reinforced their scattered men.
> Then every soldier kill his prisoners!
> Give the word through.

> —Act IV, scene vii, lines 36–38

It was a deplorable atrocity, perpetrated under a mistaken impression, for the French were in no condition to renew the battle and the prisoners might have been safely held and ransomed.

The English themselves, not inclined to let anything spoil the glory of Agincourt, nevertheless feel a little hangdog about it and try to excuse it. It was done in the heat of battle, they say, and what's more in reprisal for a French atrocity, for the story as told later was that fleeing French soldiers out of frustration at their defeat pillaged the baggage and slaughtered the boys left in charge.

Shakespeare makes use of this atrocity as excuse. Gower and Fluellen come onstage and Gower says:

> 'Tis certain there's not a boy left alive, and the cowardly rascals that ran from the battle ha' done this slaughter;
> —Act IV, scene vii, lines 5–7

Since the Boy had earlier mentioned he was among those guarding the baggage, we may assume he is now dead. That, then, is the end of Falstaff's page and of the Robin of *The Merry Wives of Windsor.*

And yet the killing of the boys is not as good an excuse for the atrocity reprisal as it might seem. It was not the French soldiers who had done this, according to the best information we have, but civilians of the area who took advantage of the battle to loot the camp.

In any case, does Shakespeare approve of the killing of the prisoners even if the excuse is as he gives it? Or does he view this as just another of the unforgivable atrocities inseparable from war? If the latter, he cannot say so directly; not in connection with the great and glorious Battle of Agincourt and the knightly hero-king Henry V. The audience would not have endured it and Shakespeare was not the type to boldly cast defiance into the teeth of an audience.

But he might be indirect about it. He has Gower say, after describing the death of the boys:

> . . . wherefore the King most worthily hath caused every soldier to cut his prisoner's throat. O, 'tis a gallant king!
> —Act IV, scene vii, lines 8–11

Surely, "worthily" is the wrong adjective. The King might much better have done it "sorrowfully" or "regretfully" or even "wrathfully." "Worthily" sounds sarcastic. Even more so does "gallant king" sound sarcastic.

War, Shakespeare seems to be saying as clearly as he dares, ruins what it touches, and even a great and merciful king is made a monster by it.

. . . Alexander the Pig . . .

Gower's remark about the killing of the prisoners and of the gallantry of King Henry is followed at once by Fluellen's estimate of the King, making use (as he always does) of ancient warriors for the purpose. Fluellen points out that King Henry was born at Monmouth (which makes him Welsh by place of birth, if not by ancestry), then asks:

> *What call you the town's name where Alexander the Pig was born?*
>
> —Act IV, scene vii, lines 13–14

Gower instantly corrects him, explaining that he means Alexander the Great, and the short-tempered Fluellen asks captiously if Pig (Big) is not equivalent to great. There is an easy laugh here, thanks to the Welsh habit of sounding *b* like *p*, but is that the only reason Shakespeare makes use of the phrase? Can he be hinting that even Alexander, the ideal warrior and the greatest of all conquerors, had his swinish aspects?

And is it an accident that Fluellen then goes on to draw parallels between Alexander and Henry?

. . . his best friend, Cleitus

There is ample room for similarities between Alexander and Henry (see page II–452). Fluellen cites none of these similarities but sinks in bathos when he can only dredge up the fact that there is a river both in Monmouth (Henry's birthplace) and Macedon (Alexander's birthplace):

> *. . . and there is salmons in both.*
>
> —Act IV, scene vii, line 32

But then Fluellen goes on to something specific and significant. He says:

> *Alexander, God knows, and you know, in his rages, and his furies, and his wraths, and his cholers, and his moods, and his displeasures, and his indignations, and also being a little intoxicates in his prains, did, in his ales and his angers, look you, kill his best friend, Cleitus.*
>
> —Act IV, scene vii, lines 35–41

The incident took place at a banquet in 327 B.C. in Maracanda (the modern Samarkand) after Persia had fallen and Alexander had reached its extreme northeastern corner. Alexander had grown dizzy with success, had heard himself hailed as a god and more than half believed it. Besides, he had drunk too much and he couldn't hold his liquor.

Alexander listened complacently while those about him praised his deeds as far superior to those of his father, Philip of Macedon.

Cleitus (or Clitus), a boyhood friend of Alexander, who had saved the King's life at the first battle fought in Asia, listened with gathering anger.

Rather drunk himself, he rose to defend Philip and denounce Alexander. In a fury, Alexander seized a spear, ran him through, and killed him.

Gower indignantly repudiates this incident as comparable to nothing in Henry's life, and Fluellen mentions the repudiation of Falstaff. The comparison is quite inept, however, but it gives rise to another thought.

Why pick out one of the most disgraceful episodes in Alexander's life for a comparison? Why stress Alexander's rage under the influence of intoxication with wine, if not, perhaps, to have us think of Henry's rage under the influence of intoxication with victory.

Is it the comparison with the killing of the prisoners that is being hinted at? Is Shakespeare (through Fluellen) trying to encourage the audience to think of it themselves without directly saying so?

It is tempting to think this, for immediately after Fluellen's speech, King Henry comes on the scene, furious (presumably at the news of the slaughter of the boys), so that the similarity to Alexander "in his rages" becomes evident. Henry says:

> *I was not angry since I came to France*
> *Until this instant.*
> —Act IV, scene vii, lines 57–58

And then, quite superfluously, but rather as though Shakespeare were laboring to make his point, Henry orders the atrocity a second time. He says:

> *. . . we'll cut the throats of those we have,*
> *And not a man of them that we shall take*
> *Shall taste our mercy.*
> —Act IV, scene vii, lines 65–67

He orders that told to the remnants of the French forces still on the field.

. . . where leeks did grow . . .

With the battle over, Fluellen approaches King Henry and says:

> *Your* [great] *grandfather of famous memory, an't please your Majesty, and your great-uncle, Edward the Black Prince of Wales, as I have read in the chronicles, fought a most prave pattle here in France.*
> —Act IV, scene vii, lines 94–98

The reference can only be to the Battle of Crécy (see page II–257). The two battles were fought in the same general area, by the way. Crécy is only about twenty miles southwest of Agincourt.

Fluellen goes on to say, concerning the battle:

> *. . . the Welshmen did good service in a garden where leeks did grow, wearing leeks in their Monmouth caps . . .*
>
> —Act IV, scene vii, lines 101–3

This casts a glow of patriotism over the matter of wearing leeks. Instead of referring it to a battle against the Saxons, it places it (quite wrongly) in a battle against the French. Furthermore, Fluellen stresses the Welsh as Monmouth men, for it was in Monmouth that Henry was born.

Consequently, when Fluellen asks the King to wear the leek on St. David's Day, Henry agrees, adding:

> *For I am Welsh, you know, good countryman.*
>
> —Act IV, scene vii, line 108

This is only in the sense that he was born in Monmouth, but of course, it is symbolic of the unity that befalls all men of the kingdom, Welsh as well as English, in the aftermath of the great victory.

But one last sting remains. Fluellen, swelling with pride over the King's acknowledgment of Welshhood, cannot resist making it look as though it is the King who is honored, not the Welsh. He says, with unconscious patronization, and even more than a little *lèse-majesté:*

> *I need not be ashamed of your Majesty, praised be God, so long as your Majesty is an honest man.*
>
> —Act IV, scene vii, lines 116–18

King Henry answers with gentle and grave courtesy, but can it be that Shakespeare is hinting, through Fluellen, that even Henry V might not always be an honest or good man and that in such a case one ought to be ashamed even of the hero-king?

. . . Alençon and myself . . .

Now Williams enters. He is the soldier who exchanged gloves with the King when the latter pretended to be a common soldier.

The King, wishing to get some amusement out of the fiery Fluellen (or, conceivably, to get back at the Welshman's condescension in wishing him an honest man?), passes to him the glove he had received from Fluellen the night before. He says to Fluellen:

*Here, Fluellen, wear thou this favor for me and stick it in thy
cap; when Alençon and myself were down together I plucked
this glove from his helm.*

—Act IV, scene vii, lines 155–58

Shakespeare is making use here of some of the Homeric details that
gathered about the battle in later legends. King Henry was said to have
fought in single battle with John, Duke of Alençon, who had been promoted to the dukedom less than a year before. The story is that King Henry
was beaten down and might have been killed if his guard had not rushed up
and killed Alençon. Henry was supposed to have tried to save Alençon's
life but the infuriated guard were beyond control.

Alençon's grandfather, Charles of Alençon, was brother of King Philip
VI of France. He had been an earlier casualty at the hands of the English,
having died at Crécy.

Fluellen wears the glove, having been told that anyone who offers to
strike him for it is a friend of Alençon's and therefore an enemy.

My Lord of Warwick . . .

Henry merely wants to be amused; he doesn't want any real trouble.
Consequently, he has someone supervise the results. He says:

*My Lord of Warwick, and my brother Gloucester,
Follow Fluellen closely at the heels.*

—Act IV, scene vii, lines 173–74

Warwick appeared in minor fashion in *Henry IV, Part Two* (see page
II–402) and his appearance in this play is even more fugitive.

Fluellen meets Williams, who strikes him. Fluellen falls instantly into a
Welsh pepper pot of anger, until the King finally separates them and owns
up to the truth.

Williams, undaunted, carries himself well and honestly against the King
himself, saying that the King presented himself as a common soldier and
therefore could not take exception to being treated as one. The King admits the justice of the argument and rewards the sturdy Williams with a
gloveful of crowns—to which Fluellen grandiosely adds a shilling.

. . . ten thousand French

The heralds have meanwhile been surveying the field of battle and making what we would today call a "body count." Among the highest-ranking
prisoners, says Exeter, is:

Charles Duke of Orleans, nephew to the King;

—Act IV, scene viii, line 78

Charles of Orléans was taken to England after his capture and remained there for twenty-five years. It was a splendid captivity for him, however. He was treated with the full honor of his rank and he spent his time in ease and comfort, writing poetry to his heart's content.

It was not till 1440 that he was released and returned to France. The young twenty-one-year-old who had been captured at Agincourt came back an elderly man (for those times) of forty-six. It was far too late for him to gain re-entry into the field of French politics, so he withdrew to private life and became a patron of literature.

In a way, though, Charles of Orléans had the last laugh (posthumously) over Henry of England. Charles's son became King of France in due time, whereas Henry's son, before he died, was not even King of England.

But that is in the future. King Henry, listening to the names of the prisoners, says:

> *This note doth tell me of ten thousand French*
> *That in the field lie slain.*

—Act IV, scene viii, lines 82–83

The list of the noble dead is given, taken right out of Holinshed, as is the number of the English dead. King Henry reads off the latter:

> *Edward the Duke of York, the Earl of Suffolk,*
> *Sir Richard Ketly, Davy Gam, esquire;*
> *None else of name; and of all other men*
> *But five-and-twenty.*

—Act IV, scene viii, lines 105–8

The figure of twenty-five English dead in combat seems incredibly low, but there have been one-sided casualty lists in later, more thoroughly documented battles. Thus, in the Battle of New Orleans, fought on January 8, 1815 (just four hundred years after Agincourt), the tables were turned on the English. They suffered over two thousand casualties fighting an American army, while the Americans lost exactly eight killed and thirteen wounded.

Still, Holinshed himself implies that the report of twenty-five English dead is unreliable and that a figure of five or six hundred is more likely. Some figures are even as high as sixteen hundred. However, it seems quite probable that the French losses outweighed those of the English by at least ten to one.

O God . . .

The listing of casualties extorts from Henry the cry:

> *O God, thy arm was here!*
> *And not to us, but to thy arm alone,*
> *Ascribe we all!*
> —Act IV, scene viii, lines 108–10

The night before, Henry had prayed that God might not remember the deposition of Richard II and thus had God answered. The sweep of the tetralogy from *Richard II* to *Henry V* might seem to go from crime to punishment to forgiveness, and England stood (or was about to stand) on the sunlit peak of victory and prosperity, clean of sin once more.

(That peak was, of course, only a temporary one. All things are temporary in history.)

. . . and to England then

With the battle over, Henry V could return to his original march to reach Calais. Of course, it was no longer as a fugitive, broken army trying to avoid the French and hide its wounds—but rather as the most gloriously victorious band of men England had ever seen.

The battle had not changed the English materially. It had not brought them more men or altered their bedraggled condition. They were still few and sick and could not remain in France as they were. What they had won, for the moment, was still only a safe passage to Calais.

But oh, the glory they carried with them. Who in England would count numbers or ask the cost now? Henry says, exultantly:

> *. . . to Calais; and to England then;*
> *Where ne'er from France arrived more happy men.*
> —Act IV, scene viii, lines 127–28

They reached Calais, finally, on October 29, four days after Agincourt, and three weeks to the day after they had left Harfleur.

. . . their conqu'ring Caesar . . .

The English army remained in Calais till November 17, resting, and then returned to England. Henry V entered London in triumph on November 23, 1415, having been away from England for three and a half months.

The speech of the Chorus that opens the fifth act describes England's response:

> How London doth pour out her citizens!
> The mayor and all his brethren in best sort—
> Like to the senators of th'antique Rome,
> With the plebeians swarming at their heels—
> Go forth and fetch their conqu'ring Caesar in;
> —Act V, Chorus, lines 24–28

The Chorus could compare it only to a Roman triumph (see page I-254), and indeed, had Henry been a general of the Roman republic and had he won a battle such as Agincourt, he would most surely have earned, and been awarded, a triumph.

. . . the general of our gracious Empress

Next, in an almost gratuitous aside, Shakespeare has the Chorus say something which succeeds in dating the first production of the play with unusual exactness. The Chorus draws a comparison between London's gaiety at Henry's return and what would follow—

> Were now the general of our gracious Empress
> (As in good time he may) from Ireland coming,
> Bringing rebellion broached on his sword,
> How many would the peaceful city quit
> To welcome him!
> —Act V, Chorus, lines 30–34

"The general of our gracious Empress" is the Earl of Essex (see page I-119), of whose party Shakespeare was a devoted member.

Essex had been put in charge of an army to suppress an Irish rebellion under Hugh O'Neill, Earl of Tyrone. Essex left England on March 27, 1599, and the play must have had its first showing in the three-month interval that followed it, for by the end of June it had become quite apparent that Essex had failed miserably.

He returned no "conqu'ring Caesar" at all, but a defeated soldier, full of blame for those whose lack of support he considered to have doomed his efforts.

Another general was sent to Ireland and succeeded where Essex had failed. Essex then grumpily rebelled against the "gracious Empress," Queen Elizabeth, and was executed for his pains, an event that must have deeply affected Shakespeare (see page I-120).

The Emperor's coming . . .

The Chorus bids the audience skip over the events of the next couple of years:

> *Now in London place him;*
> *As yet the lamentation of the French*
> *Invites the King of England's stay at home;*
> *The Emperor's coming in behalf of France*
> *To order peace between them; and omit*
> *All the occurrences, whatever chanced,*
> *Till Harry's back-return again to France.*
> —Act V, Chorus, lines 35–41

The "lamentation of the French" increased immeasurably as the result of the Battle of Agincourt. If Henry V had gained no immediate advantage in the way of actual occupied territory, he gained enormously in the way of psychology.

The Armagnacs, who had been led by the now imprisoned Charles of Orléans, bore the full brunt of the blame for the defeat, for the Burgundians had had no part in it. Had John the Fearless of Burgundy moved quickly enough after Agincourt, he might actually have gained control of Paris and with it France, so cast down was the Armagnac prestige.

However, Charles of Orléans was succeeded by Bernard VII, Count of Armagnac and Orléans' father-in-law. Since Constable D'Albret had died at Agincourt, Armagnac appointed himself the new Constable and controlled what was left of the army. Acting more quickly than John the Fearless, Armagnac seized Paris.

The Dauphin, Louis, who had sent the tennis balls to Henry, and who was so in love with his horse on the night before the battle, died in December, two months after Agincourt. His younger brother, John, became Dauphin and died in his turn in April 1417.

The mad King Charles's youngest and only surviving son (only fourteen years old at this time, and also named Charles) now became Dauphin.

Dauphin Charles remained under Armagnac control in the years that followed. In fact, there were times when the only real asset held by the Armagnacs was the Dauphin of France and the legitimacy that he represented.

Meanwhile, though, John the Fearless of Burgundy, who had not been quick enough to seize Paris, managed to hold that city under virtual siege. Doing whatever he could do to cross and thwart the Armagnacs, Burgundy seized control of the Queen of France and declared her Regent, ruling in place of the mentally incapacitated King Charles (but with Burgundy himself in real control).

France advanced closer to anarchy every day and Henry V was content to let the chaos in the land of the enemy grow for a time while he himself remained quietly at home, attending to affairs there and building up a new army for a second foray.

A second advantage accruing to Henry V as a result of the Battle of Agincourt was that it suddenly made him the most important man in Europe. So colossal a victory rang from one end of Christendom to the other. Even the Holy Roman Emperor, the greatest secular prince of the West and the temporal ruler (in theory) of all Christians who owned the Pope as spiritual head, came to visit Henry.

This Emperor was Sigismund. He was the son of one Holy Roman Emperor (Charles IV, who reigned from 1346 to 1378) and the younger brother of another (Wenceslaus, 1378–1400). He was also the brother of "good Queen Anne" of Bohemia, the first wife of Richard II (see page II–269).

He himself had become King of Hungary in 1387, but the Hungarian throne was no bed of flowers in those days. The Turkish armies were then advancing steadily in southeastern Europe, winning victories greater than that of Agincourt, and winning territories far wider and far more permanently than anything Henry V would be able to do. When Sigismund tried to lead an allied Christian army against the Turks at Nikopol on the lower Danube (in what is now northern Bulgaria), he was badly defeated.

In 1411, four years before Agincourt, Sigismund managed to get himself elected Holy Roman Emperor, but that was little improvement over his earlier crown, except in title. The Emperor had little real power and was constantly at the mercy of the powerful higher nobility of a patchwork Germany that remained disunited till the mid-nineteenth century.

The most noteworthy event of Sigismund's reign was the trial of John Huss, the Bohemian church reformer. Huss had agreed to step into the very stronghold of his enemies in order to defend his views, on Sigismund's promise that he would be safe. The promise was worthless. Huss was tried, convicted of heresy, and burned at the stake in 1414, the year before Agincourt, an act which led to years of civil war.

The Emperor was a potentially capable man, but he was hampered by the times and his reign was marked by defeat in war and dishonor at home. Nevertheless, he bore the glorious title of Emperor that had originated with Octavius Caesar (see page I–355), and nothing could erase that. In 1416 the wondering little island of England saw that this Emperor was not too proud to visit them and to meet and confer with King Henry at Canterbury and even sign a treaty with him. It was another helping of glory for King and country.

Finally, on July 23, 1417, Henry V embarked on his second invasion of France. Conditions were even better for him this second time than they had been the first. John the Fearless was now making an attempt to take Paris by force and Henry could count on being faced by demoralized and fearful Armagnacs who would have the dreaded English monsters at their throat and the Burgundians snarling at their flank.

. . . Parca's fatal web

The fifth act opens in France again and Fluellen has yet to pay back Pistol for his insulting remark about the leeks on the night before Agincourt. (Three years and a half have passed since then, but we gather that Pistol has repeated the insult since.)

It is the day after St. David's Day, and therefore March 2, 1418. In the seven months since Henry has arrived in France, he has conquered a good part of Normandy, taking city after city. None dared stand long against the hero of Agincourt, and to be sure, Henry's military leadership was excellent. This campaign is more to be admired than the one-shot stab of Agincourt, however briefly brilliant the latter may have been.

Fluellen tells Gower, indignantly, that on the previous day Pistol had approached Fluellen with bread and salt, suggesting that Fluellen eat the leek he was wearing. Fluellen, unable to answer properly at the moment, was wearing the leek again now and waiting for Pistol. When Pistol appears, Fluellen, with mock politeness, greets him as a scurvy, lousy knave.

Pistol says, grandiloquently:

> Ha, art thou bedlam [mad]? Dost thou thirst, base Trojan,
> To have me fold up Parca's fatal web?
> —Act V, scene i, lines 20–21

"Parcae" is the Roman name for the Fates (see page II–160). Pistol is thus threatening, as he did at one point in Henry IV, Part Two (see page II–398), to cause the Fates to put a close to the web of life they are spinning. In short, he is threatening to kill Fluellen.

. . . Cadwallader . . .

Fluellen is unmoved by the threat. With coldly rising anger, he suggests that Pistol eat the leek. Pistol replies:

> Not for Cadwallader and all his goats.
> —Act V, scene i, line 29

Cadwallader was the legendary King of the Celtic Britons in the sixth century. He led an expedition to the northwestern peninsula of Gaul, a region which had been called Armorica and which thereafter came to be called Brittany. "His goats" is an insulting reference to the Welsh.

That does it. With a rain of blows, Fluellen forces Pistol to eat the leek.

. . . my Doll . . .

Poor Pistol now leaves the stage for the last time, telling us of one final blow. He says:

> *News have I, that my Doll is dead i'th'spital of malady of France* [syphilis]

—Act V, scene i, lines 84–85

At first glance this would seem to refer to Doll Tearsheet, the whore of *Henry IV, Part Two* (see page II-397). In fact, early in the play, when Pistol and Nym are quarreling over the fact that the former has married Mistress Quickly, Pistol advises Nym to take Doll Tearsheet instead, and at that time Doll is referred to as being in the hospital, suffering from syphilis.

Nevertheless, it was Nell Quickly whom Pistol had married and it is very likely that "Doll" is a misprint for "Nell."

So Pistol leaves to return to England, where he plans to live as a pimp and a thief while pretending to be a wounded veteran of the French war. (What other hope for an old soldier anyway in those days, see page II-374.)

Pistol is the last breath of the Falstaff group.

. . . this meeting . . .

Better than two more years pass before the next scene, though there is no indication of that in the play.

The year 1418 had been a terrible one for France. The people of Paris had rebelled against the Armagnacs in May and June, massacring many, including Bernard of Armagnac himself. The Duke of Burgundy had little trouble, then, in forcing an entrance into Paris on July 14 (of all days) and gaining control of both the capital and the mad King.

He already had the Queen. If he could have seized the Dauphin as well, it is very likely that John the Fearless would have controlled all France outside of Normandy, which was in Henry's strong grip.

The Dauphin, however, had been seized by some of the Armagnac party who had managed to leave Paris in the midst of the disturbances and who had, with the Dauphin, retired to Bourges, 120 miles south of Paris. For years afterward, the Dauphin, ineffectual though he was, remained the center of the national resistance to the English.

Meanwhile, Henry V was completing the conquest of Normandy. He laid siege to Rouen, its largest city, the old capital of William the Conqueror (Henry's great-great-great-great-great-great-great-great-great-grandfather).

Rouen held out for seven months, enduring the extremity of privation and starvation. John the Fearless was only seventy-five miles upstream but he never made a move to help. In January 1419 the scarecrow remnants of its population had to give up.

By now the extreme danger of France made it almost an impossible luxury to continue the civil war. John the Fearless and the Dauphin were virtually forced into coming to some sort of understanding that would strengthen the French hand against the English. On July 11, 1419, they reluctantly signed an agreement.

The English were by then almost at the capital, however. They took Pontoise, only twenty miles northwest of Paris, and John the Fearless (what was it he was fearless of, one wonders) decided to abandon the capital without a fight. Taking the poor, mad French King with him, he made for Troyes, about eighty miles southeast of Paris.

The Armagnacs were sure that this was a Burgundian betrayal; that John the Fearless, immediately after having put the Armagnacs off their guard with a faithless treaty, was leaving Paris by arrangement with the English.

The furious Armagnacs asked for another meeting, which took place at Montereau, about midway between Paris and Troyes. There, on September 10, 1419, John the Fearless was struck down by one of the Armagnac faction. He was served as he himself had served Louis of Orléans a dozen years before (see page II–473).

But that made peace between Armagnacs and Burgundians impossible and it ensured the victory of Henry V. One of the French faction would have to gain a kind of miserable victory over the other by being the first to cringe to the English invaders and thus ensure getting its place in the English "new order."

The cringers were the Burgundians, and in the spring of 1420 Henry, who now controlled virtually all of northern France, including Paris itself, met with the Burgundian party in Troyes to make (or rather dictate) a peace. The second scene of the fifth act opens with a reference to this meeting.

King Henry says:

> Peace to this meeting, wherefore we are met!
> —Act V, scene ii, line 1

. . . and to our sister

Henry greets the French peace delegation in the order of rank, beginning with royalty:

> Unto our brother France and to our sister
> Health and fair time of day . . .
> —Act V, scene ii, lines 2–3

This is the first appearance of the French Queen in the play. She is Isabella of Bavaria, usually called Isabeau by the French (and Isabel in the cast of characters). She had been married to King Charles VI in 1385, when she was only fifteen years old. She was now fifty and she had had a miserable life with him after he had gone mad. She tried to take care of him and she bore him numerous children, the youngest being Katherine, who was also present at the peace conference and who, in 1420, was nineteen years old, and the Dauphin Charles, who was now seventeen and who was *not* at the conference, of course.

Isabella was a German, a foreigner, and therefore suspect to the French. Like a much later French queen of German origin, Marie Antoinette, Isabella lacked discretion and gave the gossipmongers a chance to accuse her of light behavior. With telling and retelling, her character was cut to ribbons.

Thus, when her husband was mad, she was rarely out of the presence of Louis of Orléans. There was reason for this, since Louis was the nearest approach to a central authority at that time (see page II–472). The talk, however, was that they were lovers, and there were probably not wanting those who were sure she kept the King mad by her magical arts, although in actual fact she seemed to have sought out every possible cure for his malady.

After the assassination of Louis of Orléans, when France broke apart under the strife of Armagnac and Burgundian, Isabella played a most uncertain role. She switched from side to side in an agony of uncertainty and gained the distrust of both. She ended with the Burgundians, and at the peace meeting at Troyes she played what seemed a particularly despicable part.

. . . Duke of Burgundy

Henry then extends his greetings downward:

> We do salute you, Duke of Burgundy;
> And, princes French, and peers, health to you all!
> —Act V, scene ii, lines 7–8

The Duke of Burgundy here referred to is usually known as Philip the Good. He had succeeded to the dukedom when his father, John the Fearless, was assassinated half a year before.

Since the Dauphin's party had been responsible for the assassination and since the Dauphin himself had been at the scene, the new young Duke (he was only twenty-three at this time) felt a desperate need for revenge. Reluctantly, he threw in his lot with Henry V and was ready to recognize Henry as the successor to Charles VI, rather than see the hated Dauphin gain the crown.

It is he who has arranged the meeting, and he now makes a strong plea for peace, in the eloquence of which it is not hard to detect Shakespeare's own pacifistic views.

. . . compound a boy . . .

The various members of the two parties go off to haggle over the terms of the treaty, while King Henry remains behind with fair Katherine, the French princess.

She is quite a catch, for she has only one brother living, the Dauphin Charles. If he can be disinherited and if the Salic law can be disregarded, then her son will be the next King of France; and if Henry marrys her, that son will be his too, and will therefore be King of England as well.

Henry woos her in blunt soldier's terms, making a virtue of simplicity and directness. He refers to the son they might have:

> *Shall not thou and I, between Saint Denis and Saint George,*
> *compound a boy, half French, half English, that shall go to*
> *Constantinople, and take the Turk by the beard? Shall we*
> *not? What say'st thou, my fair flower-de-luce?*
> —Act V, scene ii, lines 214–18

St. George was the patron saint of England (see page II-224) and St. Denis was the patron saint of France. (Denis is the French version of the Greek Dionysius.) According to the legend, St. Denis was the first bishop of Paris and was martyred in the third century at the age of over a hundred. The martyrdom was by way of decapitation, and the wonder tale has it that he then rose and walked a considerable distance with his head in his hands.

The flower-de-luce (more popularly called the "fleur-de-lis") is the stylized form of the lily used in heraldry. The royal coat of arms of France had such lilies thickly strewn over the shield, but Charles VI reduced them to three.

Henry visualized here a son who would unite England and France under his rule and dreamed that the united kingdom would then be strong enough to face and beat back the Turks, who, as we said, were in his time (and for a century more) marching onward with giant steps through southeastern Europe and toward its very heart.

It is hard to tell whether the reference to Constantinople is an anachronism or not. At the time of the peace conference in Troyes, Constantinople was still in Christian hands. It was almost all that was left of the old Roman Empire but in it there was still a majestic crowned monarch who called himself Roman Emperor and traced a continuous history back in time but over two thousand years. The Roman dominion had begun as but a single city, Rome itself, and now it had ended as but a single city, Constantinople.

Constantinople was ringed by the Turks and yet it held out and was to hold out for an additional generation, not falling till 1453. By Shakespeare's time it had been Turkish for a century and a half and represented all that was fearful about the Turks.

Shakespeare (who was not strong on the minutiae of dates) might have intended to have Henry speak anachronistically of Constantinople as the Turkish capital, meaning that he hoped his son would penetrate to the heart of the Turkish Empire. Or he might have meant he would go to the rescue of still Christian Constantinople.

And yet it does not matter. Poor Henry! His son was never to lead a mighty crusade against the Turks. He was to be a kindly soul who was far more like his mother's father than his own, and in the end he was to hold neither France nor England.

. . . Héritier de France

The others return. The French party has agreed to everything. The last quibble is Charles's reluctance to agree to a form whereby Henry's name is to be included along with his own in papers granting lands and titles. The manner in which Henry's name is to be included is as:

> *"Notre très cher fils Henri, Roi d'Angleterre, Héritier de France"*
>
> —Act V, scene ii, lines 351–52

This means "Our very dear son Henry, King of England, Heir to France." But this too the French agreed to at last.

In other words, the crown was preserved for the mad King during his lifetime as a pathetically puny bit of saved face. Once he was dead, Henry V, as son-in-law, would inherit.

And what of the Dauphin? He was disowned and the implication was that he was not of legitimate birth. Indeed, Queen Isabella was compelled to testify to her own adultery and was made to swear he was not true son of the King.

The Treaty of Troyes was signed on May 21, 1420, and that moment (five and a half years after Agincourt) was the peak of England's medieval grandeur.

There was even a hope at that moment that England and France might have been welded into a single land. Or, as Queen Isabella says:

> *That English may as French, French Englishmen*
> *Receive each other!*
>
> —Act V, scene ii, lines 379–80

(Alas, it was not to happen. It was not till over five hundred years more had passed, at a time when France was once again faced with an abysmal disaster, when Winston Churchill, Prime Minister of England, made a similar suggestion in 1940. That fell through too.)

It was with that hope in mind, though, that Henry took the first step, saying:

> *Prepare we for our marriage . . .*
>
> —Act V, scene ii, line 382

It is the last speech of the play and Shakespeare leaves the King at the peak of his glory.

Henry the Sixth . . .

Only the Epilogue hints at the tragedy to come. The Chorus returns for his final speech (which takes the form of a sonnet) and says:

> *Henry the Sixth, in infant bands crowned King*
> *Of France and England, did this king succeed;*
> *Whose state so many had the managing,*
> *That they lost France, and made his England bleed:*
> *Which oft our stage hath shown . . .*
>
> —Epilogue, lines 9–13

Henry V married Catherine of Valois on June 2, 1420, and took her to England half a year later. On February 23, 1421, she was crowned Queen of England in Westminster.

Henry's brother, Thomas of Clarence, remained in France as the King's viceroy. Despite the Treaty of Troyes, the war continued and was even taking on the character of a national resistance centering about the Dauphin. What's more, success was beginning to spoil the English. Some of them must truly and honestly have believed, after Agincourt, that Englishmen could defeat any number of Frenchmen, however great.

Clarence was, apparently, too careless, and on March 22, 1421, at Baugé, 140 miles southwest of Paris, he was ambushed by a large force of Frenchmen. He was killed and his troops with him, before reinforcements could come up to save him.

Henry had to rush back to France, and on June 12, 1421, he landed in Calais for his third (and last) expedition into France. He was successful as usual in his military ventures, though it took him seven months to reduce the strong point of Meaux, thirty miles east of Paris. (The French weren't so easy to defeat as all that, despite Agincourt.)

While Henry was besieging Meaux, Katherine was bearing him a son at Windsor Castle. The young prince was born on December 6, 1421, and was named Henry. (He was known as Henry of Windsor.) Mother and child came to Paris in the spring of 1422 and Henry still seemed to be in his glory.

But he had fallen sick with symptoms of dysentery during the siege of Meaux and it was getting worse. What the disease was we cannot say now but it was beyond the power of medieval medicine to cure.

Henry V died on August 31, 1422. He was thirty-five years old and he had reigned not quite ten years. Ironically, the mad King of France outlived him, so that Henry V never succeeded to the throne he had won.

Henry's son succeeded him as Henry VI of England, and when mad King Charles died a few months later he became King of France as well. It was in the reign of Henry VI that England lost what she had gained under Henry V. That sad tale was told in plays Shakespeare had written some six or seven years before and they had indeed appeared oft on the stage.

It is to them that we now turn.

36

The History of

HENRY VI, PART ONE

IF WE go by the chronology of the events within Shakespeare's plays, there are, following *Henry V*, three plays that deal with the long, turbulent, and tragic reign of Henry VI, the unfortunate son of the victorious Henry V. The three were among the very first plays written by Shakespeare, and were prepared between 1590 and 1592.

The least of the three is *Henry VI, Part One*, which shows such flaws that many Shakespearean critics think that it is not pure Shakespeare, but that the dramatist merely patched up a pre-existing play.

Some suggest that Shakespeare wrote two plays (those now called *Henry VI, Part Two* and *Henry VI, Part Three*) dealing with the English civil wars of the 1450s and 1460s. He then, perhaps on impulse, went back to an older play dealing with the still earlier events of the reign of Henry VI and made it *Henry VI, Part One* after patching it up to make it fit the other two better.

Indeed, in 1592, just about the time *Henry VI, Part One* may have been produced, Robert Greene wrote a savage satire in which one passage seems to be directed at Shakespeare. Greene's fury, some think, may have been aroused at Shakespeare's patching up of this play. Could it be that Greene was the original author and objected to the changes (as any author surely would)? We will probably never know the details or have a final answer to this question.

. . . *unto Henry's death*

Henry VI, Part One opens with the funeral of Henry V at Westminster Abbey in September 1422, two years after the events that closed *Henry V* on a note of such triumph.

The casket of the great King is brought onto the stage to funereal music, while high-placed English nobles bemoan their loss. The first to speak says:

> *Comets, importing change of times and states,*
> *Brandish your crystal tresses in the sky,*

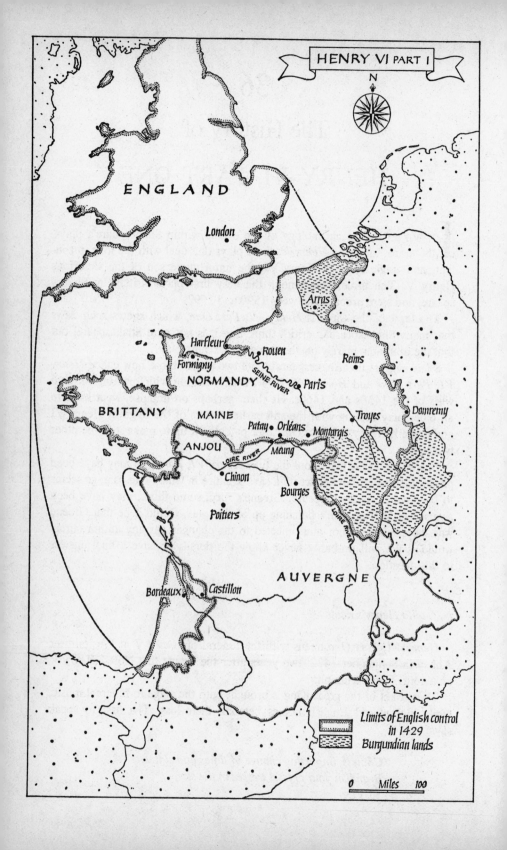

HENRY VI PART I

N

ENGLAND

London

Arras

Harfleur
Rouen
Formigny   Reims
SEINE RIVER
NORMANDY   Paris
                                              Domremy
MAINE   Troyes
BRITTANY
                Patay Orléans
ANJOU   Meung Montargis
        LOIRE RIVER
        Chinon
                Bourges
        Poitiers   LOIRE RIVER

                AUVERGNE

Bordeaux Castillon

Limits of English control
in 1429
Burgundian lands

0   Miles   100

And with them scourge the bad revolting stars
That have consented unto Henry's death!
> —Act I, scene i, lines 2–5

The speaker is John, Duke of Bedford, the older of Henry's two surviving brothers. He played a small part, as John of Lancaster, at the Battle
of Shrewsbury in *Henry IV, Part One* (see page II–364), and a larger role
against the rebels in *Henry IV, Part Two* (see page II–407).

In *Henry V* he was given the newer title of Duke of Bedford, granted
him after Henry V's accession (see page II–415). This is thus the fourth
play in which he appears.

Conjurers and sorcerers . . .

Speaking after Bedford are his younger brother Humphrey of Gloucester,
who was in charge of the mining operations at Harfleur (see page II–479)
and who was later wounded at Agincourt; and Thomas Beaufort, Duke of
Exeter, who also fought at Agincourt (see page II–487).

Exeter, in his speech, takes issue with Bedford for suggesting that the
stars (that is, Fate, or God's will) have caused Henry's death. He says:

Or shall we think the subtle-witted French
Conjurers and sorcerers that, afraid of him,
By magic verses have contrived his end?
> —Act I, scene i, lines 25–27

Actually, this begins the general theme of the play, which is designed to
explain why the French defeated the English. To patriotic Englishmen this
was a great puzzle, for with Agincourt as evidence it seemed plain that
one Englishman could defeat any number of Frenchmen. That the French
were poorly led and that they were prostrated by bad government and
civil war was ignored. That the situation was bound to change once generalship was improved and the civil war ended was also ignored.

The use of witchcraft by the French seemed a more natural explanation.
This is one of the two great causes, then, for the English defeat, and it will
be elaborated in the course of the play.

The church's prayers . . .

Speaking fourth is a churchman, who says of the dead King:

The battles of the Lord of Hosts he fought;
The church's prayers made him so prosperous.
> —Act I, scene i, lines 31–32

The one who speaks is the Bishop of Winchester, Henry Beaufort. He is the second of the three sons of John of Gaunt by his third and last wife, Catherine Swynford (see page II–319), and is therefore the older brother of Thomas of Exeter, who had delivered the previous speech.

Both Winchester and Exeter were half brothers of King Henry IV and therefore half uncles of King Henry V, who now lay in state.

Henry Beaufort had been closely associated with the government of his half brother, Henry IV, serving him as chancellor in 1403 and being appointed Bishop of Winchester, one of the oldest and richest clerical posts in England.

In 1405 he resigned his post as chancellor in order to associate himself with the part of the Prince of Wales (who was later to be Henry V), and in this showed the most pronounced facet of his character, a coldly calculating and overweening ambition. When Henry V succeeded to the crown in 1413, Winchester became chancellor once more, and in 1417 he resigned the post yet again to become a delegate to a huge and important conference of bishops in Constance in southwestern Germany. He even became cardinal for a while as a result.

While Henry V lived, Winchester's power was limited by the existence of a strong king who did not entirely trust him and who finally forced him to give up the cardinalate. With Henry V's death, however, there was going to be a scramble for power among the immediate relatives of the new King, who was still a baby. In this scramble, Winchester was going to be someone to take into account, for in addition to his very real ability, he had the prestige of high churchly office and (most important of all, perhaps) was enormously rich.

. . . an effeminate prince

The ones who were most likely to compete for power over the new King and, through him, over England, were the four men here assembled, two uncles of the new King (Bedford and Gloucester) and two great-uncles (Winchester and Exeter). Bedford and Exeter are primarily soldiers and do not wish to be involved in the cutthroat intrigue of politics.

That leaves Gloucester, who, like Winchester, is primarily a politician. Both are descendants of John of Gaunt, Gloucester a grandson and Winchester a son, but through different wives, and the rivalry between them is inveterate and to the death.

Gloucester lunges at Winchester at once, responding to the latter's comments concerning "the church's prayers." He says:

> The church! Where is it? Had not churchmen prayed,
> His thread of life had not so soon decayed.
> None do you like but an effeminate prince,

Whom, like a schoolboy, you may overawe.
— Act I, scene i, lines 33-36

The hint is that Winchester prayed for death for Henry V, rather than for victory, and had what he wished. One might indeed argue the case for that, for it was certain that Winchester could not advance his ambitions as long as Henry V lived, and he might well have had considerable animosity toward the King for making him give up the title of cardinal.

The reference by Gloucester to "an effeminate prince" is a forecast of what is to come for the new baby King. Gloucester himself could not know, of course, but the audience would know that Henry VI when he grew up was to be extremely pious and unwarlike, therefore "effeminate" and under Winchester's influence.

. . . thou art Protector

Winchester replies, bitterly:

Gloucester, whate'er we like, thou art Protector
And lookest to command the prince and realm.
Thy wife is proud . . .
— Act I, scene i, lines 37-39

By the will of Henry V, John of Bedford was made commander in chief of the armies in France and Humphrey of Gloucester was put in charge of affairs in England. He protected the person of the infant King Henry VI, and was therefore Lord Protector. As Lord Protector, Gloucester would be the logical power behind the throne, as Winchester clearly recognizes.

Unfortunately for himself, Gloucester, though as ambitious as Winchester, was neither as good a politician nor as devious a one.

(Winchester's reference to Gloucester's wife comes to nothing, but foreshadows important events in *Henry VI, Part Two.* Perhaps this is one of those inserts whereby Shakespeare tried to make this play fit the two succeeding ones.)

Thus, at the very start of the play, immediately after the mention of witchcraft, there is brought forward the second reason which Englishmen understood as bringing about the defeat in France. This was the squabbling among the lords at home; the eternal politicking that prevented full attention being paid to the war. There was at least more justification in this as an excuse for the lost war than in witchcraft.

. . . Than Julius Caesar

Bedford labors to soothe the quarrel, saying impatiently:

> *Cease, cease these jars* [quarrels] *and rest your minds in peace;*
>
> —Act I, scene i, line 44

Bedford was indeed the peacemaker, or rather, the attempted peacemaker, of the period, for he wore himself out trying to handle the French abroad and the squabbling nobles at home.

He makes an effort to continue with the solemnity of the funeral. Addressing the dead King, he says:

> *A far more glorious star thy soul will make*
> *Than Julius Caesar . . .*
>
> —Act I, scene i, lines 55–56

This is a reference to a passage in Ovid's *Metamorphoses* (see page I-8) which states that Caesar's soul was placed in the heavens as a star after his assassination.

Actually, Bedford's chief attempt at peacemaking did not come immediately at the funeral. Winchester and Gloucester's most violent quarrel, one that almost led to civil war, did force Bedford to hasten back from France to mediate it, but this took place in April 1425, two and a half years after the death of Henry V.

Compression of time is necessary in historical dramas, of course, and this alone is not to be too seriously found fault with. In *Henry VI, Part One,* however, such compression is carried to an extreme, with distortions added as well. In none of Shakespeare's other histories are the chronicles followed so badly—and that is one argument for supposing that this particular play is not Shakespeare's in essence.

Sad tidings . . .

Thus, immediately after the two causes of the loss of France—witchcraft and internal squabbling—are set forth, the consequences, in terms of defeat, are announced.

A Messenger arrives from France, crying:

> *Sad tidings bring I to you out of France,*
> *Of loss, of slaughter, and discomfiture:*
> *Guienne, Champagne, Rheims, Orleans,*
> *Paris, Guysors, Poictiers, are all quite lost.*
>
> —Act I, scene i, lines 58–61

All this seems to have happened overnight, even as Henry V is being buried. Yet Orléans, for instance, was not the site of an English defeat till 1429, seven years after Henry V's death, and the battle for it will occupy a later part of the play. As for Paris, that was not to be retaken by the French till 1437, fifteen years after Henry V's death.

The list of names is not to be taken literally, however. It merely serves to ring out a litany of defeat, the beginning of the swing of the pendulum back from Henry V's victories. The Messenger places the blame on internal squabblings and says:

> Amongst the soldiers this is mutterèd,
> That here you maintain several factions,
> And whilst a field should be dispatched and fought
> You are disputing of your generals [strategy].
>
> —Act I, scene i, lines 70–73

The Dolphin Charles . . .

A Second Messenger now arrives with additional bad news:

> The Dolphin Charles is crowned king in Rheims;
> The Bastard of Orleans with him is joined;
> Reignier, Duke of Anjou, doth take his part;
> The Duke of Alençon flieth to his side.
>
> —Act I, scene i, lines 92–95

The "Dolphin Charles" is the Dauphin who was disinherited by the Treaty of Troyes (see page II–516). Though disinherited, he did not disappear.

He remained in Bourges in central France, the city to which he had been taken when first the Burgundians and then the English had taken Paris (see page II–513). Behind him rallied that part of France which was not under the control of either the English or the Burgundians.

Charles VI of France, having reigned for forty-two years and having been mad for most of them, died on October 21, 1422, less than two months after the death of Henry V. (By that small a space of time did Henry miss out on the chance of winning the ultimate of his dreams and being actually crowned, officially, at Reims, as King of France.)

Henry's infant son, Henry VI, was crowned King of England on September 1, 1422, and was recognized as King of France by those parts of the land under English control.

The Dauphin, Charles, had himself crowned in Poitiers in November 1422 and became, theoretically, Charles VII. The nation, however, would not accept the coronation as legal until it was performed in the time-honored manner at the cathedral of Reims, and Reims was under the control of the English. (Henry VI was not crowned at Reims, either.)

Charles remained merely the Dauphin, then, until July 17, 1429, when he was finally crowned at Reims. But this took place seven years after the death of Henry V and not on the day of his funeral.

Of the others mentioned in these verses, the Bastard of Orléans is Jean, Comte de Dunois. He was an illegitimate son of that Louis of Orléans who was assassinated by John the Fearless of Burgundy (see page II–473), and a half brother, therefore, of Charles of Orléans, who had been captured at Agincourt (see page II–506).

Dunois was a capable general who joined the forces of the Dauphin in 1420, when the Treaty of Troyes was being signed. He first made his mark in 1427 (five years after Henry V's funeral) on the occasion when the English were laying siege to Montargis, sixty-five miles south of Paris.

Other French towns had been besieged to extremity without the French being able, or willing, to send relief. Harfleur, Rouen, and Meaux had been examples. This time, however, relief was sent under Dunois, and he managed the battle so well that the English experienced heavy losses and were forced to raise the siege. It was a portent of things to come.

Reignier, Duke of Anjou, is better known in history as René I, the Good. Actually, he was only thirteen years old at the time of the death of Henry V, and did not succeed to the title of Anjou until 1434. He is mentioned here not because he was important in himself as far as the progress of the war was concerned, but because he was the father of the woman who was later to become a fateful English queen.

The Duke of Alençon is John II, the son and successor of John I of Alençon, who had died at Agincourt, according to legend in single combat with Henry V (see page II–505). The younger John was likewise only thirteen at the time of Henry's death.

. . . the stout Lord Talbot . . .

Then there arrives a Third Messenger, who comes not to talk of generalities but to describe a specific battle. He says:

> I must inform you of a dismal fight
> Betwixt the stout Lord Talbot and the French.
>
> —Act I, scene i, lines 105–6

It is Talbot who is the true hero of *Henry VI, Part One*. Indeed, one might almost say that this play bears a resemblance in atmosphere and quality to the motion picture *The Green Berets* and Talbot is its John Wayne.

John Talbot was a member of an English aristocratic family, the second son of the 4th Baron Talbot. His life is a chronicle of warfare, for he was one of those who were born to battle. He fought in Wales during the reign of Henry IV, and commanded the English forces in Ireland during the great year of Agincourt.

He first went to France in 1419, four years after Agincourt, and was the fighting mainstay of the English forces there after the death of Henry V. He was the victor of some forty skirmishes and battles and, indeed, was so uniformly victorious that he seemed invincible.

His first mention in this play at this point is in connection with the crisis of the war, the siege of Orléans. This crisis began in 1428, six years after the death of Henry V, and at a time when the English (despite this first scene of the play) were still on the offensive.

. Bedford gathered some ten thousand men, who marched up to the walls of Orléans on October 12, 1428, and put it under siege. This siege, which lasted half a year, was to prove the turning point of the Hundred Years' War.

Orléans was on the middle reaches of the Loire River, seventy miles south of Paris, and halfway between Paris and Bourges, where the Dauphin held his court.

If Orléans were taken, there was little to stop the English from swarming southward. The French, who had suffered enough to break the spirit of the nation ten times over, might very well find it the last straw and the French national spirit might well have been overthrown at last (at least for a while).

At the siege were a number of important English leaders, and John Talbot, the ever victorious, was one of them. He was just about forty years old at this time.

Retiring from the siege . . .

But the siege of Orléans was broken at last under particularly remarkable circumstances, as we shall see. And in the aftermath, Talbot was *not* victorious. The Third Messenger explains:

> *The tenth of August last, this dreadful lord,*
> *Retiring from the siege of Orleans,*
> *Having full scarce six thousand in his troop,*
> *By three and twenty thousand of the French*
> *Was round encompassed and set upon.*
> —Act I, scene i, lines 110–14

The story, as the Third Messenger tells it, is that Talbot, even though outnumbered four to one, held out for three hours with Talbot wreaking personal destruction beyond imagination. (He was called "the English Achilles" by his later admirers.)

Actually, Talbot might have fought like a hero, but he had also fought like a fool. The version given here in the play has scarcely anything in common with the facts. Talbot was *not* ambushed and might easily have avoided a battle and escaped when a French force (consisting of only eight thousand men and *not* twenty-three thousand) approached him at Patay in June 1429 (and *not* August 10), some fifteen miles northwest of Orléans.

The trouble was that Talbot was humiliated at having had to retreat from Orléans, and with the odds four to three against him (*not* four to one) he decided to fight. Of course, such a keen sense of "honor" is often praised by those who are safe at home, but the Battle of Patay caused the unnecessary deaths of two thousand Englishmen, and that is a high price to pay for Talbot's wanting to pay back his humiliation.

. . . Sir John Falstaff . . .

Talbot's defeat was blamed not only on ambush by a superior force but also on treason. The Third Messenger explains that Talbot's strong fight might have won after all:

> *If Sir John Falstaff had not played the coward.*
> *He, being in the vanward, placed behind*
> *With purpose to relieve and follow them,*
> *Cowardly fled, not having struck one stroke.*
> —Act I, scene i, lines 131–34

The Sir John Falstaff mentioned here is actually Sir John Fastolfe, and the latter is the name given in other editions of this play. (It was because of this passage and another like it that Shakespeare used "Falstaff" as the name of his great comic creation in *Henry IV, Part One* and *Henry IV, Part Two,* see page II–329.)

This passage, as it happens, is sheer libel on a brave and sensible officer, who is made the goat for Talbot's folly.

Fastolfe had distinguished himself at the Battle of Agincourt and had served loyally and well as Henry V's representative in Normandy. He had also done well at the siege of Orléans, winning the "Battle of the Herrings" in February 1429. This battle got its name because an English column, which fought the battle, was bringing food supplies to the army investing Orléans. A French relief force attacked it and was driven off thanks to Fastolfe's good generalship. However, some barrels of herring were broken open in the melee and herrings were spread over the field.

Fastolfe was cocommander of the retreating English force at Patay. Being an intelligent general, and not a rakehell fighter like Talbot, he pointed out that the logical move was to hasten the retreat and avoid the French, thus saving the army for use on a more appropriate occasion. While he and Talbot were arguing, the French attacked and the opportunity for a safe retreat was lost.

To those English who were taught to believe that one Englishman was as good as ten Frenchmen, Fastolfe's advice to avoid the fight was looked on as cowardice and he was blamed for Talbot's defeat. This is an example of what those who have studied history well know: When stupidity is considered patriotism, it is unsafe to be intelligent.

A base Walloon . . .

Among the casualties is Talbot himself. Or, as the Third Messenger puts it:

> *A base Walloon, to win the Dolphin's grace,*
> *Thrust Talbot with a spear into the back,*
> —Act I, scene i, lines 137–38

A Walloon is the name given to French-speaking inhabitants of southern Belgium. In Talbot's time that area was under Burgundian control and the Walloons would not be likely to be fighting on the French side.

However, in Shakespeare's time, the Walloons, who were Catholics, tended to be on the side of the Spaniards, who were fighting the strong revolt of the Dutch Protestants, who were in turn supported by the English. Walloon might thus be used simply as a term of contempt that would be so understood by an Elizabethan audience.

. . . Lord Hungerford

Talbot has not been killed, however. The Third Messenger says:

> *. . . he lives, but is took prisoner,*
> *And Lord Scales with him and Lord Hungerford;*
> —Act I, scene i, lines 145–46

Lord Walter Hungerford had served with Henry V in France and was present at the Battle of Agincourt. In fact, it was probably he, rather than Westmoreland, who wished for ten thousand more men on the eve of the battle (see page II-495).

Talbot, Hungerford, and Scales (the last was Thomas de Scales) all survived imprisonment for many years. Scales has a small role in *Henry VI, Part Two*.

The Earl of Salisbury . . .

Despite the fact that the First Messenger announced the loss of Orléans (which the English never truly held, so that it can only mean the lifting of the siege) and the Third Messenger described a defeat of Talbot, which came only after the lifting of that siege, we are suddenly back in time and the siege of Orléans continues.

When Bedford vows to return to France forthwith with a new army, the Third Messenger says:

> So you had need, for Orleans is besieged;
> The English army is grown weak and faint;
> The Earl of Salisbury craveth supply
>
> —Act I, scene i, lines 157–59

Salisbury (Thomas de Montagu, 4th Earl of Salisbury) appeared in *Henry V* just before the Battle of Agincourt. After the death of Henry V, Salisbury became Bedford's chief lieutenant in France, and it was he who headed the besieging force of English at Orléans.

To Eltham . . .

So the mourners scatter: Bedford to raise an army and Gloucester to arrange for the new King's coronation as Henry VI. Exeter says:

> To Eltham will I, where the young king is,
> Being ordained his special governor,
>
> —Act I, scene i, lines 170–71

Eltham is an eastern suburb about eleven miles from the center of London.

Winchester, seeing Bedford busied with war and Gloucester and Exeter rushing about the baby King's business, feels left out, but he does not intend to be so for long. He mutters to himself as the crowded scene ends:

> Each hath his place and function to attend;
> I am left out; for me nothing remains.
> But long I will not be Jack out of office.
>
> —Act I, scene i, lines 173–75

Froissart, a countryman of ours . . .

The scene shifts to France, where the Dauphin and his forces are jubilant over the fact that the English, short of men and of rations, cannot long maintain the siege of Orléans.

The French attack and though they outnumber the English by the usual ten to one, they are driven back with great slaughter. (All battles are Agincourts, to hear the English legends tell it.)

Alençon says:

> *Froissart, a countryman of ours, records*
> *England all Olivers and Rowlands bred*
> *During the time Edward the Third did reign.*
> *More truly now may this be verified,*
> *For now but Samsons and Goliases*
> *It sendeth forth to skirmish.*
>
> —Act I, scene ii, lines 29–34

Jean Froissart was a French historian who visited England, Scotland, and Italy, then wrote a history entitled *Chronicles of France, England, Scotland and Spain,* which covers the history of those countries from 1325 to 1400, including the early portions of the Hundred Years' War and the battles of Edward III.

Oliver and Rowland (Roland) are the main characters in the *Song of Roland,* a legend set in Charlemagne's time. They were superhuman heroes who, like the Knights of the Round Table, could easily defeat odds of ten to one if pressed. So could such biblical strong men as Samson and Golias (Goliath), of course.

The purpose of this portion of the scene is clearly to show that Frenchmen simply could not defeat Englishmen in fair fight, even though the Englishmen might be starving, have their best fighter (Talbot) taken, and be facing a foe outnumbering them ten to one.

But in that case, why were the English defeated? The reason follows at once.

A holy maid . . .

It was witchcraft, you see.

The Bastard of Orléans, Dunois, arrives and says:

> *Be not dismayed, for succor is at hand:*
> *A holy maid hither with me I bring,*

Which by a vision sent to her from heaven
Ordained is to raise this tedious siege
And drive the English forth the bounds of France.

—Act I, scene ii, lines 50–54

The "holy maid" is, of course, Joan of Arc, one of the most amazing characters in history. If her story were told as a work of fiction it would be considered too fantastic to be plausible.

She was born in 1412 at Domrémy, 160 miles east of Paris, a village whose only claim to fame through all its history is that Joan was born there. Her name was Jeanne Darc, but this came to be spelled Jeanne D'Arc as though she were of noble birth and as though she were Joan *of* Arc, with Arc being the place of her birth. This is wrong, but it is too late to change it.

She was called Joan la Pucelle (Joan the Maid) also, because she remained a virgin and this was considered in her favor, for it made more plausible her role as a holy girl receiving inspiration from heaven. Shakespeare calls her Joan la Pucelle and her speeches are labeled "Pucelle." What's more, her birthplace is now called Domrémy-la-Pucelle. Because her most remarkable deed was in connection with the siege of Orléans, she is also called the Maid of Orléans.

In her teens she was experiencing visions and imagining herself called to save France. In 1428, when these experiences of hers finally drove her to action, the Dauphin had still not been crowned at Rheims, though six full years had passed since the death of his father. What's more, the siege of Orléans might defeat him forever. It seemed to Joan that her mission had to start at once and that she had to relieve the siege and crown the Dauphin.

The Dauphin was then at Chinon, 90 miles southwest of Orléans (not at Orléans itself, as the play makes it appear) and 270 miles from Domrémy. Joan left Domrémy in January 1429 and arrived at Chinon on February 24, 1429. She had to cross English-controlled territory to do so, and so she dressed in man's costume to avoid the kind of trouble a young girl might have in those days (or these) if she were encountered by soldiers.

. . . Thou art an Amazon

Shakespeare's treatment of Joan of Arc makes us most uncomfortable. We have long grown accustomed to treating her from the French viewpoint as a heroine and saint. (She is actually a saint, having been canonized in 1920, but this was long after Shakespeare's time, of course.)

By the English she was looked on as a witch, and when they had her in their power, they treated her as one. Shakespeare looked upon her as a witch too, and could scarcely have done anything else if he expected to keep this play on the boards. He does not hesitate to distort her story grotesquely (or to follow an already grotesquely distorted story).

Thus, in order to prove her mission to the Dauphin, he has her wield a sword and engage in single combat with him. What's more, she defeats him (a sign of witchcraft, since how else could a woman defeat a man— even if that man be merely a Frenchman). The Dauphin, beaten, cries out:

> Stay, stay thy hands! Thou art an Amazon
> And fightest with the sword of Deborah.
> —Act I, scene ii, lines 104–5

The Amazons were women warriors in Greek legend, and Deborah was a woman judge in early Israelite history who inspired a defeat of the Canaanites, though she herself bore no arms. The comparison with Deborah, though meant by Shakespeare to be ironical, is a good one.

Needless to say, no such duel took place in reality. In actual fact, once Joan arrived at the Dauphin's court, she was questioned by ecclesiastical authorities for nearly a month to test her sincerity. In the end, the churchmen advised the Dauphin to make use of her at Orléans. This did not necessarily mean that they believed her to be inspired, but they may well have thought that she could convincingly act as though she were. If the French were heartened by a maid who claimed power from heaven and if the English were equivalently disheartened, then the French might win, and what did it matter whether she were really inspired or not?

. . . Saint Martin's summer . . .

Joan goes on to reassure the French in absolute terms, saying:

> Expect Saint Martin's summer, halcyon's days,
> Since I have enterèd into these wars.
> —Act I, scene ii, lines 131–32

St. Martin's summer is what we call "Indian summer" (a name of uncertain origin), a period of warmth in November that, traditionally, follows the first frost. It is brief but while it lasts, coming as it does after the breath of winter has already made itself felt, it is infinitely appreciated and seems even warmer and calmer than it really is.

Calling it St. Martin's summer brings back the old custom of marking time by saints' days. The feast day of St. Martin of Tours is November 11 and this is the time when such a period of late warmth may well come.

"Halcyon days" is a term that dates back to Greek myth. Alcyone (or Halcyon) was married to Ceyx and they were dreadfully in love. When

Ceyx died in a shipwreck on an occasion when Alcyone, against her will, had stayed at home, she threw herself into the sea and drowned.

Both lovers were turned to kingfishers by the sympathizing gods. The Greeks went on to elaborate the fable by imagining that kingfishers lay eggs in a nest which they set floating in the sea. In memory of the ancient tragedy, the gods keep the seas calm for the sake of those eggs during the two weeks centered about the winter solstice (the last two weeks in December). These are the "halcyon days."

It seems strange that Joan should be promising the French good times in images that imply brief periods of fortune only. (After all, both St. Martin's summer and the halcyon days are followed by the real winter.) It is not, however, Joan that is promising, but Shakespeare, and undoubtedly that is all he is willing to give the French, regardless of history.

. . . Caesar and his fortune . . .

Joan's pride (for naturally Shakespeare will not show her with the becoming humility a saint would be expected to have) causes her to burst out with an overweening:

> Now am I like that proud insulting [insolent] ship
> Which Caesar and his fortune bare at once.
>
> —Act I, scene ii, lines 138–39

This refers to an episode in the life of Julius Caesar. While Caesar was being ferried across a stretch of water, the sea ran so high that the pilot, afraid for his safety, wanted to put back. Caesar, pointing forward with magnificent arrogance, said, "On, pilot, and fear not. You carry Caesar and his fortune."

The word "fortune" carries the meaning, in this case, of "good luck." Caesar believed he had been assigned triumph and success by the Fates and that it was therefore impossible for him to die until that end had been achieved. For that reason the ship could not sink, and Joan's triumphant cry compares herself to that ship.

. . . Saint Philip's daughters . . .

The Dauphin is completely won over by her utter confidence and believes her to be inspired:

> Helen, the mother of great Constantine,
> Nor yet Saint Philip's daughters, were like thee.
>
> —Act I, scene ii, lines 142–43

The Dauphin is here comparing Joan's ability to divine and foresee with that of other women in Christian legend. Helen, the mother of Constantine, was supposed to have discovered, in 326, the True Cross on which Jesus was crucified as the result of a vision.

"Saint Philip's daughters" is a reference to the biblical Book of Acts (21:9) where Philip the evangelist is said to have had "four daughters, virgins, which did prophesy."

And so the French agree not to abandon their attempts to break the siege, for Joan promises them victory.

This be Damascus . . .

While Joan of Arc was invigorating the French, civil broils among the English were being exacerbated. Gloucester is hurrying to the Tower of London to survey its stores of munitions, presumably for the French wars but possibly for his own cause, and he finds it under the control of Winchester.

The armed retainers of the two quarrel and Winchester emerges to face Gloucester in person. Winchester, as a priest, is not armed and he dares Gloucester to kill him:

> . . . *stand thou back, I will not budge a foot;*
> *This be Damascus, be thou cursèd Cain,*
> *To slay thy brother Abel, if thou wilt.*
> —Act I, scene iii, lines 38–40

Winchester is Gloucester's half uncle, a relationship close enough to make the Cain and Abel analogy a useful one. (Bolingbroke used the analogy to threaten Richard II, see page II–269.) The mention of Damascus refers to the later legend that the site on which Cain killed Abel was the place where the city of Damascus was eventually built.

The Lord Mayor of London emerges then, and carefully reads the riot act. Anyone who strikes a blow after that is breaking the law. That breaks off the quarrel, for Gloucester, like a good Englishman, says:

> *Cardinal, I'll be no breaker of the law,*
> —Act I, scene iii, line 80

The Lord Mayor, naturally portrayed as a fat, middle-aged merchant, with none of the aristocratic virtues such as the love of violence, undoubtedly raises a laugh from the audience by concluding the scene with the remark:

> *Good God, these nobles should such stomachs bear!*
> *I myself fight not once in forty year.*
>
> —Act I, scene iii, lines 90–91

Despite the fact that bloodshed has been averted on this occasion, we can be quite sure that the deadly feud between uncle and nephew will continue.

. . . like thee, Nero

Again the scene shifts to Orléans; this time to the English besiegers. Talbot is on the scene again, having been exchanged for a French prisoner.

Salisbury, the English commander, having greeted Talbot with joy, points out a certain turret grate through which he can see the French forces. He does not know that a French gunner, having discovered Salisbury's habitual use of that grate, has trained a gun on it, and left his son to be ready to use it.

The boy uses it and Salisbury drops, badly wounded. The maddened Talbot swears to avenge the leader. He says:

> *. . . I will* [avenge]; *and like thee, Nero,*
> *Play on the lute, beholding the towns burn.*
>
> —Act I, scene iv, lines 95–96

In A.D. 64 there was a great fire in Rome. This was not an uncommon occurrence in a city riddled with wooden, jerry-built slums and with only the sketchiest of fire-fighting equipment. The Emperor Nero, who was in his summer residence at Antium (see page I–236), hastened back to supervise matters and to do what he could to relieve suffering. It was six days before the fire was finally mastered.

Watching the fire one night, according to one story, Nero (who considered himself a great show business personality) strummed the lute and gloomily sang a ballad concerning the burning of Troy. It was an inappropriate, even tactless thing to do, but wasn't really wicked. Nero has, however, a bad press for a variety of reasons, including the fact that he caused Christians to be tortured afterward on the pretext that they had started the fire.

The story has therefore become current that Nero himself started the fire (he didn't) and then played and sang in delight at the sight (as now Talbot threatens to do). Usually, Nero is said to have fiddled and "to fiddle while Rome burns" expresses the height of callousness and indifference. Actually, the violin was not invented till many centuries after Nero's time, and it was the lute, as Talbot says, that Nero used.

A holy prophetess . . .

Even as Salisbury lies dying, the news comes of Joan of Arc. A Messenger arrives, saying:

> *My lord, my lord, the French have gathered head:*
> *The Dolphin, with one Joan La Pucelle joined,*
> *A holy prophetess new risen up,*
> *Is come with a great power to raise the siege.*
> —Act I, scene iv, lines 100–3

The issue is joined and the rest of the play deals largely with the combat between Talbot, the plain, brave soldier fighting for England, and Joan of Arc, the wicked witch, fighting for France.

But Shakespeare has the chronology here exactly reversed. He has Talbot captured, then Joan of Arc arrive at the French court, then Salisbury killed. Here's the way it really went:

1) Salisbury was hideously wounded by the lucky shot of the boy gunner on October 27, 1428. He was carried to Meung-sur-Loire, ten miles downstream, for treatment, and died there on November 3. The result was that English morale suffered a serious downturn.

2) Joan of Arc arrived at the French court on February 24, 1429, four months *after* the wounding of Salisbury. When she was finally allowed to go to Orléans, the French morale underwent a jubilant upturn, and on May 4, 1429, the French attack broke the English siege and sent the English into retreat. (Orléans was the Stalingrad of the Hundred Years' War.)

3) The Battle of Patay was fought during the retreat and Talbot was captured on June 29, 1429, four months *after* Joan's arrival at the French court. Talbot was kept imprisoned, by the way, for four years and was not released till 1433.

. . . thou art a witch

The first confrontation of Talbot and Joan as pictured in the play is a directly physical one at Orléans. They actually fight, and Talbot, who singlehandedly can kill droves of French soldiers, cannot kill one French girl. The conclusion is obvious and Talbot cries out:

> *Blood will I draw on thee, thou art a witch,*
> —Act I, scene v, line 6

Of course, no such duel took place. Joan of Arc went with the army and even led them, clad in armor, but she never actually fought. It was her presence that counted and the belief the soldiers had in her, not any martial deeds she could perform.

. . . France's saint

The French broke the siege, drove off the English, and entered Orléans on May 7, 1429. The turning point of the Hundred Years' War (thirteen and a half years after Agincourt) had come at last. The Dauphin, in transports of ecstasies, pours praise on Joan that is replete with classical allusions. He says:

> Divinest creature, Astraea's daughter,
> How shall I honor thee for this success?
> Thy promises are like Adonis' garden
> That one day bloomed and fruitful were the next.
>
> —Act I, scene vi, lines 4–8

Astraea was a goddess personifying justice and innocence, who lingered upon earth after the conclusion of the primeval Golden Age. Finally, men's increasing wickedness forced her away too, and she went to heaven where she was fixed among the stars as the constellation Virgo (the Virgin). Naturally Joan la Pucelle (the Virgin) would seem like her.

During the ancient agricultural festivals held in honor of Adonis (see page I-5) in midsummer, quick-growing plants were sown in plots, made to bloom in eight days, then allowed to wither. They were then thrown into the sea or river with images of the dead Adonis. This is a transparent representation of the growth and death of the plant world with the seasons, which is what the Adonis myth symbolizes. "Adonis' garden" is used for anything that quickly fulfills its promise. (It also quickly dies, so that the metaphor, like "Saint Martin's summer" earlier, is not entirely favorable.)

The Dauphin also says:

> A statelier pyramis [pyramid] to her I'll rear
> Than Rhodope's . . .
>
> —Act I, scene vi, lines 21–22

According to a Greek legend, Rhodopis (the correct spelling) was an Egyptian prostitute who built the Pyramid of Menkure out of her earnings. There is nothing to the legend, of course, but it is a most tactless allusion where virginal Joan is concerned. Undoubtedly Shakespeare did not use it by accident.

Finally, the Dauphin says:

> No longer on Saint Denis will we cry,
> But Joan La Pucelle shall be France's saint.
> > —Act I, scene vi, lines 28–29

Undoubtedly, Shakespeare meant this as the crowning example of the effeminate prince's exaggerated praise, but as it happens, it turned out to be a perfectly valid prediction.

In this day and age, when patron saints are out of fashion, there is one personage on whom Frenchmen can look back as a representation of all that is imperishable about France, of all that can rescue it from even the greatest depths of degradation, and that is Joan of Arc. She has become a symbol, not only to France, but to all the world, of a gleaming rescue at the point when all hope seems gone.

. . . the regions of Artois

Once the siege of Orléans was broken, the English tide began to recede. They never returned to Orléans. On the contrary, the French pursued the English and beat them at the Battle of Patay, the first great French victory in the open field. It broke the myth of English invincibility, and of Talbot's too.

England might then have been struck hard and Paris might have been regained by France, were it not for Joan's anxiety to have the Dauphin crowned. That was her main aim—to make Charles the legal King of France.

The Battle of Patay had opened the road. Charles and Joan led the French army to Rheims, 140 miles northeast of Orléans, and there the Dauphin was crowned on July 17, 1429, and became Charles VII, King of France.

In the play, however, in place of all this there is built up an outright falsification of history in the interest of English vanity.

At the beginning of Act II, Talbot, Bedford, and Burgundy are seen approaching Orléans in an attempt to regain what has been lost. Talbot addresses the other two:

> Lord Regent, and redoubted Burgundy,
> By whose approach the regions of Artois,
> Wallon, and Picardy are friends to us,
> > —Act II, scene i, lines 8–10

Artois, Wallon, and Picardy are regions in northeastern France, and this is a reminder that the English had beaten France mainly because part of France was on their side against the rest. It was not English valor that kept the English secure in France, so much as the Burgundian alliance, and this is not often admitted in Shakespearean history.

Actually, the Burgundian alliance had been unnecessarily weakened in the years following the death of Henry V through the ineptness of Humphrey of Gloucester, the Lord Protector.

Gloucester had, in 1423, the year after Henry V's death, married Jacqueline of Hainaut, who owned large possessions in the Netherlands. This displeased Philip of Burgundy for several reasons. In the first place, Jacqueline had previously been married to the Duke of Brabant, a kinsman of Burgundy. The lady had virtually eloped with Gloucester and had had her marriage to Brabant annulled by a dubious appeal to a Pope not recognized by all of the West. This proceeding was an insult to Burgundy, who considered his relative of Brabant to have been treated shabbily. (Brabant was Jacqueline's second husband, by the way. Her first had been the very Dauphin who had sent Henry V the tennis balls, see page II-465.)

Secondly, Gloucester greedily wanted to grab the Netherlandish territory that represented his wife's estate and landed five thousand men at Calais to fight a war in the Netherlands. This not only diverted English strength from the more important war against the Dauphin, but seriously offended Burgundy a second time, since he considered the Netherlands his own sphere of influence.

The whole thing almost led to a duel between Gloucester and Burgundy, despite Bedford's frenzied attempts at mediation. In the end the matter was settled when Gloucester's marriage was declared void in 1428. Gloucester then married Eleanor Cobham, his mistress, a relatively lowborn lady. (It was Eleanor, as we can tell from later events, whom Winchester had anachronistically referred to at Henry V's funeral when he darkly warned Gloucester, "Thy wife is proud," see page II-523.)

Burgundy's friendship for England was seriously bent by all this and England's defeat before Orléans cooled it further. Nevertheless, for the while, though the earlier enthusiasm was gone, Burgundy remained an English ally, and that was important with respect to the matter of Joan of Arc.

Coward of France . . .

Talbot explains that the French are celebrating their victory (which he attributes to sorcery, of course) and are off their guard, so that the city can be retaken by surprise attack.

Burgundy agrees with the witch theory, for he has ample reason to hate the Dauphin and take up a point of view so discreditable to him. He says:

> Coward of France! How much he wrongs his fame,
> Despairing of his own arm's fortitude,
> To join with witches and the help of hell.

> —Act II, scene i, lines 16–18

And so Orléans is (fictitiously) retaken, and the French, including Joan and the Dauphin, are made to fly the city, disgracefully, in their night-clothes.

But then Orléans is never mentioned again in the play and succeeding English feats of derring-do are always farther and farther back with no mention anywhere of how it was that all the victories place the English nearer and nearer total defeat.

. . . Scythian Tomyris . . .

With Orléans retaken, Shakespeare lays the groundwork for the (thoroughly fictitious) display of Talbot's invincibility in another respect, for he receives an invitation to visit the castle of the Countess of Auvergne, a region some 150 miles south of Orléans.

Presumably, this represents the possibility of a little love-making, and Burgundy and Bedford leer a bit at the possibility. Neither seems perturbed that Talbot is being asked to travel far into French-controlled territory. The clear-sighted Talbot, as much superior to the French ladies as to the French soldiers, lays plans of his own which are not revealed to the audience. (He calls a captain to his side and whispers to him.)

But then the lady at her appearance in the next scene reveals at once that she has formed a plot to kill Talbot. She says:

> I shall as famous be by this exploit
> As Scythian Tomyris by Cyrus' death.
>
> —Act II, scene iii, lines 5–6

Cyrus was the great conqueror who established the Persian Empire—the largest that western Asia had yet seen—in the sixth century B.C. In 529 B.C. his lust for ever more territory had led him against the hordes of the nomadic tribe of the Massagetae, which then occupied the land east of the Caspian Sea.

According to Herodotus, the tribe was governed by a queen, Tomyris. In battle against the Massagetae, Cyrus suffered his first defeat—and his last as well, for he was killed. Tomyris then located his body and cut off its head and threw it in a vat of human blood as a symbol of its insatiability for battle and blood when alive.

Shakespeare refers to Tomyris as Scythian (see page I–397), a name easily given to any nomadic tribe. Actually, the Massagetae drove out the Scythians from the trans-Caspian area and replaced them.

When Talbot arrives at the Countess' castle, she is first disappointed that he is so small of stature, and secondly she tries to arrest him.

Talbot, however, laughs and calls in his soldiers, for that was the preparation he had arranged in whispers. He arranged to have himself accompanied by a strong force, for he was not such a fool as to come at a French lady's call unaccompanied.

The French Countess falls into a state of great admiration for Talbot (something that would seem reasonable to an Elizabethan audience), and the scene ends in feasting and gaiety.

. . . a case of truth

But now comes a scene which everyone agrees is entirely Shakespeare. It was inserted to mark the genesis of the War of the Roses, the great, confused civil war that fills *Henry VI, Part Two* and *Henry VI, Part Three*. By means of this scene, plus other passages, this present play, originally a simple Talbot chronicle, becomes an almost appropriate *Henry VI, Part One*.

The fundamental excuse for the civil war is the old, old question of the succession. Who was the true successor of Richard II?

Was it a representative of the line of Henry IV, Henry V, and now Henry VI, who were all descended from John of Gaunt, the Duke of Lancaster and fourth son of Edward III? (This is the Lancastrian line.)

Or was it Edmund Mortimer, the 5th Earl of March, who was descended (on his mother's side) from Lionel of Antwerp, third son of Edward III (see page II–320)?

The cause of Mortimer had been defended by Hotspur against Lancastrian Henry IV in *Henry IV, Part One* (see page II–320) and by the Earl of Cambridge against Lancastrian Henry V in *Henry V* (see page II–466).

Now a new champion of the Mortimers has arisen, and the scene opens with a question by him.

> Great lords and gentlemen, what means this silence?
> Dare no man answer in a case of truth?
>
> —Act II, scene iv, lines 1–2

The speaker is Richard Plantagenet, son of the just mentioned Earl of Cambridge. He owns the surname because he is descended by unbroken male line from his great-grandfather Edward III Plantagenet (see page II–255).

Plantagenet's grandfather had been Edmund of Langley, who was the Duke of York in *Richard II,* and his uncle was Edward, Duke of York ("Aumerle" in *Richard II*), who died at Agincourt (see page II–500). By that time, Richard Plantagenet's father, the conspiring Earl of Cambridge (Edward of York's younger brother), had been executed. The young boy, who was only four years old at the time of Agincourt, would, ordinarily, have inherited the title and become Duke of York. As the son of a convicted traitor, however, he could not inherit and remained merely Richard Plantagenet.

Despite this denial of title, he remained on a social par with the lords of the realm and could deal with them on a footing of equality. Here he was demanding that they answer him on some point of law. What that point was is not stated anywhere in the scene but it seems reasonable to suppose that it involves the succession. Plantagenet wants to know, perhaps, whether the Mortimer line is the true pathway of descent of the English crown.

It is important to remember that the line of monarchs who were on the throne in Shakespeare's time were firmly Lancastrian in sympathy. Consequently, Shakespeare finds the chronicles of the time pro-Lancastrian and against the pretensions of the line of Mortimer. Shakespeare would absorb that point of view and would not, in any case, place anything in his plays that might be too boldly against the Establishment of his time.

Richard Plantagenet, therefore, is treated with less than justice by Shakespeare in various places. He is shown here to be raising the matter of the succession and to be laying plots to secure that succession for himself, whereas the truth of the matter seems to be that he was a loyal servant of the crown and was eventually pushed into rebellion by the incapacity of King Henry VI and the malevolence of some of those about him.

Plantagenet's case, briefly, would be this. If male ancestry only were considered, he would have no claim on the throne, for he would then be descended from Edmund of Langley, the fifth son of Edward III.

Plantagenet's father, however, had married Anne Mortimer, the younger sister of the Earl of March. If the Earl of March died without issue, then Richard Plantagenet was the son of the daughter of the son of the daughter of Lionel, the *third* son of Edward III.

Plantagenet's line is usually called the Yorkist line, both because he was descended from Edmund of Langley, Duke of York, and because he himself would eventually be Duke of York. By the marriage into the House of Mortimer, the House of York had thus developed a better claim to the throne than the House of Lancaster.

With the Yorkists representing a third son and the Lancastrians only a fourth, Richard Plantagenet could, in his own view, confidently demand a judgment from the others.

. . . the Temple Hall . . .

Plantagenet is answered, rather nervously, by one of the noblemen present, who says:

> *Within the Temple Hall we were too loud;*
> *The garden here is more convenient.*
> —Act II, scene iv, lines 3–4

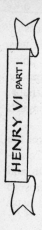

HENRY VI PART 1

HOUSE of MORTIMER-YORK

EDWARD III ●
(1312–1377)

3RD SON

5TH SON

LIONEL OF ANTWERP
(DUKE OF CLARENCE)
(1338–1368)

EDMUND OF LANGLEY
(DUKE OF YORK)
(1342–1402)

Philippa
(1355–1381)
═══ EDMUND MORTIMER
(3RD EARL OF MARCH)

EDWARD
(DUKE OF YORK)
("AUMERLE")
(1373–1415)

ROGER MORTIMER
(4TH EARL OF MARCH)
(1374–1398)

Anne Mortimer ═══ RICHARD
EARL OF CAMBRIDGE
(1375–1415)

EDMUND MORTIMER
5TH EARL OF MARCH
(1391–1425)

RICHARD
PLANTAGENET
DUKE OF YORK
(1411–)

▭ Characters in the play
● King of England
NOTE: Women's names in lower case

The Temple Hall was a favored residence for law students, so it was a good place to discuss a point of law. However, since the point under discussion could easily lead one to treasonable statements, it was indeed better to move to a more private place.

The speaker of these lines is William de la Pole, Earl of Suffolk. He spent his younger years in France, doing excellent service, first under Henry V, then under the Earl of Salisbury and the Duke of Bedford. When Salisbury was killed at Orléans, it was Suffolk who took over the command of the English army (though he does not appear in that capacity in the play's scenes dealing with the siege of Orléans—he being pushed into the background in favor of Talbot).

Suffolk was taken prisoner in the aftermath of the retreat from Orléans but was soon ransomed.

We might suppose from the fact that Suffolk is present that this scene takes place enough time after the lifting of the siege of Orléans to give him a chance to be ransomed and come back to England, so that we can say the scene is taking place in 1432. However, the scene shows no real indication of time and it is thoroughly fictitious anyway, so that any attempt at chronology is futile.

. . . wrangling Somerset . . .

Richard Plantagenet feels that if they have been silent in the Temple Hall for fear of eavesdroppers, they ought no longer be silent in the privacy of the garden. He says:

> *Then say at once if I maintained the truth;*
> *Or else was wrangling Somerset in the error?*
> —Act II, scene iv, lines 5–6

Who was Somerset? To explain that, we must return to the Beaufort family.

John of Gaunt had two sets of descendants. Through his first wife, he had given birth to Henry IV and his descendants, which, among the characters in this play, include the reigning child-king Henry VI and his uncles, John of Bedford and Humphrey of Gloucester.

Through his third wife, John of Gaunt had given birth to three sons, John Beaufort, Henry Beaufort, and Thomas Beaufort. These were all born while his third wife was still merely his mistress and were therefore illegitimate at birth. However, when John of Gaunt married that mistress, he managed to force through a decree legitimizing his children by her, though Henry IV carefully saw to it that they were declared ineligible for succession to the throne. There is some question as to whether this ineligibility was an actual decree or a later forgery, but in any case, if the line of Henry IV failed, the Beauforts would certainly put in a strong claim to the throne.

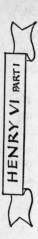

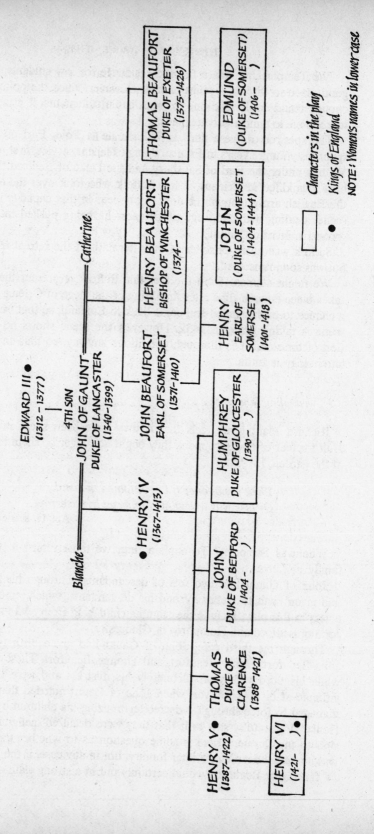

HENRY VI PART I

HOUSE of LANCASTER

EDWARD III ● (1312 – 1377)
 |
 4TH SON
 |
JOHN OF GAUNT
DUKE OF LANCASTER
(1340 – 1399)
Blanche ═══ ═══ Catherine

● HENRY IV (1367 – 1413)

JOHN BEAUFORT
EARL OF SOMERSET
(1371 – 1410)

HENRY BEAUFORT
BISHOP OF WINCHESTER
(1374 –)

THOMAS BEAUFORT
DUKE OF EXETER
(1375 – 1426)

HENRY
EARL OF
SOMERSET
(1401 – 1418)

JOHN
(DUKE OF SOMERSET)
(1404 – 1444)

EDMUND
(DUKE OF SOMERSET)
(1406 –)

HUMPHREY
DUKE OF GLOUCESTER
(1390 –)

JOHN
DUKE OF
BEDFORD
(1404 –)

THOMAS
DUKE OF
CLARENCE
(1388 – 1421)

HENRY V ● (1387 – 1422)

HENRY VI ● ☐ (1421 –)

☐ Characters in the play
● Kings of England
NOTE : Women's names in lower-case

What's more, it seemed as if the elder Lancastrian line might fail. The adult representatives, Bedford and Gloucester, had no heirs and very likely would not get any (and didn't). That would leave Henry VI, the boy-king, the last of the elder Lancastrians, and he was not of robust health.

With that in mind, where did the three Beaufort brothers stand? The youngest, Thomas, was Duke of Exeter. He died in 1426, three years before the lifting of the siege of Orléans, and left no heirs.

The middle Beaufort is Bishop of Winchester, who is very much alive, but as a churchman, will have no heirs.

The eldest Beaufort, John, was created Earl of Somerset by his half brother, Henry IV, but did not live to enjoy it long, for he died in 1410, at the age of twenty-seven or so.

John Beaufort had three sons in his turn. The eldest, Henry Beaufort, succeeded to the title of Earl of Somerset, but died in 1418 at the age of seventeen, leaving no heirs.

The other two sons were John Beaufort and Edmund Beaufort. John was the next holder of the title. He fought in France, where he spent fourteen years as a captive. He was promoted to Duke of Somerset in 1443 but died in France the next year, leaving behind only a daughter, Margaret Beaufort. The title of Somerset passed on to John's younger brother, Edmund.

It is impossible to say which brother is meant by Shakespeare's "Somerset," John or Edmund. The cast of characters calls him John Beaufort, but by the end of the play, events are described which take place after John's death and where the Somerset mentioned can only be Edmund Beaufort.

The best we can do is consider Shakespeare's "Somerset" of *Henry VI, Part One* an amalgam of John and Edmund, the brothers who represent the second Beaufort generation.

Clearly the Beauforts must be Lancastrians, for on that their claim to the throne depends. Somerset, moreover (John-Edmund Beaufort), as descendant of the oldest Beaufort brother, would be the heir to the throne on strict Lancastrian principles if Henry VI died without children, just as Richard Plantagenet would be the heir to the throne on strict Yorkist principles and ought even to replace Henry VI on that throne.

So the battle line is drawn: Richard Plantagenet versus John-Edmund of Somerset. The other nobles present are being asked to choose sides.

. . . quillets of the law

It is not hard to see that nobody present wants to choose sides. To side with Richard Plantagenet would be to commit treason or near treason, and Somerset would not forget. To side with Somerset would become treason if Plantagenet should ever succeed to the throne, and he would not forget.

Suffolk pleads lack of expertise in legal questions. Richard Plantagenet then appeals to the Earl of Warwick, who likewise weasels, saying:

> . . . *in these nice sharp quillets* [distinctions] *of the law*
> *Good faith, I am no wiser than a daw.*
> —Act II, scene iv, lines 17–18

Warwick is Richard Beauchamp, Earl of Warwick, who appeared briefly in both *Henry IV, Part Two* (see page II–402) and in *Henry V* (see page II–505).

Richard of Warwick fought at the side of Henry IV at the Battle of Shrewsbury and then spent two years on a tour of Europe, including a pilgrimage to the Holy Land. During Henry V's wars in France, Beauchamp commanded Calais. He served as ambassador to France and received the Emperor Sigismund there when the latter was traveling to England (see page II–510).

When Henry V died, his will made Warwick the tutor of his infant son, a post he held till 1437. He took young King Henry VI to France in 1430, and it was while he was there that the event took place for which he is best known in history—for it was he who supervised the trial and execution of Joan of Arc.

. . . *a white rose* . . .

Seeing that no one will speak openly, Richard Plantagenet proposes a silent test. He says:

> *Let him that is a true-born gentleman*
> *And stands upon the honor of his birth,*
> *If he suppose that I have pleaded truth,*
> *From off this brier pluck a white rose with me.*
> —Act II, scene iv, lines 27–30

Somerset follows the notion and for his side plucks a red rose.

This is supposed to explain why the White Rose was the badge of the House of York in the civil wars that eventually followed and the Red Rose the badge of the House of Lancaster.

Actually, the White Rose of York became prominent only during the civil wars and the Red Rose became prominent only after the end of those wars as a counter to the well-known White Rose.

In the next century, historians made such free use of the symbols that a legend arose concerning the origin, and it is that which Shakespeare made use of here. And it was because of that legend that the civil wars came to be known as the Wars of the Roses.

. . . grace the yeoman . . .

Now the other noblemen do take sides. Warwick plucks a white rose, for instance, and Suffolk a red rose. The quarrel grows more heated and finally, Somerset moves to leave, piercing Plantagenet as he does so with a spiteful barb, when he says to Suffolk:

> *We grace the yeoman by conversing with him.*
> —Act II, scene iv, line 81

A yeoman is a commoner, and Somerset is maintaining that since Plantagenet's father was executed for treason and Plantagenet himself is untitled, he is unfit for noblemen to talk to.

Third son . . .

Warwick defends Richard Plantagenet against the implication of non-nobility, saying of him:

> *His grandfather was Lionel Duke of Clarence,*
> *Third son to the third Edward King of England:*
> —Act II, scene iv, lines 83–84

"Grandfather" is used here as a general term, for Lionel was actually Richard's great-great-grandfather.

The emphasis on the fact that Lionel was third son is shaft enough in return, for Somerset is descended only from the fourth son.

. . . the next Parliament

When Somerset and his faction leave, Warwick consoles Plantagenet by saying:

> *This blot that they object against your house*
> *Shall be whipped out in the next Parliament*
> *Called for the truce of Winchester and Gloucester,*
> *And if thou be not then created York,*
> *I will not live to be accounted Warwick.*
> —Act II, scene iv, lines 116–20

This next Parliament spoken of here met in 1426, which makes the scene puzzling if it is taken as real instead of fictitious. In 1426 the siege of Orléans, the subject of the first act, had not yet taken place. Somerset (John) was in French imprisonment and could not be present, while his brother (Edmund) was not yet Somerset. Richard Plantagenet himself was not yet fifteen.

However, it is useless to try to unscramble the hopelessly tangled chronology of this play.

. . . the end of Edmund Mortimer

Chronology continues to suffer, for now we are taken to the Tower of London, where Edmund Mortimer is supposed to be imprisoned. He is seated in a chair, an old man, and says to a Jailer:

> *. . . these gray locks, the pursuivants* [foretellers] *of death,*
> *Nestor-like agèd in an age of care,*
> *Argue the end of Edmund Mortimer.*
> —Act II, scene v, lines 5–7

Shakespeare is quite wrong here. Presumably this is Edmund Mortimer, the 5th Earl of March, who is the rightful heir to the throne on the basis of strict legitimacy (see page II–320). He died in 1425, the year before the "next Parliament" that Warwick had just spoken of in the preceding scene. We might suppose, then, that the scene of the roses took place in 1425 just before Mortimer died, with all the anachronisms concerning Plantagenet's age and Somerset's imprisonment swallowed.

However, at the time of Mortimer's death, he was only thirty-four years old. "Nestor-like agèd"—that is, as aged as the legendary Nestor (see page I–91)—he certainly was not.

Of course, in *Henry IV, Part One* Shakespeare confused Edmund Mortimer, Earl of March, with his namesake uncle who had been captured by Owen Glendower (see page II–320). If Shakespeare means the uncle here, then that uncle, having been born in 1376, would still only have been forty-nine years old in 1425. However, he would not have been around then, for uncle Mortimer remained in Wales after his capture and died about 1409 at the age of thirty-three. Neither uncle nor nephew fits Shakespeare's picture at all.

This loathsome sequestration . . .

Edmund Mortimer is waiting for a visit from Richard Plantagenet, the son of his sister, so he can pass on his own claim to the throne. He says, referring to Richard:

Poor gentleman! his wrong doth equal mine.
Since Henry Monmouth [Henry V] *first began to reign,*
Before whose glory I was great in arms,
This loathsome sequestration have I had;
                                   —Act II, scene v, lines 22–25

For Edmund to speak of a "loathsome sequestration" (i.e., imprisonment) since Henry V first began to reign is a libel on that King. Edmund of March was indeed imprisoned by Henry IV (under conditions not too onerous), but Henry V actually set him free!

Henry V took Edmund of March with him on his first expedition to France and Edmund fought loyally at Harfleur and at succeeding battles. In 1423, after Henry V's death, Edmund was sent to Ireland and placed in charge of the English settlement there. He remained in Ireland till his death in 1425 of the plague.

He did *not* die a prisoner in the Tower of London. He died a free man and a high official of the crown.

In fact, so far from being against the line of Lancaster, it was he (it is believed by some) who informed Henry V of the treason of Richard of Cambridge, perhaps in gratitude for his freedom or in exchange for it. If so, this was rather a despicable act, since the treason was conceived for the purpose of making Edmund king.

This would also mean that the Edmund pictured here as waiting for his nephew, whose "wrong doth equal mine," is waiting for a nephew particularly wronged by Edmund himself, for it was Edmund who procured the death of the nephew's father, his own brother-in-law.

My father, Earl of Cambridge . . .

Richard Plantagenet arrives, still smarting from Somerset's slurs on his executed father, and asks Edmund Mortimer for the truth:

Therefore, good uncle, for my father's sake,
In honor of a true Plantagenet,
And for alliance' sake, declare the cause
My father, Earl of Cambridge, lost his head.
                                   —Act II, scene v, lines 51–54

Edmund Mortimer, in response, details the list of the sons of Edward III and explains that the line of Mortimer represents the rightful kings. From this point of view, of course, the Earl of Cambridge was not committing treason, but was fighting loyally for the true king against a usurper.

Richard therefore says:

. . . methinks, my father's execution
Was nothing less than bloody tyranny.
—Act II, scene v, lines 99–100

Edmund Mortimer warns Richard to proceed about his plans cautiously and then dies. With his death, Richard inherits the Mortimer estates, which are great, and automatically becomes the 6th Earl of March.

But now more than ever he needs the slur on his own position, brought about by his father's execution, wiped out. This can best be done by the recognition of his claim to the title of York at the next Parliament.

With that in mind, Richard says:

And therefore haste I to the parliament,
—Act II, scene v, line 127

Thou bastard . . .

The session of Parliament called to patch up some sort of truce between Humphrey of Gloucester and Henry of Winchester is made hideous by their quarreling. It gets so bad that their retainers, forbidden to use weapons, manage to achieve bloody results by pelting each other with rocks. (It is on this occasion that Bedford himself had to come back from France to effect a kind of compromise, though this is not dealt with in the play.)

The quarrel degenerates to personalities. When Winchester seems about to say he is as good as Gloucester, Gloucester sneers back:

As good?
Thou bastard of my grandfather!
—Act III, scene i, lines 41–42

And of course, Winchester is one of the three bastard-born Beaufort brothers (see page II–545). Since the brothers were legally legitimized, however, the use of the word seems unfair.

Others begin to take part. Somerset, the nephew of Winchester, is on his side. Warwick is on the other.

It should be mentioned that the embittered rivalry between Gloucester and Winchester involved the war in France. Gloucester, who could never forget he was brother of Henry V and had fought at Agincourt, was what we would today call a hawk. He was against anything short of complete victory in France. Winchester, determined to oppose Gloucester in everything, assumed a dovish stance and favored some sort of accommodation in France short of total victory.

Naturally the existence of a strong "peace party" in England weakened the English stand in France.

. . my tender years . . .

And now the King, Henry VI, who is presiding over the parliamentary session, intervenes, speaking for the first time in the play that is named for him. He begins:

> *Uncles of Gloucester and of Winchester,*
> —Act III, scene i, line 65

This is accurate enough. Gloucester is the King's uncle and Winchester his great-uncle. (Gloucester is about thirty-five years old at the time of the Parliament, Winchester about fifty.) The King goes on to say:

> *Believe me, lords, my tender years can tell*
> *Civil dissension is a viperous worm*
> *That gnaws the bowels of the commonwealth.*
> —Act III, scene i, lines 71–73

He is right, but his years are even more tender than one would think from this speech, for in 1426 Henry VI was only five years old. He goes on to say to the two uncles:

> *I would prevail, if prayers might prevail,*
> *To join your hearts in love and amity.*
> —Act III, scene i, lines 67–68

This is apparently a good introduction to the character of the King, for he was indeed a gentle soul who believed in the reign of love; a far too gentle soul to be King. And this was true despite the fact that every effort was made to train the royal child into what might be considered the proper aristocratic belief that the best argument is not love, but a knock on the head.

Warwick, who was in charge of the King's education, followed the stern policy of beatings for slight offenses, and Henry VI was constantly terrorized as a child.

This did not cause him to learn what he was required to learn, for he never betrayed a strong intellect. In fact, he seems to have inherited the mental instability of his mother's father, Charles VI of France (see page II–464), though this was never so extreme in Henry VI. Beating never succeeded in forcing intelligence into Henry VI, and to the end of his life he remained a gentle nonentity, lovable in his genuine piety and in his unwillingness to do harm, but an utterly incompetent king who did England more harm (unintentionally) than a strong tyrant would have done.

. . . princely Duke of York

Through royal command a hollow truce is patched up between Gloucester and Winchester, who are forced to shake hands.

With that done, the matter of Richard Plantagenet's title is taken up and
it goes through without trouble. The King says:

> *Rise, Richard, like a true Plantagenet,*
> *And rise created princely Duke of York.*
>> —Act III, scene i, lines 173–74

Richard, now of York, is vindicated, but his enemies remain. All cry
the ritual:

> *Welcome, high prince, the mighty Duke of York!*
>> —Act III, scene i, line 178

One person, however, Somerset, leader of the Lancastrian faction, says
in a muttered aside:

> *Perish, base prince, ignoble Duke of York!*
>> —Act III, scene i, line 179

. . . Henry born at Windsor . . .

All leave the stage now but Exeter, Somerset's uncle, the youngest of the
original Beaufort brothers. He is a Lancastrian by definition, but primarily he is an English general, fighting Frenchmen since Henry V's first
campaign ten years before. He sees the quarrelsome factions as fatal for
the English cause in France and says:

> *And now I fear that fatal prophecy*
> *Which in the time of Henry named the Fifth*
> *Was in the mouth of every sucking babe,*
> *That Henry born at Monmouth should win all*
> *And Henry born at Windsor lose all:*
>> —Act III, scene i, lines 196–200

No doubt there was such a prophecy. Every age sees an infinite number of prophecies of all types. Later ages remember only those prophecies
that seem to have come true, and with the retelling improve them in
order to have them fit subsequent events even better.

Exeter finds the prophecy so likely to come true

> . . . that Exeter doth wish
> His days may finish ere that hapless time.
> —Act III, scene ii, lines 201–2

Exeter got his wish. He died before the year was out, still in his late forties and while the British position in France was still at its peak. It was not till two years after Exeter's death in 1427 that there came the turning-point siege of Orléans.

With Exeter's death, Henry, Bishop of Winchester, remained the last of the original Beaufort brothers.

Cowardly knight . . .

There follows another completely fictitious scene, in which Joan of Arc and the French forces take the city of Rouen by treachery, after which good old Talbot retakes it the same day by prodigies of valor, the French being shown up as effeminate cowards at every possible chance.

None of this is so. The French did not take Rouen during Joan of Arc's short lifetime. When they finally did take it (eighteen years after Joan's death), the English did not retake it either that day or ever. What's more, the particular treachery ascribed to the French, that of having soldiers infiltrate the town in the guise of peasants, was a device actually used by the *English* in taking the town of Evreux in 1441.

There is a short passage, moreover, in which Sir John Falstaff (Fastolfe in other editions) is shown running away from the fight. A Captain calls out after him as he flees:

> *Cowardly knight, ill fortune follow thee!*
> —Act III, scene ii, line 109

This scene of cowardice is as utterly false to history as was the earlier report.

. . . stout Pendragon . . .

Bedford is on the scene too. He is old and sick now and unable to move from his chair. Nevertheless, he refuses to leave the scene of battle, saying:

> *. . . once I read*
> *That stout Pendragon in his litter sick*
> *Came to the field and vanquishèd his foes.*
> —Act III, scene ii, lines 94–96

Pendragon is Uther Pendragon, the legendary father of the legendary King Arthur. Such feats have indeed been reported in history—of Pepin of Héristal, for instance, the great-grandfather of Charlemagne. The mere presence of an admired leader, though he cannot himself strike a blow, though he be only carried in a litter, can do wonders for soldiers' morale and help bring about victory.

. . . our enemies' overthrow

Once the recapture of Rouen is completed, however, Bedford makes his last speech. He says, just before dying:

> *Now, quiet soul, depart when heaven please,*
> *For I have seen our enemies' overthrow.*
>
> —Act III, scene ii, lines 110–11

John Plantagenet, Duke of Bedford, did indeed die at Rouen. He died on September 14, 1435, however, at which time Rouen was still firmly in English hands and would remain so for another fourteen years.

What's more, far from leading the French taking of Rouen, Joan of Arc died in the city. After having been captured by the Burgundians, turned over to the English, tried and convicted of heresy, she died at the stake in Rouen on May 30, 1431, not yet twenty years old. The place where she was burned is called the Place de la Pucelle to this day.

Bedford was moderately old for that period of time, being forty-six years of age when he died. His death was a great loss to England. With Salisbury, Exeter, and Bedford all gone, the great generals of the age of Henry V had passed. Only Talbot remained, and for all that this play exaggerates him into fustian, he was indeed a resolute and indomitable fighter who never gave up, and while he lived the Hundred Years' War continued.

They set him free . . .

The gain-loss of Rouen forces Joan la Pucelle (in the play, at any rate) to other expedients. By use of honeyed words (and, no doubt, by witchcraft, in English eyes) she decides to win over Burgundy from the English alliance.

She gains a parley with him, appeals to his French patriotism, and points out that England will not, in any case, keep faith with him. She says:

> *Was not the Duke of Orleans thy foe?*
> *And was he not in England prisoner?*
> *But when they heard he was thine enemy,*

They set him free without his ransom paid,
—Act III, scene iii, lines 69–72

At this Burgundy changes sides, while Joan says, in an aside:

Done like a Frenchman: turn and turn again!
—Act III, scene iii, line 85

In this play, even the French sneer at the French.

Actually, Burgundy's turnabout came in 1435 and Joan of Arc had nothing to do with it; she had been dead for four years.

The turnabout came for much more serious reasons than a few honeyed words. In fact, from the very start England had a terrible job keeping Burgundy on their side.

Philip the Good of Burgundy did fight with the English in the fury of his rage at the assassination of his father, John the Fearless, by the Dauphin's men (see page II–513), but what he wanted was revenge on the Dauphin and no more. He was *not* interested in being chief French lackey to the English.

While the formidable Henry V was alive, Philip had to tread softly, but once the great king was dead, only a continuing series of bribes in the way of additional land kept him in line. Then, in 1423, Bedford himself had to agree to marry Philip's sister, Anne, and establish a family relationship.

Strains on the alliance continued. First there was the folly of Gloucester's marriage and his attempted war in the Netherlands (see page II–540), which the Duke of Bedford had to stop. Then there was the French recovery, the rescue of Orléans, the English defeat at Patay, the coronation of Charles VII at Rheims.

English victory no longer looked so sure and Philip could not see the profit to be gained in fighting a war that would go on forever. Then too, his sister, Anne, died in November 1432, leaving no children and there was no longer any family bond between Burgundy and Bedford.

Burgundy therefore began to push hard for a treaty of peace that would enable him and the English to keep at least some of the gains they had made in these last fifteen years. Bedford, on the other hand, still longed for total victory.

In early 1435, however, Bedford could no longer resist the pressures. He sent representatives to meet at the town of Arras, in Burgundian territory, there to treat with the Dauphin, or with King Charles VII, as he must really be called.

Yet the English could not bring themselves to give in. They would not accept the terms offered by King Charles and broke off negotiations. Philip of Burgundy shrugged his shoulders. If the English were too foolish to save half because they insisted on grasping for all, they would lose all (and they certainly did). That did not mean that Burgundy had to lose all as well. He therefore continued to negotiate on his own behalf with Charles, and Charles, eager to have Burgundy on his side against England, offered generous terms.

When Bedford died, it was not in a spirit of triumph at a fictitious victory at Rouen, as the play has it. It was in bitterness of spirit, knowing that Burgundy had left the English alliance and that England's last chance of conquering France was gone. The Treaty of Arras between Charles of France and Philip of Burgundy was signed on September 21, 1435, exactly one week after Bedford's death. The English-Burgundian alliance that had brought France to the verge of destruction had lasted only sixteen years.

But it wasn't Joan's witchcraft; it was English folly.

And did the liberation of Charles of Orléans have anything to do with it? Absolutely not!

Joan's remark that Charles of Orléans was Philip's enemy and that Charles was prisoner in England was correct. Orléans was certainly the enemy of Burgundy, since their respective fathers had been the heads of the competing factions in civil war, and since Philip's father had ordered the assassination of Charles's father.

Then, too, Charles of Orléans was indeed taken prisoner at the Battle of Agincourt and remained in England for years thereafter. He was not freed without ransom, however; he was forced to pay a very large ransom. What's more, he was not freed till 1440, nearly five years *after* Burgundy's defection.

His freedom was, in fact, the result of English squabbling at home. By 1440 the peace party under Winchester was strong indeed, in view of the way in which the English kept losing ground. It was felt that the freeing of Orléans was an easy way to make a move toward de-escalation of the war. Then too, since Humphrey of Gloucester, England's leading hawk politician, favored hanging on to Orléans as a visible reminder of the great victory at Agincourt, Winchester was all the readier to free Orléans as a blow against his great competitor.

That was indeed the way it worked. When Orléans was freed, Gloucester was staggered. He never regained the initiative and his career continued to decline steadily.

After his release, by the way, Charles of Orléans spent a quiet quarter century, divorced from politics, writing poetry, and patronizing other literary figures. He made a rich marriage (which helped pay off his ransom) and in 1462, when he was sixty-eight years old, his wife gave birth to a son who was someday to be King of France. Since even his imprisonment in England had been a gentle one, there is no denying that in many ways the lot of the loser at Agincourt was much better than that of the winner.

When I was young . . .

The endless chronological confusion continues.

We are next in Paris, where the young Henry VI has come to be crowned King of France. It was an enforced piece of pageantry. Charles VII had been crowned King of France in Reims on July 17, 1429 and however much the English might pretend to sneer at this, that coronation had a profound psychological effect.

The English could only crown Henry VI as King of France in return, but they should have done it sooner, when Reims was available to them. Now Reims was in the French grip and the English had to make Paris do. A coronation at Paris was not official, but it was all that could be done.

On April 23, 1430, then, Henry VI was brought to Calais. (It was St. George's Day, the celebration of England's patron saint, but even St. George could not retrieve the irretrievable.) On December 17, 1430, the King was taken to Paris with lavish ceremony. Though this event takes place after Bedford's death and Burgundy's defection in the play, it actually took place five years before either in real history.

Talbot is pictured as being present at the coronation, which he was *not,* for he was in French imprisonment at the time following the Battle of Patay.

King Henry responds to the presence of Talbot in most gracious fashion. Shakespeare has him say:

> *When I was young (as yet I am not old)*
> *I do remember how my father said*
> *A stouter champion never handled sword.*
> —Act III, scene iv, lines 17–19

The King was certainly "not old." At his coronation in Paris he was just past his ninth birthday. And to remember something his father said when he "was young" would make him a prodigy indeed, for he was not quite nine months old when his father died.

. . . Earl of Shrewsbury

Talbot receives his reward with a title. King Henry says:

> *We here create you Earl of Shrewsbury,*
> —Act III, scene iv, line 26

Actually, Talbot was not created Earl of Shrewsbury till 1442, a round dozen years after Henry's French coronation. The title has remained in Talbot's family down to this very day.

Not only is Talbot elevated, but the man who (according to the legend Shakespeare followed) betrayed him is degraded. When Sir John Falstaff (Fastolfe) enters, Talbot assaults him and rips the garter from his leg (this shows Falstaff to have been a Knight of the Garter, see page II–446) and denounces him as a coward.

Not all is gladsome, however, for Falstaff has entered carrying messages telling of the Duke of Burgundy's defection.

Cousin of York . . .

Yet as though to show that the defection of Burgundy and the deadly peril that this brings down upon the English causes do not prevent the English nobility from continuing to bicker, the quarrel between the White Rose and the Red breaks out again on the very day of the coronation.

King Henry tries a compromise. He puts on the red rose of Somerset in order to calm him, and then, to show York that this does not indicate any royal displeasure to himself, proceeds to appoint the latter to high office. He says:

> *Cousin of York, we institute your grace*
> *To be our Regent in these parts of France;*
>
>   —Act IV, scene i, lines 162–63

In other words, York is succeeding to the position formerly held by Bedford.

This did indeed happen. York was appointed to take charge over the French territories in January 1436, four months after Bedford's death (but five years after Henry VI's coronation in Paris).

Richard of York seems to have been completely loyal to the crown at this time. Even if he had in mind his own superior claim to the throne according to the strict tenets of legitimacy, he may well have felt that to press the claim would be impractical.

What he had in his favor was some legalistic quibbling about lines of descent which might be conclusive to lawyers but might be beyond the population generally. What the Lancastrians had was the memory of the great and conquering Henry V, and that memory was something the English people could understand very well.

Moreover, York as a child had been kindly treated by Henry V after the execution of his father for treason and he might find it difficult to desecrate the memory of that King by maintaining him to have been a usurper. The return of his title and his appointment to high office would also have a soothing effect on him.

In fact, though Shakespeare adopts the anti-York bias of his time and portrays York as scheming for the throne from the very beginning, there is no act of his until very nearly the end of his life that shows this to be true. In fact, if he were really aspiring to the throne, some of his acts, as we will see, would be inexplicable.

. . . there begins confusion

When the stage clears after the coronation, Exeter again remains behind as at the Parliament that made Richard Duke of York. Again he soliloquizes dolefully, saying:

> 'Tis much when scepters are in children's hands,
> But more when envy breeds unkind division;
> There comes the ruin, there begins confusion.
> —Act IV, scene i, lines 192–94

Exeter is correct but he is literally a voice from the grave. He was three years dead at the time of Henry's coronation in Paris, nine years dead at the time York was placed in charge of the French campaign.

The prediction of ruin and confusion came dolefully true, however. In France, Richard of York found himself unable to do anything. Talbot devastated the territories of the Duke of Burgundy wherever and whenever he could, but that won the English no friends.

What's more, Richard felt himself to be poorly supported by the home government. The Beauforts (Winchester and Somerset) gained steadily at the expense of Humphrey of Gloucester. Not only were the Beauforts head of the peace faction, but they were entirely suspicious of York. No matter how loyal he might demonstrate himself to be, they remained always conscious of his descent from Lionel and could never bring themselves to trust him. Naturally, they would not have been pleased by English victory under York, for that would have made York the darling of the English people. They would sooner lose the war than win with York.

York realized that. Paris fell to the French in 1436 soon after his appointment to the post, and in 1437 he gave up trying and asked for his recall, after he had held the post for little over a year.

York was replaced by Warwick, who could accomplish nothing either, and who died at his post in 1439. The next year, York was appointed once again and went to France most reluctantly.

This time he did remarkably well. Paris was gone and the English holdings in southwestern France were vanishing rapidly, but York and Talbot between them maintained and even strengthened the English grip on Normandy.

After 1445 there was a rather long truce between the two sides, but in the course of the truce, the French grew stronger and the English weakened, especially thanks to a marriage arranged for King Henry VI (a marriage which will be the central factor of *Henry VI, Part Two*).

In 1447 Somerset was placed in charge of the English forces in France, and now Somerset can definitely be identified. John Beaufort, the older brother, died in 1444, and Edmund, the younger brother (see page II–547), succeeded to the title in 1448. What's more, the title itself had been raised in value. In 1443 John had become Duke of Somerset, and that was what Edmund became in his turn.

In 1447, then, Edmund Beaufort, grandson of John of Gaunt and soon to be Duke of Somerset, was placed in charge of the English forces in France. (There is no indication in *Henry VI, Part One* that "Somerset" changes identities in the course of the play.)

As it happened, Somerset proved incompetent. The French swept into Normandy and took Rouen and Harfleur in 1449, cities it had taken Henry V much to capture thirty years before. Talbot himself was captured and kept prisoner a year after the fall of Rouen (which is quite a different tale from that given in the play, where Talbot retakes Rouen).

The English made a last effort. They sent a new army into Normandy. It met the French on April 15, 1450, at the village of Formigny, on the Norman coast some fifty miles west of Harfleur. But alas for England, the days of Crécys and Agincourts were over. The English no longer faced large and incompetent French armies. Actually, the French at Formigny were fewer than the English, but they had by now sharpened their efficiency in the hot forge of war and disaster. The French won, killing two thirds of the English army.

Within a year all of Normandy was French and the work of Henry V was utterly undone.

. . . the gates of Bordeaux . . .

In the scene after the coronation in Paris of King Henry, we find ourselves suddenly in Bordeaux in the southwest of France. Talbot is leading his army to the walls of the city and cries:

> Go to the gates of Bordeaux, trumpeter;
> Summon their general unto the wall.
> —Act IV, scene ii, lines 1–2

What has happened? Well, it is suddenly more than twenty years after Henry's coronation, a huge two-decade time gap that is simply sloughed off, the period during which English armies were evicted from nearly all of France. After 1451 the English controlled only Calais in the northeast and the region about Bordeaux in the southwest. They were back to where they had been before Henry V came to the throne.

Bordeaux had been English for three centuries. Richard the Lion-Heart ruled there in the twelfth century and it was much more his home than England was. Edward the Black Prince ruled there, and his son, who was later to be Richard II, was born there.

But now, in the disasters that were befalling England, even Bordeaux was threatened. The rich regions around it that had been an English empire so long melted away, and finally on June 5, 1451, Bordeaux fell to the French.

One great English captain was left, the indefatigable Talbot. Somehow the loss of Bordeaux stung the British even more than the loss of Normandy, and Talbot was sent to the southwest to retrieve the loss there.

He was nearly seventy years old by this time, but his fighting spirit was not in the least diminished.

. . . that villain Somerset

In September 1452 the English under Talbot again marched into Bordeaux, and wide areas round about declared for them.

If the English thought this was another turning point, however, they were living in a dreamland. Talbot's ancient frame could not alone bear the weight of the war, and that was all the English had—Talbot.

Charles VII (still referred to as the "Dolphin," or Dauphin, in the play, though he had been crowned a quarter century before) merely gathered his forces and marched toward Bordeaux. French reconquest was not difficult at all.

In the play there is no indication at all that the duel for Bordeaux comes so late in the game, when virtually all the rest of France has been cleared of the English. It seems to be taking place instead at a time when there are English armies in the north that ought to be marching to the aid and support of Talbot. Why did they not, then? The Shakespearean picture is that the relieving armies were two in number, one under the control of Somerset, one under that of York, and the rivalry between the two ruined Talbot.

Thus, when York hears that Charles VII is marching toward Bordeaux with overwhelming force, he can only say, petulantly:

> A plague upon that villain Somerset,
> That thus delays my promised supply
> Of horsemen . . .
> —Act IV, scene iii, lines 9–11

And then, when messengers from Talbot arrive at Somerset's army, Somerset says sullenly:

> *It is too late, I cannot send them now;*
> *This expedition was by York and Talbot*
> *Too rashly plotted.*
>
> —Act IV, scene iv, lines 1–3

My Icarus . . .

On July 14, 1453, the French were laying siege to the city of Castillon, thirty miles east of Bordeaux. Talbot hastened to its relief, as spirited as ever.

But he was Talbot—who thought that bravery was all that was required. He attacked without waiting for his artillery to come up and he was killed, together with most of his army, on July 17, 1453.

His son, another John Talbot, had joined him before the battle. Young John dies first and old Talbot, himself dying, cradles his son in his arms, and mourns:

> *. . . there died,*
> *My Icarus, my blossom, in his pride.*
>
> —Act IV, scene vii, lines 15–16

Icarus was, in the Greek myths, the son of Daedalus, the great inventor. Both were imprisoned in Crete, the King of which land they had offended. Daedalus devised wings of feathers glued to a light framework with wax, and, making use of these, he and Icarus flew out of Crete.

Daedalus had warned Icarus not to fly too high, but Icarus did not obey. He climbed into the sky too near the sun and the heat melted the wax. Away fluttered the feathers and down went Icarus into a section of the Aegean Sea north of Crete and west of Asia Minor, a section sometimes called the Icarian Sea in his honor.

Talbot himself dies, but not before delivering a line of considerable power. He says that his dead son is smiling as though to say (having died only after killing numerous Frenchmen):

> *"Had Death been French, then Death had died today."*
>
> —Act IV, scene vii, line 28

The Battle of Castillon was the last action of any consequence of the Hundred Years' War, which thus ended in utter English defeat thirty-eight years after Agincourt. There was no peace treaty, no formal conclusion. It just petered out. And all that was left to the English was Calais, which

Edward III had captured a century before, and which they were to keep for another century.

In the same year that the Hundred Years' War ended, and only a month and a half before the death of Talbot, an even more dramatic event took place. The city of Constantinople, which for eleven hundred years had been the capital of emperors who could trace their title back to the Roman Augustus (see page II-55), fell to the Turks.

It was the end of an age, both East and West. In the East, the last shadow of the ancient world was destroyed, and in the West, the warfare of the Middle Ages came to an end. Out of the ravagement of the Hundred Years' War, the modern nations of England and France were slowly to emerge.

. . . to Paris . . .

Nothing in this anachronism-haunted play shows that the Battle of Castillon ended the Hundred Years' War.

Joan of Arc appears among the victors, looking down upon the dead body of Talbot—the embodiment of French witchcraft triumphant at last over English valor. Actually, though, Joan had been dead twenty-two years by the time of Castillon.

With the battle over, the Dauphin says:

> And now to Paris, in this conquering vein:
> All will be ours, now bloody Talbot's slain.
> —Act IV, scene vii, lines 95–96

Yes, of course, except that all was theirs already.

The Earl of Armagnac . . .

The play shifts to England and it is now made to seem that the death of Talbot had so disheartened the English as to place the peace party in the ascendant.

Actually, the time moves backward several years. The peace party *is* in the ascendant, but it had been so for a decade before Talbot's death.

Henry VI's minority ended in 1437, when he was sixteen years old and Gloucester's role as Protector lost its point. The young King's piety gave Gloucester's great enemy, Winchester, particular influence over the royal youngster, who was no more able to rule than before, despite his "majority."

Gloucester's position was further shaken by his defeat in the matter of the release of Charles of Orléans (see page II-558) and by the trial of his wife for witchcraft (an event which Shakespeare pushes further ahead in time and makes an important part of *Henry VI, Part Two*).

Gloucester fought desperately to maintain the ascendancy of his own hawkish position and to save Normandy at least. Through the early 1440s he tried to arrange some marriage that would bind Henry VI to the side of a firm and aggressive foreign policy. Gloucester says to Henry:

> *The Earl of Armagnac, near knit to Charles,*
> *A man of great authority in France,*
> *Proffers his only daughter to your grace*
> *In marriage, with a large and sumptuous dowry.*
>
>   —Act V, scene i, lines 17–20

The Earl of Armagnac referred to was Jean IV, of the line of Bernard VII (see page II–473). As Charles VII grew stronger and exerted his influence more and more in southern France (the Armagnac bailiwick), Jean IV grew disaffected. He turned toward the English and Humphrey of Gloucester saw in him a new Burgundy.

Armagnac was encouraged to rebel and talk arose concerning a marriage between his daughter and King Henry in order to tie him firmly to English interests.

. . . my years are young

Henry did not like the idea suggested by Gloucester. He says:

> *Marriage, uncle! alas, my years are young,*
> *And fitter is my study and my books*
> *Than wanton dalliance with a paramour.*
>
>   —Act V, scene i, lines 21–23

By now, though (1444), his years were not so young that he might not take a wife. He was twenty-three years old.

However, he remained a child in many ways all his life. He was never able to take independent action, was always glad to be led by any stronger personality. He would indeed have preferred being left to his books and his prayers, and he was never interested in women.

But Henry was in no danger. French influence in the south grew even more rapidly than was expected, and Armagnac was slapped down. He was clearly going to be of no use to England anyway, and Humphrey's marriage project was destroyed. That was his last chance and he had lost it.

Damsel of France . . .

But the war (in the play at least) continues. The Dauphin and Burgundy, together with Joan of Arc, march toward Paris. There they will meet the English forces under Richard of York.

Before the battle, Joan's demons come onstage and leave her, presaging disaster for her. In the battle, the English win, and after York and Burgundy fight hand to hand, York captures Joan and says:

> *Damsel of France, I think I have you fast;*
> —Act V, scene iii, line 30

The germ of truth that lies beyond this monstrous fantasy is that Joan of Arc was indeed captured in the course of a campaign against Paris. That, however, was a couple of decades earlier and long before York was placed in charge of the forces in France.

After Charles VII was crowned at Reims in July 1429, Joan favored a direct attack on Paris, and forced an attempt in that direction with inadequate forces under reluctant leaders. She was wounded by an arrow through the thigh and was forced to retreat. That ruined the aura of invincibility about her, but she kept trying to force the French into aggressive action, and on May 23, 1430, Joan was captured at the city of Compiègne, forty miles northeast of Paris.

This was before the Treaty of Arras. The Burgundians were still on the side of the English and the Duke of Bedford was still alive. Far from Burgundy fighting on behalf of Joan, it was the Burgundians who captured Joan. They sold her to the English for ten thousand francs, and on January 3, 1431, the English (who were then under Warwick, not York) had her.

In a sense, then, York took Joan from Burgundy, but it was not really York who did so, but his predecessor, and he did not take her by force of arms from Joan's ally, but through purchase from Joan's enemy, and not after the Battle of Castillon, but twenty-two years before.

. . . daughter to a king

Meanwhile, Suffolk has also captured a woman prisoner in the course of the same battle. This pair of captures, as part of the same scene, is significant from a dramatic standpoint, for this second capture is of a woman who will do more harm to England than Joan of Arc had done.

Suffolk, impressed by her beauty, asks her name, and she replies:

Margaret my name, and daughter to a king,
The King of Naples . . .

—Act V, scene iii, lines 51–52

This is as badly distorted as the capture of Joan of Arc.

After the failure of Gloucester's projected Armagnac marriage, the peace party was supreme in England and men such as Winchester, Somerset, and Suffolk were in control.

When York's term of office in France expired in 1445, he was ordered back to England (as will be made clear in *Henry VI, Part Two*). This was partly because of the general enmity toward him on the part of the Beaufort family and their allies, and partly because he was too hawkish.

Suffolk then arranged a truce with France and at Arras began negotiating a marriage that would help make for a permanent peace that would perhaps leave Normandy at least in English hands.

For the purpose he chose the girl Margaret, the daughter of Reignier I (René I) of Anjou. In theory, the kingdom of Naples succeeded to him after the death of its queen, Joanna II, in 1435, but he never ruled. The Spaniards of the kingdom of Aragon, who then controlled Sicily, took over Naples as well.

René of Anjou remained titular king, however. That is, he held the title and though it brought him neither power nor income, it did carry with it social prestige. It was much easier for the English King to marry the daughter of a King of Naples than of a Count of Anjou, even if Naples was an empty title. Hence, Margaret is introduced as the "daughter to a king."

Margaret was born in 1429 and was only fifteen years old when Suffolk was negotiating the marriage. It was a good match from the standpoint of diplomacy. Not only was she of high rank, thanks to her father's titular kingdom, but she was of a family that had been loyal to the French King and therefore would be useful in urging a peace upon France—the kind of peace Suffolk and his party wanted.

To the later English chroniclers, however, Margaret was a hated Frenchwoman who, far from bringing a dowry with her, cost England provinces in exchange for the marriage. She played an unpopular role in the civil wars that followed and it was easy to blame her for everything that could not be attributed to Joan of Arc.

Her general unpopularity caused the legend makers to make everything about her unsavory and disgraceful. Thus, Suffolk is pictured in this play (which follows the legends) as falling in love with her, and then pushing through her marriage to Henry in order that he might have her as his paramour and, through her, rule both the weak English King and England itself.

Thou art no father . . .

Joan of Arc makes her last appearance now. She is on trial before the Duke of York, but this trial, like everything else concerning Joan in the play, bears no relation at all to reality, except that there *was* a trial.

To put the real facts briefly, Joan was placed on trial as a heretic on January 13, 1431, before an ecclesiastical court presided over by Pierre Cauchon, Bishop of Beauvais. The trial continued for months and Joan maintained her dignity and her resolution throughout. She was finally burned in the market place of Rouen on May 30, without ever breaking.

The final picture of Joan in the play, however, is so disgraceful and so clearly the result of unreasoning English prejudice that it, more than anything else, makes it difficult for the play ever to be staged nowadays.

In the play Joan is first made to deny her father, a shepherd, and shout:

> *I am descended of a gentler blood.*
> *Thou art no father nor no friend of mine.*
> —Act V, scene iv, lines 8–9

The self-righteous English lords affect to be shocked at Joan's action, and her father stamps off in a rage, urging that she be burned.

Joan then tries to save herself by first claiming to be a virgin, next claiming to be with child, next claiming each of three men as father of that child. She is led off, presumably to be executed.

Fortunately, this scene has never affected the general opinion of Joan among posterity. Nor did her execution in actual history long remain a blot on her memory—rather it was turned into martyrdom.

In 1450, when Charles VII re-entered Rouen, he ordered an inquiry into the trial. (After all, he had been crowned through the agency of Joan and he could scarcely have his crown ascribed to the labors of one officially declared a heretic and witch. In 1456 the inquiry was concluded, and the judgment of the trial was reversed.)

. . . a solemn peace

With Joan of Arc led off to execution—the witch to be killed—peace is signed. This is not really a peace but merely the truce arranged in 1445, accompanying the marriage arrangements with Margaret of Anjou.

In the play the description of that peace or truce is a completely chauvinistic one. King Charles, still called merely "Charles" and denied his royalty, must acknowledge King Henry as his overlord, and therefore, pre-

sumably, rightful King of France, while agreeing to pay tribute to that overlord. The scene ends, therefore, with York saying:

> *So, now dismiss your army when ye please;*
> *Hang up your ensigns, let your drums be still,*
> *For here we entertain a solemn peace.*
>
> —Act V, scene iv, lines 173–75

. . . break it . . .

If the truce of 1445 had been permanent, England would have ended a
hundred years of sporadic warfare in France with Normandy gained at
least. Whether that was worth the bloodshed and misery is extremely
doubtful, but no doubt it would have been a source of pride to the English
in later generations.

However, even as the truce is being agreed to, Alençon is whispering to
King Charles that he may

> . . . *break it when your pleasure serves.*
>
> —Act V, scene iv, line 164

Naturally, Charles could not be expected to acquiesce permanently to
the loss of Normandy, if that could be avoided. (Nor could England be
trusted, for that matter, to refrain from growing aggressive again if France
ever weakened.)

In this case the years following the truce saw France increasingly gain
strength while England continued to slide down the bickering trough to
ruin. In 1447 York, her best soldier, was sent into semiexile in Ireland to
suit the prejudices of the Lancastrians, and in 1448 Charles opened a new
offensive that broke the truce.

As described earlier (see page II–562), this led quickly to the loss of
Normandy and to the final Battle of Castillon in southwestern France.

. . . England's royal queen

It might seem reasonable to speculate that if Shakespeare were working
with an earlier play, this scene in which a truce is triumphantly signed by
the English would be a natural ending.

A final scene is, however, added, which would seem to be an appendix
to the natural conclusion; an appendix that serves as a kind of cement between this play and *Henry VI, Part Two.*

In the royal palace at London, Suffolk is describing the beautiful Margaret of Anjou to such effect that chaste King Henry is utterly won over

and his dedication to his study and his books is forgotten. He says to
Gloucester:

> . . . *my Lord Protector, give consent*
> *That Margaret may be England's royal queen.*
>> —Act V, scene v, lines 23–24

This ascribes more power to Gloucester than he had at this time, for he
is now near his final fall. However, Shakespeare deals with the fall of
Gloucester in *Henry VI, Part Two* and can give no hint of it here.

Gloucester argues against the marriage to Anjou and for Armagnac,
since Armagnac is rich and Anjou poor. Suffolk argues the kingly title and
the lady's beauty and scorns the idea that the English King will let himself
be swayed by thought of money.

And Henry, corrupted by passion, insists on having Margaret.

. . . *the youthful Paris* . . .

So it is that the play now ends in midstroke. Suffolk, who has been ordered to bring back Margaret of Anjou, delivers the last speech of the
play, after Gloucester leaves in defeat:

> *Thus Suffolk hath prevailed, and thus he goes,*
> *As did the youthful Paris once to Greece,*
>> —Act V, scene v, lines 103–4

But that is just an indication of the baleful events ahead, for Paris' mission to Greece brought back Helen of Troy (see page I–76) and eventual
destruction on the land he brought her to. And the same, or almost, was to
happen to England.

Henry VI, Part Two will begin with scarcely a jog, with the return of
Suffolk, his mission successfully completed.

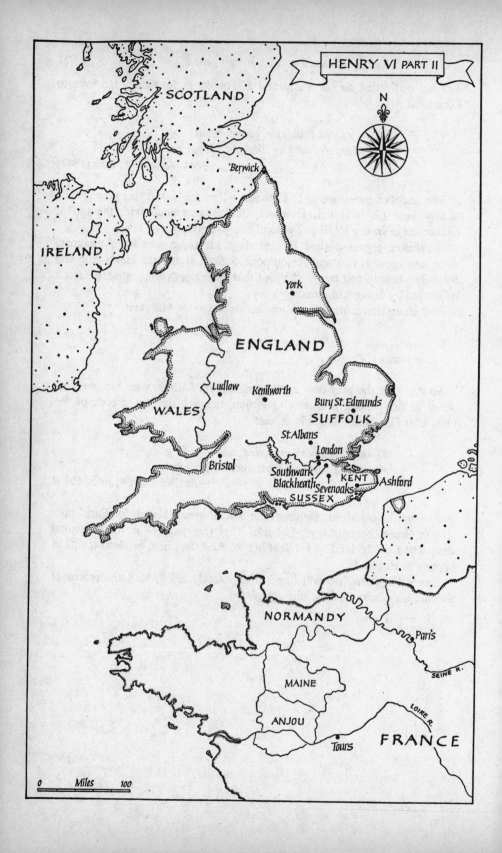

37

The History of

HENRY VI, PART TWO

HENRY VI, PART TWO begins just where *Henry VI, Part One* ends. The latter play had concluded as William de la Pole, Earl of Suffolk (see page II–545), was leaving for France to arrange the wedding of King Henry VI with Margaret of Anjou. This present play begins as Suffolk returns, the mission successfully completed.

. . . ancient city, Tours

The play opens in the royal palace in London. King Henry VI is on his throne, his nobles about him, and Suffolk addresses him:

> *I had in charge at my depart for France,*
> *As procurator [deputy] to your Excellence,*
> *To marry Princess Margaret for your Grace,*
> *So in the famous ancient city, Tours,*
> *In presence of the Kings of France and Sicil,*
> *The Dukes of Orleans, Calaber, Bretagne and Alençon,*
> *Seven earls, twelve barons, and twenty reverend bishops,*
> *I have performed my task and was espoused,*
> —Act I, scene i, lines 2–9

The marriage by proxy had taken place in Tours in central France. It is on the Loire River, about seventy miles downstream from Orléans, where the turning point of the Hundred Years' War had taken place.

The date of the marriage was April 23, 1445, and it is necessary to see in what position England and France lay in those years. Since the turning point at Orléans in 1429 (see page II–527), the English tide had been ebbing steadily. By 1444 England still held Normandy in force, together with the province of Maine immediately to its south, as well as Calais in the northeast and the region around Bordeaux in the southwest. If they could settle for that, they would still have salvaged a good deal of the conquests of Henry V.

The peace party in England, of whom Suffolk was now the chief, felt that only by arranging a treaty could these still occupied sections of France

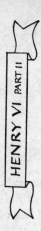

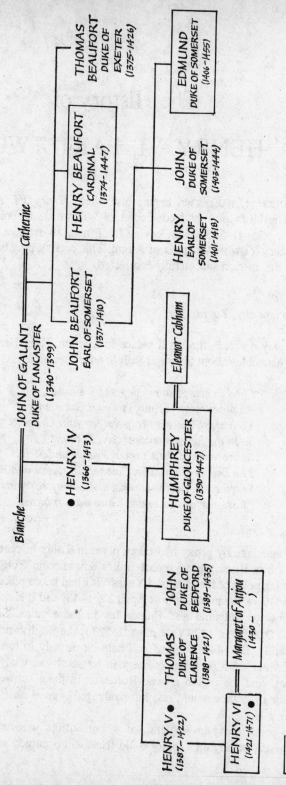

HENRY VI PART II

HOUSE of LANCASTER

Blanche == JOHN OF GAUNT
DUKE OF LANCASTER
(1340-1399)
== Catherine

• HENRY IV
(1366-1413)

JOHN BEAUFORT
EARL OF SOMERSET
(1371-1410)

HENRY BEAUFORT
CARDINAL
(1374-1447)

THOMAS BEAUFORT
DUKE OF
EXETER
(1375-1426)

HENRY
EARL OF
SOMERSET
(1401-1418)

JOHN
DUKE OF
SOMERSET
(1403-1444)

EDMUND
DUKE OF SOMERSET
(1406-1455)

HUMPHREY
DUKE OF GLOUCESTER
(1390-1447)
== Eleanor Cobham

THOMAS
DUKE OF CLARENCE
(1388-1421)

JOHN
DUKE OF BEDFORD
(1389-1435)

HENRY V •
(1387-1422)

HENRY VI •
(1421-1471)
== Margaret of Anjou
(1430 -)

▢ Characters in the play

• Kings of England

NOTE: Women's names in lower-case

be retained. Over the outcries of the remaining hawks in England, who held that the war must be continued to final victory at all costs, an approach to such a peace was made.

A ten-year truce was announced in 1444, and such a truce, if kept, would give ample time to work out a permanent peace. In order to make it more likely that the truce would be kept, Suffolk negotiated a marriage alliance between the English King Henry VI, and the French noblewoman Margaret of Anjou.

Margaret was a descendant of John II of France (the King who had lost the Battle of Poitiers to the Black Prince, see page II–257). Her father, René of Anjou, was titular King of Naples (see page II–526) and brother to the wife of the French King, Charles VII. Since Naples and Sicily were at various times in their history under the same rule (and were thus combined in 1444, except that they were under a Spanish ruler and not under René), the King of Sicil referred to in line 6 is undoubtedly the father of the bride.

Margaret, who, as you see, was the niece of the French King, was only fifteen years old at the time of her marriage.

. . . the duchy of Anjou . . .

Suffolk delivers his proxy bride to King Henry, who greets her joyfully. Suffolk next hands over a document which represents the terms of the truce he has negotiated with France.

It falls to Humphrey of Gloucester (see page II–479) to read it. Humphrey is the King's only remaining uncle and is the closest to the throne— the heir, in fact, since the King as yet has no children. He was created Lord Protector (of the King), since Henry succeeded to the throne when he was only nine months old.

Officially, he ceased being Lord Protector in 1429, when the King was seven years old, but in some ways Henry remained seven years old all his life and always needed a protector. Gloucester's influence gradually diminished, but by virtue of his relationship he remained close to the throne always and was probably long thought of as Lord Protector even after the title was no longer officially his. Shakespeare gives him that title still as this play opens, even though King Henry is now twenty-three.

As the nearest relative of the King, then, Humphrey has the honor of reading the treaty and soon comes to a passage which goes:

> *. . . That the duchy of Anjou and the county of Maine shall*
> *be released and delivered to the king her father . . .*
> —Act I, scene i, lines 50–52

Maine, as I said before, is a French province lying directly south of Normandy, while Anjou lies to the south of Maine.

There is some justice to this condition. Anjou and Maine made up the hereditary dominions of Margaret's father, René of Anjou, so he was only asking for his own.

Both provinces had been ravaged by English soldiers during the course of the Hundred Years' War, but Anjou, the more southerly of the two, was never actually occupied. Even at the height of the English offensive, Anjou remained French (despite the implication all through this play that Anjou was English-occupied).

From the dovish point of view, then, the concession was not as large as it seemed, for only Maine really had to be surrendered and this was worth it if the rest of the English-held territory could be saved.

From the hawkish point of view, however, this was base appeasement of the wicked French. Nor, they felt, could it be argued that the provinces were merely being given back to their rightful duke, who was now King Henry's father-in-law. It was quite obvious that the Duke of Anjou held no real power except that which was given him by France, and that the provinces, once ceded, would be in the grip of the French King—the great enemy of England.

And as a matter of fact, René was the last Duke of Anjou to hold even the semblance of an independent rule over his province. After his death in 1480, Anjou was united to the French crown and remained an integral part of France ever after.

. . . without having any dowry

When Gloucester (the surviving brother of conquering King Henry V, and England's leading hawk) reads the passage ceding Anjou and Maine, he is struck dumb and the paper drops from his hand. Henry Beaufort, Bishop of Winchester (see page II–522), picks it up and reads on. Winchester had been a cardinal briefly during the reign of Henry V. He had given up the office then at Henry's demands, but in 1426 he had once more secured the title. While his speeches are labeled "Winchester" in *Henry VI, Part One,* they are labeled "Cardinal" here. I will refer to him as Cardinal Beaufort in this play.

The final section of the treaty states that Margaret is

> . . . *sent over of the King of England's own proper cost and charges, without having any dowry.*
>
> —Act I, scene i, lines 60–62

Worse and worse. It was customary for a bride to bring a dowry with her. In arranging a marriage, the bride's dowry was constantly in mind, and in the case of a royal marriage, the dowry might well be some cities or a province brought under the control of the husband.

For the English (who still considered themselves a conquering people with the French as their inferiors) to be forced to take a French princess for their King without any dowry at all, and with the King even paying transportation costs and giving up two provinces in addition in a kind of reverse dowry, was too great a humiliation. From the very moment of the marriage, Margaret was unpopular in England.

In fact, the legend arose in later years (and is made use of in Shakespeare's version of history) that the surrender of these two provinces was what led inevitably to England's final loss of French dominion. Not so, however. Anjou, at least, was never England's to give up; and as for Maine, England evaded the terms of the treaty and held on as long as she could. The reverse dowry amounted to zero, therefore, and it was for other reasons that the English lost.

. . . France, 'tis ours . . .

The King accepts it all with pleasure. He, the Queen, and Suffolk leave, but the rest remain to rage and quarrel.

Gloucester, the archhawk, speaks first, crying out against the shame of the treaty and the loss it represents, after all that had been done to win France. He says it is a matter of

> Undoing all, as all had never been.
> —Act I, scene i, line 103

Cardinal Beaufort, the archdove and Gloucester's half uncle (see page II–581), denies any loss, saying:

> For France, 'tis ours; and we will keep it still [always].
> —Act I, scene i, line 106

This makes the situation seem as it was described at the end of *Henry VI, Part One,* when the truce of 1444 was being signed. The earlier play made it appear that it was France that was giving in and that King Charles had accepted the overlordship of the English King. This fantasy view is maintained at the start of this play, so that more than ever the theory is advanced that only this foolish and disadvantageous treaty designed to arrange a French marriage lost England the long war.

. . . the keys of Normandy

A more rational note is struck by another hawk, who says:

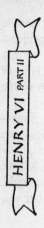

HENRY VI PART II

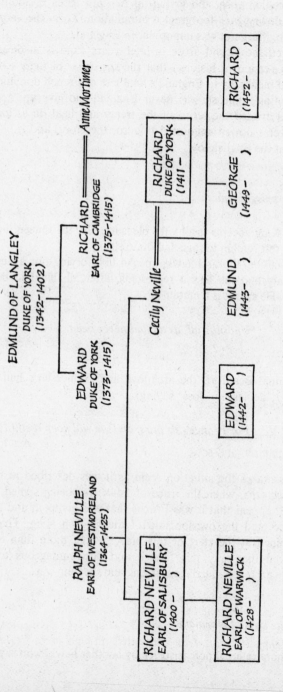

HOUSE of YORK

EDMUND OF LANGLEY
DUKE OF YORK
(1342–1402)

EDWARD
DUKE OF YORK
(1373–1415)

RICHARD ══ Anne Mortimer
EARL OF CAMBRIDGE
(1375–1415)

RICHARD ══ Cecily Neville
DUKE OF YORK
(1411–)

EDWARD
(1442–)

EDMUND
(1443–)

GEORGE
(1449–)

RICHARD
(1452–)

RALPH NEVILLE
EARL OF WESTMORELAND
(1364–1425)

RICHARD NEVILLE
EARL OF SALISBURY
(1400–)

RICHARD NEVILLE
EARL OF WARWICK
(1428–)

☐ Characters in the play

NOTE: Women's names in lower case

These counties were the keys of Normandy!
—Act I, scene i, line 114

Normandy, in north-central France, was, of all sections of France, most dear to the English aristocracy. It was from Normandy that William the Conqueror had come to establish himself in England and it was back to Normandy that most of the aristocracy could trace their lines and their ancestral estates. It almost seemed to them that Normandy was their true home.

Henry V had conquered Normandy in his second campaign in France, between 1417 and 1419 (see page II–510), and it was for that section that the English fought most fiercely. Even in 1445 that province was still firmly held. The fears that this hold would be weakened with the cession of the guarding regions to the south was a poignant one.

The speaker of this line, by the way, is the Earl of Salisbury.

There was an Earl of Salisbury in *Henry VI, Part One,* but this is not the same one. The earlier earl, Thomas de Montagu, had died in the course of the siege of Orléans (see page II–536), sixteen years before *Henry VI, Part Two* opens.

Thomas de Montagu had left no sons, but by his first wife he had an only daughter, Alice, who had in 1425 (three years before Thomas' death) married Richard Neville, a son of the Earl of Westmoreland who was a character in *Henry IV, Part One, Henry IV, Part Two,* and *Henry V* (see page II–317).

Richard Neville inherited the title after Thomas de Montagu's death, and it is Richard who is the Salisbury of this play.

. . . *Warwick, my valiant son*

Having made the remark concerning the keys of Normandy, Salisbury interrupts himself and asks:

But wherefore weeps Warwick, my valiant son?
—Act I, scene i, line 115

Again there is a possible confusion of names. In *Henry VI, Part One* we had an Earl of Warwick, who was a strong partisan on the side of Richard of York, who was in charge of the education of Henry VI, who was regent of France for a while, and who oversaw the trial and execution of Joan of Arc (see page II–548).

That Earl of Warwick is now dead. He had died in 1439 at the age of fifty-seven, six years before *Henry VI, Part Two* opens. Actually, he died before *Henry VI, Part One* concluded, though he is made to be present at the signing of the truce of 1444 in that jumbled play.

The new Earl of Warwick is the son of the Earl of Salisbury, and, like his father, is named Richard Neville.

Richard Neville of Warwick, one of the dominating figures of the next few decades, was born in 1428 and so is only seventeen years old at the time that *Henry IV, Part Two* opens. His wife was the heiress to the earldom of Warwick and it was through her that Richard gained his title (in fashion similar to that in which his father had gained *his* title). Actually, Richard didn't get the title till March 1450, five years after this play opens, so it is a bit anachronistic to call him Warwick in this first scene.

. . . myself did win them . . .

Warwick explains his tears as being over the loss of the two provinces. He says:

> *Anjou and Maine! myself did win them both;*
> *Those provinces these arms of mine did conquer:*
> —Act I, scene i, lines 119–20

This is, of course, ridiculous. This seventeen-year-old boy never fought in France, and Anjou was never conquered by anybody in that century. This seems to be a careless confusion of Richard Neville with Richard Beauchamp, the earlier Earl of Warwick of *Henry VI, Part One*.

. . . the good Duke of Gloucester

Richard of York also expresses himself against the marriage, but it is Humphrey of Gloucester who is most furious. He denounces a tax that Suffolk is pushing through Parliament to defray the expenses of the marriage and predicts that all France will be lost.

When he leaves, however, Cardinal Beaufort of Winchester renews his ancient plotting against Gloucester. He warns all within hearing that Gloucester as the heir to the throne would be displeased with any marriage that might give the King a child. Gloucester must be taken care of, then:

> *What though the common people favor him,*
> *Calling him "Humphrey, the good Duke of Gloucester."*
> —Act I, scene i, lines 158–59

Gloucester, for all his faults as a politician, was popular with the people. He was, after all, the only living brother of the great Henry V, and was therefore a perpetual reminder of those great days of conquest. He had himself fought bravely in those days and had maintained a loud patriotic stand ever since, and patriotism always sounds good.

In addition, he was renowned for his hospitality, he was a patron of scholars, and he gave large bequests to Oxford University. It is scholars who write history and in retrospect they remembered him as even better than he was, until finally the legend of "good Duke Humphrey" arose.

He being of age . . .

Another lord present, speaking now for the first time, agrees with the Cardinal's view and says of Humphrey of Gloucester:

> *Why should he then protect our sovereign,*
> *He being of age to govern of himself?*
> *Cousin of Somerset, join you with me,*
> *And altogether with the Duke of Suffolk,*
> *We'll quickly hoise Duke Humphrey from his seat.*
>
> —Act I, scene i, lines 165–69

The speaker is the Duke of Buckingham. He is another Humphrey— Humphrey Stafford—who married the heiress to the earldom of Buckingham. In 1444, just before this play opens, he was created the 1st Duke of Buckingham.

Buckingham was himself of royal blood. His mother had been the daughter of Thomas of Gloucester (see page II–264), the youngest son of Edward III. Buckingham was thus a great-grandson of that fecund monarch, and is a second cousin, once removed, of King Henry VI. He is also second cousin to Edmund Beaufort, 2nd Duke of Somerset (see page II–562), whom he here addresses as "Cousin of Somerset."

It is soon made clear, though, that the outrage at Humphrey of Gloucester's position of Protector for a King old enough to rule for himself is pure pretense. All know very well that the King cannot rule, whatever his age, and Buckingham is soon proposing to Somerset that one or the other of them will become the new Protector.

. . . thy acts in Ireland

Buckingham and Somerset leave, but York remains behind along with the father-son combination, Salisbury and Warwick. York is the most important member of the royal family who is *not* a descendant of John of Gaunt, and since he can trace his ancestry to an older brother of Gaunt (see page II–542), he has a better right to the throne, legalistically speaking, than Henry VI.

Thus, Salisbury, disapproving of the haughty bearing of Cardinal Beaufort and sympathizing with Gloucester's hawkish views, turns to York as a natural ally against the Cardinal. Salisbury says:

> . . . brother York, thy acts in Ireland,
> In bringing them to civil discipline,
> Thy late exploits done in the heart of France,
> When thou wert regent for our sovereign,
> Have made thee feared and honored of the people:
> Join we together for the public good,
>
> —Act I, scene i, lines 194–99

York had indeed done well in France in the years immediately preceding the truce and had kept England's grip on Normandy firm, and had indeed gained considerable popularity as a result. This, however, but made him all the more feared by the Lancastrians, who, with good reason, distrusted the abilities and popularity of a man who could argue a superior claim to the throne.

When his stint in France was completed, therefore, he was *not* reappointed. In fact, earlier in the scene, immediately after the fatal treaty that accompanied the marriage was read, King Henry said:

> Cousin of York, we here discharge your Grace
> From being regent i'th'parts of France,
>
> —Act I, scene i, lines 66–67

The "acts in Ireland" to which Salisbury refers in his address to York were equally noteworthy, but, however, had not yet been performed. They came later, and York's trip to Ireland will play its part eventually in the play. He did spend some time in Ireland in the early 1430s, however, though not in connection with any serious disorders there at that time.

. . . the fatal brand Althaea burned

Salisbury and Warwick then leave, and finally York is left alone onstage. Shakespeare continues to follow the anti-Yorkist feelings of his time and has York brooding on his own thwarted right to the throne. York says, addressing himself concerning the cession of the provinces:

> I cannot blame them all—what is't to them?
> 'Tis thine they give away, and not their own.
>
> —Act I, scene i, lines 220–21

In an agony of frustration at this disposal by others of what he considers his own, he says:

Methinks the realms of England, France, and Ireland
Bear that proportion to my flesh and blood
As did the fatal brand Althaea burned
Unto the Prince's heart of Calydon.
—Act I, scene i, lines 232–35

This is a reference to Meleager of Calydon, whose life would last only so long as a brand in the keeping of his mother, Althaea, remained unburned (see page II–394). Richard feels the loss of his realm will kill him just as surely as the burning of the brand would kill Meleager.

York decides, therefore, to play for the crown, biding his time and choosing his allies. He says:

Nor shall proud Lancaster usurp my right,
Nor hold the scepter in his childish fist,
—Act I, scene i, lines 244–45

Lancaster is here a reference to King Henry, whom York is denying the regal title and giving only that which he inherits from his great-grandfather, John of Gaunt, Duke of Lancaster.

York concludes that when the time is ripe:

. . . force perforce, I'll make him yield the crown,
Whose bookish rule hath pulled fair England down.
—Act I, scene i, lines 258–59

It must be repeated here, though, that there is no sign, in actual history, that York had such deep-laid plans so early in his career. As far as we may judge from his deeds in France before the truce that opens the play and his deeds in Ireland after the truce, he was utterly loyal.

. . . unto Saint Albans

The scene now shifts to the house of the Duke of Gloucester, where he is in conversation with his wife, the Duchess Eleanor.

The two are wide apart in their attitudes. Humphrey is perturbed and fearful. He has been dreaming of destruction, of being ousted from his office. Eleanor, on the other hand, has been dreaming of exaltation, of becoming queen (after all, Humphrey is heir to the throne).

Gloucester scolds her for that, but he is too good-natured not to be quickly mollified.

A Messenger then arrives, saying:

My Lord Protector, 'tis his Highness' pleasure
You do prepare to ride unto Saint Albans,

Where as the King and Queen do mean to hawk.
> —Act I, scene ii, lines 56–58

St. Albans is a town some twenty miles northwest of London's center; it is named after the first English martyr, St. Alban, who died there, according to legend, in 303. It was in St. Albans that King John II of France was held prisoner after the Battle of Poitiers, and before Henry's reign was over there were fated to be two important battles there.

. . . *new-made Duke of Suffolk*

Humphrey of Gloucester hurries off to join the King, and his Duchess promises to follow after. She lingers behind a little, however, to consult with John Hum, a dishonest priest who has been practicing on the Duchess' ambition. He has contacts with witches and sorcerers who, the Duchess thinks, will help her achieve what she wants—the royal crown. She gives him money and leaves.

Hum, remaining behind, reveals in a soliloquy that he is what we might call a double agent. He says:

> *Yet have I gold flies from another coast—*
> *I dare not say, from the rich Cardinal*
> *And from the great and new-made Duke of Suffolk.*
> > —Act I, scene ii, lines 93–95

In other words, Gloucester's opposition know of the poor Duchess' intrigues and are luring her on, hoping to destroy her, and with her, her husband as well.

In the play, Suffolk is promoted to duke immediately after bringing Margaret to England. Thus, after that fatal treaty has been read, the fatuously pleased King says to Suffolk:

> *Lord Marquess, kneel down: we here create thee*
> *First Duke of Suffolk, and girt thee with the sword.*
> > —Act I, scene i, lines 64–65

Actually, the promotion came three years later at an even more inappropriate time for Suffolk.

. . . *rightful heir to the crown*

Back at the royal palace a group of petitioners await the Protector to have him answer their pleas and judge their quarrels. Suffolk and Queen

Margaret enter instead and Suffolk insists on knowing the nature of the petitions.

One of the petitioners, an armorer's apprentice named Peter Thump, has come to lodge information against his master. He says, handing Suffolk his petition:

> *Against my master, Thomas Horner, for saying that the*
> *Duke of York was rightful heir to the crown.*
> —Act I, scene iii, lines 26–28

This, of course, was York's danger. He *was* rightful heir to the crown on the basis of strict legitimacy, and some Englishmen, displeased with the feeble rule of the King and having plenty of evidence of York's ability, were bound to remember this.

No matter how loyal York might be in reality, there was no way he could stop people from turning to him, and that in itself would suffice to feed increasing suspicion against him on the part of the Lancastrians. Eventually that suspicion would force the Lancastrians to take such actions against York as to force York into rebellion. It was all quite inevitable.

. . . bent to holiness

Queen Margaret quite naturally loses her temper over the suggestion that York is rightful King and she herself, therefore, no Queen at all. She tears up the petitions and drives the petitioners away.

Petulantly, she complains to Suffolk at the weakness of a government that stoops to listen to petitions. She is dissatisfied with so weak a King as her husband, one who is still under the thumb of a Protector. Finally, she says energetically that when she had been wooed by Suffolk on King Henry's behalf

> *I thought King Henry had resembled thee*
> *In courage, courtship and proportion:*
> *But all his mind is bent to holiness,*
> —Act I, scene iii, lines 55–57

As a matter of fact, the husband-wife situation might well have been reversed for the good of all. Margaret of Anjou, had she only been a man, would have made a strong King, while Henry, converted to a woman, would have made a perfect Queen. Unfortunately, that could not be.

Margaret, despising her husband (and undoubtedly left sexually unsatisfied by him), threw herself into party politics on her own. Naturally, as a Frenchwoman, she would be for peace with France, and she therefore espoused with all the energy of her nature the side of Suffolk and the Cardinal. She bitterly opposed the hawkish Gloucester and the equally hawkish (and dangerously competitive) York.

In this way, she lost her chance to keep the English crown above faction, dragged Henry with her into the mire of partisan politics and civil war, increased the hatred of herself on the part of all who opposed Suffolk, and sought a scapegoat for the debacle in France.

It was her passion and venom, in fact, that went far to starting the civil war soon to come, and her energy and indomitability that kept it going so long and made it so disastrous.

. . . that proud dame . . .

Queen Margaret lists the lords whom, on one pretext or another, she dislikes, but she knows who is her prime hate and it is no man at all. She says:

> Not all these lords do vex me half so much
> As that proud dame, the Lord Protector's wife:
> —Act I, scene iii, lines 77–78

This is a very natural attitude, considering that the Duchess is next in line for the queenhood and might conceivably become Queen while Margaret is still alive to anguish at being replaced. Furthermore, the Duchess was actually richer than the Queen and would undoubtedly flaunt that wealth and openly sneer at the impoverished Frenchwoman who was temporarily Queen.

Shakespeare plays up this antagonism of the two women, and yet, however correct dramatically this might be, it is utterly wrong historically. The Duchess' sad end was accomplished four years before Margaret's marriage to Henry had made her Queen. When Margaret came to England, Eleanor was already dead; Queen and Duchess were never rivals and, in fact, never met.

Yet we must follow Shakespeare's version of history, of course.

. . . Paris was besieged . . .

The court enters again, squabbling over whether Somerset is to take over what remains of the English dominions in France, or whether York is to be reappointed, after all, to his now expired post as regent in France.

When King Henry feebly tries to smooth over the quarrel, Queen Margaret jumps with relish into the fray, helping the party of the Cardinal and Suffolk denounce Humphrey of Gloucester, until the Protector, in frustration at the wolves howling at him from every direction, hastens out of the room.

Once he is gone, the Queen, pretending to mistake the Duchess for a servant, boxes her ear. The Duchess, in a towering rage, also leaves.

Humphrey of Gloucester, having mastered himself, and unaware of the gross insult to his wife, returns to plead that his fellow hawk, York, be appointed regent.

York, however, sees clearly that Gloucester is helpless and that Suffolk's party is in the ascendant. He exclaims that it will be of no use going to France. Even if he were appointed to the post, he says:

> My Lord of Somerset will keep me here
> Without discharge, money, or furniture,
> Till France be won into the Dolphin's hands.
> Last time, I danced attendance on his will
> Till Paris was besieged, famished, and lost.
> —Act I, scene iii, lines 170–74

Richard of York had been regent in France twice, from 1437 to 1439 and from 1440 to 1445. The first regency had indeed been disastrous, and York blamed that on lack of home support. It was not then, however, that Paris was taken. The French took Paris in 1436, the year before York took his post. And York's second term had been most successful and he could make no complaints about home support then. (It was the second term that had just expired.)

As it happens, though, the post falls to Somerset, for just at this point, Suffolk drags in Thomas Horner the armorer and Peter Thump the apprentice and has the latter repeat his accusation that the former had maintained York to be rightful King of England. York is furious and denounces any such belief as utterly treasonable, but it does him no good. Even Gloucester has to admit that if such opinions are being bruited about, it would be dangerous to give York a key position in France.

So it is Somerset who goes to France.

The Duke yet lives . . .

Duchess Eleanor, maddened by the blow she has received, has lost her last scruples and is now in the garden outside her house, engaged in a séance conducted by one Margery Jourdain. The Duchess wishes to learn the future in order, presumably, to adjust her behavior to that future, and for that purpose has demons called up.

As frequently happens in the Shakespearean plays, the demons called upon by black magic actually appear. In this case a Spirit becomes manifest and answers questions in oracular fashion.

The first question, put to it by Roger Bolingbroke, an astrologer patronized by Gloucester, refers to the future of the King himself. The answer comes:

> The Duke yet lives that Henry shall depose,
> But him outlive, and die a violent death.
>
> —Act I, scene iv, lines 31–32

This remark is deliberately obscure in the fashion of oracles generally, since it lends itself to a double meaning and therefore has a greater chance of being true. Thanks to the fact that English is a largely uninflected language, the first line of the prophecy can mean: "The Duke yet lives who shall depose Henry" or "The Duke yet lives who shall be deposed by Henry." It depends on which version of the first sentence is accepted before one can decide whether Duke or King shall live longer, then die a violent death.

As a matter of fact, both versions of the oracle are true or almost true (as the more sophisticated of the Elizabethan audience would know). There was a duke living who would, in a sense, depose Henry and also be deposed by Henry, and as a matter of fact, both duke and Henry would die a violent death.

By water . . .

The next question concerns the future of the Duke of Suffolk, and the answer by the Spirit is:

> By water shall he die, and take his end.
>
> —Act I, scene iv, line 34

Ambiguous, of course. Does "by water" mean near water, or by means of water and therefore by drowning? As it turns out, this is a true prediction in one fairly clear sense, and is true also in a more remote sense that doesn't appear till the event.

. . . shun castles

The final question concerns the Duke of Somerset, and the answer is:

> Let him shun castles:
> Safer shall he be upon the sandy plains
>
> —Act I, scene iv, lines 36–37

Well, does that mean that Somerset is in danger of being killed in the siege of a castle, or that he will be sent prisoner to a castle and there executed, or what? Again the actual event is far less straightforward. As is almost always the case in the fictional use of oracles, the statements that emerge are true, but useless.

. . . Aio te, Aeacida

But the net has been drawn about the Duchess. Kept fully informed by the despicable Hum, the agents of King Henry close in, allowing the séance to proceed only that they might catch her red-handed.

In the play it is York and Buckingham who trap her. York's position here is odd, since he is serving the interests of the Suffolk-Somerset clique and one would think he would have no desire to do that. And indeed, his presence is a Shakespearean invention.

York reads the three prophecies which had been written down by those at the séance as they were given and pauses to laugh at the first, which deals with the Duke and the King. He sees the obvious ambiguity as to which will depose which and says:

> Why, this is just "Aio te, Aeacida,
> Romanos vincere posse."
> —Act I, scene iv, lines 62–63

This is the oracle supposedly given to Pyrrhus, the King of Epirus, when in 282 B.C. he was preparing to cross over into Italy to attack the Romans. Translated, it says, "I tell you, descendant of Aeacus, that you the Romans can conquer."

But, both in Latin and in English, that can mean either "you can conquer the Romans" or "the Romans can conquer you." And here too, both senses had elements of correctness, for Pyrrhus did conquer the Romans in two battles, while the Romans conquered Pyrrhus in one. The Romans conquered in the last battle, however.

This description of the arrest of the Duchess is, in some respects, correct, but not in all. The attempt at witchcraft, and the arrest, took place, actually, in 1441, four years before the marriage of Henry VI and Margaret. Furthermore, York was not present at the arrest and couldn't have been. In 1441 he was in France, laboring to hold Normandy.

Nevertheless, it is good drama to have him at the arrest, if only to have him read the prophecy. For, as it happens, and as the Elizabethan audience would well know, it is York himself who is the duke in question who will, after a fashion, depose the King and who will then, after a fashion, be deposed by the King, and who will die a particularly pathetic death by violence. (This will not happen till the next play, however.)

Although by sight . . .

While the arrest of the Duchess is taking place, the King and Queen are hawking at St. Albans. The Cardinal and Gloucester are also there, quarreling viciously as usual and reaching the point of agreeing to a duel. (At the time of the Duchess' arrest, Humphrey of Gloucester is fifty years old and the Cardinal well over sixty, so that the duel would scarcely be marked by very athletic swordplay.)

There follows, then, a comic interlude in which a countryman, Saunder Simpcox, pretends a miracle, claiming to have been born blind but having suddenly become able to see.

The King is clearly shown in this scene to be a rather credulous (if well-meaning) fool, for his every remark is one of priestly piety that is clearly out of sorts with his secular position and with the non-pious mood of everyone else in the party (especially the Cardinal). Thus, on hearing that the blind man has suddenly been made to see, the King intones:

> *Great is his comfort in this earthly vale,*
> *Although by sight his sin be multiplied.*
>
> —Act II, scene i, lines 70–71

In other words, vision would expose him to temptations which would not bother him if he were blind, and his good fortune might therefore make him a greater sinner. The reference seems to be to a verse in the Gospel of St. John (9:41): "Jesus said unto them, If ye were blind, ye should have no sin: but now ye say, We see: therefore your sin remaineth."

This immediate passage actually refers to blindness in a symbolic sense. The Pharisees, whom Jesus is addressing, claimed to know the truth and to require no teaching, hence they remained sinners. If they admitted their lack of knowledge (or blindness), they would learn, and cease to sin.

The occasion for the remark, however, came after a passage earlier in the chapter in which Jesus had restored sight to a man born blind, and it was this, presumably, which brought the passage to the mind of the pious King Henry.

At Berwick . . .

The King asks the countryman where he is from, and Simpcox answers:

> *At Berwick in the north, and't like your Grace*
>
> —Act II, scene i, line 83

Berwick is on the North Sea coast of northern England, only three miles south of the Scottish border.

But now Gloucester takes over the cross-examination, the details of which Shakespeare borrows from a book entitled *Acts and Monuments of These Latter and Perilous Days*. This was written by an Englishman named John Foxe and was published in 1563. Foxe had looked up all the tales he could of people who had been persecuted, tortured, and killed for the sake of religion, so that the book promptly got its popular title of *The Book of Martyrs*.

Quietly, Gloucester lures Simpcox into identifying colors by name, something that no man blind from birth and seeing only for half an hour could possibly do. The imposter is ordered punished, though his wife cries out:

> *Alas, sir, we did it for pure need.*
> —Act II, scene i, line 157

This is important, really. The French wars had rested heavily on the English population and had brought other troubles as well. The weakness of the government under Henry VI had allowed various nobles (like Gloucester and the Cardinal, for instance) to recruit what were virtually private armies which fought one another and terrorized the populace. Furthermore, England was taking to sheep farming in a big way, and since this could be most profitably carried out on large tracts of pasturage, fields which had previously been held in common for the beasts of a town or district were now being enclosed for the special use of the nobles who owned the sheep herds.

It was decades of deterioration of the position of the English peasantry which caused the common folk to lose faith in the government and search for an alternative. The land was ripe for either revolution or civil war—or both.

Even while Gloucester is basking in the praise that follows his exposure of Simpcox, there comes the news of his wife's witchcraft and arrest. Poor Gloucester, stunned by the news, abandons all thought of fighting the Cardinal. He can only say that if his wife has indeed practiced witchcraft, the law must take its course.

. . . but for Owen Glendower . . .

Meanwhile, back in London, Richard of York is represented as once again dreaming of the throne. In secret discussions with Salisbury and Warwick, he reveals the nature of his dynastic claim and once again the tale of Edward III's seven sons is recounted, and York's descent from the third son (through his mother) as compared with Henry's descent from the fourth is once again emphasized. (It is hard to suppose that Salisbury and

Warwick are ignorant of all this, but then, the audience must be told.)
    At one point, when York comes to mention Edmund Mortimer, Earl of
March (his mother's brother), and the "rightful" successor to Richard II,
Salisbury interrupts to say:

> This Edmund, in the reign of Bolingbroke [Henry IV],
> As I have read, laid claim unto the crown;
> And, but for Owen Glendower, had been King,
> Who kept him in captivity till he died.

> —Act II, scene ii, lines 39–42

    Once again there is the old confusion. It was not the Earl of March
and heir to the throne who was captured by Owen Glendower, but his
namesake uncle (see page I–320). Here at least, though, the captured uncle is described as dying in captivity, which is true; at least, he died in
Wales, fighting for Glendower, whose son-in-law he became. In *Henry VI,
Part One* Mortimer is described as dying in the Tower of London (see
page II–552), which was true of neither uncle nor nephew.
    What Shakespeare doesn't stress is that Richard of York is married to
Cecily Neville, the sister of the Earl of Salisbury. The two men are
brothers-in-law and the Nevilles have family reasons to be Yorkists.

. . . the Duke of York a king

    Salisbury and Warwick are convinced, and hail Richard of York as King.
York urges them to go slowly and bide their time. He is even Machiavellian
enough to urge that they wait for Gloucester's destruction, predicting that
that would work to the Yorkist interest. (But, again, York's Machiavellianism is presented as part of Shakespeare's anti-Yorkist bias. There is no
justification in history for it.)
    The other two agree and Warwick says:

> My heart assures me that the Earl of Warwick
> Shall one day make the Duke of York a king.

> —Act II, scene ii, lines 79–80

    This is one of those fictional prophecies fated to come true, or almost
true. Warwick was indeed to become the bulwark of the Yorkist cause and
was in time to be known as "the King-Maker," though it was not York
whom he would make king.
    York replies:

> Richard shall live to make the Earl of Warwick
> The greatest man in England but the King.

> —Act II, scene ii, lines 82–83

Again nearly true. The time was indeed to come when Warwick would be the greatest man in England but the King, but that King would not be York himself.

. . . in Smithfield . . .

The next scene opens with King Henry passing judgment on Duchess Eleanor. Her accomplices, who are lowborn, are subjected to horrible deaths, for King Henry says:

> The witch in Smithfield shall be burnt to ashes,
> And you three shall be strangled on the gallows.
> —Act II, scene iii, lines 7–8

Smithfield is in east-central London. It was a place which had first been a site for tournaments, then for fairs, then for public executions. It is now the site of London's chief meat markets.

The witch, Margery Jourdain, was indeed burned. Of the other three, however, only Roger Bolingbroke, the astrologer, suffered the full severity of the law. He was drawn and quartered. That is, he was hanged, cut down before he was dead, and then vivisected. One of his accomplices died in prison, but the wretched informing priest, Hum, was pardoned.

. . . in the Isle of Man

As for Eleanor, her punishment was much gentler, since she was a high-placed noblewoman. King Henry says to her:

> . . . after three days' open penance done,
> Live in your country here in banishment,
> With Sir John Stanley, in the Isle of Man.
> —Act II, scene iii, lines 11–13

The Isle of Man, thirty miles long and ten miles wide, is located in the Irish Sea between northern England and northern Ireland. It had been under the rule of Scotland until Edward III took it for England.

In English hands, it was first under the control of the Montagu family (which later included, for instance, the "Salisbury" of Richard II, see page II–292, and the "Salisbury" of Henry VI, Part One, see page II–495).

The uncle of the Salisbury of Richard II sold it to William le Scrope, Earl of Wiltshire (see page II–284), who lost it for his family when he was executed in the course of Bolingbroke's rebellion. In 1406 Bolingbroke, now Henry IV, passed it on to Sir John Stanley, in whose family it has remained ever since.

It was an isolated island, sparsely settled and primitive, and served well as a kind of English Siberia.

Holden at Bury . . .

Gloucester's fall proceeds apace. His wife is condemned and the King orders him to give up his office as Protector.

After a comic interlude in which Peter Thump and Thomas Horner fight over the former's accusation of treason against the latter, the Gloucester motif is taken up again.

The wretched Duke meets his even more wretched Duchess performing her penance. Dressed in a white sheet and barefoot, the Duchess must parade through the streets of London, bearing a candle in her hand, a description of her crimes on a paper pinned on the back of the sheet, and subjected to the derision of the mob.

Gloucester tries to comfort her and she tries to warn him against further steps on the part of his enemies. Even as they speak, a Herald arrives, saying:

> *I summon your Grace to his Majesty's Parliament,*
> *Holden at Bury the first of this next month.*
>   —Act II, scene iv, lines 70–71

Shakespeare is condensing time here. The chronicle of Gloucester's fall is something like this:

(1) In 1440 Charles of Orléans was released from imprisonment over Gloucester's objections (see page II–558) and Gloucester's influence was definitely broken.

(2) In 1441 Duchess Eleanor was convicted and exiled, to Gloucester's further humiliation. She was sent to the Isle of Man, where she survived some two years, dying in 1443.

(3) In 1445 Margaret of Anjou married Henry VI and became the most inveterate of all Gloucester's enemies, all the more so since Gloucester for all his defeats and humiliations remained heir to the throne unless Margaret could produce a child.

It was not, then, till 1447, after Margaret had been married two years with no signs of a pregnancy, that it was decided that Gloucester must be put out of the way once and for all. A Parliament was called for the purpose, but it was not to meet at London. Gloucester was popular with the Londoners and to deal with him appropriately might be difficult.

Parliament was therefore assembled at Bury St. Edmunds, sixty miles northeast of London. Bury was in Suffolk, which means in the home territory of Gloucester's enemy the Duke of Suffolk.

What's more, the Parliament was called in haste and without giving

Gloucester advance notice, so that he would be unable to gather his own men in his defense. Gloucester therefore says in wonder, at hearing of the calling of Parliament:

> *And my consent ne'er asked herein before?*
> *This is close [secret] dealing. Well, I will be there.*
> —Act II, scene iv, lines 72–73

If, indeed, the Parliament had been called immediately after Gloucester's series of disasters, it would have been surprising that he would not suspect arrest and worse and that he would not take care not to go anywhere near the Parliament.

As the play stands, we must suspect Gloucester of an astonishing degree of naïveté. In historical fact, however, the Parliament was called six years after the Duchess' conviction, and Gloucester, having grown used to his own disgrace and powerlessness, might well not expect that his enemies would feel the need to take any further action against him. He would therefore appear, totally unsuspecting, at the Parliament.

. . . all is lost

Parliament meets and Gloucester is late. The Queen immediately begins denouncing him to the King as a traitor. Once again the English nobility is shown as engaged in quarrels, nothing but quarrels, and to emphasize the consequence, Somerset comes in with news. We had last seen him being appointed regent in France, but now, when the King asks for news concerning France, Somerset replies grimly:

> *. . . all your interest in those territories*
> *Is utterly bereft you: all is lost.*
> —Act III, scene i, lines 84–85

That this was eventually so was due, in large part, to the incompetence of Somerset himself. Yet Somerset's statement at this moment is premature in the light of actual history.

At the time of the Parliament at Bury in 1447, England still held Normandy and the regions around Bordeaux. It was not till the next year that the great French offensive began which swept England out of Normandy by 1450 and out of Bordeaux in 1451. It was not till 1453 that the last English effort failed and Talbot died at Castillon (see page II–564). Thus, it was to be six years yet before "all is lost."

It makes dramatic sense, nevertheless, to have Gloucester's fall come at the time of the final bankruptcy of his policy of French conquest and no retreat.

. . . high treason . . .

Now Gloucester finally appears and at once Suffolk greets him with:

> *I do arrest thee of high treason here.*
>
> —Act III, scene i, line 97

It was on February 11, 1447, the second day of Parliament, that Gloucester was arrested.

Yet the arrest was insufficient. To make the accusation stick there would have to be a trial, and there would be difficulty in making the charge of treason stick, particularly since his popularity with the commoners would make it difficult to railroad him.

Clearly, it would be most convenient for the Queen and her party to have Gloucester die somehow, and assassination is in the air.

. . . from Ireland am I come . . .

Suddenly, though, a Post arrives with more bad news from abroad. He says:

> *Great lords, from Ireland am I come amain,*
> *To signify that rebels there are up,*
> *And put the Englishmen unto the sword.*
>
> —Act III, scene i, lines 282–84

This is not surprising. Ireland had been in a state of chronic rebellion ever since the time of Edward III. With England spending all its energies for four generations in a futile attempt to conquer France, it could scarcely maintain a strong presence in Ireland.

Even a fighting machine like Talbot, the superman fighter of *Henry VI, Part One,* when he was Lord Lieutenant of Ireland from 1414 to 1419 (when Henry V was fighting at Agincourt and conquering Normandy), could do very little against the Irish.

Still, England never gave up its hold entirely, and at periodic intervals someone would be sent over to chastise the rebels.

In this case, the Suffolk faction has the brilliant idea of sending York to Ireland.

. . . all for Ireland

York's position as "rightful heir" was threatening enough to the Lancastrians. The arrest and prospective death of Gloucester would leave York one step closer to the throne, making him senior member of the royal family, next only to the King (if the Beauforts are considered ineligible to inherit the throne). It would be best to get him off the scene.

And where better than in Ireland, where his military reputation, won in France, might well perish? He himself might even die there, as his maternal grandfather, Roger Mortimer, had (see page II–320).

York has no choice but to accept. He says:

> My Lord of Suffolk, within fourteen days
> At Bristow [Bristol] I expect my soldiers;
> For there I'll ship them all for Ireland.
> —Act III, scene i, lines 327–29

Actually, things did not move as fast as all that. York managed to delay for two years the time of his leaving of England. It was not till 1449 that he sailed for Ireland.

John Cade . . .

But York (as represented by Shakespeare's prejudices) has plans of his own. He may be forced into virtual exile but he will manage to make things hot for his enemies at home just the same. For that purpose, he has a tool at hand. He says:

> I have seduced a headstrong Kentishman,
> John Cade of Ashford,
> To make commotion, as full well he can,
> Under the title of John Mortimer.
> —Act III, scene i, lines 356–59

Kent is the southeasternmost county of England (see page I–6) and Ashford is a sizable town some forty miles southeast of London. Kent had been in the forefront of the Wat Tyler insurrection seventy years before, and its people had not forgotten. Nor had things grown better since, so that Kent was ripe enough for revolt. Nevertheless, as is usually the case, those who are revolted against are certain that there would be no trouble at all were it not for outside agitators.

It is not at all likely that John Cade was an instrument of the Duke of York. To be sure, later Lancastrian propaganda, which had become official party line, so to speak, in Shakespeare's time, had it that Cade was a native Irishman who came to Kent during the period of York's stay in

Ireland. The implication is that he was sent by York, and York, in his speech, refers to Cade as having served him as a spy in Ireland:

> *Full often, like a shag-haired crafty kern,*
> *Hath he conversèd with the enemy,*
> *And undiscovered come to me again*
> *And given me notice of their villainies.*
>
> —Act III, scene i, lines 367–70

(Yet when did this happen? York was only now heading out to the civil war. On his previous stay in Ireland, he had been a young man in his early twenties and had gone only to look over his estates there; he did no fighting.)

. . . that John Mortimer . . .

Furthermore, if Cade were acting as York's agent, he would surely not represent himself as a competing claimant for the throne.

Yet York reveals the intention to have Cade call himself John Mortimer, thus pretending to be a member of the Mortimer family and legitimate heir to the throne. This would make his words carry greater weight with a peasantry who were trained all through life to respect royalty, but could scarcely serve York's own ends.

One might argue that the rights of the Mortimer family would be brought to public notice without implicating York directly. Yet it might also be argued that if the rebellion failed (as it did), the rights of the Mortimer family would be tarred with the actions of a rabble-rousing mob and York's interests would be hurt.

That York should go to such lengths fits the Machiavellian motives attributed to him by Lancastrian propaganda but makes little practical sense.

Shakespeare has York say, as though to make the Mortimer imposture more plausible:

> *For that John Mortimer, which now is dead,*
> *In face, in gait, in speech, he doth resemble:*
>
> —Act III, scene i, lines 372–73

Surely this is unnecessary. History makes it perfectly clear that it is the easiest thing in the world for any imposter, regardless of appearance, to claim to be royalty. In the centuries before photography, few commoners knew what the members of the royal family looked like. In the centuries before radio, few knew what they sounded like. Any imposture, however ridiculous, would carry conviction, if only the imposter promised to improve the lot of the people.

. . . dispatched the Duke . . .

The next scene opens, still at Bury St. Edmunds, with men running across the stage. One, the First Murderer, calls to another:

> *Run to my Lord of Suffolk; let him know*
> *We have dispatched the Duke as he commanded.*
> —Act III, scene ii, lines 1–2

Humphrey of Gloucester was, as stated earlier, arrested on February 11, 1447. He never came to trial. He was found dead in his bed on the morning of February 28.

It was, of course, maintained that Gloucester had died a natural death, and his body was displayed to show that it bore no marks. And, to be sure, at the age of fifty-six it was quite possible for Gloucester to die of a heart attack, especially considering the heavy defeats and frustrations he had endured over the past seven years.

On the other hand, the death came about so conveniently for his enemies that no one believed it was natural. The country, almost unanimously, took it for granted that Suffolk had ordered the duke's murder.

Gloucester had been popular before and, of course, in retrospect grew even more popular. Suffolk became correspondingly more unpopular. Since Gloucester left no direct heirs his estates were up for grabs. With uncommon shortsightedness (like Richard II after the death of John of Gaunt—see page II–282) Suffolk seized those estates for himself and for his family and friends. Then, in 1448, at the Queen's insistence, he was made a duke.

Surely if anything was required to make Suffolk more execrable with the people generally than to seem a murderer, it was to seem a robber of the man he had murdered. And if anything else was needed to complete his infamy in the eyes of the commons, it was the general belief that he was the Queen's lover.

It took three years after Gloucester's death for Suffolk's unpopularity to increase to the explosion point, and that point came in the aftermath of the disgrace of the loss of Normandy.

In the play, however, Normandy is depicted as lost at the time of Gloucester's arrest, and Suffolk has already been made a duke after his success in bringing Margaret of Anjou to England. It is therefore possible for Shakespeare to go immediately and dramatically from Gloucester's destruction to that of Suffolk.

. . . the commons send you word . . .

As soon as Gloucester's death is announced, King Henry faints, and when revived, is convinced the death was murder. Queen Margaret, in a long and eloquent speech, argues otherwise but fails to move him.

Warwick enters to accuse Suffolk directly as a murderer, and the quarrel degenerates into actual swordplay.

Finally, Salisbury (Warwick's father) enters to report on the common people, who have been gathering. He says to King Henry:

> *Dread Lord, the commons send you word by me,*
> *Unless Lord Suffolk straight be done to death,*
> *Or banishèd fair England's territories,*
> *They will by violence tear him from your palace,*
>
> —Act III, scene ii, lines 243–46

At once, Henry banishes Suffolk, ordering him to leave England within three days.

It was not immediately after Gloucester's death, however, but three years later, that Suffolk's turn came. When Parliament met in January 1450, Suffolk's arrest was demanded by the commons. On March 17 he was banished for five years and commanded to leave England by May 1.

. . . at point of death

Nor was Suffolk the only one of Gloucester's enemies to be ruined. Even while Suffolk is being banished, a courtier enters to announce:

> *. . . Cardinal Beaufort is at point of death;*
> *For suddenly a grievous sickness took him,*
>
> —Act III, scene ii, lines 369–70

The King hastens to his side, and as Cardinal Beaufort mumbles his last words, Henry says:

> *Lord Cardinal, if thou think'st on heaven's bliss,*
> *Hold up thy hand, make signal of thy hope.*
> *He dies and makes no sign.*
>
> —Act III, scene iii, lines 27–29

In the play, Cardinal Beaufort dies in an agony of guilt over the death of Gloucester and, as Shakespeare makes plain, goes to hell for it.

Whether the guilt really existed or not, the Cardinal (unlike Suffolk) did indeed meet his end immediately after Gloucester's death. He died in his own palace on April 11, 1447, about six weeks after Gloucester's death. He was some seventy years old at the time of his death, and was the last of all the sons of John of Gaunt—the last of all the grandsons of Edward III—to die.

Of the house of Lancaster (those descended in the male line, exclusively, from John of Gaunt) there now remained only Henry VI, Gaunt's great-grandson by his first wife, and Edmund of Somerset, Gaunt's grandson by his third wife, plus the latter's sons.

. . . by "water" I should die

As it happens, Suffolk does not quite go off to banishment. The popular fury against him grew and there were many, especially in London, who were outraged to think he was to escape death, and go off into an exile from which he might return. It looked as though all England were to be in turmoil. Perhaps to avoid this, Suffolk's ship was stopped after he had embarked on May 1, and he was taken onto a ship of war. On May 5, 1450, he was executed, presumably at the direction of a government which was throwing him to the wolves in an attempt to avoid worse. Suffolk was fifty-four years old at the time, which somehow weakens the passionate scenes in which Shakespeare depicts him taking leave of the twenty-year-old Queen.

In the play, the ship carrying a disguised Suffolk (to keep him from being murdered while he was still on his way to the ship) is indeed taken by the warship. Suffolk is handed over to a man who announces his name to be Walter Whitmore.

Suffolk is shocked and explains his start by saying:

> Thy name affrights me, in whose sound is death.
> A cunning man did calculate my birth,
> And told me that by "water" I should die:
> —Act IV, scene i, lines 33–35

This is a reference to the prediction given by the Spirit in the séance scene (which, in history, took place nine years before Suffolk's exile). "Walter" was, in medieval times, frequently pronounced "Water," so that a common shortened form was Wat, as in Wat Tyler. The common use of Wat as a first name is reflected in the common use of Watson as a surname.

Thus, Suffolk not only died by water (at sea), but by Water (at the hands of Walter).

. . . like ambitious Sylla . . .

It is plain that Suffolk faces death, but he scorns to plead for mercy. As for the Lieutenant who is in charge of the ship that has taken him, he goes through the reasons why Suffolk deserves death. Suffolk is told that he has been avaricious and gathered much of England's wealth; he has been the lover of the Queen; he has brought about Gloucester's death.

The Lieutenant says of Suffolk:

> *By devilish policy art thou grown great*
> *And like ambitious Sylla overgorged*
> *With gobbets of thy mother's bleeding heart.*
>
> —Act IV, scene i, lines 83–85

Sylla, or Sulla, was one of the generals who, in the last century of the Roman republic, helped destroy the constitution of that republic and pave the way for the foundation of the Empire. In 82 B.C. Sulla led his army against his enemies, who were then in control of the city of Rome. He was the first general actually to attack Rome with a Roman army, and in that sense, he was "overgorged with gobbets of [his] mother's bleeding heart." What's more, after his victory, Sulla confiscated the property and estates of his enemies and used these to enrich himself and his followers. This resembles the manner in which Suffolk absorbed Gloucester's estates.

A Roman sworder . . .

Suffolk still breathes defiance, pointing out that many great men in history had been killed by worthless murderers. He says:

> *A Roman sworder and banditto slave*
> *Murdered sweet Tully; Brutus' bastard hand*
> *Stabbed Julius Caesar; savage islanders*
> *Pompey the Great; and Suffolk dies by pirates.*
>
> —Act IV, scene i, lines 135–38

Tully is Cicero, who was executed by soldiers sent by Mark Antony (see page I–307). Brutus was supposed by some to have been an illegitimate son of Julius Caesar (see page I–273). Pompey was not killed by savage islanders but by more or less civilized men of the Ptolemaic kingdom of Egypt (see page I–257).

But Suffolk is killed by the men he calls pirates—because they have taken his ship on the open waters.

After he is dead, two gentlemen who had accompanied him undertake to bear his body back to London.

. . . the filth and scum of Kent

But now it is time to deal with the rebellion of Jack Cade, whom York had mentioned earlier on the occasion of his leaving for Ireland (see page II-597).

What happened was that after Suffolk's death, there was no one of the Lancastrian party left to guide the feeble King except for Somerset, and he was almost as unpopular as Suffolk, thanks to his failure in France.

The one man to whom many people turned was Richard of York. He had been competent in France, the last capable administrator of the Hundred Years' War; and what's more, he was proving competent in Ireland. He managed to quiet the rebels there and with such a mixture of firmness and gentleness that Ireland was to remain thoroughly Yorkist in sympathy through all the civil wars that were to follow.

What's more, he was the only Plantagenet (descendant of Edward III, through males exclusively) to be left outside the House of Lancaster. It didn't take bribery to make people think that York should be placed in a position of high power next to the King. The fact, then, that Yorkist feeling mounted in England after 1450 is no necessary indication that York was stirring up rebellion; it might just as well mean that the common people had the good sense required to see the obvious.

Some thirty thousand men of Kent and Sussex, under the leadership of Jack Cade (or John Cade) marched to London, then, to place their petition on York's behalf before the King. They wanted reforms in the government, and they wanted York. There was no intention of violence at the start; all was respectful, and indeed, many in the crowd were respectable small landowners whose hearts were filled with loyalty to the crown and to the mild King (though not necessarily to the foreign Queen).

Like all rebellions of farmers, peasants, and workmen, this one was vilified by chroniclers of the time, for chroniclers are usually drawn from scholars who are patronized by the aristocracy and identify with them. It is therefore difficult to get a reasonable picture of what happened. Certainly Shakespeare, who is always ready to make fun of artisans and peasants, presents the rebellion in a spirit of broad farce.

By the middle of June 1450 (some five weeks after Suffolk's execution —a sacrifice by which the Queen's party did not, after all, prevent popular disorders) Cade's army was encamped in Blackheath, south of the Thames River and about five miles east of London's center.

The court temporized, receiving petitions and answering them with every show of sympathy, while quietly gathering troops as quickly as pos-

604 THE ENGLISH PLAYS

sible. Once the troops were gathered, a detachment of soldiers was sent against the Kentishmen under two brothers named Stafford.

The petitioners, confused and frightened at the coming of armed men, and certainly not dreaming of battle, rapidly retreated back toward Kent. They were overtaken by a contingent of armed men at Sevenoaks, about twenty-three miles southeast of London.

In the play, the retreat is not mentioned. The army is pictured as meeting Cade's men while the latter are still at Blackheath, and the elder Stafford cries out to them:

> Rebellious hinds, the filth and scum of Kent,
> Marked for the gallows; lay your weapons down.
>> —Act IV, scene ii, lines 119–20

It is very common for lowborn rebels to be addressed in this fashion by the aristocrats sent against them. The theory is that the dogs have to be shown their place and that it requires only a show of firm contempt to make them turn tail and run. This works—sometimes.

And sometimes the aristocrats are torn to pieces for their pains.

. . . the Duke of Clarence' daughter . . .

In this case, Cade does not turn tail. Rather, he argues himself to be an aristocrat too, and a claimant to the throne, in fact. He says:

> . . . Edmund Mortimer, Earl of March,
> Married the Duke of Clarence' daughter, did he not?
>> —Act IV, scene ii, lines 133–34

The Duke of Clarence is Lionel of Antwerp, third son of Edward III, and his daughter was Philippa. She did indeed marry Edmund Mortimer, the 3rd Earl of March. The Staffords admit that much.

Cade goes on to explain that Philippa then had twins, which the Staffords promptly deny. The elder of these, says Cade, was stolen away by a beggar woman and grew up to be a bricklayer, and Cade himself is the son of that elder son of Edmund Mortimer.

This would make Cade a first cousin of Edmund, the 5th Earl of March (see page II–320), and prior to him in his claim to the throne. It would also make Cade first cousin, once removed, of Richard of York, and prior to him in his claim to the throne too.

Cade, however, for the sake of the King's father, Henry V, offers to make no demand for the throne but will be satisfied with merely being Lord Protector.

. . . Lord Say's head . . .

One of Cade's henchmen makes a specific demand, saying:

> *And furthermore, we'll have the Lord Say's head for selling*
> *the Dukedom of Maine.*
> —Act IV, scene ii, lines 158–59

Lord Say is James Finnes, and his full title is Lord Saye and Sele. He was a close associate of the dead Suffolk and he served Henry VI as lord chamberlain and lord treasurer. Since he was in charge of finances it seemed reasonable to blame him for high taxes. (A descendant of his was involved in the colonization of New England, and the "Say" in the name of Old Saybrook, Connecticut, comes from his name.)

There is then a battle, on June 18, in which Cade's forces actually win, killing both Staffords. To be sure, the Staffords had come up with only a vanguard of the army, the main forces of which were still behind in Blackheath.

. . . in Southwark . . .

Meanwhile, in London, softhearted King Henry is wondering how he can treat with Cade so as to avoid bloodshed, while savage Queen Margaret is hugging Suffolk's head to her bosom, and mourning.

A Messenger hastens in, and says:

> *The rebels are in Southwark: fly, my lord!*
> —Act IV, scene iv, line 27

The victory over the Staffords had a strong psychological effect. When Cade's men moved forward again, nobody cared to try to stop them. The rebels reached Southwark, just across the Thames from the heart of London, at the beginning of July.

There seemed nothing to stop them from entering London itself and it would be the height of folly to let the King be captured. Buckingham therefore says to him:

> *My gracious lord, retire to Killingworth,*
> *Until a power be raised to put them down.*
> —Act IV, scene iv, lines 39–40

Killingworth, or better, Kenilworth, is a castle located just south of

Coventry, about ninety miles northwest of London. It is best known today because of the novel *Kenilworth* by Sir Walter Scott, much of the action of which (set in Shakespeare's time, incidentally) takes place there.

As Henry makes ready to flee, a Second Messenger arrives, crying:

> *Jack Cade hath gotten London Bridge!*
> *The citizens fly and forsake their houses;*
> —Act IV, scene iv, lines 49–50

On July 3, 1450, Cade entered London without a fight. It was really a remarkable feat.

. . . to win the Tower . . .

Not only did John Cade enter London without bloodshed (by agreement with the Lord Mayor), but he endeavored to keep his men in order and to prevent damage of any sort.

In the play, on the other hand, he orders them to burn London Bridge and pull down the Tower. Actually, London could not be held for long unless the Tower could be taken, and that was firmly held by Lord Scales, who announces to the assembled citizens:

> *Such aid as I can spare you shall command,*
> *But I am troubled here with them myself:*
> *The rebels have assayed to win the Tower.*
> —Act IV, scene v, lines 7–9

Lord Scales is mentioned briefly in *Henry VI, Part One* as having been taken prisoner at the Battle of Patay with Talbot (see page II–529). That battle was twenty years in the past, but Lord Scales was still vigorous and was to live on to 1460. Indeed, at the time of Cade's rebellion, Talbot himself was still alive too. It was not till 1453, three years later, that Talbot fell at Castillon (see page II–564).

. . . because they could not read . . .

Somehow, however, Cade's men managed to get hold of Lord Say, whom the court had supposedly sent to the Tower for his own safety. How the capture was effected Shakespeare doesn't explain and neither does history.

Cade holds a mock trial of Lord Say, accusing him chiefly of encouraging literacy. Shakespeare thus pokes fun at the anti-intellectualism of the common man.

Yet one must admit that there is anti*un*intellectualism too, and that common men of Shakespeare's time might well feel that the learned placed penalties on them merely for not being learned. Thus, Cade says to Say:

> . . . *thou hast put them* [poor men] *in prison, and because they could not read thou hast hanged them* . . .
> —Act IV, scene vii, lines 45–47

This undoubtedly has reference to the famous system of "benefit of clergy" which derives from the 105th Psalm (14–15): "He [God] suffered no man to do them [His people] wrong: yea, he reproved kings for their sakes; Saying, Touch not mine anointed, and do my prophets no harm."

This passage served as a kind of shield for the priesthood against the secular power. In the Middle Ages it was used to protect priests from being tried by secular courts, since the king must do God's prophets (a term extended to cover the clergy generally) no harm. This was valuable for the clergy, since the clerical courts—before which alone they could be tried—did not pronounce the death sentence.

This "benefit of clergy" was eventually extended to all who could read (since literacy was virtually confined to the clergy in the Middle Ages). If a person convicted of murder could read a passage from the Bible, he was exempt from execution but was merely branded on the hand. A second murder, however, would mean execution. Literacy meant one murder free, in other words.

To literates, this might seem a fine thing, but to illiterates it might look uncommonly like unfair advantage on the part of those who could read. In acting against those who committed the "crime" of being literate, then, Cade's rabble were not being merely obscurantist but were getting a vague kind of revenge.

. . . in the Commentaries . . .

Lord Say attempts to defend himself, beginning:

> *Kent, in the Commentaries Caesar writ,*
> *Is termed the civil'st* [most civilized] *place of all this isle:*
> —Act IV, scene vii, lines 62–63

This is a soothing attempt at flattery.

Caesar landed in Kent when he invaded England (see page II–53), since Kent is the nearest part of the island to the Continent. Since it was nearest to the Continent, it would be that part of the island which would be most apt to trade with Gaul and to receive some influence from distant Rome. Naturally, then, Caesar would judge it to be most nearly civilized.

Henry the Fifth . . .

Despite all Lord Say can say on his own behalf, he is beheaded by Cade's men. The next day, July 4, Cade could no longer hold his men entirely in check and a few houses were pillaged. The Londoners, roused at this, began to resist and called on the help of the soldiers stationed in the Tower of London.

Cade's army spent the night across the river, and on the early morning of July 5, when they tried once again to enter London, they were met by the angry citizens of the city and were thrown back. Once that was done, the court began to break up the army by diplomacy. Promises of redress were made and a number of men, who had faith in those promises, went home.

In Shakespeare's version, Cade's men are shown as a destructive rabble who are looting London, when two men of the court, Buckingham and Clifford, enter to offer pardon and make soft promises. Clifford (the 8th Baron Westmoreland) uses another tack too, for he makes use of a magic name. He calls out:

> Who loves the King and will embrace his pardon,
> Fling up his cap, and say "God save his Majesty!"
> Who hateth him and honors not his father,
> Henry the Fifth, that made all France to quake,
> Shake he his weapon at us and pass by.
>
> —Act IV, scene viii, lines 14–18

Cade's men are strongly influenced at the mere mention of Henry V. (It is exactly this which would make York reluctant to attempt to implement his claim to the throne. The name of Henry V was still potent and until Henry VI's misrule had dissolved that potency, a rebellion based on mere legalism would have no chance.)

Cade tries to hold his forces together, but Clifford calls out the name of the great victor of Agincourt and makes a hawkish speech against France so that patriotism explodes the cause of the rebels, and Cade flees.

It was not quite that simple in actual history. After his first group broke up, Cade managed to gather enough men to make some sort of display two days later, but they quarreled among themselves and the Londoners were still firm against them. It was then that Cade gave up, quietly took to his horse, and galloped southward to the coast. No doubt he hoped to escape to France.

. . . an esquire of Kent

A thousand marks were placed on Cade's head, and in the play, Cade is forced by famine into a Kentish garden, hoping, after five days of running and starving, to make a meal. Here he is discovered by the small landowner, a model of staunch English yeomanry, who refuses to summon help but fights Cade alone, for, as he says:

> *. . . it shall ne'er be said, while England stands,*
> *That Alexander Iden, an esquire of Kent,*
> *Took odds to combat a poor famished man.*
> —Act IV, scene x, lines 44–46

Cade is struck down, mortally wounded. Only then, from Cade's dying statement, does honest Iden learn who it is he has slain, so that he cries out:

> *Is't Cade that I have slain, that monstrous traitor?*
> —Act IV, scene x, line 68

Actually, matters were not quite that heroic. Iden did indeed slay Cade in single combat, but not unwittingly, and not out of sheer desire to fight for his property. When Cade galloped southward, Iden raced hotly after him, playing a part no more noble than that of bounty hunter, for he was after the thousand-mark reward. He caught up with the fugitive, killed him, and collected.

. . . with a puissant and a mighty power

Scarcely has Henry VI, at his safe refuge in Kenilworth, heard of the breakup of Cade's army and the flight of Cade, than he gets additional news less welcome. A Messenger enters and says:

> *The Duke of York is newly come from Ireland,*
> *And with a puissant and a mighty power*
> —Act IV, scene ix, lines 24–25

Shakespeare's anti-Yorkist bias makes it appear that York has brought his army from Ireland in order to take advantage of the confusion caused by Cade's rebellion (something he had supposedly instigated).

The actuality is quite different. Cade's rebellion had been wiped out in July and York did not arrive from Ireland till September 1450. The actual facts would make it appear that York was arriving out of duty rather than out of ambition alone. It was quite plain that Henry VI could not rule and that his chief minister, Edmund of Somerset, was both unpopular and incapable.

York was senior Prince of the Blood and was heir to the throne if Henry VI should die without children (barring the doubtful claim of the Beaufort family). Why should he not have every interest to try to reorganize the government under himself as Protector? Many Englishmen would have viewed this with favor and one member of Parliament even suggested, at this time, that York be declared heir to the throne officially. (The member was put in the Tower for making the suggestion, however.)

. . . Duke Edmund to the Tower

The Lancastrians could see quite plainly that Somerset was their weak point. King Henry therefore takes the action best calculated to soothe York and, for that matter, protect Somerset. He sends Buckingham to meet York, giving him instructions to—

> . . . ask him what's the reason of these arms.
> Tell him I'll send Duke Edmund to the Tower,
> And, Somerset, we will commit thee thither,
> Until his army be dismissed from him.
> —Act IV, scene ix, lines 37–40

. . . Ajax Telamonius

Shakespeare, by attributing ambition to the crown to York, has to twist the next scene into a series of odd events. Thus, York begins the scene by announcing:

> From Ireland thus comes York to claim his right,
> And pluck the crown from feeble Henry's head.
> —Act V, scene i, lines 1–2

Then, when Buckingham arrives as emissary from the King, York finds himself helpless to proceed for no visible reason and must say in frustration:

> . . . now, like Ajax Telamonius,
> On sheep or oxen could I spend my fury.
> —Act V, scene i, lines 26–27

This is a reference to the end of Ajax (son of Telamon), who, out of ungovernable rage at having been denied the armor of the dead Achilles, went mad and slew herds of domestic animals, thinking them to be his Grecian enemies (see page I-110).

Actually, York's purpose in returning from Ireland fell far short of the crown. He marched his army into Kent, more as though exploring the feeling of the nation than attempting to rouse rebellion (though perhaps he would have rebelled if an overwhelming uprising in his behalf had developed, which it didn't), and what he found made him feel he could safely demand the end of Somerset as the power behind the throne.

Indeed, he says as much to Buckingham:

> *The cause why I have brought this army hither*
> *Is to remove proud Somerset from the King,*
> —Act V, scene i, lines 35–36

Command my eldest son . . .

Buckingham smoothly assures York that Somerset has already been sent a prisoner to the Tower, and York, accepting the assurance, dismisses his army. This is not just something Shakespeare invented; it really happened.

Now, if York had been the Machiavellian plotter Shakespeare pictures him as, if he had come to England desperately intent on seizing the throne, it passes the bounds of belief that he would so easily dismiss his army on the mere word that Somerset would be imprisoned. If, however, he were intensely loyal to the King and were intent only on becoming Protector, he might well have faith in his monarch.

Disbanding his army (this took place, in actual fact, in March 1452, a year and a half after his arrival from Ireland, and not immediately after, as the play makes it appear), York says joyously:

> *. . . let my sovereign, virtuous Henry,*
> *Command my eldest son, nay, all my sons,*
> *As pledges of my fealty and love;*
> *I'll send them all as willing as I live:*
> *Lands, goods, horse, armor, anything I have,*
> *Is his to use, so* [provided that] *Somerset may die.*
> —Act V, scene i, lines 48–53

The sons of Richard of York, whom he here refers to, and who are to play important parts in succeeding plays, have not yet made their appearance on the stage.

The sons were four in number, and in order of their birth, they were Edward, Edmund, George, and Richard. At the time York disbanded his armies, the respective ages of the first three were ten, nine, and three. The youngest, Richard, had just been born.

. . . like to Achilles' spear

It quickly appears that Somerset is not to be executed, however, and that he is not even in prison. Indeed, he comes onstage with the triumphant Margaret, whose hatred of Richard of York keeps her from dissembling any further.

York, maddened at this, throws caution to the winds. He berates Henry for his double-dealing and tells him he is not fit to be King. It is rather he himself, says York, who should be King. He says:

> *That gold* [the crown] *must round engirt these brows of mine,*
> *Whose smile and frown, like to Achilles' spear,*
> *Is able with the change to kill and cure.*
> —Act V, scene i, lines 99–101

This is one of the references to a minor legend concerning the great Greek hero Achilles (see page I–78). When the Greeks first landed in Asia Minor, they found themselves in Mysia, far from Troy, since they lacked maps. The King of Mysia, Telephus, tried to resist and was badly wounded by Achilles, who wielded a spear only he was strong enough to handle.

Telephus' wound festered and an oracle told him it could be cured only by its cause. Telephus therefore offered to guide the Greek host to Troy if Achilles would use his spear to cure the wound. Achilles agreed and scraped some of the rust from the spear into the wound, or, in an alternate version of the tale, scraped some on the ground, from which sprang the herb yarrow (*Achillea millefolium*), which served as cure.

Achilles' spear thus came to be a proverbial representation of anything that could work equally well to help or hurt, and a king, of course, can be either frowning or smiling, using the same face to kill or cure.

. . . capital treason . . .

York's speech is, to be sure, treasonable, and Somerset at once says:

> *O monstrous traitor! I arrest thee, York,*
> *Of capital treason 'gainst the King and crown:*
> —Act V, scene i, lines 107–8

Clifford enters later and goes a step further. He says of York:

He is a traitor; let him to the Tower,
And chop away that factious pate of his.
—Act V, scene i, lines 134–35

At the time York disbanded his army, he was indeed arrested, and no doubt the Lancastrians would have been glad to execute him. Practical politics dictated otherwise. York was too popular to deal with summarily and there was the recent case of Gloucester, whose death had, in the end, ruined Suffolk. There was therefore no real attempt to go to extreme measures against him, especially since he did not, in actual fact, say or do anything as openly treasonable as Shakespeare makes it appear.

Outcast of Naples . . .

York is not anxious to be a martyr either. Upon first disbanding his army, he had offered his sons as hostages for his loyalty and good behavior, and now he once again makes the offer.

Queen Margaret sneers at this and refers to—

. . . the bastard boys of York
—Act V, scene i, line 115

York then burst out in tit-for-tat invective, saying to the Queen:

O blood-bespotted Neapolitan,
Outcast of Naples, England's bloody scourge!
—Act V, scene i, lines 117–18

This makes it sound as though Queen Margaret is Italian. She is not, of course, but is thoroughly French. However, her father is titular King of Naples (see page II–568) and is kept from ruling there by the fact that a Spanish dynasty is in effective control. In that sense, the Queen is a Neapolitan and an outcast. And, of course, to the Elizabethan audience, which is accustomed to hearing Italian vice and subtlety (see page II–279) constantly contrasted with English virtue and candor, the use of an Italian-sounding epithet against Margaret would be most effective.

. . . our weapons shall

Two of York's four sons, Edward and Richard, appear, and are willing to guarantee their father's good behavior. Richard, the younger, pictured in this play and the next as a fire-eating hothead, says, concerning their method of freeing York from threatened arrest:

> *And if words will not* [suffice], *then our weapons shall.*
> —Act V, scene i, line 140

This is a remarkable speech for young Richard to make, since at the time of his father's arrest, he had just been born.

It is at this point, however, that Shakespeare skips two years without giving any indication of having done so—two years of great importance, too.

In the play, York goes straight from his position as arrested traitor without an army to sudden defiance. An army springs up from nowhere and York makes ready for war. This is quite confusing and would be inexplicable unless we could turn to history and see what really happened.

York was arrested on March 10, 1452. Since it seemed imprudent to chop off his head, the King pardoned him and sent him back to his estates. There York remained quietly for a while, convinced perhaps that events would work out in his favor and that time was on his side.

And, to be sure, three separate events took place in 1453 which were of prime importance.

First, on July 17, 1453, Talbot fought and lost the Battle of Castillon (see page II-564). That ended, at long last, the great adventure in France which Edward III had started and which Henry V had lifted to its peak. The English were out of France (except only for Calais) once and for all, and all Englishmen had to realize it. A scapegoat was needed for that and for the death of the idolized Talbot, and the natural scapegoat was the minister in power—Somerset. And he, to a large extent, deserved it.

Then, a month later, in August, King Henry's mental condition finally broke down. He had never been bright, but he had been sane. Now even that could no longer be said. He could no longer respond sensibly to statements made to him, and his condition was so plainly incompetent that the court dared not show him in public. For as long as they could, they maintained the fiction that he was well, but, of course, rumors spread.

Then, finally, in October of that same year of 1453, Queen Margaret was delivered of a baby boy. There was at once a rumor, widely believed throughout the land, that Henry was not the father of the boy. (And certainly, considering Henry's temperament, that is an easy piece of scandal to believe).

Still, believing the son of a queen to be illegitimate and proving it are two different things. No one dared make the attempt to *prove* illegitimacy (to try and to fail would be fatal to the accuser) and the infant was accepted. He was named Edward and was also made Prince of Wales, in order to make it perfectly clear he was heir to the throne.

By the end of 1453, then, the situation was this. The King's condition was bound to become known sooner or later, probably sooner, and there would have to be a Protector. Somerset had grown simply too unpopular to serve as Protector. Margaret herself now had a baby to defend and she was to bend all her energies henceforward to a single-minded effort to see to it that her young prince would someday succeed to the throne. It seemed clear, then, that she would have to swallow her pride and make a conciliatory gesture toward York. Unless she gave him an inch, the country (on hearing of Henry's condition) might compel him to take a mile—so he was recalled to a place on the council and when he demanded the removal of Somerset that demand was met and Somerset went to the Tower of London.

In February 1454 a new Parliament was opened by York and it was clearly in his interest to demonstrate to the nation why it was that the King could not open it for himself. As it happened, John Kemp, sixty-fourth Archbishop of Canterbury, had just died, and it was customary for a deputation of lords to consult with the King on possible replacements. York made sure that such a deputation was formed and that the King was forced to face it. All could see at once that Henry was mentally incompetent.

Now if York had truly been the cold-blooded schemer Shakespeare makes him out to be, if he had truly had his heart set on the throne, matters would now have been simple for him. King Henry could have been shut up as a madman and a convenient death could have been arranged for him. The infant Prince of Wales could have been declared illegitimate (who would have doubted it?) and Queen Margaret could have been imprisoned, or even executed for the treason of having been unfaithful to the King.

York would then have legally, and probably with minimum trouble, succeeded to the throne.

But as a matter of fact, York *still* shows no signs, even as late as 1454, of really having ambitions for the throne. When Henry's madness was made plain, Parliament appointed York Protector, and he accepted that position without trying to make it more. What's more, when, by the end of 1454, King Henry had recovered to the point where he could be considered sane once more, York promptly resigned his position as Protector—the act of a thoroughly loyal man.

Once again, though, York's reward for loyalty was a harsh blow. No sooner was York out of the way than King Henry (or, more likely, Queen Margaret acting in his name) made it his first business to liberate Somerset and place him in charge of the government once again.

This was very foolish of Margaret (but then she always allowed her passions to rule over her good sense—if she had any), for she couldn't possibly have done anything to worse offend the nation. The last person they wanted was the man they felt had lost France and betrayed Talbot.

Nor could she have done anything to worse offend York. It was only now that York finally felt that nothing could be done with King Henry, that only a complete revolution could save England. He saw no choice but to raise an army and thus open the Wars of the Roses. And among the chief partisans to join him now were the Earl of Salisbury and his son the Earl of Warwick.

. . . foul indigested lump

The entire two-year period—complicated politics, the loss of France, the madness of the King, the birth of an heir, the coming and going of York as Protector, the fall and rise of Somerset—is skipped by Shakespeare between one line and the next.

Instead, immediately after York's arrest and apparent utter defeat, York signals Salisbury and Warwick to enter out of nowhere and the civil wars begin.

Clifford, the most extreme of the Lancastrians, and young Richard, York's youngest son, who is to be the most extreme of the Yorkists, at once engage in a slanging match. Clifford says angrily to young Richard:

> Hence, heap of wrath, foul indigested lump,
> As crooked in thy manners as thy shape!
> —Act V, scene i, lines 157–58

Thus begins Shakespeare's portrait of young Richard, whom he ends by making one of the great villains of history. Because Shakespeare is Shakespeare, that portrait of Richard cannot be erased from the consciousness of the world, and yet it is almost totally wrong.

The anti-Yorkist bias of the Tudor dynasty under whom Shakespeare wrote and lived was directed most concentratedly, as we shall see, against this same Richard. He was vilified endlessly and shamelessly and most skillfully by Sir Thomas More, who in 1514 or thereabouts wrote *A History of Richard III*. In this book, More carefully repeated rumors designed to air the worst theories about Richard that the Tudors wanted aired, while carefully refraining from presenting them as actual statements of fact. Shakespeare drew on More's history, presenting all the vicious theories as facts.

Thus, contemporary portraits and descriptions of Richard do not indicate that he was particularly deformed in any way. He was small, perhaps, though this was more noticeable than it might otherwise have been through a comparison with his older brother Edward, who was over six feet tall, and a giant of a man by the standards of those days.

It is also possible that one of Richard's shoulders was higher than the other. More describes Richard as follows: "As he was small and little of stature so was he of body greatly deformed, the one shoulder higher than the other. . . ." He carefully gives no other instances of the way in which he was "greatly deformed."

But that is enough. Later presentations had him a hunchback, club-footed, and hideous. Hence Clifford's sneer at him as a "foul indigested lump."

Later in the scene, Clifford's son, identified here as "Young Clifford," addresses Richard as:

> *Foul stigmatic . . .*
> —Act V, scene i, line 215

One who is stigmatic carries a stigma or mark, which may be placed on his body by a branding iron as the result of his conviction of some crime, or may be there from birth. In the latter case (as was supposedly true of Richard, who was, as it was later said, born deformed) the mark was placed there by God.

Old Salisbury . . .

King Henry, in his turn, berates the Earl of Salisbury, who is the most important of the nobles who rallied to the side of York. He says:

> *Old Salisbury, shame to thy silver hair,*
> *Thou mad misleader of thy brain-sick son!*
> —Act V, scene i, lines 162–63

Salisbury is fifty-five years old at the time of the opening of the War of the Roses, which is indeed quite old for the time.

It is interesting that although Shakespeare never as much as whispers of the madness of Henry VI (any more than he did of the madness of Charles VI, see page II–464), he has Henry talk of the madness or possible madness of others. Thus, he makes Henry speak of Warwick as "brain-sick" and Salisbury as "mad" outright. Earlier in the scene Henry says of York:

> *. . . a bedlam [mad] and ambitious humor*
> *Makes him oppose himself against his King.*
> —Act V, scene i, lines 132–33

. . . turned to stone . . .

In actual history, York raised his army in Ludlow in western England, near the Welsh border. This was the traditional bailiwick of the earls of March (that is, the Mortimer family, of which York was a member on his mother's side). He then marched his men rapidly toward London, encountering the Lancastrian army at St. Albans (see page II–584) on May 22, 1455.

York offered his submission to the King on condition that Somerset be turned over to him (for execution, clearly). York, even at this late date, was thus ready to play for something less than the crown. The King (or rather, the Queen through him, for she was always obdurate) refused and battle was joined.

The Lancastrians held the town firmly, but Warwick led a portion of the army round part of the hill on which it stands and attacked suddenly from the rear, forcing an entry to the streets. Almost at once, the surprised Lancastrians gave way.

The Lancastrian army suffered some notable casualties. Shakespeare (who always treats battles in the Homeric style as successions of single combats, when he treats of them at all) has York and Clifford clash. Clifford is killed.

York leaves and Young Clifford enters and finds his father's body. He is horrified and says:

> *Even at this sight*
> *My heart is turned to stone; and while 'tis mine,*
> *It shall be stony.*
>
> —Act V, scene ii, lines 49–51

Young Clifford for the next few years was indeed to be the cruelest of the Lancastrians and was to receive the nickname "the Butcher" for that reason.

He goes on to say:

> *Henceforth, I will not have to do with pity:*
> *Meet I an infant of the house of York,*
> *Into as many gobbets will I cut it*
> *As wild Medea young Absyrtus did:*
>
> —Act V, scene ii, lines 56–59

This speech forecasts one of the most dramatic scenes of the next play.

The classical reference is to the escape of the Greek hero Jason after he had taken the Golden Fleece from the King of Colchis. The King's daughter escaped with him and took her young brother along. As they were rowed madly across the sea by Jason's crew it became obvious that the ship of the furious King was gaining on them.

Thereupon Medea cut her brother, Absyrtus, into pieces and tossed these overboard. The horrified King gathered the pieces and carried them back to Colchis for burial. Thus Jason escaped and Medea began her role as one of the great unprincipled villainesses of literature.

Young Clifford carries his dead father from the battle scene, saying:

As did Aeneas old Anchises bear,
So bear I thee upon my manly shoulders;
—Act V, scene ii, lines 62–63

When Aeneas (see page I–20) fled from burning Troy as one of its few survivors, he took his old father with him. His father was too old and palsied to walk, let alone run, and Aeneas carried him on his shoulders even though the added weight endangered his own escape. This has been held up in literature as a model of filial piety ever since.

. . . an alehouse' paltry sign

In a second single combat, young Richard kills Somerset in the streets of St. Albans.

Now, Somerset was indeed killed in the battle, but despite Shakespeare, not every death in battle is the result of single combat between balanced foes. Exactly who killed Somerset is not known, but one thing *is* known: it was not young Richard. At the time of the Battle of St. Albans, Richard was just three years old and the amount of fighting he could do was strictly limited.

Richard is shown here as fierce and brave in battle and this everyone allows him. Though his later detractors loaded him with every physical deformity and moral vice, they could not deny his bravery, and even Shakespeare doesn't go so far as to do so. Of course, the fact that Richard fights so well and so fiercely is itself evidence that he couldn't be very deformed; it is not at all likely that a clubfooted hunchback would be such a terror in battle.

The exact place of Somerset's death is significant too, for he dies under the sign of an inn. Richard says:

. . . underneath an alehouse' paltry sign,
The Castle in Saint Albans, Somerset
Hath made the wizard famous in his death.
—Act V, scene ii, lines 67–69

In the séance scene, the Spirit, asked about Somerset, had said, "Let him shun castles" (see page II–588), and, of course, with typical wizard-like ambiguity, the reference turned out not to be to a real castle, but to a sign on which a castle was painted.

Saint Albans battle . . .

At this point *Henry VI, Part Two* ends—with Somerset, York's great enemy, killed, and the pathway cleared for York to become King if he wishes. Warwick closes the play, saying:

> *. . . 'twas a glorious day:*
> *Saint Albans battle won by famous York*
> *Shall be eternized in all age to come.*
> *Sound drum and trumpets, and to London all:*
> —Act V, scene iii, lines 29–32

So the battle might have been "eternized" (i.e., immortalized in fame) if it had really settled the issue, but the Wars of the Roses were only beginning. A generation of fighting was yet to come.

So *Henry VI, Part Two* ends with York's victorious army marching toward London, and it is in London that *Henry VI, Part Three* will begin.

38

The History of

HENRY VI, PART THREE

HENRY VI, PART THREE begins just where *Henry VI, Part Two* left off—at least to all appearances. In the last speech of the earlier play, the Earl of Warwick had urged the victorious Yorkists to march from St. Albans to London. And now, as *Henry VI, Part Three* opens, the Yorkists are indeed in London—at the House of Parliament, in fact—and are discussing, one supposes, the Battle of St. Albans.

. . . the King escaped . . .

Warwick has the first word here, as he had the last in the previous play. He says:

> *I wonder how the King escaped our hands?*
> —Act I, scene i, line 1

Actually, this is the first sign that Shakespeare is once again compressing time and that more than this first battle of the Wars of the Roses is involved. The King, you see, did *not* escape after the Battle of St. Albans.

Poor Henry VI, with his insecure hold on sanity (see page II–614), was probably not too clear what the fighting in the streets of St. Albans was all about. He was slightly wounded in the neck by an arrow, and when the battle was over, the Yorkist forces discovered him hiding in a tanner's house. He was treated with all possible respect and was taken to London with the Yorkist forces.

It was quite possible for York to have deposed King Henry now and forced (or allowed) Parliament to declare him King. He did not do so. When Parliament assembled on November 12, 1455 (half a year after the Battle of St. Albans), York was satisfied to accept the post of Protector for a King who was a second time officially declared mad. The chief difference between this second bout of royal madness and the first was that then Somerset (York's deadly enemy) had been alive, even though in the Tower, and now he was dead, having been killed at St. Albans.

Therefore, though York was Protector during both the King's periods of insanity, he must have felt more secure the second time.

Nevertheless, when during the Christmas celebration in 1455 Henry VI made a public appearance and acted quite sane, York gave up the protectorship again. In February 1456 he was out of office and for a second time he had allowed the reins of government to slip from his fingers.

York's failure to make full use of his victory at St. Albans and his insistence on viewing the feeble King Henry as King in truth certainly makes York seem a loyal subject forced into rebellion by the enmity of such people as Somerset and Queen Margaret.

However, the anti-Yorkist bias of Shakespeare, which makes him present York as scheming for the throne from the very beginning, forces him to suppress the actions, just described, whereby York clearly showed his loyalty to Henry.

. . . the great Lord of Northumberland

But back to Shakespeare's version. In answer to Warwick's question, Richard of York says that the King fled after the Battle of St. Albans, abandoning his army:

> *Whereat the great Lord of Northumberland,*
> *Whose warlike ears could never brook retreat,*
> *Cheered up the drooping army; and himself,*
> *Lord Clifford, and Lord Stafford all abreast*
> *Charge our main battle's front, and, breaking in,*
> *Were by the swords of common soldiers slain.*
>
> —Act I, scene i, lines 4–9

The "great Lord of Northumberland" was Sir Henry Percy, 2nd Earl of Northumberland. He was the son of none other than Hotspur (see page II–288). The 2nd Earl was born in 1394, so that he was nine years old when his father died at the Battle of Shrewsbury.

The boy was kept in confinement by the shrewd and suspicious Henry IV, but once Henry V came to the throne, young Percy benefited by the new monarch's determination to smooth over all English quarrels so that he might safely leave for France. Young Percy, then twenty years old, was liberated and allowed to inherit his family's land, revenues, and titles.

Henry V's estimate of what ought to be done was correct in this case. The young man was grateful and the Percys no longer revolted against the House of Lancaster. The 2nd Earl was, indeed, faithful to the death, and died at the Battle of St. Albans at the age of sixty-one, an age at which he might well, and without blame, have avoided battle. (The 2nd Earl did not, by the way, play any part in *Henry VI, Part Two,* and he is mentioned here at the very start of *Henry VI, Part Three* only that he might be declared already dead.)

Lord Clifford, on the other hand, played a part in the previous play, and his death was described at its end (see page II–618). There it was attributed not to a common soldier (as is correct) but, more dramatically and incorrectly, to Richard of York himself in single combat.

Lord Stafford was Humphrey, Earl of Stafford. He was the son of Humphrey, 1st Duke of Buckingham, that Buckingham who appears in *Henry VI, Part Two* as a partisan on the Lancastrian side and who had entrapped the Duchess of Gloucester at her sorcery (see page II–589).

Lord Stafford's father . . .

York's oldest son is also present. He is Edward, Earl of March (inheriting the ill-fated title of the Mortimer family, see page II–320). Actually, he was only thirteen years old at the time of the Battle of St. Albans and he did not take part. Shakespeare makes him older, however, because, as usual, he is condensing the time lapse in the play.

Edward of March brings additional news, saying:

> *Lord Stafford's father, Duke of Buckingham,*
> *Is either slain or wounded dangerous.*
> —Act I, scene i, lines 10–11

Actually, Buckingham survived the battle and did not die till five years later at another battle. Since Shakespeare plans to skip those five years, he must be disposed of now.

. . . the Earl of Wiltshire's blood

Another chimes in, saying:

> *And, brother, here's the Earl of Wiltshire's blood,*
> *Whom I encountered as the battles joined.*
> —Act I, scene i, lines 14–15

The speaker is the Marquess of Montagu. His name is John Neville, and he is a brother of Richard of Warwick. (It is Warwick whom he is addressing, hence the "brother" in his speech.)

The Wiltshire who is here described as having died in the battle is no relation to the Wiltshire of *Richard II* (see page II–284).

This new Wiltshire was James Butler, 5th Earl of Ormonde and Earl of Wiltshire, who was associated with York during the latter's stay in Ireland. When York left Ireland in 1450, Butler remained behind, in charge of the English interests. He married a girl of the Beaufort family, which made him a relative of Somerset by marriage and tied him to the Lancastrian side. He fought against the Yorkists in both Ireland and England, and, as stated, was wounded at St. Albans.

. . . the line of John of Gaunt

The climax to this serial description of the battle comes with the arrival of none other than Richard, youngest son of York. He comes striding in with Somerset's head. He had killed Somerset at the end of *Henry VI, Part Two* and now he displays his trophy.

Since Somerset was the leader of the Lancastrian party (after the ineffectual King and his virago of a Queen), it seemed to the dazzled Yorkists that victory was indeed theirs.

One of the nobles present says, with savage sarcasm:

> *Such hope have all the line of John of Gaunt!*
> —Act I, scene i, line 19

The speaker is John Mowbray, 3rd Duke of Norfolk, now forty years old. His grandfather had been the Thomas Mowbray, 1st Duke of Norfolk, whose quarrel with Bolingbroke (son of John of Gaunt) had filled the first act of *Richard II*. John Mowbray's uncle, another Thomas Mowbray, had been allied to the Archbishop of York in *Henry IV, Part Two* and had died through the treachery of John of Lancaster, grandson of John of Gaunt.

The 3rd Duke of Norfolk thus had good family reasons for hating the descendants of John of Gaunt, and the dead Somerset, whose head he was apostrophizing, had been a grandson of John of Gaunt. Of course, all those present were perfectly aware that King Henry VI was a great-grandson of John of Gaunt, so that what Norfolk had said was clear treason.

. . . Possess it, York

Warwick does worse. Not content with speaking treason, he urges an act of treason. Pointing to the throne, the seat reserved for the King in opening Parliament, he says to York:

> *This is the palace of the fearful King,*
> *And this the regal seat. Possess it, York;*
> *For this is thine and not King Henry's heirs'.*
> —Act I, scene i, lines 25–27

York, thereupon, with the active assistance of the others (who thus

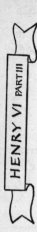

HENRY VI PART III

HOUSE of YORK

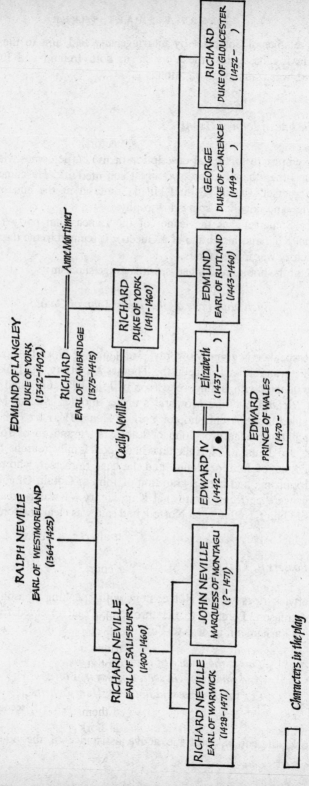

EDMUND OF LANGLEY
DUKE OF YORK
(1342–1402)

RICHARD === Anne Mortimer
EARL OF CAMBRIDGE
(1375–1415)

RICHARD
DUKE OF YORK
(1411–1460)

Cecily Neville

RALPH NEVILLE
EARL OF WESTMORELAND
(1364–1425)

RICHARD NEVILLE
EARL OF SALISBURY
(1400–1460)

RICHARD NEVILLE
EARL OF WARWICK
(1428–1471)

JOHN NEVILLE
MARQUESS OF MONTAGU
(?–1471)

EDWARD IV
(1442–   )

Elizabeth
(1437–   )

EDWARD
PRINCE OF WALES
(1470–   )

EDMUND
EARL OF RUTLAND
(1443–1460)

GEORGE
DUKE OF CLARENCE
(1449–   )

RICHARD
DUKE OF GLOUCESTER
(1452–   )

☐ Characters in the play

● Kings of England

NOTE: Women's names in lower case

share in the treasonable act), sets himself on the throne, thus making a symbolic display of himself as King.

Here is the point where five years drop out of history, for, as described earlier, the Battle of St. Albans was followed by York's loyal acceptance and return of the protectorship, with no claim upon the throne at all.

What happened?

Well, after York had resigned the protectorship for the second time in February 1456 (nine months after St. Albans), Queen Margaret took over once more. By October 1456 she had appointed strong Lancastrian partisans to all important government posts. She tried to get rid of York by sending him to Ireland again, but he avoided that post firmly. He retired to his estates and remained watchful.

The sons of the lords who had died at St. Albans were breathing fire to attack York, but the government did not quite feel ready for renewed war, and, to win time, efforts were made to win over the potentially dangerous duke and to establish some sort of conciliation. King Henry himself may have been feebly sincere about this, but to the Queen and her partisans this was merely a device that would, hopefully, put York off his guard.

Negotiations for such an accommodation were begun in October 1457 and on March 25, 1458, it was consummated. York and Warwick agreed to build a chapel to the memory of the lords who fell at St. Albans and to pay damages to their widows and children. Both sides then went together in procession to St. Paul's, with Queen Margaret and Richard of York actually walking hand in hand.

Margaret was only buying time, however. Even while the conciliation was proceeding, she was quietly collecting an army.

Her first overt action was against Warwick. Warwick had been appointed Captain of Calais (the last remaining English possession in France) in August 1455 in the aftermath of the victory at St. Albans, and he remained the only Yorkist in high position after York himself had resigned the protectorship.

Warwick was harassed by the hostile court, however, and received no financial support from them. He was therefore forced to engage in rather piratical attacks on merchant shipping, and in May 1448, two months after the conciliation, he was recalled to London to answer some complaints lodged against him by the owners of the ships he had taken.

Warwick saw clearly that the Lancastrians in control were out to break him despite the conciliation and he did not stay in London long. He conferred quickly with his father, Salisbury, and with York himself, then hastened back to Calais.

Now at last the Yorkist forces gathered themselves for the renewal of the war that Margaret was clearly preparing. York retired once more to Ludlow to raise an army and Salisbury joined him after defeating a small

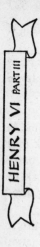

HENRY VI PART III

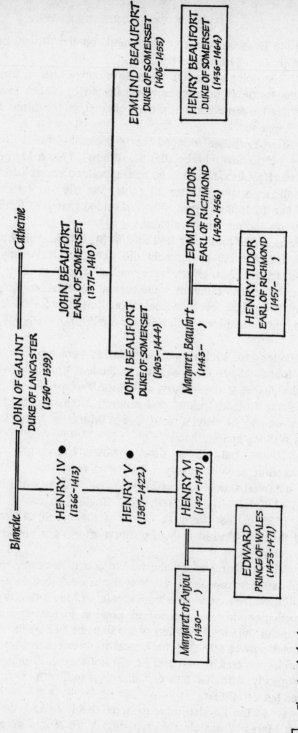

HOUSE of LANCASTER

John of Gaunt, Duke of Lancaster (1340–1399) — Catherine

Blanche — John of Gaunt, Duke of Lancaster (1340–1399)

John Beaufort, Earl of Somerset (1371–1410)

Edmund Beaufort, Duke of Somerset (1406–1455)

Henry Beaufort, Duke of Somerset (1436–1464)

John Beaufort, Duke of Somerset (1403–1444)

Margaret Beaufort (1443–) — Edmund Tudor, Earl of Richmond (1430–1456)

Henry Tudor, Earl of Richmond (1457–)

Henry IV (1366–1413) ●

Henry V (1387–1422) ●

Henry VI (1421–1471) ● — Margaret of Anjou (1430–)

Edward, Prince of Wales (1453–1471)

Characters in the play

● Kings of England

NOTE: Women's names in lower case

Lancastrian force en route. Warwick also came, with troops brought from Calais.

Thanks to Margaret's energy, however, and the time gained by conciliation with the always a little too trustful York, the Lancastrians were far better prepared than they had been four years earlier. Then it had been the Yorkists who had advanced to meet the Lancastrians near their base of operations. Now it was the Lancastrians who advanced all the way to Ludlow, and on October 13, 1459, York found himself hemmed in by the enemy army.

Nor did York have a chance to make a fight for it. During the night, most of his troops (judging, no doubt, that the Lancastrians would win) deserted him and passed over to the other side. There was nothing for the Yorkists to do but flee. Richard of York made it to Ireland, where he was popular and safe. Warwick, taking Salisbury and Edward of March with him, got safely to Calais, where *he* was popular.

For half a year afterward, Margaret and her Lancastrian supporters were supreme in England. They called a Parliament on November 29, 1459, and all the Yorkists, including Salisbury, Warwick, and York himself were declared traitors.

Margaret then tried to expand her power across the Channel by appointing a Lancastrian to replace Warwick as Captain of Calais. The new appointee was Henry Beaufort, 3rd Duke of Somerset, the son of York's great enemy who had died at St. Albans. Henry of Somerset was still a young man of twenty-three at the time. He and his two younger brothers were the last Beauforts, the last to be descended in a strictly male line from John of Gaunt, whose great-grandsons they were.

Henry of Somerset bore a hated name, however. When he tried to land in Calais, Warwick easily drove him off and the entire English fleet transferred its allegiance to the Yorkists.

With control of the sea, Warwick could sail to Dublin and back to Calais; then, having arranged matters with York, he carried a small army of fifteen hundred men to Kent toward the end of June 1460. Men flocked to his banner and what followed was more a triumphal procession than a warlike campaign.

On July 2, 1460, Warwick and his men marched unopposed into London, to the cheering of the populace. Young Edward of March, the eldest son of Richard of York, was with him, and won all hearts, for he was eighteen years old now, over six feet tall, blond, and very handsome. He was a new Richard Lion-Heart (but heterosexual) and the people went wild over him.

The Lancastrians had hastily backed away, moving northward, and Warwick, without waiting long, pursued. Warwick reached the enemy at Northampton, and on July 10, 1460, a battle was fought. This time the situation was precisely the reverse of what it had been at Ludlow nine months previously. Now it was a Lancastrian contingent, scenting defeat, that deserted, and it was the Lancastrians that were forced into retreat.

It was at this Battle of Northampton that the Duke of Buckingham, whom Edward of March claimed to have wounded at St. Albans (see page II-624), was actually killed, and it was at Northampton that Edward of March fought and not at St. Albans (when he had been too young). This is an indication of how Shakespeare condensed the two battles and skipped the time between.

King Henry was captured at Northampton, as he had been at St. Albans, and for the second time was brought back to London by triumphant Yorkists. A new Parliament was called and it dutifully followed the tide of battle, undoing all the deeds of the Lancastrian Parliament the year before and passing a new set of Yorkist resolutions.

With the Yorkists in control of London and much of the country, Richard of York came from Ireland. He entered into London with all the pageantry he could muster, marched into the House of Parliament, and thoughtfully faced the royal throne. Apparently, he was tired of accepting Margaret's word and being betrayed, and seriously considered the possibility of making himself King and settling matters. The story is that he placed a hesitant hand upon the throne as though tempted, but he did *not*, apparently, actually sit on it as Shakespeare had him do.

Earl of Northumberland . . .

It was on October 16, 1460, that Richard of York decided to declare for the kingship and demanded it of Parliament. What stood in the way was King Henry himself. He was such a pitiful, inoffensive creature that it was difficult to go against him, especially since the people generally felt he was a saint because of his piety, and blamed all the evils on the Queen and the ministers.

York therefore had to consider the possibility that in seizing the throne, the spectacle of the gentle Henry hurled ruthlessly from power might turn the hearts of men from him. Some clever device would be needed to avoid this.

Shakespeare represents the uncertainty as to the proper course of action in terms of a direct confrontation between York and the King.

Henry enters, even as York is seated on the throne, and with the King are surviving members of the Lancastrian party. Referring bitterly to York's attempt at usurpation, Henry rouses the indignation of his party by reciting the harm done them by the Yorkists. He says:

> *Earl of Northumberland, he slew thy father,*
> *And thine, Lord Clifford; and you both have vowed revenge*
> —Act I, scene i, lines 54–55

We met Lord Clifford in *Henry VI, Part Two,* where he was called "Young Clifford," since his father was "Clifford." It was Young Clifford who had promised a grisly revenge, and now, promoted to "Clifford" in this play, he will later take it.

The Earl of Northumberland who is here addressed is still another Henry Percy. He is the 3rd Earl of Northumberland, having succeeded to the title when his father died at St. Albans. The 3rd Earl had been born in 1421, the year before Henry V had died, and he was now thirty-four years old.

. . . gentle Earl of Westmoreland

Northumberland and Clifford both affirm that they do indeed want revenge. So does a third Lancastrian, who advocates an immediate attack on York, tearing him from the throne, but King Henry says:

> *Be patient, gentle Earl of Westmoreland.*
> —Act I, scene i, line 61

This is Ralph Neville, 2nd Earl of Westmoreland, grandson and namesake of the 1st Earl, who had led the forces of Henry IV in *Henry IV, Part One.* He is thus the nephew of Salisbury and the first cousin of Warwick and represents the Lancastrian side of the family. (Like all civil wars, the Wars of the Roses pitted relatives against one another.)

Cousin of Exeter . . .

Henry is certainly in no position to use force against York after the Battle of Northampton. He says, therefore, to one of his nobles who has joined Clifford and Westmoreland in demanding action:

> *Cousin of Exeter, frowns, words, and threats*
> *Shall be the war that Henry means to use.*
> —Act I, scene i, lines 72–73

Exeter is no descendant or relation of the Exeter who appears in *Henry V.* That Exeter had been the youngest of the three Beaufort sons of John of Gaunt and had held the title only for his life.

Before his day one John Holand had been 1st Duke of Exeter. His widowed mother had married the Black Prince and had become the mother of Richard II. Holand was thus elder half brother to that King and was made 1st Duke of Exeter in 1397 for helping Richard take over from Thomas of Gloucester. After Bolingbroke overthrew Richard and became

Henry IV, Holand was demoted for his share in Gloucester's death. Then, when he continued to plot against Henry IV, Holand was executed and his titles forfeited. It was for this reason that the title was available for the use of Thomas Beaufort (passing thus from the half brother of the old King to the half brother of the new).

Meanwhile the son of John Holand (also John Holand) served Henry V and later Henry VI faithfully in France, remaining a strong Lancastrian to the end, despite the nature of his father's fate, and despite the fact that he was married to Anne, a daughter of none other than Richard of York.

In 1444 his loyalty was rewarded by the restoration of his family title (Thomas Beaufort had been dead seventeen years), and once again a John Holand was Duke of Exeter. It is this Exeter that Henry VI now addresses.

. . . for this my lifetime . . .

Henry VI, as good as his word, confines himself to arguing with Richard of York, who argues back. Partisans on both sides join in, and the whole story of the succession is brought up again. Did Henry IV usurp the crown or conquer it? Were the Mortimers the real heirs or not?

The weight of the argument seems to be on the side of the Yorkists and even Henry grows uncertain. Then, when Warwick tires of the wrangling and calls in the Yorkist army, the King cries out:

> My Lord of Warwick, hear but one word;
> Let me for this my lifetime reign as king.
>
> —Act I, scene i, lines 170-71

In short, Henry is represented as volunteering to disinherit his own son provided he might rest on the throne himself.

Actually, this compromise was a shrewd move on York's part. By leaving Henry VI on the throne, York avoids an actual act of what might be considered usurpation and prevents loss of the "sympathy vote." The English public would be far less concerned with Henry's son (whom many suspected to be illegitimate, anyway). Furthermore, as Henry's heir, York would have all the power of the state and be King in fact, while poor Henry remained King only in name.

It was on October 23, 1460, that the compromise was reached, and there is a peculiar parallel with what happened just forty years earlier in 1420. Then mad King Charles VI of France had been forced to disinherit his son and accept vigorous Henry V of England as his heir (see page II-516). Henry had only to wait for the death of the sick old King—yet it was Henry who died first. Now mad King Henry VI of England (even the

Roman numeral was the same) was forced to disinherit his son and accept vigorous Richard of York as his heir. Richard had only to wait for the death of the sick old King—yet—

By means of this compromise, by the way, the Spirit's statement in the séance scene of *Henry VI, Part Two* was almost fulfilled. That statement had said that "The Duke yet lives that Henry shall depose," and Richard, Duke of York, had, in a sense, deposed Henry.

. . . disinherited thine only son

The compromise, carried through at the expense of the Prince of Wales, was a very sensible one, it would seem, and solved all problems, but one person at least would never accept it. That person was Queen Margaret. Her son, Edward, was seven years old now, and as long as he lived she would never for one moment give up the attempt to make him King eventually.

Queen Margaret had been at the Battle of Northampton, but she had managed to escape, taking her son with her. Together, they had managed to make their way to Scotland.

In the play, she now makes her appearance in London at the House of Parliament with her son, Edward of Wales. This is quite impossible, of course, since if they had been in London in 1460, they would both have been seized by the Yorkists and placed in the Tower. From there, in all probability, neither would have emerged for a long time, if ever.

Dramatically, though, the confrontation is necessary. When the Queen approaches, Exeter, who alone of the Lancastrian lords has accepted the compromise, tries to sneak away. So does the poor King, as frightened of his virago Queen as ever he was of York.

She stops them, however, and addresses her feeble husband with profound contempt, saying:

> *Hadst thou but loved him* [the Prince] *half so well as I,*
> *Or felt that pain which I did for him once,*
> *Or nourished him as I did with my blood,*
> *Thou wouldst have left thy dearest heart-blood there,*
> *Rather than have made that savage duke thine heir*
> *And disinherited thine only son.*
>
> —Act I, scene i, lines 220–25

And actually, as long as the Prince lived, Margaret never gave up. She did not hesitate to appeal to foreigners for help, and when the English failed her she did not hesitate to bring mercenaries into the land.

This made her more unpopular than ever in England, but little she cared for that. She was not an Englishwoman by birth and she had no cause to love the land in which she had found only misery.

She leaves Henry in a fury now, vowing to raise an army in the north and lead it herself.

. . . all the Northern earls and lords

The second scene of the play opens at one of York's castles. It is located near Wakefield, twenty-five miles south of York itself.

Shakespeare, with his anti-Yorkist bias, makes it appear that it is the Yorkists that are ready to break the compromise, for York's sons urge their father to make himself King outright without waiting for Henry's death.

Thus, his son Richard tempts York by saying:

> *And, father, do but think*
> *How sweet a thing it is to wear a crown,*
> *Within whose circuit is Elysium*
> *And all that poets feign of bliss and joy.*
>
> —Act I, scene ii, lines 28–31

Actually, young Richard was still only eight years old, and to make him the ringleader of the attempt to break the compromise treacherously is merely more of the vilification of which he was chief target in Shakespeare's time. (The speech has another purpose too, for it will gain a kind of grisly irony soon enough.)

Richard of York is swayed by his son's words and agrees to make the try for kingship outright when a Messenger arrives, crying:

> *The Queen with all the Northern earls and lords*
> *Intend here to besiege you in your castle:*
> *She is hard by with twenty thousand men;*
>
> —Act I, scene ii, lines 49–51

In actual history, however, York had no plans to break the compromise and no need to. He lacked nothing but the name of King, and it was surely not worth renewing a civil war just for that.

It was Queen Margaret whose hostile acts were forcing an end to the compromise. She was raising an army in the north (including Scotsmen eager for loot) and she simply had to be dealt with. Early in December 1460, then, only a month after he had been declared heir, York hurried northward. He took only a small force with him, feeling, perhaps, that the need for haste was uppermost and that a woman would be ineffective as leader of armies anyway.

He didn't know Margaret. At Wakefield, he found himself neatly trapped by a far superior force.

. . . ten to one

Richard of York might have remained in the castle and withstood a siege. A relieving army would have surely come up in time. However, he apparently could not bear the shame that would have come upon him at the word that he had been trapped and besieged by a woman.

The fire-eating young Richard (again the villain of the piece) urges battle and York allows himself to be overpersuaded, saying:

> Many a battle have I won in France,
> When as the enemy hath been ten to one.
> Why should I not now have the like success?
> —Act I, scene ii, lines 73–75

This fits in with the English legend that all battles in France were Agincourts. We can be sure, though, that York had no such impression in reality. His battles in France were not Agincourts and well he knew it.

. . . bloody Clifford . . .

Shakespeare makes it appear that York's sons Edward and Richard were with him in the castle. They weren't. Edward was with part of the Yorkist army at the city of Gloucester, 125 miles to the southwest. Eight-year-old Richard wasn't yet to the wars at all.

It was York's second son, Edmund, Earl of Rutland, who was with him, and he appears in the play only at this one point. Shakespeare's source, Edward Hall, says Edmund is twelve years old at the time and he is therefore presented in this scene as a schoolboy. Actually, he was seventeen years old, only one year younger than Edward of March, who was already a seasoned warrior.

York tried to send Edmund of Rutland out of the castle, along with his Tutor (a priest named Sir Robert Aspall, though this name is not given in the play). York did this, presumably, in the hope of saving him in case the battle was lost, but luck was against the young man. Rutland says to his Tutor:

> Ah, whither shall I fly to 'scape their hands?
> Ah, tutor, look where bloody Clifford comes!
> —Act I, scene iii, lines 1–2

Clifford's father had been slain at St. Albans (see page II–618) and Clifford had sworn to kill all members of York's family who came into his hands. At the end of *Henry VI, Part Two* he particularly threatened York's children and that served the dramatic purpose of forecasting the scene that has now come.

Is as a Fury . . .

Young Rutland pleads for his life, but Clifford says, in a rage:

> *The sight of any of the house of York*
> *Is as a Fury to torment my soul;*
> *And till I root out their accursed line*
> *And leave not one alive, I live in hell.*

—Act I, scene iii, lines 30–33

The Furies (or Erinyes, to the Greeks) were three avenging goddesses whose function it was to pursue those guilty of great crimes, filling them with dread and driving them mad. They are the personification of remorse, or the maddening pangs of awakened conscience.

Rutland still pleads. He himself has done Clifford no harm, and if his father had:

> *. . .'twas ere I was born.*

—Act I, scene iii, line 39

Not quite. Clifford's father was killed at St. Albans in 1455, and at that time Rutland was twelve years old.

. . . one son . . .

Rutland makes one final plea, saying:

> *Thou hast one son. For his sake pity me,*
> *Lest in revenge thereof, sith God is just,*
> *He be as miserably slain as I,*

—Act I, scene iii, lines 40–42

This sounds like a hindsight prophecy of something that will actually come to pass, but not so. Clifford will die in battle not long after this scene and will, indeed, leave behind one young son, Henry Clifford, about seven years old. Young Henry was brought up in obscurity in order to preserve him from Yorkist vengeance, so that he is sometimes referred to as "the shepherd lord."

After the final fall of the Yorkists, however, he came back into his own
and liv͗d to reach an age of about seventy before dying in bed.

. . . Phaëthon hath tumbled . . .

The battle was fought on December 30, 1460, and it was an utter defeat
for Richard of York, who had been badly outnumbered. The next scene
opens as York stumbles onto the stage, attempting to flee. He speaks, as he
does so, of the doughty deeds of his sons Edward and Richard as they had
attempted to rescue him, but failed. (Actually neither one was at the
battle.) He does *not* mention his brother-in-law, the Earl of Salisbury, who
had been trapped with him.

In the aftermath of the battle, Salisbury was also attempting flight. He
was taken, carried to Pontefract (where Richard II had died), and executed, dying on the last day of the year at the age of sixty.

As for York himself, he is taken on the field of battle, and Clifford,
who is among the captors, exults:

> Now Phaëthon hath tumbled from his car,
> —Act I, scene iv, line 33

The same mythic metaphor is used for the fall of York as Shakespeare
was to use some years later to describe the fall of Richard II (see page
II–297).

. . . wanton Edward . . .

Clifford would like, of course, to kill York on the spot, but savage
Margaret has better sport in mind. She intends to torture York before she
kills him and she is subtle enough to prefer mental torture to the mere
breaking of limbs.

Once he is bound and helpless she taunts him:

> Where are your mess of sons to back you now?
> The wanton Edward, and the lusty George?
> And where's that valiant crookback prodigy [monster],
> Dicky your boy . . .
> —Act I, scene iv, lines 73–76

For the first time Edward is described as "wanton." He was indeed to
become a great womanizer (though it is questionable whether he had yet
had time to prove himself one as early as 1460) and his lust was to contribute mightily to the ruin of his house.

The "valiant crookback prodigy" is, of course, young Richard, whom Shakespeare virtually never has anyone refer to without mention of his supposed deformities.

"Lusty George" is York's third son, who so far has not appeared onstage. He was born on October 21, 1449, in Dublin, while his father was serving as Lord Lieutenant of Ireland. He was only eleven years old at the time of York's capture.

Margaret then reaches the very depths of infamy when she goes on to say:

> . . . where is your darling, Rutland?
> Look, York, I stained this napkin with the blood
> That valiant Clifford, with his rapier's point,
> Made issue from the bosom of the boy;
> And if thine eyes can water for his death,
> I give thee this to dry thy cheeks withal.
>
> —Act I, scene iv, lines 78–83

Shakespeare's anti-Yorkist and pro-Lancastrian bias does not extend to the Frenchwoman Margaret. And indeed, she was so hated in England that she was the greatest asset the Yorkists had. The story of Rutland's death, as we can well imagine, was used to rouse England against her, and Rutland was made younger than he really was to increase the horror of the tale.

As the death of Humphrey of Gloucester had ruined Suffolk, so the death of Rutland was to ruin Margaret and the Lancastrian cause by losing her the last remnant of popular sympathy. And York's own end was converted into an even more pathetic tale. In this one case, Shakespeare follows the Yorkist party line, perhaps because he cannot bring himself to miss the chance of a scene of grisly perfection that no one in all history could have better handled than himself.

A crown for York . . .

Thus, Margaret is not done with her gruesome and horrible mockery. She cries out:

> A crown for York! and, lords, bow low to him.
> Hold you his hands whilst I do set it on.
>
> —Act I, scene iv, lines 94–95

A paper crown is put on York's head, while all those assembled bow low to him in mock reverence. What a commentary on York's remark in the last act of *Henry VI, Part Two* concerning the crown: "That gold must round engirt these brows of mine" (see page II–612). The imperious remark put into his mouth by Shakespeare was for this purpose put there, to forecast the moment when it would come true, with paper substituted for gold.

It is even more effective to consider now young Richard's comment just two scenes before: "How sweet a thing it is to wear a crown." York knows now how "sweet" it is and the time will come when young Richard will know as well.

What actually happened, historically, was, of course, not nearly as bad. York was found dead on the field and there was no occasion for Margaret's sadistic capering. His head was cut off and placed on the walls of York for all to see, and was then adorned with a paper crown to signify the vanity of his hopes for the succession. (That paper crown was, however, a propaganda mistake of appalling dimensions. The Yorkists built out of that crown the tale that was eventually used by Shakespeare in this play, and Margaret was pilloried for all time as a monster.)

She-wolf of France . . .

York has taken all of it dry-eyed, stunned at the disaster, but now Margaret demands his final words so that she might have the ultimate triumph of listening to his tormented wails.

York, however, can do better than that. In one final speech, the greatest in the three *Henry VI* plays, he spoils her triumph and gives her the name that marks her place in history for all time. He begins:

> *She-wolf of France, but worse than wolves of France,*
> *Whose tongue more poisons than the adder's tooth!*
> *How ill-beseeming is it in thy sex*
> *To triumph like an Amazonian trull*
> —Act I, scene iv, lines 111–14

He taunts her with her father's poverty, denies to her any beauty, virtue, or statesmanship, then says:

> *Thou art as opposite to every good*
> *As the Antipodes are unto us,*
> *Or as the South to the Septentrion.*
> *O tiger's heart wrapped in a woman's hide!*
> *How couldst thou drain the lifeblood of the child,*
> *To bid the father wipe his eyes withal,*
> *And yet be seen to bear a woman's face?*
> —Act I, scene iv, lines 134–40

The Antipodes ("opposed feet") represent the other side of the spherical earth, where the feet of the inhabitants face ours. The Septentrion ("seven stars") refers to the Big Dipper, which is always in the northern sky, so that the word is a fancy synonym for "north."

It is the powerful line "O tiger's heart wrapped in a woman's hide!" that is noteworthy here above all, however. It has an importance quite apart from anything in the play.

When the English playwright Robert Greene (see page I–147) wrote a savage satire called *A Groatsworth of Wit* in 1592, he snarlingly denounced someone he called "an upstart crow, beautified with our feathers, that with his tiger's heart wrapped in a player's hide supposes he is as well able to bombast out a blank verse as the best of you, and being an absolute Johannes-factotum is in his own conceit the only Shake-scene in a country."

Shakespeare started as an actor and began to patch up the plays in which he was appearing (to the very natural annoyance of the writers thereof). When he began producing popular plays of his own, it would naturally make men like Greene envious. What! Did a mere player think he could out-write *real* writers?

Greene did not name Shakespeare, but the semipun "Shake-scene" is enough to identify him, and if that is lacking there is that "tiger's heart wrapped in a player's hide"—one word changed of what may be the juiciest single line Shakespeare had yet written and that possibly only the year before—which gives it away completely.

. . . tigers of Hyrcania

And now York weeps at last, saying:

> *That face of his the hungry cannibals*
> *Would not have touched, would not have stained with blood;*
> *But you are more inhuman, more inexorable,*
> *O, ten times more, than tigers of Hyrcania.*
> *See, ruthless queen, a hapless father's tears:*
> *This cloth thou dipp'd'st in blood of my sweet boy,*
> *And I with tears do wash the blood away.*
> *Keep thou the napkin, and go boast of this;*
> *And if thou tell'st the heavy story right,*
> *Upon my soul, the hearers will shed tears;*
> *Yea, even my foes will shed fast-falling tears*
> *And say "Alas, it was a piteous deed!"*
> *There, take the crown, and, with the crown, my curse;*
>
> —Act I, scene iv, lines 152–64

York has turned the tables. His speech has caused Northumberland, who is present, to break down in tears himself, and Margaret must feel the truth of what York says—that from the propaganda standpoint she has been destroyed. She is from now on a she-wolf of France; she is from now on worse than a hungry cannibal, worse than a tiger of Hyrcania (Hyrcania is a wild region bordering the Caspian, noted in ancient times for its feral animals—the tales magnified by distance).

York, who was heir to the throne about six weeks altogether, is stabbed to death by Clifford and Margaret, but it is no triumph now.

And in this way, another part of the séance prophecy comes true. The Duke who has deposed Henry (see page II–588) has died a violent death.

Marched toward Saint Albans . . .

The news reaches Edward and Richard, the sons of York, and they are half mad with grief and rage at the deaths of their father and brother (and the manner of those deaths).

When Warwick enters, they fly to give him the news, but he has already heard of it and is bringing additional bad news.

After the death of York and the destruction of his small army, Margaret, her fury growing with victory, marched southward. The wild Scottish clansmen in her army, perennially angry with the English, looted to their hearts' content and Margaret made no attempt to stop them. There was no further hatred she could receive and what she wanted was only continued victory and continued revenge at whatever cost.

Warwick has nothing to say of his own father's death at Wakefield (since that was ignored by Shakespeare, who found it necessary to concentrate entirely on York), but goes on to say:

> *I, then in London, keeper of the King,*
> *Mustered my soldiers, gathered flocks of friends,*
> *And very well appointed, as I thought,*
> *Marched toward Saint Albans to intercept the Queen,*
> *Bearing the King in my behalf along;*
> —Act II, scene i, lines 111–15

Poor Henry VI, all through the Wars of the Roses (or at least that portion he lived to witness), had at no time even the feeblest shadow of a will of his own. He was merely a living flag, a symbol of royalty, to be used by whichever side controlled him. In this case, Warwick used him to indicate that he was fighting for the King, while the Queen was, by that very token, a rebel and traitor.

Before Warwick could assemble his forces after York's unexpected defeat and death, Margaret had swept all the way to St. Albans. There, on

February 17, 1461, a second battle was fought, nearly six years after the first. This time it was the Lancastrian army that rounded the flank of the opposition and fell on its rear. Warwick had to retreat quickly, leaving numerous dead. Margaret had a second victory.

Lord George . . .

By her victory at the second Battle of St. Albans, Margaret was able to retake King Henry. She allowed the abbey at St. Albans to be looted for needed money, executed several prisoners, and showed every sign of intending to enter London. The Londoners, fearing her savagery and that of her Scots, began to make desperate preparations for defense.

London was on its own too, for Warwick, with what remained of his army, was moving rapidly westward to join the forces of Edward, who now, by his father's death, was not only Earl of March, but Duke of York as well. Warwick says to Edward:

> Lord George your brother, Norfolk and myself,
> In haste, post-haste, are come to join with you;
>> —Act II, scene i, lines 138–39

George has not yet been onstage, but he is not yet twelve, after all. Still, his absence cannot be accounted for only by his youth, for Shakespeare makes all York's sons older than they are (except Rutland, whom he made younger), and George is three years older than Richard, whom Shakespeare has pictured as fighting like a hero in several battles.

Instead, the excuse used is that George was in Burgundy, and Warwick says:

> . . . for your brother, he was lately sent
> From your kind aunt, Duchess of Burgundy,
> With aid of soldiers to this needful war.
>> —Act II, scene i, lines 145–47

Shakespeare's attempt to make George's absence plausible entangles him in an anachronism. At the time of the second Battle of St. Albans, in 1461, Philip the Good (see page II–514) was still Duke of Burgundy. It was not till 1467 that he died and was succeeded by his son, Charles the Bold. Before Charles had been duke for a year, he married Margaret of York, a daughter of Richard of York. The Duchess of Burgundy was thus George's sister rather than his aunt and she did not in any case become duchess till 1468.

Making another head . . .

Warwick is careful to explain that he was hastening westward not in retreat, but merely to seize the opportunity to fight again. He explains that:

> *. . . in the marches here we heard you were,*
> *Making another head to fight again.*
> —Act II, scene i, lines 140–41

Shakespeare is here being unfair to Edward. He was doing far more than merely "making another head" (gathering new forces). He had gathered an army almost immediately the news of York's death had reached him and had been ready to fight far sooner than Warwick had been.

On February 2, 1461, Edward fought a battle against Welsh partisans of the Lancastrians at Mortimer's Cross, about a dozen miles southwest of Ludlow. He won that battle and began marching eastward to join Warwick. He was still marching when word came of Warwick's defeat at St. Albans. The two met, then, not because Warwick had retired westward, but far more because Edward was boldly pushing eastward.

By the time Edward and Warwick joined forces they were only a day or two from London. It was now February 23, 1461, a week after the second Battle of St. Albans, and Margaret's ferocious cavalry was raiding the northern edge of the city.

But news reached Margaret that Edward was marching posthaste toward her. Her own army was in disarray and she was surrounded by hostile countryside. She considered it only prudent to retire northward. She did so and the threat to London was lifted.

London went wild with joy, and to them, now, Edward was a savior dropped from heaven. When, on February 25, 1461, Edward rode into London at the head of the rescuing army, he was greeted with a hero's welcome.

. . . this brave town of York

Margaret's retreat was a long one—some 160 miles northward to York. The next scene opens outside that city, and Margaret, who is now the possessor of King Henry, shows him the sights—particularly the head of old York, still decomposing on the wall of the city. She says:

> *Welcome, my lord, to this brave town of York.*
> *Yonder's the head of that arch-enemy*
> *That sought to be encompassed with your crown.*

Doth not the object cheer your heart, my lord?

         —Act II, scene ii, lines 1–4

The sight might have satisfied Margaret's ferocity but certainly there was little else to commend it, for the Queen's victories and cruelties had by now utterly boomeranged.

A half year before, Richard of York had deemed it impolitic to seize the throne and contented himself with being heir. But now the tales of the martyred deaths of Richard of York and of his son, Edmund of Rutland, had created immense sympathy for the Yorkist side, and Margaret's wild march southward had created equal hatred for the Lancastrians. Even poor Henry's plight no longer struck a chord, for he was with Margaret and therefore party to her misdeeds.

The result was that only two months after York's death, his son was able to do what he himself could not. On March 2, 1461, a council of the nobility declared Edward King, and on March 4 the young man headed a great procession to Westminster and sat on the throne that his father (despite Shakespeare) had only dared touch. He was still not yet twenty-one years old, and now he reigned as Edward IV.

Yet King Edward could not remain in London to enjoy being King. Margaret still held the north and she would have to be defeated. The Wars of the Roses went on.

Comes Warwick . . .

Predictably, mild Henry takes no pleasure in the sight of York's dead head. He turns from all bloodshed; even regretting the bloody victories of his father, Henry V (something no one else in Shakespeare does—and perhaps this is one occasion when Shakespeare's pacifism dares speak against the great Henry's deeds directly).

Henry VI says:

> *I'll leave my son my virtuous deeds behind;*
> *And would my father had left me no more!*
> *For all the rest is held at such a rate*
> *As brings a thousand-fold more care to keep*
> *Than in possession any jot of pleasure.*

         —Act II, scene ii, lines 49–53

One gathers that the very kingship wearies Henry and that his view is quite different from that of young Richard, who felt that the crown held Elysium.

But blood must continue, for the Yorkist forces have swarmed northward on Lancastrian heels. A Messenger arrives, saying:

> *. . . with a band of thirty thousand men*
> *Comes Warwick, backing of the Duke of York,*
> *And in the towns, as they do march along,*
> *Proclaims him king . . .*
>
> —Act II, scene ii, lines 68–71

Thus, in place of a Duke of York killed for aspiring to be King comes another Duke of York who is proclaimed King.

Helen of Greece . . .

The Yorkist army arrives and there is the usual slanging match between the two sides. At one point, Edward says to Margaret:

> *Helen of Greece was fairer far than thou,*
> *Although thy husband may be Menelaus;*
> *And ne'er was Agamemnon's brother wronged*
> *By that false woman as this King by thee.*
>
> —Act II, scene ii, lines 146–49

This harks back to Suffolk's statement in the last speech of *Henry VI, Part One* to the effect that he was going to France for a Queen as Paris had gone to Greece (see page II-571). Paris had gotten the beautiful Helen, who betrayed her husband and brought ruin to her adopted country of Troy. The less beautiful Margaret, it is implied, has done the same.

But more is implied too. The accusation of Henry VI playing the part of Menelaus and of his being wronged by Margaret clearly implies the illegitimacy of the young Prince of Wales, and one can see the Yorkist line of argument. Not only is Edward rightful King of England through the line of Mortimer, but even if it were not so, Henry is incapable of rule and his son is illegitimate, and the throne is then Edward's by inheritance anyway.

Forspent with toil . . .

The two armies plunge into furious battle, the force of which becomes clear at the very beginning of the next scene, when Warwick makes his appearance onstage, crying out:

> *Forspent with toil, as runners with a race,*
> *I lay me down a little while to breathe;*
>
> —Act II, scene iii, lines 1–2

The scene is Towton, a small place about fifteen miles southwest of

York, and the battle took place on March 28, 1461. It began in a swirling snowstorm and it continued for six hours.

No careful tactics were involved. So furiously frantic were both sides that they merely fell on each other frontally and hacked away until, in all, some thirty-eight thousand Englishmen were dead on either side—a carnage far greater than any battle in France through all the Hundred Years' War.

The bloody, senseless nature of the fighting is made plain by the device of having King Henry comment on it. He sits down in a corner of the field, wishing he were dead or living the life of a harmless shepherd, and watches the particular tragedy of civil war—that members of one family might be fighting on opposite sides. He witnesses the plight of a father who has killed his son, and of a son who has killed his father.

. . . towards Berwick . . .

In the end, though, it is the Yorkists who have the victory. The Lancastrian forces are smashed completely, and Queen Margaret must flee the field. The Prince of Wales comes running onto the stage with his mother (actually, he was only eight years old at the time of the Battle of Towton), crying to King Henry:

> *Fly, father, fly! for all your friends are fled*
>
> —Act II, scene v, line 125

Queen Margaret is more specific. She says:

> *Mount you, my lord, towards Berwick post amain*
>
> —Act II, scene v, line 128

Berwick (see page II-591) is on the Scottish border. And indeed, Margaret, her son, and her husband must, in the aftermath of Towton, leg it to Scotland once again, as she had done the year before after the Battle of Northampton.

Giving no ground . . .

With royalty gone, Clifford staggers onto the stage. He is badly wounded. He has, according to the Shakespearean version of the battle, been fighting with young Richard. Whether he has or not doesn't matter, for his end came in less prosaic fashion. In the aftermath of the battle, Clifford, while removing his helmet, was accidentally struck in the throat by an arrow shot by an unknown hand.

He is onstage now to die, unrepentant to the last, and breathing the belief of all extremists always—that all misfortune comes from compromise and that only unyieldingness can win out. He says, in apostrophe to the absent King Henry:

> . . . Henry, hadst thou swayed as kings should do,
> Or as thy father and his father did,
> Giving no ground unto the house of York,
> They never then had sprung like summer flies;
>
> —Act II, scene vi, lines 14–17

Clifford dies and lies there to be taunted by his victorious Yorkist enemies. The head of York is taken down from the walls of York, and the head of Clifford is put up instead. The Butcher had survived his victims just three months.

The Earl of Northumberland (grandson of Hotspur), who had been moved to tears by York's last speech, also died at this battle.

. . . crownèd England's royal king

Edward IV had been declared King, but there had earlier been no time to go through the full ceremony, thanks to the necessity of chasing north after Margaret. Now, with the happy (for the Yorkists) outcome of the Battle of Towton, there would be time for all desirable ceremony. Warwick says to Edward:

> . . . now to London with triumphant march,
> There to be crownèd England's royal king;
>
> —Act II, scene vi, lines 87–88

The coronation of Edward, carried through with full splendor and pageantry, even though Henry VI yet lived, took place on June 29, 1461, just three months after the Battle of Towton.

. . . Duke of Gloucester

One of the King's prerogatives is the naming of peers, and Edward, after Towton, promises to make his brothers into dukes (as, indeed, he proceeded to do after the coronation). He says:

> Richard, I will create thee Duke of Gloucester;
> And George, of Clarence:
>
> —Act II, scene vi, lines 103–4

These titles are fitting. On two previous occasions Clarence had been the title given to a second son. Thus, Lionel of Antwerp (see page II–259) had been created the 1st Duke of Clarence in 1362. He was Edward III's third son, to be sure, but the second had died in infancy and Lionel was thus the second to survive to manhood. (It was from Lionel that Edward traced the descent that made him, in the Yorkist view, legitimate King, so that too militated in favor of the use of the title.)

In 1368 Lionel died without male heirs and it was not until 1412 that another Duke of Clarence was created. This was Thomas, the second son of Henry IV (see page II–361) and the younger brother of Henry V. He had died in 1421, without sons, and now it was the turn of George, second surviving son of Richard of York and younger brother of Edward IV, to be the third holder of the title.

In the same way, Gloucester had become a traditional title for a king's youngest son or brother. The first Duke of Gloucester had been Thomas of Woodstock, given the title in 1385. He was the youngest son of Edward III. The title became extinct in 1397 with Thomas' death and was revived in 1414 when Henry V made his youngest brother, Humphrey, the Duke of Gloucester. Again it became extinct, in 1447, with Humphrey's death, and now Richard was receiving it to become the third holder of the title.

Richard didn't like this, for as he says:

> Let me be Duke of Clarence, George of Gloucester;
> For Gloucester's dukedom is too ominous.
>
> —Act II, scene vi, lines 106–7

He might well say so, for the first duke, Thomas, after being nearly master of King Richard II, was finally imprisoned and assassinated (see page II–267); while the second duke, Humphrey, after being nearly master of King Henry VI, was imprisoned and assassinated (see page II–599). One might easily be suspicious enough to suspect the same fate for the third; though, as a matter of fact, Richard was not fated to follow the pattern. He did better—and worse.

However, Clarence was, in its way, an ominous title as well. The first duke, Lionel, died at the age of thirty. He was the least of those sons of Edward III who survived to manhood, and was the first to die. The second duke, Thomas, died at the age of thirty-three. He was the least of the sons of Henry IV, and the first to die. Might it not be that George would expect the same? Because that is what, in the end, he got.

In any case, Warwick impatiently derides Richard's superstitious remark and the appointments stand.

. . . in thy shoulder . . .

After Towton, Edward expresses prime gratitude to Warwick, saying:

. . . in thy shoulder do I build my seat,
And never will I undertake the thing
Wherein thy counsel and consent is wanting.
—Act II, scene vi, lines 100–2

The gratitude was deserved. It had been Warwick's energy and dash that had kept the Yorkist cause alive during its dark hours; it had been his riches and power that had been a prime factor in raising armies for York. And now that he was Earl of Salisbury (by his father's death) as well as of Warwick, he was richer and more powerful than ever.

He was thirty-three years old at the time of Edward's coronation, and provided he could be the most influential man in England after the King (whose first cousin he was), he was content to bear all the heavy burdens of the kingdom on his shoulder.

Even after the coronation, there were corners of England that required quieting, particularly in the north, and this task Warwick took upon himself. Indeed, he had family reasons for it. The Nevilles and the Percys were the great rival families of the north and that old feud had simply taken on a new name when the Nevilles became Yorkists and the Percys Lancastrians.

In the north, besides, there was still Somerset (the son of Richard of York's great enemy), who had escaped northward from Towton and was still striving to raise forces. Warwick sent his brother, John of Montagu (see page II–624) against Somerset. (Montagu had been captured at the second Battle of St. Albans and had been imprisoned, but he was freed once more after the Battle of Towton.)

On May 15, 1464, Montagu surprised Somerset at Hexham in the far north, only thirty miles from the Scottish border. There the Lancastrians were defeated once again, and Somerset was killed. Somerset had no legitimate sons and left behind two younger brothers as the last members of the Beaufort family, sprung from John of Gaunt by his third wife—at least the last male members descended through an all-male line.

All organized Lancastrian resistance came temporarily to an end thereafter, and the Nevilles crowned their victory when Montagu was given the title of Duke of Northumberland immediately after the victory at Hexham; a title which had been borne by four Percys (the first of whom had been Hotspur's father). What's more, another Neville, Warwick's brother, George, was made Archduke of York in 1465. The Nevilles thus reached the very peak of their power and were the uncrowned kings of the north.

As for Edward IV, he remained in London, enjoying himself tremendously. He liked to eat and he liked sex, and he had food and women in abundance. He was handsome and charming and it was so long since London had seen a King who was a man's man rather than a sniveling monk (as it must then have seemed to them) that Edward's self-indulgence but made him the more popular.

All seemed well for the new young King.

. . . the Lady Bona . . .

Only one Lancastrian didn't give up and wouldn't give up—Queen Margaret. Having reached Scotland after the disaster at Towton, she did her best to persuade the Scottish rulers to support her. Edward could offer Scotland larger bribes, however, and Margaret, despairing of help in the northern kingdom, took her son to France.

There she hoped to interest the French in helping her and even went so far as to offer them Calais in exchange. The French were by no means eager to start the Hundred Years' War over again and besides there was still a very dangerous conflict between France and Burgundy, for the latter duchy was stronger than ever, and France's hands were not free.

Nevertheless, Warwick quite realized that the French would be eager to help Margaret all they could. They might do so quietly and underhandedly to avoid direct implication, but even that much could be troublesome indeed for England. It was necessary, then, to neutralize the French somehow, and that might best be done by a marital alliance.

The two most recent French marital alliances had been disastrous for England. Catherine of France had married Henry V and had passed on her father's mental weakness to her son, Henry VI. Margaret of Anjou had married Henry VI and of that marriage the less said the better. Nevertheless, hope springs eternal . . .

Edward IV was young and handsome and surely somewhere in the French royal family a pleasant match could be made for him that would cement relations between England and France to the point of making Margaret's efforts useless.

In the play, Warwick says, in the immediate aftermath of the Battle of Towton, that they must go to London for Edward's coronation and:

> *From whence shall Warwick cut the sea to France,*
> *And ask the Lady Bona for thy queen.*
> —Act II, scene vi, lines 89–90

The Lady Bona is the third daughter of Amadeus VIII of Savoy and the younger sister of the French Queen. Warwick's mission came in mid-1464 after the Battle of Hexham, not immediately after Towton, as would appear in the play. Shakespeare here compresses four years of time.

. . . Lewis a prince soon won . . .

When Margaret went to France, she took her idolized son with her, but she was not concerned for Henry, whose presence would only have been an embarrassment. He was left behind in the north of England, where for some years he lurked as a fugitive, aided in secret by such Lancastrians as dared the wrath of Warwick and his adherents. Sometime in mid-1465 he was recognized by Yorkists, or possibly betrayed to them. In July 1465 he was arrested, taken to London, and placed in the Tower.

Shakespeare uses his recognition and arrest (by a pair of forest keepers —game wardens, we might say) as a means of advancing the plot somewhat, for he has Henry soliloquize on events as he wanders through the northern forests. Talking of Margaret's mission to France and of Warwick's competing embassy, he says:

> If this news be true,
> Poor queen and son, your labor is but lost;
> For Warwick is a subtle orator,
> And Lewis a prince soon won with moving words.
> —Act III, scene i, lines 31–34

"Lewis" is Louis XI, who now ruled France. His father was Charles VII (see page II–525), who reigned throughout the last thirty years of the Hundred Years' War and who lived to see the English driven out. He died in 1461, soon after the Battle of Towton.

His son, Louis XI, was crowned at Rheims on August 15, 1461, just six weeks after the coronation of Edward IV. In 1464, when Warwick was going to France, Louis had been King for four years.

Perhaps he had yet to make his mark, but Henry VI's estimate that Louis was a "prince soon won with moving words" was almost ludicrously wrong. Louis XI was one of the shrewdest men ever to sit on a throne. (He is sometimes called "the Spider King" because he was visualized as sitting in the middle of a web and controlling affairs in every direction by gentle twitches of this strand or that.) Surely neither Margaret nor Warwick nor anyone else would ever be able to win him over to anything he didn't want to do.

. . . Sir Richard Grey . . .

Meanwhile, back in London, King Edward finds he must make decisions concerning the upsetting aftermath of the civil broils. He discusses one suppliant with his younger brother Richard, saying:

> Brother of Gloucester, at Saint Albans field
> This lady's husband, Sir Richard Grey, was slain,
> His land then seized on by the conqueror.
> Her suit is now to repossess those lands;
> —Act III, scene ii, lines 1–4

The lady involved is a "commoner" in the sense that she is not of royal blood and is not related to any of the kingly lines of Europe. Nevertheless, she is of the aristocracy. Her husband was not quite "Sir Richard Grey," as this passage has it, but Sir John Grey, 7th Baron Ferrers of Groby. He had been a Lancastrian and had died at the age of twenty-nine at the second Battle of St. Albans in 1461. Having been declared guilty of treason, his property was confiscated.

Now, three years later, his widow has come begging Edward for the return of that property to the young children left behind by her husband. The widow was Elizabeth Grey, born Elizabeth Woodville, and she was the daughter of Sir Richard Woodville.

Sir Richard Woodville had been with Richard of York when the latter was head of the English forces in France, and in 1448 had earned the title of Baron Rivers for his services there. In 1450 he helped put down Cade's rebellion. What's more, about 1436 he had married Jacquetta of Luxembourg, who was the widow of the Duke of Bedford (see page II–415), who had died the year before.

Sir Richard was a Lancastrian when England split into civil war, fighting on the side of King Henry all the way through the Battle of Towton. After that battle, however, he came over to the Yorkist side, swearing fealty to Edward IV.

When Edward IV was visiting Jacquetta of Luxembourg at her manor, the lady's daughter, Elizabeth, seized the opportunity to make her request for the confiscated property.

The amorous Edward was much taken by the beautiful Elizabeth and undoubtedly would have liked to make love to her in return for granting her request. The details we don't know, though Shakespeare has a richly comic scene in which Edward tries to get Elizabeth to agree to go to bed with him while Elizabeth slips and slides in an attempt to avoid doing so without losing her suit, and brothers George and Richard make dryly ribald comments on the sidelines.

In the end, somehow, Elizabeth actually persuaded Edward to marry her, and on May 1, 1464, that marriage took place.

The marriage, into which Edward was led by infatuation, was extremely impolitic. The fact that Elizabeth was of non-royal blood was sure to displease the rest of the aristocracy, who would resent having one of themselves suddenly raised to a position higher than themselves. Furthermore, she was five years older than Edward (twenty-seven years to his twenty-two) and was a widow with three children, and that too would be found offensive by the whisperers and gossipers of the court.

Edward, who must have been terribly embarrassed, and a little uneasy, as to the reaction on the part of his nobles, kept the marriage secret for six months, even to the incredible point of not telling Warwick about it when the latter went to France to arrange for a royal bride for his royal master. (What Edward could possibly have been thinking of, we can't be sure. Perhaps he felt that Warwick's diplomacy might fall through anyway, or perhaps he thought that by delay he might have time to think of some way out of the mess.)

. . . the golden time I look for

Edward has to break off his interview with Lady Grey to attend to King Henry, who has been brought to London as a prisoner. Left alone onstage, Richard of Gloucester, the King's youngest brother, now expresses his own feelings.

The thought of Edward's marriage to anyone at all is displeasing to him because it will mean the possibility of children who will be nearer to the throne than himself. Concerning Edward, he says spitefully:

> *Would he were wasted, marrow, bones and all,*
> *That from his loins no hopeful branch may spring,*
> *To cross me from the golden time I look for!*
> —Act III, scene ii, lines 125–27

Suddenly, Shakespeare presents Richard as ambitious for the crown. This is the further working of the anti-Yorkist bias, which from this point on is most sharply concentrated on Richard, for reasons which will be clear enough as this play and the next proceed.

It is precisely because Richard's actions do not match the guilt of his later reputation that Shakespeare must have him mouth villainous speeches every once in a while. This is similar to the fashion in which Richard of York in the earlier plays was constantly being made to speak treason even though he can never be shown committing any.

Actually, at the time of Edward's marriage to Elizabeth Grey, Richard was still only twelve years old and certainly lacked the kind of ambition attributed to him here. In fact, from all that is known of Richard, he was completely and utterly faithful to his brother through all of Edward's reign.

Nevertheless, Shakespeare has Richard count up the individuals who stand between him and the crown, even if Edward did not marry or if he died without children. He says:

> *. . . between my soul's desire and me—*
> *The lustful Edward's title buried—*
> *Is Clarence, Henry, and his son young Edward,*
> *And all the unlooked-for issue of their bodies,*
> —Act III, scene ii, lines 128–31

In 1464 Henry VI still lived, as did his son Edward, Prince of Wales. In addition, of the Beaufort family, which was also descended from John of Gaunt, there were still two younger sons of Somerset. In other words, four males yet existed who were descended from John of Gaunt by way of males only.

And even if Gaunt's progeny are disregarded as having a right inferior to that of the progeny of Lionel of Clarence, and even if King Edward were to die without an heir, there still remained George of Clarence, a brother younger than Edward, but older than Richard.

. . . Love forswore me . . .

Richard feels that only the crown can content him because he cannot find consolation in love. He says:

> Why, Love forswore me in my mother's womb:
> And, for [so that] I should not deal in her soft laws,
> She did corrupt frail Nature with some bribe,
> To shrink mine arm up like a withered shrub;
> To make an envious mountain on my back,
> Where sits deformity to mock my body;
> To shape my legs of an unequal size;
> To disproportion me in every part,
> Like to a chaos, or an unlicked bear-whelp
> That carries no impression like the dam.
>
> —Act III, scene ii, lines 153–62

Here is the full list of Richard's deformities, all fictitious. Can a man with a hunchback, a withered arm, and a clubfoot fight like a demon in battle and be superlatively skillful in strenuous hand-to-hand battle, as we know from history and as is true even in Shakespeare's plays?

Richard's comparison of himself to an "unlicked bear-whelp" is the result of a nature legend that grew up out of the fact that the mother bear gives birth in the winter while she is hibernating. The cubs are unusually small at birth but have some months of security and repose in which to suckle and grow.

Careless observations of the newborn cubs gave rise to surprise at their unusual smallness compared to their mother, and even compared to the cubs themselves in the later stage in which they were usually first seen at the end of the hibernating season. The legend arose that they were born shapeless and were then licked into bear form by their mothers.

Richard, then, is here bitterly commenting that he himself was never licked into shape.

. . . the murderous Machiavel . . .

Richard therefore determines to gain the crown by any possible means
and lists the talents he knows he has for the purpose, saying:

> *I'll play the orator as well as Nestor,*
> *Deceive more slily than Ulysses could,*
> *And, like a Sinon, take another Troy.*
> *I can add colors to the chameleon,*
> *Change shapes with Proteus for advantages,*
> *And set the murderous Machiavel to school.*
> *Can I do this, and cannot get a crown?*
> *Tut, were it farther off, I'll pluck it down.*
> > —Act III, scene ii, lines 188–95

Nestor (see page I–91), Ulysses (see page I–92), and Sinon (see page
I–210) are all well-known characters in the tale of Troy, much used in literature as symbols of wisdom, shrewdness, and treason respectively.

Proteus was a sea god in Greek myths, usually pictured as an old man
who herded the sea creatures. He had the ability to foretell the future and
also the ability to change shapes at will. If anyone wanted information, he
had to sneak up on Proteus, seize him, and then hold him through all the
changes in shape he undertook—whether into a lion, a monstrous snake,
even a dancing fire. If the man in whose grasp he was held maintained his
grip steadily and boldly, Proteus would turn back into his natural shape
and give the desired information.

Proteus became the very symbol of inconstancy, therefore, and "protean"
means "changeable."

As for Machiavelli (see page II–280), he was to Elizabethans (and to
some moderns) the very epitome of Italian intrigue and deceit, so that for
Richard to claim to be able to be so much more advanced than he as to be
able to teach him was going far indeed. As a matter of fact, it goes further
than it seems, for Machiavelli was not born until five years after Edward's
marriage—the supposed occasion for Richard's present speech.

. . . the greatest part of Spain

The scene now shifts to France, where Margaret and Warwick are dis-
puting before the throne of Louis XI, Margaret begging for help to her
cause, and Warwick offering a marital alliance. The old, old arguments
over the succession are aired. Warwick boldly declares Henry VI a usurper,

implying that the entire Lancastrian line has reigned illegally, having unrightfully taken the throne from the Mortimer family.

This is disputed by an English nobleman who is present and says:

> Then Warwick disannuls great John of Gaunt,
> Which did subdue the greatest part of Spain;
> —Act III, scene iii, lines 81–82

This is a reference to Gaunt's Spanish expedition, which certainly did not "subdue the greatest part of Spain," or indeed, any part of it. It was a complete failure (see page II–263) but it suits Elizabethans, who had, only four years before, beaten off the vast Spanish Armada, to put it this way.

The speaker is John de Vere, 13th Earl of Oxford, a convinced Lancastrian and one of the few fated to survive the Wars of the Roses.

. . . your king married the Lady Grey

In the end Warwick persuades Louis XI to accept the marital alliance. This makes sense, for Louis would surely have reasoned that it was better to make friends with an apparently securely seated monarch than to lose time and effort (and court danger, too, perhaps) by siding with one the nation had rejected.

But then come letters from England, and when King Louis reads those addressed to him, he is furious, and we can scarcely blame him. He cries out:

> What! has your king married the Lady Grey?
> And now, to soothe your forgery and his,
> Sends me a paper to persuade me patience?
> Is this th'alliance that he seeks with France?
> Dare he presume to scorn us in this manner?
> —Act III, scene iii, lines 174–78

What happened was that after Edward had been married for some months, he found it no longer possible to keep the secret. It must have been obvious there was some sort of intimate relationship between the King and Lady Grey, and Lady Grey must have bitterly resented being taken to be a mistress where she was really a Queen. What's more, Edward may have begun to fear that if he kept the marriage secret any longer, he might raise a question as to the legitimacy of any sons he might have and lay the groundwork for future civil wars.

So, on September 29, 1464, a great council was held and the former Lady Grey was formally introduced as Edward's wife and, therefore, Queen of England.

The marital negotiations in France were indeed broken off and it was indeed a dreadful affront to King Louis and an even greater humiliation for Warwick.

It was an insult to Bona of Savoy as well, though she came out of it well. She went on to marry Gian Galeazzo, Duke of Milan. She survived him and then ruled Milan in the name of her young son. On the whole, her life was more successful than that of Edward's wife was fated to be.

. . . return to Henry

Warwick, thus humiliated, is maddened into seeking revenge by any means. He remembers the great deeds he has done for the house of York. He remembers the death of his father in battle for York and he even remembers disgraces he has stoically endured for his King's sake. He says:

> *Did I let pass th'abuse done to my niece?*
> —Act III, scene iii, line 188

This is a reference to a tale that King Edward, an inveterate seducer, once attempted to proposition Warwick's niece while a visitor in Warwick's home. What would have been an incredibly gross act from anyone else becomes permissible in a King, and Warwick let the matter slide.

Now, however, Edward has gone too far, and Warwick says:

> *. . . to repair my honor lost for him* [King Edward]
> *I here renounce him and return to Henry.*
> —Act III, scene iii, lines 193–94

Here again Shakespeare condenses time—six full years of it.

Warwick, humiliated by Edward's marriage, nevertheless (in actual history) had to swallow his pride. Rebellions against a King (even by Warwick) could not be brought into existence by a snap of the fingers. Warwick would have to gain confederates, gather an army, win some measure of public opinion. In short, he needed time.

Therefore, Warwick sailed back to England, to all outward appearances acquiescing in the decision of his King. In reality, he began to spin his web and to plot Edward's downfall.

He had material to work with, for Edward's marriage had hurt him in many ways. The new Queen had, after all, been daughter and wife to Lancastrians, and that offended many hitherto loyal Yorkists. Why, after all, should a Lancastrian woman be so rewarded, when worthy Yorkists were being disregarded?

It wasn't as though it were the Queen alone. She had a large family and all of them now flocked to court to be rewarded with lands, titles, and office.

Elizabeth had five brothers and seven sisters, for all of whom good marriages were now arranged and to whom fat estates fell in consequence. Her father, Sir Richard Woodville, became treasurer and then lord high constable.

All these honors had to come from somewhere, and since in the first few years of Edward's reign the Nevilles had virtually monopolized power, they began losing out now. For instance, Warwick wanted a nephew of his to marry the heiress of the Duke of Exeter, but Queen Elizabeth used her influence to secure her for her own oldest son, Thomas Grey, by her former marriage.

In proportion as the Neville family lost power in court to the swarming Woodvilles and Greys, Warwick grew more furious and more intent on revenge and more anxious to whisper in the ears of those who shared his own dislike for the new situation.

The final straw came in foreign policy. Warwick still favored some sort of alliance with France, but Edward had another idea.

France was still at odds with Burgundy. In 1467 Philip the Good (see page II–514) had died and his son, Charles the Bold, became Duke of Burgundy. Under Charles, Burgundy reached the peak of its power, and Charles's ambition was to defeat France and gain a royal title for himself. Through his entire ten-year reign, he carried on a duel with Louis XI. It was Charles's warlike ability versus Louis' patient shrewdness and it was probably this duel that kept Louis from interfering in English affairs more decisively.

As it was, England had to choose which side it was to favor, France or Burgundy—it could scarcely be friends with both, and its best bet would be to side with the eventual winner, if one could but know which the winner would be.

Warwick wanted France, but Edward, again behind his onetime supporter's back, chose Burgundy. The alliance with Burgundy was concluded in 1467, and in 1468 Edward's sister, Margaret, married Charles the Bold.

That was the very end for Warwick. If there had ever been a chance for some kind of reconciliation with Edward, that killed it.

. . . as for Clarence . . .

Warwick, in his speech to King Louis immediately after hearing of Edward's marriage (following Shakespeare's version of history), speaks of allies, saying:

> And as for Clarence, as my letters tell me,
> He's very likely now to fall from him,
> For matching more for wanton lust than honor.
>
> —Act III, scene iii, lines 208–10

Odd! After what Shakespeare has put into the mouth of Richard of Gloucester, it might seem inevitable that it would be Richard who would seize the chance to betray his brother, hoping that somehow he would be able to snatch at the crown. He would certainly do this if he were the monster he was sedulously portrayed as being in the next century. Yet actually, Richard remained staunchly faithful to his brother, despite the marriage, and never rose to the lures of Warwick.

It was George of Clarence, rather, who was the weak one. It was he who seemed to have ambition, who resented the overwhelming influence of the Queen's relatives at court. It was he, perhaps, who aspired to the crown and it was he whom Warwick was able to wean away.

Warwick had no sons, but he did have two attractive daughters, who, in addition to the undeniable beauty of their persons, were England's greatest heiresses. Warwick offered the older, Isabella, to Clarence after the final outrage of the Burgundian marriage. King Edward, not so stupid as to fail to see the danger in this marital union, forbade the marriage. Clarence stubbornly found occasion to go to Calais, and there, in July 1469, he married Isabella Warwick. After that, Warwick was sure he could count on the boy. (He was twenty years old at the time.)

The signal for open revolt was now raised. King Louis of France, once the Burgundian marriage had been put through, could only decide that Edward was going to support Charles the Bold against him, and he could have no other response than to do what he could to pull Edward down.

Warwick's influence and King Louis' discreetly offered funds raised armies in the north of England, which was crying out against the King's relatives and which had been Lancastrian not too long before. Warwick's older brother, John Neville, the new-made Duke of Northumberland, hesitated. He did not like to oppose his brother. Hastily (perhaps too hastily) Edward took back the title of Northumberland and returned it to the Percy family. If John Neville had hesitated before, he hesitated no longer. He joined the revolt.

King Edward sent an army northward to destroy the rebels, and on July 26, 1469, battle was joined at Edgecote, some twenty miles southwest of Northampton, site of the Yorkist victory ten years before.

This battle was not a Yorkist victory. The King's army was defeated, and Richard Woodville, the Queen's father, together with John Woodville, one of her brothers, were taken and executed.

Now Warwick, with his new son-in-law, Clarence, could return from Calais to England in clear triumph. Warwick had shown his power and it seemed quite evident that Edward could not remain King without him. He was the "king maker" in truth, and Edward would have to admit it.

However, Edward was actually a capable fighter and politician on his own (when he could bring himself to make the effort), and there were many who were on his side and would be glad to see the powerful Warwick taken down a notch. There was much and tedious pulling to and fro as Edward and Warwick lunged and feinted, and in April 1470 War-wick, Clarence, and their families sailed back to Calais to draw new breath.

Here too Edward was ahead of them. The Warwick party was denied admittance and the mouths of cannon aimed in their direction looked deadly. Warwick now had no choice but to make for France itself and become openly Lancastrian. Shrewd Louis XI arranged a reconciliation between Margaret of Anjou and the man who had been her greatest enemy after Richard of York himself. This took place in June 1470, so that Shakespeare, in showing Warwick to have turned Lancastrian immediately after Edward's marriage, skips (as aforesaid) six busy years.

. . . mine eldest daughter . . .

The reconciliation between Warwick and Margaret can scarcely rest on words alone, not after all that lay between them in the past. Something firmer was required, and, as it happened, Warwick, who had used one daughter for George of Clarence, had another for Margaret. He says to the tight-lipped Queen:

> This shall assure my constant loyalty,
> That if our Queen and this young Prince agree,
> I'll join mine eldest daughter and my joy
> To him forthwith in holy wedlock bands.
>
>   —Act III, scene iii, lines 240–43

Shakespeare gets the daughters wrong. The eldest daughter was Isa-bella, who had been Duchess of Clarence for a year now. It was his younger daughter, Anne, whom Warwick now arranged to marry to Ed-ward, son of Henry VI, and Prince of Wales. Prince Edward was seven-teen years old at the time.

England is safe . . .

The fourth act opens with King Edward introducing his new wife to a sullen court. His brothers, George of Clarence and Richard of Gloucester, openly express their displeasure, and Montagu (Warwick's brother) speaks of the benefits of a French alliance, now made impossible.

Edward blusters that he need not fear either France or Warwick and one courtier backs him up by saying:

> Why, knows not Montague that of itself
> England is safe, if true within itself?
>
>   —Act IV, scene i, lines 40–41

This standard piece of English patriotism is spoken by William Hastings. He was forty years old at this point; that is, a dozen years older than King Edward. He was the King's boon companion. It often happens that a young king, addicted to pleasure, finds an older, more experienced man useful to him in the making of arrangements for fun and games. Hastings served the King in this fashion and was a great favorite of his as a result.

. . . the heir of the Lord Hungerford

Naturally, Hastings is rewarded for his services as master of the revels and part-time pimp, and George of Clarence sardonically observes in response to the other's backing of the King:

> *For this one speech Lord Hastings well deserves*
> *To have the heir of the Lord Hungerford.*
> —Act IV, scene i, lines 47–48

Lord Hungerford had been briefly referred to in *Henry VI, Part One* as having been captured at the Battle of Patay (see page II–529). He had died in 1449, but by now part or all of his rich estate had been concentrated in the hands of a girl who was given to Hastings in marriage. By this marriage he could be granted the title "Baron," and could be addressed as Lord Hastings.

Envious George apparently feels that such estates should somehow be kept in the family.

. . . the heir and daughter of Lord Scales

Richard of Gloucester also objects to Edward's free and easy distribution of estates. He says to King Edward:

> *. . . methinks your Grace hath not done well*
> *To give the heir and daughter of Lord Scales*
> *Unto the brother of your loving bride.*
> —Act IV, scene i, lines 51–53

Lord Scales is also mentioned in *Henry VI, Part One* as having been taken at Patay (see page II–529). He appears briefly in *Henry VI, Part Two* as well, as commander of the Tower of London during Cade's rebellion (see page II–606). He died in 1460, leaving a daughter as his heir, and in 1461 this daughter married Anthony Woodville, Queen Elizabeth's brother, who became Lord Scales as a result.

It is unfair, however, to blame this marriage on Edward's partiality for his Queen. It took place three years *before* Edward's marriage to Elizabeth Woodville.

. . . Clarence will have the younger

Now comes the news that Warwick has defected and made an alliance with Margaret, and that the son of the latter is to marry the daughter of the former. George of Clarence, hearing this, muses concerning that marriage. Which daughter is involved, he wonders, and decides:

> Belike the elder; Clarence will have the younger.
> Now, brother king, farewell . . .
> > —Act IV, scene i, lines 118–19

There are two reversals here. George of Clarence married Warwick's daughter *before* the latter's reconciliation with Margaret. And it was the *elder* daughter that George married, not the younger.

Clarence and Somerset . . .

Shakespeare's compression of time forces quick action now. Actually, Clarence had defected long before Warwick's reconciliation with Margaret. So had Montagu. Neither would have been at King Edward's court to hear the news of that reconciliation. Now that the news has come, Shakespeare is forced to have Clarence's delayed defection take place at once. Edward just a few lines after Clarence's last speech exclaims:

> Clarence and Somerset both gone to Warwick!
> > —Act IV, scene i, line 127

Who was Somerset? Actually there was no Somerset, officially, at this time. There had been Henry Beaufort, 3rd Duke of Somerset, who had died at the Battle of Hexham in 1464. With his death, the victorious Yorkists had abolished the right of the Beaufort family to the title.

Henry Beaufort had no children, but he had two younger brothers, and one of them, Edmund, called himself 4th Duke of Somerset. This title was only recognized by the Lancastrians and he couldn't possibly have been at King Edward's court.

Pembroke and Stafford . . .

Edward at once begins his preparations. He says:

Pembroke and Stafford, you in our behalf
Go levy men, and make prepare for war.
—Act IV, scene i, lines 130–31

Pembroke was William Herbert, who had been granted the title of Earl of Pembroke by Edward in 1462.

Apparently, Shakespeare now moves back in time to a point before the Battle of Edgecote and therefore at least a year before the reconciliation of Warwick and Margaret. We can tell this because William of Pembroke died at Edgecote and by the time of the reconciliation had been dead a year.

The Stafford referred to in this passage is Sir Humphrey Stafford, a cousin of the Staffords who had been killed in the course of Cade's rebellion (see page II–604). Sir Humphrey, like Pembroke, died at Edgecote.

. . . the Thracian fatal steeds

Warwick, having made the final plunge, acted with the greatest energy. His reconciliation with Margaret had taken place in June 1470, and on September 13 he landed on the shores of southern England. King Edward was in the north attending to the disturbances which had been deliberately stirred up there by Warwick's partisans in order to cover the southern landings.

Warwick marched inland, ready for a confrontation with King Edward, who, in considerable confusion at the surprise onslaught, was marching hastily southward in disarray.

As the armies face each other somewhere in Warwickshire (according to Shakespeare), Warwick exults that Edward is ill guarded and may be taken unawares. In fact, he may even be kidnapped out of his army:

. . . as Ulysses and stout Diomede
With sleight and manhood stole to Rhesus' tents,
And brought from thence the Thracian fatal steeds,
—Act IV, scene ii, lines 19–21

This refers to an incident in the tenth book of the *Iliad*. Troy had just been reinforced by Rhesus, King of Thrace, who brought with him an excellent detachment of horsemen. Ulysses and Diomedes (see pages I–92 and I–79), sent as spies into the Trojan lines that night, came upon Rhesus' party, sleeping unguarded in their overconfidence (the Greeks had had the worse of the battle the day before). The two Greeks killed Rhesus and drove off his horses.

In later times, the story was improved by the statement that an oracle had foretold that Troy would never fall if Rhesus' horses could but once graze on the Trojan plains. That is why they are referred to as "fatal steeds," since their actions would signify the judgment of the Fates.

Warwick's plan is carried through. Edward IV is captured in his tent, while Richard of Gloucester and Lord Hastings manage to get away. Warwick does not intend to kill Edward but takes off his crown in order that he might restore it to Henry. Warwick is "king maker" indeed.

The dramatic scene does not, however, accord with history. The confrontation did not take place in Warwickshire but in Lincolnshire, close to the east coast. Edward was not captured but could see that resistance was hopeless, for Warwick was gathering troops steadily while Edward's army was falling apart through desertion. Edward decided flight was the only reasonable alternative. He made his way to the coast and took ship for Holland in October 1470.

(The year before, however, *before* Warwick's reconciliation with Margaret, King Edward had very briefly been captured by the Archbishop of York, George Neville, who was Warwick's brother. This imprisonment, from July to October 1469, which took place before King Edward was fully aware that Warwick was in open rebellion—which is why he was careless enough to be captured in the first place—Shakespeare shifts a year later for dramatic purposes.)

. . . brother Rivers . . .

Back in the London palace, Edward's Queen hears the news and says:

> *Why, brother Rivers, are you yet to learn*
> *What late misfortune is befall'n King Edward?*
> —Act IV, scene iv, lines 2–3

She is speaking to her brother Anthony Woodville, Lord Scales (see page II-661). When their father had died in the north fighting against the Neville-inspired disturbances, Scales had succeeded to the paternal title as well, and became 2nd Earl of Rivers.

Although he was unpopular among the nobility, as all the Woodvilles were, since they were jealously supposed to owe their sudden pre-eminence to their relationship to the King, Scales seems to have been a rather capable person—loyal to Edward and a devotee of the arts.

. . . Edward's offspring . . .

Elizabeth is about thirty-three years old at this time and is still quite young enough to bear children. In fact, she is pregnant at the moment and says she is avoiding emotional upset as much as possible for the sake of the health of the unborn child:

> *And I the rather wean me from despair*
> *For love of Edward's offspring in my womb.*
> > —Act IV, scene iv, lines 17–18

Since Warwick is triumphant, Elizabeth decides to fly, and it was while she was in sanctuary in Westminster Abbey that she gave birth to Edward's child on November 2, 1470.

. . . Sir William Stanley

In 1469, when Edward was really held in captivity by the Archbishop of York, Warwick was still working to a certain extent underground and trying to be in something less than open rebellion. He was not ready to go all the way and Edward was still popular enough, particularly in London, to make the imprisonment politically dangerous. It was after Edward was freed, and reasonably certain that it was Warwick's hand that had been behind the imprisonment, that Warwick and Clarence had been forced to go first to Calais and then to France.

Once they came back as open Lancastrians and with French support behind them, they had nothing to lose. Had Edward truly been captured in 1470, they would surely have placed him in the Tower and held him securely.

Shakespeare places the activity in 1470 but is forced to keep the conditions of 1469. He has the imprisonment in a Yorkshire castle and makes it a light and negligent one. It is possible to spirit the captive King out of the castle and with that purpose in mind a few die-hard Yorkists under the leadership of Richard of Gloucester arrive.

Richard, who is conducting the enterprise, and who has not yet revealed its details, says to his companions:

> *Now my Lord Hastings and Sir William Stanley,*
> *Leave off to wonder why I drew you hither,*
> > —Act IV, scene v, lines 1–2

William Stanley was of a wealthy family and he and his brother Thomas Stanley were important Yorkist leaders. Their role in the next reign was to be even more important.

Richard's plan succeeds. Edward IV is snatched out of imprisonment and is free again.

. . . Warwick, after God . . .

In London, meanwhile, Henry VI, who had spent five years in the Tower of London, was also set free. In October 1470 he was once again King, and says:

> *But, Warwick, after God, thou set'st me free,*
> —Act IV, scene vi, line 16

Thus is Warwick revenged on Edward IV.

Now the other meaning of the séance prophecy concerning the Duke and the King (see page II–588) comes true. The Duke (or the Duke's son —who is Edward IV) is deposed *by* Henry VI. The deposer was promised a violent death, and it will come for Henry VI, the King, as it had already come for Richard of York, the Duke.

. . . Earl of Richmond

All is sweetness and light for the moment. Warwick and Clarence vie to see who can be most generous in giving the other credit. Henry asks that his wife and son be sent for from France and then turns to Somerset, who is present, and inquires as to the young boy who accompanies him.

Somerset answers:

> *My liege, it is young Henry, Earl of Richmond.*
> —Act IV, scene vi, line 67

The young boy (thirteen years old at this time) is Henry Tudor, and his line of descent was a very interesting one.

The Tudor family was a Welsh family of consequence which could trace itself back to an official of the last independent Prince of Wales. The first of the family to be of importance to English history was Owen Tudor. He was a handsome young man who came to the English court soon after the death of Henry V and caught the eye of Katherine of France (see page II–476), Henry's widow.

Katherine was still only in her twenties and she can scarcely be blamed for falling in love. She secretly married Owen about 1427. The royal family was naturally displeased at the apparent liaison between them (having been married to the great conqueror, could Katherine stoop to a Welsh squire?) and Owen lived on the continuing edge of possible execution. Nevertheless, the two were happy together and though they had to live their marriage clandestinely, Katherine managed to have three sons and a daughter by her second husband.

Owen Tudor, as stepfather of Henry VI, was a good Lancastrian even though he had been placed under arrest a couple of times for his relationship with the King's mother. His wife, Katherine, had died in 1437 at the age of thirty-six, and he himself was taken prisoner at the Battle of Mortimer's Cross (see page II–643) in 1461 and beheaded afterward.

Two of Owen Tudor's sons by Katherine were of importance to English history. The oldest son was Edmund Tudor and the second was Jasper Tudor. These were half brothers to Henry VI, who treated them well, declared them of legitimate birth, knighted both in 1449, and gave them titles in 1453. Edmund became Earl of Richmond and Jasper became Earl of Pembroke.

Jasper was a doughty fighter on the Lancastrian side, having fought at the first Battle of St. Albans (see page II–618) when he was only twenty-four. He managed to get away from Mortimer's Cross, where his father had been captured and then executed, and left the country. He returned with Warwick, when Henry VI was reinstated on the throne.

As for Edmund, Jasper's older brother, he died young, in 1456. In his short life span of twenty-six years he did not have time for many feats of arms. He did have time for one important act, though. He married Margaret Beaufort, the daughter of John Beaufort, who was the "Somerset" of the scene of the roses in the Temple Garden (see page II–548) in *Henry VI, Part One*. What's more, he managed to get her pregnant before he died.

Three months after that death, on January 28, 1457, Margaret bore him a son.

This was Henry Tudor, who, on his mother's side, was thus the great-great-grandson of John of Gaunt. On his father's side, he was half nephew of Henry VI.

Throughout his boyhood, Henry Tudor (who succeeded to his father's title of Earl of Richmond) remained under the protection and care of his uncle, Jasper Tudor.

. . . England's hope . . .

King Henry calls young Henry of Richmond to him and says:

> *Come hither, England's hope. If secret powers*
> *Suggest but truth to my divining thoughts,*
> *This pretty lad will prove our country's bliss.*
>
> —Act IV, scene vi, lines 68–70

This is a dramatic moment, for the aging and feeble King seems suddenly to foresee the future. But then, even if this is not simply a legend invented after the fact, this piece of prophecy is not as wonderful as it sounds.

King Henry's heir is his son, Prince Edward, and if anything happens to Edward, next in line are the various members of the Beaufort family, of whom Henry Tudor represents the oldest branch. In short, by Lancastrian accounting, Henry Tudor is second in line to the throne and King Henry might well take note of this and hope for the best.

. . . to Burgundy

At this moment bad news arrives from the Archbishop of York. A Post says to the inquiring Warwick:

> . . . Edward is escaped from your brother,
> And fled, as he hears since, to Burgundy.
>
> —Act IV, scene vi, lines 78–79

Edward's earlier marital diplomacy now stood him in good stead. He had married his sister, Margaret, to Charles the Bold of Burgundy, and so he made his way to the court of his brother-in-law.

Charles was by no means anxious to have this refugee on his hands, feeling it would but exacerbate his troubles with France. The only way to turn the matter to profitable account was to give Edward the necessary help to get back to England. Then, if Edward managed to regain the throne, France would lose its new ally Warwick, and Burgundy would (Charles hoped) gain a grateful King. With that in mind, Charles the Bold supplied Edward liberally with men, money, and ships.

Indeed, Somerset is pictured as foreseeing this, for he says to Oxford:

> My lord, I like not of this flight of Edward's
> For doubtless Burgundy will yield him help
>
> —Act IV, scene vi, lines 89–90

Nor is Somerset sanguine as to the result, and his first care is the preservation of young Henry of Richmond for the future. He says:

> . . . Lord Oxford, to prevent the worst,
> Forthwith we'll send him [Richmond] hence to Brittany,
>
> —Act IV, scene vi, lines 96–97

As a result, young Richmond survives and lives to reappear in English history at a crucial moment.

From Ravenspurgh haven . . .

The scene shifts to York, where Edward's army is in the field. Edward says:

> *Well have we passed and now repassed the seas*
> *And brought desired help from Burgundy.*
> *What then remains, we being thus arrived*
> *From Ravenspurgh haven before the gates of York,*
> *But that we enter . . .*
> —Act IV, scene vii, lines 5–9

On March 12, 1471, about five months after he left England so hastily, Edward was back with a new army, Burgundian-financed, and landed in Ravenspurgh, where, nearly three quarters of a century before, Boling-broke had landed (see page II–287) to begin his rebellion against Richard II and start a century-long cycle of civil war.

. . . march amain to London

Once in England, Edward IV proved at his best as a general. Warwick had moved north to intercept him but Edward managed to slip past his old supporter. Warwick was left behind in frustration at Coventry while Edward raced on to London.

Shakespeare reverses matters. He has Edward's march to London come first and only later does he take up the events at Coventry.

Thus, Warwick, still in London, and apparently not yet leading an army north to try to intercept Edward, is made to say that Edward

> *Hath passed in safety through the Narrow Seas*
> *And with his troops doth march amain to London;*
> *And many giddy people flock to him.*
> —Act IV, scene viii, lines 3–5

Warwick and the others have barely left the stage, leaving Henry behind, when Edward and his men burst in. Edward cries:

> *Seize on the shamefaced* [modest] *Henry, bear him hence;*
> *And once again proclaim us King of England.*
> —Act IV, scene viii, lines 52–53

On April 11, 1471, Edward, having taken London, rode to St. Paul's, where Henry VI was seeking sanctuary. The Bishop of London delivered him up, however, and he was placed once again in the Tower. His restoration to the kingship had lasted just half a year.

. . . towards Coventry . . .

Now Shakespeare backtracks in time and takes up the events at Coventry which had actually *preceded* Edward's seizure of London. Thus, Edward, in London, is made to say:

> . . . *lords, towards Coventry bend we our course,*
> *Where peremptory Warwick now remains:*
> —Act IV, scene viii, lines 58–59

This makes it all sound as though Edward has driven Warwick out of London and is now pursuing him. Not so. We are simply backtracking in time.

. . . than Jephthah . . .

At Coventry Warwick confronts the two Yorkist brothers, Edward and Richard. Warwick is waiting for reinforcements. Indeed, Oxford arrives, as does Warwick's brother, Montagu.

But then comes George of Clarence and suddenly he turns against his father-in-law and rejoins the Yorkist cause.

Clarence is well aware of the poor figure he thus makes, having betrayed each side in turn, and tries to bluster a defense. He speaks of the oath of fidelity he has not so long ago made to Warwick and says:

> *To keep that oath were more impiety*
> *Than Jephthah, when he sacrificed his daughter.*
> —Act V, scene i, lines 90–91

This refers to the well-known tale of Jephthah in the eleventh chapter of the Book of Judges. Jephthah swore an oath before a battle with the Ammonites that if he won he would sacrifice to God the first living thing that greeted him on his return to his home. That first living thing was his daughter, and he sacrificed her—thus choosing the greater sin of human sacrifice in preference to the lesser sin of breaking a thoughtless vow to God.

This dramatic second betrayal did indeed happen near Coventry, but, as was said above, it was before Edward's taking of London and not afterward.

George had been thinking second thoughts about his alliance with Warwick after the reconciliation with Margaret. He saw Henry reinstated on the throne and his son, Prince Edward, as heir. What then would happen to George of Clarence? With what would his ambition be satisfied? When Edward returned to England, George had, moreover, the clammy feeling that his brother might win after all. George would then be left on the losing side, with exile facing him, at best, and execution at worst. When Edward evaded Warwick and skimmed past Coventry, George hastened to rejoin him before it was too late—that is, before Edward got to London and felt (possibly) that he no longer needed George.

As it happened, George switched back in time, and Edward forgave him.

. . . towards Barnet . . .

Warwick, discomfited by Clarence's defection, says to King Edward:

> *Alas, I am not cooped* [prepared] *here for defense!*
> *I will away towards Barnet presently* [at once],
> *And bid thee battle, Edward, if thou dar'st.*
> —Act V, scene i, lines 109–11

This is weak. If Warwick feels he is not prepared for defense, why does not King Edward lay siege to the town? If Edward does not, why should Warwick want to fight specifically at Barnet?

Here is what really happened. After slipping past Coventry and picking up the repentant George of Clarence, Edward dashed to London, placed King Henry in the Tower, and had himself redeclared King. But Warwick, furious, followed him as rapidly as he could.

Warwick hoped to attack Edward while he was celebrating the capture of London—a celebration which might be all the more unrestrained since Easter was very near—and catch him unprepared.

Edward, however, for once sacrificed his pleasures and did not linger. London was taken on Thursday, April 11, 1471. The next day was Good Friday, and on the day after, April 13, the day before Easter, Edward was on the move north. By nightfall he had reached Barnet, some ten miles north of London's center, and there he found the outposts of Warwick's hurrying Lancastrian army and there the battle took place.

. . . Die thou . . .

The Battle of Barnet was a gruesome one. The two armies waited tensely through the night for the dawn, but when the dawn came, it arrived with a fog that turned everything from sightless black to sightless gray.

Daring to wait no longer, the armies blundered into each other, no part knowing what the other parts were doing. On the left, Oxford the Lancastrian defeated Hastings the Yorkist. The Yorkist line broke completely there but Edward in the center and Richard on the right did not know this and therefore fought on undismayed.

In fact, Richard, pushing forward on the right, defeated the Lancastrian left under Warwick himself, and when Oxford returned from his pursuit of Hastings, Warwick's Lancastrians, panicky and trigger-happy, fearing that the men looming up from the fog were Yorkist reinforcements, met them with a shower of arrows.

That confusion meant final victory for the Yorkists after three hours of chaos, and when Warwick fell, mortally wounded, the Lancastrians were done.

In the play it is Edward himself who drags the wounded Warwick onto the stage, saying:

> So lie thou there! Die thou, and die our fear!
>> —Act V, scene ii, line 1

As Warwick lies dying, he finds that his brother Montagu, who had been fighting on his side, is already dead, for Somerset, coming upon him, says:

> Ah, Warwick! Montague hath breathed his last,
>> —Act V, scene ii, line 40

Thus, on Easter Sunday, 1471, the two Neville brothers die.

. . . a puissant power

Yet Edward's victory had been by the merest hair. Had his brother George not made his second betrayal at a crucial time, part of the *élan* of the dash to London might have been absent, and Warwick might conceivably have caught the King. And had the morning not been foggy at Barnet, Warwick might conceivably have won there.

Indeed, had Warwick been more patient and had he not attempted by his rapid march to surprise and trap Edward, he might have been better off, for he might then have caught Edward between two fires. Even as Warwick lies dying, Somerset says:

> The Queen from France hath brought a puissant power.
> Even now we heard the news.
>> —Act V, scene ii, lines 31–32

For once, this is not an example of Shakespeare condensing history.

Queen Margaret had indeed landed at Weymouth in southern England on April 14, the very Easter Sunday on which the Battle of Barnet was fought.

She had gathered together a sizable army of exiles and foreigners and had set sail for England on March 24, only twelve days after Edward's own landing at Ravenspurgh. By all odds, she ought to have arrived in ample time to supply the forces needed for Edward's final defeat, but, unfortunately for the Lancastrian cause, a series of storms and contrary winds had kept driving her back.

Even so, had Warwick waited but two more days before forcing a battle and dodged Edward's army, the news of the Queen's arrival would have reached him and the game might then have been played altogether differently.

As it was, Margaret heard of Warwick's defeat and death the day after she landed, and for a while, even her savage and indomitable spirit broke.

Hath raised in Gallia . . .

Edward too has heard of the landing of the Queen's army and that somewhat spoils the jubilation in the aftermath of the victory at Barnet. Edward says, at the close of the battle:

> *I spy a black, suspicious, threat'ning cloud*
> *That will encounter with our glorious sun*
> *Ere he attain his easeful western bed.*
> *I mean, my lords, those powers that the Queen*
> *Hath raised in Gallia have arrived our coast,*
> *And, as we hear, march on to fight with us.*
> —Act V, scene iii, lines 4–9

Actually, the Queen's army had to take time to marshal itself and gather reinforcements in England. They made their way to Bath, fifty-five miles north of Weymouth. Edward could therefore remain ten days in London, repairing his army and getting some rest. It was not till April 24, 1471, that he marched westward toward the last Lancastrian army.

. . . toward Tewksbury

Still on the battlefield of Barnet, Edward says concerning the Queen's forces:

> *We are advertised* [advised] *by our loving friends*
> *That they do hold their course toward Tewksbury.*

We, having now the best at Barnet field,
Will thither straight . . .

—Act V, scene iii, lines 18–21

Thus, Shakespeare skips the ten-day respite in London and gets on with the action.

Queen Margaret's army, marching northward in search of territory where it might entrench itself and strengthen its powers in friendly surroundings, received the news that Edward was now marching hastily toward them.

Tewkesbury (the usual present-day spelling) was the strongest position within easy reach at that time and it was there that Margaret's army made ready to fight. Tewkesbury is in western England, forty miles southwest of Coventry.

. . . Oxford to Hames Castle . . .

Shakespeare gives no details of the battle. The armies collided and fought on May 4, 1471, three weeks after Barnet. Again, the impetuous attack of Edward and Richard carried the day and once again the Lancastrians broke. A number of the Lancastrian leaders were taken.

According to Shakespeare, one was Oxford. Thus, King Edward appears onstage, the battle over, the prisoners bound, and says:

Away with Oxford to Hames Castle straight.

—Act V, scene v, line 2

That is strange. Opposition leaders, if taken alive, were generally executed as traitors after the battle. Why was this not the case with Oxford?

Actually, it was because Oxford was not at Tewkesbury. He had fought well at Barnet but then went to France. It was not till 1473, two years after Tewkesbury, which had been fought without him, that he attempted a reinvasion of England and a revival of the ruined Lancastrian cause. He was besieged in Cornwall and, after four and a half months, was forced to surrender.

Passions had lessened by then and he was imprisoned rather than executed. The imprisonment was at a Hames Castle, near Calais, for it seemed best to keep him away from English soil proper.

. . . off with his guilty head

Concerning another prisoner, matters were more straightforward. Edward IV says:

For Somerset, off with his guilty head.

—Act V, scene v, line 3

This was carried through, and Edmund Beaufort, son of the Edmund of Somerset of *Henry VI, Part Two,* was executed on May 6, 1471. His younger brother, John, had died in the course of the battle, and this meant that the family of Beaufort was extinct. There was no one left who could trace his descent to John of Gaunt and Catherine Swynford through male ancestors only.

There remained only young Henry Tudor, Earl of Richmond, a greatgrandson of John of Gaunt on his mother's side.

Take that . . .

Edward, Prince of Wales, the son of Queen Margaret and (presumably) of Henry VI, is also taken at the Battle of Tewkesbury, where, according to later pro-Lancaster accounts, he bore himself bravely.

The earliest accounts we have of the battle state that the Prince of Wales was slain in its course by some unknown hand. The later pro-Lancastrian accounts, however, have him taken prisoner.

As prisoner, he boldly maintains his right to the throne in the face of the Yorkist brothers. Angered to a pitch of unreasoning fury by Prince Edward's words, King Edward says:

Take that, the likeness of this railer [Queen Margaret] *here.*
—Act V, scene v, line 38

With that the King stabs the young man, who is eighteen years old at this time.

George of Clarence and Richard of Gloucester also stab him, and the picture is of the brave young Lancastrian prince slaughtered by a triplet of assassins. It makes for a good Lancastrian atrocity story to balance the Yorkist atrocity story of the deaths of Rutland and York (see page II-639).

But atrocity stories are usually suspect (though not always, as those who have lived through certain recent periods in German and Russian history can testify) and it is much more likely that young Prince Edward died an ordinary battlefield death that day as the early reports state and as two thousand other men did. Or, if he had been captured, it is much more likely that he would have been executed as Somerset was and it is most unlikely that the royal brothers would themselves have wielded the knives.

O, kill me too

Queen Margaret, witnessing the death of her son, breaks at last. Now all her hope is gone. Her son had been the light of her life, the one object to which all her hopes had been pinned. She was forty-one years old now and could expect no second child, and there is nothing left for her. For the first time she pleads instead of threatens; pleads for the one gift left her enemies can give her, saying:

> *O, kill me too!*
>
> —Act V, scene v, line 41

Richard of Gloucester, relentless, is perfectly willing to do so, but Edward holds him back. He fears that by killing the Prince, they have already done too much.

Actually, this dramatic scene is fictional. Queen Margaret was not taken at Tewkesbury, and even if her son were assassinated, she would not have been able to witness it. She fled the battlefield and managed to make it to Coventry, where she hid in a convent. King Edward's army passed through Coventry after the battle, however, and on May 11 Margaret was taken.

. . . a bloody supper . . .

Suddenly, in the aftermath of Tewkesbury, King Edward notices that Richard is gone. He asks after him and Clarence says that Richard has departed

> *To London, all in post* [haste]*; and, as I guess,*
> *To make a bloody supper in the Tower.*
>
> —Act V, scene v, lines 84–85

Henry VI is at the Tower of London and the implication is that Richard intends to take care of him now that Prince Edward is dead and Queen Margaret imprisoned.

Indeed, in the next scene Richard of Gloucester is at the Tower, facing the ex-King, who shrinks frightened from him, and who goes through the list of Richard's deformities which the anti-Yorkists piled upon him in later years, adding a new one:

> *Teeth hadst thou in thy head when thou wast born,*
> *To signify thou cam'st to bite the world;*
>
> —Act V, scene vi, lines 53–54

At that, Richard, angered, stabs and kills the King.

The truth, as best we know it, is this. King Edward and his triumphant Yorkist army entered London once again on May 21, 1471, two and a half weeks after Tewkesbury. The next morning Henry was found dead in the Tower. He was only forty-nine years old at the time of his death and he had been King virtually all his life without ever having held the power of the kingship for a moment. He had been ruled and guided by others, harried and chivied from this point to that, weak-minded at best, out of his mind altogether at times, and after his long misery he probably welcomed death at last.

It is, of course, asking too much of coincidence to suppose Henry's death was natural. No one doubts that King Edward had ordered the ex-King quietly murdered and one can grasp the reasons for it. As long as Henry lived he would be the center for Lancastrian uprisings, and Edward had had enough of that now. Henry VI was therefore killed for the same reasons that Richard II was killed (see page II–312), and, before him, Edward II.

What is utterly unlikely is that Richard of Gloucester, though he carried the King's order to the Tower, performed the act with his own hand. There were any number of willing daggers to do the job and there is no evidence for Richard's personal guilt except for the word of the later atrocity tellers—and those atrocity tellers heaped every obloquy on Richard in an attempt to justify the dubiously legal position of his eventual successor. (History is written by the victors.)

Clarence, beware . . .

Shakespeare follows the official anti-Yorkist, anti-Richard line and improves on it with all the power of his genius. The next play in the series will have Richard as its central character, and in it, his crimes and enormities will reach horrid heights. This is forecast in several speeches throughout this present play and is made most specific now.

Even as Richard stands over Henry's lifeless body, he says:

> *Clarence, beware. Thou keep'st me from the light;*
> *But I will sort a pitchy day for thee;*
> *For I will buzz abroad such prophecies*
> *That Edward shall be fearful of his life,*
> *And then, to purge his fear, I'll be thy death.*
> *King Henry and the Prince his son are gone:*
> *Clarence, thy turn is next . . .*
> —Act V, scene vi, lines 84–90

With King Henry's death, all the male line of John of Gaunt is gone.

Henry Tudor is *not* a Plantagenet. He is descended from Henry II, and Edward III only on his mother's side.

King Edward and his brothers, however, while claiming their throne by right of descent from Lionel of Clarence on their grandmother's side, nevertheless descend from Edmund of York on their father's side and are still Plantagenets (see page II–255). In fact, the sons of old Richard of York are the only Plantagenets left.

Young Ned . . .

As it happens, though, there is a new heir to the English throne.

In the final scene of the play, Edward IV, again seated securely on the throne and reunited with his Queen, says to her:

> *Come hither, Bess, and let me kiss my boy.*
> *Young Ned, for thee, thine uncles and myself*
> *Have in our armors watched* [remained awake] *the winter's*
> *night,*
> *Went all afoot in summer's scalding heat,*
> *That thou mightst repossess the crown in peace:*
> —Act V, scene vii, lines 15–19

Edward's first son, born while he was himself in exile, was five months old at the time of the Battle of Tewkesbury. On June 26, 1471, when he was still not yet seven months old, he was made Prince of Wales, taking the title vacated by the earlier Prince Edward, now dead.

George of Clarence and Richard of Gloucester both swear allegiance to the baby heir to the throne, but the Elizabethan audience knows well that King Edward's speech to his infant boy contains grisly dramatic irony, for he will *not* "repossess the crown in peace." And if anyone lacks that knowledge, a couple of asides from Richard make it plain that he intends harm, as will be amply revealed in the next play.

. . . waft her hence . . .

There remains only one question. What should be done with Margaret, the ex-Queen, for whom ransom money has arrived?

King Edward, in a fit of leniency, says:

> *Away with her, and waft her hence to France!*
> —Act V, scene vii, line 41

Actually, the ransom did not follow so soon. Edward kept her imprisoned for five years under circumstances that were definitely not lavish but were not actually cruel. She was only then ransomed by Louis XI of France and in 1476 returned to the France she had left as a teen-age bride thirty years before. Her period as Queen of England had been a most unhappy one for herself and for England.

And thus, with all apparently serene, *Henry VI, Part Three* ends in triumph and celebration, so that King Edward's last line—and the last line of the play—is:

> *. . . here, I hope, begins our lasting joy.*
> —Act V, scene vii, line 46

But Richard remains, a black symbol of danger, and the next play, *Richard III,* will open with him, and the most melodramatic of all Shakespeare's histories will begin.

39

The Tragedy of

RICHARD III

R ICHARD III deals with events that immediately follow *Henry VI,
Part Three,* and it is very likely that Shakespeare began work on it
as soon as he was through with the *Henry VI* trilogy. It was probably completed by 1593 at the latest.

At that time Shakespeare was still at the beginning of his career. He
had written two narrative poems, a number of sonnets, a couple of light
comedies, and the *Henry VI* trilogy, all popular and successful, but none,
as yet, a blockbuster. With *Richard III* Shakespeare finally made it big.

It is a play after the manner of Seneca, like *Titus Andronicus* (see page
I-391), which Shakespeare was also working on at the time, but infinitely
more successful.

Indeed, *Richard III* is so full of harrowing and dramatic episodes, and
Richard III himself is so successful a character, so wonderful a villain,
with so much bravery and dry humor mingled with his monstrous behavior,
that the play pleased all and made it quite plain that Shakespeare was a
new star of brilliant magnitude on the literary scene. Indeed, despite the
fact that the play is quite raw compared to the polished mastery of Shakespeare's later plays, it is still one of his most popular and successful plays
today.

. . . this sun of York

The play opens with Richard of Gloucester, youngest brother of King
Edward IV, alone on the stage. He sets the time of the scene by saying:

> *Now is the winter of our discontent*
> *Made glorious summer by this sun of York;*
> —Act I, scene i, lines 1–2

This ties in well with the final speech in *Henry VI, Part Three,* in which
Edward IV says happily that the troubles are all over and that only joy
is left.

It was in 1471 that the last serious Lancastrian threat was smashed at
Tewkesbury (see page II-674). Old King Henry VI and his son, Prince

RICHARD III

HOUSE of YORK

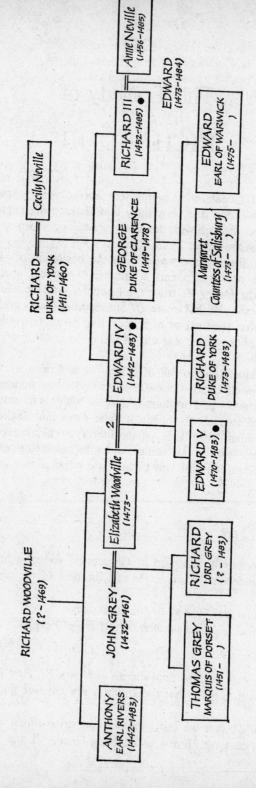

RICHARD WOODVILLE
(? - 1469)

ANTHONY
EARL RIVERS
(1442-1483)

JOHN GREY
(1432-1461)

Elizabeth Woodville
(1473-)

THOMAS GREY
MARQUIS OF DORSET
(1451-)

RICHARD
LORD GREY
(? - 1483)

EDWARD V
(1470-1483) ●

RICHARD
DUKE OF YORK
(1473-1483)

RICHARD
DUKE OF YORK
(1411-1460)

Cecily Neville

EDWARD IV
(1442-1483) ●

GEORGE
DUKE OF CLARENCE
(1449-1478)

Margaret
Countess of Salisbury
(1473-)

EDWARD
EARL OF WARWICK
(1475-)

RICHARD III
(1452-1485) ●

Anne Neville
(1456-1485)

EDWARD
(1473-1484)

☐   Characters in the play

    Kings of England

●

NOTE: Women's names in lower case

Edward, were dead immediately after that battle, and no one was left to dispute the right of King Edward to the throne.

The "sun of York" (and a sun was one of the symbols of the Yorkist house) was indeed shining.

Plots have I laid . . .

The sun of York does not satisfy Richard, however. In a speech that resembles one he had made in the earlier play (see page II–654), he explains that he is so physically deformed that the joys of peace, such as dancing and love-making, are beyond him. He will therefore confine himself to the joys of ambition, and labor to make himself a king. After all, in *Henry VI, Part Three* he waxed lyrical over the joys of being a king (see page II–634), and it is not to be wondered at that he should want those joys.

In order to become a king, he must get those out of the way who have a prior right to the throne. Among them, of course, is his older brother George of Clarence. Richard explains in his soliloquy:

> Plots have I laid, inductions [beginnings] *dangerous,*
> By drunken prophecies, libels, and dreams,
> To set my brother Clarence and the King
> In deadly hate the one against the other;
> And if King Edward be as true and just
> As I am subtile, false, and treacherous,
> This day should Clarence closely be mewed up
> About a prophecy which says that G
> Of Edward's heirs the murderer shall be.
> —Act I, scene i, lines 32–40

Shakespeare is here condensing time, for George of Clarence's break with his royal brother came in 1478, six years after the climactic Battle of Tewkesbury, despite the appearance in the first two lines of the soliloquy that it is the very morrow of the battle that is in question.

Why did the break between the brothers come? Well, it required no plot on the part of Richard, really, for George of Clarence had some of the characteristics in reality that Richard was later slanderously described as having.

It was George who was ambitious and faithless. He had deserted Edward and had sided with Warwick in 1470, and had come back to his allegiance to York, we may be sure, only out of a feeling that Warwick was going to lose and that he himself would gain more by a second double cross.

Edward had forgiven the twice faithless George but that did not prevent George from continuing to scheme for his own aggrandizement in such a way that the King was bound, eventually, to suspect his brother of aiming at the throne.

George did his best, for instance, to keep his hands on the whole enormous Warwick estate. This may have been out of mere avarice but it may also have been out of a realization of how useful wealth would be in planning a revolt. He had married Warwick's elder daughter, Isabella, in the days when he and Warwick had been friends and allies. The younger daughter, Anne, had been married to Edward, Prince of Wales, the son of old King Henry. Prince Edward was now dead and Anne was a widow; and George was determined to keep her a widow, lest some new husband insist on a half share in the Warwick estate. While Anne remained a widow, George controlled it all, and he kept the poor lady a virtual prisoner to see to it that the situation would continue.

This intentness on wealth at all costs would naturally disturb Edward.

Then there arose a new matter. Charles the Bold of Burgundy died in battle in 1477, leaving behind a twenty-year-old daughter, Mary, as his only heir. (Charles's wife had been Margaret of York, the sister of George of Clarence, see page II–642, but Mary was his daughter by a previous wife.)

Burgundy had, for over half a century, been the wealthiest nation in Europe, and under Charles it had reached its political peak, for Charles had almost defeated France and made an independent kingdom of his land. Now, with only a girl to rule Burgundy, its days seemed numbered under the pressure of France on its west and the Holy Roman Empire on its east. Unless, that is, some strong independent prince quickly married Mary and carried on where Charles the Bold had left off. George of Clarence was now a widower and he saw himself as husband of Mary and as the new Duke of Burgundy.

King Edward thoroughly disapproved of this scheme. It seemed to him that if his ambitious, faithless brother became Duke of Burgundy, with all the resources of Burgundy at his call, he would be a source of endless trouble. He would have the money to finance plots against Edward and to scheme at a double throne.

Edward therefore forbade the marriage and the two brothers became open enemies. It did not take much more for Edward to begin to suspect George of plotting his death. Two of George's henchmen were accused of trying to bring about that death by sorcery, and when George insisted they were innocent, Edward angrily had his brother arrested and thrown in the Tower of London.

Whether George was actually plotting Edward's death we cannot say, but certainly, his past and his character gave cause for suspicion and in those troubled times that was enough.

And what had been Richard's record through all this? Well, for one thing, he had remained utterly faithful to Edward in the hard times when Warwick had temporarily hurled him from the throne. He had fought with bravery and distinction at the Battles of Barnet and Tewkesbury. He had done Edward's dirty work (probably) in arranging the death of old King Henry VI in the Tower. In all respects, Richard was as much the loyal brother as George was the faithless one.

This helps explain the frustrating manner in which the characters in *Richard III* fall prey to villainous Richard, though his villainy is made to appear patent to all. In actual history, you see, he *wasn't* a villain.

Thus, consider the prophecy which helped set the King against his brother; that someone with the initial *G* would be a traitor to him. (Undoubtedly, there were prophecies extant of this sort, and of every other too, for there are astrologers and prophets everywhere and at all times, even in our own country now, and only those prophecies which come true or seem to come true are later remembered.) The King felt this applied to George of Clarence; but why not to Richard of Gloucester? The King suspected George because George deserved it; he did not suspect Gloucester because the real Gloucester's unshakable loyalty left no room for suspicion.

We can also ask ourselves whether Richard really had a hand in raising Edward's suspicions against George. There is no evidence of that at all until the later anti-Richard polemicists got to work. They say that he spoke openly in favor of his brother to the King in order to hide his secret maneuverings. The "maneuverings," however, are a later invention presented even by the polemicists as only a matter of suspicion, whereas the one *fact* they admit is that Richard defended his brother openly—which took courage.

My Lady Grey his wife . . .

Even as Richard (in Shakespeare's version) reveals his plots and villainies, George is brought onstage on his way to the Tower. This would make it January 16, 1478.

Richard expresses hearty sympathy and says:

> *Why, this it is when men are ruled by women.*
> *'Tis not the King that sends you to the Tower.*
> *My Lady Grey his wife, Clarence, 'tis she*
> *That tempers* [influences] *him to this extremity.*
> —Act I, scene i, lines 62–65

It pays Richard to rouse hostility against the Queen. In the first place, the Woodvilles (her relatives) are not popular among the aristocracy because they have monopolized so much in the way of estates and power purely on the basis of their in-law relationship to the King. Richard would gain allies, automatically, if he made himself the head of the anti-Woodville faction.

Then too, it would be wonderful for Richard if the Queen were so unpopular that people would become ready to believe that there was something wrong or irregular in her marriage to the King. Richard already implies as much by referring to her as "My Lady Grey," giving her the name she had borne before her marriage (see page II–652) as though she had no right to any other. After all, if her marriage were not a legal one, her children would be illegitimate and they would not be rightful heirs to the throne.

What's more, it is quite plausible that Queen Elizabeth would indeed be hostile to George of Clarence. When George deserted King Edward and switched to Warwick's side, it was partly because he was displeased with Edward's marriage. And if George were ambitious to be King, it could only be at the cost of Elizabeth's children. In both cases, the Queen had ample reason to hate George.

Anthony Woodeville . . .

Richard continues to insinuate his anti-Woodville venom. He says:

> *Was it not she, and that good man of worship,*
> *Anthony Woodeville her brother there,*
> *That made him send Lord Hastings to the Tower,*
> *From whence this present day he is delivered?*
>
> —Act I, scene i, lines 66–69

Anthony Woodeville, 2nd Earl Rivers (see page II–664), had, as the Queen's brother, profited greatly at court, yet he had earned that profit too. He had accompanied Edward during the latter's temporary exile (when George was fighting him) and had fought bravely for him at the Battle of Barnet.

Lord Hastings was also a favorite of the King's (see page II–661) and had been made Governor of Calais. Rivers had wanted the post for himself and that was a cause of hard feelings between them.

On the other hand, the Queen had a much more understandable reason for disliking Hastings. Although she was a loyal and fruitful wife (giving King Edward seven children, two sons and five daughters), Edward never found one woman enough and had a whole series of mistresses. It was Hastings who helped him in his extracurricular amours and the Queen could scarcely feel kindly toward Hastings in view of that.

. . . Mistress Shore

Yet Hastings was released. The King did not push matters to extremities there, and George says bitterly:

By heaven, I think there is no man secure
But the Queen's kindred, and night-walking heralds
That trudge betwixt the King and Mistress Shore.
Heard you not what an humble suppliant
Lord Hastings was to her for his delivery?
—Act I, scene i, lines 71–75

"Mistress Shore" is Jane Shore, wife of a London goldsmith. Though Edward had had many women, Jane Shore was his favorite. He took her as his mistress in 1470, at which time she was in her middle twenties, and kept her till the end of his reign.

Undoubtedly, Hastings was one of the "night-walking heralds" who helped maintain the secret contacts between King and mistress, and he may even have tasted of her himself, for he certainly kept her after the King's death. It is not surprising, then, that Hastings should turn to Jane Shore for use of her influence with the King.

The King is sickly . . .

Off goes Clarence to the Tower, Richard all concern and promising all help, but inward all glee. No sooner is Clarence gone, when Hastings, newly released and vowing vengeance gainst the Queen's party, appears. Richard asks for news and Hastings says:

The King is sickly, weak, and melancholy,
And his physicians fear him mightily.
—Act I, scene i, lines 136–37

At the time of George's imprisonment, King Edward was only thirty-six years old, certainly a young man by our standards, but he was prematurely aged even by the standards of those times.

One might argue, of course, that Edward's life had been a harrowing one, full of battles, of exiles and returns, of hasty marches and anxious fears. Even after the Battle of Tewkesbury, he had not been entirely in the clear. Although the civil wars were temporarily over, there had been a foreign campaign (which Shakespeare does not mention).

King Edward had not forgotten that Louis XI of France had helped Warwick and Queen Margaret inflict upon him the humiliation of defeat and flight (see page II–664). In 1473, two years after the Battle of Tewkesbury, Edward therefore began to plan an invasion of France in concert with Burgundy, as in the great days of Henry V. (Charles the Bold was still alive then and he was always ready to listen to any projects that might serve to harm France.)

By June 20, 1475, Edward had gathered the greatest army that England had, to that day, ever sent abroad and had landed it in Calais.

But now matters turned out differently than with Henry V in two important ways. First, Burgundy proved an utter flop. Charles was not ready
with the help he had promised.

Secondly, Louis XI was a very unusual king and Edward IV was no
match for him. Louis had no intention of fighting. Instead, he sent flattering
messages to Edward along with three hundred cartloads of wine. This
was distributed to the English soldiers, who promptly got uproariously
drunk.

After the wine came the gold. The English nobility was quite ready to
accept it (though Hastings was sufficiently nervous to draw the line at actually taking it, and suggested that it be put in his sleeve while he looked
the other way). Edward himself was bribed by the promise of a marriage,
in due time, between Louis' son and Edward's daughter. Edward was very
intent on arranging great marriages for his daughters and this pleased him.

In the end, then, the English, having come into France with a greater
army than Henry V ever had, left France without ever having struck a
blow.

Only one Englishman is recorded as having protested against this disgrace and that was none other than Richard of Gloucester. Naturally, the
later anti-Richard historians say nothing of this.

Yet it was probably not the pressures of a harried royal life that went
furthest toward making Edward prematurely old; it was rather overindul-
gence. He ate too much and grew fat; he played too much and wore out.
As Richard says of King Edward in response to Hastings' news:

> O, he hath kept an evil diet long
> And overmuch consumed his royal person.
> —Act I, scene i, lines 139–40

. . . Warwick's youngest daughter

The news is good for Richard, who looks forward to Edward's death
after that of George, something which would leave him the last remaining
son of Richard of York.

He longs for that time, as he says:

> For then I'll marry Warwick's youngest daughter.
> —Act I, scene i, line 153

Warwick's youngest daughter is Anne, the widow of Prince Edward, the
Lancastrian heir. (In *Henry VI, Part Three* Shakespeare refers to her as
the older daughter, see page II–660, but that error is corrected here.)

It was this Anne whom George was hiding, so anxious was he to keep
any part of the Warwick estate from leaving his control. Richard would,

in his turn, be very anxious to marry her in order to have a firm financial base himself. (Which is not to say Richard might not have felt affection for her as well. The fact that a woman has money doesn't make her inevitably unlikable, after all.)

King Edward was on Richard's side in this, for he wanted to reward his youngest brother's loyalty and was not at all eager to contribute to faithless George's wealth. George, however, resisted even the wish and insisted that Richard could marry Anne only if he renounced any share in the Warwick estate.

Pale ashes . . .

No sooner does Richard leave the stage than Lady Anne Neville, the very girl whom he has just mentioned, comes onstage. She has the dead body of King Henry VI with her and is mourning his death. This would make it appear that the scene is taking place very shortly after May 21, 1471, when the King was killed, and therefore nearly seven years *before* the imprisonment of George of Clarence.

Anne apostrophizes the dead King:

> *Poor key-cold figure of a holy king,*
> *Pale ashes of the house of Lancaster,*
> —Act I, scene ii, lines 5–6

She curses the man who killed the old King and, in the play, she knows that man to be Richard of Gloucester. She extends the curse by saying in her apostrophe to the corpse:

> *If ever he have wife, let her be made*
> *More miserable by the life of him*
> *Than I am made by my young lord* [her dead husband] *and*
> *thee.*
> —Act I, scene ii, lines 26–27

She then says to those who are carrying the corpse:

> *Come, now towards Chertsey with your holy load,*
> *Taken from Paul's to be interred there;*
> —Act I, scene ii, lines 29–30

After Henry's death in the Tower he was laid in state in St. Paul's Cathedral, his face left visible, in order that anyone who wished could see that it was indeed Henry and that he was indeed dead. Otherwise there would be bound to be imposters who would claim to be Henry and would gather rebels about themselves, in John Cade fashion (see page II-604).

Once that was done, the body was removed to the abbey at Chertsey, which lies twenty miles southwest of the center of London.

Ill rest betide the chamber . . .

But even as Anne is bewailing the dead King and cursing his murderer, in walks that same murderer (according to Shakespearean history) and there begins a strange courtship.

Richard dares, despite everything, to ask Anne to marry him, but when he suggests that he would like to be in her bedchamber she replies, waspishly:

> Ill rest betide the chamber where thou liest!
> —Act I, scene ii, line 112

This, in effect, is a second curse upon any wife Richard might have.

Yet in the end Anne softens and begins to respond to Richard's clever words. Richard agrees to take over the interment of the dead King, and Anne leaves.

Richard orders the corpse taken up and when asked if it is to be carried to Chertsey, he replies:

> No, to Whitefriars; there attend my coming.
> —Act I, scene ii, line 226

Whitefriars is an abbey north of the Thames.

Richard did indeed move Henry's body from Chertsey, but only in later years. Eventually, rumors began to spread that miracles were being worked at Henry's burial site. Clearly, the sympathy for a dead saint might work against the house of York and in favor of a Lancastrian pretender. Richard therefore (he was King by then) had the body moved. Where it was moved, no one can be certain, for it was never found again.

Edward her lord . . .

When Richard is once again alone onstage, he glories in his performance, feeling pride that one as ugly, as deformed, as criminal as himself should be able to win the lady over by smooth words alone. He asks sardonically:

> Hath she forgot already that brave prince,
> Edward her lord, whom I, some three months since,
> Stabbed in my angry mood at Tewksbury?
> —Act I, scene ii, lines 239–41

But it's no use asking how she could do such a thing.

In real history, Richard was not ugly and not deformed. Nor was he the type of criminal later tales made of him. He did not stab "Edward her lord," who died in battle, despite the scene in *Henry VI, Part Three* (see page II–675).

Anne, by the way, was only fifteen years old when Prince Edward died at Tewkesbury, and it is not certain that she was really married to him (he was eighteen) at the time, though she was certainly betrothed.

Naturally, this tale of Richard's wooing is not historical. Shakespeare did not even find it in any of his sources. He apparently invented it solely to produce a dramatic scene.

History's tale is almost as dramatic and much more traditionally romantic. Richard apparently penetrated his brother's estate in secret and found the Lady Anne disguised as a maid. He spirited her off and married her in 1474 when she was eighteen years old, three years after Tewkesbury (not three months) and four years before George's imprisonment.

Even so, George would not release the estate and Richard did not get his half of it until the question was brought up before Parliament. (George shows up very badly in all this, as in almost every action of his life.) In 1476 Anne gave birth to a son, the only child Richard was destined to have. Thus, at the time of George's imprisonment, not only was Richard already married, he was already a father. Richard's son never appears in the play, since there is no opportunity in that connection to vilify Richard.

Richard's half of the Warwick estate lay chiefly in the north and he succeeded to the role of the Nevilles there (see page II–649). Indeed, in the last years of Edward's reign, Richard was the hard-working and capable ruler of the north. Working always for Edward, his own loyalty remained untarnished. Between 1480 and 1483 he served the north with such efficiency and justice as to grow popular indeed. He was outstanding in war as well as in peace, for he invaded Scotland and established the English boundary there as it stands today.

. . . the trust of Richard Gloucester

The scene shifts to the palace, where Queen Elizabeth is distraught over the possibility of Edward's death. With her are three members of her family. There is her brother Anthony Woodville, Lord Rivers, who is just the King's age. There are also her two sons by her earlier marriage. One is Thomas Grey, 1st Marquis of Dorset, who is now twenty-six years old, and Richard Grey, his younger brother (referred to in the play as Lord Grey).

When the men try to comfort her with the thought that even if her husband should die, her son would be King, Queen Elizabeth replies:

> *Ah, he is young, and his minority*
> *Is put into the trust of Richard Gloucester,*

A man that loves not me, nor none of you.
> —Act I, scene iii, lines 11–13

How can Edward entrust his sons to the mercies of his evil, ruthless brother? Easily—since in history that brother was loyal, capable, and warlike. He was the natural Protector, as an earlier Gloucester had been of an earlier child-king (see page II–523).

The Prince of Wales, another Edward, was only eight years old at the time of the imprisonment of George of Clarence.

. . . Buckingham and Derby

Two courtiers approach, and Lord Grey announces them, saying:

Here come the lords of Buckingham and Derby
> —Act I, scene iii, line 17

Buckingham is Henry Stafford, 2nd Duke of Buckingham. He is the grandson of Humphrey Stafford, the 1st Duke, who played his part in *Henry VI, Part Two* as the man who entrapped and arrested Duchess Eleanor of Gloucester (see page II–589).

Buckingham's grandfather had died at the Battle of Northampton (see page II–630) in 1460, fighting on the side of Lancaster. Buckingham's father (Humphrey, Earl of Stafford) had died earlier still, in 1455, at the first Battle of St. Albans (see page II–624), also as a Lancastrian.

In 1460, then, it was young Henry, only six years old then, who inherited the ducal title. Edward IV took Henry in charge and saw to it that he grew up a firm Yorkist. In 1466, when he was still only twelve, he was married to Catherine Woodville, the sister of Queen Elizabeth, to bind him more firmly to the Yorkist cause, and to strengthen the Woodvilles with a good aristocratic connection.

Nevertheless, Buckingham was not entirely trusted. Edward IV held on to much of his ancestral estates, including the duchy of Hereford, and let him remain in obscurity. He was twenty-four at the time of George's imprisonment.

Derby is Sir Thomas Stanley. (His brother, William Stanley, is referred to in *Henry VI, Part Three* and is even onstage in the scene in which Edward IV is rescued from his imprisonment by the Archbishop of York—but is given no lines to say.)

Sir Thomas Stanley was an extraordinarily successful opportunist, for in those changeable times of civil war he managed always to shift to the winning side. He married Eleanor Neville, a sister of Warwick, just in time to be a Yorkist and to obtain high office under Edward IV. He went with the army to France in that 1475 fiasco and he fought in the north under Richard in the early 1480s. He was thirty-three at the time of George's imprisonment.

The Countess Richmond . . .

Both Buckingham and Stanley greet the Queen with polite good wishes, but the Queen turns on the latter and says peevishly:

> The Countess Richmond, good my Lord of Derby,
> To your good prayer will scarcely say "Amen."
> —Act I, scene iii, lines 20–21

After the death of his wife, Stanley married again and his second wife was none other than Margaret Beaufort, the widowed great-granddaughter of John of Gaunt and the mother of Henry Tudor, Earl of Richmond (see page II–666), who was the Lancastrian pretender to the throne. Thus, Stanley managed to keep a foot in the Lancastrian camp—and yet he got away with it, managing also to be in high office with the Yorkists until it was time for him to decide which way to make the final jump.

Small joy have I . . .

The news that Buckingham and Stanley bring is that King Edward is feeling better and wants to make peace between the warring factions at his court.

Just then, however, in comes Richard of Gloucester, with Hastings. Richard plays the role of plain, blunt-spoken gentleman, angry with the Woodvilles for having had George of Clarence thrown into the Tower. With grim irony, he taunts the Queen with having maneuvered a marriage with a King who was too young to know better. Elizabeth, feeling herself bruised and battered from every direction, cries out:

> Small joy have I in being England's Queen.
> —Act I, scene iii, line 109

Even as she says so there appears in the background none other than old Queen Margaret, the wife of dead King Henry VI. She mutters, vindictively:

> And less'ned be that small, God I beseech him!
> —Act I, scene iii, line 110

Where did she come from? What was Margaret doing at Edward's court?

In real life, she was not there. She could not be. Louis XI had ransomed her as part of the general settlement after Edward's abortive invasion of France in 1475. She had then gone back to her native land to remain there in poverty for the rest of her life. She never returned to England.

Margaret was, to be sure, alive at the time of the imprisonment of George of Clarence, but she was in France. Her appearance at the court is utterly fictitious and is designed merely to produce another dramatic scene. (Her appearance here places her in four different plays, however, since she was in all three *Henry VI* plays.)

The curse . . .

Richard and the others continue to wrangle while Margaret, unnoticed, listens. Richard accuses the Woodvilles of having been Lancastrians once, which is true (see page II–652), and they reply that they were merely being loyal to their King.

At that, Margaret finally steps forward to maintain her status as their rightful Queen even now.

At once, all turn upon her. Richard says coldly that her misfortunes are the result of

> The curse my noble father laid on thee
> When thou didst crown his warlike brows with paper
> And with thy scorns drew'st rivers from his eyes
> And then to dry them gav'st the Duke a clout [cloth]
> Steeped in the faultless blood of pretty Rutland,
> —Act I, scene iii, lines 173–77

This was indeed the great scene of *Henry VI, Part Three* (see page II–639).

. . . my quick curses

As each person present piously scolds her for that atrocity, she turns on them, in frustration, and decides to do some cursing of her own. She cries out:

> Can curses pierce the clouds and enter heaven?
> Why, then, give way, dull clouds, to my quick curses!
> Though not by war, by surfeit die your king,
> As ours by murder, to make him a king!
> Edward thy son, that now is Prince of Wales,
> For Edward our son, that was Prince of Wales,
> Die in his youth by like untimely violence!

Thyself a queen, for me that was a queen,
Outlive thy glory like my wretched self!
Long mayst thou live to wail thy children's death
And see another, as I see thee now,
Decked in thy rights as thou art stalled in mine!
Long die thy happy days before thy death,
And, after many length'ned hours of grief,
Die neither mother, wife, nor England's Queen!
Rivers and Dorset, you were standers-by,
And so wast thou, Lord Hastings, when my son
Was stabbed with bloody daggers. God I pray him
That none of you may live his natural age,
But by some unlooked accident cut off!

—Act I, scene iii, lines 194–213

If this were an actual curse, actually delivered by Margaret, at the actual time it was supposed to be delivered, it would be a most amazing performance, for it proved to be nearly entirely accurate. It was composed, however, long after the events it was supposed to predict, so that we need not marvel at her prescience. It is nevertheless a crucial part of the drama as presented by Shakespeare. The rest of the play, as a matter of fact, describes the slow working out of Margaret's curse.

The worm of conscience . . .

A strong curse would make even a rationalist uneasy, and in the sixteenth century there were few rationalists and curses were considered efficacious by almost everyone. Even the hard Richard is disturbed and he tries to quiet Margaret before she moves on to the one person as yet unmentioned —himself.

But Margaret turns on him grimly and says:

The worm of conscience still begnaw thy soul!
Thy friends suspect for traitors while thou liv'st
And take deep traitors for thy dearest friends!
No sleep close up that deadly eye of thine,
Unless it be while some tormenting dream
Affrights thee . . .

—Act I, scene iii, lines 221–26

And this curse too is slowly worked out in the play.

And when Queen Elizabeth tries to shrug off this curse of Margaret upon Richard, the ex-Queen says to the present one:

The day will come that thou shalt wish for me
To help thee curse this poisonous bunch-backed toad.
—Act I, scene iii, lines 244–45

Margaret excepts only Buckingham from her cursing, for he has neither harmed her nor stood by while others did. She tries to warn him against Richard but he scorns her; whereupon she shrieks:

O, but remember this another day,
When he shall split thy very heart with sorrow,
And say poor Margaret was a prophetess.
—Act I, scene iii, lines 298–300

And that day too will come.

Catesby, I come . . .

Margaret leaves, her dramatic function done, and a gentleman arrives to say that King Edward wants the Queen. She says:

Catesby, I come. Lords, will you go with me?
—Act I, scene iii, line 321

The person who brought the message was William Catesby, who was later to be one of Richard's loyal advisers.

. . . my executioners

Richard is left alone on the stage, yet again. He muses gleefully on his villainy, when two men enter and Richard says:

But soft! Here come my executioners.
—Act I, scene iii, line 338

Apparently, Richard is in no mind to wait upon the law to bring about the end of George of Clarence; nor is he going to chance the possible repentance of King Edward. He will have George murdered forthwith.

Actually, of course, nothing of the sort happened. The law *did* take its course, after a fashion. That is, after George had been committed to the Tower on January 16, 1478, he was tried before a jury of English peers. King Edward himself was prosecutor and in person came to demand his brother's condemnation. The peers could scarcely refuse and it was the

Duke of Buckingham who acted as "foreman of the jury" and pronounced the death sentence.

On February 7 the speaker of the House of Commons demanded that the sentence be carried out, and soon afterward it was announced that George of Clarence was dead. Obviously, he had been executed as the law had demanded.

And what had Richard of Gloucester to do with that death? Nothing at all. Except that, even according to Sir Thomas More's dreadfully prejudiced account, he openly protested the whole procedure.

. . . to cross to Burgundy

In the Tower, meanwhile, the imprisoned George of Clarence is in conversation with the Keeper, and is telling him a nightmare he had had the night before. He begins:

> *Methoughts that I had broken from the Tower*
> *And was embarked to cross to Burgundy,*
>
> —Act I, scene iv, lines 9–10

Burgundy was the natural place for him to flee, since his sister was dowager duchess there.

Richard (in George's dream) is also on board ship, and George hurtles overboard when Richard stumbles and falls against him. George's first horrified thought as he plunges into the water is:

> *O Lord, methought what pain it was to drown!*
>
> —Act I, scene iv, line 21

Eventually (in his dream) he does drown, for he says:

> *I passed, methought, the melancholy flood,*
> *With that sour ferryman which poets write of,*
> *Unto the kingdom of perpetual night.*
>
> —Act I, scene iv, lines 45–47

The sour ferryman is, of course, Charon (see page I-68).

. . . renownèd Warwick

George's dream continues after death, and, once in hell, he meets the shades of other dead men. He says:

The first that there did greet my stranger soul
Was my great father-in-law, renownèd Warwick,
Who spake aloud, "What scourge for perjury
Can this dark monarchy afford false Clarence?"

—Act I, scene iv, lines 48–51

The tale of the double perjury of George of Clarence, who first deserted his brother for Warwick at a crucial point, then Warwick for his brother at another crucial point, is told in *Henry VI, Part Three.*

Another shade approaches, crying out:

"Clarence is come, false, fleeting, perjured Clarence,
That stabbed me in the field by Tewksbury.
Seize on him, Furies, take him unto torment!"

—Act I, scene iv, lines 55–57

It is the shade of the young Prince of Wales, son of Henry VI, of course. And it is these lines which have forever pilloried George to those who are interested in this period of history, for he is almost never mentioned without some reference to "false, fleeting [fickle], perjured Clarence."

. . . the malmsey butt . . .

The murderers arrive at the Tower then, after Clarence has fallen asleep again.

In a long scene, the murderers first debate with each other whether to kill George, then, when George awakes, they debate the matter with him. The First Murderer loses patience at last and stabs him, saying:

Take that! And that! If all this will not do,
I'll drown you in the malmsey butt within.

—Act I, scene iv, lines 272–73

Malmsey is a sweet wine produced in such Mediterranean regions as Cyprus, Italy, and Spain. In it, George of Clarence experienced the pain of drowning which earlier in the scene he had described with such fear.

Was George really drowned in a barrel of wine? Surely not. While the manner of his death was kept secret and only the fact of it announced, it seems ridiculous that anything as *outré* as drowning was involved. The bit about the malmsey gained currency after George's death but what inspired it we don't know. It was too dramatic not to be spread and eventually it came to be believed.

Shakespeare uses the tale to inject not only an added bit of gruesomeness

in this horror play, but also because it inspires the poetic tale of his nightmare drowning as a bit of dramatic irony.

. . . God punish me

The second act opens with King Edward on the stage for the first (and
only) time. He appeared in *Henry VI, Part Two* as a teen-age earl, and in
Henry VI, Part Three as a vigorous, sensuous King. Now he seems a sick
old man striving to smooth the quarrels at court, presumably so that he
may leave the throne to his young son in peace.

Under the royal eye, the various factions are forced to embrace and
swear friendship; Hastings and Buckingham on one side, and the various
Woodvilles (including the Queen) on the other.

All swear their love, fulsomely. Thus, Buckingham says to the Queen:

> *Whenever Buckingham doth turn his hate*
> *Upon your Grace, but with all duteous love*
> *Doth* [not] *cherish you and yours, God punish me*
> *With hate in those where I expect most love!*
> —Act II, scene i, lines 32–35

This, as it turns out, is still additional dramatic irony, involving a self-
curse, like those of the Lady Anne.

But where is Richard of Gloucester so that he might join the love feast?
Buckingham spies him and says:

> *Here comes Sir Richard Ratcliffe and the Duke.*
> —Act II, scene i, line 46

Ratcliffe is another of the lowborn but trusted advisers of Richard.

Richard gladly adds his voice to the general reconciliation and then, at
an appropriate moment, snaps at them that George of Clarence is dead and
throws the assemblage into disarray. King Edward can only gasp:

> *Is Clarence dead? The order was reversed.*
> —Act II, scene i, line 88

Was it? Not as far as history can tell. It is inserted here only to make
it clear that Richard's is the full blame for George's death.

. . . he rescued me

King Edward bewails his brother's death, and indeed, Holinshed does say that whenever, during the rest of his reign, he had to pardon a criminal on appeal, he expressed sorrow over the fact that no one had pleaded for George's life. Shakespeare gives him the opportunity to express this sorrow now by the artificial device of having Stanley rush in to crave pardon for a henchman of his who has just committed murder.

Edward says:

> *Who told me, in the field at Tewksbury*
> *When Oxford had me down, he* [George] *rescued me*
> *And said, "Dear brother, live, and be a king"?*
> *Who told me, when we both lay in the field*
> *Frozen almost to death, how he did lap* [wrap] *me*
> *Even in his garments, and did give himself*
> *All thin and naked, to the numb-cold night?*
>
> —Act II, scene i, lines 113–19

This is all very theatrical and perhaps Edward did regret his brother's death (and perhaps he put on the show to avoid seeming a tyrant), but does this sound like George? Would he rescue the brother he had shortly before tried to destroy? Was he unselfish enough to expose himself to bitter cold for his brother's sake? Somehow that doesn't sound like the George we know, and we can all too easily suspect that this speech is included only for pathos.

Good grandam . . .

We next see onstage none other than the Duchess of York, together with the young son and daughter of George of Clarence. The son (whose speeches are ascribed to "Boy") asks:

> *Good grandam, tell us, is our father dead?*
>
> —Act II, scene ii, line 1

The Duchess of York tries to shield the children but cannot for long and is forced to admit the death. She is Cicely Neville, and she has suffered much. She is the aunt of the Earl of Warwick, who had been betrayed by her son, George, and killed in battle with her son, King Edward. She was the widow of Richard of York, who had died at Wakefield eighteen years before (see page II–639), and she is the mother of Richard of Gloucester too, and of slaughtered Edmund of Rutland.

George's son is Edward Plantagenet. His mother having been the eldest daughter of Warwick, the son inherits the title and is Earl of Warwick. Actually, he is not likely to have asked the question of his grandmother, for at the time of his father's death he was only three years old. His sister, Margaret, who also appears in this scene, was five years old.

. . . our king, is dead

The old Duchess of York bewails the treachery of her son Richard. In the play, she recognizes him throughout as a monstrous villain (though in real life she was always on good terms with him and probably felt him to be the best and most capable of her sons).

Even while the mourning proceeds, Queen Elizabeth enters with fresh cause for grief. She cries out to the Duchess:

> Edward, my lord, thy son, our king, is dead!
> —Act II, scene ii, line 40

The play makes it sound as though Edward died soon after George's death, possibly of remorse.

Not at all. Edward died on April 9, 1483, a little over five years after George's death. It was far more anger than remorse that did him in, for earlier that year Louis XI had renounced the treaty that would have married his son to Edward's daughter, and Edward was furious enough to plan another invasion.

It was not to be, however. Weakened by gluttony and debauchery, he fell ill and lingered only ten days. He was still three weeks short of his forty-first birthday at the time. And thus, for the first time, came to pass one of Queen Margaret's curses: "Though not by war, by surfeit die your king."

. . . the young prince your son . . .

A scene of wild wailing by the women and children follows, until Rivers, the Queen's brother, rather impatiently says to Elizabeth:

> Madam, bethink you like a careful mother
> Of the young prince your son. Send straight for him;
> Let him be crowned . . .
> —Act II, scene ii, lines 96–98

The young Prince, Edward, had appeared in the last scene of *Henry VI, Part Three* as a baby. At that time he was made Prince of Wales and declared heir to the throne.

In 1473, when the young Prince was only three years old, he was taken to Ludlow to be titular ruler of the borderlands (or "marches") abutting

Wales. This was the traditional estate of the Mortimer family, who were the earls of March. (Edward IV was himself Earl of March before the death of his father.) While in the west, the young Prince was placed in charge of his maternal uncle, Rivers, and his half brother, Lord Grey.

All this was supposed, eventually, to give the young Prince of Wales education in government, but those who were opposed to the Woodvilles saw in it something rather more sinister. The Prince was separated from the court and was surrounded by Woodvilles, who would surely bring him up to be strongly pro-Woodville in sympathy. By the time the young Prince succeeded to the throne, the Woodvilles would be immovable.

Of those opposed to the Woodvilles, Richard of Gloucester and Henry of Buckingham would be paramount. They represented the old nobility, and both were descended from Edward III. (Buckingham's descent was not exclusively male, however, so he was not a Plantagenet.)

If it was indeed the Woodville plan to educate the Prince of Wales in their own interest, Edward IV died too soon. The young Prince was only thirteen at the time of his father's death, too young to rule on his own. There would be needed a regent or Protector and he was not old enough to play a part in the power struggle that would now come.

. . . have comfort . . .

Even as Rivers talks of crowning the Prince, Richard enters, all sympathy and warmth, saying:

> Sister, have comfort. All of us have cause
> To wail the dimming of our shining star;
>
> —Act II, scene ii, lines 101–2

In actual history, Richard was not at court at the time of Edward's death. He was in the north, fighting the Scots successfully and upholding English honor.

As soon as he heard the news of the death, he went riding to London with a six-hundred-man escort, all wearing mourning. He supervised a magnificent funeral for his dead brother and called on all men to swear an oath of loyalty to the dead King's son, taking the oath himself first and accepting the Prince of Wales as Edward V, King of England. (Naturally, to the anti-Richard propagandists of succeeding reigns, this was profound hypocrisy, but they have no real evidence for that other than their own accusations.)

By the time Richard was back in London, however, the Woodvilles had had time to make their first moves and the new boy-king was also on his way to London with what amounted almost to an army. They were determined, apparently, to keep the royal child in a firm grip.

Clearly, the anti-Woodville faction could not allow this to happen without attempting some counter or their cause might be forever lost. Thus, after the arrangement is made, in the play, to escort the new young King to London, Buckingham says to Richard, when the two are left alone onstage:

> *My lord, whoever journeys to the Prince,*
> *For God sake let not us two stay at home;*
>> —Act II, scene ii, lines 146–47

. . . virtuous uncles . . .

The tension over who was to control the new King, the Woodvilles or the old nobility, was bound to give rise to the specter of civil war again, and Shakespeare now introduces a street scene in which a group of citizens are nervously discussing the news.

One of them, listed as Third Citizen in the speech assignations, says pessimistically:

> *Woe to the land that's governed by a child!*
>> —Act II, scene iii, line 11

This is a biblical quotation, for in Ecclesiastes 10:16 we find "Woe to thee, O land, when thy king is a child . . ." though that may have more a figurative than a literal meaning, so that what is intended is: Woe to the land whose king lacks wisdom.

The First Citizen is more optimistic. There were child-kings before whose accession did not mark immediate civil war. He says:

> *So stood the state when Henry the Sixth*
> *Was crowned in Paris but at nine months old.*
>> —Act II, scene iii, lines 16–17

(Henry VI succeeded to the throne at the age of nine months, to be sure, but he wasn't crowned at Paris till many years later, see page II–559.)

The Third Citizen points out that things were different then:

> *. . . then the King*
> *Had virtuous uncles to protect his Grace.*
>> —Act II, scene iii, lines 20–21

Actually, the comparison is a poor one, if comfort is intended. There was almost a civil war during the minority of Henry VI, and the ones at fault were those same "virtuous" uncles. At least Humphrey of Gloucester, the King's uncle, and Henry Beaufort, Bishop of Winchester, the King's great-uncle, were at odds, and their wrangling did England a great deal of damage and contributed to the loss of France (see page II–552).

Neither First nor Third Citizen seems to remember this, and instead, the First Citizen, speaking of uncles, says naïvely:

> Why, so hath this, both by his father and mother.
>
> —Act II, scene iii, line 22

But it is precisely that there are two uncles—Richard of Gloucester on the father's side and Anthony of Rivers on the mother's—that creates the problem, for they are of opposing factions.

The Third Citizen sees this at once, for he says of the uncles:

> Better it were they all came by his father,
> Or by his father there were none at all;
> For emulation [rivalry] who shall now be nearest
> Will touch us all too near . . .
>
> —Act II, scene iii, lines 23–26

. . . at Stony Stratford

In the palace, Queen Elizabeth is waiting for the arrival of her son, along with his Woodville escort. With her is the Archbishop of York, who brings news. He says:

> Last night, I hear, they lay at Stony Stratford;
> And at Northampton they do rest tonight;
> Tomorrow or next day they will be here.
>
> —Act II, scene iv, lines 1–3

The Archbishop of York is Thomas Rotherham, an English prelate who had long been a favorite of Queen Elizabeth. Through her influence, he gained a series of bishoprics, culminating in the Archbishopric of York in 1480. He also served as chancellor (the chief administrative official) from 1474 to the end of the reign of Edward IV.

If by the previous night the young King and his party were at Stony Stratford, they had traveled eighty miles southeast from Ludlow and had then been only fifty miles from London. To go to Northampton the following night would be odd, however, for Northampton is about thirteen miles due north of Stony Stratford and to go there would be to move away from London.

Actually what was happening was that Richard of Gloucester, together with Buckingham, had gone westward to meet the young King and, if possible, to wrest him from the control of the Woodvilles. This is made out to be a terribly wicked deed by the anti-Richard propagandists later on, but viewed from the standpoint of practical politics, it was natural enough.

The dying King Edward IV had named Richard as Protector and it was clear that the Woodvilles would try to nullify that. Richard was only fighting for his own. It might be ambition but it could be more than that, too; it was possible Richard considered himself more capable than the Woodvilles, and if so, it might well be argued that he was right.

Presumably, Richard was not of a mind to attack the escort directly and perhaps initiate what could degenerate into a civil war. He preferred strategy. By the time the young King and his party were at Stony Stratford, Richard and his were at Northampton.

Richard sent to Rivers and Grey, inviting them to meet him at Northampton so that they might confer on plans for the coronation. The Woodvilles chose to accept rather than to make the first move toward open hostility, and all dined together warmly at Northampton the following night.

This, apparently, is why the Archbishop places the Woodville party at Stony Stratford one night and Northampton the next.

. . . my son of York

The Dowager Duchess of York is also present when the Archbishop brings the news and with grandmotherly care expresses a hope that the King has grown sufficiently since they last saw him. Queen Elizabeth responds:

> . . . I hear no; they say my son of York
> Has almost overta'en him in his growth.
>
> —Act II, scene iv, lines 6–7

This is the first mention of Queen Elizabeth's second son, and his first appearance too, for he is also onstage. This second son, named Richard for his grandfather, is two years younger than the new King. Born in 1472, he is eleven years old now.

. . . sent to Pomfret

But now a Messenger comes hastening in with news. The young King is well, but not so with his escort. He says:

> Lord Rivers and Lord Grey are sent to Pomfret,
> And with them Sir Thomas Vaughan, prisoners.
>
> —Act II, scene iv, lines 42–43

While the pleasant night of dining had kept the Woodvilles busy, Richard's men had proceeded to Stony Stratford, where apparently they won over the Woodville escort by either threats or bribes or both. The next morning, Richard, Buckingham, and the Woodvilles rode amicably to Stony Stratford, and when they got there, Richard placed Rivers and Grey under arrest. This was on April 30, 1483, only three weeks after the death of Edward IV.

Richard and Buckingham then made their way to the place where the King himself had spent the night and bent their knees to him. This did not prevent Richard, however, from arresting Sir Thomas Vaughan, who was personal counselor to the boy-king. Vaughan had been an ardent Yorkist who had fought in many battles, but he was part of the Woodville faction and Richard would not have him.

The arrests were brutal and were carried through by treachery. This is not to be admired and yet one might very easily argue that it was Richard's prime duty to prevent civil war. He had taken the course which would wipe out the Woodville faction suddenly and without general bloodshed. Before there was time for response, it would be all over, and by cruel action against a few, he would have prevented eventual cruel action against many.

This sort of reasoning has been indulged in, in one way or another, by every strong ruler in the history of the world (something like it was, for instance, used to justify the dropping of the atom bomb on the people of Hiroshima). Its use does not make Richard admirable, of course, but neither does it make him a monster.

Queen Elizabeth recognizes the efficacy of the blow, for as soon as she hears the news, she says:

> *Ay me! I see the ruin of my house.*
>
> —Act II, scene iv, line 49

. . . we will to sanctuary

Queen Elizabeth might have faced up to the situation with courage (as old Queen Margaret would have, we can be sure). She might have outfaced Richard, demanded the release of her kinsmen, tried to raise an army, start a civil war. Or she might have tried to soothe and flatter Richard, biding her time.

She did none of these things. Fearing the worst and incapable of taking any positive action, she fled. She says to her younger son:

> *Come, come, my boy; we will to sanctuary.*
>
> —Act II, scene iv, line 66

'Elizabeth had been in sanctuary before, in Westminster Abbey, when Warwick had driven her husband out of England. She had been safe there then, for Warwick had not offered to violate sanctuary, and there she had given birth to the child who was now King. She returned to the same sanctuary now. With her she took not only the young Duke of York but also (though not mentioned in this passage) her five daughters and her remaining son by her first marriage, Dorset.

The Archbishop of York, for helping her on this occasion and for remaining loyal to the Queen who had patronized him, was relieved of his position as chancellor and was even imprisoned for a short time.

Lord Cardinal . . .

The young King, Edward V, now escorted by Richard of Gloucester, Buckingham, and their men, arrived in London on May 4, 1483. Edward V, more than a little upset by the disappearance of his Woodville relatives, wonders why his mother and brother are not there to greet him.

The reason is soon apparent when Hastings appears to explain that Queen Elizabeth and young Richard of York are in sanctuary.

This is troublesome for Richard. Queen Elizabeth herself may stay in sanctuary for all he cares. The same might be said for her daughters or her remaining Woodville son. Richard of York is another matter altogether.

The young Duke of York is next in line for the throne and is therefore a prize for anyone who meditates civil war. If Richard is to maintain the peace of England, he must control young York as well as the young King.

Buckingham therefore says:

> Lord Cardinal, will your Grace
> Persuade the Queen to send the Duke of York
> Unto his princely brother presently?
>   —Act III, scene i, lines 32–34

The Lord Cardinal here addressed is Thomas Cardinal Bouchier, who is sixty-fifth Archbishop of Canterbury. He received that office in 1454 when Henry VI was King and labored in vain to bring about a reconciliation between York and Lancaster in the early years of the Wars of the Roses. In 1461 it was he who crowned Edward of York and made him Edward IV.

. . . at the Tower

While the Archbishop of Canterbury goes off, rather reluctantly, and under some pressure from Buckingham, to perform his task, the young King asks where he will be lodging. Richard answers smoothly:

Where it seems best unto your royal self.
If I may counsel you, some day or two
Your Highness shall repose you at the Tower;
—Act III, scene i, lines 63–65

The Tower of London (see page II–305) gained a grim reputation as a place of imprisonment and execution for state prisoners—partly, in fact, because of the events in the late fifteenth century: the imprisonment and death of Henry VI and of George of Clarence, for instance.

Nevertheless, it did serve as a royal residence as well, even in the time of Edward V. When Richard suggests the Tower, he clearly wants the boy-king secure from seizure by the Woodville faction or by anyone else who might wish to dispute the government as being set up by the Protector. In that sense, the King would be held a prisoner.

On the other hand, it cannot be assumed that the King is only a prisoner simply because he is in the Tower, or that Richard, in suggesting the Tower, views it *only* as a prison.

His wit set down . . .

The mention of the Tower brings up Shakespeare's favorite historical character, and the young King talks sententiously of Julius Caesar. He says:

That Julius Caesar was a famous man.
With what his valor did enrich his wit,
His wit set down to make his valor live.
Death makes no conquest of this conqueror,
For now he lives in fame, though not in life.
—Act III, scene i, lines 84–88

It was indeed a remarkable aspect of Caesar that he made his fame as a man of thought as well as a man of action. In oratory, he was considered second, in his time, only to Cicero. As a prose writer, he was also second only to Cicero, and his *Commentaries* described his own campaigns in Gaul with great skill. In this way, he helped assure his own immortality "in fame, though not in life."

Edward V's remarks are intended to show his intelligence, to demonstrate what a King there might have been and to intensify the villainy of those who did away with him. To show that it was not only intelligence but also nobility and gallantry, young Edward is then made to say, to Buckingham:

And if I live until I be a man,

I'll win our ancient right in France again
Or die a soldier as I lived a king.
                              —Act III, scene i, lines 91–93

The English dream of French conquest died hard. It was still active through the first half of the sixteenth century. As late a king as Henry VIII invaded France with some dim notion of conquest a generation after young Edward V's brief life. It wasn't until Spain replaced France as England's chief enemy in the late sixteenth century that the long and useless dream faded.

To be sure, England fought France on a number of occasions thereafter, the final battle being that of Waterloo in 1815, but after the reign of Queen Elizabeth I, such wars did not involve dreams of continental conquest on England's part.

. . . the Duke of York

But now the Cardinal returns with the King's younger brother, and Buckingham greets them with:

Now in good time here comes the Duke of York.
                              —Act III, scene i, line 95

It seems, in the play, that it took the Cardinal little time to persuade the Queen to give up her younger son. Actually, it was a hard job that required not only cajolery, but threats. Richard had to make it clear, no doubt, that if the Queen did not give up her son, force would be used.

Again, this seems ruthless of Richard and it is ruthless. That can't be glossed over. But once again, it might be looked upon as a stroke of politics necessary to prevent any danger of civil war.

In any case, it was on June 16, 1483, fully six weeks after the young King's entrance into London, that his younger brother was released from sanctuary and was sent to join Edward V in the Tower. With that, Richard lost interest in the Queen and her other children and throughout the rest of the play they are in no particular danger.

. . . the installment of this noble duke

Richard was playing a dangerous game during the months after his brother's death. He had struck sharply and daringly, destroyed the Woodville faction, and placed himself in control of the King.

Once that was done, the very success brought new danger. There was an anti-Woodville alliance that backed Richard, but once the Woodvilles were gone would the alliance hang together? There was Hastings, for instance, who was at strong enmity with the Woodvilles, but not out of any particular love for Richard. How reliable was he now?

At some point (we don't know exactly when) Richard must have begun to feel that the post of Protector was not enough. Its power was insufficient and it was impermanent. In three years or so, young Edward V would be old enough to rule in his own name, and in those three years enemies might accumulate waiting to destroy Richard. This had happened to another Protector less than half a century before, one who had also been a Duke of Gloucester (see page II–599).

Richard might also have reasoned that England needed a strong King, and not a royal child with squabbling advisers. The record of the minority of Henry VI was not of such a nature as to bear repetition.

Then too, there's no use in trying to make Richard out to be an utter angel. The chance to be King was tempting and there were few who could resist that temptation.

But if Richard was to make himself King, whether out of pure ambition, or self-defense, or a noble concern for England's welfare, he must still make sure he had appropriate allies. The opposition must be won over or disposed of in advance or else he would become King only to preside as general on one side of a civil war, as had been the case with Edward IV.

Thus, Buckingham begins the intrigue on behalf of Richard by calling Catesby to his side. He says to him:

> *What thinkest thou? is it not an easy matter*
> *To make William Lord Hastings of our mind*
> *For the installment of this noble duke* [Richard]
> *In the seat royal of this famous isle?*
> —Act III, scene i, lines 161–64

Catesby is doubtful. He shrewdly suspects that Hastings' old friendship for Edward IV will not allow him to abandon Edward IV's son. What's more, he thinks Stanley will follow Hastings in this.

. . . *sit about the coronation*

Nevertheless, Buckingham urges Catesby to sound out Hastings, then says:

> *And summon him tomorrow to the Tower*
> *To sit about the coronation.*
> —Act III, scene i, lines 172–73

Originally, it had been planned to crown young King Edward on May 4, the day on which, in fact, he had entered London. The arrest of the Wood-villes gave Richard reason (or pretext, perhaps) to delay the coronation, in order to make sure the country was quiet.

A new date of June 22, 1483, was being considered, and this date is now approaching. It is by now less than two weeks off and something must be done quickly. If Richard is to be King he cannot wait. Once Edward V is crowned, he will be that much harder to set aside.

Give Mistress Shore . . .

As Catesby leaves to see Hastings, Richard calls after him with rough humor:

> *Tell him, Catesby,*
> *His ancient knot of dangerous adversaries* [the Woodvilles]
> *Tomorrow are let blood at Pomfret Castle,*
> *And bid my lord, for joy of this good news,*
> *Give Mistress Shore one gentle kiss the more.*
> —Act III, scene i, lines 181–85

Jane Shore, who had been mistress of the dead King, was perfectly will-ing to oblige Hastings after the King's death.

One can see Richard's purpose here. Hastings, in gratitude over the death of his enemies, might remember that Richard had been the agent for the working of this revenge and perhaps might feel he ought to help Richard in return. Richard is perfectly willing to dispose of Hastings if necessary, but, as a sensible man, he would rather have his help than his death.

The earldom of Hereford . . .

Meanwhile loyal Buckingham is to have his reward. Richard says:

> *. . . when I am king, claim thou of me*
> *The earldom of Hereford and all the movables*
> *Whereof the King my brother was possessed.*
> —Act III, scene i, lines 194–96

This is a reference to the ancestral estates which Buckingham had in-herited through his descent from the Bohun family, but which Edward IV had retained for his own use because of the Lancastrianism of Buckingham's father and grandfather.

He dreamt the boar . . .

At Lord Hastings' house, someone arrives before Catesby does. It is a Messenger with a word from Lord Stanley. The Messenger says:

> . . . *this night*
> *He* [Stanley] *dreamt the boar had rasèd off his helm.*
> —Act III, scene ii, lines 10–11

Richard's standard had a boar depicted upon it so that it was easy to refer to Richard as "the boar" (or, if one wanted to be insulting, "the hog").

The suspicious Stanley, to whom survival was a fine art, did not trust Richard, and felt that something dangerous was in the wind. He wished to warn Hastings, obliquely (anything direct would be unsafe), that Richard might be planning to cut off a few heads.

The message suggests flight but Hastings laughs at the warning. He feels that Catesby is his friend, and Richard too.

. . . this crown of mine . . .

But then comes Catesby, who loses no time in advancing the suggestion that Richard ought to be King. Whereupon Hastings says:

> *I'll have this crown of mine cut from my shoulders*
> *Before I'll see the crown so foul misplaced.*
> —Act III, scene ii, lines 43–44

That seals his fate, but he doesn't know it, and for the rest of the scene he is in high good humor, continually complimenting himself on how well off he is.

. . . Margaret's curse . . .

Before the meeting of the Tower to which Hastings is heading is shown, there is a quick shift of scene to Pomfret Castle, where, nearly a century before, Richard II died (see page II–312) and where now the Woodvilles are being led to execution. A second time, Margaret's curse is fulfilled. She had wished that those who stood by while her son was murdered at Tewkesbury be "by some unlooked accident cut off."

To be sure, her prophecy was imperfect. She had mentioned Rivers and

Dorset in that connection (for Shakespeare was following Holinshed in this respect). Dorset, however, was safe in sanctuary. It was Dorset's younger brother, Lord Grey, who was accompanying Rivers. Shakespeare might easily have changed the curse to suit this historically correct fact, but this seems to be one of the many places where Shakespeare didn't bother to make a correction.

As it is, it is Grey who remembers the curse and says:

> Now Margaret's curse is fall'n upon our heads,
> —Act III, scene iii, line 14

The exact day on which the execution took place is not certain but it is commonly said to have taken place on the day that Hastings attended the meeting at the Tower. If so, that would make it June 13, 1483, just six weeks after they were proceeding so happily to London with the young King, fully expecting to be masters of England.

. . . good strawberries . . .

Meanwhile, at the Tower, the council is meeting, with Hastings still fatuously confident of Richard's friendship. When Richard finally appears, after all are seated, he seems perfectly calm and amiable. Indeed, he engages one of the men present in apparently aimless small talk, saying:

> My Lord of Ely, when I was last in Holborn
> I saw good strawberries in your garden there.
> I do beseech you send for some of them.
> —Act III, scene iv, lines 31–33

My Lord of Ely is John Morton, an aged prelate over sixty years old. He had been a partisan on the Lancastrian side and it was not till after the Battle of Tewkesbury that he submitted to the Yorkists. He proved useful as a diplomatist to Edward IV, negotiating the treaty with Louis XI in 1475 after Edward's abortive invasion.

He was finally rewarded for his belated conversion and his usefulness by being made Bishop of Ely in 1479. His heart, however, always remained with the house of Lancaster to at least some extent, and the shrewd Richard did not trust him.

The Bishop of Ely is thought by some to have written the history of Richard III usually ascribed to More (see page II–616) or to have supplied More his source. If so, one can easily see the history can scarcely be unbiased.

. . . that harlot strumpet Shore

And yet, before the council is over, Hastings, together with Stanley and Morton of Ely, are arrested. No doubt it was done suddenly, under a show of good fellowship, as in the case of the Woodvilles, in order to paralyze any attempt at resistance. When it was done, though, it was probably done in straightforward fashion, with the usual accusation of treason.

Later legend, however, had Richard do it in deliberately sadistic fashion. After his great show of friendliness, he retires a moment, then returns in a rage, crying out that he is the victim of witchcraft. He says:

> *Look how I am bewitched. Behold, mine arm*
> *Is like a blasted sapling withered up;*
> *And this is Edward's wife, that monstrous witch,*
> *Consorted with that harlot strumpet Shore,*
> *That by their witchcraft thus have marked me.*
>
> —Act III, scene iv, lines 67–71

To the Elizabethan audience, which firmly believed that Richard was a monster, with all his features and limbs misshapen, it would be well understood that Richard's arm was withered to begin with and that by making this speech he was deliberately mocking his victims and amusing himself by making patently foolish accusations as a cause for action.

Actually, he didn't have a withered arm in the first place, so the story is patently false. Secondly, there was no need for such foolishness; a straightforward arrest was all that was necessary.

How did the story of the withered arm and witchcraft start then? Was it pure invention? Or was there a natural origin? We can speculate . . .

The fact is that Richard did arrange to have Jane Shore punished. She had not been a bad mistress as mistresses go. She had exerted no undue influence on Edward IV, and had used her power (or what power she had) neither to enrich herself unduly or to harm anyone out of spite.

Nevertheless, her existence was probably offensive in itself to Richard, who was puritanical for his times (the real Richard, not the legendary one), and he may even have blamed her for the excesses that brought his loved brother to an early grave. He therefore delivered her to an ecclesiastical court, which forced her to undergo penance, making her walk through the London streets, barefoot, in a single garment and carrying a lighted candle.

(Richard's deeper motive, if one wishes to ascribe Machiavellianism to him, may have been to blazon forth in dramatic fashion the fact that his brother the King had been notoriously wanton. This would fit in well with what was soon to be forthcoming.)

Jane Shore was punished only for her sexual offenses, but the nature of the penance was precisely that inflicted on Eleanor, Duchess of Gloucester, forty years before (see page II–594), and Eleanor had been accused of witchcraft. After a time, therefore, it was easy to suppose that Jane Shore had been accused of witchcraft too, and then that fable was easily escalated into a transparently fake excuse on the part of Richard to get at Hastings, who had become her lover after Edward's death.

Lovell and Ratcliffe . . .

Indeed, when Hastings, stunned and utterly confused at Richard's accusation, begins stumblingly to say something, Richard orders his head chopped off at once and says:

> *Lovell and Ratcliffe, look that it be done.*
> —Act III, scene iv, line 77

Francis Lovell was the third (along with Catesby and Ratcliffe) of Richard's lowborn advisers. He was made a viscount at about this time.

Lowborn advisers are generally the target of vilification by the aristocracy (see page II–276) and are blamed for all that goes wrong by a populace reluctant to grumble against the King himself. Thus, a defamatory couplet, ascribed to one William Collingbourne, was soon to circulate about the land to Richard's considerable propagandistic disadvantage, one which went: "The Rat, the Cat, and Lovell our Dog / Rule all England under the Hog."

The Rat is Ratcliffe, the Cat is Catesby, and the Hog is, of course, Richard with his boar standard.

. . . thy heavy curse

Hastings too was a stander-by at the death of Prince Edward at Tewkesbury according to Holinshed, and he too was included in the old Queen's curse, which now is fulfilled a third time, as Hastings himself says:

> *O Margaret, Margaret, now thy heavy curse*
> *Is lighted on poor Hastings' wretched head!*
> —Act III, scene iv, lines 91–92

Apparently, he died on the same day as did his Woodville enemies, though if that is so, Ratcliffe is made to be in two places at one time. It is he in the previous scene who supervises the execution of the Woodvilles, and it is he, with Lovell, who is supposed to supervise this execution now.

. . . He deserved his death

Richard does not have Stanley or Morton beheaded. The quick death of Hastings he apparently felt to be lesson enough. No one, he seems to have decided, would now be hardy enough to oppose his own assumption of the throne—not openly, at any rate.

(That, as it turned out, was a mistake on his part, for both Stanley and Ely were to betray him at crucial times. This represented still another fulfillment, a fourth, of Margaret's curse, for she had wished that Richard might "take deep traitors for thy dearest friends.")

It remained, however, for Richard to convert mere lack of opposition into enthusiastic acceptance. For that reason, in the next scene, Richard and Buckingham are shown politely explaining to the Lord Mayor of London the reason for the sudden execution of Hastings. The latter (they say) was conspiring to assassinate Richard and Buckingham.

The shocked Mayor says at this:

> *Now fair befall you! He deserved his death,*
> *And your good Graces both have well proceeded*
> *To warn false traitors from the like attempts.*
> —Act III, scene v, lines 47–49

The Lord Mayor of London at this period was Sir Edmund Shaw. He was a supporter of Richard, and, in actual fact, the Duke had a deserved popularity with the people of London at this time. This meant a good deal, since their active opposition would probably have prevented Richard from assuming the crown.

. . . the bastardy of Edward's children

Richard was working fast. The execution of Hastings and the Woodvilles had broken the baronial opposition, the seizure of the young Duke of York had deprived potential rebels of a rallying point, and now he was winning over the people.

To clinch his hold on the people, Richard launched a clever propaganda campaign aimed at the London middle class in particular. The Lord Mayor had gone to the city hall, no doubt to meet with other city officials, and Richard instructs Buckingham on just how he is to press the point. Richard says:

> *There, at your meetest vantage of the time,*
> *Infer the bastardy of Edward's children,*
> —Act III, scene v, lines 74–75

In actual fact, it does indeed seem that Richard organized a whispering campaign stressing the fact that Edward was in the habit of promising marriage to young women who seemed resistant to his blandishments. Lady Elizabeth Grey was fascinating enough and resistant enough to force him to carry out the pledge openly, so that she became Queen, but she was by no means the first to receive one.

Eleanor Butler, widowed daughter of John Talbot, Earl of Shrewsbury and hero of *Henry VI, Part One,* was one of those to whom Edward IV had promised marriage, the whispers went. Another of the sort was a Lady Elizabeth Lucy, and the whispers even went so far as to maintain that in this latter case, the King had actually gone through some private form of marriage to satisfy her, then had thrown her over. If this were so, then his later marriage to Lady Grey was invalid and his children by her were illegitimate.

There is no way of telling whether all this were true or not, and perhaps Richard would not have hesitated at this point in stretching the truth a bit, if that meant placing a strong King (himself) on the English throne.

. . . his hateful luxury

The people (particularly the comfortable and morally conservative London middle class) would be readier to believe these tales of Edward if they could be made to understand the nature of his lust. It would also serve to make the dead King more unpopular and his children less acceptable.

Thus, Richard tells Buckingham:

> *Moreover, urge his hateful luxury*
> *And bestial appetite in change of lust,*
> *Which stretched unto their servants, daughters, wives,*
> *Even where his raging eye or savage heart,*
> *Without control, lusted to make a prey.*
> —Act III, scene v, lines 80–84

This would well tie in with the punishment of Jane Shore, the most notorious of his mistresses. She was, after all, the wife of a middle-class Londoner, who had been cavalierly taken from her husband to serve the royal lust. Surely each London citizen could see himself in the role of enforced cuckold and would be offended. (And surely each citizen-wife might be offended at the thought of the danger she had undergone—or possibly at not having been picked by the roving royal eye.)

In any case, the whispering campaign was so well calculated and so cleverly pursued that public opinion veered rapidly from young Edward V to his warlike uncle.

. . . the issue was not his begot

Indeed, the later tales of the anti-Richard chroniclers make the whispering campaign reach a most monstrous pitch. Thus, Richard tells Buckingham:

> *Tell them, when that my mother went with child*
> *Of that insatiate Edward, noble York*
> *My princely father then had wars in France,*
> *And by true computation of the time*
> *Found that the issue was not his begot;*
>
> —Act III, scene v, lines 86–90

This is implausible on several counts.

First, it was unnecessary. It sufficed that Edward V and the young Duke of York were illegitimate; the illegitimacy of Edward IV would be in that case irrelevant. In fact, it would be worse, for it would cast a shadow on Richard himself. (If the mother produced one bastard, why not two?)

Second, it would involve an incredible slur on Richard's own mother, and even if he were monster enough to initiate such a slander, it would certainly offend his mother to the core. In fact, Richard, even in his role as Shakespearean villain, is a little nervous about his mother's reaction, for he tells Buckingham concerning the issue of his mother's infidelity:

> *Yet touch this sparingly, as 'twere far off,*
> *Because, my lord, you know my mother lives.*
>
> —Act III, scene v, lines 93–94

But in actual history, Richard III was always on good terms with his old mother and there is no evidence at all that she thought him a monster (as she constantly does in the play, making open reference to his vile character at every opportunity.)

Then, third, it was too easily countered. If York had thought his oldest son was a bastard, would he have placed such love and reliance on him in his final years, as he most notoriously did?

. . . to Doctor Shaw

With Buckingham gone about his business, Richard says:

> *Go Lovell, with all speed to Doctor Shaw.*
> *Go thou* [Catesby] *to Friar Penker.*
>
> —Act III, scene v, lines 103–4

The whispering campaign had to be brought out into the open and to a climax speedily indeed—before coronation time. On June 22, the day which at one time had been considered for the coronation, a friar, Dr. Ralph Shaw (a brother of the Lord Mayor), preached publicly on the bastardy of the children of Edward IV, telling the tale of the prior marriage. Friar Penker did his share in this as well.

The possible bastardy of a king, even if only through a quibbling technicality, would be a frightening thing at the time. An illegitimate king would be one who would not be king by the grace of God, and to make him a king would ensure evil for the kingdom.

. . . the brats of Clarence . . .

Left alone onstage, Richard says:

> *Now will I go to take some privy order*
> *To draw the brats of Clarence out of sight,*
> *And to give order that no manner person*
> *Have any time recourse unto the Princes.*
> —Act III, scene v, lines 106–9

The logic of events was forcing Richard further and further. If he were to become King, then the children of his dead brothers Edward IV and George of Clarence, all of whom had a better claim on the throne than himself, would have to become prisoners indeed, if only to keep them out of the exploiting hands of potential rebels.

All this was not unprecedented in English history, and indeed, in any land where the monarch does not have a clear title to the throne, those with possibly better titles are imprisoned or worse, almost as a matter of course. Thus, Henry IV, whose title to the crown was no better than Richard's, kept the young Earl of March, whose title was better, in prison throughout his reign.

Again, we are faced with acts that do not redound to Richard's credit, but (again) it was the habit of the time and Richard is merely a realistic politician, and not an unusual monster, for doing as others did.

. . . his contract by deputy . . .

The later chroniclers go into detail in recording how reluctant the citizens were to make Richard King and how many times and how crudely they had to be nudged into doing it. Thus, Buckingham returns to describe their failure to respond despite the fact that he had followed Richard's orders and mentioned

. . . his contract with Lady Lucy
And his contract by deputy in France;
—Act III, scene vii, lines 5–6

Here is something Richard had not specifically mentioned himself. Twenty years before, Warwick had gone to France to arrange a marriage between Edward IV and Bona of Savoy (see page II–650). The negotiations had broken down because of Edward's marriage to Lady Grey (something which had led eventually to the break between Edward and Warwick).

If, now, Edward had agreed to marry the Lady Bona, that too might be considered as good as a marriage in the eyes of God and it might suffice to render a later marriage invalid.

Despite all this, the commons remained unenthusiastic and Buckingham is forced to go through a long farce in which he begs Richard to become King while Richard (pretending to be deep in a pious discussion with two priests) first refuses and finally gives in almost tearfully. Buckingham at last cries out:

Then I salute you with this royal title:
Long live King Richard, England's worthy king!
—Act III, scene vii, lines 238–39

Actually, Richard was not as unpopular as the later historians pretended, or else his whispering campaign worked better than they cared to admit. On June 25, 1483, three days after the tale of the bastardy of the princes had been made the subject of open preaching, a gathering of nobles, clergy, and citizens declared Edward IV's marriage to Elizabeth Grey invalid on the grounds of previous marriage. The sons of the dead King were excluded from the throne and the crown was offered to Richard.

On June 26 he accepted and became Richard III, so that little Edward V's reign (with never a coronation) had lasted less than three months.

. . . to be crowned

Buckingham then says:

Tomorrow may it please you to be crowned?
—Act III, scene vii, line 241

Richard agrees. Actually, he was crowned not the day after his acceptance of the throne, but eleven days after, on July 6, 1483.

The coronation was carried through with great success and with no signs of trouble. Richard had obviously made up his mind to win over all hearts with liberality and geniality. Having won the throne by dubious means he might hope to drown that out in the memories of men by the deeds of a long, competent, and just reign. Surely Richard might easily hope to reign twenty years or so, since he was only thirty-one years old when he assumed the kingship, and as for competency, he had displayed that in every field. (As for precedent for living down a dubious beginning, think how Henry V's glamorous victories had utterly drowned out the memory of the rebellion and murder by which his father had gained the crown.)

Richard saw to it, for instance, that the widow and children of Hastings were well taken care of, and also the widow of Rivers. Even the widow of Oxford, an obdurate Lancastrian (see page II–656), was pensioned off.

He and his wife, Queen Anne, then proceeded to make a royal progress throughout England, and were greeted with enthusiasm wherever they went, particularly in the north, where his successful campaign against Scotland in recent years had made him very popular.

. . . live with Richmond . . .

The news that Richard has made himself King is brought to Queen Elizabeth when she tries, vainly, to see her sons in the Tower. With her is her one remaining son (by her earlier marriage), Dorset. She realizes that Richard's new position will make him all the more eager to prevent challenges from those who favor the deposed Edward V.

Distraught, she says to Dorset:

> If thou wilt outstrip death, go cross the seas
> And live with Richmond, from the reach of hell.
> —Act IV, scene i, lines 41–42

Richmond, whom we saw in *Henry VI, Part Three* as a youngster, lived in Brittany through all the years since Tewkesbury. At the time of the accession of Richard III he was a man of twenty-six, and round him all the Lancastrian remnant had rallied and, further, all those who had been Yorkists but who for one reason or another opposed Richard III.

Nor mother, wife . . .

Queen Elizabeth remembers Margaret's curse and urges Dorset to flee:

> Lest thou increase the number of the dead
> And make me die the thrall of Margaret's curse,
> Nor mother, wife, nor England's counted queen.
> —Act IV, scene i, lines 44–46

Actually, Dorset escaped Margaret's curse, which had specifically included him to be "by some unlooked accident cut off." He fled, as Elizabeth asked him to do, and he did eventually ally himself with Richmond. He was to live on to 1501, dying at last of natural causes at the age of fifty.

Queen Elizabeth, however, does indeed represent the fifth occasion on which Margaret's curse comes true. She was no longer Queen or wife, and although she remained a mother all her life (for several of her children, including her son Dorset, outlived her), she had already witnessed the death of one child, Lord Grey.

That part of Margaret's curse which says of Elizabeth, "Long mayst thou live to wail thy children's death / And see another, as I see thee now, / Decked in thy rights as thou art stalled in mine!" came only partly true. Elizabeth did live on for nine years after the death of her husband and did see another reigning as Queen. Before she died, however, she was to see her eldest daughter become Queen of England. There must have been some small compensation there.

. . . never yet one hour . . .

Richard's wife, the Lady Anne, now to be the Queen of England (whom Elizabeth will be forced to see "Decked in thy rights"), is also present. She bewails her own lot, remembering that once she had wished that Richard's wife would be made more miserable than she herself had been made by her first husband's death (see page II–689). She now realizes that she had cursed herself:

> For never yet one hour in his bed
> Did I enjoy the golden dew of sleep,
> But with his timorous dreams was still awaked.
> Besides, he hates me for my father Warwick,
> And will, no doubt, shortly be rid of me.
> —Act IV, scene i, lines 82–86

It's hard to tell what goes on between a man and wife, but there is no hard evidence to the fact that the marriage between Richard and Anne was anything but a reasonably happy one. At the time of his accession, he and Anne had been married nine years and had a seven-year-old son whom they dearly loved. Besides, no imputations of sexual immorality clung about Richard as they had about Edward IV; not even Shakespeare accuses Richard of lust.

Richard's son is not mentioned in the play, no doubt because there is no way of turning the existence of a loved son into another example of monstrosity on the part of the King.

The reference to Richard's timorous dreams harks back to Margaret's curse again, and is the sixth instance of its coming true. Margaret had said, with regard to Richard, "No sleep close up that deadly eye of thine, / Unless it be while some tormenting dream / Affrights thee. . . ."

. . . I wish the bastards dead

Richard is now King of England but he feels insecure even so. He begins to hint as much to Buckingham, his right-hand man, musing about the princes in the Tower—but Buckingham is suddenly obtuse. Finally Richard is forced to be direct, and raps out:

> *Shall I be plain? I wish the bastards dead,*
> *And I would have it suddenly performed.*
>
> —Act IV, scene ii, lines 18–19

Here approaches the climax of Richard's infamy in the eyes of the English chroniclers of the succeeding century, and the great puzzle of his reign even in legitimate history.

What happened to the princes? After Richard became King, they were never seen again, and within a month of his coronation the rumor began to go round that they were dead. Undoubtedly, they did die eventually, and the skeletons of two small bodies have been located in the Tower, bones that could very easily be their remains.

The question is: Did Richard III order them killed?

In English history, between the time of Henry II and Richard III, there were four times when a reigning monarch had been deposed and had lived on while his successor took over the robes of office. The first three cases were those of Edward II, Richard II, and Henry VI.

(1) Edward II was deposed on January 7, 1327, by a Parliament under the domination of his wife Isabella and her lover Mortimer. Edward's fifteen-year-old son succeeded as Edward III but for a time he was merely a puppet in the hands of his mother and her lover. In September 1327 Edward II was secretly murdered at the order of the ruling pair.

(2) Richard II was deposed on September 30, 1399, and his cousin succeeded as Henry IV. In February 1400 he was murdered, undoubtedly at the order of his successor (see page II–312).

In each of these two cases, the murder came in a matter of months. The reasoning, in each case, was undoubtedly that to leave a deposed monarch alive was merely to leave a center about which revolt could gather. Only the death of the ex-King could ensure the safety of his successor.

(3) Henry VI was, in a sense, deposed on March 4, 1461, when Edward IV was proclaimed King. Henry VI was not captured by the victorious Yorkists until July 1465, and he was then imprisoned in the Tower.

Edward IV did *not* follow precedent but instead let ex-King Henry live.

For five years Henry remained a live prisoner in the Tower and Edward's reward for this moderation was that when Warwick rebelled against him, he used Henry as the rallying point and restored the old King to the throne in October 1470. When Edward IV regained the throne through the battles of Barnet and Tewkesbury, he did not repeat his earlier mistake. Henry VI was killed at once.

Now Richard III was faced with a fourth situation of the sort. Edward V had reigned only a matter of weeks and had never been crowned, but surely he would serve as the center of any disaffection that might evolve. And if he died, his younger brother would succeed to that position. Richard might have felt that it was necessary for the good of the state that the princes die.

If, after those deaths, Richard then reigned long enough and well enough, they would be forgotten. It was never held against Edward III that his father had been murdered to get him the crown (though it was not Edward III himself who had been responsible). Henry IV had some trouble over the death of Richard II but he lived out a natural reign and his son and grandson succeeded him. Edward IV had a troubled reign before Henry's death and a relatively peaceful one after.

It might easily have been so with Richard too, except for one thing that made the situation unique. The ex-King and his brother were children. The enormity of killing two children was too great, and even arguments of state failed to cover the matter completely. If Richard III did order the young princes killed then even his apologists must shake their heads uneasily.

But did he?

. . . is Tyrrel

Since Buckingham, who has helped Richard at every step with his monstrous deeds (according to the Shakespeare version of history), seems to draw the line at killing the princes, Richard must find another tool.

He calls a Page and asks for some unscrupulous person, and wonder of wonders, the Page knows the very man. He says:

> His name, my lord, is Tyrrel.
>
> —Act IV, scene ii, line 40

Richard seems to have heard of the man only vaguely and when he meets him later, questions him to gauge his quality. This makes it appear as though Tyrrell is some obscure "gunman for hire."

Nothing of the sort! He was Sir James Tyrrell, a member of a distinguished family and an ardent fighter in the cause of York. He had been knighted in 1471 for his services and he served as Member of Parliament in 1477.

There is nothing in his later life to indicate he was a murderer. He served Richard III in various capacities, which would have been odd if he had supervised the murder of the princes. Richard would have wanted him out of the way lest he bear witness if that had been the case, and if Richard were the monster he was supposed to be, he would certainly have arranged to have Tyrrell killed.

He did not. Tyrrell survived Richard and lived to serve Richard's successor, Richmond (who was to reign as Henry VII). Henry VII had everything to gain from having people believe that Richard had had the princes killed, in order to plunge his predecessor into the depths of popular execration and shore up his own hold on the throne—yet he employed Tyrrell.

It was not till 1502, after Henry had reigned seventeen years, that Tyrrell fell into the royal bad graces. Tyrrell was accused of treason, arrested, and executed. Before he was executed, however, he confessed, or was forced to confess, or was reported to have confessed, that he had been placed in charge of the Tower on the day the princes were killed and that he had supervised that killing at the hands of two assassins.

Was the confession true? It is impossible to say. We can only state that it was awfully convenient for Henry VII.

There are some superapologists for Richard III who maintain that the princes were kept alive throughout Richard's short reign and were killed by Henry VII for the same reasons of state that might have motivated Richard. In that case Henry VII would badly need some sort of evidence to put the blame elsewhere.

But why Tyrrell? Why extract a confession from him rather than from someone else? Perhaps a little clever psychology was involved here.

Exactly one reigning king in English history was assassinated. That was William II, who died on August 2, 1100, with an arrow in his back during the course of a gay hunting party. It might have been an accident, but William was a hated man and everyone considered it an assassination. Exactly who did it is not certainly known either, but one man fled rather than face an inquest, and though he stoutly maintained his innocence (from abroad), common opinion made him the assassin.

And who was this man? His name was Walter Tirel and there were rumors that the family of Sir James Tyrrell was descended from this man. Could Henry VII have picked Tyrrell for the role of killer of the princes because he could rely on the populace associating this Tyrrell with the earlier Tirel?

In any case, the version put out in the report of the confession is the one that is used in Shakespeare's *Richard III* and is the one that is accepted by the world.

The boy is foolish . . .

Richard must take measures with respect to others than the young princes too. He says to Catesby:

> *Rumor it abroad*
> *That Anne my wife is very grievous sick;*
> *I will take order for her keeping close.*
> *Inquire me out some mean poor gentleman,*
> *Whom I will marry straight to Clarence' daughter.*
> *The boy is foolish, and I fear not him.*
>
> —Act IV, scene ii, lines 49–54

It is clear from this passage that (in Shakespeare's version) Richard plans to make sure his wife dies; presumably by poison. Actually, Richard's young son died in April 1484 at the age of eight, some nine months after his coronation, and not even the most extreme anti-Richard fanatic ever suggests he had anything to do with *that*. All reports indicate, rather, that Richard and Anne were overcome with grief and one might suspect it was that grief rather than any hypothetical poison that shortened the mother's life.

On March 16, 1485, Queen Anne died. She was only twenty-nine at the time of her death, but life was short in those days and there is absolutely no real evidence that Richard in any way hastened her death.

Naturally, Richard III would be concerned over Clarence's children, particularly the son, who had precedence over him to the throne, just as the royal princes had.

For that reason, Richard intends to marry the daughter, Margaret (who inherited her great-grandfather's title of Salisbury), to some individual sufficiently low in the social scale to make her and her descendants unacceptable as monarchs.

This is the sort of scheme suitable for the Richard of the legend, but it never happened. She was indeed married to a gentleman not very high in the social scale, one Sir Richard Pole, but this was not engineered by Richard III, but by his successor, Henry VII.

As for young Edward, Earl of Warwick, the only son of George of Clarence, he was kept in prison through Richard's reign. This may be regarded as a harsh act perhaps, but Richard's successor, Henry VII (made the epitome of nobility in this play), *also* kept him in prison.

Edward may have been mentally retarded, but do we know that for a fact? Shakespeare has to say so to account for the fact that monster Richard does not kill him. And why can't Richard be accused of killing him, since he is accused of so many other things he did not do? Because the actual truth of the death of Edward of Warwick is known. He was executed not at the order of Richard III, but at the order of his successor, Henry VII, in 1499.

. . . my brother's daughter

And why must Richard be rid of Anne? Through her and the Warwick connection she signified, Richard was more secure in the north than he would be without her. Actually, her death was a political blow to him as well as a personal loss.

This, however, is useless for the Richard legend. Some self-seeking motive must be found for her death, and he is made to think of the security of his throne. He says:

> I must be married to my brother's daughter,
> Or else my kingdom stands on brittle glass.
> —Act IV, scene ii, lines 59–60

The reasoning is clear. If he married Elizabeth, the oldest daughter of Edward IV, and had a son by her, that son would be a grandson of Edward IV. If Richard's own title to the throne was faulty, the son might nevertheless be accepted for his grandfather's sake.

Nevertheless, if he did so, Richard would be marrying his own niece and would be committing incest. The rumor that Richard planned to marry his niece actually spread itself after the death of the Queen. Richard, in actual history, was horrified at the suggestion and on April 11, 1485, before the Lord Mayor of London and a group of substantial citizens, he solemnly disavowed any such intention.

Just the same, the anti-Richard polemicists of the next reign pinned the intent of incest to him.

. . . the giving vein . . .

Buckingham now re-enters. He recalls that Richard has promised him the earldom of Hereford and now requests it. Richard is concerned with the threat of Richmond, recalling that Henry VI had prophesied he would someday be king (see page II–667). Buckingham keeps insisting on his reward.

Richard, angry at Buckingham's flinching away from the murder of the princes, finally flashes out at him:

> I am not in the giving vein today.
> —Act IV, scene ii, line 115

Thus, Richard reneges on his promise to his faithful henchman (faithful in all but the final demand) and forces him into the opposition. In a way, this is the seventh coming-true of Margaret's curse, for she had wished that Richard would "Thy friends suspect for traitors while thou liv'st."

But here too, Richard is maligned, for, as a matter of fact, he did turn over Hereford and its income to Buckingham within a week of his coronation.

To Brecknock . . .

The shocked Buckingham, left alone onstage, says:

> *Made I him king for this?*
> *O, let me think on Hastings, and be gone*
> *To Brecknock while my fearful head is on!*
> —Act IV, scene ii, lines 119–21

Brecknock is a county in southern Wales and its chief city is also called Brecknock (Brecon, in the modern version). The city is about 140 miles west of London, and it would seem that Buckingham feels the need of distance and wild country to keep him safe.

Actually, since Richard did indeed give him the promised reward, Buckingham did not flee for safety's sake. He fled because he turned against Richard and aimed to raise an army of sturdy Welshmen to help him overthrow the King.

Why? Nobody really knows, but that he did so because of his mistreatment at the hands of Richard is an invention of the later chroniclers.

Can it be that his experiences in helping Richard reach the throne may have put it in his mind that he was himself a descendant of Edward III and a third cousin, once removed, of Richard III? Can he have thought of the crown for himself?

Or if he did not think of this spontaneously, might it be that there existed those who put it in his mind in order to use him as a tool to overthrow Richard? The Bishop of Ely (see page II–714), who had been arrested along with Hastings a few months earlier, had been placed in the charge of Buckingham. Some suggest that the bishop artfully and eloquently fired the seeds of ambition in him and persuaded him to revolt.

We will probably never know the truth.

. . . tyrannous and bloody act . . .

Now the stage is cleared, and after an appropriate and ominous interval, Tyrrell enters, saying:

The tyrannous and bloody act is done,
The most arch [extreme] deed of piteous massacre
That ever yet this land was guilty of.
—Act IV, scene iii, lines 1–3

The princes, in other words, have been killed, and for the eighth time, Margaret's curse comes true. She had said to Queen Elizabeth: "Edward thy son, that now is Prince of Wales, / For Edward our son, that was Prince of Wales, / Die in his youth by like untimely violence!"

Now even if we set aside Tyrrell's confession in the next reign, the question still arises: Did the princes die in the Tower (no matter how and no matter by whom) during the reign of Richard III?

The answer, alas, is very likely in the affirmative. It is the one atrocity of which Richard III cannot be cleared.

The rumors of the princes' deaths arose in August 1483 and spread. By January 1484 the French government was broadcasting official accusations in this respect, anxious, as the French always were, to embarrass England politically. (Louis XI, see page II-651, died in 1483, his reign exactly spanning that of Edward IV, and was succeeded by his thirteen-year-old son, Charles VIII.)

It seems beyond question that had the princes been alive, Richard would have produced them as a matter of political necessity. Had they died of natural causes, Richard would at least have said so, even if he suspected that his enemies would refuse to believe him.

Instead, Richard stubbornly maintained a deep silence on the matter.

We can only suppose that Richard (perhaps after hearing of Buckingham's defection and fearing that the existence of the princes would accelerate the effect of the rebellion) hastily gave the order for their killing. If so, it must have greatly disturbed his conscience and perhaps he made no defense because he felt that none could be made. Perhaps he even felt that he deserved the obloquy heaped upon him. It is even possible to wonder if he felt (in the context of his times) that the death of his own son, nine months later, was a punishment for his deed.

The murder of the princes was a mistake as well as a crime. The atrocity tale did more to stir up rebellion and keep it alive than the living princes would have been able to do. What's more, the fact of that murder, unrefuted by Richard and perhaps unrefutable, made the public ready to believe all the other libels placed on poor Richard's head by his enemies in later reigns. It was possible to make Richard a monster and to attribute to him a hundred vile deeds of which he was innocent because of this one horrible act of which (whatever his motives and however he may have justified it to himself) he was probably guilty.

. . . backed with the hardy Welshmen

In Shakespeare's version, no sooner does Richard learn of the death of the princes than he receives word of Buckingham's defection. (In real history, it seems possible—though we have no evidence—that it may have been the other way around.)

Ratcliffe enters, saying:

> *Bad news, my lord. Morton* [the Bishop of Ely] *is fled to Richmond,*
> *And Buckingham, backed with the hardy Welshmen,*
> *Is in the field, and still his power increaseth.*
>
> —Act IV, scene iii, lines 46–48

By October 1483 it was plain that Buckingham was not only meditating rebellion in Wales, but was actually organizing it. Richard declared him a traitor, and on October 18, 1483, Buckingham took the field and led his Welsh army out of Wales and into England.

. . . the waning of mine enemies

The march of events is interrupted by a long scene involving the women of the play. Old Queen Margaret enters first, gloating over the manner in which the Yorkists are destroying each other. She says:

> *Here in these confines slily have I lurked*
> *To watch the waning of mine enemies.*
>
> —Act IV, scene iv, lines 3–4

This is a good trick for her. Not only had she spent the last years of the reign of Edward IV in France, so that she could not have appeared on the scene in any part of *Richard III*, but she had died in 1482, a lonely, miserable, embittered woman of fifty-three. She had died, in other words, a year before Richard III had come to the throne and too soon to see any of the fulfillments of the curse attributed to her in this play.

She is joined by her old rival, ex-Queen Elizabeth, and by her even older rival, the Dowager Duchess of York, and all three bewail their miseries. In fact, ex-Queen Elizabeth finds so much in common with ex-Queen Margaret as to say to her:

> *O thou well skilled in curses, stay awhile*
> *And teach me how to curse mine enemies!*
>
> —Act IV, scene iv, lines 116–17

Thus, Margaret's curse comes true a ninth time, for she had said to Elizabeth that "The day will come that thou shalt wish for me / To help thee curse this poisonous bunch-backed toad."

Richard himself enters, however, and manages to persuade (or to seem to have persuaded) ex-Queen Elizabeth to agree to his marriage to her daughter, the Princess Elizabeth, exactly as, at the beginning of the play, he had talked Lady Anne into marriage.

It should be repeated, though, that there is no historical evidence that such a marriage was contemplated.

. . . a puissant navy . . .

But now Ratcliffe arrives with more bad news. He says:

> Most mighty sovereign, on the western coast
> Rideth a puissant navy; to our shores
> Throng many doubtful hollow-hearted friends,
> Unarmed, and unresolved to beat them back.
> 'Tis thought that Richmond is their admiral;
>> —Act IV, scene iv, lines 433–37

Henry Tudor, Earl of Richmond, had been seeking help from his continental hosts for years. Cautiously, they had avoided committing themselves. Only now, with Buckingham in rebellion, did it seem worth the gamble to help Richmond do what Bolingbroke had once done with similar help (see page II–286).

Indeed, Richmond's attempted invasion was designed to co-operate with Buckingham's rebellion, for as Ratcliffe says concerning the ships:

> . . . there they hull [drift] expecting but the aid
> Of Buckingham to welcome them ashore.
>> —Act IV, scene iv, lines 438–39

. . . the Duke of Norfolk

Richard must take speedy action. He cries out:

> Some light-foot friend post to the Duke of Norfolk:
>> —Act IV, scene iv, line 440

The Duke of Norfolk was John Howard, first of that family to bear the title. His mother, however, was a daughter of Thomas Mowbray, the Duke of Norfolk who had fought that famous non-duel with Bolingbroke (see page II–273).

Norfolk was an ardent Yorkist, and in 1483, after Richard's accession, he was made Duke and Earl Marshal of England. He was thus the commander of Richard's army in the absence of the King himself.

. . . never will be false

Richard feels harried from all sides. He turns his mistrustful eyes on Lord Stanley, Earl of Derby and stepfather of Richmond, but Stanley says:

> Most mighty sovereign,
> You have no cause to hold my friendship doubtful.
> I never was nor never will be false.
>
> —Act IV, scene iv, lines 491-93

This is rather ironic, since Stanley was a twister and turner who never hesitated to be false to anyone, and in this way ended up always on top. What's more, despite his pious assertion, he was to be specifically false to Richard.

Richard, however, lets himself be partly convinced and asks only a hostage. He says:

> Go then and muster men; but leave behind
> Your son George Stanley.
>
> —Act IV, scene iv, lines 494-95

How could Richard, so sharp, so suspicious (in Shakespeare's version), accept the word of so confirmed a trimmer as Stanley?

But Stanley was not the only one to benefit from Richard's leniency. There were a number of disaffected Yorkists who were plotting secretly (as Stanley was) to betray Richard to Richmond, and the King seemed to detect none of them. One might almost think the killing of the princes had broken the King's spirit. He was reluctant to shed further blood.

Buckingham's army is dispersed . . .

News of continuing defection continues to come in from all directions, but then, suddenly, a Third Messenger arrives, who says:

> . . . by sudden floods and fall of waters
> Buckingham's army is dispersed and scattered,
> And he himself wand'red away alone,
>
> —Act IV, scene iv, lines 510-12

Buckingham's rebellion turned out to be abortive. His army, marching eastward, found the Wye and Severn rivers in flood and could not cross them. The few days' delay was fatal. The initial fervor of his men waned; the floods looked like heavenly disapproval and a bad omen; and the army began to disperse.

Without a single passage of arms, Buckingham found himself defeated and a fugitive.

The same bad weather also aborted Richmond's attempt to land men to co-operate with Buckingham, and a Fourth Messenger arrives to say:

> *The Britain* [Breton] *navy is dispersed by tempest.*
> —Act IV, scene iv, line 521

It was in Brittany that Richmond was living. Brittany was then under Francis II, its last semi-independent duke. He died in 1488 (five years after Richmond's abortive invasion), leaving a daughter, Anne, as his only heir. She married Charles VIII, the French King, and since then Brittany has remained an integral part of France.

To Salisbury . . .

Buckingham as fugitive was no more successful than Buckingham as rebel leader. In comes Catesby to say:

> *My liege, the Duke of Buckingham is taken.*
> —Act IV, scene iv, line 531

With grim satisfaction, Richard says:

> *Someone take order Buckingham be brought*
> *To Salisbury . . .*
> —Act IV, scene iv, lines 537–38

Richard had already reached Salisbury on his way to deal with the western rebellion. Buckingham asked for an audience with Richard, but the King refused to see his erstwhile friend and ordered him executed forthwith.

As Buckingham is led to execution, he says bitterly:

> *This is the day which in King Edward's time*
> *I wished might fall on me when I was found*
> *False to his children and his wife's allies.*
> —Act V, scene i, lines 13–15

He had sworn this at the time when the dying King Edward had attempted to reconcile the factions at the court, and he had then said that if he broke the oath, "God punish me / With hate in those where I expect most love!" He remembers also Margaret's curse, saying:

> Thus Margaret's curse falls heavy on my neck:
>
>   —Act V, scene i, line 25

Margaret had warned him to remember her words "another day, / When he [Richard] shall split thy very heart with sorrow." This is the tenth occasion on which her prophecies come true.

On November 2, 1483, Buckingham was executed. He was twenty-nine years old.

. . . landed at Milford

With Buckingham's death, the six months of confusion following the death of Edward IV came to an end, and Richard III entered a period of calm.

It was during this period that he labored to outlive the irregularities of the beginning. For instance, he went on to display his enlightened rule when Parliament was called into session. (There was, as it turned out, only a single Parliament under Richard III.) It met on January 23, 1484, and a large number of laws against unfair taxations and against too great an ease of arrest were passed.

The laws that were passed, all of them liberal, were published in English, rather than Latin, for the first time, so that all men could understand them and not scholars only. As another way of making them more available to all, they were printed. Indeed, Richard went out of his way to encourage the growth of printing in the land.

It seems quite reasonable to suppose that if Richard had only had a chance to live out a normal life span, if his son had lived, if foreign intrigue against him had ceased, he would have ended as one of the best and most popular kings the land had ever had. But it was not to be.

In this period of intended peace and justice, his son and wife died, and disaffected Yorkists continued to intrigue with Richmond.

Richard III endeavored to persuade Duke Francis of Brittany to hand over Richmond, but Richmond managed to make his way into France proper and there to find a still more powerful patron in the French government.

The French were most eager to make use of Richmond. Richard III was an able warrior and the most determined monarch England had seen since Henry V. He had objected to his brother's pusillanimous treaty with Louis XI (see page II–688) and there was reason to think that he might want to invade France once again, once his domestic troubles were settled. It was up to France, therefore, to see that those domestic troubles continued.

With French help, Richmond was finally ready to make another move, and Shakespeare skips a nearly two-year interval by having the announcement of that move made by Catesby in the same speech in which he announces Buckingham is taken (and immediately after an earlier Messenger had stated that Richmond's fleet had been dispersed by storms and had returned to Brittany—that was the first attempt).

Catesby says:

> . . . the Earl of Richmond
> Is with a mighty power landed at Milford
> —Act IV, scene iv, lines 532–33

Richmond, having left Harfleur on August 1, 1485, landed at Milford Haven (see page II–67) on August 7. Milford Haven, a Welsh port, was a good place for a landing for Richmond, who was a Tudor and therefore the descendant of a Welsh family. It was to be taken for granted that the Welsh would flock to the standards of a Welshman.

. . . Elizabeth her daughter

Meanwhile, Stanley, who is busy at his treason, is sending a message to Richmond, explaining that the fact his son is being held as hostage inhibits his actions. He says to the go-between:

> . . . say that the Queen hath heartily consented
> He should espouse Elizabeth her daughter.
> —Act IV, scene v, lines 7–8

It would appear, then, that ex-Queen Elizabeth had deceived Richard (in the play). Having seemed to concede to his demand that she agree to let him marry her daughter, she is, instead, conniving to have Richmond do so.

The marriage, as it happens, was a political necessity for Richmond. He was depending for much of his strength, not on Lancastrians, but on dissident Yorkists. These Yorkists were opposed to Richard but were not entirely overwhelmed with delight at the thought of a Lancastrian king. By agreeing to marry Princess Elizabeth, Richmond is making it possible for his son and successor to be a grandson of Edward IV. Richmond's son would then be Yorkist as well as Lancastrian and the long feud could finally be buried. And this, in fact, is what really happened.

The person to whom Stanley is talking is Sir Christopher Urswick, a chaplain who is confessor to Margaret Beaufort, mother of Richmond and wife of Stanley. In history, he did, in fact, help to carry on the negotiations that led to the marriage of Richmond and Princess Elizabeth.

Oxford . . .

Stanley asks Sir Christopher concerning the men who have lined up behind Richmond and Sir Christopher says:

> *Sir Walter Herbert, a renowned soldier;*
> *Sir Gilbert Talbot, Sir William Stanley,*
> *Oxford, redoubted Pembroke, Sir James Blunt,*
> *And Rice ap Thomas . . .*
>
> —Act IV, scene v, lines 12–15

Of these, several are worth comment.

Sir Walter Herbert was the son of William Herbert, Earl of Pembroke. The elder Herbert had appeared briefly in *Henry VI, Part Three,* was captured at the Battle of Edgecote (see page II–663), and was later executed by the Lancastrians. Despite this family grudge against the Lancastrians, Sir Walter fights for Richmond.

Sir William Stanley is the brother of the Stanley to whom Sir Christopher is speaking.

Oxford is the Lancastrian leader of *Henry VI, Part Three* who fought at Barnet and who eventually led the last forlorn attempt at Lancastrian invasion several years after Tewkesbury (see page II–674). He was imprisoned near Calais but eventually managed to escape and join Richmond.

Sir James Blunt is the grandson of Sir Walter Blunt, who appeared in *Henry IV, Part One* (see page II–373) and who died at the Battle of Shrewsbury.

From Tamworth thither . . .

Now at last Richmond appears on the scene. He is already in the center of England. He stops his march to address his men, and referring to Richard, says:

> *. . . this foul swine*
> *Is now even in the center of this isle,*
> *Near to the town of Leicester, as we learn.*
> *From Tamworth thither is but one day's march.*
>
> —Act V, scene ii, lines 12–13

Richmond, having landed in Milford Haven, marched northeastward through Wales. He was not opposed, but neither was he vigorously supported by people who undoubtedly expected him to be defeated by the warlike Richard.

When Richmond emerged from Wales and took Shrewsbury (see page II–360) without a fight on August 15, 1485, he had only four thousand men. From Shrewsbury, he marched about forty-five miles eastward to Tamworth (a town some fifteen miles northeast of modern Birmingham).

It was not till a week after Richmond's landing that Richard learned of the invasion. He marched as rapidly as he could to Leicester, twenty-five miles east of Tamworth, and by August 20 the two armies were facing each other. Richard's army was larger and better than Richmond's and Richard was far the better general.

On that basis alone, one would have expected Richard to win.

. . . here in Bosworth field

Richard at least acts confident. When he appears on the scene, he says:

> Here pitch our tent, even here in Bosworth field.
> My Lord of Surrey, why look you so sad?
> —Act V, scene iii, lines 1–2

The two armies met for actual combat in a field twelve miles west of Leicester and only three miles from the small town of Market Bosworth, which gave its name to the battle—renowned for being the last of the generation-long Wars of the Roses.

"My Lord of Surrey" is Thomas Howard, Earl of Surrey and son of John of Norfolk, who is also on the scene.

. . . Lord Northumberland

Surrey denies being downhearted, and indeed, he and his father are to fight valiantly for Richard. What Richard seems to be unaware of, however, is that some of his officers have no intention of fighting for him. There is the case of Stanley, of course, but he is not the only one.

At one point Richard asks of Ratcliffe:

> Saw'st thou the melancholy Lord Northumberland?
> —Act V, scene iii, line 68

Northumberland is the Henry Percy whose titles were temporarily given to John Neville (see page II–659) in the early part of the reign of Edward IV.

Northumberland is reported to Richard as laboring to keep up the army's morale, but he had a right to be melancholy. He was playing a double game, having sold out to Richmond, and such games are hard to play on the field of battle.

What's more, Richmond is doing his best to avail himself of the treasonable intentions of Richard's officers. He tries to establish communication with Stanley, for instance, saying to one of his own officers:

> Sweet Blunt, make some good means to speak with him
> And give him from me this most needful note.
>
> —Act V, scene iii, lines 40–41

"Jockey of Norfolk . . .

Nor can it be that Richard is entirely unwarned of all this. After the night is over (a night during which Shakespeare has all the ghosts of people whom Richard has supposedly slain appear to him in a nightmare—remember Margaret's curse—and curse him, while blessing Richmond), the Duke of Norfolk finds a note in his tent. He brings it to Richard and it reads:

> *"Jockey of Norfolk, be not so bold,*
> *For Dickon thy master is bought and sold."*
>
> —Act V, scene iii, lines 305–6

("Jockey" is a diminutive of John, "Dickon" of Richard.)

The note tells the truth, but Richard curtly dismisses it as merely enemy propaganda, designed to hurt morale.

. . . he doth deny to come

One might suppose that Richard is blind to possible treason because in his heart he wants to lose. The death of son and wife have deprived him of hope for the future, the killing of the young princes must surely lie heavy on his heart, the Elysium that Shakespeare represents him as thinking is to be found within the circuit of the crown (see page II–634) eludes him, and in his short reign all his attempts to be the just and good king have failed to keep the Hydra-head of rebellion from erupting.

Nevertheless, when the Battle of Bosworth opens on August 22, 1485, Richard fights with all his old-time generalship and bravery. As Catesby reports to Norfolk:

> *The King enacts more wonders than a man,*
>
> —Act V, scene iv, line 2

But it does no good. At a crucial moment, when Stanley is supposed to hurl his division into the fray, a Messenger arrives, saying:

> My lord, he [Stanley] *doth deny to come.*
> —Act V, scene iii, line 344

Richard furiously orders Stanley's hostage son decapitated, but in the heat of battle there is not time.

There is worse to come (though the details are not mentioned in the play). When Richard's army was counterattacked in flank, Northumberland's men could easily have swept that thrust aside, but Northumberland stood idle also.

If, of Richard's army, those who actually fought are counted, then it was Richmond who had the outnumbering forces after all.

. . . My kingdom for a horse

Richard, fighting like a giant, is nevertheless unhorsed and comes staggering onto the scene with what is (for some reason) one of the most famous lines in Shakespeare's plays. He cries:

> A horse! A horse! My kingdom for a horse!
> —Act V, scene iv, line 7

Actually, Richard might have survived. He could easily have escaped the field. Earlier kings had survived lost battles; even his brother, Edward IV, fled before Warwick and survived to return.

Catesby says to Richard:

> Withdraw, my lord; I'll help you to a horse.
> —Act V, scene iv, line 8

Richard, however, refused. He would not run to take up a life in exile as his brother had done and as Richmond had done.

We might easily imagine that he was tired of it all; tired of the politics and executions that had gotten him his crown; tired of the unending labors to win a popularity that would not come; tired of continual treason; and (perhaps) tired of the conscience he must live with over the matter of the princes.

. . . the bloody dog . . .

In the play, Richard and Richmond meet and fight (Shakespeare always decides battles by Homeric single combat) and Richard falls. Richmond says in triumph:

> *The day is ours; the bloody dog is dead.*
> —Act V, scene v, line 2

Actually, the battle came to an end when Richard, despairing, deliberately charged into a dense group of enemies, crying "Treason, treason." He hacked away, killing a number, before he was pulled off his horse and killed in his turn, at the age of thirty-two.

Richmond at once assumed the crown and became Henry VII of England.

Richard III was the last Plantagenet to rule in England, the last King who could trace his ancestry back through a continuing series of males to Henry II of England. One Plantagenet alone remained in existence and that was young Edward, son of George of Clarence, still in the Tower. This grandson of Richard of York, and great-great-great-grandson of Edward III, was to remain in prison under Henry VII as well.

. . . the White Rose and the Red

But the English people no longer worried about Plantagenets. More than anything else they wanted peace. What kept Henry VII on his throne, more than anything else (for he was a hard, cold, avaricious man, not at all the saintly character pictured by Shakespeare), was the English longing for peace at last.

Henry VII caters to this desire when he says:

> *We will unite the White Rose and the Red.*
> —Act V, scene v, line 19

By this he means his marriage to Elizabeth of York, daughter of King Edward IV. He goes on to say:

> *O, now let Richmond and Elizabeth,*
> *The true succeeders of each royal house,*
> *By God's fair ordinance conjoin together!*
> *And let their heirs, God, if thy will be so,*
> *Enrich the time to come with smooth-faced peace,*
> —Act V, scene v, lines 29–33

Henry VII eventually married Elizabeth on January 18, 1486, half a year after Bosworth, at which time she was twenty-one years old. The marriage lasted for seventeen years, since Elizabeth died in 1503. In that time, though, she bore Henry a daughter and two sons. The younger son, born on June 28, 1491, eventually succeeded to the throne as Henry VIII, and it was he who represented the union of White Rose and Red, for he was the son of Henry VII and the grandson of Edward IV.

SCOTLAND

Flodden

HENRY VIII

N

York

ENGLAND

Stoke

Leicester

Kimbolton

Ampthill

Ipswich

Dunstable

London

Calais Ardres
Guines

EMPIRE

Field of the
Cloth of Gold

Guinegate

FRANCE

0   Miles   100

40

The Famous History of the Life of

KING HENRY THE EIGHTH

SHAKESPEARE had written his last pay dealing with fifteenth-century English history in 1599. It was *Henry V*. With that, he had completed the eight plays which carried English history from 1399 to 1485, through all the turbulent quarrels over the succession that had begun with the deposition of Richard II.

That stretch of history from the death of Thomas of Gloucester in Calais to the death of Richard of Gloucester at Bosworth represented a neat section of English history, with a clear beginning, a clear ending, and a glorified peak at the Battle of Agincourt. It even had a moral (the evils of deposing a rightful king, even under provocation) and, above all, it supplied a happy ending, for after the Battle of Bosworth, England moved into an era which was, on the whole, one of peace and reconciliation.

Having completed his treatment of the fifteenth century, then, it was reasonable for Shakespeare to move on to his tragedies, his Roman plays, his bitter comedies. (One might also speculate that after 1599, with the tragedy of the revolt and execution of the Earl of Essex that soon followed (see page I–120), Shakespeare lost his taste for English history as a theme of drama. It had come too close to home.)

Yet one historical play remains to be treated; one more attempt to deal with English history. That was *Henry VIII*. It dealt with a period later than that of any other historical drama Shakespeare had written and it came at the very close of the dramatist's career. It was produced about 1612 or 1613 and many scholars do not consider it pure Shakespeare. There is a strong feeling that, like *The Two Noble Kinsmen* (which was written at about the same time), *Henry VIII* was worked at in collaboration with Fletcher (see page I–53).

Nevertheless, *Henry VIII* sounds considerably more Shakespearean than *The Two Noble Kinsmen* does, and the former is usually attributed to Shakespeare alone on the title page. What's more, *Henry VIII*, unlike *The Two Noble Kinsmen,* is usually included among editions of Shakespeare's collected works.

The events depicted in *Henry VIII* begin in 1520, so that thirty-five years have passed since the conclusion of *Richard III*. The Wars of the Roses were ended with the Battle of Bosworth and the policy of Henry VII (the "Richmond" of *Richard III*) was devoted almost entirely to the prevention of any new eruption. His aims, in other words, were just those of Richard III—peace and a strong monarchy—but Henry succeeded where Richard had failed.

Henry VII followed a deliberate policy of reconciliation. He indulged in no indiscriminate executions. He respected Parliament, went through all the necessary forms, had himself crowned on October 30, 1485, and fulfilled his promise to the anti-Richard Yorkists who had allied themselves with him by marrying Elizabeth of York (the daughter of Edward IV) on January 18, 1486.

In addition, he strengthened his own position by beginning a deliberate policy of vilification of Richard III. This successfully dimmed the possibilities of popular support for Yorkist pretenders and, in the long run, worked so well (thanks to More's biography of Richard, see page II–616, and, most of all, to Shakespeare's own play concerning him) that poor Richard was ineradicably branded for all time as the unspeakable monster he most certainly was not.

Finally, Henry VII was careful to move ruthlessly against anyone who might just possibly serve as a Yorkist rallying point. Thus, he continued to keep Edward of Warwick (the son of George of Clarence, and the last living Plantagenet) in prison.

There was another Yorkist who, however, was free and represented perhaps a greater danger than Warwick. He was John de la Pole, Earl of Lincoln, and the son of a sister of Edward IV and Richard III. When Richard's own young son had died, it was John of Lincoln, his nephew, whom he named as his successor.

John of Lincoln joined an abortive revolt led by one Lambert Simnel, who pretended to be Edward of Warwick escaped from imprisonment. The revolt was not a dangerous one and was quickly crushed at a battle at Stoke (about 110 miles north of London) in 1487. John of Lincoln was killed at the battle. Lovell (who had been one of Richard III's chief advisers, see page II–715) was also fighting on the Yorkist side and was seen fleeing from the lost battle, but was never seen again thereafter.

Simnel had been financed by Margaret of Burgundy, the dowager duchess, who was another sister of Edward IV and Richard III's (see page II–642). She remained a bitter-to-the-end opponent of the Lancastrians, a kind of mirror image of that other Margaret, the one of Anjou.

Margaret of Burgundy supported any movement against Henry VII of whatever kind. She must have known Simnel was an imposter, for instance, but that didn't matter to her. She also supported one Perkin Warbeck, who pretended to be Richard, Duke of York, Edward IV's younger son (see page II–705), and claimed to have escaped from the Tower.

Warbeck made a better try at it than Simnel had done, but in the end he was defeated and captured too. He was imprisoned in the Tower and hanged in 1499. In that same year, Edward of Warwick was also executed on general principles and the last Plantagenet was gone.

As for Margaret of Burgundy, she died in 1503 and the Yorkist cause vanished forever.

These Yorkist plots, which thus enlivened the life and reign of Henry VII, affected the English people little, and Henry, a shrewd and avaricious man, devoted himself to building up the English treasury. When he died in 1509 England was prosperous, rich, peaceful, and ready to embark on its career of world empire. It was, in fact, during the reign of Henry VII that the first English exploration of the New World began. An expedition under the leadership of the Italian explorer Giovanni Caboto (better known in English as John Cabot) discovered Newfoundland and was the first to touch the American mainland itself.

In addition to crushing the Yorkist cause by force and policy, Henry adopted it and made it part of his own dynasty. When he died, his son, another Henry, succeeded to the throne as Henry VIII. He was not only the son of Henry VII and therefore a descendant of John of Gaunt, and a Lancastrian, but he was the son of Elizabeth of York and therefore the grandson of Edward IV. In the person of Henry VIII, the houses of Lancaster and York, the Red Rose and the White, were combined.

As though to make that quite evident, Henry VIII, who became King at the age of eighteen, seemed to be Edward IV reborn. He was tall and strong, loved to wrestle and to write love ballads too. He was fair-haired and handsome, learned and affable. It is no wonder that he was enormously popular with the people—and indeed, he remained so throughout his long reign, even though his handsomeness degenerated into piglike obesity and his affability became an almost psychotic cruelty. He ended by being the sadistic tyrant in reality that Richard III was only in fable.

At the time *Henry VIII* opens, Henry VIII had been on the throne of England for eleven years.

Good morrow . . .

As the play opens in the antechamber of the palace in London, three men enter. One speaks, saying:

> *Good morrow, and well met. How have ye done*
> *Since last we saw* [each other] *in France?*
> —Act I, scene i, lines 1–2

The speaker is Edward Stafford, 3rd Duke of Buckingham, the eldest son of the Buckingham who played so important a role in *Richard III* (see page II–692), first helping that King gain the throne and then almost at once moving into revolt.

When Henry of Buckingham was executed under Richard, his son Edward (who is now speaking) was only five years old. When Richard III was defeated and killed, two years later, the new monarch, Henry VII, restored his father's title and lands to young Edward.

By the time Henry VIII succeeded to the throne, Buckingham was high in favor and one of Henry's first acts as King was to make Buckingham Lord High Constable (essentially a commander in chief of the armed forces), a post which his ancestors had held.

. . . a fresh admirer

The person addressed by Buckingham replies:

> *I thank your Grace,*
> *Healthful, and ever since a fresh admirer*
> *Of what I saw there.*

> —Act I, scene i, lines 2–4

These words are spoken by Thomas Howard, 2nd Duke of Norfolk. He is the son of "Jockey of Norfolk" (see page II–731), who was Richard's chief supporter at the Battle of Bosworth and who died at that battle. Thomas was himself at the battle and is referred to in *Richard III* by his earlier title of Earl of Surrey (see page II–737).

Thomas Howard was badly wounded at Bosworth but survived and was kept in prison till 1489. He was then released by Henry VII (who strove to conciliate where he could) and was restored to the lower title of Earl of Norfolk (not Duke). Thomas remained a loyal servant of the Tudors thereafter.

In 1513, during the reign of Henry VIII, Thomas Howard led the English army to a great victory over the Scots at Flodden, and in 1514 he was made Duke of Norfolk, thus gaining his father's full title at last.

Those suns of glory . . .

But what happened in France that caused Norfolk to be such an admirer of the events in retrospect? Buckingham wants to know too, for as he says:

> *An untimely ague*
> *Stayed me a prisoner in my chamber when*
> *Those suns of glory, those two lights of men,*
> *Met in the vale of Andren.*

> —Act I, scene i, lines 4–7

It was not only in England that a promising new king had ascended the throne. All of Western Europe was breaking out of the Middle Ages and into the full light of the Renaissance, and, as though to mark that, a number of important new young monarchs appeared on the scene.

In France, Charles VIII (see page II–729) had been on the throne at the time of the Battle of Bosworth. He had gone on, after he came of age, to fight wars in Italy that brought him into conflict with Germans and Spaniards (instead of with those traditional French enemies, the English). He died in 1498 with no sons and was succeeded by his second cousin, once removed, who reigned as Louis XII, and who was the son of the old age of Charles of Orléans, the loser at the Battle of Agincourt (see page II–506).

Louis XII continued the Italian wars and the fighting with the Spaniards and Germans. When he died in 1515, also without a son, his first cousin (once removed) succeeded as Francis I. Francis was twenty-one years old at this time, three years younger than Henry VIII.

Then, in 1516, a young man named Charles (only sixteen) began to inherit vast territories. Through his mother he was grandson of Ferdinand and Isabella of Spain, and when Ferdinand died, he became Charles I of Spain. When his own father, Maximilian, died, he also inherited territories in Burgundy and Germany. (Charles was great-great-grandson of Philip the Good, see page II–514.) Finally, in 1519, he was elected Holy Roman Emperor and was Charles V in this respect. It is as Emperor Charles V that he is remembered in European history.

Thus, in 1520, when *Henry VIII* opens, Western Europe is dominated by three young monarchs: Emperor Charles V, aged twenty; King Francis I of France, aged twenty-six; and King Henry VIII of England, aged twenty-nine.

For a whole generation now, the French had been fighting Germans and Spaniards in Italy, and now those Germans and Spaniards were united under Charles V. The great feud between France and England that had filled the fifteenth century had now been replaced by a greater feud between France and the Empire-plus-Spain that was to fill the sixteenth century.

England was, at this time, far weaker than either France or the Empire in extent of territory, in population, and in wealth, but she was important as a makeweight. By adding her own force to one side or the other she might well make victory certain for the side she favored.

At first, England, unable to free itself of its ancient enmity to France, automatically sided against her. In 1513 Henry VIII sent an army to Calais, and once again, as in the days of Edward III and Henry V, the island nation made ready to invade France. At that time, Louis XII was still King of France, Maximilian was still Emperor, and Ferdinand II was still King of Spain.

Henry VIII was no Henry V, however, and all he could do was to lay siege (and inefficient siege at that) to a few nearby French towns.

On August 16, 1513, the French prepared to get provisions into one of the besieged towns under cover of a mock battle. For the purpose, they lined up their army at Guinegate, about thirty miles southeast of Calais. (This is now in French territory, but at that time it was in Flanders, which was part of the Empire.)

As the French hoped, the English took the bait and prepared for battle. The French charged, managed to get supplies into the town, and once that was done, quickly retired. The English, however, pursued with far more energy than had been anticipated, and the French retirement was changed into a flight. Panic struck the French and the English found themselves with a considerable victory and with many prisoners, even though hardly a shot had been fired on either side. It came to be known as the "Battle of the Spurs" because of the anxiety with which the French had spurred their horses.

On September 9, only three weeks later, came the great victory over France's ally, Scotland, at Flodden.

This double triumph gave Henry VIII all the glory he wanted, and when his allies, following their own interests, seemed inclined to make peace with France, Henry felt no need for carrying on the campaign singlehanded. He therefore made a peace of his own with Louis XII, in 1514.

It is not surprising, then, that when Francis I and Charles V, as new monarchs, prepared to continue the feud of their predecessors, both should court the young English monarch who had done so well in 1513.

Francis won a spectacular propaganda victory when he persuaded Henry to come to France for what we would today call a "summit conference."

Toward the end of May 1520, Henry VIII set out on his peaceful mission to France, and during June of that year, amid fabulous pageantry, Henry VIII and Francis I met in the valley of Andren, about eight miles south of Calais.

It was these two kings to whom Buckingham refers, hyperbolically, as "Those suns of glory, those two lights of men."

'Twixt Guynes and Arde

Norfolk describes the occasion, saying:

> 'Twixt Guynes and Arde [they met].
> I was then present; saw them salute on horseback;
>
> —Act I, scene i, lines 7–8

Guynes and Arde (actually Guînes and Ardres) are two towns, five miles apart, the former west of the valley of Andren, the latter east. Guînes had been given over to the English forces, Ardres to the French.

On June 7, 1520, the two monarchs, lightly attended, rode out into the valley between to embrace and display their trust in each other.

Although in this dialogue Buckingham complains of having been confined to his quarters by illness, and Norfolk acts as though he had been an eyewitness, Shakespeare has reversed the actual roles. The truth is that Buckingham was at the festivities, the most prominent Englishman there next to the King himself. It was Norfolk who was absent. He, as victor of Flodden, was in England serving as Henry's deputy during the latter's stay in France.

All clinquant, all in gold . . .

The English and French, at this meeting, vied each with the other to impress with outer appearance; to show by visible splendor the power and glory of their respective kingdoms. As Norfolk says:

> *Today the French,*
> *All clinquant* [glittering], *all in gold, like heathen gods,*
> *Shone down the English; and tomorrow they* [the English]
> *Made Britain India: every man that stood*
> *Showed like a mine.*
> —Act I, scene i, lines 18–22

In fact, such was the elaborateness of the costume and decorations at that meeting that the place has come down in history as "the Field of the Cloth of Gold."

. . . Bevis was believed

Nor was it show only. Francis labored to keep Henry in good humor, for the French King needed Henry more than Henry needed him. Francis himself had a long nose and it was obvious that Henry was far more handsome, but the Frenchman did not mind that and deliberately let his fellow monarch shine. Francis also took the calculated risk of going unarmed into the English camp and ordered his men to fraternize freely without regard for possible treachery. The English, less trusting, kept together and maintained a certain aloofness.

There were fabulous entertainments, including tournaments in true medieval fashion, with gorgeous armor and complicated pageantry everywhere. As Norfolk says:

> *When these suns*
> *(For so they phrase 'em) by their heralds challenged*
> *The noble spirits to arms, they did perform*
> *Beyond thought's compass, that former fabulous story,*

Being now seen possible enough, got credit,
That Bevis was believed.

—Act I, scene i, lines 33–38

Bevis is a character in one of the medieval romances which *Don Quixote* satirized and killed. The romance was *Sir Bevis of Hamton* and it was filled (as all such romances were) with incredible fights, with tremendous wounds, given and taken, together with all sorts of magical byplay involving wizards and sorcerers. Norfolk's hyperbole states that so remarkable were the fights at the Field of the Cloth of Gold that even the tales of Bevis became plausible by comparison.

Actually, the fights were put-up jobs, of course. The two kings won all jousts in which they were involved, for who would have the hardihood to refuse to fall down before the royal spear or to venture to unhorse the royal person.

Only one real misadventure marred this love feast. At one point, Henry VIII, who was very proud of his wrestling ability, seized the slighter Francis suddenly, and said, "Brother, I want to wrestle with you."

If Francis had not been caught by surprise all might possibly have been well; they would have struggled for a while and ended in a draw. Francis, however, without thinking, put into play his own wrestling ability. Almost by reflex, he tripped Henry and the English King fell heavily to the ground. Henry rose, crimson with mortification, and all of Francis' flattery and diplomacy went for nothing.

It might have gone for nothing anyway, to tell the truth, for actually Charles V was not idle. All the time that Francis I had been wooing Henry with such ostentation and expense, Charles had quietly been working on the side with bribes and promises. In the end, the Field of the Cloth of Gold proved an enormous fiasco for the French, for Henry maintained a careful neutrality in the continental wars that followed, leaning toward Charles rather than Francis at odd moments when the neutrality bent.

. . . the right reverend Cardinal of York

Buckingham asks who arranged so magnificent a spectacle, and Norfolk answers:

All this was ord'red by the good discretion
Of the right reverend Cardinal of York.

—Act I, scene i, lines 50–51

The Cardinal of York referred to here is Thomas Wolsey, born about 1473 and ordained a priest in 1498. His first important position was that of tutor to the three sons of Thomas Grey, 1st Marquess of Dorset, who was the stepson of Edward IV and who appeared in *Richard III* (see page II–691) as one of the few Woodvilles who survived that reign.

Wolsey rose steadily, each of his employers being impressed by his ability and helping him onward, until he became chaplain to Henry VII. After the death of Henry VII, Wolsey became one of the most influential advisers of Henry VIII. It was he who encouraged Henry to invade France in 1513, and after the double victory at Guinegate and Flodden, it was Wolsey who negotiated what proved a most profitable peace with Louis XII of France. Wolsey was therefore rewarded with the Archbishopric of York in 1514 (a post he held *in absentia*). In 1515 the Pope made him cardinal and on December 22 of that year Henry made him Lord Chancellor.

As Cardinal of York and Lord Chancellor, Wolsey was the most powerful man in England after the King himself, and he used his position to the full. He loved wealth and power, obtained both and flaunted them pitilessly. He patronized art and literature and outshone all the nobility.

His organization of the Field of the Cloth of Gold was of a piece with his love of magnificence and it was he who cleverly saw to it that the occasion was to profit neither Francis nor Charles, really, but that England was to remain as far as possible a free agent, ready to throw her weight this way or that in order to prevent either France or the Empire from becoming too powerful. It was Wolsey who invented the notion of England as the guardian of the "balance of power," a post she was to maintain for four centuries, successfully preventing any continental conqueror, from Charles V and Francis I, right down to Hitler, from controlling all of Europe.

The devil speed him . . .

At the mention of Wolsey, Buckingham breaks out:

> *The devil speed him! No man's pie is freed*
> *From his ambitious finger.*
> > —Act I, scene i, lines 52–53

A powerful subordinate is always envied by others. When that subordinate is a man of comparatively low origins and when he ostentatiously parades his power and takes pleasure in humiliating men of higher birth than himself, that envy can rise to colossal heights.

Buckingham and Norfolk vie with each other in denouncing Wolsey's low birth and his gift of intrigue, and then the third person present, who till now has not spoken, says:

> *. . . I can see his pride*
> *Peep through each part of him.*
>
> —Act I, scene i, lines 68–69

The speaker is George Neville, Lord Abergavenny, a member of a younger branch of the family of which Richard of Warwick (see page II–580) had been the most famous representative. George Neville was married to Mary Stafford, the duke's daughter, and so was Buckingham's son-in-law.

This butcher's cur . . .

Buckingham, as a leading nobleman of the realm, is particularly outraged with Cardinal Wolsey (who now appears briefly on the scene, long enough to exchange disdainful stares with the duke) and says of him:

> *This butcher's cur is venom-mouthed . . .*
>
> —Act I, scene i, line 120

There was a rumor, spread by those who were anti-Wolsey, to the effect that his father was a butcher. Somehow, the role of butcher seems particularly lowly and bloody to an aristocrat, but in this case, the tale is almost surely false. Wolsey's father was of the middle class, a comparatively rich merchant with herds of sheep, and one who was involved in the wool trade, which in the England of the time was a thoroughly respectable occupation.

This Ipswich fellow's . . .

Buckingham, in his fury, feels that even the Field of the Cloth of Gold, which he and Norfolk have just been marveling over, is a criminal act of Wolsey's. After all, many of the English noblemen who were there had beggared themselves and ruined their estates in order to shine with the proper luxury, and for what? Nothing of value had come out of it.

In fact, Buckingham felt the King would be horrified if he knew the truth of the situation. He says:

> *I'll to the King,*
> *And from a mouth of honor quite cry down*
> *This Ipswich fellow's insolence . . .*
>
> —Act I, scene i, lines 136–38

Wolsey was born in Ipswich, a town sixty-five miles northeast of London.

. . . the Queen his aunt

Norfolk tries to calm Buckingham and prevent him from taking on an unequal fight, but Buckingham believes he has an unbeatable weapon. He says:

> *. . . Charles the Emperor,*
> *Under pretense to see the Queen his aunt*
> *(For 'twas indeed his color, but he came*
> *To whisper Wolsey) here makes visitation.*
> —Act I, scene i, lines 176–79

Ferdinand and Isabella of Spain had had two daughters, Juana and Catherine. Juana, the elder, was the mother of Emperor Charles V. Catherine, the younger, was the wife of Henry VIII. Thus, the Queen of England was the aunt of the Holy Roman Emperor.

Buckingham explains that Emperor Charles, anxious to negate the effects of the Field of the Cloth of Gold, intrigued with Wolsey and was successful in doing so. Buckingham says, triumphantly:

> *Let the King know,*
> *As soon he shall by me, that thus the Cardinal*
> *Does buy and sell his honor as he pleases,*
> *And for his own advantage.*
> —Act I, scene i, lines 190–93

In this, of course, Buckingham is being very naïve. The King is no more honest than his chancellor and the trafficking with both sides is as much part of his policy as Wolsey's.

Arrest thee of high treason . . .

Before Buckingham can put his foolish plan into action, he is forestalled. An officer enters and directs the sergeant to make an announcement. The sergeant says:

> *My lord the Duke of Buckingham, and Earl*
> *Of Hereford, Stafford, and Northampton, I*
> *Arrest thee of high treason, in the name*
> *Of our most sovereign King.*
> —Act I, scene i, lines 199–202

The officer in charge is, according to the play, named Brandon. This is a fictitious name. The actual arresting officer was Henry Marney. Abergavenny was also arrested.

. . . you have half our power

In the second scene, Henry VIII himself appears and expresses his gratitude to Wolsey for having uncovered Buckingham's treason. Before this matter can be carried onward, however, Queen Katherine enters. (She is usually known as Catherine of Aragon in the history books, but in this play her name is spelled as Katherine, and I will use that spelling too.)

The royal couple greet each other most lovingly. Indeed, when she kneels to him as a suitor, he says:

> Arise, and take place by us. Half your suit
> Never name to us: you have half our power.
> The other moiety [half] ere you ask is given.
>
> —Act I, scene ii, lines 10–13

Katherine was, at this time, thirty-six years old, six years older than her royal husband, who was now verging on thirty. Nor was she beautiful. Nevertheless, it is quite clear that Henry loved her, at least during the first dozen years of their marriage.

Her marriage into the English royal family was part of the policy of Henry VII, who felt that in this way he would gain the alliance of the rising power of Spain against the old enemy, France. The fluctuations of politics made Katherine's position in England rise and fall, however, and for a while, toward the close of Henry VII's life, it looked quite bad for her, as the old King decided to do without the Spanish alliance after all.

As soon as Henry VII died, however, the handsome young lad who succeeded as Henry VIII promptly married Katherine. He didn't have to; it might well have been to his advantage not to, and to have sought a younger bride. Despite her age and plainness, however, she appeared to Henry to be a forceful and capable woman with interests that paralleled his own. He judged that in her care he could leave the government whenever he was on his travels, and could be confident that she would do a good job.

In all this he was correct. She served as regent when he was campaigning in France, and between herself as ruler and Norfolk as general, the Scots were handily crushed.

In 1521, at the time of Buckingham's trial, the royal marriage was still strong, even to the point where Henry was scarcely even unfaithful oftener than now and then.

. . . in great grievance

Queen Katherine's suit is not for herself, but for the people. She says:

> *I am solicited, not by a few,*
> *And those of true condition, that your subjects*
> *Are in great grievance.*
>
> —Act I, scene ii, lines 18–20

This was true. Henry VIII, with all the ardor of a young king anxious to be admired, had developed an extravagant court. Wolsey, with his own hankering for wealth and magnificence, had encouraged him in this, and the conspicuous consumption of the Field of the Cloth of Gold had made things all the worse.

The money that parsimonious King Henry VII had painstakingly laid aside in the course of a careful and economical reign had vanished like snow in the munificence of his successor, and Henry VIII soon found it necessary to apply the screws to his subjects.

His subjects proved recalcitrant. In 1523, some two years after Buckingham's trial, Wolsey, in fact, had to place maximum pressure on Parliament to get them to vote new taxes.

Should without issue die . . .

Katherine openly blames the great exactions upon Cardinal Wolsey (for the two are enemies) and he protests innocence. The King orders relief for the subjects and then the council can turn to the matter of Buckingham.

The first witness against Buckingham is referred to as the Surveyor. This Surveyor was Charles Knevet (though his name is not given in the play). He is, or was, a high official of Buckingham's estates, and now he enters, prepared to give evidence against his master. He says:

> *First, it was usual with him—every day*
> *It would infect his speech—that if the King*
> *Should without issue die, he'll carry it so*
> *To make the scepter his.*
>
> —Act I, scene ii, lines 132–35

There was one flaw in King Henry's marriage, you see. Queen Katherine had given birth to four girls and two boys, yet all but one had been either

HENRY VIII

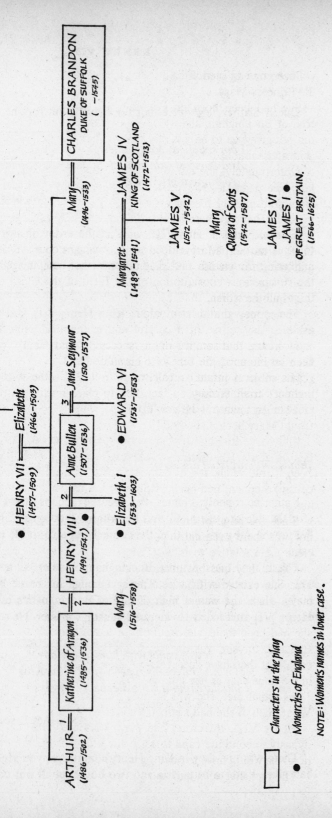

HOUSE OF TUDOR

● EDWARD IV ══ Elizabeth Woodville
  (1442–1483)   (1437–1492)

● HENRY VII ══ Elizabeth
  (1457–1509)   (1466–1505)

● ARTHUR ══¹ Katherine of Aragon ══¹ HENRY VIII ══² Anne Bullen ══³ Jane Seymour
  (1486–1502)   (1485–1536)   (1491–1547)   (1507–1536)   (1510–1537)

● Mary   ● Elizabeth I   ● EDWARD VI
  (1516–1558)   (1533–1603)   (1537–1553)

Mary ══ CHARLES BRANDON
(1496–1533)   DUKE OF SUFFOLK
                (–1545)

Margaret ══ JAMES IV
(1489–1541)   KING OF SCOTLAND
              (1472–1513)

JAMES V
(1512–1542)

Mary
Queen of Scots
(1542–1587)

● JAMES VI
  JAMES I
  OF GREAT BRITAIN.
  (1566–1625)

☐ *Characters in the play*

● *Monarchs of England*

NOTE: *Women's names in lower case.*

stillborn or had died after a very short while. The lone survivor was a girl, the Princess Mary.

She had been born on February 18, 1516, so that at the time of the trial of Buckingham she was five years old. She was not a pretty child and did not grow up to be a pretty woman, but like her mother, she was intelligent and capable.

Unfortunately, she did not make a satisfactory heir. In France, the Salic law (see page II-255) prevented a woman from sitting on the throne or from transmitting the succession to any of her descendants, male or female. In England there was no Salic law, and the female could transmit the succession. Indeed, Henry VII laid claim to the throne through the fact that his mother, Margaret Beaufort, was descended from John of Gaunt, and not through his father, who was merely a member of a family of Welsh squires.

It followed, then, that if King Henry lived long enough to allow Mary to grow up, marry, and have a son, that son would certainly succeed without trouble.

However, that son, assuming he came at all, might very well be no more than an infant at the time of his grandfather's death, and the events in the reigns of such infant successors as Henry VI and Edward V made that prospect unappetizing.

Then too, what if Henry VIII died while Mary was yet without a son? Could Mary herself succeed?

Only once in English history had a female served as monarch. This had been Matilda (the mother of Henry II, see page II-210) and that had not been a true reign, for in her time there was a civil war during which her cousin, Stephen, had been actual ruler. This one precedent was disheartening.

Since the reign of Henry II, there had been no case of a female ruling, nor was there even cause to consider the possibility. There was always a close male relative to inherit. Most of the kings left sons or, if they were childless, they had brothers or male cousins. If on any of those occasions a female existed with a better claim to the throne (if she had only been male) than the actual successor, she was ignored. For instance, when Henry VII succeeded to the throne in 1485, his mother was still alive. If she had been male, she would have taken precedence and become King of England, for she was one generation closer to John of Gaunt. Henry VII could not then have succeeded until her death, and as it happened, she died in the same year as her son, in 1509.

In actual fact, she was ignored and the crown went directly to her son. What, then, if she had not had a son?

Henry VIII, therefore, had every reason to feel that if he expected his dynasty to continue (and this was the ardent hope of every monarch, somehow) he would have to have a son. A daughter wasn't good enough.

The fact that sons had been born to him but had not lived was not only a practical disappointment but, in those superstitious times, made Henry think seriously that there might be something about the marriage that displeased heaven. As it turned out, he had other, grosser reasons to be dissatisfied and his concern about heavenly anger was often derided in later years as royal hypocrisy. And yet there might have been elements of real concern in it as well.

And what had Buckingham to do with the succession? Well, his great-great-grandmother had been Anne, the daughter of Thomas of Gloucester (see page II–264), and this made Buckingham the great-great-great-great-grandson of Edward III. What's more, his father's mother had been a Margaret Beaufort (not the mother of Henry VII, but her first cousin), and through her, he was a great-great-great-grandson of John of Gaunt. If, indeed, Henry VIII died and if Mary, as a woman, was considered inelegible for the throne, Buckingham could indeed easily be considered to be next in line.

. . . lost your office

The question is: Was the Surveyor giving true testimony?

In all likelihood, he was lying. For one thing, he had a grievance against Buckingham. Queen Katherine points this out, saying:

> *If I know you well,*
> *You were the Duke's surveyor, and lost your office*
> *On the complaint o'th'tenants.*
> —Act I, scene ii, lines 171–73

The Surveyor had been corrupt, had oppressed the tenants, and Buckingham had had the decency to side with his mistreated tenants against his own dishonest officer. The discharged employee, however, is all too likely to bear malice against his ex-employer, and any evidence he bears against him is not lightly to be trusted (though, of course, it need not necessarily be false). Moreover, Wolsey, anxious to get rid of Buckingham, is supposed to have paid Knevet well for his testimony.

. . . Sir Thomas Lovell . . .

But then, even if what the Surveyor had said is taken as true, it does not deal with a matter of outright treason. If Henry VIII dies without issue, then Buckingham might become King quite legally, and for Buckingham to look forward to such a situation with relish might argue ambition on his part, but that in itself is not treasonable. The ambition might be accompanied by a longing for the King's death and that *would* be treasonable, but how prove it?

The Surveyor sets about improving the case. He says that Buckingham had stated that

> . . . *had the King in his last sickness failed* [died],
> *The Cardinal's and Sir Thomas Lovell's heads*
> *Should have gone off.*
>
> —Act I, scene ii, lines 184–86

Sir Thomas Lovell was the official in charge of the Tower, and in those days, when the Tower was used to house prisoners of the highest importance, it was a responsible position indeed. Actually, the historic Lovell had retired in 1518, but Shakespeare has him appear throughout the play.

And yet, threatening the death of mere ministers is still not treason enough to warrant the execution of a man as highly placed as Buckingham.

About Sir William Bulmer—

The Surveyor, however, is not yet done. He says:

> *Being at Greenwich,*
> *After your Highness had reproved the Duke*
> *About Sir William Bulmer—*
>
> —Act I, scene ii, lines 188–90

Sir William Bulmer was a member of the King's personal household who had resigned to enter that of the Duke of Buckingham. We can well imagine why Bulmer might have done so. The King was a captious and tyrannical master with an uncomfortable amount of power, for with a word he could cost a man his head (and, as his later career showed, he was not at all chary about saying such a word). Buckingham, on the other hand, was a much more genial sort of man.

King Henry, however, would naturally take this as an insult. To have himself quitted for Buckingham could scarcely please him, and not only would Bulmer have earned the royal displeasure for leaving him, but Buckingham too would be in trouble for accepting him. Bulmer was forced to trial and was reduced to making no defense other than a plea for mercy, which Henry finally gave with very poor grace.

From what we know of Henry's character, taking his reign as a whole, we can well imagine that the incident rankled and that he did not forget either Bulmer or Buckingham. When the time was ripe, he would strike back.

. . . put his knife into him

The Surveyor now proceeds to complete his task. He states that Buckingham had been so angered by the risks he had run in connection with the matter of Bulmer as to make threats, saying that if he (Buckingham) had been committed to the Tower, then

> ". . . *I would have played*
> *The part my father meant to act upon*
> *Th'usurper Richard, who, being at Salisbury,*
> *Made suit to come in's presence; which if granted,*
> *As he made semblance* [pretense] *of his duty, would*
> *Have put his knife into him.*"
> —Act I, scene ii, lines 194–99

It was to Salisbury that the elder Buckingham had been brought for his execution after his abortive revolt. He had indeed asked for a final audience with Richard and had been refused (see page II–733).

This threat of assassination (if the Surveyor could be believed) was enough treason for anyone, and the King orders Buckingham to immediate trial; a trial which, in actual history, took place on May 13, 1521, nearly a year after the Field of the Cloth of Gold.

To Pepin or Clotharius . . .

The next scene (still at the palace) offers the audience a sneer at the French and their ways, something that was always popular in England. The Lord Chamberlain and Lord Sands enter and both speak with disapproval of the manner in which Englishmen have affected French fashions since the Field of the Cloth of Gold.

The Lord Chamberlain (unnamed in the play) is the aged Charles Somerset, Earl of Worcester, an illegitimate son of Henry Beaufort, 3rd Duke of Somerset, who had died nearly sixty years before at the Battle of Hexham (see page II–649).

Lord Sands is Sir William Sands, who did not actually gain the right to be called "Lord" till 1526, five years after Buckingham's trial, when Henry VIII made him a baron. In that same year he succeeded to the post of Lord Chamberlain at Charles of Worcester's death. In this play, however, there is no indication of this and Worcester remains Lord Chamberlain throughout.

One of the Chamberlain's remarks concerning the Frenchified expres-

sions affected by those Englishmen who had succumbed to foreign customs was to the effect that

> . . . *you would swear directly*
> *Their very noses had been counsellors*
> *To Pepin or Clotharius, they keep state so.*
> —Act I, scene iii, lines 8–10

Pepin was an early French monarch (see page II–455), the father of
Charlemagne. He was the first king of the Carolingian dynasty, ruling from
751 to 768.

Clotharius (or Clotaire) was a common name among the kings of the
previous dynasty, the Merovingian. The last of that name, Clotaire IV,
reigned from 717 to 719.

This backhanded reference to ancient French kings undoubtedly represents a resentful feeling of English inferiority. The French were able to
speak of great kings and powerful realms through the early centuries of
the Middle Ages, when England was riven into petty kingdoms soon to
suffer under the heel of invading Danes.

. . . Sir Thomas Bullen's daughter

As it happens, the Lord Chamberlain and Lord Sands (together with
Sir Thomas Lovell, who joins them) are on their way to a banquet being
given by Wolsey.

The banquet offers the stage the first of several chances at spectacle
granted by this play (and part of its weakness is that it is designed more as
spectacle than as drama).

There is gallant chaffing between the lords and ladies, and the King
himself, masked and in shepherd's disguise, enters with an accompanying
part. (Apparently, during the premiere performance of this play on June
29, 1613, a cannon fired as a salute to the King's entrance at this point set
fire to the Globe Theatre and burned it to the ground.)

The King finds himself attracted to a young lady who had previously
been flirting with Lord Sands. After Henry unmasks, he asks as to the
young lady's identity and the Chamberlain tells him:

> *An't please your Grace, Sir Thomas Bullen's daughter,*
> *The Viscount Rochford, one of her Highness' women.*
> —Act I, scene iv, lines 92–93

The lady is Anne Bullen (usually known in history books as Anne
Boleyn). Her father, Sir Thomas Bullen, was a prosperous merchant, and,

as a matter of fact, King Henry was already familiar with the family in a rather intimate fashion.

Although reasonably faithful to his wife till now, he did have a few flirtations, something which was taken for normal for men generally in those days, and certainly for kings. As long as he kept those flirtations discreet and did not flaunt them in the face of the court, that was all that even the most exacting wife would be expected to require.

In 1519 Henry had had a son by a lady in whom he was interested. The boy was named Henry Fitzroy (Henry "son of the King" in Norman-French), which was open enough. The King showered titles on this boy, making him Duke of Richmond, and some even thought he hoped to make the illegitimate boy his heir in default of a legitimate son. Perhaps so, for he must have been extraordinarily cherished by the King as proof that he, at least, could have a son even if Queen Katherine couldn't. Young Fitzroy died, however, before he was nineteen and that hope went glimmering.

Young Fitzroy's mother did not last long in the King's favor (no woman did, and Katherine of Aragon was the only reasonably enduring love of his life). After her, he took as his mistress, briefly, none other than Mary Bullen, elder sister of Anne Bullen.

In 1522 Anne Bullen entered the service of the court as maid of honor to Queen Katherine. It is uncertain how old Anne was at the time, somewhere between fifteen and twenty, with most historians inclining toward the younger part of the range.

She caught Henry's eye—it is not certain when—and he grew interested. This proved to be more serious than earlier flirtations, partly because he was growing more and more tired of his aging and ailing wife and partly because he was also growing more and more worried about the succession. The trial of Buckingham may have been the turning point as far as this was concerned. Even if Buckingham were framed and if Henry knew that, there was still no doubt that uncertainty as to the succession encouraged treasonous intrigues. So Henry grew desperate for a legitimate son, if not by Katherine then, somehow, by someone else.

Earl Surrey . . .

The trial of Buckingham can have only one conclusion, and he is convicted. We do not witness the trial directly but are told of it by two gentlemen. They are sure that Buckingham's conviction was the result of Wolsey's intrigues, and the First Gentleman cites evidence, saying:

> *. . . first, Kildare's attainder,*
> *Then Deputy of Ireland, who removed,*
> *Earl Surrey was sent thither, and in haste too,*
> *Lest he should help his father.*

—Act II, scene i, lines 41–44

Kildare is Gerald Fitzgerald, 9th Earl of Kildare, scion of an Irish family of Norman extraction who had held a dominating position on that island for generations. The Fitzgerald family had so long had their own way that they were only under the slightest control by the government in London. They carried on their feuds with other chieftains of either Norman or native Irish extraction, made war and peace at will, and generally kept the land in a state of turbulence.

In an effort to exert stronger central influence, Wolsey removed Kildare from office as Lord Deputy of Ireland, and replaced him with the Earl of Surrey.

The Earl of Surrey was Thomas Howard, the son and namesake of the Duke of Norfolk. In 1495 he had married Anne, a younger daughter of Edward IV, and thus became a brother-in-law of King Henry VII, who was married to Anne's older sister. Surrey's sister, Elizabeth, was the mother of Anne Bullen. Surrey was thus Anne Bullen's uncle.

Surrey's wife died in 1512 and in 1513 he married Elizabeth, the daughter of the Duke of Buckingham. Thus, at the time of Buckingham's trial, that nobleman was Surrey's father-in-law (not quite "father," as stated in the First Gentleman's speech).

Surrey was bitterly anti-Wolsey and that is probably one reason why he was sent to Ireland (as Richard of York had once been sent there by his Lancastrian foes, see page II–596). Whether the virtual exile had anything directly to do with the Buckingham trial is, however, not likely.

First, Kildare's replacement by Surrey took place in 1520, months before Buckingham was accused, and it is hard to say whether Wolsey was looking so far ahead in such detail. Besides, there was little to fear in Surrey and therefore small reason to exile him in haste. The minister was firmly backed by King Henry and the royal will was not to be flouted at any time during his reign. Thus, the person who was forced to pronounce the final sentence of condemnation was none other than Norfolk, the same man who had been so friendly with Buckingham in the first scene of this play, who was the father of Surrey and who was certainly just as bitterly anti-Wolsey as Buckingham himself.

If Norfolk could do nothing, what could Surrey have done even if he had been at the scene?

. . . poor Edward Bohun

Buckingham is led out to execution (this took place on May 17, 1521) and makes a speech maintaining his innocence. He says at one point:

> When I came hither, I was Lord High Constable
> And Duke of Buckingham; now, poor Edward Bohun.
> —Act II, scene i, lines 102–3

Actually, he was Edward Stafford, but then he was descended from the house of Bohun as well. It was Eleanor Bohun (see page II–264) who had married Thomas of Gloucester, and he was descended from that marriage. Eleanor's sister, Mary Bohun, had married Bolingbroke and was the mother of Henry V. The use of Bohun here as a family name in place of Stafford would, to an Elizabethan audience, stress Buckingham's royal descent and make more plain the real reason for his execution.

. . . a separation

Once Buckingham departs, the two gentlemen continue their conversation, and a fresh piece of gossip drives the execution out of their minds. The Second Gentleman says:

> . . . Did you not of late days hear
> A buzzing [rumor] of a separation
> Between the King and Katherine?
>
> —Act II, scene i, lines 147–49

Time is being condensed here. Buckingham's execution took place in 1521. Anne Bullen first caught the King's eye no earlier than 1522 (though it took place before the execution in the time scheme of the play), and for years it remained only an on-and-off flirtation, and perhaps did not even involve serious intimacy.

By 1527, however, two things had happened. Henry had grown increasingly interested in the fascinating Anne and increasingly anxious about the matter of an heir. Katherine was by then forty-two years old and it was just about impossible to hope that she would produce a son.

Since Katherine would not resolve the situation by obligingly dying, Henry had grown desperate enough to press for a divorce in order to make way for a second legitimate marriage and a new chance at a legitimate son.

Cardinal Campeius . . .

The Second Gentleman goes on to say:

> . . . Either the Cardinal
> Or some about him near have, out of malice
> To the good Queen, possessed him [the King] with a scruple
> That will undo her. To confirm this too,
> Cardinal Campeius is arrived, and lately;
> As all think, for this business.
>
> —Act II, scene i, lines 156–61

It was easy to blame Wolsey for all that was going badly, for he was becoming most unpopular among Englishmen generally. It was he who had tried to force Parliament to grant heavy taxes to support the King's extravagances at home and abroad. It was he who kept England to a proimperial policy that was proving a failure.

Emperor Charles V, for all the agreements worked out with him by Wolsey, did not order his foreign policy to the benefit of England. Moreover, the Emperor had specifically promised to marry Mary, the daughter of Henry VIII (and the Emperor's own first cousin), and then backed out, to the humiliation of the English court.

Wolsey might have taken stronger action to counter Charles were it not for certain personal ambitions of his own. But even those were being thwarted, and the First Gentleman sees in the moves against Katherine a revenge motive against the Queen's nephew. He says:

> 'Tis the Cardinal;
> And merely to revenge him on the Emperor
> For not bestowing on him at his asking
> The archbishopric of Toledo . . .
> —Act II, scene i, lines 161–64

Actually, Wolsey had higher ambitions still, for he wanted to be Pope. This ambition strikes us today as absolutely ridiculous, so used are we to the fact that the Pope is invariably an Italian. That, however, was not always so. Until the sixteenth century there were popes of many nations, and in 1154 an Englishman, Nicholas Breakspear, had come to the pontifical throne as Adrian IV. (He was the only Englishman to make it.)

In 1521, when Pope Leo X died, the succession depended a great deal on the influence of Charles V, and he might easily have made Wolsey Pope. He didn't. He chose a Dutchman instead, Adrian Florisze Boeyens, an aged man whose chief distinction (aside from his irreproachable virtue) was the fact that he had been the Emperor's boyhood tutor. The new Pope (the only Dutch Pope in history) reigned as Adrian VI and even this may well have frustrated Wolsey, for that might have been the very title he would have adopted in commemoration of the earlier English Pope.

But then, Adrian VI was an old man; he reigned for only a little over a year and then died. Once again, Wolsey might have been considered for the post and once again he was not. The succession fell this time upon Giulio de' Medici, a member of the famous ruling house of Florence. He reigned as Pope under the name of Clement VII and Wolsey's chance was gone forever. As a matter of fact, Adrian VI was the last of the non-Italian popes, and with Clement VII there began an unbroken line of Italian popes that has lasted through (at the moment of writing) no less than forty-four papal reigns.

By 1527, therefore, both King Henry and Wolsey were ready to abandon the Emperor and to switch to a French alliance instead, which Wolsey now negotiated (even though to the general population a French alliance was still anathema).

The switch in foreign policy fit Henry's plans for a divorce too, for as long as he was friends and allies with the Emperor, it would be difficult to break away from the Emperor's aunt. If, on the other hand, he were at war with Charles (and such a war was declared in 1528), he would have one more excuse for discarding his Queen.

Wolsey favored the divorce. He might well feel personal animosity against the Queen, but in addition he recognized the importance of the succession. He assured Henry that the divorce could be managed and that he himself would take care of it as far as the Pope was involved.

He began well, for he persuaded Pope Clement to send a representative, Cardinal Lorenz Campeggio (Campeius was the Latinized version of the name), to hear the divorce suit. Campeius arrived in London on October 7, 1528.

Undoubtedly, both Henry and Wolsey assumed that this was only a face-saving gesture on the part of the Pope and that, after a due pretense of going through the legal formalities, the divorce would be granted forthwith.

What neither Wolsey nor Henry understood clearly, apparently, was that poor Pope Clement was in a dreadful position with respect to the Emperor. An Imperial army had sacked Rome in 1527 and Charles V had control of all Italy. The Pope was virtually his prisoner and dared not antagonize him. If French armies wrested Italy from Charles, then well and good, Pope Clement might agree to let Charles's aunt be cast out. If French armies failed, Clement could do nothing—it was as straightforward as that.

. . . his brother's wife

In the next scene, the matter of the divorce is carried further in a discussion between several noblemen, including the Duke of Norfolk.

It would appear in the play that the Duke of Norfolk here is the same man who appeared in the first scene with Buckingham. Actually, the Norfolk of the first scene, the 2nd Duke, died in 1524, three years after Buckingham's execution. He was succeeded by his son and namesake, who had been the same Earl of Surrey who had been placed in charge of Ireland, and who now became the 3rd Duke of Norfolk.

Shakespeare takes no account of this succession. He keeps Norfolk throughout, with no indication that there was a change of man behind the title. He also has the younger man continue to appear in the play under his older and lesser title of Surrey.

The Chamberlain, who is also present, describes the King as immersed in sadness and explains to Norfolk:

It seems the marriage with his brother's wife
Has crept too near his conscience.

—Act II, scene ii, lines 16–17

This is the first mention in the play that Henry VIII had had a brother. This thrown-away reference is not lost on the Elizabethan audience, however, for they would know the tale well.

Henry VIII had indeed had a brother, and an older brother at that. The older brother was named Arthur and had been Prince of Wales and heir apparent to the throne of Henry VII. It was to him that Katherine was betrothed in the days when Henry VII wanted an alliance with the rising nation of Spain. The betrothal had taken place when both were children and it had been done by proxy, for Katherine remained in Spain.

In 1501, though, when Arthur was fourteen (and when his younger brother, Henry, was ten), it was decided that it was time enough for marriage and Katherine was sent for. She arrived in England on October 2, 1501, and the marriage was performed on November 14.

Arthur, however, shared the misfortune of the earlier Prince Arthur, John's nephew (see page II–240), and never lived to sit on the throne. He died of illness on April 2, 1502.

And now what was to become of the Spanish alliance? Ferdinand of Spain, Katherine's father, pushed hard for a marriage of his daughter to her dead husband's younger brother so that the dynastic connection be retained.

This was tricky for several reasons. First, it was against the rules of the church for a woman to marry each of two brothers. To be sure, one might ask whether the marriage with Arthur had been a true marriage; it had lasted only a few months and both husband and wife were quite young. The marriage might never have been sexually consummated, and, in fact, Katherine always insisted it had not been. If that were so, there would be no difficulty in getting a special dispensation from the Pope to nullify the first marriage and allow the second. Such a dispensation was indeed obtained and a new betrothal was arranged.

But now political difficulties arose. Henry of England and Ferdinand of Spain were caught up in political jockeying and Henry insisted on using Katherine as a pawn to be played against her father. When Henry VII died in 1509, Katherine was still unmarried and was even feeling the pinch of poverty. But then young Henry VIII, as soon as he was King, carried through the marriage.

Nearly twenty years later, with Katherine old, ailing, and without a son, Henry VIII regretted that hasty action of his youth. Whatever his ulterior motives, he had a legitimate religious cause, as the Bible clearly stated (Leviticus 20:21, "And if a man shall take his brother's wife, it is an unclean thing; he hath uncovered his brother's nakedness; they shall be childless.")

Of course, the Pope had given a dispensation, but perhaps the Pope had acted hastily and on inadequate ground. After all, the results proved the sin, for Henry VIII was childless in the sense that he had no male heirs. Surely the present Pope would see the justice of this argument and would undo the work of the earlier dispensation.

. . . too near another lady

The seriousness of the King's scruples might not be taken as genuine by all, for most of the court had to know by now of Henry's infatuation for Anne Bullen.

Thus, there is another gentleman present, Suffolk, who, in an aside, says of the Chamberlain's comment about the King's conscience:

> *No, his conscience*
> *Has crept too near another lady.*
> —Act II, scene ii, lines 17–18

The speaker is Charles Brandon, son of Sir William Brandon. Sir William does not have a speaking part in *Richard III* but he appears onstage. Prior to the Battle of Bosworth, he is referred to by Richmond (later Henry VII), and after the battle, he is referred to again as one of those who had been killed. According to legend, he was killed by none other than Richard III himself.

Young Charles, who was only eleven years old at the time of Bosworth, was a favorite of young Henry VIII, and in 1514 he was elevated to the title of 1st Duke of Suffolk. Charles of Suffolk was in love with Mary Tudor, sister of Henry VIII, but Mary was married to old King Louis XII of France as part of the political arrangement after the Battle of the Spurs.

Louis did not live long, however, and when Mary was widowed, she and Charles married. King Henry could scarcely be expected to approve of this, for an unmarried sister could be a very handy item for use in the marital diplomacy of the time. Still, by turning over most of the money they could get their hands on to King Henry, the young couple managed to keep the royal anger within bounds.

We need not go along entirely with Suffolk's cynical remark, however. Regardless of Henry's love for Anne, his anxiety for the succession probably came first. If Katherine had but given him a healthy son, he might still have loved Anne, but he would very likely have kept her as his mistress only and never dreamed of divorce.

The French King's sister

The Chamberlain, like the others, blames everything on Wolsey and he sees what the Cardinal is driving at. He says:

> All that dare
> Look into these affairs see this main end,
> The French King's sister.
>
> —Act II, scene ii, lines 39–41

Like Warwick before him (see page II–650), Wolsey looked upon a royal marriage as a tool of diplomacy and saw value in an alliance with France, in which marital and political would support each other. And as in the case of Warwick, the King chose to marry for love instead. Wolsey did not quite understand that Henry's feelings about Anne Bullen were strong enough to involve actual marriage.

The French princess Wolsey had his eye on was Marguerite of Navarre, the sister of King Francis I. She was a widow, for in 1509, the very year in which Henry VIII came to the throne, she had married Charles, Duc d'Alençon, a descendant of the Alençon who has a small part in *Henry VI, Part One* (see page II–526). The Duke had died in 1525 and Marguerite, widowed after sixteen years of marriage, was available.

Still, however suitable she was politically, there were certain disadvantages. She was getting on in years, for she was thirty-five, only a year younger than the King, and Henry was tired of middle-aged wives; he wanted a young Queen. He might even have argued to himself that Marguerite was past her best years for childbearing and that the marriage might be self-defeating. (As a matter of fact, though, Marguerite did marry again and gave birth to a daughter who was destined to be the mother of the great French King, Henry IV.)

. . . my new secretary

Norfolk and Suffolk try to see the King on business, but he rejects them rather savagely. He chooses, instead, to see Wolsey and Cardinal Campeius, for he is anxious to conclude the matter of the divorce.

The King greets both cardinals and then says to Wolsey:

> Prithee call Gardiner to me, my new secretary;
> I find him a fit fellow.
>
> —Act II, scene ii, lines 115–16

The reference is to Stephen Gardiner, who was just about Henry's age, and whose early life paralleled that of Wolsey. He was the son of a cloth-maker, was destined for the church, and proved a brilliant student.

Wolsey spied him as a bright young man and made him his secretary in 1525. Wolsey made use of him in the negotiations with the Pope in connection with the divorce and so well did Gardiner shine in this that Henry made him his own secretary in 1529.

. . . one Doctor Pace

Cardinal Campeius, observing Gardiner in conference with the King, asks Wolsey:

> My Lord of York, was not one Doctor Pace
> In this man's place before him?
>
> —Act II, scene ii, lines 121–22

Yes indeed. Richard Pace had served as Wolsey's secretary before Gardiner.

Campeius then warns Wolsey that there are evil rumors about Wolsey abroad, concerning all aspects of his career, even his treatment of his secretary. He says that rumor has it that Wolsey

> . . . fearing he [Pace] would rise (he was so virtuous),
> Kept him a foreign man still; which so grieved him
> That he ran mad and died.
>
> —Act II, scene ii, lines 127–29

This is an example of how Wolsey was vilified later and his deeds made more evil than they were. In the play, Wolsey does not defend himself but cynically blames Pace's troubles on his insisting on remaining virtuous.

To be sure, Wolsey did employ Richard Pace on foreign missions, having him negotiate a Swiss attack on the French when the French were the enemy, and using him as his agent in his own attempts to achieve the papacy. This was not in order to keep him from promotion by preventing him from being at court—but because he was a capable agent.

Nor did Pace go mad and die. Wolsey finally replaced him, but Pace was still alive when Cardinal Campeius was in the country. Indeed, Pace outlived Wolsey himself by six years.

. . . for Caernarvonshire . . .

We return to Anne Bullen, whom we saw only briefly at Wolsey's banquet, and who is now in a conversation with an Old Lady (unnamed). Anne virtuously pities Queen Katherine's miseries, saying that she herself would on no account be willing to be highly titled. The Old Lady dryly refuses to accept Anne's protestations. She says:

> In faith, for little England
> You'd venture an emballing [being made Queen]. I myself
> Would for Caernarvonshire . . .
>
> —Act II, scene iii, lines 46–48

Caernarvonshire is the northeasternmost county of Wales, a mountainous region that is by no means rich and that is sufficiently far from London to seem a kind of rustic wilderness.

Anne has her chance to display her sincerity almost immediately when the Chamberlain arrives with a gift from the King. The Chamberlain says to Anne:

> Ta'en of your many virtues, the King's Majesty
> Commends his good opinion of you, and
> Does purpose honor to you no less flowing
> Than Marchioness of Pembroke . . .
>
> —Act II, scene iii, lines 60–63

Anne Bullen was granted this title, in actuality, on September 1, 1532, rather later than it would appear here. In the play, the title seems to be granted while Cardinal Campeius is in England, whereas actually Anne received it three years after the cardinal had left for good.

Anne, despite her earlier protestation, accepts the title with thanks. Nor does the Chamberlain make any bawdy asides at this point as one would think he must surely do. Instead he praises Anne Bullen in an aside and says:

> . . . who knows yet
> But from this lady may proceed a gem
> To lighten all this isle?
>
> —Act II, scene iii, lines 77–79

The Chamberlain would have had to be prescient indeed to suspect this, but Shakespeare had the advantage of hindsight and played for audience applause at this point, for well he (and the audience) knew that Anne Bullen was fated to be the mother of Queen Elizabeth I.

. . . appeal unto the Pope

It is now the Queen's turn to face trial, as earlier it had been Buckingham's. The divorce trial took place on June 18, 1529, eight years after Buckingham's execution.

Katherine, alone and friendless, stands before the powerful King and his powerful minister and manages to dominate the proceedings. Refusing to answer to her name when it is called out, she denies the jurisdiction of the court over her. She proudly attests her own virtues as a wife and denounces Wolsey. Finally, she says:

> *I do refuse you* [Wolsey] *for my judge, and here,*
> *Before you all, appeal unto the Pope,*
> > —Act II, scene iv, lines 118–19

This was Katherine's trump card and she played it fearlessly. If the King, or Wolsey, or Campeius, had managed to persuade Katherine to agree to a divorce, the whole matter could have been completed without the Pope having to experience political embarrassment. Katherine need only have expressed her wish to retire to a convent, and the Pope would have given her his kindly permission to do so.

By adamantly refusing a divorce, rejecting the trial, and loudly appealing to the Pope, Katherine would force action of a different kind. It was one thing for the Pope to grant the Emperor's aunt a divorce she asked for, but quite another for him to force her out of a royal marriage against her will. The Emperor's hand, after all, was at the papal throat.

Our daughter Mary

In Queen Katherine's absence, King Henry begins a circumstantial account of how it first came to him that his marriage might be an illegitimate one. The matter began, he says:

> *. . . on certain speeches uttered*
> *By th'Bishop of Bayonne, then French ambassador,*
> *Who had been hither sent on the debating*
> *A marriage 'twixt the Duke of Orleans and*
> *Our daughter Mary.*
> > —Act II, scene iv, lines 171–75

Royal princesses were bartered on the marriage market in accordance with political expediency, of course. In 1518, when England was friendly with France, Mary was suggested as future bride for the son of French King Francis, even though she was only two years old. When England broke away from France and turned to the Empire, it was Emperor Charles who was temporarily the marital prospect. Then, on April 30, 1527, when an alliance with France was formed once more, there were the possibilities that Mary might marry, if not Francis, then his second son, Henry of Orléans (who, twenty years later, was destined to reign as King Henry II of France).

It is not unlikely that the Bishop of Bayonne, in the course of marital negotiations, would cast doubt on Mary's legitimacy as one way of lowering the value of the marriage from the French standpoint and forcing England to bid higher in other respects. One can wonder, however, whether Henry VIII might not have maneuvered the matter himself, for by then he was already revolving the possibility of divorce in his mind and it would have suited him well to have the matter brought into the open by an outsider.

My Lord of Canterbury . . .

The King, according to the story he presents the court, sought ecclesiastical opinion and finally reached the highest in the land. He says:

> *I then moved you,*
> *My Lord of Canterbury, and got your leave*
> *To make this present summons.*
> —Act II, scene iv, lines 217–19

The Archbishop of Canterbury at this time was William Warham. He had become archbishop in 1504 and it was he who crowned Henry and Katherine in 1509. He was an old man now, about eighty years old, and he had long since stepped back to let Wolsey (who, as Archbishop of York, was only second in the English hierarchy) take over.

Warham approved the divorce, for he could do no other, since he was utterly dominated by King and cardinal.

. . . well-belovèd servant, Cranmer

The papal legate, Campeius, is unmoved by Henry's recital. He has been effectively neutralized by Katherine's appeal to the Pope, for until the Pope considers that appeal, his legate can do nothing. Campeius says as much, urging an adjournment until such time as the Queen would consent to be present at the trial.

This clearly catches Henry off guard and annoys him. Presumably he had expected to continue the trial in Katherine's absence, reach a proper decision in favor of divorce, and carry on smoothly from there. Now he sees that this will not be so after all, and in an aside, he says:

> *My learned and well-belovèd servant, Cranmer,*
> *Prithee return; with thy approach, I know,*
> *My comfort comes along.*
>
> —Act II, scene iv, lines 238–40

Cranmer was a learned churchman, some two years older than the King, and was one of those who had grown interested in developments then taking place in Germany.

In that land in 1517, a certain monk named Martin Luther had challenged many aspects of the accepted theology of the Catholic Church. This had initiated what seemed at first merely a monkish dispute, of the type that often ruffled the intellectual hierarchy of the church without seriously affecting its power structure.

Through a variety of circumstances, however, Luther's doctrines spread like fire through stubble (among other reasons, because the monk made skillful use of the relatively new invention of printing to scatter his argumentative and colorfully written pamphlets far and wide). By 1520 Cranmer and other clerics were discussing these new "Lutheran" notions in England, and one of the most important of them was that the Pope had no special authority over the church as a whole and that the large edifice of tradition built up by the Catholic Church need not be accepted simply because the Pope ordered it so.

Henry VIII, who fancied himself a scholar, was highly indignant over Luther's views. In 1521 he wrote a book defending the traditional Catholic position and denouncing Luther. He insisted he wrote it himself, though many people suppose it was edited by some learned cleric. The book was taken to Rome by the Dean of Windsor and an appreciative Pope (strongly urged on by the dean) conferred upon Henry, on October 11, 1521, the title of "Defender of the Faith." (This title was retained by Henry even after he turned against the Pope, and has been held by all succeeding English monarchs down to this day.)

But now there was the matter of the divorce, and Henry was looking for help from the Pope and not finding it. His earlier conviction that the Pope was the final authority had to give way, and it was this that made Cranmer suddenly valuable to him.

It seems that in 1527 Cranmer happened to meet with a couple of the King's councillors, including Stephen Gardiner. In discussion the matter of the divorce, Cranmer took the attitude that the Pope was by no means the last word. Interested in Lutheran doctrine and sympathetic to it, Cranmer suggested that the King could take the problem to the various universities of Europe. In other words, the general opinion of the learned clerics of Christendom might support Henry, and in that case, the Pope's opinion, even if adverse, need not be allowed to carry weight.

Now, two years later, Henry snatched at this alternative as a way out of his dilemma, and he remained grateful to Cranmer for this to the end of his life.

. . . stol'n away to Rome . . .

Wolsey and Campeius do their best to persuade Katherine to submit to a trial, in order to prevent a possibly destructive confrontation between King and Pope, but Katherine, with steel-like constancy, refuses and insists on justice.

This is a serious defeat for Wolsey, and his enemies among the aristocracy gather gleefully to plot against him. Norfolk tells the others:

> . . . The King hath found
> Matter against him [Wolsey] that forever mars
> The honey of his language.
> —Act III, scene ii, lines 20–22

For one thing, the cardinal had belatedly discovered that he wasn't conducting the divorce proceedings in order to have Henry marry a French princess after all. Instead, he found that Henry had his eyes on Anne Bullen. Wolsey was horrified and the whole matter of the divorce lost its savor for him. He began to backtrack and to the cold, shrewd King that was fatal.

Suffolk says:

> The Cardinal's letters to the Pope miscarried,
> And came to th'eye o'th'King;
> —Act III, scene ii, lines 30–31

Worse yet follows, for Suffolk goes on:

> . . . Cardinal Campeius
> Is stol'n away to Rome; hath ta'en no leave;
> Has left the cause o'th'King unhandled . . .
> —Act III, scene ii, lines 56–58

The trouble was that although Henry VIII was all-powerful inside England, he had no power to influence the great events on the Continent. About the time of the trial, the French effort to wrest Italy from Charles V came to a final failure. In August 1529 France and the Empire signed a peace that left Italy in Charles's control. That meant it left Pope Clement in Charles's control too, and papal approval of Henry's divorce from Charles's aunt was now impossible.

The trial dragged on through July, but Katherine wouldn't attend, wouldn't agree to any quiet settlement, and insisted on her appeal. By July 23 the trial came to a halt. The Pope, helpless to do anything but delay, recalled Campeius, who left England. Campeius did not steal away without leave-taking, however; he had a final interview with the King on September 19.

From that moment on, Wolsey was through. He had promised Henry a divorce, but all he had obtained for Henry was a long humiliation. It was clear that Wolsey was not the man to get the King past the Pope, and it was necessary for Henry to find new tools.

. . . an archbishop

As Wolsey's stock falls, that of Cranmer rises. Cranmer feels it possible to bypass the Pope and has already been gathering opinions favorable to the King from various places. The nobles praise his labors and Suffolk says:

> . . . we shall see him
> *For it an archbishop.*
>
> —Act III, scene ii, lines 73–74

Again, time is being condensed. About two and a half years dragged on after the conclusion of the trial before Henry could actually get past the Pope. In 1532 Cranmer was sent to Germany by the King. Officially, he was to consult the Emperor, but actually he made contact with Lutheran princes, gathered Lutheran opinions, and confirmed his own sympathies to the new doctrines. Indeed, Cranmer abandoned his own celibacy and married his niece, for the Lutheran doctrines did not see any necessity for celibacy among the priesthood.

In August 1532 the old Archbishop of Canterbury died, and by March 1533 Cranmer was appointed to the vacant post and became sixty-ninth Archbishop of Canterbury.

The packet, Cromwell

Wolsey does not yet know he is out of favor. He enters with an underling and says:

> *The packet, Cromwell,*
> *Gave't you the King?*
>
> —Act III, scene ii, lines 76–77

Wolsey is speaking to Thomas Cromwell, a person of fairly low birth, whose early life is obscure until 1520, when, at the age of about thirty-five, he entered Wolsey's service. Eventually, he became Wolsey's confidential secretary.

The packet, it turns out, is the immediate occasion for Wolsey's downfall, at least in the play. The King enters and angrily gives Wolsey a paper that had accidentally found its way into the packet. It turns out to be a confidential accounting of the cardinal's property. The cardinal looks at it when the King leaves and mutters:

> 'Tis th'account
> Of all that world of wealth I have drawn together
> For mine own ends; indeed, to gain the popedom,
> And fee my friends in Rome.
>
> —Act III, scene ii, lines 210–13

The King can now use Wolsey's greed as an excuse to degrade him, for he can now undoubtedly find cause for believing in his corruption, his intrigues with Rome, and so on. Wolsey is through.

. . . *the Great Seal* . . .

Almost at once the nobles come to him and Norfolk says:

> Hear the King's pleasure, Cardinal, who commands you
> To render up the Great Seal presently
> Into our hands, and to confine yourself
> To Asher House, my Lord of Winchester's,
>
> —Act III, scene ii, lines 228–31

The Great Seal was the insignia of the Lord Chancellor's office. Wolsey was thus discharged from his position as what we would call "Prime Minister." This took place on October 17, 1529, only four months after the opening of the trial at which Wolsey was to have sat in powerful judgment over Queen Katherine.

The surrender of the Great Seal was only the development of a process that had begun earlier, however. Suffolk says:

> Because all those things you have done of late,
> By your power legative, within this kingdom,
> Fall into th'compass of a praemunire—
> That therefore such a writ be sued against you:
> To forfeit all your goods, lands, tenements,
> Chattels, and whatsoever . . .
>
> —Act III, scene ii, lines 338–43

A "Statute of Praemunire" had been passed in 1392 under Richard II. It had been designed to limit papal power in England and under it no one could deal with the Pope in certain ways without royal authority. On October 9, 1529—eight days before he had been stripped of office—Wolsey had been accused of having violated that statute, and, in consequence, forfeited almost all he owned to the King. He was allowed, however, as a gesture of royal mercy, to retain his post as Archbishop of York.

. . . *Sir Thomas More* . . .

The nobles, having amused themselves by mocking the fallen minister, leave, and Wolsey, left alone, indulges in an emotional soliloquy over the passing of his greatness. Then Cromwell enters with news, saying:

> . . . *Sir Thomas More is chosen*
> *Lord Chancellor in your place.*
>
> —Act III, scene ii, lines 393–94

Sir Thomas More was the most learned man in England in his time and was, in many respects, a most admirable person. He was an advocate of education for women and saw to it that his own daughters were fully educated.

He was a writer too, turning out a biography of Richard III in 1514, in which he intended to point a moral by contrasting a bad king, Richard, with a good one, Edward IV. (It must be remembered that Edward IV was Henry VIII's grandfather.) The biography served the purposes of Tudor propaganda and was used by Shakespeare as a source for his play *Richard III*. More never finished it and one wonders if that was because he realized it was a propaganda piece and not true history and sickened of it. Shortly afterward, he wrote *Utopia* (a word meaning "nowhere"), a picture of an ideal society—which added a word to the English language and gave rise to a genre of literature.

More was a fascinating man and Henry VIII delighted in his company. As Lord Chancellor, he was an excellent choice in many ways, for he was hard-working, kindhearted, just, and popular. He had opposed excessive taxation under Henry VII and as Speaker of the House of Commons had had the courage to stand up to Wolsey in 1523 against excessive taxation again.

In another respect, Henry was mad to appoint him. More was strongly anti-Lutheran and he could not possibly approve the divorce unless the Pope approved. If the Pope did not approve, More—a man of principle—could see no way around it and would not lift a finger to find one. When the time came that Henry *had* to ignore the Pope, More too fell from favor.

. . . in secrecy long married

Cromwell brings other news that is anachronistic, however, for again the lengthy period following the fall of Wolsey, a period full of twisting and turning before Henry can have his way, must be eliminated.

Cromwell says:

> *. . . Cranmer is returned with welcome,*
> *Installed Lord Archbishop of Canterbury.*
> —Act III, scene ii, lines 400–1

But that did not take place till March 1533, three and a half years after Wolsey's fall.

Cromwell goes on:

> *Last, that the Lady Anne,*
> *Whom the King hath in secrecy long married,*
> *This day was viewed in open as his queen,*
> —Act III, scene ii, lines 402–4

It wasn't till July 1531, however, a year and a half *after* Wolsey's fall, that Henry finally separated from Katherine and refused to see her any more. After that, Anne began to accompany the King openly, even on trips abroad. They were secretly married on January 25, 1533, and on March 28, Cranmer, now Archbishop of Canterbury, officially declared Henry's marriage to Anne legal.

. . . He will advance thee

Wolsey advises Cromwell to abandon the sinking ship and seek safety. He says:

> *Seek the King*
> *(That sun I pray may never set!)—I have told him*
> *What and how true thou art. He will advance thee;*
> —Act III, scene ii, lines 414–16

Cromwell did as he was told. An ordinary secretary might have fallen with his master, but Cromwell gained a seat in Parliament almost at once and began attempts to reach the ear of the King with plans for circumventing the Pope and for making the King himself head of the English Church. This was Cranmer's theology, but Cromwell offered himself as minister to put that theology into practice.

Henry agreed, accepted his services, and began promoting him. Eventually, Cromwell's services were such that he became a peer. In April 1540 lowborn Thomas Cromwell was made Earl of Essex.

But Wolsey is given prescience by Shakespeare. He warns Cromwell to avoid ambition and corruption, saying:

> Then if thou fall'st, O Cromwell,
> Thou fall'st a blessed martyr.
>
> —Act III, scene ii, lines 448–49

Cromwell did eventually fall. In fact, by the time he was created Earl of Essex, he had already gotten into deep trouble with Henry over a different marriage and divorce. In June 1540 he was arrested and on July 28 (only four months after his promotion to the earldom) he was executed.

However, this is well after the events with which the play concludes, and with Cromwell's fall it has nothing to do.

Had I but served my God . . .

Finally, Wolsey ends his speech with a famous remark:

> O Cromwell, Cromwell,
> Had I but served my God with half the zeal
> I served my King, he would not in mine age
> Have left me naked to mine enemies.
>
> —Act III, scene ii, lines 454–57

The statement was really made (according to legend) on his deathbed. For a while after his fall, Wolsey had lingered near London, hoping for a reconciliation with the King, and indeed, he appears to have continued to receive some proofs of lingering affection.

Wolsey was then supposed to have engaged in secret correspondence with the Pope, as well as with King Francis and Emperor Charles, hoping, possibly, to enlist their help in establishing his innocence of ever having worked with them against Henry and thus in aiding him in his planned reconciliation.

Eventually, though, he was pushed into going to York so that he could, for the first time, actually fill the post he had held so long. In April 1530 he began the trip to York.

Once there, he planned a public enthronement in November and this displeased the King. By that time tales of his secret correspondence came to light, and Henry decided Wolsey was engaged in treason. On November

4, 1530, just three days before the planned enthronement, Wolsey was arrested and ordered back to London for trial.

His health, however, was destroyed and this last journey was too much for him. He traveled slowly, but by the time he reached Leicester he was dying, and on November 29, 1530, just a year after his fall, he closed his eyes for the last time with (if the story can be believed) the famous remark about "Had I but served my God . . ." on his lips.

. . . from her coronation

The fourth act opens with two gentlemen meeting once more. They had met before (a dozen years before in real time) on the occasion of the conviction and execution of Buckingham. Now the event is a much happier one. The First Gentleman says to the Second:

> You come to take your stand here, and behold
> The Lady Anne pass from her coronation?
> —Act IV, scene i, lines 2–3

The coronation took place on May 31, 1533, immediately after Cranmer's blessing of the marriage.

. . . a late court at Dunstable . . .

The Second Gentleman asks as to the fate of Katherine, whom he can refer to now only as the Princess Dowager. The First Gentleman says:

> The Archbishop
> Of Canterbury, accompanied with other
> Learned and reverend fathers of his order,
> Held a late court at Dunstable, six miles off
> From Ampthill, where the Princess lay . . .
> —Act IV, scene i, lines 24–28

Since Henry had separated himself finally from Katherine in 1531, she had been established at Ampthill, a town forty miles north of London. In 1533 she was subjected to a second trial at Dunstable, ten miles south of Ampthill (not six), and this was quite different from the earlier trial four years before.

Again Katherine refused to appear despite repeated invitations, but this time there was no papal legate and no Pope to appeal to. Cranmer acted on his own and on May 23, 1533, he declared Henry's marriage to Katherine void. That cleared the way for his blessing of the marriage to Anne and for the coronation of the new Queen within the week.

Katherine did not give in. She refused to accept Cranmer's decision or any of the matters that followed—such as declaring her daughter, Mary, to be illegitimate. She maintained herself to be Queen to the very end, but the strain was hard on her. As the First Gentleman says:

> . . . *she was removed to Kimbolton,*
> *Where she remains now sick.*
>
> —Act IV, scene i, lines 34–35

Kimbolton is about twenty miles north of Ampthill.

He of Winchester

The description of Anne's coronation by a Third Gentleman leads to a discussion of the changes that have taken place. Gardiner, for instance, has been promoted (in 1531) from the post of the King's secretary to that of Bishop of Winchester, the wealthiest clerical position in England and the one that had once been held by Henry Beaufort (see page II–522).

The Second Gentleman points out that there is hostility among the new men of the court. He says:

> *He of Winchester* [Gardiner]
> *Is held no great good lover of the Archbishop's,*
> *The virtuous Cranmer.*
>
> —Act IV, scene i, lines 103–5

The source of the enmity is not given, but part may have been the result of Gardiner's frustrated ambition. Gardiner had had hopes for the archbishopric of Canterbury and the lesser post of Winchester was not sufficient consolation.

The Third Gentleman, however, points out that Cranmer has an ally:

> *Thomas Cromwell,*
> *A man in much esteem with th'King, and truly*
> *A worthy friend. The King has made him Master*
> *O'th'Jewel House,*
> *And one, already, of the Privy Council.*
>
> —Act IV, scene i, lines 108–12

Cromwell had succeeded Gardiner as the King's secretary, and his rapid rise thereafter was bound to displease the ambitious Gardiner.

Yet the differences between Gardiner on one side and Cromwell and

Cranmer on the other were not entirely due to jostlings of ambition. There were religious differences too.

Cromwell and Cranmer led the way in the English Reformation that followed the King's divorce. Gardiner, on the other hand, was a religious conservative who was willing to go along with the divorce but who wanted no change in Catholic doctrine.

On the whole, Henry was on Gardiner's side theologically, for the King remained "Defender of the Faith" in his heart and did not budge from Catholic doctrine except where his self-interest was at stake.

This was not only in the matter of the divorce. There was also a question of money. Henry VIII needed funds and now that he was breaking with the Pope, the rich (and in some cases, corrupt) monasteries were at his mercy. The monks were staunchly on the side of the Pope, and therefore against the divorce, and they were rich! What other crimes were necessary?

Sir Thomas More stood out against the King replacing the Pope as head of the Catholic Church, and, for his pains, he was executed on July 6, 1535, the victim of the kind of tyranny he had wrongfully ascribed to Richard III. With his death, Cromwell became supreme, under the King, and supervised the dismantling and looting of the monasteries. The King had the money he needed and the ruling groups in England shared sufficiently in the loot to gain a vested interest in maintaining the Reformation and opposing any return to Catholicism.

For the sake of the benefits he gained, then, Henry raised Cromwell and Cranmer on high and left Gardiner, with whose philosophy he really sympathized, in the rear.

. . . your name Capucius

At Kimbolton, meanwhile, Katherine is dying. She has a last visitor, and says:

> If my sight fail not,
> You should be Lord Ambassador from the Emperor,
> My royal nephew, and your name Capucius.
> —Act IV, scene ii, lines 108–10

"Capucius" is the Latinized form for "Chapuys," who was, indeed, the Imperial ambassador at Henry's court.

Katherine, for all her stubbornness in the matter of the divorce, still seemed to regard Henry with the love and respect due a husband and a king. Clinging fiercely to her rights against all the world, she was never betrayed into a single word against her cruel husband.

On her deathbed, she composed a letter to him asking for very little— that he should look after their daughter, Mary, and see to the personal welfare of the few servants who had attended her in the last years of her unhappiness and disgrace.

Henry managed to feel a last twinge of conscience at this and sent Capucius to Katherine with some consoling message. (He was safe now, after all, for she was dying.) It would seem that, in actual fact, Capucius came too late and found her dead, but according to Holinshed, he came before she had sent the letter and was the agent for taking it to the King. Shakespeare, as always, follows Holinshed.

Capucius' arrival indicated the interest the Emperor Charles was still taking in the affairs of his aunt. He could do nothing for her directly, for he was in no position to make effective war on Henry; certainly not to invade England. Nevertheless, he steadfastly refused to allow the Pope to come to any compromise with Henry, even though that meant the loss of England as far as Catholicism was concerned.

On March 23, 1534, Clement VII had at last firmly declared that the marriage between Henry and Katherine had been entirely valid. (He died half a year later, having lived through a catastrophic eleven-year period as Pope.)

Henry had to react to this and he did so strongly. On March 30 he had his Parliament formally break all ties that bound the Anglican Church to the papacy, and the King himself was established as head of the church. (A year later, More was executed for refusing to accept this.)

Now, in January 1536, with all that was precious to her—her husband and her faith—lying in ruins about her, Katherine lay dying.

. . . his young daughter

Katherine asks Capucius to take the last letter to the King:

> In which I have commended to his goodness
> The model of our chaste loves, his young daughter—
> —Act IV, scene ii, lines 131–32

The Princess Mary, daughter of Henry and Katherine, had been ten years old when the long-drawn-out affair of the divorce had begun. Her life became a miserable one thereafter. By the end of 1531 she was separated from her mother, and they were never allowed to see each other again, not even when Katherine was dying.

Mary was twenty years old at the time of her mother's death, and in her attitude she was a perfect copy of Katherine. Like her mother, Mary always refused to give up a jot of her rights. She would not recognize the divorce, would not give up her title of Princess, held firmly to the Catholic faith when Henry abandoned it.

In fact, her fierce attachment to the Catholic view (by which her mother had never ceased being Queen and she herself never ceased being Princess, as opposed to an Anglicanism which had made of her a bastard) was to lead to five tragic years for England when the traumatized girl became Queen in her turn, seventeen years after her mother's death.

Having made her final plea, then, Katherine died on January 7, 1536, at the age of fifty. Her stubbornness in the matter of the divorce ushered in long years of religious unrest in England, but perhaps they would have come anyway, for Protestant doctrines were invading the land with an intensity far beyond anything Henry himself wished to see.

The only crime of which Katherine could be accused, even by her greatest enemies, was that of failing to bear a living son.

The Queen's in labor

It was Anne Bullen's turn now to produce an heir. As the fifth act opens, Sir Thomas Lovell tells Stephen Gardiner, Bishop of Winchester:

> The Queen's in labor,
> They say, in great extremity, and feared
> She'll with the labor end.
> —Act V, scene i, lines 18–20

Anne Bullen had gotten to work at the task of producing an heir with promptness. At the time of the secret marriage, she was already pregnant and perhaps it was a missed period that made it the more necessary to marry. After all that Henry had done to supply himself with a satisfactory male heir, he could scarcely run the risk of allowing any question of illegitimacy to arise.

So it was that in early September 1533, seven months after her marriage (but over two years *before* Katherine's death, which had been described in the previous scene), Anne was in labor.

Gardiner, hearing the news, wishes the child well, but makes no effort to conceal his hostility to the Queen and to her two supporters, Cranmer and Cromwell.

. . . Is the Queen delivered

Naturally, King Henry is very anxious concerning the arrival of the heir. He comes onstage, speaks absently to others, including Cranmer, and then springs to real attention when the Old Lady (who has, presumably, been in attendance on the travailing Queen) enters. He cries to her:

> *Now by thy looks*
> *I guess thy message. Is the Queen delivered?*
> *Say "aye," and of a boy.*

> —Act V, scene i, lines 161–63

Henry could not command fate, however. The child was a girl, born on September 7, 1533, and Henry VIII was inexpressibly disappointed. He had no way of foretelling that this child was, a quarter century later, to sit on the throne and be the greatest monarch in English history. He knew only that it was another girl.

The Old Lady, perfectly aware of the bad news she was carrying, tried to make the best of it. She says it is a boy, going on to explain:

> *'Tis a girl*
> *Promises boys hereafter.*

> —Act V, scene i, lines 165–66

Alas, this was not a true prophecy. The child born that day was fated to have no sons; no children at all. She remained unmarried all her life and in legend (and even, perhaps, in reality) remained a virgin. She came to be so well known as "the Virgin Queen" that the American state of Virginia is named, in that fashion, for her.

She was, in consequence (woe to Henry's dynastic ambitions), the last of the Tudor line, of which Henry VII had been the first, so that the line endured altogether for only 118 years and only three generations. Nevertheless, James I, who succeeded Elizabeth I, was the great-grandson (through his mother) of a sister of Henry VIII and was therefore the great-great-grandson of Henry VII. All England's monarchs from the time of Henry VIII have been descendants of Henry VII, but since Elizabeth, none have been descendants of Henry VIII.

The upper Germany . . .

The next two scenes deal with Gardiner's attempt to destroy Cranmer. Gardiner accuses the Archbishop of Canterbury of heresy, and strives to secure official confirmation of this view from the council. (This took place in 1540, actually, though in the play it seems to precede the christening of the new baby princess—which took place in 1533.)

Gardiner points out the dangers of heresy and says it would lead to

> *Commotions, uproars, with a general taint*
> *Of the whole state; as of late days our neighbors,*
> *The upper Germany, can dearly witness,*

> —Act V, scene iii, lines 28–30

The reference seems to be to the Peasants' War of 1524–25. Luther had made a passionate attack on the religious establishment and was winning out. The poor peasants of the upper Rhine, assuming that this was a call for a general overhaul of the system, and long suffering unbearable economic oppression which reduced them to the levels of slaves and animals, rose in revolt.

As always, when a downtrodden and uneducated group, without sophisticated leadership, breaks into revolt, there is a general anarchy in which blind destruction is the order of the day and in which many relatively innocent and helpless people suffer. Since the peasants took vengeance on their aristocratic masters (who were the articulate members of society), their actions were presented as atrocious beyond words. When the peasants were finally beaten (as they virtually always were throughout history) and were remorselessly punished in the ratio of ten to one, there was little indignation over that, for who worries about the inarticulate robots at the bottom of the economic pyramid?

In any case, Luther was horrified over the revolt. He had depended for his support on the various German princes who saw in a break with Rome increased political power for themselves and (as in Henry's case) a flood of money from the property and lands under clerical control. But these same princes could now also see that once a revolution is started, it can spread wildly, and while they might like to rifle the church, they did not think it fun to be rifled, in turn, by their peasants.

Naturally, the church made the point that revolution was contagious (a point Gardiner now makes), and Luther, rather than see his new doctrines collapse as fearful princes drew back, decided to line up his new doctrines on the side of the political establishment. He broke out into a flood of incredible invective against the peasants, calling for their suppression by the most extreme methods. By doing this, he held the Lutheran princes in line, but he lost the peasants. The regions in which the revolt took place remain Catholic to this day.

Despite Luther's opportunism, the Peasants' War remained a horrible example to those who thought of venturing on heresy. Europe's aristocracy, unless it could move as pretty much of a unit under a strong king (as in England and in the Scandinavian countries), preferred not to stir up trouble by setting the example of a revolt against authority, and Lutheranism, which for a while had seemed likely to take over all of Western Christendom, met its limits and was restricted largely to the Teutonic countries.

. . . this new sect

Gardiner accuses Cranmer of being in sympathy with Luther's doctrines (and therefore, presumably, of subjecting England to the dangers of popular disorder), saying to him:

> *Do not I know you for a favorer*
> *Of this new sect?*
>
> —Act V, scene iii, lines 80–81

Cranmer, indeed, is about to arrested and sent to the Tower, when Henry enters, intervenes decisively, and saves the Archbishop.

While Henry VIII remained alive, his strong and autocratic hand kept diverse opinions from breaking into open conflict. Both Gardiner and Cranmer were kept under control.

After Henry's death, however, there was first a period of strong Protestant action, in which Cranmer was supreme and Gardiner was imprisoned. There next followed a time of strong Catholic reaction, in which Gardiner was supreme and Cranmer was burned at the stake.

Only with Elizabeth I was a new compromise reached and the groundwork laid for a kind of non-dogmatism in the official view of religion.

. . . a thousand thousand blessings

In the final scene in the play, Cranmer presides over the baptism of the baby, Elizabeth. He speaks prophetically (thanks to the hindsight of the dramatist), saying:

> *This royal infant—heaven still move about her!—*
> *Though in her cradle, yet now promises*
> *Upon this land a thousand thousand blessings*
> *Which time shall bring to ripeness.*
>
> —Act V, scene v, lines 17–20

Cranmer would have had to be a prophet indeed to have foreseen this. Henry certainly did not foresee it.

The birth of a girl soured the King on Anne; perhaps it made him think that heaven still frowned on him and that he had to look elsewhere. As time went on, he even began to think of divorcing Anne, and might have done so except for the general opinion that if he did, he might have to take back Katherine. This meant he had to wait for Katherine's death before doing anything about Anne.

Yet he could engage in extracurricular affairs, and he did. It was not long after Elizabeth's birth that Anne began to feel what Katherine had earlier felt.

When Katherine finally died, poor Anne was jubilant, feeling that now she was really Queen, for there was no one left to dispute the right—and besides, she was pregnant again and this time surely it would be a boy . . .

. . . covetous of wisdom . . .

Cranmer goes on in his eulogy of the baby princess, saying:

> *Saba was never*
> *More covetous of wisdom and fair virtue*
> *Than this pure soul shall be.*
> > —Act V, scene v, lines 23–25

"Saba" is a variant of "Sheba" and the reference is to the Queen of Sheba, who is described in the tenth chapter of 1 Kings as having made a long trip to Jerusalem in order to sit at the feet of the wise King Solomon and learn from him.

And the Princess Elizabeth, in the course of a perilous childhood (she too, like her older sister Mary, had to go through periods in which she was considered a bastard, and even experienced times when imprisonment and execution seemed near), received a thorough education which she completely absorbed. She spoke French, Italian, Latin, and Greek, was acquainted with classical literature, could dispute with the learned men of her court on an equal basis, and as Queen showed herself the rival, and usually the superior, intellectually and politically, of any king in Europe.

Shall star-like rise . . .

When Cranmer's eulogy passes beyond Elizabeth, it becomes ludicrous. He says of the baby:

> *So shall she leave her blessedness to one*
> *(When heaven shall call her from this cloud of darkness)*
> *Who from the sacred ashes of her honor*
> *Shall star-like rise, as great in fame as she was,*
> > —Act V, scene v, lines 43–46

This refers to Elizabeth's successor, James I (see page II–149), whom nobody could possibly recognize in this ridiculously fulsome description. But then, of course, James was on the throne at the time this play was produced and one could scarcely praise Elizabeth without making James appear the insect he was in comparison, unless one also grossly lied by praising James just as much.

With this the play ends. Henry VIII, who has not shone to advantage through much of the play, appears golden in the final act as he protects Cranmer and is happy over the princess.

But the play stops just in time, for after the death of Katherine of Aragon, Henry is in full pursuit of Jane Seymour, one of Anne's maids of honor.

Anne Bullen walked in on Henry when he was engaged in some intimate play with Jane and the Queen threw a fit. Since she was in late pregnancy, Henry, in anguish over the possible effect on her, tried to soothe her. It was to no avail. Anne went into premature labor and on January 29, 1536 (only three weeks after Katherine's death and on the very day of her official funeral), gave birth to the son Henry was looking for—but it was dead.

Henry was furious and that was the end for poor Anne. The King trumped up charges of adultery against her, had her committed to the Tower on May 2, 1536, and had her executed on May 19. She had been married to her royal husband for only three years—a sadder marriage and an unhappier end than Katherine had had.

The next day Henry married Jane Seymour, and she finally gave Henry the son he wanted on October 12, 1537, but died herself on October 24.

The remainder of Henry's reign was one long horror as he married and divorced a fourth wife, executed a fifth, and died before he could think of what to do with the sixth—all this time ruling a frightened court with absolute autocracy, and always quick to kill any who roused his ire or his suspicions.

He finally died on January 28, 1547, and was succeeded by Jane Seymour's son, then nine years old, who ruled as Edward VI. He was a sickly boy who died on July 6, 1553, only fifteen. His older sister, Mary, Katherine's daughter, followed, and initiated a five-year reign during which she uselessly and violently attempted to force England back to Catholicism.

When she died on November 17, 1588, at the age of forty-two, her twenty-five-year-old sister, Elizabeth, Anne's daughter, finally came to the throne, and there began a glorious reign that was to last forty-five years and was amply to fulfill Cranmer's words.

INDEX

Volume One

INDEX TO VOLUME ONE

INDEX

Volume Two

INDEX TO VOLUME TWO

N